(R. & H.) Sec.Reg. 4th Ed. ACB—1

American Casebook Series
Hornbook Series and Basic Legal Texts
Black Letter Series and Nutshell Series

of

WEST PUBLISHING COMPANY
P.O. Box 64526
St. Paul, Minnesota 55164–0526

Accounting

FARIS' ACCOUNTING AND LAW IN A NUTSHELL, 377 pages, 1984. Softcover. (Text)

FIFLIS, KRIPKE AND FOSTER'S TEACHING MATERIALS ON ACCOUNTING FOR BUSINESS LAWYERS, Third Edition, 838 pages, 1984. (Casebook)

SIEGEL AND SIEGEL'S ACCOUNTING AND FINANCIAL DISCLOSURE: A GUIDE TO BASIC CONCEPTS, 259 pages, 1983. Softcover. (Text)

Administrative Law

BONFIELD AND ASIMOW'S STATE AND FEDERAL ADMINISTRATIVE LAW, 826 pages, 1989. Teacher's Manual available. (Casebook)

GELLHORN AND LEVIN'S ADMINISTRATIVE LAW AND PROCESS IN A NUTSHELL, Third Edition, approximately 420 pages, 1990. Softcover. (Text)

MASHAW AND MERRILL'S CASES AND MATERIALS ON ADMINISTRATIVE LAW—THE AMERICAN PUBLIC LAW SYSTEM, Second Edition, 976 pages, 1985. (Casebook) 1989 Supplement.

ROBINSON, GELLHORN AND BRUFF'S THE ADMINISTRATIVE PROCESS, Third Edition, 978 pages, 1986. (Casebook)

Admiralty

HEALY AND SHARPE'S CASES AND MATERIALS ON ADMIRALTY, Second Edition, 876 pages, 1986. (Casebook)

MARAIST'S ADMIRALTY IN A NUTSHELL, Second Edition, 379 pages, 1988. Softcover. (Text)

SCHOENBAUM'S HORNBOOK ON ADMIRALTY AND MARITIME LAW, Student Edition, 692 pages, 1987 with 1989 pocket part. (Text)

Agency—Partnership

FESSLER'S ALTERNATIVES TO INCORPORATION FOR PERSONS IN QUEST OF PROFIT, Second Edition, 326 pages, 1986. Softcover. Teacher's Manual available. (Casebook)

HENN'S CASES AND MATERIALS ON AGENCY, PARTNERSHIP AND OTHER UNINCORPORATED BUSINESS ENTERPRISES, Second Edition, 733 pages, 1985. Teacher's Manual available. (Casebook)

REUSCHLEIN AND GREGORY'S HORNBOOK ON THE LAW OF AGENCY AND PARTNERSHIP, Second Edition, 683 pages, 1990. (Text)

SELECTED CORPORATION AND PARTNERSHIP STATUTES, RULES AND FORMS. Softcover. 727 pages, 1989.

STEFFEN AND KERR'S CASES ON AGENCY-PARTNERSHIP, Fourth Edition, 859 pages, 1980. (Casebook)

STEFFEN'S AGENCY-PARTNERSHIP IN A NUTSHELL, 364 pages, 1977. Softcover. (Text)

Agricultural Law

MEYER, PEDERSEN, THORSON AND DAVIDSON'S AGRICULTURAL LAW: CASES AND MATERIALS, 931 pages, 1985. Teacher's Manual available. (Casebook)

Alternative Dispute Resolution

KANOWITZ' CASES AND MATERIALS ON ALTERNATIVE DISPUTE RESOLUTION, 1024 pages,

---

List current as of July, 1990

Alternative Dispute Resolution—Cont'd

1986. Teacher's Manual available. (Casebook) 1990 Supplement.

RISKIN AND WESTBROOK'S DISPUTE RESOLUTION AND LAWYERS, 468 pages, 1987. Teacher's Manual available. (Casebook)

RISKIN AND WESTBROOK'S DISPUTE RESOLUTION AND LAWYERS, Abridged Edition, 223 pages, 1987. Softcover. Teacher's Manual available. (Casebook)

American Indian Law

CANBY'S AMERICAN INDIAN LAW IN A NUTSHELL, Second Edition, 336 pages, 1988. Softcover. (Text)

GETCHES AND WILKINSON'S CASES AND MATERIALS ON FEDERAL INDIAN LAW, Second Edition, 880 pages, 1986. (Casebook)

Antitrust—see also Regulated Industries, Trade Regulation

FOX AND SULLIVAN'S CASES AND MATERIALS ON ANTITRUST, 935 pages, 1989. Teacher's Manual available. (Casebook)

GELLHORN'S ANTITRUST LAW AND ECONOMICS IN A NUTSHELL, Third Edition, 472 pages, 1986. Softcover. (Text)

HOVENKAMP'S BLACK LETTER ON ANTITRUST, 323 pages, 1986. Softcover. (Review)

HOVENKAMP'S HORNBOOK ON ECONOMICS AND FEDERAL ANTITRUST LAW, Student Edition, 414 pages, 1985. (Text)

OPPENHEIM, WESTON AND MCCARTHY'S CASES AND COMMENTS ON FEDERAL ANTITRUST LAWS, Fourth Edition, 1168 pages, 1981. (Casebook) 1985 Supplement.

POSNER AND EASTERBROOK'S CASES AND ECONOMIC NOTES ON ANTITRUST, Second Edition, 1077 pages, 1981. (Casebook) 1984–85 Supplement.

SULLIVAN'S HORNBOOK OF THE LAW OF ANTITRUST, 886 pages, 1977. (Text)

Appellate Advocacy—see Trial and Appellate Advocacy

Architecture and Engineering Law

SWEET'S LEGAL ASPECTS OF ARCHITECTURE, ENGINEERING AND THE CONSTRUCTION PROCESS, Fourth Edition, 889 pages, 1989. Teacher's Manual available. (Casebook)

Art Law

DUBOFF'S ART LAW IN A NUTSHELL, 335 pages, 1984. Softcover. (Text)

Banking Law

LOVETT'S BANKING AND FINANCIAL INSTITUTIONS LAW IN A NUTSHELL, Second Edition, 464 pages, 1988. Softcover. (Text)

SYMONS AND WHITE'S TEACHING MATERIALS ON BANKING LAW, Second Edition, 993 pages, 1984. Teacher's Manual available. (Casebook) 1987 Supplement.

Business Planning—see also Corporate Finance

PAINTER'S PROBLEMS AND MATERIALS IN BUSINESS PLANNING, Second Edition, 1008 pages, 1984. (Casebook) 1990 Supplement.

Statutory Supplement. *See Selected Corporation and Partnership*

SELECTED CORPORATION AND PARTNERSHIP STATUTES, RULES AND FORMS. 727 pages, 1989. Softcover.

Civil Procedure—see also Federal Jurisdiction and Procedure

AMERICAN BAR ASSOCIATION SECTION OF LITIGATION—READINGS ON ADVERSARIAL JUSTICE: THE AMERICAN APPROACH TO ADJUDICATION, 217 pages, 1988. Softcover. (Coursebook)

CLERMONT'S BLACK LETTER ON CIVIL PROCEDURE, Second Edition, 332 pages, 1988. Softcover. (Review)

COUND, FRIEDENTHAL, MILLER AND SEXTON'S CASES AND MATERIALS ON CIVIL PROCEDURE, Fifth Edition, 1284 pages, 1989. Teacher's Manual available. (Casebook)

COUND, FRIEDENTHAL, MILLER AND SEXTON'S CIVIL PROCEDURE SUPPLEMENT. Approximately 450 pages, 1990. Softcover. (Casebook Supplement)

FEDERAL RULES OF CIVIL PROCEDURE—EDUCATIONAL EDITION. Softcover. Approximately 635 pages, 1990.

FRIEDENTHAL, KANE AND MILLER'S HORNBOOK ON CIVIL PROCEDURE, 876 pages, 1985. (Text)

KANE AND LEVINE'S CIVIL PROCEDURE IN CALIFORNIA: STATE AND FEDERAL 498 pages, 1989. Softcover. (Casebook Supplement)

Civil Procedure—Cont'd

KANE'S CIVIL PROCEDURE IN A NUTSHELL, Second Edition, 306 pages, 1986. Softcover. (Text)

KOFFLER AND REPPY'S HORNBOOK ON COMMON LAW PLEADING, 663 pages, 1969. (Text)

MARCUS, REDISH AND SHERMAN'S CIVIL PROCEDURE: A MODERN APPROACH, 1027 pages, 1989. Teacher's Manual available. (Casebook)

MARCUS AND SHERMAN'S COMPLEX LITIGATION–CASES AND MATERIALS ON ADVANCED CIVIL PROCEDURE, 846 pages, 1985. Teacher's Manual available. (Casebook) 1989 Supplement.

PARK'S COMPUTER-AIDED EXERCISES ON CIVIL PROCEDURE, Second Edition, 167 pages, 1983. Softcover. (Coursebook)

SIEGEL'S HORNBOOK ON NEW YORK PRACTICE, 1011 pages, 1978, with 1987 pocket part. (Text)

Commercial Law

BAILEY AND HAGEDORN'S SECURED TRANSACTIONS IN A NUTSHELL, Third Edition, 390 pages, 1988. Softcover. (Text)

EPSTEIN, MARTIN, HENNING AND NICKLES' BASIC UNIFORM COMMERCIAL CODE TEACHING MATERIALS, Third Edition, 704 pages, 1988. Teacher's Manual available. (Casebook)

HENSON'S HORNBOOK ON SECURED TRANSACTIONS UNDER THE U.C.C., Second Edition, 504 pages, 1979, with 1979 pocket part. (Text)

MURRAY'S COMMERCIAL LAW, PROBLEMS AND MATERIALS, 366 pages, 1975. Teacher's Manual available. Softcover. (Coursebook)

NICKLES' BLACK LETTER ON COMMERCIAL PAPER, 450 pages, 1988. Softcover. (Review)

NICKLES, MATHESON AND DOLAN'S MATERIALS FOR UNDERSTANDING CREDIT AND PAYMENT SYSTEMS, 923 pages, 1987. Teacher's Manual available. (Casebook)

NORDSTROM, MURRAY AND CLOVIS' PROBLEMS AND MATERIALS ON SALES, 515 pages, 1982. (Casebook)

NORDSTROM, MURRAY AND CLOVIS' PROBLEMS AND MATERIALS ON SECURED TRANSACTIONS, 594 pages, 1987. (Casebook)

RUBIN AND COOTER'S THE PAYMENT SYSTEM: CASES, MATERIALS AND ISSUES, 885 pages, 1989. (Casebook)

SELECTED COMMERCIAL STATUTES. Softcover. Approximately 1650 pages, 1990.

SPEIDEL'S BLACK LETTER ON SALES AND SALES FINANCING, 363 pages, 1984. Softcover. (Review)

SPEIDEL, SUMMERS AND WHITE'S COMMERCIAL LAW: TEACHING MATERIALS, Fourth Edition, 1448 pages, 1987. Teacher's Manual available. (Casebook)

SPEIDEL, SUMMERS AND WHITE'S COMMERCIAL PAPER: TEACHING MATERIALS, Fourth Edition, 578 pages, 1987. Reprint from Speidel et al., Commercial Law, Fourth Edition. Teacher's Manual available. (Casebook)

SPEIDEL, SUMMERS AND WHITE'S SALES: TEACHING MATERIALS, Fourth Edition, 804 pages, 1987. Reprint from Speidel et al., Commercial Law, Fourth Edition. Teacher's Manual available. (Casebook)

SPEIDEL, SUMMERS AND WHITE'S SECURED TRANSACTIONS: TEACHING MATERIALS, Fourth Edition, 485 pages, 1987. Reprint from Speidel et al., Commercial Law, Fourth Edition. Teacher's Manual available. (Casebook)

STOCKTON'S SALES IN A NUTSHELL, Second Edition, 370 pages, 1981. Softcover. (Text)

STONE'S UNIFORM COMMERCIAL CODE IN A NUTSHELL, Third Edition, 580 pages, 1989. Softcover. (Text)

WEBER AND SPEIDEL'S COMMERCIAL PAPER IN A NUTSHELL, Third Edition, 404 pages, 1982. Softcover. (Text)

WHITE AND SUMMERS' HORNBOOK ON THE UNIFORM COMMERCIAL CODE, Third Edition, Student Edition, 1386 pages, 1988. (Text)

Community Property

MENNELL AND BOYKOFF'S COMMUNITY PROPERTY IN A NUTSHELL, Second Edition, 432 pages, 1988. Softcover. (Text)

VERRALL AND BIRD'S CASES AND MATERIALS

Community Property—Cont'd

ON CALIFORNIA COMMUNITY PROPERTY, Fifth Edition, 604 pages, 1988. (Casebook)

Comparative Law

BARTON, GIBBS, LI AND MERRYMAN'S LAW IN RADICALLY DIFFERENT CULTURES, 960 pages, 1983. (Casebook)

GLENDON, GORDON AND OSAKWE'S COMPARATIVE LEGAL TRADITIONS: TEXT, MATERIALS AND CASES ON THE CIVIL LAW, COMMON LAW AND SOCIALIST LAW TRADITIONS, 1091 pages, 1985. (Casebook)

GLENDON, GORDON AND OSAKWE'S COMPARATIVE LEGAL TRADITIONS IN A NUTSHELL. 402 pages, 1982. Softcover. (Text)

LANGBEIN'S COMPARATIVE CRIMINAL PROCEDURE: GERMANY, 172 pages, 1977. Softcover. (Casebook)

Computers and Law

MAGGS AND SPROWL'S COMPUTER APPLICATIONS IN THE LAW, 316 pages, 1987. (Coursebook)

MASON'S USING COMPUTERS IN THE LAW: AN INTRODUCTION AND PRACTICAL GUIDE, Second Edition, 288 pages, 1988. Softcover. (Coursebook)

Conflict of Laws

CRAMTON, CURRIE AND KAY'S CASES–COMMENTS–QUESTIONS ON CONFLICT OF LAWS, Fourth Edition, 876 pages, 1987. (Casebook)

HAY'S BLACK LETTER ON CONFLICT OF LAWS, 330 pages, 1989. Softcover. (Review)

SCOLES AND HAY'S HORNBOOK ON CONFLICT OF LAWS, Student Edition, 1085 pages, 1982, with 1988–89 pocket part. (Text)

SEIGEL'S CONFLICTS IN A NUTSHELL, 470 pages, 1982. Softcover. (Text)

Constitutional Law—Civil Rights—see also Foreign Relations and National Security Law

ABERNATHY'S CASES AND MATERIALS ON CIVIL RIGHTS, 660 pages, 1980. (Casebook)

BARRON AND DIENES' BLACK LETTER ON CONSTITUTIONAL LAW, Second Edition, 310 pages, 1987. Softcover. (Review)

BARRON AND DIENES' CONSTITUTIONAL LAW IN A NUTSHELL, 389 pages, 1986. Softcover. (Text)

ENGDAHL'S CONSTITUTIONAL FEDERALISM IN A NUTSHELL, Second Edition, 411 pages, 1987. Softcover. (Text)

FARBER AND SHERRY'S HISTORY OF THE AMERICAN CONSTITUTION, 458 pages, 1990. Softcover. Teacher's Manual available. (Text)

GARVEY AND ALEINIKOFF'S MODERN CONSTITUTIONAL THEORY: A READER, 494 pages, 1989. Softcover. (Reader)

LOCKHART, KAMISAR, CHOPER AND SHIFFRIN'S CONSTITUTIONAL LAW: CASES–COMMENTS–QUESTIONS, Sixth Edition, 1601 pages, 1986. (Casebook) 1990 Supplement.

LOCKHART, KAMISAR, CHOPER AND SHIFFRIN'S THE AMERICAN CONSTITUTION: CASES AND MATERIALS, Sixth Edition, 1260 pages, 1986. Abridged version of Lockhart, et al., Constitutional Law: Cases–Comments–Questions, Sixth Edition. (Casebook) 1990 Supplement.

LOCKHART, KAMISAR, CHOPER AND SHIFFRIN'S CONSTITUTIONAL RIGHTS AND LIBERTIES: CASES AND MATERIALS, Sixth Edition, 1266 pages, 1986. Reprint from Lockhart, et al., Constitutional Law: Cases–Comments–Questions, Sixth Edition. (Casebook) 1990 Supplement.

MARKS AND COOPER'S STATE CONSTITUTIONAL LAW IN A NUTSHELL, 329 pages, 1988. Softcover. (Text)

NOWAK, ROTUNDA AND YOUNG'S HORNBOOK ON CONSTITUTIONAL LAW, Third Edition, 1191 pages, 1986 with 1988 pocket part. (Text)

ROTUNDA'S MODERN CONSTITUTIONAL LAW: CASES AND NOTES, Third Edition, 1085 pages, 1989. (Casebook) 1990 Supplement.

VIEIRA'S CONSTITUTIONAL CIVIL RIGHTS IN A NUTSHELL, Second Edition, 322 pages, 1990. Softcover. (Text)

WILLIAMS' CONSTITUTIONAL ANALYSIS IN A NUTSHELL, 388 pages, 1979. Softcover. (Text)

Consumer Law—see also Commercial Law

EPSTEIN AND NICKLES' CONSUMER LAW IN A NUTSHELL, Second Edition, 418 pages,

Consumer Law—Cont'd

1981. Softcover. (Text)

SELECTED COMMERCIAL STATUTES. Softcover. Approximately 1650 pages, 1990.

SPANOGLE AND ROHNER'S CASES AND MATERIALS ON CONSUMER LAW, 693 pages, 1979. Teacher's Manual available. (Casebook) 1982 Supplement.

Contracts

CALAMARI AND PERILLO'S BLACK LETTER ON CONTRACTS, Second Edition, approximately 450 pages, 1990. Softcover. (Review)

CALAMARI AND PERILLO'S HORNBOOK ON CONTRACTS, Third Edition, 1049 pages, 1987. (Text)

CALAMARI, PERILLO AND BENDER'S CASES AND PROBLEMS ON CONTRACTS, Second Edition, 905 pages, 1989. Teacher's Manual Available. (Casebook)

CORBIN'S TEXT ON CONTRACTS, One Volume Student Edition, 1224 pages, 1952. (Text)

FESSLER AND LOISEAUX'S CASES AND MATERIALS ON CONTRACTS—MORALITY, ECONOMICS AND THE MARKET PLACE, 837 pages, 1982. Teacher's Manual available. (Casebook)

FRIEDMAN'S CONTRACT REMEDIES IN A NUTSHELL, 323 pages, 1981. Softcover. (Text)

FULLER AND EISENBERG'S CASES ON BASIC CONTRACT LAW, Fifth Edition, approximately 1100 pages, 1990. (Casebook)

HAMILTON, RAU AND WEINTRAUB'S CASES AND MATERIALS ON CONTRACTS, 830 pages, 1984. (Casebook)

JACKSON AND BOLLINGER'S CASES ON CONTRACT LAW IN MODERN SOCIETY, Second Edition, 1329 pages, 1980. Teacher's Manual available. (Casebook)

KEYES' GOVERNMENT CONTRACTS IN A NUTSHELL, Second Edition, approximately 530 pages, 1990. Softcover. (Text)

SCHABER AND ROHWER'S CONTRACTS IN A NUTSHELL, Third Edition, approximately 438 pages, 1990. Softcover. (Text)

SUMMERS AND HILLMAN'S CONTRACT AND RELATED OBLIGATION: THEORY, DOCTRINE AND PRACTICE, 1074 pages, 1987. Teacher's Manual available. (Casebook)

Copyright—see Patent and Copyright Law

Corporate Finance

HAMILTON'S CASES AND MATERIALS ON CORPORATION FINANCE, Second Edition, 1221 pages, 1989. (Casebook)

Corporations

HAMILTON'S BLACK LETTER ON CORPORATIONS, Second Edition, 513 pages, 1986. Softcover. (Review)

HAMILTON'S CASES AND MATERIALS ON CORPORATIONS—INCLUDING PARTNERSHIPS AND LIMITED PARTNERSHIPS, Fourth Edition, approximately 1250 pages, 1990. (Casebook) 1990 Statutory Supplement.

HAMILTON'S THE LAW OF CORPORATIONS IN A NUTSHELL, Second Edition, 515 pages, 1987. Softcover. (Text)

HENN'S TEACHING MATERIALS ON THE LAW OF CORPORATIONS, Second Edition, 1204 pages, 1986. Teacher's Manual available. (Casebook)

Statutory Supplement. *See Selected Corporation and Partnership*

HENN AND ALEXANDER'S HORNBOOK ON LAWS OF CORPORATIONS, Third Edition, Student Edition, 1371 pages, 1983, with 1986 pocket part. (Text)

SELECTED CORPORATION AND PARTNERSHIP STATUTES, RULES AND FORMS. Softcover. 727 pages, 1989.

SOLOMON, SCHWARTZ AND BAUMAN'S MATERIALS AND PROBLEMS ON CORPORATIONS: LAW AND POLICY, Second Edition, 1391 pages, 1988. Teacher's Manual available. (Casebook) 1990 Supplement.

Statutory Supplement. *See Selected Corporation and Partnership*

Corrections

KRANTZ' CASES AND MATERIALS ON THE LAW OF CORRECTIONS AND PRISONERS' RIGHTS, Third Edition, 855 pages, 1986. (Casebook) 1988 Supplement.

KRANTZ' THE LAW OF CORRECTIONS AND PRISONERS' RIGHTS IN A NUTSHELL, Third Edition, 407 pages, 1988. Softcover. (Text)

ROBBINS' CASES AND MATERIALS ON POST-CONVICTION REMEDIES, 506 pages, 1982. (Casebook)

Creditors' Rights

BANKRUPTCY CODE, RULES AND OFFICIAL FORMS, LAW SCHOOL EDITION. Approximately 875 pages, 1990. Softcover.

EPSTEIN'S DEBTOR-CREDITOR RELATIONS IN A NUTSHELL, Third Edition, 383 pages, 1986. Softcover. (Text)

EPSTEIN, LANDERS AND NICKLES' CASES AND MATERIALS ON DEBTORS AND CREDITORS, Third Edition, 1059 pages, 1987. Teacher's Manual available. (Casebook)

LOPUCKI'S PLAYER'S MANUAL FOR THE DEBTOR-CREDITOR GAME, 123 pages, 1985. Softcover. (Coursebook)

NICKLES AND EPSTEIN'S BLACK LETTER ON CREDITORS' RIGHTS AND BANKRUPTCY, 576 pages, 1989. (Review)

RIESENFELD'S CASES AND MATERIALS ON CREDITORS' REMEDIES AND DEBTORS' PROTECTION, Fourth Edition, 914 pages, 1987. (Casebook) 1990 Supplement.

WHITE'S CASES AND MATERIALS ON BANKRUPTCY AND CREDITORS' RIGHTS, 812 pages, 1985. Teacher's Manual available. (Casebook) 1987 Supplement.

Criminal Law and Criminal Procedure—see also Corrections, Juvenile Justice

ABRAMS' FEDERAL CRIMINAL LAW AND ITS ENFORCEMENT, 866 pages, 1986. (Casebook) 1988 Supplement.

AMERICAN CRIMINAL JUSTICE PROCESS: SELECTED RULES, STATUTES AND GUIDELINES. 723 pages, 1989. Softcover.

CARLSON'S ADJUDICATION OF CRIMINAL JUSTICE: PROBLEMS AND REFERENCES, 130 pages, 1986. Softcover. (Casebook)

DIX AND SHARLOT'S CASES AND MATERIALS ON CRIMINAL LAW, Third Edition, 846 pages, 1987. (Casebook)

GRANO'S PROBLEMS IN CRIMINAL PROCEDURE, Second Edition, 176 pages, 1981. Teacher's Manual available. Softcover. (Coursebook)

HEYMANN AND KENETY'S THE MURDER TRIAL OF WILBUR JACKSON: A HOMICIDE IN THE FAMILY, Second Edition, 347 pages, 1985. (Coursebook)

ISRAEL, KAMISAR AND LAFAVE'S CRIMINAL PROCEDURE AND THE CONSTITUTION: LEADING SUPREME COURT CASES AND INTRODUCTORY TEXT. Approximately 725 pages, 1990 Edition. Softcover. (Casebook)

ISRAEL AND LAFAVE'S CRIMINAL PROCEDURE—CONSTITUTIONAL LIMITATIONS IN A NUTSHELL, Fourth Edition, 461 pages, 1988. Softcover. (Text)

JOHNSON'S CASES, MATERIALS AND TEXT ON CRIMINAL LAW, Fourth Edition, approximately 790 pages, 1990. Teacher's Manual available. (Casebook)

JOHNSON'S CASES AND MATERIALS ON CRIMINAL PROCEDURE, 859 pages, 1988. (Casebook) 1990 Supplement.

KAMISAR, LAFAVE AND ISRAEL'S MODERN CRIMINAL PROCEDURE: CASES, COMMENTS AND QUESTIONS, Seventh Edition, 1593 pages, 1990. (Casebook) 1990 Supplement.

KAMISAR, LAFAVE AND ISRAEL'S BASIC CRIMINAL PROCEDURE: CASES, COMMENTS AND QUESTIONS, Seventh Edition, 792 pages, 1990. Softcover reprint from Kamisar, et al., Modern Criminal Procedure: Cases, Comments and Questions, Seventh Edition. (Casebook) 1990 Supplement.

LAFAVE'S MODERN CRIMINAL LAW: CASES, COMMENTS AND QUESTIONS, Second Edition, 903 pages, 1988. (Casebook)

LAFAVE AND ISRAEL'S HORNBOOK ON CRIMINAL PROCEDURE, Student Edition, 1142 pages, 1985, with 1989 pocket part. (Text)

LAFAVE AND SCOTT'S HORNBOOK ON CRIMINAL LAW, Second Edition, 918 pages, 1986. (Text)

LANGBEIN'S COMPARATIVE CRIMINAL PROCEDURE: GERMANY, 172 pages, 1977. Softcover. (Casebook)

LOEWY'S CRIMINAL LAW IN A NUTSHELL, Second Edition, 321 pages, 1987. Softcover. (Text)

LOW'S BLACK LETTER ON CRIMINAL LAW, Revised First Edition, approximately 430 pages, 1990. Softcover. (Review)

SALTZBURG'S CASES AND COMMENTARY ON AMERICAN CRIMINAL PROCEDURE, Third Edition, 1302 pages, 1988. Teacher's Manual available. (Casebook) 1990 Supplement.

Criminal Law and Criminal Procedure—Cont'd

UVILLER'S THE PROCESSES OF CRIMINAL JUSTICE: INVESTIGATION AND ADJUDICATION, Second Edition, 1384 pages, 1979. (Casebook) 1979 Statutory Supplement. 1986 Update.

VORENBERG'S CASES ON CRIMINAL LAW AND PROCEDURE, Second Edition, 1088 pages, 1981. Teacher's Manual available. (Casebook) 1990 Supplement.

Decedents' Estates—see Trusts and Estates

Domestic Relations

CLARK'S HORNBOOK ON DOMESTIC RELATIONS, Second Edition, Student Edition, 1050 pages, 1988. (Text)

CLARK AND GLOWINSKY'S CASES AND PROBLEMS ON DOMESTIC RELATIONS, Fourth Edition. Approximately 1125 pages, 1990. Teacher's Manual available. (Casebook)

KRAUSE'S BLACK LETTER ON FAMILY LAW, 314 pages, 1988. Softcover. (Review)

KRAUSE'S CASES, COMMENTS AND QUESTIONS ON FAMILY LAW, Third Edition, 1433 pages, 1990. (Casebook)

KRAUSE'S FAMILY LAW IN A NUTSHELL, Second Edition, 444 pages, 1986. Softcover. (Text)

KRAUSKOPF'S CASES ON PROPERTY DIVISION AT MARRIAGE DISSOLUTION, 250 pages, 1984. Softcover. (Casebook)

Economics, Law and—see also Antitrust, Regulated Industries

GOETZ' CASES AND MATERIALS ON LAW AND ECONOMICS, 547 pages, 1984. (Casebook)

MALLOY'S LAW AND ECONOMICS: A COMPARATIVE APPROACH TO THEORY AND PRACTICE, Approximately 152 pages, 1990. Softcover. (Text)

Education Law

ALEXANDER AND ALEXANDER'S THE LAW OF SCHOOLS, STUDENTS AND TEACHERS IN A NUTSHELL, 409 pages, 1984. Softcover. (Text)

Employment Discrimination—see also Women and the Law

ESTREICHER AND HARPER'S CASES AND MATERIALS ON THE LAW GOVERNING THE EMPLOYMENT RELATIONSHIP, 962 pages, 1990. Teacher's Manual available. (Casebook) Statutory Supplement.

JONES, MURPHY AND BELTON'S CASES AND MATERIALS ON DISCRIMINATION IN EMPLOYMENT, (The Labor Law Group). Fifth Edition, 1116 pages, 1987. (Casebook) 1990 Supplement.

PLAYER'S FEDERAL LAW OF EMPLOYMENT DISCRIMINATION IN A NUTSHELL, Second Edition, 402 pages, 1981. Softcover. (Text)

PLAYER'S HORNBOOK ON EMPLOYMENT DISCRIMINATION LAW, Student Edition, 708 pages, 1988. (Text)

PLAYER, SHOBEN AND LIEBERWITZ' CASES AND MATERIALS ON EMPLOYMENT DISCRIMINATION LAW, Approximately 810 pages, 1990. (Casebook)

Energy and Natural Resources Law—see also Oil and Gas

LAITOS' CASES AND MATERIALS ON NATURAL RESOURCES LAW, 938 pages, 1985. Teacher's Manual available. (Casebook)

SELECTED ENVIRONMENTAL LAW STATUTES—EDUCATIONAL EDITION. Softcover. Approximately 1040 pages, 1990.

Environmental Law—see also Energy and Natural Resources Law; Sea, Law of

BONINE AND MCGARITY'S THE LAW OF ENVIRONMENTAL PROTECTION: CASES—LEGISLATION—POLICIES, 1076 pages, 1984. Teacher's Manual available. (Casebook)

FINDLEY AND FARBER'S CASES AND MATERIALS ON ENVIRONMENTAL LAW, Second Edition, 813 pages, 1985. (Casebook) 1988 Supplement.

FINDLEY AND FARBER'S ENVIRONMENTAL LAW IN A NUTSHELL, Second Edition, 367 pages, 1988. Softcover. (Text)

RODGERS' HORNBOOK ON ENVIRONMENTAL LAW, 956 pages, 1977, with 1984 pocket part. (Text)

SELECTED ENVIRONMENTAL LAW STATUTES—EDUCATIONAL EDITION. Softcover. Approximately 1040 pages, 1990.

Equity—see Remedies

Estate Planning—see also Trusts and Estates; Taxation—Estate and Gift

LYNN'S AN INTRODUCTION TO ESTATE PLANNING IN A NUTSHELL, Third Edition, 370 pages, 1983. Softcover. (Text)

Evidence

BROUN AND BLAKEY'S BLACK LETTER ON EVIDENCE, 269 pages, 1984. Softcover. (Review)

BROUN, MEISENHOLDER, STRONG AND MOSTELLER'S PROBLEMS IN EVIDENCE, Third Edition, 238 pages, 1988. Teacher's Manual available. Softcover. (Coursebook)

CLEARY, STRONG, BROUN AND MOSTELLER'S CASES AND MATERIALS ON EVIDENCE, Fourth Edition, 1060 pages, 1988. (Casebook)

FEDERAL RULES OF EVIDENCE FOR UNITED STATES COURTS AND MAGISTRATES. Softcover. Approximately 380 pages, 1990.

GRAHAM'S FEDERAL RULES OF EVIDENCE IN A NUTSHELL, Second Edition, 473 pages, 1987. Softcover. (Text)

LEMPERT AND SALTZBURG'S A MODERN APPROACH TO EVIDENCE: TEXT, PROBLEMS, TRANSCRIPTS AND CASES, Second Edition, 1232 pages, 1983. Teacher's Manual available. (Casebook)

LILLY'S AN INTRODUCTION TO THE LAW OF EVIDENCE, Second Edition, 585 pages, 1987. (Text)

MCCORMICK, SUTTON AND WELLBORN'S CASES AND MATERIALS ON EVIDENCE, Sixth Edition, 1067 pages, 1987. (Casebook)

MCCORMICK'S HORNBOOK ON EVIDENCE, Third Edition, Student Edition, 1156 pages, 1984, with 1987 pocket part. (Text)

ROTHSTEIN'S EVIDENCE IN A NUTSHELL: STATE AND FEDERAL RULES, Second Edition, 514 pages, 1981. Softcover. (Text)

Federal Jurisdiction and Procedure

CURRIE'S CASES AND MATERIALS ON FEDERAL COURTS, Fourth Edition, approximately 1125 pages, 1990. (Casebook)

CURRIE'S FEDERAL JURISDICTION IN A NUTSHELL, Third Edition, approximately 260 pages, 1990. Softcover. (Text)

FEDERAL RULES OF CIVIL PROCEDURE—EDUCATIONAL EDITION. Softcover. Approximately 635 pages, 1990.

REDISH'S BLACK LETTER ON FEDERAL JURISDICTION, 219 pages, 1985. Softcover. (Review)

REDISH'S CASES, COMMENTS AND QUESTIONS ON FEDERAL COURTS, Second Edition, 1122 pages, 1989. (Casebook) 1990 Supplement.

VETRI AND MERRILL'S FEDERAL COURTS PROBLEMS AND MATERIALS, Second Edition, 232 pages, 1984. Softcover. (Coursebook)

WRIGHT'S HORNBOOK ON FEDERAL COURTS, Fourth Edition, Student Edition, 870 pages, 1983. (Text)

Foreign Relations and National Security Law

FRANCK AND GLENNON'S FOREIGN RELATIONS AND NATIONAL SECURITY LAW, 941 pages, 1987. (Casebook)

Future Interests—see Trusts and Estates

Health Law—see Medicine, Law and

Human Rights—see International Law

Immigration Law

ALEINIKOFF AND MARTIN'S IMMIGRATION PROCESS AND POLICY, Second Edition, approximately 1100 pages, October, 1990 (Casebook)

Statutory Supplement. *See Immigration and Nationality Laws*

IMMIGRATION AND NATIONALITY LAWS OF THE UNITED STATES: SELECTED STATUTES, REGULATIONS AND FORMS. Softcover. Approximately 400 pages, 1990.

WEISSBRODT'S IMMIGRATION LAW AND PROCEDURE IN A NUTSHELL, Second Edition, 438 pages, 1989, Softcover. (Text)

Indian Law—see American Indian Law

Insurance Law

DEVINE AND TERRY'S PROBLEMS IN INSURANCE LAW, 240 pages, 1989. Softcover. Teacher's Manual available. (Course book)

DOBBYN'S INSURANCE LAW IN A NUTSHELL, Second Edition, 316 pages, 1989. Softcover. (Text)

KEETON'S CASES ON BASIC INSURANCE LAW,

Insurance Law—Cont'd

Second Edition, 1086 pages, 1977. Teacher's Manual available. (Casebook)

KEETON'S COMPUTER-AIDED AND WORKBOOK EXERCISES ON INSURANCE LAW, 255 pages, 1990. Softcover. (Coursebook)

KEETON AND WIDISS' INSURANCE LAW, Student Edition, 1359 pages, 1988. (Text)

WIDISS AND KEETON'S COURSE SUPPLEMENT TO KEETON AND WIDISS' INSURANCE LAW, 502 pages, 1988. Softcover. (Casebook)

WIDISS' INSURANCE: MATERIALS ON FUNDAMENTAL PRINCIPLES, LEGAL DOCTRINES AND REGULATORY ACTS, 1186 pages, 1989. (Casebook)

YORK AND WHELAN'S CASES, MATERIALS AND PROBLEMS ON GENERAL PRACTICE INSURANCE LAW, Second Edition, 787 pages, 1988. Teacher's Manual available. (Casebook)

International Law—see also Sea, Law of

BUERGENTHAL'S INTERNATIONAL HUMAN RIGHTS IN A NUTSHELL, 283 pages, 1988. Softcover. (Text)

BUERGENTHAL AND MAIER'S PUBLIC INTERNATIONAL LAW IN A NUTSHELL, Second Edition, 275 pages, 1990. Softcover. (Text)

FOLSOM, GORDON AND SPANOGLE'S INTERNATIONAL BUSINESS TRANSACTIONS—A PROBLEM-ORIENTED COURSEBOOK, 1160 pages, 1986. Teacher's Manual available. (Casebook) 1989 Documents Supplement.

FOLSOM, GORDON AND SPANOGLE'S INTERNATIONAL BUSINESS TRANSACTIONS IN A NUTSHELL, Third Edition, 509 pages, 1988. Softcover. (Text)

HENKIN, PUGH, SCHACHTER AND SMIT'S CASES AND MATERIALS ON INTERNATIONAL LAW, Second Edition, 1517 pages, 1987. (Casebook) Documents Supplement.

JACKSON AND DAVEY'S CASES, MATERIALS AND TEXT ON LEGAL PROBLEMS OF INTERNATIONAL ECONOMIC RELATIONS, Second Edition, 1269 pages, 1986. (Casebook) 1989 Documents Supplement.

KIRGIS' INTERNATIONAL ORGANIZATIONS IN THEIR LEGAL SETTING, 1016 pages, 1977. Teacher's Manual available. (Casebook) 1981 Supplement.

WESTON, FALK AND D'AMATO'S INTERNATIONAL LAW AND WORLD ORDER—A PROBLEM-ORIENTED COURSEBOOK, Second Edition, approximately 1305 pages, 1990. Teacher's Manual available. (Casebook) Documents Supplement.

Interviewing and Counseling

BINDER AND PRICE'S LEGAL INTERVIEWING AND COUNSELING, 232 pages, 1977. Teacher's Manual available. Softcover. (Coursebook)

BINDER, BERGMAN AND PRICE'S LAWYERS AS COUNSELORS: A CLIENT CENTERED APPROACH, Approximately 400 pages, October, 1990 Pub. Softcover. (Coursebook)

SHAFFER AND ELKINS' LEGAL INTERVIEWING AND COUNSELING IN A NUTSHELL, Second Edition, 487 pages, 1987. Softcover. (Text)

Introduction to Law—see Legal Method and Legal System

Introduction to Law Study

HEGLAND'S INTRODUCTION TO THE STUDY AND PRACTICE OF LAW IN A NUTSHELL, 418 pages, 1983. Softcover. (Text)

KINYON'S INTRODUCTION TO LAW STUDY AND LAW EXAMINATIONS IN A NUTSHELL, 389 pages, 1971. Softcover. (Text)

Judicial Process—see Legal Method and Legal System

Jurisprudence

CHRISTIE'S JURISPRUDENCE—TEXT AND READINGS ON THE PHILOSOPHY OF LAW, 1056 pages, 1973. (Casebook)

Juvenile Justice

FOX'S CASES AND MATERIALS ON MODERN JUVENILE JUSTICE, Second Edition, 960 pages, 1981. (Casebook)

FOX'S JUVENILE COURTS IN A NUTSHELL, Third Edition, 291 pages, 1984. Softcover. (Text)

Labor and Employment Law—see also Employment Discrimination, Social Legislation

FINKIN, GOLDMAN AND SUMMERS' LEGAL PROTECTION OF INDIVIDUAL EMPLOYEES, (The La-

Labor and Employment Law—Cont'd

bor Law Group). 1164 pages, 1989. (Casebook)

GORMAN'S BASIC TEXT ON LABOR LAW—UNIONIZATION AND COLLECTIVE BARGAINING, 914 pages, 1976. (Text)

LESLIE'S LABOR LAW IN A NUTSHELL, Second Edition, 397 pages, 1986. Softcover. (Text)

NOLAN'S LABOR ARBITRATION LAW AND PRACTICE IN A NUTSHELL, 358 pages, 1979. Softcover. (Text)

OBERER, HANSLOWE, ANDERSEN AND HEINSZ' CASES AND MATERIALS ON LABOR LAW—COLLECTIVE BARGAINING IN A FREE SOCIETY, Third Edition, 1163 pages, 1986. (Casebook) Statutory Supplement.

RABIN, SILVERSTEIN AND SCHATZKI'S LABOR AND EMPLOYMENT LAW: PROBLEMS, CASES AND MATERIALS IN THE LAW OF WORK, (The Labor Law Group). 1014 pages, 1988. Teacher's Manual available. (Casebook) 1988 Statutory Supplement.

Land Finance—Property Security—see Real Estate Transactions

Land Use

CALLIES AND FREILICH'S CASES AND MATERIALS ON LAND USE, 1233 pages, 1986. (Casebook) 1988 Supplement.

HAGMAN AND JUERGENSMEYER'S HORNBOOK ON URBAN PLANNING AND LAND DEVELOPMENT CONTROL LAW, Second Edition, Student Edition, 680 pages, 1986. (Text)

WRIGHT AND GITELMAN'S CASES AND MATERIALS ON LAND USE, Third Edition, 1300 pages, 1982. Teacher's Manual available. (Casebook) 1987 Supplement.

WRIGHT AND WRIGHT'S LAND USE IN A NUTSHELL, Second Edition, 356 pages, 1985. Softcover. (Text)

Legal History—see also Legal Method and Legal System

PRESSER AND ZAINALDIN'S CASES AND MATERIALS ON LAW AND JURISPRUDENCE IN AMERICAN HISTORY, Second Edition, 1092 pages, 1989. Teacher's Manual available. (Casebook)

Legal Method and Legal System—see also Legal Research, Legal Writing

ALDISERT'S READINGS, MATERIALS AND CASES IN THE JUDICIAL PROCESS, 948 pages, 1976. (Casebook)

BERCH AND BERCH'S INTRODUCTION TO LEGAL METHOD AND PROCESS, 550 pages, 1985. Teacher's Manual available. (Casebook)

BODENHEIMER, OAKLEY AND LOVE'S READINGS AND CASES ON AN INTRODUCTION TO THE ANGLO-AMERICAN LEGAL SYSTEM, Second Edition, 166 pages, 1988. Softcover. (Casebook)

DAVIES AND LAWRY'S INSTITUTIONS AND METHODS OF THE LAW—INTRODUCTORY TEACHING MATERIALS, 547 pages, 1982. Teacher's Manual available. (Casebook)

DVORKIN, HIMMELSTEIN AND LESNICK'S BECOMING A LAWYER: A HUMANISTIC PERSPECTIVE ON LEGAL EDUCATION AND PROFESSIONALISM, 211 pages, 1981. Softcover. (Text)

KEETON'S JUDGING, 842 pages, 1990. Softcover. (Coursebook)

KELSO AND KELSO'S STUDYING LAW: AN INTRODUCTION, 587 pages, 1984. (Coursebook)

KEMPIN'S HISTORICAL INTRODUCTION TO ANGLO-AMERICAN LAW IN A NUTSHELL, Third Edition, approximately 302 pages, 1990. Softcover. (Text)

REYNOLDS' JUDICIAL PROCESS IN A NUTSHELL, 292 pages, 1980. Softcover. (Text)

Legal Research

COHEN'S LEGAL RESEARCH IN A NUTSHELL, Fourth Edition, 452 pages, 1985. Softcover. (Text)

COHEN, BERRING AND OLSON'S HOW TO FIND THE LAW, Ninth Edition, 716 pages, 1989. (Text)

COHEN, BERRING AND OLSON'S FINDING THE LAW, 570 pages, 1989. Softcover reprint from Cohen, Berring and Olson's How to Find the Law, Ninth Edition. (Coursebook)

Legal Research Exercises, 3rd Ed., for use with Cohen, Berring and Olson, 229 pages, 1989. Teacher's Manual available.

ROMBAUER'S LEGAL PROBLEM SOLVING—

Legal Research—Cont'd

ANALYSIS, RESEARCH AND WRITING, Fourth Edition, 424 pages, 1983. Teacher's Manual with problems available. (Coursebook)

STATSKY'S LEGAL RESEARCH AND WRITING, Third Edition, 257 pages, 1986. Softcover. (Coursebook)

TEPLY'S LEGAL RESEARCH AND CITATION, Third Edition, 472 pages, 1989. Softcover. (Coursebook)

Student Library Exercises, 3rd ed., 391 pages, 1989. Answer Key available.

Legal Writing

CHILD'S DRAFTING LEGAL DOCUMENTS: MATERIALS AND PROBLEMS, 286 pages, 1988. Softcover. Teacher's Manual available. (Coursebook)

DICKERSON'S MATERIALS ON LEGAL DRAFTING, 425 pages, 1981. Teacher's Manual available. (Coursebook)

FELSENFELD AND SIEGEL'S WRITING CONTRACTS IN PLAIN ENGLISH, 290 pages, 1981. Softcover. (Text)

GOPEN'S WRITING FROM A LEGAL PERSPECTIVE, 225 pages, 1981. (Text)

MELLINKOFF'S LEGAL WRITING—SENSE AND NONSENSE, 242 pages, 1982. Softcover. Teacher's Manual available. (Text)

PRATT'S LEGAL WRITING: A SYSTEMATIC APPROACH, 422 pages, 1989. Teacher's Manual available. (Coursebook)

RAY AND RAMSFIELD'S LEGAL WRITING: GETTING IT RIGHT AND GETTING IT WRITTEN, 250 pages, 1987. Softcover. (Text)

SQUIRES AND ROMBAUER'S LEGAL WRITING IN A NUTSHELL, 294 pages, 1982. Softcover. (Text)

STATSKY AND WERNET'S CASE ANALYSIS AND FUNDAMENTALS OF LEGAL WRITING, Third Edition, 424 pages, 1989. Teacher's Manual available. (Text)

TEPLY'S LEGAL WRITING, ANALYSIS AND ORAL ARGUMENT, 576 pages, 1990. Softcover. Teacher's Manual available. (Coursebook)

WEIHOFEN'S LEGAL WRITING STYLE, Second Edition, 332 pages, 1980. (Text)

Legislation

DAVIES' LEGISLATIVE LAW AND PROCESS IN A NUTSHELL, Second Edition, 346 pages, 1986. Softcover. (Text)

ESKRIDGE AND FRICKEY'S CASES AND MATERIALS ON LEGISLATION: STATUTES AND THE CREATION OF PUBLIC POLICY, 937 pages, 1988. Teacher's Manual available. (Casebook) 1990 Supplement.

NUTTING AND DICKERSON'S CASES AND MATERIALS ON LEGISLATION, Fifth Edition, 744 pages, 1978. (Casebook)

STATSKY'S LEGISLATIVE ANALYSIS AND DRAFTING, Second Edition, 217 pages, 1984. Teacher's Manual available. (Text)

Local Government

FRUG'S CASES AND MATERIALS ON LOCAL GOVERNMENT LAW, 1005 pages, 1988. (Casebook)

MCCARTHY'S LOCAL GOVERNMENT LAW IN A NUTSHELL, Third Edition, approximately 400 pages, 1990. Softcover. (Text)

REYNOLDS' HORNBOOK ON LOCAL GOVERNMENT LAW, 860 pages, 1982, with 1990 pocket part. (Text)

VALENTE'S CASES AND MATERIALS ON LOCAL GOVERNMENT LAW, Third Edition, 1010 pages, 1987. Teacher's Manual available. (Casebook) 1989 Supplement.

Mass Communication Law

GILLMOR, BARRON, SIMON AND TERRY'S CASES AND COMMENT ON MASS COMMUNICATION LAW, Fifth Edition, 947 pages, 1990. (Casebook)

GINSBURG'S REGULATION OF BROADCASTING: LAW AND POLICY TOWARDS RADIO, TELEVISION AND CABLE COMMUNICATIONS, 741 pages, 1979 (Casebook) 1983 Supplement.

ZUCKMAN, GAYNES, CARTER AND DEE'S MASS COMMUNICATIONS LAW IN A NUTSHELL, Third Edition, 538 pages, 1988. Softcover. (Text)

Medicine, Law and

FURROW, JOHNSON, JOST AND SCHWARTZ' HEALTH LAW: CASES, MATERIALS AND PROBLEMS, 1005 pages, 1987. Teacher's Manual available. (Casebook) 1989 Supplement.

HALL AND ELLMAN'S HEALTH CARE LAW AND

Medicine, Law and—Cont'd

ETHICS IN A NUTSHELL, 401 pages, 1990. Softcover (Text)

KING'S THE LAW OF MEDICAL MALPRACTICE IN A NUTSHELL, Second Edition, 342 pages, 1986. Softcover. (Text)

SHAPIRO AND SPECE'S CASES, MATERIALS AND PROBLEMS ON BIOETHICS AND LAW, 892 pages, 1981. (Casebook)

SHARPE, BOUMIL, FISCINA AND HEAD'S CASES AND MATERIALS ON MEDICAL LIABILITY, Approximately 500 pages, September, 1990 Pub. (Casebook)

Military Law

SHANOR AND TERRELL'S MILITARY LAW IN A NUTSHELL, 378 pages, 1980. Softcover. (Text)

Mortgages—see Real Estate Transactions

Natural Resources Law—see Energy and Natural Resources Law, Environmental Law

Negotiation

GIFFORD'S LEGAL NEGOTIATION: THEORY AND APPLICATIONS, 225 pages, 1989. Softcover. (Text)

WILLIAMS' LEGAL NEGOTIATION AND SETTLEMENT, 207 pages, 1983. Softcover. Teacher's Manual available. (Coursebook)

Office Practice—see also Computers and Law, Interviewing and Counseling, Negotiation

HEGLAND'S TRIAL AND PRACTICE SKILLS IN A NUTSHELL, 346 pages, 1978. Softcover (Text)

STRONG AND CLARK'S LAW OFFICE MANAGEMENT, 424 pages, 1974. (Casebook)

Oil and Gas—see also Energy and Natural Resources Law

HEMINGWAY'S HORNBOOK ON OIL AND GAS, Second Edition, Student Edition, 543 pages, 1983, with 1989 pocket part. (Text)

KUNTZ, LOWE, ANDERSON AND SMITH'S CASES AND MATERIALS ON OIL AND GAS LAW, 857 pages, 1986. Teacher's Manual available. (Casebook) Forms Manual. Revised.

LOWE'S OIL AND GAS LAW IN A NUTSHELL, Second Edition, 465 pages, 1988. Softcover. (Text)

Partnership—see Agency—Partnership

Patent and Copyright Law

CHOATE, FRANCIS AND COLLINS' CASES AND MATERIALS ON PATENT LAW, INCLUDING TRADE SECRETS, COPYRIGHTS, TRADEMARKS, Third Edition, 1009 pages, 1987. (Casebook)

MILLER AND DAVIS' INTELLECTUAL PROPERTY—PATENTS, TRADEMARKS AND COPYRIGHT IN A NUTSHELL, Second Edition, approximately 440 pages, 1990. Softcover. (Text)

NIMMER'S CASES AND MATERIALS ON COPYRIGHT AND OTHER ASPECTS OF ENTERTAINMENT LITIGATION ILLUSTRATED—INCLUDING UNFAIR COMPETITION, DEFAMATION AND PRIVACY, Third Edition, 1025 pages, 1985. (Casebook) 1989 Supplement.

Products Liability

FISCHER AND POWERS' CASES AND MATERIALS ON PRODUCTS LIABILITY, 685 pages, 1988. Teacher's Manual available. (Casebook)

NOEL AND PHILLIPS' CASES ON PRODUCTS LIABILITY, Second Edition, 821 pages, 1982. (Casebook)

PHILLIPS' PRODUCTS LIABILITY IN A NUTSHELL, Third Edition, 307 pages, 1988. Softcover. (Text)

Professional Responsibility

ARONSON, DEVINE AND FISCH'S PROBLEMS, CASES AND MATERIALS IN PROFESSIONAL RESPONSIBILITY, 745 pages, 1985. Teacher's Manual available. (Casebook)

ARONSON AND WECKSTEIN'S PROFESSIONAL RESPONSIBILITY IN A NUTSHELL, 399 pages, 1980. Softcover. (Text)

MELLINKOFF'S THE CONSCIENCE OF A LAWYER, 304 pages, 1973. (Text)

PIRSIG AND KIRWIN'S CASES AND MATERIALS ON PROFESSIONAL RESPONSIBILITY, Fourth Edition, 603 pages, 1984. Teacher's Manual available. (Casebook)

ROTUNDA'S BLACK LETTER ON PROFESSIONAL RESPONSIBILITY, Second Edition, 414 pages, 1988. Softcover. (Review)

SCHWARTZ AND WYDICK'S PROBLEMS IN LE-

Professional Responsibility—Cont'd

GAL ETHICS, Second Edition, 341 pages, 1988. (Coursebook)

SELECTED STATUTES, RULES AND STANDARDS ON THE LEGAL PROFESSION. Softcover. Approximately 600 pages, 1990.

SMITH AND MALLEN'S PREVENTING LEGAL MALPRACTICE, 264 pages, 1989. Reprint from Mallen and Smith's Legal Malpractice, Third Edition. (Text)

SUTTON AND DZIENKOWSKI'S CASES AND MATERIALS ON THE PROFESSIONAL RESPONSIBILITY FOR LAWYERS, 839 pages, 1989. Teacher's Manual available. (Casebook)

WOLFRAM'S HORNBOOK ON MODERN LEGAL ETHICS, Student Edition, 1120 pages, 1986. (Text)

Property—see also Real Estate Transactions, Land Use, Trusts and Estates

BERNHARDT'S BLACK LETTER ON PROPERTY, 318 pages, 1983. Softcover. (Review)

BERNHARDT'S REAL PROPERTY IN A NUTSHELL, Second Edition, 448 pages, 1981. Softcover. (Text)

BOYER'S SURVEY OF THE LAW OF PROPERTY, Third Edition, 766 pages, 1981. (Text)

BROWDER, CUNNINGHAM, NELSON, STOEBUCK AND WHITMAN'S CASES ON BASIC PROPERTY LAW, Fifth Edition, 1386 pages, 1989. Teacher's Manual available. (Casebook)

BRUCE, ELY AND BOSTICK'S CASES AND MATERIALS ON MODERN PROPERTY LAW, Second Edition, 953 pages, 1989. Teacher's Manual available. (Casebook)

BURKE'S PERSONAL PROPERTY IN A NUTSHELL, 322 pages, 1983. Softcover. (Text)

CUNNINGHAM, STOEBUCK AND WHITMAN'S HORNBOOK ON THE LAW OF PROPERTY, Student Edition, 916 pages, 1984, with 1987 pocket part. (Text)

DONAHUE, KAUPER AND MARTIN'S CASES ON PROPERTY, Second Edition, 1362 pages, 1983. Teacher's Manual available. (Casebook)

HILL'S LANDLORD AND TENANT LAW IN A NUTSHELL, Second Edition, 311 pages, 1986. Softcover. (Text)

KURTZ AND HOVENKAMP'S CASES AND MATERIALS ON AMERICAN PROPERTY LAW, 1296 pages, 1987. Teacher's Manual available. (Casebook) 1988 Supplement.

MOYNIHAN'S INTRODUCTION TO REAL PROPERTY, Second Edition, 239 pages, 1988. (Text)

Psychiatry, Law and

REISNER AND SLOBOGIN'S LAW AND THE MENTAL HEALTH SYSTEM, CIVIL AND CRIMINAL ASPECTS, Second Edition, approximately 1127 pages, 1990. (Casebook)

Real Estate Transactions

BRUCE'S REAL ESTATE FINANCE IN A NUTSHELL, Second Edition, 262 pages, 1985. Softcover. (Text)

MAXWELL, RIESENFELD, HETLAND AND WARREN'S CASES ON CALIFORNIA SECURITY TRANSACTIONS IN LAND, Third Edition, 728 pages, 1984. (Casebook)

NELSON AND WHITMAN'S BLACK LETTER ON LAND TRANSACTIONS AND FINANCE, Second Edition, 466 pages, 1988. Softcover. (Review)

NELSON AND WHITMAN'S CASES ON REAL ESTATE TRANSFER, FINANCE AND DEVELOPMENT, Third Edition, 1184 pages, 1987. (Casebook)

NELSON AND WHITMAN'S HORNBOOK ON REAL ESTATE FINANCE LAW, Second Edition, 941 pages, 1985 with 1989 pocket part. (Text)

Regulated Industries—see also Mass Communication Law, Banking Law

GELLHORN AND PIERCE'S REGULATED INDUSTRIES IN A NUTSHELL, Second Edition, 389 pages, 1987. Softcover. (Text)

MORGAN, HARRISON AND VERKUIL'S CASES AND MATERIALS ON ECONOMIC REGULATION OF BUSINESS, Second Edition, 666 pages, 1985. (Casebook)

Remedies

DOBBS' HORNBOOK ON REMEDIES, 1067 pages, 1973. (Text)

DOBBS' PROBLEMS IN REMEDIES. 137 pages, 1974. Teacher's Manual available. Softcover. (Coursebook)

DOBBYN'S INJUNCTIONS IN A NUTSHELL, 264 pages, 1974. Softcover. (Text)

Remedies—Cont'd

FRIEDMAN'S CONTRACT REMEDIES IN A NUTSHELL, 323 pages, 1981. Softcover. (Text)

LEAVELL, LOVE AND NELSON'S CASES AND MATERIALS ON EQUITABLE REMEDIES, RESTITUTION AND DAMAGES, Fourth Edition, 1111 pages, 1986. Teacher's Manual available. (Casebook)

MCCORMICK'S HORNBOOK ON DAMAGES, 811 pages, 1935. (Text)

O'CONNELL'S REMEDIES IN A NUTSHELL, Second Edition, 320 pages, 1985. Softcover. (Text)

SCHOENBROD, MACBETH, LEVINE AND JUNG'S CASES AND MATERIALS ON REMEDIES: PUBLIC AND PRIVATE, Approximately 807 pages, 1990. Teacher's Manual available. (Casebook)

YORK, BAUMAN AND RENDLEMAN'S CASES AND MATERIALS ON REMEDIES, Fourth Edition, 1029 pages, 1985. Teacher's Manual available. (Casebook)

Sea, Law of

SOHN AND GUSTAFSON'S THE LAW OF THE SEA IN A NUTSHELL, 264 pages, 1984. Softcover. (Text)

Securities Regulation

HAZEN'S HORNBOOK ON THE LAW OF SECURITIES REGULATION, Second Edition, Student Edition, approximately 1000 pages, 1990. (Text)

RATNER'S MATERIALS ON SECURITIES REGULATION, Third Edition, 1000 pages, 1986. Teacher's Manual available. (Casebook) 1989 Supplement.

Statutory Supplement. *See Selected Securities Regulation*

RATNER'S SECURITIES REGULATION IN A NUTSHELL, Third Edition, 316 pages, 1988. Softcover. (Text)

SELECTED STATUTES, REGULATIONS, RULES, DOCUMENTS AND FORMS ON SECURITIES REGULATION. Softcover. 1272 pages, 1990.

Social Legislation

HOOD, HARDY AND LEWIS' WORKERS' COMPENSATION AND EMPLOYEE PROTECTION LAWS IN A NUTSHELL, Second Edition, 361 pages, 1990. Softcover. (Text)

LAFRANCE'S WELFARE LAW: STRUCTURE AND ENTITLEMENT IN A NUTSHELL, 455 pages, 1979. Softcover. (Text)

MALONE, PLANT AND LITTLE'S CASES ON WORKERS' COMPENSATION AND EMPLOYMENT RIGHTS, Second Edition, 951 pages, 1980. Teacher's Manual available. (Casebook)

Sports Law

SCHUBERT, SMITH AND TRENTADUE'S SPORTS LAW, 395 pages, 1986. (Text)

Tax Practice and Procedure

GARBIS, STRUNTZ AND RUBIN'S CASES AND MATERIALS ON TAX PROCEDURE AND TAX FRAUD, Second Edition, 687 pages, 1987. (Casebook)

MORGAN'S TAX PROCEDURE AND TAX FRAUD IN A NUTSHELL, Approximately 382 pages, 1990. Softcover. (Text)

Taxation—Corporate

KAHN AND GANN'S CORPORATE TAXATION, Third Edition, 980 pages, 1989. Teacher's Manual available. (Casebook)

WEIDENBRUCH AND BURKE'S FEDERAL INCOME TAXATION OF CORPORATIONS AND STOCKHOLDERS IN A NUTSHELL, Third Edition, 309 pages, 1989. Softcover. (Text)

Taxation—Estate & Gift—see also Estate Planning, Trusts and Estates

MCNULTY'S FEDERAL ESTATE AND GIFT TAXATION IN A NUTSHELL, Fourth Edition, 496 pages, 1989. Softcover. (Text)

PENNELL'S CASES AND MATERIALS ON INCOME TAXATION OF TRUSTS, ESTATES, GRANTORS AND BENEFICIARIES, 460 pages, 1987. Teacher's Manual available. (Casebook)

Taxation—Individual

DODGE'S THE LOGIC OF TAX, 343 pages, 1989. Softcover. (Text)

GUNN AND WARD'S CASES, TEXT AND PROBLEMS ON FEDERAL INCOME TAXATION, Second Edition, 835 pages, 1988. Teacher's Manual available. (Casebook) 1990 Supplement.

HUDSON AND LIND'S BLACK LETTER ON FEDERAL INCOME TAXATION, Third Edition, approximately 390 pages, 1990. Softcover. (Review)

Taxation—Individual—Cont'd

KRAGEN AND MCNULTY'S CASES AND MATERIALS ON FEDERAL INCOME TAXATION—INDIVIDUALS, CORPORATIONS, PARTNERSHIPS, Fourth Edition, 1287 pages, 1985. (Casebook)

MCNULTY'S FEDERAL INCOME TAXATION OF INDIVIDUALS IN A NUTSHELL, Fourth Edition, 503 pages, 1988. Softcover. (Text)

POSIN'S HORNBOOK ON FEDERAL INCOME TAXATION, Student Edition, 491 pages, 1983, with 1989 pocket part. (Text)

ROSE AND CHOMMIE'S HORNBOOK ON FEDERAL INCOME TAXATION, Third Edition, 923 pages, 1988, with 1989 pocket part. (Text)

SELECTED FEDERAL TAXATION STATUTES AND REGULATIONS. Softcover. Approximately 1650 pages, 1991.

SOLOMON AND HESCH'S PROBLEMS, CASES AND MATERIALS ON FEDERAL INCOME TAXATION OF INDIVIDUALS, 1068 pages, 1987. Teacher's Manual available. (Casebook)

Taxation—International

DOERNBERG'S INTERNATIONAL TAXATION IN A NUTSHELL, 325 pages, 1989. Softcover. (Text)

KAPLAN'S FEDERAL TAXATION OF INTERNATIONAL TRANSACTIONS: PRINCIPLES, PLANNING AND POLICY, 635 pages, 1988. (Casebook)

Taxation—Partnership

BERGER AND WIEDENBECK'S CASES AND MATERIALS ON PARTNERSHIP TAXATION, 788 pages, 1989. Teacher's Manual available. (Casebook)

Taxation—State & Local

GELFAND AND SALSICH'S STATE AND LOCAL TAXATION AND FINANCE IN A NUTSHELL, 309 pages, 1986. Softcover. (Text)

HELLERSTEIN AND HELLERSTEIN'S CASES AND MATERIALS ON STATE AND LOCAL TAXATION, Fifth Edition, 1071 pages, 1988. (Casebook)

Torts—see also Products Liability

CHRISTIE AND MEEKS' CASES AND MATERIALS ON THE LAW OF TORTS, Second Edition, 1264 pages, 1990. (Casebook)

DOBBS' TORTS AND COMPENSATION—PERSONAL ACCOUNTABILITY AND SOCIAL RESPONSIBILITY FOR INJURY, 955 pages, 1985. Teacher's Manual available. (Casebook) 1990 Supplement.

KEETON, KEETON, SARGENTICH AND STEINER'S CASES AND MATERIALS ON TORT AND ACCIDENT LAW, Second Edition, 1318 pages, 1989. (Casebook)

KIONKA'S BLACK LETTER ON TORTS, 339 pages, 1988. Softcover. (Review)

KIONKA'S TORTS IN A NUTSHELL: INJURIES TO PERSONS AND PROPERTY, 434 pages, 1977. Softcover. (Text)

MALONE'S TORTS IN A NUTSHELL: INJURIES TO FAMILY, SOCIAL AND TRADE RELATIONS, 358 pages, 1979. Softcover. (Text)

PROSSER AND KEETON'S HORNBOOK ON TORTS, Fifth Edition, Student Edition, 1286 pages, 1984 with 1988 pocket part. (Text)

ROBERTSON, POWERS AND ANDERSON'S CASES AND MATERIALS ON TORTS, 932 pages, 1989. Teacher's Manual available. (Casebook)

Trade Regulation—see also Antitrust, Regulated Industries

MCMANIS' UNFAIR TRADE PRACTICES IN A NUTSHELL, Second Edition, 464 pages, 1988. Softcover. (Text)

OPPENHEIM, WESTON, MAGGS AND SCHECHTER'S CASES AND MATERIALS ON UNFAIR TRADE PRACTICES AND CONSUMER PROTECTION, Fourth Edition, 1038 pages, 1983. Teacher's Manual available. (Casebook) 1986 Supplement.

SCHECHTER'S BLACK LETTER ON UNFAIR TRADE PRACTICES, 272 pages, 1986. Softcover. (Review)

Trial and Appellate Advocacy—see also Civil Procedure

APPELLATE ADVOCACY, HANDBOOK OF, Second Edition, 182 pages, 1986. Softcover. (Text)

BERGMAN'S TRIAL ADVOCACY IN A NUTSHELL, Second Edition, 354 pages, 1989. Softcover. (Text)

BINDER AND BERGMAN'S FACT INVESTIGATION: FROM HYPOTHESIS TO PROOF, 354 pages, 1984. Teacher's Manual available. (Coursebook)

Trial and Appellate Advocacy—Cont'd

CARLSON AND IMWINKELRIED'S DYNAMICS OF TRIAL PRACTICE: PROBLEMS AND MATERIALS, 414 pages, 1989. Teacher's Manual available. (Coursebook)

GOLDBERG'S THE FIRST TRIAL (WHERE DO I SIT? WHAT DO I SAY?) IN A NUTSHELL, 396 pages, 1982. Softcover. (Text)

HAYDOCK, HERR, AND STEMPEL'S FUNDAMENTALS OF PRE-TRIAL LITIGATION, 768 pages, 1985. Softcover. Teacher's Manual available. (Coursebook)

HEGLAND'S TRIAL AND PRACTICE SKILLS IN A NUTSHELL, 346 pages, 1978. Softcover. (Text)

HORNSTEIN'S APPELLATE ADVOCACY IN A NUTSHELL, 325 pages, 1984. Softcover. (Text)

JEANS' HANDBOOK ON TRIAL ADVOCACY, Student Edition, 473 pages, 1975. Softcover. (Text)

LISNEK AND KAUFMAN'S DEPOSITIONS: PROCEDURE, STRATEGY AND TECHNIQUE, Law School and CLE Edition. 250 pages, 1990. Softcover. (Text)

MARTINEAU'S CASES AND MATERIALS ON APPELLATE PRACTICE AND PROCEDURE, 565 pages, 1987. (Casebook)

NOLAN'S CASES AND MATERIALS ON TRIAL PRACTICE, 518 pages, 1981. (Casebook)

SONSTENG AND HAYDOCK'S TRIAL: THEORIES, TACTICS, TECHNIQUE, Approximately 650 pages, 1990. Softcover. (Text)

SONSTENG, HAYDOCK AND BOYD'S THE TRIALBOOK: A TOTAL SYSTEM FOR PREPARATION AND PRESENTATION OF A CASE, 404 pages, 1984. Softcover. (Coursebook)

WHARTON, HAYDOCK AND SONSTENG'S CALIFORNIA CIVIL TRIALBOOK, Law School and CLE Edition. Approximately 300 pages, 1990. Softcover. (Text)

Trusts and Estates

ATKINSON'S HORNBOOK ON WILLS, Second Edition, 975 pages, 1953. (Text)

AVERILL'S UNIFORM PROBATE CODE IN A NUTSHELL, Second Edition, 454 pages, 1987. Softcover. (Text)

BOGERT'S HORNBOOK ON TRUSTS, Sixth Edition, Student Edition, 794 pages, 1987. (Text)

CLARK, LUSKY AND MURPHY'S CASES AND MATERIALS ON GRATUITOUS TRANSFERS, Third Edition, 970 pages, 1985. (Casebook)

DODGE'S WILLS, TRUSTS AND ESTATE PLANNING–LAW AND TAXATION, CASES AND MATERIALS, 665 pages, 1988. (Casebook)

KURTZ' PROBLEMS, CASES AND OTHER MATERIALS ON FAMILY ESTATE PLANNING, 853 pages, 1983. Teacher's Manual available. (Casebook)

MCGOVERN'S CASES AND MATERIALS ON WILLS, TRUSTS AND FUTURE INTERESTS: AN INTRODUCTION TO ESTATE PLANNING, 750 pages, 1983. (Casebook)

MCGOVERN, KURTZ AND REIN'S HORNBOOK ON WILLS, TRUSTS AND ESTATES–INCLUDING TAXATION AND FUTURE INTERESTS, 996 pages, 1988. (Text)

MENNELL'S WILLS AND TRUSTS IN A NUTSHELL, 392 pages, 1979. Softcover. (Text)

SIMES' HORNBOOK ON FUTURE INTERESTS, Second Edition, 355 pages, 1966. (Text)

TURANO AND RADIGAN'S HORNBOOK ON NEW YORK ESTATE ADMINISTRATION, 676 pages, 1986. (Text)

UNIFORM PROBATE CODE, OFFICIAL TEXT WITH COMMENTS. 615 pages, 1989. Softcover.

WAGGONER'S FUTURE INTERESTS IN A NUTSHELL, 361 pages, 1981. Softcover. (Text)

WATERBURY'S MATERIALS ON TRUSTS AND ESTATES, 1039 pages, 1986. Teacher's Manual available. (Casebook)

Water Law—see also Energy and Natural Resources Law, Environmental Law

GETCHES' WATER LAW IN A NUTSHELL, Second Edition, approximately 441 pages, 1990. Softcover. (Text)

SAX AND ABRAMS' LEGAL CONTROL OF WATER RESOURCES: CASES AND MATERIALS, 941 pages, 1986. (Casebook)

TRELEASE AND GOULD'S CASES AND MATERIALS ON WATER LAW, Fourth Edition, 816 pages, 1986. (Casebook)

Wills—see Trusts and Estates

Women and the Law—see also Employment Discrimination

KAY'S TEXT, CASES AND MATERIALS ON SEX-BASED DISCRIMINATION, Third Edition, 1001 pages, 1988. (Casebook) 1990 Supplement.

THOMAS' SEX DISCRIMINATION IN A NUTSHELL, 399 pages, 1982. Softcover. (Text)

Workers' Compensation—see Social Legislation

WEST'S LAW SCHOOL ADVISORY BOARD

SECURITIES REGULATION

CASES AND MATERIALS

Fourth Edition

By

David L. Ratner
Professor of Law
University of San Francisco

Thomas Lee Hazen
Professor of Law
University of North Carolina

AMERICAN CASEBOOK SERIES®

WEST PUBLISHING CO.
ST. PAUL, MINN., 1991

50 West Kellogg Boulevard
P.O. Box 64526
St. Paul, MN 55164–0526

Library of Congress Cataloging-in-Publication Data

Ratner, David L.
Securities regulation : cases and materials / by David L. Ratner and Thomas Lee Hazen. — 4th ed.
p. cm. — (American casebook series)
Includes index.
ISBN 0–314–79326–7
1. Securities—United States—Cases. I. Hazen, Thomas Lee, 1947– . II. Title. III. Series.
KF1438.R38 1990
346.73'092—dc20
[347.30692] 90–45541
CIP

ISBN 0–314–79326–7

(R. & H.) Sec.Reg. 4th Ed. ACB

Preface

This book is intended to give prospective lawyers a feel for the concepts underlying our distinctive system for the regulation of securities transactions, and for the kinds of problems they can expect to encounter in a corporate or general business practice.

The book is divided into four Parts, dealing with (1) regulation of public offerings, (2) regulation of transactions by "insiders", (3) regulation of corporate conduct, and (4) regulation of the securities industry and markets.

Part I begins with a consideration of the disclosure requirements applicable to public offerings of securities (including the integration of 1933 and 1934 Act provisions), followed by a consideration of the civil liability provisions and how they affect the process of preparing disclosure documents. Attention is then focused on the coverage of federal law, the principal exemptions, civil liability for unregistered or exempt transactions, and state regulation of offerings.

Part II deals first with the specific liabilities for "short-swing" trading by insiders under the 1934 Act, then traces the judicial development of Rule 10b–5 and other antifraud provisions and how they are applied to the phenomenon known as "insider trading."

Part III focuses on the application of specific disclosure requirements and the antifraud provisions to corporate disclosure practices, transactions with "insiders", and mergers and acquisitions. It concludes with an intensive examination of federal and state laws applicable to takeovers and tender offers.

Part IV traces the development of the principal obligations placed on broker-dealers by the antifraud provisions, and the manner in which those obligations can be enforced. It concludes with a consideration of the regulation of broker-dealers' financial structure, of the operation of the securities markets and the self-regulatory system, and of the competition between different segments of the financial services industry.

Because this is basically a teaching book, it is designed to be illustrative rather than exhaustive, provocative rather than definitive. We have concentrated on the main roads of development, rather than trying to deal with the multitudinous questions of interpretation surrounding specific definitions or exemptions or special kinds of transactions. At the same time, the citations to primary and secondary sources, together with the selected references at the end of each section, should provide an adequate starting point for the student or lawyer who wishes to pursue a particular problem in greater detail.

In the typical law school curriculum, the course in Securities Regulation will follow a basic course in Corporations or Business Enterprises. These materials are therefore prepared on the assumption that students will have some idea of the nature of equity and debt securities, the relationships between management, directors and shareholders, and the procedures for approving corporate transactions.

Many corporations courses now give substantial attention to federal securities law, particularly in its application to "insider trading" and "corporate mismanagement." Those subjects are also covered in this book. While some teachers may choose to omit them in the Securities Regulation course, we have found that students welcome an opportunity to re-examine the problems in more systematic fashion, although the time devoted to them can be reduced where the students have already read the assigned cases in an earlier course.

The types of materials included reflect the nature of practice in different areas of securities law. The disclosure provisions involve more "office" than "courtroom" practice, so the materials are heavily weighted toward statutes, rules and administrative materials. These can be handled in class largely by working through the related Problems, and the sample Prospectus and Underwriting Agreement, included in a separate pamphlet. We have also tried in that area to give some feel for how the system actually operates, as distinguished from the way the law indicates it should operate.

In the antifraud area, on the other hand, the law has developed on a more traditional case-by-case basis. The Problems in that area are therefore designed to assist students in focusing on and analyzing the decisions in the leading cases.

In selecting materials, we have tried to include the significant steps in the development of the law in each problem area, leading (hopefully in a logical progression) from simpler to more complex situations. Securities transactions tend to be extremely complicated, and we have tried where possible to use cases in which the student can comprehend the facts sufficiently well to appreciate the issues involved. Securities opinions also tend to involve a number of separate issues, so some decisions have been divided up and redistributed under the appropriate headings.

In editing cases and other materials, we have aimed for simplicity and readability, preserving as much as possible of the "flavor" of the transaction. Substantive omissions are indicated by asterisks, but no notation has been made of omission of citations or footnotes or correction of obvious typographical errors. In view of the large proportion of securities cases in which a petition for certiorari is filed, references to denial of certiorari have been omitted, except where it has special significance. Numbered footnotes are from the original sources and have not been renumbered; lettered footnotes are ours.

The separate pamphlet accompanying this book contains Problems which we have found helpful as a basis for discussion of a substantial part of the materials (indeed, they are virtually essential for intelligent discussion of the disclosure provisions). The problems are keyed to the sections in the casebook to which they relate, as well as to the relevant provisions of the statutes, rules and forms. To give a better feel for the operation of the 1933 Act registration process, we have also included in the pamphlet the full text of a Preliminary Prospectus, as actually filed with the SEC, together with excerpts from the SEC's letter of comments and the final Prospectus, the Agreement Among Underwriters, the Purchase Agreement, and the Selected Dealer Agreement.

In putting these materials together, we have been stimulated, informed and aided by many friends in the SEC, the securities bar, and the law schools. We hope that those who use these materials—teachers, students and lawyers—will give us the benefit of their reactions and suggestions for incorporation in future editions.

DAVID L. RATNER
THOMAS LEE HAZEN

October, 1990

*

Summary of Contents

PART IV. REGULATION OF THE SECURITIES INDUSTRY AND MARKETS

*

Table of Contents

Table of Cases

The principal cases are in bold type. Cases cited or discussed in the text are roman type. Principal cases are listed under the names of both parties. Cases in which the United States, the SEC or a state is a party are listed under the name of the other party. References are to pages. Cases cited in principal cases and within other quoted materials are not included.

Table of Statutes and Rules

SECURITIES REGULATION

CASES AND MATERIALS

Fourth Edition

*

INTRODUCTION:
THE REGULATORY FRAMEWORK

Securities occupy a unique and important place in American life. They are the instruments which evidence the financial rights, and in some cases the power to control, the corporations which own the great bulk of the nation's productive facilities. They are the instruments through which business enterprises and governmental entities raise a substantial part of the funds with which to finance new capital construction. They are the instruments in which many millions of Americans invest their savings to provide for their retirement income, or education for their children, or in hopes of achieving a higher standard of living. And, inevitably, they are the instruments by which unscrupulous promoters and salesmen prey on those hopes and desires and sell worthless paper to many thousands of people every year.

The feature which distinguishes securities from most other commodities in which people deal is that they have no intrinsic value in themselves—they represent rights in something else. The value of a bond, note or other promise to pay depends on the financial condition of the promisor. The value of a share of stock depends on the profitability or future prospects of the corporation or other entity which issued it; its market price depends on how much other people are willing to pay for it, based on their evaluation of those prospects.

The distinctive features of securities give a distinctive coloration to regulation of transactions in securities, in contrast to the regulation of transactions in other types of goods. Most goods are produced, distributed and used or consumed; governmental regulation focuses on protecting the ultimate consumer against dangerous articles, misleading advertising, and unfair or non-competitive pricing practices. Securities are different.

First, securities are created, rather than produced. They can be issued in unlimited amounts, virtually without cost, since they are nothing in themselves but represent only an interest in something else. An important focus of securities regulation, therefore, is assuring that, when securities are created and offered to the public, investors have an accurate idea of what that "something else" is and how much of an interest in it the particular security represents.

Second, securities are not used or consumed by their purchasers. They become a kind of currency, traded in the so-called "secondary markets" at fluctuating prices. These "secondary" transactions far outweigh, in number and volume, the offerings of newly-created securities. A second important focus of securities regulation, therefore, is to assure that there is a continuous flow of information about the corporation or other entity which is represented by securities being actively traded in the secondary markets.

Third, since the complexity of securities invites unscrupulous people to attempt to cheat or mislead investors and traders, the securities laws contain provisions prohibiting a variety of fraudulent, manipulative or deceptive practices. These provisions have been applied to a wide range of activities, including trading on "inside information," misleading corporate publicity, and improper dealings by corporate management.

Finally, since a large industry has grown up to buy and sell securities for investors and traders, securities regulation is concerned with the regulation of people and firms engaged in that business, to assure that they do not take advantage of their superior experience and access to overreach their non-professional customers.

The Securities Markets

The facilities through which securities are traded are known as "markets". These markets may have physical locations, but in many cases are simply formal or informal systems of communication through which buyers and sellers make their interests known and consummate transactions.

There are many different markets for securities.

In terms of dollar volume, the largest market is the bond market—trading in the debt instruments issued by the United States government, by state and local governments, and by corporations. However, since the bond market attracts professional and institutional investors more than the general public, and since federal, state and local government obligations are exempt from the direct regulatory provisions of the federal securities laws, the bond markets have in recent years occupied only a small part of the attention of securities regulators.

The principal focus of securities regulation is on the markets for common stocks. There are two types of stock markets now operating in the United States—"exchange" markets and "over-the-counter" markets. An "exchange" market, of which the New York Stock Exchange (NYSE) is by far the largest, operates in a physical facility with a trading "floor" to which all transactions in a particular security are supposed to be directed. The NYSE (and, to a lesser extent, the other exchanges) has traditionally operated in a very rigid manner, prescribing the number of members, what functions each member can perform, and the minimum rate that a member must charge on all transactions. The over-the-counter (OTC) market, on the other hand, has traditionally been completely unstructured, without any physical facility, and with any qualified firm being free to engage in any types of activities with respect to any securities.

As far as the individual buyer or seller of stocks is concerned, the significant difference between an exchange and OTC transaction is the function performed by the firm with which he deals. In the case of an exchange transaction, his firm acts as a "broker"—that is, as an agent for the customer's account—and charges him a commission for its services. The only person permitted to act as a "dealer" or "make a market" in the stock on the exchange floor (that is, to buy and sell the security for his own account) is the registered "specialist" in that stock. The broker transmits the customer's order to the exchange floor where it is generally executed by buying from or selling to either the specialist or another customer whose broker has left his order on the specialist's "book."

In the OTC market, on the other hand, there is no exchange floor, only a computer and telephone communication network. Any number of firms may act as "dealers" or "market-makers" in a particular stock and may deal directly with public customers in that stock. If the firm through which a customer orders a particular stock is not a dealer in that stock, it will normally purchase it for him as broker from one of the dealers making a market in that stock. In many cases, however, the firm will solicit orders from customers in stocks in which it is making a market, selling the stock to the customer as principal at a mark-up over the price it is currently quoting to brokers. Since retail firms commonly act simultaneously as brokers in exchange-listed stocks and as dealers in OTC stocks, this may cause some confusion on the part of customers.

A firm selling stock to a customer as part of an underwritten offering of a new issue (whether of a listed or OTC stock) normally sells to the customer as principal at a fixed price (equal to or slightly below the current market price, in the case of a security which is already publicly traded). The dealer's compensation in that case comes out of the "spread" between the public offering price and the net proceeds paid to the issuer (or other person on whose behalf the distribution is being made).

Over the past two decades, two factors have substantially blurred the distinctions between exchange and OTC markets. The first is modern computer and communication technology, which enables buyers and sellers in all parts of the country to be in instantaneous and continuous communication with one another with respect to any security. This has revolutionized the operation of the over-the-counter market, and has raised serious questions about the necessity and desirability of a physical exchange "floor." At the same time, trading in common stocks, particularly those listed on the New York Stock Exchange, has been increasingly dominated by "institutional investors"—principally pension funds, mutual funds, bank trust departments, and insurance companies—with individual investors accounting for a continually decreasing percentage of trading volume. The distinctive trading practices of institutions, and the types of services they require and do not require, have put serious strains on the traditional market mechanisms and compensation structure of the Exchange, and have caused a substantial diversion of trading in NYSE-listed stocks to other markets. Current efforts within the industry and the government are focused on rationalizing the market structure and determining who can do business and on what terms in the developing "central market system".

The Securities Industry

The securities industry is characterized by great diversity, both in size and function. There are several thousand firms engaged in one or more types of securities activities, ranging from large firms engaged in brokerage, market-making, underwriting, investment advice and fund management, as well as commodities, real estate dealings and a variety of other financial service activities, down to one-man firms engaged solely in selling mutual fund shares or dealing in a few securities of solely local interest.

There are several hundred firms engaged in retail brokerage business in listed securities, and hundreds more engaged in retail activities in over-the-counter stocks. The underwriting, or investment banking, business tends to be more highly concentrated because of the substantial amounts of capital required.

There has always been a substantial failure rate among small securities firms, which commence operations during periods of high trading volume and fold when volume declines. In 1969 and 1970, however, as a result of operational breakdowns, unsound capital structures, and rapidly declining volume and prices for securities, there was an unprecedented series of failures of large NYSE member firms, almost causing the collapse of the industry. This near-collapse triggered a number of governmental studies, culminating in the imposition of new financial responsibility requirements on securities firms. It also led to efforts, which are still continuing, to devise a more rational and efficient system for the clearance and settlement of securities transactions.

Since the passage in 1933 of the Glass-Steagall Act, prohibiting banks from dealing in securities (except government bonds), the securities business has consisted of a relatively separate and well-defined group of firms. However, with the increasing tendency for individuals to make their equity investments indirectly through institutions, rather than trading directly in stock for their own account, securities firms have come increasingly into competition with banks, insurance companies, and other financial institutions. At the same time that securities firms have been offering their customers an increasing number of services that traditionally have been associated with commercial banking, commercial banks have entered many areas that formerly were reserved for investment bankers and securities firms. This competition has placed severe strains on the existing regulatory structure, under which securities firms, banks and insurance companies are regulated by different agencies with entirely different concerns and approaches.

The Regulatory System

Securities transactions are subject to regulation under both federal and state law. The federal securities laws apply to all securities transactions involving use of the mails or facilities of interstate commerce (except for securities or transactions which are specifically exempted). At the same time, however, they specifically preserve the right of the states to regulate securities transactions, so that the states remain free to supplement or duplicate federal requirements to whatever extent they choose.

Every state has some law specifically regulating transactions in securities. These laws are known as "blue sky" laws, after an early judicial opinion describing their purpose as the prevention of "speculative schemes which have no more basis than so many feet of blue sky."

While these "blue sky" laws vary greatly from state to state, they generally contain the following three types of provisions (although not all contain all three types): (a) prohibitions against fraud in the sale of securities; (b) requirements for registration of brokers and dealers; and (c) requirements for registration of securities to be sold in the state.

In 1956, the Commissioners on Uniform State Laws promulgated a Uniform Securities Act for adoption by the states. Reflecting the pre-existing pattern of state laws and the differences in regulatory philosophy among the states, the act is divided into four parts: (1) antifraud provisions, (2) broker-dealer registration provisions, (3) security registration provisions, and (4) definitions, exemptions, and administrative and liability provisions. States are thus free to adopt one, two or all of the first three parts, plus the appropriate provisions of the fourth part.

While many states have adopted most or some of the provisions of the Uniform Act, the movement toward uniformity has been hampered by several factors. (a) Some of the most important commercial states have not adopted any part of the Act. (b) Almost all the states that have adopted it have made substantial changes from the approved text. (c) State administrators and courts interpret the same language differently, producing a difference in operation that is not apparent from a reading of the laws themselves.

Nevertheless, the promulgation and adoption of the Uniform Act has produced a much more rational and consistent pattern of regulation than previously existed. This development has also been assisted by the North American Securities Administrators Association, which from time to time issues "statements of policy" on various substantive and procedural questions and indicates to what extent those policies are followed by each of its members.

In recent years, there has been some effort to coordinate state and federal regulation. The Uniform Securities Act provides a simple procedure for "registration by coordination" of an issue which is also being registered under federal law, and some states completely exempt issues registered under federal law from their own registration requirements. Efforts are also being made to coordinate the application forms and reports filed by broker-dealers registered under federal law with those required for broker-dealer registration in the states.

The Federal Securities Laws

Federal securities law basically consists of six statutes enacted between 1933 and 1940, and periodically amended in the intervening years, and one enacted in 1970. They are:

Securities Act of 1933
Securities Exchange Act of 1934
Public Utility Holding Company Act of 1935
Trust Indenture Act of 1939
Investment Company Act of 1940
Investment Advisers Act of 1940
Securities Investor Protection Act of 1970

The materials in this book relate primarily to the first two of these acts.

The *Securities Act of 1933* regulates public offerings of securities. Its basic provision is found in Section 5, which prohibits offers and sales of securities which are not registered with the Securities and Exchange Commission. Section 2 defines the terms used in the Act, and Sections 3 and 4 exempt various kinds of securities and transactions from its registration requirements. Sections 6 and 8 specify the procedure for registration, Sections 7, 10 and Schedule A prescribe the contents of the registration statement and prospectus, and Sections 11 and 12 specify civil liabilities for false or misleading statements. Section 17 prohibits fraudulent or deceptive practices in the sale of securities, and the remaining sections of the Act contain procedural and penalty provisions.

The *Securities Exchange Act of 1934* extended federal regulation to trading in securities which are already issued and outstanding. Unlike the 1933 Act, which focuses on a single regulatory provision, the 1934 Act contains a number of distinct groups of provisions, aimed at different participants in the securities trading process.

Section 4 established the Securities and Exchange Commission (SEC), and Title II transferred to it the responsibility for administration of the 1933 Act (which had originally been assigned to the Federal Trade Commission).

Sections 12, 13, 14 and 16 impose disclosure and other requirements on publicly-traded companies.

Section 12 requires any issuer which has a class of securities traded on a national securities exchange to register with the SEC. (This registration of the class of securities under the 1934 Act must be distinguished from registration of an *offering of securities* under the 1933 Act; a company which has registered a class of securities under the 1934 Act will still have to register a particular offering of securities of that class under the 1933 Act if the provisions of that Act so require.) In 1964, Section 12(g) was added, extending the registration requirements to any company which has total assets exceeding $1,000,000 and a class of equity securities with at least 500 shareholders of record.

Section 13 requires every issuer which has securities registered under Section 12 to file periodic and other reports with the SEC, and Section 14 regulates the solicitation of proxies from holders of such securities, in each case subject to rules prescribed by the SEC. Sections 13(d) and (e) and 14(d), (e) and (f), added by the "Williams Act" in 1968, regulate take-over bids, tender offers and purchases by companies of their own shares. Section 13(b)(2), added by the Foreign Corrupt Practices Act of 1977, requires every such issuer to keep accurate books and records and maintain adequate internal accounting controls.

Section 16 requires every officer, director and 10% shareholder of an issuer which has securities registered under Section 12 to report his purchases and sales of any equity securities of the issuer, and requires him to turn over to the company any profit derived from a purchase and sale of such securities within a six-month period.

Sections 9 and 10 prohibit various kinds of "manipulative or deceptive devices or contrivances" in connection with the purchase or sale of securities. Rule 10b–5, promulgated by the SEC under the general authority delegated to it in Section 10(b), has come to be a potent enforcement tool, both in SEC proceedings and private litigation.

Sections 5, 6 and 19 require national securities exchanges to register with the SEC, and authorize the SEC to suspend or discipline such exchanges and their members. Section 11 authorizes the SEC to regulate trading by exchange members for their own account.

Sections 7 and 8 authorize the Federal Reserve Board to prescribe rules governing the amount of credit that may be extended for the purchase or carrying of securities, and regulating borrowing by brokers and dealers.

Section 15 requires brokers and dealers in securities to register with the SEC, and prescribes the procedures for SEC disciplinary actions against them.

Section 15A, added by the "Maloney Act" in 1938, provides for registration with the SEC of "national securities associations" and requires any such association to exercise certain disciplinary powers over its members. The only association registered under this section is the National Association of Securities Dealers (NASD), which in general regulates activities of its members in the non-exchange, or over-the-counter (OTC) markets.

Sections 11A and 17A, added by the Securities Acts Amendments of 1975, direct the SEC to "facilitate" the establishment of a "national market system", coordinating the activities of all market makers and securities information processors, and a national system for the clearing and settlement of securities transactions, coordinating the activities of transfer agents and clearing agencies.

Section 15B, also added by the 1975 amendments, requires firms dealing solely in municipal securities to register with the SEC, and establishes a Municipal Securities Rulemaking Board to regulate their activities.

Section 15C, added in 1986, requires firms dealing solely in U.S. Government securities to register with the SEC and to comply with a regulatory system administered jointly by the SEC, the Treasury Department, and the federal banking agencies.

Section 21 authorizes the SEC to conduct investigations and to apply to the courts for injunctions and other forms of relief. Sections 20A and 21A, added in 1988 and 1984, respectively, added new enforcement weapons to curb illegal insider trading. The Insider Trading Sanctions Act of 1984 (ITSA) added § 21A, which allows the Commission to recover a civil penalty of up to three times the profits realized as a result of trading while in possession of material nonpublic information in violation of the securities laws. The Insider Trading and Securities Fraud Enforcement Act of 1988 (ITSFEA) not only clarified the scope of the SEC action under § 21A but also added § 20A, which created a private right of action by contemporaneous traders against anyone profiting from trading on the basis of material nonpublic information.

Section 30A, added by the Foreign Corrupt Practices Act of 1977, prohibits any issuer which has securities registered under § 12 from paying any bribe to an official of a foreign government. Another section of that Act extends the prohibition to all "domestic concerns."

Section 3 contains definitions, and the remaining sections of the Act contain a variety of procedural and supplementary provisions.

The *Public Utility Holding Company Act of 1935* was enacted to correct abuses which Congressional inquiries had disclosed in the financing and operation of electric and gas public utility holding company systems, and to achieve physical integration and corporate simplification of those systems. Activities under the Holding Company Act currently constitute a very small part of the SEC's work.

The *Trust Indenture Act of 1939* applies generally to public issues of debt securities in excess of $1,000,000. Even though the issue is registered under the 1933 Act, the indenture covering the securities must also be qualified under the 1939 Act, which imposes standards of independence and responsibility on the indenture trustee and requires other provisions for the protection of the security holders. Since a large part of the Act must be recited verbatim in each indenture, this Act has been a substantial source of revenue to financial printers.

The *Investment Company Act of 1940* resulted from an SEC study directed by Congress in the Holding Company Act. It gives the SEC regulatory authority over publicly-owned companies which are engaged primarily in the business of investing and trading in securities. The Act regulates the composition of the management of investment companies, their capital structure, approval of their advisory contracts and changes in investment policy, and requires SEC approval for any transactions by such companies with directors, officers or affiliates. It was amended in 1970 to impose additional controls on management compensation and sales charges. Investment companies are also subject to the disclosure requirements of the 1933 Act, when they make public offerings of their securities, and to the reporting, proxy solicitation and insider trading provisions of the 1934 Act.

The *Investment Advisers Act of 1940*, as amended in 1960, established a scheme of registration and regulation of investment advisers comparable to that contained in Section 15 of the 1934 Act with respect to broker-dealers.

The *Securities Investor Protection Act of 1970* was passed by Congress at the urging of the securities industry after the failure of a number of large securities firms in the financial crisis of 1969–70 created the risk of massive defaults on obligations to customers, leading to a loss of public confidence in securities firms generally. The Act created a non-profit membership corporation called Securities Investor Protection Corporation (SIPC) to which every broker-dealer (with limited exceptions) must belong. SIPC is managed by a board of seven directors, chosen by the government from different segments of the industry and the public, and is funded by assessments on its members and a $1 billion line of credit from the Treasury.

If SIPC determines that a member firm is in danger of failing, it may apply to a court for a decree that the firm's customers need the protection of the Act, and the appointment of a trustee to liquidate the firm. If the firm's assets are insufficient to pay the claims of all customers, SIPC must advance to the trustee funds sufficient to satisfy all such claims up to a maximum of $100,000 for each customer (but not more than $40,000 in respect of claims for cash).

The Securities and Exchange Commission

The Securities and Exchange Commission (SEC) is the agency charged with principal responsibility for the enforcement and administration of the federal securities laws. The 1934 Act provides that the SEC shall consist of five members appointed by the President for five-year terms (the term of one Commissioner expires each year), not more than three of whom shall be members of the same political party.

The Securities and Exchange Commission has passed through a number of distinct phases. From 1934 to 1941, under the leadership of its first four chairmen—Joseph P. Kennedy, James M. Landis, William O. Douglas, and Jerome N. Frank—the Commission was engaged in a struggle to establish its authority over a recalcitrant industry, and to implement Congressional directives to require full disclosure of corporate information, eliminate serious abuses in stock exchange operations, and dismantle the unsound holding company structure that dominated the public utility business. In the course of those activities it attracted to the Commission and its staff some of the ablest people in American public life.

World War II pushed the securities markets into the background, and the SEC was moved to Philadelphia to make room in Washington for agencies more directly related to the war effort. During the 1940's the Commission's major activity was dismantling and restructuring the public utility holding companies under the mandate of the 1935 Act. That job was largely completed by the early 1950's. The Commission then turned its attention to the regulation of new issues under the Securities Act of 1933 (which was significantly amended in 1954), to enforcement actions against "boiler rooms" and other unhealthy outgrowths of the post-war securities markets, and to a major scandal in the operation of the American Stock Exchange, which was completely reorganized as a result of an SEC investigation completed in 1961.

In 1961, President Kennedy, himself son of the SEC's first Chairman, appointed William L. Cary, a Columbia Law School professor, to serve as chairman of the agency. Also in 1961, Congress directed the SEC to conduct a "Special Study" of the securities markets and of the existing regulatory pattern. To conduct that study, the Commission assembled a special staff of 65 lawyers, economists and others, under the direction of Milton H. Cohen, a Chicago lawyer. The five-volume report of the Special Study, which appeared in 1963, was (and remains) the most thorough and systematic study of the workings of the American securities markets and the regulatory system. The report contained more than 175 recommendations for major and minor reforms of securities regulation. Some of these were implemented by SEC action; others were incorporated in the Securities Acts Amendments of 1964, which extended periodic disclosure requirements (previously applicable only to companies listed on stock exchanges) to several thousand large companies whose securities were traded on the OTC market. The amendments also strengthened various aspects of regulation of the people and firms engaged in the securities business.

The day that the Securities Acts Amendments of 1964 were signed into law, Cary resigned as chairman to return to teaching, and was succeeded by Manuel F. Cohen, a 20-year veteran of the SEC staff. During Cohen's record 4½-year tenure as chairman, the Commission completed its study of mutual funds, and submitted to Congress in 1967 its recommendations for additional controls on mutual fund management fees and sales charges. These recommendations, in somewhat revised form, became the basis of the Investment Company Act Amendments of 1970.

The developments set in motion under the leadership of Cary and Cohen in the 1960s have continued to evolve to the present time and can be grouped generally under three main headings—disclosure policy, enforcement activities, and regulation of the securities market.

Disclosure. In 1967, the Commission established a small study group, under the leadership of Commissioner Francis M. Wheat, to reexamine its administrative policies under the disclosure provisions of the 1933 and 1934 Acts. The report of that study, commonly known as the "Wheat Report," helped trigger a number of significant changes in disclosure policy, including the adoption of Rules 144 to 147, setting forth more objective standards for determining when various exemptions from the 1933 Act registration requirements will be available.

During the 1970s, there was increasing criticism of the SEC's disclosure policy, by economists and others, on the ground that it required the presentation of vast masses of detailed factual information that diverted investors' attention from the truly important factors that determine a company's prospects and the comparative value of its securities. William J. Casey, a former venture capitalist who served as Chairman of the Commission from 1971 to 1973, pushed through modifications of the disclosure forms to require more "soft" information about the company's plans and projections, the background and capabilities of the principal officers, and other matters. Casey also took an important step by appointing as Chief Accountant John C. ("Sandy") Burton, a Columbia University professor who pushed the accounting profession and its standard-setting bodies more vigorously than any other person who has occupied that position before or since.

Notwithstanding these changes, criticism of SEC disclosure policy continued, and in 1976 the Commission appointed an Advisory Committee on Corporate Disclosure, headed by Commissioner A.A. Sommer, Jr., "to assess the costs of the present system of corporate disclosure and to weigh those costs against the benefits it produces." The Advisory Committee's 1977 report did not satisfy advocates of the so-called "efficient market theory," who argue that market analysts process all of the available information about publicly-held companies so efficiently that most of the SEC's detailed requirements are unnecessary. It did, however, recommend substantial simplification of many disclosure items, as well as an "integrated disclosure system," in which the basic disclosure requirements under both the 1933 and 1934 Acts would be set forth in a single set of requirements and in which documents filed or disseminated under the 1934 Act could be incorporated by reference in filings required under the 1933 Act. These recommendations were substantially implemented by the Commission in a series of new forms and rules promulgated between 1980 and 1982.

Enforcement. The Commission's Division of Enforcement is responsible for investigating and bringing proceedings against securities firms, corporate officers, new business promoters and others who violate the antifraud or other provisions of federal securities law.

Over a period of 16 years, two outstanding Directors—Irving Pollack (1965–74) and Stanley Sporkin (1974–81)—made the SEC's Enforcement Division into one of the most efficient and most respected enforcement agencies in the federal government. Among the Division's most significant accomplishments are (1) the continuing campaign against "insider trading," which commenced with the *Texas Gulf Sulphur* proceeding in 1965, (2) vigorous enforcement proceedings against large stock exchange member firms, whose disciplining the Commission had previously left largely to the exchanges themselves, (3) proceedings against accountants, lawyers and other professionals based on their alleged failure to monitor their client's compliance with federal securities laws, and (4) the exposure of illegal political contributions and bribes to foreign governments by large U.S. corporations, which followed the Watergate scandal and led to the enactment of the Foreign Corrupt Practices Act. More recently, under the guidance of Enforcement Directors John Fedders (1981–1985) and Gary Lynch (1985–1989), the increased focus on insider trading has resulted in monumental penalties running into hundreds of millions of dollars against people trading in inside information about prospective takeovers.

Market Regulation. The SEC took the lead in the 1960s in exposing the bizarre reciprocal arrangements that had grown up around the New York Stock Exchange's fixed commission rate structure, paving the way for the final elimination of fixed rates in 1975. The Commission, however, was as unprepared as the industry for the operational and financial collapse that almost destroyed the securities industry in 1969–70. This fiasco led to extended Congressional hearings and ultimately to the enactment of the Securities Acts Amendments of 1975, which strengthened the SEC's supervisory authority over stock exchanges and other self-regulatory organizations. The 1975 Amendments also directed the SEC to use its powers to facilitate the creation of a "national market system" combining the various stock exchanges and the over-the-counter market into a unified trading system. However, as a result of timidity on the Commission's part and strong opposition from certain segments of the industry, little progress has been made toward this goal over the past decade. In the meantime, the most important market development has been the interpenetration of financial service markets by banks, thrift institutions, securities dealers, investment managers, commodities dealers, insurance companies and other, each of which previously operated in relatively separate and well-defined areas. Thus, a major part of the SEC's effort has been directed toward defining the "market" which it has authority and responsibility to regulate.

Market Volatility. In the 1980s, a principal focus of SEC attention has been the increased short-term volatility of the stock market (that is, large rapid increases or decreases in prices), which has coincided with a dramatic increase in the volume of trading, particularly by institutions, the development of active markets in options, futures contracts and other derivative instruments, and the use of complex trading strategies such as "index arbitrage," "program trading" and "portfolio insurance." However, while this volatility led to sharp and unnerving drops in the stock market averages in 1987 and again in 1989, neither the SEC nor any other government agency has been able to pinpoint the cause of these developments or to suggest acceptable solutions.

Evaluations of the SEC

Among lawyers, and among students of governmental process, the SEC generally enjoys a high reputation. It has been noteworthy for the level of intelligence and integrity of its staff, the flexibility and informality of many of its procedures, and its avoidance of the political and economic pitfalls in which many other regulatory agencies have found themselves trapped. Its disclosure and enforcement policies have also been credited with making an important contribution to the generally favorable reputation which American corporate securities and American securities markets enjoy, not only among American investors, but also in foreign countries.

There has also been a good deal of criticism of the agency, however, and from several different sides. It has been criticized for being too timid in its dealings with the New York Stock Exchange and other powerful segments of the industry. On the other hand, it has been criticized for being overbearing and having inadequate regard for the rights of small firms and individuals charged with violations of the law.

Economists have criticized the Commission for lack of attention to the economic consequences of its actions, and for following enforcement policies which do not promote, and may even hinder, the efficient allocation of capital. Its disclosure policies have also been criticized as not providing investors with information that is useful in making sound investment decisions. On the other hand, the agency has come under criticism by securities industry spokesmen for giving too much emphasis and publicity to wrongdoing in the industry, and not doing enough to promote the industry and help in its battles with competitors.

However, while economists, lawyers and accountants may argue interminably about ultimate effects, the SEC's administration of the federal securities laws, viewed in itself, must be judged a major accomplishment of the governmental process. The mere fact that the agency has been able to function for over 50 years without becoming a captive of the industry, without becoming hopelessly bureaucratized, and without being tarnished by any major scandals, and that it has continued to serve as a focus for the aspirations of intelligent, public-spirited observers of the securities markets, both within and without the industry, is a tribute both to the people who designed this rather unique regulatory system and to those who have made it work.

The SEC Staff

While the Commission itself is ultimately responsible for all decisions, the day-to-day administration of the Acts is largely delegated to the staff. About two-thirds of the staff is located at the Commission's head office in Washington, and the remainder in regional and branch offices in financial centers around the country. The head office staff is divided functionally into four "divisions" and a number of separate "offices."

In terms of overall size, the Commission staff reached an early peak of 1,683 employees in 1941, at the height of its activity under the Public Utility Holding Company Act. As a consequence of repeated budget cuts, the staff shrank to a low of 666 in 1955, then increased steadily to about 1,400 in 1963. It remained at that level until 1971, increased again to about 2,000 in 1975, at which level it has remained for the past fifteen years.

The two largest divisions are the Division of Corporation Finance, which is responsible for reviewing and processing the various disclosure documents filed by corporations and other issuers, and the Division of Enforcement, which is responsible for investigations of alleged violations and for the conduct of administrative and court proceedings against alleged violators.

Two smaller divisions, Market Regulation and Investment Management, assist the Commission in developing its regulatory policies over the securities markets, broker-dealer firms, and investment managers.

Of the supporting "offices", the two with the most important substantive responsibilities are the Office of General Counsel and the Office of Chief Accountant. In addition to his responsibilities for advising the Commission and its Divisions on questions of law, the General Counsel is responsible for representation of the Commission in its district and appellate court proceedings, as well as preparing the Commission's legislative proposals and its comments on legislation proposed by others. The Chief Accountant has the key role in developing the Commission's position on accounting questions and in presenting the Commission's position in deliberations of the standard-setting bodies in the accounting profession. (See section on Self-Regulation below).

The Commission and its staff have always been dominated by lawyers. A large majority of the men and women who have served as members of the Commission have been lawyers, and a predominant portion of the Commission's professional staff positions (including many non-lawyer positions) have generally been filled by lawyers.

In contrast to most other government regulatory agencies, the SEC has a very small economic staff, and engages in almost none of the rate-setting and franchise-granting activities which occupy a large part of the attention of most other regulatory agencies.

"Self-Regulation"

Rather than relying solely on regulation by the SEC, the federal securities laws reserve a uniquely important role for "self-regulation" by industry and professional groups. Stock exchanges had been regulating the activities of their members for more than 140 years prior to the passage of the Securities Exchange Act of 1934, and that Act incorporated the exchanges into the regulatory structure, subject to certain oversight powers in the SEC. In fact, in that respect, the 1934 Act might be considered a relic of the approach followed in the National Industrial Recovery Act of 1933, President Roosevelt's ill-fated attempt to impose self-regulatory "codes" on all industries, which was declared unconstitutional by the Supreme Court in 1935.

When Congress decided to impose more comprehensive regulation on the over-the-counter market, it adopted the approach already being followed with respect to the exchanges. Section 15A of the Securities Exchange Act, added by the Maloney Act in 1938, authorized the establishment of "national securities associations" to exercise self-regulatory authority over dealings in the over-the-counter market. The National Association of Securities Dealers (NASD), the only association established pursuant to that authority, regulates the OTC market in a manner roughly comparable to the regulation by the exchanges of transactions effected through their facilities.

The delegation of governmental power to industry organizations has raised complex questions as to the legal consequences of the exercise or non-exercise of that power, and as to the procedural safeguards which should attend its use. The financial debacle of the securities industry in 1969–70, combined with the inability of the various self-regulatory organizations to develop a workable national market system or an efficient system for the clearing and settlement of transactions, have raised even more serious doubts about the effectiveness and public-interestedness of the self-regulatory organizations. The Securities Acts Amendments of 1975 substantially increased the SEC's supervisory power over self-regulatory activities.

In addition to the formal delegation of authority to national securities exchanges and associations, the SEC, in at least one area—accounting—has placed principal reliance on professional accountants and their organizations in setting accounting standards for reporting companies. While the SEC has sometimes nudged the accounting profession into the adoption of stricter standards for reporting of various types of transactions, and has occasionally issued its own rules superseding those of the accounting organization, it has on the whole played a rather passive role in the task of achieving uniformity and comparability in financial reporting.

Sources of Federal Securities Law

The starting point in analyzing any question of federal securities law is of course the statutes. There is no federal "common law" of securities, and any rights or liabilities must find their source in the statutes themselves. The statutes are, however, quite sketchy or ambiguous in many important areas, so that it is necessary to resort to supplemental sources of law. These are of two kinds: rules and other statements of general applicability issued by the SEC (or self-regulatory organizations), and reports of decided cases.

The SEC has broad rule-making powers under the various statutes it administers, and has exercised its authority by prescribing at least three different kinds of rules.

One category is procedural rules, setting forth the steps to be followed in proceedings before the Commission, as well as such mundane matters as the hours the Commission is open, where papers should be filed, what size type to use, and so forth.

A second important category is the type of rule the Commission writes where Congress has given it the power to fill in the terms of the statute. For example, § 14 of the 1934 Act provides that no person shall solicit proxies from shareholders of a registered company "in contravention of such rules and regulations as the Commission may prescribe * * *." Pursuant to that authority, the SEC has adopted a detailed set of rules (Regulation 14A) prescribing the form of proxy, the contents of the proxy statement, the procedures to be followed in proxy contests and in responding to proposals submitted by shareholders, and other matters.

A third important category of rules is those defining some of the general terms used in the laws. A significant example of this definitional power is the rules adopted under the 1933 Act, defining the circumstances in which secondary offerings, mergers, non-public offerings, and intrastate offerings will be exempt from 1933 Act registration requirements.

Supplementing the SEC's rules are its forms for the various statements and reports which issuers, broker-dealers and others are required to file under the Acts. Since disclosure is such an important part of the regulatory pattern, these forms (which have the legal force of rules) play an important part in defining the extent of the disclosure obligation.

Beyond the rules and forms, the SEC goes in for a good deal of "informal law-making," setting forth the views of the Commission or its staff on questions of current concern, without stating them in the form of legal requirements. The principal media for these statements are SEC "Releases" which, as the name implies, are simply statements distributed to the press, to companies and firms registered with the Commission, and to other interested persons. While Releases are also used for the proposal and adoption of rules or to meet other formal notice requirements, they are often used to set forth Commission or staff views through general statements of policy or recitation of the position taken by the Commission in various specific cases. Examples of both types will be found in these materials.

In addition to general public statements of policy, the staff has, since the Commission's early days, been willing to respond to individual private inquiries as to whether a certain transaction could be carried out in a specified manner. These responses are known as "no-action" letters, because they customarily state that "the staff will recommend no action to the Commission" if the transaction is done in the specified manner. Prior to 1970, these letters were not made public, leading to complaints that the large law firms which frequently corresponded with the SEC had access to a considerable body of "secret law" which was unavailable to other lawyers and their clients. As a result of these complaints, as well as recommendations from the Administrative Conference of the United States, the SEC now makes these letters and responses public, adding to the burdens of lawyers who wish to make sure they have thoroughly researched a particular point.

In some areas of federal securities law, notably in the registration provisions of the 1933 Act, most of the "law" is found in the rules, forms, and policy statements of the Commission, and very little in the form of decided "cases". In other areas, however, notably under the general anti-fraud provisions of the 1934 Act, there is very little in the way of formal rules, and the law has developed in the traditional "common law" manner, with courts and other tribunals deciding each case on the basis of precedents.

In these materials, you will find reports of decisions in several different types of proceedings. The SEC itself may proceed in a number of ways if it discovers what it believes to be a violation of the law.

If the alleged violator is a broker-dealer or investment adviser required to register with it, the Commission can bring a proceeding to revoke or suspend the firm's registration or take other disciplinary action. If the alleged violator is an issuer seeking to sell securities under a 1933 Act registration statement, the Commission can bring a proceeding to suspend the effectiveness of the statement. In either case, the Commission staff acts as "prosecutor" and the Commission itself makes the final decision (after initial findings by an administrative law judge). The Commission's decision is appealable to the United States Court of Appeals in the District of Columbia or for the circuit where the registrant's principal place of business is located.

If the alleged violator is an issuer not currently making a registered public offering, or a person not registered with the Commission at all, then the Commission must go to court to obtain relief. The most common type of Commission proceeding is an application to a federal district court for an injunction against future violations. In a particularly egregious case, however, the Commission may refer the matter to the Department of Justice for prosecution as a criminal violation of the securities laws.

The Commission is not a "collection agency". It has no statutory power to require a securities law violator to make restitution to people who have been injured by his violations. In a number of injunction actions, however, the SEC has requested, and the court has granted, as "ancillary relief", an order directing the violator to pay over his "profits" to a depository for distribution to persons entitled to recovery.

A person who believes himself to have been injured by a violation of the securities laws can bring a civil action in the courts for damages. He may sue either under the specific civil liability provisions of those laws, or assert an "implied" right of action under a provision prohibiting the activity in question. In recent years, there has been an enormous expansion in the number of private damage actions under the federal securities laws, particularly those asserting an implied right of action under the general anti-fraud provisions. While many of these actions relate to distinctive securities law problems, such as misleading statements or "insider trading", a substantial number have involved allegations of corporate mismanagement which might also constitute violations of state corporation law. Plaintiffs usually bring these actions under the federal securities laws to avoid restrictive state court decisions or state procedural obstacles to stockholders' derivative suits.

Prior to 1972, the United States Supreme Court reviewed very few securities cases, and when it did, it generally construed the law broadly and gave great deference to the views of the SEC. Since the addition of Justices Powell and Rehnquist in January 1972, however, the Court has taken a very restrictive view of federal securities law, particularly with respect to implied private rights of action, and has rejected the views of the SEC in almost every case in which that agency has appeared.

Another consequence of this litigation "explosion", and the resulting uncertainties surrounding civil liability under the federal securities laws, has been increased pressure for "codification" of those laws. The American Law Institute in 1978 completed work on a nine-year project to prepare a "Federal Securities Code", designed to replace all of the federal securities laws now on the books. One of the stated purposes of the proposed Code was to give more certainty and predictability to the liability provisions, particularly those creating civil liabilities under the various laws.

This proposal was controversial on a philosophical as well as a practical level. As the Reporter for the proposed Code put it, there is a conflict in legislative drafting between "equity" and "certainty". If the various laws governing business enterprises were placed on a continuum, the antitrust laws, which consist essentially of a prohibition against "restraints of trade," interpreted by the courts on a case-by-case "common law" basis, would be at one end. At the other extreme would be the Internal Revenue Code, containing extremely detailed provisions governing every conceivable type of transaction, and even more detailed regulations covering variations of those transactions, but from which virtually all tests of "justice" or "fairness" have been eliminated.

The present federal securities laws fall somewhere between these two extremes. They are more detailed and mechanical than the antitrust laws, but not, so far at least, as detailed and mechanical as the tax laws. One of the potential dangers of codification is that it would produce a complex statute which would prove lucrative to sophisticated lawyers (because nobody else would be able to understand it), but would no longer be a useful tool for dealing with the variety of devious schemes that abound in the securities field. These are considerations you should keep in mind as you consider these materials.

Where to Find the Law

The statutory supplement to this volume contains the basic provisions of the 1933 and 1934 Acts, as well as selected rules and forms under those Acts. These selections should meet your needs in studying the materials in this book and working out the related problems. To undertake further research, however, you will have to know where the various sources of law described in the preceding section can be found.

The most comprehensive and convenient source for all of the federal securities laws, SEC rules, forms, interpretations and decisions, and court decisions on securities matters is the loose-leaf Federal Securities Law Reporter published by Commerce Clearing House (CCH). This service is kept up to date with weekly supplements, and decisions and interpretations going back to 1941 can be found in annual or bi-annual "transfer binders." Pamphlet copies of the 1933 and 1934 Acts, and of the rules and forms governing the preparation of disclosure documents under those two acts, are also available from many financial printers who specialize in the preparation of such documents.

The official version of the federal securities laws is of course found in the United States Code (and in the United States Code Annotated) as §§ 77–80 of Title 15. Unfortunately, whoever was in charge of numbering the Code decided that the sections of the 1933 Act (15 U.S.C. § 77) should be numbered §§ 77a, 77b, 77c, etc. Thus § 5(b)(1) of the Act becomes 15 U.S.C. § 77e(b)(1), and § 12(2) becomes § 77m(2). The 1934 Act is handled in similar fashion in 15 U.S.C. § 78. Since everyone connected with securities regulation uses the section numbers of the Acts, rather than the Code references, the latter are omitted throughout these materials. If you want to find a section of the 1933 or 1934 Act in the Code you can do so easily, provided you remember the alphabet and have enough fingers to count to 26 (sections of the 1934 Act after § 26 are rendered as §§ 78aa, 78bb, and so forth).

The official version of the SEC rules can be found in volume 17 of the Code of Federal Regulations. Here the numbering system is more rational. 1933 Act rules are found in 17 C.F.R. § 230 under the rule number, and 1934 Act rules can be found in 17 C.F.R. § 240 in the same manner. Thus 1933 Act Rule 144 is 17 C.F.R. § 230.144, and 1934 Act Rule 10b–5 is 17 C.F.R. § 240.10b–5.

SEC releases announcing the proposal or adoption of new rules, as well as those containing significant interpretations of the law, can be found in the Federal Register for the day on which the release was issued. Other releases are not systematically or officially published in any form other than the mimeographed releases actually distributed by the Commission, numbered serially by reference to the Act or Acts to which they related, such as Securities Act Release No. 4434. Compilations of "significant" releases under certain of the Acts are available through a number of official and unofficial compilations.

The SEC's "no-action" letters, as noted above, are now publicly available. They can be examined at the SEC office in Washington, and selected letters are published or summarized in the CCH Federal Securities Law Reporter or the BNA Securities Regulation and Law Reports (described below). Complete texts of all letters are available from several sources.

The official texts of SEC decisions in administrative proceedings brought before it are distributed as "Releases" at the time they are handed down, and are eventually printed and compiled in bound volumes of "SEC Decisions and Reports".

Useful statistical and narrative information concerning the SEC's activities can be found in the Commission's "Annual Reports" to Congress. These reports are customarily available through the GPO for several years back.

Court decisions involving the federal securities laws are generally reported promptly and in full text in the CCH Federal Securities Law Reporter. Decisions of the Courts of Appeals, of course, also appear in West's Federal Reporter, Second Series (F.2d), and the more significant District Court decisions appear in the Federal Supplement (F.Supp.). SEC briefs in cases involving the securities laws, which often contain significant statements of Commission policy, are sometimes excerpted in the CCH Reporter, but are otherwise available only by request to the Commission's Office of General Counsel.

Confirmation of the maturing of "Securities Regulation" as a field of law came in 1972, when the West Digest System established it as a separate subject matter and reclassified under the new heading all of the cases which had previously lurked in scattered key numbers under "Licenses" and other headings. Volumes 37 and 38 of the Eighth Decennial Digest, therefore, contain a compilation of all federal and state securities cases reported in the National Reporter System up to 1976.

Up-to-date compilations of the constitutions, rules and interpretations of the major stock exchanges and the NASD can be found in the loose-leaf stock exchange "Guides" and the "NASD Manual" published by CCH.

As far as state securities law is concerned, the most current and comprehensive compilation of statutes, rules and administrative and court decisions is the CCH Blue Sky Law Reporter, which contains separate sections covering the law of each of the 50 states. The securities law of any particular state can also be obtained through its published statutes, published administrative regulations (if any), and official and unofficial reports of its court decisions.

So much for the primary sources of law. Secondary sources include books, articles and current periodicals.

There are a number of books on particular aspects of securities regulation or the securities markets, which are referred to at appropriate points herein. Because of the enormous scope and complexity of, and frequent changes in, the law, however, a major portion of any secondary research into questions of current interest must focus on articles and notes, in law reviews and other publications. The number of articles and notes on legal aspects of securities regulation in recent years is truly astonishing.

In addition to articles and notes in the general law reviews published by law schools and bar associations, there are several publications devoted specifically to securities and related matters, including "Securities Regulation Law Journal," published by Warren, Gorham & Lamont, "Review of Securities Regulation," published by Standard & Poor's, and "The Business Lawyer," published by the American Bar Association's Section of Corporation, Business and Banking Law.

A number of programs on securities law for practising lawyers, generally lasting two or three days but sometimes longer, are sponsored each year by various organizations. The transcripts of some of these programs, featuring lectures and panel discussions by SEC officials, securities law specialists and others, are published in book form, and are useful sources of discussion of current problems.

Publications summarizing current developments in securities regulation on a weekly basis include Securities Regulation and Law Report, published by Bureau of National Affairs (BNA), and the summaries accompanying the weekly supplements to the CCH Federal Securities Law Reports. Of the daily newspapers, The Wall Street Journal provides the most thorough coverage, with frequent lengthier stories providing useful background information.

The Securities Bar

There are no formal prerequisites for a lawyer to engage in securities practice. The SEC's rules of practice provide that any member of the bar of any state may practice before it. There are a substantial number of lawyers specializing in securities matters, and many thousands of others who deal with securities matters in the course of their practice.

As a field of practice, securities regulation is more a series of subspecialties than a single specialty. While there are common threads of doctrine and approach which run through the entire subject, securities practice tends to be divided in roughly the same way as the division in the SEC staff—disclosure, enforcement and regulation.

Disclosure practice revolves around the preparation of the various documents that have to be filed with the SEC. Because of the great amount of time and care that goes into 1933 Act registration statements, and the substantial fees that lawyers charge for this kind of work, that has become an important sub-specialty. Legal representation of underwriters in 1933 Act offerings tends to be concentrated in a relatively small number of firms in the major financial centers. On the other hand, many lawyers who have not specialized in securities work may find themselves representing the issuer in a 1933 Act registration when a privately-owned company they have represented decides to "go public."

The second major branch of "disclosure" work grows out of general representation of publicly-owned corporations. This work may include preparation of proxy statements and other documents in connection with annual meetings or mergers, advice to corporate officers, directors and "insiders" regarding their transactions in the corporation's securities, and preparation of other documents required by the 1934 Act.

Whereas "disclosure" work falls generally into the province of the office lawyer, "enforcement" work falls more within the province of the litigator. Enforcement work may consist of representing broker-dealers or others charged by the SEC with violations of the securities laws, but it also includes representation of plaintiffs and defendants in the rapidly increasing numbers of private damage actions alleging similar violations.

A relatively small number of lawyers specialize in the "regulation" side of the SEC's activity, representing the interests of individual firms or trade groups in SEC rule-making proceedings, Congressional hearings and other policy-making activities.

In addition to the lawyers specializing in one or another branch of securities work, there are many thousands more engaged in general business practice who from time to time face a question of securities law, such as whether a particular transaction requires registration under the 1933 Act, or whether a defrauded client can get into federal court by adding a 1934 Act claim to his state law claims. The materials in this book are designed to provide a basic groundwork for the student who is thinking of specializing in the securities field, as well as a basic familiarity with the coverage and concepts of the securities laws for those who anticipate less frequent encounters with it.

One important point for every lawyer to keep in mind when doing securities work is the very broad view which the SEC and the courts are now taking with regard to the lawyer's responsibility to the investing public when advising his client on securities matters. Lawyers in securities work often do much more than simply give their client a formal opinion as to the legality of a proposed transaction or present the client's case to the SEC or the courts. Lawyers may serve on the board of directors of a client company, they are often involved in the planning and structuring of transactions, and they usually take a major role in the writing of registration statements and other disclosure documents. As a result, lawyers frequently find themselves named as defendants in proceedings brought by the SEC or private plaintiffs.

Selected References

A. *The Securities Markets*

1. *Explanations*

G. Cooke, The Stock Markets (Rev.ed.1969).

L. Engel, How to Buy Stocks (Rev. 7th ed.1982).

G. Leffler, The Stock Market (5th ed.1987).

J. Low, The Investor's Dictionary (1964).

C. Rolo & G. Nelson (eds.), The Anatomy of Wall Street: A Guide for the Serious Investor (1968).

P. Wyckoff, Dictionary of Stock Market Terms (1964).

F. Zarb & G. Kerekes (eds.), The Stock Market Handbook (1970).

2. *Exchange and Over-the-Counter Markets*

II SEC, Special Study of Securities Markets, H.Doc. No. 95, 88th Cong., 1st Sess. 35–358, 541–678 (1963).

American Stock Exchange, Amex Databook (published periodically).

New York Stock Exchange, Fact Book (published annually).

I. Friend, et al, The Over-the-Counter Securities Market (1958).

L. Loll & J. Buckley, The Over-the-Counter Securities Market (4th ed.1981).

J. Seligman, The SEC and the Future of Finance (1985).

3. *Economic Critiques*

W. Baumol, The Stock Market and Economic Efficiency (1965).

J. Lorie & M. Hamilton, The Stock Market: Theories and Evidence (2d ed.1985).

B. Malkiel, A Random Walk Down Wall Street (4th ed.1985).

S. Robbins, The Securities Markets: Operations and Issues (1966).

R. West & S. Tinic, The Economics of the Stock Market (1971).

4. *Revelations of Wall Street Practices*

H. Baruch, Wall Street: Security Risk (1971).

R. Dirks & L. Gross, The Great Wall Street Scandal (1974).

J. Brooks, Once in Golconda: A True Drama of Wall Street 1920–38 (1969); The Seven Fat Years: Chronicles of Wall Street (1958); The Go-Go Years (1973).

J. Galbraith, The Great Crash, 1929 (4th ed.1985).

G. Goodman ("Adam Smith"), The Money Game (1968); Supermoney (1972).

M. Hellerman, Wall Street Swindler: An Insider's Story of Mob Operations in the Stock Market (1977).

D. McClintick, Stealing from the Rich: The Home-Stake Oil Swindle (1977).

S. Shapiro, Wayward Capitalists: Target of the Securities and Exchange Commission (1984).

B. *Federal Regulation of Securities*

1. *Explanations*

T. Hazen, Hornbook on the Law of Securities Regulation (2d ed. 1990).

L. Loss & J. Seligman, Securities Regulation (3d ed. 1988–).

L. Loss, Fundamentals of Securities Regulation (2d ed. 1988).

D. Ratner, Securities Regulation in a Nutshell (3d ed.1988).

H. Bloomenthal, 1984 Securities Law Handbook.

E. Thomas & R. Shields, Federal Securities Act Handbook (5th ed. 1984).

2. *Origins*

R. de Bedts, The New Deal's SEC (1964).

M. Parrish, Securities Regulation and the New Deal (1970).

F. Pecora, Wall Street Under Oath (1939).

3. *Evaluations*

W. Cary, Politics and the Regulatory Agencies (1967).

R. Karmel, Regulation by Prosecution: The Securities and Exchange Commission v. Corporate America (1982).

H. Kripke, The S.E.C. and Corporate Disclosure: Regulation in Search of a Purpose (1979).

R. Posner & K. Scott, (eds.), Economics of Corporation Law and Securities Regulation (1980).

J. Seligman, The Transformation of Wall Street (1982).

Fifty Years of Federal Securities Regulation: Symposium on Contemporary Problems in Securities Regulation, 70 Va.L.Rev. 545 (1984).

C. *Commodities Markets and Regulation*

P. Johnson & T. Hazen, Commodities Regulation (2d ed. 1989).

P. Johnson, A. Peck, W. Silber, J. Stein, H. Stoll & R. Whaley, Futures Markets (A. Peck ed. 1985).

PART I

REGULATION OF OFFERINGS BY ISSUERS

CHAPTER 1

DISCLOSURE IN PUBLIC OFFERINGS

A. INTRODUCTION

A major portion of the work of the SEC (and of lawyers engaged in securities practice) is devoted to the registration of new offerings of securities under the 1933 Act. As we will see later, there are many people who feel there has been undue emphasis on this particular activity—to the detriment of other problem areas. Nevertheless, the distinctive approach and tone of American securities regulation has developed largely out of the concepts and practices in administering the Securities Act of 1933. An understanding of those concepts and practices, therefore, is essential not only to the lawyer engaged in that particular activity, but to anyone involved with any of the "disclosure" aspects of federal securities law.

---

1. The Business and Legal Context

The materials in this section are designed as a general introduction to the way in which new issues of securities are distributed to the public and how the registration process works.

In reading these materials, you may find it helpful to keep in mind two basic patterns. The first is the sequence of participation in the movement of securities from the issuer to the public:

ISSUER ⟶ UNDERWRITERS ⟶ DEALERS ⟶ PUBLIC

Of course, not every distribution follows this pattern, but it is the one on which the definitions and restrictions of the 1933 Act are based.

The second basic pattern to keep in mind is the time sequence established by the 1933 Act, by reference to the date on which the registration statement is filed and the date on which it becomes "effective":

	FILING DATE		EFFECTIVE DATE	
PRE-FILING PERIOD		WAITING PERIOD		POST-EFFECTIVE PERIOD

As you will see, the prohibitions of § 5 of the 1933 Act operate in different ways in these three periods, and have therefore had a significant influence in determining the order in which the various steps in the distribution process are carried out.

SECURITIES REGULATION

By Louis Loss and Joel Seligman

Pp. 317–372 (3d ed.1989).*

The registration and prospectus provisions of the Securities Act of 1933 can be understood—and their effectiveness evaluated—only on the background of the techniques by which securities are distributed in the United States. There are five basic "underwriting" techniques, sometimes with variations: strict or "old-fashioned" underwriting, firm-commitment underwriting, best-efforts underwriting, competitive bidding, and shelf registration.

1. Strict or "Old-Fashioned" Underwriting

Under the traditional English system of distribution—which is no longer common in that country—the issuer did not sell to an investment banking house for resale to the public, either directly or through a group of dealers. Instead, a designated "issuing house" advertised the issue and received applications and subscriptions from the public on the issuer's behalf after an announced date. When sufficient applications had been received, an announcement was made that "the lists are closed" and the issuer proceeded to allot the securities directly to the applicants or subscribers, using various methods of proration in the event of an oversubscription. Securities firms normally subscribed to new issues not for their own accounts with a view to resale at a profit, but only as brokers for the accounts of their customers. Before the public offering was thus made, the issue was "underwritten" in order to ensure that the company would obtain the amount of funds it required.

This was underwriting in the strict insurance sense. For a fee or premium, the underwriter agreed to take up whatever portion of the issue was not purchased by the public within a specified time. And just as insurance companies frequently reinsure large underwritings with other companies in order to distribute the risk, so the initial underwriter often protected himself by agreements with sub-underwriters, to which the issuer was not a party. The typical underwriting syndicate was not limited to investment bankers or so-called issuing houses. It included or even consisted entirely of insurance companies or investment trusts or other institutions, or even large individual investors who thus obtained large blocks of securities at less than the issue price. Accordingly, the underwriters planned to hold for investment any securities they might be required to take. Even the issuing houses that found themselves required to take up unsubscribed portions of issues were inclined to hold them temporarily until they found a buyer on favorable terms, instead of trying to resell them immediately, at a loss if necessary, as underwriters generally do in this country when issues get "sticky."

This method of distribution is called in the United States "strict" or "old-fashioned" or "stand-by" underwriting. It is seldom, if ever, used here except in connection with offerings to existing stockholders by means of warrants or rights. In that field, its use, with various modifications, is less common than it once was. Of the $3 billion of common stock issues registered with the SEC for cash sale for the account of the issuer in the three years 1951, 1953, and 1955 and offered through investment bankers, 59 percent were "rights offerings." In contrast, during 1971–1975, 578 listed common stock issues were registered under the Securities Act of 1933. Of these issues, 484 (83.7 percent) were not rights offerings, 56 (9.7 percent) were rights offerings with standby underwriting, and 38 (6.6 percent) were "pure" rights offerings.

* * *

2. Firm–Commitment Underwriting

For some time, the most prevalent type of underwriting has been the "firm-commitment" variety. It is not, technically, underwriting in the classic insurance sense. But its purpose and effect are much the same in that it assures the issuer of a specified amount of money at a certain time (subject frequently to specified conditions precedent in the underwriting contract) and shifts the risk of the market (at least in part) to the investment bankers. The issuer typically sells the entire issue outright to a group of securities firms, represented by one or several "manager[s]" or "principal underwriters" or "representatives." They, in turn, sometimes sell at a price differential to a "selling group" of dealers, or sell at another differential to the public. * * *

The passage of the Securities Act of 1933 made for a simplification of this system. Under the statute only negotiations between the issuer and "underwriters" are permitted before the filing of the registration statement. Until then, the securities may not be offered to the public or even to dealers who are not "underwriters" within the statutory definition. And until the actual effective date of the registration statement, no sales or contracts may be made except with underwriters. This, in practice, means that there is usually a short period (a few hours at most) between the signing of the underwriting contract and the effective date of the registration statement during which whoever is committed to purchase at a fixed price cannot legally shift his liability against a possible market decline. To protect the underwriter until the closing (usually one week later) the "market out" clause in the underwriting contract was developed.

Although the use of this clause is by no means universal, it is not considered "cricket" to take advantage of it; it typically provides that the manager of the underwriting group (or the representatives of the group) may terminate the agreement if before the date of public offering (or before the date of the closing or settlement between underwriters and issuer) the issuer or any subsidiary sustains a material adverse change, trading in the securities is suspended, minimum or maximum prices or government restrictions on securities trading are put into effect, a general banking moratorium is declared, or, in the judgment of the managing underwriter (or, alternatively, the representatives of the underwriters or a majority in interest of the several underwriters) material changes in "general economic, political or financial conditions" or the effect of international conditions on financial markets in the United States make it impracticable or inadvisable to market the securities at the specified public offering price. This clause is much broader than the traditional *force majeure* provision. Another result of the Securities Act and the stock transfer taxes enforced until 1965 was a tendency to reduce the number of transfers between groups and to enlarge the number of "underwriters" who bear the initial risk. In effect, the originating banker and the purchase and banking groups have all been combined into a single "underwriting syndicate or group."

It is difficult to generalize about firm-commitment underwriting today, because it may vary from issue to issue. Each of the leading investment banks tends to develop variations of its own. Nevertheless, certain patterns are familiar. Quite early the managing or lead underwriter specifically disclaiming any obligation gives the issuer sufficient assurance orally (or by a "letter of intent") to warrant the issuer's going ahead with the extensive work and expenses that are necessary. While letters of intent vary widely in detail, the letter normally will describe the basic structure of the proposed underwriting and will include the type of security to be offered, the size of the offering, the nature of the offering (e.g., primary, secondary, combination, or rights offering), whether the underwriting will be on a firm-commitment or best-efforts basis, the underwriters' compensation and expenses, and a contemplated price range or formula or mechanism for determining the price. The lead or managing underwriter then organizes an underwriting syndicate. Usually, invitations (normally in the form of telexes) are sent to prospective members after the registration statement is filed with the SEC. The invitations are accompanied by copies of the registration statement, a preliminary blue sky memorandum, and proofs of the basic underwriting agreement. Most major underwriters currently use a "blanket" agreement among underwriters into which underwriters are added by exchanges of telexes. The underwriting syndicate is formally created by a contract among its members, usually called the "agreement among underwriters," by which they agree to be represented in their negotiations with the issuer either by the managing or lead underwriter or by one, two, or three of their members, whom it is currently the style to call the "representatives of the underwriters." The agreement among underwriters typically grants to the managing underwriter broad authority over the offering process. The managing underwriter is authorized to "stabilize" the market by repurchasing shares in the open market, to charge each underwriter for expenses incurred by the manager, and, in the case of a "sticky" deal, to change the offering terms. The agreement also specifies the compensation of the managing underwriter, the underwriters in the syndicate, and, sometimes, the dealers. The number of shares each underwriter ultimately will be allotted for direct sale normally is specified on the date of the public offering.

Through the managing underwriter, all of the underwriters enter into an "underwriting agreement" (sometimes called a "purchase contract") directly with the issuer. The underwriting agreement normally includes the issuer's representations and warranties (e.g., the registration statement was prepared in conformity with the requirements of the Securities Act of 1933) and the obligation of the underwriters to purchase a specified number of securities on the closing date, subject to the conditions that the underwriters receive satisfactory opinions from the issuer's counsel and "comfort letters" from the independent public accountants. * * *

The method of determining the participations of the several underwriters is by no means fixed. How much a particular house gets is apt to depend on its prestige, its capital, its distributing capacity, its geographical location, whether it has any special outlets, and frequently the issuer's wishes. The participation of a given house is not necessarily related to the amount it can distribute. Some houses join the group primarily as underwriters, with a view to making a profit out of assuming their share of the risk, and they may give up most or all of their participations for sale by the representatives, for their accounts, to institutions and dealers. In other words, the amount reserved for such sale is not always prorated among the accounts of all the underwriters. Sometimes it is, but sometimes each member of the group indicates to the managing underwriter what proportion of its share it would like to have for its own retail distribution (that is, its "retention"). The portion that particular houses thus distribute at retail usually varies between 25 and 75 percent. Those underwriters who want more for their own retail distribution become selected dealers.

During the life of the underwriting syndicate, all of the underwriters and participating dealers make a concurrent public offering at a uniform (or "fixed") price with uniform concessions at each level of the distribution. The purchase price paid to the issuer and usually the initial public offering price to be paid by investors are agreed to by the issuer and managing underwriters. Dealers' concessions and discounts are determined by the managing underwriter. After the initial public offering, the manager has a right (that is not customarily used) to change the offering price, concessions, and discounts. The problem of resale price maintenance will be examined in a subsequent chapter. On occasion, there are "repurchase penalties," by which the representatives have the power to cancel the dealer's concession on securities repurchased by the representatives in the market at or below the public offering price. The theory is that the dealer did not properly perform his function of "placing" the securities if they immediately found their way back onto the market, and hence, did not earn his concession; or, as it is sometimes said, he did not "find a good home" for them.

During equity offerings (but almost never during debt issues), the managing underwriter is authorized, as the syndicate managers were before 1933, to "stabilize" the market on behalf of the underwriting group. Typically the managing underwriter places a bid for the security being underwritten at a price at or just under the public offering price. The purpose of stabilization is to "peg" or put a floor under the market to prevent the overhanging supply of securities that are being distributed from depressing the market during the distribution. Stabilization is a complicated process subject to detailed SEC regulation that will be examined in a later chapter. While the liability of each underwriter to the issuer is several, the members of the group are responsible for their proportionate shares of the underwriting expenses, including carrying costs, and they participate jointly in the stabilizing account.

Often the managing underwriter may also exercise an "overallot." The manager allots to the syndicate for sale more shares than they are obligated to purchase under the underwriting agreement as a means to protect against cancellations and to dispose of securities acquired as a result of stabilizing purchases. * * *

The difference between the price at which members of the public buy an underwritten security and the amount received by the issuer is known as the "gross spread." The spread may range in size from a fraction of 1 percent to 10 percent or more. Typically, initial public offers will have spreads of 7 to 10 percent.

The spread is normally composed of three parts. First, the management fee for the managing underwriter typically will involve approximately 20 to 25 percent of the spread. This fee is split if there is more than one managing underwriter. Second, the underwriting syndicate will receive an underwriting commission, normally about 20 percent, for assuming the risk of the issue. All of the underwriting expenses are charged against this account, including "road show" expenses, printing, counsel, stabilization, and overallotment expenses. In many instances, the primary motivation to join an underwriting syndicate is to ensure a dealer's allotment of stock. Third, the "selling concession" received for any securities sold to the public by any underwriter or dealer participating in the offering usually amounts to about 60 percent of the gross spread. For example, the underwriters may buy a million shares of stock from the issuer at $23 and sell part of them to selected dealers at $24 with a view to a public offering price of $25. If the managing underwriter received a fee of one-half the underwriting spread of $1, this would mean that for each share the managing underwriter sold to the public, it would receive the entire spread of $2 less underwriting expenses. For each share the manager sold to a dealer, it would receive the underwriting spread of $1 minus expenses. Similarly, for each share a member of the underwriting syndicate sold at retail, it would receive the entire spread of $2 less the managing underwriter's fee ($.50) and underwriting expenses.

In addition to underwriting costs (underwriters usually pay dealers out of their spread), an issuer has other expenses in connection with an underwriting. * * *

3. Best–Efforts Underwriting

Companies that are not well established are not apt to find an underwriter that will give a firm-commitment and assume the risk of distribution. Of necessity, therefore, they customarily distribute their securities through firms that merely undertake to use their best efforts. Paradoxically, this type of distribution is also preferred on occasion by companies that are so well established that they can do without any underwriting commitment, thus saving on the cost of distribution. The securities house, instead of buying the issue from the company and reselling it as principal, sells it for the company as agent; and its compensation takes the form of an agent's commission rather than a merchant's or dealer's profit. There may still be a selling group to help in the merchandising. But its members likewise do not buy from the issuer; they are subagents. This, of course, is not really underwriting; it is simply merchandising.

4. Competitive Bidding

One of the most controversial of the Commission's basic policies under the Public Utility Holding Company Act was its adoption in 1941 of a rule requiring competitive bidding in the sale of issues subject to that statute. Competitive bidding in one form or another has been the accepted method of financing by municipalities and public instrumentalities since the turn of the century. * * *

5. Shelf Registration

[See SEC Rule 415 and pp. 76, 218 below.]

* * *

6. Securities Underwriting in General

There is nothing immutable about these general methods of distribution. The investment banking industry, being very much alive, is continually studying and developing new techniques. The developments in shelf registered offerings are an illustration. Moreover, the exigencies of particular financing problems occasionally give rise to interesting modifications of the basic patterns.

Selected References

United States v. Morgan, 118 F.Supp. 621, 635–55 (S.D.N.Y.1953).

V. Carosso, Investment Banking in America: A History (1970).

I. Friend et al., Investment Banking and the New Issues Market (1967).

Dooley, The Effects of Civil Liability on Investment Banking and the New Issues Market, 58 Va.L.Rev. 776 (1972).

Douglas & Bates, Some Effects of the Securities Act Upon Investment Banking, 1 U.Chi.L.Rev. 283 (1933).

Hayes, Investment Banking: Power Structure in Flux, 49 Harv.Bus.Rev. No. 2, at 136 (Mar.–Apr.1971).

GOING PUBLIC—PRACTICE, PROCEDURE AND CONSEQUENCES

By Carl W. Schneider, Joseph M. Manko and Robert S. Kant

27 Villanova L.Rev. 1 (1981).[a]

* * *

THE REGISTRATION STATEMENT

The registration statement is the disclosure document required to be filed with the SEC in connection with a registered offering. It consists physically of two principal parts. Part I of the registration statement is the prospectus, which is the only part that normally goes to the public offerees of the securities. It is the legal offering document. Part II of the registration statement contains supplemental information which is available for public inspection at the office of the SEC.

The registration forms, Regulation S–K, Regulation S–X and the Industry Guides (when applicable) specify the information to be contained in the registration statement. Regulation S–K sets forth detailed disclosure requirements which are applicable in various contexts under the securities laws; Regulation S–X similarly sets forth financial statement requirements; and the Industry Guides require specific disclosure applicable to certain prescribed businesses such as oil and gas and banking. In addition, Regulation C sets forth certain general requirements as to the registration of securities including filing fees,

a. © Copyright 1981 by the authors. Reprinted with permission. The portions of the article reproduced below reflect revisions by the authors in 1983.

the number of copies of the registration statements and amendments to be filed, signature requirements, paper and type size and other mechanical aspects of registration.

The registration forms contain a series of "items" and instructions (generally referring to the disclosure requirements contained in Regulation S–K), in response to which disclosures must be made. But they are not forms in the sense that they have blanks to be completed like a tax return. Traditionally, the prospectus describes the company's business and responds to all the disclosures required in narrative rather than item-and-answer form. It is prepared as a brochure describing the company and the securities to be offered. The usual prospectus is a fairly stylized document, and there is a customary sequence for organizing the material.

* * *

In the typical first public offering, the items to which it is most difficult to respond, and which require the most creative effort in preparation, deal with the description of the company's business, properties, material transactions with insiders, and use of proceeds. Other matters required to be disclosed in the prospectus deal with the details of the underwriting, the plan for distributing the securities, capitalization, pending legal proceedings, competition, description of securities being registered, identification of directors and officers and their remuneration, options to purchase securities, and principal holders of securities. There are also detailed requirements concerning financial statements and financial information concerning the company's business segments.

In Part II of the registration statement is supplemental information of a more formal type which is not required to be given to each investor. Unlike the prospectus, Part II is prepared in item-and-answer form. One requirement which is sometimes troublesome calls for disclosure of recent sales of unregistered securities and a statement of the exemption relied upon. Counsel may discover that past issuances of securities violated the '33 Act. In some such cases, the result may be that the company's financial statements must reflect a very large contingent liability under the '33 Act. In some cases, past violations may be remedied by a rescission offer. If past violations have been too flagrant, the offering may have to be deferred. Part II also contains supplemental financial schedules, as well as a list of exhibits which are filed with the registration statement. Although the information in Part II normally is not seen by individual investors, sophisticated analysts and financial services may make extensive use of it, particularly the supplemental financial schedules.

In preparing a prospectus, the applicable form is merely the beginning. The forms are quite general and apply to all types of businesses, securities, and offerings except for a few industries or limited situations for which special forms have been prepared. In the course of administration over the years, the Commission has given specific content to the general disclosure requirements. It often requires disclosures on a number of points within the scope of the form but not explicitly covered by the form itself. Furthermore, in addition to the information that the form expressly requires, the company must add any information necessary to make the statements made not misleading. Thus, the prospectus may not contain a half-truth—a statement which may be literally true but is misleading in context.

The Commission's views on many matters change from time to time. SEC practitioners, both lawyers and accountants, constantly exchange news of what the Commission is currently requiring as reflected in its letters of comments.

The Commission has also evolved certain principles of emphasis in highlighting disclosures of adverse facts. It cannot prohibit an offering from being made if disclosure is adequate, but its policies on disclosure can make the offering look highly unattractive. In particular, if there are sufficient adverse factors in an offering, these are required to be set forth in detail in the very beginning of the prospectus under a caption such as "Introductory Statement" or "Risk Factors of the Offering." However, many new issues of going businesses do not require this treatment and counsel must make a judgment in each case. Some of the adverse factors which may be collected under such a heading include lack of business history; adverse business experience; operating losses; dependence upon particular customers, suppliers, and key personnel; lack of a market for the security offered; competitive factors; certain types of transactions with insiders; a low book value for the stock compared to the offering price; potential dilution which may result from the exercise of convertible securities, options, or warrants; and a small investment by the promoters compared with the public investment.

To the same end, the SEC has required that boldface reference be made to certain adverse factors on the prospectus cover page. The cover page statements must cross reference disclosures within the prospectus on such matters as high risk factors, immediate equity dilution of the public's investment, and various forms of underwriting compensation beyond the normal spread. To add to the brew, the Commission sometimes insists that certain factors be emphasized beyond what the attorneys working on the matter consider to be their true importance. A usual example is that prominent attention must be called to transactions between the company and its management. Often, matters of relative insignificance, in terms of amounts involved, are made to appear very important by the amount of space given and placement in the prospectus.

The SEC, which reviews the registration statement, has no authority to pass on the merits of a particular offering. The SEC has no general power to prohibit an offering because it considers the investment opportunity to be a poor risk. The sole thrust of the Federal statute is disclosure of relevant information. No matter how speculative the investment, no matter how poor the risk, the offering will comply with Federal law if all the required facts are disclosed. By contrast, some state securities or "blue sky" laws, which are applicable in the jurisdictions where the distribution takes place, do regulate the merits of the securities. Typically their standards are very indefinite, often expressed in terms of offerings which are "fair, just and equitable." In practice, state administrators exercise broad discretion in determining which offerings may be sold in their states.

The prospectus is a somewhat schizophrenic document, having two purposes which often present conflicting pulls. On the one hand, it is a selling document. It is used by the principal underwriters to form the underwriting syndicate and a dealer group, and by the underwriters and dealers to sell the securities to the public. From this point of view, it is desirable to present the best possible image. On the other hand, the prospectus is a disclosure document, an insurance policy against liability. With the view toward protection against liability, there is a tendency to resolve all doubts against the company and to make things look as bleak as possible. In balancing the purposes, established underwriters and experienced counsel, guided at least in part by their knowledge of the SEC staff attitudes, traditionally lean to a very conservative presentation, avoiding glowing adjectives and predictions. The layman frequently complains that all the glamor and romance has been lost. "Why can't you tell them," he says, "that we have the most aggressive and imaginative management in the industry?" It takes considerable client education before an attorney can answer this question to the client's satisfaction.

Until relatively recently, it was traditional to confine prospectuses principally to objectively verifiable statements of historic fact. It is now considered proper, and in some instances essential, to include some information in a prospectus, either favorable or adverse to the company, which is predictive or based upon opinions or subjective evaluations. However, no such "soft information" should be included in the prospectus unless it has a reasonable basis in fact and represents management's good faith judgment.

Preparing the Registration Statement

The "quarterback" in preparing the registration statement is normally the attorney for the company. Company counsel is principally responsible for preparing the non-financial parts of the registration statement. Drafts are circulated to all concerned. There are normally several major revisions before sending the job to the printer, and at least a few more printed drafts before the final filing. Close cooperation is required among counsel for the company, the underwriters' counsel, the accountants, and the printer. Unless each knows exactly what the others expect, additional delay, expense, and irritation are predictable.

It is essential for the issuer and all others involved in the financing to perceive correctly the role of company counsel. Counsel normally assists the company and its management in preparing the document and in performing their "due diligence" investigation to verify all disclosure for accuracy and completeness. Counsel often serves as the principal draftsman of the registration statement. Counsel typically solicits information both orally and in writing from a great many people, and exercises his best judgment in evaluating the information received for accuracy and consistency. Experience indicates that executives often overestimate their ability to give accurate information from their recollections without verification. It shows no disrespect, but merely the professionally required degree of healthy skepticism, when the lawyer insists on backup documentation and asks for essentially the same information in different ways and from different sources.

* * *

The authors consider it essential for the lawyers, accountants and executives to be in close coordination while the prospectus is being written. It frequently occurs that the lawyers and the accountants initially have different understandings as to the structure of a transaction, or the proper characterization or effect of an event. These differences may not be apparent readily, even from a careful reading of the registration statement's narrative text together with the financial statements. Lawyers sometimes miss the full financial implication of some important matter unless the accountants are readily available to amplify upon the draft statements and supply background information. The text is often written by counsel before the financial statements are available, based upon counsel's incorrect assumptions regarding the as yet unseen financial statement treatment of a transaction.

Experience indicates that the best and sometimes only way to flush out financial disclosure problems as well as inconsistencies between the narrative text and the financial statements is through the give and take of discussion as the structure of the offering is being determined and the draft registration statement is being reviewed. The accountant's participation in this process is often essential.

* * *

REVIEW BY THE SEC

After the registration statement is filed initially, the Commission's Division of Corporation Finance reviews it to see that it responds appropriately to the applicable form. The Division's staff almost always finds some deficiencies, which are communicated either by telephone, usually to company counsel, or through the "letter of comments" or "deficiency letter." Amendments to the registration statement are then filed in response to the comments. When the comments are reflected to the satisfaction of the SEC staff, the SEC issues an order allowing the registration statement to become effective. Only after the registration statement is effective may sales to the public take place.

There are styles and trends regarding the subjects on which staff comments tend to focus. Recent public pronouncements by the staff indicate that subjects to receive particular attention in the review process include: the required management discussion and analysis of financial condition and results of operation, liquidity, capital resources and effects of inflation; the use of proceeds; and transactions between the issuer and related parties.

If counsel, or the accountants with respect to financial comments, believe that the staff's comments are inappropriate or should not be met for some other reason, the comments will be discussed with the examiner, usually by telephone but in person if the matter is sufficiently serious. If a point cannot be resolved to counsel's satisfaction through discussions with the examiner, it is considered appropriate to request that the matter be submitted to the Branch Chief who supervises the examiner. When a significant issue is involved, higher levels of staff review may be requested if counsel remains unsatisfied. However, review should be sought at successive levels, and counsel should not leapfrog to a senior official before the subordinates have been consulted. The Commission's staff is generally reasonable in dealing with counsel's objections. However, as a practical matter, an offering cannot usually come to market unless an accommodation has been reached on all comments. Therefore, the staff usually has the last word on whether the company has adequately responded to the comments, even if the comments are not legally binding in the formal sense.

* * *

When the comment letter is received, there is a natural tendency to focus attention solely on the points raised by the Commission. However, it is most important to remember that the registration statement must be accurate as of the time it becomes effective. Accordingly, it must be reviewed carefully in its entirety just before the effective date to be sure that all statements are updated to reflect significant intervening developments, whether or not they relate to sections covered by the Commission's comments. The Commission also has a rule relating to the updating of financial statements. Generally speaking, the rule requires the most recent financial statements to be as of a date within 135 days of the date the filing is expected to become effective. The rule is phrased in terms of the issuer's expectations, suggesting that financial statements may be somewhat more than 135 days old if the issuer reasonably expected the registration statement to become effective within the 135-day period, but unanticipated delays occurred. However, the staff tends to interpret the rule as a fairly inflexible requirement that financial statements be no more than 135 days stale on the effective date. Given the inherent post-balance sheet delay required to prepare the financial statements for the filing and the further delay for SEC review, it would be prudent to anticipate that the prospectus will require financial information which is at least three months more current than the financials in the original filing.

PRE-EFFECTIVE OFFERS

Prior to the initial filing of the registration statement, no public offering, either orally or in writing, is permitted. For this purpose, the concept of offering has been given an expansive interpretation. Publicity about the company or its products may be considered an illegal offering, in the sense that it is designed to stimulate an interest in the securities, even if the securities themselves are not mentioned. A violation of this prohibition is often referred to as "gun jumping." Under a specific rule, limited announcements concerning the proposal to make a public offering through a registration statement are permitted.

In the interval between the first filing with the Commission and the effective date, the so-called "waiting period," the company and the underwriters may distribute preliminary or "red herring" prospectuses. The term "red herring" derives from the legend required to be printed in red ink on the cover of any prospectus which is distributed before the effective date of the registration statement. The legend is to the effect that a registration statement has been filed but has not become effective, and the securities may not be sold nor may offers to buy be accepted prior to the effective date.

During the waiting period between the filing of the registration statement and its effective date, the lead underwriter may escort company executives on a tour around the country—often called a "dog and pony show." The purpose of this tour is to attend meetings with prospective underwriters, who will be invited into the underwriting syndicate, and possibly also analysts and potential institutional investors.

During the waiting period, oral selling efforts are permitted but no written sales literature—that is, "free writing"—is permitted other than the red herring prospectus. Tombstone advertisements, so-called because the very limited notice of the offering which is permitted is often presented in a form resembling a tombstone, are not considered selling literature and may be published during the waiting period, although it is much more common for them to be published after the effective date. In addition, publicly-held companies must continue to make timely disclosure of factual information concerning themselves and their products during this waiting period so as not to interrupt the normal flow of information; of course, they may not do so to instigate publicity to facilitate the sale of stock. Through the use of a red herring prospectus and by making oral offers by telephone or otherwise, the underwriters may offer the security and may accept "indications of interest" from purchasers prior to the effective date. However, as indicated, no sales can be made during the waiting period.

Ideally, the investor should have the final prospectus available on which to base his decision whether to buy the security. Often this is not the case. It is theoretically possible to avoid entirely the requirements for delivering a prospectus to a purchaser without violating the law. The requirements can be avoided if the completed transaction is consummated without using the mails or any means or instruments of interstate commerce for any step from initial offer to final payment by the purchaser. In the much more typical situation, the offer and acceptance is by telephone, and the buyer first receives the final prospectus in the mail with the confirmation of the sale. He is thereby informed, assuming that he reads the prospectus and can understand it, about what he has already purchased. However, the document arrives much too late to aid in his initial decision whether to buy the security. Indeed, one commentator has dubbed it a "retrospectus." In order to counteract this, the SEC has undertaken certain steps to insure that a final prospectus or a substantially final red herring will be sent in advance of the confirmation to those indicating an interest during the waiting period.

The Underwriting Agreement

The company often signs a "letter of intent" with its managing underwriter once the selection of the underwriter has been made. If used, the letter outlines the proposed terms of the offering and the underwriting compensation. However, it expressly states that it is not intended to bind either party, except with respect to specific matters. One typical exception is a binding provision dealing with payment of one party's expenses by the other under certain conditions if the offering aborts before the letter of intent is superceded by the formal underwriting agreement.

In a "firm commitment" underwriting agreement, the underwriters agree that they will purchase the shares being offered for the purpose of resale to the public. The underwriters must pay for and hold the shares for their own account if they are not successful in finding public purchasers. This form of underwriting is almost always used by the larger underwriters, and provides the greater assurance of raising the desired funds. In the other common type of underwriting arrangement, the underwriters agree to use their "best efforts" to sell the issue as the company's agent. To the extent that purchasers cannot be found, the issue is not sold. Some best efforts agreements provide that no shares will be sold unless buyers can be found for all, while others set a lower minimum such as fifty percent. For certain special types of securities, such as tax shelter limited partnership offerings, even the major underwriters normally use the best efforts or agency underwriting relationship.

In either form of underwriting, the underwriters' obligations are usually subject to many conditions, various "outs" such as the right not to close in the event of certain specified adverse developments prior to the closing date, and compliance by the company with its numerous representations and warranties.[1] The underwriters also condition their

1. In Walk-In v. Breuer, 818 F.2d 260 (2d Cir.1987), the court affirmed a judgment of $33 million against an underwriter which refused to accept the securities at the closing, arguing that it was excused from performance by "adverse market con-

obligations upon the receipt of certain opinions of counsel and representations, sometimes called a "cold comfort letter," from the company's auditors.

The binding firm underwriting agreement normally is not signed until within twenty-four hours of the expected effective date of the registration statement—often on the morning of effectiveness. Thus, throughout the process of preparing the registration statement and during the waiting period, the company has incurred very substantial expenses with no assurance that the offering will take place. Once preparation of the registration statement has begun, however, reputable underwriters rarely refuse to complete the offering, although this can occur with some frequency, especially for small and highly speculative offerings, if there is a sharp market drop during, the waiting period. However, as indicated above, the underwriters must price the offering and organize the underwriting syndicate in relationship to market conditions prevailing at the time of the offering. Thus, if market conditions have worsened materially after the letter of intent stage, the issue must either come to the market at a price below that originally contemplated, or it must be postponed until conditions improve. Furthermore, it is not uncommon for underwriters to suggest a reduction in the size of the offering if the market conditions are unfavorable. The company may find itself in a position of accepting a less than satisfactory final proposal, regarding size and pricing of the offering, as a preferable alternative to postponement or complete abandonment of the offering. On the other hand, sharply improved market conditions may result in a higher offering price than the parties originally anticipated.

Final settlement with the underwriters usually takes place seven to ten days after the registration statement has become effective, so as to allow the underwriters time to obtain the funds from their customers. At that time, the company receives the proceeds of the sale, net of the underwriting compensation.

* * *

PRELIMINARY PREPARATION

For the average first offering, a very substantial amount of preliminary work is required which does not relate directly to preparing the registration statement as such. To have a vehicle for the offering, the business going public normally must be conducted by a single corporation or a parent corporation with subsidiaries. In most cases, the business is not already in such a neat package when the offering project commences. It is often conducted by a number of corporations under common ownership, by partnerships, or by combinations of business entities. Considerable work must be done in order to reorganize the

ditions", as provided in the underwriting agreement. The court found that the real reason for the underwriter's refusal was the fact that Walk-In stock had declined from $6 to $4 a share after the offering, and not adverse conditions in the market for securities generally.

various entities by mergers, liquidations and capital contributions. Even when there is a single corporation, a recapitalization is almost always required so that the company will have an appropriate capital structure for the public offering. A decision must be made regarding the proportion of the stock to be sold to the public. Any applicable blue sky limitations on insiders' "cheap stock" should be considered in this context, especially if the company has been organized in the relatively recent past.

Among other common projects in preparing to go public, it is often necessary to enter into, revise, or terminate employment agreements, adopt stock option plans and grant options thereunder, transfer real estate, revise leases, rewrite the corporate charter and by-laws, prepare new stock certificates, engage a transfer agent and registrar, rearrange stockholdings of insiders, draw, revise or cancel agreements among shareholders, and revamp financing arrangements.

* * *

In preparing the registration statement, there are occasionally important threshold or interpretive problems which can have a major effect on the preparation process or, indeed, on the feasibility of the offering. It is often possible to discuss such problems with the SEC staff in a pre-filing conference, although some pre-filing conference requests are denied by the staff. However, decisions to request a prefiling conference should be made with caution. Among other considerations, once a question has been asked in advance of a filing, there may be no practical alternative other than to wait for the staff's answer, which may delay a filing considerably. Frequently, the decision is made simply to proceed with the filing, resolving the threshold issue on the basis which the company considers most appropriate, in the hope that a satisfactory resolution of the problem (either the issuer's initial solution or some other) will be achieved during the review process.

TIMETABLE

Although laymen find it difficult to believe, the average first public offering normally requires two to three months of intensive work before the registration statement can be filed. One reason so much time is required is the need to accomplish the preparatory steps just referred to at the same time the registration statement is being prepared. There are many important and often interrelated business decisions to be made and implemented, and rarely are all of these questions decided definitively at the outset. Some answers must await final figures, or negotiations with underwriters, and must be held open until the last minute. Inevitably, a businessman first exposed to these considerations will change his mind several times in the interim. Furthermore, drafting of the prospectus normally begins before the financial statements are available. Almost inevitably, some rewriting must be done in the non-financial parts after the financial statements are distributed in order to blend the financial and non-financial sections together.

Laymen frequently have the frustrating feeling as the deadline approaches that everything is hopelessly confused. They are quite surprised to see that everything falls into place at the eleventh hour.

After the registration statement is filed with the Commission, the waiting period begins. It is during this interval that red herrings are distributed. The Commission reviews the registration statement and finally issues its letter of comments. There is a wide variation in the time required for the SEC to process a registration statement. Relevant factors include the level of the Commission's backlog of filings and the time of the year. There is normally a considerable rush of filings at the end of each calendar quarter, and particularly at the end of March for filings with financial statements as of December 31.

The SEC's current policy calls for the issuance of an initial letter of comments within thirty days of the filing of a registration statement, but the delay is often longer and at times has exceeded one hundred days. A recent increased number of first-time registration statements and other filings, coupled with reductions in the number of the SEC's review personnel, raised the possibility of long delays in issuing comment letters. This occurred despite various initiatives by the SEC during the past several years including the adoption of various "short-form" registration statements for certain types of companies and transactions, increases in the dollar amount of securities which could be sold without registration and the processing of certain offerings in regional offices of the SEC.

As a result, the SEC in late 1980 announced a new procedure designed to reduce delays in the review and processing of registration statements and other documents filed with it. Under the new procedure, the SEC will review offerings by public companies on a selective basis and certain registration statements of established public companies will no longer be reviewed at all. It is hoped that the new procedure will enable the SEC to reduce time delays by concentrating its resources on certain areas, including first time public offerings which will continue to receive thorough review. As of early 1983, the average time between the filing and the receipt of a comment letter for new offerings was 36 days. For repeat filings receiving full review, the average delay was 28 days, by way of comparison.

The overall time lapse between the beginning of preparation of a company's first registration statement and the final effective date may well exceed six months. Rarely will it be less than three months.

The SEC's requirements for unaudited financial statements for periods after the end of a company's last fiscal year represent another important ingredient in the timetable. In the case of a registration statement for a company going public for the first time, a company filing within forty-five days after its fiscal year end must include interim financial statements at least as current as the end of the third fiscal quarter of its most recently completed fiscal year as well as the required fiscal year end audited financial statements for the prior years; a company filing after forty-five days but within 134 days of the end of the company's most recent fiscal year end must include audited financial statements for its most recently completed fiscal year; and a company filing more than 134 days subsequent to the end of its most recent fiscal year must include interim financial statements within 135 days of the date of the filing as well as the required fiscal year end audited financial statements. The financial statements for the interim periods need not be audited, however, and the statements required are not as complete as those required for the audited periods. Of course, audited financial statements must be substituted once available in lieu of unaudited financial statements.

At the time the registration statement becomes effective, the unaudited interim financial statements must be as of a date within 135 days of the effective date, except that such financial statements may be as of the end of the third fiscal quarter of the most recently completed fiscal year if the registration statement becomes effective within forty-five days after the end of the most recent fiscal year. Audited financial statements for the most recently completed fiscal year must be included if the registration statement becomes effective between forty-five and ninety days after the end of such fiscal year.

Expenses

A major expense in going public is usually the underwriters' compensation. The underwriting cash discount or cash commission on a new issue generally ranges from 7% to 10% of the public offering price. The maximum amount of direct and indirect underwriting compensation is regulated by the National Association of Securities Dealers, Inc. (NASD), a self-regulatory agency which regulates broker-dealers. Normally, the three largest additional expenses are legal fees, accounting fees, and printing costs.

Legal fees for a first offering of at least $5,000,000 generally would be between $55,000 and $115,000, with $75,000 to $100,000 being typical. This amount includes not only the preparation of the registration statement itself, but also all of the corporate work, house cleaning and other detail which is occasioned by the public offering process. Fees for smaller offerings tend to be somewhat lower. In part, this may reflect the fact that offerings for start-up companies, which tend to be smaller in size, typically require less legal work in investigating business operations, since there are none. However, start-up offerings can be more difficult in other respects—for example, risk factors are more prevalent and minor matters may require disclosure on points which would be immaterial to an established company with a history of operations. Therefore, start-up offerings occasionally are even more demanding than offerings of larger seasoned companies.

Accounting fees can vary significantly depending on the complexity of the business, whether the financial statements to be included in the registration statement have been audited in the normal course, and the extent to which the independent accountants may be involved in the development of financial and other information to be included in the registration statement. Other factors which will cause accounting fees to vary from one registration statement to another are the extent to which the independent accountants are required to participate in meetings with counsel and underwriters' representatives and the nature and extent of procedures performed at the request of the underwriters for purposes of the "comfort letter." If there have been no prior audits and new accountants are engaged at the time of the offering, fees ranging up to $65,000 and even higher would not be unusual. * * *

Printing expenses for registration statements and various underwriting documents typically range up to $100,000, but larger charges are not unusual. * * *

For a normal first public stock offering of several million dollars, total expenses in the $175,000 to $350,000 range would be typical, exclusive of the underwriting discount or commission but inclusive of any expense allowance (whether or not accountable) payable to the underwriters. However, it should be emphasized that there are wide variations among offerings. * * *

OFFERS AND SALES OF SECURITIES BY UNDERWRITERS AND DEALERS

Securities Act Release No. 4697 (May 28, 1964).

In view of recent comments in the press concerning the rights and obligations of, and limitations on, dealers in connection with distributions of registered securities, the Commission takes this opportunity to explain the operation of Section 5 of the Securities Act of 1933 with particular reference to the limitations upon, and responsibilities of, underwriters and dealers in the offer and sale of an issue of securities prior to and after the filing of a registration statement.

The discussion below assumes that the offering is not exempt from the registration requirements of the Act and, unless otherwise stated, that the mails or facilities of interstate or foreign commerce are used.

THE PERIOD BEFORE THE FILING OF A REGISTRATION STATEMENT

Section 5 of the Securities Act prohibits both offers to sell and offers to buy a security before a registration statement is filed. Section 2(3) of the Act, however, exempts preliminary negotiations or agreements between the issuer or other person on whose behalf the distribution is to be made and any underwriter or among underwriters. Thus, negotiation of the financing can proceed during this period but neither the issuer nor the underwriter may offer the security either to investors or to dealers, and dealers are prohibited from offering to buy the securities during this period.[1] Consequently, not only may no steps be taken to form a selling group but also dealers may not seek inclusion in the selling group prior to the filing.

It should be borne in mind that publicity about an issuer, its securities or the proposed offering prior to the filing of a registration statement may constitute an illegal offer to sell. Thus, announcement of the underwriter's identity should be avoided during this period. Experience shows that such announcements are very likely to lead to illegal offers to buy. This subject will not be further discussed in this release since it has been extensively considered elsewhere.[2]

These principles, however, are not intended to restrict the normal communications between an issuer and its stockholders or the announcement to the public generally of information with respect to important business and financial developments. Such announcements are required in the listing agreements used by stock exchanges, and the Commission is sensitive to the importance of encouraging this type of communication. In recognition of this requirement of certain stock exchanges, the Commission adopted Rule 135, which permits a brief announcement of proposed rights offerings, proposed exchange offerings, and proposed offerings to employees as not constituting an offer of a security for the purposes of Section 5 of the Act.

THE PERIOD AFTER THE FILING AND BEFORE THE EFFECTIVE DATE

After the registration statement is filed, and before its effective date, offers to sell the securities are permitted but no written offer may be made except by means of a statutory prospectus. For this purpose the statutory prospectus includes the preliminary prospectus provided for in Rule 430 as well as the summary prospectus provided for in Rule 431. In addition the so-called "tombstone" advertisement permitted by Rule 134 may be used.

During the period after the filing of a registration statement, the freedom of an underwriter or dealer expecting to participate in the distribution, to communicate with his customers is limited only by the anti-fraud provisions of the Securities Act and the Securities Exchange Act, and by the fact that written offering material other than a statutory prospectus or tombstone advertisement may not be used. In other words, during this period "free writing" is illegal. The dealer, therefore, can orally solicit indications of interest or offers to buy and may discuss the securities with his customers and advise them whether or not in his opinion the securities are desirable or suitable for them. In this connection a dealer proposing to discuss an issue of securities

1. The reason for this provision was stated in the House Report on the bill as originally enacted, as follows:

"* * * Otherwise, the underwriter * * * could accept them in the order of their priority and thus bring pressure upon dealers, who wish to avail themselves of a particular security offering, to rush their orders to buy without adequate consideration of the nature of the security being offered." H.R. Report No. 85, 73rd Cong., 1st Sess. (1933), p. 11.

2. See Securities Act Release No. 3844 (1957); Carl M. Loeb, Rhoades & Co., 38 S.E.C. 843 (1959); First Maine Corporation, 38 S.E.C. 882 (1959).

with his customers should obtain copies of the preliminary prospectus in order to have a reliable source of information. This is particularly important where he proposes to recommend the securities, or where information concerning them has not been generally available. The corollary of the dealer's obligation to secure the copy is the obligation of the issuer and managing underwriters to make it readily available. Rule 460 provides that as a condition to acceleration of the effective date of a registration statement, the Commission will consider whether the persons making the offering have taken reasonable steps to make the information contained in the registration statement available to dealers who may participate in the distribution.

It is a principal purpose of the so-called "waiting period" between the filing date and the effective date to enable dealers and, through them, investors to become acquainted with the information contained in the registration statement and to arrive at an unhurried decision concerning the merits of the securities. Consistently with this purpose, no contracts of sale can be made during this period, the purchase price may not be paid or received and offers to buy may be cancelled.

THE PERIOD AFTER THE EFFECTIVE DATE

When the registration statement becomes effective oral offerings may continue and sales may be made and consummated. A copy of the final statutory prospectus must be delivered in connection with any written offer or confirmation or upon delivery of the security, whichever first occurs. Supplemental sales literature ("free writing") may be used if it is accompanied or preceded by a prospectus. However, care must be taken to see that all such material is at the time of use not false or misleading under the standards of Section 17(a) of the Act. If the offering continues over an extended period, the prospectus should be current under the standards of Section 10(a)(3). All dealers trading in the registered security must continue to employ the prospectus for the period referred to in Section 4.

---

2. *Dissemination of Information During Registration*

Section 5 of the 1933 Act has a dual thrust: (a) to prevent or restrict any public statements about the securities being offered, except those contained in the registration statement and the statutory prospectus, and (b) to assure that the information contained in the registration statement and the statutory prospectus is made available to the investing public. Unfortunately, the structure of § 5 does not clearly reflect this division; nor does it clearly reflect the distinctions between the three different periods defined by the filing date and effective date of the registration statement. As an aid to your understanding of the structure of § 5, the following diagram indicates the respective periods in which the prohibitions contained in the five subdivisions of the section are applicable:

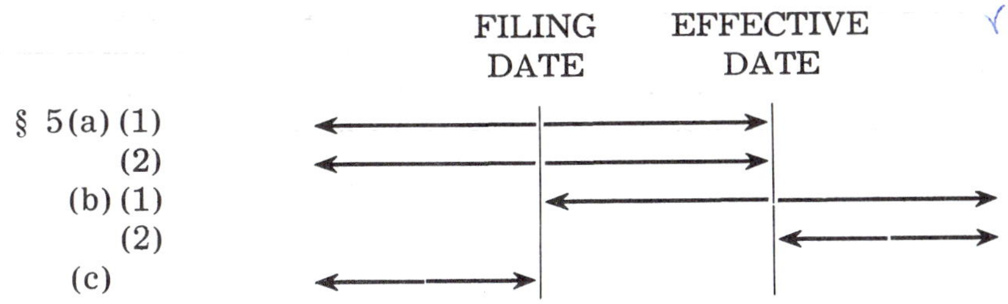

The complex structure of § 5 results from the 1954 amendments to the Securities Act. Prior to that time, the definition of "sale" in § 2(3) included offers as well as actual sales, so that § 5(a) prohibited any sales *or offers* prior to the *effective* date of the registration statement. The purpose of the 1954 amendments was to legitimate, and indeed encourage, the use of the preliminary or "red herring" prospectus to make written offers during the waiting period. Thus, § 5(c) now prohibits any *offers* prior to the *filing* of the registration statement, § 5(a) prohibits any *sales* prior to the *effective date,* § 5(b)(2) prohibits the delivery of a security after sale unless it is accompanied by the statutory prospectus, and § 5(b)(1) prohibits the use of any prospectus which does not meet the requirements of § 10 of the Act (§ 10 having also been amended in 1954 to specify what information could be omitted from the preliminary prospectus used during the waiting period).

The following materials indicate how the SEC has interpreted and undertaken to implement the provisions of § 5. An understanding of the operation of the section can only be obtained, however, by working through the questions in Problem 2 (p. 890) regarding the activities of various participants in an offering of securities.

PUBLICATION OF INFORMATION PRIOR TO OR AFTER THE EFFECTIVE DATE OF A REGISTRATION STATEMENT

Securities Act Release No. 3844 (Oct. 8, 1957).

Questions frequently are presented to the Securities and Exchange Commission and its staff with respect to the impact of the registration and prospectus requirements of Section 5 of the Securities Act of 1933 on publication of information concerning an issuer and its affairs by the issuer, its management, underwriters and dealers. Some of the more common problems which have arisen in this connection and the nature of the advice given by the Commission and its staff are outlined herein for the guidance of industry, underwriters, dealers and counsel.

A basic purpose of the Securities Act of 1933, the Securities Exchange Act of 1934 and the Investment Company Act of 1940 is to require the dissemination of adequate and accurate information concerning issuers and their securities in connection with the offer and sale of securities to the public, and the publication periodically of material business and financial facts, knowledge of which is essential to an informed trading market in such securities.

There has been an increasing tendency, particularly in the period since World War II, to give publicity through many media concerning corporate affairs which goes beyond the statutory requirements. This practice reflects a commendable and growing recognition on the part of industry and the investment community of the importance of informing security holders and the public generally with respect to important business and financial developments.

This trend should be encouraged. It is necessary, however, that corporate management, counsel, underwriters, dealers and public relations firms recognize that the Securities Acts impose certain responsibilities and limitations upon persons engaged in the sale of securities and that publicity and public relations activities under certain circumstances may involve violations of the securities laws and cause serious embarrassment to issuers and underwriters in connection with the timing and marketing of an issue of securities. These violations not only pose enforcement and administrative problems for the Commission, they may also give rise to civil liabilities by the seller of securities to the purchaser.

Absent some exemption, Section 5(c) of the Securities Act of 1933 makes it unlawful for any person directly or indirectly to make use of any means or instruments of interstate commerce or of the mails *to offer to sell* a security unless a registration statement has been filed with the Commission as to such security. * * *

It follows from the express language and the legislative history of the Securities Act that an issuer, underwriter or dealer may not legally begin a public offering or initiate a public sales campaign prior to the filing of a registration statement. It apparently is not generally understood, however, that the publication of information and statements, and publicity efforts, generally, made in advance of a proposed financing, although not couched in terms of an express offer, may in fact contribute to conditioning the public mind or arousing public interest in the issuer or in the securities of an issuer in a manner which raises a serious question whether the publicity is not in fact part of the selling effort. * * *

Instances have come to the attention of the Commission in which information of a misleading character, gross exaggeration and outright falsehood have been published by various means for the purpose of conveying to the public a message designed to stimulate an appetite for securities—a message which could not properly have been included in a statutory prospectus in conformity with the standards of integrity demanded by the statute.

Many of the cases have reflected a deliberate disregard of the provisions and purpose of the law. Others have reflected an unawareness of the problems involved or a failure to exercise a proper control over research and public relations activities in relation to the distribution of an issue of securities.

EXAMPLE # 1

An underwriter-promoter is engaged in arranging for the public financing of a mining venture to explore for a mineral which has certain possible potentialities for use in atomic research and power. While preparing a registration statement for a public offering, the underwriter-promoter distributed several thousand copies of a brochure which described in glowing generalities the future possibilities for use of the mineral and the profit potential to investors who would share in the growth prospects of a new industry. The brochure made no reference to any issuer or any security nor to any particular financing. It was sent out, however, bearing the name of the underwriting firm and obviously was designed to awaken an interest which later would be focused on the specific financing to be presented in the prospectus shortly to be sent to the same mailing list.

The distribution of the brochure under these circumstances clearly was the first step in a sales campaign to effect a public sale of the securities and as such, in the view of the Commission, violated Section 5 of the Securities Act. * * *

EXAMPLE # 5

Immediately preceding the filing of a registration statement for an issue of securities by a large industrial company, the research department of an investment banking firm distributed to a substantial number of the firm's institutional customers a brochure which referred specifically to the securities and described the business and prospects of the parent company of the prospective issuer. The business of the prospective issuer represented the principal part of the over-all operations of the total enterprise. The investment banking firm had been a principal underwriter of prior issues of securities by the parent and in accordance with policy of the firm from time to time distributed reports to its clients concerning securities of issuers which the firm had financed. It appeared, in this particular case, that the research department of the banking firm had prepared and distributed such a report to its clients without being fully aware of the activities of the underwriting department or the timing of the forthcoming offering.

The Commission advised the representatives of the issuer and the prospective underwriters that under all the circumstances, including the content, timing and distribution given to the brochure, participation of the firm in the distribution of the securities would pose difficulties from the point of view of the enforcement of the provisions of Section 5 of the Securities Act. In order to avoid any question as to violations of this provision of the Act, the banking firm did not participate in the distribution.

EXAMPLE # 6

In recognition of the problems presented, the Commission's staff frequently receives inquiries from company officials or their counsel with respect to circumstances such as the following:

The president of a company accepted, in August, an invitation to address a meeting of a security analysts' society to be held in February of the following year for the purpose of informing the membership concerning the company, its plans, its record and problems. By January a speech had been prepared together with supplemental information and data, all of which was designed to give a fairly comprehensive picture of the company, the industry in which it operates and various factors affecting its future growth. Projections of demand, operations and profits for future periods were included. The speech and the other data had been printed and it was intended that several hundred copies would be available for distribution at the meeting. In addition, since it was believed that stockholders, creditors, and perhaps customers might be interested in the talk, it was intended to mail to such persons and to a list of other selected firms and institutions copies of the material to be used at the analysts' meeting.

Later in January, a public financing by the company was authorized, preparation of a registration statement was begun and negotiation with underwriters was commenced. It soon appeared that the coming meeting of analysts, scheduled many months earlier, would be at or about the time the registration statement was to be filed. This presented the question whether, in the circumstances, delivery and distribution of the speech and the supporting data to the various persons mentioned above would contravene provisions of the Securities Act.

It seemed clear that the scheduling of the speech had not been arranged in contemplation of a public offering by the issuer at or about the time of its delivery. In the circumstances, no objection was raised to the delivery of the speech at the analysts' meeting. However, since printed copies of the speech might be received by a wider audience, it was suggested that printed copies of the speech and the supporting data not be made available at the meeting nor be transmitted to other persons.

EXAMPLE # 7

Two weeks prior to the filing of a registration statement the president of the issuer had delivered, before a society of security analysts, a prepared address which had been booked several months previously. In his speech the president discussed the company's operations and expansion program, its sales and earnings. The speech contained a forecast of sales and referred to the issuer's proposal to file with the Commission later in the month a registration statement with respect to a proposed offering of convertible subordinated debentures. Copies of the speech had been distributed to approximately 4,000 security analysts.

The Commission denied acceleration of the registration statement and requested that the registrant distribute copies of its final prospectus to each member of the group which had received a copy of the speech.

* * *

EXAMPLE # 9

An issuer was about to file a registration statement for a proposed offering on behalf of a controlling person. The timing of the issue was fixed in accommodation to the controlling person. It appeared, however, that registration would coincide with the time when the company normally distributed its annual report to security holders and others. In recognition of the problem posed, inquiry was made whether such publication and distribution of the report at such time would create any problems. The issuer was advised that, if the annual report was of the character and content normally published by the company and did not contain material designed to assist in the proposed offering, no question would be raised.

EXAMPLE # 10

A report concerning a registrant had been prepared by an engineering firm for use by prospective underwriters. The report contained a 5-year projection of earnings. It appeared that, in addition to the distribution of the report among prospective underwriters, copies of the report had been made available, after the filing of a registration statement but before it became effective, to broker-dealers, to salesmen who would be engaged in the offering and sale of the securities and to certain investors. One broker-dealer firm had made available to salesmen excerpts from the report. The Commission advised the persons responsible for the distribution of the report that in its view distribution of the report to persons other than to persons bona fide concerned with the question of considering and undertaking an underwriting commitment, contravened the provisions of Section 5.

CARL M. LOEB, RHOADES & CO.

38 S.E.C. 843 (1959).

These are consolidated proceedings pursuant to Sections 15(b) and 15A(*l*)(2) of the Securities Exchange Act of 1934 ("Exchange Act") to determine whether to revoke the registration as a broker and dealer of Carl M. Loeb, Rhoades & Co. ("Loeb Rhoades") and of Dominick & Dominick ("Dominick"), whether to suspend or expel registrants from membership in the National Association of Securities Dealers, Inc. ("NASD"), a registered securities association, and whether, under Section 15A(b)(4) of the Exchange Act, Stanley R. Grant, a partner in Loeb Rhoades, is a cause of any order of revocation, suspension or expulsion which may be issued as to that firm.

The orders for proceedings allege that commencing on September 17, 1958, registrants and Grant offered to sell shares of stock of Arvida Corporation ("Arvida") when no registration statement had been filed as to such securities, in willful violation of Section 5(c) of the Securities Act of 1933 ("Securities Act").

* * *

The Offering of Arvida Stock

Arvida was incorporated in Florida on July 30, 1958, pursuant to plans developed over the preceding 4 or 5 months to provide for the financing and development of the extensive real estate holdings of Arthur Vining Davis ("Davis") in southeastern Florida. In April 1958 each of the registrants was approached by representatives of Davis, and thereafter, in May and June 1958, as a result of discussions a plan was developed under which certain of Davis' properties would be placed in a new corporation to be financed in large part through a public offering of securities by an underwriting group proposed to be managed by registrants.

On July 8, 1958 a meeting was held in Miami to work out various aspects of the contemplated offering. At this meeting it was noted there was some concern in Florida real estate circles as to the ultimate disposition of the Davis properties and the possible effect thereof on real estate values, and it was decided to issue a press release. Grant prepared a draft release which included some description of the "great spread" of Davis' lands and mention of a proposed underwriting of the offering through Loeb Rhoades. This draft was revised by representatives of Davis so as to state merely that the major portion of the Davis land holdings was to be transferred to Arvida which would proceed with orderly development and arrange to obtain a large amount of new capital for that purpose. No mention was made of a public offering or of an underwriting or underwriters. The substance of this release appeared during the next few days in various Florida newspapers.

On September 16 and 17, 1958, meetings were held in New York at which the proposals of registrants for the financing were placed in final form and submitted to representatives of Davis for transmission to him. At this time it was decided to issue an additional press release. Grant drafted such a release on the evening of September 17 and, on September 18, submitted it to officers of Arvida, representatives of Davis, Dominick and counsel for the proposed underwriters, obtaining the approval of all of them. Later that day, Davis approved registrants' financing proposals, and public relations counsel for Loeb Rhoades was called in to arrange for distribution of the release in New York.

The release, which was issued on the letterhead of Loeb Rhoades, stated that Arvida, to which Davis was transferring his real estate, would be provided with $25 million to $30 million of additional capital through an offering of stock to the public, and that Arvida would have assets of over $100,000,000 "reflecting Mr. Davis' investment" and the public investment. It referred to a public offering scheduled within 60 days through a nationwide investment banking group headed by registrants, and to the transfer from Davis to Arvida of over 100,000 acres "in an area of the Gold Coast" in 3 named Florida counties and contained a brief description of these properties including reference to undeveloped lands and to "operating properties."

The release identified the principal officers of Arvida and stated that Arvida proposed to undertake a "comprehensive program of orderly development," under which some of the lands would be developed "immediately into residential communities" and others would be held for investment and future development as the area expands. It closed with a reference to the attraction of new industry and the place Arvida would assume in the "further growth of Southeastern Florida."

Officers of Arvida were anxious to have the release issued promptly. Public relations counsel advised Loeb Rhoades that, in order to make sure that the story appeared in 3 prominent New York newspapers, which coverage Loeb Rhoades wanted, it would be advisable, in view of newspaper deadlines, to call reporters from these papers to Loeb Rhoades' office. This was done on the afternoon of Thursday, September 18. The reporters asked certain questions which Grant undertook to answer. He disclosed that the offering price of the stock would be in the vicinity of $10 or $11 per share and gave certain information about Davis and his career but declined to answer questions concerning Davis' reasons for entering into the transaction, the extent of mortgage indebtedness, the capitalization of Arvida, its balance sheet, and the control of the corporation. His stated reason for refusing to answer these questions was that he did not wish to go beyond the release which had been approved by all interested parties.

Copies of the release were also delivered to other New York newspapers and to the principal wire services. The substance of the release and the information supplied by Grant appeared in the 3 New York newspapers on September 19, 1958, and in numerous other news media throughout the country.

A limited survey by our staff covering the 2 business days, September 19 and 22, immediately following this publicity disclosed buying interest in Arvida stock attributable to this publicity on the part of brokers, dealers, and the investing public to the extent of at least $500,000. It was later ascertained that during these 2 business days a total of 101 securities firms were recorded by Loeb Rhoades as expressing an underwriting interest in the offering. Loeb Rhoades did not accept indications of interest from individuals or prospective selling dealers during this period, but did make notations of selling group interest on September 19 and 22 by about 25 securities dealers. In addition, following the publicity, registrants received, prior to September 30, at least 58 expressions of interest from members of the public, including at least 17 specific offers to buy.

On September 22, 1958, we commenced an action in the United States District Court for the Southern District of New York against

Arvida, registrants, Grant and others, seeking an injunction against further violations of Section 5(c) of the Securities Act. On October 20, 1958, the Court denied our motion for a preliminary injunction and defendants' counter motions for dismissal, judgment on the pleadings, or summary judgment and to enjoin these broker-dealer proceedings. On December 12, 1958, the Court entered a decree permanently enjoining violation of Section 5(c) by the defendants. The defendants consented to the entry of this decree and stipulated to the findings of fact which were adopted by the Court and formed the basis for the Court's ruling. The Court concluded that, although the defendants appeared to have acted in good faith and to have had no intention to violate the Securities Act, and although they continued to deny that their activities violated the statute, their activities nevertheless constituted a violation of Section 5(c) of that Act.

Arvida filed a registration statement under the Securities Act covering its proposed offering of securities on October 27, 1958. A material amendment was filed on November 25, 1958, a further amendment was filed on December 2, 1958, and the registration statement became effective on December 10, 1958. Between December 2 and 9, 1958, the registrants pursuant to our suggestion arranged for each underwriter to furnish a copy of the November 25 and the December 2 prospectus (which were substantially the same) to all investors who were known to have expressed to such underwriter prior to October 27, 1958, any kind of interest in purchasing the securities and to whom such underwriter proposed to sell the securities.

The November 25 and the final prospectuses included in this registration statement disclosed, among other things, that the properties were encumbered by mortgage debt in the amount of $30,833,324, of which approximately $20,642,000 falls due within the next 5 years. The equity of Davis in Arvida was stated at approximately $44,827,000, represented by $6,900,000 of debentures payable to him and capital stock and surplus of $37,927,000. A substantial part of the proceeds from the financing may be required to meet mortgage indebtedness maturing in the next few years and to that extent will be unavailable to develop the properties. During the first fiscal year only $2,800,000 is budgeted for such development. Approximately 61% of the 100,650 acres owned by Arvida is located in rural areas removed from present urban development, and substantial portions of this acreage are accessible only by unpaved roads and a portion is inaccessible by automobile. Approximately 50% of the 100,650 acres are below the "flood criteria" established by local authorities as the minimum elevation at which land may be developed, and substantial fill and drainage expenses would be required for the development of this property. The operating properties of Arvida, in the aggregate, are estimated to have operated at a net loss since their respective years of acquisition.

THE IMPACT OF SECTION 5(c) OF THE SECURITIES ACT

Section 5(c) of the Securities Act, as here pertinent, prohibits offers to sell any security, through the medium of a prospectus or otherwise, unless a registration statement has been filed. Section 2(3) defines "offer to sell" to include "every attempt or offer to dispose of, or solicitation of an offer to buy, a security for value." Section 2(10) defines a "prospectus" to mean "any prospectus, notice, circular, advertisement, letter, or communication * * * which offers any security for sale * * *." These are broad definitions, and designedly so. It is apparent that they are not limited to communications which constitute an offer in the common law contract sense, or which on their face purport to offer a security. Rather, as stated by our General Counsel in 1941, they include "any document which is designed to procure orders for a security."

The broad sweep of these definitions is necessary to accomplish the statutory purposes in the light of the process of securities distribution as it exists in the United States. Securities are distributed in this country by a complex and sensitive machinery geared to accomplish nationwide distribution of large quantities of securities with great speed. Multi-million dollar issues are often oversubscribed on the day the securities are made available for sale. This result is accomplished by a network of prior informal indications of interest or offers to buy between underwriters and dealers and between dealers and investors based upon mutual expectations that, at the moment when sales may legally be made, many prior indications will immediately materialize as purchases. It is wholly unrealistic to assume in this context that "offers" must take any particular legal form. Legal formalities come at the end to record prior understandings, but it is the procedures by which these prior understandings, embodying investment decisions, are obtained or generated which the Securities Act was intended to reform.

One of the cardinal purposes of the Securities Act is to slow down this process of rapid distribution of corporate securities, at least in its earlier and crucial stages, in order that dealers and investors might have access to, and an opportunity to consider, the disclosures of the material business and financial facts of the issuer provided in registration statements and prospectuses. Under the practices existing prior to the enactment of the statute in 1933, dealers made blind commitments to purchase securities without adequate information, and in turn, resold the securities to an equally uninformed investing public. The entire distribution process was often stimulated by sales literature designed solely to arouse interest in the securities and not to disclose material facts about the issuer and its securities. It was to correct this situation that the Securities Act originally prohibited offers to sell and solicitations of offers to buy as well as sales prior to the effective date of a registration statement and imposed a 20-day waiting period between the filing and the effective date.

This entire problem was carefully reconsidered by the Congress in 1954. Both the securities industry and the Commission had been concerned by the fact that dissemination to investors during the waiting period of the information contained in a registration statement was impeded by the fear that any such dissemination might be held to constitute an illegal offer. As a result, wide dissemination of material facts prior to the time of sale, which was an important objective of the statute, was to some extent frustrated. We had attempted to deal with this problem by rules which defined distribution of preliminary or so-called "red herring" prospectuses as not constituting an "offer," and required such distribution at least to dealers as a prerequisite to acceleration of the registration statement. However, the concern that Section 5 might be violated persisted despite the permissibility of red herring prospectuses, and the desired dissemination of information was not obtained. This continuing concern is significant for present purposes and illustrates the scope and reach attributed to the prohibitions of Section 5(c).

The Congress in 1954 adopted a carefully worked out procedure to meet the problem. It is essentially as follows: (1) the strict prohibition of offers prior to the filing of a registration statement was continued; (2) during the period between the filing of a registration statement and its effective date offers but not sales may be made but written offers could be made only by documents prescribed or processed by the Commission; and (3) sales continued to be prohibited prior to the effective date. In permitting, but limiting the manner in which pre-effective written offers might be made, the Congress was concerned lest inadequate or misleading information be used in connection with the distribution of securities. We were directed to pursue a vigorous enforcement policy to prevent this from happening. In obedience to this mandate we have made clear our position that the statute prohibits issuers, underwriters and dealers from initiating a public sales campaign prior to the filing of a registration statement by means of publicity efforts which, even though not couched in terms of an express offer, condition the public mind or arouse public interest in the particular securities. Even if there might have been some uncertainty as to Congressional intent with regard to pre-effective publicity prior to 1954, none should have existed thereafter. The Congress has specified a period during which, and a procedure by which, information concerning a proposed offering may be disseminated to dealers and investors. This procedure is exclusive and cannot be nullified by recourse to public relations techniques to set in motion or further the machinery of distribution before the statutory disclosures have been made and upon the basis of whatever information the distributor deems it expedient to supply.

We accordingly conclude that publicity, prior to the filing of a registration statement by means of public media of communication, with respect to an issuer or its securities, emanating from broker-dealer firms who as underwriters or prospective underwriters have negotiated or are negotiating for a public offering of the securities of such issuer, must be presumed to set in motion or to be a part of the distribution process and therefore to involve an offer to sell or a solicitation of an offer to buy such securities prohibited by Section 5(c). Since it is unlawful under the statute for dealers to offer to sell or to offer to buy a security as to which registration is required, prior to the filing of a registration statement, dealers who are to participate in a distribution likewise risk the possibility that employment by them of public media of communication to give publicity to a forthcoming offering prior to the filing of a registration statement constitutes a premature sales activity prohibited by Section 5(c).

Turning to the facts of this case, we find that the September 19, 1958, press release and resultant publicity concerning Arvida and its securities emanated from managing underwriters contemplating a distribution of such securities in the near future as to which a registration statement had not yet been filed. We also find that the mails and instrumentalities of interstate commerce were used in the dissemination of this publicity. We further find that such release and publicity was of a character calculated, by arousing and stimulating investor and dealer interest in Arvida securities and by eliciting indications of interest from customers to dealers and from dealer to underwriters, to set in motion the processes of distribution. In fact it had such an effect.[16] It contained descriptive material concerning the properties, business, plans and management of Arvida, it included arresting references to "assets in excess of $100,000,000," and "over 100,000 acres, more than 155 square miles, in an area of the Gold Coast." Reporters were furnished with price data, and registrants were named as the managing underwriters thus permitting, if not inviting, dealers to register their interest with them.[17] We find that such activities constituted part of a selling effort by the managing underwriters.

The principal justification advanced for the September 19 release and publicity was the claim that the activities of Mr. Davis, and specifically his interests in Florida real estate, are "news" and that accordingly Section 5(c) should not be construed to restrict the freedom

16. At least 1 of the news reports following this meeting included a statement that it was unusual for underwriters to volunteer so much detail prior to registration, and also a statement that this advance detail would presumably help to intensify widespread interest in Davis' activities.

17. We reject the suggestion that the purpose of the release was merely to dispel rumors in Florida concerning the ultimate disposition of the Davis holdings. Had this been the purpose no such elaboration of detail would have been necessary, nor would there have been need to go to such effort to make sure that the material appeared in the principal financial newspapers in New York or to give it nationwide circulation. In any event, the July 8 press release seems entirely adequate to quiet any apprehension in Florida concerning the fate of the Davis properties and in fact had that effect. It was then announced that the properties were to be conveyed to Arvida which proposed to proceed with their orderly development and was arranging for necessary financing. It is significant that the July 8 release elicited public response primarily from persons interested in Florida real estate, while the September 18 release produced a reaction from investors and securities dealers. This is hardly a coincidence.

of the managing underwriters to release such publicity. We reject this contention. Section 5(c) is equally applicable whether or not the issuer or the surrounding circumstances have, or by astute public relations activities may be made to appear to have, news value.[19]

Brokers and dealers properly and commendably provide their customers with a substantial amount of information concerning business and financial developments of interest to investors, including information with respect to particular securities and issuers. Section 5, nevertheless, prohibits selling efforts in connection with a proposed public distribution of securities prior to the filing of a registration statement and, as we have indicated, this prohibition includes any publicity which is in fact a part of a selling effort. Indeed, the danger to investors from publicity amounting to a selling effort may be greater in cases where an issue has "news value" since it may be easier to whip up a "speculative frenzy" concerning the offering by incomplete or misleading publicity and thus facilitate the distribution of an unsound security at inflated prices. This is precisely the evil which the Securities Act seeks to prevent.

We realize, of course, that corporations regularly release various types of information and that a corporation in which there is wide public interest may be called upon to release more information more frequently about its activities than would be expected of lesser known or privately held enterprises. In the normal conduct of its business a corporation may continue to advertise its products and services without interruption, it may send out its customary quarterly, annual and other periodic reports to security holders, and it may publish its proxy statements, send out its dividend notices and make routine announcements to the press. This flow of normal corporate news, unrelated to a selling effort for an issue of securities, is natural, desirable and entirely consistent with the objective of disclosure to the public which underlies the federal securities laws. However, an issuer who is a party to or collaborates with underwriters or prospective underwriters in initiating or securing publicity must be regarded as participating directly or indirectly in an offer to sell or a solicitation of an offer to buy prohibited by Section 5(c).

Difficult and close questions of fact may arise as to whether a particular item of publicity by an issuer is part of a selling effort or whether it is an item of legitimate disclosure to investors unrelated to

19. It should be clear that our interpretation of Section 5(c) in no way restricts the freedom of news media to seek out and publish financial news. Reporters presumably have no securities to sell and, absent collusion with sellers, Section 5(c) has no application to them. Underwriters such as registrants are in a different position; they are in the business of distributing securities, not news. Failure to appreciate this distinction between reporters and securities distributors has given rise to a further misconception. Instances have arisen in which a proposed financing is of sufficient public interest that journalists on their own initiative have sought out and published information concerning it. Since such journalistic enterprise does not violate Section 5, our failure to question resulting publicity should not have been taken as any indication that Section 5 is inapplicable to publicity by underwriters about newsworthy offerings. Similar considerations apply to publicity by issuers.

such an effort. Some of these problems are illustrated in Securities Act Release No. 3844 above cited. This case, however, does not present such difficulties. Arvida was a new venture having, at the date of the September publicity, only 1 stockholder—Davis. There was no occasion to inform existing stockholders or investors in the trading markets concerning developments in its affairs in order that they might protect their interests or trade intelligently. We see no basis for concluding that the purpose of the release was different from its effect—the stimulation of investor and dealer interest as the first step in a selling effort.

Comparison of the September publicity with the final prospectus of Arvida illustrates the wisdom of the Congressional prohibition against pre-filing publicity. Wholly omitted from the release and withheld from reporters were the essential financial facts of capitalization, indebtedness and operating results which are so material to any informed investment decision. The great acreage owned by Arvida was stressed without disclosing that the bulk of it was in areas remote in time and distance from the development which was also stressed. Obscured also was the probable use of much of the proceeds of the financing, not to develop the properties but rather to discharge mortgage debt. As is so often the case, the impression conveyed by the whole is more significant than the individual acts of omission. From the publicity investors could, and no doubt many did, derive the impression that the risk and financing requirements of this real estate venture had been substantially satisfied by Davis and that the public was being invited to participate in reaping the fruits through early development. In fact, as clearly appears from the final prospectus, much of the risk remains to be taken and much of the financing essential to the issuer's business remains to be carried out.

What is presented in this case is no mere technical controversy as to the time and manner of public disclosure concerning significant business facts. On the contrary, the issue vitally concerns the basic principle of the Securities Act that the health of the capital markets requires that new issues be marketed upon the basis of full disclosure of material facts under statutory standards of accuracy and adequacy and in accordance with the procedural requirements of Section 5. If actual investment decisions may be brought about by press releases, then compliance with the registration requirements may be reduced to little more than a legal formality having small practical significance in the marketing of new issues.

We conclude, therefore, that registrants and Grant willfully violated Section 5(c) of the Securities Act.[21]

21. This does not mean that we find registrants and Grant to have intentionally violated the law. They assert that they acted under the mistaken impression that Section 5(c) is inapplicable to press releases concerning offerings having news value. But, as is well settled, a finding of willfulness within the meaning of Sections 15(b) and 15A(*l*)(2) of the Exchange Act does not require a finding of intention to violate the law. It is sufficient that registrants be shown to have known what they were do-

THE PUBLIC INTEREST

Since we have found willful violations of the Securities Act, we must consider whether it is in the public interest or necessary or appropriate for the protection of investors to revoke the registration of either registrant or to suspend or expel either of them from membership in the NASD. In such inquiry our concern is not only with the gravity of the violations but primarily whether under all the circumstances the public interest or investor protection calls for elimination of registrants from the securities business or their permanent or temporary exclusion from the NASD.

For the reasons discussed above we believe the violations were serious, since practices such as these may subvert to a substantial degree the essential objective of the Securities Act that investors and dealers should have the opportunity to make investment decisions upon the basis of adequate information fully disclosed under statutory standards and sanctions.

However, we have taken into account a number of mitigating factors. Registrants bear an excellent general reputation in the securities business and have never before been the subject of disciplinary proceedings by us. The Court has found that they acted in good faith and in reliance upon the opinion of counsel. These proceedings and the judgment of the Court in the injunctive action we commenced have served to place registrants and the securities industry upon unmistakable notice of their obligations in the field of publicity and forcibly to direct the attention of registrants to the consequences of improper practices in this area. There is no evidence of injury to investors since the publicity attendant upon our actions and the steps taken to disseminate the facts disclosed in the registration statement, particularly to those investors who had previously evidenced an interest, should have been adequate to dispel the effect of the unlawful release. We therefore conclude that the public interest and the protection of investors do not require that the registrations of registrants as brokers and dealers be revoked or that they be suspended or expelled from membership in the NASD.

By the Commission (Chairman Gadsby and Commissioners Orrick, Patterson, Hastings, and Sargent).

How much guidance does the *Loeb Rhoades* decision provide to issuers and underwriters with respect to prefiling publicity? Subsequent to the *Loeb Rhoades* decision, the Commission issued Rule 135 in its current form. How would the Arvida press release that was issued in *Loeb Rhoades* fare under Rule 135? Is Rule 135 exclusive or is it

ing. Thompson Ross Securities Co., 6 S.E.C. 1111, 1122–23 (1940); Hughes v. S.E.C., 174 F.2d 969, 977 (C.A.D.C.1949); The Whitehall Corporation, Exchange Act Release No. 5667 (April 2, 1958); Shuck v. S.E.C. (C.A.D.C. No. 14,208, December 1958). Registrants, of course, knew that no registration statement had been filed and the release was intentionally composed and publicized.

merely a safe harbor? Is it ever permissible in prefiling publicity to mention the price of the securities to be offered? *Cf.* Chris-Craft Industries v. Bangor Punta Corp., 426 F.2d 569 (2d Cir.1970) (indicating that Rule 135 is exclusive and discussing the impropriety of mentioning an investment banker's opinion as to the value of the securities to be offered in exchange offer).

As we will see later, there are situations in which a corporation and its officers may be *required* by the antifraud provisions of the federal securities laws to make prompt public disclosure of material facts that would affect the market price of the corporation's outstanding securities. The conflict between these requirements and the § 5 prohibition against "offers" made by means other than the statutory prospectus are considered at pages 783–786 below.

Another area of tension between the § 5(c) prohibition of offers and the need to publish information in the regular course of business arises in the context of broker-dealer recommendations. Issuers about to embark on a registered offering frequently have one or more classes of securities that are already publicly traded. Research departments and financial analysts may be following and giving recommendations with regard to these securities. When such a recommendation is made shortly before a public offering, the recommendation would appear to fall within the § 2(3) definition of "offer to sell." In order to enable securities analysts to conduct their business without running afoul of the § 5 "gun-jumping" provisions, the SEC promulgated Rules 137, 138, and 139, which exclude certain recommendations from the coverage of § 5. In studying these rules, note that the limitations on permissible recommendations vary, depending upon whether the broker-dealer making the recommendation is a participant in the distribution (Rule 139) or is not a participant and therefore not an underwriter (Rule 137; see also § 2(11)). The exclusions in Rules 137 and 138 apply during the waiting and post-effective periods as well as to the pre-filing period.

PUBLICATION OF INFORMATION PRIOR TO OR AFTER THE FILING AND EFFECTIVE DATE OF A REGISTRATION STATEMENT UNDER THE SECURITIES ACT OF 1933

Securities Act Release No. 5009 (Oct. 7, 1969).

* * *

There has been an ever increasing tendency to publicize through many media information concerning corporate affairs which goes beyond statutory requirements. This practice reflects the commendable recognition on the part of business and the investment community of the importance of informing investors and the public with respect to important business and financial developments. It has been reenforced by the policies of various self-regulatory organizations regarding timely disclosure of information which might materially affect the market for an issuer's securities.[2]

* * *

[T]he increasing obligations and incentives of corporations to make timely disclosures concerning their offerings raise a question as to a possible conflict between the obligation to make timely disclosure and the restriction on publication of information concerning an issuer which may have securities "in registration."[4] The Commission believes that such a conflict may be more apparent than real. Events resulting in a duty to make prompt disclosure under the anti-fraud provisions of the securities laws or timely disclosure policies of self-regulatory organizations at a time when a registered offering of securities is contemplated are relatively infrequent and normally may be effected in a manner which will not unduly influence the proposed offering. Disclosure of a material event would ordinarily not be subject to restrictions under Section 5 of the Securities Act if it is purely factual and does not include predictions or opinions.

The Commission recognizes that difficult and close questions will inevitably arise with respect to whether particular items of publicity are subject to restriction, and encourages issuers and their counsel to seek informal consultation with the Commission's staff which is accustomed to dealing with such questions and is usually able to give rapid and definite responses.

A number of more specific questions have been raised concerning the restrictions on circulation of information by broker-dealers, particularly during the "pre-filing" period. There appears to be some confusion as to when the restrictions on publication activities commence. Ordinarily a broker-dealer becomes subject to restrictions at any time when he commences to participate in the preparation of a registration statement or otherwise reaches an understanding with the person on whose behalf a distribution is to be made that the firm will become a managing underwriter, whether or not the terms and conditions of the underwriting have been agreed upon. Other brokers become subject to restrictions at such time as they are invited by a managing underwriter or a person on whose behalf a distribution is to be made, to participate or seeks to participate. Persons who choose to forego such underwriting in order to be free to distribute such publications should not thereafter participate in the distribution as a dealer or otherwise.

Distribution of communications containing recommendations with respect to securities which have been registered for sale from time to

2. See, e.g., New York Stock Exchange Company Manual, pages [2–1 through 2–6, revised and reprinted in 3 Fed.Sec.L.Rep. (CCH) 23,514] American Stock Exchange Guide, pages 101–108 [reprinted in 3 Fed. Sec.L.Rep. (CCH) 23,124A]

4. "In registration" is used herein to mean the entire process of registration, at least from the time an issuer reaches an understanding with the broker-dealer which is to act as managing underwriter until the completion of the offering and the period of 40 or 90 days during which dealers must deliver a prospectus. [See Section 4(3) of the 1933 Act].

time at prices prevailing in the market pose difficult questions. Usually no broker-dealer group has made arrangements with the selling shareholders for distribution of the securities. It does not appear that restrictions on the dissemination of such material are necessary until such time as a broker-dealer has reached an understanding that he will offer securities on behalf of the selling shareholder, whether or not he has technically accepted an order to sell the security.

After a particular security is "in registration," broker-dealers often do not know the extent to which they may follow up recommendations concerning the security made before the security was "in registration." If a broker-dealer is a participant in a proposed underwriting and material events occur during the "pre-filing" period, the broker should be able to make a brief, strictly factual report of these events to his customers.

After the registration statement is filed and until it becomes effective, written communications furnished to customers or others should be restricted to the preliminary prospectus ("red herring"), the summary prospectus described in Section 10(b), or the so-called "tombstone" announcements permitted under Section 2(10) of the Act or Rule 134 thereunder. Also, Rule 135 permits certain announcements of offerings before and after a registration statement is filed.

* * *

GUIDELINES FOR THE RELEASE OF INFORMATION BY ISSUERS WHOSE SECURITIES ARE IN REGISTRATION

Sec. Act Rel. No. 5180 (Aug. 16, 1971).

The Commission today took note of situations when issuers whose securities are "in registration" [1] may have refused to answer legitimate inquiries from stockholders, financial analysts, the press or other persons concerning the company or some aspect of its business. The Commission hereby emphasizes that there is no basis in the securities acts or in any policy of the Commission which would justify the practice of non-disclosure of factual information by a publicly held company on the grounds that it has securities in registration under the Securities Act of 1933 ("Act"). Neither a company in registration nor its representatives should instigate publicity for the purpose of facilitating the sale of securities in a proposed offering.

* * *

1. "In registration" is used herein to refer to the entire process of registration, at least from the time an issuer reaches an understanding with the broker-dealer which is to act as managing underwriter prior to the filing of a registration statement and the period of 40 to 90 days during which dealers must deliver a prospectus.

GUIDELINES

The Commission strongly suggests that all issuers establish internal procedures designed to avoid problems relating to the release of corporate information when in registration. As stated above, issuers and their representatives should not initiate publicity when in registration, but should nevertheless respond to legitimate inquiries for factual information about the company's financial condition and business operations. * * *

It has been suggested that the Commission promulgate an all inclusive list of permissible and prohibited activities in this area. This is not feasible for the reason that determinations are based upon the particular facts of each case. However, the Commission as a matter of policy encourages the flow of factual information to shareholders and the investing public. Issuers in this regard should:

1. Continue to advertise products and services.

2. Continue to send out customary quarterly, annual and other periodic reports to stockholders.

3. Continue to publish proxy statements and send out dividend notices.

4. Continue to make announcements to the press with respect to factual business and financial developments; i.e., receipt of a contract, the settlement of a strike, the opening of a plant, or similar events of interest to the community in which the business operates.

5. Answer unsolicited telephone inquiries from stockholders, financial analysts, the press and others concerning factual information.

6. Observe an "open door" policy in responding to unsolicited inquiries concerning factual matters from securities analysts, financial analysts, security holders, and participants in the communications field who have a legitimate interest in the corporation's affairs.

7. Continue to hold stockholder meetings as scheduled and to answer shareholders' inquiries at stockholder meetings relating to factual matters.

* * *

In the event a company publicly releases material information concerning new corporate developments during the period that a registration statement is pending, the registration statement should be amended at or prior to the time the information is released. If this is not done and such information is publicly released through inadvertence, the pending registration statement should be promptly amended to reflect such information.

The determination of whether an item of information or publicity could be deemed to constitute an offer—a step in the selling effort—in violation of Section 5 must be made by the issuer in the light of all the facts and circumstances surrounding each case. The Commission recognizes that questions may arise from time to time with respect to the release of information by companies in registration and, while the statutory obligation always rests with the company and can never be shifted to the staff, the staff will be available for consultation concerning such questions. It is not the function of the staff to draft corporate press releases. If a company, however, desires to consult with the staff as to the application of the statutory requirements to a particular case, the staff will continue to be available, and in this regard the pertinent facts should be set forth in written form and submitted in sufficient time to allow due consideration.

Note on the Distribution of Written Offering Material During the Waiting Period

As amended in 1954, § 5 permits offers, but not sales, during the waiting period between filing and effectiveness. However, § 2(10) makes any offer in writing a "prospectus", and § 5(b)(1) makes it unlawful to transmit any prospectus after the filing of the registration statement unless the prospectus contains the information called for by § 10, some of which is generally unavailable until the underwriting agreements have been signed and the offering price has been set. To meet this problem, the Act and rules provide avenues for the use of two kinds of written offering material during the waiting period—the preliminary or "red herring" prospectus, and the "tombstone ad."

Section 10(b) of the Act provides that the Commission may permit for the purposes of § 5(b)(1) the use of a prospectus which omits or summarizes some of the information required by § 10(a). Pursuant to that authority, the Commission's Rule 430 specifies what information may be omitted from a prospectus used prior to the effective date, and Item 501(c)(8) of Regulation S–K sets forth the legend that must be printed in red (whence the name "red herring") on every such preliminary prospectus. A sample preliminary prospectus is included in Appendix II.

Acting under its general definitional power in § 19, the Commission has also adopted Rule 134, providing that the term "prospectus", as defined in § 2(10), will not include a notice which contains only certain specified information about the proposed issue, and also sets forth certain legends prescribed by the rule. An example of the "tombstone ad" authorized by Rule 134 (so-called because of the brevity of its contents and the black border which typically surrounds it) is set forth on the following page.[a]

a. This advertisement, published in various newspapers on September 6, 1974, is unusual, because most "tombstone ads" that appear in the newspapers are published after the effective date (and often after the entire issue has been sold). The use of newspaper advertising to sell an industrial issue reflected the difficulty of placing a large issue of common stock (in terms of number of shares, this was believed to be the largest equity sale ever by a utility company) in the depressed stock market of 1974. After "Wall Street salesmen [had] worked on little else for a month", the issue was finally marketed on September 18, at a price of $9.50 a share (offering a yield of 14.7% on the basis of the current annual dividend of $1.40 a share). See Wall St. Journal, Sept. 19, 1974, p. 22, col. 1.

A registration statement relating to these securities has been filed with the Securities and Exchange Commission but has not yet become effective. These securities may not be sold nor may offers to buy be accepted prior to the time the registration statement becomes effective. This advertisement shall not constitute an offer to sell or the solicitation of an offer to buy nor shall there be any sale of these securities in any State in which such offer, solicitation or sale would be unlawful prior to registration or qualification under the securities laws of any such State.

Proposed New Issue expected to be offered September 18, 1974

17,500,000 Shares

The Southern Company

Common Stock

($5 par value)

The Southern Company owns all the outstanding common stocks of Alabama Power Company, Georgia Power Company, Gulf Power Company and Mississippi Power Company, each of which is an operating public utility company, and Alabama Power Company and Georgia Power Company each own 50% of the outstanding common stock of Southern Electric Generating Company. The operating affiliates supply electric service in the states of Alabama, Georgia, Florida and Mississippi, respectively, and Southern Electric Generating Company owns generating units at a large electric generating station which supplies power to Alabama Power Company and Georgia Power Company.

MORGAN STANLEY & CO. Incorporated — MERRILL LYNCH, PIERCE, FENNER & SMITH Incorporated — SALOMON BROTHERS

THE FIRST BOSTON CORPORATION — BLYTH EASTMAN DILLON & CO. Incorporated
DILLON, READ & CO. INC. — DREXEL BURNHAM & CO. Incorporated — GOLDMAN, SACHS & CO. — HALSEY, STUART & CO. INC. Affiliate of Bache & Co. Incorporated
HORNBLOWER & WEEKS-HEMPHILL, NOYES Incorporated — E. F. HUTTON & COMPANY INC. — KIDDER, PEABODY & CO. Incorporated
KUHN, LOEB & CO. — LAZARD FRERES & CO. — LEHMAN BROTHERS Incorporated
LOEB, RHOADES & CO. — REYNOLDS SECURITIES INC. — SMITH, BARNEY & CO. Incorporated
STONE & WEBSTER SECURITIES CORPORATION — WERTHEIM & CO., INC. — WHITE, WELD & CO. Incorporated
THE ROBINSON-HUMPHREY COMPANY, INC. — SHEARSON, HAMMILL & CO. Incorporated
BATEMAN EICHLER, HILL RICHARDS Incorporated — SHUMAN, AGNEW & CO., INC. — BIRR, WILSON & CO., INC.
BOETTCHER & COMPANY — CROWELL, WEEDON & CO. — SUTRO & CO. Incorporated — MORGAN, OLMSTEAD, KENNEDY & GARDNER Incorporated
WAGENSELLER & DURST, INC. — DAVIS, SKAGGS & CO., INC. — BOSWORTH, SULLIVAN & COMPANY Incorporated
FOSTER & MARSHALL INC. — HAMBRECHT & QUIST — STERN, FRANK, MEYER & FOX Incorporated — STONE & YOUNGBERG
BLACK & COMPANY, INC. — COUGHLIN AND COMPANY, INC. — PAUL KENDRICK & CO., INC.

Please send me a Preliminary Prospectus for THE SOUTHERN COMPANY

NAME .... *ADDRESS* ....
(Please Print)

TELEPHONE .... *CITY* .... *STATE* .... *ZIP* ....
(business) *(residence)*

Mail or deliver to your broker, to any of the above firms, or to Morgan Stanley & Co. Incorporated, 1251 Avenue of the Americas, New York, N. Y. 10020 or Merrill Lynch, Pierce, Fenner & Smith Incorporated, Syndicate Department, 165 Broadway, New York, N. Y. 10006 or Salomon Brothers, One New York Plaza, New York, N. Y. 10004.

[B283]

While these provisions *permit* the dissemination of written information to potential investors during the waiting period, they do not *require* it. This has given rise to the problems discussed in the following excerpts.

DISCLOSURE TO INVESTORS

(the "Wheat Report")[a] (1969).

* * *

THE DISSEMINATION OF '33 ACT PROSPECTUSES

The '33 Act seeks to inform investors through prospectuses. However, under the Act's substantive provisions the actual delivery of the prospectus to the investor may be deferred until confirmation of sale is mailed. The problem of getting the prospectus to the investor at some point before he buys remains unsolved.

This problem is especially acute in first public offerings where the prospectus is a uniquely valuable document. To the extent practicable, each prospective investor in a first public offering should receive a copy of the preliminary prospectus a reasonable time in advance of the effective date. Forty-eight hours would be deemed to be a reasonable time under the Study's proposal, which involves an amendment to Rule 460 dealing with the Commission's discretionary power to accelerate the effectiveness of '33 Act filings.

One purpose of the prospectus is to deter the fraudulent sales pitch. However, under present practice the salesman who does the actual selling during the pre-effective period may never have seen the preliminary prospectus. Moreover, he is sometimes unable to supply copies to those of his customers who want it. This problem should be dealt with by a new Commission rule establishing that

(1) Participants in underwritings should take reasonable steps to give prospectuses to all who ask for them.

(2) Each salesman who is expected to offer for sale any security as to which a registration statement has been filed should be given a copy of the preliminary prospectus and of any amended preliminary prospectus. If salesmen are expected to offer securities after the effective date, they should first receive a copy of the final prospectus.

(3) Managing underwriters should be obliged to take reasonable steps to see to it that other participants in the offering (including dealers) receive enough copies of the various versions of the prospectus to enable those participants to comply with the foregoing requirements and with the amended Rule 460. In addition, managing underwriters must furnish any dealer with prospectuses sufficient to enable such dealer to comply with post-effective delivery obligations.

* * *

---

a. See Chapter I.A.3, below for background of the Wheat Report.

PRIOR DELIVERY OF PRELIMINARY PROSPECTUS

Securities Act Release No. 4968 (Apr. 24, 1969).

The Commission again called attention to the continued high volume of registration statements filed under the Securities Act of 1933, and noted that the number of companies filing registration statements for the first time continues to mount, so that well over half of the filings now being made are by such companies. The Commission emphasized that the investing public should be aware that many such offerings of securities are of a highly speculative character and that the prospectus should be carefully examined before an investment decision is reached. It is characteristic of such speculative issues that the company has been recently organized, that the promoters and other selected persons have obtained a disproportionately large number of shares for a nominal price with the consequent dilution in the assets to be contributed by the investing public, and that the underwriters receive fees and other benefits which are high in relation to the proceeds to the issuer and which further dilute the investment values being offered.

The Commission has declared its policy in Rule 460 that it will not accelerate the effective date of a registration statement unless the preliminary prospectus contained in the registration statement is distributed to underwriters and dealers who it is reasonably anticipated will be invited to participate in the distribution of the security to be offered or sold. The purpose of this requirement is to afford all persons effecting the distribution a means of being informed with respect to the offering so that they can advise their customers of the investment merits of the security. Particularly in the case of a first offering by a nonreporting company, salesmen should obtain and read the current preliminary or final prospectus before offering the security to their clients.

The Commission also announced, in the exercise of its responsibilities in accelerating the effective date of a registration statement under Section 8(a) of the Securities Act of 1933, and particularly the statutory requirement that it have due regard to the adequacy of the information respecting the issuer theretofore available to the public, that it will consider whether the persons making an offering of securities of an issuer which is not subject to the reporting requirements of Section 13 or 15(d) of the Securities Exchange Act of 1934, have taken reasonable steps to furnish preliminary prospectuses to those persons who may reasonably be expected to be purchasers of the securities. The Commission will ordinarily be satisfied by a written statement from the managing underwriter to the effect that it has been informed by participating underwriters and dealers that copies of the preliminary prospectus complying with Rule [430] have been or are being distributed to all persons to whom it is then expected to mail confirmations of sale not less than 48 hours prior to the time it is expected to mail such confirmations. Such distribution should be by air mail if the confirmations will be sent by air mail, or a longer period to compensate for the difference in the method of mailing the prospectus should be provided. Of course, if the form of preliminary prospectus so distributed was inadequate or inaccurate in material respects, acceleration will be deferred until the Commission has received satisfactory assurances that appropriate correcting material (including a memorandum of changes) has been so distributed.

In view of the situation above discussed, the Commission proposes to invoke this acceleration policy immediately. When the Commission gains sufficient experience under this policy, it anticipates proposing appropriate revision of its rules.

In 1970, the Commission adopted Rule 15c2–8 under the 1934 Act, requiring every broker or dealer participating in an offering registered under the 1933 Act to take reasonable steps to furnish a copy of the preliminary prospectus (a) to every salesperson soliciting customers' orders for the security and (b) to any person making a written request for one. In 1982, the rule was amended to add the requirement found in Securities Act Release No. 4968 (above) that a copy of the preliminary prospectus be sent to each prospective purchaser at least 48 hours prior to mailing a confirmation of sale.

In DISKIN v. LOMASNEY, 452 F.2d 871 (2d Cir.1971), a broker wrote a letter to a customer during the waiting period offering to commit to sell 5,000 shares "at the public offering price when, as and if issued" but failed to enclose a preliminary prospectus for that security. A statutory prospectus was subsequently received by the customer prior to his agreement to purchase the security. In a private suit by the customer under § 12(1) of the 1933 Act, claiming that the securities had been sold in violation of § 5, the court ruled that an illegal offer is not cured by a subsequent legal sale. The court reasoned:

> The result here reached may appear to be harsh since [the purchaser] had an opportunity to read the final prospectus before he paid for the shares. But the 1954 Congress quite obviously meant to allow rescission or damages in the case of illegal offers as well as of illegal sales. Very likely Congress thought that, when it had done so much to broaden the methods for making legal offers during the "waiting period" between the filing and the taking effect of the registration statement, it should make sure that still other methods were not attempted. Here all [the seller] needed to have done was to accompany the September 17, 1968 letter with any one of the three [permissible waiting period offers]. * * * Very likely Congress thought a better time for meaningful prospectus reading was at the time of the offer rather than in the context of confirmation and demand for payment. In any event, it made altogether clear that an offeror of a security who had failed to follow one of the allowed paths could not achieve absolu-

tion simply by returning to the road of virtue before receiving payment.

Note on Dealers' Prospectus Delivery Obligations After the Effective Date

Section 5(b)(2), by its terms, requires that a prospectus be delivered on every sale of a security in interstate commerce. Section 4(1), however, exempts sales by anyone who is not an "issuer, underwriter or dealer." Section 4(3) exempts all sales by "dealers" (a term defined in Section 2(12)), except for two classes of sales:

a. the original sale by the dealer of the securities which are being distributed by the issuer or by or through an underwriter, no matter how long the dealer has held them (§ 4(3)(C)); and

b. resales by the dealer of securities which were sold to the public in such a distribution and reacquired by the dealer, but only if they take place within a specified period after the original public offering (§§ 4(3)(A) and (B)).

The period specified in § 4(3) for the latter class of sales is forty days in the case of securities of an issuer which has made a prior registered offering under the 1933 Act, and 90 days in the case of securities of an issuer which has not previously made a registered offering (§ 4(3), last sentence). However, the SEC, utilizing the exemptive power contained in that section, has adopted Rule 174, under which a dealer need not deliver a prospectus on any resale of a security of an issuer which is subject to the reporting requirements under the Securities Exchange Act of 1934, no matter how soon after the public offering the resale takes place. In 1988, Rule 174 was expanded to provide that, if the issuer was not previously a reporting company under the 1934 Act but becomes listed on a stock exchange or the NASDAQ system on the offering date, prospectuses need only be delivered for 25 days, rather than 90 days, after the offering date. For any issue in which dealers are required to deliver prospectuses on resale, Item 502(e) of Regulation S–K requires that the prospectus set forth the date on which the requirement terminates.

The purpose of paragraph (A) of § 4(3) is to permit dealers to trade in a security which was illegally offered to the public without registration, after a lapse of 40 days from the time the offering was made. In *Kubik v. Goldfield,* 479 F.2d 472 (3d Cir.1973), the court held that "for the purposes of determining a dealer exemption under § 4(3), a 'bona fide' offer to the public may occur when a stock first appears in the 'pink sheets', even though the stock may be 'illegally' unregistered."

If a dealer is required to deliver a prospectus a substantial time after the effective date, two questions may arise. First, § 10(a)(3) requires that any prospectus used more than nine months after the effective date be updated so that the information contained in it is not more than 16 months old. Second, whether or not nine months have elapsed, the dealer must be sure that the prospectus still contains an accurate and up-to-date description of the company. Delivery of a prospectus which is misleading at the time it is used may constitute a violation of § 17(a)(2) and subject the dealer to liability under § 12(2), even if the prospectus was completely accurate on the effective date. A prospectus can be modified or supplemented to reflect events occurring after the effective date, provided 10 copies of the modified prospectus are filed with the SEC under Rule 424(c) before it is used.

In SEC v. MANOR NURSING CENTERS, 458 F.2d 1082 (2d Cir.1972), the court held that delivery of an uncorrected prospectus, which was not an accurate statement as of the date of delivery, was a violation of § 5(b)(2), subjecting the dealer who delivered the prospectus to liability under § 12(1). The reasoning of the court in *Manor Nursing Centers* has been criticized by courts of appeals in two other circuits, which rejected the argument that use of an offering circular which has become misleading destroys the exemption provided in Regulation A or B (see p. 287 below) and thus causes a violation of § 5. SEC v. SOUTHWEST COAL AND ENERGY, 624 F.2d 1312 (5th Cir.1980); SEC v. BLAZON, 609 F.2d 960 (9th Cir.1979).

Selected References

T. Hazen, Securities Regulation §§ 2.1–2.5 (2d ed. 1990).

Chiappinelli, Gun Jumping: The Problem of Extraneous Offers of Securities, 50 U.Pitt.L.Rev. 457 (1989).

Discussion, Initial Public Offerings, 13 Inst. on. Sec. Reg. 351 (1982).

Morgan, Offers to Buy Under the Securities Act of 1933, 1982 Ariz.St.L.J. 809.

Pierce, Current and Recurrent Section 5 Gunjumping Problems, 26 Case Wes.Res.L.Rev. 370 (1976).

Schneider, Manko & Kant, Going Public—Practice, Procedure and Consequences, 27 Villanova L.Rev. 1 (1981).

Wheat & Blackstone, Guideposts for a First Public Offering, 15 Bus.Lawyer 539 (1960).

Woodside, Development of SEC Practices in Processing Registration Statements and Proxy Statements, 24 Bus.Lawyer 375 (1969).

Landis, The Legislative History of the Securities Act of 1933, 28 Geo.Wash. L.Rev. 29 (1959).

---

3. *Integration of 1933 Act and 1934 Act Disclosure Requirements*

Up to now, we have been considering the provisions of § 5 of the 1933 Act without regard to whether the issuer is already a publicly-held company subject to the disclosure requirements of the 1934 Act. As noted in the Introduction, the latter act was amended in 1964 to extend its periodic disclosure requirements to all issuers with more than 500 shareholders and more than $1 million in assets. That amendment triggered a series of efforts to achieve greater coordination of the disclosure requirements of the two acts. The history and current status of those efforts are indicated by the following materials.

"TRUTH IN SECURITIES" REVISITED

By Milton H. Cohen *

79 Harv.L.Rev. 1340 (1966).**

The first federal securities law, the Securities Act of 1933, was designed to achieve "truth in securities" in connection with public offerings. There were a few collateral provisions—general prohibitions against fraud in any offer or sale of securities and against touting for an undisclosed fee—but this first statute was essentially a narrowly focused but high-powered effort to assure full and fair disclosure on the special occasion of a public offering.

A year after this first law came the Securities Exchange Act of 1934, having as its dominant purpose the regulation of securities brokers and dealers and the securities markets in which they operate, but also providing a whole new framework of disclosure regarding securities traded in certain of those markets. However, unlike the requirements of the 1933 Act, which were (1) potentially applicable to any company, (2) but only on the occasion of a public offering, and (3) surrounded with elaborate mechanisms and sanctions to accomplish "truth in securities" on such an occasion, the disclosure requirements of the 1934 Act were (1) applicable to a more limited, albeit very important, group of issuers having securities listed and traded on an exchange, (2) on a continuous basis, (3) but with considerably less in the way of supporting mechanisms and sanctions. Moreover, in contrast to the 1933 Act's theory of registering only the actual quantity of securities proposed to be offered, the 1934 Act contemplated registration of an entire "class" of securities.

Then, thirty years later, through the Securities Act Amendments of 1964, the 1934 Act's pattern of continuous disclosure was made applicable to a much larger category of issuers—all those presumed to be the subject of active investor interest in the over-the-counter market by reason of having as many as 500 holders of record of a class of equity securities and at least one million dollars of assets. At the present time some 2,500 companies are subject to the pattern of continuous disclosure by reason of having listed securities; from 2,500 to 3,000 more are or soon will be subject to the same requirements by virtue of meeting the tests of the 1964 Amendments.

* Member of the Illinois Bar. A.B., Harvard, 1932, LL.B., 1935. Formerly Director of Special Study of Securities Markets, Securities and Exchange Commission.

It is my thesis that the combined disclosure requirements of these statutes would have been quite different if the 1933 and 1934 Acts (the latter as extended in 1964) had been enacted in opposite order, or had been enacted as a single, integrated statute—that is, if the starting point had been a statutory scheme of continuous disclosures covering issuers of actively traded securities and the question of special disclosures in connection with public offerings had then been faced in this setting. Accordingly, it is my plea that there now be created a new coordinated disclosure system having as its basis the continuous disclosure system of the 1934 Act and treating "1933 Act" disclosure needs on this foundation. * * *

Note on the American Law Institute's Federal Securities Code Project

In 1969, the Committee on Federal Regulation of Securities of the American Bar Association requested the American Law Institute to undertake the preparation of a coordinated Federal Securities Code to replace all of the present federal securities laws. The American Law Institute authorized the project, and selected Professor Louis Loss of Harvard Law School as Reporter.

Among the principal "problems" in the existing law to which the Reporter addressed his attention in the proposed Code were (1) the "complications" arising from inconsistent definitions, as well as procedural and jurisdictional provisions, in the different acts; (2) the overemphasis of the disclosure provisions on "public offerings" rather than regular reporting requirements, and (3) the "chaotic" development of civil liabilities resulting from "broad judicial implication of private rights of action" under various provisions of existing law.

The Code took approximately eight years to complete, and the final version was approved by the ALI in May 1978. Congress, however, has shown no interest in even considering the proposed Code. The chairman of the House subcommittee responsible for securities law stated in November 1983 that he "found little support for undertaking a consideration of the code as a whole." The Code has had considerable influence, however. Some of its approaches have been incorporated in new SEC rules, or picked up by the courts to resolve ambiguous provisions of current law, a process which the author of the Code has described as "cannibalizing it for spare parts."

While the ALI was pursuing the legislative route toward rationalization of the disclosure requirements, the SEC undertook to modify its own rules and procedures to achieve comparable improvements within the framework of the current law. The key step in this process was the appointment of a study group, under the direction of Commissioner Francis M. Wheat, which submitted its recommendations to the Commission in 1969:

DISCLOSURE TO INVESTORS

(the "Wheat Report") (1969).

In November, 1967, the Commission announced the formation of a small, internal study group "to examine the operation of the disclosure provisions of the Securities Act of 1933 and the Securities Exchange Act of 1934 and Commission rules and regulations thereunder."

* * *

It has been the goal of the Study to discover what could be done through the rule-making process—

(a) to enhance the degree of coordination between the disclosures required by the '33 and '34 Acts;

(b) to respond to the call for greater certainty and predictability; and

(c) to develop a consistent interpretative pattern which would help to assure that appropriate disclosures are made prior to the creation of interstate public markets in the securities of any issuer.

* * *

Historically, the Commission's efforts in the disclosure field have been concentrated in the new issue market, despite the far greater statistical importance of the trading markets. This traditional emphasis has a certain justification. The special selling effort by which new issues are normally distributed calls for countervailing measures to protect the public customer. Moreover, transactions through which new capital flows into industry can be regarded as having a more significant impact on the economy than mere trading transactions. However, it is the opinion of the Study that for the future, greater attention must be paid to those continuing disclosures which benefit the trading markets in securities. Prior to 1964, the Commission's ability to meet this need was limited. Its authority with respect to continuing disclosure reached only those issuers whose securities were listed on exchanges and those which had voluntarily registered securities under the '33 Act. Full exercise of that authority might have deterred listing. This is no longer the case, and a serious impediment to progress in disclosure policy has been removed.

* * *

For non-reporting companies, the prospectus is the only reliable source of information generally available following a registered public offering. Therefore, its dissemination should be encouraged. The 90-day post-effective prospectus delivery requirement serves that purpose. It should be retained and enforced. Different considerations apply to the post-effective delivery of prospectuses of reporting companies. Information about such companies is on file with the Commission and available to the financial community. It is questionable whether the dealer's present duty to deliver prospectuses during the 40 days following the effective date of a registration statement is particularly helpful to investors in the trading markets. If the '34 Act reports are improved as recommended in Chapter X of this report, dealers who are not acting as underwriters should be relieved from any post-effective obligation to deliver prospectuses of issuers that report under the '34 Act.

THE "GUN-JUMPING" PROBLEM

When Section 5 of the '33 Act applies, no offering can be made until a registration statement is filed; after such filing, a written offer may be made only by means of a prospectus that meets the statutory requirements. Thus, publicity which develops interest in a forthcoming registered offering may run afoul of the Act's prohibitions. However, the policy of protecting prospective buyers of new securities from undue sales pressures must be harmonized with the need to keep buyers, sellers, and holders of the issuer's outstanding securities appropriately informed.

With respect to issuer-generated publicity, present standards are sound and generally workable. They distinguish the normal flow of corporate news unrelated to an effort to sell securities from the type of publicity aimed at selling the issuer's stock. Issuers who are making or are about to make public offerings can as a general rule continue to give normal publicity to corporate events. In general, the Study agrees that projections of sales and earnings which would not be permitted in a prospectus should not be released by corporate management when a registered offering is about to take place.

Standards as to publicity generated by brokers, dealers, and investment advisers are less clear. The point in time when restrictions on such publicity commence should be made more definite. Other recommendations are summarized below:

(1) It should be specified that the gun-jumping doctrine generally applies only to the participants in the particular distribution. Assuming that securities of a reporting company are to be offered, nonparticipants who are truly independent of the participants should be under no restriction.

(2) If an issuer meets the standards for use of Form S–7, expression of opinion about its common stock should be permitted when a registration statement relating only to nonconvertible senior securities is pending, and vice versa.

(3) If a securities firm publishes a broad list of recommended securities on a regular basis, it should be permitted to include in the list a recommendation as to securities which are the subject of an underwriting in which it is a participant, subject to certain conditions which guard against abuse.

(4) Factual follow-up reporting on previously recommended securities should be permitted at any time, subject to appropriate conditions.

(5) Pre-filing distribution of market letters and industry surveys that were fully prepared and delivered to printers before the firm

reached an understanding that it would participate in the underwriting should be permitted under appropriate conditions.

In 1970, the Commission implemented these recommendations by (a) amending Rule 135 to permit announcement of an offering prior to the filing of a registration statement, (b) adopting Rules 137, 138 and 139, permitting broker-dealers to continue making recommendations regarding outstanding securities even though they may be involved in the distribution of a related security, and (c) amending Rule 174 to eliminate any requirement for delivery of a prospectus on secondary transactions in securities of issuers which are reporting companies under the 1934 Act.

In March 1982, the Commission took a major step toward integration of the 1933 and 1934 Act disclosure requirements with the adoption of an "integrated disclosure system." (Sec. Act Rel. No. 6383.) The principal elements of that system are:

(a) Inclusion of all of the disclosure requirements for the basic 1933 and 1934 Act documents in a new Regulation S–K, with the items of the various forms simply referring to the applicable items of that Regulation.

(b) Adoption of new registration forms for offerings by issuers already registered under the 1934 Act, which permit a large part of the information required in the registration statement to be incorporated by reference to the issuer's 1934 Act filings or reports to shareholders.

(c) Expansion of the opportunities for "shelf registration," under which an issuer can register under the 1933 Act securities which it contemplates offering at a later date with the time and offering terms depending on market conditions and other factors.

(d) Specification of certain circumstances to be taken into account in determining whether directors, underwriters and others have satisfied their "due diligence" obligations, particularly with respect to statements incorporated in the registration statement by reference to other documents.

The new "shelf registration" provisions, embodied in Rule 415, proved to be more controversial than the SEC had anticipated. The Rule permits an issuer to register securities for sale over a two-year period, enabling it to make an immediate offering of securities at any time by merely placing a sticker on the prospectus included in its already-effective registration statement. This avoids the delay involved in preparation of a new registration statement and the 20-day waiting period before effectiveness. The registration statement is kept up to date by the filing of post-effective amendments or the incorporation by reference of additional documents filed under the 1934 Act.

The new Rule is particularly attractive to large companies which make frequent offerings of debt securities and want to move quickly to take advantage of favorable interest rates. It was strongly opposed, however, by some of the major underwriting firms who feared that the elimination of the delay would give an advantage to firms with strong retail capabilities or, even worse, make it easier for issuers to sell directly to large institutions. In deference to their concerns, the SEC agreed to adopt the Rule on a trial basis, for a period of nine months, and to hold public hearings on its possible impact on the underwriting system.

Upon completion of these hearings, and after receipt of additional comments, the SEC adopted Rule 415 on a permanent basis, but limited its use to "traditional" types of delayed offerings and to primary offerings qualified to be registered on Form S-3 (see p. 78 below). Sec. Act Rel. No. 6499 (Nov. 17, 1983).

The 1934 Act reporting and disclosure requirements are discussed at p. 628 below.

Selected References

T. Hazen, Securities Regulation, Ch. 3 (2d ed.1990).

Banoff, Regulatory Subsidies, Efficient Markets and Shelf Registration: An Analysis of Rule 415, 70 Va.L.Rev. 135 (1984).

Cohen, The Integrated Disclosure System–Unfinished Business, 40 Bus.Law 987 (1985).

Feeney, The Saga of Rule 415: Registration for the Shelf, 9 Corp.L.Rev. 41 (1986).

Fox, Shelf Registration, Integrated Disclosure, and Underwriter Due Diligence: An Economic Analysis, 70 Va.L.Rev. 1005 (1984).

Frerichs, Underwriter Due Diligence Within the Integrated Disclosure System–If It Isn't Broken, Don't Fix It, 16 Sec.Reg.L.J. 386 (1989).

Ketels, SEC Rule 415—The New Experimental Procedures for Shelf Registration, 10 Sec.Reg.L.J. 318 (Winter 1983).

Kidwell, Marr & Thompson, Shelf Registration: Competition and Market Flexibility, 30 J. L. & Econ. 181 (1987).

Kripke, Where Are We on Securities Disclosure After the Advisory Committee Report?, 6 Sec.Reg.L.J. 99 (1978).

Rosenfeld, A Sideline View of the Disclosure Advisory Committee Report: A Response to Professor Kripke, 7 Sec.Reg.L.J. 76 (1979).

Comment, Due Diligence Under Rule 415: Is the Insurance Worth the Premium?, 38 Emory L.J. 793 (1989).

Comment, Utilization of Investment Analysis Principles in the Development of Disclosure Policy Under the Federal Securities Laws, 25 UCLA L.Rev. 292 (1977).

B. THE CONTENTS OF THE PROSPECTUS

Section 7 of the 1933 Act, by reference to Schedule A of the Act (or Schedule B, in the case of securities issued by foreign governments), prescribes the information to be included in a registration statement. Section 10(a)(1) specifies which of those items of information must be included in the prospectus furnished to purchasers.

Section 7 authorizes the Commission (a) to require any additional information to be included in a registration statement or (b) to permit the omission of certain items of information with respect to particular classes of securities or issuers. Acting under this authority, the Commission has, from time to time, promulgated a number of different forms for registering different types of offerings. The basic form for registration statements, however, is Form S–1, prescribed for use in all offerings for which no other form is authorized or prescribed.

As part of its effort (described above) to integrate the disclosure requirements of the 1933 and 1934 Acts, the Commission has adopted Regulation S–K, prescribing the disclosures to be made in documents filed under both Acts. You will therefore find, on examining Form S–1, that it refers you to Regulation S–K for the actual disclosure requirements.

Also in furtherance of its integration program, the Commission in 1982 adopted Forms S–2 and S–3, for use by issuers already registered under the 1934 Act. Form S–2, which can be used by any issuer which has been filing reports under the 1934 Act for at least three years, permits the issuer to supply the requisite information about itself by including in the registration statement and prospectus a copy of its latest annual report to shareholders and incorporating by reference its latest annual report to the Commission on Form 10–K. Form S–3 can also be used by issuers which have been filing reports under the 1934 Act for at least three years, to register (a) offerings of senior securities, secondary offerings, and certain special kinds of offerings, and (b) new offerings of equity securities if the market value of the issuer's publicly-held voting stock is at least $150 million (or $100 million if the annual trading volume of such stock is 3 million shares or more). It does not require the issuer to include in the registration statement or prospectus any information about itself, but simply to incorporate by reference its latest annual report on Form 10–K. The rationale behind these two forms is that the information already circulating in the market with respect to such issuers obviates the need for further dissemination by means of the registration statement and prospectus.

In response to pressure on the Commission to reduce the burden of registration on small issuers, the Commission in 1979 adopted a new Form S–18, for use only by issuers which are *not* registered under the 1934 Act, for cash offerings of not more than $7.5 million. It requires disclosure of the same kinds of information called for by Form S–1, but in a significantly simpler format. Form S–18 was amended in 1982 to expand its availability and to coordinate its disclosure requirements with Regulation S–K. See Sec.Act Rel. No. 6406 (June 4, 1982).

Other registration forms available for use in special situations are Form S-8, for employee stock purchase plans, Form S-11, for real estate companies, and Form S-4, for mergers and acquisitions.

There are comparable forms for foreign private issuers (F-1, F-2, F-3, and F-4). See also Form F-6 for registration of securities represented by American Depositary Receipts.

Supplementing the items and instructions in the forms and in Regulation S-K is the Commission's Regulation C, consisting of Rules 400 through 485 under the 1933 Act, which prescribes registration procedures and the general form of registration statements and prospectuses. In addition, the Commission published in 1968, and supplemented from time to time, a set of "Guides for Preparation and Filing of Registration Statements," which represented positions taken by the staff in the administration of the Act. With the exception of guides relating to specific industries, these guides were either rescinded or incorporated in Regulation S-K when the Commission adopted its integrated disclosure system in March 1982.

These rules, forms, and guides, however, are only the starting point in the preparation of a registration statement. The supposed objective of the 1933 Act is to produce a document which tells a prospective purchaser the things he really ought to know before buying a security. As the following materials indicate, however, this objective is not easy to attain. Among the factors which inhibit it are (1) the fact that it may be against the issuer's financial interest to tell investors the real weaknesses of the operation (it is much easier to prohibit a person from doing something wrong than to require him to do something well when he doesn't want to do it all), and (2) the difficulty of putting complex financial arrangements or economic factors into language simple enough for the average investor to understand.

The task is complicated further by uncertainty as to whether the principal purpose of disclosure under the federal securities laws is to protect investors against really bad deals by making sure that negative factors are emphasized, or to enable them to make rational choices among alternative respectable deals by requiring a balanced presentation of affirmative and negative factors.

---

1. *Adequacy of Disclosure*

UNIVERSAL CAMERA CORP.

19 S.E.C. 648 (1945).

This case comes before us on a motion to dismiss a stop order proceeding commenced with respect to a registration statement filed under the Securities Act of 1933 by Universal Camera Corporation (Universal). * * *

On March 19, 1945, Universal filed with the Commission a registration statement under the Securities Act of 1933. The statement related to a proposed public offering of (1) 663,500 shares of a new Class A common stock of Universal and (2) warrants, expiring December 31, 1948, for the purchase of 172,700 shares of such Class A common stock. The shares called for by the warrants would also be registered under this registration statement.

* * *

Universal was incorporated under the laws of Delaware September 29, 1937. It succeeded a New York corporation of the same name which had been incorporated in 1933. Universal's normal peace time business is the manufacture and distribution of popular priced still and motion picture cameras, projectors, film and photographic accessories.

Early in 1942 Universal virtually discontinued making these products and since then has been engaged almost exclusively in making binoculars under prime contracts for the Army and Navy. Its resumption of the manufacture of nonwar products is dependent upon the freeing of facilities from war production requirements and a relaxation of Government regulations and restrictions imposed to meet exigencies of the current national emergency. * * *

The Terms of the Offering

The registration statement covers 530,500 Class A shares to be offered to the public by Universal's present common stockholders. That is all but 1,500 of the 532,000 Class A shares which the controlling stockholders would receive (together with all of the new Class B stock and warrants for 308,400 shares of Class A stock) in exchange for the 300,000 shares of Universal's common stock which they now hold. The proceeds of sale of such Class A shares would go not to Universal but to the selling stockholders.

The registration statement covers also 133,000 Class A shares to be offered to the public by Universal itself. The proceeds of sale of such shares would go to Universal.

* * *

Speculative Character of the Shares to be Offered

The facing page of the prospectus states: "These Shares Are Offered As a Speculation."

Where the nature of the securities requires the employment of such a legend the registrant is under a duty to describe the speculative features of the offering in the registration statement and the prospectus so clearly that they will be plainly evident to the ordinary investor. This Universal failed to do. The statement as originally filed did not plainly disclose the prospective investor's relative interest in the assets, earnings or voting power of the company. Nor did it give a clear description of Universal's proposed business activities.

A. Omissions of Material Facts in Respect of the Registrant's Proposed Financial Structure

All of Universal's outstanding common stock was acquired by the present holders from Universal's predecessor for $30,000. As of December 31, 1944, it had a liquidating value of $279,438 according to Universal's books. On that basis the 532,000 shares of new Class A stock to be issued in exchange for the outstanding common would have a liquidating value of about 53 cents a share according to Universal's books.

The proceeds of Universal's sale of 133,000 Class A shares at $5 per share would increase the Class A stock's liquidating value to an aggregate of $804,423 for the 665,000 shares, or $1.21 per share according to Universal's books. The new Class B stock would have no asset value although it would have exclusive voting power.

Of their 532,000 shares of the new Class A stock, the selling stockholders propose to sell 530,500 shares to the public at $5 per share.

Through that sale they would realize $2,100,865 for the part which they propose to sell of the stock to be received in exchange for the common they originally purchased for $30,000. At the same time they would retain exclusive voting power and a 43 percent participation in earnings after preferred dividends by retaining all of the B stock also to be received in the exchange of their common. Beyond that they would still have the earning power and liquidating value represented by 1,500 shares of Class A stock not to be offered for sale, and New York Merchandise Co., Inc. would still have its 25,000 shares of preferred stock.

* * *

The omission of facts disclosing plainly the contrast between the proposed offering price and the book value of the shares to be offered would have made it practically impossible for anyone but an astute and experienced security analyst to discover, from the information as it was set out in the statement, that on the basis of the company's past earning experience it would require an accumulation of many years earnings to enable an investor, buying the Class A stock and holding it, to regain through earnings, even the difference between its book value and the price at which it was offered to him.

A disclosure which makes the facts available in such form that their significance is apparent only upon searching analysis by experts does not meet the standards imposed by the Securities Act of 1933 as we understand that Act. Elaboration of statement is usually not essential to completeness, accuracy or clarity. Indeed, with few, if any exceptions a plainly phrased, concise statement if correct and complete would provide a more effective disclosure than a more elaborate statement. The primary point is that it should be plainly understandable to the ordinary investor. * * *

Another aspect of the financial structure which the registration statement and prospectus did not adequately describe to the ordinary investor was the significance and effect of the proposed issuance of option warrants. Whatever may be the advantages of issuing warrants to underwriters and to purchasers, warrants do involve potentialities of disadvantage from the viewpoint of the issuing company's future financing.

Here it was proposed to issue warrants that would be effective for a period of more than 3 years beginning, as it would have happened, shortly after the war in Europe ceased. They were to be issued in an amount which, if all warrants were exercised, would bring in an amount of capital greater than the total liquidating value of the Class A stock that would be outstanding at the conclusion of the financing proposed in the registration statement.

In view of the amount of stock called for by the warrants proposed to be issued here, the critical period for which they would be outstanding and the large proportion of such warrants to be issued to others than public purchasers, we believe that for a fair and complete disclosure it would be requisite for Universal to state that for the life of the warrants, until December 31, 1948, the company might be deprived of favorable opportunities to procure additional equity capital, if it should be needed for the purpose of the business, and that at any time when the holders of such warrants might be expected to exercise them, the company would, in all likelihood, be able to obtain equity capital, if it needed capital then, by public sale of a new issue on terms more favorable than those provided for by the warrants.

B. Omissions and Misstatements with Respect to Registrant's Business

The original registration statement touched but lightly upon competitive conditions in the industry before the war. On the other hand it made broad general assertions concerning Universal's post-war prospects. For example, on p. 6 of the prospectus it stated:

> The Company believes that its competitive position in the postwar market will be maintained by reason of the fact that it is currently designing and preparing improved and additional photographic products which should find a ready sale.

and again at p. 8 it said:

> While other manufacturers have also gained skill and knowledge in the field of Optical Instruments in connection with their war work, the Company, by reason of its ability to successfully compete as to quality and price in the manufacture of binoculars, feels that it will be able to maintain its competitive position in the postwar market.

With respect to the first statement quoted the prospectus contained no disclosure of the extent of its progress in the development of what it described as "improved and additional photographic products." Nor were representatives of the company able to testify to a substantial basis for their opinions relative to sales prospects.

With respect to the second statement quoted it appears that the only competition the registrant has ever met in the sale of binoculars has been in sales to the government under war contracts. Obviously that is not the kind of competition in which it is likely to be engaged primarily after the war. Furthermore, the registration statement failed to state that the market for binoculars before the war was a relatively limited market.

The original prospectus made much of Universal's ability to manufacture all of its lens requirements by mass production methods by using machines it has developed. Great emphasis was placed also upon the fact that designs for such machines were donated to the government and that the machines used by other manufacturers bear the mark "built from designs donated by Universal Camera Corporation to the U.S. Government." The prospectus did not reveal, however, that these designs are not covered by patents and that, except for some relatively recent developments, competitors are well acquainted with the machines. Cf. In the Matter of Automatic Telephone Dialer, Inc., 10 S.E.C. 698 (1941).

Of like character was the failure of the prospectus to indicate in connection with statements made concerning the pending development for manufacture of a 16 mm. sound projector and a self-contained table model phonograph with automatic record changer, that in fact, in the case of the first and possibly in the case of the second, it would be necessary for Universal to obtain licenses under certain electronic patents before it would manufacture the new products if and when their development is completed. Furthermore, there was no indication of the time necessary to perfect such products for marketing.

These and other similar deficiencies indicate not only the inadequate and the misleading character of the original prospectus, they demonstrate the deficiencies of Universal's response to Item 1 of Form S–2 which calls for a disclosure of information concerning the business done and intended to be done by the registrant. * * *

In the early 1970s, the Commission substantially revised and expanded its disclosure forms to elicit more detailed information with respect to (a) the company's plan of operations (in the case of companies going public for the first time), (b) competitive conditions in the industry in which the company is engaged, and (c) dilution resulting from the disparity between the prices paid by public investors and "insiders" for their securities. The current version of these requirements can be found in Items 101(a)(2), 101(c)(x) and 506 of Regulation S–K.

FRANCHARD CORP.

42 S.E.C. 163 (1964).

CARY, CHAIRMAN: These are consolidated proceedings pursuant to Sections 8(c) and 8(d) of the Securities Act of 1933 ("Securities Act") to determine whether a stop order should issue suspending the effectiveness of three registration statements filed by Franchard Corporation, formerly Glickman Corporation ("registrant"), and whether certain post-effective amendments filed by the registrant should be declared effective. These proceedings raise important issues as to the disclosures to be required in a registration statement concerning (1) the use of substantial amounts of a company's funds for the personal benefit of its controlling person on whose business reputation public offerings of its securities were largely predicated; (2) the pledge by a dominant stockholder of his control stock; (3) the adequacy of performance of a board of directors; and (4) the unique characteristics and risk elements of a real estate company operated on a "cash flow" basis. In essence, we are concerned here with the role that can and should be performed by the disclosure requirements of the Securities Act in assisting investors to evaluate management, as well as with the most meaningful method of presenting to the investor the complexities of a cash flow real estate company's operations. * * *

I. FACTS

A. Background

Louis J. Glickman ("Glickman") has for many years been a large-scale real estate developer, operator and investor. From 1954 to 1960 he acquired control of real estate in this country and in Canada by means of "syndication" arrangements. These arrangements involved the acquisition by Glickman, through purchase, contract or option, of an interest in real estate; the organization of a legal entity, usually a limited partnership but in some instances a corporation, in which Glickman retained a controlling position, and in which interests were sold to the public for cash; and the acquisition by this entity of the property interest in question. Glickman conducted some of these syndication activities and certain other phases of his real estate business through a number of wholly owned corporations, the most important of which was Glickman Corporation of Nevada, now known as Venada Corporation ("Venada").

In May of 1960, Glickman caused registrant to be formed in order to group under one entity most of the publicly owned corporations and limited partnerships under his control. * * * Glickman established control of registrant by acquiring 450,000 of its 660,000 authorized B shares for $1 per share. He exercised a dominant role in the management of registrant's affairs as president at the time of its formation and later as its first chairman of the board. * * *

B. Glickman's Withdrawals and Pledges

Registrant's 1960 prospectus stated that Glickman had from time to time advanced substantial sums to the partnerships and corporations that were about to become subsidiaries of the registrant. It also said that he had advanced $211,000 to the registrant for the purpose of defraying its organization and registration costs and that this advance would be repaid without interest out of the proceeds of the public offering. On October 14, 1960—two days after the effective date of registrant's 1960 filing—Glickman began secretly to transfer funds from the registrant to Venada, his wholly owned corporation. Within two months the aggregate amount of these transfers amounted to $296,329. By October 2, 1961, the effective date of registrant's first 1961 filing, Glickman had made 45 withdrawals which amounted in the aggregate to $2,372,511.[8] Neither the 1961 prospectuses nor any of the effective amendments to the 1960 filing referred to these transactions.

All of registrant's prospectuses stated that Glickman owned most of its B as well as a substantial block of its A stock. On the effective date of the 1960 filing Glickman's shares were unencumbered. In the following month, however, he began to pledge his shares to finance his personal real estate ventures. By August 31, 1961, all of Glickman's B and much of his A stock had been pledged to banks, finance companies, and private individuals. On the effective dates of the two 1961 filings the loans secured by these pledges aggregated about $4,250,000. The effective interest rates on these loans ran as high as 24% annually. Glickman retained the right to vote the pledged shares in the absence of a default on the loans. The two 1961 filings made no mention of Glickman's pledges or the loans they secured.

* * *

II. ALLEGED DEFICIENCIES—ACTIVITIES OF MANAGEMENT

A. Glickman's Withdrawals of Registrant's Funds and Pledges of His Shares

Of cardinal importance in any business is the quality of its management. Disclosures relevant to an evaluation of management are particularly pertinent where, as in this case, securities are sold largely on the personal reputation of a company's controlling person. The disclosures in these respects were materially deficient. The 1960 prospectus failed to reveal that Glickman intended to use substantial amounts of registrant's

8. In most instances the amounts were returned relatively soon but were followed by fresh withdrawals. The amounts owed registrant by Glickman often exceeded $1,000,000 and on one occasion were close to $1,500,000. The withdrawals by Glickman were accomplished by transfers of funds from registrant and its subsidiaries directly to Venada and expenditures by registrant and its subsidiaries for Venada's benefit. During this period, registrant and its subsidiaries had a number of relationships with Venada which regularly required them to make payments directly to it or on its behalf. The interspersal of Glickman's unauthorized withdrawals among a large number of usual and proper disbursements on the books of registrant and its subsidiaries facilitated concealment of his activities.

funds for the benefit of Venada,[13] and the 1961 prospectuses made no reference to Glickman's continual diversion of substantial sums from the registrant. Glickman's pledges were not discussed in either the effective amendments to the 1960 filings or in the two 1961 filings.

In our view, these disclosures were highly material to an evaluation of the competence and reliability of registrant's management—in large measure, Glickman. In many respects, the development of disclosure standards adequate for informed appraisal of management's ability and integrity is a difficult task. How do you tell a "good" business manager from a "bad" one in a piece of paper? Managerial talent consists of personal attributes, essentially subjective in nature, that frequently defy meaningful analysis through the impersonal medium of a prospectus. Direct statements of opinion as to management's ability, which are not susceptible to objective verification, may well create an unwarranted appearance of reliability if placed in a prospectus. The integrity of management—its willingness to place its duty to public shareholders over personal interest—is an equally elusive factor for the application of disclosure standards.

Evaluation of the quality of management—to whatever extent it is possible—is an essential ingredient of informed investment decision. A need so important cannot be ignored, and in a variety of ways the disclosure requirements of the Securities Act furnish factual information to fill this need. Appraisals of competency begin with information concerning management's past business experience, which is elicited by requirements that a prospectus state the offices and positions held with the issuer by each executive officer within the last five years. With respect to established companies, management's past performance, as shown by comprehensive financial and other disclosures concerning the issuer's operations, furnish a guide to its future business performance. To permit judgments whether the corporation's affairs are likely to be conducted in the interest of public shareholders, the registration requirements elicit information as to the interests of insiders which may conflict with their duty of loyalty to the corporation. Disclosures are also required with respect to the remuneration and other benefits paid or proposed to be paid to management as well as material transactions between the corporation and its officers, directors, holders of more than 10 percent of its stock, and their associates.

Glickman's withdrawals were material transactions between registrant and its management, and the registration forms on which registrant's filings were made called for their disclosure. * * *

13. We reject registrant's contention that this finding cannot be made because there is no direct evidence with respect to Glickman's state of mind on the effective date of the 1960 filing. In view of the brevity of the time interval—two days—and the absence of countervailing evidence, we consider it reasonable to infer that Glickman intended to divert proceeds from registrant's offering on that date. Cf. Globe Aircraft Corporation, 26 S.E.C. 43, 48–51 (1947). Moreover, the post-effective amendments to the 1960 filing, which became effective, were materially deficient in failing to refer to Glickman's diversions. The first such amendment became effective on November 4, 1960, by which time the diversions had already begun.

A description of Glickman's activities was important on several grounds. First, publication of the facts pertaining to Glickman's withdrawals of substantial funds and of his pledges of his control stock would have clearly indicated his strained financial position and his urgent need for cash in his personal real estate ventures. * * *

Second, disclosure of Glickman's continual diversion of registrant's funds to the use of Venada, his wholly owned corporation, was also germane to an evaluation of the integrity of his management. This quality is always a material factor. * * *

Third, Glickman's need for cash as indicated by withdrawals from registrant and his substantial borrowings and pledges of registrant's shares gave him a powerful and direct motive to cause registrant to pursue policies which would permit high distribution rates and maintain a high price for registrant's A shares. * * *

Finally, the possibility of a change of control was also important to prospective investors. As we have noted, registrant's public offerings were largely predicated on Glickman's reputation as a successful real estate investor and operator. Disclosure of Glickman's secured loans, the relatively high interest rates that they bore, the secondary sources from which many of the loans were obtained, and the conditions under which lenders could declare defaults would have alerted investors to the possibility of a change in the control and management of registrant and apprised them of the possible nature of any such change.

* * *

We also cannot agree with registrant's contention that disclosure of Glickman's borrowings and pledges of registrant's stock would have been an "unwarranted revelation" of Glickman's personal affairs. An insider of a corporation that is asking the public for funds must, in return, relinquish various areas of privacy with respect to his financial affairs which impinge significantly upon the affairs of the company. That determination was made by the Congress over thirty years ago when it expressly provided in the Securities Act for disclosure of such matters as remuneration of insiders and the extent of their shareholdings in and the nature of their other material transactions with the company.

With respect to disclosure of pledged shares, registrant is not aided by pointing out that our registration forms under the Securities Act and the reports required under the Securities Exchange Act do not call for disclosure of encumbrances on a controlling stockholder's shares, and that proposals to require such disclosures in reports filed with us under the Securities Exchange Act have not been adopted. The fact that such disclosures are not required of all issuers and their controlling persons in all cases does not negate their materiality in specific cases. The registration forms promulgated by us are guides intended to assist registrants in discharging their statutory duty of full disclosure. They are not and cannot possibly be exhaustive enumerations of each and every item material to investors in the particular circumstances relevant to a specific offering. The kaleidoscopic variety of economic life precludes any attempt at such an enumeration. The preparation of a registration statement is not satisfied, as registrant's position suggests, by a mechanical process of responding narrowly to the specific items of the applicable registration form. On the contrary, Rule 408 under the Securities Act makes clear to prospective registrants that: "In addition to the information expressly required to be included in a registration statement, there shall be added such further material information, if any, as may be necessary to make the required statements in the light of the circumstances under which they were made, not misleading."

B. *Activities of Registrant's Directors*

Another issue raised in these proceedings concerns the disclosure to be required in a prospectus regarding the adequacy of performance of managerial functions by registrant's board of directors. The Division urges that the prospectuses, by identifying the members of the board of directors, impliedly represented that they would provide oversight and direction to registrant's officers. In fact, the Division argues, the board was a nullity because the directors consistently agreed to Glickman's proposals, derived their information as to the current state of registrant's finances from Glickman's sporadic oral reports, and permitted him to fix each officer's area of responsibility.

* * *

This is an issue raising fundamental considerations as to the functions of the disclosure requirements of the Securities Act. The civil liability provisions of Section 11 do establish for directors a standard of due diligence in the preparation of a registration statement—a federal rule of directors' responsibility with respect to the completeness and accuracy of the document used in the public distribution of securities. The Act does not purport, however, to define federal standards of directors' responsibility in the ordinary operations of business enterprises and nowhere empowers us to formulate administratively such regulatory standards. The diligence required of registrant's directors in overseeing its affairs is to be evaluated in the light of the standards established by state statutory and common law.

In our view, the application of these standards on a routine basis in the processing of registration statements would be basically incompatible with the philosophy and administration of the disclosure requirements of the Securities Act. * * * To generally require information in Securities Act prospectuses as to whether directors have performed their duties in accordance with the standards of responsibility required of them under state law would stretch disclosure beyond the limitations contemplated by the statutory scheme and necessitated by considerations of administrative practicality. * * *

Form S–1 was amended in 1973 to require additional information with respect to officers, directors and key employees of the registrant. Would the expanded requirements, now found in Item 401(c)–(f) of Regulation S–K, specifically call for the type of information which the Commission considered material in the *Franchard* decision?

In the late 1970s, the SEC brought actions against a number of large publicly-held corporations alleging that they had failed to disclose, in documents filed with the Commission, (a) illegal campaign contributions to candidates for political office in the United States, and/or (b) bribes to foreign officials to secure contracts with their governments or favorable treatment of corporate activities in their countries. What standard of "materiality" should be applied in determining how much disclosure of such payments should be required? Is the Commission's decision in the *Franchard* case helpful in answering that question?

SEC v. JOS. SCHLITZ BREWING CO.

452 F.Supp. 824 (E.D.Wis.1978).

GORDON, DISTRICT JUDGE.

* * *

This is an action brought by the Securities and Exchange Commission (Commission) against the Jos. Schlitz Brewing Company (Schlitz) pursuant to section 20(b) of the Securities Act of 1933, and sections 21(d) and 21(e) of the Securities Exchange Act of 1934, to restrain and enjoin Schlitz from engaging in practices alleged to violate the federal securities laws. Schlitz is a Wisconsin corporation engaged in the business of selling beer and malt beverages whose securities are registered with the Commission and are publicly traded.

The complaint sets forth three causes of action. The first cause of action alleges violations of section 17(a) of the Securities Act of 1933, and section 10(b) of the Securities Exchange Act of 1934, and Rule 10b–5. Schlitz is alleged to have failed to disclose a nationwide scheme to induce retailers of beer and malt beverages to purchase Schlitz' products by making payments or furnishing things of value of at least $3 million in violation of federal, state and local liquor laws. It is also charged that the defendant failed to disclose its alleged participation in violations of Spanish tax and exchange laws in connection with transactions with certain Spanish corporations described as affiliates. Schlitz allegedly falsified its books and records with respect to these payments and transactions. By failing to disclose these matters, Schlitz' financial statements, registration statements, periodic reports and proxy solicitation materials filed with the Commission are said to be materially false and misleading. Schlitz is also charged with aiding and abetting violations of sections 17(a) and 10(b) by the public companies which allegedly received unlawful inducement payments.

The second and third causes of action incorporate the allegations of the first cause of action and allege, respectively, violations of section 13(a) and 14(a) of the Securities Exchange Act of 1934.

* * *

Schlitz contends that the Commission lacks the jurisdiction to bring this action because the acts and practices upon which the action is predicated fall outside its regulatory jurisdiction which is limited to "acts or practices which constitute or will constitute a violation" of the federal securities laws. The inducement payments which Schlitz is alleged to have made to its customers may violate the Federal Alcohol Administration Act, the enforcement of which rests exclusively with the secretary of the treasury, through the bureau of alcohol, tobacco and firearms and the attorney general. On March 15, 1978, a federal grand jury sitting in the eastern district of Wisconsin returned an indictment charging Schlitz with, inter alia, conspiracy and substantive violations of the Federal Alcohol Administration Act. Accordingly, Schlitz contends that this action is an impermissible encroachment on and a duplication of the functions assigned by statute to the bureau of alcohol, tobacco and firearms and the attorney general.

I am unable to accept the defendant's characterization of this action as one to enforce the Federal Alcohol Administration Act. The Commission seeks by this action to enforce the disclosure requirements of the federal securities laws for the protection of shareholders and the investing public generally, a function clearly within the Commission's regulatory authority. * * * Since the basis for this action by the Commission is the alleged failure of Schlitz to disclose its potentially criminal marketing practices in its filings with the Commission, mailings to shareholders and press releases, I believe that the Commission has a rational basis for instituting this enforcement proceeding.

Attempting to demonstrate that the Commission is acting beyond its jurisdiction, Schlitz emphasizes that no statute, rule or regulation specifically requires that a corporation report its involvement in marketing or business practices that may at some future time be adjudicated to be illegal. The Commission argues in response that the reporting of such information is mandated by the philosophy of full disclosure upon which the federal securities laws are predicated.

The parties are essentially in agreement that whether Schlitz' potentially illegal activities must be disclosed depends upon whether such matter is material information. This inquiry is the focus of Schlitz' motion to dismiss for failure to state a claim upon which relief may be granted and will be discussed in that regard below. To the extent that Schlitz' motion to dismiss for lack of subject matter jurisdiction is based on the purported immateriality of the undisclosed matters, I find no basis for finding that the Commission is acting beyond its authority. The securities laws must be interpreted "not technically and restrictively, but flexibly to effectuate [their] remedial purposes." When viewed under this standard, I believe that the instant enforcement action must be sustained as a proper exercise of the Commission's jurisdiction.

* * *

Schlitz also argues that it had no obligation to disclose these allegedly improper transactions because they were not material. The parties are essentially in agreement that whether Schlitz' allegedly improper marketing practices and transactions with Spanish affiliates were material so as to be a required subject of disclosure depends upon whether there is a substantial likelihood that a reasonable person would attach importance to these matters in making investment decisions regarding Schlitz securities.

The Commission suggests several reasons why the information concerning Schlitz' allegedly improper activities is material. First, the Commission argues that this information has a direct bearing on the integrity of management. In Securities and Exchange Commission v. Kalvex, Inc., 425 F.Supp. 310, 315 (S.D.N.Y.1975), and Cooke v. Teleprompter Corp., 334 F.Supp. 467 (S.D.N.Y.1971), courts found that information of improprieties committed by corporate directors might be material to investor decisions concerning who should control the corporation. Without disputing that such information might be material to investors, Schlitz contends that the integrity of management is not at issue in this case because the complaint makes no reference to individual directors.

I am not persuaded that the omission of allegations implicating individual directors is significant. Paragraph 9(e) of the complaint alleges that Schlitz' marketing practices continued even after Schlitz was warned by the bureau of alcohol, tobacco, and firearms that such marketing practices must be terminated. I believe that the question of the integrity of management gives materiality to the matters the Commission claims should have been disclosed. * * *

The Commission also contends that the allegedly improper transactions were material from an economic standpoint. Schlitz disagrees, emphasizing that when measured against Schlitz' 1976 net sales of approximately $1 billion the alleged $3 million in payments to retailers and others would amount to only 3% of its net sales for that year.

The Commission's position is that the relatively small amount of the payments involved alone is not dispositive. In its report on questionable and illegal corporate payments and practices submitted to the Senate Housing & Urban Affairs Committee, May 12, 1976, the Commission stated, at pp. 29–30:

> "Under most circumstances, the amount of the payment is not dispositive of the materiality issue unless, of course, the payment is significant by itself. Where the size of the payment does not otherwise require disclosure, the materiality of such payments would depend on the relative economic implications of the payment to the company as a whole or to a significant line of the company's business. Thus, for example, a questionable or illegal payment that seems relatively small

in relation to corporate revenues, income or assets may assume much greater importance when one assesses the amount of business that may be dependent on or affected by it."

In addition, the Commission suggests that its discovery may reveal that the amount of payments involved was much greater than $3 million. These arguments amply demonstrate the potential materiality of the information in question.

The Commission also stresses that the allegedly illegal practices engaged in by Schlitz and its customers posed a substantial threat to their licenses to sell beer—licenses upon which many of the operations of Schlitz and its customers depend.

The parties have different views as to whether Schlitz' efforts to disclose the risk of license suspension or revocation were timely or adequate, and I am unable to resolve this dispute on the present motion. However, I am unconvinced by Schlitz' argument that the risk of license suspension was not material as a matter of law because of the infrequency of past criminal prosecutions against brewers or wholesalers for violations of the Federal Alcohol Administration Act; the complaint alleges that Schlitz was given a warning in 1973 that such practices must cease.

Schlitz also argues that some of the allegedly unlawful transactions are immaterial because the applicable statute of limitations bars a criminal prosecution for such transactions. However, even if a criminal prosecution for certain of the transactions is now barred, a matter disputed by the Commission, this does not establish the immateriality of these activities insofar as a civil action to enforce securities laws is concerned. * * *

A different approach was taken by the Court of Appeals in GAINES v. HAUGHTON, 645 F.2d 761 (9th Cir.1981), in which a shareholder alleged that failure to disclose foreign bribes by the company in a proxy statement soliciting votes for the re-election of the company's directors was a material omission under § 14(a) of the 1934 Act. The court said:

> We draw a sharp distinction * * * between allegations of director misconduct involving breach of trust or self-dealing—the nondisclosure of which is presumptively material—and allegations of simple breach of fiduciary duty/waste of corporate assets—the nondisclosure of which is never material for § 14(a) purposes. See Bertoglio v. Texas International Co., 488 F.Supp. 630, 650 (D.Del.1980); Lewis v. Valley, 476 F.Supp. 62, 65–66 (S.D.N.Y.1979) (plaintiff's § 14(a) claim based on nondisclosure of questionable foreign payments in proxy solicitations ordered dismissed because, without element of self-dealing, the undisclosed information was not material).
>
> Many corporate actions taken by directors in the interest of the corporation might offend and engender controversy among some stock-

holders. Investors share the same diversity of social and political views that characterizes the polity as a whole. The tenor of a company's labor relations policies, economic decisions to relocate or close established industrial plants, commercial dealings with foreign countries which are disdained in certain circles, decisions to develop (or not to develop) particular natural resources or forms of energy technology, and the promulgation of corporate personnel policies that reject (or embrace) the principle of affirmative action, are just a few examples of business judgments, soundly entrusted to the broad discretion of the directors, which may nonetheless cause shareholder dissent and provoke claims of "wasteful," "unethical," or even "immoral" business dealings. Should corporate directors have a duty under § 14(a) to disclose all such corporate decisions in proxy solicitations for their reelection? We decline to extend the duty of disclosure under § 14(a) to these situations. While we neither condone nor condemn these and similar types of corporate conduct (including the now-illegal practice of questionable foreign payments), we believe that aggrieved shareholders have sufficient recourse to state law claims against the responsible directors and, if all else fails, can sell or trade their stock in the offending corporation in favor of an enterprise more compatible with their own personal goals and values.

In December 1974, the Commission was ordered by a federal court, in a suit brought by an environmental public-interest group,[a] to determine whether reporting companies should be required to disclose (a) the effect of their corporate activities on the environment and (b) statistics about their equal employment practices. The basis for the decision with respect to environmental disclosure was § 102(1) of the National Environmental Policy Act (NEPA) which requires every federal agency "to the fullest extent possible" to interpret and administer federal laws "in accordance with the policies set forth" in NEPA.

In February 1975, the Commission accordingly solicited views concerning "(1) the advisability of its requiring disclosure of socially significant matters, (2) whether and on what basis these disclosures might be viewed as being material, particularly where these matters may not be considered material in an economic sense, (3) the basis and extent, if any, of the Commission's authority to require disclosure of matters primarily of social concern but of doubtful economic significance, and (4) the probable impact, if any, of such disclosure on corporate behavior." [b]

On the basis of the comments received in response to this request, the Commission in October 1975 concluded that:

(1) "economic matters were the primary concern of the Congress in prescribing the Commission's disclosure authority";

a. Natural Resources Defense Council, Inc. v. SEC, 389 F.Supp. 689 (D.D.C.1974).

b. Sec.Act Rel. No. 5569 (Feb. 11, 1975).

(2) "the discretion vested in the Commission * * * to require disclosure which is necessary or appropriate 'in the public interest' does not generally permit the Commission to require disclosure for the sole purpose of promoting social goals unrelated to those underlying [the securities] acts";

(3) "although the Commission's discretion to require disclosure is broad, its exercise of authority is limited to contexts related to the objectives of the federal securities laws."

With respect to the use that investors might make of disclosures of socially significant information, the Commission found that:

(1) "the approximately 100 participants [in the hearings] identifying themselves as investors who consider social information important * * * constitute * * * an insignificant percentage of the estimated 30 million U.S. shareholders";

(2) "those investor-participants who supported social disclosure were virtually unanimous in stating that * * * [such] information is in fact economically significant";

(3) "those investors who are interested in social disclosure would use the information more in making voting rather than investment decisions";

(4) "disclosure to investors of [environmental] information might have some indirect effect on corporate practices to the benefit of the environment."

On the basis of these conclusions, the Commission proposed to require registrants to file, as an exhibit to certain documents filed with the Commission, a list of any reports filed with other agencies that indicated that the registrant, within the past year, was not in compliance with any federal environmental standard.[c] This proposal, however, drew "almost unanimous" opposition from commentators, principally on the ground that it did not distinguish significant from insignificant violations of environmental standards. The Commission, doubting "that a definitive and universal standard can be developed to insure that only reports which relate to 'significant' noncompliance * * * would be listed," accordingly withdrew that proposal, and adopted only a requirement that registrants disclose any material estimated capital expenditures for environmental control facilities.[d]

With respect to disclosure of equal employment practices, as to which the Commission is not subject to a specific mandate comparable to that contained in NEPA, the Commission concluded that "there is no distinguishing feature which would justify the singling out of equal employment from among the myriad of other social matters in which investors may be interested" and that "disclosure of comparable non-material information regarding each of these would in the aggregate make disclosure documents wholly unmanageable * * *."

c. Sec.Act Rel. No. 5627 (Oct. 14, 1975).

d. Sec.Act Rel. No. 5704 (May 6, 1976).

The environmental group went back to court. In May 1977, the district court found that the Commission had not "engaged in serious consideration of the costs and benefits of developing standards and guidelines," and that its rejection of certain disclosure alternatives was "not rationally based" and "arbitrary and capricious." The court ordered the Commission to undertake further rulemaking proceedings and to complete them within six months.[e] On appeal, the Court of Appeals reversed, and ordered the complaint dismissed. It held that the consideration given by the Commission to the public-interest group's proposals was fully adequate to satisfy the requirements of the National Environmental Protection Act and other applicable laws.[f]

Is the SEC's position with respect to disclosure of environmental and equal employment information consistent with its position on disclosure of bribes to foreign government officials? Is the latter more closely related to the purposes of the federal securities laws? In what way? Note that the Foreign Corrupt Practices Act of 1977 added a new § 30A to the Securities Exchange Act of 1934, prohibiting any company with securities registered under that Act from bribing an official of a foreign government. The SEC therefore now has direct authority under § 21 of that Act to investigate bribery of foreign officials and to seek injunctions against violators.

An Advisory Committee on Disclosure, appointed by the SEC, recommended in November 1977 that "the Commission require disclosure of matters of social and environmental significance only if the information in question is material to informed investment or corporate suffrage decision-making or is required by laws other than securities laws." The committee also recommended that the Commission adopt the following statement of objectives:

> The Commission's function in the corporate disclosure system is to assure the public availability in an efficient and reasonable manner on a timely basis of reliable, firm-oriented information material to informed investment and corporate suffrage decision-making. The Commission should not adopt disclosure requirements which have as their principal objective the regulation of corporate conduct.

After reviewing the latter recommendation, the Commission responded:

> The Commission has carefully considered this recommendation. It does not believe, however, that the benefits to be derived from such a statement would, on balance, outweigh the difficulties which it might create. The Commission does not disagree with the general propositions advanced in the first sentence, and recognizes that, as the Committee concluded, such a statement could assist the Commission in responding to demands that the Commission take action which it believes is beyond its proper functions and responsibilities. On the other hand, it is very difficult to capture in a brief, and necessarily

e. Natural Resources Defense Council, Inc. v. SEC, 432 F.Supp. 1190 (D.D.C.1977).

f. Natural Resources Defense Council, Inc. v. SEC, 606 F.2d 1031 (D.C.Cir.1979).

general, statement, all of the considerations which, in the light of legislative provisions and history, judicial precedents and administrative policy, enter into a decision to take specific action under particular circumstances. Consequently, the Commission could become involved in unfruitful arguments, and even litigation, as to whether its response to a particular situation was consistent with the statement of objectives. The second sentence of the Committee's proposed statement illustrates this difficulty. Decisions as to required disclosure frequently do affect conduct and Congress was well aware of this consequence and thought that it would often be beneficial. Debate as to what was the Commission's primary, as distinct from secondary, objective in taking particular action is unlikely to be useful.

Sec.Act Rel. No. 5906 (Feb. 15, 1978).

Selected References

Anderson, The Disclosure Process in Federal Securities Regulation, 25 Hastings L.J. 311 (1974).

Coffee, Market Failure and the Economic Case for a Mandatory Disclosure System, 70 Va.L.Rev. 545 (1984).

Cohen, "Truth in Securities" Revisited, 79 Harv.L.Rev. 1340 (1966).

Dennis, Materiality and the Efficient Capital Market Model: A Recipe for Total Mix, 25 Wm. and Mary L.Rev. 373 (1984).

Herzel & Shepro, Setting the Boundaries for Disclosure, 16 Sec.Reg.L.J. 179 (1988).

Hewitt, Developing Concepts of Materiality and Disclosure, 32 Bus.Lawyer 887 (1977).

Hiller, Early Mandatory Disclosure Regulations, 6 Int'l Rev.L. & Econ. 229 (1986).

Jennings, Reckers, & Kreer, A Source of Insecurity: A Discussion and an Empirical Examination of Standards of Disclosure and Levels of Materiality in Financial Statements, 10 J.Corp.L. 639 (1985).

Kripke, The SEC, The Accountants, Some Myths and Some Realities, 45 N.Y.U.L.Rev. 1151 (1970).

Longstreth, SEC Disclosure Policy Regarding Management Integrity, 38 Bus.Law. 1413 (1983).

Lowenfels, Questionable Corporate Payments and the Federal Securities Laws, 51 N.Y.U.L.Rev. 1 (1976).

Manko, Environmental Disclosure, SEC v. NEPA, 31 Bus.Lawyer 1907 (1976).

Schulte, The Debatable Case for Securities Disclosure Regulation, 13 J.Corp.L. 535 (1988).

Seligman, The Historical Need for a Mandatory Corporate Disclosure System, 9 J.Corp.L. 1 (1983).

Sommer, Therapeutic Disclosure, 4 Sec.Reg.L.J. 263 (1976).

Stevenson, The SEC and the New Disclosure, 62 Cornell L.Rev. 50 (1976).

Note, Disclosure of Payments to Foreign Government Officials Under the Securities Acts, 89 Harv.L.Rev. 1848 (1976).

Note, Foreign Bribes and the Securities Acts' Disclosure Requirements, 74 Mich.L.Rev. 1222 (1976).

---

2. *Should Disclosure Documents Be Readable? And by Whom?*

THE SEC, THE ACCOUNTANTS, SOME MYTHS AND SOME REALITIES

By Homer Kripke *

45 N.Y.U.L.Rev. 1151, 1164–73 (1970).**

* * *

For nearly forty years it has been customary to begin any sympathetic discussion of the federal securities legislation with an incantation to the virtues of disclosure and the desirability of enabling the investor to make his investment on the basis of adequate and informed knowledge of the facts concerning the security. By the term "incantation" I do not mean to be supercilious about this theory as of the time the legislation was written, before we had had adequate experience with it in today's complicated financial world. The term "incantation" seems appropriate, however, for the constant repetition of the virtues of disclosure without consideration of whether disclosure continues to serve its purpose.

The conventional myth is that disclosure to the prospective investor is a good thing which he can comprehend and from which he can make an intelligent investment decision. For one commentator, therefore, a proposal that disclosure take the form of filtering information down to the investor through professionals is "a bone in the throat." Recognizing, however, that the investor will not understand a complex disclosure document and that too much information will confuse him, this view leads to the fantastic conclusion that the investor can intelligently make up his mind from a short one or two page summary which describes something as complex as a conglomerate. How anyone can suppose that a short summary would help any investor to make an intelligent informed decision is a mystery. An even greater mystery is how the SEC could properly insist that a long version of a prospectus is required for truthful disclosure and at the same time invite the investor

* Professor of Law, New York University. Professor Kripke states: "I was once Assistant Solicitor of the SEC. It is customary for current and recent employees of the SEC to preface their publications by a statement that the views expressed are not those of the Commission or its staff. But after a quarter of a century, and in the light of the nature of the views expressed, this disclaimer hardly seems necessary."

to ignore it by authorizing a shorter version as meaningful to informed investment decision.

The heart of my position is that the intelligent investor (unless he is himself a market professional) who tries to act in any informed way does so by getting at least part of his information second hand, filtered through professionals.

The concept that a prospectus enables the investor to act in informed fashion without professional aid is a delusion, and my hypothesis is that behavioral investigation will show that things do not happen that way. Yet the Wheat Report is full of statements to the effect that it was written after numerous consultations with lawyers practicing in the field and other members of the investment community. Why did not the Wheat inquiries support my hypothesis? The answer must be that if one asks the wrong question, he will get the wrong answer. The Wheat studies, written as they were by an SEC commissioner and SEC staff, could hardly have been expected to ask questions and produce answers leading to the conclusion that the Commission is engaged in misdirected effort. The inquiries had to assume that the statute would remain basically as it is, with the prospectus as an essential part and the ordinary investor who is not an analyst making wise investment decisions from a prospectus or proxy statement. It is not intended as criticism of the Wheat group to suggest that when the goal is substantial revision of the statutes, the questions asked will be different and will at least produce strong support for the writer's view that only the filtration process can produce informed investment decisions. Milton H. Cohen's brilliant article precedes the writer in reaching this conclusion.

The extent to which the official myth about wise investors making wise decisions persists in the face of substantial evidence to the contrary is striking. We all know how many waves of investment enthusiasm have taken place during which companies whose choice was "going bankrupt or going public," or strictly promotional companies without any history or immediate prospects of earnings and no history of operations, could sell securities to the public through underwriters whose marketing of the issue gave no assurance of quality. Yet the public has bought the securities avidly despite every effort of the SEC to warn them in "Introductory Statements" about speculative features of the issue, about the dilution of their money from the cheap stock and cheap warrants offered to underwriters, and about the disparity between the large percentage of stock received by the promoters for a small investment and the small percentage of stock received by the public for a large investment. Again and again, the public has rushed into these securities issues despite the SEC's requirements of disclosure.[75] It is particularly fitting that after the debacle of 1970 of many

75. The writer, however, does not see any different approach reasonably feasible for new companies who have not been part of the continuous information system provided by the Exchange Act. Any different system would be impossible to enact, and the writer does not recommend that the SEC become a capital issues committee au-

conglomerate securities issued for cash or in acquisitions in the 1960's, the conglomerate should be named as the company for which the investor should be invited to be lazy with a one or two page summary.

The Securities Act concept that an intelligent nonprofessional investor could singlehandedly make an informed investment decision from a prospectus describing a single company was never very sensible. It was reasonable only to the extent that the investor could not fail to be better off with the information and the statutory liabilities of the Act than he was in the pre-1933 period. But to whatever extent it made sense in a simpler day, it makes no sense now in the era of the continuous information system.

In the first place, many of the companies coming to market at the present time involve very advanced technologies—computers, automation, space, electronics, microwave transmission, chemicals, drugs, frozen and processed foods, etc. Any description in a prospectus sufficient to explain the company's position in specialized technologies would take far too much space. In any event, it would not be understandable to anyone but a specialist.

Second, even a company using a relatively familiar technology has hidden complexity. Take a paper company. The prospectus may disclose that its sales are X per cent kraft paper, Y per cent fine writing papers and Z per cent cartonboard. X is greater than Z. Is that good or bad? It is doubtful that these are "lines of business" for which the new divisional reporting requirements would require information on current comparative profitability, and only a "misleading omission" concept would require showing of historical changes in these rates of profitability. Nothing requires information as to comparative growth rates; in fact, the SEC is strongly opposed to any projections that would permit this information to be volunteered. Thus, the information in the prospectus leads nowhere unless the reader is a professional who is well-versed in this area.

Third, the heart of modern disclosure is accounting. As will be seen from Part II of this Article, modern accounting has become increasingly complex. The efforts of the conglomerates and other companies to put their best foot forward with such devices as "dirty poolings," partial poolings, dirty purchasing, changing accounting principles or estimates to bolster earnings and use of "funny money" to bolster earnings computed according to the incredibly complex concept of earnings per share make it impossible for any person not highly trained in current financial accounting really to understand the financial statements of any conglomerate, or indeed any company which has participated in the recent trends of acquisition and merger.

thorized to deny access to capital for issues which it thinks are uneconomical from the point of view of the public or unsafe from the point of view of investors. The harm that befalls naive investors under these circumstances is perhaps inevitable and part of the costs of a free society and of mobile capital.

Fourth, when bonds are selling on a 9 per cent yield basis, the only reason for an investor to pay more than eleven times the dividend for the common stock of a company is the expectation that the return from the investment (either from dividends or capital gain) will sometime improve. Even if the investor could reasonably conclude from the prospectus that the company would stay solvent and maintain its earnings and dividends, modern price-earnings ratios (at least until the 1969–70 stock market depression) can be justified only by a projection that earnings will increase at a substantial rate. Even a moderation of the rate of earnings increase can cause a devastating decline in market price. But the SEC will not permit the ultimate relevant information—management's earnings projections—to be furnished.

Above all, the investor's choice is never whether to sit on his cash or to make the particular investment proposed by a prospectus. The choice is always whether he should keep his cash or use it for any of the thousands of other possible investments—anything from government bonds, tax-free municipal bonds, savings banks, mutual funds, offshore funds, hedge funds, thousands of individual securities that are available on the stock exchanges and in the over-the-counter markets, or oilwells, orange groves, Black Angus cattle, real estate, even paintings or postage stamps. No prospectus can possibly give him any information which will enable him to decide the real question of whether the investment is a good one in relation to the other opportunities available. * * *

We are forced to the conclusion that the basic purpose of the Securities Act to furnish a prospectus to the individual investor on one security so that he may make an informed choice of its investment merits is based on a false assumption. A security has no investment merit except by comparison with numerous other available opportunities for investment. Any effort to rationalize the legislation must start from that reality. The individual who makes his own choice without professional help is not the individual who does or could usefully read the prospectus. The first casualties of this reasoning should be all of the efforts designed to make a prospectus short and readable by a layman. The goal is inconsistent with the reality of the complexity of modern securities and the fact that the prospectus should not really be addressed to the layman.

We return to the one other possible justification for retaining the present prospectus requirement. If an issue is being sold and the dealer is receiving something more than the usual brokerage commission, the investor arguably needs the equivalent of a prospectus to protect himself against an unusual selling push by a dealer who has a conflict of interest between his duty to his customer and his own desire to earn a significant commission. Theoretically, perhaps the customer should have the benefit of the materials with which to make an independent judgment under these circumstances. But this potential conflict of interest of the dealer has existed in the entire distribution mechanism since the beginning of the securities legislation, and there is no evidence that it has ever induced any significant number of customers to study the prospectus and other investment opportunities in lieu of accepting the advice of the dealer. * * *

Therefore, when should the current Securities Act scheme be required in the future, *i.e.,* when should a relatively complete filing be made with the SEC and when should a prospectus be prepared and handed to the investor, on a company already subject to the continuous information process? The writer's tentative answer is "never." * * *

With respect to Professor Kripke's implication that full awareness of the inadequacies of the 1933 Act disclosure scheme came about only as a result of "adequate experience with it in today's complicated financial world," consider the following excerpt from "The Federal Securities Act of 1933", by William O. Douglas and George E. Bates, 43 Yale L.J. 171 (December 1933):

> Some * * * have believed, apparently in all sincerity, that the great drop in security values in the last five years was the result of failure to tell the "truth about securities." And others have thought that with the Securities Act it would be possible to prevent a recurrence of the scandals which have brought many financiers into disrepute in recent years. As a matter of fact there are but few of the transactions investigated by the Senate Committee on Banking and Currency which the Securities Act would have controlled. There is nothing in the Act which would control the speculative craze of the American public, or which would eliminate wholly unsound capital structures. There is nothing in the Act which would prevent a tyrannical management from playing wide and loose with scattered minorities, or which would prevent a new pyramiding of holding companies violative of the public interest and all canons of sound finance. All the Act pretends to do is to require the "truth about securities" at the time of issue, and to impose a penalty for failure to tell the truth. Once it is told, the matter is left to the investor.
>
> But even the whole truth cannot be told in such simple and direct terms as to make investors discriminating. A slow educational process must precede that. Those who need investment guidance will receive small comfort from the balance sheets, statistics, contracts, and details which the prospectus reveals. Thus the effects of such an Act, though important, are secondary and chiefly of two kinds: (1) prevention of excesses and fraudulent transactions, which will be hampered and deterred merely by the requirement that their details be revealed; and (2) placing in the market during the early stages of the life of a security a body of facts which, operating indirectly through investment services and expert investors, will tend to produce more accurate appraisal of the worth of the security if it commands a broad enough market.

FEIT v. LEASCO DATA PROCESSING EQUIPMENT CORP.

332 F.Supp. 544 (E.D.N.Y.1971).

WEINSTEIN, DISTRICT JUDGE.

This case raises the question of the degree of candor required of issuers of securities who offer their shares in exchange for those of other companies in take-over operations. Defendants' registration statement was, we find, misleading in a material way. While disclosing masses of facts and figures, it failed to reveal one critical consideration that weighed heavily with those responsible for the issue—the substantial possibility of being able to gain control of some hundred million dollars of assets not required for operating the business being acquired.

Using a statement to obscure, rather than reveal, in plain English, the critical elements of a proposed business deal cannot be countenanced under the securities regulation acts. The defense that no one could be certain of precisely how much was involved in the way of releasible assets is not acceptable. The prospective purchaser of a new issue of securities is entitled to know what the deal is all about. Given an honest and open statement, adequately warning of the possibilities of error and miscalculation and not designed for puffing, the outsider and the insider are placed on more equal grounds for arms length dealing. Such equalization of bargaining power through sharing of knowledge in the securities market is a basic national policy underlying the federal securities laws.

In this class action plaintiff seeks damages resulting from alleged misrepresentations and omissions in a registration statement prepared in conjunction with a 1968 offering of a "package" of preferred shares and warrants of Leasco Data Processing Equipment Corporation (Leasco) in exchange for the common stock of Reliance Insurance Company (Reliance). He is a former shareholder of Reliance who exchanged his shares for the Leasco package. Suit was commenced in October 1969 on behalf of all Reliance shareholders who accepted the exchange offer between August 19, and November 1, 1968.

It is alleged that Leasco (1) failed to disclose an approximate amount of "surplus surplus" held by Reliance and (2) failed to fully and accurately disclose its intentions with regard to reorganizing Reliance or using other techniques for removing surplus surplus after it had acquired control. These failures, it is claimed, represented material misrepresentations or omissions in violation of Sections 11, 12(2), and 17(a) of the Securities Act of 1933. * * *

Reliance's surplus surplus is the central element in this litigation. Leasco's desire to acquire it provided much of the original impetus for the exchange offer. Lack of disclosure of facts relating to the amount of surplus surplus and Leasco's intentions concerning its use, as well as the materiality of those omissions, provide the basis of plaintiff's complaint. Finally, the method and difficulty of ascertaining its amount is critical to the defendants' affirmative defense. We cannot proceed without examining the concept.

Reliance is a fire and casualty insurance company subject to stringent regulation by the Insurance Commissioner of Pennsylvania. Such a company is required by the regulatory scheme to maintain sufficient surplus to guarantee the integrity of its insurance operations. Such "required surplus" cannot be separated from the insurance business of the company. That portion of surplus not required in insurance operations has been referred to as surplus surplus. * * *

The only statements in the prospectus with regard to surplus surplus appeared on page five. It neither mentions the amounts that Leasco's management had in mind nor suggests the importance of Reliance's possible surplus surplus. It reads:

> "The Company [Leasco] believes that this Exchange Offer is consistent with the announced intention of the Reliance management to form a holding company to become the parent of Reliance. That intention was communicated to Reliance stockholders on May 15, 1968 by A. Addison Roberts, the president of Reliance, who wrote that the holding company concept would serve the interests of Reliance and all its stockholders 'by providing more flexible operations, freedom of diversification and opportunities for more profitable utilization of financial resources.' The Company supports those objectives and intends to do all it can to promote their realization as soon as practicable. * * * Reliance will diligently pursue its previously announced intention to form a holding company which Reliance will provide with the maximum amount of funds legally available which is consistent with Reliance's present level of net premium volume." * * *

The ultimate goal of the Securities Act is, of course, investor protection. Effective disclosure is merely a means. The entire legislative scheme can be frustrated by technical compliance with the requirements of the Securities and Exchange Commission's Form S–1 for preparation of registration statements in the absence of any real intent to communicate. It is for this reason that the SEC, through its rule making power, has consistently required "clearly understandable" prospectuses. The Wheat Report at 78.

Unfortunately, the results have not always reflected these efforts. "[E]ven when an investor [is] presented with an accurate prospectus prior to his purchase, the presentation in most instances tend[s] to discourage reading by all but the most knowledgeable and tenacious." Knauss, A Reappraisal of the Role of Disclosure, 62 Mich.L.Rev. 607, 618–619 (1964). These documents are often drafted so as to be comprehensible to only a minute part of the investing public.

> "There are also the perennial questions of whether prospectuses, once delivered to the intended reader, are readable, and whether they are read. The cynic's answer to both questions is 'No'; the true believer's is 'Yes'; probably a more accurate answer than either would be:

'Yes'—by a relatively small number of professionals or highly sophisticated nonprofessionals; 'No'—by the great majority of those investors who are not sophisticated and, within the doctrine of SEC v. Ralston Purina Co., are not 'able to fend for themselves' and most 'need the protection of the Act.'" Cohen, "Truth in Securities" Revisited, 79 Harv.L.Rev. 1340, 1351–1352 (1966).

In at least some instances, what has developed in lieu of the open disclosure envisioned by the Congress is a literary art form calculated to communicate as little of the essential information as possible while exuding an air of total candor. Masters of this medium utilize turgid prose to enshroud the occasional critical revelation in a morass of dull, and—to all but the sophisticates—useless financial and historical data. In the face of such obfuscatory tactics the common or even the moderately well informed investor is almost as much at the mercy of the issuer as was his pre-SEC parent. He cannot by reading the prospectus discern the merit of the offering.

The instant case provides a useful example. Ignoring, for the moment, the alleged omissions which are the subject of the plaintiff's complaint, the passage in which Leasco's intentions with regard to surplus surplus are "disclosed" is the short excerpt set out at Part III B, supra. This revelation, while probably technically accurate with regard to Leasco's then intentions respecting surplus surplus, was hardly calculated to apprise the owner of shares of Reliance common stock that Reliance held a large pool of cash or near-cash assets which were legally and practically unnecessary for the efficient operation of the insurance business, and that Leasco intended to remove those assets "as soon as practicable." More important, it does not reveal Leasco's estimates of the extent of those assets. A conscientious effort by the issuer and its counsel would have produced a more direct, informative and candid paragraph about Leasco's intended reorganization of Reliance. They might have effectively disclosed, in understandable prose—as they did in January of 1969—the essence of the plan to the shareholders they were soliciting.

The view that prospectuses should be intelligible to the average small investor as well as the professional analyst, immediately raises the question of what substantive standard of disclosure must be maintained. The legal standard is that all "material" facts must be accurately disclosed. But to whom must the fact have material significance?

In an industry in which there is an unmistakable "trend toward a greater measure of professionalism * * * with the accompanying demand for more information about issuers" "a pragmatic balance must be struck between the needs of the unsophisticated investor and those of the knowledgeable student of finance." The Wheat Report at 9–10. There are three distinct classes of investors who must be informed by the prospectus: (1) the amateur who reads for only the grosser sorts of disclosures; (2) the professional advisor and manager who studies the prospectus closely and makes his decisions based on the insights he gains from it; and (3) the securities analyst who uses the prospectus as one of many sources in an independent investigation of the issuer.

The proper resolution of the various interests lies in the inclusion of a clearly written narrative statement outlining the major aspects of the offering and particularly speculative elements, as well as detailed financial information which will have meaning only to the expert. Requiring inclusion of such technical data benefits amateurs, as well as experts, because of the advice many small investors receive and the extent to which the market reflects professional judgments. The Wheat Report at 52. Such "[e]xpert sifters, distillers, and weighers are essential for an informed body of investors". Cohen, "Truth in Securities" Revisited, 79 Harv.L.Rev. 1340, 1353 (1966).

Mr. Justice Douglas, then teaching at Yale, commented in 1933 that:

> "[T]hose needing investment guidance will receive small comfort from the balance sheets, contracts, or compilation of other data revealed in the registration statement. They either lack the training or intelligence to assimilate them and find them useful, or are so concerned with a speculative profit as to consider them irrelevant. * * * [E]ven though an investor has neither the time, money, nor intelligence to assimilate the mass of information in the registration statement, there will be those who can and who will do so, whenever there is a broad market. The judgment of those experts will be reflected in the market price. Through them investors who seek advice will be able to obtain it." Douglas, Protecting The Investor, 23 Yale Rev. (N.S.) 508, 523–524 (1933) (quoted in The Wheat Report at 53).

The Wheat Report further notes:

> "that a fully effective disclosure policy would require the reporting of complicated business facts that would have little meaning for the average investor. Such disclosures reach average investors through a process of filtration in which intermediaries (brokers, bankers, investment advisors, publishers of investment advisory literature, and occasionally lawyers) play a vital role." The Wheat Report at 52.

> "The significance of disclosures which have an initial impact at the professional level has been heightened by recent changes in the securities business. Most important of these is the enormous growth of intermediation in investment. The relative importance of such professional money managers as bank trust departments, pension fund managers, investment counseling firms and investment advisors to mutual funds and other investment companies is greater than ever before." The Wheat Report at 54.

The significance of these observations is that the objectives of full disclosure can be fully achieved only by complete revelation of facts which would be material to the sophisticated investor or the securities professional, not just the average common shareholder. But, at the same time, the prospectus must not slight the less experienced. They are entitled to have within the four corners of the document an intelligible description of the transaction. * * *

Members of the plaintiff-class are entitled to recover money damages pursuant to Section 11 of the Securities Act of 1933. The failure to include an estimate of surplus surplus in the registration statement filed in conjunction with this exchange offer was an omission of a material fact required to be stated to prevent the statements from being misleading. * * *

Is Judge Weinstein's analysis equally applicable to registration statements filed on Form S–2 or Form S–3? Compare *Feit* with Judge Easterbrook's analysis in Wielgos v. Commonwealth Edison, at p. 120 below.

REMARKS OF HAROLD MARSH, JR., IN PANEL DISCUSSION ON DISCLOSURE IN REGISTERED SECURITY OFFERINGS

28 Bus.Lawyer 505, 527–28 (1973).*

In attempting to evaluate these condemnations of the Securities Bar and the Commission, there are several questions which need to be answered. One is obviously the question of to whom the disclosure is intended to be directed, since any communication to be effective must be tailored to the intended audience. The official position of the Commission, as reflected in the *Wheat Report* and echoed by Judge Weinstein, is that the prospectus must be completely informative both to the "unsophisticated investor" and to the "knowledgeable student of finance." In other words, the drafter of a prospectus is enjoined to be "all things to all men." Of course, if he attempts this, he runs an extreme danger, to paraphrase the same Apostle, of "saying those things which he should have left unsaid, and leaving unsaid those things which he should have said."

On the other hand, Professor Kripke denounces what he calls the "myth of the informed layman," which he asserts has colored the Commission's concept of disclosure and rendered the prospectus useless. He asserts that the prospectus should be written solely for the "professional" or "expert."

With regard to Professor Kripke's obeisance to the so-called experts in securities investment, one can, I believe, with equal justification oppose his concept of the "myth of the informed layman" with the "myth of the 'expert' expert." It would be very interesting to have some graduate student in a business college conduct a research project to determine how much of the worthless junk securities sold by conglomerates in the last few years were bought by those self-appointed "expert money managers" advising mutual funds and other institutional investors, as compared to the percentage foisted off on the general public.

It seems to me that the only common sense approach to the question of the audience to whom the disclosure should be directed is that it should be directed to those persons who are capable of understanding the transactions being described. In my opinion, this will include only a small minority of the general public and only a small minority of the self-appointed experts. But to attempt to explain to a person who is incapable of understanding is a complete waste of time. If a physicist attempted to make "full disclosure" to me regarding the theory of relativity, his attempt would be doomed to failure, whatever his talents.

Some courts seem to have adopted this common sense approach. In Shvetz v. Industrial Rayon Corporation,[23] Judge Murphy stated:

> "While it might be true that a person of limited education or nonfamiliarity with corporate finances and legal matters would find it difficult to understand many of the facets of the proposed merger, that is not the test. The statute requires the absence of false and misleading statements, as do the S.E.C. rules. Nowhere does either require that corporate reorganizations and mergers be explained in language comprehensible to school children."

This language was quoted and approved by Judge Northrop in Walpert v. Bart,[24] and inferentially by the Fourth Circuit which affirmed that case on the basis of Judge Northrop's opinion.[25] However, as indicated above, Judge Weinstein adopted lock, stock and barrel the Commission view that a prospectus must be completely intelligible to everyone.

We now, of course, have the new official position that not only must prospectuses be intelligible to school children, but they must even reach down to the kindergarten set, who have not yet graduated from finger painting. Under the recent guide adopted by the Commission, the drafter of the prospectus must draw pictures to inform the person looking at the prospectus—one cannot say the "reader," since they assume he will not or cannot read—of the percentage of the equity retained by the promoters and the percentage being sold to the public.[a]

Nowhere in the Release announcing that new artistic enterprise does the Commission even hint at what it hopes to achieve by its pie

23. 212 F.Supp. 308, 310 (S.D.N.Y.1960).

24. 280 F.Supp. 1006 (D.Md.1967).

25. 390 F.2d 877 (4th Cir.1968).

a. From 1968 through 1976, the SEC adopted a number of guides geared to increasing "readability." Among other things, these guides required the use of pie charts and bar graphs to show the percentage of the equity retained by the promoter and the percentage being sold to the public. See Sec. Act Rels. Nos. 4936, 5005, 5036, 5094, 5102, 5171, 5278, 5396, 5511, 5520, and 5692. These guides were superseded by Regulation S-K.

charts and graphs. It is impossible to believe that the Commission thinks that it will deter a purchaser from buying the stock by drawing him a picture, when he has not been dissuaded in the past by a statement to the same effect in plain English, especially since everyone knows that the reason he buys is because his broker has told him that it is going to be a "hot issue." To assert that the Commission believes that the issue which shows the larger slice of the "pie" going to the public is always the better buy for the investor would also be an insult to their intelligence. And I, for one, refuse to give any credence to the rumors that, shortly before the issuance of this Release, there were heavy purchases of the stock of compass and protractor manufacturers through the Washington brokerage houses. The only reasonable explanation of these new requirements, at least the only one that I have been able to think of, is that someone got access to the outgoing mail department of the SEC and smuggled in this Release as another put-on.

---

3. *"Hard" and "Soft" Information*

THE SEC, THE ACCOUNTANTS, SOME MYTHS AND SOME REALITIES

By Homer Kripke

45 N.Y.U.L.Rev. 1151, 1197–99 (1970).*

* * * It is quite evident that members of the financial community determine the value of a security by the capitalization of projected future income. Thus, these projections are the ultimate purpose of all disclosure, including particularly the financial disclosure. Even spokesmen for the SEC's position concede this. Yet the SEC has long taken a strong view against projections.

The SEC's basis for this goes back to the earliest days of the Securities Act and to promotional ventures where there was no sound basis for prediction. The situation is obviously entirely different when a mature company engaged in continuous financial reporting makes projections. Generalizing broadly, it is known that most sizable corporations use projections of future sales and revenues and capital needs as the basis for making very important decisions as to borrowing, building new plants, establishing new branches, ordering materials, hiring and training labor, etc. Moreover, a whole science, a branch of accounting known as budget planning, is based on projections; and libraries on economics and on business are full of texts on the subject.

But the SEC continues to take the position that projections are per se misleading, and it so states in a note to one of its proxy rules.[190]

190. [Rule] 14a-9.

Furthermore, one court, following the SEC's lead, has held that a projection was misleading just because it was a projection, entirely apart from the question whether in fact it might have been sound.[191]

That the SEC does not really think that projections are misleading is apparent from the fact that it obtained a consent injunction against a corporation which violated rule 10b–5 by supplying projections of its future income to investment analysts privately while not making them available to the public generally.[192] The incident cannot mean that the SEC thought that it was improper not to mislead the public in the same manner that the corporation misled the analysts; it can only mean that the SEC does not believe in its avowed position.

Another basis for the SEC position is stated in a widely-quoted article written by a former stalwart of the SEC Division of Corporation Finance, Harry Heller.[193] While expressly recognizing that the whole purpose of financial data is to project future earnings, he argues that no one can be an expert in prophecy. A registration statement must deal in facts, not prophecies, and leave the task of projection to each individual investor.[194]

That is nonsense to this writer. The public is certainly not as able as the management of a corporation to understand the meaning, results and implications of the complex accounting events which have occurred in any dynamic company or of differential rates of improvement or decline in the sales volume and profitability of different product lines. The problems are difficult, and the SEC is putting itself into an indefensible position by requiring divisional reporting and other full detail on the one hand, and requiring summaries in recognition of the fact that the average investor cannot grasp this kind of material on the other. The management, which has the greatest stake in the matter, and which may have spent months of labor in its projections, certainly is in a better position than the public to forecast where the company is going, and its current estimate rendered in good faith is *a fact.* Solely because a forecast is also a prophecy does not change the very important circumstance that it is a highly informed judgment, made in a rational and careful manner. The professionals get management projections informally through press conferences, speeches to analysts' societies or press releases, and these projections form the basis for professional judgment. Under its present system the SEC precludes the giving of this information equally to all investors through the documents filed with it, and does not subject them to any of the liabilities of the statutes or of administrative scrutiny.

191. Union Pac. R.R. v. Chicago & N.W. Ry., 226 F.Supp. 400, 408–10 (N.D.Ill.1964). The position of the court has been viewed with derision in R. Jennings & H. Marsh, Securities Regulation 1000–01 (2d ed. 1968).

192. SEC v. Glen Alden Corp., [1967–1969 Transfer Binder] CCH Fed.Sec.L.Rep. ¶ 92,289 (S.D.N.Y.1968).

193. Heller, Disclosure Requirements Under Federal Securities Regulation, 16 Bus.Law. 300 (1961).

194. Id. at 304–07.

The foregoing is not intended to suggest that projections could be subjected to statutory liabilities, either express or under rule 10b–5, in the same fashion as a statement of fact about last year's sales or the ownership of a building. Rather the sole factual elements of a projection should be that it represents management's view, that it was reached in a rational fashion and that it is a sincere view. Only these elements can be subject to a statutory liability, not the eventuation of the prophecy.[195]

The SEC staff would have no difficulty dealing with unreasoned or unduly optimistic projections of promotional companies, any more than it did in the early 1930's or even today with unsound estimates of mineral resources. Indeed, the absence of a projection in filed documents would warn the sophisticate that the company's estimates could not pass Commission scrutiny.

The importance of this point on projections cannot be over-estimated. If there is any hope that the public or even the professionals can make an informed investment judgment, it must start from a crystallization of all of the plethora of information into a projection for the future. The management is in the best position to make the initial estimate; on the basis of it the professional or investor could then make his own modifications. No other single change could add as much meaning to the unmanageable and unfocussed flood of facts in present Commission documents.

Again, as in the case of value, there are problems to be resolved, such as whether and when projections would be required instead of permitted and whether management must refile its projcctions whenever they are revised. But these difficulties should not be an excuse for continuation of the present totally unsound position. * * *

BEECHER v. ABLE

374 F.Supp. 341 (S.D.N.Y.1974).

MOTLEY, DISTRICT JUDGE.

These actions [under § 11 of the Securities Act of 1933] are brought on behalf of purchasers of a $75 million issue of 4¾% convertible subordinated debentures due July 1, 1991 [of Douglas Aircraft Company, Inc.]. The debentures were sold pursuant to a registration statement and prospectus filed with the Securities and Exchange Commission and which became effective July 12, 1966.

* * * Douglas was an aerospace manufacturer engaged in the manufacture of aircraft and related activities. It was a major partici-

195. I do not even suggest that we go as far as the British practice in which projections are not only used in prospectuses but the accountants attest to the bases for the forecasts and to the calculations. Willingham, Smith & Taylor, Should the CPA's Opinion Be Extended to Include Forecasts?, Financial Executive, Sept. 1970, at 80.

pant in the Government's missile and space programs and one of the principal manufacturers of jet aircraft for commercial and military use. Douglas was organized into two primary groups: the Missiles and Space Systems Group and the Aircraft Group. In April, 1967, following a financial debacle in November 1966, Douglas merged with McDonnell Company, now known as McDonnell-Douglas.

Despite a pre-tax loss of $7,517,000 and a net loss of $3,463,000 for the three months ended May 31, 1966, Douglas had a net income of $645,000 for the period November 30, 1965 through May 31, 1966, that is, the first half of fiscal 1966. However, by November 1966, the end of fiscal 1966, Douglas had sustained a net loss of $52 million. This loss was attributable to the Aircraft Division's pre-tax loss of approximately $77.0 million. The Aircraft Division's catastrophic losses were, in turn, caused by the confluence of two factors: 1) unusually long delays in the delivery of parts, particularly engines, required for the DC–8 and DC–9 aircraft and 2) the escalating costs involved in recruiting and training thousands of new, inexperienced employees who replaced skilled or recently trained Douglas workers who had been either drafted or left for other jobs in a highly fluid labor market. * * * These problems had begun to affect the Aircraft Division's operations in the early part of fiscal 1966. However, the parts shortages intensified during the second half of fiscal 1966. * * *

Plaintiffs claim that the prospectus contained material misrepresentations as follows:

(1) The projected income statement in the prospectus that "* * * it is very likely that net income, if any, for fiscal 1966 will be nominal," was, according to plaintiffs, a prediction that Douglas would break even and, as such, was a material misrepresentation of Douglas' prospects. In this connection plaintiffs argue that the prospectus falsely assured investors that Douglas would not have to correct the problems cited above and delineated in the prospectus in order to break even for fiscal 1966. Plaintiffs further argue that Douglas should have disclosed a) the assumptions underlying the forecast, and b) that previous forecasts in 1966 had failed in order to make the statement regarding profits, if any, not misleading.

(2) Douglas' statement of the use to which it would put the net proceeds of the bond issue did not accurately state the company's plans for the proceeds. Plaintiffs say Douglas used all proceeds to pay off short term bank loans but misrepresented that only a portion of the proceeds would be used to cancel these loans.

Plaintiffs also claim that failure to disclose Douglas' pre-tax loss of $7,517,000 was a material omission.

* * *

As to the first claim, the court finds and concludes herein that the statement concerning income, if any, was false in that, viewed as a prediction of break even (i.e., a little profit or a little loss) it was not highly probable that the company would break even and the statement was misleading in that it omitted to state facts necessary in order to make that prediction not misleading. It was manifestly material since it represented top management's assessment of the company's prospects despite omnipresent adversity.

The court also finds that plaintiffs satisfied their burden of proof with respect to their claims that the statement as to the use of proceeds was a material misrepresentation and failure to disclose the pre-tax loss of $7,517,000 was a material omission.

The plaintiffs' claims are examined below and the court makes the following findings as to each.

I. *"While it is not possible to determine when these factors will be corrected, it is expected that they will continue to affect the results of operations for the balance of fiscal 1966. Therefore, it is very likely that net income, if any, for fiscal 1966 will be nominal."*

Plaintiffs claim that this statement amounted to a forecast that defendant would break even in fiscal 1966 and that this is the way a reasonably prudent investor would have read the statement. Defendant claims that the statement was intended as a warning that profits, if any, for 1966 would be nominal. Moreover, says Douglas, while it did not intend to predict that it would break even in fiscal 1966, its management reasonably believed that it would incur only nominal losses. Its expectation of nominal losses was based on its in house prediction that the Aircraft Division would have a pre-tax loss of $27.8 million and that the company would have a net loss of $519,000 for the fiscal year.

The parties have stipulated that it was not illegal for defendant to make a prediction of future earnings in its prospectus. The threshold question, therefore, is whether the statement would have been interpreted by a reasonable investor merely as a warning that more than nominal profits were unlikely for fiscal 1966, as defendant has argued, or as a forecast that the company would not suffer any substantial losses, as plaintiffs contend.

The statement, of course, literally speaks only of the *improbability* of substantial earnings and *not* of the *improbability* of substantial losses. "However, a statement which is literally true, if susceptible to quite another interpretation by the reasonable investor * * * may properly * * * be considered a material misrepresentation." SEC v. First American Bank and Trust Co., 481 F.2d 673 (8th Cir.1973).

Put another way, the test is whether it is likely that an appreciable number of ordinarily prudent investors would have read the statement as a forecast that substantial losses were improbable.

The court finds that it is likely that an appreciable number of ordinarily prudent investors would have so read the passage and that such a reading was likely despite the various admonitions in the prospectus.

* * *

STANDARD OF CARE FOR EARNINGS PROJECTIONS

Since we are talking about a forecast and the parties have stipulated that forecasts in prospectuses are not illegal, the next inquiry must be whether this break-even forecast was reasonably based, as Douglas contends, or whether as plaintiffs contend, it was unreasonable to conclude that it was highly probable that substantial losses could be avoided for fiscal 1966, despite the shocking $7,500,000 pre-tax loss at the end of the second quarter.

Plaintiffs concede that an earnings forecast is not actionable merely because the facts do not turn out as predicted. Additionally, projections, unlike other statements contained in a prospectus, will not often be clearly true or false. Forecasting is an art and the weight to be attached to the many variables which should be considered in assessing a corporation's future prospects is largely a matter of judgment. However, investors are likely to attach great importance to income projections because they speak directly to a corporation's likely earnings for the future and because they are ordinarily made by persons who are well-informed about the corporation's prospects. Therefore, in view of the policy of the federal securities laws of promoting full and fair disclosure, a high standard of care must be imposed on those who, although not required to do so, nevertheless make projections.

Consequently, this court holds that an earnings forecast must be based on facts from which a reasonably prudent investor would conclude that it was highly probable that the forecast would be realized. Moreover, any assumptions underlying the projection must be disclosed if their validity is sufficiently in doubt that a reasonably prudent investor, if he knew of the underlying assumptions, might be deterred from crediting the forecast. Disclosure of such underlying assumptions is "* * * necessary to make * * * [the forecast] * * * not misleading * * *."

Factors bearing on the reasonableness of a forecast would include the corporation's record of success in forecasting earnings, the care exercised in the preparation and review of cost and sales estimates, doubts expressed by persons engaged in the process of review, the reasonableness of the underlying assumptions, and any facts not known to management which were accessible in the exercise of reasonable care.

* * *

The court, however, finds that a reasonably prudent bond purchaser would not have concluded, from the facts available to Douglas' management at the time the prospectus was issued, that it was highly probable that the forecast would be satisfied in that substantial losses would be avoided in fiscal 1966 * * *

* * *

While the court has found that defendant might reasonably have given some weight to the steps it had taken to correct its problems, the prospects of making improvements sufficient to avoid substantial losses were far too uncertain to warrant a forecast which included the suggestion that Douglas would have no substantial losses in fiscal 1966.

* * *

A reasonable, objective person would, therefore, have concluded that there was a fair possibility that some of the conditions which were beyond Douglas' control, such as failure of its engine supplier to meet its commitments, might continue to deteriorate sufficiently to offset any of the steps management had taken to improve production efficiency.

The court further finds that a reasonable investor could have read the income, if any, passage to mean that no improvement, or at least no substantial improvement, in the various adverse conditions besetting the Aircraft Division and discussed at pages 5–6 of the prospectus would be required in order for the company to avoid more than nominal losses.

While defendant has argued that the statement meant only that it was impossible to determine when the adverse factors would be resolved, rather than merely improved, a more plausible reading of the passage would be that no material changes in those factors would be necessary. In view of the court's findings above, this statement was misleading. Moreover, the statement was material since reasonable investors would be much more confident that Douglas would not have substantial losses if they had been led to believe that no substantial improvements were required to avoid such losses.

Finally, with regard to the income, if any, statement, the court finds that Douglas was required to disclose that the forecast was based on an assumption that conditions in the Aircraft Division would have to improve before the company could expect to avoid substantial losses and that earlier forecasts in 1966 had to be modified. Disclosure of these facts was required in order to make the statement about the defendant's earnings prospects not misleading.

The assumption that conditions would improve sufficiently for the company to avoid substantial losses was material since the assumption was sufficiently doubtful that reasonable investors, had they been informed of the assumption, might have been deterred from crediting the forecast.

In September 1985, Control Data Corporation canceled an offering of $300 million of securities just before the scheduled closing, because revised estimates for the current year indicated that losses by its computer division could substantially exceed profits from its other operations and cause the company to show a net loss for the year. The prospectus had estimated an operating loss for the computer division but had not projected a net loss for the parent company, and it was speculated that the underwriters had insisted on cancellation of the issue because of potential liability for inadequate disclosure in the prospectus. See Wall St. Journal, Sept. 18, 1985, p. 2, col. 2.

GUIDES FOR DISCLOSURE OF PROJECTIONS

Sec. Act Rel. No. 5992 (Nov. 7, 1978).

* * * The Commission has issued a statement indicating that it encourages certain issuers of securities to publish projected financial information in filings with the Commission or otherwise. The Commission also has authorized publication of Guides 62 and 5, "Disclosure of Projections of Future Economic Performance." The Guides are not Commission rules nor do they bear the Commission's official approval; they represent practices followed by the Division of Corporation Finance in administering the disclosure requirements of the Securities Act and the Exchange Act.

* * *

The issue of projections, economic forecasts, and other forward-looking information has been under active consideration by the Commission for several years.

On November 1, 1972, the Commission announced a public rulemaking proceeding relating to the use, both in Commission filings and otherwise, of projections by issuers whose securities are publicly traded. These hearings were ordered by the Commission for the purpose of gathering information relevant to a reassessment of its policies relating to disclosure of projected sales and earnings.

Information gathered at the hearings, held from November 10 to December 12, 1972, reinforced the Commission's observation that management's assessment of a company's future performance is of importance to investors, that such assessment should be comprehensible in light of the assumptions made and should be available, if at all, on an equitable basis to all investors. The hearings also revealed widespread dissatisfaction with the absence of guidelines or standards that issuers, financial analysts, or investors can rely on in issuing or interpreting projections.

On February 2, 1973, the Commission released a "Statement by the Commission on the Disclosure of Projections of Future Economic Performance." In this statement, the Commission determined that on the basis of the information obtained through the hearings, staff recommendations, and its experience in administering the federal securities laws, changes in its long standing policy generally not to permit the inclusion of projections in registration statements and reports filed with the Commission would assist in the protection of investors and would be in the public interest. * * *

On April 25, 1975, the Commission published a series of rule and form proposals relating to projections of future economic performance.

These proposals would have established an elaborate disclosure system for companies choosing to make public projections.

Approximately 420 letters of comment were received on these proposals. Although the majority of commentators agreed that projection information is significant, virtually all of them opposed the proposed system because they felt that the proposals would inhibit rather than foster projection communications between management and the investment community. Due to the important legal, disclosure policy, and technical issues raised by the commentators, the Commission on April 23, 1976, determined to withdraw all but one of the proposed rule and form changes regarding projections.

The Commission did, however, express its general views in the April 1976 release on the inclusion of projections in Commission filings, and authorized the publication for comment of proposed guides for the disclosure of projections in Securities Act registration statements and Exchange Act reports.

In its statement of general views, the Commission indicated that it would not object to disclosure in filings with the Commission of projections which are made in good faith and have a reasonable basis, provided that they are presented in an appropriate format and accompanied by information adequate for investors to make their own judgments.

* * *

The Commission's disclosure policy on projections and other items of soft information was among the subjects considered by the Advisory Committee on Corporate Disclosure. In its final report, issued November 3, 1977, the Advisory Committee made several recommendations for significant changes in that policy. Generally, the Committee recommended that the Commission issue a public statement encouraging companies voluntarily to disclose management projections in their filings with the Commission and elsewhere.

* * *

The Commission concurs in the Advisory Committee's recommendation and findings. * * * Accordingly, in light of the significance attached to projection information and the prevalence of projections in the corporate and investment community, the Commission has determined to follow the recommendation of the Advisory Committee and wishes to encourage companies to disclose management projections both in their filings with the Commission and in general. In order to further encourage such disclosure, the Commission has, in a separate release issued today, proposed for comment a safe-harbor rule for projection information whether or not included in Commission filings. The Commission also has determined to authorize publication of revised staff guides to assist implementation of the Advisory Committee's recommendation. * * *

In the integrated disclosure system adopted by the Commission in March 1982, the staff views set forth in Guide 62 were restated as views of the Commission and incorporated in Item 10 of Regulation S–K. At the same time, the Commission also announced a policy encouraging registrants to include in their 1933 and 1934 Act filings the ratings given to their debt securities by "nationally recognized statistical rating organizations," such as Moody's and Standard & Poor's. This policy is also set forth in Item 10 of Regulation S–K.

SAFE HARBOR RULE FOR PROJECTIONS

Sec. Act Rel. No. 6084 (June 25, 1979).

* * * The Securities and Exchange Commission today adopted a rule designed to provide a safe harbor from the applicable liability provisions of the federal securities laws for statements relating to or containing (1) projections of revenues, income (loss), earnings (loss) per share or other financial items, such as capital expenditures, dividends, or capital structure, (2) management plans and objectives for future company operations, and (3) future economic performance included in management's discussion and analysis of the summary of earnings or quarterly income statements. The rule is based upon the alternatives that were proposed in Securities Act Release No. 5993 (November 7, 1978). The rule is adopted in furtherance of the Commission's goal of encouraging the disclosure of projections and other items of forward-looking information. In a related action, the Commission is withdrawing the reference in note (a) to Rule 14a–9 to prediction of dividends as a possible example of a false or misleading statement. This release contains a brief discussion of the background of the proposed rules, the views of the commentators, and the provisions of the rule as adopted.

* * *

BURDEN OF PROOF

The Commission's proposed rule placed the burden of proof on the defendant to prove that a projection was prepared with a reasonable basis and was disclosed in good faith. The proposed rule reflected the Commission's concern as to the difficulties faced by plaintiffs since the facts are in the exclusive possession of the defendants.

The Advisory Committee rule would place the burden of proof on the plaintiff, along the lines of the Commission's existing safe harbor rules for replacement cost information and oil and gas reserve disclosures under Regulation S–X.

* * *

In view of the Commission's overall goal of encouraging projection disclosure and in light of the factors cited by the commentators, the Commission has determined to adopt the standard recommended by the Advisory Committee. * * *

Retention of Good Faith Requirement

Both the Commission's and the Advisory Committee's proposed rules require that reasonably based projections be disclosed in good faith. Several commentators believed that no objective standard exists for determining whether the "good faith" portion of the requirement has been met and that the term was ambiguous at best. Some commentators did not see how a reasonably based projection could be prepared and disclosed other than in good faith, and suggested that if a projection were found to have been prepared and disclosed with a reasonable basis, good faith disclosure is implicit.

On balance, the Commission believes that in light of the experimental nature of its program to encourage projection disclosure and the possibility of undue reliance being placed on projections, the use of a good faith standard in the rule is appropriate. The Commission also notes that there is ample precedent for the concept of good faith in other provisions of the federal securities laws.

Nature of Information Protected by the Rule

The Commission's proposed rule related only to projections of revenues, income (loss), earnings (loss) per share or other financial items. The Advisory Committee's proposed rule refers generally to statements of "management projection[s] of future company economic performance" or of "management plans and objectives for future company operations," and corresponds with that Committee's recommendation that disclosure of other types of forward-looking information beyond those items customarily projected also should be encouraged.

* * *

[T]he rule adopted today expands the items in the proposed rule to cover projections of other financial items such as capital expenditures and financing, dividends, and capital structure, statements of management plans and objectives for future company operations, and future economic performance included in management's discussion and analysis of the summary of earnings or quarterly income statements. The rule has been revised to refer specifically to these other items of forward-looking information in light of the commentators' suggestions that the broader coverage of the Advisory Committee rule be made explicit.

Disclosure of Assumptions

In Release 33–5992, the Commission emphasized the significance of disclosure of the assumptions that underlie forward-looking statements. As indicated in that release and Guide 62, disclosure of assumptions is believed to be an important factor in facilitating investors' ability to comprehend and evaluate these statements.

While the Commission has determined to follow the Advisory Committee's recommendation that disclosure of assumptions not be mandated under all circumstances, it wishes to reemphasize its position on the significance of assumption disclosure. Under certain circumstances the disclosure of underlying assumptions may be material to an understanding of the projected results. The Commission also believes that the key assumptions underlying a forward looking statement are of such significance that their disclosure may be necessary in order for such statements to meet the reasonable basis and good faith standards embodied in the rule. Because of the potential importance of assumptions to investor understanding and in order to encourage their disclosure, the rule as adopted indicates specifically that disclosed assumptions also are within its scope.

* * *

DUTY TO CORRECT

As indicated in Release 33–5992, the Commission reminded issuers of their responsibility to make full and prompt disclosure of material facts, both favorable and unfavorable, where management knows or has reason to know that its earlier statements no longer have a reasonable basis. With respect to forward-looking statements of material facts made in relation to specific transactions or events (such as proxy solicitations, tender offers, and purchases and sales of securities), there is an obligation to correct such statements prior to consummation of the transaction where they become false or misleading by reason of subsequent events which render material assumptions underlying such statements invalid. Similarly, there is a duty to correct where it is discovered prior to consummation of a transaction that the underlying assumptions were false or misleading from the outset.

Moreover, the Commission believes that, depending on the circumstances, there is a duty to correct statements made in any filing, whether or not the filing is related to a specified transaction or event, if the statements either have become inaccurate by virtue of subsequent events, or are later discovered to have been false and misleading from the outset, and the issuer knows or should know that persons are continuing to rely on all or any material portion of the statements.

This duty will vary according to the facts and circumstances of individual cases. For example, the length of time between the making of the statement and the occurrence of the subsequent event, as well as the magnitude of the deviation, may have a bearing upon whether a statement has become materially misleading.

* * *

[The new rule was adopted as Rule 175 under the Securities Act of 1933. A substantially identical rule was simultaneously adopted as Rule 3b–6 under the Securities Exchange Act of 1934.]

In what respects, if any, does the standard of liability for projections under Rule 175 differ from that set forth in *Beecher v. Able*? Would you advise a corporate client to make projections of earnings in an SEC filing in reliance on Rule 175? What potential dangers would you point out to the client if it wishes to make projections?

WIELGOS v. COMMONWEALTH EDISON

892 F.2d 509 (7th Cir.1989).

Before CUMMINGS, EASTERBROOK, and MANION, CIRCUIT JUDGES.

EASTERBROOK, CIRCUIT JUDGE.

Registration Form S–3 under the Securities Act of 1933 is reserved for firms with a substantial following among analysts and professional investors. The Securities and Exchange Commission believes that markets correctly value the securities of well-followed firms, so that new sales may rely on information that has been digested and expressed in the security's price. Registration on Form S–3 principally entails incorporation by reference of the firm's other filings, such as its comprehensive annual Form 10–K and its quarterly supplements. Firms eligible to use Form S–3 also may register equity securities "for the shelf" under Rule 415(a)(1)(x). Shelf registration allows the firm to hold stock for deferred sale. Information in the registration statement will be dated by the time of sale, but again the SEC believes that the market price of large firms accurately reflects current information despite the gap between registration and selling dates. Securities Act Release No. 6499 (1983), accompanying the permanent adoption of Rule 415. See also Basic, Inc. v. Levinson, 485 U.S. 224, 241–45 (1988), adopting the fraud-on-the-market approach to damages because capital markets efficiently establish prices that embed available information.

Commonwealth Edison Company, an electric utility in Illinois, is eligible to register its securities on Form S–3. In September 1983 the firm put three million shares of common stock on the shelf, using Rule 415. The succinct registration statement incorporated 176 pages of other filings, as Form S–3 permits. Commonwealth Edison sold the shares to the public on December 5, 1983, for the market price of $27.625. Stanley C. Wielgos bought 500 of these shares.

Commonwealth Edison operates several nuclear reactors, and at the time of the shelf registration it had five more under construction—LaSalle 2, Byron 1 and 2, and Braidwood 1 and 2. None could operate without a license, which the Nuclear Regulatory Commission does not issue unless satisfied that the reactor is safe. Problems at Three Mile Island and Chernobyl, coupled with increasing sophistication in reactor engineering and testing that has revealed shortcomings in old designs, have led the NRC to be more and more demanding in recent years, which postpones the operation of reactors under construction and increases their cost. Delay alone substantially increases cost, because utilities must pay for the capital they have used; reinspections and additional work come on top of the expenses of delay. Like other firms' reactors, Commonwealth Edison's have been afflicted with delay and cost overruns—some attributable to the benefit of hindsight (leading to more demanding regulations), some to bureaucratic error and delay, and some to shortcomings by Commonwealth Edison and its contractors in finishing the work to meet regulatory requirements.

Of the five reactors under construction in December 1983, Byron was the closest to receiving an operating license. An arm of the NRC, the Atomic Safety and Licensing Board, was considering Commonwealth Edison's request for a license. On January 13, 1984, the ASLB did something it had never done before (and has not done since): it denied the application outright, implying that Byron 1 must be dismantled. The next market day Commonwealth Edison's stock dropped to $21.50, a loss to equity investors of about $1 billion—which reflected not only the writeoff of Byron 1 (discounted by the probability that the NRC would affirm the ASLB's decision) but also the likely increase in the costs of completing the other four reactors. The NRC's Atomic Safety and Licensing Appeal Board reversed the ASLB in May 1984, and five months later the ASLB recommended that the NRC issue a license for Byron 1, which it did. Stock prices rebounded. Delay in starting Byron 1, plus the expense of re-inspections during that period, cost Commonwealth Edison more than $200 million. The Illinois Commerce Commission allowed Commonwealth Edison to add the outlay to its rate base, but the Supreme Court of Illinois disagreed. State officials later excluded the costs, and Commonwealth Edison is in the process of refunding about $200 million to its customers.

Between the ASLB's decision and its reversal, Wielgos filed this suit on behalf of all who purchased in the shelf offering, naming as defendants the issuer and its underwriters. The complaint demanded $6.125 per share, the amount equity securities declined between purchase and suit. * * *

III

In its final form the complaint contained two claims. Wielgos contended that the issuer and its underwriters violated § 11 first by underestimating the completion costs of the reactors and second by failing to reveal that the application for Byron 1's license was before the ASLB. Judge Shadur held the first claim precluded by Rule 175. The second failed because the chance of a flat turndown was so slim that the proceeding was not "material".

A

Documents incorporated by reference into the registration statement estimated the total costs of building Byron and Braidwood and the years these reactors would begin making power. Commonwealth Edison gave 1984 as the service date for Byron 1, 1985 for Byron 2 and Braidwood 1, and 1986 for Braidwood 2. It estimated the total costs of the two Byron reactors at $3.34 billion and of the two Braidwood reactors at $3.1 billion. Each projection came with a caution such as this:

> [T]he Company has under construction the additional generating units set forth below, the completion and operation of which will be subject to various regulatory approvals. These approvals may be subject to delay because of the opposition of parties who have intervened or may intervene in proceedings with respect thereto, changes in regulatory requirements or changes in design and construction of these units.

Anyone who followed Commonwealth Edison's filings would have seen that each year the firm increased the estimated costs and delayed the estimated start-up date of one or more reactors. No one had to read the fine print of a Form 10–K to recognize that higher costs and deferred completion are facts of life in the nuclear power industry; newspapers report this regularly, and the analysts who specialize in utility stocks know the story in detail.

Estimates incorporated into the September 1983 prospectus were calculated in December 1982. Commonwealth Edison updates its projections on an annual cycle; by September the December 1982 figures were stale, and Commonwealth Edison said so. Its latest quarterly report, also incorporated by reference into the registration statement, said that

> [t]he Company is in the process of conducting its annual review of the status of its construction program. While that review has not been completed, it appears likely that at the conclusion of the review the Company will announce a delay of approximately three months in the service date and a resultant cost increase for its Byron Unit 1. Any change in the service dates of the remaining generating units under construction will not be ascertained until the completion of the review.

Review began early in September 1983; in late December 1983 (after the securities had been sold) the Manager of Projects submitted his revised estimates to the firm's Expenditure Control Committee. On January 10 that Committee approved a projection increasing the costs of Byron 1 and 2 by $330 million. When the ASLB denied the application for a license at Byron 1, the firm immediately added another $100 million to the estimate, which it disclosed in a Form 8–K filed on January 17, 1984.

The statements incorporated into the prospectus were erroneous—not only in the sense that they turned out to be inaccurate but also in the sense that by early December 1983, when it sold the stock, Commonwealth Edison's internal cost estimates exceeded those in the documents on file. A material error in a prospectus usually is enough for liability. The district court granted summary judgment for the defendants, however, on the basis of Rule 175, one of many "safe harbors" established by the SEC on the authority of § 19(a) of the '33 Act. Rule 175 provides in part:

> (a) A statement within the coverage of paragraph (b) * * * which is made by or on behalf of an issuer * * * shall be deemed not to be a fraudulent statement (as defined in paragraph (d) of this

section), unless it is shown that such statement was made or reaffirmed without a reasonable basis or was disclosed other than in good faith.

(b) This rule applies to the following statements:

(1) A forward-looking statement (as defined in paragraph (e) of this section) made in a document filed with the Commission

* * *

(c) For the purpose of this rule the term "forward-looking statement" shall mean and shall be limited to:

(1) A statement containing a projection of revenues, income (loss), earnings (loss) per share, capital expenditures, dividends, capital structure or other financial items; * * *

All agree that the statements in question estimate "capital expenditures" within the meaning of Rule 175(c)(1). Because prospectuses and the 10–K and 8–K reports are documents "filed with the Commission" under Rule 175(b), they qualify for the safe harbor of Rule 175(a) "unless it is shown that such statement was made or reaffirmed without a reasonable basis or was disclosed other than in good faith." Rule 175(a) implies that once the issuer shows it has made a "forward-looking statement", the burden of persuasion concerning "reasonable basis" and "good faith" rests with the plaintiff. As the district judge observed, Wielgos has not tried to establish that Commonwealth Edison and the underwriters acted "other than in good faith". That leaves the question whether the statements had a "reasonable basis"; the district judge thought they did.

Wielgos tries to escape this by focusing on the first part of Rule 175(a), which says that covered statements "shall be deemed not to be * * * fraudulent". Liability under § 11 does not depend on "fraud", a term implying a mental element, Ernst & Ernst v. Hochfelder, 425 U.S. 185 (1976); any "untrue statement of a material fact" leads to liability for the issuer, § 11(a), and for every other signer who cannot make out a due diligence or expertise defense, § 11(b). This argument slights the language of Rule 175(a). A qualifying forward-looking statement is "deemed not to be a fraudulent statement (*as defined in paragraph (d) of this section*)" (emphasis added), and subparagraph (d) states:

> For the purpose of this rule the term "fraudulent statement" shall mean a statement which is an untrue statement of a material fact, a statement false or misleading with respect to any material fact, an omission to state a material fact necessary to make a statement not misleading, or which constitutes the employment of a manipulative, deceptive, or fraudulent device, contrivance, scheme, transaction, act, practice, course of business, or an artifice to defraud, as those terms are used in the Securities Act of 1933 or the rules or regulations promulgated thereunder.

"[F]raudulent statement" in Rule 175(a) turns out to be shorthand for all of the bases of liability in the '33 Act and its implementing rules.

Rule 175 is a safe harbor after all; qualifying statements may not be the basis of liability.

Forward-looking statements need not be correct; it is enough that they have a reasonable basis. In December 1982, when Commonwealth Edison made the estimates that Wielgos challenges, it used the best available information. Wielgos does not say otherwise. What he offers are two variations on the theme that delay disqualifies an estimate: he notes that in a world of increasing costs any estimate that was almost a year old is bound to be wrong, and he adds for good measure that Commonwealth Edison knew it. Teams of employees were revising the estimate, and by the date of sale one team had made a higher projection, although this had not been reviewed by upper levels of engineers and managers. None of this denies the issuer the shelter of Rule 175.

Commonwealth Edison made point estimates: Byron 1 and 2 will cost $3.34 billion and start in 1984 and 1985. Everyone understands that point estimates are almost certainly wrong. Things will not go exactly as predicted, and any deviation will cause the future to diverge from the estimate. Statisticians—and stock analysts—need confidence intervals to go with the maximum-likelihood estimate. Commonwealth Edison might have said, for example, that there is a two-thirds chance that the cost will fall in a given range, identifying the events that would push the cost up or down within (or outside of) that range. As new information comes to light, the firm and its observers may evaluate the consequences for themselves. Commonwealth Edison did not do this, and the projection it made did not assist anyone in estimating how likely (and how great) a departure from its point estimate would be.

Inevitable inaccuracy of a projection does not eliminate the safe harbor, however. Rule 175 does not say that projections qualify only if firms give ranges and identify the variables that will lead to departure. Like Form S-3 and the shelf registration rules, Rule 175 assumes that readers are sophisticated, can understand the limits of a projection—and that if any given reader does not appreciate its limits, the reactions of the many professional investors and analysts will lead to prices that reflect the limits of the information. A belief that investors—collectively if not individually—can look out for themselves and ought to have information that may improve the accuracy of prices even if it turns out to be fallacious in a given instance underlies the very existence of Rule 175.

Until 1978, when it adopted Rule 175, the SEC discouraged firms from making projections or commenting beyond the domain of "hard" information, such as last year's sales. See Walker v. Action Industries, Inc., 802 F.2d 703, 707 (4th Cir.1986) (describing this history); Victor Brudney, A Note on Materiality and Soft Information Under the Federal Securities Laws, 75 Va.L.Rev. 723, 753–57 (1989). It did this because statements about the future are less reliable than statements about the past. If you view investors as easily misled and unable to appreciate the uncertainty of predictions, you try to keep such information out of their hands. You will not succeed. Investors value securities because of beliefs about how firms will do tomorrow, not because of how they did yesterday. If enterprises cannot make predictions about themselves, then securities analysts, newspaper columnists, and charlatans have protected turf. There will be predictions aplenty outside the domain of the securities acts, predictions by persons whose access to information is not as good as the issuer's. When the issuer adds its information and analysis to that assembled by outsiders, the *collective* assessment will be more accurate even though a given projection will be off the mark.

Convincing the SEC of the utility of projections is one thing, and convincing enterprises that they ought to make projections is another. What's in it for them? If all estimates are made carefully and honestly, half will turn out too favorable to the firm and the other half too pessimistic. In either case the difference may disappoint investors, who can say later that they bought for too much (if the projection was too optimistic) or sold for too little (if the projection turns out to be too pessimistic). Thus the role of a safe harbor: the firm is not liable despite error.

Safe harbors are not necessarily enough. Harbors could be impossible to enter. Suppose the Commission were to require the issuer to reveal all of the data, assumptions, and methodology behind its projections, so that participants in the market could assess them fully and react appropriately. Data could be proprietary, secrets whose revelation to business rivals could damage the firm and its investors. Assumptions about the firm's own behavior could lead other firms to change theirs—for example, revealing the assumption that product line X will be discontinued at the end of the year could lead customers to stop buying it now or offer a rival a clue about how to capitalize. See Roger J. Dennis, Mandatory Disclosure Theory and Management Projections: A Law and Economics Perspective, 46 Md.L.Rev. 1197, 1211–18 (1987). The SEC therefore does not require the firm to reveal its data, assumptions, and methods. Rule 175(c)(4) allows the firm to reveal them, but their disclosure is not a condition of the safe harbor. Shelter without mandatory disclosure of the data and assumptions that may turn out to be important to evaluate the soundness depends on a belief that investors, collectively, are sophisticated. Readers may infer from what is said and what is omitted how reliable the estimate is. Firms that want to induce greater reliance may reveal more. Rule 175 leaves it to the issuer and the market to determine how much is revealed.

Commonwealth Edison made a projection but did not disclose data, assumptions, or methods. The cautions accompanying the projection were so much boilerplate. No one could have deduced from the cloud of legalese how much uncertainty the firm perceived in its estimates, and the market would have discounted them accordingly. Especially because professional analysts knew—although perhaps Wielgos did not—

that Commonwealth Edison's estimates were biased. Not wrong in the sense of inaccurate; biased in the sense of having a predictable kind of inaccuracy. Like clockwork, every January the firm increased its estimate of the cost of getting the Byron and Braidwood reactors into service. Some years the estimates went up more than others, but up they went. Lack of a normal distribution of errors could suggest the absence of a "reasonable basis" or even of "good faith". More likely, though, the pattern of errors allowed the market to infer two assumptions: that there would be no new regulations or unanticipated delays. Commonwealth Edison was estimating the costs it would experience if nothing went wrong and nothing unexpected happened. These were poor assumptions. Something always goes wrong, and in the nuclear power business the unexpected is the norm. Perhaps the firm had no way to estimate the timing and gravity of coming jolts, but if so that made the estimate less useful. Because Rule 175 does not require a firm to reveal assumptions, Commonwealth Edison did not need to tell the market it was making these.

Anyway, professional investors and analysts surely deduced what was afoot. Once they did so, they supplied their own assumptions about the likelihood that the firm will encounter trouble or that the rules will change. Issuers need not "disclose" Murphy's Law or the Peter Principle, even though these have substantial effects on business. So too issuers need not estimate the chance that a federal agency will change its rules or tighten up on enforcement. Securities laws require issuers to disclose *firm-specific* information; investors and analysts combine that information with knowledge about the competition, regulatory conditions, and the economy as a whole to produce a value for stock. Just as a firm needn't disclose that 50% of all new products vanish from the market within a short time, so Commonwealth Edison needn't disclose the hazards of its business, hazards apparent to all serious observers and most casual ones.

If Commonwealth Edison were doing significantly and unexpectedly worse than the industry as a whole—in completing its reactors or in making estimates about their costs—that might signal the presence of important, firm specific information that it would have to reveal. Wielgos does not contend that either the estimates or the performance of Commonwealth Edison fall substantially below the norms of the industry. (Half of all firms do worse than average, and finishing in the lower half does not imply a securities problem, but Wielgos does not even suggest that Commonwealth Edison is in the lower half.)

Because the estimates in question have a reasonable basis once they are understood as projecting forward from past experience rather than trying to predict what new things can go wrong, they are covered by Rule 175 unless, by the time Commonwealth Edison used the estimates by selling the stock on the basis of documents incorporating them, they "no longer [had] a reasonable basis." Wielgos observes that by December 1983 a team of employees had developed a different estimate; Commonwealth Edison responds that although the old estimate was stale, the new one was tentative and subject to review by higher echelons before release. Panter v. Marshall Field & Co., 646 F.2d 271, 291–93 (7th Cir.1981), holds that firms need not disclose tentative internal estimates, even though they conflict with published estimates, unless the internal estimates are so certain that they reveal the published figures as materially misleading. Estimates in progress in December 1983 were not of that character. Recall that the published projections included not only the one revealed in January 1983 but also the information in the quarterly report of September 1983 that the projections would be revised upward by an amount then under consideration.

Issuers need not reveal all projections. Any firm generates a range of estimates internally or through consultants. It may reveal the projection it thinks best while withholding others, so long as the one revealed has a "reasonable basis"—a question on which other estimates may reflect without automatically depriving the published one of foundation. Because firms may withhold even completed estimates, they may withhold in-house estimates that are in the process of consideration and revision. Any other position would mean that once the annual cycle of estimation begins, a firm must cease selling stock until it has resolved internal disputes and is ready with a new projection. Yet because large firm are eternally in the process of generating and revising estimates—they may have large staffs devoted to nothing else—a demand for revelation or delay would be equivalent to a bar on the use of projections if the firm wants to raise new capital. Rule 175 is designed to release enterprises from such binds.

It was no secret that the estimate prepared in December 1982 was too low. The firm said so in September 1983. Proceedings in the ASLB, including the staff's demand for reinspections of Byron 1's plumbing—costly to perform, costly because of delay—were public knowledge. The market price of the firm's stock, which Wielgos and his class paid in the shelf offering, reflected this information. Prompt incorporation of news into stock price is the foundation for the fraud-on-the-market doctrine and therefore supports a truth-on-the-market doctrine as well. Knowledge abroad in the market moderated, likely eliminated, the potential of a dated projection to mislead. It therefore cannot be the basis of liability.

B

Wielgos's remaining claim is that Commonwealth Edison and its underwriters violated § 11 by omitting from all of their filings the fact that the application for a license to operate Byron 1 was pending before the Atomic Safety Licensing Board. In the district court Wielgos argued that Item 103 of Regulation S–K—which calls for the issuer to disclose "any material pending legal proceedings" although not "ordinary routine litigation incidental to the business"—covered the license application. In this court Wielgos relies particularly on Instruction 5B to Item 103, which says that "an administrative or judicial proceeding" under any environmental laws or rules that "involves . . . capital expenditures . . . and the amount involved * * * exceeds 10 percent of the current assets of the registrant" cannot be treated as a "routine" proceeding (which needn't be disclosed). Judge Shadur did not decide whether the application is "routine"; Instruction 5B qualifies only that exception. The judge decided instead that the status of the application was not "material" * * *. It would be foolish, the judge thought, to require issuers to predict that administrative officials will make costly errors and be reversed. How do you predict blunders?

Information is material when "there is a substantial likelihood that a reasonable shareholder would consider it important". TSC Industries, Inc. v. Northway, 426 U.S. 438, 449 (1976). If Commonwealth Edison knew what the ASLB was going to do, the proceeding would have been important indeed. It didn't. Materiality depends not only on the magnitude of an effect but also on its probability. The anticipated magnitude (the size if the worst happens, multiplied by the probability that it will happen) may be small even when the total effect could be whopping. Reasonable investors do not want to know everything that could go wrong, without regard to probabilities; that would clutter registration documents and obscure important information. Issuers must winnow things to produce manageable, informative filings. * * *

Our case may be decided, however, without regard to materiality. We think that Commonwealth Edison revealed all that Item 103 requires. Its documents said that it was building five nuclear reactors, which it could not operate without licenses from the NRC. It told investors that it did not have licenses and that environmental groups were opposing its applications. What it did not say is that the application for Byron 1 was before the ASLB rather than some other part of the NRC, and that if the ASLB denied its application costs would go up while it tried to obtain a reversal. This is rather like revealing pending litigation without saying that the case is pending before a magistrate, and that costs will go up if the magistrate should make an adverse (and erroneous) but influential recommendation.

Issuers of securities must reveal firm-specific information. Investors combine this with public information to derive estimates about the securities' value. It is pointless and costly to compel firms to reprint information already in the public domain. Issuers needn't print the Code of Federal Regulations, which parcels authority among employees of the NRC. Item 103 does not call on registrants to describe the internal organization of courts or administrative bodies or even to state the status of the pending case. It says instead that the registration statement must "[d]escribe *briefly*" (emphasis added) and continues:

> Include the name of the court or agency in which the proceedings are pending, the date instituted, the principal parties thereto, a description

of the factual basis alleged to underlie the proceeding and the relief sought.

Nothing there about the status of the litigation within the tribunal, or how the tribunal is organized, or the probability that the tribunal will deliver a particular decision. Commonwealth Edison reported that it needed licenses from the NRC, and the "factual basis" for obtaining (or denying) the licenses flowed like a river through its papers. It would have been otiose to do more.

Wielgos treats the registration statement and the documents it incorporates as guarantees. They did not reveal that higher costs lay ahead; they did not predict a legally erroneous decision of the ASLB; therefore, Wielgos says, Commonwealth Edison must pay. The securities acts do not have this *ex post* perspective. Their approach is *ex ante.* Issuers and underwriters must decide what information will be useful without burying investors under a blizzard of paper. No investor absorbs sheafs of dense type, which Commonwealth Edison printed or incorporated in connection with this shelf offering. Descriptions in Form 10–K and registration statements are almost useless to individual investors. They require absorption by professional traders and investors. What these professionals need is new information specific to the issuer. Telling them over and again how the NRC works, or that costs are rising in the nuclear power industry, or even that Commonwealth Edison had run into trouble with its welds (which became known a few months before this stock was sold), has nothing to do with the accuracy of prices in the market. Investors who buy 500 shares of stock rely on the market price; Wielgos concedes that he did not read Commonwealth Edison's disclosures. Everything we can see demonstrates that the market had in its possession all significant information about Commonwealth Edison. That firm lived up to the technical requirements of Item 103. No one's interests would be served by requiring the details Wielgos demands from the privileged position of hindsight, as opposed to the "brief[ ]" description the SEC solicited.

In the course of his opinion, Judge Easterbrook indicates that materiality in an S–3 registration statement is to be judged by a different standard than in an S–1 filing. Is this consistent with the concerns of the Wheat Report and Judge Weinstein in the *Feit* case at p. 102 above?

If the estimate in *Wielgos* had been found to be an actionable material misstatement, what would the investment bankers have had to prove to establish that they acted with due diligence and therefore should not be held accountable? See Rule 176 and the discussion at pp. 221–225 below.

REMARKS OF HAROLD MARSH, JR. IN PANEL DISCUSSION ON DISCLOSURE IN REGISTERED SECURITY OFFERINGS

28 Bus.Lawyer 505, 529–30 (1973).*

* * * [M]ost of the present proposals center on the proposition that additional categories of information which Mr. Schneider has labeled "soft information" should be included. Basically, these boil down to three major categories of information, i.e., projections of future earnings, appraisals of assets, and evaluation of management. Professor Kripke has championed including both future earnings projections and appraisals as a routine matter in prospectuses, and Chairman Casey has indicated that the Securities and Exchange Commission is actively considering the possibility of permitting or requiring both projections and appraisals in prospectuses.

I think that the first thing that should be said concerning the matter of management projections of future operating results is that there may be a failure in some of the discussions of this subject to distinguish between "plans" and "expectations." No management of any company ever *plans* to lose money; and, if it did, the entire management should be instantly discharged. This, however, does not alter the fact that a large number of businesses do, in fact, lose money every year. In other words, the so-called "projections" of management are in no sense a realistic and unbiased judgment as to what the corporation is likely to achieve in the way of earnings, but represent rather the hopes of management after discounting to a large extent all unfavorable factors.

In my opinion, the routine inclusion of such projections in prospectuses would be highly dangerous, not only from the point of view of the investor who may attach too great a significance to them, but even more importantly from the point of view of the company officials who are going to be sued when the projections turn out to be erroneous. As far as I am concerned, I would not advise any client, under any circumstances, to include such projections in a prospectus unless Section 11 and Rule 10b–5 were first repealed or unless their inclusion is made mandatory by the Securities and Exchange Commission, in which event I would preface them with a statement that the Commission has forced their inclusion and that the projections are probably *wrong.*

So far as appraisals of assets are concerned, it would appear that under present law such appraisals of the assets of a business to be acquired must be included, at least under Rule 10b–5 and Section 14(a), if an acquiring corporation intends to realize any hidden values by sale or liquidation, as in the *Transamerica* case and the *Gamble-Skogmo* case. Presumably the same thing is true under Section 11 with respect to a tender offer prospectus where hidden values exist in the target company, as suggested by the *Leasco* case.

It is quite another thing, however, to say that a registrant selling securities for cash, which has no intention of liquidating or selling its fixed assets, should be permitted or required to give appraised values of assets in excess of their book value, or estimates of ore reserves which have no firm scientific basis, as Professor Kripke advocates. Mark Twain once defined a "mine" as a "hole in the ground with a liar on top." In my opinion, wholesale abandonment of the cost basis of accounting would destroy all of the very substantial improvements which have been made in financial reporting and accountability since 1933 and return us to the unbridled excesses of the 1920's. * * *

Selected References

T. Hazen, Securities Regulation § 3.7 (2d ed. 1990).

Brudney, A Note on Materiality and Soft Information Under the Federal Securities Laws, 75 Va.L.Rev. 723 (1989).

Note, Mandatory Disclosure of Corporate Projections and the Goals of Securities Regulation, 81 Colum.L.Rev. 1525 (1981).

---

4. Is Mandatory Disclosure a Good Idea?

Current criticism of the mandatory disclosure system under federal securities law is based on the same economic argument that is being used to discredit all types of regulation—that market forces will achieve the same (or better) results at lower cost. The following excerpts present two views of the current state of that issue.

MANDATORY DISCLOSURE AND THE PROTECTION OF INVESTORS

By Frank H. Easterbrook and Daniel R. Fischel

70 Va.L.Rev. 669 (1984).*

The Securities Act of 1933 and the Securities Exchange Act of 1934 have escaped the fate of many other early New Deal programs. Some of their companions, such as the National Industrial Recovery Act, were declared unconstitutional; others such as the Robinson-Patman Act, have fallen into desuetude; still others, such as Social Security, have been so changed that they would be unrecognizable to their creators. Many of the New Deal programs of regulation lost their political support and were replaced by deregulation; communications and transportation are prime examples.

The securities laws, however, have retained not only their support but also their structure. They had and still have two basic components: a prohibition against fraud, and requirements of disclosure when securities are issued and periodically thereafter. The notorious complexities of securities practice arise from defining the details of disclosure and ascertaining which transactions are covered by the disclosure requirements. There is very little substantive regulation of investments.

To be sure, the Securities and Exchange Commission (SEC) occasionally uses the rubric of disclosure to affect substance, as when it demands that insiders not trade without making "disclosures" that would make trading pointless, when it requires that a going private deal "disclose" that the price is "fair," and when it insists that the price of accelerated registration of a prospectus is "disclosure" that directors will not be indemnified for certain wrongs. Too, some amendments, such as the Williams Act provisions on tender offers, have substantive consequences. Although several of these refinements are important, they are not the principal components of regulation. The dominating principle of securities regulation is that anyone willing to disclose the right things can sell or buy whatever he wants at whatever price the market will sustain.

Why have the laws survived? Those who enacted these statutes asserted that they were necessary to eliminate fraud from the market and ensure that investors would receive the returns they expected; otherwise, the argument ran, people would withdraw their capital and the economy would stagnate. This explanation seemed especially pressing in 1933, for there had been frauds preceding the Depression and much disinvestment during. On this public interest story, the interests served by the laws are the same now as they were then, and so the laws have retained their beneficial structure.

No scholar should be comfortable with this simple tale. Fraud was unlawful in every state in 1933; we did not need a federal law to penalize lying and deceit. Fraud in the sale of education is more important to most people of moderate means (the supposed beneficiaries of the securities acts) than fraud in the sale of securities; these people have a much greater portion of their wealth invested in human capital than in the stock market. Yet there are no federal laws addressing these other assets. There were many securities frauds before 1933, and there have been many since. The Investors Overseas Services, National Student Marketing, Equity Funding, and OPM Leasing frauds of the last decade are every bit as spectacular as the frauds of the 1920s.

The modern recognition, backed up by evidence, that much legislation is the outcome of the interplay of pressure groups—and that only by accident will interest group laws serve the broader public interest—

suggests another hypothesis. The securities laws may be designed to protect special interests at the expense of investors.

The securities laws possess many of the characteristics of classic interest group legislation. Existing rules give larger issuers an edge, because many of the costs of disclosure are the same regardless of the size of the firm or the offering. Thus larger or older firms face lower flotation costs per dollar than do smaller issuers. The rules also help existing investment banks and auditing firms obtain an advantage because they acquire expertise and because rivals cannot compete by offering differentiated products. The securities laws' routinization of disclosure reduces the number of paths to the marketplace and insists that all firms give investors "the best," just as airline regulation stifled the high-density, low-fare strategies that have flourished recently.

Many lawyers are specialized in securities work, and other market professionals depend on the intricacies of the law for much revenue. Although there may be too many members of these favored groups (larger issuers, investment banks, the securities bar) for them to charge monopoly prices, the members would suffer windfall losses if existing regulations were repealed. Thus they have every incentive to support the status quo on an interest-group basis. And if the losses from existing laws are spread across a large number of people (individual investors), each of whom would benefit only slightly from abolition, the current regulation could survive even if it reduces social welfare.

Unfortunately, no one knows why some pieces of legislation are enacted and survive while others do not. The interest group explanation that might account for securities legislation also could explain airline and trucking regulation, yet these systems have been almost obliterated. Perhaps securities laws have survived because they are not predominantly interest-group legislation. But it is parlous to equate survival of legislation with public interest. Tobacco, milk, and farm price supports, for example, have survived despite the recent emphasis on deregulation. Few would seriously argue that these laws are anything other than the most naked forms of interest-group legislation.

The survival of securities regulation thus is consistent with either the interest-group or the public interest perspective. Distinguishing between the two explanations is difficult. To be sure, the dominant theme of the recent avalanche of literature in the economics of regulation is that few if any regulatory schemes can be explained as pure public interest responses to market failure. And we have no doubt that support by benefited interest groups explains much of the continued support for securities regulation. We are less confident, however, that interest-group support is the *sole* explanation for securities regulation. We think it appropriate, therefore, to search for the "public interest" justifications of those laws.

We examine in this essay the functions of legal rules against fraud and rules compelling disclosure promulgated by the national government. Our principal conclusion is that neither the supporters nor the opponents of the fraud and disclosure rules have made a very good case. Those who portray the laws as classic public-interest legislation systematically overlook how markets protect investors. Those who emphasize the power of markets often understate the costs of using markets and compare the real securities laws against hypothetical markets. The appropriate comparison is not regulation against market but one kind of regulation against another. But for the national securities laws, the regulation of securities would be in the hands of states and judges. We offer some reasons to believe that regulation in this alternative mode might be less satisfactory than the regulation we have now. Thus we are unable to reject either the interest-group or the public interest explanation of securities regulation.

* * *

MARKET FAILURE AND THE ECONOMIC CASE FOR A MANDATORY DISCLOSURE SYSTEM

By John C. Coffee, Jr.

70 Va.L.Rev. 717 (1984).*

Recent academic commentary on the securities laws has much in common with the battles fought in historiography over the origins of the First World War. The same progression of phases is evident. First, there is an orthodox school, which tends to see historical events largely as a moral drama of good against evil. Next come the revisionists, debunking all and explaining that the good guys were actually the bad. Eventually, a new wave of more professional, craftsmanlike scholars arrives on the scene to correct the gross overstatements of the revisionists and produce a more balanced, if problematic, assessment.

This same cycle is evident in the recent securities law literature. Not so long ago, academic treatment of the securities laws was clearly at the first or "motherhood" stage: to criticize the SEC was tantamount to favoring fraud. Then came the revisionists—most notably Professors Stigler, Benston, and Manne—who argued that the securities laws produced few benefits and considerable costs. According to Professor Benston, the passage of these statutes did not even significantly improve the quality of information provided to investors. These claims provoked a flurry of critical responses, both from academic critics and the SEC. Commentators have charged Professor Stigler with methodological laxness; a new literature on insider trading has suggested that such trading may create perverse incentives; and the leading historian on the SEC has effectively rebutted Professor Benston's account of market conditions prior to the passage of the Securities Exchange Act of 1934 (the '34 Act).

We therefore may be approaching a new stage, which can be called "post-revisionism." Among post-revisionism's defining characteristics are (1) a recognition of the Efficient Capital Market Hypothesis as, at the least, the best generalization by which to summarize the available empirical evidence; (2) a clearer sense of the difficulties inherent in relying on aggregate statistical evidence either to prove or rebut any broad thesis about the impact and effects of disclosure; and (3) a shift in focus from continued debate over the impact the federal securities laws had fifty years ago to an examination of contemporary market structure and the needs of investors under existing conditions.

In this typology of phases, the article by Professors Easterbrook and Fischel seems at the threshold of "post-revisionism." This categorization may overstate the degree to which they have moved beyond the simple catechism of Professors Stigler and Benston, but at least their article recognizes that the statistical studies are not clearly dispositive and that a faint possibility remains open that benefits might accrue to investors from a mandatory disclosure system. On the other hand, of the possible reasons they offer for believing that issuers might under-provide information, only one—the third party effects hypothesis—seems plausible.

In contrast, a simpler theory can justify a mandatory disclosure system. Such a theory can also explain where a disclosure system should focus. Essentially, this response will make four claims.

First, because information has many characteristics of a public good, securities research tends to be underprovided. This underprovision means both that information provided by corporate issuers will not be optimally verified and that insufficient efforts will be made to search for material information from non-issuer sources. A mandatory disclosure system can thus be seen as a desirable cost reduction strategy through which society, in effect, subsidizes search costs to secure both a greater quantity of information and a better testing of its accuracy. Although the end result of such increased efforts may not significantly affect the balance of advantage between buyers and sellers, or even the more general goal of distributive fairness, it does improve the allocative efficiency of the capital market—and this improvement in turn implies a more productive economy.

Second, a substantial basis exists for believing that greater inefficiency would exist without a mandatory disclosure system because excess social costs would be incurred by investors pursuing trading gains. Collectivization minimizes the social waste that would otherwise result from the misallocation of economic resources to this pursuit.

Third, the theory of self-induced disclosure, now popular among theorists of the firm and relied upon by Professors Easterbrook and Fischel, has only a limited validity. A particular flaw in this theory is that it overlooks the significance of corporate control transactions and assumes much too facilely that manager and shareholder interests can be perfectly aligned. In fact, the very preconditions specified by these theorists as being necessary for an effective voluntary disclosure system do not seem to be satisfied. Although management can be induced through incentive contracting devices to identify its self-interest with the maximization of share value, it will still have an interest in acquiring the shareholders' ownership at a discounted price, at least so long as it can engage in insider trading or leveraged buyouts. Because the incentives for both seem likely to remain strong, instances will arise in which management can profit by giving a false signal to the market.

Fourth, even in an efficient capital market, there remains information that the rational investor needs to optimize his securities portfolio. Such information seems best provided through a mandatory disclosure system.

None of these claims is intended, however, as a complete defense of the status quo, nor will this response address the important, but distinct, question of the utility of disclosure as a form of substantive regulation of corporate behavior through the sanction of stigmatization.

* * *

For selected references see p. 96 above.

C. CONSEQUENCES OF DEFICIENT REGISTRATION STATEMENTS

If a registration statement and prospectus filed with the SEC do not adequately set forth the information required under the 1933 Act, two types of sanctions may be applicable: (a) administrative action by the SEC, and (b) civil liability in the courts.

---

1. "Stop Orders" and "Refusal Orders"

Sections 8(d) and 8(b) of the 1933 Act prescribe the conditions under which the Commission may suspend the effectiveness of a registration statement or refuse to permit it to become effective. The Commission's policies in exercising those powers are set forth in the following excerpts from "stop order" proceedings, two of which involve registration statements whose deficiencies we examined in the preceding section.

UNIVERSAL CAMERA CORP.

19 S.E.C. 648, 658–60 (1945).

* * *

The primary remedies to forestall the offering of securities on the basis of inadequate or incorrect registration statements are provided in Section 8(b) and 8(d) of the Act. Those sections authorize the Commission after notice and opportunity for hearing to issue orders either deferring or suspending the effectiveness of registration statements found to be materially inaccurate or incomplete until they are amended in such a way as to correct their deficiencies.

It has been our practice to use sparingly the statutory authority to delay or suspend the effectiveness of deficient registration statements. Many necessary adjustments are worked out through prefiling conferences. Beyond that we have adopted the practice of informing registrants, informally, by letter, of any material questions that arise during examination of the statement once it is filed. The registrant is thereby afforded opportunity to file corrective amendments without the necessity of formal proceedings.

These practices usually have resulted in prompt correction or clarification of the statement. With relatively few exceptions, amendments worked out through such informal procedures have been found to satisfy the statutory requirements and to justify acceleration of the effective date.

Occasionally, however, the deficiencies are of such character and extent that in the judgment of the Commission they cannot adequately be dealt with informally. In such cases the Commission may deem it essential to the protection of investors, in view of the policy and purposes of the Act, to take formal steps to defer or suspend the effectiveness of the statement until the facts are developed through a hearing.

This is such a case. As we have stated above, in our opinion it would have been extremely difficult, if not practically impossible on the basis of the registration statement filed in this case, for ordinary investors to form a reasonably sound judgment concerning the nature of the securities or their relationship to Universal's capital structure or the investor's rights as a holder of such securities if he should buy them. In these circumstances we deemed it requisite in the public interest and for the protection of investors that the facts be explored through a hearing to determine whether a stop order should issue. We so directed and such a hearing was commenced.

EVENTS SINCE NOTICE OF PROCEEDING

The registration statement was filed on March 19, 1945. Its effectiveness was delayed by an amendment filed on April 5 and notice of the stop order proceedings was issued April 10.

On April 23 and May 5 Universal filed material amendments designed to correct some of the deficiencies in the original statement. On May 8, the hearing was commenced before a trial examiner. On May 24 Universal filed an additional amendment making further material changes in the statement.

We have considered the registration statement as modified by those amendments. We are satisfied that the amendments substantially correct the deficiencies cited in the notice of this proceeding except those relating to the warrants. Consequently, with that exception, the statement as amended, although in some respects no paragon of concise, lucid exposition, contains a statement of the essential facts covered by the notice in a form which we believe would enable the average investor to reach an informed decision whether to buy the stock at the price at which it is proposed to be offered.

It appears, however, that Universal is considering some modifications in the terms of the offering and will file amendments designed to make the statement describe the offering as modified, including appropriate amendments relative to any warrants that may be involved.

It appears further that counsel for Universal, at the hearing, undertook to file amendments that would defer the effectiveness of the statement until termination of the 7th War Loan Campaign and that such amendments have been filed.

CONCLUSION

Inasmuch as further amendments are to be filed to bring the statement up to date and into conformity with the terms of the offering ultimately to be made we make no determination at this time with respect to the effective date of the registration statement. That determination will be made after we have considered the amendments yet to be filed.

However, in view of the corrections accomplished by the amendments already filed we see no necessity for issuing a stop order or continuing further with this proceeding. Accordingly Universal's motion to dismiss the proceeding will be granted.

An appropriate order will issue.

DOMAN HELICOPTERS, INC.

41 S.E.C. 431 (1963).

* * *

Registrant concedes that the registration statement is deficient but argues that no stop order is warranted because this was a mere "preliminary filing" which it always intended to amend, and because the deficiencies are not of sufficient gravity to warrant a stop order. Registrant also moved to dismiss the proceedings on the ground that they were prematurely brought because the Division did not send it a letter of comment or otherwise communicate its views with respect to the deficiencies and afford registrant an opportunity to submit a curative amendment. We find no merit in either contention.

The statutory scheme does not recognize the "preliminary filing" concept that registrant now asks us to sanction nor any right to receive a letter of comment. If registrants are to be permitted to disclose as much or as little as they see fit without regard to the statutory mandate of full disclosure in their initial filings, on the theory that deficiencies can always be cured by amendment, effective administration of the Act will become impossible. The letter of comment is an informal administrative aid developed by us for the purpose of assisting those registrants who have conscientiously attempted to comply with the Act. The burden of seeing to it that a registration statement filed with us neither includes any untrue statement of a material fact nor omits to state any material fact required to be stated therein or necessary to make the facts therein not misleading always rests on the registrant itself, and it never shifts to our staff. When the Division has reason to believe that a registrant has failed to make a proper effort to shoulder this burden, it is its duty to bring such information to our attention and to recommend that we proceed in accordance with Section 8(d) of the Act.

Registrant further asks us to deem its registration statement to have been superseded by an amended registration statement that it filed after the hearings had been begun. We have on occasion in the exercise of our discretion considered assertedly curative substantive amendments filed after the institution of a stop order proceeding. But we do so only where it appears that such consideration will be in the best interest of investors and of the public. This is not such a case. Here the deficiencies were serious, a large amount of registrant's stock is outstanding in the hands of approximately 8,000 public investors, and the misleading information in the registration statement has been a matter of public record on which investors may have relied. The registrant has not, so far as the record discloses, undertaken to disseminate to its stockholders or to public investors generally information which would adequately advise them of the misleading character of the information contained in the registration statement. In such circumstances the issuance of a stop order is essential for the protection of public investors in order to dispel the misleading information publicized by the filing of the registration statement. * * *

A stop order will issue. Following the publication of this opinion and the submission of any future amendments designed to remedy the deficiencies, the Division's further views will be communicated to registrant. Thereafter the matter is to be submitted to us for appropriate action on the question of whether the stop order should be lifted and the registration statement as amended made effective.

FRANCHARD CORP.

42 S.E.C. 163 (1964).

* * *

The deficiencies we have found in registrant's effective filings are serious. Adequate disclosure of all of Glickman's unauthorized dealings with registrant's funds, of the strained state of his own finances, and of the doubtful durability of his control position would have altered the picture considerably. Omissions of so material a character would normally require the issuance of a stop order.[58]

Here, however, several factors taken together lead us to conclude that the distribution of copies of this opinion to all of registrant's past and present stockholders, as registrant has proposed, will give adequate public notice of the deficiencies in registrant's effective filings, and that neither the public interest nor the protection of investors requires the issuance of a stop order. Among those factors are Glickman's departure, the transfer of his controlling B shares to a management which has made a substantial financial commitment in registrant's securities, and registrant's voluntary disclosures to our staff prior to the initiation of these proceedings. Registrant also filed post-effective amendments to its 1960 filings which, though admittedly inadequate, represented a bona fide effort to remedy the deficiencies in its effective filings. In addition, by virtue of the important and prominent position in the industry held by registrant and Glickman and the comprehensive bulletin that registrant voluntarily sent to its stockholders on December 8, 1962, unusually extensive publicity was given to the true facts affecting registrant's affairs and to the resulting deficiencies in its effective filings.

Why did the Commission in the *Universal Camera* case proceed under Section 8(d) instead of Section 8(b)? What purpose is served by the issuance of a stop order before the registration statement becomes effective? Or after it has become effective and all the securities have been sold? What purpose is served by a stop order proceeding which is dismissed without issuance of a stop order because the registrant has corrected the inadequate filings?

---

58. Even where all of the publicly offered securities have been distributed, prospective purchasers may continue to rely on a misleading registration statement to their detriment. The issuance of a stop order is usually the most effective way of bringing the misleading character of the statement to the attention of the public. (See Oklahoma-Texas Trust v. S.E.C., 100 F.2d 888, 891 (C.A.10, 1939) affirming, 2 S.E.C. 764 (1937); Ultrasonic Corporation, 37 S.E.C. 497, 506 (1957); Globe Aircraft Corporation, 26 S.E.C. 43, 54–55 (1957); Bankers Union Life Company, 2 S.E.C. 63, 73 (1937)). It is not to be withheld merely because the issuer asserts, as registrant has here, that its future prospects might be impaired by further publicity about past activities. (See Ultrasonic Corporation, supra.) In the present case while all of the shares previously offered to the public have been sold, the 40,000 shares held by the underwriters may be the subject of a future public offering.

LAS VEGAS HAWAIIAN DEVELOPMENT CO. v. SEC

466 F.Supp. 928 (D.Hawaii 1979).

KING, DISTRICT JUDGE.

Plaintiffs Las Vegas Hawaiian Development Company (LVH), Tauri Investment Corporation (Tauri), and Alfred G. Bladen (Bladen), on November 7, 1978, filed a Complaint for Declaratory Judgment against the Securities and Exchange Commission (SEC or Commission) and its commissioners. They seek a declaration that section 8(e) of the Securities Act of 1933 cannot be utilized by the Commission to delay indefinitely the sale of securities under an effective registration statement, and that an examination of a registration statement cannot be utilized by the Commission to investigate prior transactions allegedly not within the scope of the registration statement.

* * *

On May 26, 1977, LVH filed a Form S–11 registration statement covering a proposed offering of limited partnerships in LVH. * * * A delaying amendment was attached to this registration.

By letter dated July 21, 1977, the Commission's Division of Corporation Finance forwarded to counsel for LVH sixteen pages of comments regarding the registration statement. An amended registration statement, with attached delaying amendment, was received by the Commission from LVH on December 23, 1977. The Commission's staff forwarded a second comment letter dated May 15, 1978, to counsel for LVH, discussing unresolved deficiencies, and stating that additional comments might be forthcoming.

On July 7, 1978, LVH filed a second amendment to its registration statement. This time no delaying amendment was attached. This meant that, absent Commission action, the effective date of the registration statement (as amended as of July 7, 1978) would be "the twentieth day after the filing thereof" pursuant to section 8(a) of the Securities Act of 1933.

On July 25, 1978, the Commission issued an order authorizing its staff (1) to conduct an examination, pursuant to section 8(e), to determine whether a stop order proceeding under section 8(d) was necessary with respect to LVH's proposed public offering, and (2) to conduct a private investigation of the circumstances surrounding the proposed offer, pursuant to section 20(a) of the Act of 1933 and section 21(a) of the Act of 1934.

* * *

Since then, the Commission's staff has been conducting the ordered examinations. No recommendation has been made to the Commission. The Commission has not yet considered whether to institute a stop order proceeding under section 8(d). In argument, counsel for the SEC stated that a recommendation for a section 8(d) proceeding was in process of being put together by the staff, but he could not predict when it would be completed or when the Commission might take action on the recommendation.

An effect of the Commission's July 25, 1978, order is to bring into operation the prohibition contained in section 5(c) of the Securities Act of 1933 against use of interstate communications to offer to sell or to offer to buy the registered securities "while the registration statement is the subject of * * * (prior to the effective date of the registration statement) any public proceeding or examination under section [8(e)]." Thus, although LVH's second amended registration statement became effective on the twentieth day after July 7, 1978, prior thereto, that is on July 25, 1978, it became the subject of a public examination under section 8(e) pursuant to the Commission's order of that date. As a consequence, any sales activity involving the registered securities was effectively blocked by the provisions of section 5(c).

* * *

Plaintiffs argue that the Commission is engaging in a ploy which denies LVH procedural and substantive due process. By not noticing an order delaying the effectiveness of a registration statement pursuant to section 8(d), the Commission has prevented the registrant from having a hearing.

Defendants argue that the Commission has not done anything which is reviewable. The Commission's decision to conduct a section 8(e) examination of LVH's registration statement is not a final position. The registration statement has become effective, and until the Commission notices an intention to issue a stop order, it is only conducting an examination which may or may not result in further action.

Furthermore, say defendants, a section 8(e) examination is a matter within the Commission's discretionary powers, both as to scope and length, which may not be judicially reviewed unless there is an abuse of discretion or action which exceeds the authority of the Commission, neither of which have been supported by factual allegations in the complaint.

Finally, defendants argue that plaintiffs have not exhausted their administrative remedies.

Defendants have oversimplified the situation by arguing that there is no present hardship to the plaintiffs if judicial review is withheld at this time. If the Commission's order authorizing a public examination pursuant to section 8(e) had been issued *after* the effective date of the second amended registration statement, section 5(c) would not have come into operation. LVH could then have proceeded with its sales program, even though a stop order could later issue. But the Commission's order issued *before* the effective date of the registration statement, section 5(c) is applicable, and the plaintiffs do feel the agency action in a concrete way. See Abbott Laboratories, Inc. v. Gardner, 387 U.S. 136 (1967).

While the SEC is given broad powers and wide discretion, provision is made for time limits, notices, hearings, appeals, and judicial reviews of actions that affect the issuance and sale of securities. It is not a sufficient answer to say that authorizing a section 8(e) examination is not a final Commission action, nor to say that no one has a right to register securities for public sale. A registrant does have a right to have the Commission follow the applicable statutes and regulations, and attempts by the Commission to circumvent statutorily imposed time limits may be attacked in a judicial proceeding. See SEC v. Sloan, 436 U.S. 103 (1978).

Yet Congress has not placed any time limitation on the duration of a section 8(e) examination. Nor is an order authorizing such an examination reviewable under section 9 of the Act. This leaves the registrant with whatever remedy may be had pursuant to the Administrative Procedure Act (APA).

In my opinion, a district court may, upon the petition of a registrant under the Securities Act of 1933, compel the SEC to make a determination within a reasonable time whether to notice a hearing on the issuance of a stop order under section 8(d), where the Commission has ordered an examination under section 8(e) prior to the effective date of a registration statement and the determination whether a stop order should issue has been unreasonably delayed.

The court may not compel the Commission to institute a section 8(d) proceeding. But the clear import of 5 U.S.C. § 706 is that the court may compel the SEC to either terminate a section 8(e) examination or institute a section 8(d) proceeding in a situation where the SEC's inaction has the effect of prohibiting the sale of registered securities, and when this determination has been unreasonably withheld.

* * *

Assuming the application of the APA as discussed above, must the registrant first exhaust available administrative remedies? The answer is obviously in the affirmative. Exhaustion is the rule rather than the exception. No grounds for making an exception here are alleged. But plaintiff LVH does allege that it has exhausted its administrative remedies. This is a sufficient allegation under Fed.R. Civ.P. 9(c). The Commission may respond by specifying what available administrative remedy LVH has not exhausted.

It may be noted here that it is the remedy that must be exhausted, not the petitioner, and that availability implies reasonably prompt and appropriate relief.

* * *

[The court went on to hold that LVH had not alleged sufficient facts to state a claim on which relief could be granted, and dismissed the complaint with leave to amend.]

2. *SEC Review and Denial of Acceleration*

As the foregoing excerpts indicate, the SEC has been sparing in the use of its administrative powers under §§ 8(b) and 8(d). This is not to say, however, that the SEC has played a passive role with respect to the contents of the great majority of registration statements filed with it. On the contrary, a substantial part of the time and energy of its staff has been devoted to the review of registration statements and the communication of the staff's views in "letters of comment," also known as "deficiency letters." In these informal and confidential [a] communications, which are not provided for in the Act, the staff may insist on or suggest changes, additions or deletions, or may request additional information as a prelude to further comments.

The basis of this procedure, and of the willingness of issuers to go along with it, is § 8(a) of the Act, which authorizes the Commission, subject to stated criteria, to permit a registration statement to become effective less than 20 days after filing. Because § 8(a) provides that the filing of any amendment to the registration statement starts the 20-day period running again, the SEC's willingness to "accelerate" the effective date is crucial to every issuer which wants to proceed with its offering as soon as possible after filing the amendment containing the price information with regard to the security being offered.

The following excerpts indicate the way in which the procedure has developed, as well as some of the questions that have been raised about it.

DEVELOPMENT OF S.E.C. PRACTICES IN PROCESSING REGISTRATION STATEMENTS AND PROXY STATEMENTS

By Byron D. Woodside *

24 Bus.Lawyer 375, 376–78 (1969).**

The testing time for government and business in the regulation of the securities business may fairly be said to have occurred during the

a. In January 1975, the SEC proposed a change in its rules to make comment letters and replies available as part of the public record, except to the extent that the registrant was granted confidential treatment of certain information. Sec.Act Rel. No. 5561 (Jan. 24, 1975). Four years later, the Commission announced that it was withdrawing the proposed rule. It stated that it hoped to develop a revised rule which better reflected the concerns expressed by the Supreme Court in Chrysler Corp. v. Brown, 441 U.S. 281 (1979) with respect to confidential treatment of filed materials. Sec.Act Rel. No. 6069 (May 23, 1979).

* Former Commissioner of the Securities and Exchange Commission; associated with the SEC from the time of its establishment until his retirement in April, 1967; [also first Chairman of the Securities Investor Protection Corp. from 1971 to 1973–Ed.]

period from 1933 to 1940 as the Commission and industry worked their way through the initial stages of implementing the regulatory provisions of the first two Acts. * * *

A major Commission activity under the '33 Act is the exercise of judgment and discretion to establish, in accordance with the statutory scheme, certain minimum standards as to the nature and extent of the information to be published in registration statements, and supplied to investors by means of prospectuses, and an attempt to see to it that they are followed.

The process begins with the adoption of a registration form and suitable rules and instructions as to content and procedural matters. This was done in the first instance on somewhat of a crash basis shortly after May 27, 1933. The effective date of the statute was July 27, 1933. The initial waiting period between the date of filing and the effective date prescribed by the Act was 20 days (prior to 1940 the Commission had no authority to shorten that period). A company engaged in the distribution of securities prior to July 27, and wishing to continue without interruption, thus was faced with the necessity of filing a registration statement not later than July 7 and hoping that the statement could become effective without delay on the 20th day.

On July 7, more than 80 registration statements were filed with the Federal Trade Commission—many of them by investment companies engaged in continuous offerings of their securities. There were approximately 12 to 15 persons on the staff of the newly created Securities Division when this mass of documents arrived. No one was very sure just what a registration statement should contain or what should be done with it.

Since the few people assigned to this new work could not hope to review such a volume of material quickly, the statements were assigned to various persons in different offices of the Trade Commission, and an attempt was made to check them against the requirements of the registration form and Schedule A of the Act. A substantial number of recommendations for stop order proceedings resulted.

Almost immediately there must have been a realization, on the part of those in charge, that the procedural provisions of Section 8 of the Act were too cumbrous to be useful as a means of disposing of routine business with efficiency and dispatch. Section 8(b), which contemplated an order preventing a registration statement from becoming effective, rarely could be useful, in the absence of consent, because of the short period within which notice, hearing, and order must occur. The stop order procedure under Section 8(d) was burdensome and time consuming. The formal examination or investigation authorized by Section 8(e) held no promise of expedition.

These circumstances—short staff, the desire on the part of business to proceed promptly, the willingness on the part of most to comply with the requirements, the awkwardness of the statutory administrative processes, and most important I think, the desire on the part of issuers and underwriters to avoid the risk of being second-guessed by the government after beginning a public offering—inevitably led to the conference table and informal procedures. Thus, the pre-effective deficiency letter came almost spontaneously, and by common consent, to be the principal means of communication of the Administrator's views as to apparent compliance, in the conduct of routine business. It has continued to perform this role.

The significance of "time" became apparent at once. It was clear to everyone that delay, careless or otherwise, on the part of the agency or the issuer or underwriter might be the cause of missing a market or ruining a schedule. Prolonged argumentation over less than crucial matters, or indecisiveness, could be very expensive. It was understandable, therefore, that staff recommendations, in those very early days, urging widespread use of stop order proceedings were largely rejected. Had they been followed the whole operation would have been bogged down in a morass of formal proceedings, and the worst fears of the critics would have been realized.

The Securities Act was resented and feared in the beginning. It had been predicted that business would be unable or unwilling to raise capital under its "harsh" provisions. Choking the flow of financing at the very outset by numerous Section 8 actions would have been self-defeating.

As it was, the lesson of "time" was impressed upon the consciousness of a government staff to a most unusual degree. The desire of government to make a new statute workable and acceptable had a fortunate conjunction with the desire of business to be informed, in advance of commitment if possible, of any objections, and to cooperate in making reasonable changes. "Time" and the cooperative efforts of business and government made the registration process work in those early days, and they have continued to do so.

Very early, lessons were learned which have influenced in a material way the manner in which the Commission has conducted its business under these two acts. From the beginning, industry, the bar, and the accountants were consulted on matters of rules, forms, and procedures. They were consulted and listened to and their views contributed to arriving at sensible and workable solutions. Informality marked the conduct of business in most matters. The formal investigation or administrative proceeding was reserved for the egregious case, the suspected fraud, the very careless, where good faith was doubted, or where the Commission believed some matter of principle should be explored formally and made the subject of an opinion, through which it could publicize its views.

UNIVERSAL CAMERA CORP.

19 S.E.C. 648, 656–58 (1945).

* * *

The Securities Act of 1933 indicates with definite clarity the powers and responsibilities of the Commission with respect to registration statements that do not plainly and accurately disclose the nature of the securities to be registered.

In contrast to some of the State officials and commissions, operating under state "Blue Sky" laws that authorize them to pass upon the merits of securities registered with them, it is not this Commission's function under the Securities Act to approve or disapprove securities and the statute specifically makes it unlawful to represent that the Commission has passed upon the merits of any security, or given approval to it.

It is plain that the policy Congress has established by the Securities Act and the machinery that Act creates for making its policy effective are designed to afford protection to investors, not by requiring the Commission to identify "good" and "bad" securities and forbid the sale of the latter, but by requiring those who propose to offer securities to the public to disclose plainly the facts an investor needs to know to make an informed judgment concerning the nature and quality of the securities to be offered. The Act leaves it to the investor, on the basis of the facts disclosed, to weigh the earning prospects of a registered security against the risks involved and to judge for himself whether he wishes to invest his money in it.

The Commission subjects all registration statements to careful and critical analysis. Many clarifying revisions are made as a consequence and we believe that the practice followed has been highly successful in detecting material errors and omissions that not infrequently occur in the statements as originally filed. It is plain, however, in view of the provisions of Section 23, that registration is not to be regarded as a finding by the Commission that the statement does not contain any material errors or omissions.

Where no material errors or omissions appear, the registration statement becomes effective, pursuant to Section 8(a) of the Act, on the twentieth day after it is filed, unless amendments are filed in the meantime whereby new filing dates are established. However, Section 8(a) also authorizes the Commission to make the registration effective before the twentieth day.

It is obvious from the terms of that authorization that Congress did not intend the Commission to exercise the authority casually or to grant acceleration as a matter of course. The careful definition of factors to be considered in making a determination to advance the effective date plainly indicates that the Commission's discretion is to be exercised only with full regard for the Act's purpose to provide investors with the information they need to be able to protect themselves against fraud and misrepresentation. Acceleration is to be granted only with due regard to the public interest and the protection of investors and only after taking into account:

> (1) The adequacy of the information about the issuer that was available to the public before the registration,
>
> (2) the ease with which the nature of the securities can be understood,
>
> (3) the ease with which the relationship of the securities to the capital structure of the issuer can be understood, and,
>
> (4) the ease with which the rights of holders of the securities can be understood.

This provision for acceleration was added to the Act in 1940 to relax the rigidity of the previous requirements. Its terms make plainly evident the persistent concern of Congress for the protection of investors and emphasize the intention of Congress to require that before permitting a registration to become effective the Commission must be satisfied that the information in the statement itself, together with any information previously available to the public about the issuer, will enable prospective investors to understand clearly what it is they are asked to buy.

Consistently with these provisions the Act authorizes the Commission to take steps that may be necessary to defer the public sale of any security subject to registration until the statement is cleared of material inaccuracies or omissions and contains a complete and correct statement of the information requisite to a clear understanding of the security's character and quality.

THE DIVISION OF CORPORATION FINANCE'S PROCEDURES DESIGNED TO CURTAIL TIME IN REGISTRATION UNDER THE SECURITIES ACT OF 1933

Securities Act Release No. 5231 (Feb. 3, 1972).

On November 21, 1968, the Commission issued Securities Act Release No. 4934 in which it set forth certain procedures designed to reduce the backlog of registration statements processed by the Division of Corporation Finance which had as of that date reached an unprecedented high. The Division now faces a situation similar to that which existed in the fall of 1968. For the first half of fiscal 1972, 1632 registration statements were filed as compared to 1193 for the like period in fiscal 1971. Of the fiscal 1972 filings, 632 represent first time filings by issuers which have never before been subjected to the registration process and generally require more time consuming review by the staff, as compared to 352 for the first half of fiscal 1971. The Division's workload also has been materially increased by the number of reports and other documents filed under the Securities Exchange

Act. For example, annual reports on Form 10–K in fiscal 1971 reached a level of 8,319 as compared to 6,064 in fiscal 1969. Notwithstanding this burdening workload, the Division's staff has not increased to any significant extent.

In view of the above circumstances, the Division has taken further steps as set forth below designed to curtail the time in registration. The Commission believes it appropriate to once again bring these existing procedures and the new ones to the attention of registrants, attorneys, accountants, underwriters, and others in the securities industry and to urge their cooperation in assuring that registration statements contain full and fair disclosure and are prepared in the public interest to present effective disclosure—to communicate—in order that public investors be protected.

Various Review Procedures

The Division employs four different review procedures in examining registration statements. It should be noted that the Division and not the registrant itself will determine which type of examination a registration statement will receive.

1. Deferred Review

The first category of procedures will come into operation when a supervisory staff official decides after initial analysis that the registration statement is so poorly prepared or otherwise presents problems so serious that review will be deferred since no further staff time would be justified in view of other staff responsibilities. Detailed comments will not be prepared or issued for to do so would delay the review of other registration statements which do not appear to contain comparable disclosure problems. Registrants will be duly notified. It will then be the responsibility of the particular registrant to consider whether to go forward, withdraw, or amend. Should the registrant decide to go forward without corrective steps, the staff will then make recommendations to the Commission for appropriate action.

2. Cursory Review

The second type of review involves advice to registrants that the staff has made only a cursory review of the registration statement and that no written or oral comments will be provided. In such cases, particularly with respect to companies which have never before been subject to the registration process, registrants will be requested to furnish as supplemental information letters from the chief executive officer of the issuer, the accountants, and the managing underwriter on behalf of all underwriters. These letters shall include representations that the respective persons are aware that the staff has made only a cursory rather than a detailed review of the registration statement and that such persons are also aware of their statutory responsibilities under the Securities Act. Registrants will be advised that, upon receipt of such assurances, the staff will recommend that the registration statement be declared effective. Generally with respect to a first time filing, the effective date will not be earlier than 20 days after the date of original filing.

3. *Summary Review*

The third category—summary review—involving a variation of the cursory treatment described in the preceding paragraph, will entail notification to the registrant that only a limited review of the registration material has been made and only such comments as may arise from such review will be furnished. Registrants will be requested to provide letters from the same individuals mentioned in the preceding paragraph containing similar representations. Registration statements reviewed in a summary fashion will be declared effective as described in the preceding paragraph upon receipt of both the above-mentioned assurances and upon satisfactory compliance with the limited comments of the staff.

4. *Customary Review*

In the final category of review, registration statements will receive a more complete accounting, financial and legal review.[a]

Notwithstanding the type of review applied to a registration statement, the Commission hereby again advises registrants that the statutory burden of disclosure is on the issuer, its affiliates, the underwriter, accountants and other experts; that as a matter of law this burden cannot be shifted to the staff; and that the current workload is such that the staff cannot undertake additional review and comments. Attention is directed to the case of Escott v. BarChris Construction Corporation, et al., 283 F.Supp. 643 (DC, S.D.N.Y., 1968).

The Division recognizes that due to the utilization of gradations of review, certain disclosures may appear in particular prospectuses which do not appear in others. Such differences in disclosure will not, however, preclude the staff from commenting upon the presence or absence of specific disclosures in the review of other filings. * * *

CHANGES IN REVIEW PROCEDURES IN THE DIVISION OF CORPORATION FINANCE

SEC News Digest (Nov. 17, 1980).

Beginning the week of November 17, 1980, the Division of Corporation Finance will implement new processing procedures with respect to filings made under the Securities Act of 1933 and the Securities Exchange Act of 1934 * * *. As a result, Release No. 33–5231 [p. 148 above] will no longer be in effect. Under the new procedures, certain

a. Item 501(c)(5) of Regulation S–K requires that every prospectus state on its front cover, in bold face capital letters, that the Commission has not "passed on the accuracy or adequacy of" the prospectus, and that "any representation to the contrary is a criminal offense." Would an issuer violate the law by stating that its prospectus had received a "complete accounting, financial and legal review" by the Commission's staff?

1933 Act registration statements may not be reviewed, in which cases requests for acceleration of effectiveness will be treated as confirmation by participants in the offering of their awareness of their statutory obligations under the federal securities laws.

At the time the SEC adopted selective review in 1980, the volume of 1933 and 1934 Act filings had been increasing significantly while there had been a decrease in the size of the staff available to review the filings. Although the Commission stated that the four methods of review set forth in Sec.Act Rel. No. 5231, at p. 148 above, are no longer being followed, they still provide guidance as to the procedures used by SEC staffers in reviewing 1933 Act filings.

"ACCELERATION" UNDER THE SECURITIES ACT OF 1933—A COMMENT ON THE A.B.A.'S LEGISLATIVE PROPOSAL

By Edward N. Gadsby * and Ray Garrett, Jr.**

13 Bus.Lawyer 718 (1958).***

[On] February 25, [1958], in Atlanta, Georgia, the House of Delegates of the American Bar Association adopted a resolution favoring a legislative proposal relating to the power of the Securities and Exchange Commission to grant or deny "acceleration" under the Securities Act of 1933. * * *

As the appended report indicates, the American Bar Association proposes to amend section 8(a) of the Securities Act of 1933, the first sentence of which provides that a registration statement shall become effective twenty days after filing—

> or such earlier date as the Commission may determine, having due regard to the adequacy of the information respecting the issuer theretofore available to the public, the facility with which the nature of the securities to be registered, their relationship to the capital structure of the issuer and the rights of the holders thereof can be understood, and to the public interest and the protection of investors. * * *

Under the proposed amendment if a registration statement were filed without stating the offering price, such information could be supplied by amendment on the 19th day and the statement would become effective on the 20th day without requiring any action by the Commission. On the other hand, under the present wording of the statute, such a statement would not become effective until the 39th day

* Chairman, Securities and Exchange Commission.

** Associate Executive Director, Securities and Exchange Commission. [Chairman of the SEC from 1973 to 1975.—Ed.]

after the original filing unless the Commission "accelerated" its effective date. As a practical matter since an underwriter is seldom willing to be committed to a price for any substantial length of time prior to the public offering, issuers normally request "acceleration" by the Commission. The Section's report asserts that this places in the hands of the Commission a "club" over the issuer, a power which the proponents of the statutory amendment believe the Commission should not have, even though they do admit that the "power is not being used in a manner which seriously hampers the investment banking industry."

* * *

Under the proposed amendment to the statute, an issuer would, by filing a price amendment, be able automatically to achieve an effective registration statement without regard to the standards of the statute and the Commission rules, unless the Commission were to institute stop-order proceedings. History teaches us that such a procedure would be employed and abused by the unscrupulous and irresponsible and, that while a basis for refusal to accelerate does not necessarily provide a basis for stop-order proceedings, the Commission would to a much greater degree than now be required to prepare for stop-order proceedings in any case in which adequate and fair disclosure has not been made. Issuers have little or nothing to gain by encumbering the Commission's procedures by such unnecessary burdens which could result only in slowing down our entire processes as to all issuers.

Substantively, the issuer could gain from the proposed changes only to the extent that the Commission might assert grounds for denying acceleration which it would not assert as basis for a stop-order proceeding. From the report of the Section it is evident that this is precisely the point which the proponents of the measure hope to achieve. The differences, if any, in the grounds available for Commission action under these two procedures therefore becomes significant.

The respective statutory standards under the two procedures are not identical. We have quoted above the language in section 8(a) setting forth the standards which govern our granting of acceleration. These include not only matters relating directly to disclosure but also refer to "the public interest and the protection of investors." The full and precise meaning of this very general language has never been considered by the courts. Administratively the Commission has tried not to expand these words out of context and beyond the stated purposes of the act.

In contrast, section 8(d) states that a stop-order proceeding may be begun:

> If it appears to the Commission at any time that the registration statement includes any untrue statement of a material fact or omits to state any material fact required to be stated therein or necessary to make the statements therein not misleading. * * *

Unquestionably this is more precise language, refers to more specific elements of disclosure and by its terms leaves less to Commission discretion.

In practice, however, we do not believe that the distinction amounts to very much. As the Section report recites, the Commission just last year formulated certain of its policies in acting on acceleration requests and published them in a Note to Rule 460. The Note repeats in its paragraph the standards in section 8(a) and then states five specific matters which may cause acceleration to be denied. These are, in substance, the presence of any of the following:

(a) A provision for the indemnification of directors, officers or controlling persons against liabilities arising under the act unless a specified statement is included disclosing the Commission's view that such a provision is contrary to the policy of the act, together with an undertaking to submit the question, should it arise, to an appropriate court prior to making any payment to any such person pursuant to the indemnity.

(b) A provision whereby the registrant undertakes to indemnify the underwriter, where a director, etc., of the registrant has a described affiliation with the underwriter, unless an undertaking and statement is included as in (a).

(c) A pending investigation by the Commission of the issuer or a controlling person or an underwriter under any acts administered by the Commission.

(d) An inability by an underwriter to perform his commitment without violation of the financial responsibility requirements of Rule 15C3–1 under the Securities Exchange Act of 1934.

(e) Market "manipulation" by persons connected with the offering.

The Commission believes that the policies expressed in the foregoing Note are lawful and proper under section 8(a). Their lawfulness as well as their wisdom was thoroughly debated during the hearings on the proposed Note referred to in the Section report, and the Commission, after extensive deliberation and after discarding certain other criteria whose pertinence was not so clear, concluded to proceed along the line so described.

The question remains, however, whether matters which under the Note would lead to denial of acceleration would also warrant the institution of stop-order proceedings. This question cannot be answered categorically, nor can I commit myself or my fellow commissioners as to future action in a particular instance. By far the great majority of cases which raise any problem regarding acceleration involve simple matters of factual disclosure covered by the general language of the first paragraph of the Note. In candor, it must be admitted that there might be marginal cases where the cumbersome nature of the stop-order procedure would cause limited staff manpower or sheer human inertia to tip the scales in favor of a registrant, but such instances cannot reasonably be expected to be numerous or very important.

* * *

The practitioner may occasionally feel exasperated at the practical absence of opportunity for judicial review of adverse exercise of administrative discretion, but he should reflect that in the field of public, underwritten securities offerings, it is the exigencies of the financing process rather than the law which make an appeal impracticable. Unlike, for example, Treasury rulings, in the type of offering with which the Section proposal is concerned, financing needs and arrangements cannot wait for the judicial process to work itself out. The only practical solution would seem to be the institution of some sort of a declaratory type of judicial review of Commission rules and such a provision would present such formidable difficulties as to make it impossibly complex and cumbersome.

What we have said here does not mean that the Commission is free or wants to be free to impose arbitrary and unlawful requirements or that it is insensitive to the views and interests of registrants as well as investors. The individual commissioners have always been, are now and surely will always be reasonable men who are anxious to proceed in an orderly and fair manner and who have no reason to want to act unlawfully or arbitrarily in the exercise of their duties. That they are responsive, within the limits of the statute, to the views of the industry, the bar and the accountants has been demonstrated time and again where such views appeared persuasive. This was illustrated aptly enough in the very proceedings leading to the present version of the Note to Rule 460. That the views of such groups are not always persuasive should hardly be surprising in the light of the Commission's legal responsibilities and the legislative purpose of the federal securities laws.

It would seem wiser for the members of the bar to recognize, as so many of them do, that their participation in the rule-making process and the constant interchange of views and arguments have combined with administrative flexibility and discretion to form an essential part of our legal system. Further "judicialization" of our administrative processes inevitably tends to destroy the approach which makes possible fair and efficient regulation and law enforcement. The proposed statutory amendment would unfortunately be a step in that direction.

Is there a statutory basis for the criteria originally set forth in paragraphs (a) and (b) of the Note to Rule 460 and now found in Item 512(i) of Regulation S–K? Should people who have to deal with the SEC be satisfied with the assurance that procedural safeguards are not required because the "individual commissioners have always been, are now and surely will always be reasonable men"? Consider the following reply to the above article:

"ACCELERATION" UNDER THE SECURITIES ACT OF 1933—A REPLY TO THE SECURITIES AND EXCHANGE COMMISSION

By John Mulford *

14 Bus.Lawyer 156 (1958).**

On February 25, 1958, the American Bar Association, by the unanimous vote of its House of Delegates, approved a proposed amendment to Section 8(a) of the Securities Act of 1933. The amendment provides that the filing of a price amendment to a registration statement will delay the effective date of the statement only one day instead of the twenty days now fixed by the Act. It would thus obviate the necessity for registrants to obtain the exercise of the Commission's discretionary authority to accelerate the effective date of registration statements on the filing of price amendments. This, in turn, would prevent the Commission from threatening to deny such acceleration for reasons unrelated to disclosure and thus in effect would prevent it from prohibiting public offerings of securities which contain substantive features obnoxious to the Commission. It would do so by subjecting the Commission's orders in such cases (which are not now appealable) to court review.

The proposed amendment has been attacked by the Honorable Edward M. Gadsby, Chairman of the Commission, and Ray Garrett, Jr., Esq., its Associate Director. They did not argue that more than one day was needed by the public to study the material filed in a price amendment and that therefore the amendment to the Act is in the least objectionable on its merits. Indeed they point with pride to the fact that in 88% of the most applicable cases [1] the registration statement was made effective by affirmative Commission action on the very day the price amendment was filed.

Their attack was based rather on the fact that the amendment would remove one weapon from the arsenal used by the Commission to force changes in the substantive features of public offerings of securities. They contend that this weapon (the power to deny acceleration on the filing of a price amendment and thus to prohibit particular public offerings) was intended by the Congress to be granted to the Commis-

* Member of the Philadelphia Bar and member and former chairman of the [ABA] Committee on Federal Regulation of Securities.

** Copyright 1958. Reprinted from the November 1958 issue of The Business Lawyer with the permission of the American Bar Association and its Section of Corporation, Banking and Business Law.

1. In every one of the 122 cases involving price amendments, acceleration was requested. Information on this point as to the other 244 cases is not readily available, but it would be surprising if acceleration was not requested and granted in substantially all of them. The article does not state in how many of the cases it cites registrants made substantive changes in offerings because they knew or were told that acceleration would be denied if they failed to do so. To obtain this information it would, of course, be necessary to consult counsel for each of the registrants.

sion. The relevant decisions of the courts and the legislative history of the 1940 amendment to the Securities Act which inserted the language relied on by the Commission are to the contrary.[2] * * *

Before discussing the article's objections to the proposed amendment, it is necessary to analyze the changes in practice and procedure which would result from its adoption. The case supposed below is just one example of the way the act works now and of the effect of the proposed amendment.

Paragraph (a) of the Note to Rule 460 in effect prohibits agreements to indemnify directors and officers against liabilities arising under the Act unless registrants agree to submit the question of the validity of such agreements to a court prior to performing them. Let us suppose that there is an obdurate registrant whose directors and officers insist that, unless they are indemnified by the registrant against such liability, they will not proceed with a public offering of securities. A registration statement is filed, say on January 1. In the prospectus it is clearly and prominently stated that the registrant has undertaken to provide such indemnity. On January 10 a letter of comment is received from the Commission with various suggestions, including a request to insert the agreement (spelled out in paragraph (a) of the Note to Rule 460) not to perform the indemnity agreement unless its validity has been upheld in court. The registrant refuses to make such an agreement. Today, the Commission under that part of the Note will deny acceleration on the filing of a price amendment. The order denying acceleration is not appealable to the courts.

2. Mr. Wagner: "Mr. President, I should like to offer an amendment [to the bill containing the Investment Company Act and Investment Advisers Act] which is really separate from the regulation of the investment trusts. It would liberalize the Securities Act of 1933. This, too, has been agreed upon by the National Association of Securities Dealers, Investment Bankers Association and the Securities and Exchange Commission. I have been instructed by the Committee on Banking and Currency to present the amendment. It relaxes the present provision that twenty days must elapse after an application for registration has been made before the securities may be sold.

* * *

"It is a very simple amendment. The present law is absolutely rigid and automatic. An issuer must wait twenty days after filing his registration statement before he can offer his securities for sale. The amendment vests discretion in the Securities and Exchange Commission so that an earlier date may be fixed in appropriate cases subject to appropriate standards set forth in the bill. That is all it would do." *Congressional Record, Senate,* August 8, 1940, pages 10069–70.

The amendment to the bill, which had previously passed the House, was thereupon unanimously agreed to.

Mr. Cole: [The Senate amendment is] "a relaxation of the rigid rule under which the Commission is now required to function, so that in the future registrations, if the Commission so decides, may become effective in less than the twenty day period now called for under the law." *Congressional Record, House,* August 13, 1940, page 10249.

At page 10251 the amendment was unanimously agreed to.

The foregoing is the only relevant legislative history of this amendment to Section 8(a) of the Act. Though it is not too helpful, it does make it abundantly clear that neither the Senate nor the House had any idea that, by passing the amendment, they were authorizing the Commission to pass on the merits or substantive features of particular securities or offerings. * * *

Crooker v. S.E.C., 161 F.2d 944 (C.A.1, 1947). The proposed public offering will have to be withdrawn.

Now let us suppose that the amendment to the Act is in effect. On January 12 the registrant will file its "deficiency amendment" complying with all the suggestions of the Commission except that concerned with indemnity. This amendment starts the twenty-day waiting period again. Having ascertained that the indemnity provision is the only deficiency which the Commission now has, the registrant on January 20 files a price amendment and requests acceleration. The Commission can, and we hope would, grant the request.

If the Commission refused to do so the registrant would, on February 1, the nineteenth day after the filing of the deficiency amendment, file a new price amendment. The registration statement would automatically become effective on February 2. The Commission could, however, under Section 8(d) of the Act, by notice, commence a stop order proceeding. Under Jones v. S.E.C., 298 U.S. 1, 15, 18 (1936), this would suspend the effectiveness of the registration statement and postpone the public offering. But the stop order (which must issue within fifteen days of the notice under Section 8(d)) would be appealable to a Court of Appeals under Section 9(a) of the Act. That court would have power under Section 9(b) to stay the Commission's order. Stop orders are authorized in Section 8(d) only "if it appears to the Commission at any time that the registration statement includes any untrue statement of a material fact or omits to state any material fact required to be stated therein or necessary to make the statements therein not misleading".

In the author's opinion, the court in such a case would promptly grant a stay of the Commission's order and permit the public offering to proceed as soon as it found that the only reason for the stop order was the refusal of the registrant (fully disclosed in the prospectus) to agree that its indemnity agreement would not be performed by it until after a court proceeding had established its validity. The knowledge that this procedure is available to registrants would go far to deter the Commission from denying acceleration in such a case when it was first requested.

This example shows that in most cases the registrant would still request acceleration as registrants almost invariably do today. The Commission by threatening to deny acceleration could and would continue to require registrants to comply with requirements of the Act relating to matters of disclosure. Current administrative practices of the Commission in such cases would not be changed a whit. If "unscrupulous and irresponsible" registrants failed to comply with disclosure requirements, as the article suggests, it could always issue a stop order which, of course, would not be stayed on appeal.

The procedure adopted by the obdurate registrant described above would be used only in those rare instances where the registrant and its counsel are convinced that the Commission has imposed a requirement not authorized by law as to a subject-matter so important that the registrant is willing to undergo the delay in its financing necessary to take the Commission to court. * * *

The amendment should be enacted to prevent the Commission from imposing on registrants substantive requirements unrelated to disclosure, a practice which has been aptly termed "almost administrative extortion". Coe and Coppedge, *Book Review,* 38 American Bar Association Journal 330, 332 (1952).

Indemnification provisions are not the only issue that may trigger a decision by the SEC staff to refuse acceleration for reasons unrelated to the adequacy of the disclosure in the registration statement. In 1989, a Pennsylvania corporation preparing for its initial public offering included in its certificate of incorporation a provision requiring any claim asserted by any shareholder against or on behalf of the corporation to be submitted to arbitration under the Federal Arbitration Act. The SEC staff requested, and received, an opinion of counsel that the arbitration provision was valid under Pennsylvania law. The staff then refused to accelerate the effective date of the registration statement unless the arbitration clause were removed from the charter, on the ground that acceleration would not be in the "public interest" as specified in § 8(a) and Rule 461(b). The staff declined to furnish company counsel with a written explanation for its decision, but informed counsel orally that in its view the arbitration provision (a) would deprive shareholders of access to a judicial forum, (b) would weaken shareholders' ability to recover for serious violations of the law, (c) would impair the deterrent function of private rights of action under the securities laws, (d) would undermine confidence in the securities markets, (e) would violate the anti-waiver provisions of the securities laws, and (f) was unenforceable. (The staff position on some of these questions is difficult to reconcile with the opinions of the Supreme Court in the *McMahon* and *Rodriguez* cases, pp. 954, 961 below.) When counsel requested that the question be presented to the Commission at a public meeting, the staff informed him that its position had been submitted to members of the Commission, and that none of them was prepared to reverse the staff or to order acceleration. A Freedom of Information Act request for the staff's submission to the Commission was denied on the ground that the information requested contained intra-agency communications which reflect the deliberative process. See Schneider, Arbitration in Corporate Governance Documents: An Idea the SEC Refuses to Accelerate, 4 Insights No. 5, at 21 (May 1990).

KOSS v. SEC

364 F.Supp. 1321 (S.D.N.Y.1973).

BAUMAN, DISTRICT JUDGE.

Plaintiffs, an underwriter and its president, seek a preliminary injunction restraining the Securities and Exchange Commission from "directing" issuers proposing to make public offering of their securities using plaintiff Koss Securities Corporation as underwriter to include in their offering circulars statements that the plaintiffs are respondents in an administrative proceeding pending before the Commission. Defendant now moves to dismiss pursuant to Rule 12(b) of the Federal Rules and for summary judgment pursuant to Rule 56. For the reasons that follow, I conclude that the court is not confronted with a justiciable controversy and the motion for summary judgment is, accordingly, granted.

I.

The facts are basically undisputed. Theodore Koss and his wife are the sole shareholders as well as sole directors of the corporate plaintiff, a registered broker-dealer. On September 14, 1971 the SEC launched an administrative proceeding against Koss Securities, Koss, and ten others alleging that the respondents had violated the registration requirements of the Securities Act of 1933 in selling a security and had made false and misleading statements in the process. * * *

Between February 23 and May 21, 1973 six proposed issuers intending to use Koss Securities as underwriter for Regulation A offerings received comment letters from the SEC's Regional Offices written by staffers responsible for reviewing the offering circulars. In essence, the letters requested that the circulars be amended to disclose: (1) That plaintiffs were respondents in an SEC administrative proceeding, and (2) the nature of the (as yet unproven) charges.[7] As was utterly

7. The relevant language of the letter is as follows:

> "Gentlemen:
>
> With respect to the above-captioned file, please make the appropriate changes in the following sections of the offering circular;
>
> * * *
>
> Please add the following risk factor and list it as the first paragraph of that section:
>
> "The Securities and Exchange Commission's order for public proceeding dated September 14, 1971 asserting that T. Koss and Koss Securities, among other respondents, "During the period from on or about October 1, 1969 to date, * * * wilfully violated and wilfully aided and abetted violations of Sections 5(a) and 5(c) of the Securities Act of 1933 in connection with the offer and sale of the common stock of Spectrum, Ltd. when no registration statement was in effect as to such securities".
>
> The Order also charges violations of the anti-fraud provisions of the securities laws during the same time period by both Koss and T. Koss, together with five other respondents. They are charged with having
>
> "wilfully violated and wilfully aided and abetted violations of Section 17(a) of the Securities Act and Section 10(b) of the Exchange Act and Rule 10b–5 thereunder in that, in connection with the offer to sell, sale and purchase of the common stock of Spectrum, Ltd. said persons, directly and indirectly, singly and in concert with each other and with other persons * * * employed devices, schemes and artifices to defraud, made untrus [sic] statements of material facts and omitted to state materi-

foreseeable, two of the issuers found it desirable to find another underwriter.

The damage having been done and this suit having been brought, on June 25 the Chief of the Branch of Small Issues of the Division of Corporate Finance, pursuant to an order of the Commission,[9] wrote plaintiffs' attorney saying that the staff's comment letter had been withdrawn and that no disclosure of the administrative proceeding would be required in any subsequent offering circulars. But, the letter went on, Koss would be "requested" by the appropriate regional offices to inform the issuer of any Regulation A offering naming Koss as underwriter:

> "a) of the pending public administrative proceeding and the allegations relating to Koss; b) that the responsibility for determining the materiality of the pending public administrative proceeding is that of such issuer; c) that the burden of determining whether or not to disclose such proceeding is that of such issuer; d) that such burden cannot be shifted to the Commission or the staff of the Commission; e) that disciplinary action against Koss during the offering might result in suspension of the exemption for the offering; and f) that the issuer should advise the staff in writing that it has received such advice from Koss and what the issuer's position is with respect to disclosure of these matters."

* * *

Plaintiffs contend that the staff comment letters exceeded the SEC's statutory powers * * *. Furthermore, it is contended that the comment letters violate the due process clause of the Fifth Amendment in that they reflect a prejudgment of the issues of law and fact presented in the administrative complaint and resulting in damage to Koss Securities' reputation and business. * * *

II.

The threshold question is the timeliness of judicial review in the factual context of this case,—whether, in short, the relationship of Koss with the SEC has developed to such a point that judicial intervention is appropriate. This assessment of the utility of judicial action, or of "ripeness", serves to prevent courts from entering abstract debates

al facts" with respect to several generally identified aspects of the business of Spectrum, Ltd. and its management and market activity.

The Order also asserts that for the same time period Koss failed reasonably to supervise an employee or employees subject to its supervision in violation of Section 15(b)(5)(E) of the Exchange Act.

If Theodore Koss and Koss Securities Corporation are found to have violated the Sections alleged in the Commission's order of proceeding the Administrative Law Judge could exact sanctions ranging from a mere censure to a complete bar of Theodore Koss from associating with any broker-dealer and revocation of Koss Securities Corporation's registration as a broker-dealer.

The subject proceeding is still pending.

* * *

9. The letter from the Division of Corporate Finance was written pursuant to the order of the Commission contained in its "Minute Order", issued June 25, 1973. The Commission stated that it neither approved nor disapproved the staff's comments but viewed them as raising "significant questions of administrative policy" concerning disclosure presently before the SEC.

about agency policies or reviewing agency decisions until they have been "formalized" and have caused concrete effects upon the challenging parties. Abbott Laboratories v. Gardner, 387 U.S. 136 (1967).

The question of whether judicial review is apposite to this case is not answered merely by the label—"comment letter" or "order"—which the SEC may place upon its own or its staff's communication, but rather by a functional appraisal of the consequences of the actions which plaintiffs may reasonably expect. Thus, I must evaluate "both the fitness of the issues for judicial decision and the hardship to the parties of withholding court decision." Abbott Laboratories, 387 U.S. at 149.

The simple fact is that the comment letters issued by the SEC's Regional Office staff members were withdrawn at the direction of the Commission in its Minute Order of June 25, 1973. I am not, however, persuaded that the Commission has succeeded in mooting plaintiffs' claims against its staff by apparently granting the specific relief against the staff comment letters sought in the complaint. Plaintiffs' counsel neglected to amend the complaint after the comment letters were withdrawn and the Minute Order apparently shifted the burden of disclosure from the issuers to the underwriter, and consequently, review of the Minute Order is not presently before me. Nonetheless, plaintiffs' apparently narrow request for relief looks to future activities by the SEC staff as well as to past derelictions and therefore the June 25 action does not moot plaintiffs' action, which I construe to be one to enjoin the SEC staff from subsequently issuing comment letters similar to those withdrawn.

The Commission's treatment of its staff's action indicates that internal agency checks are available to stop untoward staff conduct. The Commission is obviously prepared to exercise its own supervisory powers in scrutinizing staff errors as sharply as would this court and the existence of this careful scrutiny in the context of an ongoing administrative proceeding obviates the need for judicial review of SEC staff activity.

Another way of categorizing the events in which Koss and the SEC staff participated is that they constituted only "informal" agency activity and did not result in any definitive ruling which a court might review. * * * As the revocation of the comment letters by the Division of Corporate Finance indicates, the staff's comments did not represent the opinion of the SEC itself and thus, stopping far short of an actual threat of SEC enforcement, constituted only the informal staff advice contemplated by 17 C.F.R. § 202.1(d) (1973). * * *

Thus, the two elements of unripeness set forth in *Abbott Laboratories,* supra, are present here: the issues are unfit for judicial review because staff comment letters do not represent the opinion of the Commission itself, and no hardship will be imposed on Koss if judicial action is withheld because the SEC does not appear reluctant to oversee its staff's activities throughout the administrative proceeding.

III.

The final question I must resolve is whether the SEC's and its staff's activities concerning Mr. Koss and Koss Securities were *ultra vires*.

Koss Securities' quarrel with the SEC, in which the comment letters originated, concerned small offerings which are exempt from registration under the 1933 Act.[a] Despite the lack of registration, however, the SEC does not eschew supervision of Regulation A filings, for Rule 256 of the Regulation requires that an offering circular containing information about the offering and the issuer be filed with the Commission prior to the commencement of the offering and that it be distributed to offerees and purchasers of the securities. * * *

One of the defects in an offering statement which may provoke Commission response is the misstatement or omission of "a material fact necessary in order to make the statements made, in the light of the circumstances under which they are made, not misleading * * *" Rule 261(a)(2). The Commission did not abuse or exceed its powers in authorizing the staff to require the disclosures the June 25 letter from its Division of Corporate Finance required Koss to make to proposed issuers of securities. The fact that an administrative proceeding is pending against the underwriter of securities is material to the purchaser of securities and, a fortiori, to their issuer. Furthermore, any harm done to plaintiffs by the comment letters does not outweigh the gravity of the SEC's role in assuring full disclosure and fair dealing in securities. * * *[b]

In KIXMILLER v. SEC, 492 F.2d 641 (D.C.Cir.1974), the SEC staff refused to require an issuer to include a shareholder's proposal in the proxy material it was sending to its shareholders. The shareholder asked the Commission to reexamine the question, but the Commission expressly "declined to review the staff's position * * *." The court held that there was no "order" of the Commission which it had statutory power to review, and specifically upheld the validity of the Commission's position, expressed in its rules of practice, that "its informal procedures are ordinarily to be matters of staff activity, and will involve the Commission only when special circumstances so warrant." Under § 4A of the 1934 Act, added in 1962, the Commission has specific authority to delegate any of its functions, other than rulemaking, to specified divisions or employees of the Commission, retaining a

a. While the *Koss* case involves offering circulars in transactions exempt from registration under Regulation A, the procedures followed by the SEC in reviewing such offering circulars are substantially similar to those followed in reviewing registration statements.

b. Mr. Koss and his firm were subsequently indicted and convicted of securities fraud and mail fraud in connection with a 1970 securities offering, and their convictions were affirmed on appeal. United States v. Koss, 506 F.2d 1103 (2d Cir.1974).

discretionary right to review any actions taken pursuant to such delegation.

REMARKS OF HAROLD MARSH, JR. IN PANEL DISCUSSION ON DISCLOSURE IN REGISTERED SECURITY OFFERINGS

28 Bus.Lawyer 505, 531–32 (1973).*

Assuming that the criticisms of the usefulness of the type of disclosure presently found in most Registration Statements have some validity, and I think that few securities lawyers would assert that they are totally without foundation, the question arises as to where we went wrong. I think that this can be pinpointed with some precision. The story has often been told as to how the official in charge of the processing of 1933 Act registrations was presented with recommendations from his Staff that stop order proceedings be instituted against every single one of the more than 100 statements that were initially filed. Instead of following these recommendations, he invented the letter of comment procedure whereby the issuers were given an opportunity to rewrite their Registration Statements in the way that the SEC Staff wanted them written.

There was, however, another clear choice which he had and presumably rejected, other than instituting over 100 stop order proceedings, and that was to inform his Staff in connection with 95% to 99% of their comments that if they ever made any more asinine comments like that, they would be fired. In my opinion, the development of disclosure in registered offerings would unquestionably have been different, and very probably more useful, if the SEC Staff had stayed out of it.

It is still not too late to retrieve that error.

All that it would take is an act of will on the part of the Commission to permit the Securities Act of 1933 to operate in the manner in which it was originally written and a public announcement that the SEC Staff would never again read a Registration Statement for the purpose of issuing a "letter of comment," but would make every Registration Statement effective at any time requested by the issuer and underwriter unless a prior notice of stop order proceedings had been issued. For 39 years the Securities Bar and the SEC Staff have been attempting *jointly* to write prospectuses and, if Judge Weinstein and Professor Kripke are to be believed, all they have produced is an abortion.

Isn't it time we tried another way?

D. CIVIL LIABILITY UNDER § 11

The most powerful incentive to careful preparation of the 1933 Act registration statement is found in § 11, which sets forth the civil liabilities to purchasers with respect to any material misstatements or omissions. In contrast to the vague outlines of common law fraud liability, § 11 sets forth in great detail who may sue, what they must show, who can be held liable for how much, and the defenses and cross-claims available to various classes of defendants.

Section 11 was considered such a draconian measure at the time of its enactment that some observers thought that it would dry up the nation's underwriting business and that "grass would grow in Wall Street." It is somewhat ironic, therefore, (or perhaps simply a testimonial to the care with which people approached the task of preparing registration statements) that the first fully litigated decision interpreting the civil liability provisions of § 11 did not come until 35 years later, after more than 27,000 registration statements had become effective, covering offerings to the public of more than $384 billion of securities. When that decision, in Escott v. BarChris Construction Corp., did come down in 1968, however, it spread new waves of concern among issuers, directors, underwriters, their counsel, and accountants, as they realized that the practices that had been followed during the new-issue boom of the early 1960s simply did not measure up to the standard of "due diligence" laid down in § 11.

Because § 11 liability is a matter of such overriding concern, it is a major influence in deciding what provisions and conditions will be included in the agreement between the issuer and underwriters, and in assigning responsibilities to the various parties involved in the registration statement. Any lawyer involved in underwriting work, therefore, should have a precise knowledge of the provisions of the section, how they have been interpreted, and how they relate to the other civil liability provisions of the federal securities laws.

---

1. Who Can Sue?

BARNES v. OSOFSKY

373 F.2d 269 (2d Cir.1967).

Before LUMBARD, CHIEF JUDGE, and FRIENDLY and HAYS, CIRCUIT JUDGES.

FRIENDLY, CIRCUIT JUDGE.

Aileen, Inc. is engaged in the design, manufacture and sale of popular priced sports wear for girls and women. Prior to the fall of 1963 it had outstanding 1,019,574 common shares; 205,966 of these, most of them covered by a 1961 registration statement, were traded on the American Stock Exchange, and the balance, 813,608, were owned, in approximately equal proportions, by two officers and directors,

Osofsky and Oberlin. Pursuant to a registration statement effective September 10, 1963, a group of underwriters offered at $23.375 per share, substantially the then market price, another 200,000 shares, also to be listed on the American Exchange; 100,000 of these were an original issue, 50,000 were Osofsky's and 50,000 were Oberlin's. The prospectus reported that "Sales volume has grown from $2,120,394 in 1956 to $15,045,826 in 1962 and reached $9,826,655 for the first six months of 1963."

A press release on October 7, 1963, and a supplement to the prospectus on the following day, announced a rift in the lute. Third quarter sales had been little more than in 1962 and the volume of orders for an important spring line had not come up to expectations. The price of the stock, which had been gradually declining since late September, declined some more, reaching $15.75 by the end of October, $14.25 at the year-end, and still lower figures thereafter.

Three class actions by purchasers against the corporation, Osofsky, Oberlin, the principal underwriters and, in one instance, other officers and directors, were brought in the District Court for the Southern District of New York on November 13 and 19, 1963 and August 17, 1964, and were subsequently consolidated. The complaints in all three set forth a claim under § 11 of the Securities Act of 1933 that the registration statement and prospectus contained material misstatements and omissions, primarily in failing to disclose danger signals of which the management was aware prior to the date when the registration statement took effect. One complaint also contained a claim based on § 10(b) of the Securities Exchange Act of 1934, Rule 10b–5 and common law fraud, but this was later withdrawn. After discovery and negotiations, a settlement was agreed upon, which the District Court approved after notice and hearing, 254 F.Supp. 721 (S.D.N.Y.1966). This provided for the deposit of a fund of $775,000, 50% of which was contributed by the corporation and the remainder by the two selling stockholders in equal amounts. After payment of approved allowances, the fund was to be distributed among persons "who beneficially acquired (in his own name or otherwise) any part of the 200,000 shares * * * which was the subject of the public offering of September 10, 1963 between September 10, 1963 and August 17, 1964" and who made timely application for participation therein. Seventy-five percent of the fund, called Fund A, was to reimburse such persons for losses suffered prior to November 13, 1963; twenty-five percent, Fund B, was to reimburse them for losses thereafter. The measure of damages for Fund A was the difference between actual cost, not exceeding $23.375 per share, and the sales price for those who had sold the stock or $16.25 per share, the closing market price on November 13, for those who continued to hold it. The measure of damages for Fund B was the difference between actual cost, not exceeding $16.25 per share, and the actual sales price or $8.875 (the closing market price on August 17, 1964), whichever was higher. The judgment contained a clause barring all actions by purchasers of the 200,000 shares "founded or in any way based upon the subject matter of the pleadings of the above actions, or any of them, including any claim or claims alleged or asserted or which could have been alleged or asserted in said pleadings by virtue of the facts alleged therein."

The sole objectors to the settlement were the appellants Attilio Occhi who bought 100 shares on November 22, 1963 at about $15 per share, and Fred Zilker who bought 25 shares on September 12, 1963 for $23.375 and 50 shares on December 23 for $13.50 per share. Their objection went to the provision limiting the benefits of the settlement to persons who could establish that they purchased securities issued under the 1963 registration statement, which thus eliminated those who purchased after the issuance of the allegedly incomplete prospectus but could not so trace their purchases. Although the issue has not yet been passed upon by the special master whom Judge Ryan appointed, it appears likely that Occhi will be able to trace 50 shares which were bought on the open market and Zilker can trace 25 which were bought from an underwriter, but not the balance—all purchased on the market.

We need say little as to appellants' argument that even if § 11 of the Securities Act permits recovery only by purchasers of the issue covered by the defective registration statement as the district judge held, the court on a basis of equity should have provided for participation by others who, as a practical matter, may have suffered equally. Whether or not it would have been an abuse of discretion to have diluted a settlement so as to allow recovery by persons not legally entitled thereto, as we incline to think it would have been, surely there would be none in limiting participation to those who might have recovered had the suits been fought and won. The question thus is whether the district court was right in ruling that § 11 extends only to purchases of the newly registered shares.

Section 11(a) provides that:

> "In case any part of the registration statement, when such part became effective, contained an untrue statement of a material fact or omitted to state a material fact required to be stated therein or necessary to make the statements therein not misleading, any person acquiring such security (unless it is proved that at the time of such acquisition he knew of such untruth or omission) may, either at law or in equity, in any court of competent jurisdiction, sue"

five categories of persons therein named. The key phrase is "any person acquiring such security"; the difficulty, presented when as here the registration is of shares in addition to those already being traded, is that "such" has no referent. Although the narrower reading—"acquiring a security issued pursuant to the registration statement"—would be the more natural, a broader one—"acquiring a security of the same nature as that issued pursuant to the registration statement"—would not be such a violent departure from the words that a court could not properly adopt it if there were good reason for doing so. Appellants claim there is. Starting from the seemingly correct premise that an unduly optimistic prospectus will affect the price of shares already issued to almost the same extent as those of the same class about to be issued, they say it would therefore be unreasonable to distinguish newly registered shares from those previously traded. In addition, they contend that once it is agreed that § 11 is not limited to the original purchasers, to read that section as applying only to purchasers who can trace the lineage of their shares to the new offering makes the result turn on mere accident since most trading is done through brokers who neither know nor care whether they are getting newly registered or old shares.[1] Finally, appellants argue that it is often impossible to determine whether previously traded shares are old or new, and that tracing is further complicated when stock is held in margin accounts in street names since many brokerage houses do not identify specific shares with particular accounts but instead treat the account as having an undivided interest in the house's position. Therefore, they urge that the narrower construction offends the cardinal principle of equal treatment for persons whose entitlement is not significantly different and a "golden rule" of statutory interpretation "that unreasonableness of the result produced by one among alternative possible interpretations of a statute is reason for rejecting that interpretation in favor of another which would produce a reasonable result."

Appellants' broader reading would be inconsistent with the overall statutory scheme. The Securities Act of 1933 had two major purposes, "[t]o provide full and fair disclosure of the character of securities sold in interstate and foreign commerce and through the mails, and to prevent frauds in the sale thereof, * * *" 48 Stat. 74 (1933). These aims were "to be achieved by a general antifraud provision and by a registration provision." 1 Loss, Securities Regulation 178–79 (1961). Section 11 deals with civil liability for untrue or misleading statements or omissions in the registration statement; its stringent penalties are to insure full and accurate disclosure through registration. Since, under §§ 2(1) and 6, only individual shares are registered, it seems unlikely that the section developed to insure proper disclosure in the registration statement was meant to provide a remedy for other than the particular shares registered. In contrast both §§ 12(2) and 17, the antifraud sections of the 1933 Act, where some form of the traditional scienter requirement, dispensed with as to the issuer under § 11, is preserved, are not limited to the newly registered securities. Beyond this, the over-all limitation of § 11(g) that "In no case shall the amount recoverable under this section exceed the price at which the security was offered to the public," and the provision of § 11(e) whereby, with qualifications not here material, an underwriter's liability shall not exceed "the total price at which the securities underwritten by him and

1. Appellants note that the impracticability of determining at the moment of purchase whether old or new shares are being acquired has led dealers to comply with the requirements of § 5(b)(2) as to the delivery of a prospectus by doing this on all sales within the period established by § 4(3), see 1 Loss, Securities Regulation 259–60 (1961). While this may enable a purchaser of shares other than those registered to rely on § 12(2) upon an appropriate showing, it does not lead to the conclusion that § 11 applies.

distributed to the public were offered to the public," point in the direction of limiting § 11 to purchasers of the registered shares, since otherwise their recovery would be greatly diluted when the new issue was small in relation to the trading in previously outstanding shares.

Appellants' contention also seems to run somewhat contrary to the legislative history. Both the House and Senate versions of the present § 11, in identical language, established a conclusive presumption of reliance upon the registration statement by "every person acquiring any securities specified in such statements and offered to the public." Section 9, S. 875; Section 9, H.R. 4314, 73d Cong., 1st Sess. (1933). Both bills then continued, "In case any such statement shall be false in any material respect, any persons acquiring any securities to which such statement relates, either from the original issuer or any other person" shall have a cause of action against certain specified persons. The bills differed as to the class of people liable and their defenses. As part of a report in which § 11 in its present form was endorsed, the Managers on the part of the House noted that the only changes in § 11 were as to who was liable and their defenses. H.R.Rep. No. 152, p. 26, 73d Cong., 1st Sess. (1933).

As against this appellants seek to draw some solace from a statement in H.R.Rep. No. 85 that the remedies of § 11 were accorded to purchasers "regardless of whether they bought their securities at the time of the original offer or at some later date" and that this was within the power of Congress "to accord a remedy to all purchasers who may reasonably be affected by any statements in the registration statement." But this can be read to relate only to the extension of liability to open-market purchasers of the registered shares and the same report, in speaking of §§ 11 and 12, said that "Fundamentally, these sections entitle *the buyer of securities sold upon a registration statement* including an untrue statement or omission of a material fact to sue for recovery of his purchase price, or for damages * * *." [Emphasis added.] H.R.Rep. No. 85, p. 9.

* * *

Without depreciating the force of appellants' criticisms that this construction gives § 11 a rather accidental impact as between one open-market purchaser of a stock already being traded and another, we are unpersuaded that, by departing from the more natural meaning of the words, a court could come up with anything better. What appellants' argument does suggest is that the time may have come for Congress to reexamine these two remarkable pioneering statutes in the light of thirty years' experience, with a view to simplifying and coordinating their different and often overlapping remedies. See the provocative article by Milton H. Cohen, Truth in Securities Revisited, 79 Harv.L. Rev. 1340 (1966).

Affirmed.

Relationship to Other Remedies

What alternative remedies might be available under other sections of the 1933 and 1934 Acts on account of a misleading registration statement to a purchaser who cannot trace his securities to those offered under the registration statement? Could he sue under § 12(2) of the 1933 Act? Or under § 12(1), alleging a violation of § 5(b)(2)? Could he sue under § 10(b) of the 1934 Act? See Herman & MacLean v. Huddleston, 459 U.S. 375 (1983) (Ch. II. C. 3 below). What disadvantages would he suffer, and what advantages might he enjoy, in proceeding under one of those sections rather than Section 11? See Lanza v. Drexel & Co., 479 F.2d 1277 (2d Cir.1979), p. 209 below.

Section 11 is not the exclusive remedy for material misrepresentations in 1933 Act registration statements. On appropriate facts, an injured purchaser may be able to bring a claim under § 12(2). See pp. 358–380 below. However, a claim under § 12(2) can only be made against the dealer from whom the customer bought the security (who, if it was not an underwriter, is probably not liable because it could not have known of the misstatements) and not against the issuer or any of the other 11 defendants. See COLLINS v. SIGNETICS, 605 F.2d 110 (3d Cir.1979). Alternatively, SEC Exchange Act Rule 10b–5 may be the basis of a private suit by investors injured as a result of materially misleading registration materials. See p. 209 below.

Statute of Limitations

Section 13 of the 1933 Act establishes a two-pronged statute of limitations for actions under §§ 11 and 12. Under § 13, can a purchaser of securities registered under the Act bring a § 11 action: (a) within three years after the effective date but more than one year after the issuer had publicly announced serious reversals in its financial condition? [a] (b) within three years after the effective date but more than three years after the issuer had filed the registration statement and started making offers? [b] (c) more than three years after the effective date but within one year after the misstatements in the registration statement had first come to light? [c]

Expenses

Section 11(e) provides that in any suit brought under the Act, the court may require the plaintiff to post security for defendant's expenses, including attorney's fees. The court will generally require such an undertaking only if defendant shows "either that the plaintiff has commenced her suit in bad faith or that her claim borders on the frivolous." [d]

---

a. See Cook v. Avien, Inc., 573 F.2d 685 (1st Cir.1978).

b. See Morse v. Peat, Marwick, Mitchell & Co., 445 F.Supp. 619 (S.D.N.Y.1977).

c. See Brick v. Dominion Mortg. & Realty Trust, 442 F.Supp. 283 (W.D.N.Y. 1977).

d. Straus v. Holiday Inns, 460 F.Supp. 729 (S.D.N.Y.1978). A similar standard is

2. *Elements of the Claim*

ESCOTT v. BARCHRIS CONSTRUCTION CORP.

283 F.Supp. 643 (S.D.N.Y.1968).

McLEAN, DISTRICT JUDGE.

This is an action by purchasers of 5½ per cent convertible subordinated fifteen year debentures of BarChris Construction Corporation (BarChris). Plaintiffs purport to sue on their own behalf and "on behalf of all other and present and former holders" of the debentures. When the action was begun on October 25, 1962, there were nine plaintiffs. Others were subsequently permitted to intervene. At the time of the trial, there were over sixty.

The action is brought under Section 11 of the Securities Act of 1933. Plaintiffs allege that the registration statement with respect to these debentures filed with the Securities and Exchange Commission, which became effective on May 16, 1961, contained material false statements and material omissions.

* * *

This opinion will not concern itself with the cross-claims or with issues peculiar to any particular plaintiff. These matters are reserved for later decision. On the main issue of liability, the questions to be decided are (1) did the registration statement contain false statements of fact, or did it omit to state facts which should have been stated in order to prevent it from being misleading; (2) if so, were the facts which were falsely stated or omitted "material" within the meaning of the Act; (3) if so, have defendants established their affirmative defenses?

Before discussing these questions, some background facts should be mentioned. At the time relevant here, BarChris was engaged primarily in the construction of bowling alleys, somewhat euphemistically referred to as "bowling centers." These were rather elaborate affairs. They contained not only a number of alleys or "lanes," but also, in most cases, bar and restaurant facilities.

BarChris was an outgrowth of a business started as a partnership by Vitolo and Pugliese in 1946. The business was incorporated in New York in 1955 under the name of B & C Bowling Alley Builders, Inc. Its name was subsequently changed to BarChris Construction Corporation.

* * *

The registration statement of the debentures, in preliminary form, was filed with the Securities and Exchange Commission on March 30, 1961. A first amendment was filed on May 11 and a second on May 16. The registration statement became effective on May 16. The closing of the financing took place on May 24. On that day BarChris received the net proceeds of the financing.

applied in determining whether to award such expenses at the conclusion of the proceeding. See Klein v. Shields & Co., 470 F.2d 1344 (2d Cir.1972).

By that time BarChris was experiencing difficulties in collecting amounts due from some of its customers. Some of them were in arrears in payments due to factors on their discounted notes. As time went on those difficulties increased. Although BarChris continued to build alleys in 1961 and 1962, it became increasingly apparent that the industry was overbuilt. Operators of alleys, often inadequately financed, began to fail. Precisely when the tide turned is a matter of dispute, but at any rate, it was painfully apparent in 1962.

In May of that year BarChris made an abortive attempt to raise more money by the sale of common stock. It filed with the Securities and Exchange Commission a registration statement for the stock issue which it later withdrew. In October 1962 BarChris came to the end of the road. On October 29, 1962, it filed in this court a petition for an arrangement under Chapter XI of the Bankruptcy Act. BarChris defaulted in the payment of the interest due on November 1, 1962 on the debentures.

THE DEBENTURE REGISTRATION STATEMENT

* * *

The registration statement in its final form contained a prospectus as well as other information. Plaintiffs' claims of falsities and omissions pertain solely to the prospectus, not to the additional data.

The prospectus contained, among other things, a description of BarChris's business, a description of its real property, some material pertaining to certain of its subsidiaries, and remarks about various other aspects of its affairs. It also contained financial information. It included a consolidated balance sheet as of December 31, 1960, with elaborate explanatory notes. These figures had been audited by Peat, Marwick. It also contained unaudited figures as to net sales, gross profit and net earnings for the first quarter ended March 31, 1961, as compared with the similar quarter for 1960. In addition, it set forth figures as to the company's backlog of unfilled orders as of March 31, 1961, as compared with March 31, 1960, and figures as to the BarChris's contingent liability, as of April 30, 1961, on customers' notes discounted and its contingent liability under the so-called alternative method of financing.

Plaintiffs challenge the accuracy of a number of these figures. They also charge that the text of the prospectus, apart from the figures, was false in a number of respects, and that material information was omitted. Each of these contentions, after eliminating duplications, will be separately considered.

* * *

[The court here devotes 25 pages of the opinion to detailing and discussing the alleged inadequacies in the prospectus.]

MATERIALITY

It is a prerequisite to liability under Section 11 of the Act that the fact which is falsely stated in a registration statement, or the fact that is omitted when it should have been stated to avoid misleading, be "material." The regulations of the Securities and Exchange Commission pertaining to the registration of securities define the word as follows:

> "The term 'material', when used to qualify a requirement for the furnishing of information as to any subject, limits the information required to those matters as to which an average prudent investor ought reasonably to be informed before purchasing the security registered."

What are "matters as to which an average prudent investor ought reasonably to be informed"? It seems obvious that they are matters which such an investor needs to know before he can make an intelligent, informed decision whether or not to buy the security.

Early in the history of the Act, a definition of materiality was given in Matter of Charles A. Howard, 1 S.E.C. 6, 8 (1934), which is still valid today. A material fact was there defined as:

> "* * * a fact which if it had been correctly stated or disclosed would have deterred or tended to deter the average prudent investor from purchasing the securities in question."

The average prudent investor is not concerned with minor inaccuracies or with errors as to matters which are of no interest to him. The facts which tend to deter him from purchasing a security are facts which have an important bearing upon the nature or condition of the issuing corporation or its business.

Judged by this test, there is no doubt that many of the misstatements and omissions in this prospectus were material. This is true of all of them which relate to the state of affairs in 1961, i.e., the overstatement of sales and gross profit for the first quarter, the understatement of contingent liabilities as of April 30, the overstatement of orders on hand and the failure to disclose the true facts with respect to officers' loans, customers' delinquencies, application of proceeds and the prospective operation of several alleys.

The misstatements and omissions pertaining to BarChris's status as of December 31, 1960, however, present a much closer question. The 1960 earnings figures, the 1960 balance sheet and the contingent liabilities as of December 31, 1960 were not nearly as erroneous as plaintiffs have claimed. But they were wrong to some extent, as we have seen. Would it have deterred the average prudent investor from purchasing these debentures if he had been informed that the 1960 sales were $8,511,420 rather than $9,165,320, that the net operating income was $1,496,196 rather than $1,742,801 and that the earnings per share in 1960 were approximately 65¢ rather than 75¢? According to the unchallenged figures, sales in 1959 were $3,320,121, net operating income was $441,103, and earnings per share were 33¢. Would it have made a difference to an average prudent investor if he had known that in 1960 sales were only 256 per cent of 1959 sales, not 276 per cent; that net operating income was up by only $1,055,093, not by $1,301,698, and that earnings per share, while still approximately twice those of 1959, were not something more than twice?

These debentures were rated "B" by the investment rating services. They were thus characterized as speculative, as any prudent investor must have realized. It would seem that anyone interested in buying these convertible debentures would have been attracted primarily by the conversion feature, by the growth potential of the stock. The growth which the company enjoyed in 1960 over prior years was striking, even on the correct figures. It is hard to see how a prospective purchaser of this type of investment would have been deterred from buying if he had been advised of these comparatively minor errors in reporting 1960 sales and earnings.

Since no one knows what moves or does not move the mythical "average prudent investor," it comes down to a question of judgment, to be exercised by the trier of the fact as best he can in the light of all the circumstances. It is my best judgment that the average prudent investor would not have cared about these errors in the 1960 sales and earnings figures, regrettable though they may be. I therefore find that they were not material within the meaning of Section 11.

The same is true of the understatement of contingent liabilities in footnote 9 by approximately $375,000. As disclosed in that footnote, BarChris's contingent liability as of December 31, 1960 on notes discounted was $3,969,835 and, according to the footnote, on the alternative method of financing was $750,000, a total of $4,719,835. This was a huge amount for a company with total assets, as per balance sheet, of $6,101,085. Purchasers were necessarily made aware of this by the figures actually disclosed. If they were willing to buy the debentures in the face of this information, as they obviously were, I doubt that they would have been deterred if they had been told that the contingent liabilities were actually $375,000 higher.

This leaves for consideration the errors in the 1960 balance sheet figures which have previously been discussed in detail. Current assets were overstated by approximately $600,000. Liabilities were understated by approximately $325,000 by the failure to treat the liability on Capitol Lanes as a direct liability of BarChris on a consolidated basis. Of this $325,000 approximately $65,000, the amount payable on Capitol within one year, should have been treated as a current liability.

As per balance sheet, cash was $285,482. In fact, $145,000 of this had been borrowed temporarily from Talcott and was to be returned by January 16, 1961 so that realistically, cash was only $140,482. Trade accounts receivable were overstated by $150,000 by including Howard Lanes Annex, an alley which was not sold to an outside buyer.

As per balance sheet, total current assets were $4,524,021, and total current liabilities were $2,413,867, a ratio of approximately 1.9 to 1. This was bad enough, but on the true facts, the ratio was worse. As corrected, current assets, as near as one can tell, were approximately

$3,924,000, and current liabilities approximately $2,478,000, a ratio of approximately 1.6 to 1.

Would it have made any difference if a prospective purchaser of these debentures had been advised of these facts? There must be some point at which errors in disclosing a company's balance sheet position become material, even to a growth-oriented investor. On all the evidence I find that these balance sheet errors were material within the meaning of Section 11.

Since there was an abundance of material misstatements pertaining to 1961 affairs, whether or not the errors in the 1960 figures were material does not affect the outcome of this case except to the extent that it bears upon the liability of Peat, Marwick. That subject will be discussed hereinafter. * * *

THE CAUSATION DEFENSE

Section 11(a) provides that when a registration statement contains an untrue statement of a material fact or omits to state a material fact, "any person acquiring such security * * * may * * * sue." Section 11(e) provides that:

> "The suit authorized under subsection (a) may be to recover such damages as shall represent the difference between the amount paid for the security (not exceeding the price at which the security was offered to the public) and (1) the value thereof as of the time such suit was brought, or (2) the price at which such security shall have been disposed of in the market before suit, or (3) the price at which such security shall have been disposed of after suit but before judgment if such damages shall be less than the damages representing the difference between the amount paid for the security (not exceeding the price at which the security was offered to the public) and the value thereof as of the time such suit was brought * * *."

Section 11(e) then sets forth a proviso reading as follows:

> "Provided, that if the defendant proves that any portion or all of such damages represents other than the depreciation in value of such security resulting from such part of the registration statement, with respect to which his liability is asserted, not being true or omitting to state a material fact required to be stated therein or necessary to make the statements therein not misleading, such portion of or all such damages shall not be recoverable."

Each defendant in one form or another has relied upon this proviso as a complete defense. Each maintains that the entire damage suffered by each and every plaintiff was caused by factors other than the material falsities and omissions of the registration statement. These factors, in brief, were the decline in the bowling industry which came about because of the fact that the industry was overbuilt and because popular enthusiasm for bowling diminished.

These adverse conditions had begun before these debentures were issued, as evidenced by the growing defaults in customers' notes discounted with Talcott. Talcott did not discount any new notes for BarChris after April 1961. BarChris's financial position, as we have seen, was materially worse in May 1961 than it had been on December 31, 1960.

As time went on, conditions grew worse, both for BarChris and the industry. The receipts of alley operators diminished. New construction of alleys fell off. By 1962 it had almost ceased.

There is a wide disparity in the factual pattern of purchases and sales of BarChris debentures by the plaintiffs in this action. Some plaintiffs bought theirs when the debentures were first issued on May 16, 1961. Others bought theirs later in 1961. Still others purchased theirs at various dates in 1962, some even as late as September 1962, shortly before BarChris went into Chapter XI. In at least one instance, a plaintiff purchased debentures after BarChris was in Chapter XI.

There is a similar disparity as to sales. Some plaintiffs sold their debentures in 1961. Others sold theirs in 1962. Others never sold them.

The position taken by defendants in their affirmative defenses is an extreme one which cannot be sustained. I cannot say that the entire damage suffered by every plaintiff was caused by factors other than the errors and omissions of the registration statement for which these defendants are responsible. As to some plaintiffs, or as to part of the damage sustained by others, that may be true. The only practicable course is to defer decision of this issue until the claim of each individual plaintiff is separately considered. As stated at the outset, this opinion is devoted only to matters common to all plaintiffs. * * *

COLONIAL REALTY CORP. v. BRUNSWICK CORP., 337 F.Supp. 546 (S.D.N.Y.1971), was a suit under § 12(2) alleging that a prospectus issued by Brunswick, one of the two leading manufacturers of bowling equipment, was misleading because, among other things, it "should have predicted the saturation of the bowling market." The court held that, "even if such saturation had been proved, such hindsight predictions do not belong in prospectuses and might even result in liability for violation of SEC regulations." 337 F.Supp. at 552.

If BarChris could prove that it went bankrupt because of the subsequent decline in the bowling industry, and if it had no obligation to predict that decline, would defendants be entitled to judgment? How could plaintiffs still show that all or part of their loss resulted from the misstatements in the registration statement?

---

3. Damages

The measure of damages that plaintiffs can recover in an action under § 11 seems to be pretty clearly spelled out in § 11(e). However, difficult problems may arise in determining the meaning of that provision, as the following opinion demonstrates. To assist in your understanding of the opinion, you may wish to draw a chart showing the market price of the debentures on July 12, September 26, October 14, October 19, and February 1.

BEECHER v. ABLE

435 F.Supp. 397 (S.D.N.Y.1975).

MOTLEY, DISTRICT JUDGE: In its Findings of Fact and Conclusions of Law, dated March 20, 1974, the court found that defendant Douglas Aircraft Company, Inc. (Douglas) had on July 12, 1966 sold $75 million of its 4¾% convertible debentures due July 1, 1991 under a materially false prospectus. In particular, the court found that the break-even prediction,[a] use of proceeds section and the failure to disclose certain pre-tax losses rendered the prospectus misleading. The parties have agreed that no damages are properly attributable to the erroneous use of proceeds and pre-tax loss portions of the prospectus. Accordingly, trial of the damages sustained by plaintiffs and members of the class represented thereby, i.e., all persons who bought the convertible debentures between July 12, 1966 and September 29, 1966, was limited to those damages caused by the misleading break-even prediction in violation of § 11 of the Securities Act of 1933.

At the outset the court notes that the measurement for damages caused by violations of § 11, as set forth in the statute, is as follows:

> "11(e) * * * The suit authorized under sub-section (a) may be to recover such damages as shall represent the difference between the amount paid for the security (not exceeding the price at which the security was offered to the public) and (1) the value thereof as of the time such suit was brought, or (2) the price at which such security shall have been disposed of in the market before suit or (3) the price at which such security shall have been disposed of after suit but before judgment if such damages shall be less than the damages representing the difference between the amount paid for the security (not exceeding the price at which the security was offered to the public) and the value thereof as of the time such suit was brought: Provided, That if the defendant proves that any portion or all of such damages represents other than the depreciation in value of such security resulting from such part of the registration statement, with respect to which his liability is asserted, not being true or omitting to state a material fact required to be stated therein or necessary to make the statements therein not misleading, such portion of or all such damages shall not be recoverable."

a. The prospectus stated that "it is very likely that net income, if any, for fiscal 1966 will be nominal." The court, in an earlier opinion, see p. 114 above, held that this could be read as a prediction that Douglas would not incur substantial losses during the year. Douglas in fact sustained a net loss of $52 million for the year.

As might be anticipated from a reading of this section of the statute, the parties are in disagreement regarding the content to be given several significant terms used in § 11(e).

First, there is a dispute as to "the time such suit was brought." Secondly, there is a dispute as to the value of the debentures as of the time of suit. Third, there is sharp disagreement as to the cause or causes of the drop in the value of the debentures after September 26, 1966. Fourth, there is a dispute as to the effect of later market action on certain damage claims.

* * *

Time of Suit

The *Levy, Beecher* and *Gottesman* suits were commenced on October 14, 1966, October 19, 1966, and November 9, 1966 respectively. Plaintiffs' lead counsel has urged that October 19, 1966 be selected as the date on which suit was filed. Insofar as the closing price for the debentures on October 19, 1966 was 73, and insofar as price is some evidence of value, selection of the October 19th date—as opposed to the October 14th date, when the debentures closed higher at 75½—would tend to increase the damage award to the plaintiff class.

* * *

The court concludes that the most logical date for present purposes is October 14, 1966, the date on which the first, i.e., *Levy,* action was filed. In reaching this conclusion, the court notes that at the time of filing each of the three consolidated cases anticipated congruent classes. On October 14, 1966, when the first suit was filed, all those individuals who would eventually comprise the plaintiff class were already contemplated by the action, even though in subsequent proceedings the *Levy* class was voluntarily limited. Hence, there is no problem of selecting a date and suit which might prove under-inclusive.

* * *

In the present cases, the first date seems the most logical benchmark for measuring damages under § 11(e). In future cases the prospect of selection of the filing day of the first suit may well reduce date-shopping subsequent to the first filing and so far as possible limit the multiplicity of identical suits. Further, the certainty of the date of the first suit may shorten future damage trials, since evidence of value can be limited to one particular day.

Value as of the Time of Suit

As noted above, the value of the securities at the time of suit was sharply contested at trial. To establish "value", plaintiff asks the court first to look to the trading price on the day of suit and then to reduce that price by a sum which reflects the undisclosed financial crisis of defendant. At trial, plaintiff characterized the market for these debentures as free, open and sophisticated, marked by a heavy volume of trading on national and over-the-counter exchanges. Plaintiffs relied on trading data from July to mid-October 1966 and the testimony of their expert, Mr. Whitman, in reaching the conclusion that market price was the best evidence of maximum fair value. The reason plaintiffs urge that market price reflects maximum fair value, as opposed to value, is because the buying public was unaware of the financial crisis gripping defendant in mid-October 1966. Thus, according to plaintiff, had the buying public been aware of the crisis they would have paid less for the security.

* * *

The defendant urges the court to adopt a somewhat different approach from plaintiffs' in establishing "value" of the security at time of suit. Defendant contends that the market action of this offering was volatile and often unrelated to fair value. In particular defendant claims that on the date suit was filed the market price of the debenture was temporarily depressed by panic selling in response to the release of the defendant's disappointing third quarter earnings results. Thus, according to defendant, the market price of the debenture on the date of suit was not a reliable indicator of fair value. Defendant would have the court look to the optimistic long-range prospects of the defendant company and set a value which would not only off-set panic selling but which would reflect defendant's anticipated future gains, or the investment feature of the offering. That value, of course, would be in excess of the closing market price on October 14, 1966 of 75½.

* * *

After considering the above evidence offered by the parties with respect to "value" at the time of suit, the court makes the following observations and findings and reaches the following conclusions. Although the plaintiffs produced considerable evidence tending to show the unfavorable financial situation of defendant at the time of suit, the evidence does not convince the court that the situation was as desperate or life-threatening as it has been characterized by plaintiffs. More importantly, the court does not agree with plaintiffs that had investors known of the defendant's financial situation they would invariably have paid less for the debentures and that the court should set a value considerably below market price.

As the parties seem to agree, the market for these debentures was, in the main, a sophisticated market. As such, it no doubt was most interested in the long range investment and speculative features of this particular offering. The defendant's immediate financial troubles would likely be viewed as temporary rather than terminal by such a market. Certainly the existence of the warrant feature suggests a buying public which was future-oriented.

As defendant urged, notwithstanding the then current financial difficulties, the future of Douglas was hopeful. In particular, the substantial backlog of unfilled orders as well as the banks' continued extension of credit suggested a reasonable basis for belief in recovery. The court relies heavily on these factors in reaching the conclusion that at the time of suit the fair value of the debentures should reflect the reasonably anticipated future recovery of defendant.

* * *

Defendant also argued that the value of the debentures at the time of suit was higher than market price because on that date the market price was artificially lowered due to panic selling in response to the revelation of the third quarter earnings. The evidence strongly supports the conclusion that the market price on the day of suit was characterized by panic selling. The court relies heavily on the trading data in reaching this conclusion. In particular, these data show that following the announcement of the third quarter results the market price dropped off and continued to decline at a rate in excess of the pre-revelation rate. The sharp and continued increase in volume between revelation and mid-October suggests a market reacting to news, here presumably news of the third quarter earnings. In addition to these trading data, there was convincing expert testimony which tends to confirm the conclusion that panic selling was affecting the market price at the time of suit.

* * *

Based on the foregoing factual findings the court concludes that market price is some evidence of fair value. Using the market price as a starting point, the court further concludes that whatever amount might rightly be subtracted to account for the temporary financial crisis of defendant at time of suit, should be off-set by adding a like amount to account for the reasonable likelihood of defendant's recovery. That is, in the court's view, with respect to value at the time of suit the defendant's financial difficulties were balanced off by the defendant's probable recovery.

Finally, the court concludes that there was convincing evidence that the market price of the debentures on the day of suit was influenced by panic selling. Hence the price was somewhat below where it might have been, even in a falling market. To correct for this aberration, the court adds 9½ points to the market price of 75½ to establish a figure of 85 as fair value on the date of suit. It is expected that the figure of 85 as value represents a fair value of these debentures unaffected by the panic selling which along with other factors depressed the market price from 88 on September 26, 1966 to 75½ on October 14, 1966.

In reaching this figure the court notes that the market fell 12 points between July 12 and September 26, 1966 at an average rate of .22 per day for 54 trading days. Had that rate continued for the 14 trading days September 27 to October 14, 1966 the price of the debentures would have been at approximately 84.92. Thus, 85 seems a fair value as of October 14, 1966. The 85 figure may well have obtained in a falling market, unaffected by panic selling.

DEPRECIATION RESULTING FROM CAUSES UNRELATED TO THE FALSITY OF THE PROSPECTUS

Under the proviso in Section 11(e) the defendant has the opportunity and burden of proving that any portion or all of the damages claimed by plaintiffs represents damage other than the depreciation in value of such security resulting from that part of the registration statement with respect to which liability is asserted. At trial defendant introduced considerable evidence which was intended to demonstrate that unexpected and unforeseeable events adversely affected the Douglas debentures subsequent to the issuance of the prospectus. It was claimed that these various events largely caused the drop in the debentures and that damages otherwise arrived at should be adjusted by a factor of somewhere between 3 and 12.

* * *

In response, plaintiffs argue that the drop in the market price and value of the debentures after September 26, 1966 was caused by the revelation of the third quarter operating loss and that the losses themselves were foreseeable. * * *

Plaintiffs concede that defendant has established that the decline in market price from 100 to 88 from July 12 to September 26, 1966 (the last trading date before there was some revelation of the losses during the third quarter) resulted from increased interest rates and other general economic phenomena which were unrelated to the falsity of the prospectus forecast or other material falsities in or omissions from the prospectus. It follows therefore that no one who sold before September 27, 1966 has a claim. That is because any loss that was sustained in a pre-September 27th sale was due to a drop in market price unrelated to any falsity in the prospectus. Thus, the pre-September 27th drop caused by general market phenomenon cannot be charged against the defendant, regardless of defendant's wrong doing. As noted above, however, the cause of the decline in the market price for the debentures after the revelation is in controversy.

* * *

With respect to the causes of depreciation after the revelation the court concludes that defendant has failed to carry its burden of proving that the depreciation was caused by factors unrelated to the falsity of the prospectus. * * *

Finally the court rejects defendant's claim that depreciation resulted from unforeseen developments in the market generally and in the market for money specifically. While credit arrangements may have become more difficult to make, testimony by defendant's own witnesses establishes that at no time between July 12, 1966 and May 1967 was Douglas unable to arrange financing in order to meet its obligations in the ordinary course of business. * * *

In reaching the above conclusion the court emphasizes that unlike some commentators, the court does not believe that defendant's burden of proof of "negative causation" is "impossible." Compare, R. Jennings

& H. Marsh, Securities Regulation, Cases and Materials, 810 (1968). Indeed, the court is aware that defendants have benefitted from clearly falling markets in other similar cases. E.g., Feit v. Leasco Data Processing Equipment Co., 322 F.Supp. at 586 and Fox v. Glickman Corp., 253 F.Supp. 1005, 1010 (S.D.N.Y.1966). Here, the court's conclusions are based on an assessment of all the evidence. In the court's view, the weight of the evidence clearly establishes that the depreciation in the Douglas debentures was due to causes directly related to the falsity of the prospectus rather than the unrelated factors urged by defendant.

* * *

Effect of Later Market Action on Damage Claims of Plaintiffs Who Either Sold After 1967 or Retain Their Debentures

Defendant has brought to the court's attention the fact that the debentures regained their issue price of 100. on February 1, 1967, thereafter peaked at 145. and remained above 100. for the remainder of 1967. According to defendant, the claims of plaintiff Beecher and others who sold at a loss in 1967, and the claims of those plaintiffs who still retain their debentures should be disallowed because 1) the deleterious effects of the false prospectus were presumably spent when the debentures reached par by February 1967, 2) those plaintiffs could have and should have mitigated their damages by selling, and 3) the "negative causation" proviso of § 11(e) requires this result. The court does not agree.

As the court understands the statute, with the exception of § 11(e)(3), post-suit market action is irrelevant in establishing plaintiffs' damages. Section 11's damage formulae are explicit, comprehensive and hence, exclusive. Clause (1) covers those who never sold; clause (2) covers those who sold before suit; and clause (3) covers those who sold after suit. With respect to post-suit sellers, the impact of post-suit market action has been fully accommodated under clause (3) in which the recovery of post-suit sellers is limited to actual or realized loss.

* * *

These statutory formulae were devised for the unique situations presented by the instant cases. The usual tort out-of-pocket measure (price paid less value at the *time of purchase*) was apparently rejected by the legislature.[5] In preference, § 11(e) provides that price paid less value at *the time of suit* be awarded where a plaintiff retains the security and that the lesser of price paid minus suit value or realized loss be awarded where plaintiff made a post-suit sale. * * *

* * * Given the statutory damage formulae defendant will benefit from a post-suit sale in a rising market, should a purchaser choose to sell. Although the statute confers this benefit, a purchaser is not required to sell merely to reduce defendant's damages.

5. Section 11(e) as amended in 1934 has been described as "modified 'tort damages'." 3 Loss, Securities Regulation 1728 (2d ed. 1961).

DEBENTURE TRANSACTIONS AND DAMAGES OF A NAMED PLAINTIFF

The court makes the following findings with respect to damages sustained by the named plaintiff Lawrence J. Beecher. Plaintiff Beecher bought $5,000, in principal amount of the debentures on July 12, 1966. In two separate transactions on November 13, 1970 plaintiff Beecher sold 3,000 of the principal amount at 58¼ for a sum of $1,787.49, less a commission of $15.00 and registration fee of $.03, and 2,000 of the principal amount at 58¾ for a sum of $1,201.68 less a commission of $10.00. The gross proceeds total $2,922.50, but the realized net sale proceeds total $2,897.47 (Pl's Exh. 83). Insofar as plaintiff Beecher sold after suit but before judgment, his claims are to be measured by § 11(e)(3). Since the price which plaintiff Beecher received upon sale was less than value as determined by the court, plaintiff Beecher is entitled to the difference between amount paid and value, minus 12 points which plaintiff concedes the market had dropped between July 12 and September 26, 1966, i.e., $5,000. minus $4,250, or $750 minus $600. Thus, Mr. Beecher is entitled to damages of $150.00.

The court further finds that plaintiff Beecher's claim is typical of those of the other named plaintiffs and of the class generally, and that the damages of the remaining plaintiffs, whether they sold before suit (but after September 27, 1966), after suit or still retain the debentures, can be calculated in a similar manner. To expedite the determination of damages, the court will appoint a Special Master who will ascertain the damages suffered by the other named plaintiffs and the class generally in accordance with the findings and conclusions reached in this opinion.

Is this opinion internally consistent? Are events which occurred after October 14 relevant in determining whether the market price on that date was the real "value"? Why should the fair value at time of suit "reflect the reasonably anticipated future recovery of defendant"? Isn't that already reflected in the market price? Is the court's conclusion that defendant could not prove that the depreciation was caused by unrelated factors consistent with the upward adjustment to compensate for "panic selling"?

Section 11(e) defines the measure of damages in terms of "the difference between the amount paid for the security (not exceeding the price at which the security was offered to the public) and (1) the *value* thereof as of the time such suit was brought, or (2) the *price* at which the security shall have been disposed of." When the plaintiff sells the security, the measure is fixed by the sale price. Does the language of § 11(e)(1) indicate, as Judge Motley assumes, that *value* at the time of suit may be something other than market price? Should panic selling be taken into account under the negative causation defense?

The chart of the market price of the Douglas debentures in the *Beecher* case would look something like this:

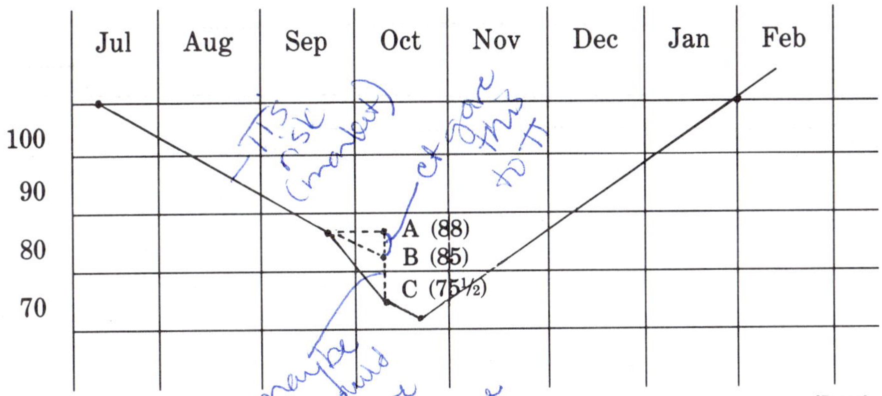

[F9682]

The court measured the damages as segment AB (the difference between the market price on September 26 and the price that the debentures would have reached by October 14 if they had continued to decline at the pre-September 26 rate). The correct measure would seem to be segment BC (the difference between the price the debentures reached after the company revealed the correct information and the price they would have reached if they had continued to decline at the previous rate, which the court found to be due to other factors).

The affirmative causation defense permits the defendant to establish that the damages fixed by § 11(e) should be reduced by "any portion or all of such damages [which] represents other than the depreciation in value of such security resulting from" the misrepresentations or omissions forming the basis of the § 11 claim. Since the panic selling in *Beecher* was caused by disclosure of the misrepresentations, why should that portion of the loss be shifted to the plaintiff?

In August 1976, the *Beecher* case, together with other related litigation, was settled for $5 million, out of which plaintiffs' attorneys were awarded fees of $1.5 million. See 435 F.Supp. 415–19 (S.D.N.Y. 1977). Based on the size of the plaintiff classes, it was estimated that claims aggregating $3.3 million would be filed by certain purchasers of Douglas common stock, and claims aggregating $2.2 million would be filed by debenture purchasers who did not sell their debentures prior to September 27, 1966. The debenture purchasers were to be allowed $30 per $1,000 debenture, or their actual loss if less. However, after publication of several notices of the settlement, the total claims filed aggregated only $1.3 million, of which $900,000 represented claims by stock purchasers and $400,000 represented claims by debenture purchasers. At this point, Douglas and plaintiffs' attorneys agreed that the payments to stock purchaser claimants should be doubled. Douglas requested that the remaining unclaimed portion of the fund be returned to it, while plaintiffs' counsel proposed that the remaining portion be awarded to the debenture purchaser claimants, raising their recovery to approximately $160 per $1,000 debenture. The district court accepted plaintiffs' position, noting that Douglas had agreed in the settlement that "no part of the fund will revert to Douglas in any eventuality." The court of appeals affirmed, holding that the $160 recovery did not constitute a windfall to the debenture purchasers, since "there was testimony at [the] trial * * * that damages to [debenture purchasers] might have been as much as $470 per debenture." Beecher v. Able, 575 F.2d 1010 (2d Cir.1978).

What should be the measure of damages in an exchange offer situation like Feit v. Leasco, p. 102 above? Considering the nature of the alleged omission in that case, should former Reliance shareholders be entitled to recover only if the Leasco securities declined in value after the exchange? What was the "amount paid" for those securities? In the actual decision, the court rejected "testimony of plaintiff's expert comparing the intrinsic rather than the market value of Leasco and Reliance" as "too speculative for purposes of assessing damages," and held that the "amount paid" was the market value of Reliance stock on the day before the exchange offer commenced. 332 F.Supp. at 585–6. Do you agree?

AKERMAN v. ORYX

810 F.2d 336 (2d Cir.1987).

Before VAN GRAAFEILAND, MESKILL and NEWMAN, CIRCUIT JUDGES.

MESKILL, CIRCUIT JUDGE:

Plaintiffs Morris and Susan Akerman and Dr. Lawrence Kuhn appeal from an order of the United States District Court for the Southern District of New York, Sofaer, J., granting summary judgment disposing of their claims under section 11 of the Securities Act of 1933 * * *.

BACKGROUND

This case arises out of a June 30, 1981, initial public offering of securities by Oryx, a company planning to enter the business of manufacturing and marketing abroad video cassettes and video discs of feature films for home entertainment. Oryx filed a registration statement and an accompanying prospectus dated June 30, 1981, with the Securities and Exchange Commission (SEC) for a firm commitment offering of 700,000 units. Each unit sold for $4.75 and consisted of one share of common stock and one warrant to purchase an additional share of stock for $5.75 at a later date.

The prospectus contained an erroneous *pro forma* unaudited financial statement relating to the eight month period ending March 31, 1981. It reported net sales of $931,301, net income of $211,815, and earnings of seven cents per share. Oryx, however, had incorrectly posted a substantial transaction by its subsidiary to March instead of April when Oryx actually received the subject sale's revenues. The prospectus, therefore, overstated earnings for the eight month period.

Net sales in that period actually totaled $766,301, net income $94,529, and earnings per share three cents.

Oryx's price had declined to four dollars per unit by October 12, 1981, the day before Oryx revealed the prospectus misstatement to the SEC. The unit price had further declined to $3.25 by November 9, 1981, the day before Oryx disclosed the misstatement to the public. After public disclosure, the price of Oryx rose and reached $3.50 by November 25, 1981, the day this suit commenced.

Plaintiffs allege that the prospectus error rendered Oryx liable for the stock price decline pursuant to sections 11 and 12(2) of the Securities Act of 1933. In July 1982, Oryx moved for summary judgment on the grounds, *inter alia,* that the misstatement was not material for purposes of establishing liability under section 11 and that the misstatement had not actually caused the price decline for purposes of damages under section 11. * * *

B. The Merits

1. Section 11 Claims

* * *

The district court determined that plaintiffs established a *prima facie* case under section 11(a) by demonstrating that the prospectus error was material "as a theoretical matter." The court, however, granted defendants' motion for summary judgment on damages under section 11(e), stating: "[Defendants] have carried their heavy burden of proving that the [Oryx stock price] decline was caused by factors other than the matters misstated in the registration statement." The precise issue on appeal, therefore, is whether defendants carried their burden of negative causation under section 11(e).

* * *

The Akermans' section 11(a) claim survived an initial summary judgment attack when the court concluded that the prospectus misstatement was material. We note, however, that the district court held that the misstatement was material only "as a theoretical matter." As described below, this conclusion weighs heavily in our judgment that the district court correctly decided that the defendants had carried their burden of showing that the misstatement did not cause the stock price to decline.

The misstatement resulted from an innocent bookkeeping error whereby Oryx misposted a sale by its subsidiary to March instead of April. Oryx received the sale's proceeds less than one month after the reported date. The prospectus, moreover, expressly stated that Oryx "expect[ed] that [the subsidiary's] sales will decline." Indeed, Morris Akerman conceded that he understood this disclaimer to warn that Oryx expected the subsidiary's business to decline.

Thus, although the misstatement may have been "theoretically material," when it is considered in the context of the prospectus' pessimistic forecast of the performance of Oryx's subsidiary, the misstatement was not likely to cause a stock price decline. Indeed, the public not only did not react adversely to disclosure of the misstatement, Oryx's price actually *rose* somewhat after public disclosure of the error.

The applicable section 11(e) formula for calculating damages is "the difference between the amount paid for the security (not exceeding the price at which the security was offered to the public) and . . . the value thereof as of the time such suit was brought." The relevant events and stock prices are:

Date	*Event*	*Oryx Stock Price*
June 30, 1981	Initial public offering	$4.75
October 15, 1981	Disclosure of error to SEC	$4.00
November 10, 1981	Disclosure of error to public	$3.25
November 25, 1981	Date of suit	$3.50

The price decline before disclosure may not be charged to defendants. See Beecher v. Able, 435 F.Supp. 397, 407 (S.D.N.Y.1975) (price decline before misstatement revealed not attributable to defendants under section 11(e)); Fox v. Glickman Corp., 253 F.Supp. 1005, 1010 (S.D.N.Y.1966) (same). At first blush, damages would appear to be zero because there was no depreciation in Oryx's value between the time of public disclosure and the time of suit.

The Akermans contended at trial, however, that the relevant disclosure date was the date of disclosure to the SEC and not to the public. Under plaintiffs' theory, damages would equal the price decline subsequent to October 15, 1981, which amounted to fifty cents per share. Plaintiffs attempted to support this theory by alleging that insiders privy to the SEC disclosure—Oryx's officers, attorneys and accountants, and underwriters and SEC officials—sold Oryx shares and thereby deflated its price before public disclosure. The district court attributed "at least possible theoretical validity" to this argument. After extensive discovery, however, plaintiffs produced absolutely no evidence of insider trading. Plaintiffs' submissions and oral argument before us do not press this theory.

The Akermans first attempted to explain the public's failure to react adversely to disclosure by opining that defendant-underwriter Moore & Schley used its position as market maker to prop up the market price. This theory apparently complemented the Akermans' other theory that insiders acted on knowledge of the disclosure to the SEC to deflate the price before public disclosure. The Akermans failed after extensive discovery to produce any evidence of insider trading and have not pressed the theory on appeal.

The district court invited statistical studies from both sides to clarify the causation issue. Defendants produced a statistical analysis of the stocks of the one hundred companies that went public contemporaneously with Oryx. The study tracked the stocks' performances for the period between June 30, 1981 (initial public offering date) and

November 25, 1981 (date of suit). The study indicated that Oryx performed at the exact statistical median of these stocks and that several issues suffered equal or greater losses than did Oryx during this period. Defendants produced an additional study which indicated that Oryx stock "behaved over the entire period . . . consistent[ly] with its own inherent variation."

Plaintiffs offered the following rebuttal evidence. During the period between SEC disclosure and public disclosure, Oryx stock decreased nineteen percent while the over-the-counter (OTC) composite index rose five percent (the first study). During this period, therefore, the OTC composite index out-performed Oryx by twenty-four percentage points. Plaintiffs also produced a study indicating that for the time period between SEC disclosure and one week after public disclosure, eighty-two of the one hundred new issues analyzed in the defendants' study outperformed Oryx's stock.

Plaintiffs' first study compared Oryx's performance to the performance of the OTC index in order to rebut a comparison offered by defendants to prove that Oryx's price decline resulted not from the misstatement but rather from an overall market decline. As previously stated, defendants' comparison indicated that the OTC index generally declined for the period between Oryx's offering date and the date of suit. The parties' conflicting comparisons, however, lack credibility because they fail to reflect any of the countless variables that might affect the stock price performance of a single company. Statistical analyses must control for relevant variables to permit reliable inferences.

The studies comparing Oryx's performance to the other one hundred companies that went public in May and June of 1981 are similarly flawed. The studies do not evaluate the performance of Oryx stock in relation to the stock of companies possessing any characteristic in common with Oryx, e.g., product, technology, profitability, assets or countless other variables which influence stock prices, except the contemporaneous initial offering dates.

* * *

Granting the Akermans every reasonable, favorable inference, the battle of the studies is at best equivocal; the studies do not meaningfully point in one direction or the other.

* * *

Defendants met their burden, as set forth in section 11(e), by establishing that the misstatement was barely material and that the public failed to react adversely to its disclosure. With the case in this posture, the plaintiffs had to come forward with "specific facts showing that there is a genuine issue for trial." Despite extensive discovery, plaintiffs completely failed to produce any evidence, other than unreliable and sometimes inconsistent statistical studies and theories, suggesting that Oryx's price decline actually resulted from the misstatement. Summary judgment was properly granted.

Damages that may be Available Under Other Sections

As the preceding material points out, the complex damage formula set forth in § 11(e) is an attempt to limit damages to the loss caused by the material misstatements and omissions and to exclude any decline in value attributable to factors not related to the § 11 violations. Section 12(2) provides for an action by a purchaser against a seller who makes material misrepresentations and omissions but is not limited to registered offerings. Section 12 provides for rescission or, if the plaintiff has sold the securities, for recissory damages. Thus, a § 12 plaintiff can recover for decline in the price of the security even though the decline had no relationship to the § 12 violation. Recall that at least one court has indicated that a § 12(1) action for rescission may also be based on a misleading prospectus since delivery of a misleading prospectus is a violation of § 5. SEC v. MANOR NURSING CENTERS, 458 F.2d 1082 (2d Cir.1972). But see SEC v. SOUTHWEST COAL & ENERGY, 624 F.2d 1312 (5th Cir.1980); SEC v. BLAZON, 609 F.2d 960 (9th Cir.1979). As is the case with § 12(2), liability under § 12(1) is limited to sellers and thus would not extend to most persons who would be liable in a § 11 action. § 12 is discussed below at pages 358–380.

Also to be compared with the measure of damages under § 11 is the applicable measure in an action under § 10(b) and Rule 10b-5 of the Exchange Act. See pp. 675–681 below.

---

4. *The "Due Diligence" Defense*

The preceding materials have dealt with the elements of a claim under § 11 and the defenses common to all parties. Section 11(a) imposes civil liabilities on: the issuer and its principal executive, financial and accounting officers (as required signers of the registration statement under § 6(a)); directors and persons designated as directors; underwriters; and "experts". Except as to the issuer, § 11(b) provides an affirmative defense to any of these persons who can demonstrate that they met a prescribed standard of diligence with respect to the information contained in the registration statement.

As you study the interpretations of this affirmative defense in the following excerpts from the *BarChris* and *Leasco* decisions, make sure you understand (1) the different "parts" into which the registration statement is divided; (2) which statements belong in which "part"; (3) the difference in the statutory standards applicable to different defendants with respect to the different "parts"; and (4) how the statutory standard is interpreted with respect to different types of defendants, such as "inside" directors, "outside" directors, lawyer-directors, underwriters, and accountants.

ESCOTT v. BARCHRIS CONSTRUCTION CORP.

283 F.Supp. 643 (S.D.N.Y.1968).

McLean, District Judge.

This is an action by purchasers of 5½ per cent convertible subordinated fifteen year debentures of BarChris Construction Corporation (BarChris). * * *

Defendants fall into three categories: (1) the persons who signed the registration statement; (2) the underwriters, consisting of eight investment banking firms, led by Drexel & Co. (Drexel); and (3) BarChris's auditors, Peat, Marwick, Mitchell & Co. (Peat, Marwick).

The signers, in addition to BarChris itself, were the nine directors of BarChris, plus its controller, defendant Trilling, who was not a director. Of the nine directors, five were officers of BarChris, i.e., defendants Vitolo, president; Russo, executive vice president; Pugliese, vice president; Kircher, treasurer; and Birnbaum, secretary. Of the remaining four, defendant Grant was a member of the firm of Perkins, Daniels, McCormack & Collins, BarChris's attorneys. He became a director in October 1960. Defendant Coleman, a partner in Drexel, became a director on April 17, 1961, as did the other two, Auslander and Rose, who were not otherwise connected with BarChris.

Defendants, in addition to denying that the registration statement was false, have pleaded the defenses open to them under Section 11 of the Act, plus certain additional defenses, including the statute of limitations. Defendants have also asserted cross-claims against each other, seeking to hold one another liable for any sums for which the respective defendants may be held liable to plaintiffs.

* * *

BarChris was an outgrowth of a business started as a partnership by Vitolo and Pugliese in 1946. The business was incorporated in New York in 1955 under the name of B & C Bowling Alley Builders, Inc. Its name was subsequently changed to BarChris Construction Corporation.

* * *

For some years the business had exceeded the managerial capacity of its founders. Vitolo and Pugliese are each men of limited education. Vitolo did not get beyond high school. Pugliese ended his schooling in seventh grade. Pugliese devoted his time to supervising the actual construction work. Vitolo was concerned primarily with obtaining new business. Neither was equipped to handle financial matters.

Rather early in their career they enlisted the aid of Russo, who was trained as an accountant. He first joined them in the days of the partnership, left for a time, and returned as an officer and director of B & C Bowling Alley Builders, Inc. in 1958. He eventually became executive vice president of BarChris. In that capacity he handled many of the transactions which figure in this case.

In 1959 BarChris hired Kircher, a certified public accountant who had been employed by Peat, Marwick. He started as controller and became treasurer in 1960. In October of that year, another ex-Peat, Marwick employee, Trilling, succeeded Kircher as controller. At approximately the same time Birnbaum, a young attorney, was hired as house counsel. He became secretary on April 17, 1961.

* * *

THE DEBENTURE REGISTRATION STATEMENT

In preparing the registration statement for the debentures, Grant acted for BarChris. He had previously represented BarChris in preparing the registration statement for the common stock issue. In connection with the sale of common stock, BarChris had issued purchase warrants. In January 1961 a second registration statement was filed in order to update the information pertaining to these warrants. Grant had prepared that statement as well.

Some of the basic information needed for the debenture registration statement was contained in the registration statements previously filed with respect to the common stock and warrants. Grant used these old registration statements as a model in preparing the new one, making the changes which he considered necessary in order to meet the new situation.

The underwriters were represented by the Philadelphia law firm of Drinker, Biddle & Reath. John A. Ballard, a member of that firm, was in charge of that work, assisted by a young associate named Stanton.

Peat, Marwick, BarChris's auditors, who had previously audited BarChris's annual balance sheet and earnings figures for 1958 and 1959, did the same for 1960. These figures were set forth in the registration statement. In addition, Peat, Marwick undertook a so-called "S-1 review," the proper scope of which is one of the matters debated here.

* * *

THE "DUE DILIGENCE" DEFENSES

Section 11(b) of the Act provides that:

"* * * no person, other than the issuer, shall be liable * * * who shall sustain the burden of proof—

* * *

(3) that (A) as regards any part of the registration statement not purporting to be made on the authority of an expert * * * he had, after reasonable investigation, reasonable ground to believe and did believe, at the time such part of the registration statement became effective, that the statements therein were true and that there was no omission to state a material fact required to be stated therein or necessary to make the statements therein not misleading; * * * and (C) as regards any part of the registration statement purporting to be made on the authority of an expert (other

than himself) * * *, he had no reasonable ground to believe and did not believe, at the time such part of the registration statement became effective, that the statements therein were untrue or that there was an omission to state a material fact required to be stated therein or necessary to make the statements therein not misleading * * *."

Section 11(c) defines "reasonable investigation" as follows:

"In determining, for the purpose of paragraph (3) of subsection (b) of this section, what constitutes reasonable investigation and reasonable ground for belief, the standard of reasonableness shall be that required of a prudent man in the management of his own property."

Every defendant, except BarChris itself, to whom, as the issuer, these defenses are not available, and except Peat, Marwick, whose position rests on a different statutory provision, has pleaded these affirmative defenses. Each claims that (1) as to the part of the registration statement purporting to be made on the authority of an expert (which, for convenience, I shall refer to as the "expertised portion"), he had no reasonable ground to believe and did not believe that there were any untrue statements or material omissions, and (2) as to the other parts of the registration statement, he made a reasonable investigation, as a result of which he had reasonable ground to believe and did believe that the registration statement was true and that no material fact was omitted. As to each defendant, the question is whether he has sustained the burden of proving these defenses. Surprising enough, there is little or no judicial authority on this question. No decisions directly in point under Section 11 have been found.

Before considering the evidence, a preliminary matter should be disposed of. The defendants do not agree among themselves as to who the "experts" were or as to the parts of the registration statement which were expertised. Some defendants say that Peat, Marwick was the expert, others say that BarChris's attorneys, Perkins, Daniels, McCormack & Collins, and the underwriters' attorneys, Drinker, Biddle & Reath, were also the experts. On the first view, only those portions of the registration statement purporting to be made on Peat, Marwick's authority were expertised portions. On the other view, everything in the registration statement was within this category, because the two law firms were responsible for the entire document.

The first view is the correct one. To say that the entire registration statement is expertised because some lawyer prepared it would be an unreasonable construction of the statute. Neither the lawyer for the company nor the lawyer for the underwriters is an expert within the meaning of Section 11. The only expert, in the statutory sense, was Peat, Marwick, and the only parts of the registration statement which purported to be made upon the authority of an expert were the portions which purported to be made on Peat, Marwick's authority.

The parties also disagree as to what those portions were. Some defendants say that it was only the 1960 figures (and the figures for prior years, which are not in controversy here). Others say in substance that it was every figure in the prospectus. The plaintiffs take a somewhat intermediate view. They do not claim that Peat, Marwick expertised every figure, but they do maintain that Peat, Marwick is responsible for a portion of the text of the prospectus, i.e., that pertaining to "Methods of Operation," because a reference to it was made in footnote 9 to the balance sheet.

Here again, the more narrow view is the correct one. The registration statement contains a report of Peat, Marwick as independent public accountants dated February 23, 1961. This relates only to the consolidated balance sheet of BarChris and consolidated subsidiaries as of December 31, 1960, and the related statement of earnings and retained earnings for the five years then ended. This is all that Peat, Marwick purported to certify. It is perfectly clear that it did not purport to certify the 1961 figures, some of which are expressly stated in the prospectus to have been unaudited.

Moreover, plaintiffs' intermediate view is also incorrect. The cross reference in footnote 9 to the "Methods of Operation" passage in the prospectus was inserted merely for the convenience of the reader. It is not a fair construction to say that it thereby imported into the balance sheet everything in that portion of the text, much of which had nothing to do with the figures in the balance sheet.

I turn now to the question of whether defendants have proved their due diligence defenses. The position of each defendant will be separately considered.

Russo

Russo was, to all intents and purposes, the chief executive officer of BarChris. He was a member of the executive committee. He was familiar with all aspects of the business. He was personally in charge of dealings with the factors. He acted on BarChris's behalf in making the financing agreements with Talcott and he handled the negotiations with Talcott in the spring of 1961. He talked with customers about their delinquencies.

Russo prepared the list of jobs which went into the backlog figure. He knew the status of those jobs. In addition to being chief executive officer of BarChris, he was a director of T-Bowl International, Inc., and the principals in St. Ann's were his friends.

It was Russo who arranged for the temporary increase in BarChris's cash in banks on December 31, 1960, a transaction which borders on the fraudulent. He was thoroughly aware of BarChris's stringent financial condition in May 1961. He had personally advanced large sums to BarChris of which $175,000 remained unpaid as of May 16.

In short, Russo knew all the relevant facts. He could not have believed that there were no untrue statements or material omissions in the prospectus. Russo has no due diligence defenses.

VITOLO AND PUGLIESE

They were the founders of the business who stuck with it to the end. Vitolo was president and Pugliese was vice president. Despite their titles, their field of responsibility in the administration of BarChris's affairs during the period in question seems to have been less all-embracing than Russo's. Pugliese in particular appears to have limited his activities to supervising the actual construction work.

Vitolo and Pugliese are each men of limited education. It is not hard to believe that for them the prospectus was difficult reading, if indeed they read it at all.

But whether it was or not is irrelevant. The liability of a director who signs a registration statement does not depend upon whether or not he read it or, if he did, whether or not he understood what he was reading.

And in any case, Vitolo and Pugliese were not as naive as they claim to be. They were members of BarChris's executive committee. At meetings of that committee BarChris's affairs were discussed at length. They must have known what was going on. Certainly they knew of the inadequacy of cash in 1961. They knew of their own large advances to the company which remained unpaid. They knew that they had agreed not to deposit their checks until the financing proceeds were received. They knew and intended that part of the proceeds were to be used to pay their own loans.

All in all, the position of Vitolo and Pugliese is not significantly different, for present purposes, from Russo's. They could not have believed that the registration statement was wholly true and that no material facts had been omitted. And in any case, there is nothing to show that they made any investigation of anything which they may not have known about or understood. They have not proved their due diligence defenses.

KIRCHER

Kircher was treasurer of BarChris and its chief financial officer. He is a certified public accountant and an intelligent man. He was thoroughly familiar with BarChris's financial affairs. He knew the terms of BarChris's agreements with Talcott. He knew of the customers' delinquency problem. He participated actively with Russo in May 1961 in the successful effort to hold Talcott off until the financing proceeds came in. He knew how the financing proceeds were to be applied and he saw to it that they were so applied. He arranged the officers' loans and he knew all the facts concerning them.

Moreover, as a member of the executive committee, Kircher was kept informed as to those branches of the business of which he did not have direct charge. He knew about the operation of alleys, present and prospective. He knew that Capitol was included in 1960 sales and that Bridge and Yonkers were included in first quarter 1961 sales despite the fact that they were not sold. Kircher knew of the infirmities in customers' contracts included in the backlog figure. Indeed, at a later date, he specifically criticized Russo's handling of the T-Bowl situation. In brief, Kircher knew all the relevant facts.

Kircher worked on the preparation of the registration statement. He conferred with Grant and on occasion with Ballard. He supplied information to them about the company's business. He read the prospectus and understood it. He knew what it said and what it did not say.

Kircher's contention is that he had never before dealt with a registration statement, that he did not know what it should contain, and that he relied wholly on Grant, Ballard and Peat, Marwick to guide him. He claims that it was their fault, not his, if there was anything wrong with it. He says that all the facts were recorded in BarChris's books where these "experts" could have seen them if they had looked. He says that he truthfully answered all their questions. In effect, he says that if they did not know enough to ask the right questions and to give him the proper instructions, that is not his responsibility.

There is an issue of credibility here. In fact, Kircher was not frank in dealing with Grant and Ballard. He withheld information from them. But even if he had told them all the facts, this would not have constituted the due diligence contemplated by the statute. Knowing the facts, Kircher had reason to believe that the expertised portion of the prospectus, i.e., the 1960 figures, was in part incorrect. He could not shut his eyes to the facts and rely on Peat, Marwick for that portion.

As to the rest of the prospectus, knowing the facts, he did not have a reasonable ground to believe it to be true. On the contrary, he must have known that in part it was untrue. Under these circumstances, he was not entitled to sit back and place the blame on the lawyers for not advising him about it.

Kircher has not proved his due diligence defenses.

BIRNBAUM

Birnbaum was a young lawyer, admitted to the bar in 1957, who, after brief periods of employment by two different law firms and an equally brief period of practicing in his own firm, was employed by BarChris as house counsel and assistant secretary in October 1960. Unfortunately for him, he became secretary and a director of BarChris on April 17, 1961, after the first version of the registration statement had been filed with the Securities and Exchange Commission. He signed the later amendments, thereby becoming responsible for the accuracy of the prospectus in its final form.

Although the prospectus, in its description of "management," lists Birnbaum among the "executive officers" and devotes several sentences to a recital of his career, the fact seems to be that he was not an executive officer in any real sense. He did not participate in the management of the company. As house counsel, he attended to legal matters of a routine nature. Among other things, he incorporated subsidiaries, with which BarChris was plentifully supplied. Among the subsidiaries which he incorporated were Capitol Lanes, Inc. which operated Capitol, Yonkers Lanes, Inc. which eventually operated Yonkers, and Parkway Lanes, Inc. which eventually operated Bridge. He was thus aware of that aspect of the business.

Birnbaum examined contracts. In that connection he advised BarChris that the T-Bowl contracts were not legally enforceable. He was thus aware of that fact.

One of Birnbaum's more important duties, first as assistant secretary and later as full-fledged secretary, was to keep the corporate minutes of BarChris and its subsidiaries. This necessarily informed him to a considerable extent about the company's affairs. Birnbaum was not initially a member of the executive committee, however, and did not keep its minutes at the outset. According to the minutes, the first meeting which he attended, "upon invitation of the Committee," was on March 22, 1961. He became a member shortly thereafter and kept the minutes beginning with the meeting of April 24, 1961.

It seems probable that Birnbaum did not know of many of the inaccuracies in the prospectus. He must, however, have appreciated some of them. In any case, he made no investigation and relied on the others to get it right. Unlike Trilling, he was entitled to rely upon Peat, Marwick for the 1960 figures, for as far as appears, he had no personal knowledge of the company's books of account or financial transactions. But he was not entitled to rely upon Kircher, Grant and Ballard for the other portions of the prospectus. As a lawyer, he should have known his obligations under the statute. He should have known that he was required to make a reasonable investigation of the truth of all the statements in the unexpertised portion of the document which he signed. Having failed to make such an investigation, he did not have reasonable ground to believe that all these statements were true. Birnbaum has not established his due diligence defenses except as to the audited 1960 figures.

AUSLANDER

Auslander was an "outside" director, i.e., one who was not an officer of BarChris. He was chairman of the board of Valley Stream National Bank in Valley Stream, Long Island. In February 1961 Vitolo asked him to become a director of BarChris. Vitolo gave him an enthusiastic account of BarChris's progress and prospects. As an inducement, Vitolo said that when BarChris received the proceeds of a forthcoming issue of securities, it would deposit $1,000,000 in Auslander's bank.

In February and early March 1961, before accepting Vitolo's invitation, Auslander made some investigation of BarChris. He obtained Dun & Bradstreet reports which contained sales and earnings figures for periods earlier than December 31, 1960. He caused inquiry to be made of certain of BarChris's banks and was advised that they regarded BarChris favorably. He was informed that inquiry of Talcott had also produced a favorable response.

On March 3, 1961, Auslander indicated his willingness to accept a place on the board. Shortly thereafter, on March 14, Kircher sent him a copy of BarChris's annual report for 1960. Auslander observed that BarChris's auditors were Peat, Marwick. They were also the auditors for the Valley Stream National Bank. He thought well of them.

Auslander was elected a director on April 17, 1961. The registration statement in its original form had already been filed, of course without his signature. On May 10, 1961, he signed a signature page for the first amendment to the registration statement which was filed on May 11, 1961. This was a separate sheet without any document attached. Auslander did not know that it was a signature page for a registration statement. He vaguely understood that it was something "for the SEC."

Auslander attended a meeting of BarChris's directors on May 15, 1961. At that meeting he, along with the other directors, signed the signature sheet for the second amendment which constituted the registration statement in its final form. Again, this was only a separate sheet without any document attached. Auslander never saw a copy of the registration statement in its final form.

At the May 15 directors' meeting, however, Auslander did realize that what he was signing was a signature sheet to a registration statement. This was the first time that he had appreciated that fact. A copy of the registration statement in its earlier form as amended on May 11, 1961 was passed around at the meeting. Auslander glanced at it briefly. He did not read it thoroughly.

At the May 15 meeting, Russo and Vitolo stated that everything was in order and that the prospectus was correct. Auslander believed this statement.

In considering Auslander's due diligence defenses, a distinction is to be drawn between the expertised and non-expertised portions of the prospectus. As to the former, Auslander knew that Peat, Marwick had audited the 1960 figures. He believed them to be correct because he had confidence in Peat, Marwick. He had no reasonable ground to believe otherwise.

As to the non-expertised portions, however, Auslander is in a different position. He seems to have been under the impression that Peat, Marwick was responsible for all the figures. This impression was not correct, as he would have realized if he had read the prospectus carefully. Auslander made no investigation of the accuracy of the prospectus. He relied on the assurance of Vitolo and Russo, and upon the information he had received in answer to his inquiries back in February and early March. These inquiries were general ones, in the nature of a credit check. The information which he received in answer to them was also general, without specific reference to the statements in the prospectus, which was not prepared until some time thereafter.

It is true that Auslander became a director on the eve of the financing. He had little opportunity to familiarize himself with the company's affairs. The question is whether, under such circumstances, Auslander did enough to establish his due diligence defense with respect to the non-expertised portions of the prospectus.

Although there is a dearth of authority under Section 11 on this point, an English case under the analogous Companies Act is of some value. In Adams v. Thrift, [1915] 1 Ch. 557, aff'd, [1915] 2 Ch. 21, it was held that a director who knew nothing about the prospectus and did not even read it, but who relied on the statement of the company's managing director that it was "all right," was liable for its untrue statements. See also In the Matter of Interstate Hosiery Mills, Inc., 4 S.E.C. 706 (1939).

Section 11 imposes liability in the first instance upon a director, no matter how new he is. He is presumed to know his responsibility when he becomes a director. He can escape liability only by using that reasonable care to investigate the facts which a prudent man would employ in the management of his own property. In my opinion, a prudent man would not act in an important matter without any knowledge of the relevant facts, in sole reliance upon representations of persons who are comparative strangers and upon general information which does not purport to cover the particular case. To say that such minimal conduct measures up to the statutory standard would, to all intents and purposes, absolve new directors from responsibility merely because they are new. This is not a sensible construction of Section 11, when one bears in mind its fundamental purpose of requiring full and truthful disclosure for the protection of investors.

I find and conclude that Auslander has not established his due diligence defense with respect to the misstatements and omissions in those portions of the prospectus other than the audited 1960 figures.

GRANT

Grant became a director of BarChris in October 1960. His law firm was counsel to BarChris in matters pertaining to the registration of securities. Grant drafted the registration statement for the stock issue in 1959 and for the warrants in January 1961. He also drafted the registration statement for the debentures. In the preliminary division of work between him and Ballard, the underwriters' counsel, Grant took initial responsibility for preparing the registration statement, while Ballard devoted his efforts in the first instance to preparing the indenture.

Grant is sued as a director and as a signer of the registration statement. This is not an action against him for malpractice in his capacity as a lawyer. Nevertheless, in considering Grant's due diligence defenses, the unique position which he occupied cannot be disregarded. As the director most directly concerned with writing the registration statement and assuring its accuracy, more was required of him in the way of reasonable investigation than could fairly be expected of a director who had no connection with this work.

There is no valid basis for plaintiffs' accusation that Grant knew that the prospectus was false in some respects and incomplete and misleading in others. Having seen him testify at length, I am satisfied as to his integrity. I find that Grant honestly believed that the registration statement was true and that no material facts had been omitted from it.

In this belief he was mistaken, and the fact is that for all his work, he never discovered any of the errors or omissions which have been recounted at length in this opinion, with the single exception of Capitol Lanes. He knew that BarChris had not sold this alley and intended to operate it, but he appears to have been under the erroneous impression that Peat, Marwick had knowingly sanctioned its inclusion in sales because of the allegedly temporary nature of the operation.

Grant contends that a finding that he did not make a reasonable investigation would be equivalent to a holding that a lawyer for an issuing company, in order to show due diligence, must make an independent audit of the figures supplied to him by his client. I do not consider this to be a realistic statement of the issue. There were errors and omissions here which could have been detected without an audit. The question is whether, despite his failure to detect them, Grant made a reasonable effort to that end.

Much of this registration statement is a scissors and paste-pot job. Grant lifted large portions from the earlier prospectuses, modifying them in some instances to the extent that he considered necessary. But BarChris's affairs had changed for the worse by May 1961. Statements that were accurate in January were no longer accurate in May. Grant never discovered this. He accepted the assurances of Kircher and Russo that any change which might have occurred had been for the better, rather than the contrary.

It is claimed that a lawyer is entitled to rely on the statements of his client and that to require him to verify their accuracy would set an unreasonably high standard. This is too broad a generalization. It is all a matter of degree. To require an audit would obviously be unreasonable. On the other hand, to require a check of matters easily verifiable is not unreasonable. Even honest clients can make mistakes. The statute imposes liability for untrue statements regardless of whether they are intentionally untrue. The way to prevent mistakes is to test oral information by examining the original written record.

There were things which Grant could readily have checked which he did not check. For example, he was unaware of the provisions of the agreements between BarChris and Talcott. He never read them. Thus, he did not know, although he readily could have ascertained, that BarChris's contingent liability on Type B leaseback arrangements was

100 per cent, not 25 per cent. He did not appreciate that if BarChris defaulted in repurchasing delinquent customers' notes upon Talcott's demand, Talcott could accelerate all the customer paper in its hands, which amounted to over $3,000,000.

As to the backlog figure, Grant appreciated that scheduled unfilled orders on the company's books meant firm commitments, but he never asked to see the contracts which, according to the prospectus, added up to $6,905,000. Thus, he did not know that this figure was overstated by some $4,490,000.

Grant was unaware of the fact that BarChris was about to operate Bridge and Yonkers. He did not read the minutes of those subsidiaries which would have revealed that fact to him. On the subject of minutes, Grant knew that minutes of certain meetings of the BarChris executive committee held in 1961 had not been written up. Kircher, who had acted as secretary at those meetings, had complete notes of them. Kircher told Grant that there was no point in writing up the minutes because the matters discussed at those meetings were purely routine. Grant did not insist that the minutes be written up, nor did he look at Kircher's notes. If he had, he would have learned that on February 27, 1961 there was an extended discussion in the executive committee meeting about customers' delinquencies, that on March 8, 1961 the committee had discussed the pros and cons of alley operation by BarChris, that on March 18, 1961 the committee was informed that BarChris was constructing or about to begin constructing twelve alleys for which it had no contracts, and that on May 13, 1961 Dreyfuss, one of the worst delinquents, had filed a petition in Chapter X.

* * *

The application of proceeds language in the prospectus was drafted by Kircher back in January. It may well have expressed his intent at that time, but his intent, and that of the other principal officers of BarChris, was very different in May. Grant did not appreciate that the earlier language was no longer appropriate. He never learned of the situation which the company faced in May. He knew that BarChris was short of cash, but he had no idea how short. He did not know that BarChris was withholding delivery of checks already drawn and signed because there was not enough money in the bank to pay them. He did not know that the officers of the company intended to use immediately approximately one-third of the financing proceeds in a manner not disclosed in the prospectus, including approximately $1,000,000 in paying old debts.

In this connection, mention should be made of a fact which has previously been referred to only in passing. The "negative cash balance" in BarChris's Lafayette National Bank account in May 1961 included a check dated April 10, 1961 to the order of Grant's firm, Perkins, Daniels, McCormack & Collins, in the amount of $8,711. This check was not deposited by Perkins, Daniels until June 1, after the financing proceeds had been received by BarChris. Of course, if Grant had knowingly withheld deposit of this check until that time, he would be in a position similar to Russo, Vitolo and Pugliese. I do not believe, however, that that was the case. I find that the check was not delivered by BarChris to Perkins, Daniels until shortly before June 1.

This incident is worthy of mention, however, for another reason. The prospectus stated on page 10 that Perkins, Daniels had "received fees aggregating $13,000" from BarChris. This check for $8,711 was one of those fees. It had not been received by Perkins, Daniels prior to May 16. Grant was unaware of this. In approving this erroneous statement in the prospectus, he did not consult his own bookkeeper to ascertain whether it was correct. Kircher told him that the bill had been paid and Grant took his word for it. If he had inquired and had found that this representation was untrue, this discovery might well have led him to a realization of the true state of BarChris's finances in May 1961.

As far as customers' delinquencies is concerned, although Grant discussed this with Kircher, he again accepted the assurances of Kircher and Russo that no serious problem existed. He did not examine the records as to delinquencies, although BarChris maintained such a record. Any inquiry on his part of Talcott or an examination of BarChris's correspondence with Talcott in April and May 1961 would have apprised him of the true facts. It would have led him to appreciate that the statement in this prospectus, carried over from earlier prospectuses, to the effect that since 1955 BarChris had been required to repurchase less than one-half of one per cent of discounted customers' notes could no longer properly be made without further explanation.

Grant was entitled to rely on Peat, Marwick for the 1960 figures. He had no reasonable ground to believe them to be inaccurate. But the matters which I have mentioned were not within the expertised portion of the prospectus. As to this, Grant was obliged to make a reasonable investigation. I am forced to find that he did not make one. After making all due allowances for the fact that BarChris's officers misled him, there are too many instances in which Grant failed to make an inquiry which he could easily have made which, if pursued, would have put him on his guard. In my opinion, this finding on the evidence in this case does not establish an unreasonably high standard in other cases for company counsel who are also directors. Each case must rest on its own facts. I conclude that Grant has not established his due diligence defenses except as to the audited 1960 figures.

The Underwriters and Coleman

The underwriters other than Drexel made no investigation of the accuracy of the prospectus. One of them, Peter Morgan, had underwritten the 1959 stock issue and had been a director of BarChris. He thus had some general familiarity with its affairs, but he knew no more than the other underwriters about the debenture prospectus. They all relied upon Drexel as the "lead" underwriter.

Drexel did make an investigation. The work was in charge of Coleman, a partner of the firm, assisted by Casperson, an associate. Drexel's attorneys acted as attorneys for the entire group of underwriters. Ballard did the work, assisted by Stanton.

On April 17, 1961 Coleman became a director of BarChris. He signed the first amendment to the registration statement filed on May 11 and the second amendment, constituting the registration statement in its final form, filed on May 16. He thereby assumed a responsibility as a director and signer in addition to his responsibility as an underwriter.

The facts as to the extent of the investigation that Coleman made may be briefly summarized. He was first introduced to BarChris on September 15, 1960. Thereafter he familiarized himself with general conditions in the industry, primarily by reading reports and prospectuses of the two leading bowling alley builders, American Machine & Foundry Company and Brunswick. These indicated that the industry was still growing. He also acquired general information on BarChris by reading the 1959 stock prospectus, annual reports for prior years, and an unaudited statement for the first half of 1960. He inquired about BarChris of certain of its banks and of Talcott and received favorable replies.

The purpose of this preliminary investigation was to enable Coleman to decide whether Drexel would undertake the financing. It did not have direct reference to any specific registration statement for at that time, of course, none had been prepared. Coleman was sufficiently optimistic about BarChris's prospects to buy 1,000 shares of its stock, which he did in December 1960.

On January 24, 1961, Coleman held a meeting with Ballard, Grant and Kircher, among others. By that time Coleman had about decided to go ahead with the financing, although Drexel's formal letter of intent was not delivered until February 9, 1961 (subsequently revised on March 7, 1961). At this meeting Coleman asked Kircher how BarChris intended to use the proceeds of the financing. In reply to this inquiry, Kircher wrote a letter to Coleman dated January 30, 1961 outlining BarChris's plans. This eventually formed the basis of the application of proceeds section in the prospectus.

Coleman continued his general investigation. He obtained a Dun & Bradstreet report on BarChris on March 16, 1961. He read BarChris's annual report for 1960 which was available in March.

By mid-March, Coleman was in a position to make more specific inquiries. By that time Grant had prepared a first draft of the prospectus, consisting of a marked-up copy of the January 1961 warrant prospectus. Coleman attended three meetings to discuss the prospectus with BarChris's representatives. The meetings were held in Perkins, Daniels' office on March 20, March 23 and March 24, 1961. Those present included Grant or his partner McCormack and Kircher for the company, and Coleman, Casperson and Ballard for the underwriters.

Logan, Peat, Marwick's manager of the 1960 audit, was present at one of the meetings.

At these discussions, which were extensive, successive proofs of the prospectus were considered and revised. At this point the 1961 figures were not available. They were put in the prospectus in May.

* * *

After Coleman was elected a director on April 17, 1961, he made no further independent investigation of the accuracy of the prospectus. He assumed that Ballard was taking care of this on his behalf as well as on behalf of the underwriters.

In April 1961 Ballard instructed Stanton to examine BarChris's minutes for the past five years and also to look at "the major contracts of the company."[23] Stanton went to BarChris's office for that purpose on April 24. He asked Birnbaum for the minute books. He read the minutes of the board of directors and discovered interleaved in them a few minutes of executive committee meetings in 1960. He asked Kircher if there were any others. Kircher said that there had been other executive committee meetings but that the minutes had not been written up.

Stanton read the minutes of a few BarChris subsidiaries. His testimony was vague as to which ones. He had no recollection of seeing the minutes of Capitol Lanes, Inc. or Biel or Parkway Lanes, Inc. He did not discover that BarChris was operating Capitol or that it planned to operate Bridge and Yonkers.

As to the "major contracts," all that Stanton could remember seeing was an insurance policy. Birnbaum told him that there was no file of major contracts. Stanton did not examine the agreements with Talcott. He did not examine the contracts with customers. He did not look to see what contracts comprised the backlog figure. Stanton examined no accounting records of BarChris. His visit, which lasted one day, was devoted primarily to reading the directors' minutes.

On April 25 Ballard wrote to Grant about certain matters which Stanton had noted on his visit to BarChris the day before, none of which Ballard considered "very earth shaking." As far as relevant here, these were (1) Russo's remark as recorded in the executive committee minutes of November 3, 1960 to the effect that because of customers' defaults, BarChris might find itself in the business of operating alleys; (2) the fact that the minutes of Sanpark Realty Corporation were incomplete; and (3) the fact that minutes of the executive committee were missing.

On May 9, 1961, Ballard came to New York and conferred with Grant and Kircher. They discussed the Securities and Exchange Commission's deficiency letter of May 4, 1961 which required the inclusion in the prospectus of certain additional information, notably net sales,

23. Stanton was a very junior associate. He had been admitted to the bar in January 1961, some three months before. This was the first registration statement he had ever worked on.

gross profits and net earnings figures for the first quarter of 1961. They also discussed the points raised in Ballard's letter to Grant of April 25. As to the latter, most of the conversation related to what Russo had meant by his remark on November 3, 1960. Kircher said that the delinquency problem was less severe now than it had been back in November 1960, that no alleys had been repossessed, and that although he was "worried about one alley in Harlem" (Dreyfuss), that was a "special situation." Grant reported that Russo had told him that his statement on November 3, 1960 was "merely hypothetical." On the strength of this conversation, Ballard was satisfied that the one-half of one per cent figure in the prospectus did not need qualification or elaboration.

As to the missing minutes, Kircher said that those of Sanpark were not significant and that the executive committee meetings for which there were no written minutes were concerned only with "routine matters."

It must be remembered that this conference took place only one week before the registration statement became effective. Ballard did nothing else in the way of checking during that intervening week.

Ballard did not insist that the executive committee minutes be written up so that he could inspect them, although he testified that he knew from experience that executive committee minutes may be extremely important. If he had insisted, he would have found the minutes highly informative, as has previously been pointed out. Ballard did not ask to see BarChris's schedule of delinquencies or Talcott's notices of delinquencies, or BarChris's correspondence with Talcott.

Ballard did not examine BarChris's contracts with Talcott. He did not appreciate what Talcott's rights were under those financing agreements or how serious the effect would be upon BarChris of any exercise of those rights.

Ballard did not investigate the composition of the backlog figure to be sure that it was not "puffy." He made no inquiry after March about any new officers' loans, although he knew that Kircher had insisted on a provision in the indenture which gave loans from individuals priority over the debentures. He was unaware of the seriousness of BarChris's cash position and of how BarChris's officers intended to use a large part of the proceeds. He did not know that BarChris was operating Capitol Lanes.

Like Grant, Ballard, without checking, relied on the information which he got from Kircher. He also relied on Grant who, as company counsel, presumably was familiar with its affairs.

The formal opinion which Ballard's firm rendered to the underwriters at the closing on May 24, 1961 made clear that this is what he had done. The opinion stated (italics supplied):

> "In the course of the preparation of the Registration Statement and Prospectus by the Company, we have had numerous conferences

with representatives of and counsel for the Company and with its auditors and we have raised many questions regarding the business of the Company. Satisfactory answers to such questions were in each case given us, and all other information and documents we requested have been supplied. We are of the opinion that the *data presented* to us are accurately reflected in the Registration Statement and Prospectus and that there has been omitted from the Registration Statement no material facts *included in such data.* Although *we have not otherwise verified* the completeness or accuracy of the information furnished to us, on the basis of the foregoing and with the exception of the financial statements and schedules (which this opinion does not pass upon), we have no reason to believe that the Registration Statement or Prospectus contains any untrue statement of any material fact or omits to state a material fact required to be stated therein or necessary in order to make the statements therein not misleading."

Coleman testified that Drexel had an understanding with its attorneys that "we expect them to inspect on our behalf the corporate records of the company including, but not limited to, the minutes of the corporation, the stockholders and the committees of the board authorized to act for the board." Ballard manifested his awareness of this understanding by sending Stanton to read the minutes and the major contracts. It is difficult to square this understanding with the formal opinion of Ballard's firm which expressly disclaimed any attempt to verify information supplied by the company and its counsel.

In any event, it is clear that no effectual attempt at verification was made. The question is whether due diligence required that it be made. Stated another way, is it sufficient to ask questions, to obtain answers which, if true, would be thought satisfactory, and to let it go at that, without seeking to ascertain from the records whether the answers in fact are true and complete?

I have already held that this procedure is not sufficient in Grant's case. Are underwriters in a different position, as far as due diligence is concerned?

The underwriters say that the prospectus is the company's prospectus, not theirs. Doubtless this is the way they customarily regard it. But the Securities Act makes no such distinction. The underwriters are just as responsible as the company if the prospectus is false. And prospective investors rely upon the reputation of the underwriters in deciding whether to purchase the securities.

There is no direct authority on this question, no judicial decision defining the degree of diligence which underwriters must exercise to establish their defense under Section 11.

There is some authority in New York for the proposition that a director of a corporation may rely upon information furnished him by the officers without independently verifying it. See Litwin v. Allen, 25 N.Y.S.2d 667 (Sup.Ct.1940).

In support of that principle, the court in Litwin (25 N.Y.S.2d at 719) quoted from the opinion of Lord Halsbury in Dovey v. Cory, [1901] App.Cas. 477, 486, in which he said:

> "The business of life could not go on if people could not trust those who are put into a position of trust for the express purpose of attending to details of management."

Of course, New York law does not govern this case. The construction of the Securities Act is a matter of federal law. But the underwriters argue that *Litwin* is still in point, for they say that it establishes a standard of reasonableness for the reasonably prudent director which should be the same as the standard for the reasonably prudent underwriter under the Securities Act.

In my opinion the two situations are not analogous. An underwriter has not put the company's officers "into a position of trust for the express purpose of attending to details of management." The underwriters did not select them. In a sense, the positions of the underwriter and the company's officers are adverse. It is not unlikely that statements made by company officers to an underwriter to induce him to underwrite may be self-serving. They may be unduly enthusiastic. As in this case, they may, on occasion, be deliberately false.

The purpose of Section 11 is to protect investors. To that end the underwriters are made responsible for the truth of the prospectus. If they may escape that responsibility by taking at face value representations made to them by the company's management, then the inclusion of underwriters among those liable under Section 11 affords the investors no additional protection. To effectuate the statute's purpose, the phrase "reasonable investigation" must be construed to require more effort on the part of the underwriters than the mere accurate reporting in the prospectus of "data presented" to them by the company. It should make no difference that this data is elicited by questions addressed to the company officers by the underwriters, or that the underwriters at the time believe that the company's officers are truthful and reliable. In order to make the underwriters' participation in this enterprise of any value to the investors, the underwriters must make some reasonable attempt to verify the data submitted to them. They may not rely solely on the company's officers or on the company's counsel. A prudent man in the management of his own property would not rely on them.

It is impossible to lay down a rigid rule suitable for every case defining the extent to which such verification must go. It is a question of degree, a matter of judgment in each case. In the present case, the underwriters' counsel made almost no attempt to verify management's representations. I hold that that was insufficient.

On the evidence in this case, I find that the underwriters' counsel did not make a reasonable investigation of the truth of those portions of the prospectus which were not made on the authority of Peat, Marwick as an expert. Drexel is bound by their failure. It is not a matter of relying upon counsel for legal advice. Here the attorneys were dealing with matters of fact. Drexel delegated to them, as its agent, the business of examining the corporate minutes and contracts. It must bear the consequences of their failure to make an adequate examination.

The other underwriters, who did nothing and relied solely on Drexel and on the lawyers, are also bound by it. It follows that although Drexel and the other underwriters believed that those portions of the prospectus were true, they had no reasonable ground for that belief, within the meaning of the statute. Hence, they have not established their due diligence defense, except as to the 1960 audited figures.[26]

The same conclusions must apply to Coleman. Although he participated quite actively in the earlier stages of the preparation of the prospectus, and contributed questions and warnings of his own, in addition to the questions of counsel, the fact is that he stopped his participation toward the end of March 1961. He made no investigation after he became a director. When it came to verification, he relied upon his counsel to do it for him. Since counsel failed to do it, Coleman is bound by that failure. Consequently, in his case also, he has not established his due diligence defense except as to the audited 1960 figures.

PEAT, MARWICK

Section 11(b) provides:

> "Notwithstanding the provisions of subsection (a) no person * * * shall be liable as provided therein who shall sustain the burden of proof—
>
> * * *
>
> "(3) that * * * (B) as regards any part of the registration statement purporting to be made upon his authority as an expert * * * (i) he had, after reasonable investigation, reasonable ground to believe and did believe, at the time such part of the registration statement became effective, that the statements therein were true and that there was no omission to state a material fact required to be stated therein or necessary to make the statements therein not misleading * * *."

This defines the due diligence defense for an expert. Peat, Marwick has pleaded it.

The part of the registration statement purporting to be made upon the authority of Peat, Marwick as an expert was, as we have seen, the 1960 figures. But because the statute requires the court to determine Peat, Marwick's belief, and the grounds thereof, "at the time such part of the registration statement became effective," for the purposes of this affirmative defense, the matter must be viewed as of May 16, 1961, and

26. In view of this conclusion, it becomes unnecessary to decide whether the underwriters other than Drexel would have been protected if Drexel had established that, as lead underwriter, it made a reasonable investigation.

the question is whether at that time Peat, Marwick, after reasonable investigation, had reasonable ground to believe and did believe that the 1960 figures were true and that no material fact had been omitted from the registration statement which should have been included in order to make the 1960 figures not misleading. In deciding this issue, the court must consider not only what Peat, Marwick did in its 1960 audit, but also what it did in its subsequent "S–1 review." The proper scope of that review must also be determined.

It may be noted that we are concerned at this point only with the question of Peat, Marwick's liability to plaintiffs. At the closing on May 24, 1961, Peat, Marwick delivered a so-called "comfort letter" to the underwriters. This letter stated:

> "It is understood that this letter is for the information of the underwriters and is not to be quoted or referred to, in whole or in part, in the Registration Statement or Prospectus or in any literature used in connection with the sale of securities."

Plaintiffs may not take advantage of any undertakings or representations in this letter. If they exceeded the normal scope of an S–1 review (a question which I do not now decide) that is a matter which relates only to the crossclaims which defendants have asserted against each other and which I have postponed for determination at a later date.

THE 1960 AUDIT

Peat, Marwick's work was in general charge of a member of the firm, Cummings, and more immediately in charge of Peat, Marwick's manager, Logan. Most of the actual work was performed by a senior accountant, Berardi, who had junior assistants, one of whom was Kennedy.

Berardi was then about thirty years old. He was not yet a C.P.A. He had had no previous experience with the bowling industry. This was his first job as a senior accountant. He could hardly have been given a more difficult assignment.

After obtaining a little background information on BarChris by talking to Logan and reviewing Peat, Marwick's work papers on its 1959 audit, Berardi examined the results of test checks of BarChris's accounting procedures which one of the junior accountants had made, and he prepared an "internal control questionnaire" and an "audit program." Thereafter, for a few days subsequent to December 30, 1960, he inspected BarChris's inventories and examined certain alley construction. Finally, on January 13, 1961, he began his auditing work which he carried on substantially continuously until it was completed on February 24, 1961. Toward the close of the work, Logan reviewed it and made various comments and suggestions to Berardi.

It is unnecessary to recount everything that Berardi did in the course of the audit. We are concerned only with the evidence relating to what Berardi did or did not do with respect to those items which I have found to have been incorrectly reported in the 1960 figures in the prospectus. More narrowly, we are directly concerned only with such of those items as I have found to be material. [The court here describes the procedures followed by Berardi, and the items he failed to discover.]

In substance, what Berardi did is similar to what Grant and Ballard did. He asked questions, he got answers which he considered satisfactory, and he did nothing to verify them. For example, he obtained from Trilling a list of contracts. The list included Yonkers and Bridge. Since Berardi did not read the minutes of subsidiaries, he did not learn that Yonkers and Bridge were intercompany sales. The list also included Woonsocket and the six T-Bowl jobs, Moravia Road, Milford, Groton, North Attleboro, Odenton and Severna Park. Since Berardi did not look at any contract documents, and since he was unaware of the executive committee minutes of March 18, 1961 (at that time embodied only in Kircher's notes), he did not learn that BarChris had no contracts for these jobs. Trilling's list did not set forth contract prices for them, although it did for Yonkers, Bridge and certain others. This did not arouse Berardi's suspicion.

Berardi noticed that there had been an increase in notes payable by BarChris. Trilling admitted to him that BarChris was "a bit slow" in paying its bills. Berardi recorded in his notes of his review that BarChris was in a "tight cash position." Trilling's explanation was that BarChris was experiencing "some temporary difficulty."

Berardi had no conception of how tight the cash position was. He did not discover that BarChris was holding up checks in substantial amounts because there was no money in the bank to cover them. He did not know of the loan from Manufacturers Trust Company or of the officers' loans. Since he never read the prospectus, he was not even aware that there had ever been any problem about loans from officers.

During the 1960 audit Berardi had obtained some information from factors, not sufficiently detailed even then, as to delinquent notes. He made no inquiry of factors about this in his S–1 review. Since he knew nothing about Kircher's notes of the executive committee meetings, he did not learn that the delinquency situation had grown worse. He was content with Trilling's assurance that no liability theretofore contingent had become direct.

Apparently the only BarChris officer with whom Berardi communicated was Trilling. He could not recall making any inquiries of Russo, Vitolo or Pugliese. As to Kircher, Berardi's testimony was self-contradictory. At one point he said that he had inquired of Kircher and at another he said that he could not recall making any such inquiry.

There had been a material change for the worse in BarChris's financial position. That change was sufficiently serious so that the failure to disclose it made the 1960 figures misleading. Berardi did not discover it. As far as results were concerned, his S–1 review was useless.

Accountants should not be held to a standard higher than that recognized in their profession. I do not do so here. Berardi's review did not come up to that standard. He did not take some of the steps which Peat, Marwick's written program prescribed. He did not spend an adequate amount of time on a task of this magnitude. Most important of all, he, was too easily satisfied with glib answers to his inquiries.

This is not to say that he should have made a complete audit. But there were enough danger signals in the materials which he did examine to require some further investigation on his part. Generally accepted accounting standards required such further investigation under these circumstances. It is not always sufficient merely to ask questions.

Here again, the burden of proof is on Peat, Marwick. I find that that burden has not been satisfied. I conclude that Peat, Marwick has not established its due diligence defense.

In LANZA v. DREXEL, 479 F.2d 1277 (2d Cir.1979), a Rule 10b–5 claim was brought by purchasers of BarChris common stock, claiming reliance on the misstatements in the registration materials. Since the common stock was not part of the registered offering, these plaintiffs could not bring suit under § 11. The Second Circuit affirmed the imposition of Rule 10b–5 liability upon three of the BarChris insiders (Russo, Vitolo, and Kircher) but dismissed the claims against Coleman and Ballard (Drexel's counsel) due to the failure to establish a conspiracy with the primary violators. Pugliese was found to be neither primarily nor secondarily liable in the Rule 10b–5 action. Secondary liability of aiders and abettors under Rule 10b–5 is discussed at pp. 455–462, 541–548 below.

Compare the standard of care required under § 11 of the 1933 Act with the "due care" defense in actions under § 12(2) of the 1933 Act. See JOHN NUVEEN & CO. v. SANDERS, 450 U.S. 1005 (1981) (Powell, dissenting), p. 376 below.

FEIT v. LEASCO DATA PROCESSING EQUIPMENT CORP.

332 F.Supp. 544 (E.D.N.Y.1971).

WEINSTEIN, DISTRICT JUDGE.

[As set forth in the portion of the opinion reproduced earlier in this Chapter, the court held that the failure to include an estimate of Reliance's "surplus surplus", in the registration statement for an exchange offer of Leasco securities to Reliance shareholders, was an omission of a material fact giving rise to civil liability under § 11. The court then turned to the question of the "due diligence" defense available to individual defendants.]

* * *

D. DUE DILIGENCE OF THE DIRECTORS—STEINBERG, SCHWARTZ & HODES

Before analyzing the due diligence defenses presented by these defendants we must consider whether they are all properly treated together. Steinberg and Schwartz are and were, respectively, Chief Executive Officer and President of Leasco—clearly "inside" directors. Hodes is a partner in the law firm which represents Leasco; he held no management office.

The leading case of Escott v. BarChris Construction Corp., 283 F.Supp. 643 (S.D.N.Y.1968) drew a distinction between directors who were officers of BarChris and its director-lawyer, Grant, who occupied a position analogous to Hodes' at Leasco. Judge McLean treated Grant as an "outside" director despite the fact that he had been a director for eight months prior to the public offering in question and had prepared the registration statement. The court then held Grant to a very high standard of independent investigation of the registration statement because of his peculiar expertise and access to information and held him liable for failure to meet that standard.

The assignment of "outside director" status to the lawyer in BarChris represented the court's conclusions on the facts peculiar to BarChris. It does not preclude a finding that "in some cases the attorney-director may be so deeply involved that he is really an insider." Folk, Civil Liabilities Under the Federal Securities Acts—the *BarChris* Case, 1 Securities L.Rev. 3, 39 (1969) (reprinted from 55 Va.L. Rev. 1 (1969)). This is the case presented by Hodes.

Hodes has been a director of Leasco since 1965—three years or more at the time of this registration statement. He participated extensively in the discussions leading up to the exchange offer for Reliance shares as early as the fall of 1967 and was constantly involved in the deal throughout both the preliminary and execution stages of the transaction. He, or a representative of his law firm, attended all meetings and was consulted on all matters pertaining to this acquisition. He was directly responsible for preparation of the registration statement and initiated all of the research regarding reorganization of Reliance and separation of its surplus surplus. He kept Leasco's Schwartz apprised of the progress on possible alternatives for Reliance. The testimony and exhibits at this trial make it clear that insofar as surplus surplus is concerned Hodes was so intimately involved in this registration process that to treat him as anything but an insider would involve a gross distortion of the realities of Leasco's management.

* * *

In BarChris the management directors were found to have known about the misrepresentations and therefore the only question of reasonable investigation arose in the context of non-insider verification of information provided by those inside directors. These standards nevertheless apply equally to insider verification of the accuracy and completeness of data and statements they propose to include in the registration statement. Inclusion or omission of an item without a reasonable investigation or verification will lead to liability for these inside directors just as surely as if they actually knew of the inaccuracy or had no reasonable belief in the accuracy.

What constitutes "reasonable investigation" and a "reasonable ground to believe" will vary with the degree of involvement of the individual, his expertise, and his access to the pertinent information and data. What is reasonable for one director may not be reasonable for another by virtue of their differing positions.

> "It was clear from the outset, however, that the duty of each potentially liable group was not the same. The House report on the bill that became the original Securities Act stated that the duty of care to discover varied in its demands upon the participants with the importance of their place in the scheme of distribution and the degree of protection that the public had a right to expect from them. It has been suggested that although inside directors might be better able to show that they undertook some investigation, the outside director could more easily demonstrate that the investigation he actually undertook was sufficient to sustain his defense." Comment, BarChris: Due Diligence Refined, 68 Colum.L.Rev. 1411, 1416 (1968).

Inside directors with intimate knowledge of corporate affairs and of the particular transactions will be expected to make a more complete investigation and have more extensive knowledge of facts supporting or contradicting inclusions in the registration statements than outside directors. Similarly, accountants and underwriters are expected to investigate to various degrees. Each must undertake that investigation which a reasonably prudent man in that position would conduct.

BarChris imposes such stringent requirements of knowledge of corporate affairs on inside directors that one is led to the conclusion that liability will lie in practically all cases of misrepresentation. Their liability approaches that of the issuer as guarantor of the accuracy of the prospectus.

> "This ruling suggests that an inside director who, either as an officer or in some other capacity, has intimate familiarity with the corporate affairs or handles major transactions, especially those as to which false statements or omissions appear in the prospectus, is least able to establish due diligence. *BarChris* indicates that for such an individual knowledge of the underlying facts precludes showing 'reasonable ground to believe' or belief in fact as to the truth of the nonexpert statements. In substance, there is a strong though theoretically rebuttable presumption that he had no reasonable ground to believe or belief in fact that the registration statement was accurate. Since an individual so situated will also have difficulty showing an absence of reasonable grounds of belief or belief in fact that expertised portions

contain no misleading statements or omissions, a similar although less weighty presumption is present there. It would be fair to say that this postulated presumption arises when the intimate connection of the individual with the affairs of the issuer is demonstrated. Such an individual comes close to the status of a guarantor of accuracy." Folk, Civil Liabilities Under the Federal Securities Acts: The *BarChris* Case, 1 Securities L.Rev. 3, 25 (1969) (reprinted from 55 Va.L.Rev. 1 (1969)).

Comment, BarChris: Due Diligence Refined, 68 Colum.L.Rev. 1411, 1420 (1968). It is with this strict standard in mind that we must approach the question of whether these three inside directors have established their defenses.

As already indicated, defendants' principal claim is that they considered including an estimate and decided against such action because of the uncertainties of computation. Steinberg and Hodes were both convinced, according to their testimony, that the estimates they had obtained were not reliable and that a reliable one could not be achieved with the data available. The key to all of their arguments is the unavailability of Reliance's management and the Pennsylvania Insurance Commissioner. We find that the director-defendants failed to fulfill their duty of reasonable investigation and that they had no reasonable ground to believe that an omission of an estimate of surplus surplus was not materially misleading. * * *

(2) Hostility of Roberts.

Defendants also argue that the management of Reliance, particularly Roberts, was so hostile to the exchange offer that the information necessary to calculate surplus surplus accurately was unavailable throughout the entire exchange offer period. They further contend that this hostility denied them standing before the Insurance Commissioner and hence his approval of a meaningful approximation. The facts of Roberts' relationship with Leasco do not support this contention.

It is true that Roberts evinced considerable hostility to both the exchange offer and Leasco prior to August 1, 1968. Peace was made on that date at a considerable financial gain to Roberts and cooperation began at once and increased in intensity.

The Court can reach but one conclusion in the face of the facts set out in Part IV B, supra—Roberts would have cooperated in the calculation of an amount of surplus surplus after August 1, 1968 if he had been asked. He testified that he could have arrived at an estimate "damn quickly" if necessary, and it is our finding based on his testimony, our observation of him on the stand, and the sense of the situation that he would have done so—or at least would have provided the information necessary for such a calculation. * * *

We find that these three defendants did not have reasonable ground to believe that omission of an estimate of surplus surplus from the registration statement was justified on the ground that they did not have access to the pertinent data on Reliance or entire to the Insurance Commissioner. Roberts would have provided both had he been asked. They ignored this fact in concluding that an accurate estimate of surplus surplus could not be developed by Leasco. They failed to exercise that high degree of care imposed upon them by Section 11.

(3) Lack of Adequate Inquiry.

Even if both of our prior conclusions regarding the lack of reasonable ground to believe in the accuracy of the registration statement were in error, these insider-defendants have nevertheless failed in their duty to reasonably investigate the accuracy of the prospectus. The uncontroverted testimony of two of the defendants themselves—Steinberg and Hodes—was that neither they nor anyone else in Leasco ever attempted to obtain a computation of surplus surplus beyond those of Leasco's Gibbs.

Surplus surplus was a crucial element of the plan to acquire Reliance. Yet, no one connected with Leasco commissioned an estimate by an insurance consultant; no one asked any Leasco employee to calculate it; Hodes never ordered one of his law firm's associates to attempt to arrive at a figure; and certainly no one made inquiry of the one man who could have easily produced a figure—Roberts.

These defendants proceeded on the assumption that they could not arrive at an accurate figure without making the attempt. They may have failed—although we do not believe they would have—but they were bound by their duties under Section 11 to attempt to verify their conclusion that it was not calculable. It is this sort of laxity and oversight to which the requirement of reasonable investigation is directed and which Judge McLean held unacceptable in *BarChris.* By assiduously proving that they never had figures other than those previously alluded to these defendants have persuaded the court that they failed to vindicate their responsibility of due diligence.

Nor can it be argued that they need not have attempted the computation or made any inquiry because such gestures would have been futile. Roberts testified that any one knowledgeable in the insurance field might have arrived at a considered figure. Section 11 requires an attempt to make use of such expertise. Hodes, Schwartz and Steinberg are liable along with the issuer, Leasco.

E. Due Diligence of the Dealer-Managers—White, Weld & Co. and Lehman Brothers

Section 11 holds underwriters to the same burden of establishing reasonable investigation and reasonable ground to believe the accuracy of the registration statement. The courts must be particularly scrupulous in examining the conduct of underwriters since they are supposed to assume an opposing posture with respect to management. The average investor probably assumes that some issuers will lie, but he probably has somewhat more confidence in the average level of morality of an underwriter who has established a reputation for fair dealing.

* * *

Dealer-managers cannot, of course, be expected to possess the intimate knowledge of corporate affairs of inside directors, and their duty to investigate should be considered in light of their more limited access. Nevertheless they are expected to exercise a high degree of care in investigation and independent verification of the company's representations. Tacit reliance on management assertions is unacceptable; the underwriters must play devil's advocate.

We find that the dealer-managers have just barely established that they reasonably investigated the surplus surplus concept as it related to Reliance and that they had reasonable ground to believe that omission of a specific figure was justified.

The evidence indicates a thorough review of all available financial data by White, Weld & Co. and its counsel. They independently examined Leasco's audit and the report of an actuary on Reliance. They made searching inquiries of Leasco's major bank. Whitney, counsel to the dealer-managers, undertook a study of Leasco's corporate minutes, records and major agreements.

Regarding surplus surplus, the dealer-managers were particularly careful in their inquiries of Leasco. Stone of White, Weld had considerable prior experience with surplus surplus. He was fully aware of the complexity of the computation problem. The Netter Report, Gibbs' Memorandum and New York Insurance Department Report were all referred to at the due diligence meetings held late in June and early in July of 1968 in New York where representatives of Leasco and the dealer-managers reviewed the proposed registration statement line by line. Based on these reports and on his own expertise, Stone briefed Whitney, lead counsel for the underwriters.

Whitney and Stone were informed by Leasco that Roberts was hostile to the exchange offer—which, in fact, was the case in early July when these meetings were held; that he would not cooperate by providing either information or an estimate of his own; and that he would not verify the approximations they already had in their possession. This assertion was reinforced by Roberts' June 24, 1968 letter to his shareholders urging them "not to act in haste" and by his May 15, 1968 letter concerning his intention to form a holding company for Reliance. Counsel for White, Weld was also aware of Hodes' June 24, 1968 telegram to Roberts requesting cooperation in the preparation of a registration statement and of Roberts' reply of July 1, indicating that Reliance would not then comply.

Based on the information supplied by Leasco and confirmed by examination of these documents, Whitney rightly concluded that as of July 5th Roberts would not cooperate either by providing an opinion, by furnishing the critical data, or by verifying the estimates included in the Netter Report and Gibbs' Memorandum. In his opinion surplus surplus could not then be calculated with any accuracy.

The underwriters did not themselves contact Roberts because they had ascertained to their satisfaction that he would not be cooperative. Throughout July, Whitney and Stone were in constant contact with Leasco representatives regarding the progress of the exchange offer. During this period they received yet further verification of Roberts' intransigence which reconfirmed Whitney's opinion and certainly could not have provided a reasonable ground to reject his earlier conclusion. First, they learned of the subsequent requests for information directed to Roberts on July 9 and July 12 and of his evasion of such inquiries on July 15. They were, of course, aware that Roberts had filed a law suit seeking to inhibit any exchange offer. Finally, any doubt which may have lingered regarding Roberts' attitude was dispelled by his July 23rd letter of opposition to his shareholders in which he discussed in detail the reasons why the offer should be rejected.

We find, therefore, that it is somewhat more probable than not that as of August 1, 1968 the dealer-managers had sufficient verification of their previous conclusion concerning the possibility of accurately computing surplus surplus. They still had reasonable ground to believe that omission of such a figure was not misleading.

The dealer-managers were, however, undoubtedly aware of the August 1st contract between the Reliance management and Leasco and absent any further verification, their failure to recognize the implications of this agreement might well create liability for the same reasons expressed in our discussion of the defenses of the directors. But Whitney was in continuous contact with Leasco after August 1st and was apparently never disabused of the notion that Roberts remained recalcitrant. This view was conclusively buttressed by receipt of a copy of a letter dated August 13, 1968 from Kenneth J. Bialkin of Wilkie, Farr & Gallagher to the SEC, set forth in Part VI, supra, stating that Reliance officials "have * * * declined to furnish information." Receipt of this letter served to reconfirm Whitney's belief that neither data nor advice would be forthcoming from Roberts. The registration statement became effective six days later, on August 19, 1968.

Though the finding might have gone the other way, on balance we conclude that the dealer-managers conducted a reasonable investigation and reasonably verified Leasco's representations that access to Reliance's management was precluded by Roberts' attitude. We note in passing that neither of the underwriters had their names on the January, 1969 Leasco prospectus which did rely on the $125 million estimate of surplus surplus.

Both White, Weld & Co. and Lehman Brothers have established their due diligence defenses with regard to this registration statement.

On the basis of the *BarChris* and *Leasco* decisions, how would you define the "due diligence" responsibilities of:

— the chief executive officer of the issuer?

— the chief financial officer?

— a director who is also an officer?

— a director who is a partner in the law firm that acts as counsel to the issuer?

— a director whose principal business activity is as an officer of another company?

— the issuer's independent accountants?

— the managing underwriter?

— the other underwriters?

— counsel to the underwriters?

What should each of them examine to satisfy their responsibilities? Which of them can delegate which responsibilities to which others?

With respect to the question left open by the court in the *BarChris* case (see note 26) as to whether all the underwriters could escape liability if the managing underwriter exercised due diligence, one court has implied that they could. In IN RE GAP STORES SECURITIES LITIGATION, 79 F.R.D. 283 (N.D.Cal.1978), the court held that the 91 underwriters of a securities issue could, on plaintiff's motion, be certified as a defendant class in an action under § 11, since "the interests of the managing and participating underwriters are nearly identical. * * * [P]roof of the due diligence of the managing underwriter will most likely exonerate the participants as well." The court noted that the SEC had taken the position that each participating underwriter "must satisfy himself that the managing underwriter makes the kind of investigation the participant would have performed if he were the manager," but felt that this "would produce an absurd result, since it would hold the participant liable for failure to investigate the manager's methods, which if he had done so would have proven to him that the manager had acted with due diligence."

Section 11(a) imposes liability on the signers of the registration statement (which includes the issuer as well as the officers specified in § 6), directors, experts, and underwriters. In most cases, § 11 defendants would not qualify as sellers of the securities so as to also be potentially liable under § 12. But what about § 10(b) and Rule 10b–5 of the Exchange Act? § 10(b) can be used to impose liability provided the defendant has acted with scienter, which imposes on plaintiff a higher burden of proof than that required by § 11. However, in LANZA v. DREXEL & CO., 479 F.2d 1277 (2d Cir.1973), the court affirmed dismissal of § 10(b) claims against individuals who were not insiders of the issuer.

On appropriate facts, § 10(b) can be used to support a claim of aiding and abetting liability. Unlike § 10(b) and SEC Rule 10b-5, §§ 11 and 12 of the 1933 Act specify who is a proper defendant. Can § 11 liability be extended to collateral participants who have been a substantial factor in creating the misleading registration materials? The language of the statute presents a strong argument in favor of a negative answer. Secondary liability of aiders and abettors under Rule 10b-5 is discussed at pp. 455-462, 541-548 below.

The integrated disclosure system implemented by the Commission in March 1982 (see p. 71 above) permits issuers using Form S-2 or S-3 to incorporate by reference in their 1933 Act registration statements information contained in their reports to shareholders and reports and other documents filed with the Commission under the 1934 Act. Liability under § 11 of the 1933 Act of course extends to the materials so incorporated and thus raises a question as to how directors, underwriters and others can meet the test of "due diligence" with respect to those materials. The Commission addressed this question in one of the releases proposing the new system:

CIRCUMSTANCES AFFECTING THE DETERMINATION OF REASONABLE INVESTIGATION UNDER SECTION 11 OF THE SECURITIES ACT

Sec. Act Rel. No. 6335 (Aug. 6, 1981).

Underwriters and others have expressed concern regarding their ability to discharge fully their responsibilities under Section 11 with respect to registration statements incorporating substantial information from periodic reports. Historically, preparation of the traditional Form S-1 registration statement began many weeks in advance of the proposed offering due to the time required to assemble and verify the information required to be set forth in the registration statement and prospectus. During this time, underwriters, directors and others conducted the necessary due diligence inquiries which, as a matter of prudence, were substantially completed before the initial filing of the registration statement. In contrast, integrated short form registration statements rely, to the maximum extent possible, on information contained in previously filed Exchange Act reports or in the annual report to security holders. Information actually set forth in the short form registration statement pertains primarily to the proposed transaction, the use of proceeds and the updating of information in incorporated documents. Preparation time is reduced sharply, as is the period of time between the issuer's decision to undertake a securities offering and the filing of the registration statement with the Commission. Some commentators are fearful that this reduction in preparation time, together with competitive pressures, will restrict the ability of responsible underwriters to conduct what would be deemed to be a reasonable investigation, pursuant to Section 11, of the contents of the registration statement. They believe that issuers may be reluctant to wait for responsible underwriters to finish their inquiry, and may be receptive to offers from underwriters willing to do less.

Some underwriters also object to utilizing information in periodic reports for registration purposes, because it has been composed by persons without consultation with the underwriters who may, in turn, be held, in the context of a registration statement, to a higher standard of civil liability than that to which the original preparers may have been subject. Moreover, there is a perception that issuers may be reluctant to modify previously filed documents in instances where the underwriters question the quality of the disclosure and that this reluctance, again coupled with competitive pressures, will hinder due diligence activities.

Moreover, because Section 11 imposes liability for omissions or misstatements of material fact in any part of the registration statement when that part became effective, there has been concern that liability could be asserted based on information in a previously filed document which was accurate when filed but which had become outdated and subsequently was incorporated by reference into a registration statement.

Proposed Rule [415], allowing shelf registration, also has caused apprehension. Commentators on the rule as initially proposed believed that insufficient consideration had been given to the responsibilities of the persons involved in a shelf registration of a primary at the market equity offering under the new proposed Rule. For example, a shelf offering on proposed Form S-3 could involve automatic incorporation by reference into the registration statement of Exchange Act reports for a substantial period of time because the offering may be made on a delayed or continuous basis. In addition, if an underwriter is brought into a shelf offering after the initial effective date of the registration statement, the late-arriving underwriter would be responsible for the accuracy of the contents of the registration statement as of the time of his entry into the transaction.

* * *

The principal goal of integration is to simplify disclosure and reduce unnecessary repetition and redelivery of information which has already been provided, not to alter the roles of participants in the securities distribution process as originally contemplated by the Securities Act. The integrated disclosure system, past and proposed, is thus not designed to modify the responsibility of underwriters and others to make a reasonable investigation. Information presented in the registration statement, whether or not incorporated by reference, must be true and complete in all material respects and verified where appropriate. Likewise, nothing in the Commission's integrated disclosure system precludes conducting adequate due diligence. This point can be demonstrated by addressing the two principal concerns which have been raised.

First, as discussed above, commentators have expressed concern about the short time involved in document preparation. There also may be a substantial reduction in the time taken for pre-effective review at the Commission. As to the latter point, however, commentators on the ABC Release themselves noted that due diligence generally is performed prior to filing with the Commission, rendering the time in registration largely irrelevant. As to the former point, there is nothing which compels an underwriter to proceed prematurely with an offering. Although, as discussed below, he may wish to arrange his due diligence procedures over time for the purpose of avoiding last minute delays in an offering environment characterized by rapid market changes, in the final analysis the underwriter is never compelled to proceed with an offering until he has accomplished his due diligence.

The second major concern relates to the fact that documents, prepared by others, often at a much earlier date, are incorporated by reference into the registration statement. Again, it must be emphasized that due diligence requires a reasonable investigation of all the information presented therein and any information incorporated by reference. If such material contains a material misstatement, or omits a material fact, then, in order to avoid liability, a subsequent document must be filed to correct the earlier one, or the information must be restated correctly in the registration statement. Nothing in the integrated disclosure system precludes such action.

The Commission specifically rejects the suggestion that the underwriter needs only to read the incorporated materials and discuss them with representatives of the registrant and named experts. Because the registrant would be the sole source of virtually all information, this approach would not, in and of itself, include the element of verification required by the case law and contemplated by the statute.

Thus, verification in appropriate circumstances is still required, and if a material misstatement or omission has been made, correction by amendment or restatement must be made. For example, a major supply contract on which the registrant is substantially dependent should be reviewed to avoid the possibility of inaccurate references to it in the prospectus. On the other hand, if the alleged misstatement in issue turns on an ambiguity or nuance in the drafted language of an incorporated document making it a close question as to whether a violation even has been committed, then the fact that a particular defendant did not participate in preparing the incorporated document, when combined with judgmental difficulties and practical concerns in making changes in prepared documents, would seem to be an appropriate factor in deciding whether "reasonable belief" in the accuracy of statements existed and thus in deciding whether to attach liability to a particular defendant's conduct.

* * *

V. Techniques of Due Diligence in an Integrated Disclosure System

Although the basic requirements of due diligence do not change in an integrated system, the manner in which due diligence may be accomplished can properly be expected to vary from traditional practice in some cases. To this end, underwriters and others can utilize various techniques. Historical models of due diligence have focused on efforts during the period of activity associated with preparing a registration statement, but the integrated disclosure system requires a broader focus. Issuers, underwriters and their counsel will necessarily be reevaluating all existing practices connected with effectuating the distribution of securities to develop procedures compatible with the integrated approach to registration.

In view of the compressed preparation time and the volatile nature of the capital markets, underwriters may elect to apply somewhat different, but equally thorough, investigatory practices and procedures to integrated registration statements. Unless the underwriter intends to reserve a specified period of time for investigation after the registration statement has been prepared but before filing, it will be necessary to develop in advance a reservoir of knowledge about the companies that may select the underwriter to distribute their securities registered on short form registration statements. To a considerable extent, broker-dealers already take this approach when they provide financial planning and investment advisory services to the investing public, as well as financial advice to companies themselves.

Extensive data about seasoned companies can be obtained with little effort. The periodic reports filed pursuant to the Exchange Act contain a wealth of information relating to subject issuer's financial performance, competitive position and future prospects. Other material developments are promptly reported on Form 8–K. Careful review of these filings on an ongoing basis not only facilitates a general familiarity with each issuer but should permit the underwriter to identify factors critical to the continuing success of the company. In many cases, the underwriters also have available analysts' reports to evaluate the issuer and its industry. With greater knowledge, the underwriter will be better prepared to question incomplete explanations, descriptions or reasoning and generally will be more sensitive to detecting and assessing material developments. The process of verification should be expedited as a result.

The issuer's investor relations program provides another opportunity for enhancing the underwriter's familiarity with the company. In particular, analysts and brokers meetings allow underwriters or potential underwriters to question members of management and to evaluate their skills and abilities. Discussion at such sessions can address recent transactions, events and economic results in relation to other companies in the same industry. When combined with the practice of furnishing detailed written analyses of material corporate events, these sessions can duplicate certain steps traditionally undertaken by the underwriter and issuer only during the preparation of the registration statement.

For directors, their continuing involvement in their company's activities must be considered. They receive reports, request information from management, meet periodically, and analyze, plan and participate in the company's business. These activities provide a strong basis for their evaluation of disclosure in a registration statement, and for considering what further due diligence is necessary on their part. In particular, their roles in reviewing the company's Form 10–K annual report and other Exchange Act filings are relevant to their due diligence for a registration statement incorporating those filings.

By developing a detailed familiarity with the company and the periodic reports it files with the Commission, the underwriter and others can minimize the number of additional tasks that must be performed in the context of a subsequent registered offering in order to meet the statutory standard of due diligence. When the short form registration statement is being prepared the underwriter's investigation then can proceed expeditiously and can be concluded at the earliest appropriate point in time. By way of comparison, a first time offering by a new or relatively unseasoned issuer requires the underwriter and other subject persons to engage in extensive data collection, analysis and independent inquiry during the preparation period for the long form registration statement.

In sum, under the Exchange Act a great deal of information about registered companies is both regularly furnished to the marketplace and also carefully analyzed by investment bankers, directors and others. Although perhaps not traditionally seen in this light, a close following of this information by investment bankers can be an important part of due diligence in the case of an underwritten offering and should expedite the remaining due diligence inquiries and verification.

Issuers eligible for short-form registration also can undertake specific steps designed to minimize the need for elaborate original investigations by underwriters immediately prior to the public distribution of newly registered securities. These actions could include (1) involvement of directors and underwriters in the preparation of the Form 10–K, (2) similar involvement by counsel for the underwriting group, (3) early discussions with underwriters about major new developments and (4) early coordination, well in advance, with respect to offerings contemplated during a given year.

The Commission subsequently adopted Rule 176, specifying certain circumstances to be taken into account in determining whether a particular person has satisfied his due diligence obligations, and Rule 412, specifying the conditions under which statements made in incorporated documents may be deemed to be modified or superseded for purposes of § 11 liability.

Are the due diligence techniques suggested by the Commission in the foregoing release realistic and feasible? Is it reasonable to expect that underwriters will be able to participate in the preparation of Form 10–K reports of all issuers whose securities they may underwrite in the future? Will the shortened preparation time and shortened waiting period give underwriters and their counsel enough time to find out about recent adverse developments which have not been disclosed in the company's 1934 Act reports?

In 1983, the Commission adopted the final version of Rule 415, which authorizes "shelf registration" of securities to be offered as much as two years after the effective date. Sec. Act Rel. No. 6499 (Nov. 17, 1983). At that time, it offered the following response to concerns about "due diligence" under the integrated disclosure system:

> Concerns expressed about the quality of disclosure also relate to underwriters' ability to conduct due diligence investigations. Commentators attribute concerns about due diligence largely to fast time schedules. Under the Rule, any underwriter may be selected to handle a particular offering. Some commentators suggest that no underwriter can afford to devote the time and expense necessary to conduct a due diligence review before knowing whether it will handle an offering and that there may not be sufficient time to do so once it is selected. These commentators also indicate that they may not have the opportunity to apply their independent scrutiny and judgment to documents prepared by registrants many months before an offering.
>
> On the other hand, registrants using the Rule indicate that procedures for conducting due diligence investigations have developed and are developing to enable underwriters to adapt to the integrated disclosure system and the shelf registration environment. They note the use of continuous due diligence programs, which employ a number of procedures, including designated underwriters' counsel. These registrants believe that underwriters' ability to conduct adequate due diligence investigations in this environment has not been impaired and, in some cases, has been enhanced.
>
> The Commission recognizes that procedures for conducting due diligence investigations of large, widely followed registrants have changed and are continuing to change. Registrants and the other parties involved in their public offerings—attorneys, accountants, and underwriters—are developing procedures which allow due diligence obligations under Section 11(b) to be met in the most effective and efficient manner possible. The anticipatory and continuous due diligence programs being implemented combine a number of procedures designed both to protect investors by assuring timely and accurate disclosure of corporate information and to recognize the separate legal status of underwriters by providing them the opportunity to perform due diligence.

The trend toward appointment of a single law firm to act as underwriters' counsel is a particularly significant development. Of course, this procedure is not new. Appointing a single law firm to act as underwriters' counsel has been done traditionally by public utility holding companies and their subsidiaries subject to the competitive bid underwriting requirements of Rule 50 under the Public Utility Holding Company Act of 1935. This technique is now being followed more broadly in the shelf registration environment and represents what the Commission believes to be a sound practice because it provides for due diligence investigations to be performed continually throughout the effectiveness of the shelf registration statement. Designation of underwriters' counsel facilitates continuous due diligence by ensuring ongoing access to the registrant on the underwriters' behalf. Recognizing the independent statutory basis on which underwriters perform due diligence, registrants cooperate with underwriters and designated counsel in making accommodations necessary for them to perform their due diligence investigation.

Other procedures registrants have developed complement the use of underwriters' counsel by presenting various opportunities for continuous due diligence throughout the shelf process. A number of registrants indicate that they hold Exchange Act report "drafting sessions." This affords prospective underwriters and their counsel an opportunity to participate in the drafting and review of periodic disclosure documents before they are filed.

Another practice is to hold so-called periodic due diligence sessions. Some registrants hold sessions shortly after the release of quarterly earnings to provide prospective underwriters and their counsel an opportunity to discuss with management the most recent financial results and other events of that quarter. Periodic due diligence sessions also include annual meetings with management to review financial trends and business developments. In addition, some registrants indicate that prospective underwriters and underwriters' counsel are able to schedule individual meetings with management at any time.

The Commission believes that the development of anticipatory and continuous due diligence techniques is consistent with the integrated disclosure system and will permit underwriters to perform due diligence in an orderly, efficient manner. Indeed, in adopting Rule 176 as part of that system, the Commission recognized that, just as different registration forms are appropriate for different companies, the method of due diligence investigation may not be the same for all registrants. Rule 176 sets forth a nonexclusive list of circumstances which the Commission believes bear upon the reasonableness of the investigation and the determination of what constitutes reasonable grounds for belief under Section 11(b) of the Securities Act. Circumstances which may be particularly relevant to an underwriter's due diligence investigation of registrants qualified to use short form registration include the type of registrant, reasonable reliance on management, the type of underwriting arrangement and the underwriter's role, and whether the underwriter participated in the preparation or review of documents incorporated by reference into the registration statement. The Commission expects that the techniques of conducting due diligence investigations of registrants qualified to use short form registration, where documents are incorporated by reference, would differ from due diligence investigations under other circumstances.

John Shad, chairman of the Commission and formerly an executive of a large brokerage firm, issued a concurring opinion expressing skepticism about the due diligence techniques suggested by his colleagues:

> The revised shelf rule offers significant advantages to issuers and their shareholders, and mitigates the risks to investors by limiting such offerings to S-3 and F-3 corporations, the largest, most creditworthy and widely followed corporations.
>
> However, concepts suggested under which underwriters might conduct due diligence investigations under the shelf rule are of limited practical value. Issuers can solicit competitive bids from underwriters and effect distributions of securities on the same day. In preparation for shelf offerings, it has been suggested that prospective issuers invite groups of underwriters and their counsel to attend several meetings a year. These would include meetings following release by the companies of their quarterly and annual reports, and when they are preparing their prospectuses, proxies, annual, quarterly and other SEC filing documents.
>
> It would be very expensive for top management executives, underwriters and their counsels to spend hundreds of thousands of hours annually attending such meetings on the speculative possibility that the individual issuer will decide to do a public offering, and that one of the underwriters attending such meetings will be the high bidder for the issue. It therefore seems likely that over time, few top management executives will attend such meetings and that investment bankers will begin sending junior observers, rather than qualified participants.
>
> It has also been suggested that the underwriters rely on due diligence reviews by attorneys hired by the issuer. It is of course the underwriter that is liable for failure to conduct an adequate due diligence investigation, and it is the underwriter's capital and reputation that are at risk if the offering is unsuccessful or performs worse than the general market following the offering.
>
> While due diligence reviews by issuer hired attorneys are useful in defending actions brought by investor-plaintiffs, this is not the principal purpose of such reviews. The principal purpose is to protect investors.
>
> Assessment of the risk of adverse market performance following an offering requires a careful due diligence investigation and the judgment of an experienced underwriter. However, the accelerated time schedules of such offerings limit the opportunity for such assessments.
>
> Issuer hired attorneys have been used in certain utility offerings. While the approach suffers the foregoing infirmities, utilities are the

most predictable of corporate enterprises. They are not subject to the vagaries to which industrial and other issuers are subject.

The bulk of shelf offerings to date have occurred during the broadest and strongest stock, bond and new issue markets in history. Investors do not seek rescission or other redress, unless the security declines in price. The test of the shelf rule will come during the next bear market.

---

5. *Indemnification and Contribution*

As we saw in the section on acceleration of the effective date of the registration statement, the SEC has taken the position that certain provisions for indemnification by the issuer against § 11 liability are against public policy and unenforceable. However, the only judicial opinion on this question came, ironically, in a case which did not arise under § 11.

GLOBUS v. LAW RESEARCH SERVICE, INC.

418 F.2d 1276 (2d Cir.1969).

Before WATERMAN, SMITH and KAUFMAN, CIRCUIT JUDGES.

IRVING R. KAUFMAN, CIRCUIT JUDGE:

This tortuous litigation raises at least two issues of great importance: are punitive damages available in private actions based on § 17(a) of the Securities Act of 1933; and, may an underwriter be indemnified by an issuer for liabilities arising out of misstatements in an offering circular of which the underwriter had actual knowledge? We hold that punitive damages may not be recovered under § 17(a) and that an underwriter may not be indemnified in a case such as this.

The plaintiffs-appellees, purchasers of the stock of Law Research Services, Inc. (LRS), initiated this action against LRS, its president Ellias C. Hoppenfeld, and the underwriter of LRS's public stock offer, Blair & Co., Granbery Marache, Inc. (Blair). They contended that the appellants violated § 17(a) of the Securities Act of 1933, § 10(b) of the Securities Exchange Act of 1934, and also committed common law fraud. The essence of their charge is that the offering circular prepared in connection with LRS's offer to sell 100,000 shares of its stock to the public under Regulation A of the Securities and Exchange Commission was misleading since it prominently featured an attractive contract between LRS and the Sperry Rand Corp. (Sperry Rand) while failing to refer to a dispute between the two companies which had led Sperry Rand to terminate some of its services to LRS and in turn caused LRS to file suit against Sperry Rand. Moreover, the plaintiffs contended that Blair's actions violated § 12(2) of the 1933 Act, and § 15(c) of the 1934 Act.

Judge Mansfield presided over a ten-day trial of these claims, to a jury in the Southern District of New York. The jury returned a verdict in favor of Blair, LRS and Hoppenfeld on the common law fraud claim but also decided that all three had violated both the Securities Act of 1933 and the Securities Exchange Act of 1934. Accordingly, the jury awarded compensatory damages to all plaintiffs totaling $32,591.14 and punitive damages against Hoppenfeld in the amount of $26,812.06 and Blair in the amount of $13,000, based on the violation of § 17(a) of the 1933 Act.

The jury was also called upon to deal with a cross-claim asserted by Blair against LRS, which rested on an indemnity clause included in the underwriting agreement, and against Hoppenfeld and a third-party defendant, Paul Wiener, Secretary-Treasurer of LRS, sounding in tort. At the same time, LRS and Hoppenfeld asserted a cross-claim against Blair, grounded on the same indemnity agreement. On all these cross-claims, the jury found for Blair.

* * *

Sperry Rand's termination of computer services and LRS's lawsuit, are the material facts which the appellees claim were omitted from the offering circular.

Blair and LRS are in complete disagreement as to whether Hoppenfeld informed its underwriter of these events. Hoppenfeld explicitly testified that he told Sanders during February 1965 that Sperry Rand had refused LRS the use of its computers. Moreover, Hoppenfeld and Johnston held a "bare diligence" meeting on February 23 to review any new developments which might affect the issue of the stock. At that time, Hoppenfeld insists he divulged to Johnston the recent legal activity.

* * *

Judge Mansfield granted the motion of LRS and Hoppenfeld to set aside the jury's verdict on the cross-claims granting indemnification to Blair. He thus struck down the indemnity agreement between the issuer and the underwriter, at least as it applied to the facts before us. Blair's cross-claim against LRS was based on a provision which compelled LRS to indemnify the underwriter for any loss arising out of an untrue statement of a material fact in the offering circular, except that Blair was not to obtain indemnification by reason of any wilful misfeasance, bad faith or gross negligence in the performance of its duties or by reason of its reckless disregard of its obligations under the agreement.[14] Its claim against Hoppenfeld and Wiener, who did not sign the

14. The text of the indemnity clause reads:

Indemnification. (a) The Company will indemnify and hold you harmless and each person, if any, who controls you within the meaning of the Securities Act, against any losses, claims, damages or liabilities, joint or several, to which you, or any such controlling person, may become subject under the Securities Act or otherwise, insofar as such losses, claims, damages or liabilities (or actions in respect thereof) arise out of or are based upon any untrue statement or alleged untrue statement of any material fact contained in the Notification, the Offering Circular, or any amendment or supplement thereto, or arise out of or are based upon the omission to state therein a

indemnification agreement in their personal capacities, rests on the theory that they were "active" wrongdoers while Blair was merely a "passive" joint tortfeasor.

The jury, by awarding compensatory and punitive damages to the plaintiffs under sections 17(a) and 10(b), necessarily found in light of the judge's charge, that Blair had actual knowledge of the material misstatements. Accordingly the court had ample basis to find Blair not deserving of recovery under the indemnity agreement itself. But it chose instead the broader ground that where there is actual knowledge of the misstatement by the underwriter and wanton indifference by Blair to its obligations, "it would be against the public policy embodied in the federal securities legislation to permit Blair and Co. * * * to enforce its indemnification agreement." Thus it is important to emphasize at the outset that at this time we consider only the case where the underwriter has committed a sin graver than ordinary negligence.

Given this state of the record, we concur in Judge Mansfield's ruling that to tolerate indemnity under these circumstances would encourage flouting the policy of the common law and the Securities Act. It is well established that one cannot insure himself against his own reckless, wilful or criminal misconduct.

Although the 1933 Act does not deal expressly with the question before us, provisions in that Act confirm our conclusion that Blair should not be entitled to indemnity from LRS. See generally Note, Indemnification of Underwriters and § 11 of the Securities Act of 1933,

material fact required to be stated therein or necessary to make the statements therein not misleading; and will reimburse you and each such controlling person for any legal or other expenses reasonably incurred by you or such controlling person in connection with investigating or defending any such loss, claim, damage, liability or action; provided, however, that the Company will not be liable in any such case to the extent that any such loss, claim, damage or liability arises out of or is based upon an untrue statement or alleged untrue statement or omission or alleged omission made in the Notification or the Offering Circular or such amendment or such supplement, in reliance upon and in conformity with written information furnished to the Company by you specifically for use in the preparation thereof and provided, further, that neither this indemnity agreement nor any of the representations or other warranties of the Company contained herein, to the extent that such agreement or any such representation or warranty requires the Company to indemnify and hold harmless against liabilities arising under the Securities Act any controlling person of or any director, officer or partner of Blair & Co., Granbery, Marache, Incorporated who, when the Notification becomes effective, is also a director of the Company, or whose election as a director of the Company upon completion of the current offering is anticipated at the time the Notification becomes effective, shall inure to the benefit of any such controlling person, director, officer or partner unless a court of competent jurisdiction shall have determined that such indemnification is not against public policy as expressed in the Securities Act. The Company shall not be required to indemnify you or any such controlling person for any payment made to any claimant in settlement of any suit or claim unless such payment is approved by the Company or by a court having jurisdiction of the controversy. Anything to the contrary in this Agreement notwithstanding, nothing herein shall protect or purport to protect you against any liability to the Company or its security holders to which you would otherwise be subject by reason of willful misfeasance, bad faith, or gross negligence in the performance of your duties or by reason of your reckless disregard of your obligations and duties under this Agreement. This indemnity agreement will be in addition to any liability which the Company may otherwise have.

72 Yale L.J. 406. For example, § 11 of the Act makes underwriters jointly liable with directors, experts and signers of the registration statement.[16] And, the SEC has announced its view that indemnification of directors, officers and controlling persons for liabilities arising under the 1933 Act is against the public policy of the Act. 17 C.F.R. § 230.460. If we follow the syllogism through to its conclusion, underwriters should be treated equally with controlling persons and hence prohibited from obtaining indemnity from the issuer. See 72 Yale, supra, at 411. But see 3 Loss, supra, at 1834 (1961).

Civil liability under section 11 and similar provisions was designed not so much to compensate the defrauded purchaser as to promote enforcement of the Act and to deter negligence by providing a penalty for those who fail in their duties. And Congress intended to impose a "high standard of trusteeship" on underwriters. Kroll, supra, at 687. Thus, what Professor Loss terms the "*in terrorem* effect" of civil liability, 3 Loss, supra, at 1831, might well be thwarted if underwriters were free to pass their liability on to the issuer. Underwriters who knew they could be indemnified simply by showing that the issuer was "more liable" than they (a process not too difficult when the issuer is inevitably closer to the facts) would have a tendency to be lax in their independent investigations. Cases upholding indemnity for negligence in other fields are not necessarily apposite. The goal in such cases is to compensate the injured party. But the Securities Act is more concerned with prevention than cure.

Finally, it has been suggested that indemnification of the underwriter by the issuer is particularly suspect. Although in form the underwriter is reimbursed by the issuer, the recovery ultimately comes out of the pockets of the issuer's stockholders. Many of these stockholders may be the very purchasers to whom the underwriter should have been initially liable. The 1933 Act prohibits agreements with purchasers which purport to exempt individuals from liability arising under the Act. The situation before us is at least reminiscent of the evil this section was designed to avoid.

GLOBUS v. LAW RESEARCH SERVICE, INC.

318 F.Supp. 955 (S.D.N.Y.1970), affirmed 442 F.2d 1346 (2d Cir.1971).

FRANKEL, DISTRICT JUDGE.

In this lawsuit, a prolific generator of nice questions, plaintiff purchasers of securities have recovered a judgment under the 1933 and 1934 Securities Acts, have been paid a reduced amount allowed by a modification on appeal, and have finally gone hence. There remains a dispute as to whether one defendant, Blair & Co., Granbery, Marache,

16. § 11 applies to full registrations. LRS's issue was under Regulation A. Compare 44 N.Y.U.L.Rev. at 229 n. 34 with Kroll, Some Reflections on Indemnification Provisions & S.E.C. Liability Insurance in the Light of BarChris and Globus, 24 Bus. L. 685 (1969).

Incorporated (Blair), having paid in full the amount of the judgment, may recover contribution from the two defendants—Law Research Service, Inc. (LRS), and Ellias C. Hoppenfeld—held jointly and severally liable with it.

* * *

As has been mentioned, the judgment in its form following the appeal left Blair, LRS and Hoppenfeld jointly and severally liable to plaintiffs.

* * *

Nevertheless, Blair alone, on May 8, 1970, paid plaintiffs the full amount of the judgment, plus interest and costs, or a total of $36,888.59, reserving any rights it might have to contribution from the others. When LRS and Hoppenfeld refused to contribute, Blair brought on the motion now before the court seeking judgment against them for one-third each of the sum paid to plaintiffs. The motion will be granted for reasons which follow.

(1) Departing from the rugged flintiness of traditional common law, the general drift of the law today is toward the allowance of contribution among joint tortfeasors. * * * Comment, Contribution Among Joint Tortfeasors, 44 Tex.L.Rev. 326, 326 n. 5 (1965) (cataloguing 24 States which have enacted statutes allowing contribution).

(2) More specifically, the securities acts underlying this case point clearly to the result Blair seeks.[2] As Judge Doyle pointed out in the *de Haas* case, supra note 2 at 815–816,

> "those sections of the [securities acts] which expressly provide for civil liability contain express provisions for contribution among intentional wrongdoers. [Citing § 11 of the 1933 Act, and §§ 9 and 18 of the 1934 Act]
>
> "Since the specific liability provisions of the Act provide for contribution, it appears that contribution should be permitted when liability is implied under Section 10(b). III Loss, Securities Regulation 1739–40, n. 178 (1961)."

This is simply a pertinent application of the general principle that the two statutes are to be administered *in pari materia*. E.g., Globus v. Law Research Service, Inc., supra, 418 F.2d at 1286.

(3) The prior decisions of Judge Mansfield and the Court of Appeals denying Blair's claim to indemnity support Blair's position now. A central ground for the ruling on indemnity was the judgment that allowing such means of absolution would dilute the deterrent impact of the securities laws, which seek "to encourage diligence, investigation and compliance with the requirements of the statute by exposing issuers and underwriters to the substantial hazard of liability for compensatory damages." Id. at 1289. The shoe is now on the other foot. If not identical, the mode of escape sought by LRS and Hop-

2. There is no basis for doubting that the subject of contribution, like indemnity (as has been held in this case), is governed here by federal law. See, e.g., de Haas v. Empire Petroleum Company, 286 F.Supp. 809, 815–816 (D.Colo.1968).

penfeld is objectionable on substantially similar grounds. They may not effectively nullify their "liability for compensatory damages" by leaving the whole of the burden to the more prompt and diligent party with which they have been cast in joint and several liability.

Blair's motion is granted. The Clerk of the Court will enter judgments for Blair against LRS and Hoppenfeld, each in the amount of $12,296.19 (the shares as computed by Blair), plus interest from May 8, 1970.

It is so ordered.

Why was the action in this case not brought under Section 11? Was the decision any different than it would have been if the action had been under Section 11?

Was the decision the one the SEC had been anticipating in requiring undertakings as to indemnification formerly found in its Note to Rule 460 and now found in Item 512(i) of Regulation S–K? (See Chapter 1.C.2.) In what respect did the court go beyond the SEC's position? In what respect did it not go as far?

In GOLDSTEIN v. ALODEX CORP., 409 F.Supp. 1201 (E.D.Pa. 1976), the court held that two outside directors were entitled to indemnification by their corporation for $44,000 in legal expenses incurred in defending against a § 11 action brought against the corporation and its directors. The action against the company was settled, but the two directors were not required to contribute to the settlement. The court found, on the basis of affidavits, that they had met the burden of showing "due diligence," that they could therefore not have been held liable under § 11, and that it would therefore not be against public policy for the corporation to indemnify them for their legal expenses. Does this case fit within the exception for "successful defense" in Item 512(i)?

As the district court pointed out on remand in *Globus*, the general rule seems to be that contribution is available in an action under Rule 10b–5. On two occasions the Supreme Court has denied the existence of an implied right to contribution for liability created under federal statutes. See Texas Industries v. Radcliff Materials, 451 U.S. 630, 639–40 (1981) (Sherman and Clayton antitrust acts); Northwest Airlines v. Transport Workers Union, 451 U.S. 77, 94–95 (1981) (Equal Pay Act of 1963 and Title VII of the 1964 Civil Rights Act). Are these cases distinguishable from those involving Rule 10b–5? Both *Texas Industries* and *Northwest Airlines* involved express statutory remedies which did not mention any right of contribution. Is the *in pari materia* analysis by Professor Loss and the court in *Globus* still viable?

Selected References

T. Hazen, Securities Regulation, ch. 7 (2d ed. 1990).

Folk, Civil Liabilities Under the Federal Securities Acts: The Bar Chris Case, 55 Va.L.Rev. 1, 199 (1969).

Freund and Hacker, Cutting Up the Humble Pie: A Practical Approach to Apportioning Litigation Risks Among Underwriters, 48 St. John's L.Rev. 461 (1974).

Heller, Weiss, Israels & Schwartz, *Bar-Chris:* A Dialogue on a Bad Case Making Hard Law (panel discussion), 57 Georgetown L.J. 221 (1968).

Kroll, Some Reflections on Indemnification Provisions and SEC Liability Insurance in the Light of *BarChris* and *Globus,* 24 Bus.Lawyer 681 (1969).

Nicholas, Integrated Disclosure System and its Impact on Underwriters' Due Diligence: Will Investors Be Protected?, 11 Sec.Reg.L.J. 3 (1983).

The *BarChris* Case (Symposium), 24 Bus.Lawyer 523 (1969).

Comment, The Role of Contribution in Determining Underwriters' Liability Under § 11, 63 Va.L.Rev. 79 (1977).

Comment, Causation of Damages Under § 11 of the Securities Act of 1933, 51 N.Y.U.L.Rev. 217 (1976).

Note, The Impact of the SEC's Shelf Registration Rule on Underwriters' Due-Diligence Investigations, 51 Geo.Wash.L.Rev. 767 (1983).

Note, Apportioning Contribution Shares Under the Federal Securities Acts: A Suggested Approach For an Unsettled Area, 50 Fordham L.Rev. 450 (1981).

Note, Section 11 in the Exchange Offer Setting: An Analysis of Feit v. Leasco, 1972 Duke L.J. 1023.

Note, Section 11 of the Securities Act: The Unresolved Dilemma of Participating Underwriters, 40 Fordham L.Rev. 869 (1972).

CHAPTER 2

COVERAGE OF THE REGULATION OF OFFERINGS

Now that we have some understanding of the requirements and consequences of registration under the 1933 Act, it is important to know when such registration is required or, to put it from the point of view of the promoter, how he can raise money from investors without going through the registration process.

As we saw, § 5 applies by its terms to every offer or sale of a "security," a term defined in § 2(1). However, it is specifically made inapplicable to certain classes of securities (or types of issues) by § 3 and to certain classes of transactions by § 4. Assuming that the issuer is not one of the special types of entities exempted by § 3(a), its principal avenues for raising money without registration are:

1. Offering and selling interests which are not "securities" within the meaning of § 2(1);

2. Offering and selling in "transactions * * * not involving any public offering" within the meaning of § 4(2);

3. Offering and selling an issue of less than $5 million in conformity with the rules promulgated by the Commission under § 3(b) or § 4(6); or

4. Offering and selling only to residents of the state in which the issuer is incorporated and doing business, as provided in § 3(a)(11).

Each of these avenues of escape from the § 5 registration requirements has its own distinctive pitfalls and restrictions, which are the subject matter of this section. In addition, we will give brief consideration to the basic coverage of state securities laws governing offerings of securities, which may be applicable in a particular case whether or not registration under § 5 is required.

A. DEFINITION OF "SECURITY"

The word "security" is defined in § 2(1). In addition to stock, bonds and "any interest or instrument commonly known as a security", it includes, among other things, any "investment contract." Comparable definitions are found in many state securities laws. These definitions have been liberally interpreted by the courts to apply to a wide range of money-raising schemes, particularly where the SEC or state regulators have sought injunctions against activities for which there was no prompt or effective relief available under other laws designed to protect the public.

Among the types of interests which have been held in certain circumstances to be "securities" are interests in oil and gas drilling programs, real estate condominiums and cooperatives, and farm lands or animals; commodity option contracts; whiskey warehouse receipts; multi-level distributorship arrangements and merchandise marketing schemes; and variable annuities and variable life insurance policies (where the amount of the benefit payments is related to the performance of a securities portfolio).

The basic approaches followed by the courts in determining whether these various types of interests constitute "securities" are illustrated by the following cases. Note that the criteria applied under federal and state law have tended to diverge slightly in recent years, although judging by the results of the cases the differences may be more semantic than substantive.

SEC v. W.J. HOWEY CO.

328 U.S. 293 (1946).

MR. JUSTICE MURPHY delivered the opinion of the Court.

This case involves the application of § 2(1) of the Securities Act of 1933 to an offering of units of a citrus grove development coupled with a contract for cultivating, marketing and remitting the net proceeds to the investor.

The Securities and Exchange Commission instituted this action to restrain the respondents from using the mails and instrumentalities of interstate commerce in the offer and sale of unregistered and nonexempt securities in violation of § 5(a) of the Act. The District Court denied the injunction, and the Fifth Circuit Court of Appeals affirmed the judgment. We granted certiorari, on a petition alleging that the ruling of the Circuit Court of Appeals conflicted with other federal and state decisions and that it introduced a novel and unwarranted test under the statute which the Commission regarded as administratively impractical.

Most of the facts are stipulated. The respondents, W.J. Howey Company and Howey-in-the-Hills Service, Inc., are Florida corporations under direct common control and management. The Howey Company owns large tracts of citrus acreage in Lake County, Florida. During the past several years it has planted about 500 acres annually, keeping half of the groves itself and offering the other half to the public "to help us finance additional development." Howey-in-the-Hills Service, Inc., is a service company engaged in cultivating and developing many of these groves, including the harvesting and marketing of the crops.

Each prospective customer is offered both a land sales contract and a service contract, after having been told that it is not feasible to invest in a grove unless service arrangements are made. While the purchaser is free to make arrangements with other service companies, the superiority of Howey-in-the-Hills Service, Inc., is stressed. Indeed, 85% of the acreage sold during the 3-year period ending May 31, 1943, was covered by service contracts with Howey-in-the-Hills Service, Inc.

The land sales contract with the Howey Company provides for a uniform purchase price per acre or fraction thereof, varying in amount only in accordance with the number of years the particular plot has been planted with citrus trees. Upon full payment of the purchase price the land is conveyed to the purchaser by warranty deed. Purchases are usually made in narrow strips of land arranged so that an acre consists of a row of 48 trees. During the period between February 1, 1941, and May 31, 1943, 31 of the 42 persons making purchases bought less than 5 acres each. The average holding of these 31 persons was 1.33 acres and sales of as little as 0.65, 0.7 and 0.73 of an acre were made. These tracts are not separately fenced and the sole indication of several ownership is found in small land marks intelligible only through a plat book record.

The service contract, generally of a 10-year duration without option of cancellation, gives Howey-in-the-Hills Service, Inc., a leasehold interest and "full and complete" possession of the acreage. For a specified fee plus the cost of labor and materials, the company is given full discretion and authority over the cultivation of the groves and the harvest and marketing of the crops. The company is well established in the citrus business and maintains a large force of skilled personnel and a great deal of equipment, including 75 tractors, sprayer wagons, fertilizer trucks and the like. Without the consent of the company, the land owner or purchaser has no right of entry to market the crop,[2] thus there is ordinarily no right to specific fruit. The company is accountable only for an allocation of the net profits based upon a check made at the time of picking. All the produce is pooled by the respondent companies, which do business under their own names.

The purchasers for the most part are non-residents of Florida. They are predominantly business and professional people who lack the knowledge, skill and equipment necessary for the care and cultivation of citrus trees. They are attracted by the expectation of substantial profits. It was represented, for example, that profits during the 1943–1944 season amounted to 20% and that even greater profits might be expected during the 1944–1945 season, although only a 10% annual return was to be expected over a 10-year period. Many of these purchasers are patrons of a resort hotel owned and operated by the Howey Company in a scenic section adjacent to the groves. The hotel's advertising mentions the fine groves in the vicinity and the attention of

2. Some investors visited their particular plots annually, making suggestions as to care and cultivation, but without any legal rights in the matter.

the patrons is drawn to the groves as they are being escorted about the surrounding countryside. They are told that the groves are for sale; if they indicate an interest in the matter they are then given a sales talk.

It is admitted that the mails and instrumentalities of interstate commerce are used in the sale of the land and service contracts and that no registration statement or letter of notification has ever been filed with the Commission in accordance with the Securities Act of 1933 and the rules and regulations thereunder.

Section 2(1) of the Act defines the term "security" to include the commonly known documents traded for speculation or investment. This definition also includes "securities" of a more variable character, designated by such descriptive terms as "certificate of interest or participation in any profit-sharing agreement," "investment contract" and "in general, any interest or instrument commonly known as a 'security.'" The legal issue in this case turns upon a determination of whether, under the circumstances, the land sales contract, the warranty deed and the service contract together constitute an "investment contract" within the meaning of § 2(1). An affirmative answer brings into operation the registration requirements of § 5(a), unless the security is granted an exemption under § 3(b). The lower courts, in reaching a negative answer to this problem, treated the contracts and deeds as separate transactions involving no more than an ordinary real estate sale and an agreement by the seller to manage the property for the buyer.

The term "investment contract" is undefined by the Securities Act or by relevant legislative reports. But the term was common in many state "blue sky" laws in existence prior to the adoption of the federal statute and, although the term was also undefined by the state laws, it had been broadly construed by state courts so as to afford the investing public a full measure of protection. Form was disregarded for substance and emphasis was placed upon economic reality. An investment contract thus came to mean a contract or scheme for "the placing of capital or laying out of money in a way intended to secure income or profit from its employment." State v. Gopher Tire & Rubber Co., 146 Minn. 52, 56, 177 N.W. 937, 938. This definition was uniformly applied by state courts to a variety of situations where individuals were led to invest money in a common enterprise with the expectation that they would earn a profit solely through the efforts of the promoter or of some one other than themselves.

By including an investment contract within the scope of § 2(1) of the Securities Act, Congress was using a term the meaning of which had been crystallized by this prior judicial interpretation. It is therefore reasonable to attach that meaning to the term as used by Congress, especially since such a definition is consistent with the statutory aims. In other words, an investment contract for purposes of the Securities Act means a contract, transaction or scheme whereby a person invests his money in a common enterprise and is led to expect profits solely from the efforts of the promoter or a third party, it being immaterial whether the shares in the enterprise are evidenced by formal certificates or by nominal interests in the physical assets employed in the enterprise. Such a definition necessarily underlies this Court's decision in Securities Exch. Commission v. C.M. Joiner Leasing Corp., 320 U.S. 344, and has been enunciated and applied many times by lower federal courts. It permits the fulfillment of the statutory purpose of compelling full and fair disclosure relative to the issuance of "the many types of instruments that in our commercial world fall within the ordinary concept of a security." H.Rep. No. 85, 73rd Cong., 1st Sess., p. 11. It embodies a flexible rather than a static principle, one that is capable of adaptation to meet the countless and variable schemes devised by those who seek the use of the money of others on the promise of profits.

The transactions in this case clearly involve investment contracts as so defined. The respondent companies are offering something more than fee simple interests in land, something different from a farm or orchard coupled with management services. They are offering an opportunity to contribute money and to share in the profits of a large citrus fruit enterprise managed and partly owned by respondents. They are offering this opportunity to persons who reside in distant localities and who lack the equipment and experience requisite to the cultivation, harvesting and marketing of the citrus products. Such persons have no desire to occupy the land or to develop it themselves; they are attracted solely by the prospects of a return on their investment. Indeed, individual development of the plots of land that are offered and sold would seldom be economically feasible due to their small size. Such tracts gain utility as citrus groves only when cultivated and developed as component parts of a larger area. A common enterprise managed by respondents or third parties with adequate personnel and equipment is therefore essential if the investors are to achieve their paramount aim of a return on their investments. Their respective shares in this enterprise are evidenced by land sales contracts and warranty deeds, which serve as a convenient method of determining the investors' allocable shares of the profits. The resulting transfer of rights in land is purely incidental.

Thus all the elements of a profit-seeking business venture are present here. The investors provide the capital and share in the earnings and profits; the promoters manage, control and operate the enterprise. It follows that the arrangements whereby the investors' interests are made manifest involve investment contracts, regardless of the legal terminology in which such contracts are clothed. The investment contracts in this instance take the form of land sales contracts, warranty deeds and service contracts which respondents offer to prospective investors. And respondents' failure to abide by the statutory and administrative rules in making such offerings, even though the failure result from a bona fide mistake as to the law, cannot be sanctioned under the Act.

This conclusion is unaffected by the fact that some purchasers choose not to accept the full offer of an investment contract by declining to enter into a service contract with the respondents. The Securities Act prohibits the offer as well as the sale of unregistered, nonexempt securities.[6] Hence it is enough that the respondents merely offer the essential ingredients of an investment contract.

We reject the suggestion of the Circuit Court of Appeals, that an investment contract is necessarily missing where the enterprise is not speculative or promotional in character and where the tangible interest which is sold has intrinsic value independent of the success of the enterprise as a whole. The test is whether the scheme involves an investment of money in a common enterprise with profits to come solely from the efforts of others. If that test be satisfied, it is immaterial whether the enterprise is speculative or non-speculative or whether there is a sale of property with or without intrinsic value. See S.E.C. v. C.M. Joiner Leasing Corp., supra, 320 U.S. 352. The statutory policy of affording broad protection to investors is not to be thwarted by unrealistic and irrelevant formulae.

Reversed.

Could a person who purchased only land from Howey, without a service contract, sue for rescission under § 12(1)?

The test laid down in the *Howey* case has been applied countless times in the more than 30 years since that case was decided, not only in defining an "investment contract" but also in defining the other kinds of instruments that are classified as "securities." Note that the definition has four elements: (1) the investment of money (2) in a common enterprise (3) with an expectation of profits (4) solely from the efforts of others.

---

1. *The Requirement of a "Common Enterprise"*

The finding of a "common enterprise" was of course central to the Court's decision in *Howey.* Subsequent decisions indicate a difference of approach among the circuits as to what type of commonality of interest will suffice to label the investment a "security."

---

6. The registration requirements of § 5 refer to sales of securities. Section 2(3) defines "sale" to include "every attempt or offer to dispose of, or solicitation of an offer to buy," a security for value.

BRODT v. BACHE

595 F.2d 459 (9th Cir.1978).

Before CHOY and SNEED, CIRCUIT JUDGES, and KELLEHER, DISTRICT JUDGE.

KELLEHER, DISTRICT JUDGE.

This case presents a question of whether a discretionary commodities trading account is an investment contract and therefore a security within the meaning of and subject to the registration requirements of the Securities Act of 1933. The District Court held that such an account was not an investment contract. We affirm.

During 1974 appellee Bergman, a registered representative of appellee Bache & Co., a national brokerage house, solicited appellants to open a commodities trading account. Although appellants knew little about the commodities market, they were persuaded by Bergman to sell their entire stock portfolio and invest the proceeds in a discretionary commodities account with Bache. Appellants sold the stock at a loss and followed Bergman's instructions to execute a form prepared by Bache to deposit the stock sale proceeds in an account with a local savings and loan association. Registered representatives of Bache were authorized to withdraw funds at their discretion from the account to finance commodities transactions, but were not required to notify the investor prior to the transactions. Notwithstanding Bergman's representations that appellants would reap sizable profits from the investments in commodities futures, appellants discovered after Bergman left Bache's employ that all of their money had been lost, and that Commonwealth Commodities Corporation, the company through which Bache had purchased the commodity option contracts, was insolvent.

* * *

The term "security" is defined in Section 2(1) of the 1933 Securities Act to mean, *inter alia,* any investment contract. The now-classic definition of an investment contract was formulated by the Supreme Court in SEC v. Howey Co.: "an investment of money in a common enterprise with profits to come solely from the efforts of others." The Supreme Court has recently restated that "the touchstone [of an investment contract] is the presence of an investment in a common venture premised on a reasonable expectation of profits to be derived from the entrepreneurial or managerial efforts of others." United Housing Foundation, Inc. v. Forman, 421 U.S. 837, 852 (1975).

The first and third elements of the investment contract test are met in the instant case. Brodt clearly made an investment of money. Accepting appellants' allegation that the account was totally discretionary, in that Bache could and did make trades without receiving the appellants' specific permission, the element of receiving return solely from the efforts of others is also satisfied. The crucial factor in the instant case is whether a common enterprise exists.

This Court has defined "common enterprise" as one in which the "fortunes of the investor are interwoven with and dependent upon the efforts and success of those seeking the investment or of third parties." SEC v. Glenn W. Turner Enterprises, Inc., 474 F.2d 476 (9th Cir.1973). This definition is inconsistent with the strict pooling requirement imposed by the Seventh Circuit. In Hirk v. Agri-Research Council, Inc., 561 F.2d 96 (7th Cir.1977) that circuit explicitly interpreted their prior decision in Milnarik v. M-S Commodities, Inc., 457 F.2d 274 (7th Cir. 1972) as requiring a pooling of investments in order to have a common enterprise. Both these cases then rejected the argument that a discretionary commodities account is a security. This pooling of interests, usually combined with a pro-rata sharing of profits, has been characterized as *horizontal* commonality.

Our definition rejects any requirement of horizontal commonality in favor of requiring only *vertical* commonality. Hector v. Wiens, 533 F.2d 429 (9th Cir.1976). The concept of vertical commonality requires that the investor and the promoter be involved in some common venture without mandating that other investors also be involved in that venture. In *Hector* this court found that a factual question existed as to whether a farmer, a feedlot operator and a bank were involved in a common enterprise. The court indicated that if *both* the farmer and the bank were dependent upon the success of the feedlot operation for the success of their investments, a common enterprise would exist.

The Fifth Circuit also seems to have adopted the concept of vertical commonality. In SEC v. Koscot Interplanetary, Inc., 497 F.2d 473, 478 (5th Cir.1974) the court held that the critical factor in the common enterprise test "is not the similitude or coincidence of investor input, but rather the uniformity of impact of the promoter's efforts." The Fifth Circuit followed *Koscot* with a case holding that a discretionary commodities trading account is an investment contract. SEC v. Continental Commodities Corp., 497 F.2d 516 (5th Cir.1974). There the court interpreted the *Koscot* treatment of common enterprise as rejecting "the proposition that the pro-rata sharing of profits is critical to a finding of commonality * * * and cast[ing] aspersions on the elevation of a pooling ingredient to exalted status in inquiries concerning a common enterprise." The Fifth Circuit again rephrased the "critical inquiry" as "whether the fortuity of the investments collectively is essentially dependent upon promoter expertise." *Id.* The court then found this test satisfied in the case of a discretionary commodities trading account because "the success of the trading enterprise as a whole and customer investments individually is contingent upon the sagacious investment counseling of Continental Commodities." * * *

A recent case in this circuit suggests that we may be applying the vertical commonality test nearly as expansively as the Fifth Circuit. In United States v. Carman, 577 F.2d 556 (9th Cir.1978), we found that the sale of Federally Insured Student Loan packages by a trade school to a credit union involved a common enterprise. Although the loans were guaranteed by the federal government, with a fixed return, the court found that there was a risk of loss, because the package included a repurchase clause and a guarantee that the school would cover any refund liability accruing from students who had not completed their school programs. Thus, a substantial risk of loss for the investor on the school's failure was sufficient to create a common enterprise, even though there was otherwise no common enterprise between the school and the credit union.

Similarly, in the instant case, the investor's return, while specifically determined by the commodities market, is also clearly affected by the expertise of the person doing the trading. *Carman* can be distinguished from the case at bar because the success or failure of Bache as a brokerage house does not correlate with individual investor profit or loss. On the contrary, Bache could reap large commissions for itself and be characterized as successful, while the individual accounts could be wiped out. Here, strong efforts by Bache will not guarantee a return nor will Bache's success necessarily mean a corresponding success for Brodt. Weak efforts or failure by Bache will deprive Brodt of potential gains but will not necessarily mean that he will suffer serious losses. Thus, since there is no direct correlation on either the success or failure side, we hold that there is no common enterprise between Bache and Brodt.

Los Angeles Trust Deed & Mortgage Exchange v. SEC, 285 F.2d 162 (9th Cir.1960), from which the *Glenn Turner* court derived its definition of common enterprise, can also be distinguished from the instant situation. That case involved the sale of second deeds of trust. The promoter, however, performed a variety of additional services for the investor, including locating the discounted trust deeds, evaluating them and servicing the deeds. In addition, a "guaranteed" return on these investments was promised. If the promoter failed, the court seemed convinced that the investor would suffer serious loss. Thus, there was the same correlation between promoter failure and investor loss that created a common enterprise in *Carman.* As noted above, that same correlation does not exist here.

Our case comes to this. Using the classic definition of *Howey,* there existed an "investment" by the appellant, the profits from which were "to come solely from the efforts of others." The investment, however, was not in a "common enterprise." It was in commodity futures. Appellant's enterprise was a "solitary" one. His profits were shared neither with other investors nor the appellee; whether his investment flourished or perished was unrelated directly to either the general financial health of the appellee or the ability of the appellee to perform a duty, the purpose of which would be "to secure" to some extent the appellant's investment. Merely furnishing investment counsel to another for a commission, even when done by way of a discretionary commodities account, does not amount to a "common enterprise."

Do the securities laws apply to a discretionary commodities account where the bulk of the broker's payment comes from a percentage of profits rather than commissions? In order for a managed commodities account to be a security must the broker share losses as well as gains?

The *Brodt* decision is limited to the concept of investment contract as defined by the *Howey* test. Is it nevertheless possible to characterize a discretionary commodities account as a security under the "risk capital" test? See Silver Hills Country Club v. Sobieski, 55 Cal.2d 811, 13 Cal.Rptr. 186, 361 P.2d 906 (1961), p. 254 below.

One issue that is not apparent from the court's decision in *Brodt* is the parallel federal regulation that is applicable to many commodities investments. The Commodity Futures Trading Commission regulates commodities futures and commodities options trading. The CFTC oversees self-regulation by the commodities exchanges on which commodities futures and options contracts are publicly traded. The CFTC also regulates commodities futures brokers, known as futures commission merchants (FCMs). The potential for overlapping jurisdiction between the SEC and CFTC has led many courts to rule that commodities accounts, including discretionary accounts, fall within the exclusive jurisdiction of the CFTC., Point Landing v. Omni Capital Int'l, 795 F.2d 415 (5th Cir.1986), *affirmed on other grounds sum nom.* Omni Capital Intl. v. Rudolph Wolff & Co., 484 U.S. 97 (1988).

Although individual commodities accounts are not subject to SEC jurisdiction, pooled accounts may be. "Commodities pools are subject to regulation by the Commodity Futures Trading Commission in much the same fashion as pooled securities investments are subject to SEC jurisdiction under the Investment Company Act of 1940. However shares of a commodities pool satisfy the *Howey* test and thus are subject to the securities laws." 1 P. Johnson & T. Hazen, Commodities Regulation 6–7 (2d Ed.1989).

Questions have arisen as to whether hybrid instruments are properly classified as "securities" or as "futures contracts". See pp. 274, 1026 below.

2. *"Investment of Money" With "Expectation of Profit"*

INTERNATIONAL BHD. OF TEAMSTERS v. DANIEL

439 U.S. 551 (1979).

MR. JUSTICE POWELL delivered the opinion of the Court.

This case presents the question whether a noncontributory, compulsory pension plan constitutes a "security" within the meaning of the Securities Act of 1933 and the Securities Exchange Act of 1934 (Securities Acts).

I

In 1954 multiemployer collective bargaining between Local 705 of the International Brotherhood of Teamsters, Chauffeurs, Warehousemen, and Helpers of America and Chicago trucking firms produced a pension plan for employees represented by the Local. The plan was compulsory and noncontributory. Employees had no choice as to participation in the plan, and did not have the option of demanding that the employer's contribution be paid directly to them as a substitute for pension eligibility. The employees paid nothing to the plan themselves.

* * *

Respondent's complaint alleged that the Teamsters, the Local, and Peick misrepresented and omitted to state material facts with respect to the value of a covered employee's interest in the pension plan. Count I of the complaint charged that these misstatements and omissions constituted a fraud in connection with the sale of a security in violation of § 10(b) of the Securities Exchange Act of 1934, and the Securities and Exchange Commission's Rule 10b–5. Count II charged that the same conduct amounted to a violation of § 17(a) of the Securities Act of 1933. Other counts alleged violations of various labor law and common-law duties. Respondent sought to proceed on behalf of all prospective beneficiaries of Teamsters pension plans and against all Teamsters pension funds.

The petitioners moved to dismiss the first two counts of the complaint on the ground that respondent had no cause of action under the Securities or Securities Exchange Acts. The District Court denied the motion. It held that respondent's interest in the Pension Fund constituted a security within the meaning of § 2(1) of the Securities Act and § 3(a)(10) of the Securities Exchange Act, because the plan created an "investment contract" as that term had been interpreted in SEC v. W.J. Howey Co. It also determined that there had been a "sale" of this interest to respondent within the meaning of § 2(3) of the Securities Act, and § 3(a)(14) of the Securities Exchange Act. It believed respondent voluntarily gave value for his interest in the plan, because he had voted on collective-bargaining agreements that chose employer contributions to the Fund instead of other wages or benefits.

The * * * Court of Appeals for the Seventh Circuit affirmed. Relying on its perception of the economic realities of pension plans and various actions of Congress and the SEC with respect to such plans, the court ruled that respondent's interest in the Pension Fund was a "security." According to the court, a "sale" took place either when respondent ratified a collective-bargaining agreement embodying the Fund or when he accepted or retained covered employment instead of seeking other work. The Court did not believe the subsequent enactment of the Employee Retirement Income Security Act of 1974 (ERISA) affected the application of the Securities Acts to pension plans, as the requirements and purposes of ERISA were perceived to be different from those of the Securities Acts. We granted certiorari, and now reverse.

II

"The starting point in every case involving the construction of a statute is the language itself." In spite of the substantial use of employee pension plans at the time they were enacted, neither § 2(1) of the Securities Act nor § 3(a)(10) of the Securities Exchange Act, which define the term "security" in considerable detail and with numerous examples, refers to pension plans of any type. Acknowledging this omission in the statutes, respondent contends that an employee's interest in a pension plan is an "investment contract," an instrument which is included in the statutory definitions of a security.

To determine whether a particular financial relationship constitutes an investment contract, "[t]he test is whether the scheme involves an investment of money in a common enterprise with profits to come solely from the efforts of others." This test is to be applied in light of "the substance—the economic realities of the transaction—rather than the names that may have been employed by the parties." Looking separately at each element of the *Howey* test, it is apparent that an employee's participation in a noncontributory, compulsory pension plan such as the Teamsters' does not comport with the commonly held understanding of an investment contract.

A. *Investment of Money*

An employee who participates in a noncontributory, compulsory pension plan by definition makes no payment into the pension fund. He only accepts employment, one of the conditions of which is eligibility for a possible benefit on retirement. Daniel contends, however, that he has "invested" in the Pension Fund by permitting part of his compensation from his employer to take the form of a deferred pension benefit. By allowing his employer to pay money into the Fund, and by contributing his labor to his employer in return for these payments, Daniel asserts he has made the kind of investment which the Securities Acts were intended to regulate.

In order to determine whether respondent invested in the Fund by accepting and remaining in covered employment, it is necessary to look at the entire transaction through which he obtained a chance to receive pension benefits. In every decision of this Court recognizing the presence of a "security" under the Securities Acts, the person found to have been an investor chose to give up a specific consideration in return for a separable financial interest with the characteristics of a security. Even in those cases where the interest acquired had intermingled security and nonsecurity aspects, the interest obtained had "to a very substantial degree elements of investment contracts * * *." In every case the purchaser gave up some tangible and definable consideration in return for an interest that had substantially the characteristics of a security.

In a pension plan such as this one, by contrast, the purported investment is a relatively insignificant part of an employee's total and indivisible compensation package. No portion of an employee's compensation other than the potential pension benefits has any of the characteristics of a security, yet these noninvestment interests cannot be segregated from the possible pension benefits. Only in the most abstract sense may it be said that an employee "exchanges" some portion of his labor in return for these possible benefits. He surrenders his labor as a whole, and in return receives a compensation package that is substantially devoid of aspects resembling a security. His decision to accept and retain covered employment must have only an extremely attenuated relationship, if any, to perceived investment possibilities of a future pension. Looking at the economic realities, it seems clear that an employee is selling his labor to obtain a livelihood, not making an investment for the future.

Respondent also argues that employer contributions on his behalf constituted his investment into the Fund. But it is inaccurate to describe these payments as having been "on behalf" of any employee. The trust agreement used employee man-weeks as a convenient way to measure an employer's overall obligation to the Fund, not as a means of measuring the employer's obligation to any particular employee. Indeed, there was no fixed relationship between contributions to the Fund and an employee's potential benefits. A pension plan with "defined benefits," such as the Local's, does not tie a qualifying employee's benefits to the time he has worked. One who has engaged in covered employment for 20 years will receive the same benefits as a person who has worked for 40, even though the latter has worked twice as long and induced a substantially larger employer contribution. Again, it ignores the economic realities to equate employer contributions with an investment by the employee.

B. Expectation of Profits From A Common Enterprise

As we observed in *Forman,* the "touchstone" of the *Howey* test "is the presence of an investment in a common venture premised on a reasonable expectation of profits to be derived from the entrepreneurial or managerial efforts of others." The Court of Appeals believed that Daniel's expectation of profit derived from the Fund's successful management and investment of its assets. To the extent pension benefits exceeded employer contributions and depended on earnings from the assets, it was thought they contained a profit element. The Fund's trustees provided the managerial efforts which produced this profit element.

As in other parts of its analysis, the court below found an expectation of profit in the pension plan only by focusing on one of its less important aspects to the exclusion of its more significant elements. It is true that the Fund, like other holders of large assets, depends to some extent on earnings from its assets. In the case of a pension fund, however, a far larger portion of its income comes from employer contributions, a source in no way dependent on the efforts of the Fund's managers. The Local 705 Fund, for example, earned a total of $31 million through investment of its assets between February 1955 and January 1977. During this same period employer contributions totaled $153 million. Not only does the greater share of a pension plan's income ordinarily come from new contributions, but unlike most entrepreneurs who manage other people's money, a plan usually can count on increased employer contributions, over which the plan itself has no control, to cover shortfalls in earnings.

The importance of asset earnings in relation to the other benefits received from employment is diminished further by the fact that where a plan has substantial preconditions to vesting, the principal barrier to an individual employee's realization of pension benefits is not the financial health of the Fund. Rather, it is his own ability to meet the Fund's eligibility requirements. Thus, even if it were proper to describe the benefits as a "profit" return on some hypothetical investment by the employee, this profit would depend primarily on the employee's efforts to meet the vesting requirements, rather than the Fund's investment success. When viewed in light of the total compensation package an employee must receive in order to be eligible for pension benefits, it becomes clear that the possibility of participating in a plan's asset earnings "is far too speculative and insubstantial to bring the entire transaction within the Securities Acts."

* * *

[The Court went on to hold that nothing in the legislative history evidenced any Congressional intent to subject noncontributory pension plans to the securities laws, and that the 1974 enactment of the Employee Retirement Income Security Act (ERISA) to regulate the types of abuse revealed in this case removed any doubt on that score.]

V

We hold that the Securities Acts do not apply to a noncontributory, compulsory pension plan. Because the first two counts of respondent's complaint do not provide grounds for relief in federal court, the District Court should have granted the motion to dismiss them. The judgment below is therefore

Reversed.

In BLACK v. PAYNE, 591 F.2d 83 (9th Cir.1979), an employee of the State of California alleged that his interest in the state's Public Employees Retirement System (PERS), to which employees were required to make contributions, was a "security", and that misstatements by the state in inducing employees to apply for benefits violated the anti-fraud provisions of federal securities law. The court rejected his contention:

> In International Brotherhood of Teamsters v. Daniel, the Supreme Court determined that participation in a noncontributory, compulsory

private pension plan did "not comport with the commonly held understanding of an investment contract," and thus did not implicate the federal securities laws. * * *

Although PERS is contributory, Black's participation therein does not involve a "reasonable expectation of profits" to be derived from the efforts of others. The California legislature's purpose in enacting PERS was not to provide an investment opportunity. Under state law participation in PERS is considered a part of the employee's compensation for service to the state. Moreover, PERS benefits are determined by a statutory formula and not by the income or "profit" made by PERS. And as a non-profit operation, any income earned by PERS must either be credited to contributions or held in reserve against later deficiencies. Further, Black's participation in PERS was compulsory as an incident to his employment; he thus did not "choose" to participate because of a reasonable expectation of profit from the effort of others. Finally, as a state program PERS lacks the element of economic risk usually associated with investments. Because the key factor indicating an investment—the reasonable expectation of entrepreneurial profit—is absent here, we conclude that Black's participation in PERS does not constitute an "investment contract" or "security" within the meaning of the federal securities laws.[4]

* * *

Real Estate Interests. The sale of condominium units in a resort area or other real estate development raises questions as to the expectation of profit, the commonality of the enterprise, and the efforts of the promoter. In a 1973 release, the SEC took the position that the offering of condominium units in conjunction with any of the following arrangements would be viewed as an offering of securities:

> 1. The condominiums, with any rental arrangement or other similar service, are offered and sold with emphasis on the economic benefits to the purchaser to be derived from the managerial efforts of the promoter, or a third party designated or arranged for by the promoter, from rental of the units.
>
> 2. The offering of participation in a rental pool arrangement; and
>
> 3. The offering of a rental or similar arrangement whereby the purchaser must hold his unit available for rental for any part of the year, must use an exclusive rental agent or is otherwise materially restricted in his occupancy or rental of his unit.

Sec.Act Rel. No. 5347 (Jan. 4, 1973).

In HOCKING v. DUBOIS, 885 F.2d 1449 (9th Cir.1989), the plaintiff purchased a condominium unit from the prior owner and then entered into the optional rental pool arrangement maintained by the manager of the development (the prior owner had not participated in the

4. Because of our conclusion supra, we need not determine if Black's participation in PERS might satisfy the "investment of money" component of the *Howey* test.

arrangement). The trial court ordered summary judgment for the defendant, finding that no security existed. The Ninth Circuit reversed and remanded, ruling that depending upon resolution of issues of fact, the arrangement could be classified as a security.

3. *"Solely From the Efforts of Others"*

SEC v. AQUA-SONIC PRODUCTS

687 F.2d 577 (2d Cir.1982).

Before FRIENDLY, KAUFMAN and PIERCE, CIRCUIT JUDGES.

FRIENDLY, CIRCUIT JUDGE:

Defendants Martin Hecht and Inventel Corporation appeal from a judgment of the United States District Court for the Southern District of New York, declaring that they had violated §§ 5(a), 5(c), and 17(a) of the Securities Act of 1933, § 10(b) of the Securities Exchange Act of 1934, and Rule 10b–5 under the latter act, and enjoining them against future violations. Defendants concede that if the licenses they were promoting were "investment contracts", and therefore "securities" within the meaning of § 2(1) of the 1933 Act and § 3(a)(10) of the 1934 Act, the securities laws were violated in that no registration was effected and the promotional materials omitted material information and contained material misrepresentations. We affirm the district court's holding that the licensing scheme was an investment contract and therefore a security within the 1933 and 1934 Acts.

I. BACKGROUND

This case concerns a plan to manufacture and distribute new dental devices termed Steri Products. Inventor Arthur Kuris conceived of an improvement of the Cavitron—a device that employs ultrasonic waves to dislodge plaque in the course of dental prophylaxis—which would use sterile water in place of tap water in order to reduce the risk of contamination. Kuris had discussions with one of his friends, M. Joshua Aber, a lawyer, and two of Aber's partners, Leon Schekter and defendant Hecht. The latter three formed a professional corporation called Schekter, Aber and Hecht, P.C. (SAH), and together the group established four corporations: Aqua-Sonic and Ultrasonic, New York corporations; Dentasonic, a Netherlands Antilles corporation; and Inventel, a Delaware corporation.

* * *

The proposed method of operation was that Aqua-Sonic would sell licensees the right to sell Steri Products in certain geographical regions. Ultrasonic was described to potential licensees as an optional sales agent. * * *

If a licensee accepted the "Offer to Act as Sales Agent", Ultrasonic would be responsible for all sales of Steri Products for the benefit of that licensee. Under the Ultrasonic sales agency agreement, the licensee retained the right to cancel at any time upon ninety days written notice, ultimate control over pricing and other conditions relating to orders, and the right to inspect the relevant records of Ultrasonic. However, Ultrasonic was authorized to perform all significant marketing functions, such as finding customers, taking orders, collecting proceeds, and paying expenses and taxes. Additionally, Ultrasonic was authorized to reduce the sales price unilaterally so long as its commission on the sale was reduced in the same amount. Prospective licensees were informed that "by entering into the proposed Sales Agency Agreement * * * you will derive substantial tax advantages in connection with your acquisition of a license."

Franchises for over one hundred territories were available. The fee for a typical territory was $159,500: $9,150 to be paid in cash upon the granting of the license; $9,150 in the form of a 7% negotiable promissory note due January 15, 1979; and $141,200 by a 6% nonrecourse promissory note due January 1, 1985, but requiring prepayment based upon a portion of the proceeds from the sale of Steri Products.

* * *

The Aqua-Sonic licenses were marketed throughout the United States. Hecht contacted attorneys, accountants and financial planners and recruited people to sell Aqua-Sonic licenses on commission. Some of these individuals were financial consultants for some of the investors who ultimately purchased the licenses. Between May 1 and December 31, 1978, Aqua-Sonic investments were sold to 50 licensees for approximately $12,100,000, of which $900,000 was in cash and recourse notes.

All 50 licensees entered into Ultrasonic sales agency agreement. None of these licensees had any experience selling dental products. In most cases, the territories of the licenses were not close to the licensee's residence. The promotional materials did not offer or advise of the existence of any sales agent other than Ultrasonic.

* * *

The venture ultimately collapsed when mechanical difficulties prevented the timely manufacture of Steri Products. The SEC then brought this action against Aqua-Sonic, Ultrasonic, Dentasonic, Hersch, Hecht, Aber, Schekter and Inventel, seeking an injunction against future violations of the registration and antifraud provisions of the securities laws.

We thus must determine whether the enterprise described above constitutes the offering of an investment contract under the rule established in the leading case of SEC v. W.J. Howey Co.

It is not contested that the scheme here at issue involves "an investment of money in a common enterprise" with the expectation of profit. Rather, defendants claim that the licensees undertook important obligations, that the sales agency agreement was optional, and that even under that agreement the licensees retained significant rights, such that it cannot be said that they expected profits to be derived *solely* from the efforts of others.

The Commission argues that the Court's use of the term "solely" in *Howey* is not to be taken literally. The Ninth Circuit ruled some years ago that the "the word 'solely' should not be read as a strict or literal limitation on the definition of an investment contract [since] * * * [i]t would be easy to evade[, for example,] by adding a requirement that the buyer contribute a modicum of effort." SEC v. Glenn W. Turner Enterprises, Inc., 474 F.2d 476, 482 (1973). This was shortly followed by the Fifth Circuit in SEC v. Koscot Interplanetary, Inc., 497 F.2d 473, 479–84 (1974), where Judge Gewin made a comprehensive survey of the cases in the courts of appeals and the district courts, pointed out that in the *Gopher Tire & Rubber* case cited by Justice Murphy in *Howey* the investors were required to make some efforts, and referred to one of the state cases cited in fn. 4 to the *Howey* opinion, Stevens v. Liberty Packing Corp., 111 N.J.Eq. 61, 161 A. 193 (1932), as having envisioned even more substantial investor participation. The Fifth Circuit has recently said:

> the Supreme Court has altogether omitted the word "solely" in its most recent formulation of the investment contract definition. In United Housing Foundation, Inc. v. Forman, * * *, the Court quoted the investment contract definition from *Howey* and restated it as "an investment in a common venture premised on a reasonable expectation of profits to be derived from the entrepreneurial or managerial efforts of others." * * *.

Williamson v. Tucker, 645 F.2d 404, 418–19 (1981). If this was intended to mean that the Supreme Court had already performed the necessary surgery on the *Howey* opinion, it would read too much into *Forman* since the Court there explicitly reserved the question whether "solely" should be taken literally. However, given the Court's repeated directions to consider investment schemes in light of their economic realities and the ease of circumvention if the "solely" language in *Howey* were to be taken literally, as well as the history summarized in *Koscot,* we think that if faced with the question the Court would not insist on applying that language literally but would consider whether, under all the circumstances, the scheme was being promoted primarily as an investment or as a means whereby participants could pool their own activities, their money and the promoter's contribution in a meaningful way.

As a first step in the analysis it is useful to consider whether the allegedly optional nature of the sales agency agreements removes them from the concept of investment contracts. It has long been understood that the mere existence of such an option is not inconsistent with the entire scheme's being an investment contract. Defendants assert that a major difference between their offering and that in *Howey* is that in the latter it was not economically feasible for an investor to refuse the option. Although the Court noted this, it must be remembered that

15% of the acreage sold in the scheme in that case was not covered by the optional service contracts. Thus it appears that the Court focused not on whether it was somehow possible for an investor to profit without accepting the option, or whether the investor had a bare theoretical right to reject the option, but rather on whether the typical investor who was being solicited would be expected under all the circumstances to accept the option, thus remaining passive and deriving profit from the efforts of others.

Similarly, in the instant case, while it cannot be said with certainty that prospective licensees would be wholly unable to benefit without taking advantage of the sales agency agreement, it can hardly be said that realistically the agency agreement was a mere option.

* * *

The offering materials presented the license and agency agreements as a package, although within the package each was described separately and each required separate signatures. Moreover, the promotional materials indicated that additional tax benefits would accrue to investors taking advantage of the option. This is particularly important when the license agreement itself was promoted largely for the tax advantages it offered, suggesting that the prospective licensees who could be expected to be attracted to the offering in the first instance would be ones that would find the agency agreement desirable for the same reasons. * * * This was not mere coincidence. The record does not indicate that any attempts were made to locate such purchasers. Hecht's leading salesman was an insurance agent and financial and tax consultant; other salesmen included a salesman in investment opportunities and an accountant. Thus, the defendants recruited salesmen who could be expected to and did contact typical passive investors, not persons with experience in the distribution of dental supplies. While it is true that in determining whether the offering is an investment contract courts are to examine the offering from an objective perspective, and therefore the acceptance of the sales agency option by all 50 licensees is not decisive, this result is precisely what the defendants must have expected from their behavior.

Defendants' other major argument relies heavily upon the Fifth Circuit's dicta in *Williamson:*

> In each case the actual control exercised by the purchaser is irrelevant. So long as the investor has the right to control the asset he has purchased, he is not dependent on the promoter or on a third party for "those essential managerial efforts which affect the failure or success of the enterprise."

[I]f it would circumvent the purposes of the securities laws to exonerate defendants who had the guile to insert the requirement that the buyer contribute a modicum of effort, it would be an even greater affront to the policies of these laws to exempt schemes that preserved the mere right to provide some effort.

This is not to suggest that if it was reasonable to expect investors to exercise their retained rights under the sales agency agreement in a nontrivial manner the scheme would still be an investment contract. However, in the case of the Aqua-Sonic offering, this simply was not the case. All of the preceding analysis indicating that licensees would have been expected to take the sales agency option equally suggests that they would not be likely to terminate the option and take over distribution for themselves shortly thereafter. Adding to the implausibility of such an expectation is the fact that licensees were obligated for the full price of the 8-year sales agency agreement upon acceptance; none of this fee was refundable upon termination. While it is not inconceivable that there might have been some licensees who would have made some efforts at some point in time, this is insufficient to defeat the conclusion that the scheme was an investment contract.

We recognize that to write a rule precisely defining the line between contracts such as those here at issue and the typical franchise agreement, whether for Cadillacs, Coca-Cola or Kentucky Fried Chicken, may be impossible. Decision will necessarily turn on the totality of the circumstances, not on any single one. This is a situation where, in the words of Justice Holmes, "lines are pricked out by the gradual approach and contact of decisions on the opposing sides." But we have not the slightest doubt on which side of the line this case falls. Defendants sought to attract the passive investor for whose benefit the securities laws were enacted. His retention of some legal rights over distribution does not render it unnecessary for him to have the benefits of the disclosures provided in registration statements or the protection of the antifraud provisions. If, by contrast, the reasonable expectation was one of significant investor control, a reasonable purchaser could be expected to make his own investigation of the new business he planned to undertake and the protection of the 1933 and 1934 Acts would be unnecessary. We thus conclude that in light of the economic realities of this case and the precedents in the Supreme Court, in the state courts prior to adoption of the 1933 Act, and in the courts of appeals thereafter, the Aqua-Sonic scheme was an "investment contract" and therefore a "security".

The judgment of the District Court is affirmed.

SEC v. GLENN W. TURNER ENTERPRISES, INC., 474 F.2d 476 (9th Cir.1973), was an SEC action for an injunction against Dare to Be Great, Inc., the purveyor of self-improvement plans, called "Adventures", which consisted largely of tape recordings, written materials, group sessions, and the right to sell such plans to others. The court found that the scheme was "a gigantic and successful fraud." The only question was whether it was a "security" within the meaning of the 1933 Act, since the profits did not "come solely from the efforts of others. * * * [T]he investor, or purchaser, must himself exert some efforts if he is to realize a return on his initial cash outlay. He must find prospects * * * and at least some of them must then purchase a plan if he is to realize that return."

The court held, however, that "in light of the remedial nature of the legislation, the statutory policy of affording broad protection to the public, and the Supreme Court's admonitions that the definition of securities should be a flexible one, the word 'solely' should not be read as a strict or literal limitation on the definition of an investment contract * * *. Rather we adopt a more realistic test, whether the efforts made by those other than the investor are the undeniably significant ones, those essential managerial efforts which affect the failure or success of the enterprise." The court held that the plans were "securities" within the meaning of the 1933 Act. A similar result was reached with respect to another Turner scheme in SEC v. KOSCOT INTERPLANETARY, INC., 497 F.2d 473 (5th Cir.1974).

Is an interest in a limited partnership a security? In GOODMAN v. EPSTEIN, 582 F.2d 388, 406–08 (7th Cir.1978), limited partners brought an action for damages against the general partners for misrepresentation under the federal securities laws. The court noted that numerous other courts, as well as the SEC, had recognized "that the very legal requirements for a limited partnership necessitate its including all of the attributes of a 'security' in the interest bestowed on one of the limited partners." As to whether the return to be realized by Freeman, one of the limited partners, was to come "solely from the efforts of others," the court concluded that "[w]hile Freeman's alleged participation in arranging financing or his relative proximity to the 'management circle' may have been relevant and highly significant to the issue of Freeman's knowledge * * * of the operation, and while it may have been sufficient to cloud the jury's perception in this test for the existence of a security * * *, it was certainly insufficient to overcome the simple facts that Freeman, as a Limited Partner, was prohibited, by law, from taking part in the management of the corporation and that the defendants made no showing that Freeman had actually participated in any of the essential management decisions affecting the basic direction of the partnership."

In contrast to the situation of limited partnerships, most courts have held that a general partnership interest is not normally a security, because of the management powers granted to the partners by the Uniform Partnership Act. In RIVANNA TRAWLERS v. THOMPSON, 840 F.2d 236 (4th Cir.1988), the court summarized the present state of the law as follows:

> The critical issue on this appeal is whether appellants' general partnership interests in RTU meet the third prong of the *Howey* test—that is, the expectation of profits derived solely from the efforts of others. General partnerships ordinarily are not considered investment contracts because they grant partners—the investors—control over significant decisions of the enterprise. In [Williamson v. Tucker, 645

F.2d 404 (5th Cir.1981)], a leading case, the Fifth Circuit identified a narrow exception to the strong presumption that a general partnership is not a security. The court stated that:

> * * * a partnership can be an investment contract only when the partners are so dependent on a particular manager that they cannot replace him *or otherwise* exercise ultimate control.
>
> Only when this degree of dependence by the partners exists is there an investment contract. Moreover, the court emphasized that "[t]he delegation of rights and duties—standing alone—does not give rise to the sort of dependence on others which underlies the third prong of the *Howey* test." In other words, the mere choice by a partner to remain passive is not sufficient to create a security interest. The critical inquiry is, "whether the powers possessed by the [general partners] in the [partnership agreement] were so significant that, regardless of the degree to which such powers were exercised, the investments could not have been premised on a reasonable expectation of profits to be derived from the management efforts of others."
>
> We agree with the Fifth Circuit, as well as the other circuits that appear to have embraced the *Williamson* reasoning, that only under certain limited circumstances can an investor's general partnership interest be characterized as an investment contract. A court must examine the partnership agreement and circumstances of a particular partnership to determine the reality of the contractual rights of the general partners. When, however, a partnership agreement allocates powers to the general partners that are specific and unambiguous, and when those powers are sufficient to allow the general partners to exercise ultimate control, as a majority, over the partnership and its business, then the presumption that the general partnership is not a security can only be rebutted by evidence that it is not possible for the partners to exercise those powers. As the district court stated, "[e]ven when general partners do not individually have decisive control over major decisions, they do have the sort of influence which generally provides them with access to important information and protection against a dependence on others."

See also, e.g., Matek v. Murat, 862 F.2d 720 (9th Cir.1988) ("bright-line" rule should not be applied; whether a general partnership interest is a security depends upon the economic realities of the particular transaction—the court found that the partnership interests were not securities).

In L & B HOSPITAL VENTURES v. HEALTHCARE INTERNATIONAL, 894 F.2d 150 (5th Cir.1990), a group of psychiatrists who were limited partners in a psychiatric treatment facility brought suit under the securities laws against the general partner and others. The court held that a question of fact existed as to whether the limited partners had managerial capacity or whether they were dependent on the managerial efforts of the general partner so as to make the limited partnership interests "investment contracts."

An alternative test for determining whether a franchise or similar arrangement constitutes a "security" is the so-called "risk capital" test, which has been utilized in a number of decisions interpreting state securities laws and which derives from the decision of the California Supreme Court in SILVER HILLS COUNTRY CLUB v. SOBIESKI, 55 Cal.2d 811, 13 Cal.Rptr. 186, 361 P.2d 906 (1961).

In WIEBOLDT v. METZ, 355 F.Supp. 255 (S.D.N.Y.1973), the "risk capital" test was described as follows:

> Broadly speaking, according to the "risk capital" approach, a franchise is a security if the franchisee's monetary contribution to the enterprise constitutes part of its initial capitalization, while his personal participation in its activities does not give him any effective control over it. The theory behind the test is that, under those circumstances, the profit-making potential of his investment is essentially realized by the franchisor and the *Howey* test that "profits [are] to come solely from the efforts of others" is satisfied.

The basic "risk capital" approach has not received uniform application. One commentator seems to have concluded from it that, since "a franchisee could not exist without the success of the entire common enterprise franchise system, which is operated and controlled solely by the franchisor, and, furthermore, that the franchisee's profits depend thereon," all franchises should be treated as securities. B. Goodwin, Franchising in the Economy: The Franchise Agreement as a Security under Securities Acts, Including 10b–5 Considerations, 24 The Business Lawyer 1311, 1319 (1969). This approach was rejected by Mr. Steak, Inc. v. River City Steak, Inc., 324 F.Supp. 640, 646 (D.Colo.1970), aff'd, 460 F.2d 666, 670–71 (10th Cir.1972). We agree that its adoption "would work an unwarranted extension of the Securities Act."

On the other hand, the original exponent of the "risk capital" test, the California Attorney General, has, on the basis of *Silver Hills,* distinguished three types of franchises:

> "1. Where the franchisee participates only nominally in the franchised business in exchange for a share of the profits.
>
> "2. Where the franchisee participates actively in the franchised business and where the franchisor agrees to provide certain goods and services to the franchisee.
>
> "3. Where the franchisee participates actively in the franchised business and where the franchisor agrees to provide certain goods and services to the franchisee, but where the franchisor intends to secure a substantial portion of the initial capital that is needed to provide such goods and services from the fees paid by the franchisee or franchisees." 49 Ops.Cal.Atty.Gen. 124 (1967).

Under the California approach, types 1 and 3, but not 2 constitute securities.

As to type 3, which we shall call the "initial capitalization" approach, it is clear from the analysis accompanying the Attorney

General's opinion that the initial capital referred to is the franchisor's not the franchisee's. R.W. Jennings and H. Marsh, Securities Regulation (2d ed.) 254 (1968). This follows logically from the fact that the question for decision is what type of investment the franchisee is making in the franchisor's operation. However active the franchisee may be with regard to his franchised business, if the price he pays for it contributes to the franchisor's initial capital, he may be considered a passive investor as to the latter. As the analysis of the California Attorney General states:

> "Following this reasoning, it would seem that the franchised business operated by the franchisee and the franchisor's business of supplying the franchisee with goods and services are separate 'business ventures' and that the venture in which the franchisee participates is not the same venture for which he supplies the risk capital."

This approach was viewed with favor in *Mr. Steak,* but its application was limited by the court "to situations where exceptionally high risk, speculative franchises are involved."

There appears to be increasing support for use of the risk capital approach. See, e.g., Simon Oil Co. v. Norman, 789 F.2d 780, 781–82 (9th Cir.1986); Home Guaranty Insurance Corp. v. Third Financial Services, Inc., 667 F.Supp. 577 (M.D.Tenn.1987).

---

4. *"Stock" and "Notes"*

The previous cases deal with "investment contracts." To what extent does the *Howey* test apply to specifically identified investments such as "stock" and "notes"?

In UNITED HOUSING FOUNDATION, INC. v. FORMAN, 421 U.S. 837 (1975), plaintiffs alleged violations of the antifraud provisions of the 1933 and 1934 Acts in connection with the sale of "stock" in a non-profit cooperative housing corporation, which they were required to purchase in order to obtain apartments in Co-op City, a government-supported housing project. The Supreme Court held, 6–3, that the stock was not a "security" within the meaning of either Act. The majority first rejected the argument that anything called "stock" was automatically a "security", holding that this stock had none of the characteristics "that in our commercial world fall within the ordinary concept of a security" and that "the inducement to purchase was solely to acquire subsidized low-cost living space; it was not to invest for profit." The majority then held that the stock was not an "investment contract" because there was no "expectation of profit". Neither the deductibility of a part of the maintenance charges for tax purposes nor the opportunity to obtain an apartment at a cost substantially below the going rental charges for comparable space was considered a "profit" under the *Howey* test, and the possibility of income from the rental of commercial space in the housing project was considered "far too speculative and insubstantial" in this case to bring the transaction under the securities laws. The majority added that, even if they were inclined to "abandon the element of profits" and to "adopt the 'risk capital' approach articulated by the California Supreme Court in Silver Hills Country Club v. Sobieski", as urged by plaintiffs, they would not apply it in the present case because the purchasers "take no risk in any significant sense. If dissatisfied with their apartments, they may recover their initial investments in full." Justices Brennan, Douglas and White dissented, arguing that the financial incentives dismissed by the majority were "expectations of profit" under the *Howey* test.

In MARINE BANK v. WEAVER, 455 U.S. 551 (1982), the Supreme Court held that a bank certificate of deposit should not be considered a security subject to the antifraud provisions of the securities laws, since "the holders of bank certificates of deposit are abundantly protected under the federal banking laws." The Court also held in that case that an agreement by the plaintiff to pledge the certificate of deposit as guarantee for a loan by the bank to a third party, in exchange for a 50% share of the third party's profit, $100 per month, and a right to use the third party's barn and pasture, was not a "security." The Court noted that the term "investment contract" had generally been applied to instruments which could be publicly traded, and that "a unique agreement, negotiated one-on-one by the parties, is not a security."

Starting in 1981, a number of courts, following the lead of the Seventh Circuit in FREDERIKSEN v. POLOWAY, 637 F.2d 1147, held that the sale of 100% of a business enterprise, effected by a transfer of all the stock of the enterprise, is not a sale of securities, since the stock is "passed incidentally as an indicia of ownership of the business assets." Other courts, however, rejected this approach, finding no evidence of congressional intent to exempt such transactions. The issue reached the Supreme Court in 1985.

LANDRETH TIMBER CO. v. LANDRETH

471 U.S. 681 (1985).

JUSTICE POWELL delivered the opinion of the Court.

This case presents the question whether the sale of all of the stock of a company is a securities transaction subject to the antifraud provisions of the federal securities laws (the Acts).

I

Respondents Ivan K. Landreth and his sons owned all of the outstanding stock of a lumber business they operated in Tonasket, Washington. The Landreth family offered their stock for sale through both Washington and out-of-state brokers. Before a purchaser was found, the company's sawmill was heavily damaged by fire. Despite the fire, the brokers continued to offer the stock for sale. Potential purchasers were advised of the damage, but were told that the mill would be completely rebuilt and modernized.

Samuel Dennis, a Massachusetts tax attorney, received a letter offering the stock for sale. On the basis of the letter's representations concerning the rebuilding plans, the predicted productivity of the mill, existing contracts, and expected profits, Dennis became interested in acquiring the stock. He talked to John Bolten, a former client who had retired to Florida, about joining him in investigating the offer. After having an audit and an inspection of the mill conducted, a stock purchase agreement was negotiated, with Dennis the purchaser of all of the common stock in the lumber company. Ivan Landreth agreed to stay on as a consultant for some time to help with the daily operations of the mill. Pursuant to the terms of the stock purchase agreement, Dennis assigned the stock he purchased to B & D Co., a corporation formed for the sole purpose of acquiring the lumber company stock. B & D then merged with the lumber company, forming petitioner Landreth Timber Co. Dennis and Bolten then acquired all of petitioner's Class A stock, representing 85% of the equity, and six other investors together owned the Class B stock, representing the remaining 15% of the equity.

After the acquisition was completed, the mill did not live up to the purchasers' expectations. Rebuilding costs exceeded earlier estimates, and new components turned out to be incompatible with existing equipment. Eventually, petitioner sold the mill at a loss and went into receivership. Petitioner then filed this suit seeking rescission of the sale of stock and $2,500,000 in damages, alleging that respondents had widely offered and then sold their stock without registering it as required by the Securities Act of 1933. Petitioner also alleged that respondents had negligently or intentionally made misrepresentations and had failed to state material facts as to the worth and prospects of the lumber company, all in violation of the Securities Exchange Act of 1934.

Respondents moved for summary judgment on the ground that the transaction was not covered by the Acts because under the so-called "sale of business" doctrine, petitioner had not purchased a "security" within the meaning of those Acts. The District Court granted respondents' motion and dismissed the complaint for want of federal jurisdiction. It acknowledged that the federal statutes include "stock" as one of the instruments constituting a "security," and that the stock at issue possessed all of the characteristics of conventional stock. Nonetheless, it joined what it termed the "growing majority" of courts that had held that the federal securities laws do not apply to the sale of 100% of the stock of a closely held corporation. Relying on United Housing Foundation, Inc. v. Forman, 421 U.S. 837 (1975), and SEC v. W.J. Howey Co.,

328 U.S. 293 (1946), the District Court ruled that the stock could not be considered a "security" unless the purchaser had entered into the transaction with the anticipation of earning profits derived from the efforts of others. Finding that managerial control of the business had passed into the hands of the purchasers, and thus, that the transaction was a commercial venture rather than a typical investment, the District Court dismissed the complaint.

The United States Court of Appeals for the Ninth Circuit affirmed the District Court's application of the sale of business doctrine. It agreed that it was bound by United Housing Foundation v. Forman, supra, and SEC v. W.J. Howey Co., supra, to determine in every case whether the economic realities of the transaction indicated that the Acts applied. Because the Courts of Appeals are divided over the applicability of the federal securities laws when a business is sold by the transfer of 100% of its stock, we granted certiorari. We now reverse.

II

It is axiomatic that "[t]he starting point in every case involving construction of a statute is the language itself." Section 2(1) of the 1933 Act defines a "security" as including

> "any note, stock, treasury stock, bond, debenture, evidence of indebtedness, certificate of interest or participation in any profit-sharing agreement, collateral-trust certificate, preorganization certificate or subscription, transferable share, investment contract, voting-trust certificate, certificate of deposit for a security, fractional undivided interest in oil, gas, or other mineral rights, * * * or, in general, any interest or instrument commonly known as a 'security,' or any certificate of interest or participation in, temporary or interim certificate for, receipt for, guarantee of, or warrant or right to subscribe to or purchase, any of the foregoing." [1]

As we have observed in the past, this definition is quite broad, and includes both instruments whose names alone carry well-settled meaning, as well as instruments of "more variable character [that] were necessarily designated by more descriptive terms," such as "investment contract" and "instrument commonly known as a 'security.'" The face of the definition shows that "stock" is considered to be a "security" within the meaning of the Acts. As we observed in United Housing Foundation, Inc. v. Forman, most instruments bearing such a traditional title are likely to be covered by the definition.

As we also recognized in *Forman,* the fact that instruments bear the label "stock" is not of itself sufficient to invoke the coverage of the Acts. Rather, we concluded that we must also determine whether

1. We have repeatedly ruled that the definitions of "security" in § 3(a)(10) of the 1934 Act and § 2(1) of the 1933 Act are virtually identical and will be treated as such in our decisions dealing with the scope of the term. Marine Bank v. Weaver, 455 U.S. 551, 555, n. 3 (1982); United Housing Foundation, Inc. v. Forman, 421 U.S. 837, 847, n. 12 (1975).

those instruments possess "some of the significant characteristics typically associated with" stock, recognizing that when an instrument is both called "stock" and bears stock's usual characteristics, "a purchaser justifiably [may] assume that the federal securities laws apply." We identified those characteristics usually associated with common stock as (i) the right to receive dividends contingent upon an apportionment of profits; (ii) negotiability; (iii) the ability to be pledged or hypothecated; (iv) the conferring of voting rights in proportion to the number of shares owned; and (v) the capacity to appreciate in value.[2]

Under the facts of *Forman,* we concluded that the instruments at issue there were not "securities" within the meaning of the Acts. That case involved the sale of shares of stock entitling the purchaser to lease an apartment in a housing cooperative. The stock bore none of the characteristics listed above that are usually associated with traditional stock. Moreover, we concluded that under the circumstances, there was no likelihood that the purchasers had been misled by use of the word "stock" into thinking that the federal securities laws governed their purchases. The purchasers had intended to acquire low-cost subsidized living space for their personal use; no one was likely to have believed that he was purchasing investment securities.

In contrast, it is undisputed that the stock involved here possesses all of the characteristics we identified in *Forman* as traditionally associated with common stock. Indeed, the District Court so found. Moreover, unlike in *Forman,* the context of the transaction involved here—the sale of stock in a corporation—is typical of the kind of context to which the Acts normally apply. It is thus much more likely here than in *Forman* that an investor would believe he was covered by the federal securities laws. Under the circumstances of this case, the plain meaning of the statutory definition mandates that the stock be treated as "securities" subject to the coverage of the Acts.

Reading the securities laws to apply to the sale of stock at issue here comports with Congress' remedial purpose in enacting the legislation to protect investors by "compelling full and fair disclosure relative to the issuance of 'the many types of instruments that in our commercial world fall within the ordinary concept of a security.'" Although we recognize that Congress did not intend to provide a comprehensive federal remedy for all fraud, we think it would improperly narrow Congress' broad definition of "security" to hold that the traditional stock at issue here falls outside the Acts' coverage.

III

Under other circumstances, we might consider the statutory analysis outlined above to be a sufficient answer compelling judgment for petitioner. Respondents urge, however, that language in our previous

2. Although we did not so specify in *Forman,* we wish to make clear here that these characteristics are those usually associated with common stock, the kind of stock often at issue in cases involving the sale of a business. Various types of preferred stock may have different characteristics and still be covered by the Acts.

opinions, including *Forman,* requires that we look beyond the label "stock" and the characteristics of the instruments involved to determine where application of the Acts is mandated by the economic substance of the transaction. Moreover, the Court of Appeals rejected the view that the plain meaning of the definition would be sufficient to hold this stock covered, because it saw "no principled way," to justify treating notes, bonds, and other of the definitional categories differently. We address these concerns in turn.

A

It is fair to say that our cases have not been entirely clear on the proper method of analysis for determining when an instrument is a "security." * * *

This so-called "*Howey* test" formed the basis for the second part of our decision in *Forman,* on which respondents primarily rely. As discussed above, the first part of our decision in *Forman* concluded that the instruments at issue, while they bore the traditional label "stock," were not "securities" because they possessed none of the usual characteristics of stock. We then went on to address the argument that the instruments were "investment contracts." Applying the *Howey* test, we concluded that the instruments likewise were not "securities" by virtue of being "investment contracts" because the economic realities of the transaction showed that the purchasers had parted with their money not for the purpose of reaping profits from the efforts of others, but for the purpose of purchasing a commodity for personal consumption.

Respondents contend that *Forman* and the cases on which it was based[4] require us to reject the view that the shares of stock at issue here may be considered "securities" because of their name and characteristics. Instead, they argue that our cases require us in every instance to look to the economic substance of the transaction to determine whether the *Howey* test has been met. According to respondents, it is clear that petitioner sought not to earn profits from the efforts of others, but to buy a company that it could manage and control. Petitioner was not a passive investor of the kind Congress intended the Acts to protect, but an active entrepreneur, who sought to "use or consume" the business purchased just as the purchasers in *Forman* sought to use the apartments they acquired after purchasing shares of stock. Thus, respondents urge that the Acts do not apply.

4. Respondents also rely on Tcherepnin v. Knight, 389 U.S. 332 (1967), and Marine Bank v. Weaver, 455 U.S. 551 (1982), as support for their argument that we have mandated in every case a determination of whether the economic realities of a transaction call for the application of the Acts. It is sufficient to note here that these cases, like the other cases on which respondents rely, involved unusual instruments that did not fit squarely within one of the enumerated specific kinds of securities listed in the definition. *Tcherepnin* involved withdrawable capital shares in a state savings and loan association, and *Weaver* involved a certificate of deposit and a privately negotiated profit sharing agreement. See Marine Bank v. Weaver, supra, at 557, n. 5, for an explanation of why the certificate of deposit involved there did not fit within the definition's category "certificate of deposit, for a security."

We disagree with respondents' interpretation of our cases. First, it is important to understand the contexts within which these cases were decided. All of the cases on which respondents rely involved unusual instruments not easily characterized as "securities." Thus, if the Acts were to apply in those cases at all, it would have to have been because the economic reality underlying the transactions indicated that the instruments were actually of a type that falls within the usual concept of a security. In the case at bar, in contrast, the instrument involved is traditional stock, plainly within the statutory definition. There is no need here, as there was in the prior cases, to look beyond the characteristics of the instrument to determine whether the Acts apply.

Contrary to respondents' implication, the Court has never foreclosed the possibility that stock could be found to be a "security" simply because it is what it purports to be. In SEC v. C.M. Joiner Leasing Corp., the Court noted that "we do nothing to the words of the Act; we merely accept them * * *. In some cases, [proving that the documents were securities] might be done by proving the document itself, which on its face would be a note, a bond, or a share of stock." Nor does *Forman* require a different result. Respondents are correct that in *Forman* we eschewed a "literal" approach that would invoke the Acts' coverage simply because the instrument carried the label "stock." *Forman* does not, however, eliminate the Court's ability to hold that an instrument is covered when its characteristics bear out the label.

Second, we would note that the *Howey* economic reality test was designed to determine whether a particular instrument is an "investment contract," not whether it fits within *any* of the examples listed in the statutory definition of "security." Our cases are consistent with this view. * * * Moreover, applying the *Howey* test to traditional stock and all other types of instruments listed in the statutory definition would make the Acts' enumeration of many types of instruments superfluous.

Finally, we cannot agree with respondents that the Acts were intended to cover only "passive investors" and not privately negotiated transactions involving the transfer of control to "entrepreneurs." The 1934 Act contains several provisions specifically governing tender offers, disclosure of transactions by corporate officers and principal stockholders, and the recovery of short-swing profits gained by such persons. Eliminating from the definition of "security" instruments involved in transactions where control passed to the purchaser would contravene the purposes of these provisions. Furthermore, although § 4(2) of the 1933 Act exempts transactions not involving any public offering from the Act's registration provisions, there is no comparable exemption from the antifraud provisions. Thus, the structure and language of the Acts refute respondents' position.

B

We now turn to the Court of Appeals' concern that treating stock as a specific category of "security" provable by its characteristics means that other categories listed in the statutory definition, such as notes, must be treated the same way. Although we do not decide whether coverage of notes or other instruments may be provable by their name and characteristics, we do point out several reasons why we think stock may be distinguishable from most if not all of the other categories listed in the Acts' definition.

Instruments that bear both the name and all of the usual characteristics of stock seem to us to be the clearest case for coverage by the plain language of the definition. First, traditional stock "represents to many people, both trained and untrained in business matters, the paradigm of a security." Thus persons trading in traditional stock likely have a high expectation that their activities are governed by the Acts. Second, as we made clear in *Forman,* "stock" is relatively easy to identify because it lends itself to consistent definition. Unlike some instruments, therefore, traditional stock is more susceptible of a plain meaning approach.

Professor Loss has agreed that stock is different from the other categories of instruments. He observes that it "goes against the grain" to apply the *Howey* test for determining whether an instrument is an "investment contract" to traditional stock. L. Loss, Fundamentals of Securities Regulation 211–212 (1983). As Professor Loss explains,

> "It is one thing to say that the typical cooperative apartment dweller has bought a home, not a security; or that not every installment purchase 'note' is a security; or that a person who charges a restaurant meal by signing his credit card slip is not selling a security even though his signature is an 'evidence of indebtedness.' But *stock* (except for the residential wrinkle) is so quintessentially a security as to foreclose further analysis."

We recognize that in SEC v. C.M. Joiner Leasing Corp., the Court equated "notes" and "bonds" with "stock" as categories listed in the statutory definition that were standardized enough to rest on their names. Nonetheless, in *Forman,* we characterized *Joiner's* language as dictum. As we recently suggested in a different context in Securities Industry Association v. Board of Governors, 468 U.S. ___ (1984), "note" may now be viewed as a relatively broad term that encompasses instruments with widely varying characteristics, depending on whether issued in a consumer context, as commercial paper, or in some other investment context. We here expressly leave until another day the question whether "notes" or "bonds" or some other category of instrument listed in the definition might be shown "by proving [only] the document itself." We hold only that "stock" may be viewed as being in a category by itself for purposes of interpreting the scope of the Acts' definition of "security."

IV

We also perceive strong policy reasons for not employing the sale of business doctrine under the circumstances of this case. * * *

More importantly, however, if applied to this case, the sale of business doctrine would also have to be applied to cases in which less than 100% of a company's stock was sold. This inevitably would lead to difficult questions of line-drawing. The Acts' coverage would in every case depend not only on the percentage of stock transferred, but also on such factors as the number of purchasers and what provisions for voting and veto rights were agreed upon by the parties. As we explain more fully in Gould v. Ruefenacht, decided today as a companion to this case, coverage by the Acts would in most cases be unknown and unknowable to the parties at the time the stock was sold. These uncertainties attending the applicability of the Acts would hardly be in the best interests of either party to a transaction. Respondents argue that adopting petitioner's approach will increase the workload of the federal courts by converting state and common law fraud claims into federal claims. We find more daunting, however, the prospect that parties to a transaction may never know whether they are covered by the Acts until they engage in extended discovery and litigation over a concept as often elusive as the passage of control.

V

In sum, we conclude that the stock at issue here is a "security" within the definition of the Acts, and that the sale of business doctrine does not apply. The judgment of the United States Court of Appeals for the Ninth Circuit is therefore

Reversed.

JUSTICE STEVENS, dissenting.

In my opinion, Congress did not intend the antifraud provisions of the federal securities laws to apply to every transaction in a security described in § 2(1) of the 1933 Act.

* * *

The legislative history of the 1933 and 1934 Securities Acts makes clear that Congress was primarily concerned with transactions in securities that are traded in a public market. * * *

I believe that Congress wanted to protect investors who do not have access to inside information and who are not in a position to protect themselves from fraud by obtaining appropriate contractual warranties.

At some level of analysis, the policy of Congress must provide the basis for placing limits on the coverage of the Securities Acts. The economic realities of a transaction may determine whether "unusual instruments" fall within the scope of the Act, and whether an ordinary commercial "note" is covered. The negotiation of an individual mortgage note, for example, surely would not be covered by the Act, although a note is literally a "security" under the definition. The marketing to the public of a large portfolio of mortgage loans, however, might well be.

I believe that the characteristics of the entire transaction are as relevant in determining whether a transaction in "stock" is covered by the Act as they are in transactions involving "notes," "investment contracts," or the more hybrid securities. Providing regulations for the trading of publicly listed stock—whether on an exchange or in the over-the-counter market—was the heart of Congress' legislative program, and even private sales of such securities are surely covered by the Acts. I am not persuaded, however, that Congress intended to cover negotiated transactions involving the sale of control of a business whose securities have never been offered or sold in any public market. In the latter cases, it is only a matter of interest to the parties whether the transaction takes the form of a sale of stock or a sale of assets, and the decision usually hinges on matters that are irrelevant to the federal securities laws such as tax liabilities, the assignability of Government licenses or other intangible assets, and the allocation of the accrued or unknown liabilities of the going concern. If Congress had intended to provide a remedy for every fraud in the sale of a going concern or its assets, it would not have permitted the parties to bargain over the availability of federal jurisdiction.

In short, I would hold that the antifraud provisions of the federal securities laws are inapplicable unless the transaction involves (i) the sale of a security that is traded in a public market; or (ii) an investor who is not in a position to negotiate appropriate contractual warranties and to insist on access to inside information before consummating the transaction. Of course, until the precise contours of such a standard could be marked out in a series of litigated proceedings, some uncertainty in the coverage of the statute would be unavoidable. Nevertheless, I am persuaded that the interests in certainty and predictability that are associated with a simple "bright-line" rule are not strong enough to "justify expanding liability to reach substantive evils far outside the scope of the legislature's concern."

In the companion case of GOULD v. RUEFENACHT, 471 U.S. 701 (1985), involving the application of the "sale of business" doctrine to the sale of a 50% stock interest in a business corporation, the Court reached the same result as in *Landreth,* on substantially similar grounds. The Court also adverted to the additional problem of determining what percentage of the stock would constitute a "controlling" interest, when less than 100% was being sold. Justice Stevens again dissented.

For another expression of concern about the application of the federal securities laws to local, essentially private transactions, see Judge Posner's decision in Trecker v. Skag, at p. 473 below.

REVES v. ERNST & YOUNG

110 S.Ct. 945 (1990).

JUSTICE MARSHALL delivered the opinion of the Court.

This case presents the question whether certain demand notes issued by the Farmer's Cooperative of Arkansas and Oklahoma are "securities" within the meaning of § 3(a)(10) of the Securities Exchange Act of 1934. We conclude that they are.

I

The Co–Op is an agricultural cooperative that, at the time relevant here, had approximately 23,000 members. In order to raise money to support its general business operations, the Co–Op sold promissory notes payable on demand by the holder. Although the notes were uncollateralized and uninsured, they paid a variable rate of interest that was adjusted monthly to keep it higher than the rate paid by local financial institutions. The Co–Op offered the notes to both members and nonmembers, marketing the scheme as an "Investment Program." Advertisements for the notes, which appeared in each Co–Op newsletter, read in part: "YOUR CO–OP has more than $11,000,000 in assets to stand behind your investments. The Investment is not Federal [sic] insured but it is . . . Safe . . . Secure . . . and available when you need it." App. 5 (ellipses in original). Despite these assurances, the Co–Op filed for bankruptcy in 1984. At the time of the filing, over 1,600 people held notes worth a total of $10 million.

After the Co–Op filed for bankruptcy, petitioners, a class of holders of the notes, filed suit against Arthur Young & Co., the firm that had audited the Co–Op's financial statements (and the predecessor to respondent Ernst & Young). Petitioners alleged, inter alia, that Arthur Young had intentionally failed to follow generally accepted accounting principles in its audit, specifically with respect to the valuation of one of the Co–Op's major assets, a gasohol plant. Petitioners claimed that Arthur Young violated these principles in an effort to inflate the assets and net worth of the Co–Op. Petitioners maintained that, had Arthur Young properly treated the plant in its audits, they would not have purchased demand notes because the Co–Op's insolvency would have been apparent. On the basis of these allegations, petitioners claimed that Arthur Young had violated the antifraud provisions of the 1934 Act as well as Arkansas' securities laws.

Petitioners prevailed at trial on both their federal and state claims, receiving a $6.1 million judgment. Arthur Young appealed, claiming that the demand notes were not "securities" under either the 1934 Act or Arkansas law, and that the statutes' antifraud provisions therefore did not apply. A panel of the Eighth Circuit, agreeing with Arthur Young on both the state and federal issues, reversed. Arthur Young & Co. v. Reves, 856 F.2d 52 (1988). We granted certiorari to address the federal issue and now reverse the judgment of the Court of Appeals.

II

A

This case requires us to decide whether the note issued by the Co-Op is a "security" within the meaning of the 1934 Act. Section 3(a)(10) of that Act is our starting point * * * Congress' purpose in enacting the securities laws was to regulate investments, in whatever form they are made and by whatever name they are called.

A commitment to an examination of the economic realities of a transaction does not necessarily entail a case-by-case analysis of every instrument, however. Some instruments are obviously within the class Congress intended to regulate because they are by their nature investments. * * * *Landreth Timber* does not signify a lack of concern with economic reality; rather, it signals a recognition that stock is, as a practical matter, always an investment if it has the economic characteristics traditionally associated with stock. Even if sparse exceptions to this generalization can be found, the public perception of common stock as the paradigm of a security suggests that stock, in whatever context it is sold, should be treated as within the ambit of the Acts.

We made clear in *Landreth Timber* that stock was a special case, explicitly limiting our holding to that sort of instrument. Although we refused finally to rule out a similar per se rule for notes, we intimated that such a rule would be unjustified. Unlike "stock," we said, " 'note' may now be viewed as a relatively broad term that encompasses instruments with widely varying characteristics, depending on whether issued in a consumer context, as commercial paper, or in some other investment context." While common stock is the quintessence of a security and investors therefore justifiably assume that a sale of stock is covered by the Securities Acts, the same simply cannot be said of notes, which are used in a variety of settings, not all of which involve investments. Thus, the phrase "any note" should not be interpreted to mean literally "any note," but must be understood against the backdrop of what Congress was attempting to accomplish in enacting the Securities Acts.[1]

Because the *Landreth Timber* formula cannot sensibly be applied to notes, some other principle must be developed to define the term "note." A majority of the Courts of Appeals that have considered the issue have adopted, in varying forms, "investment versus commercial" approaches that distinguish, on the basis of all of the circumstances

1. An approach founded on economic reality rather than on a set of per se rules is subject to the criticism that whether a particular note is a "security" may not be entirely clear at the time it is issued. Such an approach has the corresponding advantage, though, of permitting the SEC and the courts sufficient flexibility to ensure that those who market investments are not able to escape the coverage of the Securities Acts by creating new instruments that would not be covered by a more determinate definition. One could question whether, at the expense of the goal of clarity, Congress overvalued the goal of avoiding manipulation by the clever and dishonest. If Congress erred, however, it is for that body, and not this Court, to correct its mistake.

surrounding the transactions, notes issued in an investment context (which are "securities") from notes issued in a commercial or consumer context (which are not).

The Second Circuit's "family resemblance" approach begins with a presumption that any note with a term of more than nine months is a "security." See, e.g., Exchange Nat'l Bank of Chicago v. Touche Ross & Co., 544 F.2d 1126, 1137 (2d Cir.1976). Recognizing that not all notes are securities, however, the Second Circuit has also devised a list of notes that it has decided are obviously not securities. Accordingly, the "family resemblance" test permits an issuer to rebut the presumption that a note is a security if it can show that the note in question "bear[s] a strong family resemblance" to an item on the judicially crafted list of exceptions, or convinces the court to add a new instrument to the list. See, e.g., Chemical Bank v. Arthur Andersen & Co., 726 F.2d 930, 939 (2d Cir.1984).

In contrast, the Eighth and District of Columbia Circuits apply the test we created in SEC v. W.J. Howey Co., 328 U.S. 293 (1946), to determine whether an instrument is an "investment contract" to the determination whether an instrument is a "note." Under this test, a note is a security only if it evidences "(1) an investment; (2) in a common enterprise; (3) with a reasonable expectation of profits; (4) to be derived from the entrepreneurial or managerial efforts of others." Arthur Young & Co. v. Reves, 856 F.2d, at 54.

We reject the approaches of those courts that have applied the *Howey* test to notes; *Howey* provides a mechanism for determining whether an instrument is an "investment contract." The demand notes here may well not be "investment contracts," but that does not mean they are not "notes." To hold that a "note" is not a "security" unless it meets a test designed for an entirely different variety of instrument "would make the Acts' enumeration of many types of instruments superfluous," and would be inconsistent with Congress' intent to regulate the entire body of instruments sold as investments.

The other two contenders—the "family resemblance" and "investment versus commercial" tests—are really two ways of formulating the same general approach. Because we think the "family resemblance" test provides a more promising framework for analysis, however, we adopt it. The test begins with the language of the statute; because the Securities Acts define "security" to include "any note," we begin with a presumption that every note is a security.[2] We nonetheless recognize that this presumption cannot be irrebutable. As we have said, Con-

2. The Second Circuit's version of the family resemblance test provided that only notes with a term of more than nine months are presumed to be "securities." See supra, at 6. No presumption of any kind attached to notes of less than nine months duration. The Second Circuit's refusal to extend the presumption to ALL notes was apparently founded on its interpretation of the statutory exception for notes with a maturity of nine months or less. Because we do not reach the question of how to interpret that exception, see infra, at 13, we likewise express no view on how that exception might affect the presumption that a note is a "security."

gress was concerned with regulating the investment market, not with creating a general federal cause of action for fraud. In an attempt to give more content to that dividing line, the Second Circuit has identified a list of instruments commonly denominated "notes" that nonetheless fell without the "security" category. See Exchange Nat. Bank, supra, at 1138 (types of notes that are not "securities" include "the note delivered in consumer financing, the note secured by a mortgage on a home, the short-term note secured by a lien on a small business or some of its assets, the note evidencing a 'character' loan to a bank customer, short-term notes secured by an assignment of accounts receivable, or a note which simply formalizes an open-account debt incurred in the ordinary course of business (particularly if, as in the case of the customer of a broker, it is collateralized)"); Chemical Bank, supra, at 939 (adding to list "notes evidencing loans by commercial banks for current operations").

We agree that the items identified by the Second Circuit are not properly viewed as "securities." More guidance, though, is needed. It is impossible to make any meaningful inquiry into whether an instrument bears a "resemblance" to one of the instruments identified by the Second Circuit without specifying what it is about *those* instruments that makes *them* non-"securities." Moreover, as the Second Circuit itself has noted, its list is "not graven in stone," and is therefore capable of expansion. Thus, some standards must be developed for determining when an item should be added to the list.

An examination of the list itself makes clear what those standards should be. In creating its list, the Second Circuit was applying the same factors that this Court has held apply in deciding whether a transaction involves a "security." First, we examine the transaction to assess the motivations that would prompt a reasonable seller and buyer to enter into it. If the seller's purpose is to raise money for the general use of a business enterprise or to finance substantial investments and the buyer is interested primarily in the profit the note is expected to generate, the instrument is likely to be a "security." If the note is exchanged to facilitate the purchase and sale of a minor asset or consumer good, to correct for the seller's cash-flow difficulties, or to advance some other commercial or consumer purpose, on the other hand, the note is less sensibly described as a "security." Third, we examine the reasonable expectations of the investing public: The Court will consider instruments to be "securities" on the basis of such public expectations, even where an economic analysis of the circumstances of the particular transaction might suggest that the instruments are not "securities" as used in that transaction. Finally, we examine whether some factor such as the existence of another regulatory scheme significantly reduces the risk of the instrument, thereby rendering application of the Securities Acts unnecessary. See, e.g., *Marine Bank,* 455 U.S., at 557–559, and n. 7.

We conclude, then, that in determining whether an instrument denominated a "note" is a "security," courts are to apply the version of the "family resemblance" test that we have articulated here: a note is presumed to be a "security," and that presumption may be rebutted only by a showing that the note bears a strong resemblance (in terms of the four factors we have identified) to one of the enumerated categories of instrument. If an instrument is not sufficiently similar to an item on the list, the decision whether another category should be added is to be made by examining the same factors.

B

Applying the family resemblance approach to this case, we have little difficulty in concluding that the notes at issue here are "securities." Ernst & Young admits that "a demand note does not closely resemble any of the Second Circuit's family resemblance examples." Nor does an examination of the four factors we have identified as being relevant to our inquiry suggest that the demand notes here are not "securities" despite their lack of similarity to any of the enumerated categories. The Co–Op sold the notes in an effort to raise capital for its general business operations, and purchasers bought them in order to earn a profit in the form of interest.[3] Indeed, one of the primary inducements offered purchasers was an interest rate constantly revised to keep it slightly above the rate paid by local banks and savings and loans. From both sides, then, the transaction is most naturally conceived as an investment in a business enterprise rather than as a purely commercial or consumer transaction.

As to the plan of distribution, the Co–Op offered the notes over an extended period to its 23,000 members, as well as to nonmembers, and more than 1,600 people held notes when the Co–Op filed for bankruptcy. To be sure, the notes were not traded on an exchange. They were, however, offered and sold to a broad segment of the public, and that is all we have held to be necessary to establish the requisite "common trading" in an instrument.

The third factor—the public's reasonable perceptions—also supports a finding that the notes in this case are "securities". We have consistently identified the fundamental essence of a "security" to be its character as an "investment." The advertisements for the notes here characterized them as "investments," and there were no countervailing factors that would have led a reasonable person to question this characterization. In these circumstances, it would be reasonable for a prospective purchaser to take the Co–Op at its word.

3. We emphasize that by "profit" in the context of notes, we mean "a valuable return on an investment," which undoubtedly includes interest. We have, of course, defined "profit" more restrictively in applying the Howey test to what are claimed to be "investment contracts." See, e.g., Forman, 421 U.S., at 852 ("[P]rofit" under the Howey test means either "capital appreciation" or "a participation in earnings"). To apply this restrictive definition to the determination whether an instrument is a "note" would be to suggest that notes paying a rate of interest not keyed to the earning of the enterprise are not "notes" within the meaning of the Securities Acts.

Because the Howey test is irrelevant to the issue before us today, we decline to extend its definition of "profit" beyond the realm in which that definition applies.

Finally, we find no risk-reducing factor to suggest that these instruments are not in fact securities. The notes are uncollateralized and uninsured. Moreover, unlike the certificates of deposit in *Marine Bank,* supra, which were insured by the Federal Deposit Insurance Corporation and subject to substantial regulation under the federal banking laws, and unlike the pension plan in Teamsters v. Daniel, which was comprehensively regulated under the Employee Retirement Income Security Act of 1974, the notes here would escape federal regulation entirely if the Acts were held not to apply.

The court below found that "[t]he demand nature of the notes is very uncharacteristic of a security," on the theory that the virtually instant liquidity associated with demand notes is inconsistent with the risk ordinarily associated with "securities." This argument is unpersuasive. Common stock traded on a national exchange is the paradigm of a security, and it is as readily convertible into cash as is a demand note. The same is true of publicly traded corporate bonds, debentures, and any number of other instruments that are plainly within the purview of the Acts. The demand feature of a note does permit a holder to eliminate risk quickly by making a demand, but just as with publicly traded stock, the liquidity of the instrument does not eliminate risk all together. Indeed, publicly traded stock is even more readily liquid than are demand notes, in that a demand only eliminates risk when and if payment is made, whereas the sale of a share of stock through a national exchange and the receipt of the proceeds usually occur simultaneously.

We therefore hold that the notes at issue here are within the term "note" in § 3(a)(10).

III

Relying on the exception in the statute for "any note * * * which has a maturity at the time of issuance of not exceeding nine months," respondent contends that the notes here are not "securities," even if they would otherwise qualify. Respondent cites Arkansas cases standing for the proposition that, in the context of the state statute of limitations, "[a] note payable on demand is due immediately." Respondent concludes from this rule that the "maturity" of a demand note within the meaning of § 3(a)(10) is immediate, which is, of course, less than nine months. Respondent therefore contends that the notes fall within the plain words of the exclusion and are thus not "securities."

* * * If it is plausible to regard a demand note as having an immediate maturity because demand *could* be made immediately, it is also plausible to regard the maturity of a demand note as being in excess of nine months because demand *could* be made many years or decades into the future.

Given this ambiguity, the exclusion must be interpreted in accordance with its purpose. As we have said, we will assume for argument's sake that petitioners are incorrect in their view that the exclusion is intended to exempt only commercial paper. Respondent presents no competing view to explain why Congress would have enacted respondent's version of the exclusion, however, and the only theory that we can imagine that would support respondent's interpretation is that Congress intended to create a bright-line rule exempting from the 1934 Act's coverage *all* notes of less than nine months' duration, because short-term notes are, as a general rule, sufficiently safe that the Securities Acts need not apply. As we have said, however, demand notes do not necessarily have short terms. In light of Congress' broader purpose in the Acts of ensuring that investments of all descriptions be regulated to prevent fraud and abuse, we interpret the exception not to cover the demand notes at issue here. Although the result might be different if the design of the transaction suggested that both parties contemplated that demand would be made within the statutory period, that is not the case before us.

IV

For the foregoing reasons, we conclude that the demand notes at issue here fall under the "note" category of instruments that are "securities" under the 1933 and 1934 Acts. We also conclude that, even under a respondent's preferred approach to § 3(a)(10)'s exclusion for short-term notes, these demand notes do not fall within the exclusion. Accordingly, we reverse the judgment of the Court of Appeals and remand the case for further proceedings consistent with this opinion.

JUSTICE STEVENS, concurring.

While I join the Court's opinion, an important additional consideration supports my conclusion that these notes are securities notwithstanding the statute's exclusion for currency and commercial paper that has a maturity of no more than nine months. The Courts of Appeals have been unanimous in rejecting a literal reading of that exclusion. They have instead concluded that "when Congress spoke of notes with a maturity not exceeding nine months, it meant commercial paper, not investment securities."

In my view such a settled construction of an important federal statute should not be disturbed unless and until Congress so decides. "[A]fter a statute has been construed, either by this Court or by a consistent course of decision by other federal judges and agencies, it acquires a meaning that should be as clear as if the judicial gloss had been drafted by the Congress itself." * * *

[Chief Justice Rehnquist, with whom Justice White, Justice O'Connor, and Justice Scalia join, joined Part II of the Court's opinion, holding that the note was a security, but dissented from the Court's finding that it was not covered by the statutory exemption for a note having "a maturity at the time of issuance of not exceeding nine months."]

---

5. *Hybrid Securities*

A. *A Brief Primer on options and futures*

It is possible to invest in "put" and "call" options on individual securities whereby investors, rather than buying a security outright, are able to enter into an option contract to either buy or sell the security at a designated exercise price (or "strike price") prior to a predetermined expiration date.

When purchasing a call option, the option holder is taking a "bullish" position in the underlying security—that is, he or she is hoping that the price will rise; conversely the seller of a call option is betting that the price will not rise. A call option is a contract between the writer of the option (i.e., the seller) and the option holder (i.e., the purchaser) under which the holder of the call option has the right to "call" the underlying stock away from the option writer at the exercise price at any time prior to the expiration date. The pricing of a call option is based on the relationship of the current market price of the underlying security to the exercise price on the option. Publicly traded options on securities have expiration dates that are tied to the third Friday of the designated month. Hence, an ABC Corp. $40 March 1990 call option would give the owner (i.e., buyer) of the option the right to purchase 100 shares of ABC stock at $40 per share (plus applicable commission) any time prior to the close of trading on the third Friday in March, 1990. A call option is "in the money" when the exercise price is at or below the current market price of the underlying security.

In contrast to the purchaser of a call option, the purchaser of a put option is hoping that the price of the security will fall. A put option is a contract under which the option holder (i.e. the purchaser) has the right to sell the underlying stock to the option writer (i.e. the seller of the option) at the designated exercise price any time prior to the expiration date. A put option is "in the money" when the exercise price is at or above the current market price for the underlying security.

Options can be used for taking leveraged "long" or "short" positions in the underlying securities. A "long" position exists when an investor owns a security (or an option to buy the security); an investor has a "short" position when he or she has obligations of sale with regard to securities that he or she does not own. Thus, for example, when an investor sells a call option without owning the underlying security, he or she has taken a "short" position since in the event that the call option is exercised, the option writer will have to purchase the security in order to satisfy the option obligation. It is possible to take the same investment stance without the use of options simply by selling short—i.e. selling the securities without owning them and then borrowing securities from a broker in order to fulfill the delivery obligation.[1]

In addition to using options to take a leveraged position in the underlying security, investors can use options as a hedge against their other investments. Consider the following example: an investor owning 1000 shares of ABC Co. stock, which is currently trading at $12 per share, may want to limit the risk of a price decline. In such a case an appropriate hedge strategy would be to buy put options with an exercise price of $10 per share. This would guarantee that, any time until the expiration date, the investor could sell the stock for $10 per share. Buying the puts will cause the investor to incur the cost of the premium that the market has placed on the put and thereby increases his or her total cost but limits the risk of loss.

Options trading is not limited to individual securities. Today, investors can utilize various investment strategies by investing in index options and index futures. An index option operates much like an option on a particular security except that rather than involving the right to purchase or sell a security, it involves the right to purchase or sell a basket of stocks the aggregate price of which determines the applicable dollar amount. An index future has similar investment potential but rather than merely an option, creates a contractual delivery obligation. However, the delivery obligation is illusory since investment positions in futures contracts are generally "closed out" by purchasing an off-setting contract.

Futures contracts have traditionally been used in the trading of commodities, but more recently have expanded into stock index and other financial futures. See generally P. Johnson & T. Hazen, Commodities Regulation ch. 1 (2d ed. 1989). The mechanics of a futures contract are as follows. A June gold futures contract obligates the seller (i.e., writer) to deliver a designated amount of gold to the purchaser on a specified delivery date at a specified price. Futures contracts are priced in reference to the current price of the underlying commodity and the investment community's prediction as to the likelihood of price increases or decreases. Originally, futures contracts were conceived of as a way for farmers and other merchants to hedge their positions (e.g., by selling corn futures against the crops in the ground). However, today the futures markets are dominated by investors. Less than five percent of all futures contracts are satisfied by delivery since more than 95% of the delivery obligations are extinguished by a market process known as *offset* whereby the investor purchases (or sells) an off-setting contract prior to the delivery date. Stock index futures operate the same as future contracts on hard commodities except that the delivery obligation is not defined in terms of the

1. As is the case when writing uncovered (or "naked") call options, when selling short, the margin rules require that the investor have a certain amount of security on deposit with the broker.

underlying basket of securities but rather is for an amount of cash to be determined by reference to the applicable index.

Although stock index futures involve risks generally associated with securities (and securities options), they are regulated by the Commodity Futures Trading Commission. As is discussed in more detail at p. 1023 below, there have been repeated jurisdictional battles between the SEC and the CFTC over the regulation of derivative financial investments.

B. Hybrid investments as "securities"

The proliferation of new hybrid investment instruments has led to increasing jurisdictional tension between the SEC and CFTC. See p. 1023 below. Futures contracts that are derivative of securities are regulated by the CFTC. In 1989, securities exchanges authorized the listing of index participation units (the value of which depended upon an underlying stock index which is computed according to the value of a designated "basket" of securities. Clearly, these index participation units more closely resemble securities than commodities. Whether these units are securities was considered by the Seventh Circuit Court of Appeals in a decision which is excerpted below and reproduced more fully at p. 1026 below.

CHICAGO MERCANTILE EXCHANGE v. SEC

883 F.2d 537 (7th Cir.1989).

Before BAUER AND EASTERBROOK, CIRCUIT JUDGES, and FAIRCHILD, SENIOR CIRCUIT JUDGE.

EASTERBROOK, CIRCUIT JUDGE.

The Commodity Futures Trading Commission has authority to regulate trading of futures contracts (including futures on securities) and options on futures contracts. The Securities and Exchange Commission has authority to regulate trading of securities and options on securities. If an instrument is both a security and a futures contract, the CFTC is the sole regulator because "the Commission shall have exclusive jurisdiction with respect to . . . transactions involving . . . contracts of sale (and options on such contracts) for future delivery of a group or index of securities (or any interests therein or based upon the value thereof)." If, however, the instrument is both a futures contract and an option on a security, then the SEC is the sole regulator because "the [CFTC] shall have no jurisdiction to designate a board of trade as a contract market for any transaction whereby any party to such transaction acquires any put, call, or other option on one or more securities . . . including any group or index of such securities, or any interest therein or based on the value thereof."

The CFTC regulates futures and options on futures; the SEC regulates securities and options on securities; jurisdiction never overlaps. Problem: The statute does not define either "contracts . . . for future delivery" or "option"—although it says that " 'future delivery' . . . shall not include any sale of any cash commodity for deferred shipment or delivery." Each of these terms has a paradigm, but newfangled instruments may have aspects of each of the prototypes. Our case is about such an instrument, the index participation (IP). We must decide whether tetrahedrons belong in square or round holes.

* * *

Securities usually arise out of capital formation and aggregation (entrusting funds to an entrepreneur), while futures are means of hedging, speculation, and price revelation without transfer of capital. So one could think of the distinction between the jurisdiction of the SEC and that of the CFTC as the difference between regulating capital formation and regulating hedging. Congress conceived the role of the CFTC in that way when it created the agency in 1974 to assume functions that had been performed by the Department of Agriculture but which were no longer thought appropriate for that Department as futures markets expanded beyond commodities into financial instruments. Unfortunately, the distinction between capital formation and hedging falls apart when it comes time to allocate the regulation of options.

A call option is a promise by the writer to deliver the underlying instrument at a price fixed in advance (the "strike price") if the option is exercised within a set time. The buyer pays a price (the "premium") in advance for the opportunity; the writer may or may not own the instrument he promises to deliver. Call options are written "out of the money"—that is, the exercise price exceeds the market price at the outset. The writer will make money if by the time the option expires the market price is less than the strike price plus the premium (plus the interest earned on the premium in the interim); the buyer of the option hopes that the market price will rise above the strike price by enough to cover the premium, the time value of money, and the transactions costs of executing the option. Options play valuable roles in price discovery, and they also allow the parties to adjust the net riskiness of their portfolios. Writers of call options reduce the risk they bear if the market falls while limiting gains if the market rises; buyers hope for large proportional gains if the market rises while accepting the likelihood that the options will turn out to be worthless. Options are side deals among investors, which do not augment an entrepreneur's coffers (except to the extent greater liquidity and opportunities to adjust risk increase social marginal propensity to invest). Unlike financial and index futures, options call for delivery of the underlying instrument—be it a share of stock or a futures contract.

The SEC consistently has taken the position that options on securities should be regulated as securities. For some years the CFTC maintained that options on securities should be regulated as futures because options are extrinsic to capital formation and because it is almost always possible to devise an option with the same economic attributes as a futures contract (and the reverse).

* * *

Unless Congress changes the allocation of jurisdiction between the agencies, the question a court must resolve is . . .: is the instrument a futures contract? If yes, then the CFTC's jurisdiction is exclusive, unless it is also an option on a security, in which case the SEC's jurisdiction is exclusive. So long as an instrument is a futures contract (and not an option), whether it is also a "security" is neither here nor there.

[The court went on to hold that since the index participations were "futures contracts," they were subject to regulation only by the CFTC even if they also were "securities."]

Other varieties of hybrid investments include those issued by financial institutions, such as life insurance policies and annuities, "shares" in savings and loan associations, and certificates of deposit in banks. When such institutions issue investments that involve investment risks akin to those involved with securities generally, they will fall within the definition of "securities." Thus, when the rate of return on such instruments varies with the profitability of the institution or a portfolio of securities, they will be considered "securities." The Supreme Court has held in two decisions that "variable annuities" issued by insurance companies are "securities" required to be registered under the 1933 Act. SEC v. VARIABLE ANNUITY LIFE INS. CO., 359 U.S. 65 (1959); SEC v. UNITED BENEFIT LIFE INS. CO., 387 U.S. 202 (1967). See also Marine Bank v. Weaver, p. 256 above (certificate of deposit is not a security). Even if found to be a "security," a hybrid instrument issued by a financial institution may nevertheless be exempt from 1933 Act registration. See Sec. Act § 3(a)(2), (5), (8); Sec. Exch. Act § 3(a)(12); and TCHEREPNIN v. KNIGHT, p. 277 below (savings and loan association's withdrawable capital shares held "securities" under the 1934 Act although exempted from the 1933 Act).

---

6. *Exempt Securities*

Section 3(a) of the 1933 Act and Section 3(a)(12) of the 1934 Act contain lists of "exempted securities". In general, an "exempted security" is not subject to the registration and disclosure requirements of the particular statute, but may be subject to the general anti-fraud and civil liability provisions. Note that while provisions of the 1933 Act do not apply to exempted securities "except as * * * expressly provided" (see, for example, Sections 12(2) and 17(c)), provisions of the 1934 Act do apply to exempted securities unless their operation is specifically excluded (see, for example, Sections 12(a) and 15(a)(1)).

The most important class of "exempted securities" under Section 3(a)(2) of the 1933 Act and Section 3(a)(12) of the 1934 Act are obligations issued or guaranteed by the United States government or by state or local governments (including tax-exempt industrial development bonds). The 1933 Act (but not the 1934 Act) also exempts securities issued by banks, religious and other charitable organizations, savings and loan associations, and motor carriers subject to regulation by the Interstate Commerce Commission, as well as bankruptcy certificates, and insurance policies and annuity contracts.

Most of the specialized types of investment instruments issued by financial institutions, such as life insurance policies and annuities, "shares" in savings and loan associations, or certificates of deposit in banks, are specifically exempted from the registration provisions (but not the antifraud provisions) of the federal securities laws. See Sec.Act § 3(a)(2), (5), (8); Sec.Ex.Act § 3(a)(12). There is some question as to whether the traditional forms of these instruments would be deemed to be "securities" even in the absence of such exemption. See SEC v. Variable Annuity Life Ins. Co., 359 U.S. 65 (1959); SEC v. United Benefit Life Ins. Co., 387 U.S. 202 (1967). The Supreme Court has also held that withdrawable capital shares issued by a savings and loan association are "securities" for the purposes of the antifraud provisions of the 1934 Act, even though they are specifically exempted from the registration provisions of the 1933 Act. Tcherepnin v. Knight, 389 U.S. 332 (1967).

In 1986, the SEC adopted a new Rule 151, exempting from the 1933 Act registration requirements any annuity contract, issued by an insurance company, which "is not marketed primarily as an investment" and on which the insurer assumes the investment risk, i.e., guarantees the principal amount of the payments and credits a specified rate of interest which is not changed more than once a year.

Short-term (less than 9-month maturity) notes issued for working capital purposes and commonly known as "commercial paper" are "exempted securities" under Section 3(a)(3) of the 1933 Act and are not a "security" under Section 3(a)(10) of the 1934 Act. This latter provision, however, did not prevent the Seventh Circuit from holding short-term notes to be "securities" for 1934 Act purposes.[a]

The 1933 Act also exempts from its provisions certain "classes" of securities which are in reality transaction exemptions. Among these are securities issued in exchange for other securities (Sections 3(a)(9) and (10)) or in intrastate offerings (Section 3(a)(11)), as well as in small offerings made in compliance with SEC rules under Section 3(b).

Certain of these exemptions have been deleted or restricted in light of demonstrated abuses. The collapse of Penn Central Company in 1970 led to a reexamination of the exemption for securities of common carriers registered with the ICC, and the Railroad Revitalization Act of

a. Sanders v. John Nuveen & Co., Inc., 463 F.2d 1075 (7th Cir.1972).

1976 eliminated the 1933 Act exemption for securities issued by railroads (other than equipment trust certificates).[b] The Securities Exchange Act was amended in 1974 to require the banking agencies, which administer that Act's disclosure requirements with respect to bank securities, to conform their regulations to those of the SEC, unless different treatment could be justified.[c] The Securities Acts Amendments of 1975 required firms that deal solely in state and local government securities to register with the SEC and to comply with rules laid down by a newly-created Municipal Securities Rulemaking Board.[d]

The Municipal Securities Rulemaking Board does not have jurisdiction over dealers in securities issued by the United States government. There was no comparable regulation for government securities dealers until 1986. Following the insolvency of a number of government securities dealers, Congress enacted § 15C of the 1934 Act which requires registration of government securities dealers with the SEC. The government securities dealer registration requirements more closely parallels that of broker-dealers generally than of municipal securities dealers. In view of the interest of the federal government in the qualifications of those who deal in its securities, § 15C gives the Treasury Department significant rule-making powers over their activities. In addition, banks are major dealers in U.S. government securities, and regulation of their activities is delegated by § 15C to their "appropriate regulatory agencies" (as defined in § 3(a)(34)) rather than to the SEC.

Application of the securities laws to certain kinds of "exempt" securities may raise difficult constitutional questions. In SEC v. World Radio Mission, 544 F.2d 535 (1st Cir.1976), a religious organization claimed that an SEC action for an injunction against its sale of "loan plans" violated its freedom of religion under the First Amendment. The court held, however, that, since the loan plans were marketed to the general public and by appeal to economic motives rather than purely religious motives, they were outside the scope of First Amendment protection.

In City of Philadelphia v. SEC, 434 F.Supp. 281 (E.D.Pa.1977), a municipality alleged that a preliminary investigation by the SEC into alleged fraud in the issuance of its securities was an impermissible infringement on state sovereignty under the decision in National League of Cities v. Usery, 426 U.S. 833 (1976). The court held that the city had standing to challenge the SEC, but that the indirect harm to the city's credit caused by the existence of the investigation was not a

b. Sec. Act § 3(a)(6), as amended by P.L. 94–210, § 308, 90 Stat. 56 (1976); see H.Rep. No. 94–725, at 65–68 (1975).

c. Sec.Ex.Act § 12(i), as amended by P.L. 93–495, § 105(b), 88 Stat. 1503 (1974).

d. Sec.Ex.Act § 15B, added by P.L. 94–29, § 13, 89 Stat. 131 (1975).

direct enough interference with state or local government functions to bring the *Usery* rule into play.

Selected References

A. *General Sources*

T. Hazen, Securities Regulation § 1.5 (2d ed. 1990).

Arnold, "When Is a Car a Bicycle?" And Other Riddles: The Definition of a Security Under the Federal Securities Laws, 33 Clev.St.L.Rev. 449 (1984–85).

Arnold, The Definition of a Security Under the Federal Securities Laws Revisited, 34 Clev.St.L.Rev. 249 (1985–86).

Carney, Defining a Security: The Addition of a Market–Oriented Contextual Approach to Investment Contract Analysis, 13 Emory L.J. 311 (1984).

Chang, Meaning, Reference, and Reification in the Definition of a Security, 19 U.C.D.L.Rev. 403 (1986).

Coffey, The Economic Realities of a "Security": Is There a More Meaningful Formula?, 18 Case W. Res.L.Rev. 367 (1967).

Hannan & Thomas, The Importance of Economic Reality and Risk in Defining Federal Securities, 25 Hastings L.J. 219 (1974).

Karjala, Realigning Federal and State Roles in Securities Regulation Through the Definition of Security, 1982 U.Ill.L.Rev. 413.

Rosin, Historical Perspectives on the Definition of a Security, 28 S.Tex.L. Rev. 575 (1987).

Steinberg & Kaulbach, The Supreme Court and the Definition of "Security": The "Context" Clause, "Investment Contract" Analysis, and their Ramifications, 40 Vand.L.Rev. 489 (1987).

B. *Employee Benefit Plans*

Stzandbury & Bedol, Interests in Employee Benefit Plans as Securities: Daniel and Beyond, 8 Sec.Reg.L.J. 226 (1980).

C. *Franchises, Syndications, etc.*

Campbell, Racing Syndicates as Securities, 74 Ky.L.J. 691 (1985–86).

Freedman, Analysis of the Franchise Agreement Under Federal Securities Laws, 27 Syr.L.Rev. 919 (1976).

D. *Futures and Options as "Securities"*

Bromberg, Securities Law—Relationship to Commodities Law, 35 Bus.Law. 787 (1980).

Gilberg, Regulation of New Financial Instruments Under the Federal Securities and Commodities Laws, 39 Vand.L.Rev. 1599 (1986).

Markham & Gilberg, Stock and Commodity Options—Two Regulatory Approaches and Their Conflicts, 47 Alb.L.Rev. 741 (1983).

Note, Discretionary Commodity Accounts as Securities: An Application of the Howey Test, 53 Fordham L.Rev. 639 (1984).

E. *Notes as "Securities"*

Glidden, When Are Loans Security Transactions? A Proposed Test, 13 Sec. Reg.L.J. 212 (1985).

Gordon, Common Enterprise and Multiple Investors: A Contractual Theory for Defining Investment Contracts and Notes, 1988 Colum.Bus.L.Rev. 635.

Sonnenshein, Federal Securities Law Coverage of Note Transactions: The Antifraud Provisions, 35 Bus.Law. 1567 (1980).

F. *Partnership Interests as "Securities"*

Levinson, General Partnership Interests and the Securities Act of 1933: Recent Judicial Developments, 10 Ohio N.U.L.Rev. 463 (1983).

Long, Partnership, Limited Partnership and Joint Venture Interests as Securities, 37 Mo.L.Rev. 581 (1972).

Note, General Partnership Interests as Securities Under the Federal Securities Laws: Substance Over Form, 54 Fordham L.Rev. 303 (1985).

G. *Insurance Products as "Securities"*

Mason & Roth, SEC Regulation of Life Insurance Products—On the Brink of the Universal, 15 Conn.L.Rev. 505 (1983).

H. *Real Estate Interests as "Securities"*

Morgenstern, Real Estate Joint Venture Interests as Securities: The Implications of Williamson v. Tucker, 59 Wash.U.L.Q. 123 (1982).

Rosenbaum, The Resort Condominium and the Federal Securities Laws—A Case Study in Governmental Inflexibility, 60 Va.L.Rev. 785 (1974).

I. *Risk Capital Test*

Carney & Fraser, Defining a "Security": Georgia's Struggle with the "Risk Capital" Test, 30 Emory L.J. 73 (1981).

Note, Securities Regulation: Risk Capital—Twenty Years After Silver Hills, 35 Okla.L.Rev. 436 (1982).

J. *Stock as a "Security"*

Edwards, A New Literalism? Rejection of the Sale of Business Doctrine, 30 St. Louis U.L.J. 427 (1986).

Fitzgibbon, What is a Security? A Redefinition Based on Eligibility to Participate in the Financial Markets, 64 Minn.L.Rev. 893 (1980).

O'Brien & Moye, The Sale of Business Doctrine: Landreth Adds New Life to Anti-Fraud Provisions of the Securities Acts, 11 Vt.L.Rev. 1 (1986).

B. EXEMPTIONS FOR OFFERINGS BY ISSUERS

If the interest being offered is a security, then it must be registered under the 1933 Act unless an exemption is available under § 3 or § 4. (Note, however, that while an interest which is not a "security" is not subject to any of the provisions of the federal securities law, an offering of securities which is exempted by § 3 or 4 from the provisions of § 5 is still subject to the general anti-fraud provisions of §§ 17 and 12(2)[a] of the 1933 Act as well as the anti-fraud provisions of the 1934 Act.)

There are several important facts a lawyer must keep in mind in deciding whether an exemption is available and evaluating the consequences if it turns out not to have been available.

First, the SEC and the courts have taken the position that a transaction is presumed *not* to be exempt from the registration requirements unless the issuer carries the burden of proving that an exemption is available.

Second, the availability of an exemption is generally determined by applying the tests to the entire offering, rather than to the sale to a particular purchaser. Furthermore, the "integration" doctrine may result in a series of allegedly separate offerings being considered a single offering. Also, the entire offering must comply with a single exemption; it is not sufficient if part of the offering complies with one exemption and the other part complies with a different exemption.

Third, if an offering is found not to qualify for an exemption, any purchaser can sue to recover his or her purchase price under § 12(1) on the ground that the sale violated § 5(a). Generally, the purchaser can sue even if the particular sale to him or her complied with the terms of the exemption.

Fourth, some of the statutory exemptions are available whether or not the SEC takes any action to implement them (although the SEC may adopt rules defining the statutory terms or establishing criteria which will be deemed to satisfy them); others are available only to the extent the SEC adopts implementing rules.

---

1. *"Non-public" Offerings—§ 4(2)*

The most important exemption for an ordinary corporate issuer wishing to raise money without registration is the exemption in § 4(2) for "transactions by an issuer not involving any public offering." Very large amounts of securities have been sold pursuant to this exemption. The vast bulk of these offerings, however, consists of "private placements" of large blocks of securities with institutional investors—typically the sale of notes or debentures to one or more insurance companies or pension funds. The SEC has generally raised no objections to the consummation of these transactions in reliance on the § 4(2)

a. Except as to securities exempted by § 3(a)(2).

exemption, since the purchasers are customarily in a position to insist upon the issuer providing them with information more extensive than that contained in a registration statement and to give them other protections not available to purchasers in a registered public offering.

The private offering exemption is of course available for any other kind of offering which meets its basic criteria. Two areas where it has been effectively utilized are in offerings to key employees of the issuing company and in exchange offers to acquire the stock of closely-held companies.

The area of greatest difficulty has been the use of the § 4(2) exemption for promotional offerings to limited numbers of people. Restrictive interpretations by the SEC and the courts as to the manner in which, and the persons to whom, a "non-public" offering could be made, coupled with strict liability under § 12(1) if the terms of the exemption were not strictly complied with, made many lawyers dubious as to whether the § 4(2) exemption could ever be safely used in this situation.

SEC v. RALSTON PURINA CO.

346 U.S. 119 (1953).

MR. JUSTICE CLARK, delivered the opinion of the Court.

Section 4(2) of the Securities Act of 1933 exempts "transactions by an issuer not involving any public offering" from the registration requirements of § 5. We must decide whether Ralston Purina's offerings of treasury stock to its "key employees" are within this exemption. On a complaint brought by the Commission under § 20(b) of the Act seeking to enjoin respondent's unregistered offerings, the District Court held the exemption applicable and dismissed the suit. The Court of Appeals affirmed. The question has arisen many times since the Act was passed; an apparent need to define the scope of the private offering exemption prompted certiorari.

Ralston Purina manufactures and distributes various feed and cereal products. Its processing and distribution facilities are scattered throughout the United States and Canada, staffed by some 7,000 employees. At least since 1911 the company has had a policy of encouraging stock ownership among its employees; more particularly, since 1942 it has made authorized but unissued common shares available to some of them. Between 1947 and 1951, the period covered by the record in this case, Ralston Purina sold nearly $2,000,000 of stock to employees without registration and in so doing made use of the mails.

In each of these years, a corporate resolution authorized the sale of common stock "to employees * * * who shall, without any solicitation by the Company or its officers or employees, inquire of any of them as to how to purchase common stock of Ralston Purina Company." A memorandum sent to branch and store managers after the resolution was adopted, advised that "The only employees to whom this stock will be available will be those who take the initiative and are interested in buying stock at present market prices." Among those responding to these offers were employees with the duties of artist, bakeshop foreman, chow loading foreman, clerical assistant, copywriter, electrician, stock clerk, mill office clerk, order credit trainee, production trainee, stenographer, and veterinarian. The buyers lived in over fifty widely separated communities scattered from Garland, Texas, to Nashua, New Hampshire and Visalia, California. The lowest salary bracket of those purchasing was $2,700 in 1949, $2,435 in 1950 and $3,107 in 1951. The record shows that in 1947, 243 employees bought stock, 20 in 1948, 414 in 1949, 411 in 1950, and the 1951 offer, interrupted by this litigation, produced 165 applications to purchase. No records were kept of those to whom the offers were made; the estimated number in 1951 was 500.

The company bottoms its exemption claim on the classification of all offerees as "key employees" in its organization. Its position on trial was that "A key employee * * * is not confined to an organization chart. It would include an individual who is eligible for promotion, an individual who especially influences others or who advises others, a person whom the employees look to in some special way, an individual, of course, who carries some special responsibility, who is sympathetic to management and who is ambitious and who the management feels is likely to be promoted to a greater responsibility." That an offering to all of its employees would be public is conceded.

The Securities Act nowhere defines the scope of § 4(2)'s private offering exemption. Nor is the legislative history of much help in staking out its boundaries. The problem was first dealt with in § 4(1) of the House Bill, H.R. 5480, 73d Cong., 1st Sess., which exempted "transactions by an issuer not with or through an underwriter; * * *." The bill, as reported by the House Committee, added "and not involving any public offering." H.R.Rep. No. 85, 73d Cong., 1st Sess. 1. This was thought to be one of those transactions "where there is no practical need for * * * [the bill's] application or where the public benefits are too remote." Id., at 5. The exemption as thus delimited became law. It assumed its present shape with the deletion of "not with or through an underwriter" by § 203(a) of the Securities Exchange Act of 1934, 48 Stat. 906, a change regarded as the elimination of superfluous language. H.R.Rep. No. 1838, 73d Cong., 2d Sess. 41.

Decisions under comparable exemptions in the English Companies Acts and state "blue sky" laws, the statutory antecedents of federal securities legislation have made one thing clear—to be public, an offer need not be open to the whole world. In Securities and Exchange Comm. v. Sunbeam Gold Mines Co., 9 Cir.1938, 95 F.2d 699, 701, this point was made in dealing with an offering to the stockholders of two corporations about to be merged. Judge Denman observed that:

"In its broadest meaning the term 'public' distinguishes the populace at large from groups of individual members of the public segregated because of some common interest or characteristic. Yet such a distinction is inadequate for practical purposes; manifestly, an offering of securities to all red-headed men, to all residents of Chicago or San Francisco, to all existing stockholders of the General Motors Corporation or the American Telephone & Telegraph Company, is no less 'public', in every realistic sense of the word, than an unrestricted offering to the world at large. Such an offering, though not open to everyone who may choose to apply, is none the less 'public' in character, for the means used to select the particular individuals to whom the offering is to be made bear no sensible relation to the purposes for which the selection is made. * * * To determine the distinction between 'public' and 'private' in any particular context, it is essential to examine the circumstances under which the distinction is sought to be established and to consider the purposes sought to be achieved by such distinction."

The courts below purported to apply this test. The District Court held, in the language of the Sunbeam decision, that "The purpose of the selection bears a 'sensible relation' to the class chosen," finding that "The sole purpose of the 'selection' is to keep part stock ownership of the business within the operating personnel of the business and to spread ownership throughout all departments and activities of the business." The Court of Appeals treated the case as involving "an offering, without solicitation, of common stock to a selected group of key employees of the issuer, most of whom are already stockholders when the offering is made, with the sole purpose of enabling them to secure a proprietary interest in the company or to increase the interest already held by them."

Exemption from the registration requirements of the Securities Act is the question. The design of the statute is to protect investors by promoting full disclosure of information thought necessary to informed investment decisions. The natural way to interpret the private offering exemption is in light of the statutory purpose. Since exempt transactions are those as to which "there is no practical need for * * * [the bill's] application," the applicability of § 4(1) should turn on whether the particular class of persons affected need the protection of the Act. An offering to those who are shown to be able to fend for themselves is a transaction "not involving any public offering."

The Commission would have us go one step further and hold that "an offering to a substantial number of the public" is not exempt under § 4(2). We are advised that "whatever the special circumstances, the Commission has consistently interpreted the exemption as being inapplicable when a large number of offerees is involved." But the statute would seem to apply to a "public offering" whether to few or many.[11]

11. See Viscount Sumner's frequently quoted dictum in Nash v. Lynde, "'The public' * * * is of course a general word. No particular numbers are prescribed. Anything from two to infinity may serve: perhaps even one, if he is intended to be

It may well be that offerings to a substantial number of persons would rarely be exempt. Indeed nothing prevents the commission, in enforcing the statute, from using some kind of numerical test in deciding when to investigate particular exemption claims. But there is no warrant for superimposing a quantity limit on private offerings as a matter of statutory interpretation.

The exemption, as we construe it, does not deprive corporate employees, as a class, of the safeguards of the Act. We agree that some employee offerings may come within § 4(2), e.g., one made to executive personnel who because of their position have access to the same kind of information that the act would make available in the form of a registration statement.[12] Absent such a showing of special circumstances, employees are just as much members of the investing "public" as any of their neighbors in the community. Although we do not rely on it, the rejection in 1934 of an amendment which would have specifically exempted employee stock offerings supports this conclusion. The House Managers, commenting on the Conference Report, said that "the participants in employees' stock-investment plans may be in as great need of the protection afforded by availability of information concerning the issuer for which they work as are most other members of the public." H.R.Rep. No. 1838, 73d Cong., 2d Sess. 41.

Keeping in mind the broadly remedial purposes of federal securities legislation, imposition of the burden of proof on an issuer who would plead the exemption seems to us fair and reasonable. Agreeing, the court below thought the burden met primarily because of the respondent's purpose in singling out its key employees for stock offerings. But once it is seen that the exemption question turns on the knowledge of the offerees, the issuer's motives, laudable though they may be, fade into irrelevance. The focus of inquiry should be on the need of the offerees for the protections afforded by registration. The employees here were not shown to have access to the kind of information which registration would disclose. The obvious opportunities for pressure and imposition make it advisable that they be entitled to compliance with § 5.

Reversed.

THE CHIEF JUSTICE and MR. JUSTICE BURTON dissent.

---

the first of a series of subscribers, but makes further proceedings needless by himself subscribing the whole." [1929] A.C. 158, 169.

12. This was one of the factors stressed in an advisory opinion rendered by the Commission's General Counsel in 1935. "I also regard as significant the relationship between the issuer and the offerees. Thus, an offering to the members of a class who should have special knowledge of the issuer is less likely to be a public offering than is an offering to the members of a class of the same size who do not have this advantage. This factor would be particularly important in offerings to employees, where a class of high executive officers would have a special relationship to the issuer which subordinate employees would not enjoy." 11 Fed.Reg. 10952.

Section 4(2) exempts "transactions by an *issuer* not involving any public offering." The exemption therefore is not available to persons other than issuers. Assume, for example, that the issuer's president and vice president both qualify as purchasers under the *Ralston Purina* test. The issuer can rely on the § 4(2) exemption in offering stock to both the president and vice president. However, what if the issuer sells the stock to the president who three years later decides to sell to the vice president. This second transaction is by the president, not by the issuer. Does this mean that it is not exempt? See § 4(1) and the discussion of the "section 4(1½)" exemption at pages 345–350 below.

The *Ralston Purina* decision highlights a number of factors that are relevant in determining the availability of the § 4(2) exemption. As the following SEC materials indicate, investor sophistication has become significant in determining the availability of the § 4(2) exemption. See especially former Rule 146 and its successor Rule 506. Does the statutory language of § 4(2) properly provide a basis for such a requirement? Does the *Ralston Purina* decision provide a basis for a sophistication requirement?

Can there be a public offering to only one purchaser? Consider an issuer which offers a substantial amount of its stock to a worker on the assembly line who had just won a million dollar lottery. While the *Ralston Purina* test would not appear to be satisfied, is it proper to read the statute to mean that an offer to one person can be a public offering? See footnote 11 on p. 284, above. The language of § 4(2) should be compared to the many state blue sky laws which exempt an offering to less than a specified number of offerees or purchasers without regard to the offerees' or purchasers' sophistication.

NON-PUBLIC OFFERING EXEMPTION

Securities Act Release No. 4552 (Nov. 6, 1962).

The Commission today announced the issuance of a statement regarding the availability of the exemption from the registration requirements of Section 5 of the Securities Act of 1933 afforded by the Section 4(2) of the Act for "transactions by an issuer not involving any public offering," the so-called "private offering exemption." Traditionally, Section 4(2) has been regarded as providing an exemption from registration for bank loans, private placements of securities with institutions, and the promotion of a business venture by a few closely related persons. However, an increasing tendency to rely upon the exemption for offerings of speculative issues to unrelated and uninformed persons prompts this statement to point out the limitations on its availability.

Whether a transaction is one not involving any public offering is essentially a question of fact and necessitates a consideration of all surrounding circumstances, including such factors as the relationship between the offerees and the issuer, the nature, scope, size, type and manner of the offering.

The Supreme Court in S.E.C. v. Ralston Purina Co., 346 U.S. 119, 124, 125 (1953), noted that the exemption must be interpreted in the light of the statutory purpose to "protect investors by promoting full disclosure of information thought necessary to informed investment decisions" and held that "the applicability of Section 4[(2)] should turn on whether the particular class of persons affected need the protection of the Act." The Court stated that the number of offerees is not conclusive as to the availability of the exemption, since the statute seems to apply to an offering "whether to few or many." However, the Court indicated that "nothing prevents the Commission, in enforcing the statute, from using some kind of numerical test in deciding when to investigate particular exemption claims." It should be emphasized, therefore, that the number of persons to whom the offering is extended is relevant only to the question whether they have the requisite association with and knowledge of the issuer which make the exemption available.

Consideration must be given not only to the identity of the actual purchasers but also to the offerees. Negotiations or conversations with or general solicitations of an unrestricted and unrelated group of prospective purchasers for the purpose of ascertaining who would be willing to accept an offer of securities is inconsistent with a claim that the transaction does not involve a public offering even though ultimately there may only be a few knowledgeable purchasers.

A question frequently arises in the context of an offering to an issuer's employees. Limitation of an offering to certain employees designated as key employees may not be a sufficient showing to qualify for the exemption. As the Supreme Court stated in the *Ralston Purina* case: "The exemption as we construe it, does not deprive corporate employees, as a class, of the safeguards of the Act. We agree that some employee offerings may come within Section 4(2), e.g., one made to executive personnel who because of their position have access to the same kind of information that the Act would make available in the form of a registration statement. Absent such a showing of special circumstances, employees are just as much members of the investing 'public' as any of their neighbors in the community." The Court's concept is that the exemption is necessarily narrow. The exemption does not become available simply because offerees are voluntarily *furnished* information about the issuer. Such a construction would give each issuer the choice of registering or making its own voluntary disclosures without regard to the standards and sanctions of the Act.

The sale of stock to promoters who take the initiative in founding or organizing the business would come within the exemption. On the other hand, the transaction tends to become public when the promoters begin to bring in a diverse group of uninformed friends, neighbors and associates.

The size of the offering may also raise questions as to the probability that the offering will be completed within the strict confines of the exemption. An offering of millions of dollars to non-institutional and non-affiliated investors or one divided, or convertible, into many units would suggest that a public offering may be involved.

When the services of an investment banker, or other facility through which public distributions are normally effected, are used to place the securities, special care must be taken to avoid a public offering. If the investment banker places the securities with discretionary accounts and other customers without regard to the ability of such customers to meet the tests implicit in the *Ralston Purina* case, the exemption may be lost. Public advertising of the offerings would, of course, be incompatible with a claim of a private offering. Similarly, the use of the facilities of a securities exchange to place the securities necessarily involves an offering to the public.

An important factor to be considered is whether the securities offered have come to rest in the hands of the initial informed group or whether the purchasers are merely conduits for a wider distribution. Persons who act in this capacity, whether or not engaged in the securities business, are deemed to be "underwriters" within the meaning of Section 2(11) of the Act. If the purchasers do in fact acquire the securities with a view to public distribution, the seller assumes the risk of possible violation of the registration requirements of the Act and consequent civil liabilities.[3] * * *

INTEGRATION OF OFFERINGS

A determination whether an offering is public or private would also include a consideration of the question whether it should be regarded as a part of a larger offering made or to be made. The following factors are relevant to such question of integration: whether (1) the different offerings are part of a single plan of financing, (2) the offerings involve issuance of the same class of security, (3) the offerings are made at or about the same time, (4) the same type of consideration is to be received, (5) the offerings are made for the same general purpose.

What may appear to be a separate offering to a properly limited group will not be so considered if it is one of a related series of offerings. A person may not separate parts of a series of related transactions, the sum total of which is really one offering, and claim that a particular part is a non-public transaction. Thus, in the case of offerings of fractional undivided interests in separate oil or gas properties where the promoters must constantly find new participants for

3. See Release No. 33–4445. [With respect to resale of securities purchased in private placements, see Chapter 2.B.4.]

each new venture, it would appear to be appropriate to consider the entire series of offerings to determine the scope of this solicitation.

As has been emphasized in other releases discussing exemptions from the registration and prospectus requirements of the Securities Act, the terms of an exemption are to be strictly construed against the claimant who also has the burden of proving its availability. Moreover, persons receiving advice from the staff of the Commission that no action will be recommended if they proceed without registration in reliance upon the exemption should do so only with full realization that the tests so applied may not be proof against claims by purchasers of the security that registration should have been effected. Finally, Sections 12(2) and 17 of the Act, which provide civil liabilities and criminal sanctions for fraud in the sale of a security, are applicable to the transactions notwithstanding the availability of an exemption from registration.

Two decisions by the Fifth Circuit in 1971 and 1972 raised serious doubts in the minds of many lawyers as to whether § 4(2) could ever be relied on to exempt the raising of equity capital from a small group of friends or business associates. In HILL YORK CORP. v. AMERICAN INT'L FRANCHISES, INC., 448 F.2d 680 (5th Cir.1971), the court held that defendants had violated the 1933 Act by selling $65,000 worth of securities to 13 "sophisticated businessmen and lawyers" without registering the offering under the Act. In holding the § 4(2) exemption unavailable, the court relied principally on the fact that the purchasers were not supplied with information comparable to what a registration statement would have contained, and that the defendants did not introduce any evidence as to the number and nature of persons to whom the offer was made, other than the actual purchasers.

In SEC v. CONTINENTAL TOBACCO CO., 463 F.2d 137 (5th Cir. 1972), the SEC, relying heavily on the Fifth Circuit's language in the *Hill York* case, persuaded the court of appeals to reverse a district court holding that an offering of common stock to 38 professional and business people was exempt under § 4(2). While the actual decision of the court of appeals did not go as far as it did in *Hill York* in restricting the scope of the private offering exemption, some of the language in the SEC's appeal briefs led many lawyers to conclude that in the Commission's view there could never be a private offering of equity securities to individuals. This, in turn, intensified the pressure for a more "objective" test of what constitutes a "private" offering exempt from 1933 Act registration requirements.

Securities Act Release No. 4552, page 286 above, raises the question of integrating two purportedly separate offerings into one. The integration problem is not limited to the § 4(2) exemption. See, e.g., the discussion of the intrastate exemption at pages 309–324 below. The SEC applies the five-factor test to integration problems generally. In addition, Rule 502(a) establishes a safe harbor for Regulation D offerings.

Integration may also be a problem when an exempt transaction is followed by a public offering (or vice versa). If the two offerings are integrated then the offers to the public will most likely make the exemption unavailable. The offers in the purportedly exempt transaction will not comply with the prospectus requirements and in turn may affect the validity of the public offering.

Can an issuer, planning on a public offering, raise seed money prior to the public offering through a nonpublic offering? See Rule 152 and SEC no-action letters to Vintage Group, Incorporated (April 11, 1988); The Immune Response Corporation (Nov. 2, 1987); Vulture Petroleum Corp. (Dec. 31, 1986).

Letters From a Kentucky Lawyer

The following correspondence indicates the need for simplified tests and procedures for exempting essentially local offerings from 1933 Act registration requirements. The first letter (names changed to preserve anonymity) was received by the SEC's regional office in Chicago in 1963, from a lawyer in a small town in Kentucky, apparently in response to an inquiry from the SEC:

Dear Sirs:

Mr. Abner Hawkins, president of Mountainville Auto Auctions, Inc., has handed me your letter of January 12, to which please refer.

I set up the corporation for these fellows. It has an authorized capital of $50,000, 500 shares of $100 par value. They have bought themselves a lot and are aiming to put up a place where used cars are auctioned off. There is one other such place doing same business in this county already. The boys' intentions are to sell stock only to used car dealers. The auction is to be where dealers only can purchase cars. To keep the stock from getting out of the hands of used car dealers, there was placed on the stock certificates the words "This stock certificate cannot be transferred without consent of Board of Directors", or words to that effect. It is not their intention to sell to the general public at all. It was to be an auction lot owned by, run by, and for the benefit of used car dealers. I know this for a fact, because I set in on several of their meetings when they started the corporation last April. Of course, I suppose they could sell stock to the public if they took a mind to. There is nothing in their charter forbidding it. But the whole idea was that if a used car dealer owned stock in this company, then he would naturally bring his cars there to auction them off. So, sale of stock was to be to used car dealers in order to promote business profit. Selling to somebody not a dealer would not get them anymore business.

Now I will frankly tell you that I am a country lawyer. There are a dozen lawyers in this town, and I would not give two cents for what all of us put together know about Federal laws. The reason is that each one of the regulatory or administrative agencies of the govt. has got its own books of rules and regulations, and if a lawyer here had them he would be needing a barn to put them in, and he would be bankrupt from buying them. So, most of us gave up on Federal law long ago. All I've got is a $3 book on bankruptcy. If some poor fellow comes in with a Federal Problem, I tell him to write his Congressman. There may be a copy of the Securities Act of 1933, referred to in your letter, in this town, but I don't know who would have it, and I sure don't.

So, if the Mountainville Auto Auction boys are doing something you don't like, you let me know what it is and I will tell them to quit it. Or, if there are some papers you want them to fill out, please send them to me and I will try to get them filled out right for them and send them back to you.

I can't figure how you ever heard of this little outfit. I think their competitors must have written to you. Maybe you could also check on their competitors, though I am sure that nobody is intentionally violating any Federal law.

Your early reply will be appreciated, and you may be assured of complete cooperation.

Yours,

/s/ J.M. Turnbull

In response, the SEC apparently sent its standard package of 1933 Act, Regulations and Releases. Six weeks later it received the following reply:

Dear Sirs:

I thank you for your letter of January 22, 1963, and I regret that I have taken so long to reply.

It does appear that the stock offering might not have been entirely intrastate, and that therefore registration is required unless exempted. I have wended my way through all the material you sent me, and I think I fairly comprehend the substance of Release Nos. 4434, 4554, 4450, 4470, and the Securities Act of 1933. However, I must confess that "General Rules and Regulations under the Securities Act of 1933" is the most incomprehensible document that has ever come to my hand. When I graduated from law school, I got the highest grade on the state bar exam, I had an I.Q. of 137, and I still can't read this damn thing and make any sense out of it. I think the reason is that it constantly refers from one paragraph to another causing the reader to jump back and forth until he loses not only his place but his train of thought.

I presume that this stock issue is exempt under section 257 as an offering not in excess of $50,000. If you all wish to pursue this matter further, please send me some blank forms to fill out.

Yours,

/s/ J.M. Turnbull

In response to requests for more certainty as to when an offering is public, the Commission in 1974 adopted a new Rule 146, under which an offering was not deemed to be "public" within the meaning of § 4(2) if (a) the securities were purchased by not more than 35 persons (not counting purchasers of more than $150,000 worth); (b) there was no general solicitation or advertising; (c) the securities were offered and sold only to persons meeting certain criteria of investment experience and ability to bear the risk; (d) the offerees were furnished with information comparable to that contained in a registration statement, and (e) steps were taken to assure that the securities could not be resold except in accordance with the rules governing resales.

Rule 146 provided a degree of certainty by specifying what information should be *furnished* to purchasers to satisfy the test rather than requiring that they have *access* to information by virtue of their relationship to the issuer. However, the Rule was extremely complex and technical, and many issuers continued to rely on the statutory exemption provided by § 4(2). The Fifth Circuit, which had created much of the uncertainty about § 4(2), modified its interpretation of that section to correspond more closely to the Rule 146 approach:

DORAN v. PETROLEUM MGMT. CORP.

545 F.2d 893 (5th Cir.1977).

Before GOLDBERG, DYER and SIMPSON, CIRCUIT JUDGES.

GOLDBERG, Circuit Judge: In this case a sophisticated investor who purchased a limited partnership interest in an oil drilling venture seeks to rescind. The question raised is whether the sale was part of a private offering exempted by § 4(2) of the Securities Act of 1933, from the registration requirements of that Act. We hold that in the absence of findings of fact that each offeree had been furnished information about the issuer that a registration statement would have disclosed or that each offeree had effective access to such information, the district court erred in concluding that the offering was a private placement. Accordingly, we reverse and remand.

I. FACTS

Prior to July 1970, Petroleum Management Corporation (PMC) organized a California limited partnership for the purpose of drilling and operating four wells in Wyoming. The limited partnership agreement provided for both "participants," whose capital contributions were to be used first to pay all intangible expenses incurred by the partnership, and "special participants," whose capital contributions were to be applied first to pay tangible drilling expenses.

PMC and Inter-Tech Resources, Inc., were initially the only "special participants" in the limited partnership. They were joined by four "participants." As found by the district court, PMC contacted only four other persons with respect to possible participation in the partnership. All but the plaintiff declined.

* * *

The court below found that the offer and sale of the "special participant" interest was a private offering because Doran was a sophisticated investor who did not need the protection of the Securities Acts.

* * *

II. The Private Offering Exemption

* * *

The defendants do not contest the existence of the elements of plaintiff's prima facie case but raise an affirmative defense that the relevant transactions came within the exemption from registration found in § 4(2). Specifically, they contend that the offering of securities was not a public offering. The defendants, who of course bear the burden of proving this affirmative defense, must therefore show that the offering was private.

This court has in the past identified four factors relevant to whether an offering qualifies for the exemption. * * * The relevant factors include the number of offerees and their relationship to each other and the issuer, the number of units offered, the size of the offering, and the manner of the offering. Consideration of these factors need not exhaust the inquiry, nor is one factor's weighing heavily in favor of the private status of the offering sufficient to ensure the availability of the exemption. Rather, these factors serve as guideposts to the court in attempting to determine whether subjecting the offering to registration requirements would further the purposes of the 1933 Act.

* * *

In the case at bar, the defendants may have demonstrated the presence of the latter three factors. A small number of units offered, relatively modest financial stakes, and an offering characterized by personal contact between the issuer and offeree free of public advertising or intermediaries such as investment bankers or securities exchanges—these aspects of the instant transaction aid the defendants' search for a § 4(2) exemption.

Nevertheless, with respect to the first, most critical, and conceptually most problematic factor, the record does not permit us to agree that the defendants have proved that they are entitled to the limited sanctuary afforded by § 4(2). We must examine more closely the importance of demonstrating both the number of offerees and their relationship to the issuer in order to see why the defendants have not yet gained the § 4(2) exemption.

A. The Number of Offerees

Establishing the number of persons involved in an offering is important both in order to ascertain the magnitude of the offering and in order to determine the characteristics and knowledge of the persons thus identified.

* * *

In the case at bar, the record indicates that eight investors were offered limited partnership shares in the drilling program—a total that would be entirely consistent with a finding that the offering was private.

The defendants attempt to limit the number of offerees even further, however. They argue that Doran was the sole offeree because all others contacted by PMC were offered "participant" rather than "special participant" interests. The district court, which did not issue a finding of fact or conclusion of law with respect to this argument, appears to have assumed that there were eight offerees.

* * *

In considering the number of offerees solely as indicative of the magnitude or scope of an offering, the difference between one and eight offerees is relatively unimportant. Rejecting the argument that Doran was the sole offeree is significant, however, because it means that in considering the need of the offerees for the protection that registration would have afforded we must look beyond Doran's interests to those of all his fellow offerees. Even the offeree-plaintiff's 20–20 vision with respect to the facts underlying the security would not save the exemption if any one of his fellow offerees was blind.

B. The Offerees' Relationship to the Issuer

Since SEC v. Ralston Purina, courts have sought to determine the need of offerees for the protections afforded by registration by focusing on the relationship between offerees and issuer and more particularly on the information available to the offerees by virtue of that relationship. Once the offerees have been identified, it is possible to investigate their relationship to the issuer.

The district court concluded that the offer of a "special participant" interest to Doran was a private offering because Doran was a sophisticated investor who did not need the protections afforded by registration. It is important, in light of our rejection of the argument that Doran was the sole offeree, that the district court also found that all four "participants" and all three declining offerees were also sophisticated investors with regard to oil ventures.

* * *

1. The role of investment sophistication

The lower court's finding that Doran was a sophisticated investor is amply supported by the record, as is the sophistication of the other offerees. Doran holds a petroleum engineering degree from Texas A & M University. His net worth is in excess of $1,000,000. His holdings of approximately twenty-six oil and gas properties are valued at $850,000.

Nevertheless, evidence of a high degree of business or legal sophistication on the part of all offerees does not suffice to bring the offering within the private placement exemption. We clearly established that proposition in Hill York Corp. v. American International Franchises, Inc. We reasoned that "if the plaintiffs did not possess the information requisite for a registration statement, they could not bring their sophisticated knowledge of business affairs to bear in deciding whether or not to invest * * *." Sophistication is not a substitute for access to the information that registration would disclose.

* * *

In short, there must be sufficient basis of accurate information upon which the sophisticated investor may exercise his skills. Just as a scientist cannot be without his specimens, so the shrewdest investor's acuity will be blunted without specifications about the issuer. For an investor to be invested with exemptive status he must have the required data for judgment.

2. The requirement of available information

* * *

The requirement that all offerees have available the information registration would provide has been firmly established by this court as a necessary condition of gaining the private offering exemption.

* * *

In Hill York Corp. v. American International Franchises, Inc., this court approved jury instructions that "correctly stated the ultimate test. * * * that every offeree had to have information equivalent to which a registration statement would disclose." In subsequent cases we have adhered to that test. See Woolf v. S.D. Cohn & Co., 515 F.2d at 613; SEC v. Continental Tobacco Co., 463 F.2d at 158–61; Henderson v. Hayden, Stone Inc., 461 F.2d at 1071. Because the district court failed to apply this test to the case at bar, but rather inferred from evidence of Doran's sophistication that his purchase of a partnership share was incident to a private offering, we must remand so that the lower court may determine the extent of the information available to each offeree.

More specifically, we shall require on remand that the defendants demonstrate that all offerees, whatever their expertise, had available the information a registration statement would have afforded a prospective investor in a public offering. * * *

C. On Remand: The Issuer-Offeree Relationship

In determining on remand the extent of the information available to the offerees, the district court must keep in mind that the "availability" of information means either disclosure of or effective access to the relevant information. The relationship between issuer and offeree is most critical when the issuer relies on the latter route.

* * *

1. Disclosure or access: a disjunctive requirement

That our cases sometimes fail clearly to differentiate between "access" and "disclosure" as alternative means of coming within the private offering exemption is, perhaps, not surprising. Although the *Ralston Purina* decision focused on whether the offerees had "access" to the required information, the holding that "the exemption question turns on the knowledge of the offerees," could be construed to include possession as well as access. Such an interpretation would require disclosure as a necessary condition of obtaining a private offering notwithstanding the offerees' access to the information that registration would have provided.

Both the Second and the Fourth Circuits, however, have interpreted *Ralston Purina* as embodying a disjunctive requirement.

* * *

The cases in this circuit are not inconsistent with this view. In Woolf v. S.D. Cohn & Co., supra, 515 F.2d at 612–13, we admittedly read *Continental* as "requiring that there be disclosure of the information registration would have revealed to each offeree * * *." Because the court in *Continental* found neither disclosure to all offerees of the information registration would provide nor their access to such information, however, the case does not hold that when sophisticated offerees have access to the requisite information by virtue of their privileged relationship to the issuer, actual disclosure is nonetheless necessary. Only if the defendants in *Continental* had demonstrated that all offerees were sophisticated and that all had access to the relevant information, but the court had nevertheless required actual disclosure, could *Continental* foreclose the view we express in the case at bar.

Woolf refers to Rule 146 as a "useful frame of reference to an appellate court in assessing the validity of § 4(2) exemptions claimed * * * prior to its effective date." Since *Woolf* elsewhere notes specifically that Rule 146 would permit the issuer to show either access or disclosure, it is inconceivable that the court in *Woolf* would establish more stringent requirements for this circuit or would interpret *Continental* to establish such requirements. Rather, *Woolf* observes correctly that Rule 146 does not purport to be an exclusive definition of the circumstances under which the exemption is available, implying that there will be a class of placements that do not satisfy the more stringent criteria of the Rule 146 safe harbor but are nevertheless to be accorded private status.

Although Rule 146 cannot directly control the case at bar, we think its disjunctive requirement that the private offering claimant may show either "access" or "disclosure" expresses a sound view that this court has in fact implicitly accepted. * * *

IV. Conclusion

An examination of the record and the district court's opinion in this case leaves unanswered the central question in all cases that turn on the availability of the § 4(2) exemption. Did the offerees know or have a realistic opportunity to learn facts essential to an investment judgment? We remand so that the trial court can answer that question.

* * *

We are conscious of the difficulty of formulating black letter law in this area because of the multiplicity of security transactions and their multifarious natures. Securities regulation is often a matter of the hound chasing the hare as issuers devise new ways to issue their securities and the definition of a security itself expands. We do not want the private offering exemption to swallow the Securities Act, and we must resolve doubtful cases against the private placement claimant and in favor of the Act's paramount value of disclosure. By the same token, we must heed the existence and purposes of the exemption, and be cautious lest we discourage private avenues for raising capital. Our present emphasis on the availability of information as the *sine qua non* of the private offering is an attempt to steer a middle course.

SEC v. MURPHY

626 F.2d 633 (9th Cir.1980).

Before Merrill and Ferguson, Circuit Judges, and Smith, District Judge.

Ferguson, Circuit Judge.

* * *

Stephen Murphy formed Intertie, a California company that provided financing, construction, and management of cable television systems, in December, 1971, and he was its president and director until February, 1974, when he became vice-president, treasurer and director. In May, 1975, he resigned from these positions after an unsuccessful proxy fight, but he regained control of the company in August, 1975, and became chairman of the board.

Intertie's business involved the promotion of approximately 30 limited partnerships to which it sold cable television systems. Most commonly, Intertie would buy a cable television system, making a cash down payment and financing the remainder, and then sell it to a partnership for a cash down payment and non-recourse promissory notes in favor of Intertie and lease it back from the partnership. Murphy was the architect of this financing scheme, by which Intertie took in approximately $7.5 million from 400 investors. Intertie engaged International Securities Corporation (ISC), a securities brokerage firm, to sell most of these partnership interests, and it agreed that ISC would receive a 10 percent sales commission. ISC's president, Jack

Glassford, and ISC shared a three percent commission override. From this three percent, starting in the summer of 1974, Murphy received a one-half percent commission on the sales of partnership interests.

Under ISC's sales program, representatives contacted potential investors to interest them in purchasing limited partnership shares in cable television systems. An ISC sales representative was usually the general partner in the venture. Intertie and ISC did not register the limited partnership interests as securities but relied on the private offering exemption of § 4(2) of the Securities Act, and on Rule 146, which provides a "safe harbor" for private placements that meet certain specified conditions.

Intertie took no steps to assure that the offering and sale were directed only to a small number of sophisticated, informed investors; in fact, it did not even number its memoranda so that it could monitor the volume of offers made. Moreover, Murphy in his deposition stated that he felt that information on qualifications of investors was often inadequate. Intertie relied on ISC to comply with the securities laws and agreed by letter to take whatever steps ISC requested for compliance. There was no written contract allocating this responsibility to ISC, however. Neither Intertie nor ISC assured that offeree representatives that the investors used were capable of providing informed advice, even though Murphy doubted the competence of many of the offeree representatives he met.[3] Some of the representatives were salesmen for ISC and a few acted as both salesman and general partner for a partnership.

* * *

Murphy participated heavily in the offerings. He prepared or reviewed Intertie's offering memoranda and sales brochures and sometimes revised language written by Intertie's lawyers; he drafted other materials for distribution to offerees of limited partnership interests; he met with ISC salesmen and with potential investors and their representatives, if any, to give them information about Intertie; and he presented the Intertie investment plan at sales seminars with broker-dealers.

* * *

In 1975, the SEC brought suit against Murphy and other defendants, charging violations of the registration and fraud provisions of the securities laws, and seeking injunctive relief. * * *

The district court granted summary judgment for the SEC on the registration count, finding a violation of § 5(a) and (c) of the 1933 Act, which forbid offers and sales of securities in interstate commerce unless a registration statement is in effect for the security.

The defendant argues that the court's grant of summary judgment on the registration count was inappropriate because there were disput-

3. When asked at his SEC deposition about the offeree representatives, Murphy said: "Some are extremely competent and know the questions to ask and pursue it and ask it and others * * * God help the investors is kind of my feeling about the offeree representatives."

ed facts material to the following issues; whether the limited partnership interests were securities, whether the securities were exempt from registration, whether the transactions were covered by the securities laws, and whether his activities were sufficient to subject him to liability.

* * *

A. Elements of a Section 5 Violation

Section 5 of the 1933 Act forbids the offer or sale of unregistered securities in interstate commerce, but § 5 does not apply if the securities are exempt from registration as a private offering, § 4(2), or are not offered or sold in a transaction by an issuer, underwriter or dealer, § 4(1).

1. Security

Murphy argues on appeal that the shares in limited partnerships in the cable television systems were not securities. That argument is disingenuous. An investment contract is a security. Under the test for an investment contract established in SEC v. W.J. Howey Co., a limited partnership generally is a security, Goodman v. Epstein, because by definition, it involves investment in a common enterprise with profits to come solely from the efforts of others. In SEC v. Glenn W. Turner Enterprises, Inc., this court held that it would not confine the *Howey* test to situations where the term "solely from the efforts of others" applied literally, but would find that element satisfied when "the efforts made by those other than the investor are the undeniably significant ones, those essential managerial efforts which affect the failure or success of the enterprise." Here the investors had no managerial role whatsoever: the limited partnership interests clearly are securities.

2. Unregistered and Sold in Interstate Commerce

Murphy admitted in the pretrial order that the limited partnership interests were not registered, and he offered nothing to rebut the SEC's evidence that the securities were offered and sold in interstate commerce.

3. Not Exempt from Registration

Murphy contends, however, that the limited partnership interests were exempt from registration under the private offering exemption in § 4(2) of the 1933 Act, or under Rule 146, which each exempt certain private placements.

* * *

A court assessing the availability of a private offering exemption focuses upon the issuer and the offerees, paying particular attention to the relationship between the two. * * * The problem in this case, as the SEC conceded at oral argument, is that it is not clear who was the issuer of the securities at suit.

As defined in the 1933 Act, "'issuer' means every person who issues or proposes to issue any security." In a corporate offering, the issuer generally is the company whose stock is sold. Here there is no company issuing stock, but instead, a group of individuals investing funds in an enterprise for profit, Cal.Corp.Code § 15006(1), and receiving in return an entitlement to a percentage of the proceeds of the enterprise. That entitlement, a partnership share, is similar to a share of stock, however; and, just as a share of stock is considered issued by the corporation, so should a partnership share be considered issued by the partnership.

* * *

In determining that a security qualifies as a private offering, then, we must make sure that the offerees are provided with or given access to the information that is material to their investment decision. * * * In a limited partnership setting, information about the issuer—the partnership—would be of no value if the partnership did not predate the investor's entry into the venture, and it might be of little value even if the partnership did have a history of operation. In the latter case, information about the partnership's previous record would be material, but it would not, alone, be sufficient. The information crucial to the investment decision would be that concerning the entity which was responsible for the success or failure of the enterprise.

* * *

Here, Murphy himself conceded that information about Intertie's finances was material to the decision whether to invest in a limited partnership that Intertie promoted. Given the realities of Intertie's financing scheme, that concession was unavoidable. Intertie developed the partnership offering plan and assumed a major role in engaging investors. It engineered and operated the systems from which the investors would receive their returns. It managed many of the partnerships and it prepared tax forms for most of them. Without generating new capital through continued partnership offerings, Intertie could not meet its obligations on the systems sold to previous investors.

For all these reasons, Intertie clearly held the key to success or failure of the partnerships. Accordingly, Intertie was the entity about which the investors needed information, and, therefore, it is properly considered the issuer of the securities for purposes of determining the availability of a private offering exemption.

* * * [O]ur holding today does not mean that anyone who has information material to an investment decision is transformed into an issuer. We hold only that when a person organizes or sponsors the organization of limited partnerships and is primarily responsible for the success or failure of the venture for which the partnership is formed, he will be considered an issuer for purposes of determining the availability of the private offering exemption.

a. Private Offering Exemption: § 4(2)

* * *

(1.) The Number of Offerees

The *Ralston Purina* decision made it clear that there was no rigid limit to the number of offerees to whom an issuer could make a private offering. Nonetheless, while the number of offerees, itself, is not decisive, "the more offerees, the more likelihood that the offering is public." Murphy introduced no evidence below to suggest that the number of offerees was small or that there was even any attempt to monitor the number of offerees at all.

The SEC introduced Murphy's deposition, in which he stated that offering memoranda were not numbered. Apparently, then, no one knows how many offerees ISC contacted on any of the partnership offerings. Once the SEC provided evidence that there was no control placed on the number of offerees, it was incumbent upon Murphy, in opposing summary judgment, to rebut that evidence. Without introducing evidence on the number of offerees, Murphy could not satisfy even the small burden imposed on a party resisting summary judgment.

Moreover, the SEC contends that we should look at the number of offerees not on an individual system basis, but in the aggregate. It argues that each offering of limited partnership interests was part of an overall plan for financing Intertie's operations and that, therefore, the offerings should be considered integrated.

In Securities Act Release No. 4552 (Nov. 6, 1962), the Commission set out five factors to be used in determining whether to consider apparently separate offerings as one integrated offering. These factors guide our evaluation. The factors are: (a) whether the offerings are part of a single plan of financing; (b) whether the offerings involve issuance of the same class of securities; (c) whether the offerings are made at or about the same time; (d) whether the same kind of consideration is to be received; and (e) whether the offerings are made for the same general purposes.

Applying these factors to the undisputed facts, we conclude that the offerings of limited partnership interests must be considered integrated. We reach this conclusion despite the difficulty detailed above in determining who was the issuer of the securities in question. As we explained in the introduction to this section of the opinion, supra, Intertie is not technically the issuer of the securities here. Nonetheless, because Murphy developed the scheme for selling partnership shares as a financing mechanism for Intertie, which was responsible for the success or failure of the ventures, we must look to Intertie in evaluating the listed factors.

All but the third factor militate in favor of finding integration. The separation in time from one system offering to the next suggests that the offerings were not integrated, but that factor is heavily outweighed by the remaining considerations. Clearly, the offerings were all made for the same general purpose: they were part of one financing plan which Murphy aptly described, "to give dollars to the cable operating company that could be used at a cost they could live with." To the extent that we can define classes of securities that are not stocks or bonds, the securities at issue here—all limited partnership interests—are of the same class. Finally, the consideration for all partnership shares was the same, cash and notes secured by the particular cable systems purchased.

Thus, factually and legally, the trial court on summary judgment was bound to conclude that the offerings were integrated. While the trial court did not make a specific finding or conclusion on the issue of integration, we must infer that it considered the offerings to be integrated, since it concluded that Intertie was the issuer and that the offerings constituted one placement and the offerees only one group. When we look at the number of purchasers in the aggregate, as we must, their number—400—clearly suggests a public offering rather than a private placement.

(2.) The Sophistication of the Offerees

It was also incumbent upon Murphy to introduce evidence to rebut the inferences of lack of investor sophistication that the court could have drawn from Murphy's deposition testimony. His statement that 60 percent of the investors used offeree representatives suggests at least that the majority of the purchasers, if not the majority of the offerees, lacked the sort of business acumen necessary to qualify as sophisticated investors. Moreover, Murphy's admission that offeree representatives who were also salesmen and general partners in the cable systems did not disclose this relationship to prospective investors suggests the inadequacy of the representatives. His further testimony that some of the offeree representatives whom he met were incompetent reveals both that the investors needed the protections of the Act and that Murphy and Intertie were not concerned about investor sophistication. Intertie did not obtain information about the investors in the limited partnerships, nor did it insist that ISC do so. Murphy merely stated that Intertie relied on ISC to qualify the investors, but he did not produce evidence suggesting that ISC actually took any such steps.

Because the SEC introduced little evidence on the sophistication question, Murphy's burden in resisting summary judgment on this issue was not a great one. Nevertheless, he failed to adduce any evidence on the issue of investor sophistication and, therefore, failed to meet even his limited burden.

(3.) The Size and Manner of the Offering

If an offering is small and is made directly to the offerees "rather than through the facilities of public distribution such as investment bankers or the securities exchanges," a court is more likely to find that it is private. The SEC's evidence shows that the amounts invested in individual systems varied, but that the purchase price for several of the systems was more than $1 million each. Viewed individually, these offerings cannot automatically be labeled small; and there is reason to believe that they should not be viewed individually in any case. When we consider the placements as one integrated offering, we are confronted with a sale of $7.5 million in securities. Without question, that is a sizeable offering, and it is one that we are inclined to consider as public, absent a significant showing that the investors did not need the protection of the Act.

(4.) The Relationship Between the Issuer and the Offerees

A court may only conclude that the investors do not need the protection of the Act if all the offerees have relationships with the issuer affording them access to or disclosure of the sort of information about the issuer that registration reveals. * * * Included in this information is the use of investor funds, the amount of direct and indirect commissions, and accurate financial statements. * * *

The SEC introduced Murphy's testimony that he often refused to provide financial information about Intertie. Murphy also testified that no one disclosed the one-half percent commission that he received or any of the commission above 10 percent that was paid.

Thus, other considerations aside, because the offerees clearly lacked access to financial information about Intertie, we would have to sustain the court's entry of summary judgment on this ground alone.

b. Private Offering Exemption: Rule 146

The offers and sales also were not exempt under Rule 146, adopted by the SEC in 1974. The Rule requires that the issuer and any person who offers or sells securities on his behalf have "reasonable grounds to believe" that the offeree is capable of evaluating the prospective investment or able to bear the economic risk. Rule 146(d)(1). If the offeree becomes a purchaser, he either must be capable of evaluating the investment or he must have a competent advisor and be able to bear the economic risk. Rule 146(d)(2). The discussion above resolves these issues against the defendant. Moreover, each offeree must have access to the kind of information required in Schedule A of the 1933 Act. Rule 146(e)(1). No one furnished the offerees here with such information, and no one provided them access to Intertie's financial statements. In addition, contrary to the requirements of Rule 146(a), the issuer had no reasonable grounds to believe: (1) that offeree representatives were not affiliates or employees of the issuer of the securities; and (2) that the material relationships between the offeree representatives and the issuer had been disclosed to the offerees in writing. Thus, the trial court correctly found that the SEC was entitled to prevail as a matter of law on Murphy's claimed Rule 146 exemption.

In MARY S. KRECH TRUST v. LAKES APARTMENTS, 642 F.2d 98 (5th Cir.1981), an issuer which took the following steps was held to have taken adequate precautions to be entitled to the § 4(2) exemption:

1. The issuer and underwriters compiled a select list of sales representatives who had prior experience with similar offerings.

2. The select group of sales representatives were provided a project fact sheet to help them determine which of their customers would be suitable for the investment.

3. If a broker had an interested customer he or she could obtain a copy of the offering materials only after the broker was questioned as to the customer's suitability.

4. Offerees (who were prescreened) were required to fill out offeree questionnaires requiring them to set out their net worth and financial sophistication (including past experience with similar investments).

5. The completed offeree questionnaires were then reviewed centrally and only after approval would an offer be made.

6. All qualified offerees were given the offering materials and had time to read the materials and ask questions.

Selected References

T. Hazen, Securities Regulation § 4.22 (2d ed.1990).

E. Shapiro & C. Wolf, The Role of Private Placements in Corporate Finance (1972).

Cohn, Securities Markets for Small Issuers: The Barrier of Federal Solicitation and Advertising Prohibitions, 38 U.Fla.L.Rev. 1 (1986).

Deaktor, Integration of Securities Offerings, 31 U.Fla.L.Rev. 465 (1979).

Daugherty, Rethinking the Ban on General Solicitation, 38 Emory L.J. 67 (1989).

Fletcher, Sophisticated Investors Under the Federal Securities Laws, 1988 Duke L.J. 1081.

Integration of Securities Offerings: Report of the Task Force on Integration, 41 Bus.Law 595 (1986).

Lipson & Scharfman, General Solicitations in Exempt Offerings, 20 Rev. Sec. & Commod.Reg. 8 (Jan. 14, 1987).

Marsh, Who Killed The Private Offering Exemption? A Legal Whodunit, 71 Nw.U.L.Rev. 470 (1976).

Schneider, The Statutory Law of Private Placements, 14 Rev.Sec.Reg. 869 (1981).

Section 4(2) and Statutory Law—A Position Paper of the Federal Regulation of Securities Committee, 31 Bus.Lawyer 483 (1975).

Note, Securities Regulation: Integration of Securities Offerings, 34 Okla.L. Rev. 864 (1981).

Comment, Private Placement Exemptions Outside Rule 146, 25 Emory L.J. 899 (1976).

---

2. *Limited Offerings—§ 3(b) and Regulation D*

Rule 146 was extremely complex and technical, and there were many complaints that it was too burdensome on small and growing businesses seeking to raise capital in non-public offerings. The SEC accordingly turned to another section of the 1933 Act to provide relief in these cases. Section 3(b) authorizes the SEC, "by rules and regulations," to exempt offerings, not exceeding a specified dollar amount, when it finds that registration is not necessary "by reason of the small amount involved or the limited character of the public offering." The dollar limit has been periodically raised by Congress from its initial level of $100,000, the most recent increase coming in 1980 and raising the limit from $2 million to the present level of $5 million. Under this authority, the Commission has adopted a number of rules providing exemptions for certain specialized kinds of offerings.

For many years, the principal exemption under § 3(b) for offerings of ordinary securities was Regulation A, consisting of Rules 251–263. As amended by the Commission in 1953, however, Regulation A was not so much an exemption as a simplified form of registration, involving the filing of an "offering circular" (similar in basic form to a statutory prospectus) with a regional office of the SEC. In August 1981, the disclosure requirements for Regulation A offering circulars were substantially modified. However, the Commission announced at the same time that, in view of the widespread acceptance of Form S–18 (the simplified registration form for offerings of up to $7.5 million) and the substantial similarity between the disclosures required by Form S–18 and Regulation A, it was considering the feasibility of eliminating Regulation A. The only significant advantages of Regulation A to a prospective issuer are that it does not require any audited financial statements and does not subject the issuer to periodic reporting requirements under § 15(d) of the 1934 Act. See Sec.Act Rels. Nos. 6339, 6340 (Aug. 7, 1981).

To provide a simple exemption for very small offerings by issuers who could not meet the technical requirements of Rule 146, the Commission in 1975 adopted Rule 240 pursuant to § 3(b). Under that rule, an issuer could sell up to $100,000 of securities in any 12-month period, provided it did not wind up with more than 100 beneficial owners of its securities.

Rule 240 was only useful for extremely small offerings, and the Commission followed it up in 1980 with a new Rule 242, also under the authority of § 3(b). Under Rule 242, an issuer could sell up to $2 million of securities to an unlimited number of "accredited persons" (defined to include certain types of institutions and any person buying at least $100,000 of securities) without requiring that any specific information be furnished to the purchasers. The offering could also include sales to not more than 35 "non-accredited persons," provided they were furnished with information comparable to that contained in a Form S–18 registration statement.

Also in 1980, Congress added a new § 4(6) to the 1933 Act, exempting any offering of not more than $5 million made solely to "accredited investors" (defined to include specified types of institutions and other classes of investors that the SEC might specify by rule).

These developments set the stage for the coordination of the private offering and small offering exemptions in a new Regulation D. In 1982, the Commission took a major step in simplifying and coordinating the exemptions for limited offerings by repealing Rules 146, 240 and 242, and adopting in their place a new Regulation D, composed of Rules 501 through 506.

Definitions. Rule 501 defines the terms used in Regulation D. The most important of these is the term "accredited investor," which is defined to include (1) any bank, savings and loan association, credit union, insurance company, investment company, or employee benefit plan, (2) any business development company, (3) any charitable or educational institution with assets of more than $5 million, as well as corporations, partnerships, and business trusts with more than $5 million in assets, (4) any director, executive officer or general partner of the issuer, (5) any person with a net worth of more than $1 million, and (6) any person with an annual income of more than $200,000 (or annual joint spousal income of $300,000).

Rule 502 sets forth certain conditions applicable to all offerings under Regulation D:

Integration. Offerings that are separated in time by more than six months are not deemed to be parts of a single offering. Whether offerings within six months of each other will be considered part of a single offering depends on application of the five factors traditionally employed by the SEC: whether the offerings (1) are part of a single plan of financing, (2) involve the same class of security, (3) are made at or about the same time, (4) involve the same type of consideration, and (5) are made for the same general purpose.

Information. If an issuer sells securities under Rule 504 or to accredited investors only, there are no specific requirements for furnishing information to offerees or purchasers. If securities are sold to non-accredited purchasers under Rule 505 or 506, the following information must be furnished to all purchasers:

> If the issuer is not registered under the 1934 Act, the information that would be contained in a registration statement on Form S–18 or, if the offering exceeds $5 million, the information that would be contained in a registration statement on the form the issuer would be entitled to use. For offerings under $2 million the informational requirements can be satisfied by supplying the information required by Regulation A (supplemented by a certified balance sheet).
>
> If the issuer is registered under the 1934 Act, its most recent annual report to shareholders and proxy statement, or the information contained in its most recent annual report to the Commission, plus specified updating and supplemental information.

Manner of Offering and Limitations on Resale. No general solicitation or general offering is permitted. Securities sold pursuant to Regulation D are considered to have been purchased in a non-public offering and cannot be resold without registration unless an exemption is available under § 4(1) or Rule 144 (see Ch. 2.B.4., below). The issuer must take certain specified precautions to insure that the purchasers do not make resales.

Notice. Under Rule 503, notices of any sales pursuant to Regulation D must be filed with the Commission. Rule 507 renders Regulation D unavailable if the issuer, its predecessors, or affiliates have been subject to a court order or decree for noncompliance with Rule 503's notice requirement. Rule 507(b) permits the Commission to waive this disqualification. Failure to file Rule 503 notices will not by itself destroy the exemption.

Rule 504. Under Rule 504, an issuer can sell an aggregate of $1 million of securities in any twelve-month period to any number of purchasers, accredited or non-accredited, with no requirements for furnishing of any information to the purchasers, except that not more than $500,000 can be offered without registration under a state securities law. If the offering is made only in states where it must be registered under state law and a disclosure document delivered to purchasers before the sale, the Rule 502 restrictions on the manner of offering and resales by purchasers do not apply. The exemption is available to all issuers except investment companies and companies registered under the 1934 Act.

Rule 505. Under Rule 505, an issuer can sell up to $5 million of securities in any 12-month period to any number of accredited investors and up to 35 other purchasers. If there are any non-accredited purchasers, the information prescribed by Rule 502 must be furnished to all purchasers. The exemption is available to any issuer other than an investment company or an issuer that would be disqualified by Rule 252 from using Regulation A.

Rule 506. Under Rule 506, an issuer can sell an unlimited amount of securities to any number of accredited investors and up to 35 other purchasers. Prior to the sale, the issuer must reasonably believe that each non-accredited investor, or his "purchaser representative" (a term defined in Rule 501) has such knowledge or experience in financial and business matters that he is capable of evaluating the merits and risks of the prospective investment. If there are any non-accredited purchasers, the information prescribed by Rule 502 must be furnished to all purchasers. The exemption is available to all issuers.

Note that offerings complying with Rule 504 or 505 are exempted from registration pursuant to § 3(b) of the Act, while offerings complying with Rule 506 (which may amount to more than $5 million) are deemed to be transactions not involving any public offering within the meaning of § 4(2). Also note that Rule 506 is not the exclusive method of complying with § 4(2); offerings which do not meet all of the Rule's requirements may still be exempt under § 4(2) as interpreted by the courts and the SEC.

Rule 508. Rule 508 provides that "insignificant deviations" from Regulation D's requirements will not destroy the exemption so long as the issuer made a reasonable and good faith effort to comply and the deviation did not pertain to a term or condition designed to protect the complaining party.

Section 4(6). The Commission also adopted a new Rule 215, defining the term "accredited investor" for purposes of § 4(6) to include the various categories of purchasers listed in Rule 501. Section 4(6) is thus an alternative exemption for an offering of up to $5 million made solely to accredited investors.

Exemption for Employee Compensation Plans

In 1988, the Commission adopted a § 3(b) exemption for certain employee compensation plans. Rule 701 exempts employee stock compensation plans (ranging from $500,000 to $5 million annually) provided that the issuer is neither a 1934 Act reporting company nor a registered investment company. Issuers relying on the Rule 701 exemption are not precluded from relying on other exemptions as well. See preliminary note 3.

There are five preconditions to the Rule 701 exemption:

1. *Issuer Qualification.* The exemption is not available to issuers whose securities are traded on a national exchange or the more active over-the-counter markets. The exemption is only available to the issuer and thus cannot be used by affiliates or anyone else reselling the securities on the issuer's behalf. Rule 703(T) provides that the exemption is not available to an issuer where it, its predecessors, or its affiliates are subject to a court order enjoining violations of Rule 702's notification requirements. However, this disqualification may be waived by the Commission upon a showing of good cause.

2. *Qualified Plans.* The Rule 701 exemption can be used for stock purchase plans, option plans, bonus plans, stock appreciation rights, profitsharing, thrift, incentive, or similar plans. Rule 701(b)(1) permits issuers to offer securities pursuant to a written contract or written compensation plan to its employees, directors, general partners, trustees, officers, consultants, or advisors. The exemption is not available for compensation of underwriters or most promoters. See Preliminary Note 5 ("[I]n view of the primary purpose of the rule, which is to provide an exemption from the registration requirements of the Act for securities issued in compensatory circumstances, the rule is not available for plans or schemes to circumvent this purpose, such as to raise capital").

3. *Limitation on Amount.* The maximum amount of securities that can be offered within a twelve month period pursuant to a compensation plan varies from $500,000 to $5 million, depending upon the size of the company and number of shares already outstanding. Rule 701(b)(5) establishes a $500,000 limit with two alternative means of raising that limit up to the $5 million dollar ceiling of § 3(b).

4. *Notification Requirements.* Rule 702(T) requires that the issuer give notice of all sales pursuant to a Rule 701 exemption. The notice is to be filed on Form 701 at the Commission's office in Washington, D.C. within thirty days of any sale that places the aggregate sales within a twelve month period above $100,000.

5. *Restrictions on Resale.* Securities acquired pursuant to a Rule 701 offering are deemed to be restricted securities within the meaning of Rule 144. See pp. 343–345 below.

Integration Doctrine not Applicable. Rule 701(b)(6) contains an express exclusion from the integration doctrine. Unlike the other § 3(b) exemptions (Regulation A, Rule 504, and Rule 505) securities sold pursuant to other § 3(b) exemptions need not be counted in the $5 million ceiling.

Applicability of Antifraud Provisions and State Law. In Preliminary Note 1, the Commission points out that the Rule 701 exemption does not limit the issuer's disclosure obligations under the antifraud provisions. Similarly, Preliminary Note 2 explains that the Rule 701 exemption does not affect the need to comply with state law registration requirements.

Selected References

T. Hazen, Securities Regulation §§ 4.17–4.22 (2d ed.1990).

Donahue, New Exemptions from the Registration Requirements of the Securities Act of 1933: Regulation D, 10 Sec.Reg.L.J. 235 (1982).

Warren, A Review of Regulation D: The Present Exemption Regimes for Limited Offerings Under the Securities Act of 1933, 33 Am.U.L.Rev. 355 (1984).

Note, Regulation D: Coherent Exemptions for Small Businesses Under the Securities Act of 1933, 24 Wm. & Mary L.Rev. 121 (1982).

Computer Exercise

Hazen, Small Issues Exemptions, published by The Center for Computer Assisted Legal Instruction.

---

3. *Intrastate Offerings*

Section 3(a)(11) of the 1933 Act exempts from the registration requirements of that Act "any security which is part of an issue offered and sold only to persons resident within a single State * * * where the issuer of such security is * * * a corporation incorporated by and doing business within such State * * *." This exemption for intrastate offerings raises many of the same questions as the exemption for non-public offerings in § 4(2). There are similar problems as to whether the offering should be "integrated" with other offerings, whether the securities sold have "come to rest" in the hands of the purchasers, and in the total loss of the exemption whenever there is a single offer or sale to an ineligible person. The key difference is that while the focus of § 4(2) is on the number and nature of the offerees and their access to relevant information, the focus of § 3(a)(11) is simply on whether they are "residents" of the state (plus the additional requirement that the corporation be "doing business" in the state).

The pattern of development in this area has also been similar. Court decisions and SEC statements created increasing uncertainty as to whether the exemption could ever be safely relied upon. This resulted in demands for the promulgation of more "objective" standards, culminating in the adoption of SEC Rule 147, which purports to supply those standards.

While the non-public offering and intrastate offering exemptions may be alternative routes to avoid registration in any particular situation, they cannot be combined. In other words, a corporation cannot offer securities to the general public in its home state and simultaneously offer the same securities to a limited number of residents of other states to whom a private offering could be made. The offering must comply completely with one or the other exemption; it cannot straddle them.

SECTION 3(A)(11) EXEMPTION FOR LOCAL OFFERINGS

Securities Act Release No. 4434 (Dec. 6, 1961).

The meaning and application of the exemption from registration provided by Section 3(a)(11) of the Securities Act of 1933, as amended, have been the subject of court opinions, releases of the Securities and Exchange Commission [Release Nos. 33–1459 (1937) and 33–4386 (1961)], and opinions and interpretations expressed by the staff of the Commission in response to specific inquiries. This release is published to provide in convenient and up-to-date form a restatement of the principles underlying Section 3(a)(11) as so expressed over the years and to facilitate an understanding of the meaning and application of the exemption.

General Nature of Exemption

Section 3(a)(11), as amended in 1954, exempts from the registration and prospectus requirements of the Act:

"Any security which is a part of an issue offered and sold only to persons resident within a single State or Territory, where the issuer of such security is a person resident and doing business within, or, if a corporation, incorporated by and doing business within, such State or Territory."

The legislative history of the Securities Act clearly shows that this exemption was designed to apply only to local financing that may practicably be consummated in its entirety within the State or Territory in which the issuer is both incorporated and doing business. As appears from the legislative history, by amendment to the Act in 1934, this exemption was removed from Section 5(c) and inserted in Section 3, relating to "Exempted Securities", in order to relieve dealers of an unintended restriction on trading activity. This amendment was not intended to detract from its essential character as a transaction exemption.

"Issue" Concept

A basic condition of the exemption is that the *entire issue* of securities be offered and sold exclusively to residents of the state in question. Consequently, an offer to a non-resident which is considered a part of the intrastate issue will render the exemption unavailable to the entire offering.

Whether an offering is "a part of an issue", that is, whether it is an integrated part of an offering previously made or proposed to be made, is a question of fact and depends essentially upon whether the offerings are a related part of a plan or program. Thus the exemption should not be relied upon in combination with another exemption for the different parts of a single issue where a part is offered or sold to non-residents.

The determination of what constitutes an "issue" is not governed by state law. Shaw v. U.S., 131 F.2d 476, 480 (C.A.9, 1942). Any one or more of the following factors may be determinative of the question of integration: (1) are the offerings part of a single plan of financing; (2) do the offerings involve issuance of the same class of security; (3) are the offerings made at or about the same time; (4) is the same type of consideration to be received, and (5) are the offerings made for the same general purpose.

Moreover, since the exemption is designed to cover only those security distributions, which, as a whole, are essentially local in character, it is clear that the phrase "sold only to persons resident" as used in Section 3(a)(11) cannot refer merely to the initial sales by the issuing corporation to its underwriters, or even the subsequent resales by the underwriters to distributing dealers. To give effect to the fundamental purpose of the exemption, it is necessary that the entire issue of securities shall be offered and sold to, and come to rest only in the hands of residents within the state. If any part of the issue is offered or sold to a non-resident, the exemption is unavailable not only for the securities so sold, but for all securities forming a part of the issue, including those sold to residents. It is incumbent upon the issuer, underwriter, dealers and other persons connected with the offering to make sure that it does not become an interstate distribution through resales. It is understood to be customary for such persons to obtain assurances that purchases are not made with a view to resale to non-residents.

DOING BUSINESS WITHIN THE STATE

In view of the local character of the Section 3(a)(11) exemption, the requirement that the issuer be doing business in the state can only be satisfied by the performance of substantial operational activities in the state of incorporation. The doing business requirement is not met by functions in the particular state such as bookkeeping, stock record and similar activities or by offering securities in the state. Thus, the exemption would be unavailable to an offering by a company made in the state of its incorporation of undivided fractional oil and gas interests located in other states even though the company conducted other business in the state of its incorporation. While the person creating the fractional interests is technically the "issuer" as defined in Section 2(4) of the Act, the purchaser of such security obtains no interest in the issuer's separate business within the state. * * * So also, a Section 3(a)(11) exemption should not be relied upon for each of a series of corporations organized in different states where there is in fact and purpose a single business enterprise or financial venture whether or not it is planned to merge or consolidate the various corporations at a later date.

RESIDENCE WITHIN THE STATE

Section 3(a)(11) requires that the entire issue be confined to a single state in which the issuer, the offerees and the purchasers are residents. Mere presence in the state is not sufficient to constitute residence as in the case of military personnel at a military post. The mere obtaining of formal representations of residence and agreements not to resell to non-residents or agreements that sales are void if the purchaser is a non-resident should not be relied upon without more as establishing the availability of the exemption. * * *

RESALES

From these general principles it follows that if during the course of distribution any underwriter, any distributing dealer (whether or not a member of the formal selling or distributing group), or any dealer or other person purchasing securities from a distributing dealer for resale were to offer or sell such securities to a non-resident, the exemption would be defeated. In other words, Section 3(a)(11) contemplates that the exemption is applicable only if the entire issue is distributed pursuant to the statutory conditions. Consequently, any offers or sales to a non-resident in connection with the distribution of the issue would destroy the exemption as to all securities which are a part of that issue, including those sold to residents regardless of whether such sales are made directly to non-residents or indirectly through residents who as part of the distribution thereafter sell to non-residents.

This is not to suggest, however, that securities which have actually come to rest in the hands of resident investors, such as persons purchasing without a view to further distribution or resale to non-residents, may not in due course be resold by such persons, whether directly or through dealers or brokers, to non-residents without in any way affecting the exemption. The relevance of any such resales consists only of the evidentiary light which they might cast upon the factual question whether the securities had in fact come to rest in the hands of resident investors. If the securities are resold but a short time after their acquisition to a non-resident this fact, although not conclusive, might support an inference that the original offering had not come to rest in the state, and that the resale therefore constituted a part of the process of primary distribution; a stronger inference would arise if the purchaser involved were a security dealer. It may be noted that the non-residence of the underwriter or dealer is not pertinent so long as the ultimate distribution is solely to residents of the state.

Use of the Mails and Facilities of Interstate Commerce

The intrastate exemption is not dependent upon non-use of the mails or instruments of interstate commerce in the distribution. Securities issued in a transaction properly exempt under this provision may be offered and sold without registration through the mails or by use of any instruments of transportation or communication in interstate commerce, may be made the subject of general newspaper advertisement (provided the advertisement is appropriately limited to indicate that offers to purchase are solicited only from, and sales will be made only to, residents of the particular state involved), and may even be delivered by means of transportation and communication used in interstate commerce, to the purchasers. Similarly, securities issued in a transaction exempt under Section 3(a)(11) may be offered without compliance with the formal prospectus requirements applicable to registered securities. Exemption under Section 3(a)(11), if in fact available, removes the distribution from the operation of the registration and prospectus requirements of Section 5 of the Act. It should be emphasized, however, that the civil liability and anti-fraud provisions of Sections 12(2) and 17 of the Act nevertheless apply and may give rise to civil liabilities and to other sanctions applicable to violations of the statute.

Conclusion

In conclusion, the fact should be stressed that Section 3(a)(11) is designed to apply only to distributions genuinely local in character. From a practical point of view, the provisions of that section can exempt only issues which in reality represent local financing by local industries, carried out through local investment. Any distribution not of this type raises a serious question as to the availability of Section 3(a)

(11). Consequently, any dealer proposing to participate in the distribution of an issue claimed to be exempt under Section 3(a)(11) should examine the character of the transaction and the proposed or actual manner of its execution by all persons concerned with it with the greatest care to satisfy himself that the distribution will not, or did not, exceed the limitations of the exemption. Otherwise the dealer, even though his own sales may be carefully confined to resident purchasers, may subject himself to serious risk of civil liability under Section 12(1) of the Act for selling without prior registration a security not in fact entitled to exemption from registration.

SEC v. McDONALD INVESTMENT CO.

343 F.Supp. 343 (D.Minn.1972).

NEVILLE, DISTRICT JUDGE.

The question presented to the court is whether the sale exclusively to Minnesota residents of securities, consisting of unsecured installment promissory notes of the defendant, a Minnesota corporation, whose only business office is situate in Minnesota, is exempt from the filing of a registration statement under § 3(a)(11) of the 1933 Securities Act, when the proceeds from the sale of such notes are to be used principally, if not entirely, to make loans to land developers outside of Minnesota. Though this is a close question, the court holds that such registration is required and the defendants have not satisfied their burden of proving the availability of an exemption under the Act; this despite the fact that the securities have heretofore been duly registered with the Securities Commissioner of the State of Minnesota for whom this court has proper respect.

Plaintiff, the Securities and Exchange Commission, instituted this lawsuit pursuant to § 20(b) of the 1933 Securities Act. The defendants are McDonald Investment Company, a Minnesota corporation, and H.J. McDonald, the company's president, treasurer, and owner of all the company's outstanding common stock. Plaintiff requests that the defendants be permanently enjoined from offering for sale and selling securities without having complied with the registration requirements of Section 5 of the Act.

Plaintiff and defendants have stipulated to the following pertinent facts: The defendant company was organized and incorporated in the State of Minnesota on November 6, 1968. The principal and only business office from which the defendants conduct their operations is located in Rush City, Minnesota, and all books, correspondence, and other records of the company are kept there.

Prior to October 19, 1971, the defendants registered an offering for $4,000,000 of its own installment notes with the Securities Division of the State of Minnesota pursuant to Minnesota law. The prospectus offering these installment notes became effective on October 19, 1971 by a written order of the Minnesota Commissioner of Securities making the registration and prospectus effective following examination and review by the Securities Division. Sales of the installment notes, according to the amended prospectus of January 18, 1972, are to be made to Minnesota residents only. Prior to the institution of this action, the defendants were enjoined from their past practices of selling, without Securities and Exchange Commission registration, notes secured by lien land contracts and first mortgages on unimproved land located at various places in the United States, principally Arizona. The defendant company is said to have sold $12,000,000 of such to some 2,000 investors. The present plan contemplates that those purchasing defendant company's securities henceforth will have only the general unsecured debt obligation of the company, though the proceeds from the installment notes will be lent to land developers with security taken from them in the form of mortgages or other liens running to the defendant corporation. The individual installment note purchasers will not, however, have any direct ownership or participation in the mortgages or other lien security, nor in the businesses of the borrowers.

* * *

The plaintiff predicates its claim for a permanent injunction on the ground that the defendants will be engaged in a business where the income producing operations are located outside the state in which the securities are to be offered and sold and therefore not available for the 3(a)(11) exemption. Securities and Exchange Commission v. Truckee Showboat, 157 F.Supp. 824 (S.D.Cal.1957); Chapman v. Dunn, 414 F.2d 153 (6th Cir.1969). While neither of these cases is precisely in point on their facts, the rationale of both is clear and apposite to the case at bar.

In *Truckee* the exemption was not allowed because the proceeds of the offering were to be used primarily for the purpose of a new unrelated business in another state, i.e., a California corporation acquiring and refurbishing a hotel in Las Vegas, Nevada. Likewise, in *Dunn* the 3(a)(11) exemption was unavailable to an offering by a company in one state, Michigan, of undivided fractional oil and gas interests located in another state, Ohio. The *Dunn* court specifically stated at page 159:

> "* * * in order to qualify for the exemption of § 3(a)(11), the issuer must offer and sell his securities only to persons resident within a single State and the issuer must be a resident of that same State. *In addition to this, the issuer must conduct a predominant amount of his business within this same State.* This business which the issuer must conduct within the same State refers to the income producing operations of the business in which the issuer is selling the securities * * *." [Emphasis added]

This language would seem to fit the instant case where the income producing operations of the defendant, after completion of the offering, are to consist entirely of earning interest on its loans and receivables invested outside the state of Minnesota. While the defendant will not participate in any of the land developer's operations, nor will it own or control any of the operations, the fact is that the strength of the installment notes depends perhaps not legally, but practically, to a large degree on the success or failure of land developments located outside Minnesota, such land not being subject to the jurisdiction of the Minnesota court. The investor obtains no direct interest in any business activity outside of Minnesota, but legally holds only an interest as a creditor of a Minnesota corporation, which of course would be a prior claim on the defendant's assets over the shareholder's equity, now stated to be approximately a quarter of a million dollars.

This case does not evidence the deliberate attempt to evade the Act as in the example posed by plaintiff of a national organization or syndicate which incorporates in several or many states, opens an office in each and sells securities only to residents of the particular state, intending nevertheless to use all the proceeds whenever realized in a venture beyond the boundaries of all, or at best all but one of the states. See Securities & Exchange Commission v. Los Angeles Trust Deed & Mortgage Exchange, 186 F.Supp. 830, 871 (S.D.Cal.1960), aff'd 285 F.2d 162 (9th Cir.1960). Defendant corporation on the contrary has been in business in Minnesota for some period of time, is not a "Johnny come lately" and is not part of any syndicate or similar enterprise; yet to relieve it of the federal registration requirements where none or very little of the money realized is to be invested in Minnesota, would seem to violate the spirit if not the letter of the Act. * * *

Defendant notes that agreements with land developers will by their terms be construed under Minnesota law; that the income producing activities will be the earning of interest which occurs in Minnesota; that the Minnesota registration provides at close proximity all the information and protection that any investor might desire; that whether or not registered with the Securities and Exchange Commission, a securities purchaser has the protection of [§ 12(2)] which attaches liability to the issuer whether or not registration of the securities are exempted for fraudulent or untrue statements in a prospectus or made by oral communications; that plaintiff blurs the distinction between sale of securities across state lines and the operation of an intrastate business; and that if injunction issues in this case it could issue in any case where a local corporation owns an investment out of the particular state in which it has its principal offices and does business such as accounts receivable from its customers out of state. While these arguments are worthy and perhaps somewhat more applicable to the facts of this case than to the facts of *Truckee* and *Chapman,* supra, on balance and in carrying out the spirit and intent of the Securities Act of 1933, plaintiff's request for a permanent injunction should be granted.

BUSCH v. CARPENTER

827 F.2d 653 (10th Cir.1987).

Before SEYMOUR and TACHA, CIRCUIT JUDGES, and WEINSHIENK, DISTRICT JUDGE.

SEYMOUR, CIRCUIT JUDGE.

Paul and Linda Busch brought this action under [§ 12 of the Securities Act of 1933] against Craig Carpenter, George Jensen, and Ronald Burnett to recover the purchase price of shares of stock in Sonic Petroleum, Inc. Plaintiffs alleged that the stock had not been registered as required by [§ 5], and that the stock did not qualify for the intrastate offering exemption set out in [§ 3(a)(11)].[1]

* * *

I.

BACKGROUND

The undisputed facts are briefly as follows. Sonic was incorporated in Utah on October 2, 1980. The three defendants were officers and directors of Sonic at its inception. Carpenter was president until May 1981, and a director and officer through June 26, 1981, the date on which plaintiffs bought their shares. Jensen was vice president and a director through June 26. Burnett was secretary and a director until May 1981. During October and November of 1980, Sonic publicly offered and sold shares of Sonic stock to Utah residents through Olsen & Company, Inc. Although Sonic complied with Utah state registration requirements, it did not file a registration statement under federal securities law, relying on the exemption from registration provided for intrastate offerings. Sonic, which had no prior operating history at the time of this offering, was incorporated in Utah and purportedly organized to acquire, extract, and market natural resources such as oil, gas, and coal. Although the company had not undertaken this activity in Utah or anywhere else, it maintained its corporate office, books, and records in Utah at the time of the initial offering. It is not disputed that the offering of 25,000,000 shares of Sonic was sold for $500,000 entirely to Utah residents.

In late March or early April of 1981, Carpenter was contacted by William Mason, an Illinois oil and gas promoter, about a merger of Sonic with Mason's operations in Illinois. Sonic and Mason reached an agreement, effective May 25, 1981, under which Sonic issued Mason a controlling block of stock and acquired an Illinois drilling corporation privately owned by Mason. * * * Shortly after Mason Oil was formed, William Mason drew $351,126 from the remainder of the

1. Plaintiffs also alleged that defendants had violated Rule 147, which is a "safe harbor" provision establishing the circumstances in which the SEC will not challenge the applicability of the intrastate offering exemption. The district court held that defendants' failure to comply with Rule 147 did not preclude them from establishing that they were nonetheless entitled to the exemption. Plaintiffs do not raise this ruling as error on appeal.

$435,000 net proceeds of the original Sonic offering and deposited it in Illinois. This money was not used in Utah.

In May 1981, Mason and Carpenter set up Norbil Investments, a brokerage account in Utah, so that Mason and his friends could buy shares of the company's stock. Plaintiffs, who are California residents, bought their stock through Norbil. Plaintiffs also presented evidence of purchases through Norbil of stock by other non-residents between May and August 1981.

II.

THE INTRASTATE OFFERING EXEMPTION

Congress enacted the Securities Act of 1933 "to protect investors by promoting full disclosure of information thought necessary to informed investment decisions." * * * However, Congress also recognized that the protections of the 1933 Act were not essential for those securities that could be supervised effectively by the states. * * *

In light of the 1933 Act's broad remedial purpose, its exemption provisions are to be narrowly construed. Once a plaintiff makes out a prima facie case that the securities offered or sold were not registered, the defendant bears the burden of demonstrating its entitlement to an exemption.

A. Coming to Rest

The district court ruled that the resale of stock to non-residents occurred after the issued securities had come to rest in Utah and concluded that the public offering was therefore consummated in Utah within the meaning of section 3(a)(11). On appeal, plaintiffs contend that the court's ruling was erroneous and that the circumstances of the resale defeated the intrastate exemption.

In order to fall within the intrastate exemption, initial sales to state residents must be bona fide. The intrastate exemption becomes unavailable whenever sales or purchases by an issuer, an intermediary, or a subsequent purchaser circumvent the federal securities laws. The SEC has consistently maintained that a distribution of securities must have "actually come to rest in the hands of resident investors—persons purchasing for investment and not with a view to further distribution or for purposes of resale." We agree.

During the proceedings below, plaintiffs contended that the resale to non-residents within seven months of the initial offering in and of itself precluded the application of the intrastate offering exemption. The Amicus [Securities & Exchange Commission] raises a new argument on appeal, contending that because defendants had the burden to show their right to the exemption, they had the burden below to present evidence that the original buyers bought with investment intent. The Amicus argues that without such a showing, summary judgment for defendants was improper. Plaintiffs have abandoned their claim that resale alone was enough to defeat the exemption.

They now join in the Amicus argument, and rely on that argument to assert that they are entitled to summary judgment.

We reject the Amicus' argument. The intrastate offering exemption requires that the issue be "offered and sold only to persons resident within a single State." In our view, a seller seeking summary judgment makes a prima facie showing that the offering was consummated within a state by showing that the stock was sold only to residents of that state. We disagree with Amicus that, in order to be entitled to summary judgment, the issuer should be required to disprove all the possible circumstances that might establish the stock has not come to rest. It seems more logical to us to impose on the other party the burden of producing some contrary evidence on this issue when the seller claiming the exemption has satisfied the facial requirement of the statute. In the face of defendants' undisputed showing that all of the original buyers were Utah residents, plaintiffs were therefore required to produce evidence that the stock had not come to rest but had been sold to people who intended to resell it out of state.

The evidence fails to suggest that any of Sonic's publicly offered shares were issued under questionable circumstances. * * * Norbil served as a conduit for over-the-counter purchases made by Olsen & Company on behalf of Mason and various acquaintances. Although Carpenter did collect from buyers, pay Olsen, and transfer the stock certificates to their new owners, there is simply no indication that those who sold through Norbil had not originally purchased their stock for investment purposes. * * * Accordingly, the trial court did not err in concluding that no genuine question of fact was raised on whether the issue had come to rest in the hands of Utah residents.

B. *Doing Business*

Plaintiffs alternatively contend that defendants were not entitled to the intrastate offering exemption because the corporate issuer was not doing business in Utah as required by section 3(a)(11). There is no dispute that the newly formed company, not yet operational, maintained its offices, books, and records in Salt Lake City. The decisive issue concerns whether, under the circumstances of this case, Sonic's failure to invest a portion of the proceeds from its initial public offering in Utah could defeat the intrastate exemption.

Although neither the statute nor its legislative history defines the doing business requirement, courts have uniformly held that it refers to activity that actually generates revenue within an issuer's home state. The leading case is Chapman v. Dunn, 414 F.2d 153 (6th Cir.1969), which involved a company that maintained its offices and issued stock in Michigan while operating its sole productive venture, an oil and gas business, in Ohio. The *Chapman* court reasoned that "doing business" in the context of securities regulation connotes substantially more activity than that which would warrant exercising personal jurisdiction in ordinary civil suits. Effective supervision of stock offerings, the court added, can entail on-site inspections, familiarity with local economic conditions, and sometimes reliance upon judicial process. State oversight of business operations located elsewhere could often prove cumbersome, costly, and ineffective. The *Chapman* court therefore approved the SEC's view that the intrastate exemption applies only in cases of local financing for local industries. The court held that "doing business" refers to income-producing activity, and that an issuer must conduct a "predominant amount" of that activity within its home state.

Cases involving somewhat different facts have reached the same result. SEC v. Truckee Showboat, Inc., 157 F.Supp. 824 (S.D.Cal.1957), involved a California corporation that planned to use the proceeds of an intrastate stock offering to acquire and operate a Nevada hotel. Although the company had not begun operations beyond maintaining its books and records in California, the intent to invest proceeds elsewhere sufficed to defeat a claim of exemption. In SEC v. McDonald Investment Co., 343 F.Supp. 343 (D.Minn.1972), an established Minnesota corporation that maintained its offices there while doing business elsewhere, planned to invest the proceeds from a local offering in unspecified, out-of-state real estate ventures. The court recognized that although the company operated outside of Minnesota, all land development agreements would be governed by Minnesota law, and interest income would be earned in Minnesota. Even so, because exemptions from registration are to be narrowly construed, the court reasoned that only local industries may be properly excused. Finally, in SEC v. Asset Management Corp., Fed.Sec.L.Rep. (CCH) ¶ 97,278, at 96,970 (S.D.Ind. 1979), a case similar to *Truckee* but involving coal leases rather than a hotel, the court flatly limited the intrastate exemption to cases of "local financing by local industries."

These cases make clear that an issuer cannot claim the exemption simply by opening an office in a particular state. Conducting substantially all income-producing operations elsewhere defeats the exemption, as do the plans of recently organized companies to invest the net proceeds of initial public offerings only in other states. Doing business under the 1933 Act means more than maintaining an office, books, and records in one state.

Viewing the evidence and drawing reasonable inferences most favorably to plaintiffs, a fact issue exists regarding whether Sonic's plans for the use of proceeds are distinguishable from the issuers' plans in *Truckee* and *Asset Management.* Here the corporation never did more than maintain its office, books, and records in Utah. This was not sufficient to make a prima facie showing of compliance with the intrastate offering exemption. While its prospectus stated that no more than twenty percent of all proceeds would be used outside of Utah, Sonic nonetheless transferred essentially all of its assets to Mason in Illinois. The record contains no evidence, moreover, of any prior efforts whatever at locating investment opportunities within Utah. These considerations support a reasonable inference that Sonic may have been intending all along to invest its assets outside the state.

Although Carpenter and Mason may have been strangers to one another, this fact alone fails to dispel the possibility that Sonic had been seeking and perhaps investigating other business operations out of state. If so, and we intimate no view on this unresolved fact question, the intrastate exemption would be unavailable.

* * *

The foregoing cases address the scope of the statutory exemption. As described in the following release, Rule 147 contains a safe harbor for issuers seeking to rely on the intrastate exemption.

NOTICE OF ADOPTION OF RULE 147

Securities Act Release No. 5450 (Jan. 7, 1974).

The Securities and Exchange Commission today adopted Rule 147 which defines certain terms in, and clarifies certain conditions of, Section 3(a)(11) of the Securities Act of 1933 ("the Act"). * * *

In developing the definitions in, and conditions of, Rule 147 the Commission has considered the legislative history and judicial interpretations of Section 3(a)(11) as well as its own administrative interpretations. The Commission believes that adoption of the rule, which codifies certain of these interpretations, is in the public interest, since it will be consistent with the protection of investors and provide, to the extent feasible, more certainty in determining when the exemption provided by that Section of the Act is available. Moreover, the Commission believes that local businesses seeking financing solely from local sources should have objective standards to facilitate compliance with Section 3(a)(11) and the registration provisions of the Act, and that the rule will enable such businesses to determine with more certainty whether they may use the exemption in offering their securities. * * *

Section 3(a)(11) was intended to allow issuers with localized operations to sell securities as part of a plan of local financing. Congress apparently believed that a company whose operations are restricted to one area should be able to raise money from investors in the immediate vicinity without having to register the securities with a federal agency. In theory, the investors would be protected both by their proximity to the issuer and by state regulation. Rule 147 reflects this Congressional intent and is limited in its application to transactions where state regulation will be most effective. The Commission has consistently taken the position that the exemption applies only to local financing provided by local investors for local companies. To satisfy the exemption, the entire issue must be offered and sold exclusively to residents of the state in which the issuer is resident and doing business. An offer or sale of part of the issue to a single non-resident will destroy the exemption for the entire issue.

Certain basic questions have arisen in connection with interpreting Section 3(a)(11). They are:

1. what transactions does the Section cover;

2. what is "part of an issue" for purposes of the Section;

3. when is a person "resident within" a state or territory for purposes of the Section; and

4. what does "doing business within" mean in the context of the Section?

The courts and the Commission have addressed themselves to these questions in the context of different fact situations, and some general guidelines have been developed. Certain guidelines were set forth by the Commission in Securities Act Release No. 4434 and, in part, are reflected in Rule 147. However, in certain respects, as pointed out below, the rule differs from past interpretations.

THE TRANSACTION CONCEPT

Although the intrastate offering exemption is contained in Section 3 of the Act, which Section is phrased in terms of exempt "securities" rather than "transactions," the legislative history and Commission and judicial interpretations indicate that the exemption covers only specific transactions and not the securities themselves. Rule 147 reflects this interpretation.

THE "PART OF AN ISSUE" CONCEPT

The determination of what constitutes "part of an issue" for purposes of the exemption, i.e. what should be "integrated," has traditionally been dependent on the facts involved in each case. The Commission noted in Securities Act Release 4434 that "any one or more of the following factors may be determinative of the question of integration:

"1. are the offerings part of a single plan of financing;

"2. do the offerings involve issuance of the same class of security;

"3. are the offerings made at or about the same time;

"4. is the same type of consideration to be received; and

"5. are the offerings made for the same general purpose."

In this connection, the Commission generally has deemed intrastate offerings to be "integrated" with those registered or private offerings of the same class of securities made by the issuer at or about the same time.

The rule as initially proposed would have done away with the necessity for such case-by-case determination of what offerings should be integrated by providing that all securities offered or sold by the issuer, its predecessor, and its affiliates, within any consecutive six month period, would be integrated. As adopted, the rule provides in Subparagraph (b)(2) that, for purposes of the rule only, certain offers and sales of securities, discussed below, will be deemed not to be part of an issue and therefore not be integrated, but the rule does not otherwise define "part of an issue." Accordingly, as to offers and sales not within (b)(2), issuers who want to rely on Rule 147 will have to determine whether their offers and sales are part of an issue by applying the five factors cited above.

THE "PERSON RESIDENT WITHIN" CONCEPT

The object of the Section 3(a)(11) exemption, i.e., to restrict the offering to persons within the same locality as the issuer who are, by reason of their proximity, likely to be familiar with the issuer and protected by the state law governing the issuer, is best served by interpreting the residence requirement narrowly. In addition, the determination of whether all parts of the issue have been sold only to residents can be made only after the securities have "come to rest" within the state or territory. Rule 147 retains these concepts, but provides more objective standards for determining when a person is considered a resident within a state for purposes of the rule and when securities have come to rest within a state.

THE "DOING BUSINESS WITHIN" REQUIREMENT

Because the primary purpose of the intrastate exemption was to allow an essentially local business to raise money within the state where the investors would be likely to be familiar with the business and with the management, the doing business requirement has traditionally been viewed strictly. First, not only should the business be located within the state, but the principal or predominant business must be carried on there. Second, substantially all of the proceeds of the offering must be put to use within the local area.

Rule 147 reinforces these requirements by providing specific percentage amounts of business that must be conducted within the state, and of proceeds from the offering that must be spent in connection with such business. In addition, the rule requires that the principal office of the issuer be within the state. * * *

Operation of Rule 147

Rule 147 will operate prospectively only. The staff will issue interpretative letters to assist persons in complying with the rule, but will consider requests for "no action" letters on transactions in reliance on Section 3(a)(11) outside the rule only on an infrequent basis and in the most compelling circumstances.

The rule is a nonexclusive rule. However, persons who choose to rely on Section 3(a)(11) without complying with all the conditions of the rule would have the burden of establishing that they have complied with the judicial and administrative interpretations of Section 3(a)(11) in effect at the time of the offering. The Commission also emphasizes that the exemption provided by Section 3(a)(11) is not an exemption from the civil liability provisions of Section 12(2) or the antifraud provisions of Section 17 of the Act or of Section 10(b) of the Securities

Exchange Act of 1934. The Commission further emphasizes that Rule 147 is available only for transactions by issuers and is not available for secondary offerings.

In view of the objectives and policies underlying the Act, the rule would not be available to any person with respect to any offering which, although in technical compliance with the provisions of the rule, is part of a plan or scheme by such person to make interstate offers or sales of securities. In such cases, registration would be required. In addition, any plan or scheme that involves a series of offerings by affiliated organizations in various states, even if in technical compliance with the rule, may be outside the parameters of the rule and of Section 3(a)(11) if what is being financed is in effect a single business enterprise.

* * *

The Commission, acting pursuant to the Securities Act of 1933, particularly Section 3(a)(11) and 19(a) thereof, hereby adopts Rule 147 effective for issues of securities commenced on or after March 1, 1974.

Selected References

T. Hazen, Securities Regulation § 4.12 (2d ed.1990).

Cummings, The Intrastate Exemption and the Shallow Harbor of Rule 147, 69 Nw.U.L.Rev. 167 (1974).

Dicken, Rule 147: Those Hard to Find No-Action Letters, 17 Cap.U.L.Rev. 17 (1987).

Gardiner, Intrastate Offering Exemption: Rule 147—Progress or Stalemate, 35 Ohio St.L.J. 340 (1974).

Long, A Lawyer's Guide to the Intrastate Exemption and Rule 147, 24 Drake L.Rev. 471 (1975).

---

4. "Secondary" Transactions

The determination of when a person other than the issuer may be required to have securities registered under the 1933 Act in order to sell them is governed largely by the definition of the term "underwriter" in § 2(11) of that Act. Section 4(1) of the Act exempts from the registration requirements "transactions by any person other than an issuer, *underwriter,* or dealer," so that any sale by an "underwriter" requires registration.

The § 4(1) exemption should be read in conjunction with the § 4(4) exemption for unsolicited broker's transactions. See Ira Haupt & Co., p. 329 below. "Issuer" is defined in § 2(4). See the discussion of "issuer" in SEC v. Murphy, p. 297 above. "Dealer" is defined in § 2(12). While the definition of "dealer" in the 1933 Act includes brokers, a separate definition of "broker" can be found in § 3(a)(4) of the 1934 Act.

There are three ways in which one can become a statutory underwriter:

1) Direct or Indirect participation in a selling effort, See *SEC v. Chinese Consol. Benev. Ass'n,* below;

2) Purchasing securities from an issuer or a control person with a view to distribution, see *United States v. Sherwood,* below; and

3) Selling for an issuer or a control person, see *Ira Haupt & Co.,* p. 329 below and *United States v. Wolfson,* p. 338 below.

SEC v. CHINESE CONSOLIDATED BENEVOLENT ASSOC., 120 F.2d 738 (2d Cir.1941). The Republic of China authorized the issuance of a total of $550 million in government bonds. The defendant was a nonprofit association in New York which organized a committee to solicit funds for the bond offering. The committee received $600,000 for the bonds. The defendant association forwarded the money to China and the bonds were sent to defendant which in turn distributed them to the individual purchasers. Neither the defendant association nor any of its members received any remuneration for these activities. The S.E.C. sought an injunction claiming that this was a public offering. The defendant relied on the § 4(1) exemption, claiming that it was neither an issuer, underwriter, nor dealer and thus its activities were exempt. The Second Circuit reversed the district court's granting of defendant's motion to dismiss and further directed that an injunction be issued. The Second Circuit reasoned that the defendant was an essential cog in the public offering and thus it was an underwriter within the meaning of § 2(11). Judge Swan dissented, contending that as a result of the court's decision a newspaper editorial endorsing the bonds would make the newspaper an underwriter.

The definition of "underwriter" in § 2(11) includes many persons other than the securities dealers who perform the traditional underwriting function in a public offering of securities by a corporation. The following case indicates the two basic ways in which a sale of securities by an individual may be found to involve an "underwriter" for the purposes of § 4(1).

UNITED STATES v. SHERWOOD

175 F.Supp. 480 (S.D.N.Y.1959).

SUGARMAN, DISTRICT JUDGE.

By order to show cause filed February 6, 1959, the United States of America moves for an order adjudging Robert Maurice Sherwood to be in criminal contempt for not obeying a final decree of permanent injunction entered against him * * *.

The application for the order to show cause alleges *inter alia* that:

"1. On September 23, 1958 the Securities and Exchange Commission filed in this Court a complaint * * * This action complained of sales of the common capital stock of Canadian Javelin Limited in violations of both the registration and fraud provisions of the Securities Act of 1933 and the anti-market manipulation provisions of the Securities Exchange Act of 1934.

"2. On November 24, 1958, United States District Judge Sidney Sugarman, sitting in the Southern District of New York, issued a permanent injunction enjoining Robert Maurice Sherwood and others from, among other things, * * * violations of the registration provisions of the Securities Act of 1933, in the offer and sale of common shares of Canadian Javelin Limited.

"3. On November 24, 1958, Robert Maurice Sherwood through his American Counsel, Simpson Thacher and Bartlett, by Albert C. Bickford, a partner, consented to the entry of this final decree of permanent injunction. * * *

"4. It was clearly stated both in open court and in conferences leading to the acceptance of the consent, that all of the Canadian Javelin Limited shares received by Robert Maurice Sherwood from Canadian Javelin Limited, the issuer, or from John Christopher Doyle, a control person of the issuer, were and would remain control shares in Sherwood's hands, and could not be offered and sold without full registration with the Securities and Exchange Commission or, at the very least, without a request for and receipt of a so called no action letter from the Securities and Exchange Commission based on an acceptable change of circumstances, which letter in turn would be required to be filed with the Court as a basis for an application for modification of the permanent injunction, to release any shares covered in such no action letter.

"5. No registration statement covering shares of Canadian Javelin Limited has ever been filed with the Securities and Exchange Commission, and none has ever been in effect.

"6. * * * no request for modification of the permanent injunction was ever addressed to this Court.

"7. Since November 24, 1958 * * * Robert Maurice Sherwood has offered and sold more than 8,000 shares of Canadian Javelin Limited, by orders executed in the United States, to members of the public in the United States for about $125,000, in an almost daily marketing operation. More than 4,000 additional shares were offered and sold in Canada during this same period by the defendant Robert Maurice Sherwood.

"8. These shares were all shares received by Robert Maurice Sherwood from John Christopher Doyle who in turn received them from the issuer. * * *"

Of the quoted facts alleged in the petition herein the trial of the contempt prosecution established these: the civil action for injunction commenced by the Securities and Exchange Commission; the consent of the defendant Sherwood to a final injunction; sales of numerous shares of Canadian Javelin Limited in the United States by the defendant Sherwood without the filing of a registration statement with the Securities and Exchange Commission.

The prosecution's contentions are basically that:

(1) Sherwood, by consenting to the injunction of November 24, 1958 undertook not to sell in the United States, until a registration statement was filed, the Canadian Javelin Limited shares which he did thereafter sell.

(2) Even if the defendant's undertaking was not to sell the shares he took through Doyle unless and until a registration thereof was required and filed, such registration thereof was required and Sherwood is in contempt for selling the shares without the filing of a registration statement.

The first contention of the prosecution cannot be sustained. A reading of the language of the injunction, to which Sherwood gave his consent, in the light of all the testimony and exhibits presented showing the genesis thereof, demonstrates that in so far as is here pertinent, Sherwood undertook to refrain from selling, offering to sell, or transporting Canadian Javelin Limited shares *only if a registration statement should then be required* and not be filed as is suggested by the second contention.

* * *

That the post-decree sales were made from the block of shares received by Sherwood from Doyle under the September 2, 1954 agreement was proven. The crucial issue therefore is, "Were the shares of Canadian Javelin Limited sold by Sherwood required to be registered before sale thereof by him?"

The prosecution theory is alternatively, first, that a registration statement was required to be filed because Sherwood was a statutory underwriter when he acquired his shares because he purchased them from an issuer with a view to distribution thereof, or second, that Sherwood was required to file a registration statement because when he made the sales complained of, he was a "control person".

The evidence does not sustain the second charge that Sherwood was at the time of the sales a "control person". To the contrary, although Sherwood dominated 8% of the total issued stock, he was unable to secure a representation on the board of directors, he had had a falling-out with John Christopher Doyle, who appears to have been the dominant figure in the management of Canadian Javelin Limited, and Sherwood was unable to free the bulk of his shares for distribution until Doyle consented thereto. Furthermore, no statutory or case authority has been cited nor has any been found to sustain the prosecutor's broad contention that "the shares of Canadian Javelin, Ltd., held by the defendant, Robert Maurice Sherwood, received by him from John Christopher Doyle, an admitted control person of Canadian Javelin, Ltd., and sold by Sherwood both prior to and subsequent to the final decree of November 24, 1958, were control shares from the time of their issuance; remained in their status as control shares during the period that Sherwood and Doyle were working together 'in the interests of the company'; and remain control shares from then to this very day." The court knows of no authority for a holding that shares once owned by "control" persons retain "control" characteristics in the hands of subsequent owners.

As to the first contention, that Sherwood was a statutory underwriter, on this record I am not satisfied beyond a reasonable doubt that at the time Sherwood took his shares from the issuer through Doyle, he purchased them with a view to the distribution thereof.

Defendant points to the long period between his purchase of and the first sale from his block of Canadian Javelin Limited shares. From this, he argues that:

> "From such behavior, it is impossible to infer the intention to distribute, *at the time of acquisition,* that it is necessary under the Act to qualify Sherwood as an underwriter within the meaning of the Act. His retention of the shares for a minimum of two full years after he personally had obtained physical possession of them belies any inference that he had originally acquired them 'with a view to distribution,' and is inconsistent with any such intention."

On the proof before me it appears that Sherwood took the unrestricted ownership of the block of shares out of which the post-decree sales were made in September 1955 when they were delivered to his agents, Lombard & Odier. No sales or other transactions were made out of this block until September 1957. The passage of two years before the commencement of distribution of any of these shares is an insuperable obstacle to my finding that Sherwood took these shares with a view to distribution thereof, in the absence of any relevant evidence from which I could conclude he did not take the shares for investment. No such evidence was offered at the trial. In fact, the only reference to Sherwood's intention with regard to the block of stock which he received appears when government counsel was cross-examining Sherwood's Canadian counsel, Courtois. The testimony, if anything, indicates Sherwood's intention not to sell his stock. Courtois' testimony on this score is as follows:

> "A. I remember asking Mr. Sherwood if he had any intention of selling any of his shares or disposing of his holdings in Canadian Javelin.
>
> "Q. And what was his answer?
>
> "A. His answer was no because he said for the time being he had a large block and he thought as such it had some value. * * *"

This decision, of course, is not to be deemed a finding that the shares of Canadian Javelin Limited stock owned by Sherwood are not subject to registration under the Securities Act of 1933, nor is it a finding that future transfer of that stock by defendant would not constitute contempt.

This decision is merely a finding *that on this record* the prosecution has not proven, beyond a reasonable doubt, that the accused's transactions were violative of the decree of this court.

The motion to punish Robert Maurice Sherwood for contempt of this court's decree of November 24, 1958 is denied and it is so ordered.

SEC v. GUILD FILMS CO., 279 F.2d 485 (2d Cir.1960). Guild Films issued to W–R Corporation 400,000 shares of Guild Films stock, plus promissory notes, in exchange for certain film properties. W–R Corporation signed a statement of investment intent in order that Guild Films could avoid registration in reliance on the § 4(2) non-public offering exemption. Hal Roach, Jr., who controlled W–R Corporation, used the Guild shares as collateral for loans he had obtained from two banks. When Roach defaulted, the banks, in good faith, foreclosed by selling the stock. Guild Films refused to transfer the shares on its books, on the ground that the sale would violate the 1933 Act. The banks sued in state court, which ordered that Guild Films make the transfer since the § 4(2) exemption would still be available to the banks.

The SEC sought an injunction in federal court; the injunction was granted. The court found that the sale would violate the 1933 Act because:

1. The pledgee banks knew that they were receiving unregistered stock and that the issuer had forbidden transfer, and

2. The banks knew that it was likely that it would be necessary to sell the stock because of Roach's financial situation.

Cf. Rubin v. United States, 449 U.S. 424 (1981), at p. 472 below, holding that a pledge is a sale under § 17(a) of the 1933 Act. Would the banks in the *Guild Films* situation be able to sell their shares under Rule 144?

IRA HAUPT & CO.

23 S.E.C. 589 (1946).

Findings and Opinion of the Commission

This proceeding was instituted under Sections 15(b) and 15A(*l*)(2) of the Securities Exchange Act of 1934 to determine whether Ira Haupt & Co. ("Respondent") willfully violated Section 5(a) of the Securities Act of 1933 and, if so, whether the revocation of its registration as a broker-dealer and its expulsion or suspension from membership in the National Association of Securities Dealers, Inc. ("NASD"), a registered securities association, would be in the public interest.

The alleged violation of Section 5(a) is based on respondent's sale, for the accounts of David A. Schulte, a controlled corporation of

Schulte's, and the David A. Schulte Trust (sometimes hereinafter referred to collectively as the "Schulte interests"), of approximately 93,000 shares of the common stock of Park & Tilford, Inc., during the period November 1, 1943, to June 1, 1944. It is conceded that the Schulte interests were in control of Park & Tilford during this period, that the sales were effected by use of the mails and instrumentalities of interstate commerce, and that the stock was not covered by a registration statement under the Securities Act.

* * *

Since the early 1920's David A. Schulte, a director and president of Park & Tilford, Inc., has maintained various accounts with respondent. Substantial blocks of securities were bought and sold in these accounts, including Park & Tilford common stock. * * *

On November 30, 1943, there were 243,731 shares of Park & Tilford common stock outstanding. Of this amount, the public held 18,249 shares or 9 percent; Schulte owned 54,510 shares or 22 percent directly; the 1924 Corporation, controlled by Schulte, held 4,853 shares or 2 percent; and 165,119 shares or 67 percent were held by the David A. Schulte Trust ("the Trust"), which Schulte created for his family and friends and whose trustees were his three sons. It is conceded that the Schulte interests, holding over 90 percent of the common stock, controlled Park & Tilford, Inc.

On or about December 14, 1943, Schulte called Haupt to his office. George Ernst, counsel for Schulte, was also present. Haupt testified that at this meeting Schulte told him that:

> * * * the Park & Tilford Company are going to announce a plan, a liquor plan * * * Mr. George Ernst spoke up and said that in the announcement of this liquor plan very likely the stock would become terribly active, or very active and that Mr. Schulte would like to have an orderly market and that they were contemplating putting in a hundred shares of stock to sell every quarter or half point or point, what they decide, would that create an orderly market. I said I think it would take a little more stock than that, due to the fact that if somebody came in to the crowd to buy a couple of thousand shares of stock it would put the market up 3 or 4 dollars. So George Ernst turned to Mr. Schulte and says I think Mr. Haupt might have something there, what do you think of making the order 2 or 3 hundred shares. So Mr. Schulte said, well, I will consider it, and if I am ready to do anything, Mr. Haupt, I will phone down to Mr. Scherk [Respondent's order clerk]. On the morning of December 15 he telephoned down to Mr. Herbert Scherk an order to sell 200 shares of stock at 59 and every quarter up.

At about this time, 33,362 shares of the stock were on deposit in Schulte's stock accounts with Haupt.

On the morning of December 15, Schulte publicly announced that Park & Tilford was contemplating a distribution of whiskey at cost to its shareholders. In 2 days, the stock advanced $13\frac{1}{4}$ points, from $57\frac{5}{8}$

to a closing price of 70⅞ on December 16; during those 2 days Schulte sold 15,700 shares through respondent.

The price declined between December 18, 1943, and January 19, 1944, and Schulte sold only 200 shares while purchasing 3,300 shares.

When the price began rising on January 20, Schulte resumed selling. By the end of January, he disposed of 5,900 shares at 60¾ to 76½. In February 14,553 shares, including the 4,853 shares held by the 1924 Corporation, were sold at 72¼ to 80¾; 11,800 shares were sold in March at prices ranging from 75 to 83; 4,400 shares were sold in April; and 1,042 were sold in May at 89½ to 95½. All sales were effected by respondent for the account of Schulte or the 1924 Corporation on orders to sell a specific number of shares at a limited price.

On February 24 Reinach was called to a conference with Arthur Schulte (son of David A. Schulte and a trustee of the Trust) and George Ernst to discuss a proposed sale of 50,000 shares by Respondent for the account of the Trust. * * * In accordance with the discussion, the Trust sent respondent a revised letter dated February 25, 1944, which was received on March 7. This letter read in part as follows:

> You are hereby authorized to sell for the account of the undersigned * * * up to but not in excess of 50,000 shares of Park & Tilford, Inc. common stock at $80 per share or better. We will not hold you responsible for sales at or above $80 which are not executed for our account.

By letter dated March 31, the number of shares to be sold for the Trust was increased from 50,000 shares to 73,000 shares. The increased number was to be sold subject to the same authority and conditions as the original 50,000 shares.

Pursuant to this authorization respondent sold 38,900 shares for the account of the Trust: 8,000 shares between March 23 and March 31 at 80¼ to 86¾; 4,700 shares in April; and 26,200 shares in May at prices of 84 to 98.

On May 26 Park & Tilford offered to sell to stockholders at a reduced price six cases of whiskey for each share of stock. On that day the stock reached a high of 98¼. On May 31 the Office of Price Administration limited the negotiability of the purchase rights and the maximum profits on the resale of the liquor. That day the price of the stock dropped 10⅛ points. It reached a low of 30⅝ in June. Neither Schulte nor the Trust sold any stock in June.

All told, respondent sold approximately 93,000 shares of stock for the account of the Schulte interests, from December 15, 1943, to May 31, 1944. In the period between November 30, 1943, and May 31, 1944, Schulte's holdings were reduced from 54,510 shares or 22 percent to 2,410 shares or 1 percent; the 1924 Corporation's holdings of 4,853 shares or 2 percent were reduced to zero; and the Trust's holdings were reduced from 165,119 shares or 67 percent to 115,344 [a] shares or 53 percent. During the same period, the public's holdings were increased from 18,249 shares or 8 percent to 115,344 or 46 percent.

It was further stipulated that during the period between December 15, 1943, and May 31, 1944, 10 customers' men and/or registered representatives of Haupt solicited 21 of their customers who purchased approximately 4,000 shares of the stock and that Hyman Federman, respondent's chief statistician, prepared a written analysis of the stock for a customer who purchased 100 shares at 84½ on the basis of this analysis.

* * *

Counsel for the staff contends that the foregoing facts show a willful violation of Section 5(a) of the Securities Act. Respondent asserts that its transactions were exempt from registration and that, in any event, it lacked the requisite intent for a "willful" violation.

* * *

THE ISSUES INVOLVED

It is conceded that respondent's transactions in Park & Tilford stock for the account of the Schulte interests constitute a violation of Section 5(a) unless an exemption was applicable to such transactions. Respondent contends that one or more of the following exemptions was applicable: * * *

Section 4(3) which exempts

> transactions by a dealer (including an underwriter no longer acting as an underwriter in respect of the security involved in such transaction), except transactions within one year after the first date upon which the security was bona fide offered to the public * * * by or through an underwriter * * * and except transactions as to securities constituting the whole or part of an unsold allotment to or subscription by such dealer as a participant in the distribution of such securities * * * by or through an underwriter.;

and Section 4(4) which exempts

> Brokers' transactions, executed upon customers' orders on any exchange or in the over-the-counter market, but not the solicitation of such orders.

The applicability of the foregoing exemptions involves the following subissues:

> (1) Was Respondent an "underwriter" as that term is defined in Section 2(11)? * * *
>
> (3) Is the brokerage exemption of Section 4(4) available to an underwriter who effects a distribution of an issue for the account of a controlling stockholder through the mechanism of a stock exchange?

* * *

a. So in original. Should presumably be 125,977.

1. *Was Respondent an "Underwriter"?*

Section 2(11) defines an "underwriter" as

> any person who * * * sells for an issuer in connection with, the distribution of any security * * * As used in this paragraph the term "issuer" shall include * * * any person * * * controlling * * * the issuer * * *

The purpose of the last sentence of this definition is to require registration in connection with secondary distributions through underwriters by controlling stockholders. This purpose clearly appears in the House Report on the Bill which states that it was intended:

> to bring within the provisions of the bill redistribution whether of outstanding issues or issues sold subsequently to the enactment of the bill. All the outstanding stock of a particular corporation may be owned by one individual or a select group of individuals. At some future date they may wish to dispose of their holdings and to make an offer of this stock to the public. Such a public offering may possess all the dangers attendant upon a new offering of securities. Wherever such a redistribution reaches significant proportions, the distributor would be in the position of controlling the issuer and thus able to furnish the information demanded by the bill. This being so, the distributor is treated as equivalent to the original issuer and, if he seeks to dispose of the issue through a public offering, he becomes subject to the act.

It is conceded that the Schulte interests controlled Park & Tilford and the respondent was, therefore, "selling for" a person in control of the issuer. However, respondent denies that these sales were effected "in connection with the distribution of any security." It asserts that at no time did it intend, nor was it aware that Schulte intended, a distribution of a large block of stock. It emphasizes that, in connection with the sales by which Schulte disposed of approximately 52,000 shares over a period of 6 months, each order was entered by Schulte to maintain an orderly market and was limited to 200 to 300 shares at a specific price; that the authority to sell 73,000 shares for the Trust was dependent upon a market price of at least 80; that the total amount which would be sold was never fixed or ascertained, and that consequently it did not intend to sell in connection with a distribution.

"Distribution" is not defined in the Act. It has been held, however, to comprise "the entire process by which in the course of a public offering the block of securities is dispersed and ultimately comes to rest in the hands of the investing public." In this case, the stipulated facts show that Schulte, owning in excess of 50,000 shares, had formulated a plan to sell his stock over the exchange in 200 share blocks "at 59 and every quarter up" and that the trust, holding 165,000 shares, specifically authorized the sale over the exchange of 73,000 shares "at $80 per share or better." A total of 93,000 shares was in fact sold by respondent for the account of the Schulte interests pursuant to these authorizations. We think these facts clearly fall within the above quoted definition and constitute a "distribution." We find no validity in the argument that a predetermination of the precise number of shares which are to be publicly dispersed is an essential element of a distribution. Nor do we think that a "distribution" loses its character as such merely because the extent of the offering may depend on certain conditions such as the market price. Indeed, in the usual case of an offering at a price, there is never any certainty that all or any specified part of the issue will be sold. And where part of an issue is outstanding, the extent of a new offering is almost always directly related to variations in the market price. Such offerings are not any less a "distribution" merely because their precise extent cannot be predetermined.

Nor can we accept respondent's claim that it was not aware of the distribution intended by the Schulte interests. The record shows that respondent was informed of the extent of Schulte's holdings and of his plan to sell 200 share blocks "at 59 and every quarter up." And, in the case of the Trust, respondent received its express authorization to sell up to 73,000 shares "at $80 per share or better" and affirmatively undertook to sell this block subject only to the contingency that the market reach the specified figure. Once sales were made under these authorizations we believe the foregoing facts, in themselves, show that respondent was an underwriter selling for the Schulte interests in connection with the distribution of Park & Tilford stock. But even if we assume that the nature of the contingency and respondent's belief as to the possibility of its fulfillment are relevant in determining the existence of a "distribution" and respondent's status, the facts in this case show that respondent had every reason to believe that the distribution would in fact take place.

* * *

We conclude from the foregoing facts that respondent was selling for the Schulte interests, controlling stockholders of Park & Tilford, in connection with the distribution of their holdings in the stock and was, therefore, an "underwriter" within the meaning of the Act. * * *

3. Is the Brokerage Exemption of Section 4(4) Available to an Underwriter Who Effects a Distribution of an Issue for the Account of a Controlling Stockholder Through the Mechanism of a Stock Exchange?

Respondent's final argument on this phase of the case is that * * * even though respondent may be found to be an underwriter, its transactions fall within Section 4(4) which exempts "brokers' transactions, executed upon customers' orders on any exchange * * * but not the solicitation of such orders." Counsel for the staff takes the position, first that Section 4(4) can never apply to exempt the transactions of an underwriter engaged in a distribution for a controlling stockholder and, second, that, even if Section 4(4) can apply in such a situation, its applicability in the present case is destroyed by activities of respondent which exceeded the normal functions of a broker and by the further fact that respondent engaged in the solicitation of customers' orders.

* * *

We find nothing in the language or legislative history of Section 4(4) to compel the exemption of this type of secondary distribution and the consequent overriding of the general objectives and policy of the Act. On the contrary, there are affirmative indications that Section 4(4) was meant to preserve the distinction between the "trading" and "distribution" of securities which separates the exempt and non-exempt transactions under Section 4(1). * * *

From the foregoing, it is apparent that transactions by an issuer or underwriter and transactions by a dealer during the period of *distribution* (which period for purposes of administrative practicality is arbitrarily set at one year) [a] must be preceded by registration and the use of a prospectus. It is likewise apparent that Congress intended that, during this period, persons other than an issuer, underwriter, or dealer should be able to *trade* in the security without use of a prospectus. Since such persons would carry on their trading largely through the use of brokers (who are included in the general definition of dealers), such trading through brokers without the use of a prospectus could be permitted during the first year after the initial offering only if there were a special exemption for dealers acting as brokers. The importance of this special exemption is emphasized in the case where a stop order might be entered against a registration statement. For, although such a stop order was intended to and would operate to stop all *distribution* activities, it would also result in stopping all *trading* by individuals through dealers acting as brokers unless a special exemption were provided for brokers. It was in recognition of this fact and to permit a dealer to act as a broker for an individual's trading transactions, while the security is being distributed and during the period of a stop order, that Section 4(4) was enacted. * * *

To summarize: Section 4(4) permits individuals to sell their securities through a broker in an ordinary brokerage transaction, during the period of distribution or while a stop order is in effect, without regard to the registration and prospectus requirements of Section 5. But the process of distribution itself, however carried out, is subject to Section 5.

What we have said also disposes of Respondent's argument that Section 4(4) would be rendered meaningless if it were interpreted not to apply to an underwriter "acting as a broker." * * *

---

a. Prior to 1954, a dealer was required to deliver a prospectus on all sales within one year after the offering, rather than within 40 or 90 days, as now provided in § 4(3).

SECURITIES REGULATION

By Louis Loss and Joel Seligman

Pp. 1465–71 (3d ed. 1989).*

May an affiliate (who is not an underwriter or dealer) sell securities without limit as long as he or she does so through unsolicited brokers' transactions?

Until 1946, the Commission followed this line: The fact that a broker effects an isolated transaction for an affiliate of the issuer does not make the broker an underwriter, even though he is selling for an "issuer" within the meaning of § 2(11). Consequently, the broker's part of the transaction is exempt under § 4(4), and the affiliate's part is exempt under § 4(1) because the affiliate is neither an issuer nor an underwriter nor a dealer. This assumes, however, that the broker does not exceed ordinary brokerage functions. If he does, he becomes an underwriter, with the result that his part of the transaction loses the § 4(4) exemption and the affiliate's part loses the § 4(1) exemption. What constitutes ordinary brokerage functions is a question of fact. Presumably the delegation of unusual discretion as to the time and manner of executing the affiliate's order, or the payment of more than a customary brokerage commission, would be fatal. And, although solicitation would normally seem to be part of the ordinary brokerage function, any solicitation that destroys the § 4(4) exemption for the broker's part of the transaction destroys also the § 4(1) exemption for the affiliate's part. The caveat was always added, however, that a broker engaged in distributing any substantial block of securities would probably be compelled to perform functions beyond those normally exercised by brokers.

This caveat seemed adequate to draw the line between sporadic trading and secondary distributions until the "bull" market of 1945 and 1946. It became apparent, however, that large blocks of securities could be sold in that market without solicitation or any particular sales effort. For example, in a series of three orders entered between late December 1945 and May 1946, the Commission granted exemptions under the Holding Company Act for the sale by The United Corporation on the New York Stock Exchange of a total of almost 600,000 shares of the common stock of its subsidiary, Columbia Gas & Electric Co. Since there was clear control and no registration statement had been filed under the Securities Act, it was obvious from the Commission's silence that exemption was assumed under §§ 4(1) and 4(4).

A few months later, in the *Haupt* case, the Commission repudiated the implications of these orders and restated its position under § 4(4).

* * *

Although it could not be convincingly argued for a moment that Congress did not intend this kind of distribution to be subject to the registration requirement, the absence of any precise line between a nonexempt secondary distribution and the kind of brokerage transaction on behalf of an affiliate of an issuer that might still come within the brokerage exemption caused a good deal of concern among the brokerage fraternity. The argument was occasionally heard that, since "distribution" was supposed to be synonymous with "public offering," no broker could feel safe any longer in executing an order to sell 100 shares of stock on behalf of some officer or director of a corporation who might conceivably be deemed to be a member of a controlling group.

The upshot was the Commission's adoption eight years later, in 1954, of Rule 154, which defined the term *brokers' transactions* in § 4(4) to include transactions by a broker acting as agent for a person in a control relationship with the issuer if, in addition to otherwise meeting the conditions of that section, he was "not aware of circumstances indicating that his principal is an underwriter in respect of the securities or that the transactions are part of a distribution of securities on behalf of his principal." And by way of "a ready guide for routine cases involving trading as distinguished from distributing transactions," the Rule provided that there was not deemed to be a "distribution" if the transaction in question and all other sales of the same class of securities by or on behalf of the same person within the preceding six months did not exceed approximately 1 percent of the shares or units of an over-the-counter security and, in the case of a security traded on an exchange, the lesser of that amount or the aggregate reported volume of exchange trading during any week within the preceding four weeks. Whether transactions exceeding this formula constituted a "distribution" would depend on whether they involved an amount that was "substantial in relation to the number of shares or units of the security outstanding and the aggregate volume of trading in such security."

In 1969 the Wheat Report broadly surveyed problems concerning secondary distributions and brokers' transactions. Its specific criticism of Rule 154 was a narrow one:

> Under the present Rule 154, if the broker selling for the account of a controlling person is unaware of circumstances indicating that his principal is engaged in making a distribution, the broker escapes liability even though his principal may have violated the '33 Act. If, however, the broker sells securities for the account of a shareholder who is, in fact, an underwriter of the securities under Section 2(11), the broker, however innocent, is also an underwriter. No rule exists which grants the broker absolution in such a case. It is the Study's recommendation that Rule 154 be revised to protect a broker under both sets of circumstances if, after reasonable inquiry of his customer, he has no grounds for believing and does not believe that the customer's sale amounts to a "distribution" under [proposed] Rule 162.

In 1972, the Commission adopted Rule 144, simultaneously rescinding Rule 154, to deal with the problems of both secondary distributions and brokerage transactions. Rule 144(g) specifically defines brokers' transactions in § 4(4) expressly for the purposes of Rule 144; implicitly, it is the current Commission interpretation of § 4(4).

UNITED STATES v. WOLFSON

405 F.2d 779 (2d Cir.1968).

Before MOORE, WOODBURY and SMITH, CIRCUIT JUDGES.

WOODBURY, SENIOR CIRCUIT JUDGE:

It was stipulated at the trial that at all relevant times there were 2,510,000 shares of Continental Enterprises, Inc., issued and outstanding. The evidence is clear, indeed is not disputed, that of these the appellant Louis E. Wolfson himself with members of his immediate family and his right hand man and first lieutenant, the appellant Elkin B. Gerbert, owned 1,149,775 or in excess of 40%. The balance of the stock was in the hands of approximately 5,000 outside shareholders. The government's undisputed evidence at the trial was that between August 1, 1960, and January 31, 1962, Wolfson himself sold 404,150 shares of Continental through six brokerage houses, that Gerbert sold 53,000 shares through three brokerage houses and that members of the Wolfson family, including Wolfson's wife, two brothers, a sister, the Wolfson Family Foundation and four trusts for Wolfson's children sold 176,675 shares through six brokerage houses.

Gerbert was a director of Continental. Wolfson was not, nor was he an officer, but there is ample evidence that nevertheless as the largest individual shareholder he was Continental's guiding spirit in that the officers of the corporation were subject to his direction and control and that no corporate policy decisions were made without his knowledge and consent. Indeed Wolfson admitted as much on the stand. No registration statement was in effect as to Continental; its stock was traded over-the-counter.

The appellants do not dispute the foregoing basic facts. They took the position at the trial that they had no idea during the period of the alleged conspiracy, stipulated to be from January 1, 1960, to January 31, 1962, that there was any provision of law requiring registration of a security before its distribution by a controlling person to the public. On the stand in their defense they took the position that they operated at a level of corporate finance far above such "details" as the securities laws; as to whether a particular stock must be registered. They asserted and their counsel argued to the jury that they were much too busy with large affairs to concern themselves with such minor matters and attributed the fault of failure to register to subordinates in the Wolfson organization and to failure of the brokers to give notice of the need. Obviously in finding the appellants guilty the jury rejected this defense, if indeed, it is any defense at all.

* * *

The appellants argue that they come within [the § 4(1)] exemption for they are not issuers, underwriters or dealers. At first blush there would appear to be some merit in this argument. The immediate difficulty with it, however, is that § 4(1) by its terms exempts only "transactions," not classes of persons, and ignores § 2(11) of the Act which defines an "underwriter" to mean any person who has purchased from an issuer with a view to the distribution of any security, or participates directly or indirectly in such undertaking unless that person's participation is limited to the usual and customary seller's commission, and then goes on to provide:

> "As used in this paragraph the term 'issuer' shall include, in addition to an issuer, any person directly or indirectly *controlling* or controlled by *the issuer,* or any person under direct or indirect common control with the 'issuer.'" (Italics supplied.)

In short, the brokers provided outlets for the stock of issuers and thus were underwriters. Wherefore the stock was sold in "transactions by underwriters" which are not within the exemption of § 4(1), supra.

But the appellants contend that the brokers in this case cannot be classified as underwriters because their part in the sales transactions came within § 4(4), which exempts "brokers' transactions executed upon customers' orders on any exchange or in the over-the-counter market but not the solicitation of such orders."[1] The answer to this contention is that § 4(4) was designed only to exempt the brokers' part in security transactions. Control persons must find their own exemptions.

There is nothing inherently unreasonable for a broker to claim the exemption of § 4(4), supra, when he is unaware that his customer's part in the transaction is not exempt. Indeed, this is indicated by the definition of "brokers' transaction" in Rule 154 which provides:

> "(a) The term 'brokers' transaction' in Section 4(4) of the act shall be deemed to include transactions by a broker acting as agent for the account of any person controlling, controlled by, or under common control with, the issuer of the securities which are the subject of the transaction where:
>
> "(4) The broker is *not aware* of circumstances indicating * * * that the transactions are part of a distribution of securities on behalf of his principal."

And there can be no doubt that appellants' sale of over 633,000 shares (25% of the outstanding shares of Continental and more than 55% of their own holdings), was a distribution rather than an ordinary brokerage transaction. See Rule 154(6) which defines "distribution" for

1. It is undisputed that the brokers involved in this case did not solicit orders from the appellants.

the purpose of paragraph (a) generally as "substantial" in relation to the number of shares outstanding and specifically as a sale of 1% of the stock within six months preceding the sale if the shares are traded on a stock exchange.

Certainly if the appellants' sales, which clearly amounted to a distribution under the above definitions had been made through a broker or brokers with knowledge of the circumstances, the brokers would not be entitled to the exemption. It will hardly do for the appellants to say that because they kept the true facts from the brokers they can take advantage of the exemption the brokers gained thereby.

The appellants' argument that §§ 4 and 5 of the Act are unconstitutionally vague does not call for extended discussion. It will suffice to say that the appellants' defense was not that they misunderstood or misinterpreted the statute but that it was beneath their notice and they knew nothing about it. Under these circumstances we need say no more than that any possible uncertainty in the statute need not trouble us now. There will be time enough to consider that question when raised by someone whom it concerns.

The further argument of the appellants that the concept of "control" stock is unconstitutionally vague and indefinite was considered and rejected in United States v. Re, 336 F.2d 306, 316 (2d Cir.1964). And as already pointed out Wolfson himself on the stand admitted that he was in control of Continental within the ordinary and accepted meaning of that term. * * *

Affirmed.

After Wolfson's conviction in this case, he sued one of his brokers for the damages he had suffered, alleging that the broker had willfully and fraudulently misrepresented to him that he could engage in the sales of Continental stock without violating federal securities laws. The court gave judgment for defendant, holding that, under the doctrine of collateral estoppel, Wolfson's conviction estopped him from asserting he was unaware of the law at the time of the sale. "From this Court's examination of the record in Wolfson's criminal case, it is abundantly clear that Wolfson's knowledge of the registration requirements in connection with his sale of Continental stock was an exhaustively litigated issue, and that the jury's verdict against Wolfson necessarily rests upon a finding that Wolfson's claims of ignorance were insufficient to create a reasonable doubt of his criminal culpability." WOLFSON v. BAKER, 444 F.Supp. 1124, 1130 (M.D.Fla.1978), affirmed 623 F.2d 1074 (5th Cir.1980).

DISCLOSURE TO INVESTORS

(the "Wheat Report") (1969).

CHAPTER VI—SECONDARY DISTRIBUTIONS AND BROKERS' TRANSACTIONS

When can securities that have been purchased in non-public transactions from issuers and from controlling persons be reoffered publicly without registration? Present doctrine in this field turns on the private purchaser's state of mind. The resulting emphasis on subjective factors causes unacceptable uncertainty and administrative difficulty. "How long do I have to hold" is the question most frequently raised in requests for "no-action" letters. The answer often depends upon cloudy concepts which have arisen over the years, such as "change of circumstances" and "fungibility."

The consequences of this uncertainty are damaging to the healthy administration of the '33 Act. They include: (1) an increasing burden of requests for no-action letters and interpretative advice, (2) substantial inconsistency in advice given by private lawyers to their clients, which frequently puts careful and experienced counsel at a marked disadvantage, (3) wide leeway for the unscrupulous, and (4) the existence of formidable problems of proof in the enforcement of the law.

Various alternative solutions examined by the Study are outlined in the body of the chapter. The best of these, in the Study's view, would be the adoption of new rules (to take effect prospectively) which would, to the extent practicable, replace present subjective tests with objective ones. It is believed that the Commission has authority to adopt such rules, an opinion in which the Commission's General Counsel concurs.

A central feature of the proposed new rules would be a definition of the term "distribution" in Section 2(11) of the '33 Act. The new definition would apply both to the sale of securities on behalf of controlling persons and to sales by persons who have purchased their securities in private offerings. In developing such a definition the Study focused its inquiry (in the words of Justice Clark) on "* * * the need of the offerees for the protections afforded by registration." When securities held by a controlling person are sold, or when securities sold privately by the issuer are resold, under what circumstances do investors need the protection of registration?

It was concluded that a sensible answer to this question could only be found by drawing a distinction between companies which file regular, informative reports on their affairs with the Commission under Sections 13 or 15(d) of the '34 Act (so-called "reporting companies") and companies which do not. If there has been no full disclosure of a company's business, earnings and financial condition (or if, despite the fact that the company is a reporting company, its reports appear to be defective or out of date), then a sale to the public of that company's securities ought to be accompanied by the disclosures afforded by '33 Act registration. Conversely, if a company has registered a class of its securities with the Commission under the '34 Act and is maintaining the currency of the information in that original registration statement through up-to-date periodic reports to the Commission, then it ought to be possible to permit secondary sales of its securities to the public without the filing of a '33 Act registration statement except (1) where the quantity of those securities to be sold exceeds an amount which the trading market could normally be expected to absorb within a reasonable period of time, or (2) where, in order to move the securities from private into public hands, arrangements for the solicitation of buying customers, or selling incentives exceeding the commissions paid in ordinary trading transactions, are required.

Objective tests were needed to determine what sales are consistent with ordinary trading. Here, a precedent was available to the Study. The draftsmen of the present version of Rule 154 sought a similar objective. That rule was designed to separate the routine trading transaction from the transaction involving the disposition of a large block of securities by means of extra selling incentives.

The Study reached the conclusion that the general framework of Rule 154 is valid as applied to the securities of reporting companies, at least until the Commission can assess the results of an initial period of experience with improved '34 Act reporting. * * *

If such a definition of "distribution" is to be workable both for sales on behalf of controlling persons and for sales of privately placed securities, one problem must be solved. The use of ostensible private purchasers as conduits for the sale of securities to the public without registration must be prevented. To solve this problem, a short mandatory holding period is essential, during which the private purchaser is at risk. (A controlling stockholder who acquired his shares in the trading market would not be subject to any holding period.) All who consulted with the Study recognized the need for such a holding period, but views as to its appropriate length differed appreciably. Some favored a period of six months. Others strongly believe that the period should be two years. The Study recommends a period of one year. During the holding period, a private purchaser could not resell publicly without registration, unless Regulation A, or another Section 3 exemption, is available. He could, of course, always sell in transactions which are not public offerings. * * *

The essence of the proposed new definition of "distribution" is as follows:

First, non-public transactions are excluded from the term "distribution" and do not require registration of the securities involved.

Second, any public offering of the securities of an issuer which is *not* subject to appropriate reporting requirements is a "distribution."

Third, a public offering of the securities of an issuer which is subject to the reporting requirements and is not delinquent in its filings is not a "distribution" (and no registration of the securities is required) if the amounts involved and the method of sale are within the standards for "ordinary trading" outlined in the preceding paragraphs.

The framework of statutory provisions and Commission rules into which the proposed new definition of "distribution" would fit is, in simplest outline, as follows:

(1) Any security acquired directly or indirectly from its issuer, or from any person in a control relationship with its issuer, in a transaction or series of transactions none of which was a public offering or other public disposition, would be defined as a "restricted security."

(2) Any person who disposes of a "restricted security" in a "distribution" would be an "underwriter."

(3) Transactions by an "underwriter" are not exempt from registration under the '33 Act. * * *

The SEC's response to the Wheat Report recommendations was the adoption in 1972 of Rule 144, which applies a relatively objective (if rather complex) set of rules to both types of "underwriter" transactions. The Rule has been heavily utilized, and substantially liberalized, over the years. Under Rule 144, any sale of securities by an "affiliate" of the issuer (i.e., securities acquired from the issuer in a non-public transaction), must comply with the following requirements:

(1) A person's sales under Rule 144 during any three-month period may not exceed the greater of (a) 1% of the total number of units of the security outstanding and (b) the average weekly trading volume for the preceding four weeks.

(2) If the person acquired the securities from the issuer or affiliate of the issuer in a non-public transaction, he or she must have held them for at least two years before reselling them. (Securities are not considered fungible for this purpose; securities held for more than two years may be sold, even if the seller has recently acquired additional securities of the same class from the issuer.) In 1990, the Commission amended rule 144 to provide that the two-year holding period runs from the time the securities were purchased from the issuer or an affiliate of the issuer. Accordingly, there now is a tacking of holding periods for nonaffiliates who purchase securities from a nonaffiliate.

(3) The issuer must be subject to, and in current compliance with, the periodic reporting requirements of the 1934 Act, or there must otherwise be publicly available information comparable to that which would be found in such reports.

(4) The securities must be sold in ordinary brokerage transactions, or transactions directly with a "market maker," not involving any special remuneration or solicitation.

(5) A notice of each sale must be filed with the SEC at the time the order is placed with the broker.

The most significant liberalization of the Rule came in October 1983, when the Commission amended paragraph (k) to remove all of the restrictions of the Rule from resales of restricted securities by any person who has held those securities for at least three years and has not been an affiliate of the issuer for at least three months. This liberalization enables investors who have provided venture capital to a closely-held company to resell all of their securities publicly after a three-year holding period, even though the company has not made any information publicly available under either the 1933 or the 1934 Act.

The Commission gave the following rationale for its decision:

> In September 1982, the Commission hosted the first annual SEC Government–Business Forum on Small Business Capital Formation (the "Forum"). Approximately 175 persons with an interest in small business met to discuss the problems small businesses face in raising capital and developed 37 recommendations in the areas of taxation, securities, credit and access to institutional investors, designed to facilitate the capital formation process. With regard to the regulatory scheme concerning the resale of restricted securities, the participants at the Forum felt that certain provisions of Rule 144 may deter investment in small business and recommended that the rule be amended to allow non-affiliates to resell restricted securities freely after a holding period of three years.
>
> While a company which is required to file periodic reports pursuant to the Securities Exchange Act of 1934 fulfills the information requirement of Rule 144 so long as the company is current in its reports, small companies not in the reporting system must make certain information available on a continuing basis to security holders, broker-dealers, market makers, financial statistical services and other interested persons. Participants at the Forum felt that this requirement unduly restricts resales of securities of small companies. Investors generally have no right to demand that the company make such information publicly available. Moreover, many small companies do not have the financial or personnel resources to compile, print and distribute the required information on a regular basis as contemplated by the "publicly available" requirement. As a result, the small business community believes that potential investors often choose not to purchase in a private offering of a small issuer's securities because of the reduced liquidity of their investment.
>
> The Commission believes that the comments by the Forum participants have merit. Section 2(11) of the Securities Act does not contain any specific reference to the need for current public information as a determinant of underwriter status, and it seems appropriate not to impose a current information requirement after a person has demonstrated, through a holding period of three years, that it is unlikely he bought his securities from the issuer with a view to distribution. Accordingly, while an information requirement may be necessary and appropriate in certain circumstances as a condition for the safe harbor provided by Rule 144, it appears unduly restrictive to apply the requirement on an indefinite basis to non-affiliates. In view of the

significant burdens which such a requirement can impose on small public companies, and the resultant proscription on resales by non-affiliates who have met the holding period when the company is unable to meet the information requirement, the three year holding period for non-affiliates appears to be an adequate standard. For companies whose securities are traded, Rule 15c2–11 under the Exchange Act currently requires brokers who initiate trading in a security through the submission or publication of priced quotations in quotation media to maintain certain minimum current information about the issuer of the security and to make such information available to investors upon request.

Are you persuaded? Does this amendment permit a company to make a public offering without going through the registration process? Or does Rule 15c2–11 (discussed at p. 932 below) afford adequate protection by preventing dealers from making a market in such securities?

The Section "4(1½)" Exemption for Resales by Purchasers

The § 4(2) nonpublic offering exemption is limited by its terms to "transactions by an issuer" and thus is not available for private resales by purchasers who acquired their securities from the issuer. Consider, for example, a private placement by Issuer Co.; S and B both qualify as purchasers under § 4(2) but B does not have adequate funds to make a purchase. S purchases stock in a transaction that qualifies for the § 4(2) exemption. One year later, S decides to sell her stock and learns that B now has sufficient cash on hand. Since S has not held the stock for two years, she cannot take advantage of Rule 144. Similarly, S cannot be certain that she has satisfied the requirements of the § 4(1) exemption. Assuming that the issuer is willing to make current information available to B, there would seem no reason to require registration of S's sale to B as the only alternative to waiting until Rule 144's two-year holding period has elapsed.

Since, in the foregoing example, the issuer could validly issue shares directly to B as a qualified private placement purchaser, why should S not be able to take advantage of a similar exemption? The answer is the statutory limitation of § 4(2) to transactions by an issuer. It can be argued, however, that § 4(1) would support such an exemption. In the above example, S clearly is not an issuer or a dealer, so in order to qualify for the exemption, she must be able to demonstrate that she is not an underwriter. It would appear that a resale which is not a "public offering" within the meaning of § 4(2) is not properly classified as a "distribution" and as such the seller is not an "underwriter" under § 2(11). Accordingly, the proper basis for any exemption for the seller in the foregoing example is § 4(1), while the requirements that must be satisfied are derived from the parameters of § 4(2).

There is considerable support for what has become known as the "§ 4(1½) exemption." Although not expressly contained in the statute nor formally adopted by the Commission, support for the so-called "§ 4(1½) exemption" can be found in SEC no action letters,[1] SEC interpretative releases,[2] the courts,[3] and the commentators.[4] The absence of a formal SEC rule or interpretative release explaining the exemption means that it is difficult to ascertain the precise scope of the exemption. The SEC has recognized that the exemption is available to affiliates of the issuer and should equally apply to nonaffiliates.[5]

The elements of the "§ 4(1½) exemption" are as follows: First, the purchaser must have access to the current information about the issuer similar to the types of information that would be made available through a registration statement. This requirement emanates from § 4(2). In addition to the requirement that a purchaser have access to current information about the issuer, the purchaser must meet § 4(2) qualifications. See pp. 281–304 above. Any general solicitation of purchasers will destroy the § 4(2) exemption and thus would be equally fatal to the § 4(1½) exemption. Finally, if too many § 4(1½) sales take place within a given time frame, there is the possibility that a distribution will be found to exist.

In ACKERBERG v. JOHNSON, 892 F.2d 1328 (8th Cir.1989), Ackerberg bought unregistered Vertimag shares from Johnson in March of 1984. He brought suit under § 12(1) claiming that the shares should have been registered. Although talking in terms of § 4(1), the court's opinion implicitly accepts the rationale underlying the § 4(1½) exemption:

> * * * Johnson argues that he is entitled to an exemption under § 4(1) of the 1933 Act, which provides that the registration require-

1. E.g., Sidney Stahl (SEC No Action Letter available April 23, 1981); Illinois Capital Investment Corp. (SEC No Action Letter available May 17, 1976); Elwill Development, Ltd. (SEC No Action Letter available Jan. 18, 1975).

2. Sec.Act Rel. No. 33–6188 n. 178, CCH Fed.Sec.L.Rep. ¶ 1051 (SEC Feb. 1, 1980); Sec.Act Rel. No. 33–5452, CCH Fed.Sec.L. Rep. ¶ 79,633 at p. 83,698 (SEC Feb. 1, 1974).

3. E.g., Stoppelman v. Owens, CCH Fed. Sec.L.Rep. ¶ 91,511 at pp. 98,779–80 (D.D.C. 1984); Neuwirth Investment Fund, Ltd. v. Swanton, 422 F.Supp. 1187 (S.D.N.Y.1975); Value Line Income Fund, Inc. v. Marcus, CCH Fed.Sec.L.Rep. ¶ 91,523 (S.D.N.Y. 1965). Cf. Acme Propane, Inc. v. Tenexco, Inc., 844 F.2d 1317 (7th Cir.1988) (indicating in passing that the § 4(1½) exemption might be available).

4. See ABA Committee on Federal Regulation of Securities, The Section "4(1½)" Phenomenon: Private Resales of Restricted Securities, 34 Bus.Law.1961 (1971); Olander & Jacks, The Section 4(1½) Exemption—Reading Between the Lines of the Securities Act of 1933, 15 Sec.Reg.L.J. 339 (1988); Schneider, Section 4(1½)—Private Resales of Restricted or Control Securities, 49 Ohio St.L.J. 501 (1988); Titus, Secondary Trading—Stepchild of the Securities Laws, 20 Conn.L.Rev. 595 (1988); Comment, Reinterpreting the "Section 4(1½)" Exemption From Securities Registration: The Investor Protection Requirement, 6 U.S.F.L.Rev. 681 (1982).

5. Sec.Act Rel. No. 33–6188 n. 178, CCH Fed.Sec.L.Rep. ¶ 1051 (SEC Feb. 1, 1980); Sidney Stahl (SEC No Action Letter available April 23, 1981); See Olander & Jacks, The Section 4(1½) Exemption—Reading Between the Lines of the Securities Act of 1933, 15 Sec.Reg.L.J. 339 (1988).

ments of the 1933 Act, shall not apply to "transactions by any person other than an issuer, underwriter, or dealer."[6]

* * *

The parties do not seriously argue that Johnson was an issuer or a dealer. Clearly he is neither. Rather, Ackerberg contends that Johnson is an underwriter within § 4(1).

When considering whether Johnson is an underwriter, it is helpful to consider that the § 4(1) exemption is meant to distinguish "between distribution of securities and trading in securities." L. Loss & J. Seligman, 2 Securities Regulation 627 (3d ed. 1989) (quoting H.R.Rep. No. 85, 73d Cong., 1st Sess. 15 (1933)).

* * * The congressional intent in defining "underwriter" was to cover all persons who might operate as conduits for the transfer of securities to the public. T. Hazen, The Law of Securities Regulation § 4.24, at 141 (1985) (quoting H.R.Rep. No. 85, 73d Cong., 1st Sess. 13–14 (1933)).

* * * Given the statutory definition of "underwriter," the exemption should be available if: (1) the acquisition of the securities was not made "with a view to" distribution; or (2) the sale was not made "for an issuer in connection with" a distribution. See ABA Report, The Section "4(1½)" Phenonemen: Private Resales of "Restricted Securities, 34 Bus.Law.1961, 1975 (July 1979); Hazen, The Law of Securities Regulation at § 4.23, at 138. Relevant to both inquiries are whether the securities have come to rest in the hand of the security holder and whether the sale involves a public offering.

We begin by considering whether the securities were acquired by Johnson with a view to their distribution. * * * Johnson held his shares for at least four years before selling them to Ackerberg, a period well in excess of the usual two years required to find that the securities have come to rest.

Our second inquiry is whether the resale was made "for an issuer in connection with" a distribution. Whether the sale was "for an issuer" can also be determined by whether the shares have come to rest. * * *

6. It is clear that the applicable and appropriate exemption to be applied in this case is § 4(1). To the extent that Ackerberg argues that both Johnson and the PJH defendants rely on a "§ 4(1½)" exemption, he misunderstands the nature of a § 4(1) exemption. While the term "§ 4(1½) exemption" has been used in the secondary literature, see, e.g., ABA Report, The Section "4(1½)" Phenomenon: Private Resales of "Restricted" Securities, 34 Bus. Law.1961 (July 1979); Schneider, Section 4(1½)—Private Resales of Restricted or Control Securities, 49 Ohio St.L.J. 501 (1988), the term does not properly refer to an exemption other than § 4(1). Rather, the term merely expresses the statutory relationship between § 4(1) and § 4(2). That is, the definition of underwriter, found in § 2(11), depends on the existence of a distribution, which in turn is considered the equivalent of a public offering. Section 4(2) contains the exemption for transactions not involving a public offering. Any analysis of whether a party is an underwriter for purposes of § 4(1) necessarily entails an inquiry into whether the transaction involves a public offering. While the term "4(1½) exemption" adequately expresses this relationship, it is clear that the exemption for private resales of restricted securities is § 4(1). We need not go beyond the statute to reach this conclusion.

To determine whether the sale was made "in connection with" a distribution, however, requires that we consider directly the meaning of "distribution," and thus whether the resale involved a public offering. The definition of "distribution" as used in § 2(11) is generally considered to be synonymous with a public offering. * * *

The case law is equally clear that a public offering is defined not in quantitative terms, but in terms of whether the offerees are in need of the protection which the Securities Act affords through registration. Thus, the Supreme Court held in SEC v. Ralston Purina, 346 U.S. 119 (1953) that the proper focus is on the need of the offerees for information.

Since exempt transactions are those as to which "there is not practical need for [the bill's] application," the applicability of [the private placement exemption] should turn on whether the particular class of persons affected needs the protection of the Act. An offering to those who are shown to be able to fend for themselves is a transaction "not involving any public offering." Id. at 125. This circuit has followed *Ralston Purina* by finding that a public offering "turns on the need of the offerees for the protections afforded by registration. . . . If the offerees have access to such information, registration is unnecessary, and the section 4(2) exemption should apply."

That "distribution" should be read in terms of "public offering," and the need of the offerees for information, makes sense in light of the purpose of the 1933 Act as construed by this circuit. We held in *Van Dyke* that "[t]he design of the Act is to protect investors by promoting full disclosure of information thought necessary to make informed investment decisions." Moreover, the parties in this case do not dispute that Ackerberg is a sophisticated investor, not in need of the protections afforded by registration under the 1933 Act. As earlier stated, Ackerberg read and signed a subscription agreement in which he represented that: he had the knowledge and experience in investing to properly evaluate the merits and risks of his purchase of Vertimag securities; he was able to bear the economic risk of the investment in Vertimag securities; he was given full and complete information regarding Vertimag Systems Corporation; he knew that the securities were not registered under the 1933 Act, and were being sold pursuant to exemptions from the 1933 Act; and he knew that the sale was being made in reliance on his representations in the subscription agreement. Ackerberg further represented that his net worth was substantial, and the record clearly shows that Ackerberg is, if not a conscientious investor, at least a prolific one. We, therefore, have no trouble finding that Ackerberg is a sophisticated investor and not in need of the protections afforded by registration under the 1933 Act. Hence, this case involves no public offering, and thus no distribution. Absent a distribution, Johnson cannot be an underwriter within § 4(1), and is, therefore, entitled to that exemption.

Note on Rule 144A

In response to requests for a codification of the "§ 4(1½)" exemption, the SEC in 1988 proposed a new Rule 144A, which it then adopted, in revised form, in April 1990. Sec.Act Rel. No. 6862 (Apr. 23, 1990). As adopted, however, rule 144A does not deal with the question involved in the *Ackerberg* case—a resale by an individual purchaser to another individual who might have qualified as a purchaser in the original offering. What the Rule does is to permit unlimited resales of securities that have never been registered under the 1933 Act, as long as all such sales are made to a specific class of large institutional investors.

Rule 144A, like Rule 144, classifies certain offers and sales as not involving a distribution, so that persons participating in such offers and sales are not considered "underwriters." Essentially, the exemption covers any sale to a "qualified institutional buyer," which is defined as any institution (including insurance companies, investment companies, employee benefit plans, banks, and savings and loan associations) that owns more than $100 million worth of securities of unaffiliated issuers and, in the case of banks and savings and loans, has a net worth of at least $25 million.

In addition to direct transactions among these classes of institutions, the Rule also permits securities dealers to participate in transactions, either as purchasers for their own account, provided they themselves own at least $10 million worth of securities of unaffiliated issuers, or as agents for qualified institutions. Indeed, the Rule contemplates the formation of an active trading market in Rule 144A securities, in which qualified institutions and dealers can enter bids and offers. Simultaneously with the adoption of Rule 144A, the SEC approved the establishment by the National Association of Securities Dealers (NASD) of a screen-based computer and communication system called PORTAL (Private Offerings, Resales and Trading through Automated Linkages) to facilitate secondary trading of Rule 144A securities.

Rule 144A only applies to sales of securities of a class that is *not* listed on a U.S. stock exchange or traded in the NASDAQ system. With respect to securities issued by companies subject to the 1934 Act reporting requirements, or by foreign issuers, use of the Rule is not conditioned on the provision or availability of any information about the issuer. With respect to securities of other issuers, however, the Rule is only available if the prospective purchaser has received from the issuer a brief statement of the nature of the issuer's business and certain specified financial statements.

This information requirement for non-reporting domestic companies drew a sharp dissent from Commissioner Fleischman. He complained that these requirements would make the Rule unavailable to many "emerging growth companies" for whose benefit the Rule was supposedly adopted. He also argued that, since sales under the rule can only be made to qualified institutional buyers who are presumed to be able to fend for themselves, the information requirement is unnecessary, noting that under Regulation D, governing initial offerings by issuers, there is no information requirement as long as all sales are made to institutional buyers.

The adoption of Rule 144A and the establishment of the PORTAL system create the potential for an active trading market in foreign securities and in unregistered debt and equity issues of domestic issuers, limited to a designated class of large institutions and dealers. The SEC has also indicated that it will consider expanding the availability of the Rule as experience is gained about its operation.

Selected References

S. Goldberg, Private Placements and Restricted Securities (1978 ed.).

D. Goldwasser, A Guide to Rule 144 (2d ed. 1978).

T. Hazen, Securities Regulation §§ 4.22–4.26.1 (2d ed. 1990).

Campbell, Defining "Control" in Secondary Distributions, 18 B.C.Ind. & Comm.L.Rev. 37 (1976).

Casey, SEC Rule 144 Revisited, 43 Brooklyn L.Rev. 571 (1977).

Fogelson, Rule 144: A Summary Review, 37 Bus.Law. 1519 (1982).

Linde, The Resale of Restricted and Control Securities Under SEC Rule 144: The First Five Years, 8 Seton Hall L.Rev. 157 (1977).

Olander & Jacks, The Section 4(1½) Exemption—Reading Between the Lines of the Securities Act of 1933, 15 Sec.Reg.L.J. 339 (1988).

Schneider, Resales of Restricted or Control Securities, 49 Ohio St.L.J. 501 (1988).

The Section "4(1½)" Phenomenon: Private Resales of Restricted Securities—Report of the Committee on Federal Regulation of Securities, 34 Bus.Law. 1961 (1979).

---

5. *Reorganizations and "No–Sale" Transactions*

When two companies combine by means of a statutory merger or consolidation, state corporation law generally requires that the transaction must be approved by the shareholders of one or both of the companies. If one of the companies is a publicly-held company registered under § 12 of the 1934 Act, it must solicit proxies from its shareholders in accordance with the SEC "proxy rules" adopted under § 14 of that Act. See Ch. 6.A below.

For almost 40 years after the enactment of the Securities Act of 1933, the SEC took the position that the solicitation of shareholder votes for approval of a merger, sale of assets, or reclassification of securities was not a "sale" within the meaning of § 2(3) and therefore did not require registration under that Act. This position led to a number of problems and anomalies in the application of disclosure requirements. See pp. 352–357 below.

Sections 3(a)(9) and 3(a)(10) exempt certain types of business combinations. Section 3(a)(9) exempts securities issued to existing security holders in exchange for other securities of the same issuer. Section 3(a)(10) exempts certain court or administratively supervised business reorganizations. In addition, § 3(a)(7) exempts certificates issued pursuant to court approval under the Federal Bankruptcy Act.

Section 3(a)(9) exempts voluntary exchanges between the issuer and its existing security holders provided there is neither direct or indirect remuneration paid for solicitation efforts. In Securities Act Release No. 646 (Feb. 3, 1936) the Commission stated that § 3(a)(9) does not apply where the exchange is a first step in a scheme to evade registration. Cf. SEC v. Datronics Engineers, p. 355 below. Accordingly, if an exchange with existing security holders is followed by a significant number of resales, the § 3(a)(9) exemption will not be available, and the selling shareholders may be considered "underwriters" under § 2(11). See Sec.Act Rel. No. 2029 (Aug. 8, 1939).

Section 3(a)(10) provides an exemption for certain judicially or administratively approved reorganizations. In order to qualify for the § 3(a)(10) exemption, the hearing must be open and must consider the fairness of the transaction. See Securities Act Release No. 312 (March 15, 1935). Absent another exemption, all resales to members of the public must be registered under the 1933 Act.

These provisions have been used by imaginative promoters to avoid the 1933 Act's registration requirements. One technique involves the use of "no sale" distributions which are described in the SEC Release below and are exemplified in the decisions that follow.

APPLICATION OF THE SECURITIES ACT OF 1933 AND THE SECURITIES EXCHANGE ACT OF 1934 TO SPIN OFFS OF SECURITIES AND TRADING IN THE SECURITIES OF INACTIVE OR SHELL CORPORATIONS

Securities Act Rel. No. 4982 (July 2, 1969).

The Securities and Exchange Commission today made publicly known its concern with the methods being employed by a growing number of companies and persons to effect distributions to the public of unregistered securities in possible violation of the registration requirements of the Securities Act of 1933 and of the anti-fraud and anti-manipulative provisions of the Securities Act of 1933 and the Securities Exchange Act of 1934. The methods employed can take and in fact have taken a variety of patterns.

I

Frequently, the pattern involves the issuance by a company, with little, if any, business activity, of its shares to a publicly-owned company in exchange for what may or may not be nominal consideration. The publicly-owned company subsequently spins off the shares to its shareholders with the result that active trading in the shares begins with no information on the issuer being available to the investing public. Despite this lack of information, moreover, the shares frequently trade in an active market at increasingly higher prices. Under such a pattern, when the shares are issued to the publicly-owned or acquiring company, a sale takes place within the meaning of the Securities Act and if the shares are then distributed to the shareholders of the acquiring company, that company may be an underwriter within the meaning of Section 2(11) of the Act as a person "who purchased from an issuer with a view to * * * the distribution of any security" or as a person who "has a direct or indirect participation in any such undertaking."

While the distribution of the shares to the acquiring company's shareholders may not, in itself, constitute a distribution for the purposes of the Act, the entire process, including the redistribution in the trading market which can be anticipated and which may indeed be a principal purpose of the spin off, can have that consequence. It is accordingly the Commission's position that the shares which are distributed in certain spin offs involve the participation of a statutory underwriter and are thus, in those transactions, subject to the registration requirements of the Act and subsequent transactions in the shares by dealers, unless otherwise exempt, would be subject to the provisions of Section 5 requiring the delivery of a prospectus during the forty or ninety day period set forth in Section 4(3).

The theory has been advanced that since a sale is not involved in the distribution of the shares in a spin off that registration is not required and that even if it is required, no purpose would be served by filing a registration statement and requiring the delivery of a prospectus since the persons receiving the shares are not called upon to make an investment judgment.

This reasoning fails, however, to take into account that there is a sale by the issuer and the distribution thereafter does not cease at the point of receipt by the initial distributees of the shares but continues into the trading market involving sales to the investing public at large. Moreover, it ignores what appears to be primarily the purpose of the spin off in numerous circumstances which is to create quickly, and without the disclosure required by registration, a trading market in the shares of the issuer. Devices of this kind, contravene the purpose, as well as the specific provisions, of the Act which, in the words of the statutory preamble, are "to provide full and fair disclosure of the character of the securities sold in interstate and foreign commerce and through the mails, and to prevent frauds in the sale thereof." In the circumstances of a spin off, when the shares are thereafter traded in the absence of information about the issuer, the potential for fraud and deceit is manifest.

This release does not attempt to deal with any problems attributable to more conventional spin offs, which do not involve a process of purchase of securities by a publicly-owned company followed by their spin off and redistribution in the trading markets. * * *

II

Another pattern has come to the Commission's attention in which certain promoters have acquired corporations which have ceased active operations, or which have little or no assets ("shell corporations"), and which have a substantial number of shares outstanding, generally in the hands of the public. Thereafter the promoters have engaged in activities to quickly increase the market value of their shareholdings. For example, in some cases promoters have initiated a program of acquisitions, transferring assets of dubious value to the "shell corporations" in exchange for substantial amounts of newly issued shares. This activity is frequently accompanied by publicity containing exaggerated or misleading statements and designed to stimulate interest of public investors in the company's shares in violation of the anti-fraud provisions of the Securities Exchange Act of 1934. Thereafter the market prices of these securities have risen sharply under circumstances which bear no relationship to the underlying financial condition and business activities of the company. In some of these cases the promoters or other corporate insiders, take advantage of the market activity and the price rise which they have generated, have sold their shares at the inflated prices to the public in violation of the registration and anti-fraud provisions of the Federal securities laws. Similar activities have also been noted in a number of cases involving shares which a publicly held company has spun off to its shareholders.

III

The activities discussed above generally can only be successfully accomplished through the efforts of brokers and dealers. Accordingly, brokers and dealers are cautioned to be particularly mindful of their obligations under the registration and anti-fraud provisions of the Federal securities laws with respect to effecting transactions in such securities. In this connection, where a broker or dealer receives an order to sell securities of a little-known, inactive issuer, or one with respect to which there is no current information available except possibly unfounded rumors, care must be taken to obtain sufficient information about the issuer and the person desirous of effecting the trade in order to be reasonably assured that the proposed transaction complies with the applicable requirements. Moreover, before a broker or dealer induces or solicits a transaction he should make diligent inquiry concerning the issuer, in order to form a reasonable basis for his recommendation, and fully inform his customers of the information so obtained, or in the absence of any information, of that fact.

Former § 3(a)(1) of the 1933 Act provided an exemption from registration for securities issued or bona fide offered to the public prior to the effective date of the Act.[1] In SEC v. A.G. BELLIN SECURITIES, 171 F.Supp. 233 (S.D.N.Y.1959), the SEC sought an injunction against an unregistered offering claimed to be exempt under § 3(a)(1). Defendants had sought a company whose stock could be purchased and resold to the public without registration under the 1933 Act. They located a closely held and inactive mining company which had originally issued its shares in 1931. After authorizing additional shares, the defendants planned a new offering and claimed an exemption from registration under § 3(a)(1). The court issued the injunction, reasoning:

> It is clear that the stock here involved was not sold, disposed of or bona fide offered to the public. Moreover even if it be considered to have been "disposed of" by issuance of all but one share [to B and S], they under the statute were "issuers" since they controlled the "issuer" Pacific Gold Placers, Incorporated. Josephson clearly purchased the stock either for himself or his clients, if any with a view to its distribution. Accordingly he, under section 2(11), became an "underwriter" whose "new offering" of the stock was not exempt from registration.

In the *Ira Haupt* case, at p. 329 above, the respondent also made the same argument as defendants in the *Bellin* case—that the sales by Schulte were exempt under former § 3(a)(1) because the shares he was selling had been issued prior to the enactment of the 1933 Act. The SEC held the exemption unavailable because the "distribution" of a controlling block constituted a "new offering" through an underwriter within the meaning of § 3(a)(1). The Commission also noted from its records that, of the 243,731 Park & Tilford shares outstanding, 31,246 had been issued more than 60 days after enactment of the 1933 Act, and that "this fact, in itself, would make § 3(a)(1) inapplicable" (assuming, of course, that Schulte could not trace his shares to those issued prior to 1933). Because of its apparent obsolescence, § 3(a)(1) was repealed in 1987 as part of a series of technical amendments to the federal securities laws.

Consider the impact of the *Bellin* and *Ira Haupt* rationale beyond the context of the § 3(a)(1) exemption. For example, assume that in 1985, Moneybags acquires fifteen percent of a public company on the open market. In 1989, Moneybags decides to sell his shares on the open market. Must these sales be registered?

1. The exemption covered "[a]ny security which, prior to or within sixty days after the enactment of this title, has been sold or disposed of by the issuer or bona fide offered to the public, but this exemption shall not apply to any new offering of such security by an issuer or underwriter subsequent to such sixty days . . ."

Similarly, consider the plight of the unsuccessful corporate raider: In early 1990, Raider acquires 35% of Target Co. stock in a tender offer but then is rebuffed by Target management. Can Raider simply sell his stock through a broker? Does the Target management's response, preclude Raider from being characterized as a control person? See United States v. Sherwood, p. 325 above.

SEC v. DATRONICS ENGINEERS, INC.

490 F.2d 250 (4th Cir.1973).

Before BRYAN, SENIOR CIRCUIT JUDGE, and FIELD and WIDENER, CIRCUIT JUDGES.

BRYAN, SENIOR CIRCUIT JUDGE: The Securities and Exchange Commission in enforcement of the Securities Act of 1933, § 20(b), and the Securities Exchange Act of 1934, § 21(e), sought a preliminary injunction to restrain Datronics Engineers, Inc., its officers and agents, as well as related corporations, from continuing in alleged violation of the registration and antifraud provisions of the Acts. The breaches are said to have been committed in the sale of unregistered securities, § 5 of the 1933 Act, and by the employment of false representations in their sale, § 10(b) of the 1934 Act, and Rule 10b–5 of the Commission.

Summary judgment went for the defendants, and the Commission appeals. We reverse.

Specifically, the complaint charged transgressions of the statutes by Datronics, assisted by the individual defendants, in declaring, and effectuating through the use of the mails, "spin-offs" to and among its stockholders of the unregistered shares of stock owned by Datronics in other corporations. With exceptions to be noted, and since the decision on appeal rests on a motion for summary judgment, there is no substantial dispute on the facts. Datronics was engaged in the construction of communications towers. Its capital stock was held by 1000 shareholders and was actively traded on the market. All of the spin-offs occurred within a period of 13 months—from November 1, 1968 to December 31, 1969—and the spun-off stock was that of nine corporations, three of which were wholly owned subsidiaries of Datronics and six were independent corporations.

The pattern of the spin-offs in each instance was this: Without any business purpose of its own, Datronics would enter into an agreement with the principals of a private company. The agreement provided for the organization by Datronics of a new corporation, or the utilization of one of Datronic's subsidiaries, and the merger of the private company into the new or subsidiary corporation. It stipulated that the principals of the private company would receive the majority interest in the merger-corporation. The remainder of the stock of the corporation would be delivered to, or retained by, Datronics for a nominal sum per share. Part of it would be applied to the payment of the services of

Datronics in the organization and administration of the proposed spin-off, and to Datronics' counsel for legal services in the transaction. Datronics was bound by each of the nine agreements to distribute among its shareholders the rest of the stock.

Before such distribution, however, Datronics reserved for itself approximately one-third of the shares. Admittedly, none of the newly acquired stock was ever registered; its distribution and the dissemination of the false representations were accomplished by use of the mails.

I. Primarily, in our judgment each of these spin-offs violated § 5 of the Securities Act, in that Datronics caused to be carried through the mails an unregistered security "for the purpose of sale or for delivery after sale." Datronics was actually an issuer, or at least a co-issuer, and not exempted from § 5 by § 4(1) of the Act, as "any person other than an issuer".

Datronics and the other appellees contend, and the District Court concluded, that this type of transaction was not a sale. The argument is that it was no more than a dividend parceled out to stockholders from its portfolio of investments. A noteworthy difference here, however, is that each distribution was an obligation. Their contention also loses sight of the definition of "sale" contained in § 2 of the 1933 Act. * * *

As the term "sale" includes a "disposition of a security", the dissemination of the new stock among Datronics' stockholders was a sale. However, the appellees urged, and the District Court held, that this disposition was not a statutory sale because it was not "for value", as demanded by the definition. Here, again, we find error. Cf. Securities and Exchange Commission v. Harwyn Industries Corp., 326 F.Supp. 943, 954 (S.D.N.Y.1971). Value accrued to Datronics in several ways. First, a market for the stock was created by its transfer to so many new assignees—at least 1000, some of whom were stockbroker-dealers, residing in various States. Sales by them followed at once—the District Judge noting that "[i]n each instance dealing promptly began in the spun-off shares". This result redounded to the benefit not only of Datronics but, as well, to its officers and agents who had received some of the spun-off stock as compensation for legal or other services to the spin-off corporations. Likewise, the stock retained by Datronics was thereby given an added increment of value. The record discloses that in fact the stock, both that disseminated and that kept by Datronics, did appreciate substantially after the distributions.

This spurious creation of a market whether intentional or incidental constituted a breach of the securities statutes. Each of the issuers by this wide spread of its stock became a publicly held corporation. In this process and in subsequent sales the investing public was not afforded the protection intended by the statutes. Further, the market and the public character of the spun-off stock were fired and fanned by the issuance of shareholder letters announcing future spin-offs, and by information statements sent out to the shareholders.

Moreover, we think that Datronics was an underwriter within the meaning of the 1933 Act. * * * Clearly, in these transactions the merger-corporation was an issuer; Datronics was a purchaser as well as a co-issuer; and the purchase was made with a view to the distribution of the stock, as commanded by Datronics' preacquisition agreements. By this underwriter distribution Datronics violated § 5 of the 1933 Act—sale of unregistered securities. * * *

WIDENER, CIRCUIT JUDGE, concurring: I concur in the issuance of the temporary injunction because I believe the existence of the agreements between Datronics and the various companies whose stock found its way to the market through Datronics, on account of the agreements, with no apparent business purpose which has been expressed to us, other than the creation of a public market for the stock, points to the fact that Datronics may have been a willing cat's-paw in a device or scheme to avoid the statute. * * *

With so much of the opinion as holds that Datronics may be an underwriter within the meaning of the statute, I agree. The word "distribution" as used in the statute has not been defined to require value. * * *

Another impediment to the use of shell corporations to avoid registration of spin-off transactions is the SEC rule dealing with over-the-counter quotations. Rule 15c2–11, which is discussed more fully at p. 932 below, prohibits broker-dealers from providing price quotations in over-the-counter securities unless either (1) the issuer is a 1934 Act reporting company or (2) the broker-dealer has made available specified financial information about the issuer. The effect of the rule is to preclude price quotes for companies about which no public information is publicly available.

Selected References

Greene & Junewicz, A Reappraisal of Current Regulation of Mergers and Acquisitions, 132 U.Pa.L.Rev. 647–739 (1984).

Ash, Reorganizations and Other Exchanges Under § 3(a)(10), 75 Nw.U.L. Rev. 1–95 (1980).

Heyman, Implications of Rule 145 Under the Securities Act of 1933, 53 B.U.L.Rev. 785 (1973).

Schneider & Manko, Rule 145: An Analysis and Appraisal, 5 Rev.Sec.Reg. 811, 911 (1972–73).

Comment, Business Combinations and Registration Requirements: SEC Rule 145, 47 N.Y.U.L.Rev. 929 (1972).

Note, Registration of Stock Spin–Offs Under the Securities Act of 1933, 1980 Duke L.J. 965.

Lorne, The Portfolio Spin-Off and Securites Regulation, 52 Tex.L.Rev. 918 (1974).

Long, Control of the Spin-Off Device Under the Securities Act of 1933, 25 Olka.L.Rev. 317 (1972).

Orlanski, Going Public Through the Backdoor and the Shell Game, 58 Va. L.Rev. 1451 (1972).

C. CIVIL LIABILITY UNDER § 12

Section 12 of the 1933 Act imposes civil liability on sellers of securities in two situations: where a security is sold in violation of § 5 (i.e., in an unregistered, non-exempt transaction) or where a security is sold by means of an oral or written communication which has a material misstatement or omission. In contrast to the complex provisions in § 11 relating to plaintiffs and defendants, § 12 simply provides that the person who "offers or sells" the security is "liable to the person purchasing such security from him."

PINTER v. DAHL

486 U.S. 622 (1988).

JUSTICE BLACKMUN delivered the opinion of the Court.

* * *

The controversy arises out of the sale prior to 1982 of unregistered securities (fractional undivided interests in oil and gas leases) by petitioner Billy J. "B.J." Pinter to respondents Maurice Dahl and Dahl's friends, family, and business associates. Pinter is an oil and gas producer in Texas and Oklahoma, and a registered securities dealer in Texas. Dahl is a California real estate broker and investor, who, at the time of his dealings with Pinter, was a veteran of two unsuccessful oil and gas ventures. * * *

After investing approximately $310,000 in the properties, Dahl told the other respondents about the venture. Except for Dahl and respondent Grantham, none of the respondents spoke to or met Pinter or toured the properties. Because of Dahl's involvement in the venture, each of the other respondents decided to invest about $7,500.

Dahl assisted his fellow investors in completing the subscription-agreement form prepared by Pinter. Each letter-contract signed by the purchaser stated that the participating interests were being sold without the benefit of registration under the Securities Act, in reliance on Securities and Exchange Commission Rule 146. In fact, the oil and gas interests involved in this suit were never registered with the Commission. Respondents' investment checks were made payable to Black Gold Oil Company. Dahl received no commission from Pinter in connection with the other respondents' purchases.

When the venture failed and their interests proved to be worthless, respondents brought suit against Pinter in the United States District Court for the Northern District of Texas, seeking rescission under § 12(1) of the Securities Act, for the unlawful sale of unregistered securities.

* * *

The District Court, after a bench trial, granted judgment for respondent-investors. The court concluded that Pinter had not proved that the oil and gas interests were entitled to the private-offering exemption from registration. Accordingly, the court ruled that, because the securities were unregistered, respondents were entitled to rescission pursuant to § 12(1). * * *

A divided panel of the Court of Appeals for the Fifth Circuit affirmed.

* * *

The Court of Appeals * * * considered whether Dahl was himself a "seller" of the oil and gas interests within the meaning of § 12(1), for if he was, the court assumed, he could be held liable in contribution for the other plaintiffs' claims against Pinter. Citing Fifth Circuit precedent, the court described a statutory seller as "(1) one who parts with title to securities in exchange for consideration or (2) one whose participation in the buy-sell transaction is a substantial factor in causing the transaction to take place." While acknowledging that Dahl's conduct was a "substantial factor" in causing the other plaintiffs to purchase securities from Pinter, the court declined to hold that Dahl was a "seller" for purposes of § 12(1). Instead, the court went on to refine its test to include a threshold requirement that one who acts as a "promoter" be "motivated by a desire to confer a direct or indirect benefit on someone other than the person he has advised to purchase."

* * *

Because of the importance of the issues involved to the administration of the federal securities law, we granted certiorari.

* * *

In determining whether Dahl may be deemed a "seller" for purposes of § 12(1), such that he may be held liable for the sale of unregistered securities to the other investor-respondents, we look first at the language of § 12(1). That statute provides, in pertinent part: "Any person who * * * offers or sells a security" in violation of the registration requirement of the Securities Act "shall be liable to the person purchasing such security from him." This provision defines the class of defendants who may be subject to liability as those who offer or sell unregistered securities. But the Securities Act nowhere delineates who may be regarded as a statutory seller, and the sparse legislative history sheds no light on the issue. The courts, on their part, have not defined the term uniformly.

At the very least, however, the language of § 12(1) contemplates a buyer-seller relationship not unlike traditional contractual privity. Thus, it is settled that § 12(1) imposes liability on the owner who passed title, or other interest in the security, to the buyer for value. Dahl, of course, was not a seller in this conventional sense, and therefore may be held liable only if § 12(1) liability extends to persons other than the person who passes title.

A

In common parlance, a person may offer or sell property without necessarily being the person who transfers title to, or other interest in, that property. We need not rely entirely on ordinary understanding of the statutory language, however, for the Securities Act defines the operative terms of § 12(1). Section 2(3) defines "sale" or "sell" to include "every contract of sale or disposition of a security or interest in a security, for value," and the terms "offer to sell," "offer for sale," or "offer" to include "every attempt or offer to dispose of, or solicitation of an offer to buy, a security or interest in a security, for value." Under these definitions, the range of persons potentially liable under § 12(1) is not limited to persons who pass title. The inclusion of the phrase "solicitation of an offer to buy" within the definition of "offer" brings an individual who engages in solicitation, an activity not inherently confined to the actual owner, within the scope of § 12. * * *

Determining that the activity in question falls within the definition of "offer" or "sell" in § 2(3), however, is only half of the analysis. The second clause of § 12(1), which provides that only a defendant "from" whom the plaintiff "purchased" securities may be liable, narrows the field of potential sellers. Several courts and commentators have stated that the purchase requirement necessarily restricts § 12 primary liability to the owner of the security. * * *

We do not read § 12(1) so restrictively. The purchase requirement clearly confines § 12 liability to those situations in which a sale has taken place. Thus, a prospective buyer has no recourse against a person who touts unregistered securities to him if he does not purchase the securities. The requirement, however, does not exclude solicitation from the category of activities that may render a person liable when a sale has taken place. A natural reading of the statutory language would include in the statutory seller status at least some persons who urged the buyer to purchase. For example, a securities vendor's agent who solicited the purchase would commonly be said, and would be thought by the buyer, to be among those "from" whom the buyer "purchased," even though the agent himself did not pass title.

The Securities Act does not define the term "purchase." The soundest interpretation of the term, however, is as a correlative to both "sell" and "offer," at least to the extent that the latter entails active solicitation of an offer to buy. This interpretation is supported by the history of the phrase "offers or sells," as it is used in § 12(1). As enacted in 1933, § 12(1) imposed liability on "[a]ny person who sells a security." The statutory definition of "sell" included "offer" and the activities now encompassed by that term, including solicitation. The words "offer or" were added to § 12(1) by the 1954 amendments to the

Securities Act, when the original definition of "sell" in § 2(3) was split into separate definitions of "sell" and "offer" in order to accommodate changes in § 5. Since "sells" and "purchases" have obvious correlative meanings, Congress' express definition of "sells" in the original Securities Act to include solicitation suggests that the class of those from whom the buyer "purchases" extended to persons who solicit him. The 1954 amendment to § 12(1) was intended to preserve existing law, including the liability provisions of the Act. Hence, there is no reason to think Congress intended to narrow the meaning of "purchased from" when it amended the statute to include "solicitation" in the statutory definition of "offer" alone.

* * *

An interpretation of statutory seller that includes brokers and others who solicit offers to purchase securities furthers the purposes of the Securities Act—to promote full and fair disclosure of information to the public in the sales of securities. The solicitation of a buyer is perhaps the most critical stage of the selling transaction. It is the first stage of a traditional securities sale to involve the buyer, and it is directed at producing the sale. In addition, brokers and other solicitors are well positioned to control the flow of information to a potential purchaser, and, in fact, such persons are the participants in the selling transaction who most often disseminate material information to investors. Thus, solicitation is the stage at which an investor is most likely to be injured, that is, by being persuaded to purchase securities without full and fair information. Given Congress' overriding goal of preventing this injury, we may infer that Congress intended solicitation to fall under the mantle of § 12(1).

Although we conclude that Congress intended § 12(1) liability to extend to those who solicit securities purchases, we share the Court of Appeals' conclusion that Congress did not intend to impose rescission based on strict liability on a person who urges the purchase but whose motivation is solely to benefit the buyer. * * * The language and purpose of § 12(1) suggest that liability extends only to the person who successfully solicits the purchase, motivated at least in part by a desire to serve his own financial interests or those of the securities owner. If he had such a motivation, it is fair to say that the buyer "purchased" the security from him and to align him with the owner in a rescission action.

B

Petitioner is not satisfied with extending § 12(1) primary liability to one who solicits securities sales for financial gain. Pinter assumes, without explication, that liability is not limited to the person who actually parts title with the securities, and urges us to validate, as the standard by which additional defendant-sellers are identified, that version of the "substantial factor" test utilized by the Fifth Circuit before the refinement espoused in this case. Under that approach, grounded in tort doctrine, a nontransferor § 12(1) seller is defined as one "whose participation in the buy-sell transaction is a substantial factor in causing the transaction to take place." The Court of Appeals acknowledged that Dahl would be liable as a statutory seller under this test.

We do not agree that Congress contemplated imposing § 12(1) liability under the broad terms petitioner advocates. There is no support in the statutory language or legislative history for expansion of § 12(1) primary liability beyond persons who pass title and persons who "offer," including those who "solicit" offers. Indeed, § 12's failure to impose express liability for mere participation in unlawful sales transactions suggests that Congress did not intend that the section impose liability on participants collateral to the offer or sale.

The deficiency of the substantial-factor test is that it divorces the analysis of seller status from any reference to the applicable statutory language and from any examination of § 12 in the context of the total statutory scheme. Those courts that have adopted the approach have not attempted to ground their analysis in the statutory language. Instead, they substitute the concept of substantial participation in the sales transaction, or proximate causation of the plaintiff's purchase, for the words "offers or sells" in § 12. The "purchase from" requirement of § 12 focuses on the defendant's relationship with the plaintiff-purchaser. The substantial-factor test, on the other hand, focuses on the defendant's degree of involvement in the securities transaction and its surrounding circumstances. Thus, although the substantial-factor test undoubtedly embraces persons who pass title and who solicit the purchase of unregistered securities as statutory sellers, the test also would extend § 12(1) liability to participants only remotely related to the relevant aspects of the sales transaction. Indeed, it might expose securities professionals, such as accountants and lawyers, whose involvement is only the performance of their professional services, to § 12(1) strict liability for rescission. The buyer does not, in any meaningful sense, "purchas[e] the security from" such a person.

Further, no congressional intent to incorporate tort law doctrines of reliance and causation into § 12(1) emerges from the language or the legislative history of the statute. Indeed, the strict liability nature of the statutory cause of action suggests the opposite. By injecting these concepts into § 12(1) litigation, the substantial-factor test introduces an element of uncertainty into an area that demands certainty and predictability. As the Fifth Circuit has conceded, the test affords no guidelines for distinguishing between the defendant whose conduct rises to a level of significance sufficient to trigger seller status, and the defendant whose conduct is not sufficiently integral to the sale. * * * We find it particularly unlikely that Congress would have ordained *sub silentio* the imposition of strict liability on such an unpredictably defined class of defendants.

* * *

The substantial-factor test reaches participants in sales transactions who do not even arguably fit within the definitions set out in

§ 2(3); it "would add a gloss to the operative language of [§ 12(1)] quite different from its commonly accepted meaning." * * * Being merely a "substantial factor" in causing the sale of unregistered securities is not sufficient in itself to render a defendant liable under § 12(1).

C

We are unable to determine whether Dahl may be held liable as a statutory seller under § 12(1). The District Court explicitly found that "Dahl solicited each of the other plaintiffs (save perhaps Grantham) in connection with the offer, purchase, and receipt of their oil and gas interests." * * * It is not clear, however, that Dahl had the kind of interest in the sales that make him liable as a statutory seller. * * * Accordingly, further findings are necessary to assess Dahl's liability.

Is it significant that the *Pinter* decision was made in the context of a § 12(1) transaction? Is there any basis for applying a different test of who is a seller in an action under § 12(2)? Subsequent cases have applied the same test to § 12(2). Thus, for example, people who solicit purchasers are subject to liability under § 12(2) as well as under § 12(1). In re Craftmatic, 890 F.2d 628 (3d Cir.1989). See also Wilson v. Ruffa & Hanover, 872 F.2d 1124 (2d Cir.1989) (law firm not liable under § 12(2) in wake of *Pinter*); Capri v. Murphy, 856 F.2d 473 (2d Cir.1988) (general partners of issuer were "sellers" under § 12(2)).

The Court in *Pinter* limited its discussion to the meaning of seller in determining the scope of primary liability under § 12. Would it be possible to expand the scope of persons liable by the imposition of secondary liability under aiding and abetting principles? See discussion of aiding and abetting at pp. 455–462, 541–548 below. Permitting aiding and abetting liability would seem counter to the thrust of the Court's reasoning.

Another issue under § 12 is its applicability to people taking positions in options and other derivative investments. It has been held, for example, that an option seller is not a purchaser under § 12(2). Panek v. Bogucz, 718 F.Supp. 1228 (D.N.J.1989).

In *Pinter,* the Supreme Court also considered the availability of the *in pari delicto* defense in actions under § 12(1). Under that doctrine, a plaintiff cannot recover if he was equally at fault with the defendant. In Bateman Eichler v. Berner, p. 932 below, the Court had held that the defense was available in an action under Rule 10b–5. In *Pinter,* the court of appeals held that the defense was not available in a § 12(1) action because that section imposes "strict liability", unlike Rule 10b–5, which creates liability only for intentional misconduct. The Supreme Court disagreed, holding that the defense was available in private actions under any provision of the federal securities laws, and went on to specify how the tests laid down in *Bateman Eichler* would apply in an action under § 12(1):

> Under the first prong of the *Bateman Eichler* test, as we have noted above, a defendant cannot escape liability unless, as a direct result of the plaintiff's own actions, the plaintiff bears at least substantially equal responsibility for the underlying illegality. The plaintiff must be an active, voluntary participant in the unlawful activity that is the subject of the suit. * * *
>
> In the context of a private action under § 12(1), the first prong of the *Bateman Eichler* test is satisfied if the plaintiff is at least equally responsible for the actions that render the sale of the unregistered securities illegal—the issuer's failure to register the securities before offering them for sale, or his failure to conduct the sale in such a manner as to meet the registration exemption provisions. As the parties and the Commission agree, a purchaser's knowledge that the securities are unregistered cannot, by itself, constitute equal culpability, even where the investor is a sophisticated buyer who may not necessarily need the protection of the Securities Act. * * *
>
> Under the second prong of the *Bateman Eichler* test, a plaintiff's recovery may be barred only if preclusion of suit does not offend the underlying statutory policies. The primary purpose of the Securities Act is to protect investors by requiring publication of material information thought necessary to allow them to make informed investment decisions concerning public offerings of securities in interstate commerce. * * *
>
> In our view, where the § 12(1) plaintiff is primarily an investor, precluding suit would interfere significantly with effective enforcement of the securities laws and frustrate the primary objective of the Securities Act. The Commission, too, takes this position. Because the Act is specifically designed to protect investors, even where a plaintiff actively participates in the distribution of unregistered securities, his suit should not be barred where his promotional efforts are incidental to his role as an investor. Thus, the *in pari delicto* defense may defeat recovery in a § 12(1) action only where the plaintiff's role in the offering or sale of nonexempted, unregistered securities is more as a promoter than as an investor.
>
> Whether the plaintiff in a particular case is primarily an investor or primarily a promoter depends upon a host of factors, all readily accessible to trial courts. These factors include the extent of the plaintiff's financial involvement compared to that of third parties solicited by the plaintiff; the incidental nature of the plaintiff's promotional activities; the benefits received by the plaintiff from his promotional activities; and the extent of the plaintiff's involvement in the planning stages of the offering (such as whether the plaintiff has arranged an underwriting or prepared the offering materials).

Note on Civil Liability for Non-Exempt Offerings

If an unregistered offer or sale of securities does not qualify for an exemption under Section 3 or 4 of the 1933 Act, it violates Section 5, and Section 12(1) entitles a purchaser to rescind the transaction and recover his purchase price.

In DISKIN v. LOMASNEY, 452 F.2d 871 (2d Cir.1971), the plaintiff received a written offer that was in violation of the prospectus requirements. The plaintiff subsequently received a statutory prospectus before the sale was consummated. The court nevertheless held that plaintiff could sue under § 12(1) for the illegal offer even though the sale was legal. See also Doran v. Petroleum Management Corp., p. 292 above, where the court noted in a section 12(1) action "Even the plaintiff's 20–20 vision with respect to the facts underlying the security would not save the exemption if any of his fellow offerees was blind."

In HENDERSON v. HAYDEN, STONE, INC., 461 F.2d 1069 (5th Cir.1972), plaintiff, who "can only be described as a sophisticated investor," sued under Section 12(1) to rescind his purchase of $180,000 worth of stock out of a total offering of $300,000. The court rejected defendants' argument that the transaction did not involve a public offering, in view of their failure to produce clear evidence as to the number of other offerees and their relationship to the issuer. The court also rejected defendant's argument that plaintiff was estopped to recover under the particular circumstances:

> "[A]lthough Henderson is certainly not the average innocent investor, nevertheless allowing him to recover clearly will not frustrate the legislative purpose. * * * In any event, the concomitant of the legislative purpose is affirmatively served here. Congress sought to encourage sellers of securities to register those securities prior to any sales or offers to sell. By allowing recoveries such as the one in this case, unregistered sales are discouraged."

Are you persuaded? Or are you sympathetic to the suggestion that "the Commission adopt a rule creating an issuer's defense against Section 12(1) liability arising out of an innocent and immaterial failure to comply with the terms of an exemption * * *. If a particular sale of securities to a given purchaser complied with all of the conditions of a Rule implementing an exemption, or otherwise met all the standards for availability of the exemption apart from such Rule, such purchaser would not have a right to rescind under Section 12(1) solely because of an innocent and immaterial defect in the offer or sale to other persons as part of the same transaction." Schneider & Zall, Section 12(1) and the Imperfect Exempt Transaction: the Proposed I and I Defense, 28 Bus.Lawyer 1011, 1013 (1973). Does the Commission have power to adopt such a rule with respect to non-public offerings? With respect to intrastate offerings?

In 1989, the Commission adopted Rule 508, under which failure to comply with a condition or requirement of Regulation D that is insignificant with respect to the offering as a whole will not result in the loss of the exemption if the issuer can show a good faith reasonable attempt to comply. A purchaser in such an offering would be barred from suing under § 12(1) only if the failure to comply was insignificant with respect to the sale to him or her as well as to the offering as a whole.

What can an issuer do if it discovers it has inadvertently made an offer that should have been registered under the 1933 Act?

MEYERS v. C & M PETROLEUM PRODUCERS, INC.

476 F.2d 427 (5th Cir.1973).

Before COLEMAN, MORGAN and RONEY, CIRCUIT JUDGES.

COLEMAN, CIRCUIT JUDGE: * * *

C & M Petroleum Producers, Inc., is a Georgia corporation with its principal office and place of business in Jesup, Georgia. The corporation was organized for the purpose of buying and selling mineral leases in gas and oil wells in Ohio. The Company began to offer to sell and deliver these securities to certain residents of Georgia and Florida. The purchasers-appellants paid C & M a total of $23,750 for their interests in the wells. Although no registration statement has been filed with the Securities and Exchange Commission as required by § 5 of the Securities Act of 1933, the mails, telephone, and other means of interstate transportation and communication were employed by C & M in these offers, sales, and deliveries.

Being informed of non-compliance with the registration requirements of the Securities Act of 1933 and the Georgia Securities Act of 1957, C & M wrote purchasers-appellants on May 27, 1969, advising them of the status of the matter and offering to repurchase their interests in the wells. The letter stated:

> "We are advised that as a result of having sold you an interest in the above mentioned gas wells, we are in violation of the Georgia Securities Act of 1957 as amended and the Securities Act of 1933 as amended. These Statutes provide that we should have registered this interest as a security before offering it to you for sale. Consequently, in view of our violation of the Georgia and Federal Statutes, we hereby offer to repurchase from you said interest for the sum of money paid by you for said interest, less any monies received by you therefrom. This offer to repurchase the above described interest from you shall terminate ten days after the date hereof. In other words, you have ten days to decide whether you want to keep your interest or not. Enclosed is a copy of this letter on which you are requested to indicate your preference. You will also find herewith a stamped, self-addressed envelope

in order that you may return the enclosed copy to us promptly. Very truly yours, C & M Petroleum Producers, Incorporated. Herman Morris.

"1. I desire that my interest be repurchased ( ).

"2. I do not desire that my interest be repurchased ( ).

"If we have not received a reply within ten days, we will assume that you wish to keep your interest in the referred well or wells."

The purchasers did not accept this proposal. Their attorney wrote C & M that he felt it impossible to determine the feasibility of accepting or rejecting the purchase offer unless first given data which would reflect the actual value of the securities. This clearly meant that the purchasers did not wish to surrender the securities if they were worth more than had been paid for them. The letter raised no other impediment to the return of the stock. It indicated an unwillingness to accept the remedy provided by the statute.

The purchasers took no further action and the ten day period expired. C & M then revoked the offer to repurchase.

Thereafter, the purchasers received and accepted $1,472.91 in income from the wells.

On December 23, 1969, the purchasers brought suit to recover the consideration paid for the securities, with interest, less the income received therefrom.

As already stated, the District Court allowed into evidence C & M's ten day repurchase offer as bearing on whether the purchasers had waived their rights under §§ 5 and 12(1) of the Securities Act of 1933. The jury found that the purchasers-appellants had waived their rights and judgment was entered for C & M.

Appellants assert two grounds for reversal: that the defense of waiver is not available in a suit arising under § 12(1) of the Act, and that the repurchase offer itself violated the registration requirements of the Act.

Since, except for the self-imposed ten day limitation, the C & M letter was an offer to provide the remedy prescribed by statute, we find no merit in the second argument.

This leaves remaining only the contention that by the express provisions of the Securities Act mere waiver was not, and could not be, a defense to this suit.

* * *

[Section 14 of the Securities Act of 1933] provides that:

> "Any condition, stipulation, or provision binding any person acquiring any security to waive compliance with any provision of this sub-chapter or of the rules and regulations of the Commission shall be void."

Can–Am Petroleum v. Beck, 10 Cir., 1964, 331 F.2d 331, was a case in which undivided interests in oil and gas leases had been sold in violation of §§ 5 and 12 of the Act. The Court held that the remedial aspects of the Securities Act cannot be waived, either directly or indirectly, citing Wilko v. Swan, 346 U.S. 427 (1953). The appellees here, defendants in the court below, sought to establish a waiver in the manner and form already set forth. Contrary to the general rule applicable to other transactions, this has been expressly prohibited by the Congress for the purpose of making the Act as effective as possible.

If C & M had unconditionally tendered the refund of the purchase price together with interest, less income received from the securities, coupled with a demand for the return of the securities, and had the purchasers rejected such an unconditional tender and demand they would have impaled themselves upon such an estoppel as recognized by the Court of Appeals for the Ninth Circuit in the cases of Straley v. Universal Uranium and Milling Corporation, 1961, 289 F.2d 370, and Royal Air Properties, Inc. v. Smith, 1964, 312 F.2d 210. What the appellees did was to make an *offer* to repay the purchase price and accept return of the securities, but they imposed their own ten day limitation upon the acceptance of the offer. When the offer was not accepted within the prescribed time the sellers cancelled it, restoring the parties to the position they occupied before the offer was made. While, as the jury found, this could be enough to establish a waiver, it was not enough to create an estoppel, lacking, as it did, an unconditional tender and demand. * * *

Our holding in this case is that while the defendants-appellees established a waiver, the statute permits none.

RONEY, CIRCUIT JUDGE (specially concurring):

I concur in the decision that the failure of the purchasers to accept the repurchase offer of the sellers did not constitute an effective waiver of rights under the statute. The matter is completely within the control of Congress, which provided that

> *Any* condition, stipulation, or provision binding any person acquiring any security to waive compliance with any provision of this subchapter or of the rules and regulations of the Commission shall be *void.* (Italics added)

Since apparently an intentional, formal, written waiver executed either before or after the acquisition of securities is void, *a fortiori* any waiver that might be inferred from less formal acts must also be void. * * *

Is it so clear that § 14 applies to situations of this kind? Could it be interpreted to apply only to waivers given before or at the time of purchase? On the other hand, if § 14 is applicable, should a seller be able to avoid its impact by casting his rescission offer in the form of an "unconditional tender and demand"? [a]

---

a. See Bromberg, Curing Securities Law Violations: Rescission Offers and Other Techniques, 1 J.Corp.L. 1 (1975).

While a claim under § 12(1) is based on noncompliance with § 5 of the Act, § 12(2) addresses material misstatements and omissions of fact. Section 12(2) has given rise to a number of interpretive issues.

Even where the person being sued under § 12(2) is clearly the "seller," some causal connection must be shown between the alleged misrepresentation and the sale. In JACKSON v. OPPENHEIM, 533 F.2d 826 (2d Cir.1976), Oppenheim, who owned 20% of the stock of Chelsea House, prepared a memorandum setting forth his objections to the Chelsea House management and listing the steps he considered necessary for the company's survival. Jackson did not receive a copy of this memorandum.

> Our view is that appellant has wholly failed to prove a cause of action under Section 12(2) because he has not shown that the securities involved here were offered for sale or sold "by means of a prospectus or oral communication" containing a misstatement or misleading statement. There was in fact no statement whatever made by Oppenheim regarding his stock subsequent to his verbal agreement with Steinberg's intermediary to sell for $3 per share. Oppenheim made absolutely no representations to the intermediary or other buyers in connection with the sale. The only communication upon which appellant can rely is his March 13, 1970, discussion with appellee regarding deficiencies in the Chelsea House management. Yet it is undisputed that no sale was contemplated or discussed at the March 13 meeting. While appellant need not prove that the alleged "misleading nature" of his March 13, 1970 discussion with appellee "caused" the eventual purchase of Oppenheim's stock by Jackson, he must still prove that the challenged sale was effected "by means of" the communication viewed as a whole. That is to say, the communication as a whole must have been instrumental in the sale of Oppenheim's shares of Chelsea House stock. * * * While appellant need not show that the alleged misleading communication had a "decisive effect" on his decision to buy, he must show it at least stands in some causal relationship to that decision. Since the evidence is clear that the challenged communication was neither intended nor perceived as instrumental in effecting the sale, there is no liability under Section 12(2).

If the alleged misstatement is made in connection with the sale, however, it is not necessary for the buyer to prove that he relied on it. In JOHNS HOPKINS UNIV. v. HUTTON, 422 F.2d 1124 (4th Cir.1970), the court said:

> Hutton next contends that the element of "causation" presents a genuine issue of fact precluding summary judgment. LaPiere's representations, Hutton says, did not cause Hopkins to buy the production payment. On the contrary, the argument runs, Hopkins made its purchase because of information it received from its own advisers and from Trice and also because of Trice's guarantee. Under Section 12(2), however, a buyer need not prove that he relied on the misstatement or omission. "To say that purchaser reliance is a prerequisite to seller

liability is to import something into the statute which is not there." Woodward v. Wright, 266 F.2d 108, 116 (10th Cir.1959).

See also, e.g., Currie v. Cayman, 835 F.2d 780 (11th Cir.1988).

A few decisions have ruled that § 12(2) applies only to distributions or "batch offerings" and not to ordinary aftermarket transactions. McCowan v. Dean Witter Reynolds, CCH Fed.Sec.L.Rep. ¶ 94,423 (S.D. N.Y.1989); Ralph v. Prudential–Bache Securities, 692 F.Supp. 1322 (S.D.Fla.1988); SSH Co. v. Shearson Lehman Brothers, 678 F.Supp. 1055 (S.D.N.Y.1987). But see Scotch v. Mosley, 709 F.Supp. 95, 97 (M.D. Pa.1988):

> The Supreme Court has repeatedly stated that the starting point in every case involving construction of the federal securities laws is the language of the statute itself. See, e.g., Pinter v. Dahl, 108 S.Ct. at 2075. [S]ection 12(2) is not limited by its terms to initial offerings and the court's language in *Pinter* would seem to go against such a restrictive reading. * * *
>
> In addition, while it is true that the 1933 Act was *primarily* concerned with regulating the distribution of new securities, its scope is not so limited. * * * Based on these authorities, the court agrees that, rather than arbitrarily limiting section 12(2) to initial offerings, it should apply section 12(2) to open market purchases subject only to the limitations imposed by the "seller" requirement.

FRANKLIN SAVINGS BANK v. LEVY

551 F.2d 521 (2d Cir.1977).

Before MULLIGAN, VAN GRAAFEILAND and MESKILL, CIRCUIT JUDGES.

MULLIGAN, CIRCUIT JUDGE:

This is an appeal from a judgment of the United States District Court for the Southern District of New York entered on January 13, 1976 following a nine-day bench trial before the Hon. Charles M. Metzner, District Judge. Defendants-appellants, Goldman, Sachs & Co. and its general partners (Goldman, Sachs), were found to have violated § 12(2) of the Securities Act of 1933, and § 10(b) of the Securities Exchange Act of 1934, and the Securities Exchange Commission Rule 10b–5. The violations were based on a sale by Goldman, Sachs to plaintiff-appellee Franklin Savings Bank of New York (Franklin) of a Penn Central Transportation Company (Penn Central) note. A judgment of $500,000 with interest and costs, was entered in favor of Franklin.

Goldman, Sachs is a leading commercial paper dealer and was the exclusive dealer for Penn Central's notes. Dealers act as principals, buying from the issuer at one interest rate and selling to investors at a slightly lower rate. This "spread" constitutes the dealer's compensation. The commercial paper dealt in by Goldman, Sachs consisted of short-term, unsecured promissory notes of industrial or finance corporations. Since the interest rates on the paper are only fractionally different from rates available on other money market instruments such as Treasury bills, the differential only becomes significant in investments of ninety days or less when large sums are involved. In 1969 and 1970 the average commercial paper transaction involved notes having a total face amount in excess of one million dollars. It was a Goldman, Sachs' policy not to make sales under $100,000. This was neither a market nor an investment vehicle in which widows and orphans sought refuge.

New York State enacted a statute, N.Y.Banking Law § 235.12–a (McKinney 1971), effective June 1, 1968, which allowed savings banks to invest in commercial paper. Such banks were only permitted to purchase paper which an independent rating service designated by the State Banking Board had given its highest rating. The National Credit Office (NCO), a subsidiary of Dun & Bradstreet, an approved service, had rated the Penn Central paper "prime", its highest rating, on August 1, 1968.

Soon after the passage of this law, Goldman, Sachs advised Franklin in writing of the services which the investment bank offered in the commercial paper field. The parties transacted business several times before March 16, 1970 when Franklin purchased from Goldman, Sachs a Penn Central note with a face value of $500,000 and a maturity date of June 26, 1970. The price paid by Franklin was $487,958.33. On June 21, 1970 Penn Central filed its reorganization petition in bankruptcy with the United States District Court for the Eastern District of Pennsylvania and is still in reorganization. Franklin tendered the note and payment was never received.

Penn Central was formed on February 1, 1968 by the merger of the New York Central and Pennsylvania Railroads. It was the nation's largest railroad and sixth largest nonfinancial corporation. By the time the bankruptcy occurred, there was outstanding $82,530,000 of commercial paper which Penn Central had been unable to either refinance or roll over and which was not supported by bank credit lines. Goldman, Sachs, the nation's largest commercial paper dealer, had sold all of this paper to approximately 60 lenders.

On February 4, 1970 Penn Central's financial statements for both the year 1969 and its last quarter were publicly announced. The loss for the year was $56.3 million, ten times greater than that of the previous year. In the fourth quarter, the company had lost $13.2 million. Disturbed by this news, Goldman, Sachs arranged a meeting with representatives of Penn Central for February 6. The day before the scheduled conference, Robert Wilson, a Goldman, Sachs general partner and a named defendant, called Jonathan O'Herron, a Penn Central vice president, attempting to convince Penn Central to buy back some of the approximately $15 million of Penn Central paper that the investment bank had in its inventory.

Wilson and the late Gustave Levy, another Goldman, Sachs general partner and a defendant, attended the February 6 meeting on behalf of the dealer. Penn Central was represented by O'Herron and David Bevan, chairman of that company's finance committee. Penn Central reported that its projected losses for 1970 would be no greater than its 1969 losses. Goldman, Sachs told O'Herron and Bevan that it would place a $5 million limit on the amount of Penn Central paper it would carry in its inventory. It also urged Penn Central to get 100% bank line coverage of its outstanding commercial paper; at that time, the bank line coverage was only 50%. On February 9, Penn Central bought back $10 million worth of paper from Goldman, Sachs.

Brown Brothers Harriman & Co., an investment banking firm which had purchased as much as 15% of Penn Central's commercial paper, on February 5, 1970 removed that company from its approved list.

In finding Goldman, Sachs violated § 10(b) of the 1934 Act and § 12(2) of the 1933 Act, the district court found that both the buy back of February 9 and the removal of Penn Central from the Brown Brothers approved list were material facts which affected the quality and credit worthiness of the note. The failure of Goldman, Sachs to disclose these facts was found to create liability under both acts.

I. 1933 Act

A. *Jurisdiction*

For jurisdiction under § 12(2) of the 1933 Act, the statute requires that the security be sold "by the use of any means or instruments of transportation or communication in interstate commerce or of the mails." It can not be disputed that the Penn Central note is a security within § 12(2).[6] As the court found below, the sales here consisted primarily of the manual delivery of the note and the receipt of payment, neither of which occasioned the use of the mails. After the delivery of the note and the receipt of payment however, Goldman, Sachs mailed a letter to Franklin on March 16, 1970 confirming the sale. The confirmation slip contained the discount date, the name of the purchaser, the full amount of the note, the discount rate and amount, the maturity date of the note, the net discounted price and delivery instructions. The note itself only revealed its face value and maturity date. On the same day Franklin mailed a letter to the Savings Bank Trust Company, its agent bank, authorizing and directing it to receive the note from Goldman, Sachs and to charge Franklin's account in the sum of $487,958.33. Again on March 16 the Savings

6. Although notes with a maturation period of less than nine months and securities issued by a common carrier are exempted securities under § 3(a)(3), (6) of the 1933 Act they are despite this exemption explicitly included within the coverage of § 12(2).

Bank Trust Company mailed a letter to Franklin confirming that the note had been received by its depository, Chemical Bank New York Trust Company, and to complete the paperwork the latter bank mailed a letter to Franklin confirming that its account had been debited in the amount of $487,958.33. The district court found jurisdiction on the basis of either the first or fourth of the mailings described. While all of these mailings were instructional or confirmatory and the actual delivery of the note and payment were achieved manually and without the use of the mails, we find that they were within the statutory language and were sufficient to provide jurisdiction.[7] The record establishes that while manual delivery may be usual in transactions of this nature in New York City, written confirmations are important not only for internal record keeping purposes of the banking institutions involved but for their regulatory agencies as well.

Appellants claim that § 12(2) literally provides for jurisdiction only if the cause of action arises in this case against one who offers or sells a security by the use of the mails. * * * However, it has been generally held that the mailing of a letter which simply confirms a prior sale constitutes an appropriate basis for jurisdiction under the 1933 Act.[8]

* * * We conclude that there was sufficient use of the mails here to find jurisdiction under § 12(2) of the 1933 Act.

7. In light of this determination it is unnecessary to address appellee's additional contention that an intrastate telephone call is a sufficient basis for 1933 Act jurisdiction.

8. United States v. Porter, 441 F.2d 1204, 1211 (8th Cir.1971); Moses v. Michael, 292 F.2d 614, 618 (5th Cir.1961); Creswell-Keith, Inc. v. Willingham, 264 F.2d 76, 78–80 (8th Cir.1959); Schillner v. H. Vaughan Clarke & Co., 134 F.2d 875, 877 (2d Cir.1943); United States v. Benigno, [Current Binder] CCH Fed.Sec.L. Rep. ¶ 95,812 (S.D.N.Y. Oct. 6, 1976); Welch Foods Inc. v. Goldman, Sachs & Co., 398 F.Supp. 1393, 1396 (S.D.N.Y.1974); A. Jacobs, The Impact of Rule 10b–5 at § 3.01[c] ("The better rule * * * is that the jurisdictional means [specified in § 12(2)] (such as the mails) need only be involved at some stage of the transaction and do not have to transmit the misleading prospectus or oral communication.")

The only contrary authority cited by appellants is 3 L. Loss, Securities Regulation 1525 (1961), "Of course, since the mails or interstate facilities must be used in some manner *for the purpose of executing the fraud,* it does not suffice to show that they were used after the completion of the scheme." (Emphasis in the original.) However, this statement was derived from cases construing the mail fraud statutes and not the 1933 Act. This court has already commented on the problems involved in using the mail fraud statutes as a guide to reading the 1933 Act. "The analogy is not an apt one because it ignores the fundamental fact that the purpose of the mail fraud statutes is to protect against the 'use of the United States mails in furtherance of * * * [the] schemes,' * * * while the evil at which the Securities Act is directed is the fraud in the sale of securities." United States v. Cashin, supra, 281 F.2d at 674 (citations omitted). While this rejection was directed at an analogy for venue purposes, it is also instructive on the issue of jurisdiction.

B. Merits

Section 12(2) imposes liability upon:

Any person who—

(2) offers to sell or sells a security * * * by means of a prospectus or oral communication, which includes an untrue statement of a material fact or omits to state a material fact necessary in order to make the statements, in the light of the circumstances under which they were made, not misleading (the purchaser not knowing of such untruth or omission), and who shall not sustain the burden of proof that he did not know, and in the exercise of reasonable care could not have known, of such untruth or omission * * *.

In finding that there was a violation of § 12(2) the district court's opinion made only this reference:

> In view of the understanding between the parties as to the basis upon which the notes were being sold, which amounts to a statement of a material fact, Goldman, Sachs is also liable under Section 12(2).

In the preceding paragraph of its opinion in finding § 10(b) liability under the 1934 Act, the court referred to Goldman, Sachs' failure to disclose certain material facts. Thus it appears that Judge Metzner's basis for finding § 12(2) liability was the failure to disclose the same facts upon which he based § 10(b) liability. Those omitted facts principally relied upon by the court below are as follows:

(1) On February 6, 1970 Goldman, Sachs advised Penn Central that it would place a limit of $5 million on the paper of Penn Central which it would carry in its inventory. Penn Central paper had been running up to $20 million of the dealer's inventory. On February 9, Penn Central bought back $10 million of its paper reducing the amount of it in Goldman, Sachs' inventory to below $5 million. While recognizing that Goldman, Sachs had urged that there were valid business reasons for this policy Judge Metzner found that no other inventories were reduced by Goldman, Sachs.

(2) On February 5, 1970 Penn Central's commercial paper was removed from the approved list of Brown Brothers Harriman & Co. It had held as much as 15% of the Penn Central paper through purchases from Goldman, Sachs and it now ceased purchasing this paper.

* * *

Appellants argue that they could not have violated § 12(2) of the 1933 Act on the findings made below. Their argument basically is that, as found below, the representation of Goldman, Sachs was that the notes were credit worthy and high quality and that this constitutes merely an opinion only actionable if that opinion was dishonestly or recklessly held. The only authority cited for this proposition is Myzel v. Fields, 386 F.2d 718, 734 n. 8 (8th Cir.1967). However that case involved § 10(b) of the 1934 Act and not § 12(2) of the 1933 Act. Moreover, the footnote relied upon simply recites the charge of the trial court in that case. Appellants admit that § 12(2) imposes liability where there is a failure on the part of the seller to exercise reasonable care. At the same time it is now recognized that under Ernst & Ernst v. Hochfelder, 425 U.S. 185 (1976) an intent to defraud criterion is imposed by § 10(b) and Rule 10b–5. We do not understand therefore why the latter standard should be applied to § 12(2).

The distinction between liability for the misrepresentation of a fact and the mere expression of an opinion is appreciated if at times difficult to make. We have been loath, however, to permit a broker-dealer to escape liability under § 10(b) of the 1934 Act by recourse to the fact-opinion dichotomy. We have held that where a broker-dealer makes a representation as to the quality of the security he sells, he impliedly represents that he has an adequate basis in fact for the opinion he renders. Hanly v. Securities & Exchange Commission, 415 F.2d 589, 596–97 (2d Cir.1969). We see no reason why that theory is not at least equally appropriate in cases involving § 12(2) of the 1933 Act.

Here Goldman, Sachs became an exclusive source of the Penn Central notes in issue. It was a professional vendor admittedly recommending this paper for sale to an institution authorized by statute only to invest in prime paper. Such an undertaking implies that Goldman, Sachs had conducted an ongoing investigation of Penn Central's financial condition. If Goldman, Sachs failed to exercise reasonable professional care in assembling and evaluating the financial data, particularly in view of the worsening condition of Penn Central, then its representation that the paper was credit worthy and high quality was untrue in fact and misleading no matter how honestly but mistakenly held. This view does not render Goldman, Sachs an insurer as appellants claim—liable for some catastrophe beyond its control. Rather, it in fact makes the dealer responsible to Franklin if it is unable to shoulder the burden of establishing that it was not reasonable for it to have determined on March 16, 1970 that the quality of the paper it was purveying was less than that represented. In our view this constitutes a proper construction of § 12(2). On remand the district court will address itself to that issue and conduct such further evidentiary hearings, if any, as in its discretion it may determine to be necessary.

* * *

VAN GRAAFEILAND, CIRCUIT JUDGE, concurring in part and dissenting in part:

I concur with the majority that the judgment appealed from must be reversed and the matter remanded. However, I do not agree that the proper test of defendants' liability under § 12(2) is whether they exercised reasonable professional care in evaluating financial data.

Although § 12(2) is often spoken of as a negligence statute, this description is not completely accurate. Before defendants can be put to the burden of showing that they exercised reasonable care, plaintiff must first establish that they made an untrue statement of a "material fact" or omitted to state a "material fact" necessary in order to make the statements not misleading.

Construing an expression of opinion so as to make it a statement of fact requires some rather fancy legal footwork. This result has been accomplished most gracefully where the opinion is a forecast of future earnings. Where the statement in question is a pure expression of opinion, as distinguished from a forecast, it is a contradiction in terms to call it a statement of fact. The "material fact" in such instance is that the speaker honestly holds the opinion which he has expressed. In Hanly v. SEC, 415 F.2d 589, 596–97 (2d Cir.1969), we held that a securities dealer implicitly represents that he has an adequate basis for his opinions. However, in that SEC initiated action we merely tracked the language of SEC releases No. 34–6721 and No. 33–4445, issued February 2, 1962; and we specifically stated that this "implied warranty" may not be as rigidly enforced in a private action for damages.

In the instant case, events subsequent to plaintiff's purchase have proven that the defendants' opinion, implied rather than expressed, concerning the credit-worthiness of Penn Central paper was probably in error and that defendants' potential exposure is tremendous, running into many millions of dollars. Requiring defendants to prove, "in the bright gleam of hindsight", that they exercised reasonable professional care in arriving at their erroneous opinion, places upon them an almost insurmountable burden. The better rule, I submit, would place upon the defendants the burden of proving that their opinion was based upon a review of the pertinent available data and was held honestly and in good faith. If the defendants' opinion was thus held honestly and in good faith, there was no misstatement of a material fact; and there is no need to reach the issue of negligence.

It is seldom that the purchaser of stock does not secure from his broker some expression of opinion concerning the wisdom of the purchase. If each such opinion is construed to be a statement of material fact, the next substantial break in the securities market may well put most brokers out of business. While it is possible that "[r]epresentations as to value, soundness and worth of securities * * *" may, in some instances, show much more than "* * * the mistaken judgment of [an] honest man * * *," Holmes v. United States, 134 F.2d 125, 133 (8th Cir.1943), the proper measure of culpability should not be whether other dealers might reasonably have arrived at another judgment.

JOHN NUVEEN & CO. v. SANDERS

450 U.S. 1005 (1981).

On petition for writ of certiorari to the United States Court of Appeals for the Seventh Circuit.

March 23, 1981. The petition for a writ of certiorari is denied.

JUSTICE STEVENS took no part in the consideration or decision of this petition.

JUSTICE POWELL, with whom JUSTICE REHNQUIST joins, dissenting.

This securities controversy, which has been in litigation for 11 years, involves sales of commercial paper in the 1960's. The Court of Appeals for the Seventh Circuit has heard the case four times on various issues over the years, and the present petition for certiorari is the third to come before the Supreme Court. The Court today denies further review, and it is indeed long past time that this litigation should come to rest. I dissent from the denial of certiorari, however, because I believe that the Court of Appeals has seriously misapplied the Securities Act of 1933. Its decision could affect adversely the efficiency of the Nation's short-term financing markets.

Petitioner is a broker and dealer registered with the Securities and Exchange Commission (SEC). In the late 1960's petitioner undertook to sell the short-term promissory notes—commercial paper—of Winter & Hirsch, Inc. (W & H), a consumer finance company. Relying on (i) the company's certified financial statements, (ii) responses to inquiries from banks, and (iii) a brief inspection of company records, petitioner issued a "Commercial Paper Report," similar to a prospectus, on W & H commercial paper. The Report reviewed the data in certified financial statements and noted that "[t]he ratio of debt to capital funds came to 311%—Excellent! * * * Bad debts charged off came to $375,000 and recoveries in relation were $173,000—46%, an excellent showing." Respondents and other customers of petitioner made purchases.

Unknown to petitioner and to the public W & H at the time was in serious financial trouble. W & H officers had conspired with auditors from the certified public accounting firm of Lieber, Bleiweis & Co. to tamper with the company's financial statements to make the company appear profitable. Its financial statement for 1968 showed that W & H had earned $500,000; in fact, it had lost about $1 million.

When the fraud was discovered in 1970, officials from W & H and Lieber, Bleiweis, were convicted of federal fraud charges. Holders of W & H commercial paper were paid about 65 cents on the dollar. A class of plaintiffs, respondents here, sued under a variety of theories to recover the remainder. The issue presently before the Court concerns liability under § 12(2) of the Securities Act of 1933. * * *

The District Court held that petitioner was liable under § 12(2) because it had failed to use "reasonable care" when it issued the misleading Report and recommended orally to some individuals that they buy W & H paper. The Court of Appeals affirmed. *Sanders IV*, 619 F.2d 1222 (7 Cir.1980). It reasoned that petitioner had failed to use "reasonable care" because petitioner had not made a reasonable *investigation* of W & H's financial health. Instead, petitioner had relied principally on the certified financial statements. Its independent investigation consisted of inquiries to banks and a one-day spot check of company records. The Court of Appeals thought that petitioner also should have examined the company's tax returns, its minute books, and the work papers of the independent accountants.

II

Although the opinion of the Court of Appeals is not explicit, it appears to impose a duty of "reasonable investigation" rather than § 12(2)'s requirement of "reasonable care."

A

Section 11(a) of the 1933 Act imposes liability on certain persons for selling securities in a registered public offering pursuant to a materially false or misleading registration statement. A registered offering is the class of financial transactions for which Congress prescribed the most stringent regulation. The standard of care imposed on an underwriter is that it must have "had, after *reasonable investigation,* reasonable grounds to believe and did believe" that the registration statement was accurate.

Liability in this case was not imposed on petitioner under § 11, but under § 12(2). Under that section, it is necessary for sellers to show only that they "did not know, and in the exercise of *reasonable care* could not have known," that their statements were false or misleading. (Emphasis added.)

In providing standards of care under the 1933 Act, Congress thus used different language for different situations. "Reasonable *investigation*" is required for registered offerings under § 11, but nothing more than "mer[e] * * * 'reasonable *care*' " is required by § 12(2). The difference in language is significant, because in the securities acts Congress has used its words with precision. "Investigation" commands a greater undertaking than "care."

In a brief filed in this case with the Court of Appeals, the SEC expressly stated that the standard of care under § 12(2) is less demanding than that prescribed by § 11:

> "[I]t would be inconsistent with the statutory scheme to apply precisely the same standards to the scope of an underwriter's duty under Section 12(2) as the case law appropriately has applied to underwriters under Section 11. Because of the vital role played by an underwriter in the distribution of securities, and because the registration process is integral and important to the statutory scheme, we are of the view that a higher standard of care should be imposed on those actors who are critical to its proper operations. Since Congress has determined that registration is not necessary in certain defined situations, we believe that it would undermine the Congressional intent—that issuers and other persons should be relieved of registration—if the same degree of investigation were to be required to avoid potential liability whether or not a registration statement is required."

The Court of Appeals' opinion may be read as holding that petitioner's duty of "reasonable care" under § 12(2) required it independently to *investigate* the accuracy and completeness of the certified financial statements. It was customary, however—and in my view entirely reasonable—for petitioner to rely on these statements as accurately reflecting W & H's financial condition. Even under § 11 of the Act, an underwriter is explicitly absolved of the duty to investigate with respect to "any part of the registration statement purporting to be made on the authority of an expert" such as a certified accountant if "he had no reasonable ground to believe, and did not believe" that the information therein was misleading. This provision is in the Act because, almost by definition, it *is* reasonable to rely on financial statements certified by public accountants. Yet, in this case, the Court of Appeals nevertheless seems to have imposed the higher duty prescribed by § 11 to investigate, but denied petitioner the right to rely on "the authority of an expert" that also is provided by § 11.

B

The Solicitor General at this Court's request has filed a brief *amicus curiae.* He does not embrace the decision of the Court of Appeals, but nevertheless suggests that we deny certiorari because, *inter alia,* courts in the future "will undoubtedly recognize" that the decision in this case is confined to its "unusual fact situation."

If it were clear that the decision fairly must be read as thus limited, I would not dissent from denial of certiorari. My concern is that the opinion of the Court of Appeals will be read as recognizing no distinction between the standards of care applicable under §§ 11 and 12(2), and particularly as casting doubt upon the reasonableness of relying upon the expertise of certified public accountants. Dealers may believe that they must undertake extensive independent financial investigations rather than rely on the accuracy of the certified financial statements. If this is so, the efficiency of the short-term financial markets will be impaired. I would grant certiorari.

Selected References

T. Hazen, Securities Regulation §§ 7.2, 7.5 (2d ed. 1990).

Goodwin, The Effect of Pinter v. Dahl on Participant Liability Under Section 12 of the Securities Act of 1933, 19 Cumb.L.Rev. 191 (1989).

O'Hara, Erosion of the Privity Requirement in Section 12(2) of the Securities Act of 1933: The Expanded Meaning of Seller, 31 UCLA L.Rev. 921 (1984).

Prentice & Thompson, The Legal Blitz Against Accountants: An Analysis of Section 12, 76 Ky.L.J. 345 (1987–88).

Prentice, Section 12 of the Securities Act of 1933: The Case of the Overly Eager Investor, 23 New Eng.L.Rev. 697 (1988–89).

Prentice, Section 12 of the 1933 Act: Establishing the Statutory Seller, 40 Ala.L.Rev. 417 (1989).

Reece, Would Someone Please Tell Me the Definition of the Term, "Seller": The Confusion Surrounding Section 12(2) of the Securities Act of 1933, 14 Del.J.Corp.L. 35 (1989).

Schneider, Section 12 of the Securities Act of 1933: The Privity Requirement in the Contemporary Securities Law Perspective, 51 Tenn.L.Rev. 235 (1984).

Note, Secondary Liability Under Section 12(2) of the Securities Act of 1933, 78 Nw.U.L.Rev. 832 (1983).

Gruenbaum, Avoiding the Protections of the Federal Securities Laws: The Anti–Waiver Provision, 20 Santa Clara L.Rev. 49 (1980).

D. STATE REGULATION OF OFFERINGS

As noted in the Introduction, § 18 of the 1933 Act specifically preserves the right of the states to regulate offerings of securities. Every state has some law specifically regulating securities transactions. These laws are known as "blue sky" laws, after an early judicial opinion describing their purpose as the prevention of "speculative schemes which have no more basis than so many feet of blue sky."

While these "blue sky" laws vary greatly from state to state, they generally contain the following three types of provisions (although not all contain all three types); (a) prohibitions against fraud in the sale of securities; (b) requirements for registration of brokers and dealers; and (c) requirements for registration of securities to be sold in the state.

In 1956, the Commissioners on Uniform State Laws promulgated a Uniform Securities Act (USA) for adoption by the states. Reflecting the pre-existing pattern of state laws and the differences in regulatory philosophy among the states, the act is divided into four parts; (1) antifraud provisions, (2) broker-dealer registration provisions, (3) security registration provisions, and (4) definitions, exemptions, and administrative and liability provisions. States are thus free to adopt one, two or all of the first three parts, plus the appropriate provisions of the fourth part.

While more than 30 states have adopted most or some of the provisions of the Uniform Act, the movement toward uniformity has been hampered by several factors. (a) Some of the most important commercial states, including New York, California, Illinois and Texas, have not adopted any part of the Act. (b) Almost all the states that have adopted it have made substantial changes from the approved text. (c) State administrators and courts interpret the same language differently, producing a difference in operation that is not apparent from a reading of the laws themselves.

Nevertheless, the promulgation and adoption of the Uniform Act has produced a much more rational and consistent pattern of regulation than previously existed. This development has also been assisted by the North American Securities Administrators Association (NASAA), an association of state and provincial securities administrators, which from time to time issues "statements of policy" on various substantive and procedural questions and indicates to what extent those policies are followed by each of its members.

In 1985, the Commissioners promulgated a revised Uniform Securities Act, modified for the stated purposes of (1) updating licensing and registration procedures to reflect new federal and state developments, (2) expediting the registration process for seasoned issuers, and (3) strengthening the powers of state securities administrators. Section references in this note are to the 1985 version of the Act.

Note on State Registration Requirements

With the exception of the New England and Middle Atlantic states, most of which have only rudimentary provisions for the registration of securities, almost every state requires that some affirmative action be taken to register securities before they can be sold in the state. This means that an underwriting syndicate making a national distribution of a new issue must take steps to "blue sky" the issue in more than 40 states in addition to complying with the federal Securities Act of 1933.

(a) Procedures

Most states which require registration of securities issues provide two alternative methods of registration: "filing" and "qualification." Some states provide a third method: registration by "coordination" for issues simultaneously being registered with the SEC.

Securities may generally be registered by "filing" only if they meet certain tests for stability and earnings coverage. See Uniform Securities Act (USA) § 302. Registration is accomplished by filing a statement showing compliance with the statutory test, plus a description of the securities being registered and the terms of the offering. The registration automatically becomes effective within a prescribed period. Prior to 1985 the Uniform Act spoke in terms of registration by "notification" which becomes effective after a specified period unless the state administrator takes action to prevent it. The former version, which is still in effect in many states, thus permitted the Securities Administrator to pass on the merits of securities so registered.

Registration by "coordination" is substantially similar to registration by "notification" except that the only information normally required to be filed is a copy of the prospectus filed with the SEC under the 1933 Act.

Registration by "qualification" is the method generally prescribed for those issues which do not meet the tests prescribed for registration by other methods. The issuer must file a statement containing information roughly comparable to that required in a 1933 Act registration statement, and registration does not become effective until the administrator takes action to approve it.

(b) Standards

In contrast to the 1933 Act, under which the SEC has no power to approve or disapprove the sale of securities, most state laws authorize the administrator to deny an application for registration, even though the facts regarding the security and the issuer are fully disclosed. The standards for granting or denying an application range from those which authorize denial only on grounds of "fraud" to those which authorize the administrator to bar any issue unless he finds its terms to be "fair, just and equitable." Interpretations of these vague standards also vary greatly from state to state. The 1985 Uniform Act offers alternative wordings for adoption by the states, authorizing denial of registration if the administrator finds either that the offering would "tend to work a fraud upon purchasers" or that it is "unfair, unjust or inequitable," as well as in situations where it "would be made with unreasonable amounts of" underwriting compensation, promoters' profits, or options. USA § 306(a)(5), (6). The associations of North American Securities Administrators and Midwest Securities Administrators have also issued a number of "Statements of Policy", indicating what levels of compensation or other arrangements with insiders would be considered unfair in determining whether registration of a particular issue should be granted.

(c) Exemptions

Most states exempt from their registration requirements the principal types of securities exempted from the 1933 Act—government securities, instruments issued by various types of institutions, and securities issued by companies subject to special regulatory statutes (such as banks and common carriers). In addition, most states exempt one important class of securities which are not exempt from the 1933 Act—namely, those listed on major stock exchanges or on NASDAQ. See USA §§ 401(a)(7), (8).

Private Placements. Traditionally, most state statutes did not contain exemptions comparable to the 1933 Act exemption for "transactions by an issuer not involving any public offering", although many had exemptions for "isolated transactions" or "pre-organization subscriptions." The 1985 Uniform Act exempts offerings which involve no general solicitation and result in sales to no more than 25 purchasers in the state who are purchasing for investment and not for resale. USA § 402(11). The "accredited investor" concept in Regulation D finds a counterpart in state provisions which commonly exempt sales to broker-dealers or other financial or institutional investors. See USA § 402(10). The North American Securities Administrators Association in 1983 promulgated a "Uniform Limited Offering Exemption," which has been adopted by more than 20 states, under which any offering which meets the tests of the SEC's Regulation D is also exempt from the state's registration requirements.

Secondary Transactions. State securities laws do not embrace the "underwriter" concept of 1933 Act § 2(11), which has given rise to so much difficulty in determining when a person other than the issuer must register securities for sale under federal law. Most state laws have an exemption for "isolated non-issuer transactions" and for other non-issuer sales of securities registered under § 12 of the 1934 Act or listed in "standard manuals" (such as Moody's and Standard & Poor's). See USA § 402(2), (3). Under the Uniform Act, a registration of securities remains in effect for one year (unless suspended or revoked), and "all outstanding securities of the same class * * * are considered to be registered for the purpose of any non-issuer transaction" during that period. USA § 305(i).

Interstate Offerings. The federal exemption for intrastate offerings in § 3(a)(11) of the 1933 Act finds a counterpart in provisions found in several state laws, notably those of New York and New Jersey, which exempt all offerings registered with the SEC and thus apply *only* to intrastate public offerings. See N.Y. Gen.Bus.Law § 359–ff; N.J.Stat. Ann. 49:3–60.

(d) Sanctions for Violations

Most state laws provide for a range of sanctions against persons who violate the registration or antifraud provisions. The Uniform Act authorizes the administrator to conduct investigations, issue subpoenas and bring injunction actions, in addition to imposing criminal penalties for violations. USA §§ 601–604. The weak point of these provisions is that most states have a very small staff engaged in administration and enforcement of their securities laws, so that as a practical matter the only significant sanction against violators is the threat of civil liability.

(e) Civil Liabilities

The traditional state securities law generally provides that any sale "made in violation of any provision" of the law is "voidable", and that the purchaser is entitled to rescind the transaction and recover his purchase price. The types of violations which give rise to this right of rescission may include many technical violations as well as a failure to register or a violation of the anti-fraud provisions. Thus, an issuer or broker-dealer making a public distribution runs the risk that a technical failure to comply with any provision of the securities law of a particular state will give all purchasers in that state an absolute right to the refund of their investment if the security declines in value. Enforceability is facilitated in many states by a requirement that issuers or broker-dealers post a surety bond for satisfaction of their liabilities.

The Uniform Act departs from the "voidability" concept to follow the approach of § 12 of the 1933 Act. Any person who offers or sells a security (1) in violation of the registration requirements or certain other important provisions, or (2) by means of a misstatement or omission of a material fact, is made liable to refund the purchase price upon tender of the security or to pay damages to the purchaser if he no longer owns it. USA § 605.

Persons Liable. Many state laws impose civil liability not only on the "seller", but also on any persons, or specified classes of persons, who "participate" or "aid" in the sale. The Uniform Act imposes liability on partners, officers and directors of the seller, whether or not they aid in the sale, and on other employees, broker-dealers and agents who "materially aid in the sale", subject in each case to a defense of "due diligence". USA § 605(d).

Most state securities laws apply to any offer or sale of securities in the state, but contain no explicit provisions defining when an offer or sale is made "in the state". Since many securities transactions involve a buyer in one state and a seller in another, difficult problems arise in determining (a) to which transactions the law of a particular state applies, and (b) which state law governs the validity of a transaction which has contacts with more than one state. For example, is an advertisement in a newspaper published in State A but also circulated in State B an "offer" in State B? If a broker in State A makes an offer by telephone to a customer in State B, who accepts the offer by mailing a check to the broker in State A, is the transaction voidable if the broker and the security were registered in State A but not in State B?

Keep in mind that the consequences of a sale made in violation of state registration requirements may not be as serious as the consequences of a sale in violation of federal registration requirements. If neither the issuer nor the underwriters are doing business within a particular state, there may be very little that the state regulatory authorities can do to them,[a] and, if the illegal sales in a particular state only constitute a small part of the total issue, civil liability will generally be limited to the portion of the issue sold in that state.

Applicable Law. Since most civil actions under the blue sky laws are in the nature of actions for rescission, courts traditionally tended to look to the conflict of laws principles applicable to contract claims, and to hold that the contract was not voidable if it was valid under the law

a. In Travelers Health Ass'n v. Virginia, 339 U.S. 643 (1950), the Supreme Court held that the Due Process Clause of the Constitution did not bar Virginia from issuing a cease and desist order under its blue sky law against a Nebraska association which solicited Virginia residents by mail and encouraged Virginia members to submit the names of their friends to the association's home office. Justices Minton and Jackson, dissenting, argued that the appeal should be dismissed, since Virginia had taken no action which could result in a taking of the association's property without due process, and that they could see "no reason why Virginia may not go through this shadow-boxing performance in order to publicize the activities of appellants in Virginia and notify its citizens that appellants have not qualified under the Securities Law."

of the state where the contract was made or to be performed. See, e.g., Robbins v. Pacific Eastern Corp., 8 Cal.2d 241, 65 P.2d 42 (1937). Under this approach, an issuer or broker-dealer could offer and sell securities to residents of a state with a "strict" blue sky law—without complying with the terms of that law—simply by making sure that the contract was technically made and performed in its own state. A more recent approach, however, is to hold that, when a customer is solicited in his home state, the securities law of that state must be complied with, no matter where the transaction is technically consummated.

GREEN v. WEIS, VOISIN, CANNON, INC.

479 F.2d 462 (7th Cir.1973).

Before MURRAH, SENIOR CIRCUIT JUDGE, and KILEY and SPRECHER, CIRCUIT JUDGES.

SPRECHER, CIRCUIT JUDGE: This appeal is concerned primarily with the meaning of the words "sale" or "sell" in the Illinois Securities Act.

Plaintiffs appealed from grants of summary judgments for defendants in a diversity action seeking rescission of stock purchases because of the failure of defendants to comply with the registration requirements of the Illinois Securities Act. Ill.Rev.Stat., ch. 121½, §§ 137.1 et seq. The state of Illinois, which filed a brief as amicus curiae, also urged reversal on the ground that the trial court's construction of Illinois law would emasculate the protection accorded Illinois citizens by the Illinois Securities Act.

Each of the plaintiffs in No. 72–1441 purchased five thousand shares of the common stock of London Ben, Inc., in March, 1969. The purchase price for the stock in each case was $11,000. Defendants are London Ben and Weis, Voisin, Cannon, Inc., the underwriter and agent for the sale of the London Ben stock.

The facts surrounding these sales are not disputed. All of the plaintiffs are residents of Chicago, Illinois or its suburbs. Each of the plaintiffs, except Nathan Rosenstone, was solicited in Illinois by defendant Weis, Voisin in oral and written communications. Each of the plaintiffs received, in Chicago, an investment letter and selling circular of London Ben, offering to sell the stock of London Ben. The investment letter and selling circular were sent by Weis, Voisin from its Chicago offices. Each of the plaintiffs accepted the offer to purchase by signing the investment letter and sending it, with a check, to the Weis, Voisin offices in Chicago.

* * *

Section 137.12 of Ill.Rev.Stat., ch. 121½, states that it is a violation of Illinois law to "sell any security except in accordance with the provisions of this Act" or to "fail to file with the Secretary of State any application, report or document required to be filed under the provisions of this Act * * *." Section 137.13 provides that "every sale of a security made in violation of the provisions of this Act shall be voidable at the election of the purchaser."

The district court's decision finding that the sale of securities to these plaintiffs did not take place in Illinois is premised upon the fact that after plaintiffs' checks and investment letters were received in Chicago by Weis, Voisin, the checks were forwarded by the defendant to its New York offices and deposited in its New York bank account. The confirmations and stock certificates were also issued to the plaintiffs from New York. The district court concluded from these facts that the actual sale of securities took place in New York and that the broad definition of sale in § 137.2–5 was irrelevant since the "sale" plaintiffs were attempting to rescind was the completed sale which was only concluded when the defendants "accepted" plaintiffs' offer to buy in New York.

The term "sale" as defined in the Illinois Securities Act cannot be so limited. The language of the statute specifically encompasses the sale of London Ben stock to these plaintiffs. Section 137.2–5 provides:

> " 'Sale' or 'sell' shall have the full meaning of that term as applied by or accepted in courts of law or equity, and shall include every disposition, or attempt to dispose, of a security for value. 'Sale' or 'sell' shall also include a contract to sell, an exchange, an attempt or an offer to sell, an option of sale or a solicitation of an offer to buy, directly or indirectly; * * * "

The defendants in this case offered to sell the securities in question in solicitations made to persons all but one of whom were in the state at the time of the solicitation, by representatives in Illinois, received acceptances of their offer in Illinois from persons all but one of whom were in Illinois at the time of the mailing of the acceptance, and mailed confirmations and stock certificates to Illinois residents at their Illinois addresses. Whether or not a common law definition of sale would therefore place the consummation of the sale in New York is therefore irrelevant to the statutory definition. Defendants became subject to the statute at least when they successfully completed the sale of London Ben stock after soliciting offers to buy in Illinois. To construe the language of the statute otherwise would permit an issuer or dealer to solicit sales at will in Illinois without complying with the statute, so long as an act entirely within the seller's control such as placing the proceeds in a bank account or issuing stock certificates, was performed at or from some other place. Illinois residents should not be so helpless in obtaining protection through their own state legislature or dependent upon the possibility of aid from the laws of another state, particularly when they might be unable to even determine which state would be the state of sale at the time they accepted the offer to purchase.

* * *

There is no constitutional infirmity in this construction. The Supreme Court long ago upheld the constitutionality of state blue sky laws in Hall v. Geiger–Jones Co., 242 U.S. 539 (1917); Caldwell v. Sioux Falls Stock Yards Co., 242 U.S. 559 (1917); and Merrick v. N.W. Halsey & Co., 242 U.S. 568 (1917). The Supreme Court has also upheld specifically the right of a state to regulate solicitations of its citizens by a corporation outside the state. Bothwell v. Buckbee, Mears Co., 275 U.S. 274 (1927).

As noted by the court at the end of the opinion in *Green,* the Supreme Court has had occasion to consider the constitutionality of state blue sky laws. In MERRICK v. N.W. HALSEY, 242 U.S. 568 (1917), the court held, without discussion, that application of a state's blue sky laws to offers directed into the state by an out-of-state broker-dealer was not an unconstitutional interference with interstate commerce. Subsequently, in TRAVELERS HEALTH ASS'N v. VIRGINIA, 339 U.S. 643 (1950), the Court, in a five-to-four ruling, rejected a claim that the Due Process Clause precluded Virginia from issuing an order under its blue sky law ordering a Nebraska association to cease and desist from soliciting Virginia residents by mail. See note a on p. ___ above.

More recently the Court has had occasion to consider the constitutionality of state laws regulating tender offers. See pp. 811–828 below.

PAULOS v. BEST SECURITIES, INC.

260 Minn. 283, 109 N.W.2d 576 (1961).

THOMAS GALLAGHER, JUSTICE.

Plaintiff, a Minnesota resident, instituted this action against Best Securities Incorporated, a New York corporation, not qualified to do business in Minnesota or having a place of business here, and certain of its officers and agents, none of whom were physically present here, for violation of Minn.St. 80.07,[1] 80.12, subd. 1,[2] and 80.18,[3] in the sale of certain common stocks to plaintiff.

1. Minn.St. 80.07 provides in part: "No securities, except * * * [exceptions not applicable here] shall be offered for sale or sold within the state unless such securities have been registered * * *."

2. Minn.St. 80.12, subd. 1, provides in part: "No broker or dealer shall offer for sale, sell or profess the business of selling, any securities unless or until he shall have been licensed as a broker or dealer as hereinafter provided; * * *."

3. Minn.St. 80.18 provides in part: "No person shall himself, or by or through others, or as agent or otherwise, publish, circulate, distribute, or cause to be published, circulated, or distributed, in any manner, any circular, prospectus, printed matter, document, pamphlet, advertisement through any medium, or other matter, pertaining to any securities which have not been registered as herein provided; * * *.

"No circular, prospectus, advertisement, printed matter, document, pamphlet, leaflet, or other matter * * * containing or constituting an offer to sell any securities required to be registered in compliance with the provisions of sections 80.08 and 80.09, or rendering advice with relation thereto, shall be published, circulated, distributed, or caused to be published, circulated, or distributed, in any manner unless and until such advertising matter shall

Pursuant to § 80.14, subd. 1,[4] service of process upon the defendants was made by leaving a copy of the summons and complaint for each of them with the commissioner of securities for the State of Minnesota as defendants' attorney for such service. No answers were interposed and subsequently plaintiff entered a default judgment against all of the defendants in the sum of $6,399.58.

This is an appeal from an order quashing such service and vacating the judgment. In a memorandum attached to the order, the trial court stated:

> "It appears conclusively that the defendant corporation is a New York corporation and that the other defendants named in said action also reside outside of the State of Minnesota, and that they have never been engaged within the State of Minnesota in the sale of securities. It appears conclusively that the defendants never registered nor attempted to register the stocks which they subsequently sold to the plaintiff in this case. It further appears that they never appointed the Commissioners of Securities as their agent for the service of summons in this State. It further appears that they never through any agents within the State of Minnesota * * * carried on their operations to sell stocks. It appears conclusively that the sales here involved were based almost entirely on and arose out of telephone communications had between the defendants in New York and the plaintiff in the State of Minnesota. There appears to have been a small amount of mail matter passed between the parties also. In the light of the foregoing facts it seems too clear for serious argument that the sales here in question were in fact New York sales and that the defendants did nothing to subject them to any penalties under Minnesota law.
>
> * * *
>
> "Under the factual situation here presented it is not possible to properly serve process upon the defendants through the Commissioner of Securities of the state of Minnesota * * *. Garber vs. Bancamerica-Blair Corp., 205 Minn. 275, 285 N.W. 723."

Plaintiff contends that defendants' violations of §§ 80.07, 80.12, subd. 1, and 80.18 in effect constituted defendants' appointment of the Minnesota commissioner of securities as their attorney for the service

have been submitted in duplicate to the commission and approved by it."

4. Minn.St. 80.14, subd. 1, provides: "Every non-resident person shall, before having any securities registered or being licensed * * * appoint the commissioner of securities * * * his true and lawful attorney upon whom may be served all legal process in any action * * *.

"The commission of any act which constitutes a violation of sections 80.05 to 80.27 by any nonresident person who has not theretofore appointed the commissioner of securities his attorney in compliance with the first paragraph of this section shall be conclusively deemed an irrevocable appointment by such person of the commissioner of securities * * * as his true and lawful attorney upon whom may be served all legal process in any action * * * involving such violation, * * *.

"Service of process under this section shall be made by delivering a copy thereof to the commissioner of securities * * * accompanied by one additional copy for each person so served, and by the mailing by the commissioner of a copy thereof by registered mail, not later than the business day following the day of such service, to each person so served * * * at his last known address * * *."

of process and subjected them to the jurisdiction of the Minnesota courts under § 80.14, subd. 1; and further that as to Best Securities its actions with reference to its sales to plaintiff of common stocks not registered here constituted "doing business" here as defined in § 303.13, subd. 1(3),[6] so as to afford the Minnesota courts a valid basis for jurisdiction of both the subject matter of the action and of this defendant.

It is not disputed that none of the individual defendants ever maintained offices or were physically present in this state during the transactions described; that neither Best Securities nor any of its officers or agents were ever present here during such transactions; that Best Securities was not at any time qualified to do business here as a foreign corporation; that plaintiff, a St. Paul attorney, was at no time present in New York during the transactions described; and that all communications between plaintiff and defendants were either by mail or by telephone.

The facts upon which plaintiff claims Minnesota courts acquired jurisdiction are as follows: Initially defendants mailed plaintiff a letter entitled "OUR INVITATION TO YOU" in which they proposed to send plaintiff a weekly periodical designated "Best's News & Views," which purported to analyze news stories relative to stock market action. In response thereto plaintiff mailed to defendants a printed card which defendants had enclosed in their communication to plaintiff requesting that defendants mail plaintiff the regular issues of the periodical described. These periodicals which plaintiff subsequently received contained descriptions and information relative to certain corporations whose shares, though unregistered here and unlisted on any exchange, could be purchased through defendants. Included therein was Alaska International Corporation, a company engaged in various oil and development activities, stock in which defendants were offering for sale as indicated.

Subsequently, numerous long distance telephone conversations ensued between the parties. As a result of these conversations and the correspondence between the parties, plaintiff at various times between June 2, 1959, and February 9, 1960, purchased from defendants as brokers a total of 3,495 shares of Alaska International Corporation's common stock for the sum of $5,791.25. To pay for this plaintiff mailed his checks from St. Paul to defendants in New York. There defendants credited plaintiff's account with the shares of stock thus purchased, all

6. Minn.St. 303.13, subd. 1(3), provides in part: "If a foreign corporation makes a contract with a resident of Minnesota to be performed in whole or in part by either party in Minnesota * * * *such acts shall be deemed to be doing business in Minnesota by the foreign corporation* and shall be deemed equivalent to the appointment by the foreign corporation of the secretary of the State of Minnesota and his successors to be its true and lawful attorney upon whom may be served all lawful process in any actions or proceedings against the foreign corporation arising from or growing out of such contract or tort." (Italics supplied.)

of which were delivered to plaintiff except 800 shares covered by the last order.

On March 24, 1960, defendants called plaintiff from New York and advised him to sell his shares of Alaska International Corporation which he had purchased through them, as it had fallen in value to .625 per share—plaintiff's shares accordingly then having a total value of but $2,266.50. At the same time, defendants urged him to authorize them to use the proceeds of the contemplated sale for the purchase of stock in some other corporation which they represented as brokers. Later this same day they reported to plaintiff that they had sold all of his stock in Alaska International Corporation and had credited his account with $2,183.50. This sum is still held by them.

1. We are of the opinion that plaintiff's substituted service of process upon the defendants under § 80.14, subd. 1, as above described, was valid and gave the district court jurisdiction of both the subject matter of the action described in the complaint and of the defendants named therein. The provisions of § 80.14, subd. 1, authorizing such service, were enacted by L.1941, c. 547, § 11, following decisions in Garber v. Bancamerica–Blair Corp., 205 Minn. 275, 285 N.W. 723, and Sivertsen v. Bancamerica–Blair Corp., D.C.D.Minn., 43 F.Supp. 233. Prior to that time the governing statutes (Mason St.1927, §§ 3996–1 to 3996–28) contained no provision for the involuntary appointment of the commissioner of securities as attorney for service of process on nonresidents operating here in violation of Minnesota statutes relative to the sale of securities in Minnesota. Under § 80.14, subd. 1, as amended, a nonresident's violation of any of the provisions of §§ 80.05 to 80.27 is conclusively deemed an *irrevocable* appointment of the commissioner of securities by such nonresident as his true and lawful attorney for service of legal process in any action involving such violation. Here plaintiff alleged that defendants were guilty of violation of §§ 80.07, 80.12, subd. 1, and 80.18, and accordingly it would follow that under § 80.14, subd. 1, they became subject to the jurisdiction of the Minnesota courts through service of process upon the commissioner of securities.

2. That provisions relative to substituted service upon nonresidents of a state similar to those included in § 80.14, subd. 1, are valid has been established by a number of decisions of the United States Supreme Court. McGee v. International Life Ins. Co., 355 U.S. 220; International Shoe Co. v. State of Washington, 326 U.S. 310.

* * *

3. It seems clear that the instant case falls within the foregoing principles, and that thereunder § 80.14, subd. 1, must be construed as valid. The facts as to defendants' contacts and actions with reference to plaintiff, a Minnesota resident, and in offering for sale and selling to him the shares of stock described do not vary greatly from those involved in McGee v. International Life Ins. Co., supra. Likewise, it cannot be denied that here Minnesota has a manifest interest in

providing an effective means of redress for its residents against nonresidents involved in selling securities to them in violation of legislation designed for their protection. It must follow that plaintiff's service of process upon the commissioner of securities as defendants' attorney was valid and proper and subjected defendants as well as the subject matter of the action to the jurisdiction of the Minnesota court.

4. Insofar as Best Securities is concerned, it may be said that under § 303.13, subd. 1(3), above quoted, its actions as above described constituted "doing business" in Minnesota. This section provides that a foreign corporation shall be deemed as "doing business" here if it enters into a contract with a resident, which contract is to be performed in whole or in part within the state. Obviously, the acts of Best Securities in promoting and consummating a series of stock sales to plaintiff in Minnesota, through repeated long distance telephone and mail communications, would fall within this definition. Certainly plaintiff's payments for such shares and their ultimate delivery to him were acts, some part of which at least were to be performed in Minnesota. It would follow that under § 303.13, subd. 1(3), such actions were sufficient to give the Minnesota court jurisdiction of Best Securities as a foreign corporation doing business here.

Order appealed from is reversed and judgment ordered reinstated.

In BLACK & COMPANY, INC. v. NOVA–TECH, INC., 333 F.Supp. 468 (D.Or.1971), plaintiffs were residents of Oregon who purchased, through an Oregon broker, shares of a California corporation which had not been registered for sale in Oregon. They sued the California corporation, its officers and directors, and its corporate counsel, a California law firm. The court held that the members of the law firm were properly subject to service of process under the Oregon "long-arm" statute if they "participated" in the illegal sales. With respect to the constitutional issue, the court said:

> Service of process in these cases is also consistent with due process. Service of process is valid if: (1) the defendant purposefully avails himself of the privilege of acting within the forum state or of causing important consequences in that state; (2) the cause of action arises from the consequences of defendants' activities with regard to the forum state; and (3) jurisdiction over the defendant does not offend judicial standards of fairness and substantial justice. McGee v. International Life Ins. Co., 355 U.S. 220 (1957); Hanson v. Denckla, 357 U.S. 235 (1958); State ex rel. White Lumber Sales, Inc. v. Sulmonetti, 252 Or. 121, 448 P.2d 571 (1968).
>
> The presence in Oregon of the unregistered securities satisfied the first requirement.

For jurisdictional purposes, a defective security should be no different from a defective product. Both carry dangerous consequences for the unsuspecting consumer. Constitutionally, it is no less fair to obtain long-arm jurisdiction over the seller and participants in the sale in Oregon of illegal securities than it is to serve local process upon the out-of-state manufacturer of a defective product sold in Oregon.

In each case, the cause of action arises from the consequences of defendants' activities which had predictable results in Oregon, and personal jurisdiction over these defendants does not offend reasonable standards of fair play and substantial justice. See, e.g., Dijulio v. Digicon, 325 F.Supp. at 966. * * *

There is no constitutional infirmity in the service of process * * *.

AN OPEN ATTACK ON THE NONSENSE OF BLUE SKY REGULATION

By Rutheford B. Campbell, Jr.

10 J.Corp.L. 553, 563–67 (1985).*

B. Merit Regulation

From the very inception of modern blue sky laws, certain commentators have stoutly defended merit regulation. In the early 1920's, commissioner Dolley went on record by loudly extolling the success of his application of merit standards in Kansas. More recently, some administrators from the states have written in law reviews attempting to demonstrate the efficacy of merit regulation. This writer is convinced, however, that in today's world merit regulation simply is not worth its cost to society.

Merit regulation generally empowers state securities commissioners to deny registration if the offering does not meet the substantive standards contained in the particular state's securities act. Although the standards applied by the various states involve, as one commentator observed, "a confusing array of substantive tests", the standards typically are designed to insure the fair treatment of investors by protecting investors from exploitation at the hands of promoters and underwriters.

A major portion of merit regulation, therefore, is designed to insure that the original owners of the company (i.e., those who own the company prior to the public offering) do not retain an unfairly large portion of the company after the proposed offering is completed. In this regard, a number of states will deny registration if the commissioner concludes that stock has previously been purchased by insiders at prices that are unfairly low.

Although states have developed various criteria to deal with the acquisition of "cheap stock" by promoters, a typical formula will result in the denial of registration if there is an "unreasonable" amount of cheap stock going to promoters. As one would imagine, states have differing tests for determining whether the prior sale to promoters was "cheap," whether the amount was "unreasonable" and whether the prior issuance was so distant that it was not to be considered a problem.

Some states apply merit criteria that focus on the price paid for stock by the new investors and, accordingly, will deny registration in the event the commissioner determines the price to the public is excessive or unfair. This, of course, is merely a corollary to the limitation on cheap stock, since both are intended to insure a fair division of the company between the promoters and the new investors. Again, states apply different formulas to determine whether or not the new shareholders are paying too much for their stock. Some states will consider a price excessive if it is in excess of some predetermined multiple of the company's recent earnings. Other states determine the excessiveness by the dilution suffered by the new shareholders at the time of their investment.

* * *

The substantive standards of merit regulations are also designed to protect public investors from exploitation at the hands of underwriters. The Uniform Securities Act, for example, permits the commissioner to deny registration if he finds that "the offering . . . has unreasonable amounts of underwriters' and sellers' discounts, commissions, or other compensation." As in the case of the merit standards aimed at promoters, these constraints on underwriters are designed to keep the underwriters from grabbing too much of the proceeds of the offering or too much of the company.

* * *

There seems to be no reason to doubt the conclusion that regulators can recognize deals that are risky and that, in such instances, investors will suffer no loss if the regulators deny permission to make the offering. This does not, however, resolve the more fundamental issue of whether society benefits from denying issuers access to public financing in such situations.

It is not difficult to identify the pernicious impact of merit regulation. To the extent that merit regulation is used to deny issuers the right to register their securities, that pernicious impact can be significant. Simply stated, merit regulation unnecessarily constrains the freedom of people to do business as they see fit, discourages entrepreneurial initiative and impedes the flow of capital to its most efficient use.

By denying registration under existing merit standards, a state government is refusing promoters, underwriters and investors the right to do business and allocate risks and rewards of an enterprise in a way that each has determined to be in its own best interest. This is exceedingly presumptuous and paternalistic on the part of regulators and represents a significant compromise in the right one has (or at least should have) to remain free from unnecessary governmental intrusion. One should be denied the right to conduct his affairs as he sees fit only if the benefits of such regulation outweigh the adverse consequences of the regulation, and that is not the case in the application of merit standards.

In addition, merit regulation is inconsistent with the very essence of a capitalistic system. If any capitalistic system is going to work, entrepreneurial initiative must be encouraged. Investors, promoters and underwriters must be encouraged to evaluate which enterprises society desires and allowed to divide the enterprises in a way that provides each with sufficient rewards to justify his participation.

Obviously one does not encourage a promoter to take the risk of forming and financing a new enterprise if regulators are permitted to limit the rewards a promoter can keep in the event the deal is successful. Just as obviously one does not encourage new enterprises by allowing regulators to limit the rewards underwriters can receive for their selling efforts. Capital formation and entrepreneurial initiative can be promoted only by allowing participants the possibility of rewards sufficient to justify their efforts.

Related to this is the question of who should control the flow and use of capital in this country. This author is convinced that the efficient use of capital requires that the market make this determination. When one decides to invest his capital, he has determined that the potential reward justifies the risk of the capital. This means, in an economic sense, that the investor believes (and is willing to risk his capital on the belief) that his capital will be used efficiently, since society, as a result of the utility derived from the enterprise, will reward the investor sufficiently to pay him for the use of his capital. Without a clear and significant reason, regulators should not be permitted to interfere with this process. Capital should be permitted to flow into those enterprises and uses that the market demands.

In discussing the possible benefits to society of merit regulation, it is essential that one avoid an overly emotional, knee-jerk analysis. One should be suspicious of attempts to justify merit regulation on the basis that it saves the unprotected and unsophisticated investor from squandering his life's savings on some dishonest promoter's fraudulent scheme. Professor Bloomenthal has convincingly argued that merit regulation is no serious impediment to the perpetration of fraud. Promotors with fraud on their minds can either neglect any attempt to comply with state securities laws or, alternatively, comply with those laws and then waste, mismanage or steal the proceeds of the offering. Obviously merit regulation cannot, and one would assume is not intended to, prevent such abuses. Rather, remedies in those situations must come from the disclosure and antifraud provisions of the applicable laws and from state fiduciary laws.

* * *

* * * People who invest in schemes that would not pass muster under merit regulations are people who are otherwise unhappy with the rates of return that are being paid by banks and similar institutions. Indeed, one could argue in these circumstances that the only effect of merit regulation is to protect investors from their own stupidity and greed. Society should not be asked to pay much for this.

WHO SPEAKS FOR THE INVESTOR? AN EVALUATION OF THE ASSAULT ON MERIT REGULATION

By Hugh H. Makens

13 U.Balt.L.Rev. 435 (1984).*

I. Introduction

* * *

When a state applies merit regulation in its registration process, it is attempting to channel investment capital into offerings that will give investors a better chance to earn a return on their investment. The exclusive goal of merit regulation, therefore, is a very specific form of investor protection. Recently, with the shift in emphasis to a more deregulatory environment, a trend has developed toward the realization that an administrator may have a dual obligation, involving both investor protection and consideration of the overall economic climate for business in determining the manner of application of the securities laws.

* * *

Merit regulation has a significant impact primarily on public corporations in which insiders retain significant ownership or voting control. The effect of merit regulation on the problems created by the separation of ownership and control is seen most vividly in the restrictions on officer and director compensation. The states restrict this compensation by objecting to excessive warrants and options, cheap stock, and loans to insiders. Some forms of compensation are curtailed to ensure promoter commitment to the project, provide for an orderly secondary market, and increase the amount of capital actually going to the project. Anyone familiar with securities offerings would identify these as basic objectives that underwriters, investment advisors, and attorneys should seek to achieve in structuring an offering for an issuing entity. Much of the quarrel with these objectives thus relates not to the propriety of the objectives but rather to the specific limitations imposed in their name.

Issuers whose offerings do not fit within merit constraints must either modify the terms of the offering or face denial of the application for registration. The customary procedure, however, is for the administrator to negotiate with the registrant, a process that results in either registration or voluntary withdrawal of the application.

* * *

The administrator assumes the role of investor's advocate because the investor is not in a position to negotiate the terms of an offering on his own behalf and because the underwriter is often unable to negotiate favorable terms for the investor without risk of losing the underwriting. The administrator may initially assume, often correctly, that the lead underwriter will provide only a minimum level of due diligence and fairness negotiation. Through application of the merit standards, the administrator seeks to establish a level of minimum fairness to the investor. These standards attempt to ensure that sufficient funds are placed into a project to permit the success of the enterprise, to prevent self-dealing that would strip the enterprise of vital capital resources, and to provide the investor with a means of self-help if the transaction fails because of managerial wrong-doing.

* * *

Perhaps the most important aspect of merit regulation is the securities industry's voluntary compliance with published rules and guidelines. Insofar as the premises underlying merit standards are valid, many companies include these protections without reference to the guidelines or rules because it is in their self-interest to do so. In contrast, other issuers will comply with merit standards only because they realize that without compliance they will face substantial problems in meeting blue sky requirements. The net result, however, is that many of the merit standards become industry standards, honed in a competitive environment over time. The development of an industry standard has a dramatic effect on all offerings, public and private. In the real estate field, for example, the controversial offerings of the early 1970's, as modified in response to merit concerns, have become the models for most of today's offerings. The ripple effect of merit regulation thus goes far beyond culling out the fraudulent or weak offerings. This vital element of merit regulation has been ignored by all of the commentators.

* * *

In some states, merit regulation today is under siege. * * *

For example, it has been argued that market forces should govern the sale of securities, and that as long as "full disclosure" is provided, no further regulation is necessary or appropriate, particularly the paternalistic regulation implicit in the use of merit standards. Some contend that inexperienced or untrained securities examiners and administrators lack the expertise needed for intelligent evaluation of most offerings. It has been argued that the efficient working of the market will provide adequate investor protection, and that merit regulation is unnecessary. Similarly, it has been said that the best allocation of scarce state securities regulatory resources is fighting fraud through enforcement, not fighting reams of prospectuses used in offerings in which little if any fraud may be involved. The net effect of these arguments may lead to the suggestion that the federal disclosure system provides adequate protection in public offerings and that state review is redundant, except perhaps in the case of wholly intrastate offerings.

* * *

The opponents of merit regulation can marshal philosophical arguments and provide specific examples of the failure of merit review as to particular issues, but they have not yet produced any strong basis for the claim that the merit system produces more social costs than social benefits. No regulatory system works perfectly, and the suggestion that a few failures destroy the value of the system is as ridiculous as suggesting that merit regulation is justified by the existence of a few frauds. An evaluation of merit regulation cannot be made on the basis of isolated instances on either side of the equation.

* * *

The direct costs of merit regulation are obvious: filing fees, attorney's fees for blue sky work, and mailing expenses. In my experience, these costs represent a miniscule percentage of the money raised and are not in themselves a sufficient basis for challenging merit regulation or blue sky regulation in its entirety. * * *

The most significant cost of merit regulation is perhaps that of time. Clearance with multiple states may take several weeks because some states are faced with substantial backlogs. Because time is often of the essence for first-time corporate issuers and for real estate or other programs requiring the purchase of specific properties, these delays may be very costly. This factor is difficult to quantify but it is a pervasive concern of issuers and their counsel.

A second major cost is more elusive. This is the expense to business created by the need to restructure an offering to comply with merit guidelines. This kind of forced restructuring happens frequently, but it is not clear whether or to what extent this possibility actually "kills" potential public offerings. Because it is difficult to quantify these costs, policy makers should exercise caution before concluding that this cost of merit regulation outweighs its benefits to society.

Against these costs must be weighed the benefits of merit regulation. The central benefit, of course, is investor protection. A simple reference to the concept of "investor protection" is misleading since there are multiple categories of investors who require differing amounts of protection.

* * *

It is perhaps fair to say that new issues are customarily sold to rather than bought by the public investor. This inherent market pressure, when viewed in light of the varieties of competing securities products, the lack of informed and critical analysis of new issues, the paucity of information that is provided by most registered representatives to their customers, and the inadequacy of many due diligence reviews, creates a substantial need for investor protection. Merit administrators fulfill the function of asking the questions and seeking the underlying information that should have been asked and sought by underwriters. That, however, is only part of the blue sky process. By applying merit standards, regulators perform the function that neither the market, the underwriter, nor the brokerage firm can perform on a consistent basis: ensuring fair treatment of the public investor. By performing these interrelated functions of eliciting material disclosures and regulating the substantive fairness of the offering, the merit regulators try to speak for the investor.

Selected References

J. Mofsky, Blue Sky Restrictions on New Business Promotions (1971).

Bartell, Federal–State Relations Under the Federal Securities Code, 32 Vand.L.Rev. 457 (1979).

Brandi, Securities Practitioners and Blue Sky Laws: A Survey of Comments and a Ranking of States by Stringency of Regulation, 10 J.Corp. L. 689 (1985).

Brandi, The Silver Lining in Blue Sky Laws: The Effect of Merit Regulation on Common Stock Returns and Market Efficiency, 12 J.Corp.L. 713 (1987).

Buchanan & Stevenson, Developments in Litigation and Enforcement Under State Securities Laws, 40 Bus.Law. 669 (1985).

Carpenter & Stevenson, Blue Sky Litigation, 44 Bus.Law 575 (1989).

Goodkind, Blue Sky Law: Is There Merit in the Merit Requirements?, 1976 Wisc.L.Rev. 79.

Hainsfurther, Summary of Blue Sky Exemptions Corresponding to Regulation D, 38 Southwestern L.J. 989 (1984).

Jennings, Childers & Kudla, Federalism to an Advantage: The Demise of State Blue Sky Laws Under the Uniform Securities Act, 19 Akron L.Rev. 395 (1986).

Karmel, Blue–Sky Merit Regulation: Benefit to Investors or Burden on Commerce?, 53 Brooklyn L.Rev. 105 (1987).

Long, The Conflict of Laws Provision of the Uniform Securities Act, 31 Okla.L.Rev. 781 (1978).

Long, State Securities Regulation: An Overview, 32 Okla.L.Rev. 541–82 (1979).

Shapiro & Sachs, Blue Sky Law and Practice: An Overview, 4 U.Baltimore L.Rev. 1 (1974).

Warren, Legitimacy in the Securities Industry: The Role of Merit Regulation, 53 Brooklyn L.Rev. (1987).

Warren, Reflections on Dual Regulation of Securities: A Case Against Preemption, 25 B.C.L.Rev. 495 (1984).

Report on State Merit Regulation of Securities Offerings, 41 Bus.Law 785 (1986).

*

PART II

REGULATION OF TRANSACTIONS BY "INSIDERS"

In the first part of this book, we looked principally at transactions by issuers—the corporations or other entities that created the securities. In this part, we examine the regulation of transactions by corporate "insiders"—directors, officers, employees, major stockholders, and others.

In considering the obligations of these insiders, there are three provisions of the federal securities laws to be kept in mind. The first, already considered in Part I, is § 5 of the 1933 Act, which becomes applicable to certain sales by these insiders because of the definition of "underwriter" found in § 2(11) of that Act. The second is § 16 of the 1934 Act, which imposes reporting requirements and civil liabilities on officers, directors and major stockholders of companies registered under the 1934 Act. The third is the antifraud provisions of the 1934 Act, particularly § 10(b) and Rule 10b–5, which have been construed to prohibit trading by corporate insiders on the basis of material nonpublic information.

CHAPTER 3

LIABILITY OF "INSIDERS" FOR "SHORT-SWING" PROFITS

Section 16 of the Securities Exchange Act of 1934 is part of the complex of provisions (§§ 13, 14 and 16) applicable to companies required to register under § 12 of the Act. Section 16 requires officers, directors and major shareholders of those companies to file reports with the SEC when they purchase or sell any securities of the company, and imposes civil liability on them for any profits realized on a purchase and sale within a period of six months. Section 16 is not really a disclosure requirement; its ostensible purpose was to discourage those persons from profiting from the use of "inside information." The statute, however, imposes liability in certain specified circumstances, regardless of whether the person trading had access to any such information. The courts, in interpreting these provisions, have alternated between the "objective" approach, in which liability is imposed on any transaction which fits within the literal terms of the statute, and the "pragmatic" approach, in which the language of the statute is interpreted to apply only if the transaction in question could possibly lend itself to the types of speculative abuse that the statute was designed to prevent.

Section 16 does not *prohibit* officers, directors and 10% shareholders from trading in the stock of their companies; it simply authorizes the company (or a shareholder suing on its behalf) to recover the "profits" realized from such trading. The SEC, therefore, has no enforcement responsibilities under § 16. It does, however, have power to adopt rules and regulations exempting transactions from the liability provisions if it finds them to be "not comprehended within the purpose of" § 16(b). Pursuant to this authority, the Commission has adopted a large number of rules defining terms and exempting particular persons or transactions. In 1988, the Commission proposed a complete rewriting of these rules, incorporating many substantive changes. Sec.Ex.Act Rel. No. 26333 (Dec. 2, 1988). After receiving comments, the Commission reproposed the rules in revised form. Sec.Ex.Act Rel. No. 27148 (Aug. 18, 1989). The effect that these rules will have on prior decisions and doctrines is noted at the appropriate places in these materials.

SMOLOWE v. DELENDO CORP.

136 F.2d 231 (2d Cir.1943).

Before SWAN, CHASE, and CLARK, CIRCUIT JUDGES.

CLARK, CIRCUIT JUDGE.

The issue on appeal is solely one of the construction and constitutionality of § 16(b) of the Securities Exchange Act of 1934, rendering directors, officers, and principal stockholders liable to their corporation for profits realized from security tradings within any six months' period. Plaintiffs, Smolowe and Levy, stockholders of the Delendo Corporation, brought separate actions under this statute on behalf of themselves and other stockholders for recovery by the Corporation—joined as defendant—against defendants Seskis and Kaplan, both directors and president and vice-president respectively of the Corporation.

* * *

The named defendants had been connected with the Corporation (whose name was Oldetyme Distillers Corporation until after the transactions here involved) since 1933, and each owned around 12 per cent (approximately 100,000 shares) of the 800,000 shares of $1 par value stock issued by the Corporation and listed on the New York Curb Exchange. The Corporation had negotiated for a sale of all its assets to Schenley Distillers Corporation in 1935–1936; but the negotiations were then terminated because of Delendo's contingent liability for a tax claim of the United States against a corporation acquired by it, then in litigation.

* * *

Negotiations with Schenley's were reopened on April 11 [, 1940] and were consummated by sale on April 30, 1940, for $4,000,000 plus the assumption of certain of the Corporation's liabilities. Proceedings for dissolution of the Corporation were thereupon initiated and on July 16, 1940, an initial liquidating dividend of $4.35 was paid.

During the six months here in question from December 1, 1939, to May 30, 1940, Seskis purchased 15,504 shares for $25,150.20 and sold 15,800 shares for $35,550, while Kaplan purchased 22,900 shares for $48,172 and sold 21,700 shares for $53,405.16. Seskis purchased 584 shares on the Curb Exchange and the rest from a corporation: he made the sale at one time thereafter to Kaplan at $2.25 per share—15,583 shares in purported satisfaction of a loan made him by Kaplan in 1936 and 217 shares for cash. Kaplan's purchases, in addition to the stock received from Seskis, were made on the Curb Exchange at various times prior to April 11, 1940; he sold 200 shares on February 15, and the remaining shares between April 16 and May 14, 1940 (both to private individuals and through brokers on the Curb). Except as to 1,700 shares, the certificates delivered by each of them upon selling were not the same certificates received by them on purchases during the period. The district court held the transactions within the statute and by matching purchases and sales to show the highest profits held

Seskis for $9,733.80 and Kaplan for $9,161.05 to be paid to the Corporation. Both the named defendants and the Corporation have appealed.

* * *

The controversy as to the construction of the statute involves both the matter of substantive liability and the method of computing "such profit." The first turns primarily upon the preamble, viz., "For the purpose of preventing the unfair use of information which may have been obtained by such beneficial owner, director, or officer by reason of his relationship to the issuer." Defendants would make it the controlling grant and limitation of authority of the entire section, and liability would result only for profits from a proved unfair use of inside information. We cannot agree with this interpretation.

We look first to the background of the statute. Prior to the passage of the Securities Exchange Act, speculation by insiders—directors, officers, and principal stockholders—in the securities of their corporation was a widely condemned evil. While some economic justification was claimed for this type of speculation in that it increased the ability of the market to discount future events or trends, the insiders' failure to disclose all pertinent information gave them an unfair advantage of the general body of stockholders which was not to be condoned. Twentieth Century Fund, Inc., The Security Market, 1935, 297, 298. By the majority rule, aggrieved stockholders had no right to recover from the insider in such a situation. And although some few courts enforced a fiduciary relationship and the United States Supreme Court in Strong v. Repide, 213 U.S. 419, announced a special-circumstances doctrine whereby recovery would be permitted if all the circumstances indicated that the insider had taken an inequitable advantage of a stockholder, even these remedies were inadequate because of the heavy burden of proof imposed upon the stockholders.

The primary purpose of the Securities Exchange Act—as the declaration of policy in § 2 makes plain—was to insure a fair and honest market, that is, one which would reflect an evaluation of securities in the light of all available and pertinent data. Furthermore, the Congressional hearings indicate that § 16(b), specifically, was designed to protect the "outside" stockholders against at least short-swing speculation by insiders with advance information. It is apparent too, from the language of § 16(b) itself, as well as from the Congressional hearings, that the only remedy which its framers deemed effective for this reform was the imposition of a liability based upon an objective measure of proof. This is graphically stated in the testimony of Mr. Corcoran, chief spokesman for the draftsmen and proponents of the Act, in Hearings before the Committee on Banking and Currency on S. 84, 72d Cong., 2d Sess., and S. 56 and S. 97, 73d Cong., 1st and 2d Sess., 1934, 6557: "You hold the director, irrespective of any intention or expectation to sell the security within six months after, because it will be absolutely impossible to prove the existence of such intention or expectation, and you have to have this crude rule of thumb, because you cannot undertake the burden of having to prove that the director intended, at the time he bought, to get out on a short swing."

A subjective standard of proof, requiring a showing of an actual unfair use of inside information, would render senseless the provisions of the legislation limiting the liability period to six months, making an intention to profit during that period immaterial, and exempting transactions wherein there is a bona fide acquisition of stock in connection with a previously contracted debt. It would also torture the conditional "may" in the preamble into a conclusive "shall have" or "has." And its total effect would be to render the statute little more of an incentive to insiders to refrain from profiteering at the expense of the outside stockholder than are the common-law rules of liability; it would impose a more stringent statute of limitation upon the party aggrieved at the same time that it allowed the wrongdoer to share in the spoils of recovery.

Had Congress intended that only profits from an actual misuse of inside information should be recoverable, it would have been simple enough to say so.

* * *

The present case would seem to be of the type which the statute was designed to include. Here it is conceded that the defendants did not make unfair use of information they possessed as officers at the time of the transactions. When these began they had no offer from Schenley's. But they knew they were pressing the tax suit; and they, of course, knew of the corporate offer to settle it which re-established the offer to purchase and led to the favorable sale. It is naive to suppose that their knowledge of their own plans as officers did not give them most valuable inside knowledge as to what would probably happen to the stock in which they were dealing. It is difficult to find this use "unfair" in the sense of illegal; it is certainly an advantage and a temptation within the general scope of the legislature's intended prohibition.

The legislative history of the statute is perhaps more significant upon a determination of the method of computing profits—defendants' second line of attack upon the district court's construction of the statute. They urge that even if the statute be not construed to impose liability only for unfair use of inside information, in any event profits should be computed according to the established income tax rule which first looks to the identification of the stock certificate, and if that is not established, then applies the presumption which is hardly more than a rule of administrative convenience of "first in, first out."

* * *

Defendants seek support for their position from the Senate hearings, where, in answer to Senator Barkley's comment, "All these transactions are a matter of record. It seems to me the simple way would be to charge him with the actual profit," Mr. Corcoran responded: "It is the same provision you have in the income tax law. Unless you can prove the actual relationship between certificates, you take the highest price sold and the lowest price bought." This was an incorrect statement of the income tax law. The rule there is first in, first out, regardless of price, wherever the stock actually purchased and sold is not identifiable. But this does show the rule the proponents had in mind, even though its source is erroneously stated. Analysis will show that the income tax rules cannot apply without defeating the law almost completely. Under the basic rule of identifying the stock certificate, the large stockholder, who in most cases is also an officer or director, could speculate in long sales with impunity merely by reason of having a reserve of stock and upon carefully choosing his stock certificates for delivery upon his sales from this reserve. Moreover, his profits from any sale followed by a purchase would be practically untouchable, for the principle of identity admits of no gain without laboring proof of a subjective intent—always a nebulous issue—to effectuate the connected phases of this type of transaction. In consequence the statute would be substantially emasculated. We cannot ascribe to it a meaning so inconsistent with its declared purpose.

Once the principle of identity is rejected, its corollary, the first-in, first-out rule, is left at loose ends. * * * Its application would render the large stockholder with a backlog of stock not immediately devoted to trading immune from the Act. Further, we should note that it does not fit the broad statutory language; a purchase followed immediately by a sale, albeit a transaction within the exact statutory language, would often be held immune from the statutory penalty because the purchase would be deemed by arbitrary rule to have been made at an earlier date; while a sale followed by purchase would never even be within the terms of the rule.[20] We must look elsewhere for an answer to our problem of finding a reasonable and workable interpretation of the statute in the light of its admitted purpose.

Another possibility might be the striking of an average purchase price and an average sale price during the period, and using these as bases of computation. What this rule would do in concrete effect is to allow as offsets all losses made by such trading. * * * Even had the statutory language been more uncertain, this rule seems one not to be favored in the light of the statutory purpose. Compared to other possible rules, it tends to stimulate more active trading by reducing the

20. Defendants suggest, albeit rather obliquely, an intermediate rule limiting the application of the principle only to stock purchased and sold during the chosen six months' period. On the surface this would appear to prevent complete emasculation of the statute, since it assumes to prevent use of an investment backlog. Actually it makes a rule of most uncertain incidence; thus here it would leave the recovery against Seskis untouched, but reduce that against Kaplan by roughly two-thirds. These uncertain results would be increased, of course, if the period during which the officer actually continued his trading was greater than six months; consider its chance application to say, a fourteen months' period, which might be divided up into three, or even four, six-month periods starting at different times. And once the general income tax rule is rejected (as we have seen it must be), there is surely no basis for developing this original and uncertain gloss upon it, since it does not aid the statutory intent or fit the statutory language.

chance of penalty; thus Kaplan, with his more involved trading, benefits by the rule, whereas Seskis, who bought substantially at one time and sold as a whole, does not. Its application to a case where trading continued more than six months might be most uncertain, depending upon how the beginning of each six months' period was ascertained. It is not a clear-cut taking of "any profit" for the corporation, and we agree with the district court in rejecting it.

The statute is broadly remedial. Recovery runs not to the stockholder, but to the corporation. We must suppose that the statute was intended to be thorough-going, to squeeze all possible profits out of stock transactions, and thus to establish a standard so high as to prevent any conflict between the selfish interest of a fiduciary officer, director, or stockholder and the faithful performance of his duty. The only rule whereby all possible profits can be surely recovered is that of lowest price in, highest price out—within six months—as applied by the district court. We affirm it here, defendants having failed to suggest another more reasonable rule.

* * *

Agreeing, therefore, with the district court's interpretation of the statute and ascertainment of the profits, we turn to the constitutional issue raised by this appeal. Defendants make three claims here: denial of due process of law; that the statute attempts to regulate intrastate transactions; that it improperly delegates legislative authority.

First, the statute as interpreted does not infringe due process guaranties. It was enacted only upon a considered finding, supported by ample evidence, of the abuses of inside speculation. In effect it was but a new approach to the common-law attitude which had long recognized the reasonableness of enforcing a level of conduct upon fiduciaries "higher than that trodden by the crowd." See Meinhard v. Salmon, 249 N.Y. 458, 464, 164 N.E. 545, 546, 62 A.L.R. 1. It would not have been unreasonable here to prohibit all short-swing speculation by corporate fiduciaries. Surely no complaint can be heard of measures less harsh than criminal prohibition. That the evil might have been stamped out by still more lenient measures—a possibility, however, which defendants have failed to make real by concrete suggestion—is without our concern, for in the imposition of penalties Congress has a wide discretion.

* * *

That transactions on national security exchanges have taken on an interstate character, justifying regulation under the commerce clause, is now beyond doubt. Defendants contend, however, that private sales, such as some of those here transacted, are purely intrastate activities, immune to Congressional regulation. But private sales affect stock quotations on national security exchanges—and thus interstate commerce—no less than the production of an acre of wheat affects the price and market conditions of wheat transported between the states, cf. Wickard v. Filburn, 317 U.S. 111; and no less than the ownership of securities by a holding company whose subsidiaries are engaged in interstate commerce affects the service those companies render, cf. North American Co. v. Securities and Exchange Commission, 2 Cir., 133 F.2d 148.

The final constitutional objection is that the statute delegates an undefined and, therefore, unlawful authority to the Commission to grant exemptions. The Commission has promulgated no regulation injurious to defendants, and we are asked to make an abstract determination upon the face of the statute. The request is premature. In any event we think the delegation so clearly lawful that there is no reason to wait for a future more pointed argument. Guiding the Commission in the exercise of an actually limited authority is the quite adequate standard—illustrated by two specific statutory exemptions—that its regulations be consistent with the expressed purpose of the statute. The delegation serves no other than the commendable functions of relieving the statute from imposing undue hardship and of giving it flexibility in administration.

The total recovery against defendants accruing to the corporation is $18,894.85, plus costs of $38.93. By this, plaintiffs will be benefited only to the extent of about $3, since they own but 150 shares of a total of 800,000. Upon their petition, however, the district court awarded them $3,000 for counsel fees, together with their expenses of $78.98 payable out of the funds accruing to the corporation.

While it is well settled that in a stockholder's or creditor's representative action to recover money belonging to the class the moving party is entitled to lawyer's fees from the sum recovered, this was not strictly an action for money belonging to either class, but for a penalty payable to the corporation. Ordinarily the corporate issuer must bring the action; and only upon its refusal or delay to do so, as here, may a security holder act for it in its name and on its behalf. But this in effect creates a derivative right of action in every stockholder, regardless of the fact that he has no holdings from the class of security subjected to a short-swing operation or that he can receive no tangible benefits, directly or indirectly, from an action because of his position in the security hierarchy. And a stockholder who is successful in maintaining such an action is entitled to reimbursement for reasonable attorney's fees on the theory that the corporation which has received the benefit of the attorney's services should pay the reasonable value thereof.

* * *

While the allowance made here was quite substantial, we are not disposed to interfere with the district court's well-considered determination. Since in many cases such as this the possibility of recovering attorney's fees will provide the sole stimulus for the enforcement of § 16(b), the allowance must not be too niggardly.

Is the court's method of computing "profit realized" by matching the highest price sales with the lowest price purchases during a six-month period really the "only rule" by which the statutory objective could be realized? Or does it go too far? Should the defendant be held liable for "profits realized" if he actually had a net loss on his total trading in the stock during a six-month period?

To understand the effect of Smolowe, consider a situation in which a director makes the following purchases and sales:

March 1	:	purchases	200 shares at $40
April 1	:	sells	100 shares at $20
May 1	:	purchases	100 shares at $35
June 1	:	sells	200 shares at $50
July 1	:	purchases	100 shares at $45
August 1	:	sells	100 shares at $40

What would be his "profit realized" under the rule laid down in *Smolowe* and how much profit did he actually make?

Note that Section 16(b) does not *prohibit* purchases and sales by directors, officers and 10% shareholders, but simply permits the corporation to recover the profit realized from any such purchases and sale within a six-month period. The corporate management will seldom be interested in bringing suit against its own members; therefore enforcement of the section results largely from derivative suits brought by shareholders of the corporation. Since the benefit to any individual shareholder is likely to be infinitesimal, as the *Smolowe* case indicated, the only incentive for bringing such actions is the fee which the court awards the lawyer, and which is paid by the corporation as the beneficiary of the recovery. The information which a lawyer needs to make his case under Section 16(b) is found in the reports which directors, officers and 10% shareholders are required to file with the SEC under Section 16(a) whenever they acquire or dispose of securities of the corporation. To make the lawyers' job easier, the forms were amended in 1972 to require disclosure of the price at which securities were bought or sold (for some unknown reason, this information was not previously required). See Securities Exchange Act Release No. 9500 (Feb. 23, 1972). Approximately 100,000 insider trading reports are filed annually with the SEC.

The deterrent or punitive impact of § 16(b) can be significantly affected by the tax treatment of the payments which the insider is required to make to the corporation. Prior to 1961, the Internal Revenue Service took the position that a payment under § 16(b) was in the nature of a penalty and not deductible from the insider's income. In 1961, the IRS reversed that position and ruled that 16(b) payments would be deductible. Rev.Rul. 61–115, 1961–1 Cum.Bull. 46. The question whether they were deductible as an ordinary loss or as a capital loss would be determined by reference to "the income tax significance of the capital stock dealings giving rise to the payment." This formulation has caused problems in the situation where liability is based on a sale followed by a purchase within six months. The Tax Court has held in a series of such cases that since the purchase which gives rise to the liability is not a taxable event, the insider is entitled to deduct his payment as an ordinary loss, related to the maintenance of his position with the corporation. See William M. Mitchell, 52 T.C. 170 (1969). This position has been consistently rejected by the Courts of Appeals, which have held the payments to be capital losses, in order to avoid the "windfall" to the insider if his "profit" was taxed at capital gain rates but he was entitled to a deduction at ordinary rates on his repayment. See, e.g., Cummings v. Comm'r, 506 F.2d 449 (2d Cir.1974). One judge in the *Cummings* case argued that the payment in the sale-purchase situation should not be deductible from income at all, but should be added to the basis of the shares purchased, thus reducing the capital gain when those shares are sold.

A. PERSONS SUBJECT TO LIABILITY

Section 16 imposes liability only on a specifically-defined group—anyone who "is a director or officer of the issuer" or who "is directly or indirectly the beneficial owner of more than 10 per centum of any class of equity security which is registered pursuant to section 12" of the 1934 Act. Nevertheless, difficulties have arisen in determining who falls within the defined categories.

---

1. *"Officers" and "Directors"*

C.R.A. REALTY v. CROTTY

878 F.2d 562 (2d Cir. 1989).

Before OAKES, CHIEF JUDGE, and TIMBERS and MESKILL, CIRCUIT JUDGES.

TIMBERS, CIRCUIT JUDGE:

The essential question presented by this appeal is whether an employee's functions, rather than his title, determine whether he is an "officer" within the meaning of § 16(b) of the Securities Exchange Act of 1934. The district court held that the employee's functions were determinative. We agree. We affirm.

Appellant C.R.A. Realty Corp. appeals from a judgment entered December 27, 1988 in the Southern District of New York, Robert L. Carter, District Judge, dismissing after trial appellant's complaint which alleged that appellee Joseph R. Crotty (Crotty), an "officer" of appellee United Artists Communications, Inc. (United Artists or the company) engaged in short-swing trading in United Artists' securities in violation of § 16(b) of the Securities Exchange Act of 1934, which prohibits short-swing trading in the securities of a company by any director, officer or 10% shareholder of the company. The district court held that Crotty was not an "officer" within the meaning of § 16(b)—

despite his position as a corporate vice-president—because he was "a middle management employee of United Artists whose duties did not provide access to any confidential information about the company's financial plans or future operations".

Appellant asserts on appeal that the district court erred in holding that Crotty was not an officer because (1) Crotty's lack of access to confidential or inside information is irrelevant since § 16(b) imposes strict liability on *any* officer engaging in short-swing trading regardless of whether he has access to inside information, and (2) in the alternative, appellant demonstrated in the district court that Crotty had access to inside information.

For the reasons which follow, we affirm.

I.

* * *

Appellant is an organization incorporated to act as a private attorney general to purchase stock and commence actions against corporate officials for violations of the federal securities laws. During the period in question, appellant owned 10 shares of United Artists, then a nationwide distributor and exhibitor of motion pictures. Crotty, a vice-president of United Artists, was the head film buyer of its western division, a territory encompassing six western states.

Crotty was first employed by United Artists in December 1969. He became head film buyer for the western division in 1980. He was elected a vice-president of United Artists in 1982 and continued to serve as head film buyer for the western division. As head film buyer, he obtained movies to be shown at the 351 movie screens in the western division theaters. He supervised their distribution. This included negotiating and signing agreements pursuant to which United Artists obtained movies for exhibition, supervising the distribution of the movies to the company's theaters, and settling contracts after the movies had been shown in the theaters. Crotty also had some supervisory responsibility for advertising in his division.

Crotty supervised a staff of 30 people. He had virtually complete and autonomous control of film buying in the western division. He was required to consult with higher authority only if he wanted to exceed a certain limit on the amount of the cash advance paid to a distributor for the exhibition of a particular movie. This occurred no more than two or three times a year. The gross revenue from Crotty's division routinely was about 35–36% of United Artists' gross revenue from movie exhibition, or around 15–18% of the company's total gross revenue.

The short-swing transactions here involved took place between December 19, 1984 and July 24, 1985. During this period Crotty purchased 7500 shares of United Artists and sold 3500 of its shares. He realized a large profit which appellant seeks to recover on behalf of United Artists. Following an unsuccessful demand on United Artists that it proceed against Crotty to recover this profit, appellant commenced the instant action against appellees pursuant to § 16(b). Following trial, the district court entered a judgment which dismissed the complaint. The court held that, although Crotty was a vice-president of United Artists, he was not an officer within the purview of § 16(b) because he had no access to inside information regarding the company's financial plans or future operations. This appeal followed.

II.

Section 16(b) * * * "imposes a strict prophylactic rule with respect to insider, short-swing trading". Any corporate official within the statutory meaning of an "officer" who engages in short-swing trading automatically will be required to surrender any profit from the trading, "without proof of actual abuse of insider information, and without proof of intent to profit on the basis of such information". This objective test was chosen by Congress because of the difficulty of proving whether a corporate insider actually abused confidential information to which he had access or purchased or sold an issuer's stock with the intention of profiting from such information. Since the statute imposes strict liability, it is to be applied only when doing so "best serves the congressional purpose of curbing short-swing speculation by corporate insiders".

Appellant challenges the district court's holding by asserting that Crotty automatically was an officer within the meaning of § 16(b) by virtue of his title of vice-president of United Artists. The district court, however, held that it was Crotty's actual duties at the time of the short-swing trading—rather than his corporate title—that determined whether he was an officer within the meaning of § 16(b). We believe that the district court's holding was correct.

Appellant's starting point in challenging the district court's holding is the Securities and Exchange Commission rule which defined the term "officer" in the 1934 Act as including a vice-president of an issuer.[2] Appellant asserts that, since Crotty is a vice-president of United Artists, this rule places him within the purview of § 16(b). We believe it is significant, however, that the SEC itself does not believe that this rule should be rigidly applied in determining who is an officer within the meaning of § 16. For example, two SEC releases show that the Commission does not consider an employee's title as an officer to bring the employee automatically under § 16.[3] We do not believe that

2. SEC Rule 3b–2 states:

"The term 'officer' means a president, *vice-president,* secretary, treasurer or principal financial officer, comptroller or principal accounting officer, and any person routinely performing corresponding functions with respect to any organization whether incorporated or unincorporated." (emphasis added).

3. In proposing new rules in this Release to clarify the term "officer" under § 16, the SEC stated:

"If applied literally, the Rule 3b–2 definition of 'officer' can be too broad in the context of Section 16; *of particular concern is the inclusion of all vice presidents in the definition.* Many businesses give the title of vice president to employees who do not have significant managerial or policymaking duties and are not privy to inside information.

The reporting and short-swing profit recovery provisions of Section 16 *were intended to apply to those officers who*

Rule 3b–2 requires us to hold that Crotty is an officer within the purview of § 16(b) merely by virtue of his title as a vice-president of the company.

Moreover the district court's holding is consistent with the law of this Circuit. It relied primarily on Colby v. Klune, 178 F.2d 872 (2 Cir. 1949). In *Colby* we held that a corporate employee who did not hold the title of a corporate officer nevertheless could be an officer within the meaning of § 16(b) if he "perform[ed] important executive duties of such character that he would be likely, in discharging these duties, to obtain confidential information about the company's affairs that would aid him if he engaged in personal market transactions".

* * *

Three other circuits have followed a similar functional approach in determining the liability of officers under § 16(b). Although the Ninth Circuit generally views an issuer's designation of one of its employees as a corporate officer as automatically bringing him within § 16(b), National Medical Enterprises, Inc. v. Small, 680 F.2d 83, 84 (9 Cir.1982) (per curiam), it recognizes an exception if the title is honorary or ceremonial. Id.; Merrill Lynch, Pierce, Fenner & Smith, Inc. v. Livingston, 566 F.2d 1119, 1122–23 (9 Cir.1978) (title of vice-president raises an inference that employee has access to inside information that may be overcome if title is shown to be merely honorary). Two other Circuits generally follow our functional approach. Winston v. Federal Exp. Corp., 853 F.2d 455, 456–57 (6 Cir.1988); Gold v. Sloan, 486 F.2d 340, 351 (4 Cir.1973).

The general approach established by our Court in *Colby* is consistent with that of the Supreme Court in § 16(b) cases in which the Court has emphasized that potential access to inside information is the key to finding liability, rather than rigid application of statutory designations. * * *

It is significant that the approach set forth in *Colby* implements the objective standard established by § 16(b). *Colby*'s approach will require more proof that an employee is an officer under § 16(b) than merely showing that the employee holds a title as a corporate officer. We emphasize, however, that all that is required by *Colby* is that a plaintiff establish that it is more likely than not that the employee's duties gave him access to inside information. A plaintiff need not show that the employee actually obtained inside information or used it to his advantage.

We hold that it is the duties of an employee—especially his potential access to inside information—rather than his corporate title which determine whether he is an officer subject to the short-swing trading restrictions of § 16(b) of the 1934 Act.

have routine access to material non-public information, not those with particular titles."

III.

We turn next to the district court's finding that Crotty's duties did not give him access to inside information concerning United Artists. Since we hold that this finding was supported by substantial evidence and was not clearly erroneous, we discuss it only briefly.

The evidence indicated that Crotty's appointment as a vice-president—two years after he became a head film buyer—was essentially honorary. The appointment was accompanied by no raise in pay or change in responsibilities. Viewing his responsibilities both before and after the appointment, Crotty had no access to inside information such as the financial or operational plans of United Artists. He was not a director of the company, never attended a directors meeting, and never received any information from the Board of Directors that was not available to the general public.

* * *

IV.

To summarize:

We hold that it is the actual functions of an employee—particularly his access to inside information—and not his corporate title that determine whether he is an officer within the purview of § 16(b) of the 1934 Act; Crotty's title of vice-president did not make him an officer. We also hold that the district court's finding that Crotty had no access to inside information is not clearly erroneous.

Affirmed.

MESKILL, CIRCUIT JUDGE, dissenting:

I respectfully dissent.

The plain language of both section 16(b) of the Securities Exchange Act of 1934, and the applicable Securities and Exchange Commission (SEC) regulation, Rule 3b–2, contains no exception that exempts appellee Crotty from liability in this case. * * *

While these provisions clearly leave room to construe as officers those who do not possess the titles of officers, they do not permit the reverse inference.

Where the language of a statute is clear, as it is in this case, any extraneous considerations, such as the statute's legislative history, are irrelevant to an analysis of the statute's meaning. * * *

Simply put, the majority's interpretation of section 16(b) writes the word "officer" out of the statute. At the very least, the statute should create a presumption that an officer has access to inside information. The majority opinion, however, gives only lip service to the words of the statute and the SEC's own regulation interpreting those words. Crotty is a vice president of UA, and as such he should be liable for the profit he made in the short-swing transactions at issue here.

* * *

There is, however, a second reason why I believe the district court's decision should be reversed. Even under the majority's reading of the statute and regulation, Crotty is an insider. * * *

The facts clearly show that Crotty was in a position not only to bind UA through the execution of major contracts, but also to obtain information that could be useful in making investment decisions before that information was generally known either within the company, within the industry or to the general public. * * * If an employee's functions provide the employee with access to inside information, that employee falls within the purview of these laws. * * *

The SEC's new rules, as originally proposed in 1988, would have limited the coverage of § 16 to officers who "perform policy-making functions" by defining "officer" to mean the same thing as the term "executive officer" in Rule 3b–7. However, the revised rules promulgated in 1989 would include not only executive officers, but also principal financial officers, controllers or principal accounting officers, and officers of the issuer's parent who perform policy making functions for the issuer. In promulgating the revised rules, the Commission specifically endorsed the Second Circuit's statement in *Crotty* that "it is the duties of an employee * * * rather than his corporate title which determine whether he is an officer subject to * * * § 16(b)."

WHITING v. DOW CHEMICAL COMPANY

523 F.2d 680 (2d Cir.1975).

Before GIBBONS, GURFEIN and MESKILL, CIRCUIT JUDGES.

GURFEIN, CIRCUIT JUDGE:

This appeal presents a difficult and important question of first impression in this court concerning the interpretation of § 16(b) of the Securities Exchange Act of 1934, as it applies to the matching transactions of a corporate insider and his spouse. The issue is whether a corporate director may be held to have "realized profit" within the meaning of § 16(b) as a result of a matching of his wife's sales and his own purchase of his company's securities within the statutory six-month period.

In a thorough opinion after a non-jury trial, Judge Ward dismissed the complaint of Macauley Whiting, a director of Dow Chemical Company ("Dow"), which sought a declaratory judgment that he was not liable to Dow under § 16(b) and awarded judgment to Dow on its counterclaim for the profits realized. 386 F.Supp. 1130 (S.D.N.Y.1974). We affirm.

I

Helen Dow Whiting sold an aggregate of 29,770 shares of Dow stock for $1.6 million during September and November of 1973 at an average price of $55–$56. In December 1973 her husband, appellant Macauley Whiting, exercised an option to purchase 21,420 Dow shares for $520,000 at a price of $24.3125. He exercised the option with funds he borrowed from his wife, which were part of the proceeds of her sales of the Dow stock in the preceding two months.

Macauley Whiting has been a director of Dow since 1959. His wife of thirty years is a granddaughter of the founder of Dow, and acquired substantial amounts of Dow stock over the years by gift and inheritance, and these assets are segregated from appellant's. On the other hand, Judge Ward found that "the resources of both husband and wife are significantly directed toward their common prosperity, and they easily communicate concerning matters which relate to that prosperity." Moreover, the Whitings' separate accounts are managed by the same financial advisors. The Whitings file joint tax returns, and their common financial planning has included Mrs. Whiting's use of her husband's annual gift tax exclusion to make charitable gifts and gifts to trusts established for their six children.

Mrs. Whiting's personal wealth and income—primarily consisting of dividends and capital gains derived from her Dow holdings—is considerably larger than that of her husband. Although Judge Ward found that Mr. Whiting contributes virtually his entire salary toward family expenses, he also found that Mrs. Whiting is primarily responsible for the considerable costs incurred in the style of living the Whitings have chosen to pursue. It is her dividend income, for example, which has provided for education of the Whitings' children, which defrays medical expenses, which maintains a family vacation home, and which pays real estate taxes on the Whitings' property.

Mrs. Whiting's sales of the Dow stock in September and November of 1973 were made pursuant to a long-term investment plan, arranged by the Whitings and their financial advisor, which was designed to diversify the holdings of the family and to obtain tax benefits. The court found that the Whitings discussed the general philosophy to govern the management of Mrs. Whiting's estate, and, in early 1972, agreed on a major shift in their philosophy. They then discharged their long-time investment advisor. Desiring to pursue a more aggressive investment program, the Whitings in late 1972 retained new investment counselors, Smith, Barney & Company, Inc. ("Smith Barney"), and new tax, accounting and estate planning advisors, Goldstein, Golub, Kessler & Company ("Goldstein"). As had been the case with their previous financial advisor, the Whitings continued to maintain formal segregation of their investment accounts, but these accounts were managed jointly as discretionary accounts under the supervision of one person at Smith Barney.

Since January 1966, in the Form 3 and 4 reports he was required to make as a Dow director pursuant to § 16(a), Mr. Whiting regularly reported his wife's Dow stock as "directly owned" by him, and never disclaimed ownership as he might have pursuant to SEC regulations, a procedure of which he was made aware by Dow's counsel. Under SEC Rule 144(a)(2)(i), effective April 15, 1972, Mrs. Whiting as a "relative or spouse" was herself required to report her sales of Dow stock. From the outset Smith Barney advised the Whitings that it considered Mrs. Whiting to be a "control" person of Dow by reason of Mr. Whiting's position as a Dow director. The Whitings acquiesced in such treatment, and Mrs. Whiting, thereafter, regularly filed Form 144 reports with the SEC covering her sales of Dow stock.

Judge Ward found that not only did Mr. and Mrs. Whiting use the same financial advisors, but both were present at many meetings with these advisors; they had a "general philosophy" concerning the management of the family estates. He also found that Mrs. Whiting upon occasion "consults her husband concerning the desirability of certain investments in areas of his expertise," but that "Mr. Whiting does not communicate with his wife concerning the affairs of [Dow]." 386 F.Supp. at 1132.

* * *

As we have seen, Goldstein advised the Whitings on October 29 that Mr. Whiting should finance the exercise of his option by means of an intrafamily loan from his wife. Mr. Whiting explored the possibility of obtaining a personal loan through Harris Bank of Chicago, and he was quoted an interest rate of 1/4% to 1/2% over the then prevailing prime lending rate of about 10%. Ultimately, for reasons not revealed by the record but apparent from the circumstances, Mr. Whiting informed the Harris Bank that "[w]e have been able to get the cash required *from sale of stock* and will not need the loan at this time" (emphasis added). The "sale of stock" to which Mr. Whiting referred was the very sale of Dow stock by Mrs. Whiting now at issue. Appellant borrowed the $520,000 he needed to exercise his option from his spouse and used it for that purpose. The loan was at 7% interest, and no repayment terms were specified.

II

It is strange that more than forty years of experience with Section 16(b) has yielded practically no judicial guidance on Section 16(b) liability concerning attribution of transactions by the spouse of a director. * * * The decision below proceeded on the assumption that, under the circumstances related, appellant was the "beneficial owner" of the securities sold by the wife.

Cases where the husband simply buys stock and puts the shares in his wife's name are relatively simple; so, too, perhaps where he has sole control of her account. The difficulty arises when, as here, the securities are incontestably the wife's, but where the husband obtains benefits, nevertheless, from the dividends and proceeds of sale through the wife's supplying the larger share of family expenses. The problem is compounded by the action of both spouses in managing both the sales and the exercise of the option jointly, and further by the use of the proceeds of sale for the exercise of the option.

* * *

The Securities and Exchange Commission has variously required the reporting of securities owned by the spouse of an insider when the insider had received "benefits substantially equivalent to ownership" by reason of his spouse's holdings or when the insider has the right to revest title to such shares in himself. There appears to be no judicial decision squarely in support of the Commission's interpretation though there can be little doubt that the second part of the definition, not applicable here, is correct.

The question is whether the term "beneficial owner[ship]" includes securities from which the spouse has shared "benefits substantially equivalent to ownership." See SEC Securities Exchange Act Release No. 7793 (Jan. 19, 1966).

In a traditional sense, in the absence of a statutory definition, a beneficial owner would be a person who does not have the legal title to the securities but who is, nevertheless, the beneficiary of a trust or a joint venture, or is a shareholder in a corporation which owns the shares. In the normal equity sense, Mr. Whiting would not be the beneficial owner of his wife's separate estate.

The Commission's definition seeks to go further to include situations where the insider indirectly benefits from the dividends though he does not own the shares. The theory is that such an insider would be tempted to pass on inside information to the holder of the stock from which he, himself, "benefits" and thus falls within the class intended by Congress.

* * *

"Beneficial owner" is the language of § 16(a) and we have been told to read the words of § 16(b) not literally. In the broader sense, we think the term should be read more expansively than it would be in the law of trusts. For purposes of the family unit, shares to which legal title is held by one spouse may be said to be "beneficially owned" by the other, the insider, if the ordinary rewards of ownership are used for their joint benefit. These rewards are generally the dividend income as well as the capital gains on sale and the power to dispose of the shares to their children by gift or upon death.

While we cannot earmark the proceeds of Mrs. Whiting's particular sales as going to household and family support, we know from the findings that the larger part of their joint maintenance came from her estate, the bulk of it in Dow stock. We also know that they engaged in joint estate planning. So that while it is true that if they ever separated, Mrs. Whiting would take her Dow shares, it is also true that while they continue to live as a married couple, there is hardly anything Mrs. Whiting gets out of the ownership that appellant does not share.

While the case is harder than if it had been Mr. Whiting who had put the shares in his wife's name originally, the mischief that "inside information" will be used is just as great.

In the words of the present Chief Justice, "[i]n addition to the intent and purpose of the legislation which we must glean from the statute as a whole rather than from isolated parts, we must consider the results which would flow from each of the two interpretations contended for. If we find one interpretation tends to carry out and the other to defeat the purposes of the statute, the resolution of the issue becomes simple." Adler v. Klawans, 267 F.2d at 844.

Turning to the specific facts, while there was no exclusive "control" by appellant over his wife's separate investments generally, there was sufficient evidence to establish that the questioned transactions were part of a common plan, jointly managed by husband and wife.

* * *

If, then, appellant is "the beneficial owner" of his wife's securities of the issuer for § 16(b) purposes, how does one interpret the statutory language of § 16(b) "any profit realized by *him*" (emphasis added).

If we hold that he is a "beneficial owner" he must be chargeable with all the profits or none, in the absence of a way to measure benefit. Cf. Blau v. Lehman, supra, 286 F.2d at 791. It is fiction, of course, to say that he will get all the profit for himself, but here the prophylaxis comes in. The whole profit is "his" profit, "realized by him" because the shares are "his" by the statutory "beneficial owner" concept as applied, and because he is a person in a position to obtain inside information.

This may be a case where innocents were trapped by the statute and its gloss. If Mr. Whiting had not exercised his option until June 1974, just before it expired, he would have incurred no § 16(b) liability, for the six months from the time of Mrs. Whiting's last sale in November 1973 would have expired. But the threat of a new tax bill in 1974 apparently made him exercise the option in 1973. The path of this harsh statute is strewn with such possibly innocent victims. But to allow immunity here would open the door to patent abuse which Congress sought to prevent by a catch-all type of statute, at least where the purchase and sale aspects of the transaction are not subject to dispute.

The judgment is affirmed.

In CBI v. HORTON, 682 F.2d 643 (7th Cir.1982), the court held that a sale made by a director could not be matched against subsequent purchase by him as trustee of a trust for his children, since the benefit to his children was not "profit realized by him" within the meaning of the statute.

The SEC's new rules, as originally proposed in 1988, would have automatically deemed an insider to be the beneficial owner of securities held by a member of his immediate family sharing the same residence. However, as revised in 1989, the rules merely provide a "rebuttable presumption" that he is the beneficial owner of such securities.

The question whether the holdings of one person can be considered as "beneficially" owned by another person can also arise in the case of related corporations or other entities. In MAYER v. CHESAPEAKE, 877 F.2d 1154 (2d Cir.1989), seven companies with interlocking stockholdings, all controlled by Victor Posner, owned an aggregate of 23% of the stock of Peabody. One of those companies, APL, purchased and then sold about 12% of Peabody's stock within a six-month period. Plaintiff argued that APL's profit should be calculated by matching its sale against all of its purchases, even those made before it became a 10% stockholder, because the shares owned by all the Posner companies should be aggregated in determining 10% ownership. However, the court held that, since APL was a publicly-held company in which the Posner interests held only 56% of the stock, none of the other Posner companies, nor Posner himself, could be considered the "beneficial" owners of the Peabody shares held by APL. Thus, § 16(b) liability could attach only to the shares purchased by APL after *it* became a 10% stockholder. A similar result was reached in C.R.A. REALTY v. GOODYEAR, 705 F.Supp. 972 (S.D.N.Y.1989), with respect to two partnerships with overlapping ownership.

The SEC's proposed new rules would change this situation significantly by providing that "beneficial ownership" for purposes of § 16 would be determined by the criteria used under § 13(d) of the Act, which requires reports from all persons who own more 5% of the stock of a reporting company. The § 13(d) criteria are considerably broader than those that have hitherto been applied under § 16 (see pp. 757–58 below).

FEDER v. MARTIN MARIETTA CORP.

406 F.2d 260 (2d Cir.1969).

Before WATERMAN, SMITH and HAYS, CIRCUIT JUDGES.

WATERMAN, CIRCUIT JUDGE.

Plaintiff-appellant, a stockholder of the Sperry Rand Corporation ("Sperry") after having made the requisite demand upon Sperry which was not complied with, commenced this action pursuant to § 16(b) of the Securities Exchange Act of 1934, to recover for Sperry "short-swing" profits realized upon Sperry stock purchases and sales by the Martin Marietta Corporation ("Martin"). Plaintiff alleged that George M. Bunker, the President and Chief Executive of Martin Marietta, was deputized by, or represented, Martin Marietta when he served as a member of the Sperry Rand Board of Directors and therefore during his membership Martin Marietta was a "director" of Sperry Rand within the meaning of Section 16(b). The United States District Court for the Southern District of New York, Cooper, J., sitting without a jury, finding no deputization, dismissed plaintiff's action. 286 F.Supp. 937 (S.D.N.Y.1968). We hold to the contrary and reverse the judgment below.

The purpose of § 16(b) as succinctly expressed in the statute itself is to prevent "unfair use of information" by insiders and thereby to protect the public and outside stockholders. The only remedy which the framers of § 16(b) deemed effective to curb insider abuse of advance information was the imposition of a liability based upon an objective measure of proof. Thus, application of the act is not conditional upon proof of an insider's intent to profit from unfair use of information, or upon proof that the insider was privy to any confidential information. Rather, Section 16(b) liability is automatic, and liability attaches to any profit by an insider on any short-swing transaction embraced within the arbitrarily fixed time limits of the statute.

The judicial tendency, especially in this circuit, has been to interpret Section 16(b) in ways that are most consistent with the legislative purpose, even departing where necessary from the literal statutory language. But the policy underlying the enactment of § 16(b) does not permit an expansion of the statute's scope to persons other than directors, officers, and 10% shareholders. Through the creation of a legal fiction, however, our courts have managed to remain within the limits of § 16(b)'s literal language and yet have expanded the Act's reach.

In Rattner v. Lehman, 193 F.2d 564 (2 Cir.1952), Judge Learned Hand in his concurring opinion planted the seed for a utilization of the theory of deputization upon which plaintiff here proceeds. In discussing the question whether a partnership is subject to Section 16(b) liability whenever a partner is a director of a corporation whose stock the partnership traded, Judge Hand stated:

> I agree that § 16(b) does not go so far; but I wish to say nothing as to whether, if a firm deputed a partner to represent its interests as a director on the board, the other partners would not be liable. True, they would not even then be formally "directors"; but I am not prepared to say that they could not be so considered; for some purposes the common law does treat a firm as a jural person. 193 F.2d at 567.

The Supreme Court in Blau v. Lehman, 368 U.S. 403, 408–410 (1962), more firmly established the possibility of an entity, such as a partnership or a corporation, incurring Section 16(b) liability as a "director" through the deputization theory. Though the Court refused to reverse the lower court decisions that had held no deputization, it stated:

> Although admittedly not "literally designated" as one, it is contended that Lehman is a director. No doubt Lehman Brothers, though a partnership, could for purposes of § 16 be a "director" of Tide Water and function through a deputy * * *. 368 U.S. at 409.

In Marquette Cement Mfg. Co. v. Andreas, 239 F.Supp. 962, 967 (SDNY 1965), relying upon Blau v. Lehman, the availability of the deputization theory to impose § 16(b) liability was again recognized.

In light of the above authorities, the validity of the deputization theory, presumed to be valid here by the parties and by the district court, is unquestionable. Nevertheless, the situations encompassed by its application are not as clear. The Supreme Court in Blau v. Lehman intimated that the issue of deputization is a question of fact to be settled case by case and not a conclusion of law. Therefore, it is not enough for appellant to show us that inferences to support appellant's contentions should have been drawn from the evidence. Rather our review of the facts and inferences found by the court below is imprisoned by the "unless clearly erroneous" standard. Fed.R.Civ.P. 52(a). In the instant case, applying that standard, though there is some evidence in the record to support the trial court's finding of no deputization, we, upon considering the entire evidence, are left with the definite and firm conviction that a mistake was committed. Consequently, we reverse the result reached below.

Bunker served as a director of Sperry from April 29, 1963 to August 1, 1963, when he resigned. During the period December 14, 1962 through July 24, 1963, Martin Marietta accumulated 801,300 shares of Sperry stock of which 101,300 shares were purchased during Bunker's directorship. Between August 29, 1963 and September 6, 1963, Martin Marietta sold all of its Sperry stock. Plaintiff seeks to reach, on behalf of the Sperry Rand Corporation, the profits made by Martin Marietta from the 101,300 shares of stock acquired between April 29 and August 1, all of which, of course, were sold within six months after purchase. * * *

[The court here summarizes the evidence as to whether Bunker was acting as Martin Marietta's deputy on the Sperry Board.]

In summary, it is our firm conviction that the district court erred in apportioning the weight to be accorded the evidence before it. The control possessed by Bunker, his letter of resignation, the approval by the Martin Board of Bunker's directorship with Sperry, and the functional similarity between Bunker's acts as a Sperry director and the acts of Martin's representatives on other boards, as opposed to the factors relied upon by the trial court, are all definite and concrete indicatives that Bunker, in fact, was a Martin deputy, and we find that indeed he was.

The trial court's disposition of the case obviated the need for it to determine whether § 16(b) liability could attach to the corporate director's short-swing profits realized after the corporation's deputy had ceased to be a member of the board of directors of the corporation whose stock had been so profitably traded in. It was not until after Bunker's resignation from the Sperry Board had become effective that Martin Marietta sold any Sperry stock. The issue is novel and until this case no court has ever considered the question. We hold that the congressional purpose dictates that Martin must disgorge all short-swing profits made from Sperry stock purchased during its Sperry directorship and sold after the termination thereof if sold within six months of purchase.

Relying upon the congressional objectives sought to be accomplished by the passage of § 16(b), this court, in Adler v. Klawans, 267 F.2d 840 (2 Cir.1959), held that § 16(b) imposes liability to surrender his short-swing profits upon a person who is a director at the date of sale, whether or not he was a director at the date of purchase. The court explained:

> This [the language of § 16(b) itself] makes plain the intent of Congress to reach a "purchase and sale" or "sale and purchase" within a six month period by someone within one of the proscribed categories, i.e., one who was a director, officer or beneficial owner *at some time.* The conventional rules of construction applied to this latter portion of the statute alone are not sufficient to resolve the issue. Appellant presents an arguable interpretation of the statute which would limit its reach to transactions in which the person is a director or officer at both ends of the transaction. If Congress had made such profits the subject of a criminal penalty—as presumably it could—appellant's argument would carry much weight for we would be obliged to construe it strictly. For reasons which will be developed more fully hereafter we construe this statute to be remedial, not penal, and hence subject to that interpretation most consistent with the legislative purpose as that can be discerned from the statute itself and by resort to its history if that be needed.

It must be emphasized, of course, that the statute evidences a clear legislative intent to treat corporate directors and officers in one category of insiders and 10% shareholders in another. The act expressly sets forth that the liability of a 10% shareholder to surrender his short-swing profits is conditional upon his being such both at the time of purchase and at the time of sale, but there is no such limitation in the case of officers and directors.

Our decision in *Adler,* however, did not require us to consider the validity of Rule X–16A–10 of the Securities Exchange Commission, which reads:

> Any transaction which has been or shall be exempted by the Commission from the requirements of section 16(a) shall, in so far as it is otherwise subject to the provisions of section 16(b), be likewise exempted from section 16(b).

On the form provided by the SEC for a director to file his statement of changes in stock ownership, the Commission further clarifies a director's obligation to report under § 16(a), as follows:

FORM 4

1. Persons Required to File Statements.

Statements on this form are required to be filed by each of the following persons:

> (a) Every person who at any time during any calendar month was (i) directly or indirectly the beneficial owner of more than 10 percent of any class of equity securities (other than exempt securities) listed and registered on a national securities exchange, or (ii) a director or officer of the company which is the issuer of such securities, and who during such month had any change in his beneficial ownership of any class of equity securities of such company * * *.

In *Adler,* this court read this last rule to require a director to report all "changes in his ownership" irrespective of whether the ownership was established "by a director while a director." Indeed, § 16(a) itself expressly imposes its requirements on every person "who is a director" or who "becomes such * * * director." Thus, by finding that § 16(a)'s reporting rules extend to a director who became such after the acquisition of securities, we were able to avoid deciding whether Rule X–16A–10 constituted a proper exercise of the Commission's power.

Congress has vested the Commission with broad power to promulgate rules and regulations exempting transactions from the coverage of § 16(b). But, as this court has commented on a previous occasion, the promulgation of rules is not a matter solely within the expertise of the SEC and beyond the scope of judicial review. The Commission's authority, according to the statute, is subject to the limitation that the transactions the SEC exempts are "not comprehended within the purpose" of § 16(b). We must determine, therefore, whether the Commission by exempting from § 16(b) liability any transaction not required to be reported under § 16(a) exceeded the authority delegated to it by Congress.

To be sure, the congressional belief that inside information could be abused, the belief that prompted the prophylactic enactment of § 16(b), is just as germane to the situation when a person is a director only at the time of purchase as when he is a director only at the time of sale. For, in the case of a director who resigns his directorship before the sale it is possible for both the purchase and sale to have been unfairly motivated by insider knowledge; whereas if the purchase were made prior to the directorship only the sale could be motivated by inside information. Clearly, therefore, a "short swing" sale or purchase by a resigning director must be a transaction "comprehended within the purpose of" § 16(b), and to the extent Rule X–16A–10 exempts such a transaction from § 16(b) the Rule is invalid.

Martin Marietta Corporation has urged, in opposition to this approach, that in the *Adler* case this court, in dictum, approved of Rule X–16A–10 when we said:

> We agree that, if he is exempt from the Section 16(a) reporting requirement, he would be exempt under Rule X–16A–10 from the accounting requirements of Section 16(b).

However, the quoted statement was made in an opinion holding that liability under § 16(b) was established. Similarly, the contexts in which other courts have said that § 16(b) must be read in conjunction with § 16(a) in order to determine § 16(b) liability have all also involved an affirmative, rather than a negative, finding of § 16(b) liability.

Arguably, however, § 16(b) itself, as well as, arguably, the SEC regulations, limits liability to only those persons encompassed within the meaning of subsection (a), for subsection (b) applies to "such beneficial owner, director, or officer," and, when literally read, this language probably means only such beneficial owner, director, or officer as described in subsection (a). So semanticizing, it would follow that if a person has no duty to report pursuant to § 16(a) he ought not to be required to relinquish his short-swing profits under § 16(b). SEC Form 4, however, which governs the reporting provision of § 16(a) seems to extend the reporting requirement to ex-directors so as to include the calendar month during which their directorships terminate. Consequently, even if we found Rule X–16A–10 to be a valid Rule, there is no difficulty in finding that liability under § 16(b) can attach to ex-directors for transactions executed within the calendar month of their resignations. Unlike Rule X–16A–10, Form 4 is entirely consistent with and in furtherance of the legislative purpose of § 16.

While Form 4 represents a proper exercise by the Commission of its rule-making power it is arbitrarily inadequate. For example, it would permit a director of a corporation to purchase its stock within six months prior to September 3, during his directorship, resign on August 31, sell the stock on September 2, and not have any obligation to report the sales transaction, but if he had resigned on September 1 he would have had a duty to report the September 2 transaction. Such an arbitrary rule provides an unnecessary loophole in the effective operation of the statutory scheme. While we do not here determine the effect of Form 4 on the scope of § 16(a), we do point out that the Form 4 reporting requirement here mentioned extends § 16(b) putative liability to the extent of that requirement. Therefore, inasmuch as Form 4, a valid exercise of the SEC's power, has already extended § 16(b) to cover, in part, an ex-director's activities, a less arbitrarily defined reporting requirement for ex-directors is but a logical extension of § 16(b) coverage, would be a coverage in line with the congressional aims, and would afford greater assurance that the lawmakers' intent will be effectuated. In view of the foregoing, we hold that § 16(b) applies to a sale of corporate stock by a former director of that corporation if the stock were purchased by him (or purchased by any jural person that had "deputized" him) during the time he was a director and the sale was made within six months after purchase.

Under the well-established rule, profits for § 16(b) purposes are computed by arbitrarily matching purchases with sales in order to obtain the maximum amount of profits. As the briefs do not agree as to the exact amount of the profits Martin Marietta made and do not give us all the relevant data for us to make a correct determination, and as, additionally, the trial court has discretion in connection with an award of interest in a § 16(b) suit, we remand the case to the district court with instructions to proceed with these determinations.

Reversed and remanded.

The SEC's proposed new rules under § 16 do not undertake to define the term "director" beyond the definition found in § 3(a)(7) of the Act, nor do they attempt to codify the case law relating to "deputization," which the Commission viewed as "best left to a case-by-case determination."

After the decision in *Feder,* the SEC amended Rule 16a–1 by adding paragraphs (d) and (e). These paragraphs require a director or officer to file a report with respect to a transaction which took place while he was not a director or officer if it occurs within six months prior to the first transaction, or within six months after the last transaction, effected while he was a director or officer.

In LEVY v. SEATON, 358 F.Supp. 1 (S.D.N.Y.1973), defendant purchased and sold shares of General Motors during the six-month period following his resignation as a director of the corporation. The court held that the transactions were not required to be reported under Section 16(a) (because Rule 16a–1(e) only requires a report of such a transaction if it occurred within six months of a transaction prior to the date of his resignation) and were therefore exempt from 16(b) liability by virtue of Rule 16a–10.

In WINSTON v. FEDERAL EXPRESS, 853 F.2d 455 (6th Cir.1988), Winston resigned as an officer of the company on August 25, but his resignation was not to be effective until September 30 to enable him to exercise a stock option which would not become exercisable until September 25. He exercised the option on September 30, and resold the stock less than six months later. The court held him liable under § 16(b). Since he conceded that he exercised substantial executive responsibilities and had access to inside information until August 25, the fact that he ceased to perform any duties for the company after that date would not relieve him from liability unless he could produce "substantial evidence" to overcome the presumption that he continued to have access to confidential information until the effective date of his resignation.

---

2. *10% Shareholders*

CHEMICAL FUND, INC. v. XEROX CORP.

377 F.2d 107 (2d Cir.1967).

Before LUMBARD, CHIEF JUDGE, and MEDINA and KAUFMAN, CIRCUIT JUDGES.

LUMBARD, CHIEF JUDGE.

The principal issue on this appeal is whether Chemical Fund, the owner of more than ten percent of Xerox Convertible Debentures, is liable for short-swing trading profits as a "beneficial owner of more than 10 per centum of any class of any equity security" within the meaning of section 16 of the Securities Exchange Act of 1934. We think not. As Chemical Fund at no time would have owned more than 2.72 percent of Xerox common stock had it chosen to convert all its Debentures into common stock, we hold it was not liable for the profits realized from the purchase of Debentures and the sales of common stock within six months of such purchases. Accordingly, we reverse the judgment of the district court and direct that summary judgment be entered in favor of Chemical Fund on its complaint and that the counterclaim of Xerox be dismissed.

Chemical Fund brought this suit against Xerox for declaratory judgment in the Western District of New York in November 1963 after it had filed certain forms with the Securities and Exchange Commission and a claim for short-swing profits had been asserted against it. Xerox filed an answer and counterclaimed for profits received by Chemical Fund from its transactions. In June 1965 both parties moved for summary judgment. The district court in April 1966 granted summary judgment to Xerox for $153,972.43, without interest, and dismissed Chemical Fund's complaint.

Chemical Fund appeals from the dismissal of its complaint for declaratory judgment and from the judgment in favor of Xerox on the counterclaim. * * *

The facts are undisputed. Chemical Fund, organized in 1938, is an open-end diversified investment company, registered under the Investment Company Act of 1940.

In November 1963 it had about 60,000 shareholders and owned securities of 62 corporations, one of which was Xerox. Since 1954 Chemical Fund has held an investment in Xerox common stock, of which it owned 91,000 shares, 2.36 percent of the 3,851,844 shares outstanding, in early December 1962. It also acquired 4½ percent Xerox Convertible Subordinated Debentures due May 1, 1981 after they were issued in 1961; in early December 1962 it held $1,486,000 of a total of $15,072,400 principal amount of the Debentures. Each $1,000 Debenture was convertible into approximately 9.5 shares of common stock and was protected against dilution of the conversion right, but carried no voting rights or participation in the equity of Xerox.

In December 1962 Chemical Fund, pursuant to a program designed to increase its secured position and improve its yield from its Xerox investment without sacrificing its ability to take advantage of the continuing appreciation of Xerox common stock, commenced to sell some of its Xerox common stock and to purchase Xerox Debentures convertible into the same number of shares of common. The yield on the Debentures was approximately 2.8 percent of the November 30, 1962 mean market price of $1,607.50, compared to a yield on the common of some .66 percent of the mean price of $150.62. From December 4 through 20, 1962, and again from April 24 through August 2, 1963, the Fund purchased $318,000 principal amount of Debentures, convertible into 3029 shares of Xerox common, and during this period it sold 3000 shares of common stock. After the Fund had purchased $11,000 principal amount of Debentures on December 4 and again on December 12, 1962, it held more than 10 percent of the outstanding Convertible Debentures. It continued to hold more than 10 percent of the outstanding Debentures until November 22, 1963, after Xerox had called the Debentures for redemption, when it converted all its Debentures, $1,804,000 in principal amount, into 17,180.95 shares of common stock.

Judge Burke in computing profits matched purchases of Debentures from December 12, 1962 through August 2, 1963, against sales of common stock within a six-month period. As the market price of Xerox common was at all times substantially above the conversion price, the right of conversion caused the price of the Debentures to fluctuate with the market price of the common. Because of the constantly rising price of the common stock, matching the highest sales with the lowest purchases, resulted in a "profit" of $153,972.43, even though, as the district court noted, the series of transactions as a whole resulted in a substantial net loss because of the premium paid for the higher yield and senior position of the Debentures.

The Securities Exchange Act provides in section 16 that a corporation to which it applies may recover profits realized by an officer, director, or "beneficial owner of more than 10 per centum of any class of any equity security" of the corporation from purchases and sales of such equity securities within any period of less than six months. Section 16(b) states that recovery of such profits was allowed: "For the purpose of preventing the unfair use of information which may have been obtained by such beneficial owner * * * by reason of his relationship to the issuer * * *." It is conceded that the Debentures are securities as defined in section 3(a)(10) of the Act, and that they are equity securities because they are convertible into common stock. Under the definition in section 3(a)(11), it is apparent that a Convertible Debenture is an "equity security" only because of its convertible nature, since an "equity security" is defined as "any stock or similar security; or any security convertible * * * into such a security * * * or any such warrant or right * * *."

Thus the question is: are the Debentures by themselves a "class of any equity security," or does the class consist of the common stock augmented, as to any beneficial holder in question, by the number of shares into which the Debentures it owns are convertible? We think that the Debentures are not a class by themselves; the total percentage of common stock which a holder would own following a hypothetical conversion of the Debentures it holds is the test of liability under section 16(b). The history of the legislation, the stated purpose of the Act, and the anomalous consequences of any other meaning all support this conclusion.

Nothing in the hearings which preceded passage of the Act in 1934 would indicate that the owners of Debentures as such ought to be considered as "insiders." Indeed, S. 2693, 73d Cong.2d Sess. (1934) as introduced included bondholders as insiders, and was later revised to exclude them from the application of section 16. The hearings did disclose instances where directors, officers and large stockholders profited through receiving information before it had become public knowledge. See, e.g., S.Rep. No. 792, 73d Cong., 2d Sess. 9 (1934). Thus it is that section 16 is specifically concerned with "directors, officers and principal stockholders," and has adopted a rule that any stockholder owning more than 10 percent of an equity security is presumed to be an insider who will receive information regarding the company before it is made public. The reason that officers, directors and 10 percent stockholders have been held to account for profits on short-swing transactions is because they are the people who run the corporation, and who are familiar with its day to day workings. This is necessarily so of officers and directors, and there was ample basis for concluding that stockholders owning more than 10 percent of the voting stock of the company, if not in control, would be closely advised, as their votes usually elected the directors who in turn elected the officers, where these were not elected directly by the stockholders.

But there is no reason whatever to believe that any holder of any Convertible Debentures would, by reason of such holding, normally have any standing or position with the officers, directors or large stockholders of a company so that such holder of Debentures would be the recipient of any inside information. There is no provision which gives a holder of the Debentures any standing beyond that of a creditor entitled to certain specified payments of interest at stated intervals, and possessing numerous rights all of which are specifically spelled out in the trust indenture pursuant to which the Debentures were issued.

To hold that the beneficial owner of 10 percent or more of the Debentures is liable under section 16(b) would here impose a liability on an owner who by conversion of all his Debentures would obtain less than one-half of one percent of Xerox common stock. At the same time a holder of as much as 9 percent of Xerox common stock would not be liable. Thus Chemical Fund, able to command only 2.72 percent of Xerox common, would be liable for short-swing profits, although the holder of 9 percent of the common, more than three times Chemical Fund's total potential holding, would not be liable. We do not believe that Congress could have meant to apply the provisions of the Act to any holder of Convertible Debentures whose possible equity position following full conversion of its Debentures would be less than 10 percent of the class of equity stock then outstanding.

The Securities and exchange Commission contends that the general legal and financial usage of the word "class" compels the conclusion that Chemical Fund was subject to section 16, citing Ellerin v. Massachusetts Mut. Life Ins. Co., 270 F.2d 259 (2 Cir.1959). But this Court referred to the common meaning of "class" in that case because there was no prior case law, statutory history, or legislative definition to guide it. Here the purpose of section 16 to impose liability on the basis of actual or potential control is clear, and we should give it effect.

The Commission further argues that a holding that Chemical Fund did not hold more than 10 percent of any class of equity security would conflict with its long-standing administrative interpretation reflected in [Rule] 16–a–2, which sets forth the manner in which 10 percent ownership is to be determined and which refers specifically, *inter alia,* to "the class of voting trust certificates or certificates of deposit." As with a Convertible Debenture, it is solely the right to convert a voting trust certificate and certificate of deposit into a "stock or similar security" that brings these interests within the statutory definition of "equity security." The Commission's ruling may well be justified in that some of the most glaring instances of abuse prior to the passage of section 16 were committed through the use of stock pools and combinations, see, e.g., S.Rep. No. 792, 73d Cong., 2d Sess. 8–9 (1934), and voting trust certificates provide a vehicle for the exercise of actual control over a corporation by a relatively small block of common stock. But while the Commission's position may be tenable with respect to voting trust certificates, we are not persuaded that it should apply to Convertible Debentures, for the reasons we have stated. We note, however, that the Commission, apparently recognizing that unnecessary harshness would result from its own interpretation, took the further position that a class of voting trust certificates or certificates of deposit is deemed to consist not only of the voting trust certificates or certificates of deposit then outstanding, but of the total amount of certificates issuable with respect to the total amount of outstanding equity securities of the class which may be deposited under the voting trust agreement or deposit agreement, whether or not all of such outstanding securities have been so deposited. The size of the class is therefore necessarily related to the equity securities which underly it, as here we find the Convertible Debentures are related to the common stock of Xerox.

Lastly, the argument is made that Chemical Fund in substance admitted the applicability of section 16 when it filed Forms 3 and 4 with the Commission on September 17, 1963, after its directors were advised on August 14, 1963, that a possible question under the section existed, but did not file a disclaimer as permitted by [Rule] 16a–3, which expressly declares "that the filing of such statement shall not be construed as an admission that such person is, for the purposes of Section 16 of the Act, the beneficial owner of any equity securities covered by the statement." The short answer to this argument is that there was no dispute as to whether or not Chemical Fund was the beneficial owner of the securities in question. Failure to file such a disclaimer cannot fairly be read to dispose of the question of statutory interpretation presented in this case.

In view of our holding that Chemical Fund was not subject to section 16, we do not pass on the remaining issues raised by the parties.

We reverse the judgment of the district court and direct that summary judgment be entered in favor of Chemical Fund on its complaint and that the counterclaim be dismissed.

B. TRANSACTIONS GIVING RISE TO LIABILITY

If a person is found to fall within one of the categories covered by § 16, the next question is whether there has been a "purchase" and "sale." The exercise of an option or a conversion privilege, or the exchange of one security for another, either in a merger or a voluntary transaction, may or may not fall within the statute, depending on the circumstances.

BERSHAD v. McDONOUGH

428 F.2d 693 (7th Cir.1970).

Before SWYGERT, CHIEF JUDGE, CUMMINGS, CIRCUIT JUDGE, and GRANT, DISTRICT JUDGE.

CUMMINGS, CIRCUIT JUDGE.

This appeal is from a summary judgment in favor of the plaintiff, a common stockholder in the Cudahy Company of Phoenix, Arizona. Plaintiff brought this action under Section 16(b) of the Securities Exchange Act of 1934 to recover for Cudahy's benefit the "short-swing" profits coming to defendant from his and his wife's purchase and sale of 272,000 shares of Cudahy common stock.

On March 15 and 16, 1967, defendant Bernard P. McDonough and his wife Alma, who reside in Parkersburg, West Virginia, each purchased 141,363 shares of Cudahy common stock at $6.75 per share, totaling over 10% of the outstanding common stock of Cudahy. Soon after the purchase, McDonough was elected to the Cudahy Board of Directors and named Chairman of the Board. At the same time, Donald E. Martin and Carl Broughton, business associates of McDonough, were elected to the Cudahy Board.

On July 20, 1967, in Parkersburg, West Virginia, Mr. and Mrs. McDonough and Smelting Refining and Mining Co. ("Smelting") entered into a formal "option agreement" granting Smelting the right to purchase 272,000 shares of the McDonoughs' Cudahy stock. Smelting paid $350,000 upon execution of the agreement, which set the purchase price for the shares of $9 per share, or a total of $2,448,000. The option was exercisable on or before October 1, 1967. The $350,000 was to be applied against the purchase price but was to belong to the McDonoughs if Smelting failed to exercise the option. Accompanying this "option" was an escrow agreement under which the McDonoughs' 272,000 shares of Cudahy stock were placed in escrow with their lawyer. They also simultaneously granted Smelting an irrevocable proxy to vote their 272,000 shares of stock until October 1, 1967.

A day or two after the documents were signed, Mr. McDonough and Carl Broughton, his business associate, acceded to the request of Smelting and agreed to resign from the Cudahy Board if Smelting representatives were put on the Board. Both of them resigned as directors on July 25, 1967. About that time, five nominees of Smelting were placed on the Cudahy Board. Smelting subsequently wrote the McDonoughs on September 22, 1967, that it was exercising its option. The closing took place in Parkersburg five days later, with the $2,098,000 balance of the purchase price being paid to the McDonoughs through the escrow agent. From their sales, Mr. and Mrs. McDonough realized a profit of $612,000.

In the court below, defendant contended that under West Virginia law the July 20 agreement constituted an option contract with Smelting, and not a contract for the sale of the Cudahy stock. A stock option, he argued, does not qualify as a "sale or contract for sale" for purposes of applying the rule of Section 16(b) of the Securities Exchange Act of 1934. The district court, however, took another view of the transaction. In a thoughtful memorandum opinion, the trial judge looked beyond the formal wording of the July 20 "option" and concluded that the transaction between the McDonoughs and Smelting "amounted to a sale or a contract of sale" within the terms of the Securities Exchange Act. Since this event occurred less than six months after the McDonoughs had purchased the Cudahy stock, under Section 16(b) summary judgment for $612,000, together with interest, was entered for plaintiff. We affirm.

Section 16(b) was designed to prevent speculation in corporate securities by "insiders" such as directors, officers and large stockholders. Congress intended the statute to curb manipulative and unethical practices which result from the misuse of important corporate information for the personal aggrandizement or unfair profit of the insider. Congress hoped to insure the strict observance of the insider's fiduciary duties to outside shareholders and the corporation by removing the profit from short-swing dealings in corporate securities. Conversely,

Congress sought to avoid unduly discouraging bona fide long-term contributions to corporate capital. * * *

Under Section 3(a)(14) of the Act, the "sales" covered by Section 16(b) are broadly defined to include "any contract to sell or otherwise dispose of" any security. Construction of these terms is a matter of federal law, and "[w]hatever the terms 'purchase' and 'sale' may mean in other contexts," they should be construed in a manner which will effectuate the purposes of the specific section of the Act in which they are used. Applying this touchstone, courts have generally concluded that a transaction falls within the ambit of Section 16(b) if it can reasonably be characterized as a "purchase" or "sale" without doing violence to the language of the statute, and if the transaction is of a kind which can possibly lend itself to the speculation encompassed by Section 16(b).

The phrase "any purchase and sale" in Section 16(b) is therefore not to be limited or defined solely in terms of commercial law of sales and notions of contractual rights and duties. Applicability of this Section may depend upon the factual circumstances of the transaction, the sequence of relevant transactions, and whether the insider is "purchasing" or "selling" the security. By the same token, we conclude transactions subject to speculative abuses deserve careful scrutiny. The insider should not be permitted to speculate with impunity merely by varying the paper form of his transactions. The commercial substance of the transaction rather than its form must be considered, and courts should guard against sham transactions by which an insider disguises the effective transfer of stock.

The considerations thus guiding the application of Section 16(b) provide substantial support for coverage of an insider's sale of an option within six months of his purchase of the underlying security. The utility of various stock options as a tool of speculation is well recognized. As noted in Booth v. Varian Associates, 334 F.2d 1, 4 (1st Cir. 1964).

> "Options, conversions and similar devices have lent themselves quite readily to the abuses uncovered in the Congressional investigation antedating the Act, and in order to give maximum support to the statute courts have attempted to include these transactions by characterizing them as purchases or sales."

The insider's sale of options in his stock is well adapted to speculation and abuse of inside information whether or not the option is subsequently exercised. The sale of the right to purchase the underlying security is itself a means of realizing a profit from that security. The right to purchase stock at a given price under specified circumstances, although clearly not identical to the rights attendant upon ownership of the stock itself, derives from and is dependent upon the value of the underlying security. Sale of such purchase rights provides an easy vehicle for the use of inside information in extracting profits from the stock itself. Where the option is ultimately exercised, moreover, the exact date of exercise may be unimportant to the substance of the transaction from the point of view of the insider-vendor, since he can exploit his position in the corporation by setting the terms of sale in the option. In addition, parties frequently provide that the option price shall be considered a retroactive down payment of the purchase price of the stock sold upon exercise of the option. Under such circumstances, it may be reasonable to hold the parties to their own treatment of the transaction and date the "sale" of the stock at the purchase of the option rather than its exercise.

It is unnecessary, however, to rely solely upon these considerations to conclude that the McDonoughs' "sale" of the Cudahy stock to Smelting took place well in advance of the exercise of the option on September 22. The circumstances of the transactions clearly indicate that the stock was effectively transferred, for all practical purposes, long before the exercise of the option. The $350,000 "binder" ostensibly paid for the option represented over 14% of the total purchase price of the stock. Granting the magnitude of the sale contemplated, the size of the initial commitment strongly suggests that it "was not just a binder." The extent of that payment represented, if not the exercise of the option, a significant deterrent to the abandonment of the contemplated sale. In addition, the reverse side of the "Option Agreement" contained provisions for the transfer of the Cudahy stock, endorsed in blank, to an escrow agent pending completion of the transaction. At the same time, the McDonoughs delivered an irrevocable proxy to Smelting to vote the 272,000 shares at any regular or special shareholders' meetings. Within a few days, McDonough and one of his associate directors resigned and were replaced by representatives of Smelting's interests, including the Chairman of the Board of Directors of Smelting, and the president and director of that corporation. Significantly, only a few days after the expiration of the six-month period from the McDonoughs' purchase of the Cudahy stock, Smelting formally exercised its option and, on the same day that Smelting mailed its notification, the McDonoughs executed the necessary stock powers.

Defendant finally contends that these facts were insufficient to support the district court's grant of summary judgment in favor of plaintiff. We cannot accept this contention. The question in this case, unlike Blau v. Allen, 163 F.Supp. 702, 705 (S.D.N.Y.1958), involves the determination not of the existence of the sale, but the date to be ascribed to the transfer under Section 16(b). The basic facts in this case are undisputed and far exceed those present in Allen. We conclude that as a matter of law, the sale was effectively accomplished within the six-month period contemplated by Section 16(b). Consequently, the motion for summary judgment was properly granted.

Affirmed.

The acquisition and exercise of options, the acquisition and conversion of convertible securities, and the receipt of stock pursuant to employee stock option, bonus or purchase plans have all raised difficult questions under § 16(b). The SEC's new rules deal extensively with these questions and modify many of the pre-existing rules and interpretations.

Note on the Application of § 16(b) to Takeover Bids

The situation that has caused the greatest difficulty in recent years in the interpretation of § 16(b) has been that of the unsuccessful bidder in a takeover attempt. Assume the following situation:

Company A formulates a plan to take over Target Company. It starts off by acquiring more than 10% of Target's stock, either by block purchases, open market purchases, or a public tender offer, at an average price of $25 a share. Target management opposes the takeover attempt, and arranges a merger with Company B, under which Target shares are exchanged for securities of B having a market value of $30 a share. A does not own enough shares to block the merger, and it is consummated. A has no desire to hold securities of B (which may even be one of its major competitors), and sells them for $28 a share. The entire series of transactions takes place in a period of less than six months.

If the purchase which made A a 10% shareholder of Target can be matched against A's disposition of the Target shares in exchange for B shares on the merger, A has made a "profit" of $5 a share for § 16(b) purposes. Even if the merger is not considered a "sale", A may be considered to have made a profit of $3 a share when it sold the B shares which it acquired in exchange for its Target shares. To add insult to injury, the recovery under § 16(b), which would normally have gone to Target Company, goes to Company B, which has succeeded to all of Target's rights under the merger. B is thus able to obtain A's holdings of Target shares at A's cost, rather than at the higher price it offered other Target shareholders in order to "top" A's bid.

This possibility is more than theoretical. In 1970, the Second Circuit held (in a case involving an arranged merger of two controlled companies, rather than an unsuccessful takeover bid) that the purchase which made a person a 10% shareholder could be matched against a subsequent sale, and that the disposition of shares in a merger was a "sale" because it involved the surrender of an interest in one enterprise in exchange for a smaller percentage interest in the combined enterprise.[a] The defendant in that case was held liable for "profits" of more than $7,900,000. NEWMARK v. RKO GENERAL, 425 F.2d 348 (2d Cir.1970).

a. In an earlier decision, Blau v. Lamb, 363 F.2d 507 (2d Cir.1966), the court had held that the conversion of convertible preferred stock into common stock was not a "sale" for § 16(b) purposes because of the "economic equivalence" between the shares of common stock he received and the shares of convertible preferred stock he surrendered. In *Newmark,* the court distinguished Blau v. Lamb on the ground that the shares in the merged company were not the economic equivalent of the shares in the constituent companies.

The situation of the unsuccessful takeover bidder was clearly not the kind of "abuse" Congress had in mind in enacting § 16(b). One such company importuned the SEC to adopt a rule exempting "forced mergers" from the definition of "sale" pursuant to its power to exempt transactions "not comprehended within the purpose" of the section.[b] The SEC, however, concerned about the scope and possible consequences of such a rule, declined.[c]

The first unsuccessful takeover case to reach the Supreme Court was RELIANCE ELECTRIC CO. v. EMERSON ELECTRIC CO., 404 U.S. 418 (1972). Emerson had acquired 13.2% of the stock of Dodge Mfg. Co. in a tender offer. Dodge then arranged a defensive merger with Reliance. Before the merger was consummated, Emerson sold its Dodge stock. To minimize its possible § 16(b) liability, however, it sold the stock in two steps. First, it sold enough stock to reduce its holdings to 9.96%. Then, in the following month, it sold the remainder. It contended that the second sale did not give rise to liability because it was no longer a 10% shareholder at the time of that sale. The Court of Appeals accepted this argument, and the Supreme Court, in a 4–3 decision, agreed. The majority held that Emerson had met the technical requirements of the statute and that its intent to evade liability was irrelevant. The dissenters argued that "the spirit of the Act" required a presumption that such a "split sale" was part of a single plan of disposition for purposes of § 16(b) liability.

Ironically (in light of later events), Emerson could not raise in the Supreme Court the issue of whether it should be excused from liability altogether because it was not a 10% shareholder at the time it made its original purchase. The Court of Appeals, following the weight of precedent, had held that the purchase which makes a person a 10% shareholder can be matched against subsequent purchases, and Emerson, satisfied with having escaped three-quarters of its potential liability through the split sale, did not appeal that portion of the decision.

A year after its decision in *Reliance,* the Supreme Court was faced with a more complicated situation in KERN COUNTY LAND CO. v. OCCIDENTAL PETROLEUM CORP., 411 U.S. 582 (1973). Occidental acquired more than 20% of the stock of Kern at a price of $83.50 a share pursuant to a tender offer. Kern opposed Occidental's bid and negotiated a merger with Tenneco. Occidental lacked the votes to block the merger, and its efforts to prevent the merger by litigation were unsuccessful. To protect itself against being locked into a minority position in Tenneco after the merger, Occidental negotiated an agreement with Tenneco giving Tenneco an option to buy the Tenneco shares which Occidental would receive in the merger, at a price of $105 a share. In an effort to avoid § 16(b) liability, the option could not be exercised by Tenneco until a date six months and one day after the completion of Occidental's tender offer. A $10 per-share nonrefundable down payment on the option was designed to assure that it would be in Tenneco's interest to exercise the option by paying the

b. SEC Rule 16b–7 does exempt certain mergers from § 16(b), but only if they are between a parent company and a subsidiary of which the parent previously owned more than 85% of the stock.

c. See Kern County Land Co. v. Occidental Petroleum Corp., 411 U.S. 582, 588–89 (1973).

remainder of the price as long as the market price of the shares did not drop below $95 a share. The merger was consummated, the option was exercised on schedule, and Tenneco then sued Occidental for its $17 million profit on the transaction.

The district court held that the grant of the option and the exchange of Kern shares for Tenneco shares on the merger were both "sales" under § 16(b), and ordered Occidental to disgorge its profit. The Court of Appeals for the Second Circuit held that neither the option nor the exchange was a "sale", and ordered summary judgment for Occidental. The Supreme Court, in a 6–3 decision, affirmed the Court of Appeals.

In reaching its decision, the Supreme Court used an interesting blend of the "pragmatic" and "objective" approaches to § 16(b).[d] With respect to the exchange of stock pursuant to the merger, the Court took the "pragmatic" approach that, while some merger transactions might give rise to § 16(b) liability, Occidental should not be held liable because of "the involuntary nature of [its] exchange" and because its "outside" position meant there was an "absence of the possibility of speculative abuse of inside information." With respect to the option, on the other hand, the Court took the "objective" position that, since Occidental could not force Tenneco to exercise the option if the stock price dropped below $95 a share, it had not obtained the assurance of profit that is normally incident to a "sale". Again, as in *Reliance,* the Supreme Court did not reach the question of whether the purchase that made Occidental a 10% shareholder could be matched against subsequent sales, since the Court of Appeals had decided the case in Occidental's favor on other grounds and had therefore deemed it unnecessary to decide that question.

A subsequent decision of the Court of Appeals for the Second Circuit carried the Supreme Court's *Kern County* approach a step further. AMERICAN STANDARD, INC. v. CRANE CO., 510 F.2d 1043 (2d Cir.1974), cert. denied 421 U.S. 1000 (1975), involved a contest for control of Westinghouse

d. The Supreme Court described the "objective" and "pragmatic" approaches in the following terms in footnote 26 to its *Kern County* opinion:

> Several decisions have been read as to apply a so-called "objective" test in interpreting and applying § 16(b). See, e.g., Smolowe v. Delendo Corp., 136 F.2d 231 (C.A.2), cert. denied, 320 U.S. 751 (1943); Park & Tilford v. Schulte, 160 F.2d 984 (C.A.2), cert. denied, 332 U.S. 761 (1947); Heli–Coil Corp. v. Webster, 352 F.2d 156 (C.A.3, 1965). Under some broad language in those decisions, § 16(b) is said to be applicable whether or not the transaction in question could possibly lend itself to the types of speculative abuse that the statute was designed to prevent. By far the greater weight of authority is to the effect that a "pragmatic" approach to § 16(b) will best serve the statutory goals. See, e.g., Roberts v. Eaton, 212 F.2d 82 (C.A.2), cert. denied, 348 U.S. 827 (1954); Ferraiolo v. Newman, 259 F.2d 342 (C.A.6, 1958), cert. denied, 359 U.S. 927 (1959); Blau v. Max Factor & Co., 342 F.2d 304 (C.A.9), cert. denied, 382 U.S. 892 (1965); Blau v. Lamb, 363 F.2d 507 (C.A.2, 1966), cert. denied, 385 U.S. 1002 (1967); Petteys v. Butter, 367 F.2d 528 (C.A.8, 1966), cert. denied, 385 U.S. 1006 (1967). For a discussion and critical appraisal of the various "approaches" to the interpretation and application of § 16(b), see Lowenfels, Section 16(b): A New Trend in Regulating Insider Trading, 54 Corn.L.Q. 45 (1969); Note, Stock Exchanges Pursuant to Corporate Consideration: A Section 16(b) "Purchase or Sale?," 117 U.Pa.L. Rev. 1034 (1969); Note, Reliance Electric and 16(b) Litigation: A Return to the Objective Approach?, 58 Va.L.Rev. 907 (1972); Gadsby & Treadway, Recent Developments Under Section 16(b) of the Securities Exchange Act of 1934, 17 N.Y.L.Forum 687 (1971).

Air Brake Co. After Crane had acquired 32% of Air Brake's stock, Air Brake, over Crane's objections, was merged into Standard and Crane became an unwilling holder of more than 10% of a new class of convertible preferred stock of Standard, its major competitor in the plumbing business. Crane promptly sold the Standard preferred stock for about $10 million more than it had paid for the Air Brake stock. The Second Circuit held that Crane was not liable under § 16(b). First, the exchange of stock pursuant to the merger was not a "sale" of the Air Brake stock, under the reasoning of the Supreme Court in *Kern County.* Second, if the merger exchange was not a sale of the Air Brake stock, it would be "anomalous" to hold that it was a purchase of the Standard stock that could be matched against the subsequent sale of that stock. Third, the sale of Standard stock could not be matched against the purchase of Air Brake stock because they were not securities of the same "issuer", as provided in the language of the statute.

In 1976, the issue that had evaded review finally came before the Supreme Court. In FOREMOST–McKESSON v. PROVIDENT SECURITIES CO., 423 U.S. 232 (1976), which involved not a takeover but the purchase and resale of a large block of convertible debentures, the Supreme Court construed the provision exempting transactions by 10% shareholders who were "not such both at the time of the purchase and sale, or the sale and purchase," as meaning that the purchase which makes a person a 10% shareholder cannot be matched against a subsequent sale to establish liability. The Court found support for its construction of the statute in

> the distinction Congress recognized between short-term trading by mere stockholders and such trading by directors and officers. The legislative discourse revealed that Congress thought that all short-swing trading by directors and officers was vulnerable to abuse because of their intimate involvement in corporate affairs. But trading by mere stockholders was viewed as being subject to abuse only when the size of their holdings afforded the potential for access to corporate information. These different perceptions simply reflect the realities of corporate life.
>
> It would not be consistent with this perceived distinction to impose liability on the basis of a purchase made when the percentage of stock ownership requisite to insider status had not been acquired. To be sure, the possibility does exist that one who becomes a beneficial owner by a purchase will sell on the basis of information attained by virtue of his newly acquired holdings. But the purchase itself was not one posing dangers that Congress considered intolerable, since it was made when the purchaser owned no shares or less than the percentage deemed necessary to make one an insider. Such a stockholder is more analogous to the stockholder who never owns more than 10% and thereby is excluded entirely from the operation of § 16(b), than to a director or officer whose every purchase and sale is covered by the statute. While this reasoning might not compel our construction of the exemptive provision, it explains why Congress may have seen fit to draw the line it did. Cf. Adler v. Klawans, 267 F.2d 840, 845 (C.A.2 1959).

Does this distinction make sense? If § 16(b) should not be applied to a 10% stockholder in this situation, why should it be applied to a person who purchases stock, then becomes a director, then sells (the situation in Adler v. Klawans, discussed at p. 423 above)?

The *Foremost* rule also raises problems when applied to the situation of a sale followed by a repurchase, to which the exception is, by its terms, equally applicable. Assume that a holder of more than 10% of a company's shares learns, by virtue of his position, that the company is about to suffer a serious reverse. He sells his entire holdings, then buys back an equivalent number of shares at a much lower price after the company's reverses are publicly disclosed. This would seem to be precisely the kind of situation § 16(b) was intended to reach. The Court in *Foremost* was careful to limit its holding to the situation of a purchase followed by a sale, but a distinction is hard to draw under the language of the statute.

The *Reliance–Kern County–Foremost* line of cases has certainly solved the problems of defeated takeover bidders (perhaps even oversolved them). In the course of deciding *Reliance* and *Kern County,* however, the Supreme Court made a lot of law that is probably undesirable in the general administration of § 16(b) and turned out to be largely unnecessary in light of the subsequent decision in *Foremost.* Indeed, the holding in *Reliance* weakens the protection which the *Foremost* rule provides for takeover bidders. Where they acquire more than 10% of a company's stock in a series of prearranged transactions, they would like to argue for *Foremost* purposes that the entire series of transactions was the "purchase" that made them 10% shareholders. But *Reliance,* by implication, forecloses that argument and would expose them to liability on all transactions after they had reached the 10% level.

There is an alternative approach to the "timing" problem, which would be more consonant with the philosophy of § 16(b). The thrust of that section is to prevent someone from taking advantage of presumed access to inside information by engaging in a *matched* purchase and sale, or sale and purchase. The only person who can take such advantage is one who was in the prescribed status *prior to the first of the two transactions.* The solution, therefore, is to provide that a person subject to liability—whether an officer, director or 10% shareholder—is liable only if he engages in a purchase and sale, or sale and purchase, within a six-month period during which he occupied the prescribed status prior to the first of the two transactions. This would resolve the unsuccessful takeover problem (subject to the complication created by the *Reliance* decision) as well as the *Levy v. Seaton* problem described at p. 426 above.

It would also facilitate resolution of the problem of a director of a merged company who sells the stock of the surviving company which he receives in the merger. In GOLD v. SLOAN, 486 F.2d 340 (4th Cir.1973), defendant Scurlock was a director of Atlantic and owned about 20% of its common stock. He was on bad terms with Atlantic's management, and took no part in the negotiations which led to a merger of Atlantic into Susquehanna. As a director of Atlantic, however, he voted in favor of the merger, which was approved by a 4–3 vote of the Atlantic directors. Pursuant to the terms of the merger agreement, he became a director of

Susquehanna upon consummation of the merger, in addition to receiving Susquehanna stock in exchange for his Atlantic stock. Within six months after the merger, while still a director of Susquehanna, he made cash sales of Susquehanna stock in the open market.

In an action under § 16(b) to recover Scurlock's profit on the acquisition and sale of Susquehanna stock, the court of appeals held, 2–1, that he was not liable because his acquisition was not a "purchase." The majority felt that, under the Supreme Court's decision in the *Kern County* case, the merger was not a "purchase" on Scurlock's part because he did not take part in the negotiations and had no access to inside information about the terms of the merger. (The court held unanimously that the chief executive officer of Atlantic, who had conducted the merger negotiations on behalf of Atlantic and was also a defendant in the action, had "purchased" the Susquehanna stock he received in the merger, and was liable for the profit on a subsequent sale within six months.) The dissenting judge argued that Scurlock's lack of access to inside information prior to the merger was irrelevant, since he was a director of Susquehanna from the time of the merger until the time of his sale, and therefore was presumed under the statute to have access to inside information about Susquehanna which he could utilize in timing his *sales.* The dissenter felt that the limitation imposed by the Supreme Court in *Kern County* was appropriate there because the merger was a "closing disposition" of defendant's stock, while in this case the merger was an "opening acquisition."

An additional obstacle to § 16(b) actions in takeover situations is that there may not be any shareholder with standing to sue. Assume that Company A is merged into Company B, and that D was an officer, director or 10% shareholder of Company A who had acquired his A shares less than six months before the merger and disposed of them at a profit. After the merger, there are no longer any A shareholders. Can a shareholder of B bring suit under § 16(b) on B's behalf? In NEWMARK v. RKO, 425 F.2d 348 (2d Cir.1970), the Second Circuit held that a B shareholder could sue in this situation, even though she had never been a shareholder of A. Decisions in two other circuits have gone the other way. In PORTNOY v. KAWECKI, 607 F.2d 765 (7th Cir.1979), the court held that while A's right of action would vest in B, a shareholder of B was not a shareholder of the "issuer" of the securities in which D traded, and therefore lacked standing. And in LEWIS v. McADAM, 762 F.2d 800 (9th Cir.1985), a case in which A was merged into a wholly-owned subsidiary of B, the court held that a shareholder of B lacked standing because he was not even a shareholder of the company which had succeeded to A's rights. However, in MENDELL v. GOLLUST, 909 F.2d 724 (2d Cir.1990), the Second Circuit adhered to its position that a shareholder does not lose standing in this situation.

The new rules initially proposed by the SEC in 1988 would have extended standing to former beneficial owners who were compelled to dispose of their securities because of a business combination resulting in the issuer's becoming a non-reporting company (i.e., a wholly-owned subsidiary of another company). The Commission was concerned that otherwise "potential § 16(b) defendants in the acquired companies are shielded from liability, unless the parent decides to sue the former insiders of its subsidiary," which would "undercut the policing function played by shareholders in § 16(b) actions." However, in its 1989 revised proposal, the Commission, without explanation, drew back from this position and proposed instead that standing should extend only to former security holders who had filed suit before surrendering their securities. In the typical situation in which the "sale" by the insider occurs at the time the company ceases to be publicly-held, who will play the "policing function" with which the Commission was concerned in its 1988 release?

TEXAS INT'L AIRLINES v. NATIONAL AIRLINES

714 F.2d 533 (5th Cir.1983).

Before GARZA, POLITZ and JOHNSON, CIRCUIT JUDGES.

JOHNSON, CIRCUIT JUDGE: Texas International (TI) appeals the grant of summary judgment for National Airlines (National) holding TI liable to National under section 16(b) of the Securities Exchange Act of 1934 (the Exchange Act) for the "short swing profits" made on the sale of 121,000 shares of National common stock.

* * *

The three factors which trigger section 16(b) liability were all present—TI was a ten percent beneficial owner of National that purchased and sold National stock within a six-month period. The district court, therefore, found TI subject to automatic section 16(b) liability to National for the short swing profits TI made on the sale. On appeal, TI argues that equity bars any recovery by National and, in the alternative, that proof of "nonaccess" to inside information should be decisive in a section 16(b) inquiry. This Court affirms the grant of summary judgment for National.

On March 14, 1979, during an attempt by TI to gain control of National, TI purchased 121,000 shares of National common stock in open market brokerage transactions. On March 14, the date of the purchase, TI was a beneficial owner of more than ten percent of National's common stock. On July 28, 1979, within six months of the March 14 purchase, TI and Pan American World Airways, Inc. (Pan Am) entered into a stock purchase agreement whereby TI agreed to sell 790,700 shares of National common stock to Pan Am at $50 per share. The closing was held on July 30, 1979. Under the matching rules of section 16(b) the 790,700 shares sold by TI on July 28, 1979 are deemed to include the 121,000 shares purchased by TI in March.

On September 6, 1978, National and Pan Am had entered into a merger agreement which provided for the merger of National into Pan Am contingent upon certain conditions and, in connection with the merger, for the exchange by Pan Am of not less than $50 in cash for each share of National common stock, other than the shares held by Pan Am. On May 16, 1979, National stockholders approved the merger agreement dated September 6, 1978, as amended. TI, as a National stockholder, stood to receive $50 per share for its National stock if and when the merger closed. For whatever reason, TI decided not to wait until the merger went through to negotiate for the disposition of its holdings to Pan Am. It was not until after the July 28, 1979 sale by TI of its National stock to Pan Am that the National–Pan Am merger was effectuated.

On August 2, 1979, only five days after TI sold its National stock to Pan Am, TI sought declaratory relief that it was not liable to National under section 16(b) for profits realized on the purchase and sale of National common stock. In the alternative, TI sought to reduce its short swing profits by deducting expenses it allegedly incurred in connection with the purchase and sale of its National stock. On September 26, 1979, National counterclaimed, seeking recovery of TI's short swing profits under section 16(b). National moved for summary judgment on November 24, 1980.

On May 11, 1981, the district court granted National's motion in part, finding that TI's purchase and sale of the 121,000 shares of National stock constituted a violation of section 16(b). The district court squarely rejected TI's contention that the control contest situation rendered the transaction at issue "unorthodox" within the meaning of Kern County Land Co. v. Occidental Petroleum Corp. In reaching its conclusion that TI was liable under section 16(b), the district court stated that no court has exempted the type of transaction at issue here—a cash-for-stock transaction—from the automatic application of section 16(b).

* * *

On May 10, 1982, the district court issued its final judgment, dismissing TI's complaint for declaratory judgment and awarding National the sum of $1,149,195 on its counterclaim, together with prejudgment interest and costs.

* * *

TI urges this Court to create an exception to automatic section 16(b) liability in cases where a defendant can prove that, notwithstanding its ownership of over ten percent of the stock of the issuer, the defendant had no access to inside information concerning the issuer. According to TI, the classic example of such a case is a sale of stock in the hostile takeover context. Application of section 16(b) in this type of case, argues TI, does not serve congressional goals—Congress intended short-swing profits to be disgorged only when the particular transaction serves as a vehicle for the realization of these profits based upon access to inside information.

TI's argument is unsupported by the legislative history of section 16(b). Although the abuse Congress sought to curb was speculation by stockholders with inside information, "the only method Congress deemed effective to curb the evils of insider trading was a *flat rule* taking the profits out of a *class of transactions* in which the possibility of abuse was believed to be intolerably great." In explaining the necessity for a "crude rule of thumb" to Congress, Thomas Corcoran, a principal draftsman of the Act, stated: "You have to have a general rule. In particular transactions it might work a hardship, but those transactions that are a hardship represent the sacrifice to the necessity of having a general rule." The Supreme Court explained the necessity for the flat rule or "objective approach" of the statute in Reliance Electric Company v. Emerson Electric Company, *quoting Bershad v. McDonough,* 428 F.2d 693, 696 (7th Cir.1970):

> In order to achieve its goals, Congress chose a relatively arbitrary rule capable of easy administration. The objective standard of Section 16(b) imposes strict liability upon substantially all transactions occurring within the statutory time period, regardless of the intent of the insider or the existence of actual speculation. This approach maximized the ability of the rule to eradicate speculative abuses by reducing difficulties in proof. Such arbitrary and sweeping coverage was deemed necessary to insure the optimum prophylactic effect.

* * *

This Court is in agreement with the statements of legislative purpose as expressed by the Supreme Court in *Emerson Electric* and *Kern County*—the mechanical application of section 16(b) to the specified class of transactions is necessary in order to guarantee that the abuse at which the statute is aimed will be effectively curbed.

In *Kern County* the Supreme Court approved an extremely narrow exception to the objective standard of section 16(b). The Court held that when a transaction is "unorthodox" or "borderline," the courts should adopt a pragmatic approach in imposing section 16(b) liability which considers the opportunity for speculative abuse, i.e., whether the statutory "insider" had or was likely to have access to inside information.

TI engages in an analogy between the hostile and adversary situation that existed between the target company and the putative insider in *Kern County* and the adversary relationship between TI and National in the instant case. Even assuming the alleged parallelism between the adversary situations in the two cases and assuming that TI could prove that it neither had nor was likely to have access to inside information by virtue of its statutory "insider" status, no valid basis for an exception to section 16(b) liability on these facts is perceived. The Supreme Court in *Kern County* inquired into whether the transaction had the potential for abuse of inside information only because the transaction fell under the rubric of "unorthodox" or "borderline." In *Kern County,* Occidental, a shareholder in Kern County Land Company (Old Kern) converted its shares in Old Kern into shares of the acquiring corporation pursuant to a merger. The Supreme Court clearly distinguished the unorthodox transaction—a conversion of securities—before it from the traditional cash-for-stock transaction in the instant case: "traditional cash-for-stock transactions * * * are clearly within the purview of § 16(b)."

TI lays frontal attack on the unorthodox transaction test as fundamentally flawed, principally because the form of consideration received—cash or stock—has nothing to do with whether inside information was or might have been used. What this attack fails to consider, however, is the significance of the factor of voluntariness in the Supreme Court's decision. The Court's sole concern was not that cash-for-stock sales present a greater opportunity for abuse of inside information than do stock-for-stock sales. Rather, language in the Supreme Court's opinion indicates that traditional cash-for-stock sales were excluded from the concept of unorthodox transactions because of their voluntary nature;

> The critical fact is that the exchange took place and was required pursuant to a merger * * *.
>
> Occidental could, of course, have disposed of its shares of Old Kern for cash before the merger was closed. Such an act would have been a section 16(b) sale and would have left Occidental with a prima facie section 16(b) liability * * *. But the *involuntary nature* of Occidental's exchange, when coupled with the absence of the possibility of speculative abuse of inside information, convinces us that section 16(b) should not apply to transactions such as this one.

In the instant case, TI voluntarily entered into the stock purchase agreement with Pan Am before the National–Pan Am merger was effectuated. Despite the alleged lack of access to inside information and therefore the possibility of speculative abuse, the volitional character of the exchange is sufficient reason to trigger applicability of the language of section 16(b). For whatever reason, after the National–Pan Am merger had been approved, TI decided to take the initiative for the course of subsequent events into its own hands rather than wait for the merger to become accomplished. These circumstances do not warrant the creation of an exception to automatic section 16(b) liability.

* * *

CONCLUSION

This Court finds no valid justification for deviation from the express terms of section 16(b) or the case law interpreting it. The judgment of the district court is affirmed.

GARZA, CIRCUIT JUDGE, dissenting: I respectfully dissent. The majority opinion is highly persuasive and its interpretation of Kern County Land Co. v. Occidental Petroleum Corp., is certainly consistent with the "weight" of the law as it exists.

However, due to the particular facts of this case I would extend the rationale of *Kern County,* supra.

Section 16(b) provides that a statutory insider must surrender to the issuing corporation any profit realized from the purchase and sale of an equity security of the issuer within a period less than six months.

The statute itself states that it was enacted "for the purpose of preventing the unfair use of information which may have been obtained by [a statutory insider] * * * by reason of his relationship to the issuer." The statute itself is a strict liability statute designed to deter insiders from exploiting information not generally available to others in order to secure quick profits.

In *Kern County,* supra, the Supreme Court recognized that the nature of certain "unorthodox" transactions were such that a narrow exception to the otherwise strict liability rule was permissible. The facts of this case, I believe, would bring it within that narrow exception to the otherwise strict liability rule.

Texas International (TI) correctly argues that there are many similarities between the present case and that presented to the Supreme Court in *Kern County.* The putative "insider" in both cases was a party seeking to institute a "hostile" takeover of the issuer. It is evident from the record in this case that in both cases the party seeking takeover had no "inside information" upon which it could obtain short swing profits. In both cases the statutory stockholder failed in its attempt to take over the target company. The Supreme Court recognized in *Kern County* that after the merger agreement was approved, Occidental had no choice but to take action to protect its own interest.

In this case TI moved to protect its own interest when it agreed to sell its stock to the takeover company, Pan American World Airways, Inc. (Pan Am), after it became apparent that TI had lost the takeover battle. Unfortunately for TI, the sale took place forty-eight days before the statutory period had run.

Admittedly, the forced merger present in *Kern County* distinguishes that case from the present one. However, the facts of this case present a scenario, which favors extension of the "unorthodox" exception.

Like Occidental, no one can argue that TI actually made use of inside information to obtain any short swing profits. The reason for the existence of § 16(b) is in no way promoted by its application to the present transaction. Furthermore, TI's sale of stock was to the parent corporation for the purpose of protecting its own interests and cooperating in the merger transaction which Pan Am was attempting to effectuate.

The record clearly evidences that at the time of the sale by TI to Pan Am, no present or past shareholders of National Airlines had in any way been monetarily damaged by TI's purchase and sale of stock. In fact, it can be argued that the attempted takeover of National by TI helped to increase the value of National Airlines' stock. TI did not receive a higher price for the stock than any other shareholder. *All* shareholders of National Airlines received $50 per share.

Application of § 16(b) in this case serves only to permit Pan Am to avoid that portion of its contract with TI in which it agreed to pay $50 per share. The award in this case is nothing more than a "windfall" to Pan Am as the successor of National Airlines.

There is language in *Kern County* which, at first glance, as held by the majority opinion, appears to foreclose TI's present argument. At one point in that opinion the court stated:

> *Although traditional cash-for-stock transactions* that result in a purchase and sale or a sale and purchase within the six-month statutory period *are clearly within the purview of § 16(b),* the courts have wrestled with the question of inclusion or exclusion of certain "unorthodox" transactions.

TI's sale was clearly a "cash-for-stock" transaction; however, the situation before us, like *Kern County,* involved a hostile takeover which failed. The "hostile" takeover situation is hardly the "traditional cash-for-stock sale" which § 16(b) was designed to encompass. Rather, it is more of a "borderline" or "unorthodox" transaction and the above language can arguably be used to support such a finding.

The majority opinion cites the following language in *Kern County:*

> Occidental could, of course, have disposed of its shares of Old Kern for cash before the merger was closed. Such an act would have been a § 16(b) sale and would have left Occidental with a prima facie § 16(b) liability. It was not, therefore, a realistic alternative for Occidental * * *.

in holding that this language forecloses TI's argument; however, it is unclear whether it would have made a difference to the Supreme Court if the disposition of shares had been to the takeover company or a third party.

I agree that if Occidental in *Kern County* or TI in this case had sold its shares after the merger agreement to a third party, § 16(b) would have been clearly implicated. On the other hand, such is not the case if the sale was to the takeover company itself and the statutory insider, TI, received no more than any other shareholder of the issuer. In the case before us, no potential for abuse would have arisen or could arise and it is unclear from the court's statement quoted above, if it was referring to a disposition of shares to a third party or to any party including the takeover company. My view is that the above language need not foreclose TI's argument. TI did what every other shareholder of National Airlines had to do and the fact that it did it forty-eight days before the six-month period expired should not work to the detriment of TI and as a windfall to Pan Am who bought the shares for the price stated in the merger agreement.

In summary then, I would hold that the "spirit" of *Kern County* suggests that in an "unorthodox" transaction as the one before us, where the policies of § 16(b) are in no way implemented (and in fact, where such rule permits a party to void an otherwise legal contract) liability against the statutory "insider" should not be enforced.

Under the facts of the case before us, the hostile takeover scenario is more closely analogous to the "unorthodox" transaction rather than the "traditional" cash-for-stock sale.

Under similar situations I would not make any distinction between a cash-for-stock and a stock-for-stock sale.

Accordingly, I would hold that § 16(b) was not applicable to TI and I would reverse the court below.

"Within Any Period of Less Than Six Months"

Liability is imposed under § 16(b) only when there is a purchase and sale "within any period of less than six months." What does that mean? If a person purchases stock on March 15, what is the first day on which she can sell without incurring liability? September 16? September 15? September 14? In STELLA v. GRAHAM–PAIGE, 132 F.Supp. 100 (S.D. N.Y.1955), the court defined the six-month period by taking the date on which the stock was purchased, finding the corresponding date six months later, and then subtracting one day to determine the date on which the six-month period terminates. In the above example, therefore, the six-month period would end on September 14, and the purchaser could sell on that date without incurring liability because that period would constitute exactly six months, not less than six months. In JAMMIES v. NOWINSKI, 700 F.Supp. 189 (S.D.N.Y.1988), the court was faced with a situation in which the defendant purchased stock on October 31 and sold it on the following April 29? Is he liable? (Problem: April has only 30 days; what is the "corresponding date"?)

"Profit Realized"

The "profit realized" is generally determined by subtracting the purchase price, plus related expenses, from the purchase price. However, where the sale or purchase is part of a larger transaction, there can be problems in ascertaining the "price," as the following case indicates:

HERRMAN v. STEINBERG

812 F.2d 63 (2d Cir. 1987).

Before KEARSE and ALTIMARI, CIRCUIT JUDGES, and STEWART, DISTRICT JUDGE.

STEWART, DISTRICT JUDGE:

The cross-appeals before us concern a new variable in the calculation of short swing profit subject to section 16(b) of the Securities and Exchange Act of 1934. * * *

Plaintiffs Jeffrey W. Herrmann and Linda J. Herrmann ("the Herrmanns") are stockholders who brought this action on behalf of Walt Disney Productions Corporation ("Disney") to recover profit realized on the sale of 100 Disney shares bought and sold within a six month period by defendants Saul P. Steinberg, Reliance Group Holdings, Inc., and Reliance Insurance Company (referred to collectively herein as "Reliance"). Reliance conceded below that it is liable under section 16(b) to Disney for short swing profits realized on the 100 shares. Both parties appeal the District Court's calculation of these profits.

BACKGROUND

Reliance began to acquire large amounts of Disney stock beginning in March 1984. By early May 1984, Reliance had become a beneficial owner of more than 10% of Disney's outstanding common stock, bringing Reliance within the ambit of section 16(b).[2] Reliance purchased an additional 100 shares of Disney stock on June 1, 1984, paying $6,460 ($64.50 per share, plus $10 in brokerage commissions). In its June 8, 1984 13D statement filed with the Securities and Exchange Commission—and in letters delivered that day to Disney's directors—Reliance announced its intention to take over Disney through a tender offer for additional Disney shares sufficient to increase its holdings to at least 49%. Reliance also reiterated its previously stated intention to seek the removal of Disney's directors through a proxy contest.

At some point, presumably before its June 8 announcement, Reliance formed a new corporation to carry out its tender offer. The new corporation required total financing of $1,525,000,000. Loan commitments were obtained by Reliance's investment bankers, Drexel Burnham Lambert Incorporated ("Drexel"), from various sources, and Reliance paid these sources fees in proportion to their various commitments. In addition, Reliance compensated Drexel for its financial services. Other costs incurred in anticipation of the tender offer included public relations, legal, and proxy solicitation expenses.

On the evening of June 8—the same day that Reliance announced its tender offer—Disney offered to buy back all of its stock held by Reliance. After some negotiating, the parties entered into an agreement on June 11, 1984, in which Reliance agreed to cancel its inchoate tender offer and sell its 4,198,333 shares of Disney stock for $297,367,926.40 ("purchase price"). In addition to the purchase price, Disney paid Reliance $28 million as reimbursement for expenses incurred in preparing for the aborted tender offer. Apparently, this $28 million was also rendered in part to reimburse Reliance for actual purchases of shares, as discussed below.

How to factor this $28 million into the calculation of Reliance's short swing profit is the central issue on appeal.

The district court found that the expenses reimbursed had been incurred by Reliance for its own benefit and thus were not "incidental" to the sale. The court stated that the transaction fell within a blanket rule that tender offer expenses are not deductible from short swing profit. Accordingly, the district court added the $28 million to the purchase price, arriving at a per share sale price of $77.50 per share.

2. The plaintiffs in this case do not dispute that the May 1, 1984 purchase of 1,000,000 shares that pushed Reliance over the 10% ownership threshold was a single block trade. Therefore, for the purposes of this case the only shares subject to section 16(b) are the 100 shares purchased after the May 1 transaction.

Multiplying this $77.50 by one hundred and subtracting from that amount the $6,460 paid by Reliance for the 100 shares, the court calculated that Reliance had realized $1,290 in short swing profit. A judgment in this amount was entered for the plaintiffs.

The Herrmanns assert that the $28 million (which they call a "greenmail kicker") should be considered profit solely on the 100 share transaction, and that the court below erred in assigning only a pro rata share of the $28 million to the purchase price of the 100 shares. The Herrmanns admit that it is difficult to ascertain exactly what Disney received in consideration for its $28 million. In the face of this uncertainty, they assert that the district court should have awarded all of the $28 million to Disney as short swing profit, erring on the side of maximum penalty for Reliance's excursion into "greenmail."

Reliance contends that the district court erred in ignoring the legal consequences of its conclusion that the $28 million was reimbursement for the abandoned tender offer. Reliance argues that short swing profit does not include payments made to reimburse a party for takeover expenses unless those expenses were incurred in the purchase and sale of stock violative of section 16(b). Since the proposed tender offer had nothing to do with the 100 shares subject to section 16(b), Reliance reasons, the tender offer did not help it realize illicit short swing profits.

We hold that the district court erred in its treatment of the $28 million. The district court did not find a sufficient connection between the $28 million and the purchase and sale of the shares subject to 16(b) to justify its inclusion of the $28 million in the calculation of short swing profits. However, when the district court examines on remand the role of the $28 million in the Disney–Reliance transaction, such a connection may be revealed. We vacate the judgment and remand for further fact finding on the question of damages.

DISCUSSION

We begin by breaking down the expenses "reimbursed" by Disney's $28 million payment into two types: expenses incurred in the actual purchase of shares and those incurred in the preparation of the abandoned tender offer. * * *

The evidence suggests that some of the $28 million was intended as reimbursement for expenses incurred in the actual purchase of shares. The June 11, 1984 agreement between Disney and Reliance describes the $28 million as "reimbursement of . . . estimated out-of-pocket costs and expenses incurred in connection with its *actual* and contemplated purchases of Shares." * * *

Non-incidental expenses incurred in purchasing section 16(b) stock are not deductible from short swing profits. We will describe how to include such expenses in the calculation of Reliance's short swing profits after discussing the proper treatment of the remaining portion of the $28 million: that portion that was reimbursement for expenses incurred in the abandoned tender offer ("tender offer reimbursement").

The district court apparently assumed that the tender offer reimbursement should be included in the short swing profits realized by Reliance because of the types of expenses being reimbursed. "[T]ender offer expenses that an unsuccessful bidder incurs for its own benefit, such as commitment fees, investment banking fees, public relations fees, and legal fees, are not deductible expenses." However, the cases cited by the district court in support of this proposition concern expenses that were incurred in buying the stocks that were subject to section 16(b). It was this close connection between the takeover expenses reimbursed and the purchase and sale violative of section 16(b) that was dispositive in Texas International Airlines v. National Airlines, Inc., 714 F.2d at 540–42 and Lane Bryant, Inc. v. Hatleigh Corp., 517 F.Supp. at 1202. Such a connection is not present in this case, where the money spent by Reliance on the abandoned tender offer did not yield a single share.

Yet it would be simplistic to divorce the abandoned tender offer completely from Disney's purchase of Reliance's holdings and hence from the realization of short swing profit that resulted from that purchase. A more realistic picture of the transaction is revealed when the focus is shifted from the nature of the expenses reimbursed to what Disney received in return for its money. Disney's objective in entering into negotiations with Reliance was to ward off its takeover threat. Success depended on neutralizing the two components of that threat: Reliance's substantial holdings of Disney stock and its announced tender offer. Reliance and Disney structured their agreement to make it appear that all Disney received in consideration for the $28 million was the end of one component of the takeover threat, i.e., the tender offer. However, this discrete treatment has an appearance of artificiality. When the relationship between the tender offer and Reliance's substantial stock holdings are examined on remand, the district court may determine that some portion of the $28 million was paid by Disney as consideration for Reliance's sale of its Disney shares.

While the record before us is incomplete, it is at least possible that Disney would not have paid $28 million to end Reliance's tender offer if Reliance had not also agreed to sell its Disney holdings. From Disney's standpoint, the takeover threat would not have disappeared if Reliance had agreed solely to withdraw its tender offer. Reliance could still have purchased Disney stock by other means, or it could have sold its entire block of shares to another suitor. On the other hand, it would make little sense for Reliance to go forward with a tender offer after having just sold its Disney holdings, amounting to approximately 11% of Disney's outstanding stock, to its takeover target. For these reasons, the district court may decide to attribute at least some portion of the tender offer reimbursement to Reliance's agreement to sell the company its shares.

On remand, the finder of fact must determine what portion of the tender offer reimbursement (if any) was paid by Disney as consideration for Reliance's sale of its Disney shares. This amount can be calculated by subtracting from $28 million the amount that Disney would have paid Reliance to withdraw the tender offer if Reliance had not also agreed to sell its substantial stock holdings. While the determination of this amount must await resolution at trial, it appears unlikely that Disney would ascribe no value to ending the tender offer. Disney's offer to negotiate appears to have come only after the tender offer announcement, suggesting that Reliance's sizable stock position alone was insufficient to bring Disney to the bargaining table. Moreover, ending the immediate tender offer threat—even for a short period—would have given Disney valuable time to prepare defenses to a takeover.

CONCLUSION

The decision of the district court is vacated and the case is remanded. On remand, the district court should add to the $297,367,926.40 purchase price paid by Disney: 1) any part of the $28 million that was reimbursement for expenses incurred in the actual purchase of shares and 2) that portion of the $28 million that was paid in consideration for Reliance's sale of its Disney holdings. As it did below, the district court should divide this amount by the total number of Disney shares sold by Reliance to Disney, resulting in a per-share purchase price. Multiplying this amount by 100 and subtracting the $6,460 that Reliance paid for the 100 shares subject to 16(b) will yield the short swing profit to be disgorged by Reliance.

Selected References

T. Hazen, Securities Regulation §§ 12.2–12.7 (2d ed. 1990).

Black & Barton, Section 16(b) of the Exchange Act: An Archaic Insider Trading Statute in Need of Reform, 12 Sec.Reg.L.J. 203 (1984).

Cohn, Stock Appreciation Rights and the SEC: A Case of Questionable Rulemaking, 79 Colum.L.Rev. 66–104 (1979).

Jacobs, An Analysis of Section 16 of the Securities Exchange Act of 1934, 32 N.Y.L.Sch.L.Rev. 209 (1987).

Lang & Katz, Section 16(b) and "Extraordinary" Transactions: Corporate Reorganizations and Stock Options, 49 Notre Dame Lawyer 705 (1974).

Ribstein, The Application of Section 16(b) to Tender Offers, 31 S.W.L.J. 503 (1977).

Wentz, Refining a Crude Rule: The Pragmatic Approach to § 16(b), 70 Nw. U.L.Rev. 221 (1975).

Comment, Short–Swing Profits in Failed Takeover Bids—The Role of Section 16(b), 59 Wash.L.Rev. 895 (1984).

Note, Mismatching Convertible Debentures and Common Stock Under Section 16(b), 1985 Duke L.J. 1057.

CHAPTER 4

THE JURISPRUDENCE OF THE "ANTIFRAUD" PROVISIONS

Some of the most important developments in federal securities law have come about through interpretation and elaboration of the "antifraud" provisions found in those laws—generalized prohibitions against such evils as "fraud or deceit" or "manipulative or deceptive devices or contrivances."

Provisions of this type are found in § 17 of the Securities Act of 1933, §§ 9, 10, 14 and 15 of the Securities Exchange Act of 1934, and § 206 of the Investment Advisers Act of 1940. Because § 10(b) of the 1934 Act has the broadest jurisdictional reach, it is the provision most frequently invoked, but many of the doctrines developed under it are also applicable to the other sections and rules.

A. ELEMENTS OF A CLAIM UNDER RULE 10B–5

One of the most serious abuses in the securities markets on which Senate investigators focused in their 1933 hearings was the operation of "pools" which ran up the prices of securities on an exchange by series of well-timed transactions, then unloaded their holdings on the public just before the price dropped. Accordingly, §§ 9 and 10(a) of the 1934 Act prohibit a variety of manipulative activities with respect to exchange-listed securities, and § 10(b) contains a catch-all provision permitting the SEC to prohibit by rule any "manipulative or deceptive device or contrivance" with respect to any security.

Section 10(b) makes it unlawful for any person to use the mails or facilities of interstate commerce:

> "To use or employ, in connection with the purchase or sale of any security * * * any manipulative or deceptive device or contrivance in contravention of such rules and regulations as the Commission may prescribe as necessary or appropriate in the public interest or for the protection of investors."

Note that § 10(b) by its terms does not make anything unlawful unless the Commission has adopted a rule prohibiting it.

In 1942, the Commission was presented with a situation in which the president of a company was buying shares from the existing shareholders at a low price by misrepresenting the company's financial condition. While § 17(a) of the Securities Act of 1933 prohibited fraud and misstatements in the sale of securities, there was no comparable provision prohibiting such practices in connection with the purchase of securities. The SEC's Assistant Solicitor accordingly lifted the operative language out of § 17(a), made the necessary modifications, added the words "in connection with the purchase or sale of any security," and presented the product to the Commission as Rule 10b-5. The following excerpt describes the birth of the Rule.

REMARKS OF MILTON V. FREEMAN *

22 Bus.Lawyer 922 (1967).**

* * * [S]ince people keep talking about 10b-5 as my rule, and since I have told a lot of people about it, I think it would be appropriate for me now to make a brief statement of what actually happened when 10b-5 was adopted, where it would be written down and be available to everybody, not just the people who are willing to listen to me.

It was one day in the year 1943, I believe. I was sitting in my office in the S.E.C. building in Philadelphia and I received a call from Jim Treanor who was then the Director of the Trading and Exchange Division. He said, "I have just been on the telephone with Paul Rowen," who was then the S.E.C. Regional Administrator in Boston, "and he has told me about the president of some company in Boston who is going around buying up the stock of his company from his own shareholders at $4.00 a share, and he has been telling them that the company is doing very badly, whereas, in fact, the earnings are going to be quadrupled and will be $2.00 a share for this coming year. Is there anything we can do about it?" So he came upstairs and I called in my secretary and I looked at Section 10(b) and I looked at Section 17, and I put them together, and the only discussion we had there was where "in connection with the purchase or sale" should be, and we decided it should be at the end.

We called the Commission and we got on the calendar, and I don't remember whether we got there that morning or after lunch. We passed a piece of paper around to all the commissioners. All the commissioners read the rule and they tossed it on the table, indicating approval. Nobody said anything except Sumner Pike who said, "Well," he said, "we are against fraud, aren't we?" That is how it happened.

* * * I never thought that twenty-odd years later it would be the biggest thing that had ever happened. It was intended to give the Commission power to deal with this problem. It had no relation in the Commission's contemplation to private proceedings. How it got into

* Attorney and Assistant Solicitor, SEC, 1934-46.

private proceedings was by the ingenuity of members of the private Bar starting with the *Kardon* case. It has been developed by the private lawyers, the members of the Bar, with the assistance or, if you don't like it, connivance of the federal judiciary, who thought this was a very fine fundamental idea and that it should be extended. Recently we have seen among the people who have joined the private Bar in extending it the staff of the Securities Exchange Commission, and I think that this is something that you can think of as either a good thing or a bad thing.

Myself, I tend to think that judges do not extend principles that do not appeal to their basic sense of fairness and equity. I would be inclined to say that whether the development comes from a rule or from a congressional adoption, the result would be in broad outline approximately the same.

Since its adoption, Rule 10b–5 has been invoked in countless SEC and private proceedings, and applied to almost every conceivable kind of situation. It has spawned a formidable outpouring of legal scholarship, including two complete books and innumerable law review articles. But before examining systematically this body of jurisprudence of Rule 10b–5, it is necessary to have in mind certain basic features of the rule:

1. It applies to any purchase or sale by any person of any security. There are no exemptions. It applies to securities which are registered under the 1934 Act, or which are not so registered. It applies to publicly-held companies, to closely-held companies, to any kind of entity which issues something that can be called a "security." It even applies to "exempted securities", as defined in § 3(a)(12), (including federal, state and local government securities) which are specifically exempted from certain other provisions of the Act. Because of this broad scope, the rule may be invoked in many situations in which alternative remedies are made available (or are not made available) by applicable provisions of federal securities laws or state securities or corporation laws. Thus there is often a question as to the extent to which Rule 10b–5 should be available to by-pass procedural or substantive restrictions in other laws.

2. It is an "antifraud" provision. It was adopted by the SEC under authority of a section designed to prohibit "any manipulative or deceptive device or contrivance," and two of its three operative clauses are based on the concept of "fraud" or "deceit".

3. It is worded as a prohibition; except for the provisions of the Insider Trading Sanctions Act of 1984, see p. 624 below, there are no express provisions in the securities laws prescribing any civil liability for its violation. However, as far back as 1946, the courts took the position that they would follow the normal tort rule that a person who violates a legislative enactment is liable in damages if he invades an

interest of another person that the legislation was intended to protect. Kardon v. National Gypsum Co., 69 F.Supp. 512 (E.D.Pa.1946).

In the 1960's and early 1970's, many federal appellate courts and district courts developed expansive interpretations of Rule 10b–5 (and other antifraud provisions of the securities laws). They applied it to impose liability for negligent as well as deliberate misrepresentations, for breaches of fiduciary duty by corporate management, and for failure by directors, underwriters, accountants and lawyers to prevent wrongdoing by others. In private actions for damages, the courts were willing to imply a private right of action for anyone whose losses were even remotely connected with the alleged wrongdoing, or even in someone who had suffered no loss if his suit would help to encourage compliance with the law. The Supreme Court aided and abetted this development, giving an expansive reading to the terms "fraud" and "purchase or sale" and to the "connection" that had to be found between them.

Starting in 1975, a new conservative majority on the Supreme Court has sharply reversed this trend, in a series of decisions giving a narrow reading to the terms of Rule 10b–5 and other antifraud provisions, and limiting the situations in which a private right of action will be implied.

The tone of these recent Supreme Court decisions is even more important than their actual holdings. They cast doubt on the continued vitality of many of the expansive decisions of the preceding 15 years, even those that have not been specifically overruled. This fact should be kept in mind in evaluating the decisions which follow.

There are three separate clauses in Rule 10b–5, not arranged in a very logical order. Clauses (1) and (3) speak in terms of "fraud" or "deceit" while clause (2) speaks in terms of misstatements or omissions. It is generally assumed, however, that clause (3), which prohibits "any act, practice, or course of business which operates or would operate as (a) a fraud or deceit (b) upon any person (c) in connection with (d) the purchase or sale (e) of any security," has the broadest scope. Each of the elements of this formulation has given rise to interpretive questions, as illustrated by the following cases.

---

1. *"Fraud or Deceit"*

ERNST & ERNST v. HOCHFELDER

425 U.S. 185 (1976).

MR. JUSTICE POWELL delivered the opinion of the Court.

The issue in this case is whether an action for civil damages may lie under § 10(b) of the Securities Exchange Act of 1934 and Securities and Exchange Commission Rule 10b–5, in the absence of an allegation of intent to deceive, manipulate, or defraud on the part of the defendant.

I

Petitioner, Ernst & Ernst, is an accounting firm. From 1946 through 1967 it was retained by First Securities Company of Chicago (First Securities), a small brokerage firm and member of the Midwest Stock Exchange and of the National Association of Securities Dealers, to perform periodic audits of the firm's books and records. In connection with these audits Ernst & Ernst prepared for filing with the Securities and Exchange Commission (the Commission) the annual reports required of First Securities under § 17(a) of the 1934 Act. It also prepared for First Securities responses to the financial questionnaires of the Midwest Stock Exchange (the Exchange).

Respondents were customers of First Securities who invested in a fraudulent securities scheme perpetrated by Leston B. Nay, president of the firm and owner of 92% of its stock. Nay induced the respondents to invest funds in "escrow" accounts that he represented would yield a high rate of return. Respondents did so from 1942 through 1966, with the majority of the transactions occurring in the 1950's. In fact, there were no escrow accounts as Nay converted respondents' funds to his own use immediately upon receipt. These transactions were not in the customary form of dealings between First Securities and its customers. The respondents drew their personal checks payable to Nay or a designated bank for his account. No such escrow accounts were reflected on the books and records of First Securities, and none was shown on its periodic accounting to respondents in connection with their other investments. Nor were they included in First Securities' filings with the Commission or the Exchange.

This fraud came to light in 1968 when Nay committed suicide, leaving a note that described First Securities as bankrupt and the escrow accounts as "spurious." Respondents subsequently filed this action for damages against Ernst & Ernst [3] in the United States District Court for the Northern District of Illinois under § 10(b) of the 1934 Act. The complaint charged that Nay's escrow scheme violated § 10(b) and Commission Rule 10b–5,[4] and that Ernst & Ernst had "aided and abetted" Nay's violations by its "failure" to conduct proper audits of First Securities. As revealed through discovery, respondents' cause of

3. The first count of the complaint was directed against the Exchange, charging that through its acts and omissions it had aided and abetted Nay's fraud. Summary judgment in favor of the Exchange was affirmed on appeal. Hochfelder v. Midwest Stock Exchange, 503 F.2d 364 (C.A.7), cert. denied, 419 U.S. 875 (1974).

4. Immediately after Nay's suicide the Commission commenced receivership proceedings against First Securities. In those proceedings all of the respondents except two asserted claims based on the fraudulent escrow accounts. These claims ultimately were allowed in SEC v. First Securities Co., 463 F.2d 981, 986 (C.A.7 1972), cert. denied, 409 U.S. 880 (1973), where the court held that Nay's conduct violated § 10(b) and Rule 10b–5, and that First Securities was liable for Nay's fraud as an aider and abettor. The question of Ernst & Ernst's liability was not considered in that case.

action rested on a theory of negligent nonfeasance. The premise was that Ernst & Ernst had failed to utilize "appropriate auditing procedures" in its audits of First Securities, thereby failing to discover internal practices of the firm said to prevent an effective audit. The practice principally relied on was Nay's rule that only he could open mail addressed to him at First Securities or addressed to First Securities to his attention, even if it arrived in his absence. Respondents contended that if Ernst & Ernst had conducted a proper audit, it would have discovered this "mail rule." The existence of the rule then would have been disclosed in reports to the Exchange and to the Commission by Ernst & Ernst as an irregular procedure that prevented an effective audit. This would have led to an investigation of Nay that would have revealed the fraudulent scheme. Respondents specifically disclaimed the existence of fraud or intentional misconduct on the part of Ernst & Ernst.

After extensive discovery the District Court granted Ernst & Ernst's motion for summary judgment and dismissed the action. The court rejected Ernst & Ernst's contention that a cause of action for aiding and abetting a securities fraud could not be maintained under § 10(b) and Rule 10b–5 merely on allegations of negligence. It concluded, however, that there was no genuine issue of material fact with respect to whether Ernst & Ernst had conducted its audits in accordance with generally accepted auditing standards.

The Court of Appeals for the Seventh Circuit reversed and remanded, holding that one who breaches a duty of inquiry and disclosure owed another is liable in damages for aiding and abetting a third party's violation of Rule 10b–5 if the fraud would have been discovered or prevented but for the breach.[7] The court reasoned that Ernst & Ernst had a common-law and statutory duty of inquiry into the adequacy of First Securities' internal control system because it had contracted to audit First Securities and to prepare for filing with the Commission the annual report of its financial condition required under § 17 of the 1934 Act and Rule 17a–5. The Court further reasoned that respondents were beneficiaries of the statutory duty to inquire[9] and the related

7. In support of this holding, the Court of Appeals cited its decision in Hochfelder v. Midwest Stock Exchange, supra, where it detailed the elements necessary to establish a claim under Rule 10b–5 based on a defendant's aiding and abetting a securities fraud solely by inaction. See n. 3 supra. In such a case the plaintiff must show "that the party charged with aiding and abetting had knowledge of or, but for the breach of a duty of inquiry, should have had knowledge of the fraud, and that possessing such knowledge the party failed to act due to an improper motive or breach of a duty of disclosure." Id., at 374. The court explained in the instant case that these "elements constitute a flexible standard of liability which should be amplified according to the peculiarities of each case." 503 F.2d at 1104. In view of our holding that an intent to deceive, manipulate, or defraud is required for civil liability under § 10(b) and Rule 10b–5, we need not consider whether civil liability for aiding and abetting is appropriate under the section and the rule, nor the elements necessary to establish such a cause of action.

9. The court concluded that the duty of inquiry imposed on Ernst & Ernst under § 17(a) was "grounded on a concern for the protection of investors such as [respondents]," without reaching the question whether the statute imposed a "direct du-

duty to disclose any material irregularities that were discovered. The court concluded that there were genuine issues of fact as to whether Ernst & Ernst's failure to discover and comment upon Nay's mail rule constituted a breach of its duties of inquiry and disclosure, and whether inquiry and disclosure would have led to the discovery or prevention of Nay's fraud.

We granted certiorari to resolve the question whether a private cause of action for damages will lie under § 10(b) and Rule 10b–5 in the absence of any allegation of "scienter"—intent to deceive, manipulate, or defraud.[12] We conclude that it will not and therefore we reverse.

* * *

A

Section 10(b) makes unlawful the use or employment of "any manipulative or deceptive device or contrivance" in contravention of Commission rules. The words "manipulative or deceptive" used in conjunction with "device or contrivance" strongly suggest that § 10(b) was intended to proscribe knowing or intentional misconduct.

In its *amicus curiae* brief, however, the Commission contends that nothing in the language "manipulative or deceptive device or contrivance" limits its operation to knowing or intentional practices.[18] In support of its view, the Commission cites the overall congressional purpose in the 1933 and 1934 Acts to protect investors against false and deceptive practices that might injure them. The Commission then reasons that since the "effect" upon investors of given conduct is the same regardless of whether the conduct is negligent or intentional, Congress must have intended to bar all such practices and not just

ty" to the respondents. The court held that Ernst & Ernst owed no common-law duty of inquiry to respondents arising from its contract with First Securities since Ernst & Ernst did not specifically foresee that respondents' limited class might suffer from a negligent audit.

* * *

12. In this opinion the term "scienter" refers to a mental state embracing intent to deceive, manipulate, or defraud. In certain areas of the law recklessness is considered to be a form of intentional conduct for purposes of imposing liability for some act. We need not address here the question whether, in some circumstances, reckless behavior is sufficient for civil liability under § 10(b) and Rule 10b–5.

Since this case concerns an action for damages we also need not consider the question whether scienter is a necessary element in an action for injunctive relief under § 10(b) and Rule 10b–5.

18. The Commission would not permit recovery upon proof of negligence in all cases. In order to harmonize civil liability under § 10(b) with the express civil remedies contained in the 1933 and 1934 Acts, the Commission would limit the circumstances in which civil liability could be imposed for negligent violation of Rule 10b–5 to situations in which (i) the defendant knew or reasonably could foresee that the plaintiff would rely on his conduct, (ii) the plaintiff did in fact so rely, and (iii) the amount of the plaintiff's damages caused by the defendant's conduct was definite and ascertainable. The Commission concludes that the present record does not establish these conditions since Ernst & Ernst could not reasonably have foreseen that the financial statements of First Securities would induce respondents to invest in the escrow accounts, respondents in fact did not rely on Ernst & Ernst's audits, and the amount of respondents' damages was unascertainable. Respondents accept the Commission's basic analysis of the operative language of the statute and rule, but reject these additional requirements for recovery for negligent violations.

those done knowingly or intentionally. The logic of this effect-oriented approach would impose liability for wholly faultless conduct where such conduct results in harm to investors, a result the Commission would be unlikely to support. But apart from where its logic might lead, the Commission would add a gloss to the operative language of the statute quite different from its commonly accepted meaning. The argument simply ignores the use of the words "manipulative," "device," and "contrivance," terms that make unmistakable a congressional intent to proscribe a type of conduct quite different from negligence.[20] Use of the word "manipulative" is especially significant. It is and was virtually a term of art when used in connection with securities markets. It connotes intentional or willful conduct designed to deceive or defraud investors by controlling or artificially affecting the price of securities.[21]

* * * In view of the language of § 10(b) which so clearly connotes intentional misconduct, and mindful that the language of a statute controls when sufficiently clear in its context, further inquiry may be unnecessary. We turn now, nevertheless, to the legislative history of the 1934 Act to ascertain whether there is support for the meaning attributed to § 10(b) by the Commission and respondents.

B

Although the extensive legislative history of the 1934 Act is bereft of any explicit explanation of Congress' intent, we think the relevant portions of that history support our conclusion that § 10(b) was addressed to practices that involve some element of scienter and cannot be read to impose liability for negligent conduct alone.

* * *

Neither the intended scope of § 10(b) nor the reasons for the changes in its operative language are revealed explicitly in the legislative history of the 1934 Act, which deals primarily with other aspects of the legislation. There is no indication, however, that § 10(b) was intended to proscribe conduct not involving scienter. The extensive hearings that preceded passage of the 1934 Act touched only briefly on § 10, and most of the discussion was devoted to the enumerated devices that the Commission is empowered to proscribe under § 10(a). The most relevant exposition of the provision that was to become § 10(b) was by Thomas G. Corcoran, a spokesman for the drafters. Corcoran indicated:

20. Webster's Int'l Dictionary (2d ed. 1934) defines "device" as "[t]hat which is devised, or formed by design; a contrivance; an invention; project; scheme; often a scheme to deceive; a strategem; an artifice," and "contrivance" in pertinent part as "[a] thing contrived or used in contriving; a scheme, plan, or artifice." In turn, "contrive" in pertinent part is defined as "[t]o devise; to plan; to plot * * * [t]o fabricate * * * design; invent * * * to scheme * * *." The Commission also ignores the use of the terms "[t]o use or employ," language that is supportive of the view that Congress did not intend § 10(b) to embrace negligent conduct.

21. Webster's Int'l Dictionary, supra, defines "manipulate" as " * * * to manage or treat artfully or fraudulently; as to *manipulate* accounts * * *. 4. *Exchanges.* To force (prices) up or down, as by matched orders, wash sales, fictitious reports * * *; to rig."

"Subsection (c) [§ 9(c) of H.R. 7852—later § 10(b)] says, 'Thou shalt not devise any other cunning devices.' * * *

"Of course subsection (c) is a catchall clause to prevent manipulative devices. I do not think there is any objection to that kind of clause. The Commission should have the authority to deal with new manipulative devices."

* * *

It is difficult to believe that any lawyer, legislative draftsman, or legislator would use these words if the intent was to create liability for merely negligent acts or omissions. Neither the legislative history nor the briefs supporting respondents identify any usage or authority for construing "manipulative [or cunning] devices" to include negligence.

* * *

C

* * *

The Commission argues that Congress has been explicit in requiring willful conduct when that was the standard of fault intended, citing § 9 of the 1934 Act, which generally proscribes manipulation of securities prices. * * * From this the Commission concludes that since § 10(b) is not by its terms explicitly restricted to willful, knowing, or purposeful conduct, it should not be construed in all cases to require more than negligent action or inaction as a precondition for civil liability.

The structure of the Acts does not support the Commission's argument. In each instance that Congress created express civil liability in favor of purchasers or sellers of securities it clearly specified whether recovery was to be premised on knowing or intentional conduct, negligence, or entirely innocent mistake. For example, § 11 of the 1933 Act unambiguously creates a private action for damages when a registration statement includes untrue statements of material facts or fails to state material facts necessary to make the statements therein not misleading.

* * * The express recognition of a cause of action premised on negligent behavior in § 11 stands in sharp contrast to the language of § 10(b), and significantly undercuts the Commission's argument.

We also consider it significant that each of the express civil remedies in the 1933 Act allowing recovery for negligent conduct is subject to significant procedural restrictions not applicable under § 10(b). * * * [T]hese procedural limitations indicate that the judicially created private damage remedy under § 10(b)—which has no comparable restrictions—cannot be extended, consistently with the intent of Congress, to actions premised on negligent wrongdoing. Such extension would allow causes of action covered by § 11, § 12(2), and § 15 to be brought instead under § 10(b) and thereby nullify the effectiveness of the carefully drawn procedural restrictions on these express actions. We would be unwilling to bring about this result absent substantial support in the legislative history, and there is none.

D

We have addressed, to this point, primarily the language and history of § 10(b). The Commission contends, however, that subsections (2) and (3) of Rule 10b-5 are cast in language which—if standing alone—could encompass both intentional and negligent behavior. These subsections respectively provide that it is unlawful "[t]o make any untrue statement of a material fact or to omit to state a material fact necessary in order to make the statements made, in light of the circumstances under which they were made, not misleading * * *" and "to engage in any act, practice, or course of business which operates or would operate as a fraud or deceit upon any person. * * *" Viewed in isolation the language of subsection (2), and arguably that of subsection (3), could be read as proscribing, respectively, any type of material misstatement or omission, and any course of conduct, that has the effect of defrauding investors, whether the wrongdoing was intentional or not.

We note first that such a reading cannot be harmonized with the administrative history of the rule, a history making clear that when the Commission adopted the rule it was intended to apply only to activities that involved scienter. More importantly, Rule 10b-5 was adopted pursuant to authority granted the Commission under § 10(b). The rulemaking power granted to an administrative agency charged with the administration of a federal statute is not the power to make law. Rather, it is " 'the power to adopt regulations to carry into effect the will of Congress as expressed by the statute.' " Thus, despite the broad view of the Rule advanced by the Commission in this case, its scope cannot exceed the power granted the Commission by Congress under § 10(b). For the reasons stated above, we think the Commission's original interpretation of Rule 10b-5 was compelled by the language and history of § 10(b) and related sections of the Acts.

MR. JUSTICE BLACKMUN, with whom MR. JUSTICE BRENNAN joins, dissenting.

Once again—see Blue Chip Stamps v. Manor Drug Stores—the Court interprets § 10(b) of the Securities Exchange Act of 1934, and the Securities and Exchange Commission's Rule 10b-5, restrictively and narrowly and thereby stultifies recovery for the victim. This time the Court does so by confining the statute and the Rule to situations where the defendant has "scienter," that is, the "intent to deceive, manipulate, or defraud." Sheer negligence, the Court says, is not within the reach of the statute and the Rule, and was not contemplated when the great reforms of 1933, 1934, and 1942 were effectuated by Congress and the Commission.

Perhaps the Court is right, but I doubt it. The Government and the Commission doubt it too, as is evidenced by the thrust of the brief filed by the Solicitor General on behalf of the Commission, as *amicus curiae.* The Court's opinion, ante, to be sure, has a certain technical consistency about it. It seems to me, however, that an investor can be victimized just as much by negligent conduct as by positive deception, and that it is not logical to drive a wedge between the two, saying that Congress clearly intended the one but certainly not the other.

No one questions the fact that the respondents here were the victims of an intentional securities fraud practiced by Leston B. Nay. What is at issue, of course, is the petitioner-accountant firm's involvement and that firm's responsibility under Rule 10b–5. The language of the Rule * * * seems to me, clearly and succinctly, to prohibit negligent as well as intentional conduct of the kind proscribed, to extend beyond common law fraud, and to apply to negligent omission and commission. This is consistent with Congress' intent, repeatedly recognized by the Court, that securities legislation enacted for the purpose of avoiding frauds be construed "not technically and restrictively, but flexibly to effectuate its remedial purposes."

On motion for summary judgment, therefore, the respondents' allegations, in my view, were sufficient, and the District Court's dismissal of the action was improper to the extent that the dismissal rested on the proposition that suit could not be maintained under § 10(b) and Rule 10b–5 for mere negligence. The opposite appears to be true, at least in the Second Circuit, with respect to suits by the SEC to enjoin a violation of the Rule. I see no real distinction between that situation and this one, for surely the question whether negligent conduct violates the Rule should not depend upon the plaintiff's identity. If negligence is a violation factor when the SEC sues, it must be a violation factor when a private party sues. And, in its present posture, this case is concerned with the issue of violation, not with the secondary issue of a private party's judicially created entitlement to damages or other specific relief.

The critical importance of the auditing accountant's role in insuring full disclosure cannot be overestimated. The SEC has emphasized that in certifying statements the accountant's duty "is to safeguard the public interest, not that of his client." "In our complex society the accountant's certificate and the lawyer's opinion can be instruments for inflicting pecuniary loss more potent than the chisel or the crowbar." In this light, the initial inquiry into whether Ernst & Ernst's preparation and certification of the financial statements of First Securities Company of Chicago were negligent, because of the failure to perceive Nay's extraordinary mail rule, and in other alleged respects, and thus whether Rule 10b–5 was violated, should not be thwarted.

But the Court today decides that it is to be thwarted; and so once again it rests with Congress to rephrase and to re-enact, if investor victims, such as these, are ever to have relief under the federal securities laws that I thought had been enacted for their broad, needed, and deserving benefit.

The Supreme Court, in Note 12 to its opinion, left open two important questions: (1) whether "scienter" means an intent to deceive, or whether recklessness may suffice; and (2) whether scienter must be alleged in an SEC injunctive action under Rule 10b–5.

In a decision subsequent to *Hochfelder,* the Seventh Circuit held that "reckless" misrepresentation of earnings figures was sufficient to create civil liability under 10b–5. SUNDSTRAND CORP. v. SUN CHEMICAL CORP., 553 F.2d 1033 (7th Cir.1977). The court also held that a partner in an investment banking firm, who acted as a broker in the transaction and thereby acquired a "quasi-fiduciary" common law duty to disclose material facts relating to the proposed transaction, could be held civilly liable for "reckless omission of material facts upon which the plaintiff put justifiable reliance." The court defined "reckless" omission as "a highly unreasonable omission, involving not merely simple, or even inexcusable, negligence, but an extreme departure from the standards of ordinary care, and which presents a danger of misleading buyers or sellers that is either known to the defendant or is so obvious that the actor must have been aware of it." Id. at 1044, quoting from Franke v. Midwestern Okla. Development Authority, 428 F.Supp. 719 (W.D.Okla.1976). However, in a still later decision, the same court warned that "the definition of 'reckless behavior' should not be a liberal one lest any discerning distinction between 'scienter' and 'negligence' be obliterated for these purposes. We believe 'reckless' in these circumstances comes closer to being a lesser form of intent than merely a greater degree of ordinary negligence." SANDERS v. JOHN NUVEEN & CO., 554 F.2d 790 (7th Cir.1977). Recklessness has also been accepted as meeting the scienter requirement in other circuits. See HACKBART v. HOLMES, 675 F.2d 1114 (10th Cir.1982).

In McLEAN v. ALEXANDER, 599 F.2d 1190 (3d Cir.1979), the court held that the appropriate standard of scienter in a lawsuit against an accounting firm under Rule 10b–5 was "that the defendant lacked a genuine belief that the information disclosed was accurate and complete in all material respects." The court went on to say that "plaintiff need not produce direct evidence of the defendant's state of mind" but that circumstantial evidence, such as a "showing of shoddy accounting practices amounting at best to a 'pretended audit' " might suffice.

With respect to the question whether the SEC must establish that a defendant acted with scienter in order to obtain an injunction against him under Rule 10b–5, the Court held in AARON v. SEC, 446 U.S. 680 (1980), that "the rationale of *Hochfelder* ineluctably leads to the conclusion that scienter is an element of a violation of § 10(b) and Rule 10b–5, regardless of the identity of the plaintiff or the nature of the relief sought."

In the *Aaron* case, the SEC also alleged that the defendant had violated § 17(a) of the 1933 Act, from which the language of Rule 10b–5 is taken. With respect to that section, the Court held that scienter must be shown to establish a violation of § 17(a)(1), but not of § 17(a)(2) or (3). The Court found the language of § 17(a)(2) "devoid of any suggestion whatsoever of a scienter requirement," while § 17(a)(3) "focuses on the *effect* of particular conduct on members of the investing public, rather than the culpability of the person responsible." This decision means that the language of clause (3) of Rule 10b–5 has a different meaning than the comparable language in § 17(a)(3), lending additional significance to the (as yet unresolved) question whether there is any implied private right of action under § 17(a).

Selected References

T. Hazen, Securities Regulation § 13.4 (2d ed. 1990).

Berner & Franklin, Scienter and SEC, Rule 10b–5 Injunctive Actions: A Reappraisal in Light of *Hochfelder,* 51 N.Y.U.L.Rev. 769 (1976).

Bucklo, The Supreme Court Attempts to Define Scienter Under Rule 10b–5: Ernst & Ernst v. Hochfelder, 29 Stan.L.Rev. 213 (1977).

Cox, Ernst & Ernst v. Hochfelder: A Critique and an Evaluation, 28 Hastings L.J. 569 (1977).

Haimoff, Holmes Looks at *Hochfelder* and 10b–5, 32 Bus.Lawyer 147 (1976).

Milich, Securities Fraud Under Section 10(b) and Rule 10b–5: Scienter, Recklessness and the Good Faith Defense, 11 J.Corp.L. 179 (1986).

Thel, The Original Conception of Section 10(b) of the Securities Exchange Act of 1934, 42 Stan.L.Rev. 385 (1990).

---

2. *"Upon Any Person"*

HOOPER v. MOUNTAIN STATES SECURITIES CORP.

282 F.2d 195 (5th Cir.1960).

Before RIVES, CHIEF JUDGE, and CAMERON and BROWN, CIRCUIT JUDGES.

JOHN R. BROWN, CIRCUIT JUDGE.

In this civil action seeking relief for violation of § 10(b) of the Securities Exchange Act, and Rule X–10B–5 promulgated by the SEC, the principal question is whether a corporation misled by fraud in the issuance of its stock in return for spurious assets is a seller. Is the transaction a sale? The District Court on motion to dismiss the complaint thought not.

* * *

The argument against allowing recovery to a corporation issuing its own stock in exchange for a consideration, cash or property, runs somewhat this way. It is recognized that § 10(b) is not self-executing.

It only makes unlawful that which SEC forbids by "such rules and regulations as the Commission may prescribe as necessary or appropriate." But since the test of necessity or appropriateness is "the public interest or for the protection of investors," regulation X–10B–5 can give rise to a private right only in the event the "seller" or "purchaser" is an "investor." The forensic climax is that whatever else it might be, such an issuing corporation is not an investor.

But this argument is an artificial application of the concept that violation of a legislative standard gives those intended to be protected a private right of action provided the injury sustained is other than that suffered by the public generally. See, generally, Restatement of Torts, §§ 286–288. The SEC had ample power to promulgate this regulation. It had two bases—"in the public interest" or "for the protection of investors." Each fully justified the regulation. Its validity does not therefore depend on its being issued "for the protection of investors."

* * *

Certainly a person who parts with stock owned by him as the result of fraudulent practices wrought on him by his purchaser sustains an adverse impact that differentiates him from the damage suffered by the public generally. It is not essential, therefore, that for an issuing corporation to come under § 10(b) and Rule X–10B–5 it have the status of an "investor" as such.

Freed of any implied limitation of "investor" status, does such corporation otherwise come within the section and the rule?

Certainly the regulation uses language which would comprehend an issuing corporation. It makes it unlawful for "any person * * * to employ any * * * scheme * * * to defraud, to make an untrue statement * * * or, to engage in any act * * * which operates * * * as a fraud or deceit upon any person * * *." See note 3, supra. The Act supplies its own definition to make a "person" encompass "a corporation." § 3(a)(9). If an issuing corporation is not within the regulation, it is not because it is not a "person." This means, then, that to exclude it from X–10B–5 it must be because there is no "sale of any security" and hence the issuer is not a "seller." Again, the first hurdle encountered is the wording of the statute. In the plainest of language it provides that "the term 'security' means * * * any * * * stock * * * or right to * * * purchase * * * any [stock]." § (3)(a)(10). What Consolidated issued was its own stock certificates in the usual form. This stock was a security within the statute and regulation and was the subject of the transaction between Consolidated and Mid–Atlantic.

The effort to escape the impact of X–10B–5 finally boils down to the assertion that the transfer of this admitted security could not have been a "sale." As before, the statute is remarkably rich in the legislative determination of critical terms. The Act provides that "the terms 'sale' and 'sell' each include any contract to sell or otherwise dispose of." § 3(a)(14). Certainly the transactions between Consolidated and the apparent transferee, Mid–Atlantic, had many earmarks of a sale. Mid–Atlantic had properties which it ostensibly valued highly. It was willing to trade these properties as consideration for the Consolidated stock. Consolidated, on the other hand, had its own stock which had a marketability of $1 per share. To the corporation it had the same economic value as would the proceeds received from a public issue of like shares to acquire property which it desired and which it had been led to believe was valuable. Before the transaction Consolidated had 700,000 shares of stock. After the transaction it no longer had the stock, but it had, or thought it had, the property. If this is not a sale in the strict common law traditional sense, it certainly amounted to an arrangement in which Consolidated "otherwise dispose[d] of" its stock. § 3(a)(14).

* * * Considering the purpose of this legislation, it would be unrealistic to say that a corporation having the capacity to acquire $700,000 worth of assets for its 700,000 shares of stock has suffered no loss if what it gave up was $700,000 but what it got was zero. * * *

In UNITED STATES v. NAFTALIN, 441 U.S. 768 (1979), the Supreme Court upheld the criminal conviction under § 17(a)(1) of the 1933 Act of a "professional investor" who made "short sales" of stock while falsely representing to brokers that he owned the stock he directed them to sell. The defendant argued that § 17(a) applies only to frauds directed against investors, and not to those directed against brokers, who were the only victims of his actions. The Supreme Court held that the language of § 17(a)(1), prohibiting "any device, scheme, or artifice to defraud," does not indicate any such limitation, and that, while investor protection was a principal objective of the Act, Congress was also motivated by an effort "to achieve a high standard of business ethics in every facet of the securities industry" and a "desire to protect ethical businessmen."

---

3. "In Connection With"

SUPERINTENDENT OF INSURANCE v. BANKERS LIFE & CASUALTY CO.

404 U.S. 6 (1971).

MR. JUSTICE DOUGLAS delivered the opinion of the Court.

Manhattan Casualty Company, now represented by petitioner, New York's Superintendent of Insurance, was, it is alleged, defrauded in the sale of certain securities in violation of the Securities Act of 1933, and of the Securities Exchange Act of 1934. The District Court dismissed the complaint, and the Court of Appeals affirmed, by a divided bench.

It seems that Bankers Life, one of the respondents, agreed to sell all of Manhattan's stock to one Begole for $5,000,000. It is alleged that Begole conspired with one Bourne and others to pay for this stock, not out of their own funds, but with Manhattan's assets. They were alleged to have arranged, through Garvin, Bantel—a note brokerage firm—to obtain a $5,000,000 check from respondent Irving Trust, although they had no funds on deposit there at the time. On the same day they purchased all the stock of Manhattan from Bankers Life for $5,000,000 and as stockholders and directors, installed one Sweeny as president of Manhattan.

Manhattan then sold its United States Treasury bonds for $4,854,552.67.[1] That amount, plus enough cash to bring the total to $5,000,000, was credited to an account of Manhattan at Irving Trust and the $5,000,000 Irving Trust check was charged against it. As a result, Begole owned all the stock of Manhattan, having used $5,000,000 of Manhattan's assets to purchase it.

* * *

Manhattan was the seller of Treasury bonds and, it seems to us, clearly protected by § 10(b) of the Securities Exchange Act, which makes it unlawful to use "in connection with the purchase or sale" of any security "any manipulative or deceptive device or contrivance" in contravention of the rules and regulations of the Securities and Exchange Commission.

There certainly was an "act" or "practice" within the meaning of Rule 10b–5 which operated as "a fraud or deceit" on Manhattan, the seller of the Government bonds. To be sure, the full market price was paid for those bonds; but the seller was duped into believing that it, the seller, would receive the proceeds. We cannot agree with the Court of Appeals that "no investor [was] injured" and that the "purity of the security transaction and the purity of the trading process were unsullied."

Section 10(b) outlaws the use "in connection with the purchase or sale" of any security of "any manipulative or deceptive device or contrivance." The Act protects corporations as well as individuals who are sellers of a security. Manhattan was injured as an investor through a deceptive device which deprived it of any compensation for the sale of its valuable block of securities.

The fact that the fraud was perpetrated by an officer of Manhattan and his outside collaborators is irrelevant to our problem. For § 10(b) bans the use of any deceptive device in the "sale" of any security by "any person." And the fact that the transaction is not conducted through a securities exchange or an organized over-the-counter market is irrelevant to the coverage of § 10(b). Hooper v. Mountain States Securities Corp., 5 Cir., 282 F.2d 195, 201. Likewise irrelevant is the

1. Manhattan's Board of Directors was allegedly deceived into authorizing this sale by the misrepresentation that the proceeds would be exchanged for a certificate of deposit of equal value.

fact that the proceeds of the sale that were due the seller were misappropriated. As the Court of Appeals for the Fifth Circuit said in the *Hooper* case, "considering the purpose of this legislation, it would be unrealistic to say that a corporation having the capacity to acquire $700,000 worth of assets for its 700,000 shares of stock has suffered no loss if what it gave up was $700,000 but what it got was zero." 282 F.2d, at 203.

The Congress made clear that "disregard of trust relationships by those whom the law should regard as fiduciaries, are all a single seamless web" along with manipulation, investor's ignorance, and the like. H.R.Rep. No. 1383, 73d Cong., 2d Sess., p. 6. Since practices "constantly vary and where practices legitimate for some purposes may be turned to illegitimate and fraudulent means, broad discretionary powers" in the regulatory agency "have been found practically essential." Id., at 7. Hence we do not read § 10(b) as narrowly as the Court of Appeals; it is not "limited to preserving the integrity of the securities markets" (430 F.2d, at 361), though that purpose is included. Section 10(b) must be read flexibly, not technically and restrictively. Since there was a "sale" of a security and since fraud was used "in connection with" it, there is redress under § 10(b), whatever might be available as a remedy under state law.

We agree that Congress by § 10(b) did not seek to regulate transactions which comprise no more than internal corporate mismanagement. But we read § 10(b) to mean that Congress meant to bar deceptive devices and contrivances in the purchase or sale of securities whether conducted in the organized markets or face-to-face. And the fact that creditors of the defrauded corporate buyer or seller of securities may be the ultimate victims does not warrant disregard of the corporate entity. The controlling stockholder owes the corporation a fiduciary obligation—one "designed for the protection of the entire community of interests in the corporation—creditors as well as stockholders." Pepper v. Litton, 308 U.S. 295.

The crux of the present case is that Manhattan suffered an injury as a result of deceptive practices touching its sale of securities as an investor. As stated in Shell v. Hensley, 430 F.2d 819, 827 (5th Cir. 1970):

> "When a person who is dealing with a corporation in a securities transaction denies the corporation's directors access to material information known to him, the corporation is disabled from availing itself of an informed judgment on the part of its board regarding the merits of the transaction. In this situation the private right of action recognized under Rule 10b–5 [9] is available as a remedy for the corporate disability."

9. It is now established that a private right of action is implied under § 10(b). See 6 L.Loss, Securities Regulation 3869–73 (1969 Supp.); 3 L.Loss, Securities Regulation 1763 et seq. 1961). Cf. Tcherepnin v. Knight, 389 U.S. 332; J.I. Case v. Borak, 377 U.S. 426.

In its opinion affirming the dismissal of the complaint, the Court of Appeals had stated:

> What distinguishes the fraud perpetrated on Manhattan in this case from one cognizable under Rule 10b-5 is that the sole object was to obtain possession of Manhattan's government bonds for the personal use of the perpetrators. No doubt the deception was successful, for had the board known that Sweeny and his associates intended to misappropriate the proceeds for their own use it undoubtedly would not have authorized their sale. But that deception did not infect the subsequent sales transaction. With respect to the terms of the sale itself neither the purchaser nor the seller of the bonds was deceived or defrauded.

Does the Supreme Court adequately answer this point? Is it a violation of Rule 10b-5 when an officer of a corporation steals securities which he has caused the corporation to purchase? What if the corporation gives him money to purchase securities, but he steals the money and never purchases the securities? See Superintendent of Ins. v. Freedman, 443 F.Supp. 628 (S.D.N.Y.1977).

In KETCHUM v. GREEN, 557 F.2d 1022 (3d Cir.1977), the court held that alleged fraud in procuring plaintiffs' votes for the election of directors was not "in connection with" the redemption of plaintiffs' shares after the directors had removed them as officers of the corporation. Other courts have also read the clause restrictively, holding that misappropriation of corporate funds which occurs some time after the funds were received from a sale of securities is not "in connection with" the sale. In re Investors Funding, 523 F.Supp. 533 (S.D.N.Y.1980); Rochelle v. Marine Midland, 535 F.2d 523 (9th Cir.1976).

In SEC v. TEXAS GULF SULPHUR, 401 F.2d 833 (2d Cir.1968), the Commission charged that Texas Gulf Sulphur Company had violated Rule 10b-5 by issuing a press release which painted a misleadingly gloomy picture of a recent ore discovery. The question was whether the press release was "in connection with" any purchase or sale, since the company had not traded in its own stock after issuing the release. The court said:

> [I]t seems clear from the legislative purpose Congress expressed in the Act, and the legislative history of Section 10(b) that Congress when it used the phrase "in connection with the purchase or sale of any security" intended only that the device employed, whatever it might be, be of a sort that would cause reasonable investors to rely thereon, and, in connection therewith, so relying, cause them to purchase or sell a corporation's securities. There is no indication that Congress intended that the corporations or persons responsible for the issuance of a misleading statement would not violate the section unless they engaged in related securities transactions or otherwise acted with wrongful motives; indeed, the obvious purposes of the Act to protect the investing public and to secure fair dealing in the securities markets would be seriously undermined by applying such a gloss onto the legislative language. Absent a securities transaction by an insider it is almost impossible to prove that a wrongful purpose motivated the

issuance of the misleading statement. The mere fact that an insider did not engage in securities transactions does not negate the possibility of wrongful purpose; perhaps the market did not react to the misleading statement as much as was anticipated or perhaps the wrongful purpose was something other than the desire to buy at a low price or sell at a high price. * * *

Accordingly, we hold that Rule 10b–5 is violated whenever assertions are made, as here, in a manner reasonably calculated to influence the investing public, e.g., by means of the financial media, if such assertions are false or misleading or are so incomplete as to mislead irrespective of whether the issuance of the release was motivated by corporate officials for ulterior purposes.

---

4. *"The Purchase or Sale"*

In the *Hooper* case, p. 464 above, the court held that the issuance by a corporation of its own shares was a "sale" under Rule 10b–5. The first Supreme Court decision interpreting the Rule dealt with its applicability to a merger transaction.

SEC v. NATIONAL SECURITIES

393 U.S. 453 (1969).

MR. JUSTICE MARSHALL delivered the opinion of the Court.

This case raises some complex questions about the Securities and Exchange Commission's power to regulate the activities of insurance companies and of persons engaged in the insurance business. The Commission originally brought suit in the United States District Court for the District of Arizona, pursuant to § 21(e) of the Securities Exchange Act of 1934. It alleged violations of § 10(b) of the Act, and of the Commission's Rule 10b–5. According to the amended complaint, National Securities and various persons associated with it had contrived a fraudulent scheme centering on a contemplated merger between National Life & Casualty Insurance Co. (National Life), a firm controlled by National Securities, and Producers Life Insurance Co. (Producers).

* * *

The Commission was denied temporary relief, and shortly thereafter Producers' shareholders and the Arizona Director of Insurance approved the merger. The two companies were formally consolidated into National Producers Life Insurance Co. on July 9, 1965. Thereafter, the Commission amended its complaint to seek additional relief * * *. The court ruled that the relief requested was either barred by § 2(b) of the McCarran–Ferguson Act, or was beyond the scope of § 21(e) of the Securities Exchange Act. The Ninth Circuit affirmed, relying on the McCarran–Ferguson Act. Upon application by the

Commission, we granted certiorari because of the importance of the questions raised to the administration of the securities laws.

Insofar as it is relevant to this case, § 2(b) of the McCarran–Ferguson Act provides that "[n]o Act of Congress shall be construed to invalidate, impair, or supersede any law enacted by any State for the purpose of regulating the business of insurance * * * unless such Act specifically relates to the business of insurance * * *." Respondents contend that this Act bars the present suit since the Arizona Director of Insurance found that the merger was not "[i]nequitable to the stockholders of any domestic insurer" and not otherwise "contrary to law," as he was required to do under the state insurance laws. If the Securities Exchange Act were applied, respondents argue, these laws would be "superseded." * * * The first question posed by this case is whether the relevant Arizona statute is a "law enacted * * * for the purpose of regulating the business of insurance" within the meaning of the McCarran–Ferguson Act. Even accepting respondents' view of Arizona law, we do not believe that a state statute aimed at protecting the interests of those who own stock in insurance companies comes within the sweep of the McCarran–Ferguson Act. Such a statute is not a state attempt to regulate "the business of insurance," as that phrase was used in the Act.

* * *

Respondents argue that there are alternative grounds on which the lower courts' action in granting judgment on the pleadings can be sustained. They contend that the complaint fails to allege a "purchase or sale" of securities within the meaning of § 10(b) and the Commission's Rule 10b–5, and that in any case Rule 10b–5 does not apply to misrepresentations in connection with the solicitation of proxies.

* * * For the statute and the rule to apply, the allegedly proscribed conduct must have been "in connection with the purchase or sale of any security." The relevant definitional sections of the 1934 Act are for the most part unhelpful; they only declare generally that the terms "purchase" and "sale" shall include contracts to purchase or sell. Consequently, we must ask whether respondents' alleged conduct is the type of fraudulent behavior which was meant to be forbidden by the statute and the rule.

According to the amended complaint, Producers' shareholders were misled in various material respects prior to their approval of a merger. The deception furthered a scheme which resulted in their losing their status as shareholders in Producers and becoming shareholders in a new company. Moreover, by voting in favor of the merger, each approving shareholder individually lost any right under Arizona law to obtain an appraisal of his stock and payment for it in cash. Whatever the terms "purchase" and "sale" may mean in other contexts, here an alleged deception has affected individual shareholders' decisions in a way not at all unlike that involved in a typical cash sale or share exchange. The broad antifraud purposes of the statute and the rule would clearly be furthered by their application to this type of situation. Therefore we conclude that Producers' shareholders "purchased" shares in the new company by exchanging them for their old stock.

* * *

In INTERNATIONAL CONTROLS CORP. v. VESCO, 490 F.2d 1334 (2d Cir.1974), ICC alleged that Vesco, its former president, had fraudulently induced ICC's board of directors to approve a spin-off to ICC shareholders of the shares of an ICC subsidiary which owned a Boeing 707 aircraft. Vesco's alleged motive for the spin-off was to assure his continued ability to use the 707 for his personal convenience by transferring it to a separate entity of which all the directors were personal associates of his.

Defendants argued that ICC had no claim under Rule 10b–5, since the spin-off was not a "sale" of a security, no consideration having passed to ICC in the transaction. The court held, however, 2–1, that, in light of the "umbrella of protection placed over securities transactions by § 10(b)", ICC must be deemed to be a "seller" of securities. The court acknowledged that decisions holding a spin-off to be a "sale" for 1933 Act purposes, where the purpose was to create a public market in the securities being distributed, were inapposite, since in this case ICC received no benefits whatever. However, it noted that § 10(b) was designed to protect creditors as well as shareholders, and that ICC's creditors were adversely affected when the corporation's asset base was eroded by the distribution of the subsidiary's securities. Judge Mulligan, dissenting, could find no basis in precedent for the majority's position, believing that it "not only strains, but flatly contradicts, the words of the statute."

In re PENN CENTRAL SECURITIES LITIGATION, 494 F.2d 528, (3d Cir.1974). Plaintiffs, former shareholders in the Penn Central Railroad, argued that a reorganization plan in which they surrendered their shares in the railroad in exchange for shares of a holding company, which simultaneously became the owner of 100% of the stock of the railroad, was a "purchase" and "sale" within the meaning of § 10(b). The court found that the reorganization plan "was in effect an 'internal corporate management' decision which only incidentally involved an exchange of shares" rather than "a major corporate restructuring requiring the same kind of investment decision by the shareholders as would a proposed merger with a separate existing corporation." It held that neither (a) the alleged loss of shareholder appraisal rights, (b) the inability of the shareholders to participate in the railroad's bankruptcy proceedings, nor (c) the added potential for diversification by the holding company, was a sufficient change in the shareholders' interests to bring the transaction within the scope of § 10(b).

In RUBIN v. UNITED STATES, 449 U.S. 424 (1981), the Supreme Court held that fraud in connection with a pledge of securities to a bank violated § 17(a) of the 1933 Act. The Court held that a pledge was a "sale" within the meaning of § 2(3) of that Act, which defines "sale" to include "every contract of sale *or disposition* of a security *or interest in a security,* for value." Would a pledge be considered a "sale" under § 10(b) and Rule 10b-5, in light of the narrower definition found in § 3(a)(14) of the 1934 Act? In MALLIS v. FDIC, 568 F.2d 824 (2d Cir. 1977), the court held a pledge to be a "sale" for purposes of § 10(b), relying on decisions holding a pledge to be a "sale" under the 1933 Act, without discussing the difference in language. The Supreme Court granted certiorari to review the question, but then dismissed the writ in light of concessions made by the plaintiff at oral argument. BANKERS TRUST v. MALLIS, 435 U.S. 381 (1978).

---

5. *"Of Any Security"*

As noted above, there are no jurisdictional limits on the application of Rule 10b-5; it applies to transactions in "any security," whether publicly traded or not. One judge has recently expressed strong dissatisfaction with this broad reading of the Rule.

TRECKER v. SCAG

679 F.2d 703 (7th Cir.1982).

POSNER, CIRCUIT JUDGE, concurring.

I join Chief Judge Cummings' excellent opinion without reservations, and write separately only to express my doubts whether this case really belongs in the federal courts. I do not mean that we do not have jurisdiction; I mean that perhaps we should not have jurisdiction.

The dispute out of which this case arises is local. Wisconsin is the home of Messrs. Scag and Trecker and of their corporation, Wisconsin Marine, Inc.—the home, that is to say, of all the disputants except Ransomes, which while named as a defendant is not accused of any wrongdoing. And Wisconsin Marine is a closely held corporation. Its stock is not traded on any organized exchange—in fact is not freely traded at all. The basis of federal jurisdiction over the lawsuit is Scag's use of the mails in his dealings with Ransomes, but the federal government has no substantive interest in local transactions just because the parties happen to send letters to each other. The theory of the suit is that Scag defrauded Trecker by failing to inform him of the deal with Ransomes (which showed that Trecker's stock was worth more than Trecker knew), thereby inducing Trecker to redeem his stock for less than its true worth. This is common law fraud, a matter traditionally of state rather than federal law—but anyway Wisconsin has a statute similar to Rule 10b-5. Wis.Stat.Ann. § 189.18. Moreover, as in so many Rule 10b-5 cases, the legal issues on this appeal are issues of, or entwined with, state law: whether Trecker could under

Wisconsin law have abandoned his redemption suit if he had known of the negotiations with Ransomes (as Chief Judge Cummings' opinion explains, unless Trecker could have abandoned the suit Scag's failure to inform him of the deal with Ransomes could not have been a material omission); and whether Wisconsin's statute of limitations, which governs this Rule 10b–5 private action because there is no applicable federal statute of limitations, has run.

If I thought Congress really wanted the federal courts to decide lawsuits of this sort, involving primarily local law applied to local disputes between local residents, I would bow to its desire without protest, for there is no constitutional obstacle to federal jurisdiction. But I cannot believe that this consequence was intended when Congress enacted section 10(b) of the Securities Exchange Act of 1934. Section 10(b) makes it unlawful to use the mails "To use or employ, in connection with the purchase or sale of any security * * *, any manipulative or deceptive device or contrivance in contravention of such rules and regulations as the Commission may prescribe as necessary or appropriate in the public interest or for the protection of investors." This grant of rulemaking authority was taken up in 1942 when the SEC issued Rule 10b–5, which defines the term "deceptive device" to include "any act, practice, or course of business which operates or would operate as a fraud or deceit upon any person, in connection with the purchase or sale of any security." The Securities Exchange Act does not expressly create a private right of action for violations of rules promulgated under section 10(b), but the courts early on implied a right of action and the Supreme Court confirmed it in a footnote in Superintendent of Ins. v. Bankers Life & Cas. Co. And so we arrive at federal jurisdiction in a case such as the present, a garden-variety squabble among shareholders in a closely held corporation, which could not even be maintained as a diversity action because of the lack of complete diversity among the parties.

Rule 10b–5 was defensible as a catch-all prohibition of deceptive devices when the enforcement of the rule was confined to the SEC. Like every other government agency, the SEC has a limited budget, which prevents it from bringing anything like all the cases that are within the potential reach of the statutes and rules that it enforces. But no budget constraint limits private damage actions; such an action will be brought so long as the expected damages exceed, however, slightly, the expected cost of the litigation to the plaintiff. The SEC's budget constraint, which probably would deter it from enforcing Rule 10b–5 in cases where state remedies are adequate, ceased to constrain Rule 10b–5 actions when the courts authorized private actions.

The resulting displacement of state substantive law and state court jurisdiction in an area remote from any federal concern that might arise from federal regulation of the securities markets could not have been foreseen by the framers of the Securities Exchange Act. But there is little if anything that the lower federal courts can do to arrest or retard the unintended federalization of corporation law by Rule 10b–5. In Santa Fe Indus., Inc. v. Green, 430 U.S. 462 (1977), the Supreme Court put some brakes on Rule 10b–5 actions by confining the concept of fraud, in the statute and the rule, to deception; unfairness is no longer enough. But as the present case * * * illustrates, the fact that deception is shown, while enough to bring Rule 10b–5 into play, does not turn a spat between two shareholders of a closely held corporation into a "federal case" in any real sense. And although *Green* is not the only limiting interpretation of Rule 10b–5 that has been made it is hard to see how a rule that applies to "the purchase or sale of any security" could be judicially amended to read "the purchase or sale of any publicly traded security."

* * *

I note that an alternative theory for Trecker to a Rule 10b–5 violation was abuse by Scag of his positions as majority shareholder, director, and officer, which created fiduciary obligations on his part toward the plaintiff that Scag, it may be argued, breached. I do not want to prejudge the plaintiff's rights under Wisconsin law, but only to point out that he might actually get more complete relief in a suit under Wisconsin law than in this federal suit. True, he could have joined a state law claim with his federal claim under the doctrine of pendent jurisdiction, but since the exercise of pendent jurisdiction is discretionary, he could not have been sure that the federal court would retain a state law claim.

When asked at the oral argument of this appeal why he had not brought this suit in state court, plaintiff's counsel stated that there were no cases under Wisconsin's counterpart to Rule 10b–5 —all the case development had been federal. This just shows that the expansion of federal jurisdiction under Rule 10b–5, an expansion barely checked by decisions such as *Green,* has stultified the development of state law in an area where there is no reason to displace state by federal authority. This is not what Congress intended to happen when it enacted section 10(b) in 1934; I regret that we cannot enforce its actual intentions.

B. LIABILITY FOR ANTIFRAUD VIOLATIONS

---

1. *Governmental Sanctions*

Any person who violates the antifraud provisions of the 1934 Act is subject to criminal prosecution under § 32 of the Act. In addition, if the violator is a broker-dealer, its registration may be revoked or suspended in an administrative proceeding before the SEC under § 15(b)(4). In situations where the violator is not registered with the SEC, and the violation is not serious enough to warrant criminal prosecution, the SEC is empowered by § 21(d) to go into federal court to obtain an injunction against any future violations of the law. The grounds on which the courts will issue such injunctions have been a matter of some controversy.

In RONDEAU v. MOSINEE PAPER CORP., 422 U.S. 49 (1975), p. 750 below, the Supreme Court held that a private party was not entitled to injunctive relief under § 13(d) of the 1934 Act unless it could "satisfy the traditional prerequisites of extraordinary equitable relief by establishing irreparable harm". The Court did not indicate that any such requirement would apply to SEC injunctive actions, which of course are specifically authorized by § 21(d)(1) of the Act. In the course of the Securities Acts Amendments of 1975, the SEC persuaded the Senate to amend § 21(d)(1) to entitle the Commission to apply for an injunction whenever it appears that a person "has engaged" (as well as when he "is engaged or is about to engage") in a violation, and to provide that an injunction should be issued when the Commission had made "such showing" (rather than "a proper showing"). S. 249, 94th Cong., 1st Sess. (1975). A committee of prominent securities lawyers wrote to the Senate–House Conference Committee, protesting that the proposed change had not been discussed in the committee reports on the legislation, that it would impair the traditional discretion of the courts in determining whether or not to issue an injunction, and that it would convert the SEC injunction into an "automatic branding device" rather than a remedial enforcement weapon. See BNA Sec.Reg. & L.Rep. No. 302, at A–1, H–1 (1975). The Conference Committee deleted the proposed change and retained the existing language of § 21(d)(1). H.Rep. No. 94–229, at 102 (1975).

The current judicial attitude with respect to the SEC's right to an injunction in disciplinary proceedings was summed up by Judge Friendly in SEC v. COMMONWEALTH CHEMICAL, 574 F.2d 90 (2d Cir. 1978):

> It is fair to say that the current judicial attitude toward the issuance of injunctions on the basis of past violations at the SEC's request has become more circumspect than in earlier days. Experience has shown that an injunction, while not always a "drastic remedy" as appellants contend, often is much more than the "mild prophylactic" described by the court in SEC v. Capital Gains Research Bureau, 375 U.S. 180, 193 (1963). In some cases the collateral consequences of an injunction can be very grave. The Securities Act and the Securities Exchange Act speak, after all, of enjoining "any person [who] is engaged or about to engage in any acts or practices" which constitute or will constitute a violation. Except for the case where the SEC steps in to prevent an ongoing violation, this language seems to require a finding of "likelihood" or "propensity" to engage in future violations. As said by Professor Loss, "[t]he ultimate test is whether the defendant's past conduct indicates * * * that there is a reasonable likelihood of further violation in the future." Our recent decisions have

emphasized, perhaps more than older ones, the need for the SEC to go beyond the mere facts of past violations and demonstrate a realistic likelihood of recurrence. See SEC v. Universal Major Industries, 546 F.2d 1044, 1048 (2 Cir.1976), SEC v. Parklane Hosiery, 558 F.2d 1083 (2 Cir.1977), and SEC v. Bausch & Lomb, Inc., 565 F.2d 8, 18 (2 Cir.1977) where the court went so far as to say "[T]he Commission cannot obtain relief without positive proof of a reasonable likelihood that past wrongdoing will recur."

Judge Friendly indicates in the *Commonwealth* opinion that "the collateral consequences of an injunction can be very grave." The Supreme Court added to the gravity of the consequences in PARKLANE HOSIERY CO. v. SHORE, 439 U.S. 322 (1979). It held that when a defendant in an SEC injunction action was found to have issued a false and misleading statement, he was estopped from denying that the statement was false and misleading in a subsequent private action for damages. The Court held that the doctrine of collateral estoppel foreclosed the defendant from relitigating the issue, and that this foreclosure did not violate defendant's Seventh Amendment right to a jury trial.

In October 1990, Congress added substantially to the SEC's enforcement powers by enacting the Securities Enforcement Remedies and Penny Stock Reform Act. Among the important changes made by that Act are provisions (a) authorizing the SEC to issue cease-and-desist orders, and to impose fines or order disgorgement of profits in administrative proceedings, (b) increasing the fines for deliberate or reckless violations of the securities laws, (c) permitting the courts to bar violators from serving as officers or directors of publicly-held corporations, and (d) requiring additional disclosures by dealers in "penny stocks" (see pp. 937–41 below).

Selected References

T. Hazen, Securities Regulation § 9.5 (2d ed. 1990).

Hazen, Administrative Enforcement: An Evaluation of the SEC's Use of Injunctions and Other Enforcement Methods, 31 Hast.L.J. 427–72 (1979).

Jacobs, Judicial and Administrative Remedies Available to the SEC for Breaches of Rule 10b–5, 53 St. Johns L.Rev. 397 (1979).

Mathews, Litigation and Enforcement of SEC Administrative Enforcement Proceedings, 29 Cath.U.L.Rev. 215 (1980).

---

2. *Implication of a Private Right of Action*

The antifraud provisions of the federal securities laws are worded as prohibitions; no express private right of action is given to a person injured by a violation. However, beginning in 1946, federal courts began to *imply* the existence of a private right of action, utilizing basic common law principles.

KARDON v. NATIONAL GYPSUM CO.

69 F.Supp. 512 (E.D.Pa.1946).

KIRKPATRICK, DISTRICT JUDGE.

This complaint, in substance, charges a conspiracy, participated in by the three defendants, and certain fraudulent misrepresentations and suppressions of the truth in pursuance of the conspiracy, as a result of which the plaintiffs were induced to sell their stock in two corporations to the Slavins, two of the defendants, for far less than its true value.

* * *

It is not, and cannot be, questioned that the complaint sets forth conduct on the part of the Slavins directly in violation of the provisions of Sec. 10(b) of the Act and of Rule X–10B–5 which implements it. It is also true that there is no provision in Sec. 10 or elsewhere expressly allowing civil suits by persons injured as a result of violation of Sec. 10 or of the Rule. However, "The violation of a legislative enactment by doing a prohibited act, or by failing to do a required act, makes the actor liable for an invasion of an interest of another if; (a) the intent of the enactment is exclusively or in part to protect an interest of the other as an individual; and (b) the interest invaded is one which the enactment is intended to protect. * * *" Restatement, Torts, Vol. 2, Sec. 286. This rule is more than merely a canon of statutory interpretation. The disregard of the command of a statute is a wrongful act and a tort.

Of course, the legislature may withhold from parties injured the right to recover damages arising by reason of violation of a statute but the right is so fundamental and so deeply ingrained in the law that where it is not expressly denied the intention to withhold it should appear very clearly and plainly. The defendants argue that such intention can be deduced from the fact that three other sections of the statute (Sections 9, 16 and 18) each declaring certain types of conduct illegal, all expressly provide for a civil action by a person injured and for incidents and limitations of it, whereas Sec. 10 does not. The argument is not without force. Were the whole question one of statutory interpretation it might be convincing, but the question is only partly such. It is whether an intention can be implied to deny a remedy and to wipe out a liability which, normally, by virtue of basic principles of tort law accompanies the doing of the prohibited act. Where, as here, the whole statute discloses a broad purpose to regulate securities transactions of all kinds and, as a part of such regulation, the specific section in question provides for the elimination of all manipulative or deceptive methods in such transactions, the construction contended for by the defendants may not be adopted. In other words, in view of the general purpose of the Act, the mere omission of an express provision for civil liability is not sufficient to negative what the general law implies.

The other point presented by the defendants is that, under the general rule of law, civil liability for violation of a statute accrues only to a member of a class (investors) for whose special benefit the statute was enacted an argument applied to both Sec. 10 and to Rule X–10B–5. Sec. 10 prohibits deceptive devices "in contravention of such rules and regulations as the Commission may prescribe as necessary or appropriate in the public interest or for the protection of investors." I cannot agree, however, that "investors" is limited to persons who are about to invest in a security or that two men who have acquired ownership of the stock of a corporation are not investors merely because they own half of the total issue.

Apart from Sec. 10(b), I think that the action can also be grounded upon Sec. 29(b) of the Act which provides that contracts in violation of any provision of the Act shall be void. Here, unlike the point just discussed, the question is purely one of statutory construction. It seems to me that a statutory enactment that a contract of a certain kind shall be void almost necessarily implies a remedy in respect of it. The statute would be of little value unless a party to the contract could apply to the Courts to relieve himself of obligations under it or to escape its consequences. * * * And * * * such suits would include not only actions for rescission but also for money damages.

National's contention that the complaint fails to state a cause of action against it cannot be sustained. * * *

The question whether the courts should imply a private right of action under Rule 10b–5 did not reach the Supreme Court for 25 years after the *Kardon* decision. When the question did come before the Court in 1971 in Superintendent of Insurance v. Bankers Life & Casualty Co., p. 466 above, the Court simply stated in a footnote, with a citation to Professor Loss' treatise, that "it is now established that a private right of action is implied under § 10(b)." There was no discussion of the basis for this implication.

In 1979, the Supreme Court, having adopted a more negative attitude toward implied private rights of action, implicitly rejected the rationale underlying the *Kardon* decision by noting that "the Court has been especially reluctant to imply causes of action under statutes that create duties on the part of persons for the benefit of the public at large." The Court described the *Superintendent of Insurance* case as a "deviat[ion] from this pattern" in which "the Court explicitly acquiesced in the 25-year-old acceptance by the lower federal courts of a 10b-5 cause of action." Cannon v. University of Chicago, 441 U.S. 677 (1979).

Seven years before it first considered the question of a private right of action under Rule 10b-5, however, the Supreme Court had considered the availability of a private right of action under § 14 of the 1934 Act, and set forth its rationale for concluding that such a right of action did exist.

J.I. CASE CO. v. BORAK

377 U.S. 426 (1964).

MR. JUSTICE CLARK delivered the opinion of the Court.

This is a civil action brought by respondent, a stockholder of petitioner J.I. Case Company, charging deprivation of the pre-emptive rights of respondent and other shareholders by reason of a merger between Case and the American Tractor Corporation. It is alleged that the merger was effected through the circulation of a false and misleading proxy statement by those proposing the merger. The complaint was in two counts, the first based on diversity and claiming a breach of the directors' fiduciary duty to the stockholders. The second count alleged a violation of § 14(a) of the Securities Exchange Act of 1934 with reference to the proxy solicitation material. The trial court held that as to this count it had no power to redress the alleged violations of the Act but was limited solely to the granting of declaratory relief thereon under § 27 of the Act. * * * We consider only the question of whether § 27 of the Act authorizes a federal cause of action for rescission or damages to a corporate stockholder with respect to a consummated merger which was authorized pursuant to the use of a proxy statement alleged to contain false and misleading statements violative of § 14(a) of the Act.

I.

Respondent, the owner of 2,000 shares of common stock of Case acquired prior to the merger, brought this suit based on diversity jurisdiction seeking to enjoin a proposed merger between Case and the American Tractor Corporation (ATC) on various grounds, including breach of the fiduciary duties of the Case directors, self-dealing among the management of Case and ATC and misrepresentations contained in the material circulated to obtain proxies. The injunction was denied and the merger was thereafter consummated. Subsequently successive amended complaints were filed and the case was heard on the aforesaid two-count complaint. The claims pertinent to the asserted violation of the Securities Exchange Act were predicated on diversity jurisdiction as well as on § 27 of the Act. They alleged: that petitioners, or their predecessors, solicited or permitted their names to be used in the solicitation of proxies of Case stockholders for use at a special stockholders' meeting at which the proposed merger with ATC was to be voted upon; that the proxy solicitation material so circulated was false and misleading in violation of § 14(a) of the Act and Rule 14a–9 which the Commission had promulgated thereunder, that the merger was approved at the meeting by a small margin of votes and was thereafter consummated; that the merger would not have been approved but for the false and misleading statements in the proxy solicitation material; and that Case stockholders were damaged thereby.

* * *

II.

It appears clear that private parties have a right under § 27 to bring suit for violation of § 14(a) of the Act. Indeed, this section specifically grants the appropriate District Courts jurisdiction over "all suits in equity and actions at law brought to enforce any liability or duty created" under the Act. The petitioners make no concessions, however, emphasizing that Congress made no specific reference to a private right of action in § 14(a); that, in any event, the right would not extend to derivative suits and should be limited to prospective relief only. In addition, some of the petitioners argue that the merger can be dissolved only if it was fraudulent or non-beneficial, issues upon which the proxy material would not bear. But the causal relationship of the proxy material and the merger are questions of fact to be resolved at trial, not here. We therefore do not discuss this point further.

III.

While the respondent contends that his Count 2 claim is not a derivative one, we need not embrace that view, for we believe that a right of action exists as to both derivative and direct causes.

The purpose of § 14(a) is to prevent management or others from obtaining authorization for corporate action by means of deceptive or inadequate disclosure in proxy solicitation. * * * These broad remedial purposes are evidenced in the language of the section which makes it "unlawful for any person * * * to solicit or to permit the use of his name to solicit any proxy or consent or authorization in respect of any security * * * registered on any national securities exchange in contravention of such rules and regulations as the Commission may prescribe as necessary or appropriate in the public interest *or for the protection of investors.*" (Italics supplied.) While this language makes no specific reference to a private right of action, among its chief purposes is "the protection of investors," which certainly implies the availability of judicial relief where necessary to achieve that result.

The injury which a stockholder suffers from corporate action pursuant to a deceptive proxy solicitation ordinarily flows from the damage done the corporation, rather than from the damage inflicted directly upon the stockholder. The damage suffered results not from the deceit practiced on him alone but rather from the deceit practiced on the stockholders as a group. To hold that derivative actions are not within the sweep of the section would therefore be tantamount to a denial of private relief. Private enforcement of the proxy rules provides a necessary supplement to Commission action. As in antitrust treble damage litigation, the possibility of civil damages or injunctive relief serves as a most effective weapon in the enforcement of the proxy requirements. The Commission advises that it examines over 2,000 proxy statements annually and each of them must necessarily be expedited. Time does not permit an independent examination of the facts set out in the proxy material and this results in the Commission's acceptance of the representations contained therein at their face value, unless contrary to other material on file with it. Indeed, on the allegations of respondent's complaint, the proxy material failed to disclose alleged unlawful market manipulation of the stock of ATC, and this unlawful manipulation would not have been apparent to the Commission until after the merger.

We, therefore, believe that under the circumstances here it is the duty of the courts to be alert to provide such remedies as are necessary to make effective the congressional purpose. * * * It is for the federal courts "to adjust their remedies so as to grant the necessary relief" where federally secured rights are invaded. "And it is also well settled that where legal rights have been invaded, and a federal statute provides for a general right to sue for such invasion, federal courts may use any available remedy to make good the wrong done." Section 27 grants the District Courts jurisdiction "of all suits in equity and actions at law brought to enforce any liability or duty created by this title * * *." In passing on almost identical language found in the Securities Act of 1933, the Court found the words entirely sufficient to fashion a remedy to rescind a fraudulent sale, secure restitution and even to enforce the right to restitution against a third party holding assets of the vendor.

* * *

Nor do we find merit in the contention that such remedies are limited to prospective relief. This was the position taken in Dann v. Studebaker–Packard Corp., 6 Cir., 288 F.2d 201, where it was held that the "preponderance of questions of state law which would have to be interpreted and applied in order to grant the relief sought. * * * is so great that the federal question involved * * * is really negligible in comparison." But we believe that the overriding federal law applicable here would, where the facts required, control the appropriateness of redress despite the provisions of state corporation law, for it "is not uncommon for federal courts to fashion federal law where federal rights are concerned."

* * *

Moreover, if federal jurisdiction were limited to the granting of declaratory relief, victims of deceptive proxy statements would be obliged to go into state courts for remedial relief. And if the law of the State happened to attach no responsibility to the use of misleading proxy statements, the whole purpose of the section might be frustrated.

Furthermore, the hurdles that the victim might face (such as separate suits, as contemplated by Dann v. Studebaker–Packard Corp., supra, security for expenses statutes, bringing in all parties necessary for complete relief, etc.) might well prove insuperable to effective relief.

IV.

Our finding that federal courts have the power to grant all necessary remedial relief is not to be construed as any indication of what we believe to be the necessary and appropriate relief in this case. We are concerned here only with a determination that federal jurisdiction for this purpose does exist. Whatever remedy is necessary must await the trial on the merits.

The other contentions of the petitioners are denied.

Affirmed.

The rationale of the *Borak* decision, which was the first Supreme Court decision implying a private right of action under federal securities law, has been significantly undermined by more recent decisions of the Court. In TOUCHE ROSS v. REDINGTON, 442 U.S. 560 (1979), the Court refused to imply a private right of action under the record-keeping requirements of § 17 of the 1934 Act.

> [Plaintiffs] argue that our decision in *Borak* requires implication of a private cause of action under § 17(a). * * * [They] emphasize language in *Borak* that discusses the remedial purposes of the 1934 Act and § 27 of the Act, which, *inter alia,* grants to federal district courts the exclusive jurisdiction of violations of the Act and suits to enforce any liability or duty created by the Act or the rules and regulations thereunder. They argue that Touche Ross has breached its duties under § 17(a) and the rules adopted thereunder and that in view of § 27 and of the remedial purposes of the 1934 Act, federal courts should provide a damage remedy for the breach.
>
> The reliance of [plaintiffs] on § 27 is misplaced. Section 27 grants jurisdiction to the federal courts and provides for venue and service of process. It creates no cause of action of its own force and effect; it imposes no liabilities. The source of plaintiffs' right must be found, if at all, in the substantive provisions of the 1934 Act which they seek to enforce, not in the jurisdictional provision. The Court in *Borak* found a private cause of action implicit in § 14(a). We do not now question the actual holding of that case, but we decline to read the opinion so broadly that virtually every provision of the securities acts gives rise to an implied private cause of action.
>
> The invocation of the "remedial purposes" of the 1934 Act is similarly unavailing. Only last Term, we emphasized that generalized references to the "remedial purposes" of the 1934 Act will not

justify reading a provision "more broadly than its language and the statutory scheme reasonably permit." * * * To the extent our analysis in today's decision differs from that of the Court in *Borak,* it suffices to say that in a series of cases since *Borak* we have adhered to a stricter standard for the implication of private causes of action, and we follow that stricter standard today. The ultimate question is one of congressional intent, not one of whether this Court thinks that it can improve upon the statutory scheme that Congress enacted into law.

Justice Powell, dissenting in CANNON v. UNIVERSITY OF CHICAGO, 441 U.S. 677 (1979), was even more critical of the *Borak* decision:

> [In *Borak*] the Court held that a private party could maintain a cause of action under § 14(a) of the Securities Exchange Act of 1934, in spite of Congress' express creation of an administrative mechanism for enforcing that statute. I find this decision both unprecedented and incomprehensible as a matter of public policy. The decision's rationale, which lies ultimately in the judgment that "[p]rivate enforcement of the proxy rules provides a necessary supplement to Commission action," ignores the fact that Congress, in determining the degree of regulation to be imposed on companies covered by the Securities Exchange Act, already had decided that private enforcement was unnecessary. More significant for present purposes, however, is the fact that *Borak,* rather than signaling the start of a trend in this Court, constitutes a singular and, I believe, aberrant interpretation of a federal regulatory statute.

With respect to the availability of a private right of action for damages for violations of the antifraud provisions of § 206 of the Investment Advisers Act, the Supreme Court held in TRANSAMERICA MORTGAGE ADVISORS, INC. v. LEWIS, 444 U.S. 11 (1979) (5–4 decision) that no such right could be implied from the language of the Act or the legislative history. The Court did find, however, that § 215 of the Act, which provides that contracts made in violation of the Act "shall be void * * * as regards the rights of" the violator, implied the availability of an equitable suit for rescission or restitution or injunctive relief. The four dissenters argued that the decision "cannot be reconciled with our decisions recognizing implied private actions for damages under securities laws with substantially the same language," i.e. § 10(b) of the 1934 Act and Rule 10b–5.

Three years after the *Transamerica* decision, however, the Supreme Court held, again in a 5–4 decision, that a private right of action *could* be implied under the antifraud provisions of the Commodity Exchange Act. MERRILL LYNCH v. CURRAN, 456 U.S. 353 (1982). While the majority in the *Merrill Lynch* case relied on certain peculiarities in the legislative history of the Commodity Exchange Act, the dissenters found the decision flatly inconsistent with *Transamerica.* Indeed, the only apparent reason for the different result in the two cases is that

Justice Blackmun switched sides, since the lineup of the other eight justices remained the same.

In AARON v. SEC, 446 U.S. 680 (1980), the Supreme Court held that scienter need not be shown to establish a violation of clause (2) or (3) of § 17(a) of the 1933 Act, even though it must be shown to establish a violation of the corresponding clauses of Rule 10b–5. This has lent greater significance to the question (not yet addressed by the Supreme Court) whether there is a private right of action under § 17(a). The current state of the law was summarized in LANDRY v. ALL AMERICAN, 688 F.2d 381 (5th Cir.1982):

> Unquestionably, the most far reaching of the issues we resolve today is whether § 17(a) of the federal Securities Act of 1933 creates an implied private cause of action. While *res nova* in this Circuit, the controversy over this issue is by no means new. Of the circuits which have expressly addressed the issue, four have ruled that a private cause of action may be implied, while one has ruled that it may not. But while a clear majority view exists, few circuit court decisions have analyzed the issue in depth. In fact, as one learned commentator has observed, the existence of the § 17(a) private remedy "seems to be taken for granted." 6 L. Loss, Securities Regulation 3913 (2nd ed. Supp.1969).
>
> Most of these cases trace their creation of a private cause of action back to Chief Judge Friendly's concurring opinion in SEC v. Texas Gulf Sulphur Co. Judge Friendly's opinion was primarily concerned with establishing that negligence in the drafting of a press release should not be the basis of civil liability under Rule 10b–5(2). In his discussion of the origins of Rule 10b–5, however, Judge Friendly stated in dicta that while he had considerable doubt as to whether a private remedy under § 17(a) was ever intended, "there seemed little practical point in denying the existence of such an action under § 17" "[o]nce it had been established * * * that an aggrieved buyer has a private action under § 10(b) of the 1934 Act." As subsequent decisions have revealed, this seed fell on very fertile ground. The lack of a clearly articulated standard, however, has resulted in the fragmentation of the district courts with respect to this issue. Nor can it be said that a general consensus exists among the commentators.
>
> Perhaps the main reason for the somewhat awkward development of the law under § 17(a) of the 1933 Act is the fact that it has traditionally lived in the shadow of another area of securities law: Rule 10b–5. Rule 10b–5, adopted under § 10(b) of the Securities and Exchange Act of 1934, is substantially identical to § 17(a). When the judiciary recognized a private cause of action under Rule 10b–5 shortly after its promulgation, cases that might have fit a § 17(a) cause of action were instead decided under Rule 10b–5. This was true even when a plaintiff pleaded a cause of action under both.
>
> In 1976, however, the Supreme Court severely limited the Rule 10b–5 cause of action in Ernst & Ernst v. Hochfelder. There the Court established that allegations of the defendant's scienter are an essential

element of the plaintiff's cause of action under Rule 10b–5. The Court based its holding on the language of § 10(b) of the 1934 Act, asserting that the narrower language of that section constrained the reach of the broader Rule 10b–5 language.

The law under § 17(a), however, is not so distinct. In Aaron v. SEC, the Supreme Court was faced with the question of whether the SEC was required to establish scienter as an element of a civil enforcement action to enjoin violations of § 10(b) and Rule 10b–5 of the 1934 Act, and § 17(a) of the 1933 Act. While the Court decided that scienter was a necessary prerequisite under the 1934 Act, * * * [it held] that the language of § 17(a) requires scienter under § 17(a)(1), but not under § 17(a)(2) or § 17(a)(3).

The question of whether a private cause of action should be implied under § 17(a) operates against a backdrop of long-developing and varied judicial formulations of the circumstances under which implication is appropriate. The most recent test stems from the Supreme Court's decision of Cort v. Ash, 422 U.S. 66 (1975). In *Cort,* the Supreme Court unanimously refused to imply a private cause of action for damages against corporate directors and in favor of stockholders for purported violations of a criminal statute prohibiting corporations from making certain campaign contributions. In rejecting the plaintiff's theory that implication was appropriate for violations of this criminal statute, Justice Brennan outlined the following four-part test for determining when a private remedy should be implied:

> First, is the plaintiff "one of the class for whose *especial* benefit the statute was enacted,"—that is, does the statute create a federal right in favor of the plaintiff? Second, is there any indication of legislative intent, explicit or implicit, either to create such a remedy or to deny one? Third, is it consistent with the underlying purposes of the legislative scheme to imply such a remedy for the plaintiff? And finally, is the cause of action one traditionally relegated to state law, in an area basically the concern of the States, so that it would be inappropriate to infer a cause of action based solely on federal law?

Application of the modified *Cort* test to § 17(a) of the 1933 Act leads this Court to believe that a private cause of action is not implied. * * *

An alternative to implying a private right of action from a statutory prohibition itself, under general principles of tort law, is to imply a right of rescission from § 29(b) of the 1934 Act, which provides that any contract made in violation of the Act "shall be void." The contours of this right of rescission are discussed in the following opinion:

REGIONAL PROPERTIES v. FINANCIAL AND REAL ESTATE CONSULTING CO.

678 F.2d 552 (5th Cir.1982).

Before BROWN, COLEMAN and RUBIN, CIRCUIT JUDGES.

ALVIN B. RUBIN, CIRCUIT JUDGE:

Two real estate developers and their affiliated corporations entered into a number of agreements with a securities broker whereby the broker agreed to structure limited partnerships and market the limited partnership interests. The developers discovered that the broker had never registered as a broker-dealer with the SEC and had thus violated the Securities Exchange Act in selling the partnership interests, although the time when they learned of this is disputed. The major question presented is whether, under these circumstances, the developers were entitled to rescind their agreements with the broker under the contract-voiding provision contained in the Act. We hold that the developers were entitled to bring such an action and established a *prima facie* case for relief, but that the district court erred in failing to rule upon the broker's asserted defenses. We, therefore, remand the case so that the district court may consider and rule upon these defenses.

* * *

II. REGIONAL'S SECTION 29(B) CLAIMS.

Section 29(b) provides, "[e]very contract made in violation of any provision of [the Act] * * *, and every contract * * * the performance of which involves the violation of * * * any provision of [the Act] * * *, shall be void * * * as regards the rights of any person who, in violation of any such provision * * * shall have made or engaged in the performance of any such contract * * *." Although it has been a part of the Act since its passage in 1934, it has been invoked infrequently. See Gruenbaum & Steinberg, Section 29(b) of the Securities Exchange Act of 1934: A Viable Remedy Awakened, 48 Geo.Wash. L.Rev. 1, 1–3 & n. 5 (1979) [hereinafter cited as *Viable Remedy*]. It does not in terms give a party to a contract made in violation of the section a private cause of action to rescind the contract. If it authorizes such an action by implication, the following questions must also be addressed: (1) What are the elements of the cause of action? (2) What defenses, if any, are available against the claim? and (3) What relief is available to a successful claimant?

A. Does Section 29(b) Provide for a Private Cause of Action?

Without expressly considering whether section 29(b) implies a private cause of action, courts have uniformly either held or assumed that such suits can be brought. In the only Fifth Circuit case interpreting section 29(b), Eastside Church of Christ v. National Plan, Inc., 391 F.2d 357 (5th Cir.1968), the issuer of certain bonds sued a purchaser of the bonds under section 29(b) to have the contract of sale rescinded on the ground that the purchaser had violated the Act by not being a registered broker-dealer when it made the purchase. We prefaced our discussion of the points raised on appeal by stating that section 29(b) "contemplates civil suit for relief by way of rescission and damages * * *." Therefore, at least since 1968, it has been the rule of this circuit that a private cause of action can be founded upon section 29(b).

Language in two subsequent Supreme Court decisions tends to affirm this view. In Mills v. Electric Auto-Lite Co., 396 U.S. 375 (1970), the Court stated, in dicta, that the interests of the "innocent party" to a contract are protected by section 29(b)'s "giving him the right to rescind." More recently, in Transamerica Mortgage Advisors, Inc. (TAMA) v. Lewis, 444 U.S. 11 (1979), the Court was called upon to determine whether section 215(b) of the Investment Advisers Act, which is nearly identical to section 29(b) of the (Securities Exchange) Act, provides a private cause of action. In answering that question in the affirmative, the Court stated:

> By declaring certain contracts void, § 215 by its terms necessarily contemplates that the issue of voidness under its criteria may be litigated somewhere. At the very least Congress must have assumed that § 215 could be raised defensively in private litigation to preclude the enforcement of an investment advisers contract.
>
> But the legal consequences of voidness are typically not so limited. A person with the power to void a contract ordinarily may resort to a court to have the contract rescinded and to obtain restitution of consideration paid * * *. Moreover, the federal courts in general have viewed such language as implying an equitable cause of action for rescission or similar relief.
>
> For these reasons we conclude that when Congress declared in § 215 that certain contracts are void, it intended that the customary legal incidents of voidness would follow, including the availability of a suit for rescission * * *, and for restitution.

Therefore, based upon our (implicit) holding in *Eastside Church,* and the supporting language in *Mills* and holding in *TAMA,* it must be considered as settled that section 29(b), by implication, does provide a private, "equitable cause of action for rescission or similar relief."

B. The Elements of a Section 29(b) Cause of Action.

In *Eastside Church,* supra, we rejected the defendants' argument that a section 29(b) plaintiff must prove a causal connection between its harm and the defendants' violation of the Act. The "Act," we said, "requires only that the [complainant] be in the class of persons the Act was designed to protect * * *." * * * Although we did not define the phrase, "class of persons the Act was designed to protect," the plaintiff in *Eastside Church* was obviously a member of it as the issuer of the bonds that were sold under the contract.

We indicated that there was one other requirement, contractual privity. The issuer in *Eastside Church* had not dealt directly with the purchaser-defendant, but had instead delivered the bonds to its agent for their sale. When it was pointed out that the agent might have purchased for his own account some of the bonds he thus received before he in turn sold them to the purchaser-defendant, we held that the defendant was "liable only on those purchases which were made from [the agent] acting [as such] * * * and not from [the agent] individually."

To summarize, then, a person can avoid a contract under section 29(b) if he can show that (1) the contract involved a "prohibited transaction," (2) he is in contractual privity with the defendant, and (3) he is "in the class of persons the Act was designed to protect."

* * *

Contractual privity, the first element of the cause of action, is established beyond dispute. In fact, Regional and Financial were the only parties to the contracts. Regional also satisfied the second element, proof that "prohibited transactions occurred." Section 29(b) does not render void only those contracts that "by their terms" violate the Act. If the Act were so limited, it would lead immediately to the inquiry, "What would such a contract look like?" A statute that voided only contracts by which persons have agreed in express terms to violate the Act would be so narrow as to be a waste of the congressional time spent in its enactment.

The situation here is in all essentials identical to that in *Eastside Church.* Regional sought to avoid certain contracts, perfectly lawful on their face, the performance of which by Financial resulted in a violation of the Act. That these contracts, under different circumstances, *could* have been performed without violating the Act is immaterial. Considering the language of section 29(b), our holding in *Eastside Church,* and the dicta in *Mills,* we conclude that Regional proved the existence of "prohibited transactions," i.e., ones proscribed by section 29(b).

The final element of a section 29(b) cause of action under *Eastside Church* is proof that the complainant was a "member of the class of persons the Act was designed to protect." * * *

Section 29(b) renders certain contracts void. It does not limit that invalidity to contracts between issuers and sellers or to those between issuers and investors. The contracts involved here were between the general partners and a partnership that held itself out to be a qualified broker. Neither any investor nor the issuer was privy to it. Yet, as we have just held, they were precisely the kind of contracts "performance of which involve[d] the violation of" a provision of the Act, specifically, section 15(a)(1). If a party to these contracts could not attack them, it would be yet more difficult to find reason to permit assault by the nonparty issuers and investors whom, according to Financial, the Act was designed to protect.

* * *

C. The Defenses to a Section 29(b) Cause of Action.

Having thus decided that Regional did make out a *prima facie* case under section 29(b), we next must determine whether there exist defenses to such an action and, if so, whether Financial succeeded in proving any. Although the question of the availability of defenses to a section 29(b) action was not discussed in *Eastside Church,* we have no hesitation in holding that there are such defenses and that they, in fact, encompass all the traditional equitable defenses.

The starting points for our discussion are the propositions, too elementary to require citation, that, historically, a suit to void a contract sounded in equity, and that, in suits in equity, equitable defenses, such as laches, estoppel, etc., may be raised. While actions to void a securities broker's contract obviously stem from statute rather than a traditional equitable right, they are equitable in nature. The Ninth circuit has stated in the leading case on this subject:

> Since courts generally interpret statutes in the context of the common law and Congress has not specifically denied the availability of these defenses, we see no reason why the ordinary [equitable] defenses of estoppel and waiver should not be applicable.

Royal Air Properties, Inc. v. Smith, 312 F.2d 210, 214 (9th Cir.1962). Though that court mentioned only the defenses of estoppel and waiver, because those were the only ones raised by the defendant, we see no reason why the same reasoning would not allow any of the equitable defenses to be pleaded and proved by a section 29(b) defendant.

* * *

Therefore, because it would be anomalous to hold that, while one equitable defense is available, the others are not, we join with virtually all other courts that have decided this issue and hold that all equitable defenses are available in a section 29(b) cause of action.

* * *

In the *Regional Properties* case, the court held that, in a suit seeking rescission under § 29(a), it is not necessary that the plaintiff show any causal connection between the harm it suffered and the defendant's violation of the Act. When the suit is brought under the "implied private right of action" theory, however, the situation is very different. In those cases, courts have generally held that the plaintiff must show both "transaction causation," i.e., that the fraud caused the plaintiff to enter into the transaction, and "loss causation," i.e., that the transaction caused the loss to the plaintiff. See, e.g., Schlick v. Penn–Dixie, p. 726 below. More recently, some courts have gone further and required that the plaintiff demonstrate that the loss was a result of the facts which were misrepresented by the defendant:

BASTIAN v. PETREN

892 F.2d 680 (7th Cir.1990).

Before BAUER, CHIEF JUDGE, POSNER, CIRCUIT JUDGE, and ESCHBACH, SENIOR CIRCUIT JUDGE.

POSNER, CIRCUIT JUDGE.

In 1981 the plaintiffs invested $600,000 in oil and gas limited partnerships promoted by the defendants. The plaintiffs allege that, had it not been for the offering memoranda's misrepresentations and misleading omissions concerning the defendants' competence and integrity, the plaintiffs would not have invested in these partnerships, which by 1984 were worthless. The original complaint charged violations of Rule 10b–5 of the Securities and Exchange Commission, and the RICO statute, and sought damages equal to the investment. The district judge dismissed this complaint, but without prejudice, on the defendants' motion under Fed.R.Civ.P. 12(b)(6) to dismiss for failure to state a claim. 681 F.Supp. 530 (N.D.Ill.1988). With respect to the RICO charge he found only a minor technical deficiency easily curable by filing an amended complaint. With respect to the Rule 10b–5 charge he found a more serious deficiency: a failure to allege "loss causation"—that is, that if the facts had been as represented by the defendants the value of the limited partnerships would not have declined. * * *

The plaintiffs argue that they should not be required to allege that, but for the circumstances that the fraud concealed, the investment that they were induced by the fraud to make would not have lost its value. They say it should be enough to allege that they would not have invested but for the fraud; for if they had not invested, they would not have lost their money, and the fraud was therefore the cause of their loss. They say they have no idea why their investment was wiped out and it does not matter; the defendants, being responsible for the disaster by having used fraud to induce the investment, must not be allowed to get off scot-free just because the plaintiffs do not know how the investment would have fared in the marketplace had the facts about the defendants' competence and integrity been as represented. As a fallback position the plaintiffs argue that the defendants should have the burden of proving what part (if any) of the loss would have occurred even if the defendants had been as competent and honest as represented.

Rule 10b–5 is not a complete scheme for remedying securities fraud. Indeed, it is just a declaration that securities fraud is unlawful. The right to bring a private action for damages that the rule has been held to confer is an implied right, and its dimensions and incidents are a common law growth nourished by analogies from the law of torts. All Rule 10b–5 does is supply the foundation upon which federal judges have built a federal common law of securities fraud. It would be surprising therefore if the rules that have evolved over many years to establish the contours of common law actions for fraud and other intentional torts were entirely inapplicable to suits under Rule 10b–5, and of course they are not.

Indeed what securities lawyers call "loss causation" *is* the standard common law fraud rule, merely borrowed for use in federal securities fraud cases. It is more fundamental still; it is an instance of the common law's universal requirement that the tort plaintiff prove causation. No hurt, no tort. * * *

The plaintiffs alleged that they invested in the defendants' limited partnerships because of the defendants' misrepresentations, and that their investment was wiped out. But they suggest no reason *why* the investment was wiped out. They have alleged the cause of their entering into the transaction in which they lost money but not the cause of the transaction's turning out to be a losing one. It happens that 1981 was a peak year for oil prices and that those prices declined steadily in the succeeding years. When this happened the profitability of drilling for oil (and gas, which generally is produced with it) in the continental United States plummeted. * * * If the defendants had come clean in their offering memoranda, then we may assume—because the plaintiffs allege, and the case was dismissed on the complaint—that the plaintiffs would not have invested in the defendants' limited partnerships. But there were plenty of other oil and gas limited partnerships they could have invested in. They wanted to invest in oil and gas limited partnerships; they only wanted to be sure that the general partners were honest and competent people. Yet to be honest and competent is not to be gifted with prevision. If the alternative oil and gas limited partnerships to which these plaintiffs would have turned had the defendants leveled with them were also doomed, despite competent and honest management, to become worthless, the plaintiffs were not hurt by the fraud; it affected the place but not the time or amount of their loss.

To satisfy Rule 11 all that the plaintiffs had to do was to obtain evidence from persons knowledgeable about oil and gas ventures in the early 1980s that many or most oil and gas ventures had succeeded notwithstanding the downturn in price after 1981. Perhaps if the plaintiffs had conducted such a search they would have discovered, contrary to our speculation (and it is just that), that oil and gas ventures managed by competent and honest businessmen *had* survived the drop in oil prices. If so, this would support an inference that if the defendants had been as competent and honest as they represented themselves to be, they would not have lost the plaintiffs' $600,000. The plaintiffs' unwillingness to make this allegation in their amended complaint suggests to us that they may have made inquiry of experts in the oil and gas industry and discovered that the cause of the disaster was unrelated to the competence and honesty of the defendants.

If the plaintiffs would have lost their investment regardless of the fraud, any award of damages to them would be a windfall. Other sections of the securities laws, such as section 12(2) of the 1933 Act, permit windfall recoveries, but we do not see how this helps the plaintiffs. Those sections deal with other conduct and some of them contain restrictions on liability that Rule 10b–5 does not. * * * No social purpose would be served by encouraging everyone who suffers an investment loss because of an unanticipated change in market conditions to pick through offering memoranda with a fine-tooth comb in the hope of uncovering a misrepresentation. Defrauders are a bad lot and should be punished, but Rule 10b–5 does not make them insurers against national economic calamities. If the defendants' oil and gas ventures failed not because of the personal shortcomings that the defendants concealed but because of industry-wide phenomena that destroyed all or most such ventures, then the plaintiffs, given their demonstrated desire to invest in such ventures, lost nothing by reason of the defendants' fraud and have no claim to damages.

We have treated the question whether loss causation is an element of a claim for damages under Rule 10b–5 from the ground up because there is no controlling precedent in the Supreme Court or in this circuit, and because there are cases on both sides of the question in the other circuits, though they greatly preponderate in favor of the requirement and such conflict as there is appears to be within rather than among circuits. Our cases either state in dictum, or assume, that the requirement does exist. We have tried to explain why it should exist, and now we add a note on its scope which suggests that some of the cases that express disagreement with the doctrine may be reconcilable with it. Suppose a broker gives false assurances to his customer that an investment is risk-free. In fact it is risky, the risk materializes, the investment is lost. Here there can be no presumption that but for the misrepresentation the customer would have made an equally risky investment. On the contrary, the fact that the broker assured the customer that the investment was free of risk suggests that the customer was looking for a safe investment. Liability in such a case is therefore consistent with nonliability in a case such as the present. The plaintiffs in the present case were not told that oil and gas partnerships are risk-free. They knew they were assuming a risk that oil prices might drop unexpectedly. They are unwilling to try to prove that anything beyond the materializing of that risk caused their loss.

* * *

Selected References

Aiken, Availability of an Implied Civil Cause of Action Under Section 17(a) of the Securities Act of 1933, 9 N.C.J.Int'l L. & Com.Reg. 207 (1984).

Ashford, Implied Causes of Action Under Federal Laws: Calling the Court Back to *Borak,* 79 Nw.U.L.Rev. 227 (1984).

Hazen, Allocation of Jurisdiction Between the State and Federal Courts for Private Remedies Under the Federal Securities Laws, 60 N.C.L.Rev. 707 (1982).

Schneider, Implying Private Rights and Remedies under the Federal Securities Acts, 62 N.C.L.Rev. 853 (1984).

Note, A Plea for Consistency: Refusing Implication of a Private Right of Action Under Section 17(a) of the Securities Act of 1933, 62 N.Y.U.L. Rev. 116 (1987).

Note, Section 17(a) of the Securities Act of 1933: Implication of a Private Right of Action, 29 UCLA L.Rev. 244 (1981).

---

3. *Overlap With Other Provisions*

Recognition of a private right of action for fraudulent misstatements under Rule 10b–5 of course raises the possibility that such an action may be brought where the misstatement is covered by another, more specific, provision of federal securities law. The Supreme Court considered this question in its opinion in SEC v. NATIONAL SECURITIES, 393 U.S. 453 (1969), another part of which appears at p. 470 above:

> Respondents' alternative argument that Rule 10b–5 does not cover misrepresentations which occur in connection with proxy solicitations can be dismissed rather quickly. Section 14 of the 1934 Act, and the rules adopted pursuant to that section, set up a complex regulatory scheme covering proxy solicitations. At the time of the conduct charged in the complaint, these provisions did not apply to respondents; the 1964 amendments to the Securities Exchange Act would have made them applicable later if certain conditions relating to state regulation had not been met. But the existence or nonexistence of regulation under § 14 would not affect the scope of § 10(b) and Rule 10b–5. The two sections of the Act apply to different sets of situations. Section 10(b) applies to all proscribed conduct in connection with a purchase or sale of any security; § 14 applies to all proxy solicitations, whether or not in connection with a purchase or sale. The fact that there may well be some overlap is neither unusual nor unfortunate. Nor does it help respondents that insurance companies may often be exempt from federal proxy regulation under the 1964 amendments. The securities laws' exemptions for insurance companies and insurance activities are carefully limited. None is applicable to the Rule 10b–5 situation with which we are confronted, and we do not have the power to create one. Congress may well have concluded that the Commission's general antifraud powers over purchases and sales of securities should continue to apply to insurance securities, even though the more detailed regulation of proxy solicitations—which may often be conducted in connection with the managerial activities of insurance companies—was left to the States. Accordingly, we find no bar to the application of Rule 10b–5 to respondents' misstatements in their proxy materials.

The *National Securities* case, however, involved an overlap with § 14 of the 1934 Act, which also contains no express private right of action. The question is more difficult when the misstatement would also give rise to an express private right of action under § 11 of the 1933 Act or § 18 of the 1934 Act. In that situation, Rule 10b–5 can be used to circumvent some of the limitations written into the express civil liability provision.

HERMAN & MacLEAN v. HUDDLESTON

459 U.S. 375 (1983).

JUSTICE MARSHALL delivered the opinion of the Court.

These consolidated cases raise two unresolved questions concerning Section 10(b) of the Securities Exchange Act of 1934. The first is whether purchasers of registered securities who allege they were defrauded by misrepresentations in a registration statement may maintain an action under Section 10(b) notwithstanding the express remedy for misstatements and omissions in registration statements provided by Section 11 of the Securities Act of 1933. The second question is whether persons seeking recovery under Section 10(b) must prove their cause of action by clear and convincing evidence rather than by a preponderance of the evidence.

I

In 1969 Texas International Speedway, Inc. ("TIS"), filed a registration statement and prospectus with the Securities and Exchange Commission offering a total of $4,398,900 in securities to the public. The proceeds of the sale were to be used to finance the construction of an automobile speedway. The entire issue was sold on the offering date, October 30, 1969. TIS did not meet with success, however, and the corporation filed a petition for bankruptcy on November 30, 1970.

In 1972 plaintiffs Huddleston and Bradley instituted a class action in the United States District Court for the Southern District of Texas on behalf of themselves and other purchasers of TIS securities. The complaint alleged violations of Section 10(b) of the Securities Exchange Act of 1934 ("the 1934 Act") and SEC Rule 10b–5 promulgated thereunder. Plaintiffs sued most of the participants in the offering, including the accounting firm, Herman & MacLean, which had issued an opinion concerning certain financial statements and a pro forma balance sheet that were contained in the registration statement and prospectus. Plaintiffs claimed that the defendants had engaged in a fraudulent scheme to misrepresent or conceal material facts regarding the financial condition of TIS, including the costs incurred in building the speedway.

II

The Securities Act of 1933 and the Securities Exchange Act of 1934 "constitute interrelated components of the federal regulatory scheme governing transactions in securities." The Acts created several express private rights of action, one of which is contained in Section 11 of the

1933 Act. In addition to the private actions created explicitly by the 1933 and 1934 Acts, federal courts have implied private remedies under other provisions of the two laws. Most significantly for present purposes, a private right of action under Section 10(b) of the 1934 Act and Rule 10b–5 has been consistently recognized for more than 35 years. The existence of this implied remedy is simply beyond peradventure.

The issue in this case is whether a party should be barred from invoking this established remedy for fraud because the allegedly fraudulent conduct would apparently also provide the basis for a damage action under Section 11 of the 1933 Act. The resolution of this issue turns on the fact that the two provisions involve distinct causes of action and were intended to address different types of wrongdoing.

Section 11 of the 1933 Act allows purchasers of a registered security to sue certain enumerated parties in a registered offering when false or misleading information is included in a registration statement. The section was designed to assure compliance with the disclosure provisions of the Act by imposing a stringent standard of liability on the parties who play a direct role in a registered offering. If a plaintiff purchased a security issued pursuant to a registration statement, he need only show a material misstatement or omission to establish his *prima facie* case. Liability against the issuer of a security is virtually absolute, even for innocent misstatements. Other defendants bear the burden of demonstrating due diligence.

Although limited in scope, Section 11 places a relatively minimal burden on a plaintiff. In contrast, Section 10(b) is a "catchall" antifraud provision, but it requires a plaintiff to carry a heavier burden to establish a cause of action. While a Section 11 action must be brought by a purchaser of a registered security, must be based on misstatements or omissions in a registration statement, and can only be brought against certain parties, a Section 10(b) action can be brought by a purchaser or seller of "*any* security" against "*any* person" who has used "*any* manipulative or deceptive device or contrivance" in connection with the purchase or sale of a security. However, a Section 10(b) plaintiff carries a heavier burden than a Section 11 plaintiff. Most significantly, he must prove that the defendant acted with scienter, i.e., with intent to deceive, manipulate, or defraud.

Since Section 11 and Section 10(b) address different types of wrongdoing, we see no reason to carve out an exception to Section 10(b) for fraud occurring in a registration statement just because the same conduct may also be actionable under Section 11. Exempting such conduct from liability under Section 10(b) would conflict with the basic purpose of the 1933 Act: to provide greater protection to purchasers of registered securities. It would be anomalous indeed if the special protection afforded to purchasers in a registered offering by the 1933 Act were deemed to deprive such purchasers of the protections against manipulation and deception that Section 10(b) makes available to all persons who deal in securities.

While some conduct actionable under Section 11 may also be actionable under Section 10(b), it is hardly a novel proposition that the Securities Exchange Act and the Securities Act "prohibit some of the same conduct." United States v. Naftalin, 441 U.S. 768, 778 (1979) (applying Section 17(a) of the 1933 Act to conduct also prohibited by Section 10(b) of the 1934 Act in an action by the SEC). " 'The fact that there may well be some overlap is neither unusual nor unfortunate.' " Ibid., quoting SEC v. National Securities, Inc., 393 U.S. 453, 468 (1969). In savings clauses included in the 1933 and 1934 Acts, Congress rejected the notion that the express remedies of the securities laws would preempt all other rights of action. Section 16 of the 1933 Act states unequivocally that "[t]he rights and remedies provided by this subchapter shall be in addition to any and all other rights and remedies that may exist at law or in equity." Section 28(a) of the 1934 Act contains a parallel provision. These provisions confirm that the remedies in each Act were to be supplemented by "any and all" additional remedies.

This conclusion is reinforced by our reasoning in Ernst & Ernst v. Hochfelder, which held that actions under Section 10(b) require proof of scienter and do not encompass negligent conduct. In so holding, we noted that each of the express civil remedies in the 1933 Act allowing recovery for negligent conduct is subject to procedural restrictions not applicable to a Section 10(b) action. We emphasized that extension of Section 10(b) to negligent conduct would have allowed causes of action for negligence under the express remedies to be brought instead under Section 10(b), "thereby nullify[ing] the effectiveness of the carefully drawn procedural restrictions on these express actions." In reasoning that scienter should be required in Section 10(b) actions in order to avoid circumvention of the procedural restrictions surrounding the express remedies, we necessarily assumed that the express remedies were not exclusive. Otherwise there would have been no danger of nullification. Conversely, because the added burden of proving scienter attaches to suits under Section 10(b), invocation of the Section 10(b) remedy will not "nullify" the procedural restrictions that apply to the express remedies.

This cumulative construction of the remedies under the 1933 and 1934 Acts is also supported by the fact that, when Congress comprehensively revised the securities laws in 1975, a consistent line of judicial decisions had permitted plaintiffs to sue under Section 10(b) regardless of the availability of express remedies. In 1975 Congress enacted the "most substantial and significant revision of this country's Federal securities laws since the passage of the Securities Exchange Act in 1934." When Congress acted, federal courts had consistently and routinely permitted a plaintiff to proceed under Section 10(b) even where express remedies under Section 11 or other provisions were available. In light of this well-established judicial interpretation, Congress' decision to leave Section 10(b) intact suggests that Congress ratified the cumulative nature of the Section 10(b) action.

A cumulative construction of the securities laws also furthers their broad remedial purposes. In enacting the 1934 Act, Congress stated that its purpose was "to impose requirements necessary to make [securities] regulation and control reasonably complete and effective." In furtherance of that objective, Section 10(b) makes it unlawful to use "*any* manipulative or deceptive device or contrivance" in connection with the purchase or sale of any security. The effectiveness of the broad proscription against fraud in Section 10(b) would be undermined if its scope were restricted by the existence of an express remedy under Section 11. Yet we have repeatedly recognized that securities laws combating fraud should be construed "not technically and restrictively, but flexibly to effectuate [their] remedial purposes." SEC v. Capital Gains Research Bureau, 375 U.S. 180, 195 (1963). Accord: Superintendent of Insurance v. Bankers Life & Cas. Co., 404 U.S. 6, 12 (1971); Affiliated Ute Citizens v. United States, 406 U.S. 128, 151 (1972). We therefore reject an interpretation of the securities laws that displaces an action under Section 10(b).

Accordingly, we hold that the availability of an express remedy under Section 11 of the 1933 Act does not preclude defrauded purchasers of registered securities from maintaining an action under Section 10(b) of the 1934 Act. To this extent the judgment of the court of appeals is affirmed.

III

In a typical civil suit for money damages, plaintiffs must prove their case by a preponderance of the evidence.

* * *

The Court of Appeals nonetheless held that plaintiffs in a Section 10(b) suit must establish their case by clear and convincing evidence. The Court of Appeals relied primarily on the traditional use of a higher burden of proof in civil fraud actions at common law. Reference to common law practices can be misleading, however, since the historical considerations underlying the imposition of a higher standard of proof have questionable pertinence here.

* * *

A preponderance-of-the-evidence standard allows both parties to "share the risk of error in roughly equal fashion." Any other standard expresses a preference for one side's interests. The balance of interests in this case warrants use of the preponderance standard. On the one hand, the defendants face the risk of opprobrium that may result from a finding of fraudulent conduct, but this risk is identical to that in an action under Section 17(a), which is governed by the preponderance-of-the-evidence standard. The interests of defendants in a securities case do not differ qualitatively from the interests of defendants sued for violations of other federal statutes such as the antitrust or civil rights laws, for which proof by a preponderance of the evidence suffices. On the other hand, the interests of plaintiffs in such suits are significant. Defrauded investors are among the very individuals Congress sought to protect in the securities laws. If they prove that it is more likely than not that they were defrauded, they should recover.

The Supreme Court has not specifically passed on the question whether a plaintiff can sue under Rule 10b–5 for misstatements in a document filed under the 1934 Act, as to which there would be an express right of action under § 18. Several courts of appeals, however, have held that such an action can be brought, utilizing reasoning similar to that of the Supreme Court in the *Huddleston* case. See ROSS v. A.H. ROBINS, 607 F.2d 545 (2d Cir.1979); WACHOVIA BANK v. NATIONAL STUDENT MARKETING, 650 F.2d 342 (D.C.Cir.1980).

One important reason that plaintiffs have turned to Rule 10b–5 rather than the express liability provisions of the 1933 and 1934 Acts in suing for misstatements in filed documents is the rather short statute of limitations applicable to those provisions—suit must generally be brought within three years of the transaction and within one year from the time the plaintiff discovered or should have discovered the misstatement. In actions under Rule 10b–5, on the other hand, the courts, under prevailing federal doctrines, have tended to look to the state statutes of limitations applicable to "analogous" claims in the state where the violation occurred. This has led to a large expenditure of judicial resources and a haphazard set of rules that makes very little sense. Recently, however, there have been indications that the courts may be moving toward a different approach, as the following opinion indicates:

DAVIS v. BIRR, WILSON

839 F.2d 1369 (9th Cir.1988).

Before ALDISERT, SKOPIL and SCHROEDER, CIRCUIT JUDGES.

PER CURIAM:

Davis appeals from the district court's grant of summary judgment in favor of Birr, Wilson & Company. The single issue on appeal is whether Davis' section 10(b) action is barred by the statute of limitations. We affirm.

These claimed violations of section 10(b) of the Securities Exchange Act of 1934, are subject to California's three-year statute of limitations for fraud. The statute of limitations begins to run when the plaintiff has actual knowledge of the fraud or knowledge of facts sufficient to put a reasonable person on notice.

* * *

ALDISERT, CIRCUIT JUDGE, concurring:

Although I join in the per curiam opinion of the court, I write separately to suggest that the Supreme Court has now sent signals that a uniform limitations period should be established nationwide for cases brought under section 10(b) of the Securities Exchange Act of 1934, and its nubile offspring, Rule 10b–5. I think that it is both timely and appropriate for this court to adopt a clear-cut limitations period because of the rapidly accelerating growth of securities transactions in the states and territories that fall within this court's extensive jurisdiction.

I.

I recognize that the Supreme Court has yet to rule on the applicable limitations period for a section 10(b) and Rule 10b–5 action. The absence of a uniform limitations period in such actions has been described by Judge Easterbrook as "one tottering parapet of a ramshackle edifice. Deciding what features of state periods of limitation to adopt for which federal statutes wastes untold hours." Norris v. Wirtz, 818 F.2d 1329, 1332 (7th Cir.1987). Judge Easterbrook has lamented:

> Never has the process been more enervating than in securities law. There are many potentially analogous state statutes, with variations for different kinds of securities offenses and different circumstances that might toll the period of limitations. Both the bar and scholars have found the subject vexing and have pleaded, with a unanimity rare in the law, for help. As the ABA's Committee on Federal Regulation of Securities observed, the courts of appeals disagree on every possible question about limitations periods in securities cases. Only Congress or the Supreme Court can bring uniformity and predictability to this field[.]

Yet we first must review the reasoning and holdings of our cases setting forth the present limitations period in section 10(b) cases.

In the seminal case of Fratt v. Robinson, 203 F.2d 627, 635 (9th Cir. 1953), the court declared, strangely enough, that actions based on section 10(b) "do not arise out of nor upon a statute," but instead are based upon state tort fraud precepts. Accordingly, the court determined that Washington's three-year statute of limitations for fraud applies to section 10(b) actions brought in that state. In Royal Air Properties, Inc. v. Smith, 312 F.2d 210, 214 (9th Cir.1962), we recognized that "[i]n an action brought under section 10(b) of the Securities Exchange Act of 1934 there is no federal statute of limitations," and, without offering any additional reasoning, simply said that in *Fratt* "we applied the applicable state statute of limitations" to such actions. In Hecht v. Harris, Upham & Co., 430 F.2d 1202, 1210 (9th Cir.1970), we simply noted that in a section 10(b) case brought in California, the state's limitations period for fraud applied, citing only *Royal Air Properties* and *Fratt.* Speaking for the court in Robuck v. Dean Witter & Co., 649 F.2d 641 (9th Cir.1980), Judge Goodwin noted that in a section 10(b) case, it was possible that two limitations periods could be applied to a single complaint brought in California: three years for a count sounding in fraud; two years for one charging lack of "due diligence." * * *

The law in this court, borrowing state limitations periods for section 10(b) cases, was in tune with that of all courts of appeals, because all of us were marching to the drum beat then set by the Supreme Court—where the federal statute is silent, borrow from that state limitations period that most resembles the federal cause of action. But the Court has now changed the beat. We are now marching to a different drummer since the recent trilogy of Agency Holding Corp. v. Malley–Duff & Assocs., Inc., ___ U.S. ___ (1987), Wilson v. Garcia, 471 U.S. 261 (1985), and DelCostello v. International Bhd. of Teamsters, 462 U.S. 151 (1983).

II.

In Agency Holding Corp. v. Malley–Duff Assocs., Inc., the Court provided us with a formula to approach the problem we face today. In *Malley–Duff,* the Court stated that "[a]lthough it has been suggested that federal courts always should apply the state statute of limitations most analogous to each individual case whenever a federal statute is silent on the proper limitations period, *a clear majority of the Court [in DelCostello] rejected such a single path.*" The Court then outlined the procedure to be followed in determining the appropriate statute of limitations for a federal claim. The first step involves characterizing the federal claim; this is generally a question of federal law. In this initial step, we must determine whether all claims arising out of the federal statute should be characterized in the same way, or whether they should be evaluated differently depending upon the varying factual circumstances and legal theories presented in each individual case.

Once this characterization is made, the next inquiry is whether a federal or state statute of limitations should be used. The Supreme Court has held that the Rules of Decision Act, 28 U.S.C. § 1652, requires application of state statutes of limitations to federal statutory actions not covered by an express limitations period unless "a timeliness rule drawn from elsewhere in federal law should be applied." In some circumstances, the characterization of a federal claim has led the Court to conclude that "state statutes of limitations can be unsatisfactory vehicles for the enforcement of federal law. In those instances, it may be inappropriate to conclude that Congress would choose to adopt state rules at odds with the purpose or operation of federal substantive law." * * *

Because the Court has condemned a practice of dealing with section 10(b) and Rule 10b–5 that involves "a shifting and highly fact-oriented disposition," I think it is sending an impressive message that we should adopt a uniform limitations period in these cases rather than try to color match each case with shifting state fraud statutes of limitations. See Friedlander v. Troutman, Sanders, Lockerman, 788 F.2d 1500, 1505

(11th Cir.1986) (adopting a uniform limitations period for all section 10(b) and Rule 10b–5 claims).

III.

This court's practice of borrowing state fraud limitations periods in section 10(b) suits demonstrates the attractiveness of a uniform statute of limitations. The states and territories that fall within the jurisdiction of the Court of Appeals for the Ninth Circuit have adopted a wide diversity of limitations periods for common law fraud. Alaska, Oregon, and Montana have set a two-year limitations period for fraud. Arizona, California, Idaho, Nevada, Washington, and Guam have established a three-year statute. Finally, Hawaii and the Marianas have adopted a six-year limitations period.

In looking for the one most appropriate statute of limitations for section 10(b) and Rule 10b–5 claims, we must not make the error of equating private rights of action under section 10(b) and Rule 10b–5 with available common law fraud actions. The Supreme Court instructs that section 10(b) and Rule 10b–5 actions and common law fraud suits are two distinct breeds. * * * Moreover, the antifraud provisions of the securities laws are not coextensive with common law doctrines of fraud. "Indeed, an important purpose of the federal securities statutes was to rectify perceived deficiencies in the available common-law protections by establishing higher standards of conduct in the securities industry." * * * It is therefore clear that, far from being a mirror image or a reasonable facsimile of common law fraud, actions brought under section 10(b) and Rule 10b–5 appear to be *sui generis.*

IV.

I suggest that the federal schema of limitations expressly set forth in the Securities Exchange Act of 1934 "clearly provides a closer analogy than available state statutes," and that "the federal policies at stake [in section 10(b) and Rule 10b–5 actions] and the practicalities of litigation make [the federal] rule a significantly more appropriate vehicle for interstitial lawmaking." I now turn to those sections of federal securities law that are companion provisions to section 10(b).

Congress provided for statutes of repose in numerous provisions of the Securities Acts. The Securities Act of 1933 extended to the purchaser two years from the date of discovery of the fraud, but in no event more than 10 years after the sale. When Congress enacted the Securities Exchange Act of 1934, it amended the 1933 limitations statute and specified a new statute of limitations for each of the express rights of action it created.

The express periods of limitations added or amended in 1934 allow the plaintiff to file an action no later than one year after the plaintiff discovers the facts, and in no event more than three years after the transaction in question. One exception, the unlawful profit statute, section 16(b), sets two rather than three years as the period of repose.

There are reasons for these specific periods of repose in the 1934 Act. In Norris v. Wirtz, 818 F.2d 1329, 1332 (7th Cir.), the court noted:

> The legislative history in 1934 makes it pellucid that Congress included statutes of repose because of fear that lingering liabilities would disrupt normal business and facilitate false claims. It was understood that the three-year rule was to be absolute.

* * *

Both section 10(b) and its companion provisions—§ 9(e) (manipulation of security prices); § 16(b) (profits from purchase and sale of securities within six months); § 18(c) (liability for misleading statements in any application, report, or filed document); and § 29(b) (validity of contract provisions in violation of Act or regulations thereunder)—are aimed at the same objectives. All of these companion provisions, except section 16(b), have a uniform federal limitations period. * * * All aim to compensate the same type of injury. All are designed to fill a void in the common law and to create remedies that would be uniform throughout our nation's commercial universe, instead of being subjected to the vagaries of independent and diverse state statutory regulations.

* * *

The necessity for uniform federal remedies in security cases would seem to demand recourse to a uniform federal statute of limitations. A broker in Phoenix, an issuer in San Francisco, a purchaser in Montana, an accountant in Portland, and a lawyer in Honolulu should be subject to the same statute of limitations for actions based on section 10(b) or Rule 10b–5. Again with a nod to Cicero, you simply should not have a different Securities Act limitations period for Rome, New York, and Athens, Georgia (*Non erit alia lex Romae, alia Athenis*). And since uniformity is not found in the diverse body of state tort limitations periods, we are impelled inexorably to look to federal limitations for borrowing purposes.

* * *

V.

I therefore suggest that the express limitations sections of the Securities Exchange Act of 1934 provide the preferable source of limitations borrowing here.

* * *

When Congress has created a right to sue in securities matters, it has declared a limitations period no longer than three years. I think that the proper period of limitations for a section 10(b) and Rule 10b–5 action should be one year after the plaintiff discovers the facts, and in no event more than three years after the transaction in question.

In a subsequent case arising in the Third Circuit, the Court of Appeals, *en banc*, in an opinion by Judge Aldisert, followed his reasoning in the *Davis* case and held that actions under Rule 10b–5 are governed by the statute of limitations found in other provisions of the federal securities laws. In re DATA ACCESS SYSTEMS, 843 F.2d 1537 (3d Cir.1988).

In 1988, Congress passed the Insider Trading and Securities Fraud Enforcement Act, which establishes a five-year statute of limitations for actions brought by private plaintiffs under new § 20A of the 1934 Act. This section requires plaintiffs to show that defendants violated the prohibitions against insider trading found in the Act or rules thereunder (principally Rule 10b–5; see p. 624 below). How would this affect the implementation of the approach endorsed by Judge Aldisert in the *Davis* and *Data Access* cases? In CERES v. GEL, 714 F.Supp. 679 (S.D. N.Y.1989), the court held that the § 20A statute of limitations was not the appropriate statute to apply to offenses not involving misappropriation or wrongful use of inside information.

Selected References

Aldave, "Neither Unusual Nor Unfortunate": The Overlap of Rule 10b–5 with the Express Liability Sections of the Securities Acts, 60 Tex.L. Rev. 719 (1982).

Crespi, The Availability After Carpenter of Private Rights of Action Under Rule 10b–5 Based Upon the Misappropriation of Information Concerning Acquisitions, 26 Am.Bus.L.J. 709 (1989).

Sachs, Exclusive Federal Jurisdiction for Implied Rule 10b–5 Actions: The Emperor Has No Clothes, 49 Ohio St. L.J. 559 (1988).

Siegel, Interplay Between the Implied Remedy Under Section 10(b) and the Express Causes of Action of the Federal Securities Laws, 62 B.U.L.Rev. 385 (1982).

Steinberg, Propriety and Scope of Cumulative Remedies Under the Federal Securities Laws, 67 Cornell L.Rev. 557 (1982).

Wang, Is a Seller's Rule 10b–5 Cause of Action Automatically Transferable to the Buyer?, 1988 Colum.Bus.L.Rev. 129.

---

4. *Standing to Sue*

In one of the earliest appellate court decisions interpreting Rule 10b–5, the Second Circuit held that only a person who had purchased or sold securities had standing to sue under the Rule. Birnbaum v. Newport Steel, 193 F.2d 461 (2d Cir.1952). The issue reached the Supreme Court in 1975, affording the Court its first opportunity to set forth a new conservative approach toward interpretation of the antifraud provisions.

BLUE CHIP STAMPS v. MANOR DRUG STORES

421 U.S. 723 (1975).

MR. JUSTICE REHNQUIST delivered the opinion of the Court.

This case requires us to consider whether the offerees of a stock offering, made pursuant to an antitrust consent decree and registered under the Securities Act of 1933, may maintain a private cause of action for money damages where they allege that the offeror has violated the provisions of Rule 10b–5 of the Securities and Exchange Commission, but where they have neither purchased nor sold any of the offered shares.

I

In 1963 the United States filed a civil antitrust action against Blue Chip Stamp Company ("Old Blue Chip"), a company in the business of providing trading stamps to retailers, and nine retailers who owned 90% of its shares. In 1967 the action was terminated by the entry of a consent decree. The decree contemplated a plan of reorganization whereby Old Blue Chip was to be merged into a newly formed corporation "New Blue Chip." The holdings of the majority shareholders of Old Blue Chip were to be reduced, and New Blue Chip, one of the petitioners here, was required under the plan to offer a substantial number of its shares of common stock to retailers who had used the stamp service in the past but who were not shareholders in the old company. Under the terms of the plan, the offering to nonshareholder users was to be proportional to past stamp usage and the shares were to be offered in units consisting of common stock and debentures.

The reorganization plan was carried out, the offering was registered with the SEC as required by the 1933 Act, and a prospectus was distributed to all offerees as required by § 5 of that Act. Somewhat more than 50% of the offered units were actually purchased. In 1970, two years after the offering, respondent, a former user of the stamp service and therefore an offeree of the 1968 offering, filed this suit in the United States District Court for the Central District of California. Defendants below and petitioners here are Old and New Blue Chip, eight of the nine majority shareholders of Old Blue Chip, and the directors of New Blue Chip (collectively called "Blue Chip").

Respondent's complaint alleged, *inter alia,* that the prospectus prepared and distributed by Blue Chip in connection with the offering was materially misleading in its overly pessimistic appraisal of Blue Chip's status and future prospects. It alleged that Blue Chip intentionally made the prospectus overly pessimistic in order to discourage respondent and other members of the allegedly large class whom it represents from accepting what was intended to be a bargain offer, so that the rejected shares might later be offered to the public at a higher price. The complaint alleged that class members because of and in reliance on the false and misleading prospectus failed to purchase the offered units. Respondent therefore sought on behalf of the alleged class some $21,400,000 in damages representing the lost opportunity to purchase the units; the right to purchase the previously rejected units at the 1968 price, and in addition, it sought some $25,000,000 in exemplary damages.

The only portion of the litigation thus initiated which is before us is whether respondent may base its action on Rule 10b–5 of the Securities and Exchange Commission without having either bought or sold the shares described in the allegedly misleading prospectus.

* * *

Section 10(b) of the 1934 Act does not by its terms provide an express civil remedy for its violation. Nor does the history of this provision provide any indication that Congress considered the problem of private suits under it at the time of its passage. Similarly there is no indication that the Commission in adopting Rule 10b–5 considered the question of private civil remedies under this provision.

Despite the contrast between the provisions of Rule 10b–5 and the numerous carefully drawn express civil remedies provided in both the Acts of 1933 and 1934, it was held in 1946 by the United States District Court for the Eastern District of Pennsylvania that there was an implied private right of action under the Rule. Kardon v. National Gypsum Co., 69 F.Supp. 512 (1946). This Court had no occasion to deal with the subject until 20–odd years later, and at that time we confirmed with virtually no discussion the overwhelming consensus of the district courts and courts of appeals that such a cause of action did exist.

Within a few years after the seminal *Kardon* decision the Court of Appeals for the Second Circuit concluded that the plaintiff class for purposes of a private damage action under § 10(b) and Rule 10b–5 was limited to actual purchasers and sellers of securities. Birnbaum v. Newport Steel Corp., 193 F.2d 461 (1952).

The Court of Appeals in this case did not repudiate *Birnbaum;* indeed, another panel of that court (in an opinion by Judge Ely) had but a short time earlier affirmed the rule of that case. Mount Clemmons Industries v. Bell, 464 F.2d 339 (C.A.9 1972). But in this case a majority of the Court of Appeals found that the facts warranted an exception to the *Birnbaum* rule. For the reasons hereinafter stated, we are of the opinion that *Birnbaum* was rightly decided, and that it bars respondent from maintaining this suit under Rule 10b–5.

III

The panel which decided *Birnbaum* consisted of Chief Judge Swan and Judges Learned Hand and Augustus Hand: the opinion was written by the latter. Since both § 10(b) and Rule 10b–5 proscribed only fraud "in connection with the purchase or sale" of securities, and since the history of § 10(b) revealed no congressional intention to extend a private civil remedy for money damages to other than defrauded purchasers or sellers of securities, in contrast to the express civil remedy provided by § 16(b) of the 1934 Act, the court concluded that the plaintiff class in a Rule 10b–5 action was limited to actual purchasers and sellers.

Just as this Court had no occasion to consider the validity of the *Kardon* holding that there was a private cause of action under Rule 10b–5 until 20–odd years later, nearly the same period of time has gone by between the *Birnbaum* decision and our consideration of the case now before us. As with *Kardon,* virtually all lower federal courts facing the issue in the hundreds of reported cases presenting this question over the past quarter century have reaffirmed *Birnbaum's* conclusion that the plaintiff class for purposes of § 10(b) and Rule 10b–5 private damage action is limited to purchasers and sellers of securities.

In 1957 and again in 1959, the Securities and Exchange Commission sought from Congress amendment of § 10(b) to change its wording from "in connection with the purchase or sale of any security" to "in connection with the purchase or sale of, *or any attempt to purchase or sell,* any security." (Emphasis added.)

* * * In the words of a memorandum submitted by the Commission to a congressional committee, the purpose of the proposed change was "to make section 10(b) also applicable to manipulative activities in connection with any attempt to purchase or sell any security." Opposition to the amendment was based on fears of the extension of civil liability under § 10(b) that it would cause. Neither change was adopted by Congress.

The longstanding acceptance by the courts, coupled with Congress' failure to reject *Birnbaum's* reasonable interpretation of the wording of § 10(b), wording which is directed towards injury suffered "in connection with the purchase or sale" of securities, argues significantly in favor of acceptance of the *Birnbaum* rule by this Court.

Available extrinsic evidence from the texts of the 1933 and 1934 Acts as to the congressional scheme in this regard, though not conclusive, supports the result reached by the *Birnbaum* court.

* * * [W]e would by no means be understood as suggesting that we are able to divine from the language of § 10(b) the express "intent of Congress" as to the contours of a private cause of action under Rule 10b–5. When we deal with private actions under Rule 10b–5, we deal with a judicial oak which has grown from little more than a legislative acorn. Such growth may be quite consistent with the congressional enactment and with the role of the federal judiciary in interpreting it, but it would be disingenuous to suggest that either Congress in 1934 or the Securities and Exchange Commission in 1942 foreordained the present state of the law with respect to Rule 10b–5. It is therefore proper that we consider, in addition to the factors already discussed, what may be described as policy considerations when we come to flesh out the portions of the law with respect to which neither the congres-

sional enactment nor the administrative regulations offer conclusive guidance.

* * *

A great majority of the many commentators on the issue before us have taken the view that the *Birnbaum* limitation on the plaintiff class in a Rule 10b–5 action for damages is an arbitrary restriction which unreasonably prevents some deserving plaintiffs from recovering damages which have in fact been caused by violations of Rule 10b–5. The Securities and Exchange Commission has filed an *amicus* brief in this case espousing that same view. We have no doubt that this is indeed a disadvantage of the *Birnbaum* rule, and if it had no countervailing advantages it would be undesirable as a matter of policy, however much it might be supported by precedent and legislative history. But we are of the opinion that there are countervailing advantages to the *Birnbaum* rule, purely as a matter of policy, although those advantages are more difficult to articulate than is the disadvantage.

There has been widespread recognition that litigation under Rule 10b–5 presents a danger of vexatiousness different in degree and in kind from that which accompanies litigation in general.

* * *

We believe that the concern expressed for the danger of vexatious litigation which could result from a widely expanded class of plaintiffs under Rule 10b–5 is founded in something more substantial than the common complaint of the many defendants who would prefer avoiding lawsuits entirely to either settling them or trying them. These concerns have two largely separate grounds.

The first of these concerns is that in the field of federal securities laws governing disclosure of information even a complaint which by objective standards may have very little chance of success at trial has a settlement value to the plaintiff out of any proportion to its prospect of success at trial so long as he may prevent the suit from being resolved against him by dismissal or summary judgment. The very pendency of the lawsuit may frustrate or delay normal business activity of the defendant which is totally unrelated to the lawsuit.

* * *

The second ground for fear of vexatious litigation is based on the concern that, given the generalized contours of liability, the abolition of the *Birnbaum* rule would throw open to the trier of fact many rather hazy issues of historical fact the proof of which depended almost entirely on oral testimony.

* * *

In considering the policy underlying the *Birnbaum* rule, it is not inappropriate to advert briefly to the tort of misrepresentation and deceit, to which a claim under § 10b–5 certainly has some relationship. Originally under the common law of England such an action was not available to one other than a party to a business transaction. That limitation was eliminated in Pasley v. Freeman, 3 Term Rep. 51, 100

Eng.Rep. 450 (1789). Under the earlier law the misrepresentation was generally required to be one of fact, rather than opinion, but that requirement, too, was gradually relaxed. Lord Bowen's famous comment in Edgington v. Fitzmaurice, that "the state of a man's mind is as much a fact as the state of his digestion," 1882, L.R. 29 Ch.Div. 359, suggests that this distinction, too, may have been somewhat arbitrary. And it has long been established in the ordinary case of deceit that a misrepresentation which leads to a refusal to purchase or to sell is actionable in just the same way as a representation which leads to the consummation of a purchase or sale. Butler v. Watkins, 13 Wall. 456, 20 L.Ed. 629 (1871). These aspects of the evolution of the tort of deceit and misrepresentation suggest a direction away from rules such as *Birnbaum.*

But the typical fact situation in which the classic tort of misrepresentation and deceit evolved was light years away from the world of commercial transactions to which Rule 10b–5 is applicable. The plaintiff in *Butler,* supra, for example, claimed that he had held off the market a patented machine for tying cotton bales which he had developed by reason of the fraudulent representations of the defendant. But the report of the case leaves no doubt that the plaintiff and defendant met with one another in New Orleans, that one presented a draft agreement to the other, and that letters were exchanged relating to that agreement. Although the claim to damages was based on an allegedly fraudulently induced decision not to put the machines on the market, the plaintiff and the defendant had concededly been engaged in the course of business dealings with one another, and would presumably have recognized one another on the street had they met.

In today's universe of transactions governed by the Securities Exchange Act of 1934, privity of dealing or even personal contact between potential defendant and potential plaintiff is the exception and not the rule. The stock of issuers is listed on financial exchanges utilized by tens of millions of investors and corporate representations reach a potential audience, encompassing not only the diligent few who peruse filed corporate reports or the sizable number of subscribers to financial journals, but the readership of the Nation's daily newspapers. Obviously neither the fact that issuers or other potential defendants under Rule 10b–5 reach a large number of potential investors, or the fact that they are required by law to make their disclosures conform to certain standards, should in any way absolve them from liability for misconduct which is proscribed by Rule 10b–5.

But in the absence of the *Birnbaum* rule, it would be sufficient for a plaintiff to prove that he had failed to purchase or sell stock by reason of a defendant's violation of Rule 10b–5. The manner in which the defendant's violation caused the plaintiff to fail to act could be as a result of the reading of a prospectus, as respondent claims here, but it could just as easily come as a result of a claimed reading of information contained in the financial pages of a local newspaper. Plaintiff's proof would not be that he purchased or sold stock, a fact which would be capable of documentary verification in most situations, but instead that he decided *not* to purchase or sell stock. * * *

There is strong evidence that application of the *Birnbaum* rule to preclude suit by the disappointed offeree of a registered 1933 Act offering under Rule 10b–5 furthers the intention of Congress as expressed in the 1933 Act.

Sections 11 and 12 of the 1933 Act provide express civil remedies for misrepresentations and omissions in registration statements and prospectuses filed under the Act, as here charged, but restrict recovery to the offering price of shares actually purchased:

> "To impose a greater responsibility would unnecessarily restrain the conscientious administration of honest business with no compensating advantage to the public." H.R.Rep. No. 85, 73d Cong., 1st Sess., 9 (1933).

* * *

There is thus ample evidence that Congress did not intend to extend a private cause of action for money damages to the nonpurchasing offeree of a stock offering registered under the 1933 Act for loss of the opportunity to purchase due to an overly pessimistic prospectus.

* * *

Reversed.

MR. JUSTICE POWELL, with whom MR. JUSTICE STEWART and MR. JUSTICE MARSHALL join, concurring.

Although I join the opinion of the Court, I write to emphasize the significance of the tests of the Acts of 1933 and 1934 and especially the language of § 10(b) and Rule 10b–5.

I

The starting point in every case involving construction of a statute is the language itself. The critical phrase in both the statute and the rule is "in connection with the *purchase* or *sale* of any security." Section 3(a)(14) of the 1934 Act provides that the term "sale" shall "include any contract to sell or otherwise dispose of" securities. There is no hint in any provision of the Act that the term "sale," as used in § 10(b), was intended—in addition to its long-established legal meaning—to include an "offer to sell." Respondent, nevertheless, would have us amend the controlling language in § 10(b) to read:

> "* * * in connection with the purchase or sale of, or an offer to sell, any security."

Before a court properly could consider taking such liberty with statutory language there should be, at least, unmistakable support in the history and structure of the legislation. None exists in this case.

* * *

II

Mr. Justice Blackmun's dissent charges the Court with "a preternatural solicitousness for corporate well-being and a seeming callousness toward the investing public." Our task in this case is to construe a statute. In my view, the answer is plainly compelled by the language as well as the legislative history of the Securities Acts. But even if the language is not "plain" to all, I would have thought none could doubt that the statute can be read fairly to support the result the Court reaches. Indeed, if one takes a different view—and imputes callousness to all who disagree—he must attribute a lack of legal and social perception to the scores of federal judges who have followed *Birnbaum* for two decades.

The dissenting opinion also charges the Court with paying "no heed to the unremedied wrong" arising from the type of "fraud" that may result from reaffirmance of the *Birnbaum* rule. If an issue of statutory construction is to be decided on the basis of assuring a *federal* remedy—in addition to state remedies—for every perceived fraud, at least we should strike a balance between the opportunities for fraud presented by the contending views. It may well be conceded that *Birnbaum* does allow some fraud to go unremedied under the federal Securities Acts. But the construction advocated by the dissent could result in wider opportunities for fraud. As the Court's opinion makes plain, abandoning the *Birnbaum* construction in favor of the rule urged by the dissent would invite any person who failed to purchase a newly offered security that subsequently enjoyed substantial market appreciation to file a claim alleging that the offering prospectus understated the company's potential. The number of possible plaintiffs with respect to a public offering would be virtually unlimited. As noted above, an honest offeror could be confronted with subjective claims by plaintiffs who had neither purchased its securities nor seriously considered the investment. It frequently would be impossible to refute a plaintiff's assertion that he relied on the prospectus, or even that he made a decision not to buy the offered securities. A rule allowing this type of open-ended litigation would itself be an invitation to fraud.

MR. JUSTICE BLACKMUN, with whom MR. JUSTICE DOUGLAS and MR. JUSTICE BRENNAN join, dissenting.

Today the Court graves into stone *Birnbaum's* arbitrary principle of standing. For this task the Court, unfortunately, chooses to utilize three blunt chisels: (1) reliance on the legislative history of the 1933 and 1934 Securities Acts, conceded as inconclusive in this particular context; (2) acceptance as precedent of two decades of lower court decisions following a doctrine, never before examined here, that was pronounced by a justifiably esteemed panel of that Court of Appeals regarded as the "Mother Court" in this area of the law, but under entirely different circumstances; and (3) resort to utter pragmaticality and a conjectural assertion of "policy considerations" deemed to arise in distinguishing the meritorious Rule 10b–5 suit from the meretricious one. In so doing, the Court exhibits a preternatural solicitousness for corporate well-being and a seeming callousness toward the investing public quite out of keeping, it seems to me, with our own traditions and the intent of the securities laws.

The plaintiffs' complaint—and that is all that is before us now—raises disturbing claims of fraud. It alleges that the directors of "New Blue Chip" and the majority shareholders of "Old Blue Chip" engaged in a deceptive and manipulative scheme designed to subvert the intent of the 1967 antitrust consent decree and to enhance the value of their own shares in a subsequent offering.

* * *

From a reading of the complaint in relation to the language of § 10(b) of the 1934 Act and of Rule 10b–5, it is manifest that plaintiffs have alleged the use of a deceptive scheme "in connection with the purchase or sale of any security." To my mind, the word "sale" ordinarily and naturally may be understood to mean not only a single, individualized act transferring property from one party to another, but also the generalized event of public disposal of property through advertisement, auction, or some other market mechanism. Here, there is an obvious, indeed a court-ordered, "sale" of securities in the special offering of New Blue Chip shares and debentures to former users. Yet the Court denies these plaintiffs the right to maintain a suit under Rule 10b–5 because they do not fit into the mechanistic categories of either "purchaser" or "seller." This, surely, is anomaly, for the very purpose of the alleged scheme was to inhibit these plaintiffs from ever acquiring the status of "purchaser." Faced with this abnormal divergence from the usual pattern of securities frauds, the Court pays no heed to the unremedied wrong or to the portmanteau nature of § 10(b).

* * *

Instead of the artificiality of *Birnbaum,* the essential test of a valid Rule 10b–5 claim, it seems to me, must be the showing of a logical nexus between the alleged fraud and the sale or purchase of a security. It is inconceivable that Congress could have intended a broadranging antifraud provision, such as § 10(b), and, at the same time, have intended to impose, or be deemed to welcome, a mechanical overtone and requirement such as the *Birnbaum* doctrine. The facts of this case, if proved and accepted by the factfinder, surely are within the conduct that Congress intended to ban. Whether these particular plaintiffs, or any plaintiff, will be able eventually to carry the burdens of proving fraud and of proving reliance and damage—that is, causality and injury—is a matter that should not be left to speculations of "policy" of the kind now advanced in this forum so far removed from witnesses and evidence.

In a number of appellate court decisions before the Supreme Court's decision in *Blue Chip,* the courts held that a person who was forced to exchange his securities for cash or other securities in connection with a merger or similar transaction had standing to sue under Rule 10b–5 as a "forced seller" if he could show that the transaction was effected by means of fraudulent misstatements. See, e.g., VINE v. BENEFICIAL, 374 F.2d 627 (2d Cir.1967). Courts have continued to recognize this "forced seller" exception after *Blue Chip.* See, e.g., ALLEY v. MIRAMON, 614 F.2d 1372 (5th Cir.1980).

---

5. *Responsibilities of Attorneys and Other Professionals*

As we saw in the materials on § 11 of the 1933 Act, the securities laws do not impose any specific liabilities on lawyers *as such.* By virtue of the central role that lawyers have assumed in the disclosure process, however, there has been a developing tendency, in SEC and court decisions, to hold lawyers responsible for misstatements in disclosure documents or for securities transactions which violate the law. This responsibility is of course in addition to whatever liability lawyers may incur to their clients under common law principles for negligence in the performance of their legal work.

(a) Elements of the Obligation

SEC v. NATIONAL STUDENT MARKETING CORP.

457 F.Supp. 682 (D.D.C.1978).

BARRINGTON D. PARKER, DISTRICT JUDGE:

This opinion covers the final act in a civil proceeding brought by the Securities and Exchange Commission (Commission or SEC) seeking injunctive sanctions against numerous defendants as a result of their participation in alleged securities laws violations relating to the National Student Marketing Corporation (NSMC) securities fraud scheme. The original defendants included the corporation and certain of its officers and directors; the accounting firm of Peat, Marwick, Mitchell & Co. (Peat Marwick) and two of its partners; several officers and directors of Interstate National Corporation (Interstate); the law firm of White & Case and one of its partners; and the law firm of Lord, Bissell & Brook (LBB) and two of its partners. The majority of these defendants are not now before the Court. As discovery progressed during the pre-trial stages of this litigation, NSMC and other principal defendants consented to the entry of final judgments of permanent injunction or otherwise reached a resolution of the charges against them. The only defendants remaining are Lord, Bissell & Brook; its two partners, Max E. Meyer and Louis F. Schauer; and Cameron Brown, a former president and director of Interstate, and presently a director of and consultant to NSMC.

The focal point of the Commission's charges against these defendants is the corporate merger of Interstate with NSMC on October 31, 1969. The principal question presented is whether the defendants violated or aided and abetted the violation of the antifraud provisions of the federal securities laws in two instances: (1) consummation of the NSMC merger; and (2) the immediately following sale of newly acquired NSMC stock by former Interstate principals, including certain of the defendants. These transactions are alleged to have occurred despite the prior receipt by the defendants of information which revealed that NSMC's interim financial statements, used in securing shareholder approval of the merger and available to the investing public generally, were grossly inaccurate and failed to show the true condition of the corporation. The information was included in a comfort letter prepared by NSMC's accountants. The Commission contends that these violations demonstrate a reasonable likelihood of future misconduct by the defendants, thereby justifying the requested permanent injunctive relief.

* * *

I. BACKGROUND

* * *

The Merger Agreement [signed on August 15, 1969] set forth fully the terms and conditions of the understanding between the two corporations. Among other things, both corporations represented and warranted that the information "contained in Interstate's and NSMC's Proxy Statements relating to the transactions contemplated by this Agreement will be accurate and correct and will not omit to state a material fact necessary to make such information not misleading" and that the financial statements included among the provisions "are true and correct and have been prepared in accordance with generally accepted accounting principles consistently followed throughout the periods involved." NSMC specifically referred to its 1968 year-end and May 31, 1969, nine-month financial statements and represented that those statements:

> fairly present the results of the operations of NSMC and its subsidiaries for the periods indicated, subject in the case of the nine month statements to year-end audit adjustments.

The Agreement also provided several conditions precedent to the obligations of the two corporations to consummate the merger. One required the receipt by NSMC of an opinion letter from Interstate's counsel LBB to the effect, *inter alia,* that Interstate had taken all actions and procedures required of it by law and that all transactions in connection with the merger had been duly and validly taken, to the best knowledge of counsel, in full compliance with applicable law; a similar opinion letter was required to be delivered from NSMC's counsel to Interstate. Another condition was the receipt by each company of a "comfort letter" from the other's independent public accountants. Each letter was required to state: (1) that the accountants had no reason to believe that the unaudited interim financial statements for the company in question were not prepared in accordance with accounting principles and practices consistent with those used in the previous year-end audited financials; (2) that they had no reason to believe that any material adjustments in those financials were required in order fairly to present the results of operations of the company; and (3) that the company had experienced no material adverse change in its financial position or results of operations from the period covered by its interim financial statement up to five business days prior to the effective date of the merger. Although setting forth these specific conditions to consummation of the merger, the final paragraph of the Agreement also provided that:

> Anything herein to the contrary notwithstanding and notwithstanding any stockholder vote of approval of this Agreement and the merger provided herein, this Agreement may be terminated and abandoned by mutual consent of the Boards of Directors of NSMC and Interstate at any time prior to the Effective Date and the Board of Directors of any party may waive any of the conditions to the obligations of such party under this Agreement.

Finally, the Agreement specified that "[t]he transactions contemplated herein shall have been consummated on or before November 28, 1969."

Both NSMC and Interstate utilized proxy statements and notices of special stockholder meetings to secure shareholder approval of the proposed merger. Interstate's materials included a copy of the Merger Agreement and NSMC's Proxy Statement; the latter contained NSMC's financial statements for the fiscal year ended August 31, 1968, and the nine-month interim financial statement for the period ending May 31, 1969. Interstate shareholders were urged to study the NSMC Proxy Statement:

> The NSMC Proxy Statement contains a description of each company, relevant financial statements, comparative per share data and other information important to your consideration of the proposed merger. You are urged to study the NSMC Proxy Statement, hereby incorporated as part of this Proxy Statement, prior to voting your shares.

The boards of both companies recommended approval of the merger and at special shareholder meetings that approval was secured by large majorities.

In mid-October, Peat Marwick began drafting the comfort letter concerning NSMC's unaudited interim financials for the nine-month period ended May 31, 1969. As issued by NSMC, those financials had reflected a profit of approximately $700,000.

Soon after beginning work on the comfort letter, Peat Marwick representatives determined that certain adjustments were required with respect to the interim financials. Specifically, the accountants proposed that a $500,000 adjustment to deferred costs, a $300,000 writeoff of unbilled receivables, and an $84,000 adjustment to paid-in capital be made retroactive to May 31 and be reflected in the comfort letter delivered to Interstate. Such adjustments would have caused NSMC to show a loss for the nine-month period ended May 31, 1969, and the company as it existed on May 31 would have broken even for fiscal 1969. Although Peat Marwick discussed the proposed adjustments with representatives of NSMC, neither the accountants nor NSMC informed Interstate of the adjustments prior to the closing. A draft of the comfort letter, with the adjustments, was completed on October 30 and on the next day, the morning of the closing, it was discussed among senior partners of Peat Marwick.

The closing meeting for the merger was scheduled at 2 p.m. on Friday, October 31, at the New York offices of White & Case. Brown, Meyer and Schauer were present in addition to Interstate directors Bach, Allison and Tate. The representatives of NSMC included Randell, Joy, John G. Davies, their attorney [Marion J. Epley III, a partner in White & Case,] and other White & Case associates.

Although Schauer had had an opportunity to review most of the merger documents at White & Case on the previous day, the comfort letter had not been delivered. When he arrived at White & Case on the morning of the merger, the letter was still not available, but he was informed by a representative of the firm that it was expected to arrive at any moment.

The meeting proceeded. When the letter had not arrived by approximately 2:15 p.m., Epley telephoned Peat Marwick's Washington office to inquire about it. Anthony M. Natelli, the partner in charge, thereupon dictated to Epley's secretary a letter which provided in part:

> [N]othing has come to our attention which caused us to believe that:
>
> 1. The National Student Marketing Corporation's unaudited consolidated financial statements as of and for the nine months ended May 31, 1969:
>
> a. Were not prepared in accordance with accounting principles and practices consistent in all material respects with those followed in the preparation of the audited consolidated financial statements which are covered by our report dated November 14, 1968;
>
> b. Would require any material adjustments for a fair and reasonable presentation of the information shown except [that the $884,000 of adjustments referred to above should have been reflected in the earnings for the nine months ended May 31, 1969.]

Epley delivered one copy of the typed letter to the conference room where the closing was taking place. Epley then returned to his office.

Schauer was the first to read the unsigned letter. He then handed it to Cameron Brown, advising him to read it. Although there is some dispute as to which of the Interstate representatives actually read the letter, at least Brown and Meyer did so after Schauer. They asked

Randell and Joy a number of questions relating to the nature and effect of the adjustments. The NSMC officers gave assurances that the adjustments would have no significant effect on the predicted year-end earnings of NSMC and that a substantial portion of the $500,000 adjustments to deferred costs would be recovered. Moreover, they indicated that NSMC's year-end audit for fiscal 1969 had been completed by Peat Marwick, would be published in a couple of weeks, and would demonstrate that NSMC itself had made each of the adjustments for its fourth quarter. The comfort letter, they explained, simply determined that those adjustments should be reflected in the third quarter ended May 31, 1969, rather than the final quarter of NSMC's fiscal year. Randell and Joy indicated that while NSMC disagreed with what they felt was a tightening up of its accounting practices, everything requested by Peat Marwick to "clean up" its books had been undertaken.

At the conclusion of this discussion, certain of the Interstate representatives, including at least Brown, Schauer and Meyer, conferred privately to consider their alternatives in light of the apparent nonconformity of the comfort letter with the requirements of the Merger Agreement. Although they considered the letter a serious matter and the adjustments as significant and important, they were nonetheless under some pressure to determine a course of action promptly since there was a 4 p.m. filing deadline if the closing were to be consummated as scheduled on October 31. Among the alternatives considered were: (1) delaying or postponing the closing either to secure more information or to resolicit the shareholders with corrected financials; (2) closing the merger; or (3) calling it off completely.

The consensus of the directors was that there was no need to delay the closing. The comfort letter contained all relevant information and in light of the explanations given by Randell and Joy, they already had sufficient information upon which to make a decision. Any delay for the purpose of resoliciting the shareholders was considered impractical because it would require the use of year-end figures instead of the stale nine-month interim financials. Such a requirement would make it impossible to resolicit shareholder approval before the merger upset date of November 28, 1969, and would cause either the complete abandonment of the merger or its renegotiation on terms possibly far less favorable to Interstate. The directors also recognized that delay or abandonment of the merger would result in a decline in the stock of both companies, thereby harming the shareholders and possibly subjecting the directors to lawsuits based on their failure to close the merger. The Interstate representatives decided to proceed with the closing. They did, however, solicit and receive further assurances from the NSMC representatives that the stated adjustments were the only ones to be made to the company's financial statements and that the 1969 earnings would be as predicted. When asked by Brown whether the closing could proceed on the basis of an unsigned comfort letter, Meyer responded that if a White & Case partner assured them that this was in fact the comfort letter and that a signed copy would be forthcoming from Peat Marwick, they could close. Epley gave this assurance. Meyer then announced that Interstate was prepared to proceed, the closing was consummated, and a previously arranged telephone call was made which resulted in the filing of the Articles of Merger at the Office of the Recorder of Deeds of the District of Columbia. Large packets of merger documents, including the required counsel opinion letters, were exchanged. The closing was solemnized with a toast of warm champagne.

* * *

Following the acquisition of Interstate and several other companies NSMC stock rose steadily in price, reaching a peak in mid-December. However, in early 1970, after several newspaper and magazine articles appeared questioning NSMC's financial health, the value of the stock decreased drastically. Several private lawsuits were filed and the SEC initiated a wide-ranging investigation which led to the filing of this action.

II. The Present Action

The Court has jurisdiction of this proceeding under § 22(a) of the Securities Act of 1933 (1933 Act) and § 27 of the Securities Exchange Act of 1934 (1934 Act). * * * Specifically, the Commission alleges that the defendants, both as principals and as aiders and abettors, violated § 10(b) of the 1934 Act, Rule 10b–5 promulgated thereunder, and § 17(a) of the 1933 Act, through their participation in the Interstate/NSMC merger and subsequent stock sales by Interstate principals, in each instance without disclosing the material information revealed by the Peat Marwick comfort letter.

The Commission, in what appears to be typical fashion, makes little effort to distinguish between principals and aiders and abettors in its charges against the defendants. Although the significance of the distinction between primary and secondary liability may be dwindling in light of recent developments, the distinction nonetheless provides a means by which the violations can be specified and the defendants' conduct qualified. Thus, the Court will attempt to sort through the SEC allegations and delineate which charge principal violations of the antifraud provisions and which charge aiding and abetting.

The Commission charges Brown and Meyer with responsibility for proceeding with the merger of Interstate and NSMC. Since shareholder approval of the merger was secured in part on the basis of the nine-month financials which the comfort letter indicated were inaccurate, the SEC contends that Brown and Meyer should have refused to close until the shareholders could be resolicited with corrected financials. The Commission also charges the two directors with effecting the sale of NSMC stock following merger, without first disclosing the information contained in the comfort letter. These allegations clearly constitute charges of principal violations of the antifraud provisions. In addition, Brown is specifically charged with aiding and abetting sales of

NSMC stock by Interstate principals through his issuance, with Schauer's assistance, of the Rule 133 letter to NSMC.

Numerous charges, all of which appear to allege secondary liability, are leveled against the attorney defendants. Schauer is charged with "participating in the merger between Interstate and NSMC," apparently referring to his failure to interfere with the closing of the merger after receipt of the comfort letter. Such inaction, when alleged to facilitate a transaction, falls under the rubric of aiding and abetting. See Kerbs v. Fall River Industries, Inc., 502 F.2d 731, 739–40 (10th Cir. 1974). Both Schauer and Meyer are charged with issuing false opinions in connection with the merger and stock sales, thereby facilitating each transaction, and with acquiescence in the merger after learning the contents of the signed comfort letter. The Commission contends that the attorneys should have refused to issue the opinions in view of the adjustments revealed by the unsigned comfort letter, and after receipt of the signed version, they should have withdrawn their opinion with regard to the merger and demanded resolicitation of the Interstate shareholders. If the Interstate directors refused, the attorneys should have withdrawn from the representation and informed the shareholders or the Commission. The SEC specifically characterizes the attorneys' conduct in issuing the Rule 133 opinion as aiding and abetting, and because their alleged misconduct with regard to the merger also appears sufficiently removed from the center of that transaction, it too will be considered under a charge of secondary liability. And finally, LBB is charged with vicarious liability for the actions of Meyer and Schauer with respect to the attorneys' activities on behalf of the firm.

Since any liability of the alleged aiders and abettors depends on a finding of a primary violation of the antifraud provisions, the Court will first address the issues relating to the Commission's charges against the principals. If the evidence presented demonstrates that there was a violation in either instance the Court will then proceed to discuss whether the conduct of the various defendants also constituted aiding and abetting.

* * * [T]he Court finds that Brown and Meyer violated § 10(b), Rule 10b–5, and § 17(a) through their participation in the closing of the Interstate/NSMC merger and through their sales of NSMC stock immediately following the merger, in each instance without first disclosing the material information contained in the unsigned comfort letter.

IV. Aiding and Abetting

The Court must now turn to the Commission's charges that the defendants aided and abetted these two violations of the antifraud provisions. The violations themselves establish the first element of aiding and abetting liability, namely that another person has committed a securities law violation. The remaining elements, though not set forth with any uniformity, are essentially that the alleged aider and abettor had a "general awareness that his role was part of an overall activity that is improper, and [that he] knowingly and substantially assisted the violation."

The Commission's allegations of aiding and abetting by the defendants seem to fall into four basic categories: (1) the failure of the attorney defendants to take any action to interfere in the consummation of the merger; (2) the issuance by the attorneys of an opinion with respect to the merger; (3) the attorneys' subsequent failure to withdraw that opinion and inform the Interstate shareholders or the SEC of the inaccuracy of the nine-month financials; and (4) the issuance by the attorneys and Brown of an opinion and letter, respectively, concerning the validity of the stock sales under Rule 133. The SEC's position is that the defendants acted or failed to act with an awareness of the fraudulent conduct by the principals, and thereby substantially assisted the two violations. The Court concurs with regard to the attorneys' failure to interfere with the closing, but must conclude that the remaining actions or inaction alleged to constitute aiding and abetting did not substantially facilitate either the merger or the stock sales.

As noted, the first element of aiding and abetting liability has been established by the finding that Brown and Meyer committed primary violations of the securities laws. Support for the second element, that the defendants were generally aware of the fraudulent activity, is provided by the previous discussion concerning scienter. With the exception of LBB, which is charged with vicarious liability, each of the defendants was actually present at the closing of the merger when the comfort letter was delivered and the adjustments to the nine-month financials were revealed. Each was present at the Interstate caucus and the subsequent questioning of the NSMC representatives; each knew of the importance attributed to the adjustments by those present. They knew that the Interstate shareholders and the investing public were unaware of the adjustments and the inaccuracy of the financials. Despite the obvious materiality of the information, each knew that it had not been disclosed prior to the merger and stock sale transactions. Thus, this is not a situation where the aider and abettor merely failed to discover the fraud, or reasonably believed that the victims were already aware of the withheld information. The record amply demonstrates the "knowledge of the fraud, and not merely the undisclosed material facts," that is required to meet this element of secondary liability.

The final requirement for aiding and abetting liability is that the conduct provide knowing, substantial assistance to the violation. In addressing this issue, the Court will consider each of the SEC's allegations separately. The major problem arising with regard to the Commission's contention that the attorneys failed to interfere in the closing of the merger is whether inaction or silence constitutes substantial assistance. While there is no definitive answer to this question, courts have been willing to consider inaction as a form of substantial assistance when the accused aider and abettor had a duty to disclose.

Woodward v. Metro Bank of Dallas, 552 F.2d at 97; see Kerbs v. Fall River Industries, Inc., 502 F.2d at 740; Brennan v. Midwestern United Life Ins. Co., 417 F.2d 147, 154 (7th Cir.1969). Although the duty to disclose in those cases is somewhat distinguishable, in that they contemplate disclosure to an opposing party and not to one's client, they are sufficiently analogous to provide support for a duty here.

Upon receipt of the unsigned comfort letter, it became clear that the merger had been approved by the Interstate shareholders on the basis of materially misleading information. In view of the obvious materiality of the information, especially to attorneys learned in securities law, the attorneys' responsibilities to their corporate client required them to take steps to ensure that the information would be disclosed to the shareholders. However, it is unnecessary to determine the precise extent of their obligations here, since it is undisputed that they took no steps whatsoever to delay the closing pending disclosure to and resolicitation of the Interstate shareholders. But, at the very least, they were required to speak out at the closing concerning the obvious materiality of the information and the concomitant requirement that the merger not be closed until the adjustments were disclosed and approval of the merger was again obtained from the Interstate shareholders. Their silence was not only a breach of this duty to speak, but in addition lent the appearance of legitimacy to the closing. The combination of these factors clearly provided substantial assistance to the closing of the merger.

Contrary to the attorney defendants' contention, imposition of such a duty will not require lawyers to go beyond their accepted role in securities transactions, nor will it compel them to "err on the side of conservatism, * * * thereby inhibiting clients' business judgments and candid attorney-client communications." Courts will not lightly overrule an attorney's determination of materiality and the need for disclosure. However, where, as here, the significance of the information clearly removes any doubt concerning the materiality of the information, attorneys cannot rest on asserted "business judgments" as justification for their failure to make a legal decision pursuant to their fiduciary responsibilities to client shareholders.

The Commission also asserts that the attorneys substantially assisted the merger violation through the issuance of an opinion that was false and misleading due to its omission of the receipt of the comfort letter and of the completion of the merger on the basis of the false and misleading nine-month financials. The defendants contend that a technical reading of the opinion demonstrates that it is not false and misleading, and that it provides accurate opinions as to Interstate's compliance with certain corporate formalities. Of concern to the Court, however, is not the truth or falsity of the opinion, but whether it substantially assisted the violation. Upon consideration of all the circumstances, the Court concludes that it did not.

Contrary to the implication made by the SEC, the opinion issued by the attorneys at the closing did not play a large part in the consummation of the merger. Instead, it was simply one of many conditions to the obligation of NSMC to complete the merger. It addressed a number of corporate formalities required of Interstate by the Merger Agreement, only a few of which could possibly involve compliance with the antifraud provisions of the securities laws. Moreover, the opinion was explicitly for the benefit of NSMC, which was already well aware of the adjustments contained in the comfort letter. Thus, this is not a case where an opinion of counsel addresses a specific issue and is undeniably relied on in completing the transaction. Compare SEC v. Coven, 581 F.2d 1020 (2d Cir.1978); SEC v. Spectrum, Ltd., 489 F.2d 535 (2d Cir. 1973). Under these circumstances, it is unreasonable to suggest that the opinion provided substantial assistance to the merger.

The SEC's contention with regard to counsel's alleged acquiescence in the merger transaction raises significant questions concerning the responsibility of counsel. The basis for the charge appears to be counsel's failure, after the merger, to withdraw their opinion, to demand resolicitation of the shareholders, to advise their clients concerning rights of rescission of the merger, and ultimately, to inform the Interstate shareholders or the SEC of the completion of the merger based on materially false and misleading financial statements. The defendants counter with the argument that their actions following the merger are not subject to the coverage of the securities laws.

The filing of the complaint in this proceeding generated significant interest and an almost overwhelming amount of comment within the legal profession on the scope of a securities lawyer's obligations to his client and to the investing public. The very initiation of this action, therefore, has provided a necessary and worthwhile impetus for the profession's recognition and assessment of its responsibilities in this area. The Court's examination, however, must be more limited. Although the complaint alleges varying instances of misconduct on the part of several attorneys and firms, the Court must narrow its focus to the present defendants and the charges against them.

Meyer, Schauer and Lord, Bissell & Brook are, in essence, here charged with failing to take any action to "undo" the merger. The Court has already concluded that counsel had a duty to the Interstate shareholders to delay the closing of the merger pending disclosure and resolicitation with corrected financials, and that the breach of that duty constituted a violation of the antifraud provisions through aiding and abetting the merger transaction. The Commission's charge, however, concerns the period following that transaction. Even if the attorneys' fiduciary responsibilities to the Interstate shareholders continued beyond the merger, the breach of such a duty would not have the requisite relationship to a securities transaction, since the merger had already been completed. It is equally obvious that such subsequent action or inaction by the attorneys could not substantially assist the merger.

* * *

Thus, the Court finds that the attorney defendants aided and abetted the violation of § 10(b), Rule 10b–5, and § 17(a) through their participation in the closing of the merger.

V. Appropriateness of Injunctive Relief

Although the Commission has proved past violations by the defendants, that does not end the Court's inquiry. Proof of a past violation is not a prerequisite to the grant of injunctive relief, nor by itself necessarily sufficient to justify such relief, but it may, in combination with other factors, warrant an inference of future misconduct by the charged party.

* * *

The Commission has not demonstrated that the defendants engaged in the type of repeated and persistent misconduct which usually justifies the issuance of injunctive relief.

* * *

Further, it is difficult to characterize the violations presented here as either "willful, blatant, and often completely outrageous," or as the "garden variety fraud" urged by the Commission. * * *

Finally, the Commission asserts that an injunction is necessary because the professional occupations of the defendants provide significant opportunities for further involvement in securities transactions. It notes that Brown holds positions as a director and as a consultant with NSMC, and that Meyer, Schauer and LBB continue to be involved in various corporate activities, including securities transactions, as part of their legal practice. While these opportunities distinguish the present defendants from those who, because they completely lack such opportunities, should not be subject to the threat of an injunction, they do not alone justify relief. In fact, various circumstances indicate that this factor is not as one-sided as the Commission suggests. Although Brown retains his positions with NSMC, he is in effect virtually retired: the likelihood of his being involved in a securities transaction, other than as an investor, seems quite small. While the attorney defendants are more likely to be so involved, that fact is countered somewhat by their professional responsibilities as attorneys and officers of the court to conform their conduct to the dictates of the law. The Court is confident that they will take appropriate steps to ensure that their professional conduct in the future comports with the law.[75]

75. The Commission contends that the defendants' failure to recognize the seriousness of their misconduct, by continuing to maintain that their actions were lawful and proper, demonstrates the need for an injunction. The Court, however, considers the defendants' conduct in this regard as simply putting the SEC to its burden of making a proper showing that injunctive relief is warranted. In the absence of more egregious conduct, such as dilatoriness or bad faith, the defendants will not be penalized for fully defending this action.

After considering the "totality of circumstances" presented here, the Court concludes that the Securities and Exchange Commission has not fulfilled its statutory obligation to make a "proper showing" that injunctive relief is necessary to prevent further violations by these defendants. Accordingly, judgment will be entered for the defendants and the complaint will be dismissed.

As the court notes, the SEC actions against White & Case and one of its partners, Marion J. Epley, were settled.[a] Epley agreed that he would not practice before the SEC or advise clients with respect to filings under the securities laws for a period of 180 days. He also consented to the entry of a permanent injunction against him, barring him from violating the anti-fraud provisions of the securities laws in any transaction in which a document required to be delivered under an agreement "is delivered in a form which does not conform in all material respects with the applicable terms of the agreement."

No injunction was entered against White & Case, and the SEC stipulated that it would not take any disciplinary action against the firm. White & Case, however, undertook to "adopt, effectuate and maintain procedures in connection with its representation of clients" in securities matters, and delivered a letter to the SEC, "confirming its present procedures, [which] the Commission has neither approved nor disapproved." These procedures included the following:

> "1. Prior to the undertaking by the Firm of corporate representation as principal outside counsel of a prospective client having securities registered under the Federal Securities Laws (a) such representation will be considered by a committee of partners of the Firm charged with the review and approval of any such new representation, and (b) if the Firm has ascertained that the representation of such prospective client by its prior principal outside counsel was terminated by such counsel,[b] due inquiry will be made of such prospective client as to the reasons for the change and the prospective client will be requested to release such prior counsel from any obligation of confidentiality for purposes of discussion with the Firm of the proposed representation. Appropriate documentation reflecting the results of any such inquiry will be maintained by the Firm and will be available on a continuing basis to lawyers actively participating in the Firm's representation of the client.
>
> "2. Prior to the undertaking by the Firm of corporate representation as principal outside counsel of a prospective client having securities registered under the Federal Securities Laws, the responsible partner will determine whether, within the preceding two years, the prospective client has filed a Report on Form 8–K with respect to any

a. SEC v. National Student Marketing Corp., CCH Fed.Sec.L.Rep. ¶ 96,027 (D.D.C.1977).

b. The firm of Covington & Burling had resigned as NSMC's outside counsel in 1968, being replaced by White & Case.

change of independent public accountants.[c] Where such a change has occurred and the Report on Form 8–K is considered by the aforementioned committee of partners to indicate that an inquiry of the prior independent public accountants is appropriate, such an inquiry will be made by the responsible partner and the prospective client will be asked to direct the prior accountants to respond to said inquiry by this Firm. Appropriate documentation reflecting the results of any such inquiry will be maintained by the Firm and will be made available on a continuing basis to lawyers actively participating in the Firm's representation of the client.

"3. In connection with any transactions involving the issuance of securities to the public where the Firm represents the issuer of the securities, the Firm will not deliver any opinion in connection with the issuance of such securities if it has knowledge that (i) any material representation or warranty made by or on behalf of the client is not true and correct in material respects, in the light of the circumstances under which it was made, or (ii) there has been any material adverse change which would render any such representation or warranty, in the light of the circumstances under which it was made, false or misleading as of the date of consummation of the transaction, unless in either case the client has taken appropriate corrective action.

"4. If during the course of any transaction involving the issuance of securities to the public where the Firm represents the issuer of the securities, the Firm becomes aware of any materially false or misleading representation or warranty by or on behalf of the client concerning the financial condition, results of operations, prospects, properties or assets of the client or any of its subsidiaries, the Firm will advise the client of the client's disclosure obligations under the Federal Securities Laws and, if the client does not take appropriate action to comply with such obligations, the responsible partner will consider with at least two other partners of the Firm the need for the Firm to withdraw from employment or take other appropriate action.

"5. In connection with any transaction involving the issuance of securities to the public where the Firm represents the issuer of the securities and the terms of such transaction call for the delivery of a document which by its terms deals with the client's general financial condition, if another party to the transaction elects to waive the delivery of such document or to accept such document in a form which does not conform in all material respects with the applicable terms of the agreement, the Firm will not deliver any opinion in connection with the issuance of such securities unless and until the partner responsible for the matter has consulted with and obtained the concurrence of at least two other partners of the Firm in the delivery of such opinion.

"6. In connection with any transaction involving the issuance of securities to the public where the Firm represents the issuer or underwriters of the securities, (a) any registration statement under the

c. The firm of Arthur Anderson & Co. had resigned as NSMC's outside auditor in 1968, being replaced by Peat, Marwick, Mitchell & Co.

> Securities Act of 1933 (other than on Form S–8 or Form S–16 as to which the Firm believes that the procedure is not as a matter of policy necessary in every instance) prepared for use in such transaction will be reviewed before the effective date of such registration statement, in substantially the form filed or to be filed with the Commission, by a second partner of the Firm who is experienced in securities matters and who is not directly otherwise working on the transaction, and (b) any opinion delivered by the Firm with respect to such transaction will reasonably identify the matters upon which the Firm is rendering an opinion and will generally describe the nature of the review upon which the opinion is based."

The most controversial aspect of the SEC's position in the *National Student Marketing* case was the assertion in its complaint that the attorneys for NSMC and Interstate had participated in a fraudulent scheme when they "failed to refuse to issue their opinions * * * and failed to insist that the financial statements be revised and shareholders be resolicited, and failing that, to cease representing their respective clients and, under the circumstances, notify the plaintiff Commission concerning the misleading nature of the nine month financial statements."

As you can see from the opinion, Judge Parker did not deal directly with the question of a lawyer's obligation to notify the Commission that his client has filed incorrect statements with it. To what extent does the SEC position go beyond the American Bar Association's Disciplinary Rule 7–102(B)(1), which in 1969 provided that:

> A lawyer who receives information clearly establishing that his client has, in the course of the representation, perpetrated a fraud upon a person or tribunal shall promptly call upon his client to rectify the same, and if his client refuses or is unable to do so, he shall reveal the fraud to the affected person or tribunal.

In February 1974, the ABA amended the above rule to add at the end the words: "except when the information is protected as a privileged communication." Its stated reason was that the previous language "had the unacceptable result * * * of requiring a lawyer in certain instances to reveal privileged communications which he also was duty-bound not to reveal according to the law of evidence." ABA Ethics Opinion 341 (1975).

Does the revised language conflict with the position taken by the SEC in *National Student Marketing?* At the annual meeting of the ABA House of Delegates in August 1975, the following resolution was unanimously adopted:

> 1. The confidentiality of lawyer-client consultations and advice and the fiduciary loyalty of the lawyer to the client, as prescribed in the American Bar Association's Code of Professional Responsibility ("CPR"), are vital to the basic function of the lawyer as legal counselor because they enable and encourage clients to consult legal counsel freely, with assurance that counsel will respect the confidentiality of

the client's communications and will advise independently and in the client's best interest without conflicting loyalties or obligations.

2. This vital confidentiality of consultation and advice would be destroyed or seriously impaired if it is accepted as a general principle that lawyers must inform the SEC or others regarding confidential information received by lawyers from their clients even though such action would not be permitted or required by the CPR. Any such compelled disclosure would seriously and adversely affect the lawyers' function as counselor, and may seriously and adversely affect the ability of lawyers as advocates to represent and defend their clients' interest.

3. In light of the foregoing considerations, it must be recognized that a lawyer cannot, consistently with his essential role as legal adviser, be regarded as a source of information concerning possible wrong-doing by clients. Accordingly, any principle of law which, except as permitted or required by the CPR, permits or obliges a lawyer to disclose to the SEC otherwise confidential information, should be established only by statute after full and careful consideration of the public interests involved, and should be resisted unless clearly mandated by law.

The SEC position in *National Student Marketing* is that a lawyer has an obligation to inform the SEC if his client refuses to disclose material facts in a filed document. If a lawyer furnishes such information to the SEC, is he also required, or permitted, to make it available to private parties who sue his client (or former client) for violation of the securities laws? Or is he barred from making such disclosure by Ethical Consideration 4–1 of the Code of Professional Responsibility, which "require[s] the preservation by the lawyer of confidences and secrets of one who has employed or sought to employ him"? Does it make any difference if the lawyer furnishes the information to the plaintiff in an effort to demonstrate that there was no basis for naming him as a defendant in the action? See Meyerhofer v. Empire Fire Ins. Co., 497 F.2d 1190 (2d Cir.1974).

In March 1979, an SEC administrative law judge ordered two partners in the New York law firm of Brown, Wood, Ivey, Mitchell & Petty suspended from practice before the Commission for periods of one year and nine months, respectively. The basis for the suspension, which arose from the lawyers' representation of National Telephone Company, was that they had:

(a) violated, and aided and abetted violations of, Rule 10b–5 by participating in the preparation of a misleading press release and a misleading 8–K report, and by failing to take steps to correct a false and misleading statement sent to shareholders or to see that adequate disclosure was made; and

(b) engaged in unethical and improper professional conduct by failing to inform National's board of directors concerning management's unwillingness to make disclosure of material facts affecting National's financial condition.[a]

On review of the decision by the administrative law judge, the Commission reversed his findings and held that there was no basis for sanctions under Rule 2(e).[b]

With respect to the charge of aiding and abetting National Telephone's violations of Rule 10b–5, the Commission held that "a finding of *willful aiding and abetting* within the meaning of Rule 2(e) requires a showing that respondents were aware or knew that their role was part of an activity that was improper or illegal." The Commission concluded that the evidence was "insufficient to establish that either respondent acted with sufficient knowledge and awareness or recklessness" to satisfy that test.

With respect to the charge of engaging in unethical and improper professional conduct, the Commission felt that it "should not establish new rules of conduct and impose them retroactively upon professionals who acted at the time without reason to believe that their conduct was unethical or improper," and that the "responsibilities of lawyers who become aware that their client is engaging in violations of the securities laws have not been so firmly and unambiguously established that we believe all practicing lawyers can be held to an awareness of generally recognized norms." To deal with future cases, the Commission set forth the following views:

> The Commission is of the view that a lawyer engages in "unethical or improper professional conduct" under the following circumstances: When a lawyer with significant responsibilities in the effectuation of a company's compliance with the disclosure requirements of the federal securities laws becomes aware that his client is engaged in a substantial and continuing failure to satisfy those disclosure requirements, his continued participation violates professional standards unless he takes prompt steps to end the client's noncompliance. The Commission has determined that this interpretation will be applicable only to conduct occurring after the date of this opinion.
>
> We do not imply that a lawyer is obliged, at the risk of being held to have violated Rule 2(e), to seek to correct every isolated disclosure action or inaction which he believes to be at variance with applicable disclosure standards, although there may be isolated disclosure failures that are so serious that their correction becomes a matter of primary professional concern. It is also clear, however, that a lawyer is not privileged to unthinkingly permit himself to be co-opted into an ongoing fraud and cast as a dupe or a shield for a wrongdoing client.
>
> Initially, counselling accurate disclosure is sufficient, even if his advice is not accepted. But there comes a point at which a reasonable lawyer must conclude that his advice is not being followed, or even sought in good faith, and that his client is involved in a continuing

a. In re Carter, Adm.Proc. No. 3–5464. BNA Sec.Reg. & L.Rep. No. 494, at F–1 (Mar. 7, 1979) (initial decision).

b. In re Carter, Sec.Ex.Act Rel. No. 17597 (Feb. 28, 1981).

course of violating the securities laws. At this critical juncture, the lawyer must take further, more affirmative steps in order to avoid the inference that he has been co-opted, willingly or unwillingly, into the scheme of nondisclosure.

The lawyer is in the best position to choose his next step. Resignation is one option, although we recognize that other considerations, including the protection of the client against foreseeable prejudice, must be taken into account in the case of withdrawal. A direct approach to the board of directors or one or more individual directors or officers may be appropriate; or he may choose to try to enlist the aid of other members of the firm's management. What is required, in short, is some prompt action that leads to the conclusion that the lawyer is engaged in efforts to correct the underlying problem, rather than having capitulated to the desires of a strong-willed, but misguided client.

In October 1981, the SEC solicited public comments on a proposal to adopt the standard set forth in the first paragraph of the above excerpt from its opinion in the *Carter* case as a "Standard of Conduct Constituting Unethical or Improper Professional Practice Before the Commission," The ABA Section of Corporation, Banking and Business law submitted a statement strongly criticizing the proposal on the merits and also urging that the SEC had no statutory power to regulate the conduct of lawyers in that manner.

In the meantime, the ABA was engaged in a complete revision of its Code of Professional Responsibility. In the course of that revision, the ABA's ethics commission suggested a new guideline that would have encouraged lawyers to speak out if their clients were engaged in securities fraud or other kinds of irregular financial transactions. At its annual meeting in 1983, however, the ABA rejected this proposal and amended the Code in a way that actually limited the pre-existing obligation of lawyers to "blow the whistle" on their clients in these situations. Under Rule 1.16 of the ABA's new Model Rules of Professional Conduct, a lawyer *may* withdraw from representing a client if "the client persists in a course of action involving the lawyer's services that the lawyer reasonably believes is criminal or fraudulent." However, under Rule 1.6, the lawyer may reveal information relating to representation of a client only "to prevent the client from committing a criminal act that the lawyer believes is likely to result in imminent death or substantial bodily harm."

SEC v. FRANK, 388 F.2d 486 (2d Cir.1968). The SEC obtained a district court order enjoining Nylo–Thane, its officers, and its attorney, Frank, from making further misrepresentations concerning the company's business. Frank, who had represented Nylo–Thane in the preparation of a Regulation A offering circular which the SEC had held to be misleading, appealed from the issuance of an injunction against him.

* * * His position, broadly stated, was that the portion of the offering circular alleged to misrepresent the additive had been prepared by the officers of Nylo–Thane and that his function had been that of a scrivener helping them to place their ideas in proper form. * * *

Although Frank makes much of this being the first instance in which the Commission has obtained an injunction against an attorney for participation in the preparation of an allegedly misleading offering circular or prospectus, we find this unimpressive. A lawyer has no privilege to assist in circulating a statement with regard to securities which he knows to be false simply because his client has furnished it to him. At the other extreme it would be unreasonable to hold a lawyer who was putting his client's description of a chemical process into understandable English to be guilty of fraud simply because of his failure to detect discrepancies between their description and technical reports available to him in a physical sense but beyond his ability to understand. The instant case lies between these extremes. The SEC's position is that Frank had been furnished with information which even a non-expert would recognize as showing the falsity of many of the representations, notably those implying extensive and satisfactory testing at factories and indicating that all had gone passing well at the test by the Army Laboratories. If this is so, the Commission would be entitled to prevail; a lawyer, no more than others, can escape liability for fraud by closing his eyes to what he saw and could readily understand. Whether the fraud sections of the securities laws go beyond this and require a lawyer passing on an offering circular to run down possible infirmities in his client's story of which he has been put on notice, and if so what efforts are required of him, is a closer question on which it is important that the court be seized of the precise facts, including the extent, as the SEC claimed with respect to Frank, to which his role went beyond a lawyer's normal one.

The court of appeals held that the district court had not made adequate findings of fact, and remanded the case for further proceedings.

The following excerpts are from a January 1974 speech entitled "The Emerging Responsibilities of the Securities Lawyer" by A.A. Sommer, Jr., a member of the SEC and a former chairman of the ABA Committee on Federal Regulation of Securities:

Attorneys have since the earliest days of the federal securities laws been at the heart of the scheme that developed in response to those laws. While their formal participation mandated by the '33 and '34 Acts was limited—the only reference to counsel was in Item (23) of Schedule A to the 1933 Act which required the inclusion in registration statements of "the names and addresses of counsel who have passed on the legality of the issue * * * "—nonetheless, the registration statement has always been a lawyer's document and with very, very rare exceptions the attorney has been the field marshal who coordinated the activities of others engaged in the registration process, wrote (or at least rewrote) most of the statement, made the judgments with regard to the inclusion or exclusion of information on the grounds of materiality, compliance, with registration form requirements, necessities of avoiding omission of disclosure necessary to make those matters stated not misleading. The auditors have been able to point to clearly identifiable parts of the registration statements as their responsibility and they have successfully warded off efforts to extend their responsibility beyond the financial statements with respect to which they opine. With the exception of the financial statements, virtually everything else in the registration statement bears the imprint of counsel.

Counsel have been involved in many other ways with the federal securities laws. They are frequently called upon to give opinions with respect, principally, to the availability of exemptions from the requirements for registration and use of a statutory prospectus. None would deny the importance of these opinions: millions upon millions of dollars of securities have been put into the channels of commerce—not just sold once, but permanently into the trading markets—in reliance upon little more than the professional judgment of an attorney. In many, perhaps most, instances these opinions have been confined to questions concerning the technical availability of the exemption and have not been concerned with questions of disclosure, compliance with the somewhat amorphous mandates of Rule 10b–5 and other anti-fraud provisions of the federal securities laws.

* * *

In a word, and the word is Professor Morgan Shipman's, the professional judgment of the attorney is often the "passkey" to securities transactions. If he gives an opinion that an exemption is available, securities get sold; if he doesn't give the opinion, they don't get sold. If he judges that certain information must be included in a registration statement, it gets included (unless the client seeks other counsel or the attorney crumbles under the weight of client pressure); if he concludes it need not be included, it doesn't get included.

Securities lawyers have since the adoption of the 1933 Act stoutly urged that they play a limited role in this process, even to the point of continuing to insist, despite the requirement of Form S–1, among others, that there be submitted as a part of the registration statement an opinion of counsel concerning the legality of the securities being registered, that they are in no way "experts" within the meaning of Section 11. Beyond that, they have gloried in the occasional judicial acknowledgment of the limitations of their role. How often have we been reminded that in Escott v. BarChris Judge McLean specifically rejected the suggestion that the attorneys involved in the preparation of the contested registration statement were experts with respect to all of it except the financial statements and concluded that some of the attorneys had liability only because of their roles as director and officer of the issuer?

We are consistently reminded that historically the attorney has been an advocate, that his professional ethics have over the years defined his function in those terms, that such a role includes unremitting loyalty to the interests of his client (short of engaging in or countenancing fraud). Whenever the effort is made to analogize the responsibilities of the attorney to those of the independent auditor, one is reminded that the federal securities law system conceives of the auditor as independent and defines his role specifically, whereas the attorney is not and cannot be independent in the same sense in which an auditor is independent. It has been asserted by very eminent counsel that, "The law, so far, [this was in 1969] is very clear. The lawyers' responsibility is exclusively to their own client." If this distinction is clear to lawyers, it is less clear to others. Last week two of the most eminent leaders of the accounting profession asked me why it was that the attorneys named in the Commission's *National Student Marketing* complaint were not indicted while the auditors were. This sort of inquiry is increasingly asked, not only by auditors, but others as well.

I would suggest that the security bar's *conception* of its role too sharply contrasts with the *reality* of its role in the securities process to escape notice and attention—and in such situations the reality eventually prevails. Lawyers are not paid in the amounts they are to put the representations of their clients in good English, or give opinions which assume a pure state of facts upon which any third year law student could confidently express an opinion.

* * *

I would suggest that in securities matters (other than those where advocacy is clearly proper) the attorney will have to function in a manner more akin to that of the auditor than to that of the advocate. This means several things. It means he will have to exercise a measure of independence that is perhaps uncomfortable if he is also the close counselor of management in other matters, often including business decisions. It means he will have to be acutely cognizant of his responsibility to the public who engage in securities transactions that would never have come about were it not for his professional presence. It means he will have to adopt the healthy skepticism toward the representations of management which a good auditor must adopt. It means he will have to do the same thing the auditor does when confronted with an intransigent client—resign.

Selected References

Hazard & Leiman, Liability of Attorneys Involved in the Preparation of Disclosure Documents, 13 Inst. on Sec.Reg. 265, 277 (1982).

Jenkins, Attorney Liability Under the Federal Securities Laws, 2 J.Corp.L. 505 (1977).

Johnson, The Dynamics of SEC Rule 2(e): A Crisis for the Bar, 1975 Utah L.Rev. 629.

Karmel, Attorneys' Securities Laws Liabilities, 27 Bus.Lawyer 1153 (1972).

Lorne, The Corporate and Securities Adviser, the Public Interest, and Professional Ethics, 76 Mich.L.Rev. 423 (1978).

Parker, Attorney Liability Under the Federal Securities Laws After Ernst & Ernst v. Hochfelder, 10 Loyola LA L.Rev. 521 (1977).

Shipman, The Need for SEC Rules to Govern the Duties and Civil Liabilities of Attorneys Under the Federal Securities Statutes, 34 Ohio State L.J. 231 (1973).

Small, An Attorney's Responsibilities Under Federal and State Securities Laws, 61 Calif.L.Rev. 1189 (1973).

Sonde, The Responsibility of Professionals Under the Federal Securities Laws, 68 Nw.U.L.Rev. 1 (1973).

Symposium, Lawyers' Responsibilities and Liabilities Under the Securities Laws, 11 Colum.J.L. & Soc.Prob. 99 (1974).

(b) SEC Administrative Sanctions

TOUCHE ROSS & CO. v. SEC

609 F.2d 570 (2d Cir.1979).

Before: KAUFMAN, CHIEF JUDGE, TIMBERS and GURFEIN, CIRCUIT JUDGES.

TIMBERS, CIRCUIT JUDGE:

One of the most urgent problems of our day is the responsibility of the courts and other government bodies to prescribe high standards of conduct for their members and for those who practice before them. An indispensable corollary of this responsibility is the right—indeed, the duty—to discipline those who fail to conform to the high standards of conduct which have been prescribed.

We are called upon today to determine (1) whether the Securities and Exchange Commission ("SEC" or "Commission"), pursuant to one of its Rules of Practice which has been in effect for more than forty years, may conduct an administrative proceeding to determine whether certain professionals—in this case, accountants—should be censured or suspended from appearing or practicing before the Commission because of alleged unethical, unprofessional or fraudulent conduct in their audits of the financial statements of two corporations; and (2) if the Commission is authorized to conduct such an administrative proceeding, whether it should be permitted to conclude it before the accountants resort to the courts. For the reasons below, we hold that both questions must be answered in the affirmative.

I.

On September 1, 1976—more than two and one-half years ago—the SEC, pursuant to Rule 2(e) of its Rules of Practice,[1] entered an order which provided for a public administrative proceeding against the

1. Rule 2(e) of the SEC's Rules of Practice in relevant part provides:

"(e) *Suspension and disbarment.* (1) The Commission may deny, temporarily

accounting firm of Touche Ross & Co. and three of its former partners, Edwin Heft, James M. Lynch and Armin J. Frankel. The firm and the three partners, all appellants, will be referred to collectively as "Touche Ross" or "appellants".

The proceeding was instituted to determine whether appellants had engaged in unethical, unprofessional or fraudulent conduct in their audits of the financial statements of Giant Stores Corporation and Ampex Corporation.

The Commission's order alleged that Touche Ross and the individual appellants, in examining the companies' financial statements, had failed to follow generally accepted accounting standards and had no reasonable basis for their opinions regarding the financial statements of these companies. The order also recited that, if these allegations were found to be true, they tended to show that Touche Ross and the individual appellants had engaged in improper professional conduct and willfully had violated, and had aided and abetted violations of, §§ 5, 7, 10 and 17(a) of the Securities Act of 1933 and §§ 10(b) and 13 of the Securities Exchange Act of 1934, and rules and regulations thereunder.

In view of the nationwide accounting practice of Touche Ross, the SEC decided that it would be in the public interest to institute a public proceeding and to order a hearing at which Touche Ross would be afforded an opportunity to present a defense to these charges. The Commission then would have been in a position to determine whether the substantive allegations were true and, if so, whether Touche Ross and the individual appellants should be disqualified, either temporarily or permanently, from appearing and practicing before the Commission.

No administrative hearings have ever been held in this case.

On October 12, 1976, Touche Ross commenced the instant action for declaratory and injunctive relief in the Southern District of New York, naming as defendants the Commission and four of its members in their official capacities. By this action, Touche Ross sought a permanent injunction against the on-going administrative proceeding which had been instituted against them by the SEC pursuant to Rule 2(e). Touche Ross also sought a declaratory judgment that Rule 2(e) had been promulgated "without any statutory authority"; that the Rule 2(e) administrative proceeding had been instituted against them "without authority of law"; and, in any event, since the SEC does not constitute an impartial forum for the adjudication of the issues raised in the SEC's

or permanently, the privilege of appearing or practicing before it in any way to any person who is found by the Commission after notice of and opportunity for hearing in the matter (i) not to possess the requisite qualifications to represent others, or (ii) to be lacking in character or integrity or to have engaged in unethical or improper professional conduct, or (iii) to have willfully violated, or willfully aided and abetted the violation of any provision of the Federal securities laws, or the rules and regulations thereunder."

Rule 2(e) order, that such administrative proceedings would deny Touche Ross due process of law.

* * *

II.

[W]e turn first to the question whether appellants must exhaust their administrative remedies before resorting to the courts to assert their claims.

* * *

Appellants' principal claim on the instant appeal is that the Commission is acting without authority and beyond its jurisdiction in proceeding against them pursuant to Rule 2(e). They also contend that the administrative proceedings should be enjoined because the Commission is "biased", as indicated by the institution of public rather than nonpublic proceedings; they argue that, because the proceedings are public, they will not be given a fair and impartial hearing in accordance with due process.

If the claim of bias were the only basis for appellants' demand for injunctive relief, it would be unnecessary for us to go further than to hold, with respect to that claim, that exhaustion of administrative remedies is required.

* * *

Appellants, however, go further and contend that the SEC, in promulgating Rule 2(e), acted in excess of its statutory authority and now is proceeding against them without jurisdiction.

* * *

* * * While the Commission's administrative proceeding is not "plainly beyond its jurisdiction", nevertheless to require appellants to exhaust their administrative remedies would be to require them to submit to the very procedures which they are attacking.

Moreover, the issue is one of purely statutory interpretation. Further agency action is unnecessary to enable us to determine the validity of Rule 2(e). There is no need for the exercise of discretion on the part of the agency nor for the application of agency expertise. While the Commission has the power to declare its own rule invalid, it is unlikely that further proceedings would produce such a result. Accordingly, we now turn to the merits of that question.

III.

Section 23(a)(1) of the 1934 Act, authorizes the Commission to "make such rules and regulations as may be necessary or appropriate to implement the provisions of this title for which [it is] responsible or for the execution of the functions vested in [it] by this title * * *." Pursuant to this general rulemaking authority, the Commission adopted and subsequently has amended Rule 2(e) of its Rules of Practice, the relevant part of which is set forth above.

The current Rule and its predecessors have been in effect for over forty years. It has been the basis for a number of disciplinary proceedings brought against professionals—including accountants and attorneys—during this forty year period.

Although the mere fact that the Rule is of long standing does not relieve us of our responsibility to determine its validity, it is noteworthy that no court has ever held that the Rule is invalid. * * *

Appellants concede that there is no express statutory prohibition against promulgation of the Rule. They contend, however, that the statutory scheme negates any implied authority that the SEC may discipline accountants pursuant to Rule 2(e). Specifically, they point to § 27 of the 1934 Act, which provides that the district courts "shall have exclusive jurisdiction of violations of this chapter." Viewed in conjunction with other statutory provisions which authorize the SEC to commence proceedings in the district courts to enjoin what the Commission believes to be violations of the Acts, appellants argue that these provisions indicate that Congress intended that only the courts should adjudicate violations of the Acts. Absent express Congressional authorization for the Commission to adjudicate such violations—so the argument goes—the Commission is without power to promulgate its disciplinary Rule.

We reject appellants' argument for several reasons. First, it is clear that the SEC is not attempting to usurp the jurisdiction of the federal courts, to deal with "violations" of the securities laws. The Commission, through its Rule 2(e) proceeding, is merely attempting to preserve the integrity of its own procedures, by assuring the fitness of those professionals who represent others before the Commission. Indeed, the Commission has made it clear that its intent in promulgating Rule 2(e) was not to utilize the rule as an additional weapon in its enforcement arsenal, but rather to determine whether a person's professional qualifications, including his character and integrity, are such that he is fit to appear and practice before the Commission.

* * *

The chief purpose of the 1933 Act was to "provide investors with full disclosure of material information concerning public offerings of securities in commerce." One of the mechanisms designed to implement this policy of full disclosure was the requirement that a registration statement be filed with the Commission before a security could be sold to the public. In connection with the filing requirements, the Commission was given broad authority to regulate the contents of the filings, including the authority to prescribe the form and method of preparing financial statements, to define accounting terms, and to require that financial statements be certified by an independent public accountant.

The role of the accounting and legal professions in implementing the objectives of the disclosure policy has increased in importance as the number and complexity of securities transactions has increased. By the very nature of its operations, the Commission, with its small staff and limited resources, cannot possibly examine, with the degree of close scrutiny required for full disclosure, each of the many financial statements which are filed. Recognizing this, the Commission necessarily must rely heavily on both the accounting and legal professions to perform their tasks diligently and responsibly. Breaches of professional responsibility jeopardize the achievement of the objectives of the securities laws and can inflict great damage on public investors. As our Court observed in United States v. Benjamin, 328 F.2d 854 (2d Cir. 1964), "In our complex society the accountant's certificate and the lawyer's opinion can be instruments for inflicting pecuniary loss more potent than the chisel or the crowbar."

Rule 2(e) thus represents an attempt by the SEC essentially to protect the integrity of its own processes. If incompetent or unethical accountants should be permitted to certify financial statements, the reliability of the disclosure process would be impaired.

These concerns have led courts to reject challenges to the authority of other agencies to discipline attorneys practicing or appearing before them. In Goldsmith v. Board of Tax Appeals, 270 U.S. 117 (1926), the Supreme Court upheld the power of the Board of Tax Appeals to adopt rules of practice for professionals appearing before it as a necessary adjunct to the Board's power to protect the integrity of its administrative procedures and the public in general. * * *

Similarly, in Herman v. Dulles, 205 F.2d 715, 716 (D.C.Cir.1953), the Court of Appeals for the District of Columbia Circuit held that, since the International Claims Commission had been given the "express authority to 'prescribe such rules and regulations as may be necessary to enable it to carry out its functions'", it therefore had implied authority to prescribe rules setting standards of practice and adopting procedures for disciplining attorneys who failed to conform to those standards.

Appellants attempt to distinguish *Goldsmith* and *Herman* from the instant case on the ground that the agencies involved in those cases exercised only "judicial functions", whereas the SEC, according to appellants, is authorized to act only as an enforcement agency. Assuming arguendo the correctness of appellants' restrictive description of the SEC's functions, it is uniformly accepted that many agencies properly combine the functions of prosecutor, judge and jury. Indeed, the Supreme Court has held that a hearing conducted by such a body does not automatically constitute a violation of due process. Appellants nevertheless argue—we think facetiously—that permitting the SEC to discipline attorneys who appear before it would be equivalent to empowering United States Attorneys to disbar lawyers who represent clients in criminal prosecutions in the federal courts. Aside from the obviously inapt analogy, this contention at most merely suggests the possibility that the power to discipline may be abused; it is wide of the mark of suggesting a reason for invalidating the Commission's rule.

* * *

Accordingly, we hold that the district court properly refused to enjoin the Commission from proceedings against Touche Ross pursuant to Rule 2(e). We affirm the judgment dismissing the action. In view of our holding that Rule 2(e) represents a valid exercise of the Commission's rulemaking power, appellants must exhaust their administrative remedies before the SEC before they attempt to obtain judicial review of their other claims, including their claim that the Commission is acting with bias and will not afford them a fair hearing in accordance with due process.

KAUFMAN, CHIEF JUDGE (with whom TIMBERS, CIRCUIT JUDGE, joins), concurring:

I concur fully in the splendid opinion of Judge Timbers. I wish simply to underscore one salient fact.

The corollary of the doctrine of exhaustion of administrative remedies is the precept that judicial review of final agency action is always available.

* * *

Our opinion today affirms the ability of the SEC to ensure that the professionals who practice before it—on whose probity the viability of the regulatory process depends—meet the highest ethical standards. The assertion of that authority is consistent with the underlying purposes of the securities laws, and manifests the wisdom of the congressional decision to vest wide rulemaking authority in the Commission. But in recognition that any power may be misused, dispassionate panels of Article III judges stand ready to correct the occasional excesses and errors that are an inevitable part of the administrative process.

After this decision, Touche Ross settled the SEC proceeding, agreeing to accept a censure by the SEC and to undergo a peer review of its audit procedures. Sec.Ex.Act Rel. No. 15978 (June 27, 1979). At the time of the *Touche Ross* decision, all proceedings under Rule 2(e) were non-public unless the Commission directed otherwise. In 1988, the Rule was amended to provide that all such proceedings shall be public unless the Commission directs otherwise.

In KIVITZ v. SEC, 475 F.2d 956 (D.C.Cir.1973), the Commission imposed a two-year suspension on an attorney who had purportedly participated five years earlier in an arrangement to split his fees with laymen who allegedly could provide political influence to secure Commission clearance of a registration statement. The court of appeals reversed the Commission order and ordered the proceedings dismissed, on the ground that Kivitz had "been saddled by adverse evidence which never should have been received against him," and that the Commission's findings of fact were not supported by "substantial evidence" as required by § 25 of the 1934 Act. The court noted that the case involved disbarment of a lawyer, which is not a "specialty developed in the administration of the Act entrusted to the agency" but is "an area we know something about."

In EMANUEL FIELDS, Sec.Act Rel. No. 5404 (June 18, 1973), an attorney against whom the SEC had obtained four injunctions was permanently disqualified by the Commission, pursuant to its Rule 2(e), from appearing or practicing before it. In response to Fields' argument that the Commission had no authority to disqualify him from appearing before it as long as he was a qualified member of the New York Bar, the Commission said:

> [There is] a basic flaw in Field's argument that only the courts of New York which made him a lawyer in the first place can deprive him of the right to practice here. That argument assumes, among other things, that the standards of character and integrity that the New York courts consider adequate for their purposes ought to be and are necessarily controlling here. This fallacious position overlooks the peculiarly strategic and especially central place of the private practicing lawyer in the investment process and in the enforcement of the body of federal law aimed at keeping that process fair. Members of this Commission have pointed out time and time again that the task of enforcing the securities laws rests in overwhelming measure on the bar's shoulders. These were statements of what all who are versed in the practicalities of securities law know to be a truism, i.e., that this Commission with its small staff, limited resources, and onerous tasks is peculiarly dependent on the probity and the diligence of the professionals who practice before it. Very little of a securities lawyer's work is adversary in character. He doesn't work in courtrooms where the pressure of vigilant adversaries and alert judges checks him. He works in his office where he prepares prospectuses, proxy statements, opinions of counsel, and other documents that we, our staff, the financial community, and the investing public must take on faith. This is a field where unscrupulous lawyers can inflict irreparable harm on those who rely on the disclosure documents that they produce. Hence we are under a duty to hold our bar to appropriately rigorous standards of professional honor. To expect this vital function to be performed entirely by overburdened state courts who have little or no contact with the matters with which we deal would be to shirk that duty.

To what extent does a lawyer's responsibility for "enforcing the securities laws" limit his right, or duty, to represent the interests of his client? See Freedman, A Civil Libertarian Looks at Securities Regulation, 35 Ohio St.L.J. 280 (1974).

In addition to the possibility of being subjected to disciplinary action under SEC Rule 2(e), an attorney who participates in the preparation of disclosure documents which are subsequently found to be false or misleading may also face penalties under § 15(c)(4) of the 1934 Act. That section empowers the Commission, if it finds that a person was the "cause" of a company failing to comply with the disclosure provisions of 12, 13 or 14 of the Act, "due to an act or omission the person knew or should have known would contribute to the failure to comply," to issue an order requiring that person "to comply, or to take steps to effect compliance" with those provisions.

In 1987, the Commission brought a proceeding under § 15(c)(4) against George Kern, a partner in the New York law firm of Sullivan & Cromwell, alleging that he was the "cause" of the failure of Allied Stores Corporation to amend its Schedule 14D–9 filed with the Commission to reflect the commencement of negotiations leading to a possible merger or sale of the company's assets. Kern argued (a) that the negotiations had not yet reached the point at which they would be deemed "material" under existing precedents, (b) that the words "knew or should have known" in the section meant that he could only be found liable if he had acted willfully or recklessly, and (c) that he could not be held liable for advice given as a lawyer because the Commission had not established that his actions amounted to legal malpractice.

The administrative law judge rejected all of these contentions, finding (a) that the negotiations were material, (b) that negligence on the part of the person causing the violation was sufficient to meet the "should have known" standard, and (c) that the standards applicable to legal malpractice actions did not apply to Commission proceedings under § 15(c)(4). On this last question, the ALJ stated: [1]

> It appears from the record that during the relevant period Kern found himself in the center of a complex and fast-changing series of negotiations which required him to exercise his authority to have Allied comply with the disclosure requirements of Rule 14d–9. In the usual relationship of lawyer and client Kern would have had only the responsibility of giving legal advice to Macioce or other officers of Allied who in turn would have made the decisions whether amendments to Allied's Schedule 14D–9 were required. When Kern accepted discretionary authority to make those decisions he also accepted the responsibility the Allied officers had for compliance with Rule 14d–9 and cannot be heard now to complain that his legal judgments are being second-guessed in these proceedings. Were the law otherwise, corporate officials could find a safe harbor from accountability by giving discretionary authority to discharge their responsibility for compliance with disclosure requirements to a lawyer who in turn would be immune from action under Section 15(c)(4) unless his misconduct were so egregious as to also warrant disciplinary action under Rule 2(e) of the Commission's Rules of Practice. Delegation of authority by corporate officers to counsel to comply with Sections 12, 13, 14 or 15(d) of the Exchange Act would be encouraged, with Section 15(c)(4) becoming an ineffectual enforcement tool. Moreover, if a "cause" happens to be a person who is also counsel to the person out of compliance, adoption of Kern's approach to responsibility would create

1. In the matter of George C. Kern, Jr., Admin. Proc. File No. 3–6869, CCH Fed. Sec.L.Rep. ¶ 84,342, at p. 89,592 (1987).

a two-tiered standard for enforcement of Section 15(c)(4), one for the "cause," who happens to be a lawyer, the other for a non-lawyer "cause." Such distinction would be at odds with the statutory language of Section 15(c)(4) which calls to account any person, not just a non-lawyer, who is a "cause."

With respect to the appropriate remedy, the ALJ rejected the argument by the Commission staff that the Commission could issue an order that Kern comply with §§ 12, 13 and 14 in connection with the representation of other clients in the future. He held that § 15(c)(4) only contemplated an order respecting compliance by the company that had violated the provisions, and that, since Kern no longer had any power to influence Allied's actions in this matter, no order should be issued.

Kern appealed the ALJ's decision to the full Commission, which heard oral argument on it in June 1989.

Selected References

Barber, Lawyer Duties in Securities Transactions Under Rule 2(e): The Carter Opinions, 1982 B.Y.U.L.Rev. 513–44.

Siedel, Rule 2(e) and Corporate Officers, 39 Bus.Law. 455 (1984).

Note, SEC Disciplinary Proceedings Against Attorneys Under Rule 2(e), 79 Mich.L.Rev. 1270 (1981).

(c) Civil Liability

STOKES v. LOKKEN

644 F.2d 779 (8th Cir.1981).

Before BRIGHT, HENLEY and ARNOLD, CIRCUIT JUDGES.

ARNOLD, CIRCUIT JUDGE.

This is an appeal from the entry of summary judgment by the District Court in favor of Lawrence Lokken, a lawyer, and his former law firm. Henson & Tully (we will refer to these parties in the singular as "Lokken") on claims of negligent misrepresentation and aiding and abetting violations of federal and state securities laws. We affirm.

This action was brought against Continental Financial Corporation, Continental Coin Exchange, and Numisco Sales Company (referred to collectively as "CFC") on February 11, 1975. * * *

CFC was engaged in the marketing of precious metals, including the sale of gold and silver on margin accounts. * * *

Lokken's involvement with this suit arises out of CFC's request that Touche, Ross undertake an audit of CFC for the fiscal year ending

August 31, 1973. In the course of conducting this audit, Touche, Ross sent a standard auditor's letter to Henson & Tully, because the firm had previously done some legal work for CFC. In response to this request Lokken sent a letter dated September 14, 1973, which noted the possibility of securities-law claims relating to the margin transactions, but gave the opinion that the margin transactions did not amount to the sale of securities. The relevant portion of the letter reads as follows:

> Continental Coin Exchange Inc. sells coins in bulk in transactions which conceivably could be characterized as sales of securities and hence made in violation of federal and state securities laws. If the sales do constitute sales of a security, substantial liabilities to customers could arise. It is our opinion that the sales in question do not involve the sale of a security.

Although Lokken had previously performed some services of a limited nature for CFC, only the conduct associated with the September 14, 1973, letter is alleged to be in violation of the securities laws. Lokken had no further involvement with any CFC concerns.

Some time after the Touche, Ross audit was completed, CFC complied an advertising brochure, entitled "The Silver Book." The Silver Book extolled the virtues of investing in silver through CFC and presented information about CFC's financial condition, including a reference to a favorable Touche, Ross audit opinion. The Silver Book made no mention of Lokken, nor is there any specific indication in the record that Lokken had reason to know that the Touche, Ross audit would be reproduced in advertising literature.

* * *

ALLEGED AIDING AND ABETTING OF VIOLATIONS OF § 10(B) AND RULE 10B–5.

The courts of appeals have formulated a three-part test that must be met before aiding and abetting liability is imposed. If proof of any part is lacking, there can be no liability. The three prerequisites are:

> (1) the existence of a securities law violation by the primary party (as opposed to the aiding and abetting party);
>
> (2) "knowledge" of the violation on the part of the aider and abettor; and
>
> (3) "substantial assistance" by the aider and abettor in the achievement of the primary violation.

* * *

(1) *The Primary Violation.* There is no dispute that the first element has been satisfied. The court in *Jenson* found that CFC violated the federal securities laws, and that finding is not in controversy on this appeal.

(2) *Knowledge of the Violation.* The Supreme Court in *Ernst & Ernst v. Hochfelder,* held that a finding of scienter—intent to deceive, manipulate, or defraud—is a prerequisite to § 10(b) liability. *Hoch-*

felder clearly eliminates negligence as a possible basis for a finding of liability, but leaves open the question whether recklessness could be sufficient under certain circumstances.

Since *Hochfelder,* the courts of appeals have generally concluded that recklessness, in some form, can satisfy the scienter requirement. This Court has not yet decided what degree of knowledge will satisfy the scienter requirement. * * * We do not believe it necessary in this opinion to canvass the matter fully and announce a comprehensive standard adequate to govern all cases. For here the actor's conduct falls short of any reasonable formulation of the requisite legal standard.

A brief review of the allegations and evidence submitted to the District Court makes clear that Lokken did not act with the quality of intent required to sustain civil liability. As corporate counsel Lokken incorporated CFC, drafted some agreements, and advised CFC, in a limited way, on its corporate activities. Then, after receiving a standard auditor's request, Lokken responded with an opinion letter that was based on facts concerning CFC's manner of operations supplied by CFC's President, Richard V. Marteson, and limited legal research conducted in August of 1972 on whether the sale of bags of coins constituted the sale of securities. Appellants allege that Lokken relied on advice he solicited over the phone from a Mr. Sedgwick of the Minnesota Securities Division to the effect that the margin transactions were not securities. Such reliance is said to be improper, especially in light of the availability of a statutory procedure for the issuance of interpretive opinions by the Commissioner of Securities. In essence Lokken's research, both legal and otherwise, that was the basis of his opinion letter is alleged to be so grossly negligent that it amounts to recklessness, thus satisfying the scienter requirement.

These allegations still fall short of the state of mind that § 10(b) and Rule 10b–5 require. Language in *Ernst & Ernst v. Hochfelder* is particularly telling on this point. There the court said:

> There is no indication that Congress intended anyone to be made liable [under Rule 10b–5] unless he acted other than in good faith. The catchall provision of § 10(b) should be interpreted no more broadly.

Lokken's conduct in this matter cannot be considered other than in good faith. Indeed, no one claims that he *knew* his legal advice was incorrect. Lokken's opinion letter was a product of good-faith reliance on the facts as he had been given them. Further, Mr. Lokken's opinion was a qualified one, fully noting the possibility that others might disagree, and contingent liabilities result. * * * Lokken's actions cannot be regarded as so reckless that an inference of bad faith might reasonably be made.

(3) *Substantial Assistance.* When proof is lacking on any one part of the three-part test for an aiding-and-abetting violation of § 10(b), there can be no liability. We discuss the proof of substantial assistance only for the purpose of explaining a point made above, although briefly. The point is that the individual parts of the three-part test are not

considered in isolation, but rather in relation to one another, especially the elements of scienter and substantial assistance. For example, where there is a minimal showing of substantial assistance, a greater showing of scienter is required.

* * *

In the present case, the amount of assistance rendered by Lokken is minimal at most. Lokken took no part in the preparation of The Silver Book, nor does the brochure refer to his opinion letter. While Touche, Ross may have relied on the opinion letter to some extent when giving its clean audit report, such reliance is hardly proof of substantial assistance, considering the hedging nature of the opinion and the fact that another attorney, Mr. Efron, also alerted Touche, Ross to the potential securities problem. In short, Lokken's involvement was only tangential. This circumstance strengthens our conviction of the correctness of the District Court's entry of summary judgment on the § 10(b)—Rule 10b–5 aiding-and-abetting claim.

BARKER v. HENDERSON

797 F.2d 490 (7th Cir.1986).

Before CUMMINGS, CHIEF JUDGE, and EASTERBROOK and RIPPLE, CIRCUIT JUDGES.

EASTERBROOK, CIRCUIT JUDGE.

For several years Michigan Baptist Foundation, Inc., built and operated a retirement village in Florida. It sold lifetime leases to the apartments in Estero Woods Village (the Project). In order to finance the Project until it could receive revenue from the leases, the Foundation issued bonds secured by its interest in the land and ongoing construction. Many of the bonds were sold in small amounts to people who, we assume, were unsophisticated and unable to afford losing their investments. In October 1976 Lee County Bank, the Trustee for the bonds, refused to participate in further issues. The Foundation then sold unsecured notes for another 17 months, until, at the request of state officials, a state court enjoined the sale of further instruments. The total sales exceed $7 million in principal. None of the bonds or notes were registered under the Securities Act of 1933. We shall assume that the materials used to sell the bonds and notes omitted essential information about the risks involved in the Project.

The purchasers of bonds between January 1974 and October 1976, and of notes between November 1976 and March 1978, are the plaintiffs in this suit under § 10(b) of the Securities Exchange Act of 1934, and the SEC's Rule 10b–5. * * *

Henderson, Franklin, Starnes & Holt (the Law Firm) furnished legal advice to the Foundation and its predecessors in interest (collectively the Foundation) from 1971 through 1976. Taylor, Edenfield, Gilliam & Wiltshire (the Accounting Firm) furnished accounting services during the same period. The district court reviewed the voluminous materials produced during discovery and wrote a lengthy opinion explaining why neither the Law Firm nor the Accounting Firm was sufficiently involved in the sale of the securities to be liable for any of the Foundation's sins. * * * The plaintiffs' case against the two Firms is essentially that (a) the Firms sent the Foundation down the wrong path, failing at the outset to insist that it register the securities and disclose the risks involved; (b) the Firms knew of the Foundation's continued solicitation of funds but did not "blow the whistle"; (c) the Firms induced the Trustee to lend implied support to the securities through October 1976 by acting as Trustee.

* * *

There is no direct evidence that either Firm acted with intent to deceive any purchaser of the Foundation's securities. There is indeed no evidence that either Firm saw any of the Foundation's selling documents during the period 1974–78 until after the document had been placed in use. There is no serious claim that either Firm intentionally or recklessly gave bad advice to the Foundation. The Accounting Firm was fired after catching a problem in the Foundation's internal affairs. A jury might conclude that the Law Firm was negligent in drafting a "loose" indenture and in obtaining belated releases of the mortgage on the land, but negligence does not establish the necessary scienter, and neither of these errors (if they were errors) was the subject of a scheme to defraud. The securities laws do not impose liability for ordinary malpractice, even though that malpractice may diminish the value of the issuer and thus of the issuer's securities. (We do not say whether there was malpractice here.)

The plaintiffs insist that the Firms *must* have known that the Foundation's selling documents were inaccurate and, because they did not do anything to stop the sales and answered queries from the Trustee, they *must* have had the necessary mental state. If this were enough to establish scienter, however, the scienter doctrine would not do anything to distinguish liability under § 10(b) and Rule 10b–5 from the presumptive or absolute liability under §§ 11, 12, 15, and 20. A plaintiff's case against an aider, abetter, or conspirator may not rest on a bare inference that the defendant "must have had" knowledge of the facts. The plaintiff must support the inference with some reason to conclude that the defendant has thrown in his lot with the primary violators.

Law firms and accountants may act or remain silent for good reasons as well as bad ones, and allowing scienter or conspiracy to defraud to be inferred from the silence of a professional firm may expand the scope of liability far beyond that authorized in *Ernst & Ernst* and *Herman & MacLean.* If the plaintiff does not have direct evidence of scienter, the court should ask whether the fraud (or cover-up) was in the interest of the defendants. Did they gain by bilking the buyers of the securities? In this case the Firms did not gain. They received none of the proceeds from the sales. They did not receive fees for rendering advice in connection with the sales to the plaintiffs. Both Firms billed so little time to the Foundation between 1974 and 1976 (and none after October 1976) that it is inconceivable that they joined a venture to feather their nests by defrauding investors. They had nothing to gain and everything to lose. There is no sound basis, therefore, on which a jury could infer that the Firms joined common cause with other offenders or aided and abetted a scheme with the necessary state of mind.

The district court also held that the Firms had not committed any forbidden act, had not participated in a scheme to defraud by remaining silent when there was a duty to speak. This, too, is a correct conclusion. Neither lawyers nor accountants are required to tattle on their clients in the absence of some duty to disclose.

The extent to which lawyers and accountants should reveal their clients' wrongdoing—and to whom they should reveal—is a question of great moment. There are proposals to change the rules of legal ethics and the SEC's regulations governing accountants. The professions and the regulatory agencies will debate questions raised by cases such as this one for years to come. We express no opinion on whether the Firms did what they should, whether there was malpractice under state law, or whether the rules of ethics (or other fiduciary doctrines) ought to require lawyers and accountants to blow the whistle in equivalent circumstances. We are satisfied, however, that an award of damages under the securities laws is not the way to blaze the trail toward improved ethical standards in the legal and accounting professions. Liability depends on an *existing* duty to disclose. The securities law therefore must lag behind changes in ethical and fiduciary standards. The plaintiffs have not pointed to any rule imposing on either Firm a duty to blow the whistle.

NICEWARNER v. BLEAVINS, 244 F.Supp. 261 (D.Colo.1965), was a suit under § 12(1) of the 1933 Act to recover the purchase price of securities sold without registration under that Act. One defendant, Hudson, was an attorney who, the court found, was "present * * * at every turn" in the transaction, "but always in the capacity of attorney for Lingenfelter. * * * Hudson had reason to anticipate a public offering; he knew that no registration statement was in effect; he should have known that the assignments were securities; he * * * could have foreseen the use of the mails or of interstate facilities; and he could see that the Nicewarners needed the protection of the Act." Nevertheless, the court held that Hudson "was not a party to the sale" for the purposes of § 12(1), and that while "he might have prevented the sale, * * * failure to do so in these circumstances does not render one a seller or an offeror."

In GOODMAN v. KENNEDY, 18 Cal.3d 335, 556 P.2d 737 (1976), the California Supreme Court held that a lawyer who negligently advised his clients that they could sell certain shares in a company they controlled, without jeopardizing the company's exemption under Regulation A, could not be held liable to the purchasers of the shares for losses suffered when the SEC suspended the exemption because of the violations.

The present defendant had no relationship to plaintiffs that would give rise to his owing plaintiffs any duty of care in advising his clients that they could sell the stock without adverse consequences. There is no allegation that the advice was ever communicated to plaintiffs and hence no basis for any claim that they relied upon it in purchasing or retaining the stock.

* * *

Plaintiffs contend, however, that because the advice related to a possible sale of stock by defendant's clients, defendant's duty of care in giving the advice extended to anyone to whom the sale might be made.

* * *

[P]laintiffs argue that defendant's advice was "intended to affect" them as purchasers and that harm to them was foreseeable from the adverse effect of the sale upon the value of the stock contrary to the erroneous assurances embodied in the negligent advice. However, plaintiffs were not persons upon whom defendant's clients had any wish or obligation to confer a benefit in the transaction. Plaintiffs' only relationship to the proposed transaction was that of parties with whom defendant's clients might negotiate a bargain at arm's length. Any buyers' "potential advantage" from the possible purchase of the stock "was only a collateral consideration of the transaction" and did not put such potential buyers into any relationship with defendant as "intended beneficiaries" of his clients' anticipated sales.

To make an attorney liable for negligent confidential advice not only to the client who enters into a transaction in reliance upon the advice but also to the other parties to the transaction with whom the client deals at arm's length would inject undesirable self-protective reservations into the attorney's counselling role. The attorney's preoccupation or concern with the possibility of claims based on mere negligence (as distinct from fraud or malice) by any with whom his client might deal "would prevent him from devoting his entire energies to his client's interests". The result would be both "an undue burden on the profession" and a diminution in the quality of the legal services received by the client.

Justices Mosk and Tobriner dissented:

Until relatively recent times, the absence of privity of contract precluded a person other than a client from recovering for the professional negligence of an attorney or an accountant. The rationale underlying this rule can be traced to an opinion by Judge Cardozo in Ultramares Corporation v. Touche (1931) 255 N.Y. 170, 174 N.E. 441, which involved the liability of a firm of accountants to a creditor who had extended credit to a corporation in reliance on a balance sheet of the corporation prepared by the defendant indicating that the corporation had substantial assets. * * *

Since *Ultramares* there has been a steady erosion of the privity requirement in malpractice actions, and California has been in the forefront of jurisdictions extending the scope of professional liability to third persons.

* * *

Defendant contends that his advice to his client was not intended to affect plaintiffs because at the time the advice was rendered plaintiffs had no connection with the corporation. While it is true that when defendant rendered his advice he was not certain the corporation would issue the additional shares and, of course, could not know the identity of prospective purchasers, there can be no doubt he knew that if his advice was followed those who purchased the stock would be affected thereby. The mere fact that he did not know their identity cannot be decisive. Nor is there any question that it was reasonably foreseeable if the advice was incorrect the purchasers of the stock would be injured.

The complaint leaves something to be desired in specifying the relationship between defendant's negligence and the injury suffered by plaintiffs, but liberally construed, it can be read to allege that the corporation issued the additional shares as the result of defendant's advice, which in turn caused the commission to suspend the Regulation A exemption, resulting in impairment of the value of the stock and the inability of plaintiffs to sell their shares. * * *

I conclude that defendant should be held to owe a duty to plaintiffs. I disagree with the majority's conclusion that the imposition of liability in this case will result in an undue burden upon the legal profession.

* * *

In this case the class of persons certain to be damaged by the attorney's negligent advice to his client was reasonably foreseeable and the damage was an inexorably direct consequence of the negligent act.

In WACHOVIA BANK v. NATIONAL STUDENT MARKETING CORP., 461 F.Supp. 999 (D.D.C.1978), the court held that a bank which purchased $5 million of NSMC debentures in December 1969 (two months after the Interstate closing) was entitled to assert a claim against NSMC's attorneys and accountants under § 17(a) of the 1933 Act and § 10(b) of the 1934 Act, but then held that the particular claim was barred by the applicable statute of limitations.

Selected References

Note, Secondary Liability of Attorneys for Securities Laws Violations—The Need for a Single Standard of Attorney Conduct, 30 Wayne L.Rev. 65 (1983).

Note, Attorneys and Participant Liability Under § 12(2) of the Securities Act of 1933, 1982 Ariz.St.L.J. 529.

Knepper, Liability of Lawyer–Directors, 40 Ohio St.L.J. 341 (1979).

CHAPTER 5

INSIDER TRADING

The preceding discussion of the general jurisprudence of Rule 10b–5 and the other antifraud provisions tends to obscure the fact that they are applied to a wide variety of situations. Each of these situations has its own special attributes which create distinctive problems in the interpretation of the applicable rules. One of the most important applications of Rule 10b–5 is its use as a sanction against "insider trading"—purchases or sales by persons who have access to information which is not available to those with whom they deal or to traders generally.

A. ELEMENTS OF THE VIOLATION

Early applications of the rule focused on the situation with which it was specifically designed to deal—purchases in direct transactions by a company or its officers without disclosure of material favorable information about the company's affairs. Ward La France Truck Corp., 13 S.E.C. 373 (1943); Speed v. Transamerica Corp., 99 F.Supp. 808 (D.Del. 1951). In this context, it was available to supplement state common law, which in most states did not afford a remedy to the aggrieved seller in this situation in the absence of affirmative misstatements or "special circumstances."

In a series of administrative decisions and injunctive proceedings, commencing in 1961, the SEC greatly broadened the applicability of Rule 10b–5 as a general prohibition against any trading on "inside information" in anonymous stock exchange transactions as well as in face-to-face dealings. However, subsequent decisions of the Supreme Court have cast doubt on some of the doctrines developed in those decisions.

CADY, ROBERTS & CO.

40 S.E.C. 907 (1961).

By CARY, CHAIRMAN.

This is a case of first impression and one of signal importance in our administration of the Federal securities acts. It involves a selling broker who executes a solicited order and sells for discretionary accounts (including that of his wife) upon an exchange. The crucial question is what are the duties of such a broker after receiving nonpublic information as to a company's dividend action from a director who is employed by the same brokerage firm.

These proceedings were instituted to determine whether Cady, Roberts & Co. ("registrant") and Robert M. Gintel ("Gintel"), the selling broker and a partner of the registrant, willfully violated the "anti-fraud" provisions of Section 10(b) of the Securities Exchange Act of 1934 ("Exchange Act"), Rule 10b–5 issued under that Act, and Section 17(a) of the Securities Act of 1933 ("Securities Act") and, if so, whether any disciplinary action is necessary or appropriate in the public interest. The respondents have submitted an offer of settlement which essentially provides that the facts stipulated by respondents shall constitute the record in these proceedings for the purposes of determining the occurrence of a willful violation of the designated anti-fraud provisions and the entering of an appropriate order, on the condition that no sanction may be entered in excess of a suspension of Gintel for 20 days from the New York Stock Exchange.[3]

The facts are as follows:

Early in November 1959, Roy T. Hurley, then President and Chairman of the Board of Curtiss–Wright Corporation, invited 2,000 representatives of the press, the military and the financial and business communities to a public unveiling on November 23, of a new type of internal combustion engine being developed by the company. On November 24, 1959, press announcements concerning the new engine appeared in certain newspapers. On that day Curtiss–Wright stock was one of the most active issues on the New York Stock Exchange, closing at 35¼, up 3¼ on a volume of 88,700 shares. From November 6 through November 23, Gintel had purchased approximately 11,000 shares of Curtiss–Wright stock for about 30 discretionary accounts of customers of registrant. With the rise in the price on November 24, he began selling Curtiss–Wright shares for these accounts and sold on that day a total of 2,200 shares on the Exchange.

The activity in Curtiss–Wright stock on the Exchange continued the next morning, November 25, and the price rose to 40¾, a new high for the year. Gintel continued sales for the discretionary accounts and, between the opening of the market and about 11:00 a.m., he sold 4,300 shares.

On the morning of November 25, the Curtiss–Wright directors, including J. Cheever Cowdin ("Cowdin"), then a registered representative of registrant,[4] met to consider, among other things, the declaration

3. The offer of settlement, submitted pursuant to Section 5(b) of the Administrative Procedure Act and Rule 8 of our Rules of Practice, further provides that respondents also waive a hearing and a recommended decision by a hearing examiner and agree to participation by our Division of Trading and Exchanges in the preparation of our findings and opinion.

4. Mr. Cowdin, who died in September 1960, was a registered representative of the registrant from July 1956 until March 1960, and was also a member of the board of directors of Curtiss–Wright, having first been elected in 1929.

of a quarterly dividend. The company had paid a dividend, although not earned, of $.625 per share for each of the first three quarters of 1959. The Curtiss–Wright board, over the objections of Hurley, who favored declaration of a dividend at the same rate as in the prior quarters, approved a dividend for the fourth quarter at the reduced rate of $.375 per share. At approximately 11:00 a.m., the board authorized transmission of information of this action by telegram to the New York Stock Exchange. The Secretary of Curtiss–Wright immediately left the meeting room to arrange for this communication. There was a short delay in the transmission of the telegram because of a typing problem and the telegram, although transmitted to Western Union at 11:12 a.m., was not delivered to the Exchange until 12:29 p.m. It had been customary for the company also to advise the Dow Jones News Ticker Service of any dividend action. However, apparently through some mistake or inadvertence, the Wall Street Journal was not given the news until approximately 11:45 a.m. and the announcement did not appear on the Dow Jones ticker tape until 11:48 a.m.

Sometime after the dividend decision, there was a recess of the Curtiss–Wright directors' meeting, during which Cowdin telephoned registrant's office and left a message for Gintel that the dividend had been cut. Upon receiving this information, Gintel entered two sell orders for execution on the Exchange, one to sell 2,000 shares of Curtiss–Wright stock for 10 accounts, and the other to sell short 5,000 shares for 11 accounts. Four hundred of the 5,000 shares were sold for three of Cowdin's customers. According to Cowdin, pursuant to directions from his clients, he had given instructions to Gintel to take profits on these 400 shares if the stock took a "run-up." These orders were executed at 11:15 and 11:18 a.m. at 40¼ and 40⅜, respectively.[6]

When the dividend announcement appeared on the Dow Jones tape at 11:48 a.m., the Exchange was compelled to suspend trading in Curtiss–Wright because of the large number of sell orders. Trading in Curtiss–Wright stock was resumed at 1:59 p.m. at 36½, ranged during the balance of the day between 34⅛ and 37, and closed at 34⅞.

Violation of Anti–Fraud Provisions

So many times that citation is unnecessary, we have indicated that the purchase and sale of securities is a field in special need of regulation for the protection of investors. To this end one of the major purposes of the securities acts is the prevention of fraud, manipulation

6. Subsequently, but prior to 11:48 a.m., Gintel sold 2,000 shares of Curtiss–Wright stock for a mutual fund which had a large position in this stock. A securities analyst for the investment manager of this fund who came into Gintel's office that morning about 11 o'clock testified that he had been concerned about the possible Curtiss–Wright dividend action and, on behalf of the fund, had delivered to Curtiss–Wright a letter urging that the dividend not be reduced. Both Gintel and the analyst stated that Gintel did not furnish any information regarding the dividend action. The analyst, by telephone from registrant's office, did advise the investment manager of the fund to sell Curtiss–Wright stock. The fund placed orders for and sold about 11,300 shares, including the 2,000 sold through Gintel, who had previously not handled any transactions for the fund.

or deception in connection with securities transactions. Consistent with this objective, Section 17(a) of the Securities Act, Section 10(b) of the Exchange Act and Rule 10b–5, issued under that Section, are broad remedial provisions aimed at reaching misleading or deceptive activities, whether or not they are precisely and technically sufficient to sustain a common law action for fraud and deceit. Indeed, despite the decline in importance of a "Federal rule" in the light of Erie R. Co. v. Tompkins, the securities acts may be said to have generated a wholly new and far-reaching body of Federal corporation law.

* * *

Section 17 and Rule 10b–5 apply to securities transactions by "any person." Misrepresentations will lie within their ambit, no matter who the speaker may be. An affirmative duty to disclose material information has been traditionally imposed on corporate "insiders," particularly officers, directors, or controlling stockholders. We, and the courts, have consistently held that insiders must disclose material facts which are known to them by virtue of their position but which are not known to persons with whom they deal and which, if known, would affect their investment judgment. Failure to make disclosure in these circumstances constitutes a violation of the anti-fraud provisions.[13] If, on the other hand, disclosure prior to effecting a purchase or sale would be improper or unrealistic under the circumstances, we believe the alternative is to forego the transaction.

The ingredients are here and we accordingly find that Gintel willfully violated Sections 17(a) and 10(b) and Rule 10b–5. We also find a similar violation by the registrant, since the actions of Gintel, a member of registrant, in the course of his employment are to be regarded as actions of registrant itself. It was obvious that a reduction in the quarterly dividend by the Board of Directors was a material fact which could be expected to have an adverse impact on the market price of the company's stock. The rapidity with which Gintel acted upon receipt of the information confirms his own recognition of that conclusion.

We have already noted that the anti-fraud provisions are phrased in terms of "any person" and that a special obligation has been traditionally required of corporate insiders, e.g., officers, directors and controlling stockholders. These three groups, however, do not exhaust the classes of persons upon whom there is such an obligation. Analytically, the obligation rests on two principal elements; first, the existence of a relationship giving access, directly or indirectly, to information

13. Speed v. Transamerica Corp., 99 F.Supp. 808, 828–829 (D.Del.1951); Kardon v. National Gypsum Co., 73 F.Supp. 798, 800 (E.D.Penn.1947); Ward LaFrance Truck Corp., 13 S.E.C. 373, 380, 381 (1943).

Although the "majority" state rule apparently does not impose an affirmative duty of disclosure on insiders when dealing in securities, an increasing number of jurisdictions do impose this responsibility either on the theory that an insider is generally a fiduciary with respect to securities transactions or "special facts" may make him one. See, e.g., Strong v. Repide, 213 U.S. 419, 29 S.Ct. 521 (1909); Hobart v. Hobart Estate Co., 26 Cal.2d 412, 159 P.2d 958 (1945); Hotchkiss v. Fischer, 136 Kan. 530, 16 P.2d 531 (1932).

intended to be available only for a corporate purpose and not for the personal benefit of anyone,[15] and second, the inherent unfairness involved where a party takes advantage of such information knowing it is unavailable to those with whom he is dealing. In considering these elements under the broad language of the anti-fraud provisions we are not to be circumscribed by fine distinctions and rigid classifications. Thus our task here is to identify those persons who are in a special relationship with a company and privy to its internal affairs, and thereby suffer correlative duties in trading in its securities. Intimacy demands restraint lest the uninformed be exploited.

The facts here impose on Gintel the responsibilities of those commonly referred to as "insiders." He received the information prior to its public release from a director of Curtiss–Wright, Cowdin, who was associated with the registrant. Cowdin's relationship to the company clearly prohibited him from selling the securities affected by the information without disclosure. By logical sequence, it should prohibit Gintel, a partner of registrant.[17] This prohibition extends not only over his own account, but to selling for discretionary accounts and soliciting and executing other orders. In somewhat analogous circumstances, we have charged a broker-dealer who effects securities transactions for an insider and who knows that the insider possesses non-public material information with the affirmative duty to make appropriate disclosures or dissociate himself from the transaction.

The three main subdivisions of Section 17 and Rule 10b–5 have been considered to be mutually supporting rather than mutually exclusive. Thus, a breach of duty of disclosure may be viewed as a device or scheme, an implied misrepresentation, and an act or practice, violative of all three subdivisions. Respondents argue that only clause (3) may be applicable here. We hold that, in these circumstances, Gintel's conduct at least violated clause (3) as a practice which operated as a fraud or deceit upon the purchasers. Therefore, we need not decide the scope of clauses (1) and (2).

We cannot accept respondents' contention that an insider's responsibility is limited to existing stockholders and that he has no special duties when sales of securities are made to non-stockholders. This approach is too narrow. It ignores the plight of the buying public—wholly unprotected from the misuse of special information.

15. A significant purpose of the Exchange Act was to eliminate the idea that the use of inside information for personal advantage was a normal emolument of corporate office. See Sections 2 and 16 of the Act; H.R.Rep. No. 1383, 73rd Cong., 2d Sess. 13 (1934); S.Rep. No. 792, 73rd Cong., 2d Sess. 9 (1934); S.E.C., Tenth Annual Report 50 (1944).

17. See 3 Loss, Securities Regulation. 1450–1 (2d ed., 1961). Cf. Restatement. Restitution, Section 201(2) 1937). Although Cowdin may have had reason to believe that news of the dividend action had already been made public when he called registrant's office, there is no question that Gintel knew when he received the message that the information was not yet public and was received from a director.

Neither the statutes nor Rule 10b–5 establish artificial walls of responsibility. Section 17 of the Securities Act explicitly states that it shall be unlawful for any person in the offer or sale of securities to do certain prescribed acts. Although the primary function of Rule 10b–5 was to extend a remedy to a defrauded seller, the courts and this Commission have held that it is also applicable to a defrauded buyer.[22] There is no valid reason why persons who *purchase* stock from an officer, director or other person having the responsibilities of an "insider" should not have the same protection afforded by disclosure of special information as persons who *sell* stock to them. Whatever distinctions may have existed at common law based on the view that an officer or director may stand in a fiduciary relationship to existing stockholders from whom he purchases but not to members of the public to whom he sells, it is clearly not appropriate to introduce these into the broader anti-fraud concepts embodied in the securities acts.

Respondents further assert that they made no express representations and did not in any way manipulate the market, and urge that in a transaction on an exchange there is no further duty such as may be required in a "face-to-face" transaction.[24] We reject this suggestion. It would be anomalous indeed if the protection afforded by the anti-fraud provisions were withdrawn from transactions effected on exchanges, primary markets for securities transactions. If purchasers on an exchange had available material information known by a selling insider, we may assume that their investment judgment would be affected and their decision whether to buy might accordingly be modified. Consequently, any sales by the insider must await disclosure of the information.

Cases cited by respondents in which relief was denied to purchasers or sellers of securities in exchange transactions are distinguishable. The action here was instituted by the Commission, not by individuals. The cited cases concern private suits brought against insiders for violation of the anti-fraud rules. They suggest that the plaintiffs may not recover because there was lacking a "semblance of privity" since it was not shown that the buyers or sellers bought from or sold to the insiders. These cases have no relevance here as they concern the remedy of the buyer or seller *vis-a-vis* the insider. The absence of a remedy by the private litigant because of lack of privity does not absolve an insider from responsibility for fraudulent conduct.

Respondents argue that any requirement that a broker-dealer in exchange transactions make disclosure of "adverse factors disclosed by

22. See Ellis v. Carter, 291 F.2d 270 (C.A.9, 1961); Matheson v. Armbrust, 284 F.2d 670 (C.A.9, 1960), cert. denied, 365 U.S. 870 (1961); Fischman v. Raytheon, 188 F.2d 783 (C.A.2, 1951). See Securities Exchange Act Release No. 3634. We note that, in 16 F.R. 7928, August 11, 1951, the Commission struck the words "by a purchaser" from the title of Rule 10b–5 (then X10B–5) so as to read "Employment of manipulative and deceptive devices."

24. It is interesting to note that earlier attacks on the applicability of Rule 10b–5 rested on the contention that it applied only to exchange transactions or other transactions on an organized security market.

his analysis" would create uncertainty and confusion as to the duties of those who are constantly acquiring and analyzing information about companies in which they or their clients are interested. Furthermore, it is claimed, substantial practical difficulties would be presented as to the manner of making disclosures.

There should be no quandary on the facts here presented. While there may be a question as to the materiality and significance of some corporate facts and as to the necessity of their disclosure under particular circumstances, that is not this case. Corporate dividend action of the kind involved here is clearly recognizable as having a direct effect on the market value of securities and the judgment of investors. Moreover, knowledge of this action was not arrived at as a result of perceptive analysis of generally known facts, but was obtained from a director (and associate) during the time when respondents should have known that the board of directors of the issuer was taking steps to make the information publicly available but before it was actually announced.

Furthermore, the New York Stock Exchange has recognized that prompt disclosure of important corporate developments, including specifically dividend action, is essential for the benefit of stockholders and the investing public and has established explicit requirements and recommended procedures for the immediate public release of dividend information by issuers whose securities are listed on the Exchange. The practical problems envisaged by respondents in effecting appropriate disclosures in connection with transactions on the Exchange are easily avoided where, as here, all the registered broker-dealer need do is to keep out of the market until the established procedures for public release of the information are carried out instead of hastening to execute transactions in advance of, and in frustration of, the objectives of the release.

Finally, we do not accept respondents' contention that Gintel was merely carrying out a program of liquidating the holdings in his discretionary accounts—determined and embarked upon prior to his receipt of the dividend information. In this connection, it is further alleged that he had a fiduciary duty to these accounts to continue the sales, which overrode any obligations to unsolicited purchasers on the Exchange.

The record does not support the contention that Gintel's sales were merely a continuance of his prior schedule of liquidation. Upon receipt of the news of the dividend reduction, which Gintel knew was not public, he hastened to sell before the expected public announcement all of the Curtiss-Wright shares remaining in his discretionary accounts, contrary to his previous moderate rate of sales. In so doing, he also made short sales of securities which he then allocated to his wife's account and to the account of a customer whom he had never seen and with whom he had had no prior dealings. Moreover, while Gintel undoubtedly occupied a fiduciary relationship to his customers, this relationship could not justify any actions by him contrary to law. Even if we assume the existence of conflicting fiduciary obligations, there can be no doubt which is primary here. On these facts, clients may not expect of a broker the benefits of his inside information at the expense of the public generally. The case of *Van Alstyne, Noel & Co.,*[32] cited by respondents, not only fails to support their position but on the contrary itself suggests that a confidential relationship with one person cannot be relied upon as overriding a duty not to defraud another. In that case, we held that a broker-dealer's sales of a company's securities to customers through misleading statements and without revealing material facts violated anti-fraud provisions, notwithstanding the broker-dealer's assertion that the information concealed from investors had been obtained in confidence from the company and so could not be revealed.

The Public Interest

All the surrounding circumstances and the state of mind of the participants may be taken into consideration in determining what sanctions should appropriately be imposed here.

It is clear that Gintel's conduct was willful in that he knew what he was doing.[34] However, there is no evidence of a preconceived plan whereby Cowdin was to "leak" advance information of the dividend reduction so that Gintel could use it to advantage before the public announcement; on the contrary, the evidence points to the conclusion that Cowdin probably assumed, without thinking about it, that the dividend action was already a matter of public information and further that he called registrant's office to find out the effect of the dividend news upon the market. The record, moreover, indicates that Gintel's conduct was a spontaneous reaction to the dividend news, that he intended primarily to benefit existing clients of Cady, Roberts & Co. and that he acted on the spur of the moment and so quickly as to preclude the possibility of review by registrant or of his own more deliberate consideration of his responsibilities under the securities acts.

Gintel has been fined $3,000 by the New York Stock Exchange in connection with the instant transactions. The publication of this opinion, moreover, will in itself serve as a further sanction upon Gintel and registrant and will also induce a more careful observance of the requirements of the anti-fraud provisions in the area in question. Furthermore, registrant had no opportunity to prevent Gintel's sponta-

32. 33 S.E.C. 311 (1952).

34. * * * Gintel has stressed that he did not communicate with or advise any of his other accounts to trade in Curtiss-Wright stock or make any trades for himself (other than the excess short position taken in his wife's account) upon receiving the dividend information, thus in effect indicating that he recognized the impropriety of using what he knew was inside information not publicly known. When asked why he had not disclosed the fact that the dividend had been cut, Gintel answered: "Well, the only answer I can think of to give is that I didn't want to tell him or anybody that what I had accidentally learned from a director of the company * * * I had obtained the information from a director of the company in this manner."

neous transactions and no contention has been made that its procedures for handling accounts did not meet proper standards. Under all the circumstances we conclude that the public interest and the protection of investors will be adequately and appropriately served if Gintel is suspended from the New York Stock Exchange for 20 days and if no sanction is imposed against the registrant. Accordingly, we accept respondents' offer of settlement.

Commissioners WOODSIDE and COHEN join in the above opinion. COMMISSIONER FREAR dissents in part (see below).

COMMISSIONER FREAR, dissenting in part:

I agree that the facts disclosed by the record submitted in connection with the offer of settlement show willful violations of the antifraud provisions of the Securities Acts, and I concur in the views enunciated in the part of the Commission's Findings and Opinion dealing with such violations. However, in my opinion those facts and violations require the imposition of a greater sanction than the 20-day suspension of Gintel from membership on the New York Stock Exchange, which is the maximum permitted under the offer of settlement, and I would accordingly reject the offer.

SEC v. TEXAS GULF SULPHUR CO.

401 F.2d 833 (2d Cir.1968).

Before LUMBARD, CHIEF JUDGE, and WATERMAN, MOORE, FRIENDLY, SMITH, KAUFMAN, HAYS, ANDERSON and FEINBERG, CIRCUIT JUDGES.

WATERMAN, CIRCUIT JUDGE.

This action was commenced in the United States District Court for the Southern District of New York by the Securities and Exchange Commission (the SEC) pursuant to Sec. 21(e) of the Securities Exchange Act of 1934 (the Act), against Texas Gulf Sulphur Company (TGS) and several of its officers, directors and employees, to enjoin certain conduct by TGS and the individual defendants said to violate Section 10(b) of the Act, and Rule 10b–5 (the Rule), promulgated thereunder, and to compel the rescission by the individual defendants of securities transactions assertedly conducted contrary to law. The complaint alleged (1) that defendants Fogarty, Mollison, Darke, Murray, Huntington, O'Neill, Clayton, Crawford, and Coates had either personally or through agents purchased TGS stock or calls thereon from November 12, 1963 through April 16, 1964 on the basis of material inside information concerning the results of TGS drilling in Timmins, Ontario, while such information remained undisclosed to the investing public generally or to the particular sellers; (2) that defendants Darke and Coates had divulged such information to others for use in purchasing TGS stock or calls [3] or recommended its purchase while the information was undis-

3. A "call" is a negotiable option contract by which the bearer has the right to buy from the writer of the contract a certain number of shares of a particular stock

closed to the public or to the sellers * * *. The case was tried at length before Judge Bonsal of the Southern District of New York, sitting without a jury. Judge Bonsal in a detailed opinion decided, *inter alia,* that the insider activity prior to April 9, 1964 was not illegal because the drilling results were not "material" until then; that Clayton and Crawford had traded in violation of law because they traded after that date; that Coates had committed no violation as he did not trade before disclosure was made * * *. 258 F.Supp. 262, at 292–296 (SDNY 1966). Defendants Clayton and Crawford appeal from that part of the decision below which held that they had violated Sec. 10(b) and Rule 10b–5 and the SEC appeals from the remainder of the decision which dismissed the complaint against defendants TGS, Fogarty, Mollison, Holyk, Darke, Stephens, Kline, Murray, and Coates.

* * *

During the period of drilling in Timmins, the market price of TGS stock fluctuated but steadily gained overall. On Friday, November 8, when the drilling began, the stock closed at 17⅜; on Friday, November 15, after K–55–1 had been completed, it closed at 18. After a slight decline to 16⅜ by Friday, November 22, the price rose to 20⅞ by December 13, when the chemical assay results of K–55–1 were received, and closed at a high of 24⅛ on February 21, the day after the stock options had been issued. It had reached a price of 26 by March 31, after the land acquisition program had been completed and drilling had been resumed, and continued to ascend to 30⅛ by the close of trading on April 10, at which time the drilling progress up to then was evaluated for the April 12th press release. On April 13, the day on which the April 12 release was disseminated, TGS opened at 30⅛, rose immediately to a high of 32 and gradually tapered off to close at 30⅞. It closed at 30¼ the next day, and at 29⅜ on April 15. On April 16, the day of the official announcement of the Timmins discovery, the price climbed to a high of 37 and closed at 36⅜. By May 15, TGS stock was selling at 58¼.

I. The Individual Defendants

A. Introductory

* * *

Rule 10b–5 was promulgated pursuant to the grant of authority given the SEC by Congress in Section 10(b) of the Securities Exchange Act of 1934. By that Act Congress purposed to prevent inequitable and unfair practices and to insure fairness in securities transactions generally, whether conducted face-to-face, over the counter, or on exchanges, see 3 Loss, Securities Regulation 1455–56 (2d ed. 1961). The Act and the Rule apply to the transactions here, all of which were consummated on exchanges.

at a fixed price on or before a certain agreed-upon date.

Whether predicated on traditional fiduciary concepts, see, e.g., Hotchkiss v. Fisher, 136 Kan. 530, 16 P.2d 531 (Kan.1932), or on the "special facts" doctrine, see, e.g., Strong v. Repide, 213 U.S. 419 (1909), the Rule is based in policy on the justifiable expectation of the securities marketplace that all investors trading on impersonal exchanges have relatively equal access to material information, see Cary, Insider Trading in Stocks, 21 Bus.Law. 1009, 1010 (1966), Fleischer, Securities Trading and Corporation Information Practices: The Implications of the Texas Gulf Sulphur Proceeding, 51 Va.L.Rev. 1271, 1278–80 (1965). The essence of the Rule is that anyone who, trading for his own account in the securities of a corporation has "access, directly or indirectly, to information intended to be available only for a corporate purpose and not for the personal benefit of anyone" may not take "advantage of such information knowing it is unavailable to those with whom he is dealing," i.e., the investing public. Matter of Cady, Roberts & Co., 40 SEC 907, 912 (1961). Insiders, as directors or management officers are, of course, by this Rule, precluded from so unfairly dealing, but the Rule is also applicable to one possessing the information who may not be strictly termed an "insider" within the meaning of Sec. 16(b) of the Act. Cady, Roberts, supra. Thus, anyone in possession of material inside information must either disclose it to the investing public, or, if he is disabled from disclosing it in order to protect a corporate confidence, or he chooses not to do so, must abstain from trading in or recommending the securities concerned while such inside information remains undisclosed. So, it is here no justification for insider activity that disclosure was forbidden by the legitimate corporate objective of acquiring options to purchase the land surrounding the exploration site; if the information was, as the SEC contends, material, its possessors should have kept out of the market until disclosure was accomplished. Cady, Roberts, supra at 911.

B. Material Inside Information

An insider is not, of course, always foreclosed from investing in his own company merely because he may be more familiar with company operations than are outside investors. An insider's duty to disclose information or his duty to abstain from dealing in his company's securities arises only in "those situations which are essentially extraordinary in nature and which are reasonably certain to have a substantial effect on the market price of the security if [the extraordinary situation is] disclosed." Fleischer, Securities Trading and Corporate Information Practices: The Implications of the Texas Gulf Sulphur Proceeding, 51 Va.L.Rev. 1271, 1289.

Nor is an insider obligated to confer upon outside investors the benefit of his superior financial or other expert analysis by disclosing his educated guesses or predictions. The only regulatory objective is that access to material information be enjoyed equally, but this objective requires nothing more than the disclosure of basic facts so that outsiders may draw upon their own evaluative expertise in reaching their own investment decisions with knowledge equal to that of the insiders.

This is not to suggest, however, as did the trial court, that "the test of materiality must necessarily be a conservative one, particularly since many actions under Section 10(b) are brought on the basis of hindsight," in the sense that the materiality of facts is to be assessed solely by measuring the effect the knowledge of the facts would have upon prudent or conservative investors. As we stated in List v. Fashion Park, Inc., 340 F.2d 457, 462, "The basic test of materiality * * * is whether a *reasonable* man would attach importance * * * in determining his choice of action in the transaction in question. Restatement, Torts § 538(2)(a); accord Prosser, Torts 554–55; I Harper & James, Torts 565–66." (Emphasis supplied.) This, of course, encompasses any fact " * * * which in reasonable and objective contemplation *might* affect the value of the corporation's stock or securities * * *." List v. Fashion Park, Inc., supra at 462, quoting from Kohler v. Kohler Co., 319 F.2d 634, 642 (7 Cir.1963). (Emphasis supplied.) Such a fact is a material fact and must be effectively disclosed to the investing public prior to the commencement of insider trading in the corporation's securities. The speculators and chartists of Wall and Bay Streets are also "reasonable" investors entitled to the same legal protection afforded conservative traders. Thus, material facts include not only information disclosing the earnings and distributions of a company but also those facts which affect the probable future of the company and those which may affect the desire of investors to buy, sell, or hold the company's securities.

In each case, then, whether facts are material within Rule 10b–5 when the facts relate to a particular event and are undisclosed by those persons who are knowledgeable thereof will depend at any given time upon a balancing of both the indicated probability that the event will occur and the anticipated magnitude of the event in light of the totality of the company activity. Here, notwithstanding the trial court's conclusion that the results of the first drill core, K–55–1, were "too 'remote' * * * to have had any significant impact on the market, i.e., to be deemed material," knowledge of the possibility, which surely was more than marginal, of the existence of a mine of the vast magnitude indicated by the remarkably rich drill core located rather close to the surface (suggesting mineability by the less expensive open-pit method) within the confines of a large anomaly (suggesting an extensive region of mineralization) might well have affected the price of TGS stock and would certainly have been an important fact to a reasonable, if speculative, investor in deciding whether he should buy, sell, or hold. After all, this first drill core was "unusually good and * * * excited the interest and speculation of those who knew about it."

Our disagreement with the district judge on the issue does not, then, go to his findings of basic fact, as to which the "clearly erroneous" rule would apply, but to his understanding of the legal standard applicable to them. Our survey of the facts found below conclusively establishes that knowledge of the results of the discovery hole, K–55–1, would have been important to a reasonable investor and might have affected the price of the stock.[12] On April 16, The Northern Miner, a trade publication in wide circulation among mining stock specialists, called K–55–1, the discovery hole, "one of the most impressive drill holes completed in modern times." Roche, a Canadian broker whose firm specialized in mining securities, characterized the importance to investors of the results of K–55–1. He stated that the completion of "the first drill hole" with "a 600 foot drill core is very very significant * * * anything over 200 feet is considered very significant and 600 feet is just beyond your wildest imagination." He added, however, that it "is a natural thing to buy more stock once they give you the first drill hole." Additional testimony revealed that the prices of stocks of other companies, albeit less diversified, smaller firms, had increased substantially solely on the basis of the discovery of good anomalies or even because of the proximity of their lands to the situs of a potentially major strike.

Finally, a major factor in determining whether the K–55–1 discovery was a material fact is the importance attached to the drilling results by those who knew about it. In view of other unrelated recent developments favorably affecting TGS, participation by an informed person in a regular stock-purchase program, or even sporadic trading by an informed person, might lend only nominal support to the inference of the materiality of the K–55–1 discovery; nevertheless, the timing by those who knew of it of their stock purchases and their purchases of *short-term* calls—purchases in some cases by individuals who had never before purchased calls or even TGS stock—virtually compels the inference that the insiders were influenced by the drilling results. This insider trading activity, which surely constitutes highly pertinent evidence and the only truly objective evidence of the materiality of the K–55–1 discovery, was apparently disregarded by the court below in favor of the testimony of defendants' expert witnesses, all of whom "agreed that one drill core does not establish an ore body, much less a mine," 258 F.Supp. at 282–283. Significantly, however, the court below, while relying upon what these defense experts said the defendant insiders *ought* to have thought about the worth to TGS of the K–55–1 discovery, and finding that from November 12, 1963 to April 6, 1964 Fogarty, Murray, Holyk and Darke spent more than $100,000 in

12. We do not suggest that material facts must be disclosed immediately; the timing of disclosure is a matter for the business judgment of the corporate officers entrusted with the management of the corporation within the affirmative disclosure requirements promulgated by the exchanges and by the SEC. Here, a valuable corporate purpose was served by delaying the publication of the K–55–1 discovery. We do intend to convey, however, that where a corporate purpose is thus served by withholding the news of a material fact, those persons who are thus quite properly true to their corporate trust must not during the period of non-disclosure deal personally in the corporation's securities or give to outsiders confidential information not generally available to all the corporation's stockholders and to the public at large.

purchasing TGS stock and calls on that stock, made no finding that the insiders were motivated by any factor other than the extraordinary K–55–1 discovery when they bought their stock and their calls. No reason appears why outside investors, perhaps better acquainted with speculative modes of investment and with, in many cases, perhaps more capital at their disposal for intelligent speculation, would have been less influenced, and would not have been similarly motivated to invest if they had known what the insider investors knew about the K–55–1 discovery.

Our decision to expand the limited protection afforded outside investors by the trial court's narrow definition of materiality is not at all shaken by fears that the elimination of insider trading benefits will deplete the ranks of capable corporate managers by taking away an incentive to accept such employment. Such benefits, in essence, are forms of secret corporate compensation, see Cary, Corporate Standards and Legal Rules, 50 Calif.L.Rev. 408, 409–10 (1962), derived at the expense of the uninformed investing public and not at the expense of the corporation which receives the sole benefit from insider incentives. Moreover, adequate incentives for corporate officers may be provided by properly administered stock options and employee purchase plans of which there are many in existence. In any event, the normal motivation induced by stock ownership, i.e., the identification of an individual with corporate progress, is ill-promoted by condoning the sort of speculative insider activity which occurred here; for example, some of the corporation's stock was sold at market in order to purchase short-term calls upon that stock, calls which would never be exercised to increase a stockholder equity in TGS unless the market price of that stock rose sharply.

The core of Rule 10b–5 is the implementation of the Congressional purpose that all investors should have equal access to the rewards of participation in securities transactions. It was the intent of Congress that all members of the investing public should be subject to identical market risks,—which market risks include, of course the risk that one's evaluative capacity or one's capital available to put at risk may exceed another's capacity or capital. The insiders here were not trading on an equal footing with the outside investors. They alone were in a position to evaluate the probability and magnitude of what seemed from the outset to be a major ore strike; they alone could invest safely, secure in the expectation that the price of TGS stock would rise substantially in the event such a major strike should materialize, but would decline little, if at all, in the event of failure, for the public, ignorant at the outset of the favorable probabilities would likewise be unaware of the unproductive exploration, and the additional exploration costs would not significantly affect TGS market prices. Such inequities based upon unequal access to knowledge should not be shrugged off as inevitable in our way of life, or, in view of the Congressional concern in the area, remain uncorrected.

We hold, therefore, that all transactions in TGS stock or calls by individuals apprised of the drilling results of K–55–1 were made in violation of Rule 10b–5. * * *

In BASIC v. LEVINSON, 485 U.S. 224 (1988), the Supreme Court expressly adopted for Rule 10b–5 purposes the standard of materiality it had previously adopted for proxy statements in TSC v. Northway, p. ___ below namely, whether "there is a substantial likelihood that a reasonable shareholder would consider [the omitted fact] important in deciding how to vote." The *Basic* case involved the question whether the company had violated Rule 10b–5 by failing to disclose negotiations that might possibly lead to a merger. The Supreme Court held that the appropriate test of materiality in that kind of uncertain situation was the one laid down in *Texas Gulf Sulphur,* namely "a balancing of both the indicated probability that the event will occur and the anticipated magnitude of the event in light of the totality of the company activity."

INVESTORS MANAGEMENT CO., INC.

44 S.E.C. 633 (1971).

[By the Commission:]

This is a limited review on our own motion of the hearing examiner's initial decision in these proceedings pursuant to Section 15(b) of the Securities Exchange Act of 1934 ("Exchange Act") and Section 203(e) of the Investment Advisers Act of 1940. The examiner found that the respondents willfully violated or aided and abetted violations of the antifraud provisions of Section 17(a) of the Securities Act of 1933 and Section 10(b) of the Exchange Act and Rule 10b–5 thereunder in the sale of stock of Douglas Aircraft Co., Inc., without disclosing to the purchasers material information as to a reduction in Douglas' earnings which they had received from the prospective managing underwriter of a proposed Douglas debenture offering. Merrill Lynch, Pierce, Fenner & Smith, Inc. ("Merrill Lynch").[1] The examiner ordered that those respondents be censured.

Factual Background

The following summarizes the principal facts which were found by the hearing examiner and are described in detail in his initial decision.

In 1966 Douglas was a leading producer of commercial transport aircraft and its common stock was actively traded on the New York Stock Exchange and the Pacific Coast Stock Exchange. Immediately prior to the events described below, many analysts had viewed Douglas'

1. Merrill Lynch and fourteen of its officers and employees had been named as respondents in the order for proceedings. They submitted an offer of settlement, and pursuant thereto we found violations of the stated antifraud provisions and imposed certain sanctions. Merrill Lynch, Pierce, Fenner & Smith, Inc. et al., Securities Exchange Act Release No. 8459 (November 25, 1968).

earnings outlook as favorable, and the company itself estimated that per share earnings would be $4 to $4.50 for 1966 and $8 to $12 for 1967. On June 20, 1966, Douglas informed the Merrill Lynch vice-president in charge of the proposed underwriting of Douglas debentures of substantially reduced Douglas earnings and earnings estimates. It advised that it had a loss in May, that earnings for the first six months of 1966 were expected to be only 49¢ per share, it would about break even for 1966, and it expected 1967 earnings to be only $5 to $6. The next day, June 21, this information was relayed to Merrill Lynch's senior aerospace analyst, who gave it to two salesmen in Merrill Lynch's New York Institutional Sales Office. The latter informed three other Merrill Lynch employees and the five employees began imparting it to decision-making investment personnel of respondents, which were investment companies or partnerships with substantial capital or the advisers or managers for such interests. All of the respondents knew that Merrill Lynch was the prospective underwriter of the anticipated public offering of Douglas debentures, and some of them had indicated to Merrill Lynch an interest in buying debentures in such offering. Most of them had shortly before purchased Douglas stock.

Upon receiving the unfavorable Douglas earnings information between June 21 and June 23, respondents on those days sold a total of 133,400 shares of Douglas stock from existing long positions, which constituted virtually all of their holdings of Douglas stock, and sold short 21,100 shares, for an aggregate price of more than $13,300,000. The price of Douglas stock, which had a high of 90 on June 21, rose to 90½ the next day, apparently because of an optimistic newspaper article on the aerospace industry, and fell to 76 when Douglas publicly announced the disappointing earnings figures on June 24. On the following trading day, when those figures received further publicity the price of Douglas stock fell to 69, and subsequently declined to a low of 30 in October 1966.

As set forth below, the circumstances under which the information from Merrill Lynch was received and Douglas shares sold by the various respondents were similar in their essential aspects, although in some cases they differed in certain respects.

Respondent Madison Fund, an investment company, had purchased 6,000 shares of Douglas stock in early June 1966 on the basis of a favorable assessment of Douglas' earnings prospects for its second quarter and for 1966, and on June 13 had advised Merrill Lynch of its interest in purchasing Douglas debentures in the anticipated public offering. However, on June 21, within 15 minutes of being advised of the adverse Douglas earnings figures by one of the Merrill Lynch employees, it placed an order with Merrill Lynch for the sale of all those shares, which was executed that day. Respondent Investors Management Co., Inc. ("IMC") acted as investment adviser to several mutual funds, two of which had on its recommendation purchased 100,000 and 21,000 shares of Douglas stock, respectively, between

January and April 1966. On the afternoon of June 21 and the morning of June 22, one of the Merrill Lynch salesmen called the IMC vice-presidents who were the fund managers for the two funds and told them that Douglas would have disappointing earnings for the first six months and break even for 1966. After an unsuccessful effort to verify that information with a Merrill Lynch analyst, IMC advised the two funds to sell all their Douglas shares, and part of the shares were sold on June 22 and the balance over the next three trading days. Respondent Van Strum & Towne, Inc., which was the investment adviser to the Channing Growth Fund, had also considered the Douglas stock to be a desirable acquisition as late as June 20, when it caused that fund to buy 1,500 shares. On June 22, while attending a luncheon for professional investors, the firm's president overheard remarks implying that Douglas would have no earnings. When on making inquiry he was told that a portfolio manager for a large fund had received similar information from Merrill Lynch, he called a Merrill Lynch employee and was given the new Douglas earnings figures. He thereupon caused the 1,500 shares of Douglas stock to be sold that day.

Respondents William A.M. Burden & Co., a family investment partnership, and Burden Investors Services, Inc., which acted as investment adviser to other members of the Burden family, had on the advice of a broker purchased a total of 11,000 shares of Douglas stock on the morning of June 21. That afternoon, one of the Merrill Lynch salesmen informed a principal Burden partner that Douglas' earnings for May were very disappointing, that its quarterly earnings would be down, and that its earnings for 1966 would be "flat". Inquiries to three analysts did not produce any verification of the information, although at the June 22 luncheon for professional investors the Burden partner heard rumors that Douglas' earnings would be very disappointing. Early on June 23, the broker on whose advice the Douglas shares had been purchased reported that he had just been cautioned about the Douglas situation and he recommended the sale of those shares. Such sale was effected later that day.

* * *

It is clear that * * * the conduct of respondents in this case came within the ambit and were violative of the antifraud prohibitions of the securities laws. All the requisite elements for the imposition of responsibility were present on the facts found by the examiner. We consider those elements to be that the information in question be material and non-public; that the tippee, whether he receives the information directly or indirectly, know or have reason to know that it was non-public and had been obtained improperly by selective revelation or otherwise, and that the information be a factor in his decision to effect the transaction.[18] We shall discuss these elements in turn in light of the

18. Our formulation would clearly attach responsibility in a situation where the recipient knew or had reason to know the information was obtained by industrial espionage, commercial bribery or the like. We also consider that there would be potential responsibility, depending on an evaluation of the specific facts and circum-

contentions that have been presented by the parties and pertinent considerations under the securities laws.

With respect to materiality, we held in our findings with regard to Merrill Lynch in these proceedings that the information as to Douglas' earnings that it divulged was material because it "was of such importance that it could be expected to affect the judgment of investors whether to buy, sell or hold Douglas stock [and, i]f generally known, * * * to affect materially the market price of the stock." Among the factors to be considered in determining whether information is material under this test are the degree of its specificity, the extent to which it differs from information previously publicly disseminated, and its reliability in light of its nature and source and the circumstances under which it was received. While the test would not embrace information as to minor aspects or routine details of a company's operations, the information received by the respondents from Merrill Lynch was highly significant since it described a sharp reversal of Douglas' earnings realization and expectations. Although all respondents did not receive identical information, in each instance the information received was specific and revealed the existence and significant extent of the adverse earnings developments. Such extraordinary information could hardly help but be important to a reasonable investor in deciding whether he should buy, sell or hold Douglas stock. The information's significance was immediately clear; it was not merely one link in a chain of analytical information.[20]

Respondents are not aided by their claim that as far as the earnings projections were concerned such projections in the aerospace industry are uncertain. Douglas was an established company with a history of operations and its adverse earnings projections were short-term and of such specific importance as would necessarily affect the judgment of investors to buy, sell or hold the company's securities. Moreover, the fact that respondents acted immediately or very shortly after receipt of the information to effect sales and short sales of Douglas stock, is in itself evidence of its materiality.

The requirement that the information divulged be non-public was also satisfied here. Information is non-public when it has not been disseminated in a manner making it available to investors generally. Although during the first half of 1966 some aerospace analysts had indicated pessimism concerning Douglas' earnings prospects, and there were adverse rumors circulating in the financial community on June 21, 22 and 23 regarding Douglas' earnings, the information conveyed to

stances, where persons innocently come into possession of and then use information which they have reason to know is intended to be confidential. Our test would not attach responsibility with respect to information which is obtained by general observation or analysis.

20. The probability of the accuracy of the information was strongly indicated by the fact that it was highly adverse and, as all the respondents knew, the informant was engaged in acting for Douglas as prospective managing underwriter of an offering seeking to raise new funds from the public at a time when it was thus in the company's and the underwriter's interest to promote a favorable earnings picture.

respondents by Merrill Lynch personnel was much more specific and trustworthy than what may have previously been known to those analysts or could be said to have been general knowledge. The rumors circulated at the June 22 luncheon, which was attended by about 50 representatives of professional investors, to the effect that Douglas' earnings would be disappointing and that it was having production problems and would not be able to meet its delivery schedules, did not, as respondents urge, reflect public knowledge of the earnings information disclosed by Merrill Lynch. Unlike that information, the rumors did not include specific figures of actual and projected earnings and were not attributed to a corporation-informed source. Moreover, even if the rumors had contained the more specific data, their circulation among the limited number of investors present at the luncheon could not constitute the kind of public disclosure that would suffice to place other investors in an equal position in the marketplace. It was not until after Douglas had issued its press release that the earnings data became available to the investing public.

The specific Douglas earnings information imparted to respondents having thus been of the material and non-public character bringing it within the scope of the antifraud provisions, we turn to the question of the awareness on the part of respondents that is required to establish a violation. As has been indicated, in our opinion the appropriate test in that regard is whether the recipient knew or had reason to know that the information was non-public and had been obtained improperly by selective revelation or otherwise. We reject the contentions advanced by respondents that no violation can be found unless it is shown that the recipient himself occupied a special relationship with the issuer or insider corporate source giving him access to non-public information, or, in the absence of such relationship, that he had actual knowledge that the information was disclosed in a breach of fiduciary duty not to reveal it.

We consider that one who obtains possession of material, nonpublic corporate information, which he has reason to know emanates from a corporate source, and which by itself places him in a position superior to other investors, thereby acquires a relationship with respect to that information within the purview and restraints of the antifraud provisions. Both elements are here present as they were in the *Cady Roberts* case. When a recipient of such corporate information, knowing or having reason to know that the corporate information is non-public, nevertheless uses it to effect a transaction in the corporation's securities for his own benefit, we think his conduct cannot be viewed as free of culpability under any sound interpretation or application of the antifraud provisions.

Considerations of both fairness and effective enforcement demand that the standard as to the requisite knowledge be satisfied by proof that the recipient had reason to know of the non-public character of the information, and that it not be necessary to establish actual knowledge of that fact or, as suggested by respondents, of a breach of fiduciary duty. The imposition of responsibility where one has reason to know of the determinative factors in violative conduct is in keeping with the broad remedial design of the securities laws and has been applied under other of their provisions as well as the antifraud provisions. That standard is clearly appropriate in the situation where it is shown that the respondent received and made use of information that was material and non-public. In such situation, the question of whether the recipient had the requisite "reason to know" is properly determinable by an examination of all the surrounding circumstances, including the nature and timing of the information, the manner in which it was obtained, the facts relating to the informant, including his business or other relation to the recipient and to the source of his information, and the recipient's sophistication and knowledge of related facts.

In this case, it is clear that respondents had the knowledge requisite to a finding of violation of Rule 10b–5. They knew Merrill Lynch, from whom they obtained the Douglas information, was the prospective underwriter of the company's securities. As professionals in the securities industry, they knew that underwriters customarily receive non-public information from issuers in order to make business judgments about the proposed public offering. Although such information is not publicly disclosed, it may be conveyed to the prospective underwriter by the issuer for a valid corporate purpose; however, the prospective underwriter, as we have previously held, may not properly disclose or use the information for other than that purpose. Under the circumstances there can be no doubt that respondents, all of whom were sizeable existing or potential customers of Merrill Lynch, knew or had reason to know that they were selectively receiving non-public information respecting Douglas from Merrill Lynch.[25]

Respondents cannot successfully argue that their obligations under the antifraud provisions were any less because they were "remote tippees" who received their information from Merrill Lynch salesmen who were themselves "tippees." It would appear that the corporate insider position that Merrill Lynch in effect occupied by virtue of its role in assisting Douglas in its corporate financing functions would embrace anyone in its organization who obtained and transmitted the Douglas information, and not merely those in its underwriting division. But even if respondents are viewed as indirect recipients of the Douglas information, the same criteria for finding a violation of the antifraud provisions by the respondents properly apply. Although the case of such an indirect recipient may present more questions of factual proof of the requisite knowledge, the need for the protections of those provisions in the tippee area is unaffected. While there are some

25. Some of the respondents have pointed out that they received the information from Merrill Lynch without solicitation by them. While under some circumstances a finding with respect to whether the recipient knew or had reason to know that information was non-public might be affected by whether or not it had been solicited by him, it did not under the facts of this case, as the examiner held.

express restraints on transactions by traditional insiders, such as the prohibition against short-swing trading under the Exchange Act and the requirement for registration under the Securities Act of securities received from the issuer which they desire to sell, they do not apply to other persons who receive and act upon non-public information. In addition, the ability of a corporate insider to take action with the benefit of non-public information may be limited by his position in the company and his own personal resources. However, others may have a greater capacity to act, particularly those who, like the respondents here, are engaged in professional securities activities and have not only access to or advisory functions with respect to substantial investment funds but also the sophistication to appraise and capitalize upon the market effect of the information.[26]

We appreciate the concerns that have been expressed about the need to facilitate the free flow of information throughout the financial community. We have consistently required or encouraged the broadest possible disclosure of corporate information so as to provide public investors and their professional financial advisers with the most accurate and complete factual basis upon which to make investment decisions. We also recognize that discussions between corporate management and groups of analysts which provide a forum for filling interstices in analysis, for forming a direct impression of the quality of management, or for testing the meaning of public information, may be of value.[27] In some cases, however, there may be valid corporate reasons for the nondisclosure of material information. Where such reasons exist, we would not ordinarily consider it a violation of the antifraud provisions for an issuer to refrain from making public disclosure. At the same time we believe it necessary to ensure that there be no improper use of undisclosed information for non-corporate purposes.

Turning next to the requirement that the information received be a factor in the investment decision, we are of the opinion that where a transaction of the kind indicated by the information (e.g., a sale or short sale upon adverse information) is effected by the recipient prior to its public dissemination, an inference arises that the information was such a factor. The recipient of course may seek to overcome such inference by countervailing evidence. Respondents did not meet that burden in this case.[28]

26. The instant case is illustrative of the potential magnitude of tippee trading. As noted above, the information concerning the change in the Douglas earnings picture precipitated sales of Douglas stock with a value of more than $13,300,000 by the respondents as to whom the examiner found violations.

27. See New York Stock Exchange Company Manual A–20: "The competent analyst depends upon his professional skills and broad industry knowledge in making his evaluations and preparing his reports and does not need the type of inside information that could lead to unfairness in the marketplace." See also Haack, Corporate Responsibility to the Investing Public, CCH Fed.Sec.L.Rep. ¶ 77,554 at 83,173: "If during the course of discussion [between the issuer and analyst], some important information is divulged that has not yet been published—information which could affect the holdings or investment decision of any stockholder—that information should be made the subject of an immediate and comprehensive news release."

28. The examiner rejected contentions by various of the respondents that their sales of Douglas stock were motivated by factors other than the Merrill Lynch infor-

We do not find persuasive the claim made by respondents that as persons managing funds of others they had a fiduciary duty to their clients to sell their Douglas stock upon learning of the poor Douglas earnings, and that a failure to do so might have subjected them to liability for breach of such duty. The obligations of a fiduciary do not include performing an illegal Act,[29] and respondents could have sold the Douglas stock in a legal manner if they had secured the public disclosure of the information by Douglas.[30] And there is no basis for the stated concern that a fiduciary who refrains from acting because he has received what he believes to be restricted information would be held derelict if it should later develop that the information could in fact have been acted upon legally. If that belief is reasonable, his non-action could not be held improper.

CONCLUSION

We find no reason for disturbing the hearing examiner's conclusion that each of the respondents be censured. Although the facts in this case may be novel in certain respects, the findings of violation here do not represent an impermissible application of new standards, as respondents have claimed. The ambit of the antifraud provisions is necessarily broad so as to embrace the infinite variety of deceptive conduct. The inherent unfairness of the transactions effected by respondents on the basis of the non-public information imparted to them from an inside source should have been evident to respondents.

Accordingly, it is ordered that the imposition by the hearing examiner of the sanction of censure upon the above-captioned respondents be and it hereby is, affirmed.

mation. Van Strum had contended that its decision to sell Douglas stock two days after its purchase was based on an "unconfirmed rumor" that cast doubt on the assumption which formed the basis of its decision to buy the stock; the Jones respondents contended that their short sales of June 22, 1966 resulted from "a careful, painstaking analysis of Douglas made over a period of years"; Fleschner–Becker contended that it sold Douglas short as a result of the stream of bearish information on Douglas and because of its own analysis that production problems would have an adverse effect on Douglas' earnings; and the Burden respondents stress that they did not act for several days after receiving the information and not until after they were advised to do so by the broker who originally recommended purchase of their Douglas shares.

On the other hand, in dismissing the proceedings with respect to one respondent, an adviser to a large investment fund, the examiner credited its defense that a junior analyst who received the Merrill Lynch information and thereupon recommended sale of all Douglas holdings to his superior, who made the investment decisions for the fund, did not advise his superior of such receipt, and that other considerations led to the fund's sales. We consider it appropriate to observe that in future cases we would view as suspect and subject to close scrutiny a defense that there was no internal communication of material non-public information and its source by a member of a broker-dealer firm or other investment organization who received it, where a transaction of the kind indicated by it was effected by his organization immediately or closely thereafter. A showing of such receipt and transaction prior to the time the information became public should in itself constitute strong evidence of knowledge by the one who effected the transaction and by the firm.

29. See Cady Roberts, supra. Restatement of Trusts, 2d (1959) § 166. Scott on Trusts (3d ed. 1967) § 166.

30. Since respondents did not disclose to their immediate purchasers of Douglas securities the non-public information they had received from Merrill Lynch, we need not decide whether it would have nonetheless constituted a violation of the antifraud provisions had they done so.

By the COMMISSION (CHAIRMAN CASEY and COMMISSIONERS OWENS, HERLONG and NEEDHAM), COMMISSIONER SMITH concurring in the result.

COMMISSIONER SMITH, concurring in the result:

The Commission here spells out, in effect, four questions to be asked in determining the applicability of Rule 10b–5 to an inside information trading case: One, was the information material? Two, was the information non-public? Three, was the person effecting the transaction an insider or, if not an insider but a "tippee", did he know or have reason to know that the information "was non-public and had been obtained improperly by selective revelation or otherwise"? And four, was the information "a factor" in the person's decision to effect the transaction?

* * * I think the nexus of the special relationship between Merrill Lynch and Douglas and respondents' knowledge of that relationship as the source of the information is essential to the case. * * * I would therefore have framed the third test in terms of the respondents knowing or having reason to know that the material non-public information became available to them in breach of a duty owed to the corporation not to disclose or use the information for non-corporate purposes. Such knowledge, in effect, renders the tippee a participant in the breach of duty when he acts on the basis of the information received. I would hope that is what the majority means by "improperly obtained".

* * *

I also have difficulty with the expression of the causation test. The Commission's staff in this case, and in *Cady Roberts* and *Texas Gulf,* accepted the burden of proving that the inside information was the motivating factor, and not just a factor, in the decision to effect the transaction. The burden was satisfied in each of these cases and it is evidently not an unduly difficult one to meet in the proper case—especially where a transaction of the kind indicated by the inside information is effected within a relatively short period of time after its receipt, and there is the inference (which I consider appropriate) that the information substantially contributed to the recipient's decision to buy or sell. The majority's opinion may appear to do violence to the traditional concept of causation, but I do not read its requirement that the information be "a factor" as, for instance, encompassing situations where a firm decision to effect a transaction had clearly been made prior to the receipt of the information and the information played no substantial role in the investment decision.

In SLADE v. SHEARSON, HAMMILL & CO., INC., CCH Fed.Sec.L. Rep. ¶ 94,329 (S.D.N.Y.1974), plaintiff alleged that Shearson had solicited customer purchases of Tidal Marine stock at a time when it was in possession of material non-public adverse information which it had received from Tidal Marine in its capacity as an investment banker for that company. Shearson moved for summary judgment, arguing that under the SEC's interpretations of Rule 10b–5, "even if Shearson's corporate finance department had known this non-public information, it was precluded from using it to prevent the solicitation of purchases by its retail sales force until the information was made public." The court denied the motion, holding that prior decisions under Rule 10b–5 held only that inside information could not be disclosed to favored customers, and that its fiduciary obligations to its customers required it to refrain from making affirmative recommendations under the circumstances. The district court then certified to the court of appeals the following question: "Is an investment banker/securities broker who receives adverse material nonpublic information about an investment banking client precluded from soliciting customers for that client's securities on the basis of public information which (because of its possession of inside information) it knows to be false or misleading?" The court of appeals, after hearing oral argument and receiving briefs from the parties, the SEC, and representatives of other segments of the securities industry, concluded that what it had before it was "not one legal question * * * but a complexity of interlocking questions the answers to which may vastly affect the operations of one of the most important financial businesses in the country * * *." The court accordingly concluded that it should await further development of the facts at a trial on the merits, and dismissed the certification as improvidently granted. 517 F.2d 398 (2d Cir.1974). The case was subsequently settled for $1,725,000. 79 F.R.D. 309 (S.D.N.Y.1978).

What would you advise a brokerage firm to tell its salesmen when its underwriting department comes into possession of material nonpublic adverse information about a company on which it has an outstanding "buy" recommendation?

In SEC v. GEON INDUSTRIES, INC., 531 F.2d 39 (2d Cir.1976), Geon's chief executive officer had allegedly given information about a prospective merger to a stockbroker. The court held that both the officer and the stockbroker had violated Rule 10b–5, even though the SEC was unable to provide any direct evidence of "tipping" because "[the stockbroker] asserted his privilege against self-incrimination and [the officer] claimed inability to recall the subject matter of most of their numerous talks." The court held that the "circumstantial evidence" of telephone conversations followed by purchases of stock justified the trial judge in inferring that inside information was communicated.

The preceding decisions all involved people who traded on the basis of material undisclosed information *about the issuer of the securities.* There is another category of information that may raise similar problems—namely information with regard to the intention of another person to purchase or sell, or recommend the purchase or sale, of that security. Examples would be a decision by a mutual fund advisor to have the fund acquire or dispose of a large position in a particular stock, or the preparation by a large retail brokerage firm of a highly favorable or unfavorable report on a particular company which it plans to mail out to its customers, or the determination by one company to make a tender offer for the stock of another. Any of these events, when it comes to pass, is likely to have a significant effect on the market price of the stock, and a person who buys or sells with advance knowledge of this "market information" enjoys an arguably "unfair" advantage over other persons trading in the market.

CHIARELLA v. UNITED STATES

445 U.S. 222 (1980).

MR. JUSTICE POWELL delivered the opinion of the Court.

The question in this case is whether a person who learns from the confidential documents of one corporation that it is planning an attempt to secure control of a second corporation violates § 10(b) of the Securities Exchange Act of 1934 if he fails to disclose the impending takeover before trading in the target company's securities.

I

Petitioner is a printer by trade. In 1975 and 1976, he worked as a "markup man" in the New York composing room of Pandick Press, a financial printer. Among documents that petitioner handled were five announcements of corporate takeover bids. When these documents were delivered to the printer, the identities of the acquiring and target corporations were concealed by blank spaces or false names. The true names were sent to the printer on the night of the final printing.

The petitioner, however, was able to deduce the names of the target companies before the final printing from other information contained in the documents. Without disclosing his knowledge, petitioner purchased stock in the target companies and sold the shares immediately after the takeover attempts were made public. By this method, petitioner realized a gain of slightly more than $30,000 in the course of 14 months. Subsequently, the Securities and Exchange Commission (Commission or SEC) began an investigation of his trading activities. In May 1977, petitioner entered into a consent decree with the Commission in which he agreed to return his profits to the sellers of the shares. On the same day, he was discharged by Pandick Press.

In January 1978, petitioner was indicted on 17 counts of violating § 10(b) of the Securities Exchange Act of 1934 (1934 Act) and SEC Rule 10b–5. After petitioner unsuccessfully moved to dismiss the indictment, he was brought to trial and convicted on all counts.

The Court of Appeals for the Second Circuit affirmed petitioner's conviction. 588 F.2d 1358 (1978). We granted certiorari, and we now reverse.

II

Section 10(b) of the 1934 Act, prohibits the use "in connection with the purchase or sale of any security * * * [of] any manipulative or deceptive device or contrivance in contravention of such rules and regulations as the Commission may prescribe." Pursuant to this section, the SEC promulgated Rule 10b–5 which provides in pertinent part:

> "It shall be unlawful for any person, directly or indirectly, by the use of any means or instrumentality of interstate commerce, or of the mails or of any facility of any national securities exchange,
>
> "(a) To employ any device, scheme, or artifice to defraud, [or]
>
> * * *
>
> "(c) To engage in any act, practice, or course of business which operates or would operate as a fraud or deceit upon any person, in connection with the purchase or sale of any security."

This case concerns the legal effect of the petitioner's silence. The District Court's charge permitted the jury to convict the petitioner if it found that he wilfully failed to inform sellers of target company securities that he knew of a forthcoming takeover bid that would make their shares more valuable. In order to decide whether silence in such circumstances violates § 10(b), it is necessary to review the language and legislative history of that statute as well as its interpretation by the Commission and the federal courts.

Although the starting point of our inquiry is the language of the statute, Ernst & Ernst v. Hochfelder, 425 U.S. 185, 197 (1976), § 10(b) does not state whether silence may constitute a manipulative or deceptive device. Section 10(b) was designed as a catchall clause to prevent fraudulent practices. 425 U.S., at 202, 206. But neither the legislative history nor the statute itself affords specific guidance for the resolution of this case. When Rule 10b–5 was promulgated in 1942, the SEC did not discuss the possibility that failure to provide information might run afoul of § 10(b).

The SEC took an important step in the development of § 10(b) when it held that a broker-dealer and his firm violated that section by selling securities on the basis of undisclosed information obtained from a director of the issuer corporation who was also a registered representative of the brokerage firm. In Cady, Roberts & Co., 40 S.E.C. 907 (1961), the Commission decided that a corporate insider must abstain from trading in the shares of his corporation unless he has first disclosed all material inside information known to him. The obligation to disclose or abstain derives from

> "[a]n affirmative duty to disclose material information[, which] has been traditionally imposed on corporate 'insiders,' particularly officers, directors, or controlling stockholders. We, and the courts have consistently held that insiders must disclose material facts which are known to them by virtue of their position but which are not known to persons with whom they deal and which, if known, would affect their investment judgment."

The Commission emphasized that the duty arose from (i) the existence of a relationship affording access to inside information intended to be available only for a corporate purpose, and (ii) the unfairness of allowing a corporate insider to take advantage of that information by trading without disclosure.[8]

That the relationship between a corporate insider and the stockholders of his corporation gives rise to a disclosure obligation is not a novel twist of the law. At common law, misrepresentation made for the purpose of inducing reliance upon the false statement is fraudulent. But one who fails to disclose material information prior to the consummation of a transaction commits fraud only when he is under a duty to do so. And the duty to disclose arises when one party has information "that the other [party] is entitled to know because of a fiduciary or other similar relation of trust and confidence between them."[9] In its *Cady, Roberts* decision, the Commission recognized a relationship of trust and confidence between the shareholders of a corporation and those insiders who have obtained confidential information by reason of their position with that corporation. This relationship gives rise to a duty to disclose because of the "necessity of preventing a corporate insider from * * * tak[ing] unfair advantage of the uninformed minority stockholders." Speed v. Transamerica Corp., 99 F.Supp. 808, 829 (Del.1951).

The federal courts have found violations of § 10(b) where corporate insiders used undisclosed information for their own benefit. E.g., SEC v. Texas Gulf Sulphur Co. The cases also have emphasized, in accordance with the common-law rule, that "[t]he party charged with failing to disclose market information must be under a duty to disclose it." Frigitemp Corp. v. Financial Dynamics Fund, Inc., 524 F.2d 275, 282 (CA2 1975). Accordingly, a purchaser of stock who has no duty to a prospective seller because he is neither an insider nor a fiduciary has been held to have no obligation to reveal material facts. See General Time Corp. v. Talley Industries, Inc., 403 F.2d 159, 164 (CA2 1968).

* * *

Thus, administrative and judicial interpretations have established that silence in connection with the purchase or sale of securities may operate as a fraud actionable under § 10(b) despite the absence of

8. In *Cady, Roberts,* the broker-dealer was liable under § 10(b) because it received nonpublic information from a corporate insider of the issuer. Since the insider could not use the information, neither could the partners in the brokerage firm with which he was associated. The transaction in *Cady, Roberts* involved sale of stock to persons who previously may not have been shareholders in the corporation. The Commission embraced the reasoning of Judge Learned Hand that "the director or officer assumed a fiduciary relation to the buyer by the very sale; for it would be a sorry distinction to allow him to use the advantage of his position to induce the buyer into the position of a beneficiary although he was forbidden to do so once the buyer had become one." Quoting Gratz v. Claughton, 187 F.2d 46, 49 (CA2).

9. Restatement (Second) of Torts § 551(2)(a) (1976). See James & Gray, Misrepresentation—Part II, 37 Md.L.Rev. 488, 523–527 (1978). As regards securities transactions, the American Law Institute recognizes that "silence when there is a duty to * * * speak may be a fraudulent act." ALI. Federal Securities Code § 262(b) (Prop.Off.Draft 1978).

statutory language or legislative history specifically addressing the legality of nondisclosure. But such liability is premised upon a duty to disclose arising from a relationship of trust and confidence between parties to a transaction. Application of a duty to disclose prior to trading guarantees that corporate insiders, who have an obligation to place the shareholder's welfare before their own, will not benefit personally through fraudulent use of material, nonpublic information.[12]

In this case, the petitioner was convicted of violating § 10(b) although he was not a corporate insider and he received no confidential information from the target company. Moreover, the "market information" upon which he relied did not concern the earning power or operations of the target company, but only the plans of the acquiring company. Petitioner's use of that information was not a fraud under § 10(b) unless he was subject to an affirmative duty to disclose it before trading. In this case, the jury instructions failed to specify any such duty. In effect, the trial court instructed the jury that petitioner owed a duty to everyone; to all sellers, indeed, to the market as a whole. The jury simply was told to decide whether petitioner used material, nonpublic information at a time when "he knew other people trading in the securities market did not have access to the same information."

The Court of Appeals affirmed the conviction by holding that "[*a*]*nyone* —corporate insider or not—who regularly receives material nonpublic information may not use that information to trade in securities without incurring an affirmative duty to disclose." Although the court said that its test would include only persons who regularly receive material, nonpublic information, its rationale for that limitation is unrelated to the existence of a duty to disclose. The Court of Appeals, like the trial court, failed to identify a relationship between petitioner and the sellers that could give rise to a duty. Its decision thus rested solely upon its belief that the federal securities laws have "created a system providing equal access to information necessary for reasoned and intelligent investment decisions." The use by anyone of material information not generally available is fraudulent, this theory suggests, because such information gives certain buyers or sellers an unfair advantage over less informed buyers and sellers.

This reasoning suffers from two defects. First, not every instance of financial unfairness constitutes fraudulent activity under § 10(b). See Santa Fe Industries, Inc. v. Green, [p. 686 below]. Second, the element required to make silence fraudulent—a duty to disclose—is absent in this case. No duty could arise from petitioner's relationship

12. "Tippees" of corporate insiders have been held liable under § 10(b) because they have a duty not to profit from the use of inside information that they know is confidential and know or should know came from a corporate insider. Shapiro v. Merrill Lynch [casebook p. 462]. The tippee's obligation has been viewed as arising from his role as a participant after the fact in the insider's breach of a fiduciary duty. Subcommittees of American Bar Association Section of Corporation, Banking, and Business Law, Comment Letter on Material, Non–Public Information (Oct. 15, 1973), reprinted in BNA, Securities Regulation & Law Report No. 233, pp. D–1, D–2 (Jan. 2, 1974).

with the sellers of the target company's securities, for petitioner had no prior dealings with them. He was not their agent, he was not a fiduciary, he was not a person in whom the sellers had placed their trust and confidence. He was, in fact, a complete stranger who dealt with the sellers only through impersonal market transactions.

We cannot affirm petitioner's conviction without recognizing a general duty between all participants in market transactions to forgo actions based on material, nonpublic information. Formulation of such a broad duty, which departs radically from the established doctrine that duty arises from a specific relationship between two parties, should not be undertaken absent some explicit evidence of congressional intent.

As we have seen, no such evidence emerges from the language or legislative history of § 10(b). Moreover, neither the Congress nor the Commission ever has adopted a parity-of-information rule. Instead the problems caused by misuse of market information have been addressed by detailed and sophisticated regulation that recognizes when use of market information may not harm operation of the securities markets. For example, the Williams Act limits but does not completely prohibit a tender offeror's purchases of target corporation stock before public announcement of the offer. Congress' careful action in this and other areas contrasts, and is in some tension, with the broad rule of liability we are asked to adopt in this case.

Indeed, the theory upon which the petitioner was convicted is at odds with the Commission's view of § 10(b) as applied to activity that has the same effect on sellers as the petitioner's purchases. "Warehousing" takes place when a corporation gives advance notice of its intention to launch a tender offer to institutional investors who then are able to purchase stock in the target company before the tender offer is made public and the price of shares rises. In this case, as in warehousing, a buyer of securities purchases stock in a target corporation on the basis of market information which is unknown to the seller. In both of these situations, the seller's behavior presumably would be altered if he had the nonpublic information. Significantly, however, the Commission has acted to bar warehousing under its authority to regulate tender offers after recognizing that action under § 10(b) would rest on a "somewhat different theory" than that previously used to regulate insider trading as fraudulent activity.

We see no basis for applying such a new and different theory of liability in this case. As we have emphasized before, the 1934 Act cannot be read "'more broadly than its language and the statutory scheme reasonably permit.'" Section 10(b) is aptly described as a catchall provision, but what it catches must be fraud. When an allegation of fraud is based upon nondisclosure, there can be no fraud absent a duty to speak. We hold that a duty to disclose under § 10(b) does not arise from the mere possession of nonpublic market information. The contrary result is without support in the legislative history of § 10(b) and would be inconsistent with the careful plan that Congress has enacted for regulation of the securities markets.

IV

In its brief to this Court, the United States offers an alternative theory to support petitioner's conviction. It argues that petitioner breached a duty to the acquiring corporation when he acted upon information that he obtained by virtue of his position as an employee of a printer employed by the corporation. The breach of this duty is said to support a conviction under § 10(b) for fraud perpetrated upon both the acquiring corporation and the sellers.

We need not decide whether this theory has merit for it was not submitted to the jury. * * *

* * *

The jury instructions demonstrate that petitioner was convicted merely because of his failure to disclose material, nonpublic information to sellers from whom he bought the stock of target corporations. The jury was not instructed on the nature or elements of a duty owed by petitioner to anyone other than the sellers. Because we cannot affirm a criminal conviction on the basis of a theory not presented to the jury, we will not speculate upon whether such a duty exists, whether it has been breached, or whether such a breach constitutes a violation of § 10(b).

The judgment of the Court of Appeals is reversed.

MR. JUSTICE STEVENS, concurring.

Before liability, civil or criminal, may be imposed for a Rule 10b–5 violation, it is necessary to identify the duty that the defendant has breached. Arguably, when petitioner bought securities in the open market, he violated (a) a duty to disclose owed to the sellers from whom he purchased target company stock and (b) a duty of silence owed to the acquiring companies. I agree with the Court's determination that petitioner owed no duty of disclosure to the sellers, that his conviction rested on the erroneous premise that he did owe them such a duty, and that the judgment of the Court of Appeals must therefore be reversed.

The Court correctly does not address the second question: whether the petitioner's breach of his duty of silence—a duty he unquestionably owed to his employer and to his employer's customers—could give rise to criminal liability under Rule 10b–5. Respectable arguments could be made in support of either position. On the one hand, if we assume that petitioner breached a duty to the acquiring companies that had entrusted confidential information to his employers, a legitimate argument could be made that his actions constituted "a fraud or a deceit" upon those companies "in connection with the purchase or sale of any security." On the other hand, inasmuch as those companies would not be able to recover damages from petitioner for violating Rule 10b–5 because they were neither purchasers nor sellers of target company securities, see Blue Chip Stamps v. Manor Drug Stores, [p. 505 above], it could also be argued that no actionable violation of Rule 10b–5 had occurred. I think the Court wisely leaves the resolution of this issue for another day.

I write simply to emphasize the fact that we have not necessarily placed any stamp of approval on what this petitioner did, nor have we held that similar actions must be considered lawful in the future. Rather, we have merely held that petitioner's criminal conviction cannot rest on the theory that he breached a duty he did not owe.

I join the Court's opinion.

MR. JUSTICE BRENNAN, concurring in the judgment.

The Court holds, correctly in my view, that "a duty to disclose under § 10(b) does not arise from the mere possession of nonpublic market information." Prior to so holding, however, it suggests that no violation of § 10(b) could be made out absent a breach of some duty arising out of a fiduciary relationship between buyer and seller. I cannot subscribe to that suggestion. On the contrary, it seems to me that Part I of The Chief Justice's dissent correctly states the applicable substantive law—a person violates § 10(b) whenever he improperly obtains or converts to his own benefit nonpublic information which he then uses in connection with the purchase or sale of securities.

While I agree with Part I of The Chief Justice's dissent, I am unable to agree with Part II. Rather, I concur in the judgment of the majority because I think it clear that the legal theory sketched by The Chief Justice is not the one presented to the jury. * * *

MR. CHIEF JUSTICE BURGER, dissenting.

I believe that the jury instructions in this case properly charged a violation of § 10(b) and Rule 10b–5, and I would affirm the conviction.

I

As a general rule, neither party to an arm's-length business transaction has an obligation to disclose information to the other unless the parties stand in some confidential or fiduciary relation. See W. Prosser, Law of Torts § 106 (2d ed. 1955). This rule permits a businessman to capitalize on his experience and skill in securing and evaluating relevant information; it provides incentive for hard work, careful analysis, and astute forecasting. But the policies that underlie the rule also should limit its scope. In particular, the rule should give way when an informational advantage is obtained, not by superior experience, foresight, or industry, but by some unlawful means.

* * * I would read § 10(b) and Rule 10b–5 to encompass and build on this principle: to mean that a person who has misappropriated nonpublic information has an absolute duty to disclose that information or to refrain from trading.

* * *

II

The Court's opinion, as I read it, leaves open the question whether § 10(b) and Rule 10b–5 prohibit trading on misappropriated nonpublic information. Instead, the Court apparently concludes that this theory of the case was not submitted to the jury. * * *

The Court's reading of the District Court's charge is unduly restrictive. Fairly read as a whole and in the context of the trial, the instructions required the jury to find that Chiarella obtained his trading advantage by misappropriating the property of his employer's customers. * * *

In any event, even assuming the instructions were deficient in not charging misappropriation with sufficient precision, on this record any error was harmless beyond a reasonable doubt. Here, Chiarella, himself, testified that he obtained his informational advantage by decoding confidential material entrusted to his employer by its customers. He admitted that the information he traded on was "confidential," not "to be use[d] * * * for personal gain." * * *

In sum, the evidence shows beyond all doubt that Chiarella, working literally in the shadows of the warning signs in the printshop, misappropriated—stole to put it bluntly—valuable nonpublic information entrusted to him in the utmost confidence. He then exploited his ill-gotten informational advantage by purchasing securities in the market. In my view, such conduct plainly violates § 10(b) and Rule 10b–5. Accordingly, I would affirm the judgment of the Court of Appeals.

MR. JUSTICE BLACKMUN, with whom MR. JUSTICE MARSHALL joins, dissenting.

Although I agree with much of what is said in Part I of the dissenting opinion of The Chief Justice, I write separately because, in my view, it is unnecessary to rest petitioner's conviction on a "misappropriation" theory. The fact that petitioner Chiarella purloined, or, to use The Chief Justice's word, "stole," information concerning pending tender offers certainly is the most dramatic evidence that petitioner was guilty of fraud. He has conceded that he knew it was wrong, and he and his co-workers in the printshop were specifically warned by their employer that actions of this kind were improper and forbidden. But I also would find petitioner's conduct fraudulent within the meaning of § 10(b), and Rule 10b–5, even if he had obtained the blessing of his employer's principals before embarking on his profiteering scheme. Indeed, I think petitioner's brand of manipulative trading, with or without such approval, lies close to the heart of what the securities laws are intended to prohibit.

The Court continues to pursue a course, charted in certain recent decisions, designed to transform § 10(b) from an intentionally elastic "catchall" provision to one that catches relatively little of the misbehavior that all too often makes investment in securities a needlessly risky business for the uninitiated investor. * * *

I, of course, agree with the Court that a relationship of trust can establish a duty to disclose under § 10(b) and Rule 10b–5. But I do not agree that a failure to disclose violates the Rule only when the responsibilities of a relationship of that kind have been breached. * * * Both the SEC and the courts have stressed the insider's misuse of secret knowledge as the gravamen of illegal conduct. The Court, I think, unduly minimizes this aspect of prior decisions.

Cady, Roberts & Co., which the Court discusses at some length, provides an illustration. In that case, the Commission defined the category of "insiders" subject to a disclose-or-abstain obligation according to two factors:

> "[F]irst, the existence of a relationship giving access, directly or indirectly, to information intended to be available only for a corporate purpose and not for the personal benefit of anyone, and second, the inherent unfairness involved where a party takes advantage of such information knowing it is unavailable to those with whom he is dealing."

The Commission, thus, regarded the insider "relationship" primarily in terms of *access* to nonpublic information, and not merely in terms of the presence of a common-law fiduciary duty or the like. This approach was deemed to be in keeping with the principle that "the broad language of the anti-fraud provisions" should not be "circumscribed by fine distinctions and rigid classifications," such as those that prevailed under the common law. The duty to abstain or disclose arose, not merely as an incident of fiduciary responsibility, but as a result of the "inherent unfairness" of turning secret information to account for personal profit. This understanding of Rule 10b–5 was reinforced when Investors Management Co., 44 S.E.C. 633, 643 (1971), specifically rejected the contention that a "special relationship" between the alleged violator and an "insider" source was a necessary requirement for liability.

A similar approach has been followed by the courts. In SEC v. Texas Gulf Sulphur Co., the court specifically mentioned the common-law "special facts" doctrine as one source for Rule 10b–5, and it reasoned that the rule is "based in policy on the justifiable expectation of the securities marketplace that all investors trading on impersonal exchanges have relatively equal access to material information."

* * * Although I am not sure I fully accept the "market insider" category created by the Court of Appeals, I would hold that persons having access to confidential material information that is not legally available to others generally are prohibited by Rule 10b–5 from engaging in schemes to exploit their structural informational advantage through trading in affected securities. To hold otherwise, it seems to me, is to tolerate a wide range of manipulative and deceitful behavior. * * *

Whatever the outer limits of the Rule, petitioner Chiarella's case fits neatly near the center of its analytical framework. He occupied a relationship to the takeover companies giving him intimate access to concededly material information that was sedulously guarded from public access. The information, in the words of Cady, Roberts & Co., was "intended to be available only for a corporate purpose and not for the personal benefit of anyone." Petitioner, moreover, knew that the information was unavailable to those with whom he dealt. And he took full, virtually riskless advantage of this artificial information gap by selling the stocks shortly after each takeover bid was announced. By any reasonable definition, his trading was "inherent[ly] unfai[r]." This misuse of confidential information was clearly placed before the jury. Petitioner's conviction, therefore, should be upheld, and I dissent from the Court's upsetting that conviction.

The *Chiarella* decision leaves open the question whether a violation of Rule 10b–5 can be based on a breach of duty to the person from whom the insider obtained his information. In UNITED STATES v. NEWMAN, 664 F.2d 12 (2d Cir.1981), the court of appeals upheld the indictment of a stock trader who passed on confidential information about proposed takeovers which he had obtained from two employees of investment banking firms that were advising the companies planning the takeovers. The indictment charged that the acts of the two employees operated as a fraud on the investment banking firms and their clients, and that the stock trader had aided and abetted that fraud. The court held (a) that the defendant's conduct could constitute a criminal violation of Rule 10b–5 despite the fact that neither the investment bankers nor their clients were purchasers or sellers in any transaction with any of the defendants, (b) that the use of the information defrauded the investment bankers by "sullying their reputations as safe repositories of client confidences" and defrauded the investment bankers' clients by artificially inflating the price of the target companies' securities, and (c) that the fraud was "in connection with" a purchase or sale of securities because "the sole purpose" of the misappropriation of information was to purchase shares of the target companies. One judge dissented on the ground that the Supreme Court decisions in *Chiarella* and in Blue Chip Stamps v. Manor Drug Stores, casebook p. 537, "seem to evince a trend to confine the scope of § 10(b) to practices harmful to participants in actual purchase-sale transactions."

In the subsequent case of SEC v. MATERIA, 745 F.2d 197 (2d Cir. 1984), the court of appeals, utilizing the "misappropriation" theory, upheld an injunction against an employee of a financial printing firm on facts essentially similar to those in *Chiarella*. The Supreme Court denied certiorari. In 1988, the Supreme Court considered the question again in a case involving a Wall Street Journal reporter who had tipped friends to purchase stocks which he was planning to recommend in his column. He was prosecuted on the ground that he had "misappropriated" this information from the Journal, and his conviction was upheld by the Second Circuit. The Supreme Court unanimously affirmed his conviction for violation of the mail fraud statute, but his conviction for violation of Rule 10b–5 was affirmed by a 4–4 vote without opinion. CARPENTER v. UNITED STATES, 484 U.S. 19 (1987).

DIRKS v. SEC

463 U.S. 646 (1983).

JUSTICE POWELL delivered the opinion of the Court.

Petitioner Raymond Dirks received material nonpublic information from "insiders" of a corporation with which he had no connection. He disclosed this information to investors who relied on it in trading in the shares of the corporation. The question is whether Dirks violated the antifraud provisions of the federal securities laws by this disclosure.

I

In 1973, Dirks was an officer of a New York broker-dealer firm who specialized in providing investment analysis of insurance company securities to institutional investors. On March 6, Dirks received information from Ronald Secrist, a former officer of Equity Funding of America. Secrist alleged that the assets of Equity Funding, a diversified corporation primarily engaged in selling life insurance and mutual funds, were vastly overstated as the result of fraudulent corporate practices. Secrist also stated that various regulatory agencies had failed to act on similar charges made by Equity Funding employees. He urged Dirks to verify the fraud and disclose it publicly.

Dirks decided to investigate the allegations. He visited Equity Funding's headquarters in Los Angeles and interviewed several officers and employees of the corporation. The senior management denied any wrongdoing, but certain corporation employees corroborated the charges of fraud. Neither Dirks nor his firm owned or traded any Equity Funding stock, but throughout his investigation he openly discussed the information he had obtained with a number of clients and investors. Some of these persons sold their holdings of Equity Funding securities, including five investment advisers who liquidated holdings of more than $16 million.

While Dirks was in Los Angeles, he was in touch regularly with William Blundell, the Wall Street Journal's Los Angeles bureau chief. Dirks urged Blundell to write a story on the fraud allegations. Blundell did not believe, however, that such a massive fraud could go undetected and declined to write the story. He feared that publishing such damaging hearsay might be libelous.

During the two-week period in which Dirks pursued his investigation and spread word of Secrist's charges, the price of Equity Funding stock fell from $26 per share to less than $15 per share. This led the New York Stock Exchange to halt trading on March 27. Shortly thereafter California insurance authorities impounded Equity Funding's records and uncovered evidence of the fraud. Only then did the Securities and Exchange Commission (SEC) file a complaint against Equity Funding and only then, on April 2, did the Wall Street Journal publish a front-page story based largely on information assembled by Dirks. Equity Funding immediately went into receivership.

The SEC began an investigation into Dirks' role in the exposure of the fraud. After a hearing by an administrative law judge, the SEC found that Dirks had aided and abetted violations of § 17(a) of the Securities Act of 1933, § 10(b) of the Securities Exchange Act of 1934, and SEC Rule 10b–5, by repeating the allegations of fraud to members of the investment community who later sold their Equity Funding stock. The SEC concluded: "Where 'tippees'—regardless of their motivation or occupation—come into possession of material 'information that they know is confidential and know or should know came from a corporate insider,' they must either publicly disclose that information or refrain from trading." Recognizing, however, that Dirks "played an important role in bringing [Equity Funding's] massive fraud to light," the SEC only censured him.

Dirks sought review in the Court of Appeals for the District of Columbia Circuit. The court entered judgment against Dirks "for the reasons stated by the Commission in its opinion."

* * *

In view of the importance to the SEC and to the securities industry of the question presented by this case, we granted a writ of certiorari. We now reverse.

In the seminal case of *In re Cady, Roberts & Co.,* the SEC recognized that the common law in some jurisdictions imposes on "corporate 'insiders,' particularly officers, directors, or controlling stockholders" an "affirmative duty of disclosure * * * when dealing in securities." The SEC found that not only did breach of this common-law duty also establish the elements of a Rule 10b–5 violation, but that individuals other than corporate insiders could be obligated either to disclose material nonpublic information before trading or to abstain from trading altogether. In *Chiarella,* we accepted the two elements set out in *Cady Roberts* for establishing a Rule 10b–5 violation: "(i) the existence of a relationship affording access to inside information intended to be available only for a corporate purpose, and (ii) the unfairness of allowing a corporate insider to take advantage of that information by trading without disclosure." * * *

III

We were explicit in *Chiarella* in saying that there can be no duty to disclose where the person who has traded on inside information "was not [the corporation's] agent, * * * was not a fiduciary, [or] was not a person in whom the sellers [of the securities] had placed their trust and confidence." Not to require such a fiduciary relationship, we recognized, would "depar[t] radically from the established doctrine that duty arises from a specific relationship between two parties" and would amount to "recognizing a general duty between all participants in market transactions to forgo actions based on material, nonpublic information." This requirement of a specific relationship between the shareholders and the individual trading on inside information has created analytical difficulties for the SEC and courts in policing tippees who trade on inside information. Unlike insiders who have independent fiduciary duties to both the corporation and its shareholders, the typical tippee has no such relationships.[14] In view of this absence, it has been unclear how a tippee acquires the *Cady, Roberts* duty to refrain from trading on inside information.

A

The SEC's position, as stated in its opinion in this case, is that a tippee "inherits" the *Cady, Roberts* obligation to shareholders whenever he receives inside information from an insider:

This view differs little from the view that we rejected as inconsistent with congressional intent in *Chiarella*. In that case, the Court of Appeals agreed with the SEC and affirmed Chiarella's conviction, holding that " '[*a*]*nyone* —corporate insider or not—who regularly receives material nonpublic information may not use that information to trade in securities without incurring an affirmative duty to disclose.' " Here, the SEC maintains that anyone who knowingly receives nonpublic material information from an insider has a fiduciary duty to disclose before trading.[15]

14. Under certain circumstances, such as where corporate information is revealed legitimately to an underwriter, accountant, lawyer, or consultant working for the corporation, these outsiders may become fiduciaries of the shareholders. The basis for recognizing this fiduciary duty is not simply that such persons acquired nonpublic corporate information, but rather that they have entered into a special confidential relationship in the conduct of the business of the enterprise and are given access to information solely for corporate purposes. When such a person breaches his fiduciary relationship, he may be treated more properly as a tipper than a tippee. See Shapiro v. Merrill Lynch, Pierce, Fenner & Smith, Inc., 495 F.2d 228, 237 (CA2 1974) (investment banker had access to material information when working on a proposed public offering for the corporation). For such a duty to be imposed, however, the corporation must expect the outsider to keep the disclosed nonpublic information confidential, and the relationship at least must imply such a duty.

15. Apparently, the SEC believes this case differs from *Chiarella* in that Dirks' receipt of inside information from Secrist, an insider, carried Secrist's duties with it, while Chiarella received the information without the direct involvement of an insider and thus inherited no duty to disclose or abstain. The SEC fails to explain, however, why the receipt of nonpublic information from an insider automatically carries with it the fiduciary duty of the insider. As we emphasized in *Chiarella,* mere possession of nonpublic information does not give rise to a duty to disclose or abstain; only a specific relationship does that. And we do not believe that the mere receipt of information from an insider creates such a special relationship between the tippee and the corporation's shareholders.

Apparently recognizing the weakness of its argument in light of *Chiarella,* the SEC attempts to distinguish that case factually as involving not "inside" information, but rather "market" information, i.e., "information generated within the company relating to its assets or earnings." Brief for Respondent 23. This Court drew no such distinction in *Chiarella* and, as the Chief Justice noted, "[i]t is clear that § 10(b) and Rule 10b–5 by their terms and by their history make no such distinction." 445 U.S., at 241, n. 1, 100 S.Ct., at 1121, n. 1 (dissenting opinion). See ALI Fed.Sec.Code

In effect, the SEC's theory of tippee liability in both cases appears rooted in the idea that the antifraud provisions require equal information among all traders. This conflicts with the principle set forth in *Chiarella* that only some persons, under some circumstances, will be barred from trading while in possession of material nonpublic information.

* * *

Imposing a duty to disclose or abstain solely because a person knowingly receives material nonpublic information from an insider and trades on it could have an inhibiting influence on the role of market analysts, which the SEC itself recognizes is necessary to the preservation of a healthy market. It is commonplace for analysts to "ferret out and analyze information,"[18] and this often is done by meeting with and questioning corporate officers and others who are insiders. And information that the analysts obtain normally may be the basis for judgments as to the market worth of a corporation's securities. The analyst's judgment in this respect is made available in market letters or otherwise to clients of the firm. It is the nature of this type of information, and indeed of the markets themselves, that such information cannot be made simultaneously available to all of the corporation's stockholders or the public generally.

B

The conclusion that recipients of inside information do not invariably acquire a duty to disclose or abstain does not mean that such tippees always are free to trade on the information. The need for a ban on some tippee trading is clear. Not only are insiders forbidden by their fiduciary relationship from personally using undisclosed corporate information to their advantage, but they may not give such information to an outsider for the same improper purpose of exploiting the information for their personal gain. * * *

Thus, some tippees must assume an insider's duty to the shareholders not because they receive inside information, but rather because it has been made available to them *improperly.* And for Rule 10b–5 purposes, the insider's disclosure is improper only where it would violate his *Cady, Roberts* duty. Thus, a tippee assumes a fiduciary duty

§ 1603. Comment (2)(j) (Proposed Official Draft 1978).

18. On its facts, this case is the unusual one. Dirks is an analyst in a broker-dealer firm, and he did interview management in the course of his investigation. He uncovered, however, startling information that required no analysis or exercise of judgment as to its market relevance. Nonetheless, the principle at issue here extends beyond these facts. The SEC's rule—applicable without regard to any breach by an insider—could have serious ramifications on reporting by analysts of investment views.

Despite the unusualness of Dirks' "find," the central role that he played in uncovering the fraud at Equity Funding, and that analysts in general can play in revealing information that corporations may have reason to withhold from the public, is an important one. Dirks' careful investigation brought to light a massive fraud at the corporation. And until the Equity Funding fraud was exposed, the information in the trading market was grossly inaccurate. But for Dirks' efforts, the fraud might well have gone undetected longer.

to the shareholders of a corporation not to trade on material nonpublic information only when the insider has breached his fiduciary duty to the shareholders by disclosing the information to the tippee and the tippee knows or should know that there has been a breach. As Commissioner Smith perceptively observed in *Investors Management Co.:* "[T]ippee responsibility must be related back to insider responsibility by a necessary finding that the tippee knew the information was given to him in breach of a duty by a person having a special relationship to the issuer not to disclose the information * * *." Tipping thus properly is viewed only as a means of indirectly violating the *Cady, Roberts* disclose-or-abstain rule.[21]

C

In determining whether a tippee is under an obligation to disclose or abstain, it thus is necessary to determine whether the insider's "tip" constituted a breach of the insider's fiduciary duty.

* * *

[T]he test is whether the insider personally will benefit, directly or indirectly, from his disclosure. Absent some personal gain, there has been no breach of duty to stockholders. And absent a breach by the insider, there is no derivative breach.

* * *

The SEC argues that, if inside-trading liability does not exist when the information is transmitted for a proper purpose but is used for trading, it would be a rare situation when the parties could not fabricate some ostensibly legitimate business justification for transmitting the information. We think the SEC is unduly concerned. In determining whether the insider's purpose in making a particular disclosure is fraudulent, the SEC and the courts are not required to read the parties' minds. Scienter in some cases is relevant in determining whether the tipper has violated his *Cady, Roberts* duty. But to determine whether the disclosure itself "deceive[s], manipulate[s], or defraud[s]" shareholders, the initial inquiry is whether there has been a breach of duty by the insider. This requires courts to focus on objective criteria, i.e., whether the insider receives a direct or indirect personal benefit from the disclosure, such as a pecuniary gain or a reputational benefit that will translate into future earnings.

* * *

21. We do not suggest that knowingly trading on inside information is ever "socially desirable or even that it is devoid of moral considerations." Dooley, Enforcement of Insider Trading Restrictions, 66 Va.L.Rev. 1, 55 (1980). Nor do we imply an absence of responsibility to disclose promptly indications of illegal actions by a corporation to the proper authorities—typically the SEC and exchange authorities in cases involving securities. Depending on the circumstances, and even where permitted by law, one's trading on material nonpublic information is behavior that may fall below ethical standards of conduct. But in a statutory area of the law such as securities regulation, where legal principles of general application must be applied, there may be "significant distinctions between actual legal obligations and ethical ideals."

There are objective facts and circumstances that often justify such an inference. For example, there may be a relationship between the insider and the recipient that suggests a *quid pro quo* from the latter, or an intention to benefit the particular recipient. The elements of fiduciary duty and exploitation of nonpublic information also exist when an insider makes a gift of confidential information to a trading relative or friend. The tip and trade resemble trading by the insider himself followed by a gift of the profits to the recipient.

* * *

IV

Under the inside-trading and tipping rules set forth above, we find that there was no actionable violation by Dirks. It is undisputed that Dirks himself was a stranger to Equity Funding, with no pre-existing fiduciary duty to its shareholders. He took no action, directly or indirectly, that induced the shareholders or officers of Equity Funding to repose trust or confidence in him. There was no expectation by Dirks' sources that he would keep their information in confidence. Nor did Dirks misappropriate or illegally obtain the information about Equity Funding. Unless the insiders breached their *Cady, Roberts* duty to shareholders in disclosing the nonpublic information to Dirks, he breached no duty when he passed it on to investors as well as to the Wall Street Journal.

It is clear that neither Secrist nor the other Equity Funding employees violated their *Cady, Roberts* duty to the corporation's shareholders by providing information to Dirks. The tippers received no monetary or personal benefit for revealing Equity Funding's secrets, nor was their purpose to make a gift of valuable information to Dirks. As the facts of this case clearly indicate, the tippers were motivated by a desire to expose the fraud. In the absence of a breach of duty to shareholders by the insiders, there was no derivative breach by Dirks. Dirks therefore could not have been "a participant after the fact in [an] insider's breach of a fiduciary duty."

V

We conclude that Dirks, in the circumstances of this case, had no duty to abstain from use of the inside information that he obtained. The judgment of the Court of Appeals therefore is

Reversed.

JUSTICE BLACKMUN, with whom JUSTICE BRENNAN and JUSTICE MARSHALL join, dissenting.

The Court today takes still another step to limit the protections provided investors by § 10(b) of the Securities Exchange Act of 1934. The device employed in this case engrafts a special motivational requirement on the fiduciary duty doctrine. This innovation excuses a knowing and intentional violation of an insider's duty to shareholders if the insider does not act from a motive of personal gain. Even on the extraordinary facts of this case, such an innovation is not justified.

I

As the Court recognizes, the facts here are unusual. After a meeting with Ronald Secrist, a former Equity Funding employee, on March 7, 1973, petitioner Raymond Dirks found himself in possession of material nonpublic information of massive fraud within the company. In the Court's words, "[h]e uncovered * * * startling information that required no analysis or exercise of judgment as to its market relevance." In disclosing that information to Dirks, Secrist intended that Dirks would disseminate the information to his clients, those clients would unload their Equity Funding securities on the market, and the price would fall precipitously, thereby triggering a reaction from the authorities.

Dirks complied with his informant's wishes. Instead of reporting that information to the Securities and Exchange Commission (SEC or Commission) or to other regulatory agencies, Dirks began to disseminate the information to his clients and undertook his own investigation. One of his first steps was to direct his associates at Delafield Childs to draw up a list of Delafield clients holding Equity Funding securities. On March 12, eight days before Dirks flew to Los Angeles to investigate Secrist's story, he reported the full allegations to Boston Company Institutional Investors, Inc., which on March 15 and 16 sold approximately $1.2 million of Equity securities. As he gathered more information, he selectively disclosed it to his clients. To those holding Equity Funding securities he gave the "hard" story—all the allegations; others received the "soft" story—a recitation of vague factors that might reflect adversely on Equity Funding's management.

Dirks' attempts to disseminate the information to nonclients were feeble, at best. On March 12, he left a message for Herbert Lawson, the San Francisco bureau chief of The Wall Street Journal. Not until March 19 and 20 did he call Lawson again, and outline the situation. William Blundell, a *Journal* investigative reporter based in Los Angeles, got in touch with Dirks about his March 20 telephone call. On March 21, Dirks met with Blundell in Los Angeles. Blundell began his own investigation, relying in part on Dirks' contacts, and on March 23 telephoned Stanley Sporkin, the SEC's Deputy Director of Enforcement. On March 26, the next business day, Sporkin and his staff interviewed Blundell and asked to see Dirks the following morning. Trading was halted by the New York Stock Exchange at about the same time Dirks was talking to Los Angeles SEC personnel. The next day, March 28, the SEC suspended trading in Equity Funding securities. By that time, Dirks' clients had unloaded close to $15 million of Equity Funding stock and the price had plummeted from $26 to $15. The effect of Dirks' selective dissemination of Secrist's information was that Dirks' clients were able to shift the losses that were inevitable due to the Equity Funding fraud from themselves to uninformed market participants.

II

A

No one questions that Secrist himself could not trade on his inside information to the disadvantage of uninformed shareholders and purchasers of Equity Funding securities. Unlike the printer in *Chiarella,* Secrist stood in a fiduciary relationship with these shareholders. As the Court states, corporate insiders have an affirmative duty of disclosure when trading with shareholders of the corporation. This duty extends as well to purchasers of the corporation's securities.

The Court also acknowledges that Secrist could not do by proxy what he was prohibited from doing personally. But this is precisely what Secrist did. Secrist used Dirks to disseminate information to Dirks' clients, who in turn dumped stock on unknowing purchasers. Secrist thus intended Dirks to injure the purchasers of Equity Funding securities to whom Secrist had a duty to disclose. Accepting the Court's view of tippee liability, it appears that Dirks' knowledge of this breach makes him liable as a participant in the breach after the fact.

B

The Court holds, however, that Dirks is not liable because Secrist did not violate his duty; according to the Court, this is so because Secrist did not have the improper purpose of personal gain. In so doing, the Court imposes a new, subjective limitation on the scope of the duty owed by insiders to shareholders. The novelty of this limitation is reflected in the Court's lack of support for it.

* * *

C

The fact that the insider himself does not benefit from the breach does not eradicate the shareholder's injury. It makes no difference to the shareholder whether the corporate insider gained or intended to gain personally from the transaction; the shareholder still has lost because of the insider's misuse of nonpublic information. The duty is addressed not to the insider's motives, but to his actions and their consequences on the shareholder. Personal gain is not an element of the breach of this duty.

* * *

[T]he breach consists in taking action disadvantageous to the person to whom one owes a duty. In this case, Secrist owed a duty to purchasers of Equity Funding shares. The Court's addition of the bad purpose element to a breach of fiduciary duty claim is flatly inconsistent with the principle of *Mosser.* I do not join this limitation of the scope of an insider's fiduciary duty to shareholders.[13]

13. Although I disagree in principle with the Court's requirement of an improper motive, I also note that the requirement adds to the administrative and judicial burden in Rule 10b–5 cases. Assuming the validity of the requirement, the SEC's approach—a violation occurs when the insider knows that the tippee will trade with the information, Brief for SEC 31—can be seen as a presumption that the insider

III

The improper purpose requirement not only has no basis in law, but it rests implicitly on a policy that I cannot accept. The Court justifies Secrist's and Dirks' action because the general benefit derived from the violation of Secrist's duty to shareholders outweighed the harm caused to those shareholders, in other words, because the end justified the means. Under this view, the benefit conferred on society by Secrist's and Dirks' activities may be paid for with the losses caused to shareholders trading with Dirks' clients.

* * *

IV

In my view, Secrist violated his duty to Equity Funding shareholders by transmitting material nonpublic information to Dirks with the intention that Dirks would cause his clients to trade on that information. Dirks, therefore, was under a duty to make the information publicly available or to refrain from actions that he knew would lead to trading. Because Dirks caused his clients to trade, he violated § 10(b) and Rule 10b–5. Any other result is a disservice to this country's attempt to provide fair and efficient capital markets. I dissent.

In STATE TEACHERS v. FLUOR, 592 F.Supp. 592 (S.D.N.Y.1984), the court elaborated on the *Dirks* criteria by holding that a tippee can be held liable only if the information was passed to the tippee for the personal benefit of the tipper, and if the tippee knew or had reason to know that the tipper had satisfied all the elements of tipper liability.

Under the *Dirks* approach, can a tippee ever be held liable for taking advantage of inside information in a situation like *Investors Management,* where the company source acted properly in disclosing the information because of a pre-existing relationship (in that case, issuer and underwriter)? One court has held that the tippee in that kind of situation may acquire the status of a "temporary insider," subjecting it to the same duties as the person from whom it obtained the information. SEC v. LUND, 570 F.Supp. 1397 (C.D.Cal.1983).

gains from the tipping. The Court now requires a case-by-case determination, thus prohibiting such a presumption.

The Court acknowledges the burdens and difficulties of this approach, but asserts that a principle is needed to guide market participants. I fail to see how the Court's rule has any practical advantage over the SEC's presumption. The Court's approach is particularly difficult to administer when the insider is not directly enriched monetarily by the trading he induces. For example, the Court does not explain why the benefit Secrist obtained—the good feeling of exposing a fraud and his enhanced reputation—is any different from the benefit to an insider who gives the information as a gift to a friend or relative. Under the Court's somewhat cynical view, gifts involve personal gain. See ibid. Secrist surely gave Dirks a gift of the commissions Dirks made on the deal in order to induce him to disseminate the information. The distinction between pure altruism and self-interest has puzzled philosophers for centuries; there is no reason to believe that courts and administrative law judges will have an easier time with it.

Can a remote tippee shield himself from liability by not inquiring as to the source of information he receives from another tippee? In SEC v. MUSELLA, 678 F.Supp. 1060 (S.D.N.Y.1988), remote tippees, who were experienced stock market investors, "made a deliberate decision not to ask [the intermediate tippee] about the confidential sources they were quite certain [he] had." The court held that the requisite scienter was shown: "I cannot accept that conscious avoidance of knowledge defeats scienter in a stock fraud case."

In 1980, the SEC, acting under § 14(e) of the 1934 Act, which prohibits "any fraudulent, manipulative, or deceptive acts or practices in connection with any tender offer," adopted Rule 14e–3, which prohibits any person who is in possession of material information relating to a tender offer [other than the offeror itself] which he knows or has reason to know is (a) nonpublic and (b) has been acquired directly or indirectly from the offeror, the issuer or any persons acting on their behalf, to purchase or sell any securities which are the subject of the offer. Would Rule 14e–3 apply to Chiarella or to the various people involved in the *Newman* case? If so, is it a valid exercise of the Commission's power under § 14(e), in light of the Supreme Court's interpretation of the words "fraud," "manipulation" and "deception" in *Chiarella?*

The first appellate court consideration of this question came in UNITED STATES v. CHESTMAN, 903 F.2d 75 (2d Cir.1990). In that case, Ira Waldbaum and his family, who owned 51% of the stock of Waldbaum, Inc., entered into an agreement to sell all their stock to the A & P supermarket chain for $50 a share, on condition that A & P then make a tender offer for the remaining stock at the same price. Before the agreement was publicly announced, Ira told his sister Shirley, who in turn told her daughter Susan, who in turn told her husband Keith, each one telling the other not to tell anyone outside the family because that "could ruin the sale." Keith testified that he called his broker Chestman and told him that he "had some definite, some accurate information" that Waldbaum was being sold at a "substantially higher" price than the current market and asked Chestman "what he thought I should do." Chestman was aware that Keith was married to Waldbaum's niece. During that morning, Chestman purchased 11,000 shares of Waldbaum stock for himself and his discretionary accounts at prices ranging from $24.65 to $26 a share. When the tender offer was announced later that day, the price of Waldbaum stock rose to $49 a share. Chestman was convicted of violations of Rule 10b–5 and Rule 14e–3. On appeal, a panel of the Second Circuit unanimously reversed his conviction under Rule 10b–5:

> Evidence that Keith Loeb revealed the critical information in breach of a duty of trust and confidence known to Chestman is essential to the imposition of liability upon Chestman as aider/abettor, Materia, 745 F.2d at 201, or as tippee, Dirks, 463 U.S. at 660. Such evidence is lacking here. Although Chestman was aware that Loeb was a member of the Waldbaum family and may well have gathered that the "definite" and "accurate" information furnished by Loeb was

> not generally available, there simply is no evidence that he knew that Loeb was breaching a confidential relationship by imparting the information to him. The government can point to nothing in the record demonstrating actual or constructive knowledge on the part of Chestman that Keith Loeb was pledged to secrecy by Susan Loeb, who was pledged to secrecy by Shirley Witkin, who was pledged to secrecy by Ira Waldbaum. Loeb testified on direct examination that he could not recall describing the information as confidential, and there is no evidence that he ever alluded to the source of his information. Cf. Materia, 745 F.2d at 202. It is impossible to attribute knowledge of confidentiality to Chestman in view of the attenuated passage of the information and in the absence of any showing that the information retained any kind of confidentiality in the hands of Keith Loeb.

Chestman argued that his conviction under Rule 14e–3 should be reversed on the ground that the SEC exceeded its authority under § 14(e) by adopting a rule which imposes liability for trading without finding either misappropriation of information or a fiduciary duty to people on the other side of the market. The three-judge panel voted 2–1 to reverse the conviction, but split three ways on the question of the validity of Rule 14e–3. Judge Miner voted to uphold the validity of the rule, and the conviction, on the ground that Congress gave the SEC broader powers under § 14(e) than under § 10(b), including "a broad congressional mandate to prescribe all 'means reasonably designed' to prevent manipulative acts, including the regulation of nondeceptive activities." Judge Mahoney thought that the conviction should be reversed because § 14(e) only gave the SEC the authority to apply the legal principles developed under Rule 10b–5 to the "novel area" of tender offers, "rather than to constitute an authorization for the Commission to redefine the meaning of the terms 'fraudulent, deceptive or manipulative' as established by authoritative Supreme Court interpretations of § 10(b) and Rule 10b–5, upon which § 14(e) is concededly modeled." Judge Carman thought that the Rule could be held valid on the ground that "in promulgating Rule 14e–3 shortly after the *Chiarella* decision, the SEC seeking to implement the will of Congress as expressed in § 14(e) can be presumed to have contemplated that the rule would be read to include commonly accepted principles and elements associated with fraud," but that Chestman's conviction would have to be reversed because the trial judge had not instructed the jury that all the elements of fraud, including scienter and a knowing breach of duty, would have to be found to support a conviction.

The *Chestman* decision, by further complicating the question of what constitutes illegal "insider trading," has precipitated new calls for a statutory definition of the offense. In August 1990, the Second Circuit agreed to reconsider the *Chestman* decision *en banc*.

In 1985, Sanford Weill, former CEO of Shearson and former President of American Express, was interested in becoming CEO of

BankAmerica. He had secured a commitment from Shearson to invest $1 billion in BankAmerica if his negotiations were successful. Weill discussed his plans, and the Shearson commitment, with his wife, who discussed them with her psychiatrist, Dr. Willis. Between January 14 and February 6, Dr. Willis purchased 13,000 shares of BankAmerica stock. On February 20, BankAmerica announced that Weill had sought to become its CEO but that BankAmerica was not interested. The next day Dr. Willis sold all his BankAmerica shares for a profit of approximately $27,500. Has Dr. Willis violated Rule 10b–5, as interpreted by the Second Circuit in the *Chestman* case? See UNITED STATES v. WILLIS, CCH Fed.Sec.L.Rep. ¶ 95,232, 737 F.Supp. 269 (S.D. N.Y.1990). Is it relevant that the "Hippocratic Oath," relating to the practice of medicine, concludes with the following words:

> Whatsoever things I see or hear concerning the life of men, in my attendance on the sick or even apart therefrom, which ought not to be noised abroad, I will keep silence thereon, counting such things to be as sacred secrets.

The decisions by the Supreme Court in the *Chiarella* and *Dirks* cases raise a further complication. If an insider or tippee is found to have no pre-existing fiduciary duty to persons on the other side of the market, so that the violation of Rule 10b–5 results solely from a breach of duty to the person from whom the information was obtained, can anyone sue to recover the wrongdoer's profit?

B. CIVIL LIABILITY

As noted above, a violation of Rule 10b–5 has been held to give rise to a private right of action by a person who can show that the violator invaded an interest of his which the rule was designed to protect. As applied to insider trading, this doctrine has raised difficult questions. The nature of the questions differs depending on (a) whether the transaction involves direct dealings or is effected through the impersonal facilities of an exchange, and (b) whether the right is being asserted by the person on the other side of the transaction or by or on behalf of the corporation.

Keep in mind that Rule 10b–5 does not prohibit "insider trading" in those terms, but actions which operate as a "fraud or deceit" on some person. To recover in an action of "deceit" at common law, plaintiff had to establish (a) that defendant had made a false representation of fact (b) with knowledge of its falsity (or without sufficient basis of information to make it) and (c) with the intention to induce plaintiff to act in reliance on the misrepresentation, and (d) that plaintiff had acted in reasonable reliance on the misrepresentation and (e) suffered damage as a result.[1] As you read the following cases and materials,

1. See W. Prosser, Torts 523 (2d ed. 1955).

consider how far the cause of action for "deceit" under Rule 10b–5 differs from its common law predecessor.

LIST v. FASHION PARK, INC.

340 F.2d 457 (2d Cir.1965).

Before SWAN, WATERMAN and MOORE, CIRCUIT JUDGES.

WATERMAN, CIRCUIT JUDGE.

Plaintiff brought suit in the United States District Court for the Southern District of New York, seeking damages of $160,293 from numerous individual, partnership, and corporate defendants. The suit was based upon alleged violations of Section 10(b) of the Securities Exchange Act, and Rule 10b–5, promulgated thereunder by the Securities and Exchange Commission.

* * *

The crucial facts of the case are for the most part undisputed. Fashion Park is a manufacturer and distributor of men's clothing with headquarters in Rochester, New York. The company had not been prospering for several years preceding the events of this suit, and its factory employees were working only part-time. In September and October, 1960, the manager of the union which represented Fashion Park's employees warned the president and the chairman of the board, Fashion Park's majority shareholders, that he would take a substantial number of employees away from Fashion Park if he could induce another clothing manufacturer to settle in Rochester. In response to this threat, the president of Fashion Park called a directors' meeting for November 4, 1960. Among the directors who attended was defendant Lerner, a minority shareholder.

At the meeting the union manager reiterated his plan to withdraw 300 to 350 employees, and urged the board to consider selling Fashion Park. He told the board that he knew of someone who might be interested in buying the company, but he neither disclosed the name of his prospective purchaser nor any potential purchase terms. The directors then adopted a resolution to the effect that the company seek to negotiate a sale or a merger. Ten days later, the union manager revealed to the president of Fashion Park that the prospective purchaser was Hat Corporation of America, but this information was not relayed to defendant Lerner until the following month. Negotiations between Fashion Park and Hat Corporation began on November 22, 1960, a preliminary understanding was announced on December 7, 1960, and the formal contract of sale was signed on February 3, 1961. By one of the contractual provisions, Hat Corporation agreed to offer $50 per share to all minority shareholders of Fashion Park.

Plaintiff, an experienced and successful investor, had purchased 5100 shares of Fashion Park stock in January, 1959 at $13.50 per share. About November 11, 1960, with the advice of his broker, he authorized the sale of his stock at a net price to him of not less than $18 per share. At that time, defendants Lerner and H. Hentz & Co., as well as another director of Fashion Park, were bidding for Fashion Park stock through the National Quotation Bureau sheets. Plaintiff's broker knew that two directors were bidding for the company's stock, but he did not think it important to disclose this fact to plaintiff, and plaintiff had not sought to learn whether Fashion Park directors were bidding for the stock.

On November 16, 1960, plaintiff's broker called H. Hentz & Co. to invite a purchase of plaintiff's stock at $20 per share. Defendant William P. Green, the partner in H. Hentz & Co. who handled the transaction, contacted Lerner and Beaver Associates to ask if they would like to participate in the purchase. (Green and his brother, defendant Bernard A. Green, are partners in Beaver Associates.) After intensive negotiations between plaintiff's broker and William P. Green, and among Green, Lerner, and Beaver Associates, the sale of the 5100 shares was consummated on November 17, 1960 at $18.50 per share. 4300 shares went to Lerner, 400 to William P. Green and his daughter, and 400 to Beaver Associates. Within two weeks after the transaction, Lerner disposed of part or all of his interest in 3137 of the shares, at an average profit of about $1 per share. At the time of the transaction, William P. Green knew that Lerner was a director of Fashion Park; he may not have known of the resolution of November 4, 1960 to sell or merge the company. Neither plaintiff nor his broker knew that H. Hentz & Co. were brokers for a Fashion Park director who was one of the purchasers of the stock, or that the company's management was considering the sale of the company.

Plaintiff brought suit on February 24, 1961, claiming the difference between the price ($18.50) at which he sold his 5100 shares of Fashion Park stock and the price ($50) which Hat Corporation subsequently offered to Fashion Park's minority shareholders. He alleged that defendants had conspired to buy his stock and then to sell it at a substantial profit, and that they had failed to disclose to him material facts in their possession which would have affected his decision to sell his stock. Insofar as is pertinent to this appeal, the undisclosed facts, alleged to be material, upon which plaintiff relied to support his allegations, were that one of the buyers of his stock was a director of Fashion Park, and that the Fashion Park board, with a potential purchaser on the horizon, had resolved to sell or merge the company. In the opinion dismissing the complaint, the trial court held that there was insufficient evidence of a conspiracy, that plaintiff would have sold even if he had known that one of the buyers was a director of Fashion Park, and that the undisclosed possibility that Fashion Park might be sold was not a material fact.

Plaintiff appeals from the decision of the trial court rejecting his claim that he was damaged by defendants' nondisclosures. * * * We affirm the decision of the trial court * * *.

The general principles governing suits such as this were definitively set forth in the often cited case of Speed v. Transamerica Corp., 99 F.Supp. 808, 828–829 (D.Del.1951), aff'd, 235 F.2d 369 (3 Cir.1956):

> "It is unlawful for an insider, such as a majority stockholder, to purchase the stock of minority stockholders without disclosing material facts affecting the value of the stock, known to the majority stockholder by virtue of his inside position but not known to the selling minority stockholders, which information would have affected the judgment of the sellers. The duty of disclosure stems from the necessity of preventing a corporate insider from utilizing his position to take unfair advantage of the uninformed minority stockholders. It is an attempt to provide some degree of equalization of bargaining position in order that the minority may exercise an informed judgment in any such transaction."

Moreover, "a broker who purchases on behalf of an insider and who has knowledge of inside information would seem to be under the same obligation to disclose as the insider who purchases directly." III Loss, Securities Regulation 1452 (2 ed. 1961).

At the outset, defendant Lerner contends that the courts have never applied Rule 10b–5 in a civil suit involving total non-disclosure. By "total non-disclosure" defendant presumably means that there was no significant communication bearing upon value by buyer to seller except for offer, counteroffer, acceptance, or rejection. The trial judge made no findings relative to this contention, but we are prepared to assume with defendant that, in the sense defendant uses the term, there was a total non-disclosure by defendants to plaintiff.

Although there may be no square holdings in civil suits under Rule 10b–5 involving total non-disclosure, there are ample dicta to the effect that "lack of communication between defendant and plaintiff does not eliminate the possibility that Rule 10b–5 has been violated." Cochran v. Channing Corp., 211 F.Supp. 239, 243 (S.D.N.Y.1962); see Speed v. Transamerica Corp., supra, 99 F.Supp. at 829. Apparently there are no dicta to the contrary in any of the cases. Furthermore, in the leading case of Strong v. Repide, 213 U.S. 419 (1909), the Supreme Court found common law fraud by an insider in the purchase of stock from a minority shareholder, even though "perfect silence was kept" by the defendant. Surely we would suppose that Rule 10b–5 is as stringent in this respect as the federal common law rule which preceded it.

The doctrine for which defendant Lerner contends would tend to reinstate the common law requirement of affirmative misrepresentation. Such a tendency contravenes the purpose of Rule 10b–5 in cases like this, as enunciated in Speed v. Transamerica Corp., supra, which precludes not only the conveyance of half truths by the buyer which actually misled the seller, but, as well, failure by the buyer to disclose the full truth so as to put the seller in an equal bargaining position with the buyer. Moreover, the effect of adopting such a doctrine would be automatically to exempt many impersonal transactions. This effect would be contrary to the intent of Congress, as set forth in Section 2 of the Securities Exchange Act, which was to regulate "transactions in securities as commonly conducted upon securities exchanges [as well as] over-the-counter markets."

It may well be that suits under Rule 10b–5 involving total non-disclosure cannot be brought pursuant to clause (2) of the rule. III Loss, Securities Regulation 1439. Contra, Speed v. Transamerica Corp., supra. Perhaps, as defendant Lerner contends, they cannot be brought pursuant to clause (1) either. Joseph v. Farnsworth Radio & Television Corp., 99 F.Supp. 701, 706 (S.D.N.Y.1951), aff'd 198 F.2d 883 (2 Cir. 1952). Contra, III Loss, Securities Regulation 1439. But we fail to see that it makes any difference which clause of Rule 10b–5 is relied on by plaintiff, and no reason for requiring a choice here has been pointed out to us.

Because there is much disagreement and confusion among the parties concerning the meaning and applicability of "reliance" and "materiality" under Rule 10b–5, we think it advisable first to set forth the well known and well understood common law definitions of these terms and the reasons for the rules in which the terms are incorporated. Insofar as is pertinent here, the test of "reliance" is whether "the misrepresentation is a substantial factor in determining the course of conduct which results in [the recipient's] loss." Restatement, Torts § 546 (1938); accord, Prosser, Torts 550 (2 ed. 1955); I Harper & James, Torts 583–84 (1956). The reason for this requirement, as explained by the authorities cited, is to certify that the conduct of the defendant actually caused the plaintiff's injury. The basic test of "materiality," on the other hand, is whether "a reasonable man would attach importance [to the fact misrepresented] in determining his choice of action in the transaction in question." Restatement, Torts § 538(2)(a); accord, Prosser, Torts 554–55; I Harper & James, Torts 565–66. Thus, to the requirement that the *individual plaintiff* must have acted upon the fact misrepresented, is added the parallel requirement that a *reasonable man* would also have acted upon the fact misrepresented.

The parties to this suit apparently agree that the requirement that a misrepresentation be material is carried over into civil cases under Rule 10b–5 involving non-disclosure by an insider. Moreover, the meaning of the term is ostensibly the same as at common law. III Loss, Securities Regulation 1431. "Materiality" encompasses those facts "which in reasonable and objective contemplation might affect the value of the corporation's stock or securities * * * " Kohler v. Kohler Co., 319 F.2d 634, 642 (7 Cir.1963).

Disagreement centers on the applicability and meaning of the requirement that reliance be placed upon the misrepresentation. Our examination of the authorities satisfies us that this requirement also is carried over into civil suits under Rule 10b–5. Plaintiff also relies on the fact that in Speed v. Transamerica Corp., 99 F.Supp. 808, 833, the court allowed a class action by the defrauded sellers, from which fact he infers that no inquiry into the reasons why each seller transferred his stock is required by Rule 10b–5. However, a comparison of that decision with the opinion in an earlier phase of the same suit, Speed v. Transamerica Corp., 5 F.R.D. 56, 60, shows that a class action was allowed only because the court was convinced that all members of the class had relied on defendant's misrepresentation.

This interpretation of Rule 10b–5 is a reasonable one, for the aim of the rule in cases such as this is to qualify, as between insiders and outsiders, the doctrine of *caveat emptor*—not to establish a scheme of investors' insurance. Assuredly, to abandon the requirement of reliance would be to facilitate outsiders' proof of insiders' fraud, and to that extent the interpretation for which plaintiff contends might advance the purposes of Rule 10b–5. But this strikes us as an inadequate reason for reading out of the rule so basic an element of tort law as the principle of causation in fact. Plaintiff's citation of decisions by the Securities and Exchange Commission, and commentary thereon, does not persuade us otherwise. Cady, Roberts & Co., Sec.Ex.Act Rel. 6668, p. 9 (1961); III Loss, Securities Regulation 1438–39 n. 30. The aim of administrative proceedings under Rule 10b–5 is to deter misconduct by insiders, rather than to compensate their victims. That, because of the peculiar circumstances of the particular outsiders involved, no harm actually results from the misconduct is ordinarily irrelevant to this preventive purpose. But see III Loss, Securities Regulation 1764.

On the other hand, we do not agree with certain overtones in the opinion of the trial court concerning the meaning of "reliance" in a case of non-disclosure under Rule 10b–5. The opinion intimates that the plaintiff must prove he actively relied on the silence of the defendant, either because he consciously had in mind the negative of the fact concealed, or perhaps because he deliberately put his trust in the advice of the defendant. Such a requirement, however, would unduly dilute the obligation of insiders to inform outsiders of all material facts, regardless of the sophistication or naivete of the persons with whom they are dealing. Connelly v. Balkwill, 174 F.Supp. 49, 59 (N.D.Ohio 1959), aff'd, 279 F.2d 685 (6 Cir.1960), must be read in light of the fact that the prime defendant in that case was not an insider.

The proper test is whether the plaintiff would have been influenced to act differently than he did act if the defendant had disclosed to him the undisclosed fact. Speed v. Transamerica Corp., 99 F.Supp. 808, 829; Kardon v. National Gypsum Co., 73 F.Supp. 798, 800 (E.D.Pa.1947). To put the matter conversely, insiders "are not required to search out details that presumably would not influence the person's judgment with whom they are dealing." Kohler v. Kohler Co., supra, 319 F.2d at 642. This test preserves the common law parallel between "reliance" and "materiality," differing as it does from the definition of "materiality" under Rule 10b–5 solely by substituting the individual plaintiff for the reasonable man. Of course this test is not utterly dissimilar from the one hinted at by the trial court. That the outsider did not have in mind the negative of the fact undisclosed to him, or that he did not put his trust in the advice of the insider, would tend to prove that he would not have been influenced by the undisclosed fact even if the insider had disclosed it to him.

The trial court concluded that plaintiff would have sold his stock even if he had known that defendant Lerner, an insider, was one of the buyers. The trial court based this result upon its findings that plaintiff is an experienced and successful investor in securities; that he actively solicited the sale to defendants; that he did not ask his broker whether any insiders were bidding for stock in the corporation; that his broker knew two directors were bidding but did not think it necessary to inform plaintiff of this; that the only restriction plaintiff placed on his broker related to price; and that his broker suggested that five points would be a nice profit, to which plaintiff agreed. From these facts, the trial court presumably inferred that plaintiff was so desirous of "the potential five point profit he would make" and so reliant on knowledge acquired through "his many dealings in the securities field" that the identity of the buyer would have been of little or no concern to him.

We cannot say that the finding of the trial court was clearly erroneous.[4]

The trial court also concluded that adoption of the November 4, 1960 resolution, and the setting in which it occurred, were not material facts that should have been disclosed to plaintiff. This result was based in part on the undisputed facts that at the time the resolution was adopted the Fashion Park directors only had before them the statement of the union manager that he knew of some unidentified person who would be interested in buying Fashion Park; that by the time plaintiff sold his stock on November 17, 1960 nothing more had occurred except that the president of Fashion Park had learned the name of the potential purchaser; and that within two weeks after he bought plaintiff's stock defendant Lerner disposed of part or all of his interest in 3137 of his 4300 shares at an average profit of only about $1 per share. The trial court presumably inferred from these facts that the prospects for "a sale of Fashion Park" and for a sale at a price "profitable to shareholders," insofar as Lerner and the other defendants apprehended them to be at the time they purchased plaintiff's stock, were too remote to have influenced the conduct of a reasonable investor.

Here too, the finding of the trial court was not clearly erroneous.

* * *

In AFFILIATED UTE CITIZENS v. UNITED STATES, 406 U.S. 128 (1972), plaintiffs had sold shares in Ute Development Corporation, representing their interest in assets required to be distributed to the

4. In view of this result, we express no opinion on the totally novel question of whether failure by an insider to disclose his identity can ever be a violation of Rule 10b-5. * * *

mixed-blood members of the Ute tribe under the Ute Partition Act. Their complaint alleged that two employees of the bank in which the shares were deposited, in arranging for sales of these shares by mixed-bloods to whites, had failed to disclose their own interests in the transactions or the fact that the shares were selling at substantially higher prices in transactions between whites. The court of appeals held that there was no violation of Rule 10b–5 unless the record disclosed evidence of reliance by the sellers on misrepresentation of material fact by the two employees. The Supreme Court reversed:

> It is no answer to urge that, as to some of the petitioners, these defendants may have made no positive representation or recommendation. The defendants may not stand mute while they facilitate the mixed-bloods' sales to those seeking to profit in the non-Indian market the defendants had developed and encouraged and with which they were fully familiar. The sellers had the right to know that the defendants were in a position to gain financially from their sales and that their shares were selling for a higher price in that market.
>
> Under the circumstances of this case, involving primarily a failure to disclose, positive proof of reliance is not a prerequisite to recovery. All that is necessary is that the facts withheld be material in the sense that a reasonable investor might have considered them important in the making of this decision. This obligation to disclose and this withholding of a material fact establish the requisite element of causation in fact.

The preceding cases all involved direct face-to-face dealings, or at least transactions in which the parties could be easily identified. When the transactions take place on an anonymous market, such as a stock exchange, there are far greater difficulties in determining to whom an "insider" should be held liable, and for how much.

JOSEPH v. FARNSWORTH RADIO & TELEVISION CORP., 99 F.Supp. 701 (S.D.N.Y.1951), aff'd, 198 F.2d 883 (2d Cir.1952). Plaintiffs, who had purchased Farnsworth stock in stock exchange transactions in November and December 1948, brought an action under Rule 10b–5 against certain officers and directors of the corporation. They alleged that defendants had (a) sold Farnsworth stock between March and October 1948 without disclosing adverse information about Farnsworth's financial condition, and (b) caused Farnsworth to issue a misleading financial statement in November 1948, falsely reflecting Farnsworth's financial condition at October 31 and its earnings for the preceding six months. Plaintiffs did not allege that they relied on the misleading financial statement. The trial judge framed the issue as follows:

> May A, who purchased stock of the F Corporation on November 12th and B, who likewise purchased stock of the same corporation on December 13th, each on a national stock exchange and each at a price

higher than he would have paid therefor had he known the true financial condition of F, recover from C, D and E, the directors and officers of the corporation, the difference between that paid and that which would have been paid had C, D and E disclosed, between the previous March 19th and October 30th when they were unloading their own stock in F, that F was in a straitened financial condition?

The court, noting that it was not passing on "the rights of those who bought the individual defendants' stock between March 19 and October 30, 1948," held that a "semblance of privity between the vendor and purchaser of the security * * * seems to be requisite and it is entirely lacking here." The complaint was dismissed.

The court of appeals affirmed, 2–1, on the basis of the opinion below. Judge Frank dissented, arguing that there was no requirement of privity in fraud actions, even at common law. While recognizing the common law requirement "that the person relying upon a misrepresentation be within the ambit of persons whom the defendant actually intended to defraud," he noted that "liability has been imposed [in negotiable instrument cases] where plaintiffs have relied on intentional misrepresentations though the defendant had no intent to influence the particular person or class of persons." He concluded that in light of the legislative history of § 10(b) and Rule 10b–5, the narrow limitation should be rejected in actions brought under those provisions.

SHAPIRO v. MERRILL LYNCH

495 F.2d 228 (2d Cir.1974).

Before: DANAHER, LUMBARD and TIMBERS, CIRCUIT JUDGES.

TIMBERS, CIRCUIT JUDGE:

This appeal presents important questions, some of first impression, involving the scope of the antifraud provisions of the federal securities laws in their application to transactions on a national securities exchange when material inside information has not been disclosed.

Specifically, the questions presented are (1) whether Section 10(b) of the Securities Exchange Act of 1934 and Rule 10b–5 were violated by a prospective managing underwriter of a debenture issue and the underwriter's officers, directors and employees when they divulged material inside information to the underwriter's customers for the purpose of protecting the latters' investments in the stock of the issuer; (2) whether the same antifraud provisions of the securities laws were violated by the underwriter's customers when they traded in the stock of the issuer without disclosing the material inside information which had been divulged to them by the underwriter; and (3) whether those referred to above, if they did violate the antifraud provisions of the securities laws, are liable in damages to those persons who during the same period purchased stock in the same company in the open market without knowledge of the material inside information. In short, this case involves the liability of non-trading "tippers" and trading "tippees" under Section 10(b) and Rule 10b–5.

* * *

[This case involved the same fact situation as the *Investors Management* case, p. 564 above. Plaintiffs were two investors who had purchased an unspecified number of shares of Douglas common stock on the New York Stock Exchange during the four-day period when the institutions that had received a tip from Merrill Lynch that Douglas earnings would be sharply reduced were selling an aggregate of 165,000 shares of Douglas (approximately one-half of all sales of Douglas stock during that period). The court held that Merrill Lynch and the selling institutions had violated Rule 10b–5 by passing on, or trading on the basis of, material non-public information.]

We turn next to the remaining major legal question presented: assuming that defendants did violate the antifraud provisions of the securities laws by trading in or recommending trading in Douglas common stock (as we have held above), whether they are liable in a private action for damages to plaintiffs who during the same period purchased Douglas stock in the open market without knowledge of the material inside information which was in the possession of defendants.

The essential argument of defendants on this question is that, even if they did violate Section 10(b) and Rule 10b–5, their conduct did not "cause" damage to plaintiffs; that it was Douglas' precarious financial condition, not defendants' securities law violations, which precipitated the sudden, substantial drop in the market price of Douglas stock and hence the losses sustained by plaintiffs; that, since plaintiffs had no prior or contemporaneous knowledge of defendants' actions, they would have purchased Douglas stock regardless of defendants' securities law violations; and that, since defendants' sales were unrelated to plaintiffs' purchases and all transactions took place on anonymous public stock exchanges, there is lacking the requisite connection between defendants' alleged violations and the alleged losses sustained by plaintiffs.

The short, and we believe conclusive, answer to defendants' assertion that their conduct did not "cause" damage to plaintiffs is the "causation in fact" holding by the Supreme Court in Affiliated Ute Citizens v. United States, 406 U.S. 128, 153–54 (1972), upon the authority of which we conclude that the requisite element of causation in fact has been established here by the uncontroverted facts that defendants traded in or recommended trading in Douglas stock without disclosing material inside information which plaintiffs as reasonable investors might have considered important in making their decision to purchase Douglas stock.

* * *

As one branch of their absence of causation argument, defendants contend that there was no privity between themselves and plaintiffs. We hold here, as we have held before, that privity between plaintiffs and defendants is not a requisite element of a Rule 10b–5 cause of action for damages. * * * As the Tenth Circuit stated in Mitchell v. Texas Gulf Sulphur Co., 446 F.2d 90, 101 (1971), "[p]erhaps the first step is to realize that the common law requirement of privity has all but vanished from 10b–5 proceedings while the distinguishable 'connection' element is retained." * * * In short, causation as an element of a Rule 10b–5 cause of action can be established notwithstanding lack of privity.

As a further refinement of their absence of causation argument, defendants contend that, even if privity between plaintiffs and defendants is not required, it is still necessary to show a "connection" between defendants' non-disclosure conduct and plaintiffs' purchase of Douglas stock—in the sense that the former induced the latter—before a Rule 10b–5 claim can be established. It is true that prior to the Supreme Court decision in *Affiliated Ute* the so-called connection requirement was stated in terms of causation and reliance. For example, we have noted that the reason for the requirement of reliance "is to certify that the conduct of the defendant actually caused the plaintiff's injury", List v. Fashion Park, Inc., supra, 340 F.2d at 462, and we have held that "[t]o the extent that reliance is necessary for a finding of a 10b–5 violation in a non-disclosure case * * *, the test is properly one of tort 'causation in fact.'" Chasins v. Smith, Barney & Co., 438 F.2d at 1172. While the concepts of reliance and causation have been used interchangeably in the context of a Rule 10b–5 claim, the proper test to determine whether causation in fact has been established in a non-disclosure case is "whether the plaintiff would have been influenced to act differently than he did act if the defendant had disclosed to him the undisclosed fact." List v. Fashion Park, Inc., supra, 340 F.2d at 463.

Even on the basis of the pre-*Affiliated Ute* decisions discussed above, therefore, we would reject defendants' essential causation argument, namely, that, absent an allegation that plaintiffs' purchase of Douglas stock was induced by defendants' non-disclosure of material inside information, the requisite element of causation is lacking. On the contrary, the Rule 10b–5 causation in fact requirement is satisfied by plaintiffs' allegation that they would not have purchased Douglas stock if they had known of the information withheld by defendants.

* * *

As applied to the instant case, [the] holding in *Affiliated Ute* surely warrants our conclusion that the requisite element of causation in fact has been established by the admitted withholding by defendants of material inside information which they were under an obligation to disclose, such information being clearly material in the sense that plaintiffs as reasonable investors might have considered it important in making their decision to purchase Douglas stock.

Defendants argue that the *Affiliated Ute* rule of causation in fact should be confined to the facts of that case which involved face-to-face transactions. We disagree. That rule is dependent not upon the character of the transaction—face-to-face versus national securities exchange—but rather upon whether the defendant is obligated to disclose the inside information. Here, as we have held above, defendants were under a duty to the investing public, including plaintiffs, not to trade in or to recommend trading in Douglas stock without publicly disclosing the revised earnings information which was in their possession. They breached that duty. Causation in fact therefore has been established.

* * *

For the reasons set forth above, we hold that defendants are liable in this private action for damages to plaintiffs who, during the same period that defendants traded in or recommended trading in Douglas common stock, purchased Douglas stock in the open market without knowledge of the material inside information which was in the possession of defendants.

Finally, having held that all defendants violated Section 10(b) and Rule 10b–5 and that they are liable to plaintiffs in this private action for damages, we leave to the district court the appropriate form of relief to be granted, including the proper measure of damages. * * * Among the questions to be determined which will have an important bearing on the form of relief is whether the action is to be maintained as a class action and, if so, the parameters of the class; as to this, the district court understandably was unable to make a determination on the facts presented by the pleadings. Another closely related question bearing upon the relief to be granted as to which the district court had insufficient data upon which to make a determination is just when Douglas' news release regarding its revised earnings forecast on the morning of June 24, 1966 became effectively disseminated, especially in the light of SEC v. Texas Gulf Sulphur Co., 401 F.2d 833, 854, n. 18 (2 Cir.1968). Other questions bearing upon the appropriate form of relief which must await trial include the extent of the selling defendants' trading in Douglas stock, whether such trading effectively impaired the integrity of the market, what compensation if any was paid by the selling defendants to Merrill Lynch for the inside information, what profits or other benefits were realized by defendants, what expenses were incurred and what losses were sustained by plaintiffs, and what should be the difference, if any, in the extent of liability imposed on the individual defendants and the selling defendants, respectively. Moreover, we do not foreclose the possibility that an analysis by the district court of the nature and character of the Rule 10b–5 violations committed may require limiting the extent of liability imposed on either class of defendants.

In leaving to the district court the fashioning of appropriate relief, including the proper measure of damages, we are not unmindful of the arguments pressed upon us by all defendants that the resulting judgment for damages may be very substantial in amount—in the words of defendants' counsel, a "Draconian liability". This is an additional reason for leaving to the district court the appropriate form of relief to be granted—a determination that can best be made after an evidentiary hearing and on the basis of appropriate findings of fact. * * *

On remand, the district court determined that the action could proceed as a class action, and that the class should include "all persons who purchased Douglas stock in the open market without the benefit of inside information from the time of the first allegedly illegal sale by a defendant, June 21, 1966, through June 24, 1966, the day of Douglas' public announcement of the information." The court's rationale was that once the insiders' duty to "abstain or disclose" was breached, they were liable to all purchasers until "the public is restored to its position of equal access by circulation of the material information," Shapiro v. Merrill Lynch, CCH Fed.Sec.L.Rep. ¶ 95,377 (S.D.N.Y.1975).

Does this make sense? If, as the court says, an insider's duty is to "abstain or disclose," why can he not terminate his liability after one transgression by thereafter abstaining rather than disclosing?

In WILSON v. COMTECH TELECOMMUNICATIONS CORP., 648 F.2d 88 (2d Cir.1981), the Second Circuit drew back from the approach taken by the district court in *Shapiro,* and held that an investor who purchased stock about a month after the insiders sold, but before full disclosure was made by the company, had no claim under Rule 10b–5:

> In *Shapiro,* this court held insider sellers subject to a duty to disclose only to those who purchased the stock "during the same period" as the insider's sales. To be sure, the district court on remand interpreted this language to refer to the period of time from the defendant's trades to the public disclosure of the inside information, but the entire period in that case was only four days. To extend the period of liability well beyond the time of the insider's trading simply because disclosure was never made could make the insider liable to all the world.

This problem of "Draconian liability" led the Sixth Circuit to reject the idea of any civil liability in this situation. In Fridrich v. Bradford, 542 F.2d 307 (6th Cir.1976), the court held that insiders who bought in the open market on the basis of non-public information were not liable to persons selling in the open market during the same period on the ground that "defendants' act of trading with third persons was not causally connected with any claimed loss by plaintiffs who traded on the impersonal market and who were otherwise unaffected by the wrongful acts of the insider." *Affiliated Ute* was distinguished on the basis of the face-to-face dealings and the pre-existing relationship between the parties.

The Second Circuit, however, dealt with the damage question in a different way:

ELKIND v. LIGGETT & MYERS

635 F.2d 156 (2d Cir.1980).

Before MANSFIELD and NEWMAN, CIRCUIT JUDGES.

MANSFIELD, CIRCUIT JUDGE.

This case presents a number of issues arising out of what has become a form of corporate brinkmanship—non-public disclosure of business-related information to financial analysts. The action is a class suit by Arnold B. Elkind on behalf of certain purchasers (more fully described below) of the stock of Liggett & Myers, Inc. (Liggett) against it. They seek damages for alleged failure of its officers to disclose certain material information with respect to its earnings and operations and for their alleged wrongful tipping of inside information to certain persons who then sold Liggett shares on the open market.

After a non-jury trial Judge Constance Baker Motley held in post-trial findings and conclusions that Liggett did not violate Section 10(b) of the Securities Exchange Act of 1934, or Rule 10b–5 promulgated thereunder, by failing prior to July 18, 1972, to release figures showing a substantial downturn in earnings or to correct erroneous projections of financial analysts which it had allegedly fostered. The court found, however, that on July 10, 1972, and July 17, 1972, officers of Liggett disclosed material inside information to individual financial analysts, leading to sale of Liggett stock by investors to whom this information was conveyed. Damages were computed on the basis of the difference between the price which members of the plaintiff class (uninformed buyers of Liggett stock between the time of the first tip and subsequent public disclosure) paid and what the stock sold for after the later disclosure. * * *

* * *

We * * * conclude that the tip of July 10 was not material and was not accompanied by the requisite scienter to furnish the basis for liability under Rule 10b–5. The tip of July 17, however, was material and made with scienter. We turn, then, to the computation of damages.

This case presents a question of measurement of damages which we have previously deferred, believing that damages are best addressed in a concrete setting. See Shapiro v. Merrill Lynch. We ruled in *Shapiro* that defendants selling on inside information would be liable to those who bought on the open market and sustained "substantial losses" during the period of insider trading.

The district court looked to the measure of damages used in cases where a buyer was induced to purchase a company's stock by materially misleading statements or omissions. In such cases of fraud by a fiduciary intended to induce others to buy or sell stock the accepted measure of damages is the "out-of-pocket" measure. This consists of the difference between the price paid and the "value" of the stock when bought (or when the buyer committed himself to buy, if earlier). Except in rare face-to-face transactions, however, uninformed traders on an open, impersonal market are not induced by representations on the part of the tipper or tippee to buy or sell. Usually they are wholly unacquainted with and uninfluenced by the tippee's misconduct. They trade independently and voluntarily but without the benefit of information known to the trading tippee.

In determining what is the appropriate measure of damages to be awarded to the outside uninformed investor as the result of tippee-trading through use of information that is not equally available to all investors it must be remembered that investors who trade in a stock on the open market have no absolute right to know inside information. They are, however, entitled to an honest market in which those with whom they trade have no confidential corporate information.

Recognizing the foregoing, we in *Shapiro* suggested that the district court must be accorded flexibility in assessing damages, * * *. We thus gave heed to the guidance provided by the Supreme Court in *Affiliated Ute* to the effect that "Congress intended securities legislation enacted for the purpose of avoiding frauds to be construed 'not technically and restrictively, but flexibly to effectuate its remedial purposes.'"

Within the flexible framework thus authorized for determining what amounts should be recoverable by the uninformed trader from the tipper and tippee trader, several measures are possible. First, there is the traditional out-of-pocket measure used by the district court in this case. For several reasons this measure appears to be inappropriate. In the first place, as we have noted, it is directed toward compensating a person for losses directly traceable to the defendant's fraud upon him. No such fraud or inducement may be attributed to a tipper or tippee trading on an impersonal market. Aside from this the measure poses serious proof problems that may often be insurmountable in a tippee-trading case. The "value" of the stock traded during the period of nondisclosure of the tipped information (i.e., the price at which the market would have valued the stock if there had been a disclosure) is hypothetical. Expert testimony regarding that "value" may, as the district court found in the present case, be entirely speculative.

* * *

An equally compelling reason for rejecting the theory is its potential for imposition of Draconian, exorbitant damages, out of all proportion to the wrong committed, lining the pockets of all interim investors and their counsel at the expense of innocent corporate stockholders. Logic would compel application of the theory to a case where a tippee sells only 10 shares of a heavily traded stock (e.g., IBM), which then drops substantially when the tipped information is publicly disclosed. To hold the tipper and tippee liable for the losses suffered by every open market buyer of the stock as a result of the later decline in value of the stock after the news became public would be grossly unfair.

While the securities laws do occasionally allow for potentially ruinous recovery, we will not readily adopt a measure mandating "large judgments, payable in the last instance by innocent investors [here, Liggett shareholders], for the benefit of speculators and their lawyers," unless the statute so requires.

An alternative measure would be to permit recovery of damages caused by erosion of the market price of the security that is traceable to the tippee's wrongful trading, i.e., to compensate the uninformed investor for the loss in market value that he suffered as a direct result of the tippee's conduct. Under this measure an innocent trader who bought Liggett shares at or after a tippee sold on the basis of inside information would recover any decline in value of his shares caused by the tippee's trading. * * *

This causation-in-fact approach has some disadvantages. It allows no recovery for the tippee's violation of his duty to disclose the inside information before trading. Had he fulfilled this duty, others, including holders of the stock, could then have traded on an equal informational basis. Another disadvantage of such a measure lies in the difficult if not impossible burden it would impose on the uninformed trader of proving the time when and extent to which the integrity of the market was affected by the tippee's conduct. * * * Moreover, even assuming market erosion caused by this trading to be provable and that the uninformed investor could show that it continued after his purchase, there remains the question of whether the plaintiff would not be precluded from recovery on the ground that any post-purchase decline in market price attributable to the tippee's trading would not be injury to him as a purchaser, i.e., "in connection with the purchase and sale of securities," but injury to him as a stockholder due to a breach of fiduciary duty by the company's officers, which is not actionable under § 10b of the 1934 Act or Rule 10b–5 promulgated thereunder. For these reasons, we reject this strict direct market-repercussion theory of damages.

A third alternative is (1) to allow any uninformed investor, where a reasonable investor would either have delayed his purchase or not purchased at all if he had had the benefit of the tipped information, to recover any post-purchase decline in market value of his shares up to a reasonable time after he learns of the tipped information or after there is a public disclosure of it but (2) limit his recovery to the amount gained by the tippee as a result of his selling at the earlier date rather than delaying his sale until the parties could trade on an equal informational basis. Under this measure if the tippee sold 5,000 shares at $50 per share on the basis of inside information and the stock thereafter declined to $40 per share within a reasonable time after public disclosure, an uninformed purchaser, buying shares during the interim (e.g., at $45 per share) would recover the difference between his purchase price and the amount at which he could have sold the shares on an equal informational basis (i.e., the market price within a reasonable time after public disclosure of the tip), subject to a limit of $50,000, which is the amount gained by the tippee as a result of his trading on the inside information rather than on an equal basis. Should the intervening buyers, because of the volume and price of their purchases, claim more than the tippee's gain, their recovery (limited to that gain) would be shared *pro rata.*

This third alternative, which may be described as the disgorgement measure, has in substance been recommended by the American Law Institute in its 1978 Proposed Draft of a Federal Securities Code, §§ 1603, 1703(b), 1708(b), 1711(j). It offers several advantages. To the extent that it makes the tipper and tippees liable up to the amount gained by their misconduct, it should deter tipping of inside information and tippee-trading. On the other hand, by limiting the total recovery to the tippee's gain, the measure bars windfall recoveries of exorbitant amounts bearing no relation to the seriousness of the misconduct. It also avoids the extraordinary difficulties faced in trying to prove traditional out-of-pocket damages based on the true "value" of the shares purchased or damages claimed by reason of market erosion attributable to tippee trading. A plaintiff would simply be required to prove (1) the time, amount, and price per share of his purchase, (2) that a reasonable investor would not have paid as high a price or made the purchase at all if he had had the information in the tippee's possession, and (3) the price to which the security had declined by the time he learned the tipped information or at a reasonable time after it became public, whichever event first occurred. He would then have a claim and, up to the limits of the tippee's gain, could recover the decline in market value of his shares before the information became public or known to him. In most cases the damages recoverable under the disgorgement measure would be roughly commensurate to the actual harm caused by the tippee's wrongful conduct. In a case where the tippee sold only a few shares, for instance, the likelihood of his conduct causing any substantial injury to intervening investors buying without benefit of his confidential information would be small. If, on the other hand, the tippee sold large amounts of stock, realizing substantial profits, the likelihood of injury to intervening uninformed purchasers would be greater and the amount of potential recovery thereby proportionately enlarged.

We recognize that there cannot be any perfect measure of damages caused by tippee-trading. The disgorgement measure, like others we have described, does have some disadvantages. It modifies the principle that ordinarily gain to the wrongdoer should not be a prerequisite to liability for violation of Rule 10b–5. It partially duplicates disgorgement remedies available in proceedings by the SEC or others. Under some market conditions such as where the market price is depressed by wholly unrelated causes, the tippee might be vulnerable to heavy damages, permitting some plaintiffs to recover undeserved windfalls. In some instances the total claims could exceed the wrongdoer's gain, limiting each claimant to a *pro rata* share of the gain. In other situations, after deducting the cost of recovery, including attorneys' fees, the remainder might be inadequate to make a class action worthwhile. However, as between the various alternatives we are persuaded, after weighing the pros and cons, that the disgorgement measure, despite some disadvantages, offers the most equitable resolution of the difficult problems created by conflicting interests.

In the present case the sole Rule 10b–5 violation was the tippee-trading of 1,800 Liggett shares on the afternoon of July 17, 1972. Since the actual preliminary Liggett earnings were released publicly at 2:15 P.M. on July 18 and were effectively disseminated in a Wall Street Journal article published on the morning of July 19, the only outside purchasers who might conceivably have been damaged by the insider-trading were those who bought Liggett shares between the afternoon of July 17 and the opening of the market on July 19. Thereafter all purchasers bought on an equal informational footing, and any outside purchaser who bought on July 17 and 18 was able to decide within a reasonable time after the July 18–19 publicity whether to hold or sell his shares in the light of the publicly-released news regarding Liggett's less favorable earnings.

The market price of Liggett stock opened on July 17, 1972, at $55\frac{5}{8}$, and remained at substantially the same price on that date, closing at $55\frac{1}{4}$. By the close of the market on July 18 the price declined to $52\frac{1}{2}$ per share. Applying the disgorgement measure, any member of the plaintiff class who bought Liggett shares during the period from the afternoon of July 17 to the close of the market on July 18 and met the reasonable investor requirement would be entitled to claim a *pro rata* portion of the tippee's gain, based on the difference between their purchase price and the price to which the market price declined within a reasonable time after the morning of July 19. By the close of the market on July 19 the market price had declined to $46\frac{3}{8}$ per share. The total recovery thus would be limited to the gain realized by the tippee from the inside information, i.e., 1,800 shares multiplied by approximately $9.35 per share.[29]

The *Elkind* approach has also been applied in an SEC action seeking disgorgement of profits from insider trading. The court rejected the SEC argument that defendant should be required to disgorge

29. Since, as previously pointed out, the tipped information was not as adverse as the bad news ultimately disclosed, the defendants could plausibly argue that the tippee's gain (and therefore the limit of plaintiffs' recovery) should be only the difference between the price at which he sold and the hypothetical price to which the stock would have declined if the tip had been disclosed. While that approach would make sense if a tippee were held liable for the out-of-pocket losses of all plaintiffs, we think that when only a disgorgement measure of damages is used, a tippee who trades is liable for the entire difference between the price at which he sold and the price the stock reached after the tip became known. By trading on tipped information, the tippee takes the risk that by the time the tip is disclosed the market price may reflect disclosure of information more adverse than the tip and other adverse market conditions.

the difference between what he paid for the stock and what he sold it for two years later. SEC v. MacDONALD, 699 F.2d 47 (1st Cir.1983).

MOSS v. MORGAN STANLEY

719 F.2d 5 (2d Cir.1983).

Before MANSFIELD, MESKILL and KEARSE, CIRCUIT JUDGES.

MESKILL, CIRCUIT JUDGE:

This appeal spotlights two issues of significance for the litigation of federal securities fraud claims: (1) whether a shareholder who unwittingly sold stock of a "target" company on the open market prior to public announcement of a tender offer has a cause of action for damages under section 10(b) of the Securities Exchange Act of 1934, and rule 10b–5 promulgated thereunder against a person who purchased "target" shares on the basis of material nonpublic information which he acquired from the tender offeror's investment adviser; and (2) whether this same unwitting shareholder can recover treble damages under the Racketeer Influenced and Corrupt Organizations Act, 18 U.S.C. §§ 1961 et seq. (RICO), on the ground that he was injured by an unlawful "enterprise" conducting a "pattern of racketeering activity" comprised of "fraudulent" securities transactions.

The district court held that the shareholder failed to state a cause of action under both the 1934 Act and RICO. We agree for the reasons stated below.

Affirmed.

BACKGROUND

The chain of events that culminated in this action began in the latter months of 1976 with tender offer discussions between Warner–Lambert Company (Warner) and Deseret Pharmaceutical Company (Deseret). On November 23, 1976 Warner retained the investment banking firm of Morgan Stanley & Co. Incorporated, a subsidiary of Morgan Stanley Inc. (Morgan Stanley), to assess the desirability of acquiring Deseret, to evaluate Deseret's stock and to recommend an appropriate price per share for the tender offer.

One of the individual defendants in this action, E. Jacques Courtois, Jr., was then employed by Morgan Stanley in its mergers and acquisitions department. In that capacity Courtois acquired knowledge of Warner's plan to purchase Deseret stock. On November 30, 1976 Courtois informed defendant Adrian Antoniu, an employee of Kuhn Loeb & Co., of the proposed tender offer and urged him to purchase Deseret stock. Antoniu in turn informed James M. Newman, a stockbroker, that Warner intended to bid for Deseret. Pursuant to an agreement with Antoniu and Courtois, Newman purchased 11,700 shares of Deseret stock at approximately $28 per share for his and their accounts. Newman also advised certain of his clients to buy Deseret stock.

Trading was active in Deseret shares on November 30, 1976, with approximately 143,000 shares changing hands. Michael E. Moss, the plaintiff in this action, was among the active traders, having sold 5,000 shares at $28 per share. On the following day, December 1, 1976, the New York Stock Exchange halted trading in Deseret stock pending announcement of the tender offer. Trading remained suspended until December 7, 1976 when Warner publicly announced its tender offer for Deseret stock at $38 per share. Newman and the other defendants tendered their shares to Warner and reaped a substantial profit.

On August 5, 1982 Moss commenced this action on his own behalf and on behalf of the class of investors who sold stock in Deseret on November 30, 1976. He contended that "members of the class have been substantially damaged in that they sold Deseret stock prior to the public announcement of the Warner tender offer at prices substantially below [those] offered by Warner." The amended complaint stated three causes of action: (1) Moss sought to recover damages from Newman for allegedly violating section 10(b) of the 1934 Act and rule 10b–5 thereunder by purchasing Deseret shares with knowledge of the imminent tender offer and without disclosing such information to Deseret shareholders; (2) Moss sought to recover damages from Morgan Stanley on the ground that as a "controlling person" under section 20(a) of the 1934 Act, Morgan Stanley should be derivatively liable for Courtois' wrongdoing; and (3) pursuant to RICO, Moss sought to recover treble damages from Newman on the ground that he engaged in "at least two acts of fraud in connection with the purchase and sale of securities and as such [his actions represented] a pattern of racketeering activity within the meaning of RICO."

* * *

DISCUSSION

I. Section 10(b) Liability

A. Introduction

It is well settled that traditional corporate "insiders"—directors, officers and persons who have access to confidential corporate information—must preserve the confidentiality of nonpublic information that belongs to and emanates from the corporation. Consistent with this duty, the "insider" must either disclose nonpublic corporate information or abstain from trading in the securities of that corporation. The individual defendants in this case—Courtois, Antoniu and Newman—having acquired confidential information through Warner's investment adviser and having no direct relationship with Deseret, could not be traditional corporate "insiders."

However, in a number of decisions the Supreme Court has extended the "duty of disclosure" requirement to nontraditional "insiders"—persons who have no special access to corporate information but who do have a special relationship of "trust" and "confidentiality" with the issuer or seller of the securities. Moss sought to include the defendants in this category of nontraditional "insiders" and argued that they necessarily violated section 10(b) and rule 10b–5 by purchasing Deseret stock without publicly disclosing their knowledge of the impending tender offer. After finding that none of the defendants occupied a position of "trust" with respect to Moss, the district court held that none of the defendants owed him such a "duty of disclosure." In light of the Supreme Court's decisions in *Chiarella* which recently articulated the standard for analyzing violations of section 10(b) and rule 10b–5, we agree with the district court's dismissal of plaintiff's federal securities law claim.

* * *

C. Application of Chiarella

In applying *Chiarella*'s "fiduciary standard" to this case, Judge Pollack concluded that Newman owed no "duty of disclosure" to plaintiff Moss and hence could not be liable for a section 10(b) or rule 10b–5 violation. We agree. Like Chiarella, both Courtois and Newman were "complete stranger[s] who dealt with the sellers [of Deseret stock] only through impersonal market transactions." However, in this appeal plaintiff continues to insist, *arguendo,* that if civil "liability is premised upon a duty to disclose arising from a relationship of trust and confidence between parties to a transaction," then he occupied such a position of "trust" with respect to the defendants. He suggests three sources for the defendants' "duty of disclosure."

1. United States v. Newman

Moss first argues that because Courtois owed a "fiduciary duty" to his employer, Morgan Stanley, and to Morgan Stanley's client, Warner, then Newman (standing in Courtois' shoes) owed a separate duty of disclosure to Deseret shareholders. Plaintiff claims that our decision in United States v. Newman, 664 F.2d 12 (2d Cir.1981), supports this circuitous linking of liability. We disagree.

In *Newman* we held that Courtois' and Antoniu's securities transactions constituted a breach of their fiduciary duty of confidentiality and loyalty to their employers (Morgan Stanley and Kuhn Loeb & Co., respectively) and thereby provided the basis for *criminal* prosecution under section 10(b) and rule 10b–5. Indeed, the district court at Newman's trial specifically charged the jury that "the law is clear that Mr. Newman had no obligation or duty to the people from whom he bought the stock to disclose what he had learned, and, thus, he could not have defrauded these people as a matter of law." Nothing in our opinion in *Newman* suggests that an employee's duty to "abstain or disclose" with respect to his employer should be stretched to encompass an employee's "duty of disclosure" to the general public. * * * Thus, the district court was correct in concluding that "plaintiff cannot hope to piggyback upon the duty owed by defendants to Morgan Stanley and

Warner. There is no 'duty in the air' to which any plaintiff can attach his claim."

2. *"Insider" Trading*

Plaintiff's next attempt to find a source for Newman's duty to disclose is to argue that Morgan Stanley and its employee Courtois were "insiders" of Deseret and therefore owed a duty to Deseret shareholders. Moss asserts that Morgan Stanley and Courtois were transformed into "insiders" upon their receipt of confidential information from Deseret during tender offer negotiations in this "friendly takeover." Such an argument fails both as a matter of fact and law.

First, the complaint contains no factual assertions that Morgan Stanley or Courtois received *any* information from Deseret. Nor does it allege that Newman traded on the basis of information derived from the issuer or seller of Deseret stock. Rather, the complaint was premised solely on the theory that Newman traded on the basis of information originating from "Warner's plan to acquire Deseret stock."

Yet, even if we overlook the complaint's facial deficiencies, plaintiff's theory fails as a matter of law. In Walton v. Morgan Stanley & Co., 623 F.2d 796 (2d Cir.1980), we held that an investment banker, representing an acquiring company, does not owe a fiduciary duty to the target simply because it received confidential information during the course of tender offer negotiations. In *Walton,* Kennecott Copper Corporation retained Morgan Stanley to advise it about the possible acquisition of Olinkraft, Inc. In the course of negotiations, Olinkraft furnished Morgan Stanley with "inside" information which was to be kept confidential. Although Kennecott ultimately elected not to bid, Morgan Stanley purchased Olinkraft shares for its own account based on the "confidential" information. In rejecting Olinkraft's claim that Morgan Stanley violated section 10(b) by breaching a fiduciary duty owed to Olinkraft, we held that Morgan Stanley had engaged in arm's length bargaining with the target. Morgan Stanley did not become the target's fiduciary simply upon receipt of confidential information. We noted that "we have not found any [cases] that consider[ ] one in Morgan Stanley's position [investment adviser to the 'shark'] to stand in a fiduciary relationship to one in Olinkraft's [the target]." * * *

Relying on *Walton,* Judge Pollack properly concluded that "unless plaintiffs can set forth facts that turn the negotiations from arm's length bargaining into a fiduciary relationship, they cannot claim that Morgan Stanley owed them a fiduciary duty." We recognize that with only "the complaint and the appellee's motion to dismiss, we do not have the benefit of findings of fact about whatever communication occurred between Olinkraft [Deseret], the potential target, and Morgan Stanley, the financial advisor to the potential acquirer: how the communication proceeded, what understandings were reached, what assumptions or expectations the trade's practice would justify." Yet Moss' complaint is patently deficient. It is barren of any factual allegations that might establish a fiduciary relationship between Morgan Stanley and Deseret. The complaint shows only that Morgan Stanley was retained by Warner and represented Warner's interest in the tender offer negotiations with Deseret. The district court correctly found that the complaint did not allege a section 10(b) or rule 10b–5 claim premised on Morgan Stanley's "insider" status.

3. Broker–Dealer Duty

Plaintiff's final attempt to establish a cognizable duty between himself and the defendants is to argue that Newman violated rule 10b–5 because as a registered broker-dealer he owed a general duty to the market to disclose material nonpublic information prior to trading. Moss relies on the District of Columbia Circuit's decision in Dirks v. SEC, 681 F.2d 824 (D.C.Cir.1982), to support his argument. Such reliance is misplaced. In *Dirks,* the SEC censured a broker-dealer for tipping his clients about irregularities at Equity Funding Corporation of America before he publicly disclosed evidence of corporate fraud. The Circuit Court did not consider whether a broker-dealer's nondisclosure of nonpublic information gives rise to civil liability under section 10(b) or rule 10b–5. In fact, the D.C. Circuit made clear that a "private action for damages might raise questions of standing, causation, and appropriate remedy not pertinent [in *Dirks*]." Moreover, in the Supreme Court's recent reversal of *Dirks,* the Court expressly declined to consider Judge Wright's "novel theory" that "Dirks acquired a fiduciary duty by virtue of his position as an employee of a broker-dealer." Therefore, neither the D.C. Circuit's nor the Supreme Court's decision in *Dirks* lends any support to the plaintiff's argument.

We find nothing in the language or legislative history of section 10(b) or rule 10b–5 to suggest that Congress intended to impose a *special duty of disclosure* on broker-dealers simply by virtue of their status as market professionals. * * * Indeed, to impose such a duty "could have an inhibiting influence on the role of market analysts, which the SEC itself recognizes is necessary to the preservation of a healthy market."

* * *

The defendants in this case—Courtois and his tippees Antoniu and Newman—owed no duty of disclosure to Moss. In working for Morgan Stanley, neither Courtois nor Newman was a traditional "corporate insider," and neither had received any confidential information from the target Deseret. Instead, like Chiarella and Dirks, the defendants were "complete stranger[s] who dealt with the sellers [of Deseret stock] only through impersonal market transactions."

Since Moss failed to demonstrate that he was owed a duty by any defendant, he has failed to state a claim for damages under section 10(b) or rule 10b–5.

D. "Misappropriation" Theory of Disclosure

In addition to arguing that he satisfied the *Chiarella* "duty to disclose" standard, Moss alternatively argues that the district court misread *Chiarella.* He contends that *Chiarella* establishes *only* that "a duty to disclose under § 10(b) does not arise from the mere possession of nonpublic market information." Moss urges us to recognize an exception to *Chiarella* and allow a section 10(b) cause of action against any person who trades on the basis of nonpublic "misappropriated" information.

Both Moss and the SEC premise their "misappropriation" theory on Justice Burger's dissent in *Chiarella:*

> I would read § 10(b) and Rule 10b–5 to encompass and build on this principle: to mean that a person who has misappropriated nonpublic information has an absolute duty to disclose that information or to refrain from trading.

* * * In essence, Moss' theory is that any person who "misappropriates" information owes a general duty of disclosure to the entire marketplace. He asserts that this Court's recognition of the "misappropriation theory" is necessary to effectuate the remedial purposes of the securities laws.

While we agree that the general purpose of the securities laws is to protect investors, the creation of a new species of "fraud" under section 10(b) would "depart[ ] radically from the established doctrine that duty arises from a specific relationship between two parties * * * [and] should not be undertaken absent some explicit evidence of congressional intent."

* * *

In effect, plaintiff's "misappropriation" theory would grant him a windfall recovery simply to discourage tortious conduct by securities purchasers. Yet, the Supreme Court has made clear that section 10(b) and rule 10b–5 protect investors against *fraud;* they do not remedy every instance of undesirable conduct involving securities. As defendants owed no duty of disclosure to plaintiff Moss, they committed no "fraud" in purchasing shares of Deseret stock. * * * We find that plaintiff's "misappropriation" theory clearly contradicts the Supreme Court's holding in both *Chiarella* and *Dirks* and therefore conclude that the complaint fails to state a valid section 10(b) or rule 10b–5 cause of action.

* * *

III. RICO

A. Introduction

In Count II of the amended complaint, plaintiff Moss alleged that defendant Newman's unlawful purchase and sale of Deseret stock constituted a violation of RICO, 18 U.S.C. § 1962(c), thereby subjecting him to civil liability under 18 U.S.C. § 1964(c). The district court dismissed plaintiff's RICO claim on the grounds that the complaint failed to include several allegations "essential" to pleading a RICO claim. We affirm the district court's dismissal of the RICO count, but do not endorse the court's reasons for doing so.

B. Threshold Defect in the Complaint

To state a claim for damages under RICO a plaintiff has two pleading burdens. First, he must allege that the defendant has violated the substantive RICO statute, 18 U.S.C. § 1962 commonly known as "criminal RICO." In so doing, he must allege the existence of seven constituent elements: (1) that the defendant (2) through the commission of two or more acts (3) constituting a "pattern" (4) of "racketeering activity" (5) directly or indirectly invests in, or maintains an interest in, or participates in (6) an "enterprise" (7) the activities of which affect interstate or foreign commerce. Plaintiff must allege adequately defendant's violation of section 1962 before turning to the second burden—i.e., invoking RICO's civil remedies of treble damages, attorneys fees and costs. To satisfy this latter burden, plaintiff must allege that he was "injured in his business or property *by reason of* a violation of section 1962." Moss' complaint fails to carry either pleading burden.

Section 1962

Plaintiff's complaint fails to allege one of the elements needed to state a violation of section 1962—that defendant Newman engaged in "racketeering activity." Section 1961(5) defines "pattern of racketeering activity" as at least two acts of "racketeering activity" occurring within ten years of each other. In turn, section 1961(1)(D) defines "racketeering activity" to include "any offense involving fraud * * * in the sale of securities." Plaintiff sought to satisfy both the "pattern" and "racketeering" elements of RICO by alleging that "[d]efendants' actions as set forth herein in this Complaint constitute at least two acts of fraud in connection with the purchase and sale of securities and as such represent a pattern of racketeering activity within the meaning of RICO." Thus, the complaint clearly relies on Newman's allegedly "fraudulent" securities transactions with respect to Deseret stock as the predicate acts of "racketeering" that form the "pattern" underpinning plaintiff's RICO claim. Such allegations of fraud would ordinarily satisfy RICO's "racketeering activity" pleading prerequisite.

However, in section I of this opinion, we held that plaintiff Moss' pleadings had failed *as a matter of law* to state a claim that Newman had *defrauded* him in violation of section 10(b) and rule 10b–5. In affirming the district court's grant of Newman's 12(b)(6) motion to dismiss, we dismissed plaintiff's claim of "securities fraud" from the complaint. In addition, the district court's dismissal of plaintiff's section 14(e), rule 14(e)–3 and common law fraud claims was never appealed. Therefore, since the complaint contains no *valid* allegation of "fraud," to underpin the "predicate acts" of "racketeering," it necessarily must fail.

* * *

C. District Court Dismissal of RICO

We now turn to the remaining rationales offered by the district court to support its dismissal of plaintiff's RICO claim. The district court dismissed the RICO claim on the grounds that plaintiff had failed to allege several elements essential to pleading such a claim. Most notably, the court found that the complaint failed to allege (1) the existence of an "enterprise" and that this "enterprise" was economically independent from defendants' "pattern of racketeering activity," and (2) that the "enterprise," or any of the defendants, had a tie to "organized crime." We do not agree with the district court's assessment that these omissions required dismissal of the complaint.

1. Civil RICO

The district court's opinion is replete with expressions of concern about the broad scope of civil RICO. The court began its analysis by noting that "[t]he Racketeer Influenced and Corrupt Organizations Act, part of the Organized Crime Control Act of 1970, was designed in a multifaceted campaign against the pervasive presence of organized crime infiltrated in American business and trade," and then cautioned that "[t]he statutory language and recent Supreme Court and Second Circuit precedent, if carefully applied, can be extraordinarily effective in limiting RICO to its intended scope and filtering out many RICO claims that are just efforts to claim treble damages for ordinary violations of criminal or tort laws." The court continued, "The sweep of the statute does not embrace ordinary violators charged in common law fraud actions or federal securities law violations as the predicate offenses for RICO relief," and finally concluded that "there is nothing in the legislative history to suggest that Congress intended to create a private right of action for treble damages for violations of substantive statutes by ordinary business[es] or parties."

We sympathize with the district court's concerns. However, it is not the "[judiciary's] role to reassess the costs and benefits associated with the creation of a dramatically expansive * * * tool for combating organized crime." In this regard we agree with the author of the Note, Civil RICO: The Temptation and Impropriety of Judicial Restriction, 95 Harv.L.Rev. 1101, 1120–21 (1982):

> Courts should not be left to impose liability based on their own tacit determination of which defendants are affiliated with organized crime. Nor should they create standing requirements that would preclude liability in many situations in which legislative intent would compel it. Complaints that RICO may effectively federalize common law fraud and erode recent restrictions on claims for securities fraud are better addressed to Congress than to courts.

Although we appreciate the concerns motivating the district court to limit RICO's scope, we believe that the court misinterpreted the elements essential to pleading a RICO cause of action.

2. Organized Crime

The district court stated that "application of RICO should be restricted sharply to organized crime and the enterprises on which its talons have fastened. Thus, courts in the Southern District and elsewhere have held that RICO claims for damages could be maintained only if there was a tie to organized crime."

It is true that RICO's legislative history states that it was enacted to provide "enhanced sanctions and new remedies to deal with the unlawful activities of those engaged in organized crime." The language of the statute, however, does not premise a RICO violation on proof or allegations of any connection with organized crime.

The *Moss* case is one of a large number of cases in which plaintiffs have added a claim under RICO, which permits recovery of treble damages, to their fraud claims under federal securities law. The holding in *Moss,* that RICO is not limited to situations involving organized crime, was followed by the Supreme Court, in a 5–4 decision. SEDIMA v. IMREX, 473 U.S. 479 (1985). The Supreme Court held that a civil suit under RICO did not require either (a) a prior conviction of the defendant on criminal charges, or (b) a showing of injury from the kind of "racketeering" activity at which RICO was principally directed, i.e., organized crime. The four dissenters felt that this interpretation "validates the federalization of broad areas of state common law of frauds, and it approves the displacement of well-established federal remedial provision." With specific respect to securities law, the dissenters stated:

> In addition to altering fundamentally the federal-state balance in civil remedies, the broad reading of the civil RICO provision also displaces important areas of federal law. For example, one predicate offense under RICO is "fraud in the sale of securities." By alleging two instances of such fraud, a plaintiff might be able to bring a case within the scope of the civil RICO provision. It does not take great legal insight to realize that such a plaintiff would pursue his case under RICO rather than do so solely under the Securities Act of 1933 or the Securities Exchange Act of 1934, which provide both express and implied causes of action for violations of the federal securities laws. Indeed, the federal securities laws contemplate only compensatory damages and ordinarily do not authorize recovery of attorney's fees. By invoking RICO, in contrast, a successful plaintiff will recover both treble damages and attorney's fees.
>
> More importantly, under the Court's interpretation, the civil RICO provision does far more than just increase the available damages. In fact, it virtually eliminates decades of legislative and judicial development of private civil remedies under the federal securities laws. Over the years, courts have paid close attention to matters such as standing, culpability, causation, reliance and materiality, as well as the definitions of "securities" and "fraud." All of this law is now an endangered species because plaintiffs can avoid the limitations of the securities laws merely by alleging violations of other predicate acts. For example, even in cases in which the investment instrument is not a "security" covered by the federal securities laws, RICO will provide a treble damage remedy to a plaintiff who can prove the required pattern of mail or wire fraud. Before RICO, of course, the plaintiff could not have recovered under federal law for the mail or wire fraud violation.

Similarly, a customer who refrained from selling a security during a period in which its market value was declining could allege that, on two occasions, his broker recommended by telephone, as part of a scheme to defraud, that the customer not sell the security. The customer might thereby prevail under civil RICO even though, as neither a purchaser nor a seller, he would not have had standing to bring an action under the federal securities laws.

Liability to the Corporation

One element of the obligation under Rule 10b–5 to refrain from trading on inside information is "the existence of a relationship giving access to information intended to be available only for a corporate purpose and not for the personal benefit of anyone." Cady Roberts & Co., supra. It would therefore seem that the company (or a shareholder suing derivatively on its behalf) should have a right of action under Rule 10b–5 to recover the insider's trading profits, at least where the information he used was intended solely for corporate purposes. However, one significant court-imposed limitation on private rights of action under Rule 10b–5, reaffirmed by the Supreme Court in *Blue Chip,* is that the person bringing the action must be a "purchaser" or "seller" of securities in the transaction in question. The courts have accordingly held that the issuer may not sue to recover an insider's trading profits under Rule 10b–5. See e.g., Davidge v. White, 377 F.Supp. 1084 (S.D. N.Y.1974).

There are, however, three alternative ways in which the insider's profits may be recovered by the corporation. First, they may be recoverable under § 16(b). However, this will only apply if the insider is an officer, director or 10% shareholder, and if there was a matching purchase and sale within a six-month period.

Second, where the SEC brings an injunctive action against an insider for trading in violation of Rule 10b–5, it may request, and the court may grant, as "ancillary relief", a decree ordering the defendant to turn over his profits to the company, "subject to disposition in such manner as the court may direct." See SEC v. Texas Gulf Sulphur Co., 312 F.Supp. 77 (S.D.N.Y.1970), affirmed 446 F.2d 1301 (2d Cir.1971); SEC v. Golconda Mining Co., 327 F.Supp. 257 (S.D.N.Y.1971).

Third, in certain states, a corporation may be able to recover insider trading profits of its officers or directors under common law agency principles of fiduciary duty. See Diamond v. Oreamuno, 24 N.Y.2d 494, 301 N.Y.S.2d 78, 248 N.E.2d 901 (1969); Brophy v. Cities Service Co., 31 Del.Ch. 241, 70 A.2d 5 (1949); Restatement, Second, Agency § 388, Comment c. However, other courts have rejected this approach, holding that the corporation has no right to recover unless it suffered actual damage. See Freeman v. Decio, 584 F.2d 186 (7th Cir. 1978); Schein v. Chasen, 313 So.2d 739 (Fla.1975).

Liability to Persons on the Same Side of the Market

Almost all of the private actions based on insider trading have been brought by people who were on the other side of the market (i.e., those who were selling while the insider was buying, or vice versa). However, at least one commentator has suggested that in many cases of open-market insider trading, the people who are hurt by such trading are not the people on the other side of the market (who, if they intended to trade anyway, may actually have received a *better* price than they would have received if the insider had not been trading). The people who are hurt are those who intended to trade on the same side of the market as the insider and who, because of the market effect of the insider's trades, have to pay more or receive less for their stock than they would have paid or received in the absence of such trading.[1]

The paradigm situation in which a claim of this type could be made is the hostile takeover. A bidder is planning a hostile takeover of a company, at a 50% premium over the current market price. Insiders learn about the bidder's plans, and purchase large amounts of stock in the market, causing the price to rise. The bidder has to pay more for the target company than it had expected. Does it have standing to sue the insiders for its damages under Rule 10b–5? It is a purchaser, as required by the Supreme Court's holding in *Blue Chip,* but it is not a party to the transactions in which the insiders participated.

Two cases arising out of the Ivan Boesky—Dennis Levine insider trading operation have shed some, but not much, light on this question. In FMC v. BOESKY, 852 F.2d 981 (7th Cir.1988), FMC Corporation was planning a recapitalization in which it would buy up all of its publicly-held stock. Boesky bought a large number of FMC shares, allegedly causing the market price to rise and forcing FMC to offer a higher price to its stockholders. FMC sued Boesky under Rule 10b–5. The district court dismissed the claim on the ground that FMC had no standing to sue under Article III of the U.S. Constitution, since it had suffered no damage. The court felt that a payment by a corporation to its own shareholders could not result in damage to the corporation because the shareholders are the owners of the corporation. The Court of Appeals reversed, holding that FMC had been damaged by the misappropriation of its proprietary information about its own plans, and remanded the case to the district court without passing on any of the statutory issues.

In LITTON v. LEHMAN, 709 F.Supp. 438 (S.D.N.Y.1989), Litton was planning a bid to acquire all the stock of Itek for $40 a share, and retained Lehman Brothers as its investment banker. Levine, who worked for Lehman, and his associates purchased an aggregate of 60,000 shares of Itek in the open market over a six-week period. Litton subsequently acquired Itek for $48 a share, and sued Levine and his associates to recover the extra amount it had to pay. The defendants

1. Wang, Trading on Material Non–Public Information on Impersonal Stock Markets: Who Is Harmed, and Who Can Sue Whom Under SEC Rule 10b–5, 54 So. Cal.L.Rev. 1217 (1981).

did not contest Litton's standing to sue under Rule 10b–5. However, the court granted summary judgment to defendants on the 10b–5 claim on the ground that there was no evidence that defendants' purchases "caused" Litton to pay the higher price. The court found that Itek's directors would probably have rejected any offer of less than $48 a share, based on their evaluation of the "inherent value" of Itek rather than the market price of its shares, and that, since Litton was only interested in a "friendly" takeover, it could not have acquired Itek for less than that price even if defendants had not traded.

New Statutory Penalties and Liabilities

In view of the prevailing uncertainty as to the availability of a private damage remedy for insider trading and as to the adequacy of existing penalties in deterring insider trading, the SEC urged Congress to enact stiffer sanctions. Congress responded with two pieces of legislation, the Insider Trading Sanctions Act of 1984 (ITSA) and the Insider Trading and Securities Fraud Enforcement Act of 1988 (ITSFEA), adding new §§ 20A and 21A to the 1934 Act.

Under § 21A, if any person violates the 1934 Act or any rule thereunder by trading while in possession of material nonpublic information, or by communicating such information in connection with a securities transaction, the SEC can go to court to seek a civil penalty equal to three times the amount of the profit gained or the loss avoided by the illegal transaction. "Profit" or "loss" is defined as the difference between the purchase or sale price and the value of the security a reasonable period after public dissemination of the nonpublic information. The SEC may seek such a penalty both against the person who committed the violation and on any person who "controlled" the violator (which, in most cases will mean the firm with which the violator is associated). The penalty imposed on the "controlling person" cannot exceed $1 million and can only be imposed if the SEC establishes that such person knowingly or recklessly failed to take appropriate steps or establish adequate procedures to prevent such violations. The amount of the penalty is reduced by any amount the defendant is required to disgorge in an injunction action brought by the Commission under § 21(d).

To provide an incentive for people to "blow the whistle" on insider trading, § 21A(e) provides that up to 10% of any civil penalty recovered by the SEC may, in the SEC's discretion, be paid as a bounty to any person or persons who provide information leading to the imposition of the penalty. In June 1989, the SEC issued rules and guidelines governing the award of these bounties. See Rules 61–68 of SEC Rules of Practice, 17 C.F.R. § 201.61–68, and Sec.Ex.Act Rel. No. 26994 (June 30, 1989).

Under § 20A, any person who violates the 1934 Act or any rule thereunder by trading while in possession of material nonpublic information is liable to any person who was "contemporaneously" trading the same security on the other side of the market. (This in effect reverses the result in Moss v. Morgan Stanley, p. 613 above.) Liability under this Section also extends to any person who communicates material nonpublic information and to any person who "controls" the violator, and is similarly reduced by the amount of any disgorgement in an injunction action brought by the SEC.

An action under either § 20A or § 21A may be brought up to five years after the last violation, a considerably longer statute of limitations than is found in other specific civil liability provisions of the federal securities laws (see pp. 499–504 above).

During the hearings on the 1984 Act, Congress was urged to define more precisely the kind of insider trading that would give rise to liability. However, faced with irreconcilable differences between the SEC and industry views, Congress finally opted to define the offense simply by reference to existing law.

The 1988 amendment also modified § 32 of the 1934 Act to increase the maximum criminal penalty for violation of the Act from $100,000 to $1 million, in the case of individuals, and from $500,000 to $2.5 million, in the case of other entities.

Selected References

Insider Trading

T. Hazen, Securities Regulation § 13.9 (2d ed. 1990).

D. Langevoort, Insider Trading Regulation (1988).

H. Manne, Insider Trading and the Stock Market (1966).

Brudney, Insiders, Outsiders, and Informational Advantages under the Federal Securities Laws, 93 Harv.L.Rev. 322 (1979).

Cox, Insider Trading and Contracting: A Critical Response to the "Chicago School," 1986 Duke L.J. 628 (1986).

Cox & Fogarty, Bases of Insider Trading Law, 49 Ohio St.L.J. 353 (1988).

Haddock & Macey, A Coasian Model of Insider Trading, 80 Nw.U.L.Rev. 1449 (1986).

Macey, Ethics, Economics and Insider Trading: Ayn Rand Meets the Theory of the Firm, 11 Harv.J.L. & Pub.Pol. 785 (1988).

Wang, Trading on Material Non–Public Information on Impersonal Stock Markets, 54 So.Cal.L.Rev. 1217 (1981).

RICO

T. Hazen, Securities Regulation § 19.3 (2d ed. 1990).

Lynch, RICO: The Crime of Being a Criminal, 87 Colum.L.Rev. 661 (1987).

McArthur & White, Civil RICO after *Sedima:* The New Weapon Against Business Fraud, 23 Houst.L.Rev. 743 (1986).

*

PART III

REGULATION OF CORPORATE CONDUCT

In this portion of the book, we examine the application of the federal securities laws to activities of publicly-held corporations other than the public offering of their securities. We will focus principally on four areas: corporate disclosure requirements; transactions between corporations and their managements or controlling shareholders; mergers and acquisitions; and takeovers and tender offers. In each of these areas there is an interplay between specific statutory provisions and rules and the more general "antifraud" provisions discussed in Chapter 4.

CHAPTER 6

CORPORATE DISCLOSURE REQUIREMENTS

A. SPECIFIC DISCLOSURE REQUIREMENTS

One principal thrust of the Securities Exchange Act of 1934 was to assure the public availability of adequate information about companies with publicly-traded stocks. As amended in 1964, the Act's disclosure requirements apply not only to companies with securities listed on national securities exchanges, but also to all companies with more than 500 shareholders and more than $1,000,000 of assets. § 12(a), (g). Certain special types of issuers are exempted, including investment companies, § 12(g)(2)(B), and insurance companies if they are subject to comparable state requirements, § 12(g)(2)(G). Banks are subject to the requirements, but administration and enforcement with respect to them are vested in the federal banking agencies rather than the SEC. § 12(i). About 9,000 companies are currently subject to 1934 Act disclosure requirements, of which about 3,000 have securities listed on exchanges and about 6,000 have securities traded solely in the over-the-counter market. As part of its effort to reduce administrative burdens on small companies, the SEC in April 1982 adopted a new rule exempting any issuer with less than $3,000,000 of assets from the Act's disclosure requirements. In 1986, Rule 12g–1 was amended to extend the exemption to issuers with up to $5,000,000 of assets.

The specific requirements for disclosure of information about the issuing company are found in §§ 12, 13, and 14. § 12 requires the filing of a detailed statement about the company when it first registers under the 1934 Act, and § 13 requires a registered company to file with the SEC "such annual reports * * * and such quarterly reports * * * as the Commission may prescribe."

The basic reports required to be filed with the SEC under § 13 are (a) an annual report on Form 10–K, (b) a quarterly report on Form 10–Q, and (c) a current report on Form 8–K for any month in which certain specified events occur.

In October 1970, the Commission substantially revised its forms for registration and reporting under Sections 12 and 13 of the 1934 Act. Form 10, the general form for initial registration of a class of securities under Section 12, was revised to make its disclosures correspond more closely to those required in a 1933 Act registration statement or a proxy statement under Section 14 of the 1934 Act. Sec.Ex.Act Rel. No. 8996 (Oct. 14, 1970). Form 10–K, the general form of annual report for companies registered under the 1934 Act, was revised "to provide on an annual basis information which, together with that contained in the proxy or information statement sent to security holders, will furnish a reasonably complete and up-to-date statement of the business and operations of the registrant." Sec.Ex.Act Rel. No. 9000 (Oct. 21, 1970). A new form 10–Q was adopted, under which registered companies must file quarterly reports containing summarized financial information for each of the first three quarters of their fiscal years. Sec.Ex.Act Rel. No. 9004 (Oct. 28, 1970).

In 1977, the Commission took a further step toward conforming the disclosure requirements under the 1934 Act to those under the 1933 Act by adopting a new Regulation S–K. Sec.Act Rel. No. 5893 (Dec. 23, 1977). Regulation S–K, which was substantially expanded in 1982, now sets forth virtually all of the substantive disclosure requirements applicable to documents filed under either the 1933 Act or the 1934 Act. It thus serves as an important link in the integration of 1933 and 1934 Act disclosure requirements.

Section 14 makes it unlawful for a company registered under the 1934 Act to solicit proxies from its shareholders "in contravention of such rules and regulations as the Commission may prescribe as necessary or appropriate in the public interest or for the protection of investors." Under this authority, the Commission has promulgated detailed regulations prescribing the form of proxy and the information to be furnished to shareholders in the accompanying "proxy statement," with special provisions relating to shareholder proposals, proxy contests, and other matters. In 1964, the reach of § 14 was broadened by the addition of § 14(c), under which a company, even if it does not solicit proxies from its shareholders in connection with a meeting, must furnish them with information "substantially equivalent" to that which would be required if it did solicit proxies.

The "proxy rules" promulgated by the SEC under § 14 thus serve as an important instrument of disclosure in connection with the annual meeting of shareholders for the election of directors (as well as special meetings called to obtain approval of mergers or other significant corporate changes). Their impact has been further broadened by the inclusion of references to the annual report (the non-statutory one) which a company normally sends to its shareholders after the close of the fiscal year and before the annual meeting.

Rule 14a–3, as first adopted by the Commission in 1942, required every registered company, when soliciting proxies for its annual meeting for election of directors, to furnish each shareholder with an annual report "containing such financial statements for the last fiscal year as will, in the opinion of the management, adequately reflect the financial position and operations of the issuer." Such financial statements, however, "may be in any form deemed suitable by the management." Sec.Ex.Act Rel. No. 3347 (1942). In 1964, the rule was amended to require that the financial statements in the annual report to shareholders be audited, and that there be a notation of any material differences between such financial statements and those filed with the Commission. Sec.Ex.Act Rel. No. 7324 (1964). In 1967 it was further amended to require comparative financial statements for the past *two* fiscal years, rather than just the past year. Sec.Ex.Act Rel. No. 8029 (1967).

With respect to non-financial information, the Commission in 1965 amended the rule to require a company, in its first annual report to shareholders after it became subject to the proxy rules, to include such information as to the business done by the company as will "indicate the general nature and scope of the business." Sec.Ex.Act Rel. No. 7508 (1965). In 1974, this provision was substantially expanded to require a registered company to include in *each* annual report to shareholders "a summary of the issuer's operations for the last five fiscal years and a management analysis thereof; a brief description of the issuer's business; a lines of business breakdown for the issuer's last five fiscal years; the identification of the issuer's directors and executive officers and the disclosure of each such person's principal occupation or employment and of the name and principal business of any organization by which such person is so employed; and the identification of the principal market in which securities entitled to vote at the meeting are traded and a statement of the market price ranges of such securities and dividends paid on such securities for each quarterly period during the issuer's two most recent fiscal years." Sec.Ex.Act Rel. No. 11079 (Oct. 31, 1974).

An SEC Advisory Committee on Corporate Disclosure noted in 1977 that while the annual and quarterly reports filed with the SEC were more complete, the writing style in the reports distributed to shareholders was more readable. It accordingly recommended that registrants be encouraged to use their annual and quarterly reports to shareholders as filing documents in lieu of preparing separate 10–K and 10–Q reports. The Commission responded by issuing guidelines for combining annual and quarterly reports with the information required by the forms to satisfy the requirements of § 13. Sec.Ex.Act Rel. No. 13639 (June 17, 1977).

In 1980–81, the Commission took several additional steps toward integrating the annual and quarterly reports to shareholders with the reports required to be filed at the SEC. First, it amended Rule 14a–3 to expand the categories of information required to be included in the annual report to shareholders. Second, it required that certain of that information be presented in accordance with the provisions of Regulation S–K (the general regulation governing disclosure in 1933 and 1934 Act filings). Third, it substantially revised the Form 10–K annual reporting form and the Form 10–Q quarterly reporting form to permit much of the information required by those forms to be incorporated by reference to the company's annual and quarterly reports to shareholders. Sec.Ex.Act Rels. Nos. 17114 (Sept. 2, 1980), 17524 (Feb. 9, 1981).

At the same time, the commission also adopted a controversial requirement that the Form 10–K annual report be signed not only by the company, but also by its principal executive, financial and accounting officers and by at least a majority of the board of directors (the same as the signature requirements applicable to a 1933 Act registration statement). The Commission stated that it did "not believe that this expansion [would] have substantial legal effect, [since] in the commission's view the persons who would be required to sign the revised form are presently legally responsible for the information content of the existing form." Sec.Ex.Act Rel. No. 16496 (Jan. 15, 1980). The Commission's stated reason for imposing the new signature requirement was that "just as its rules and the administrative focus of the Division of Corporation Finance are being realigned to reflect the shift in emphasis toward relying on periodic disclosure under the Exchange Act, so too the attention of the private sector, including management, directors, accountants, and attorneys, must also be refocused towards Exchange Act filings if a sufficient degree of discipline is to be instilled in the system to make it work." Sec.Ex.Act Rel. No. 17114 (Sept. 2, 1980).

A company with a relatively small number of shareholders may find these disclosure requirements unduly burdensome. Under § 12(g)(4) of the 1934 Act, a company may terminate its registration if its shares are held of record by fewer than 300 persons. One method frequently used to reduce the number of shareholders below 300 is a reverse stock split (for example, one new share for each 1,000 shares outstanding) with holders of fractional shares being paid off in cash. In 1987, Bacardi Corp. attempted to accomplish deregistration in this manner. However, a dissident shareholder who held 238,000 shares transferred them to 238 separate trusts, each of which held one new share after the reverse split, thus increasing the number of record holders to more than 300. In February 1990, an SEC administrative law judge held that there was no basis for concluding that the trusts were fictitious or non-existent persons, denied Bacardi's request to terminate its registration, and ordered Bacardi to file all of its past-due reports under § 13. In Re Bacardi, Admin.Proc. No. 3–7019, 22 BNA Sec.Reg. & L.Rep. 274 (1990).

Note on the Proxy Rules

Section 14(a) of the 1934 Act gives the SEC virtually a "blank check" to write rules governing the solicitation of proxies for shareholder meetings. Since the subject of proxy solicitation has become intimately intertwined with questions relating to shareholder action, it is generally treated at considerable length in the course on Corporation Law, rather than in Securities Regulation. The following is a brief summary of the major features of the proxy rules.

Section 14 makes it unlawful for a company registered under § 12 to solicit proxies from its shareholders "in contravention of such rules and regulations as the Commission may prescribe as necessary or appropriate in the public interest or for the protection of investors." In 1964, the reach of § 14 was broadened by the addition of § 14(c), under which a company, even if it does not solicit proxies from its shareholders in connection with a meeting, must furnish them with information "substantially equivalent" to that which would be required if it did solicit proxies. Under § 14(f), added in 1968, a corporation must also make disclosures to shareholders when a majority of its board of directors is replaced by action of the directors, without a shareholders' meeting, in connection with the transfer of a controlling stock interest.

Disclosure. Under this authority, the Commission has promulgated detailed regulations prescribing the form of proxy and the information to be furnished to shareholders. Prior to every meeting of its security holders, a registered company must furnish each of them with a "proxy statement" containing the information specified in Schedule 14A, together with a form of proxy on which the security holder can indicate his approval or disapproval of each proposal expected to be presented at the meeting. Rules 14a–3, 4. Where securities are registered in the names of brokers, banks or nominees, the company must inquire as to the beneficial ownership of the securities, furnish sufficient copies of the proxy statement for distribution to all of the beneficial owners, and pay the reasonable expenses of such distribution. Rule 14a–3(d).

Definitive copies of the proxy statement and form of proxy must be filed with the SEC at the time they are first mailed to security holders. In addition, if the proxy solicitation relates to any matters other than election of directors, approval of accountants, or shareholder proposals, preliminary copies of both documents must be filed with the SEC ten days before they are to be mailed. Rule 14a–6. Although the proxy statement does not have to become "effective" in the same manner as a 1933 Act registration statement (see § 8 supra), the SEC will often comment on, and insist on changes in, the proxy statement before it is mailed.

Proxy Contests. The SEC proxy rules apply to all solicitations of proxies, consents or authorizations from security holders, by the management or anyone else, subject to exceptions specified in Rule 14a–2. When there is a contest with respect to election or removal of directors, Rule 14a–11 imposes special procedural requirements, and calls for the filing with the Commission of additional information specified in Schedule 14B.

Shareholder Proposals. Under Rule 14a–8, if a security holder of a registered company gives timely notice to the management of his intention to present a proposal for action at a forthcoming meeting, the management must include the proposal, with a supporting statement of not more than 500 words, in its proxy statement and afford security holders an opportunity to vote for or against it in the management's proxy. To be eligible to have such a proposal included, the security holder must own at least $1,000 worth, or 1%, of the securities entitled to be voted at the meeting.

This rule has been extensively utilized by proponents of "shareholder democracy," to require inclusion of proposals relating to management compensation, conduct of annual meetings, shareholder voting rights, and similar matters. It has also been utilized by persons opposed to the Vietnam war, discrimination, pollution, and other evils, to attempt to force changes in company policies that affect those matters.

Since management generally resists the inclusion of shareholder proposals, the provisions of the rule specifying the kinds of proposals that can be omitted have been the subject of constant controversy and frequent change. As presently in effect, Rule 14a–8(c) permits management to exclude a proposal if, among other things, it

(1) is under governing state law, not a proper subject for action by security holders;

(2) would require the company to violate any law;

(3) is contrary to the SEC proxy rules;

(4) relates to redress of a personal claim or grievance;

(5) relates to operations which account for less than 5% of the company's business;

(6) is beyond the company's power to effectuate;

(7) deals with the company's ordinary business operations;

(8) relates to an election to office;

(9) is counter to a management proposal;

(10) has been rendered moot;

(11) is duplicative of another proposal included in the proxy statement; or

(12) is substantially similar to a proposal previously submitted during the past five years, which received affirmative votes from less than a specified percentage of the shares voted.

In case of a dispute between management and a shareholder as to whether a particular proposal may be excluded from the proxy statement, the decision in the first instance is for the SEC. The Commission initially took the position that its refusal to direct a company to include a proposal is not an "order" subject to judicial review under § 25, but one court disagreed. MEDICAL COMMITTEE v. SEC, 432 F.2d 659 (D.C.Cir.1970), vacated as moot, 404 U.S. 403 (1972). However, the Commission subsequently discovered that it could avoid judicial review by delegating to its staff the power to decide individual cases, and declining to review the staff decision. KIXMILLER v. SEC, 492 F.2d 641 (D.C.Cir.1974).

Note on Suspension of Trading Under the 1934 Act

If a company fails to file its required reports under the 1934 Act, or files reports containing material inaccuracies, the SEC can go to court for an injunction under § 21(d). It can also take action on its own to suspend trading in the security if there is insufficient information available to permit informed trading.

Under Sections 12(j) and (k) of the Securities Exchange Act, the SEC has the power to revoke or suspend the registration of a security under the Act, thus in effect prohibiting any trading in that security on an exchange or in the over-the-counter market. Section 12(j), which is relatively rarely used, authorizes the Commission to revoke the registration of a security, or suspend it for up to 12 months, if, after notice and opportunity for hearing, the Commission finds that the issuer has violated any provision of the Act.

Section 12(k), which is much more frequently invoked, authorizes the Commission to suspend trading in a security "summarily" (i.e., without any notice or hearing) for a period not exceeding ten days "if in its opinion the public interest and the protection of investors so require." The legislative history of the predecessor of § 12(k) indicates that it was intended to permit the suspension of trading "when fraudulent or manipulative practices * * * have deprived [a] security of a fair and orderly market, or when some corporate event has made informed trading impossible and has created conditions in which investors are likely to be deceived." [a]

Generally, the Commission requires the issuance of a statement clarifying the issuer's business and financial situation as a condition of lifting a suspension of trading. The following example is taken from a Commission release announcing the termination of a suspension of trading and quoting from a letter sent by the company to its shareholders: [b]

> Robert C. Wade, president of Santa Fe International, Inc., a Colorado corporation, today issued the following statement in order to clarify numerous unfounded rumors concerning the company and to provide current information concerning its business operations, financial condition, and assets.
>
> Santa Fe International, Inc. (formerly Santa Fe Uranium & Oil Co., Inc.), was organized in 1955 and it is capitalized at 10,000,000 shares of common capital stock authorized and outstanding with a par value of 1¢ per share. * * *
>
> The following rumors concerning Santa Fe have been circulating, none of which are true. They are absolutely *false.* We do not have two former governors of Colorado on our board of directors. We are not operating a silver mine. We are not being taken over by an insurance company. We do not have the food and beverage concessions on the ship Queen Mary located at Long Beach, California. We are absolutely not contemplating the purchase of the ship Queen Elizabeth. We are not contemplating building a ski lodge near Georgetown, Colorado. The corporate management will inform the Stockholders, in writing, of any developments which would change the status of the corporation, and we will not be responsible for unfounded rumors and false information from any other source.
>
> As of February 1, 1968, the company, based upon unaudited financial statements, had current assets consisting of cash in the sum of $7.80. As of such date, the company's current liabilities far exceeded its limited current assets. * * *

a. S.Rep. No. 379, 88th Cong., 1st Sess., at 66 (1963).

b. Sec.Ex.Act Rel. No. 8284 (March 20, 1968).

While § 12(k) speaks in terms of a suspension for not more than ten days, the Commission for many years asserted, and exercised, its power to issue successive ten-day suspension orders over periods of several years while it conducted an investigation of an issuer's affairs. In 1978, however, the Supreme Court put a stop to this practice. In SEC v. SLOAN, 436 U.S. 103 (1978), a case involving 37 successive ten-day suspension orders, the Court held that the SEC has no such power under the statute:

> * * * We note that this is not a case where the Commission, discovering the existence of a manipulative scheme affecting CJL stock, suspended trading for 10 days and then, upon the discovery of a second manipulative scheme or other improper activity unrelated to the first scheme, ordered a second 10–day suspension. Instead it is a case in which the Commission issued a series of summary suspension orders lasting over a year on the basis of evidence revealing a single, though likely sizable, manipulative scheme. Thus, the only question confronting us is whether, even upon a periodic redetermination of "necessity," the Commission is statutorily authorized to issue a series of summary suspension orders based upon a single set of events or circumstances which threaten an orderly market. This question must, in our opinion, be answered in the negative.
>
> The first and most salient point leading us to this conclusion is the language of the statute. Section 12(k) authorizes the Commission "summarily to suspend trading in any security * * * *for a period not exceeding ten days* * * *." The Commission would have us read the underscored phrase as a limitation only upon the duration of a single suspension order. So read, the Commission could indefinitely suspend trading in a security without any hearing or other procedural safeguards as long as it redetermined every 10 days that suspension was required by the public interest and for the protection of investors. While perhaps not an impossible reading of the statute, we are persuaded it is not the most natural or logical one. The duration limitation rather appears on its face to be just that—a maximum time period for which trading can be suspended for any single set of circumstances.
>
> Apart from the language of the statute, which we find persuasive in and of itself, there are other reasons to adopt this construction of the statute. In the first place, the power to summarily suspend trading in a security even for 10 days, without any notice, opportunity to be heard or findings based upon a record, is an awesome power with a potentially devastating impact on the issuer, its shareholders, and other investors. A clear mandate from Congress, such as that found in § 12(k), is necessary to confer this power. No less clear a mandate can be expected from Congress to authorize the Commission to extend, virtually without limit, these periods of suspension. But we find no such unmistakable mandate in § 12(k). Indeed, if anything, that section points in the opposite direction.
>
> Other sections of the statute reinforce the conclusion that in this area Congress considered summary restrictions to be somewhat drastic and properly used only for very brief periods of time. When explicitly longer term, though perhaps temporary, measures are to be taken

against some person, company or security, Congress invariably requires the Commission to give some sort of notice and opportunity to be heard. * * *

Justices Brennan and Marshall, concurring, were even more vehement about the SEC's actions:

The Court's opinion does not reveal how flagrantly abusive the Securities and Exchange Commission's use of its § 12(k) authority has been. That section authorizes the Commission "summarily to suspend trading in any security * * * for a period not exceeding ten days * * *." As the Court says, this language "is persuasive in and of itself" that 10 days is the "maximum time period for which trading can be suspended for any single set of circumstances." But the Commission has used § 12(k), or its predecessor statutes to suspend trading in a security for up to 13 *years*. And, although the 13–year suspension is an extreme example, the record is replete with suspensions lasting the better part of a year. I agree that § 12(k) is clear on its face and that it prohibits this administrative practice. But even if § 12(k) were unclear, a 13–year suspension, or even a one-year suspension as here, without notice or hearing so obviously violates fundamentals of due process and fair play that no reasonable individual could suppose that Congress intended to authorize such a thing.

* * *

Moreover, the SEC's procedural implementation of its § 12(k) power mocks any conclusion other than that the SEC simply could not care whether its § 12(k) orders are justified. So far as this record shows, the SEC never reveals the reasons for its suspension orders.[1] To be sure, here respondent was able long after the fact to obtain some explanation through a Freedom of Information Act request, but even the information tendered was heavily excised and none of it even purports to state the reasoning of the Commissioners under whose authority § 12(k) orders issue.[2] Nonetheless, when the SEC finally agreed to give respondent a hearing on the suspension of Canadian Javelin stock, it required respondent to state, in a verified petition, (that is, *under oath*) why he thought the unrevealed conclusions of the SEC to be wrong. This is obscurantism run riot.

1. The only document made public by the SEC at the time it suspends trading in a security is a "Notice of Suspension of Trading." Numerous copies of this notice are included in the Appendix and each contains only the boilerplate explanation:

"It appearing to the Securities and Exchange Commission that the summary suspension of trading in such securities on such exchange and otherwise than on a national securities exchange is required in the public interest and for the protection of investors; [therefore, trading is suspended]."

2. In each instance, the explanation consists only of memoranda from the SEC's Division of Enforcement *to* the Commission. In at least one instance, the memorandum post-dates the public notice of suspension. In no case is there a memorandum *from* the Commission explaining its action. The Court apparently assumes that the memoranda of the Division of Enforcement adequately explain the Commission's action, although the basis for any such assumption is not apparent. Moreover, since the recommendations portion of each memoranda is excised, presumably as permitted (but not required) by exemption 5 of the Freedom of Information Act, there is no statement of reasons in any traditional sense in any of the memoranda.

Accordingly while we today leave open the question whether the SEC could tack successive 10-day suspensions if this were necessary to meet first one and then a different emergent situation, I for one would look with great disfavor on any effort to tack suspension periods unless the SEC concurrently adopted a policy of stating its reasons for each suspension. Without such a statement of reasons, I fear our holding today will have no force since the SEC's administration of its suspension power will be reviewable, if at all, only by the circuitous and time-consuming path followed by respondent here.

In the wake of the *Sloan* decision, the SEC's use of trading suspensions dropped dramatically. From a level of more than 100 trading suspensions in each of the years 1973 to 1977, it dropped to about 23 a year in 1979 to 1981, and since 1982 has averaged less than 10 a year.

B. APPLICABILITY OF RULE 10b-5

The provisions of §§ 12, 13 and 14 of the 1934 Act require specific disclosures in specified documents at regular intervals or on specified occasions; they do not purport to govern the voluntary disclosures made by companies through reports to shareholders, press releases or other means. However, in the *Texas Gulf Sulphur* case, p. 469 above, the court held that any statement by a publicly-held company which would affect the judgment of investors as to the value of its securities was deemed to be "in connection with" the market transactions taking place in those securities, and therefore within the ambit of Rule 10b-5. Any report, brochure, press release or other communication, therefore, which misstates or omits a material fact may give rise to liability under clause (2) or (3) of the Rule.

Since the Supreme Court decisions in *Hochfelder* and *Aaron*, pp. 455, 463 above, it is clear that there can be no liability under Rule 10b-5 unless the company acted with the requisite degree of *scienter* in making the misstatement. A large number of actions have been brought against companies under the Rule, alleging intentional misstatements in their annual or quarterly reports, press releases, or other documents. There is some residual uncertainty, however, as to whether or when a company may violate the Rule by (a) failing to make a statement concerning changes in its situation, or (b) failing to correct misstatements about the company being made by others.

FINANCIAL INDUSTRIAL FUND v. McDONNELL DOUGLAS CORP., 474 F.2d 514 (10th Cir.1973). On the basis of the facts described in the *Investors Management* case at p. 564 above, a mutual fund which had purchased 80,000 shares of Douglas common stock on June 22 and 23, 1966, sued Douglas for the loss it suffered after Douglas reported reduced earnings on June 24. The theory of the complaint was that

Douglas had withheld the announcement of reduced earnings beyond the point in time at which the relevant facts were available to it. The trial was held before a jury, which rendered a verdict for the plaintiff in the amount of $712,500. Douglas' motion for judgment n.o.v. was denied, and Douglas appealed:

Defendant Douglas argues that the elements of an action under Rule 10b–5 were not shown. Specifically, defendant urges that the plaintiff failed to show facts to meet the scienter standards or requirements, which were applicable to a complaint alleging a failure to issue the special earnings statement at an earlier time.

* * * [T]he information about which the issues revolve must be "available and ripe for publication" before there commences a duty to disclose. To be ripe under this requirement, the contents must be verified sufficiently to permit the officers and directors to have full confidence in their accuracy. It also means, as used by the Second Circuit, that there is no valid corporate purpose which dictates the information be not disclosed. As to the verification of the data aspect, the hazards which arise from an erroneous statement are apparent, especially when it has not been carefully prepared and tested. It is equally obvious that an undue delay not in good faith, in revealing facts, can be deceptive, misleading, or a device to defraud under Rule 10b–5.

* * *

To prevail the plaintiff in this silence case had the burden of proof to establish that it exercised due care in making its stock purchase, that the defendant failed to issue the special earnings statement when sufficient information was available for an accurate release (or could have been collected by the exercise of due diligence), and to show there existed a duty owed by the defendant to the plaintiff to so disclose as to do otherwise would be a violation of Rule 10b–5, and upon inaction under such showing plaintiff relied to its detriment. The defendant as a separate defense could show either good faith or the exercise of good business judgment in its acts or inaction. The evaluation of the significance of the change in defendant's earnings as it might affect the corporation, its stockholders, or persons considering the purchase of stock, called for the exercise of discretion, and upon a showing of the exercise of due care in the gathering and consideration of the facts, a presumption arose that the evaluation made was in the exercise of good business judgment although subsequent events might show the decision to have been in error.

* * *

Under the standards herein set out, the trial court should have granted the motion of defendant Douglas for judgment notwithstanding the verdict. We have considered the evidence most favorable to the plaintiff, and have given it the benefit of all reasonable inferences which may be drawn from the evidence. The evidence as to Douglas, as indicated above, shows the presence of a strong motive to delay the publication of figures showing a decline in earnings, but there is no proof that there was such a delay within the legal standards set forth above. There was speculation and innuendo, but no facts. Thus under the standards heretofore set forth by this court and herein described, the trial court should have granted defendant's motion for judgment n.o.v.

In STATE TEACHERS v. FLUOR CORP., 654 F.2d 843 (2d Cir. 1981), the court held that a corporation was not liable to stockholders who sold stock after the corporation was awarded a major construction contract but before the contract was made public. The court held that the corporation had not violated Rule 10b-5 either (a) by withholding announcement of the award (which it was contractually obligated to keep confidential until a later date) or (b) by failing to request the New York Stock Exchange to suspend trading in its stock when the stock price and trading volume suddenly increased sharply. The court also declined, under the circumstances, to imply a private right of action for violation of the provisions of the New York Stock Exchange Company Manual requiring prompt disclosure of significant developments.

In STAFFIN v. GREENBERG, 672 F.2d 1196 (3d Cir.1982), the court refused to hold a company liable for failing to disclose material events, stating that "plaintiffs have not called our attention to any case, including *TGS,* which imposed any duty of disclosure under the Federal Securities Laws on a corporation which is *not* trading in its own stock and which has *not* made a public statement."

In ELKIND v. LIGGETT & MYERS, 635 F.2d 156 (2d Cir.1980), the court was faced with an allegation by shareholders that "Liggett, by virtue of its alleged cultivation of favorable reports and forecasts by analysts, incurred an obligation to disclose its less optimistic internal predictions."

> We have no doubt that a company may so involve itself in the preparation of reports and projections by outsiders as to assume a duty to correct material errors in those projections. This may occur when officials of the company have by their activity, made an implied representation that the information they have reviewed is true or at least in accordance with the company's views. Cf. Kerbs v. Fall River Industries, 502 F.2d 731, 739–40 (10th Cir.1974); Green v. Jonhop, 358 F.Supp. 413, 418–20 (D.Or.1973); Moerman v. Zipco, 302 F.Supp. 439, 446 (E.D.N.Y.1969), *affd. per curiam,* 422 F.2d 871 (2d Cir.1970).
>
> After reviewing the facts of this case, however, we find no reason to reverse as clearly erroneous the district court's finding that Liggett did not place its imprimatur, expressly or impliedly, on the analysts' projections. The company did examine and comment on a number of reports, but its policy was to refrain from comment on earnings forecasts. Testimony at trial indicated that the analysts knew they were not being made privy to the company's internal projections. While the evidence leaves little doubt that Liggett made suggestions as to factual and descriptive matters in a number of the reports it reviewed, the record does not compel the conclusion that this conduct carried a suggestion that the analysts' projections were consistent with Liggett's internal estimates. Nor has plaintiff demonstrated that

Liggett left uncorrected any *factual* statements which it knew or believed to be erroneous. Thus, Liggett assumed no duty to disclose its own forecasts or to warn the analysts and the public) that their optimistic view was not shared by the company.

While we find no liability for non-disclosure in this aspect of the present case, it bears noting that corporate pre-release review of the reports of analysts is a risky activity, fraught with danger. Management must navigate carefully between the "Scylla" of misleading stockholders and the public by implied approval of reviewed analyses and the "Charybdis" of tipping material inside information by correcting statements which it knows to be erroneous. A company which undertakes to correct errors in reports presented to it for review may find itself forced to choose between raising no objection to a statement which, because it is contradicted by internal information, may be misleading and making that information public at a time when corporate interests would best be served by confidentiality.

In recent years, the most frequently-litigated issue of corporate disclosure has been the liability of a corporation to purchasers or sellers of its stock for failing to make prompt disclosure of negotiations for mergers or acquisitions. In GREENFIELD v. HEUBLEIN, 742 F.2d 751 (3d Cir.1984), the court held that there was no duty to disclose merger negotiations until an "agreement in principle" on the price and structure of the transaction had been reached. The issue reached the Supreme Court for review in 1988.

BASIC v. LEVINSON

485 U.S. 224 (1988).

JUSTICE BLACKMUN delivered the opinion of the Court.

This case requires us to apply the materiality requirement of § 10(b) of the Securities Exchange Act of 1934, (1934 Act), and the Securities and Exchange Commission's Rule 10b–5, promulgated thereunder, in the context of preliminary corporate merger discussions. We must also determine whether a person who traded a corporation's shares on a securities exchange after the issuance of a materially misleading statement by the corporation may invoke a rebuttable presumption that, in trading, he relied on the integrity of the price set by the market.

I

Prior to December 20, 1978, Basic Incorporated was a publicly traded company primarily engaged in the business of manufacturing chemical refractories for the steel industry. As early as 1965 or 1966, Combustion Engineering, Inc., a company producing mostly alumina-based refractories, expressed some interest in acquiring Basic, but was deterred from pursuing this inclination seriously because of antitrust concerns it then entertained. In 1976, however, regulatory action opened the way to a renewal of Combustion's interest. The "Strategic Plan," dated October 25, 1976, for Combustion's Industrial Products Group included the objective: "Acquire Basic Inc. $30 million."

Beginning in September, 1976, Combustion representatives had meetings and telephone conversations with Basic officers and directors, including petitioners here, concerning the possibility of a merger. During 1977 and 1978, Basic made three public statements denying that it was engaged in merger negotiations.[4] On December 18, 1978, Basic asked the New York Stock Exchange to suspend trading in its shares and issued a release stating that it had been "approached" by another company concerning a merger. On December 19, Basic's board endorsed Combustion's offer of $46 per share for its common stock, and on the following day publicly announced its approval of Combustion's tender for all outstanding shares.

Respondents are former Basic shareholders who sold their stock after Basic's first public statement of October 21, 1977, and before the suspension of trading in December 1978. Respondents brought a class action against Basic and its directors, asserting that the defendants issued three false or misleading public statements and thereby were in violation of § 10(b) of the 1934 Act and of Rule 10b-5. Respondents alleged that they were injured by selling Basic shares at artificially depressed prices in a market affected by petitioners' misleading statements and in reliance thereon.

The District Court adopted a presumption of reliance by members of the plaintiff class upon petitioners' public statements that enabled the court to conclude that common questions of fact or law predominated over particular questions pertaining to individual plaintiffs. The District Court therefore certified respondents' class. On the merits, however, the District Court granted summary judgment for the defendants. It held that, as a matter of law, any misstatements were immaterial: there were no negotiations ongoing at the time of the first statement, and although negotiations were taking place when the

4. On October 21, 1977, after heavy trading and a new high in Basic stock, the following news item appeared in the Cleveland Plain Dealer:

"[Basic] President Max Muller said the company knew no reason for the stock's activity and that no negotiations were under way with any company for a merger. He said Flintkote recently denied Wall Street rumors that it would make a tender offer of $25 a share for control of the Cleveland-based maker of refractories for the steel industry."

On September 25, 1978, in reply to an inquiry from the New York Stock Exchange, Basic issued a release concerning increased activity in its stock and stated that

"management is unaware of any present or pending company development that would result in the abnormally heavy trading activity and price fluctuation in company shares that have been experienced in the past few days."

On November 6, 1978, Basic issued to its shareholders a "Nine Months Report 1978." This Report stated:

"With regard to the stock market activity in the Company's shares we remain unaware of any present or pending developments which would account for the high volume of trading and price fluctuations in recent months."

second and third statements were issued, those negotiations were not "destined, with reasonable certainty, to become a merger agreement in principle."

The United States Court of Appeals for the Sixth Circuit affirmed the class certification, but reversed the District Court's summary judgment, and remanded the case. The court reasoned that while petitioners were under no general duty to disclose their discussions with Combustion, any statement the company voluntarily released could not be " 'so incomplete as to mislead.' " In the Court of Appeals' view, Basic's statements that no negotiations were taking place, and that it knew of no corporate developments to account for the heavy trading activity, were misleading. With respect to materiality, the court rejected the argument that preliminary merger discussions are immaterial as a matter of law, and held that "once a statement is made denying the existence of any discussions, even discussions that might not have been material in absence of the denial are material because they make the statement made untrue."

The Court of Appeals joined a number of other circuits in accepting the "fraud-on-the-market theory" to create a rebuttable presumption that respondents relied on petitioner's material misrepresentations, noting that without the presumption it would be impractical to certify a class under Fed.Rule Civ.Proc. 23(b)(3).

We granted certiorari to resolve the split among the Courts of Appeals as to the standard of materiality applicable to preliminary merger discussions, and to determine whether the courts below properly applied a presumption of reliance in certifying the class, rather than requiring each class member to show direct reliance on Basic's statements.

* * *

The Court previously has addressed various positive and common-law requirements for a violation of § 10(b) or of Rule 10b–5. The Court also explicitly has defined a standard of materiality under the securities laws, see TSC Industries v. Northway, 426 U.S. 438 (1976), concluding in the proxy-solicitation context that "[a]n omitted fact is material if there is a substantial likelihood that a reasonable shareholder would consider it important in deciding how to vote." Acknowledging that certain information concerning corporate developments could well be of "dubious significance," the Court was careful not to set too low a standard of materiality; it was concerned that a minimal standard might bring an overabundance of information within its reach, and lead management "simply to bury the shareholders in an avalanche of trivial information—a result that is hardly conducive to informed decisionmaking." It further explained that to fulfill the materiality requirement "there must be a substantial likelihood that the disclosure of the omitted fact would have been viewed by the reasonable investor as having significantly altered the 'total mix' of information made available." We now expressly adopt the *TSC Industries* standard of materiality for the § 10(b) and Rule 10b-5 context.

III

The application of this materiality standard to preliminary merger discussion is not self-evident. Where the impact of the corporate development on the target's fortune is certain and clear, the *TSC Industries* materiality definition admits straightforward application. Where, on the other hand, the event is contingent or speculative in nature, it is difficult to ascertain whether the "reasonable investor" would have considered the omitted information significant at the time. Merger negotiations, because of the ever-present possibility that the contemplated transaction will not be effectuated, fall into the latter category.

A

Petitioners urge upon us a Third Circuit test for resolving this difficulty. Under this approach, preliminary merger discussions do not become material until "agreement-in-principle" as to the price and structure of the transaction has been reached between the would-be merger partners. See Greenfield v. Heublein, 742 F.2d 751, 757 (3d Cir. 1984). By definition, then, information concerning any negotiations not yet at the agreement-in-principle stage could be withheld or even misrepresented without a violation of Rule 10b-5.

Three rationales have been offered in support of the "agreement-in-principle" test. The first derives from the concern expressed in *TSC Industries* that an investor not be overwhelmed by excessively detailed and trivial information, and focuses on the substantial risk that preliminary merger discussions may collapse: because such discussions are inherently tentative, disclosure of their existence itself could mislead investors and foster false optimism. The other two justifications for the agreement-in-principle standard are based on management concerns: because the requirement of "agreement-in-principle" limits the scope of disclosure obligations, it helps preserve the confidentiality of merger discussions where earlier disclosure might prejudice the negotiations; and the test also provides a usable, brightline rule for determining when disclosure must be made.

None of these policy-based rationales, however, purports to explain why drawing the line at agreement-in-principle reflects the significance of the information upon the investor's decision.

* * *

We therefore find no valid justification for artificially excluding from the definition of materiality information concerning merger discussions, which would otherwise be considered significant to the trading decision of a reasonable investor, merely because agreement-in-principle as to price and structure has not yet been reached by the parties or their representatives.

B

The Sixth Circuit explicitly rejected the agreement-in-principle test, as we do today, but in its place adopted a rule that, if taken literally, would be equally insensitive, in our view, to the distinction between materiality and the other elements of an action under Rule 10b–5:

> "When a company whose stock is publicly traded makes a statement, as Basic did, that 'no negotiations' are underway, and that the corporation know of 'no reason for the stock's activity,' and that 'management is unaware of any present or pending corporate development that would result in the abnormally heavy trading activity,' information concerning ongoing acquisition discussions becomes material *by virtue of the statement denying their existence.*
>
> "In analyzing whether information regarding merger discussions is material such that it must be affirmatively disclosed to avoid a violation of Rule 10b–5, the discussions and their progress are the primary considerations. However, once a statement is made denying the existence of any discussions, even discussions that might not have been material in absence of the denial are material because they make the statement made untrue."

C

Even before this Court's decision in *TSC Industries,* the Second Circuit had explained the role of the materiality requirement of Rule 10b–5, with respect to contingent or speculative information or events, in a manner that give that term meaning that is independent of the other provisions of the Rule. Under such circumstances, materiality "will depend at any given time upon a balancing of both the indicated probability that the event will occur and the anticipated magnitude of the event in light of the totality of the company activity." SEC v. Texas Gulf Sulphur Co., 401 F.2d, at 849. Interestingly, neither the Third Circuit decision adopting the agreement-in-principle test nor petitioners here take issue with this general standard. Rather, they suggest that with respect to preliminary merger discussions, there are good reasons to draw a line at agreement on price and structure.

* * *

Whether merger discussions in any particular case are material therefore depends on the facts. Generally, in order to assess the probability that the event will occur, a factfinder will need to look to indicia of interest in the transaction at the highest corporate levels. Without attempting to catalog all such possible factors, we note by way of example that board resolutions, instructions to investment bankers, and actual negotiations between principals or their intermediaries may serve as indicia or interest. To assess the magnitude of the transaction to the issuer of the securities allegedly manipulated, a factfinder will need to consider such facts as the size of the two corporate entities and of the potential premiums over market value. No particular event or factor short of closing the transaction need be either necessary or sufficient by itself to render merger discussions material.[17]

As we clarify today, materiality depends on the significance the reasonable investor would place on the withheld or misrepresented information. The fact-specific inquiry we endorse here is consistent with the approach a number of courts have taken in assessing the materiality of merger negotiations. Because the standard of materiality we have adopted differs from that used by both courts below, we remand the case for reconsideration of the question whether a grant of summary judgment is appropriate on this record.

* * *

THE CHIEF JUSTICE, JUSTICE SCALIA, and JUSTICE KENNEDY took no part in the consideration or decision of this case.

JUSTICE WHITE, with whom JUSTICE O'CONNOR joins, concurring in part and dissenting in part.

I join Parts I–III of the Court's opinion, as I agree that the standard of materiality we set forth in TSC Industries v. Northway, should be applied to actions under § 10(b) and Rule 10b–5. * * *

In the *Greenfield* case, the corporation, in response to an inquiry from the New York Stock Exchange, had made a statement that it "was aware of no reason that would explain the activity in its stock in trading on the Exchange." The Third Circuit held that this was not a materially misleading statement, even though the corporation knew that it was engaged in merger discussions, if the corporation had no reason to believe that any non-public information about these discussions had been "leaked" to traders. Judge Higginbotham dissented strongly from this portion of the opinion, and the SEC indicated its disagreement with the position taken by the court. The Supreme Court did not directly address the issue in the *Basic* case.

C. CIVIL LIABILITY FOR MISSTATEMENTS

Section 18 of the 1934 Act purports to make a company liable in damages to any person who buys or sells stock in reliance on a

17. To be actionable, of course, a statement must also be misleading. Silence, absent a duty to disclose, is not misleading under Rule 10b–5. "No comment" statements are generally the functional equivalent of silence.

It has been suggested that given current market practices, a "no comment" statement is tantamount to an admission that merger discussions are underway. That may well hold true to the extent that issuers adopt a policy of truthfully denying merger rumors when no discussions are underway, and of issuing "no comment" statements when they are in the midst of negotiations. There are, of course, other statement policies firms could adopt; we need not now advise issuers as to what kind of practice to follow, within the range permitted by law. Perhaps more importantly, we think that creating an exception to a regulatory scheme founded on a prodisclosure legislative philosophy, because complying with the regulation might be "bad for business," is a role for Congress, not this Court.

misleading statement in any application, report or other document that the company has filed with the SEC under the Act. The limitations on recovery under § 18, however as indicated by the following materials, have made the section virtually a "dead letter."

HEIT v. WEITZEN

402 F.2d 909 (2d Cir.1968).

Before MEDINA, MOORE and HAYS, CIRCUIT JUDGES.

MEDINA, CIRCUIT JUDGE.

[Plaintiffs, who had purchased Belock securities in the open market, sued Belock under §§ 10(b) and 18(a) of the 1934 Act, alleging that they had purchased in reliance on misleading statements and omissions in Belock's annual report to stockholders and in its report filed with the SEC on Form 10–K. The trial court dismissed the claim under § 18(a) on the ground that none of the reports on which the claims were predicated were "filed" with the SEC as required by that section.]

Plaintiffs * * * have contended that they relied on various documents which were "filed" within the meaning of Section 18. The documents in question are the "10K report" for the fiscal year ended October 31, 1964 and Belock's annual report for the same year, which was filed with the American Stock Exchange.

Judge Sugarman correctly ruled that the copies of the annual report submitted to the SEC were not "filed" documents within the meaning of Section 18. Rule 14a–3(c) of the Regulations under the Securities Exchange Act of 1934, as it read when the 1964 financial statements were issued on or about February 4, 1965 provided:

> Four copies of each annual report sent to security holders pursuant to this section shall be mailed to the Commission * * *. The annual report is not deemed to be "soliciting material" or to be "filed" with the Commission or subject to this regulation otherwise than as provided in this section, or to the liabilities of section 18 of the Act, except to the extent that the issuer specifically requests that it be treated as a part of the proxy soliciting material or incorporates it in the proxy statement by reference.

The above exemption provision, in addition to exempting the annual report filed with the SEC from the status of a "filed" document, also exempts the annual report filed with the American Stock Exchange from the coverage of Section 18. This result is required by the specific language of the second sentence of the above provision which contains several independent exemption clauses. Thus, the annual report is neither considered to be "filed with the Commission" nor subject to "the liabilities of section 18 of the Act." The latter phrase covers the alleged filing with the American Stock Exchange.

Although Fischman v. Raytheon, 188 F.2d 783 (2d Cir.1951) held that Section 18(a) applied to "documents" filed with a national securities exchange, the effect of the above regulation is to withdraw annual reports from the category of "filed" documents. The SEC has the power to prescribe rules that "may be necessary for the execution of the functions vested in" it by the Securities Exchange Act, Section 23(a), and in the performance of this duty the Commission may properly determine which filings are to be deemed "filings" for the purposes of Section 18. Therefore, the only possible "filed" document remaining is the "10K report" which is submitted to the SEC. We think it clear that the 10K report is a "filed" document within the meaning of Section 18.

* * *

The opinion of the District Court is unclear and we are unable to determine whether Judge Sugarman intended to hold that the 10K report was not a "filed" document. Appellees contend that Judge Sugarman ignored plaintiffs' claims based on form 10K simply because on oral argument appellants conceded that they could not allege or prove actual knowledge of and reliance upon any Belock 10K report. Appellants have denied making this concession. Reliance on the actual 10K report is an essential prerequisite for a Section 18 action and constructive reliance is not sufficient. Therefore, although under the liberal pleading provisions of the Federal Rules of Civil Procedure, the *Heit* and *Volk* complaints might well be considered broad enough to cover the allegation that they relied on misrepresentations contained in 10K reports, we believe it advisable to remand these cases to the District Court for a reconsideration of the question of leave to amend.

As this case indicates, a distinction is drawn, for purposes of § 18 liability, between the annual report on Form 10–K, which is filed with the Commission pursuant to § 13, and the annual report to shareholders, copies of which must be mailed to the Commission under Rule 14a–3.

If a false or misleading statement of a material fact is made both in a 10–K report filed with the SEC and in an annual report distributed to stockholders, can a stockholder who saw the statement in the annual report and relied upon it in purchasing or selling the stock meet the "reliance" test of § 18(a)? Can he meet the "price effect" test by showing that the market price was affected by the dissemination of the statement in the annual report?

The answer given thus far by the courts, at least to the first question, appears to have been negative. Several district courts have held that under § 18(a) the plaintiffs must allege "eyeball reliance" on the filed document; reliance on similar statements in other documents is insufficient.

In ROSS v. A.H. ROBINS, 607 F.2d 545 (2d Cir.1979), the court ruled that, in order to succeed under § 18(a), plaintiff must prove both knowledge of and reliance upon the materially misleading information in filed documents. The court in *Ross* also ruled that the remedies under §§ 10(b) and 18(a) are cumulative. See also HERMAN & MacLEAN v. HUDDLESTON, 459 U.S. 375 (1983); WACHOVIA BANK v. NATIONAL STUDENT MARKETING, 650 F.2d 342 (D.C.Cir.1982); pp. 494–99 above.

Is availability of the § 18(a) remedy really that significant even if the "eyeball" test has been satisfied? Who is liable under § 18(a)? What is the standard of culpability? How does it compare with the due diligence test in § 11 of the 1933 Act? With the *scienter* requirement under § 10(b) of the 1934 Act?

Because of these limitations on actions under § 18(a), the principal concern of the people involved in the preparation of corporate disclosure documents is the possible liability of the corporation, and others, under Rule 10b–5, to all investors who bought or sold after the corporation had issued a statement which is found to be incorrect or misleading.

The key question in determining whether a company will face civil liability for intentional misstatements in its published documents under Rule 10b–5 is whether the court will permit shareholders to bring a class action, since it will be relatively unusual for any single purchaser or seller to have a sufficient claim to warrant an individual action. Determination of this issue involves a number of questions, including commonality of issues of law and fact, interpretation of the reliance requirement, and determining the appropriate measure of damages.

BLACKIE v. BARRACK

524 F.2d 891 (9th Cir.1975).

Before TUTTLE, KOELSCH and BROWNING, CIRCUIT JUDGES.

KOELSCH, CIRCUIT JUDGE:

These are appeals from an order conditionally certifying a class in consolidated actions for violation of Section 10(b) of the Securities and Exchange Act of 1934, and Rule 10b–5 promulgated thereunder.

The litigation is a product of the financial troubles of Ampex Corporation. The annual report issued May 2, 1970, for fiscal 1970, reported a profit of $12 million. By January 1972, the company was predicting an estimated $40 million loss for fiscal 1972 (ending April 30, 1972). Two months later the company disclosed the loss would be much larger, in the $80 to $90 million range; finally, in the annual report for fiscal 1972, filed August 3, 1972, the company reported a loss of $90 million, and the company's independent auditors withdrew certification of the 1971 financial statements, and declined to certify those for 1972, because of doubts that the loss reported for 1972 was in fact suffered in that year.

Several suits were filed following the 1972 disclosures of Ampex's losses. They were consolidated for pre-trial purposes. The named plaintiffs in the various complaints involved in these appeals purchased Ampex securities during the 27 month period between the release of the 1970 and 1972 annual reports, and seek to represent all purchasers of Ampex securities during the period. The corporation, its principal officers during the period, and the company's independent auditor are named as defendants. The gravamen of all the claims is the misrepresentation by reason of annual and interim reports, press releases and SEC filings of the financial condition of Ampex from the date of the 1970 report until the true condition was disclosed by the announcement of losses in August of 1972.

The plaintiffs moved for class certification shortly after filing their complaints in 1972; after extensive briefing and argument the district judge entered an order on April 11, 1974, conditionally certifying as a class all those who purchased Ampex securities during the 27 month period. The defendants filed notices of appeal from the order of certification on May 9 and 10, 1974.

* * *

* * * The district judge is required by Fed.R.Civ.P. 23(c)(1) to determine "as soon as practicable after the commencement of an action brought as a class action * * * whether it is to be so maintained." * * *

Defendants question this suit's compliance with each of the various requirements of Rule 23(a) and (b)(3) [18] except numerosity (understandably, as it appears that the class period of 27 months will encompass the purchasers involved in about 120,000 transactions involving some 21,000,000 shares). However, all of defendants' contentions can be resolved by addressing 3 underlying questions: 1) whether a common question of law or fact unites the class; 2) whether direct individual proof of subjective reliance by each class member is necessary to

18. Rule 23 provides in part:

"(a) Prerequisites to a Class Action. One or more members of a class may sue or be sued as representative parties on behalf of all only if (1) the class is so numerous that joinder of all members is impracticable, (2) there are questions of law or fact common to the class, (3) the claims or defenses of the representative parties are typical of the claims or defenses of the class, and (4) the representative parties will fairly and adequately protect the interests of the class.

"(b) Class Actions Maintainable. An action may be maintained as a class action if the prerequisites of subdivision (a) are satisfied, and in addition:

* * *

"(3) the court finds that the questions of law or fact common to the members of the class predominate over any questions affecting only individual members, and that a class action is superior to other available methods for the fair and efficient adjudication of the controversy. The matters pertinent to the findings include: (A) the interest of members of the class in individually controlling the prosecution or defense of separate actions; (B) the extent and nature of any litigation concerning the controversy already commenced by or against members of the class; (C) the desirability or undesirability of concentrating the litigation of the claims in the particular forum; (D) the difficulties likely to be encountered in the management of a class action."

establish 10b–5 liability in this situation; and 3) whether proof of liability or damages will create conflicts among class members and with named plaintiffs sufficient to make representation inadequate? We turn to the first issue.

1. COMMON QUESTIONS OF LAW OR FACT.

The class certified runs from the date Ampex issued its 1970 annual report until the company released its 1972 report 27 months later. Plaintiffs' complaint alleges that the price of the company's stock was artificially inflated because:

> "the annual reports of Ampex for fiscal years 1970 and 1971, various interim reports, press releases and other documents (a) overstated earnings, (b) overstated the value of inventories and other assets, (c) buried expense items and other costs incurred for research and development in inventory, (d) misrepresented the companies' current ratio, (e) failed to establish adequate reserves for receivables, (f) failed to write off certain assets, (g) failed to account for the proposed discontinuation of certain product lines, (h) misrepresented Ampex's prospects for future earnings."

The plaintiffs estimate that there are some 45 documents issued during the period containing the financial reporting complained of, including two annual reports, six quarterly reports, and various press releases and SEC filings.

Because the alleged misrepresentations are contained in a number of different documents, each pertaining to a different period of Ampex's operation, the defendants argue that purchasers throughout the class period do not present common issues of law or fact. They reason that proof of 10b–5 liability will require inspection of the underlying set of facts to determine the falsity of the impression given by any particular accounting item presented; that the underlying facts fluctuate as the business operates (i.e., inventory is bought and sold, accounts are paid off and created); thus, proof of the actionability of a current accounting representation or omission will apply only to those who purchased while a financial report was current; from which they conclude no common question is presented and a class is improper.

We disagree. The overwhelming weight of authority holds that repeated misrepresentations of the sort alleged here satisfy the "common question" requirement. Confronted with a class of purchasers allegedly defrauded over a period of time by similar misrepresentations, courts have taken the common sense approach that the class is united by a common interest in determining whether a defendant's course of conduct is in its broad outlines actionable, which is not defeated by slight differences in class members' positions, and that the issue may profitably be tried in one suit. * * * Those views are consistent with the views of the Advisory Committee on the Rule: "[A] fraud perpetrated on numerous persons by the use of similar misrepresentations may be an appealing situation for a class action * * *." The availability of the class action to redress such frauds has been consistently upheld, in large part because of the substantial role that the deterrent effect of class actions plays in accomplishing the objectives of the securities laws. See III Loss, Securities Regulation 1819 (2d ed. 1961) ("the ultimate effectiveness of [the security anti-fraud laws] may depend on the applicability of the class action device").

While the nature of the interrelationship and the degree of similarity which must obtain between different representations in order to come within the outer boundaries of the "common course of conduct" test is somewhat unclear, the test is more than satisfied when a series of financial reports uniformly misrepresent a particular item in the financial statement. In that situation, the misrepresentations are "interrelated, interdependent, and cumulative"; "[l]ike standing dominoes * * * one misrepresentation * * * cause[s] subsequent statements to fall into inaccuracy and distortion when considered by themselves or compared with previous misstatements."

Precisely such a situation is alleged here in at least three respects—the failure to create adequate reserves for uncollectible accounts receivable and for contractually guaranteed royalty payments, and the overstatement of inventory. The 1972 Annual Report shows writedowns of $31.9 million as provision for royalty guarantees, $11.8 million for uncollectible accounts receivable, and $15 million for inventory. Plaintiffs allege that the writedowns had roots tracing back to the beginning of the class period, an allegation somewhat borne out by the auditors' withdrawal of certification of the 1971 report because of uncertainty that the huge losses reported in 1972 were the product of 1972 business operations, and not attributable to earlier years. Plaintiffs contend that the company's financial reports throughout the period uniformly and fraudulently failed to establish reserves in amounts adequate to satisfy accepted accounting principles, injuring all purchasers of the consequently inflated stock.

* * *

Defendants nevertheless contend that a class is improper because each purchaser must depend on proof of a different set of accounting facts to establish the inadequacy of the reserves at the time he bought. Defendants misconceive the requirement for a class action; all that is required is a common issue of law *or* fact. Even were we to assume that the reserves were at some points during the period adequate, the class members still would be united by a common interest in the application to their unique situation of the accounting and legal principles requiring adequate reserves—i.e., by a common question of law. Here, however, in light of the progressive deterioration of Ampex's financial position and the magnitude of the losses at the end of the period, even the fact that reserves were in reality inadequate throughout much if not all of the period may not be in serious dispute; rather, the question will be whether the inadequacy was in some sense culpable because the contingencies which proved them inadequate were foreseen or foreseeable.

* * *

2. Predominance and Reliance.

Defendants contend that any common questions which may exist do not predominate over individual questions of reliance and damages.

The amount of damages is invariably an individual question and does not defeat class action treatment. Moreover, in this situation we are confident that should the class prevail the amount of price inflation during the period can be charted and the process of computing individual damages will be virtually a mechanical task.

Individual questions of reliance are likewise not an impediment—subjective reliance is not a distinct element of proof of 10b–5 claims of the type involved in this case.

The class members' substantive claims either are, or can be, cast in omission or non-disclosure terms—the company's financial reporting failed to disclose the need for reserves, conditions reflecting on the value of the inventory, or other facts necessary to make the reported figures not misleading. The Court has recognized that under such circumstances

> "involving primarily a failure to disclose, positive proof of reliance is not a prerequisite to recovery. All that is necessary is that the facts withheld be material in the sense that a reasonable investor might have considered them important in the making of this decision. This obligation to disclose and this withholding of a material fact establish the requisite element of causation in fact."

Affiliated Ute Citizens of Utah v. United States, 406 U.S. 128, 153–154 (1972).

Moreover, proof of subjective reliance on particular misrepresentations is unnecessary to establish a 10b–5 claim for a deception inflating the price of stock traded in the open market. Proof of reliance is adduced to demonstrate the causal connection between the defendant's wrongdoing and the plaintiff's loss. We think causation is adequately established in the impersonal stock exchange context by proof of purchase and of the materiality of misrepresentations, without direct proof of reliance. Materiality circumstantially establishes the reliance of some market traders and hence the inflation in the stock price—when the purchase is made the causational chain between defendant's conduct and plaintiff's loss is sufficiently established to make out a prima facie case.

Defendants argue that proof of causation solely by proof of materiality is inconsistent with the requirement of the traditional fraud action that a plaintiff prove directly both that the reasonable man would have acted on the misrepresentation (materiality), and that he himself acted on it, in order to establish the defendant's responsibility for his loss, which justifies the compensatory recovery.

We disagree. The 10b–5 action remains compensatory; it is not predicated solely on a showing of economic damage (loss causation). We merely recognize that individual "transactional causation" can in these circumstances be inferred from the materiality of the misrepresentation, and shift to defendant the burden of disproving a prima facie case of causation. Defendants may do so in at least 2 ways: (1) by disproving materiality or by proving that, despite materiality, an insufficient number of traders relied to inflate the price; and (2) by proving that an individual plaintiff purchased despite knowledge of the falsity of a representation, or that he would have, had he known of it.

That the prima facie case each class member must establish differs from the traditional fraud action, and may, unlike the fraud action, be established by common proof, is irrelevant; although derived from it, the 10b–5 action is not coterminous with a common law fraud action.

Here, we eliminate the requirement that plaintiffs prove reliance directly in this context because the requirement imposes an unreasonable and irrelevant evidentiary burden. A purchaser on the stock exchanges may be either unaware of a specific false representation, or may not directly rely on it; he may purchase because of a favorable price trend, price earnings ratio, or some other factor. Nevertheless, he relies generally on the supposition that the market price is validly set and that no unsuspected manipulation has artificially inflated the price, and thus indirectly on the truth of the representations underlying the stock price—whether he is aware of it or not, the price he pays reflects material misrepresentations. Requiring direct proof from each purchaser that he relied on a particular representation when purchasing would defeat recovery by those whose reliance was indirect, despite the fact that the causational chain is broken only if the purchaser would have purchased the stock even had he known of the misrepresentation. We decline to leave such open market purchasers unprotected. The statute and rule are designed to foster an expectation that securities markets are free from fraud—an expectation on which purchasers should be able to rely.

Thus, in this context we think proof of reliance means at most a requirement that plaintiff prove directly that he would have acted differently had he known the true facts. That is a requirement of proof of a speculative negative (I would not have bought had I known) precisely parallel to that held unnecessary in *Affiliated Ute* and *Mills* (I would not have sold had I known). We reject it here for the same reasons. Direct proof would inevitably be somewhat pro-forma, and impose a difficult evidentiary burden, because addressed to a speculative possibility in an area where motivations are complex and difficult to determine. That difficulty threatens to defeat valid claims—implicit in *Affiliated Ute* is a rejection of the burden because it leads to underinclusive recoveries and thereby threatens the enforcement of the securities laws. Here, the requirement is redundant—the same causal nexus can be adequately established indirectly, by proof of materiality coupled with the common sense that a stock purchaser does not ordinarily seek to purchase a loss in the form of artificially inflated stock. Under those circumstances we think it appropriate to eliminate the burden.

* * *

C. CONFLICTS.

Defendants' final major argument is that conflicts among class members preclude class certification. They contend that the interests of class members in proving damages from price inflation (and hence the existence and materiality of misrepresentations subsumed in proving inflation) irreconcilably conflict, because some class members will desire to maximize the inflation existing on a given date while others will desire to minimize it. For example, they posit that a purchaser early in the class period who later sells will desire to maximize the deflation due to an intervening corrective disclosure in order to maximize his out of pocket damages, but in so doing will conflict with his purchaser, who is interested in maximizing the inflation in the price he pays. We agree that class members might at some point during this litigation have differing interests. We altogether disagree, for a spate of reasons, that such potential conflicts afford a valid reason at this time for refusing to certify the class.

Defendants' position depends entirely on adoption of the out of pocket loss measure of damages, rather than a rescissory measure. Under the out of pocket standard each purchaser recovers the difference between the inflated price paid and the value received, plus interest on the difference. If the stock is resold at an inflated price, the purchaser-seller's damages, limited by § 28(a) of the Act to "actual damages," must be diminished by the inflation he recovers from his purchaser. Thus, he is interested in proving that some intervening event, such as a corrective release, had diminished the inflation persisting in the stock price when he sold.

While out of pocket loss is the ordinary standard in a 10b–5 suit, it is within the discretion of the district judge in appropriate circumstances to apply a rescissory measure, or to allow consequential damages. It is for the district judge, after becoming aware of the nature of the case, to determine the appropriate measure of damages in the first instance; the possible creation of potential conflicts by that decision does not render the class inappropriate now. The Rule provides the mechanism of subsequent creation of subclasses, Rule 23(c)(4), to deal with latent conflicts which may surface as the suit progresses. As a result, courts have generally declined to consider conflicts, particularly as they regard damages, sufficient to defeat class action status at the outset unless the conflict is apparent, imminent, and on an issue at the very heart of the suit.

Here, the conflict, if any, is peripheral, and substantially outweighed by the class members' common interests. Even assuming *arguendo* that the out of pocket standard applies, the class is proper. Every class member shares an overriding common interest in establishing the existence and materiality of misrepresentations. The major portion of the inflation alleged is attributed to causes which allegedly persisted throughout the class period. It will be in the interest of each class member to maximize the inflation from those causes at every point in the class period, both to demonstrate the *sine qua non*—liability—and to maximize his own potential damages—the more the stock is inflated, the more every class member stands to recover. Moreover, because the major portion of the inflation is attributed to causes persisting throughout the period, interim corrective disclosures (of which there appear to have been only two or three) do not necessarily bring predisclosure purchasers into conflict with post-disclosure purchasers. Because both share an interest in maximizing overall inflation, the latter purchaser will no doubt strive to show a substantial market effect from disclosure of the lesser (or partial) causes of inflation to maximize the inflation attributable to more serious causes persisting when he bought—a showing which will increase the recovery of the earlier purchaser. In that light, any conflicting interests in tracing fluctuations in inflation during the class period are secondary, and do not bar class litigation to advance predominantly common interests. Courts faced with the same situation have repeatedly, either explicitly or implicitly, rejected defendants' position, for the potential conflict is present in most prolonged classes involving a series of misrepresentations.

RIFKIN v. CROW

574 F.2d 256 (5th Cir.1978).

Before GEWIN, RONEY and HILL, CIRCUIT JUDGES.

RONEY, CIRCUIT JUDGE:

In this Rule 10b–5 securities case, plaintiff appeals from the district court's grant of summary judgment for defendants. The court's decision was based on a lack of "some element of general reliance by plaintiff" on the reports released by defendants. In his deposition testimony which was before the district court, plaintiff specifically averred that he relied on the reports disseminated by defendants, which were allegedly misleading in their treatment of sales to a subsidiary and of research and development expenses. Holding that the district court erroneously concluded that there was no issue of fact as to reliance, and that it misapplied our case of Simon v. Merrill Lynch, Pierce, Fenner & Smith, Inc., 482 F.2d 880 (5th Cir.1973), which turned on a finding of lack of any reliance on a broker's advice, we reverse.

I. FACTS

Plaintiff Michael Rifkin brought this class action suit pursuant to § 10(b) of the Securities Exchange Act of 1934 and Rule 10b–5 promulgated thereunder. Named as defendants were Recognition Equipment, Inc.; nine of its officers and directors; its affiliate, Corporation S; and its accountants, Price Waterhouse & Co. Plaintiff sought to recover damages suffered by himself and all persons who purchased Recognition common stock on the open market between October 31, 1969 and July 1, 1971 at prices allegedly inflated by misleading financial and other statements disseminated by Recognition, some of which were certified by defendant Price Waterhouse. Plaintiff alleges that Recognition was able to show a profit in 1969 only by improperly capitalizing millions of dollars worth of research and development expenses, and by not consolidating Recognition's financial statements with those of its 49%-owned affiliate, Corporation S, to which Recognition made substantial sales.

* * *

II. Issues of Fact

A. *As to Reliance*

The district court erred in holding that there was no genuine issue of fact regarding the lack of "some element of general reliance by plaintiff." * * *

In his deposition, Rifkin specifically stated that he relied on the 1969 Annual Report and other statements emanating directly and indirectly from Recognition in making his seven purchases of Recognition stock in the period in question. He summarized his detailed deposition testimony about his reliance by saying that:

> I read every document I received from the Company, and to the extent I read it, I relied on it.

* * *

In addition, * * * Rifkin stated that in making his purchases he relied on the fact that the market price of a stock reflects the company's financial statements and its inherent value:

> If the price of the stock reflects, and I believe it does, if the price of a stock reflects the financial statements which are circulated to the investment community and if the financial statements are over-stated, inflated, it would be reasonable to believe that the price of the stock was over-stated. I think that a buyer of a security has a right to rely on the fact that the stock value bears some reasonable relationship to the financial statements circulated in the investment market. * * * [Investors] are entitled to rely on the fairness of a price set by the general investment community and that that price has been established as bearing a reasonable relationship to the earnings and balance sheets and if the earnings and balance sheets are over-stated, why their reliance and expectation of paying a fair price is just not borne out.

Thus, plaintiff's testimony, if accepted by a trier of fact, would support recovery under even the most restricted reliance requirement.

III. Simon v. Merrill Lynch and Rule 10b-5's Reliance Requirement

While we do not know for certain how the facts will develop on further proceedings, we have concluded that, in light of the parties' contentions, it is highly unlikely that *Simon* will be a controlling or dispositive precedent as to the law in this case. That decision held a 10b–5 cause of action foreclosed because there was no "general reliance" on the stockbroker's alleged misrepresentations. Further analysis here may be helpful to the district court on remand to put *Simon* in proper context, *vis-a-vis* this case and the law of reliance as it has developed in the other circuits.

Simon brought his 10b–5 action against Merrill Lynch, alleging he had purchased common stock in a computer corporation because of misrepresentations and omissions made by Merrill Lynch. After a bench *trial,* the district court concluded that Simon had failed to prove his case against Merrill Lynch. Simon appealed, and we affirmed. Our disposition was clearly based on the fact that the district judge, as trier of fact, found that Simon *had not relied* on any Merrill Lynch representations.

* * *

Simon argued that the trial court's finding of nonreliance was "not dispositive," because Simon read Affiliated Ute Citizens v. United States, 406 U.S. 128 (1972), as holding that reliance need not be proved in nondisclosure cases. We rejected Simon's argument on the basis of the facts before us, that is, that the district judge had found that Simon was not relying on any information from Merrill Lynch in making his purchases.

* * *

In *Ute,* a bank purchased stock from a group of unsophisticated investors without disclosing that the stock was selling at a higher price on a secondary market made by the bank. The Court of Appeals for the Tenth Circuit denied recovery because the record failed to disclose evidence that the plaintiffs relied on any misstatements made by the bank. The Supreme Court reversed, holding that

> [u]nder the circumstances of this case, involving primarily a failure to disclose, positive proof of reliance is not a prerequisite to recovery. All that is necessary is that the facts withheld be material in the sense that a reasonable investor might have considered them important in the making of this decision.

Thus, *Ute* simply did not address the *Simon* situation where there was positive proof that the plaintiff did not rely on anything defendant did.

After *Ute,* the reliance requirement has varied somewhat in articulation from circuit to circuit, but a general pattern seems to have emerged: where a 10b–5 action alleges defendant made positive misrepresentations of material information, proof of reliance by the plaintiff upon the misrepresentation is required. Upon an absence of proof on the issue, plaintiff loses. On the other hand, where a plaintiff alleges deception by defendant's nondisclosure of material information, the *Ute* presumption obviates the need for plaintiff to prove actual reliance on the omitted information. Upon a failure of proof on the issue, defendant loses. But this presumption of reliance in nondisclosure cases is not conclusive. If defendant can prove that plaintiff did not rely, that is, that plaintiff's decision would not have been affected even if defendant had disclosed the omitted facts, then plaintiff's recovery is barred. *Simon,* therefore, employs a reliance standard no different from that generally applied in other federal courts.

The above analysis tends to demonstrate that *Simon* may well be inapplicable to this case. On remand, when the facts are fully developed, it will first be necessary for the district court to "characterize" the case, as a "misrepresentation" or an "omission" case. If the court determines that this is a misrepresentation case, then the more stringent reliance requirement would apply, and Rifkin would need to prove that he relied on defendants' misrepresentations. If, on the other hand, the district court determines that this is an omission case, Rifkin would be entitled to the *Ute* presumption of reliance, and without more, he could prevail on the reliance issue unless, as in *Simon,* defendants prove that plaintiff did not rely. Since the alleged misstatements were in the official financial statements of the company itself, defendants may be hard pressed to demonstrate that these statements played no part in the investment decisions of an investor such as Rifkin.

Simon would also be inapplicable should the facts so develop as to present a "fraud on the market" theory of action. Rifkin testified that he relied on the market to properly reflect in market value the financial condition of a company as accurately set forth in the company's statements. The inaccuracies and omissions of the statements caused a distortion in the market which Rifkin claims misled him as to the fair market value of the stock. In further support of his claim, Rifkin submitted an affidavit from a securities expert, who concluded that the alleged misstatements "had a material inflationary impact on the price at which Recognition stock traded during the period" in question.

In cases involving similar "fraud on the market" claims, the Second and Ninth Circuits have held that a plaintiff need not show individual reliance upon the particular misrepresentations or omissions made by a defendant.[4] * * * A defendant can rebut this presumption of reliance in two ways: by proving that an insufficient number of traders relied to inflate the stock's price, or by proving that the plaintiff purchased despite knowledge of the misrepresentation or omission or that he would have purchased had he known of it.

This Circuit has not yet decided whether reliance should be presumed in "fraud on the market" situations. Without full development of the facts, we need not now decide whether such a theory will be recognized in this Circuit.

---

4. Blackie v. Barrack, 524 F.2d 891, 906–907 (9th Cir.1975); Schlick v. Penn–Dixie Cement Corp., 507 F.2d 374, 381 (2d Cir.1974). * * *

In SHORES v. SKLAR, 647 F.2d 462 (5th Cir.1981), a purchaser of revenue bonds sued various persons involved with the issuance of the bonds, alleging that they "had fabricated a materially misleading offering circular to induce an industrial development board to issue, and the public to buy, fraudulently marketed bonds." He admitted that he had not read or relied on the offering circular, and indeed was not even aware of its existence. The Fifth Circuit, in a 12–10 *en banc* decision, upheld his claim under Rule 10b–5. The court construed his claim to allege, not that he paid too much for the bonds because of the misleading statements (in which event he would have had to prove reliance), but that the bonds would not have been marketable at all without the fraudulent scheme of which the offering circular was a part. It held that "the securities laws allow an investor to rely on the integrity of the market to the extent that the securities it offers to him for purchase are entitled to be in the market place." The dissenters argued that this holding was inconsistent with the holding in *Rifkin* and a misapplication of the *Blackie* "fraud on the market" theory.

In PANZIRER v. WOLF, 663 F.2d 365 (2d Cir.1981), the court upheld a claim based on allegedly misleading statements in an annual report. Plaintiff had not seen the annual report but purchased stock on the basis of a newspaper article which she claimed would have presented the company in a less favorable light had the annual report been accurate. The court held that this "secondary reliance" was sufficient. "When the plaintiff acts upon information from those working in or reporting on the securities markets, and where that information is circulated after a material misrepresentation or omission, plaintiff has stated a sufficient claim of reliance on the misstatement or omission." The Supreme Court granted certiorari, then vacated and remanded for dismissal on grounds of mootness. Price Waterhouse v. Panzirer, 459 U.S. 1027 (1982).

In 1988, the "fraud on the market" theory came before the Supreme Court for review.

BASIC v. LEVINSON

485 U.S. 224 (1988).

JUSTICE BLACKMUN delivered the opinion of the Court.

This case requires us to * * * determine whether a person who traded a corporation's shares on a securities exchange after the issuance of a materially misleading statement by the corporation may invoke a rebuttable presumption that, in trading, he relied on the integrity of the price set by the market.

[The facts are set forth in the portion of the opinion reproduced at p. 640 above.]

* * *

IV

A

We turn to the question of reliance and the fraud-on-the-market theory. Succinctly put:

> "The fraud on the market theory is based on the hypothesis that, in an open and developed securities market, the price of a company's stock is determined by the available material information regarding the company and its business. * * * Misleading statements will therefore defraud purchasers of stock even if the purchasers do not directly rely on the misstatements. * * * The causal connection between the defendants' fraud and the plaintiffs' purchase of stock in such a case is no less significant than in a case of direct reliance on misrepresentations." Peil v. Speiser, 806 F.2d 1154, 1160–1161 (3d Cir. 1986).

Our task, of course, is not to assess the general validity of the theory, but to consider whether it was proper for the courts below to apply a rebuttable presumption of reliance, supported in part by the fraud-on-the-market theory.

This case required resolution of several common questions of law and fact concerning the falsity or misleading nature of the three public statements made by Basic, the presence or absence of scienter, and the materiality of the misrepresentations, if any. In their amended complaint, the named plaintiffs alleged that in reliance on Basic's statements they sold their shares of Basic stock in the depressed market created by petitioners. Requiring proof of individualized reliance from each member of the proposed plaintiff class effectively would have prevented respondents from proceeding with a class action, since individual issues then would have overwhelmed the common ones. The District Court found that the presumption of reliance created by the fraud-on-the-market theory provided "a practical resolution to the problem of balancing the substantive requirement of proof of reliance in securities cases against the procedural requisites of [Fed.Rule Civ. Proc.] 23." The District Court thus concluded that with reference to each public statement and its impact upon the open market for Basic shares, common questions predominated over individual questions, as required by Fed.Rule Civ.Proc. 23(a)(2) and (b)(3).

Petitioners and their *amici* complain that the fraud-on-the-market theory effectively eliminates the requirement that a plaintiff asserting a claim under Rule 10b–5 prove reliance. They note that reliance is and long has been an element of common-law fraud, and argue that because the analogous express right of action includes a reliance requirement, see, *e.g.*, § 18(a) of the 1934 Act, as amended, so too must an action implied under § 10(b).

We agree that reliance is an element of a Rule 10b–5 cause of action. Reliance provides the requisite causal connection between a defendant's misrepresentation and a plaintiff's injury. There is, however, more than one way to demonstrate the causal connection. Indeed, we previously have dispensed with a requirement of positive proof of reliance, where a duty to disclose material information had been breached, concluding that the necessary nexus between the plaintiffs' injury and the defendant's wrongful conduct had been established. Similarly, we did not require proof that material omissions or misstatements in a proxy statement decisively affected voting, because the proxy solicitation itself, rather than the defect in the solicitation materials, served as an essential link in the transaction.

The modern securities markets, literally involving millions of shares changing hands daily, differ from the face-to-face transactions contemplated by early fraud cases, and, our understanding of Rule 10b-5's reliance requirement must encompass these differences.

* * *

B

Presumptions typically serve to assist courts in managing circumstances in which direct proof, for one reason or another, is rendered difficult. The courts below accepted a presumption, created by the fraud-on-the-market theory and subject to rebuttal by petitioners, that persons who had traded Basic shares had done so in reliance on the integrity of the price set by the market, but because of petitioners' material misrepresentations that price had been fraudulently depressed. Requiring a plaintiff to show a speculative state of facts, i.e., how he would have acted if omitted material information had been disclosed, or if the misrepresentation had not been made, would place an unnecessarily unrealistic evidentiary burden on the Rule 10b-5 plaintiff who has traded on an impersonal market.

* * *

The presumption is also supported by common sense and probability. Recent empirical studies have tended to confirm Congress' premise that the market price of shares traded on well-developed markets reflects all publicly available information, and, hence, any material misrepresentations. It has been noted that "it is hard to imagine that there ever is a buyer or seller who does not rely on market integrity. Who would knowingly roll the dice in a crooked crap game?" Indeed, nearly every court that has considered the proposition has concluded that where materially misleading statements have been disseminated into an impersonal, well-developed market for securities, the reliance of individual plaintiffs on the integrity of the market price may be presumed. Commentators generally have applauded the adoption of one variation or another of the fraud-on-the-market theory. An investor who buys or sells stock at the price set by the market does so in reliance on the integrity of that price. Because most publicly available information is reflected in market price, an investor's reliance on any public material misrepresentations, therefore, may be presumed for purposes of a Rule 10b-5 action.

C

The Court of Appeals found that petitioners "made public, material misrepresentations and [respondents] sold Basic stock in an impersonal, efficient market. Thus the class, as defined by the district court, has established the threshold facts for proving their loss." The court acknowledged that petitioners may rebut proof of the elements giving rise to the presumption, or show that the misrepresentation in fact did not lead to a distortion of price or that an individual plaintiff traded or would have traded despite his knowing the statement was false.

Any showing that severs the link between the alleged misrepresentation and either the price received (or paid) by the plaintiff, or his decision to trade at a fair market price, will be sufficient to rebut the presumption of reliance. For example, if petitioners could show that the "market makers" were privy to the truth about the merger discussions here with Combustion, and thus that the market price would not have been affected by their misrepresentations, the causal connection would be broken: the basis for finding that the fraud had been transmitted through market price would be gone. Similarly, if, despite petitioners' allegedly fraudulent attempt to manipulate market price, news of the merger discussions credibly entered the market and dissipated the effects of the misstatements, those who traded Basic shares after the corrective statements would have no direct or indirect connection with the fraud. Petitioners also could rebut the presumption of reliance as to plaintiffs who have divested themselves of their Basic shares without relying on the integrity of the market. For example, a plaintiff who believed that Basic's statements were false and that Basic was indeed engaged in merger discussions, and who consequently believed that Basic stock was artificially underpriced, but sold his shares nevertheless because of other unrelated concerns, e.g., potential antitrust problems, or political pressures to divest from shares of certain businesses, could not be said to have relied on the integrity of a price he knew had been manipulated.

* * *

THE CHIEF JUSTICE, JUSTICE SCALIA, and JUSTICE KENNEDY took no part in the consideration or decision of this case.

JUSTICE WHITE, with whom JUSTICE O'CONNOR joins, concurring in part and dissenting in part.

I join Parts I–III of the Court's opinion, as I agree that the standard of materiality we set forth in TSC Industries v. Northway, should be applied to actions under § 10(b) and Rule 10b–5. But I dissent from the remainder of the Court's holding because I do not agree that the "fraud-on-the-market" theory should be applied in this case.

I

Even when compared to the relatively youthful private cause-of-action under § 10(b), the fraud-on-the-market theory is a mere babe. Yet today, the Court embraces this theory with the sweeping confidence usually reserved for more mature legal doctrines. In so doing, I fear that the Court's decision may have many adverse, unintended effects as it is applied and interpreted in the years to come.

A

At the outset, I note that there are portions of the Court's fraud-on-the-market holding with which I am in agreement. Most importantly, the Court rejects the version of that theory, heretofore adopted by some courts, which equates "causation" with "reliance," and permits recovery by a plaintiff who claims merely to have been harmed by a material misrepresentation which altered a market price, notwithstanding proof that the plaintiff did not in any way *rely* on that price. I agree with the Court that if Rule 10b–5's reliance requirement is to be left with any content at all, the fraud-on-the-market presumption must be capable of being rebutted by a showing that a plaintiff did not "rely" on the market price.

* * *

B

But even as the Court attempts to limit the fraud-on-the-market theory it endorses today, the pitfalls in its approach are revealed by previous uses by the lower courts of the broader versions of the theory. Confusion and contradiction in court rulings are inevitable when traditional legal analysis is replaced with economic theorization by the federal courts.

* * *

For while the economists' theories which underpin the fraud-on-the-market presumption may have the appeal of mathematical exactitude and scientific certainty, they are—in the end—nothing more than theories which may or may not prove accurate upon further consideration. Even the most earnest advocates of economic analysis of the law recognize this. Thus, while the majority states that, for purposes of reaching its result it need only make modest assumptions about the way in which "market professionals generally" do their jobs, and how the conduct of market professionals affects stock prices, I doubt that we are in much of a position to assess which theories aptly describe the functioning of the securities industry.

Consequently, I cannot join the Court in the effort to reconfigure the securities laws, based on recent economic theories, to better fit what it perceives to be the new realities of financial markets. I would leave this task to others more equipped for the job than we.

C

At the bottom of the Court's conclusion that the fraud-on-the-market theory sustains a presumption of reliance is the assumption that individuals rely "on the integrity of the market price" when buying or selling stock in "impersonal, well-developed market[s] for securities." Even if I was prepared to accept (as a matter of common sense or general understanding) the assumption that most persons buying or selling stock do so in response to the market price, the fraud-on-the-market theory goes further. For in adopting a "presumption of reliance," the Court *also* assumes that buyers and sellers rely—not just on the market price—but on the "*integrity*" of that price. It is this aspect of the fraud-on-the-market hypothesis which most mystifies me.

To define the term "integrity of the market price," the majority quotes approvingly from cases which suggest that investors are entitled to " 'rely on the price of a stock as a reflection of its value.' " But the meaning of this phrase eludes me, for it implicitly suggests that stocks have some "true value" that is measurable by a standard other than their market price. While the Scholastics of Medieval times professed a means to make such a valuation of a commodity's "worth," I doubt that the federal courts of our day are similarly equipped.

Even if securities had some "value"—knowable and distinct from the market price of a stock—investors do not always share the Court's presumption that a stock's price is a "reflection of [this] value." Indeed, "many investors purchase or sell stock because they believe the price *inaccurately* reflects the corporation's worth." If investors really believed that stock prices reflected a stock's "value," many sellers would never sell, and many buyers never buy (given the time and cost associated with executing a stock transaction). As we recognized just a few years ago: "[I]nvestors act on inevitably incomplete or inaccurate information, [consequently] there are always winners and losers; but those who have 'lost' have not necessarily been defrauded." Yet today, the Court allows investors to recover who can show little more than that they sold stock at a lower price than what might have been.

I do not propose that the law retreat from the many protections that § 10(b) and Rule 10b–5, as interpreted in our prior cases, provide to investors. But any extension of these laws, to approach something closer to an investor insurance scheme, should come from Congress, and not from the courts.

II

Congress has not passed on the fraud-on-the-market theory the Court embraces today. That is reason enough for us to abstain from doing so. But it is even more troubling that, to the extent that any view of Congress on this question can be inferred indirectly, it is contrary to the result the majority reaches.

A

In the past, the scant legislative history of § 10(b) has led us to look at Congress' intent in adopting other portions of the Securities Act when we endeavor to discern the limits of private causes of action under Rule 10b–5. A similar undertaking here reveals that Congress flatly rejected a proposition analogous to the fraud-on-the-market theory in adopting a civil liability provision of the 1934 Act.

Section 18 of the Act expressly provides for civil liability for certain misleading statements concerning securities. When the predecessor of this section was first being considered by Congress, the initial draft of the provision allowed recovery by any plaintiff "who shall have purchased or sold a security the price of which may have been affected by such [misleading] statement." Thus, as initially drafted, the precursor to the express civil liability provision of the 1934 Act would have permitted suits by plaintiffs based solely on the fact that the price of the securities they bought or sold was *affected* by a misrepresentation: a theory closely akin to the Court's holding today.

Yet this provision was roundly criticized in congressional hearings on the proposed Securities Act, because it failed to include a more substantial "reliance" requirement. Subsequent drafts modified the original proposal, and included an express reliance requirement in the final version of the Act.

* * *

B

A second congressional policy that the majority's opinion ignores is the strong preference the securities laws display for widespread public disclosure and distribution to investors of material information concerning securities. This congressionally-adopted policy is expressed in the numerous and varied disclosure requirements found in the federal securities law scheme.

Yet observers in this field have acknowledged that the fraud-on-the-market theory is at odds with the federal policy favoring disclosure.

* * *

It is no surprise, then, that some of the same voices calling for acceptance of the fraud-on-the-market theory also favor dismantling the federal scheme which mandates disclosure. But to the extent that the federal courts must make a choice between preserving effective disclosure and trumpeting the new fraud-on-the-market hypothesis, I think Congress has spoken clearly—favoring the current pro-disclosure policy. We should limit our role in interpreting § 10(b) and Rule 10b–5 to one of giving effect to such policy decisions by Congress.

III

Finally, the particular facts of this case make it an exceedingly poor candidate for the Court's fraud-on-the-market theory, and illustrate the illogic achieved by that theory's application in many cases.

Respondents here are a class of sellers who sold Basic stock between October, 1977 and December 1978, a fourteen-month period. At the time the class period began, Basic's stock was trading at $20 a share (at the time, an all-time high); the last members of the class to sell their Basic stock got a price of just over $30 a share. It is indisputable that virtually every member of the class made money from his or her sale of Basic stock.

The oddities of applying the fraud-on-the-market theory in this case are manifest. First, there are the facts that the plaintiffs are sellers and the class period is so lengthy—both are virtually without precedent in prior fraud-on-the-market cases. For reasons I discuss in the margin, I think these two facts render this case less apt to application of the fraud-on-the-market hypothesis.

Second, there is the fact that in this case, there is no evidence that petitioner's officials made the troublesome misstatements for the purpose of manipulating stock prices, or with any intent to engage in underhanded trading of Basic stock. Indeed, during the class period, petitioners do not appear to have purchased or sold *any* Basic stock whatsoever. I agree with *amicus* who argues that "[i]mposition of damages liability under Rule 10b–5 makes little sense . . . where a defendant is neither a purchaser nor a seller of securities." In fact, in previous cases, we had recognized that Rule 10b–5 is concerned primarily with cases where the fraud is committed by one trading the security at issue. And it is difficult to square liability in this case with § 10(b)'s express provision that it prohibits fraud "*in connection with* the purchase or sale of any security."

Third, there are the peculiarities of what kinds of investors will be able to recover in this case. As I read the District Court's class certification order, there are potentially many persons who did not purchase Basic stock until *after* the first false statement (October 1977), but who nonetheless *will* be able to recover under the Court's fraud-on-the-market theory. Thus, it is possible that a person who heard the first corporate misstatement and *disbelieved* it—i.e., someone who purchased Basic stock thinking that petitioners' statement was false—may still be included in the plaintiff-class on remand. How a person who undertook such a speculative stock-investing strategy—and made $10 a share doing so (if he bought on October 22, 1977, and sold on December 15, 1978)—can say that he was "defrauded" by virtue of his reliance on the "integrity" of the market price is beyond me. And such speculators may not be uncommon, at least in this case.

Indeed, the facts of this case lead a casual observer to the almost inescapable conclusion that many of those who bought or sold Basic stock during the period in question flatly disbelieved the statements which are alleged to have been "materially misleading." Despite three statements denying that merger negotiations were underway, Basic stock hit record-high after record-high during the 14–month class period. It seems quite possible that, like Casca's knowing disbelief of Caesar's "thrice refusal" of the Crown, clever investors were skeptical of petitioners' three denials that merger talks were going on. Yet such investors, the savviest of the savvy, will be able to recover under the Court's opinion, as long as they now claim that they believed in the "integrity of the market price" when they sold their stock (between September and December, 1978). Thus, persons who bought after hearing and relying on the *falsity* of petitioner's statements may be able to prevail and recover money damages on remand.

And who will pay the judgments won in such actions? I suspect that all too often the majority's rule will "lead to large judgments, payable in the last analysis by innocent investors, for the benefit of speculators and their lawyers." This Court and others have previously recognized that "inexorably broadening . . . the class of plaintiff[s] who may sue in this area of the law will ultimately result in more harm than good." Yet such a bitter harvest is likely to be reaped from the seeds sewn by the Court's decision today.

IV

In sum, I think the Court's embracement of the fraud-on-the-market theory represents a departure in securities law that we are ill-suited to commence—and even less equipped to control as it proceeds. As a result, I must respectfully dissent.

IN RE APPLE COMPUTER

886 F.2d 1109 (9th Cir.1989).

Before FARRIS, BOOCHEVER and HALL, CIRCUIT JUDGES.

FARRIS, CIRCUIT JUDGE:

This is an appeal from three orders which together granted summary judgment against plaintiffs on all of their claims under the Securities Exchange Act of 1934. Plaintiffs allege that Apple Computer Inc. and its top officers misled the market about the capabilities and prospects of a novel office computer and disk-drive system. They claim that they purchased Apple stock in reliance on the artificially high stock price resulting from Apple's misrepresentations, and that they suffered actionable damages when the true facts about the computer became known and Apple's stock price fell by almost 75%. The trial court granted summary judgment on the grounds that each of Apple's alleged misstatements was either immaterial or made without scienter. We affirm in part, reverse in part, and remand.

BACKGROUND

Apple is a publicly-traded company which manufactures computers and computer peripherals. The individual defendants were officers and directors of Apple at the time of the events complained of—November 12, 1982 through September 23, 1983. During the six months immediately preceding this "class period," Apple's common stock traded in a range of between $11 and $30 per share.

In 1982, Apple was readying a computer named "Lisa" and a compatible disk-drive named "Twiggy" for commercial release. Apple's previous successes, most notably the "Apple II," had been in the home computer market. With Lisa, Apple hoped to service the computer needs of medium-size to large corporations. Lisa contained a number of technological innovations which later proved to be commercially viable when incorporated into the "Macintosh" home computer. For example, Lisa pioneered use of the "mouse"—a hand-held device which allows the operator to communicate with the computer without using the keyboard—and "icons"—graphic displays of the computer's functions. However, Lisa and Twiggy themselves proved to be unsuccessful commercially. Apple replaced Twiggy with another disk-drive system before actual sales of Lisa began. Apple discontinued Lisa altogether shortly after the close of the class period.

The named plaintiffs represent a certified class of persons who purchased Apple stock during the class period. They allege that Apple and its top officers made a number of highly positive statements about Lisa and Twiggy during the class period. For example, on November 29, 1982, Apple issued a press release introducing Twiggy, and claiming that "[i]t represents three years of research and development and has undergone extensive testing and design verification during the past year." In a *Business Week* article published on January 31, 1983, Apple's former Chairman of the Board, Steven P. Jobs, is quoted as stating: "I don't think we will have any problem selling all the Lisas we can build." In a Wall Street Journal article published on April 14, 1983, Jobs is quoted as stating: "Lisa is going to be phenomenally successful in the first year out of the chute." Plaintiffs attribute volatility in Apple's common stock price to these optimistic statements. Apple's stock price soared during the class period, reaching a high of almost $63 per share, and bottomed out at a bit over $17 per share shortly after the class period when Apple disclosed news of Lisa's disappointing sales.

Plaintiffs claim that Apple's officers recklessly ignored a number of problems with Lisa and Twiggy which tended to undermine their public optimism. First, internal tests conducted by Apple indicated some slowness and unreliability in Twiggy's information-processing capabilities. Second, communications among Apple's insiders revealed concern that Lisa could not be made compatible with the IBM computer products which dominated the office computer market. Third, there was also concern within Apple that independents would not design software for Lisa. Finally, before beginning actual sales, Apple submitted Lisa prototypes for use by potential customers on a trial basis, and for the inspection of industry analysts and the press. As a result of this test-marketing, Apple received generally enthusiastic reports, and built up a backlog of over 10,000 pre-shipment orders. However, the press and many of the targeted customers raised questions about the wisdom of Lisa's proposed $9,995 retail price. In light of these problems, plaintiffs claim that Apple's unqualified optimism was false and misleading, and actionable under Section 10(b) of the Securities Exchange Act and Rule 10b–5 enacted thereunder.

Although plaintiffs allege that Apple did not fairly and adequately inform the market about Lisa's prospects, many of the risks and underlying problems were widely publicized. For example, the same *Business Week* article which quotes Jobs as stating his belief that Apple would have little trouble selling Lisa also states: "One indication of how uncertain Apple's prospects are is that expert estimates of how many Lisas the company will sell are all over the lot—from 2,000 to 30,000." The article also questions whether independent software writers would support Lisa, and whether the $9,995 price tag was realistic. Similarly the *Wall Street Journal* article in which Jobs predicts that Lisa will be "phenomenally successful" is entitled "Some Warm Up to Apple's 'Lisa,' but Eventual Success is Uncertain." The article details Apple's difficulties in achieving IBM-compatibility, in attracting independent software suppliers, and in raising consumer interest at $9,995. On the other hand, both articles and many others identified by the parties report positive evaluations of Lisa by many large corporations—a number of which expressed interest in purchasing the machine.

In three separate orders, the trial court granted Apple summary judgment against plaintiffs on their entire case. With respect to two of the alleged misstatements, the court held that there was no genuine issue as to scienter. The court held that the remainder of the statements were either not misleading or immaterial as a matter of law, since the information necessary to make the statements not misleading was adequately reported by the press.

On appeal, plaintiffs argue that the trial court misapplied the standard for materiality in a fraud on the market case. They claim that, notwithstanding the press' attention to Lisa's shortcomings, Apple's omissions were material because a reasonable investor would place greater weight on the opinions of corporate insiders. Plaintiffs also argue that evidence of sales of Apple stock during the class period raises a genuine issue as to the defendants' good faith, and evidence that Lisa would be a commercial failure raises a genuine issue as to whether defendants' optimism had a reasonable basis. Finally, plaintiffs argue that the trial court invaded the province of the jury by either ignoring or discrediting the testimony of plaintiffs' expert that Apple's nondisclosures were material and the evidence of volatility in Apple's common stock price.

* * *

SECTION 10(B) LIABILITY UNDER A FRAUD ON THE MARKET THEORY

Rule 10b–5, enacted under Section 10(b), makes it unlawful "[t]o make any untrue statement of fact or to omit to state a material fact necessary to make the statements made, in light of all the circumstances in which they were made, not misleading." The most obvious example of a false or misleading statement is a misrepresentation of historic fact. The statement that "Apple began volume shipments June One of its new $10,000 Lisa Computer," for example, may be actionable if volume shipments did not in fact begin until the middle of June, if the inaccuracy is material, and if it was made recklessly or in bad faith.

Most of the statements challenged by plaintiffs are projections or general expressions of optimism, as opposed to simple representations of historic fact. The "truth" of such statements as the prediction that

"Lisa is going to be phenomenally successful" and the assertion that "we are very pleased with the market acceptance and orders to date" presents more subjective issues. Nonetheless, projections and general expressions of optimism may be actionable under the federal securities laws. See, e.g., Marx v. Computer Sciences Corp., 507 F.2d 485, 489–92 (9th Cir.1974); G & M Inc. v. Newbern, 488 F.2d 742, 745–46 (9th Cir. 1973). A projection or statement of belief contains at least three implicit factual assertions: (1) that the statement is genuinely believed, (2) that there is a reasonable basis for that belief, and (3) that the speaker is not aware of any undisclosed facts tending to seriously undermine the accuracy of the statement. A projection or statement of belief may be actionable to the extent that one of these implied factual assertions is inaccurate.

Plaintiffs bring their claim under the so-called "fraud on the market" theory first recognized by this court in Blackie v. Barrack. In the usual claim under Section 10(b), the plaintiff must show individual reliance on a material misstatement. Under the fraud on the market theory, the plaintiff has the benefit of a presumption that he has indirectly relied on the alleged misstatement, by relying on the integrity of the stock price established by the market. The Supreme Court has recently considered a corporate insider's liability for affirmative misrepresentatives under the fraud on the market theory. Basic, Inc. v. Levinson, 108 S.Ct. 978 (1988). This case raises similar issues with regard to misleading predictions or statements of belief.

Liability for Failure to Disclose Material Risks

The most closely controverted issue in this case is whether the defendants' optimistic statements about Lisa and Twiggy are shielded from liability because of the press' documentation of the relevant risks. The trial court held that disclosures by the press rendered the defendants' omissions immaterial. Ordinarily, omissions by corporate insiders are not rendered immaterial by the fact that the omitted facts are otherwise available to the public. Where a plaintiff alleges actual reliance on a particular statement, it does not matter that the *market* is aware of the facts necessary to make the statement not misleading. The plaintiff may be misled into believing that the stock has been incorrectly valued by the market.

The situation is different in a fraud on the market case. In a fraud on the market case, the plaintiff claims that he was induced to trade stock not by any particular representations made by corporate insiders, but by the artificial stock price set by the market in light of statements made by the insiders as well as all other material public information. Provided that they have credibly entered the market through other means, the facts allegedly omitted by the defendant would already be reflected in the stock's price; the mechanism through which the market discovered the facts in question is not crucial.

The point is best illustrated by way of example. Assume that only two "facts" are relevant to Lisa's prospects, and assume that both facts are equally "true": (1) Apple's Chairman of the Board believes that Lisa will be phenomenally successful, and (2) a number of potential customers have balked at Lisa's proposed $9,995 retail price. Where both facts are transmitted to the market with roughly equal intensity and credibility, the market will receive complete and accurate information. Informed investors will invest in light of an accurate appreciation of the relevant risks. Those investors who know only of the Chairman's optimism may overvalue Apple stock; those who know only of the problems with the suggested retail price may undervalue the stock. However, it is a basic assumption of the securities laws that the partially-informed investors will cancel each other out, and that Apple's stock price will accurately reflect all relevant information.[3] Particular individuals who hear only one of the two facts may receive a distorted impression of Lisa, and thus may have an actionable claim. But the *market*, and any individual who relies only on the price established by the market, will not be misled.

In a recent opinion, the Supreme Court has explicitly embraced this line of reasoning. In *Basic,* a would-be class of stock holders alleged that corporate insiders fraudulently depressed the price of the corporation's stock by falsely denying that they were engaged in merger negotiations. Defendants opposed class certification on the theory that questions of individual reliance on the alleged misstatements predominated over common questions. The trial court overcame that obstacle to class certification by holding that all members of the putative class were entitled to a presumption that they relied on the stock price established by the market, which in turn reflected the alleged misstatements. The Supreme Court approved the trial court's adoption of the fraud on the market theory. However, it stressed that the presumption of reliance could be rebutted by a showing that information sufficient to correct the defendants' alleged misstatements was transmitted through market price in the same fashion as the misstatements themselves. * * *

We conclude that in a fraud on the market case, the defendant's failure to disclose material information may be excused where that information has been made credibly available to the market by other sources. The issue with regard to the bulk of Apple's misstatements is whether, in light of the press' documentation of Lisa's risks, a rational jury could nonetheless find a "substantial likelihood" that full disclosures by Apple would have "significantly altered the 'total mix' of information made available." TSC Industries, Inc. v. Northway, Inc.

With respect to two of the challenged statements, there are genuine issues of material fact. In a November 29, 1982 press release, Apple stated that Twiggy "ensures greater integrity of data than the other high density drives by way of a unique, double-sided

3. "Recent empirical studies have tended to confirm Congress' premise that the market price of shares traded on well-developed markets reflects all publicly available information. . . ." *Basic,* 108 S.Ct. at 991. See In re LTV Securities Litigation, 88 F.R.D. 134, 144 (N.D.Tex. 1980) (citing studies).

mechanism designed and manufactured by Apple." (Statement 4). Apple also claimed that Twiggy "represents three years of research and development and has undergone extensive testing and design verification during the past year." (Statement 5). At the time these optimistic statements were made, internal tests conducted by Apple indicated slowness and unreliability in Twiggy's information-processing capabilities. Approximately two weeks before the press release was issued, the Apple division responsible for production of Lisa warned top executives that "[a]s of now, the Twiggy reliability would lead us to DELAY THE INTRODUCTION OF LISA BY MANY MONTHS." On December 6, 1982, Steven Jobs expressed "virtually zero confidence" in the division that was responsible for the design and development of Twiggy.

There is at least a triable issue of whether Twiggy's technical problems were material facts tending to undermine the unqualified optimism of Statements 4 and 5. Unlike the information about Lisa's market risks, these problems were not made known to the market by the press or by anyone else. However, the November 29, 1982 press release stated that Twiggy would not be available until the following spring. Apple has produced affidavits from several market experts stating that when a computer industry product is announced for future availability, the market fully understands that the product is still in the development stage. Apple therefore claims that the market did not understand Statements 4 and 5 as implying that Twiggy was ready to perform, and that the technical problems Apple was encountering did not materially undermine the optimistic press release.

Whether this argument has merit is a question which should be decided by the jury. The expert affidavits introduced by Apple never state definitively that the market as a whole was aware that there was a problem with Twiggy. There is a difference between knowing that any product-in-development may run into a few snags, and knowing that a particular product has already developed problems so significant as to require months of delay. We are unable to say as a matter of law that Apple's failure to disclose Twiggy's technical problems had no misleading effect on market price.

The remainder of the challenged statements involved Lisa, or Apple generally, rather than Twiggy. Although many of these statements failed to disclose material risks, we agree with the trial court that there are no genuine issues of fact under a fraud on the market theory. The press portrayed Lisa as a gamble, with the potential for either enormous success or enormous failure. At least twenty articles stressed the risks Apple was taking, and detailed the underlying problems producing those risks. Many of the optimistic statements challenged by plaintiffs appeared in those same articles, essentially bracketed by the facts which plaintiffs claim Apple wrongfully failed to disclose. The market could not have been made more aware of Lisa's risks.

We stress the limits of our holding. Scrutiny by the press will not ordinarily excuse the type of unqualified exuberance expressed by Apple and its officers in this case. Even in a fraud on the market case, corporate insiders are not relieved of their duty to disclose material information where that information has received only brief mention in a few poorly-circulated or lightly-regarded publications. The investing public justifiably places heavy reliance on the statements and opinions of corporate insiders. In order to avoid Rule 10b–5 liability, any material information which insiders fail to disclose must be transmitted to the public with a degree of intensity and credibility sufficient to effectively counter-balance any misleading impression created by the insiders' one-sided representations. *See Basic,* 108 S.Ct. at 992 (the presumption that a fraudulent statement has been transmitted through market price may be rebutted by a showing that "corrective statements" have "*credibly* entered the market") (emphasis added). That standard has been met in this case because of the press' intense, sustained focus on Lisa and her risks.

Plaintiffs argue that summary judgment is nonetheless inappropriate because their claim of materiality was supported by evidence of stock price movements, and by the testimony of plaintiffs' expert. The evidence of stock price movement does not raise a genuine issue of material fact. The crucial issue with regard to most of the optimistic statements is whether the statements were misleading because they *omitted* material information. Dramatic price movements in response to an optimistic statement would provide a strong indication that the statement itself was material, but would not suggest that material information tending to undermine the statement has not been made available to the market. An entirely plausible explanation would be that the market was persuaded by Apple's optimism notwithstanding the known risks. In that case, the optimistic statement could still result in liability if the statement was not genuinely believed, or if that belief lacked a reasonable basis. *See Marx,* 507 F.2d at 490–91. But the evidence of stock price movements provides no rational basis for determining whether Lisa's risks were adequately conveyed to the public, and therefore is not enough to get plaintiffs to the jury on the first theory of liability in *Marx.*

More problematic is the testimony by plaintiffs' expert to the effect that the investment community pays special attention to the statements of corporate management and that Apple's nondisclosures were therefore material. As a general rule, summary judgment is inappropriate where an expert's testimony supports the nonmoving party's case. However, where the evidence is as clear as that in this record, the court is not required to defer to the contrary opinion of plaintiffs' "expert." It does not require any special competence to read the pertinent press reports and conclude that Lisa's risks were adequately conveyed to the public.

Scienter

With regard to the great bulk of the statements challenged by the plaintiffs, we have held that the publicity surrounding Lisa was sufficient to shield Apple from liability for failing to disclose material risks. Apple alternatively argues that it is nonetheless entitled to summary judgment because there is no rational basis in the record for concluding that any of the challenged statements was made with the requisite scienter. We have interpreted scienter to include recklessness.

Except for statements four and five, we agree with Apple. The significant technological flaws in Twiggy raise a genuine issue of material fact as to these statements' recklessness. However, plaintiffs produced no evidence controverting defendants' good faith basis for making the other statements. Each of Apple's officers filed an affidavit stating that he acted in good faith belief that his optimistic statements were accurate and not misleading. Apple's massive investment in Lisa demonstrates this good faith. Apple's officers also had a reasonable basis for their optimism about Lisa, given the novelty of Lisa's technology, the positive responses Apple had received from its test-marketing and from the press, and the substantial backlog of pre-shipment orders. Plaintiffs contend that much of the evidence available to Apple suggested that Lisa's prospects were bleak. The results of Apple's test marketing, its internal studies, and reports by the press all may have suggested that Lisa was a gamble. But none of these sources suggested that optimism was unrealistic. Granting them every reasonable inference, plaintiffs can only show that Lisa's prospects were uncertain. Such a showing is insufficient to support liability as a matter of law. See Ernst & Ernst v. Hochfelder (a defendant may not be found liable under Rule 10b–5 "unless he acted other than in good faith").

Plaintiffs also point to evidence that defendants collectively sold about 8% of their Apple holdings valued at roughly $84 million during the class period. Plaintiffs claim that these sales are inconsistent with Apple's expressed optimism, and raise a genuine issue as to the defendants' good faith. Insider trading in suspicious amounts or at suspicious times is probative of bad faith and scienter. See, e.g., Goldman v. Belden, 754 F.2d 1059, 1070 (2d Cir.1985). However, the pattern of stock trading by Apple's insiders is insufficient to raise an issue for the jury. The defendants collectively sold a slightly greater number of shares during an equal period of time just before the class period than they did during the class period. Uncontradicted deposition testimony from several of the defendants provided credible and wholly innocent explanations for the stock sales, ranging from long-standing programs of periodic divestment, to the need to free cash to meet matured tax liabilities. These unrebutted explanations are sufficient to defeat any inference of bad faith. * * *

Any remote inference of bad faith arising from the defendants' stock sales is completely dispelled by the defendants' overall pattern of conduct. Throughout the class period, the defendants continued to stake much of Apple's future on the success of Lisa, pouring millions of dollars into product development, market research, and promotions. At the same time, defendants retained the great bulk of their Apple holdings, and held on in the face of a decline in value of almost 75% following disclosure of Lisa's disappointing sales. The most that can be said of the evidence in this case is that while defendants bet quite heavily on Lisa, they did not put *all* of their eggs in the same basket. We cannot conclude that this conduct is so inconsistent with the defendants' expressed optimism as to raise a triable issue regarding the defendants' good faith.

* * *

CONCLUSION

Plaintiffs have raised genuine issues of material fact in support of their claims that the optimistic statements about Twiggy were materially misleading. We remand so that plaintiffs can present these claims to a jury. However, there are no triable issues with regard to the remainder of plaintiffs' claims. Defendants have conclusively established that all material information tending to undermine their optimistic statements about Lisa had credibly entered the market. There is no rational basis for concluding that the defendants did not genuinely and reasonably believe that these statements were accurate. The trial court properly granted summary judgment.

In addition to the issue of what type of reliance must be shown by plaintiffs in a class action based on misleading corporate statements, there are also difficult questions in determining how to measure the damages suffered by various members of the class, as indicated by the following opinion.

GREEN v. OCCIDENTAL PETROLEUM CORP.

541 F.2d 1335 (9th Cir.1976).

Before DUNIWAY, KILKENNY and SNEED, CIRCUIT JUDGES.

PER CURIAM.

Plaintiffs filed several lawsuits, which were transferred to the district court below, against defendant Occidental Petroleum ("Occidental") and other defendants alleging violations of the federal securities laws due to allegedly misleading financial statements and other reports. * * * As the district judge found:

> The gravamen of each complaint appears to be that the principal defendants violated Section 10(b) of the 1934 Act by utilizing improper accounting practices and issuing press releases and quarterly reports to

shareholders in which the profits of Occidental were overstated, or that other misleading information was given, with the result that the market price of Occidental securities was artifically inflated.

* * *

[The court held that the allowance of class certification was proper under F.R.C.P. Rule 23(b)(3), which permits a class action if "the court finds that the questions of law or fact common to the members of the class predominate over any questions affecting only individual members * * *."]

SNEED, CIRCUIT JUDGE (concurring in part).

* * *

As I view it, the district court abused its discretion if the Rule 23(b)(3) certification was based on the assumption that the rescissory measure of damages would be the proper measure. * * *

I.

An Assumption That the Rescissory Measure of Damages Would Be Used Would Make Certification an Abuse of Discretion

My starting point is that the class members in this case did not deal face to face with the corporate defendant. Rather they purchased in the open market. Whatever these purchasers "lost" did not directly accrue to the defendant. Such benefits as did accrue very likely were tangential and not closely correlated to the purchasers' "losses." It follows that the proper measure of damages is what the purchasers lost as a result of the defendant's wrong, not what the defendant gained.

The rescissory measure of damages does not properly measure that loss. The reason is that it permits a defrauded purchaser to place upon the defendant the burden of any decline in the value of the stock between the date of purchase and the date of disclosure of the fraud even though only a portion of that decline may have been proximately caused by the defendant's wrong. The other portion is the result of market forces unrelated to the wrong. Moreover, this decline is unrelated both to any benefits derived by the defendant from his fraud and to the blameworthiness of his conduct.

* * *

This measure (the difference between the purchase price and the value of the stock as of the date of disclosure) works justly when a defrauded *seller* proceeds after an *increase* in value of the stock against a fraudulent buyer who is unable to return the stock he fraudulently purchased. His inability to return the stock should not deprive the injured seller of the remedy of restitution. Under these circumstances it is appropriate to require the fraudulent buyer to account for his "ill-gotten profits" derived from an increase in the value of the stock following his acquisition of the stock. *See* Janigan v. Taylor, 344 F.2d 781 (1st Cir.1965). *See also,* Affiliated Ute Citizens v. United States,

406 U.S. 128 (1972). Only in this manner can the seller be put in the position he occupied before the contract was made.

* * *

The obligations of a corporate defendant in an open market setting such as in this case are not rooted in a contract of sale. The corporate defendant sold nothing to the aggrieved purchaser. The purchaser acquired his stock from others in the open market. The misrepresentations of the corporate defendant did not result in a shift of the risks of loss in the value of the stock from it to the misled purchaser. There exists no undertaking on the part of the corporate defendant to assume responsibility for the purchaser's loss. The rescissory measure of damages, if used in these circumstances, cannot rest on the theory of restitution. The corporate defendant can return no purchase price because it never received the price. If such a measure is proper it must be because it is necessary to give effect to rule 10b–5.

* * * To impose upon the defendant the burden of restoring *all* investment losses by those who held their stock until disclosure burdens the defendant with certain losses which it neither caused nor with respect to which it assumed a responsibility. I cannot believe rule 10b–5 contemplates a civil penalty so unpredictable in its scope. Nor do I believe that the rescissory measure is appropriate for purchasers who sold before disclosure date. The rescissory measure permits in those instances a recovery of all investment losses between the dates of purchase and sale.

I acknowledge, however, that management of the class in this and similar cases would be simplified by use of the rescissory measure of damages. Each plaintiff retaining his stock to the disclosure date would be required to prove only his purchase price while the disclosure date value would be applicable to all such class members alike. Purchasers selling before disclosure need only prove their purchase and sale price. The price of simplification is, however, too high. Wrongdoing defendants should not be mulcted to make simple the management of a class proceeding under rule 10b–5. To certify a class on the assumption that only by such means is the class manageable would constitute, in my opinion, an abuse of discretion.

II.

An Assumption That the Out-of-Pocket Measure Would Be Used Would Make Certification Not an Abuse of Discretion.

The trial court's certification in this case may have proceeded on a different assumption. That is, its view may have been that damages should be determined by the so-called out-of-pocket measure. This measure fixes recovery at the difference between the purchase price and the value of the stock at the date of purchase. This difference is proximately caused by the misrepresentations of the defendant. It measures precisely the extent to which the purchaser has been required to invest a greater amount than otherwise would have been necessary.

It furthers the purpose of rule 10b–5 without subjecting the wrongdoer to damages the incidence of which resembles that of natural disasters. A certification on this assumption is neither arbitrary nor capricious although it does complicate the management of the class.

Complications result because it becomes necessary to establish, for the period between the date of the misrepresentations and the date of disclosure, data which when arranged on a chart will form, on the one hand, a "price line" and, on the other, a "value line." The price line will reflect, among other things, the effect of the corporate defendant's wrongful conduct. The establishment of these two lines will enable each class member purchaser who has not disposed of his stock prior to disclosure of the misrepresentations to compute his damages by simply subtracting the true value of his stock on the date of his purchase from the price he paid therefor. Fixing the value line for the entire period involved in this case is obviously a more difficult and complex task than would be establishing the price at the date of disclosure of the misrepresentations and the price at all relevant dates prior to disclosure. However, such intimations as have been reflected in the briefs and oral argument suggest that establishing the required value line is practicable. In any event, in my view the attempt is necessary if class certification in this case is to survive.

* * *

III.

Application of the Out-of-Pocket Measure To Purchasers Who Sell Before Disclosure.

What has been said to this point regarding the out-of-pocket measure of damages has assumed that all class members held their stock until disclosure of the misrepresentations. The spread between the price and value lines *at the date of purchase* provides the proper measure of recovery. Purchasers during the period in question who sell before disclosure present a somewhat more difficult issue.

The difficulty springs from uncertainty about whether the spread between the price and value lines remained constant during the entire period. Assuming for the moment that the spread remained constant, class member purchasers who sold before disclosure have recovered from the open market the "cost" of the misrepresentations. * * *

The spread between the price and value lines may not remain constant, however. The spread, or value of the misrepresentations, may increase or decrease as a result of market forces operating on the misrepresentations. To illustrate, a false representation that the corporation has discovered oil will increase in value if the price of oil goes up subsequent to the misrepresentation. Expressed in terms of price and value lines, the spread between the lines increases causing the lines to diverge. A decline in the price of oil, on the other hand, will reduce the value of the misrepresentation and cause the lines to converge.

These changes in the spread are, to repeat, irrelevant to the purchaser who holds his stock until after disclosure. Nor should a *divergence* be material to a purchaser who sells before disclosure. The increased value of the misrepresentation is recouped in the market place just as is the original value of the misrepresentation. A *convergence* of the price and value lines, however, presents a different question with respect to the purchaser who sells before disclosure. From the market he recoups only a portion of the original value of the misrepresentation for which he paid full value. The unrecovered portion should be recoverable from the corporate wrongdoer, even when the purchaser resells at a price greater than his cost.

The advantage of convergence of price and value lines to purchasers who sell before disclosure creates a conflict between them and certain other purchasers. The former will be interested in narrowing the spread between the price and value lines on the date of his sale, while purchasers who bought on the date the former sold will be interested in increasing the spread. All purchasers who held their stock until disclosure are interested in establishing as wide a spread as possible on each date of purchase. These interests may require the creation of sub-classes; they do not, however, make class certification an arbitrary or capricious act.

IV.

Recovery Under Out-of-Pocket Measure Possible Where Sales Price Exceeds Purchase Price.

The out-of-pocket measure of damages, which I regard as the only measure which justifies class certification in this case, permits a recovery by purchasers who sold for a price greater than they paid for the stock. Thus, purchasers who disposed of their stock after disclosure are entitled to recover the difference between the price and value of the stock on the date of their purchase even though they ultimately sold the stock for more than they paid for it. Nor is a recovery of this amount precluded by the fact that the stock has never been sold. Purchasers who sold before disclosure, entitled to recovery because of a convergence of the price and value lines subsequent to their purchase, also may recover even though their selling price exceeded their purchase price.

The reason for these results is that the "cost" of the misrepresentations should be recovered from the wrongdoer to the extent not recovered in the open market. After disclosure, or a sale prior to disclosure following convergence of the price and value lines, recovery in the open market is impossible. The wrongdoer should compensate the purchasers for these losses no longer recoverable from the market. This obligation should not be satisfied by appropriating a portion of each purchaser's investment gains. This would be the consequence of denying any recovery so long as a purchaser's selling price exceeded the purchase price. To permit such an appropriation by a wrongdoer is no more just than to charge the wrongdoer with investment losses not proximately caused by his misrepresentations. The out-of-pocket measure employed properly is the only way to avoid these twin evils.

Assuming that the trial court's certification of the class was based on an intention to apply properly the out-of-pocket measure of damages, I concur in the result reached in the Court's opinion.

If the district court, on remand, applies Judge Sneed's formula, what difficulties will it face which would not be present if it applied the "rescissory measure of damages"?

To explain the workings of his suggested formula, Judge Sneed, in footnotes to his opinion, posited the following situation:

A corporation announces the discovery of X barrels of oil when in fact it discovered no oil at all. Assume the value of X barrels of oil amounts to $10 per share. After the announcement, the stock sells in the market at $150 a share. At this point, P purchases a share. Its "true value" is $140 ($150 – $10). Subsequently, an oil embargo is imposed by the OPEC, raising the assumed value of the corporation's "discovery" to $25 per share. The market price of the stock rises to $165 per share. In due course, the falsity of the corporation's announcement is revealed, and the stock drops to $140 a share. How much should P recover? How much should he recover if he purchased the stock at $165 while the market was at that level?

Assume that instead of the OPEC embargo, there was a massive oil discovery in Alaska, reducing the assumed value of the corporation's "discovery" to $5 per share and the market price to $145. On discovery of the falsity, the market price again drops to $140. How much should P recover? How much should he recover if he sold at $145 while the market was at that level? Should he recover anything if the market price rose from $145 to $155 for reasons unrelated to the "discovery," and P sold at $155?

How realistic is this example? Recall and consider the actual situation in Beecher v. Able, at p. 176 above.

After remand, the *Green* case was settled, with Occidental and its accountants agreeing to pay approximately $12 million into a settlement fund to be distributed to persons who purchased Occidental stock between July 31, 1969 and March 5, 1971. Each such purchaser was entitled to claim a loss of 3% of the gross purchase price of any such stock which he resold during that period, and 15% of any such stock which he did not resell during that period. If the aggregate amount of claims filed was greater than, or less than, the settlement fund, the recovery by each claimant was to be reduced, or increased, on a pro rata basis. Notice of Settlement Hearing, Wall St. Journal, Apr. 16, 1979, p. 26, col. 3. Is this method of computing the amount that can be recovered by each purchaser consistent with the approach urged by Judge Sneed?

Selected References

T. Hazen, Securities Regulation §§ 13.6, 13.10 (2d ed. 1990).

Symposium, Affirmative Disclosure Obligations Under the Securities Laws, 46 Md.L.Rev. 908 (1987).

Bauman, Rule 10b–5 and the Corporation's Affirmative Duty to Disclose, 67 Geo.L.Rev. 935 (1979).

Black, Fraud on the Market: A Criticism of Dispensing with Reliance Requirements in Certain Open Market Transactions, 62 N.C.L.Rev. 435 (1984).

Block, Barton & Garfield, Affirmative Duty to Disclose Material Information Concerning Issuer's Financial Condition and Business Plans, 40 Bus.Law. 1243 (1985).

Cornell & Morgan, Using Finance Theory to Measure Damages in Fraud on the Market Cases, 37 U.C.L.A.L.Rev. 883 (1990).

Macey & Miller, Good Finance, Bad Economics: An Analysis of the Fraud-on-the-Market Theory, 42 Stan.L.Rev. 1059 (1990).

Sheffey, Securities Law Responsibilities of Issuers to Respond to Rumors and other Publicity, 57 Notre Dame Law. 755 (1982).

Wilkinson, The Affirmative Duty to Disclose After Chiarella and Dirks, 10 J.Corp.L. 581 (1985).

Note, The Fraud-on-the-Market Theory and the Efficient Market Hypothesis: Applying A Consistent Standard, 14 J.Corp.L. 443 (1989).

Note, An Unwise Extension of the Fraud-on-the-Market Theory, 67 N.C.L. Rev. 1161 (1989).

CHAPTER 7

TRANSACTIONS WITH INTERESTED PARTIES

A. "FRAUD ON THE CORPORATION"

When officers, directors or controlling shareholders of a corporation cause the corporation to enter into a transaction with them, the transaction may be subject to attack under state corporation law as "self-dealing." When the transaction involves the sale or purchase of securities, it may also be subject to attack under Rule 10b–5. In the *Hooper* case, p. 464 above, the Fifth Circuit held that a corporation which was defrauded into issuing its securities for an inadequate consideration was a person entitled to the protection of Rule 10b–5. Subsequent cases have explored the difficult problems in applying Rule 10b–5 when the persons alleged to have defrauded the corporation are its own directors or controlling shareholders.

RUCKLE v. ROTO AMERICAN CORP., 339 F.2d 24 (2d Cir.1964) was a derivative action on behalf of a corporation, alleging that a majority of the directors withheld material information from the remaining directors in connection with the approval of the issuance of shares to affiliates of the president of the corporation. The Second Circuit, per Medina and Lumbard, JJ., held that the failure to disclose such information to the remaining directors constituted a "fraud" on the corporation within the meaning of Rule 10b–5. The court said:

> We note at the outset that in other contexts, such as embezzlement and conflict of interest, a majority or even the entire board of directors may be held to have defrauded their corporation. When it is practical as well as just to do so, courts have experienced no difficulty in rejecting such cliches as the directors constitute the corporation and a corporation, like any other person, cannot defraud itself.
>
> If, in this case, the board defrauded the corporation into issuing shares either to its members or others, we can think of no reason to say that redress under Rule 10b–5 is precluded, though it would have been available had anyone else committed the fraud. There can be no more effective way to emasculate the policies of the federal securities laws than to deny relief solely because a fraud was committed by a director rather than by an outsider.

Marshall, J., concurred in the result.

Three weeks after the decision in the *Ruckle* case, the Second Circuit decided O'NEILL v. MAYTAG, 339 F.2d 764 (1964), a derivative action on behalf of National Airlines, alleging that its directors caused it to reacquire its own shares from another airline at a premium price in order to eliminate a threat to their control of National. The Second Circuit, per Lumbard and Marshall, JJ., held that while the acts alleged might constitute a breach of fiduciary duty under state law, "no cause of action is stated under Rule 10b–5 unless there is an allegation of facts amounting to deception." The court distinguished *Ruckle* on the ground that in *Ruckle* "there was a clear allegation of deception in connection with the sale of securities, and the fact that the alleged deception occurred within the corporate structure did not by itself avoid liability under Rule 10b–5." Hays, J., dissented.

PAPPAS v. MOSS

393 F.2d 865 (3d Cir.1968).

Before KALODNER, GANEY and SEITZ, CIRCUIT JUDGES.

SEITZ, CIRCUIT JUDGE.

* * *

Plaintiffs below asserted claims against the defendants under the New Jersey common law and under the Securities Exchange Act of 1934 as amended. Each claim is based on alleged wrongful acts of the defendants in connection with the sale of 64,534 additional shares of Hydromatics stock to themselves and to outsiders (who were not sued) in private placement transactions at a price so far below the contemporaneous fair value for the shares as to amount to fraud.

* * *

Prior to the issuance of the shares here involved, Hydromatics, Inc. had 500,000 authorized shares of common stock of which some 288,000 shares were issued and outstanding, plus 30,000 shares reserved for issuance under a stock option plan. In 1960 all of these shares were listed for trading on the American Stock Exchange.

At all times here pertinent the defendants constituted the board of directors of Hydromatics and all except one were officers thereof. The one non-officer director was also named as a defendant in his capacity as trustee of the Company's Profit–Sharing and Retirement Trust. Prior to the stock sale in dispute, the defendants owned in the aggregate 170,957 shares. In addition, the trustee of the Profit Sharing Trust held 1,100 shares. Thus, the individual defendants controlled 172,057 out of a total of 288,000 outstanding shares.

By resolution dated December 21, 1961, the defendants by board action unanimously authorized the issuance of up to 100,000 shares of Hydromatics common stock at a price of $6.00 per share to themselves and to a limited number of additional purchasers.

* * *

Plaintiff contends that there was substantial proof and indeed findings of fact which showed a direct violation of Rule 10b–5 arising from fraud and misrepresentations by defendants. Defendants argue that even if the plaintiff's allegations concerning fraud and misrepresentation were proved, they could not constitute violations of the Rule. They contend that "violations [of 10b–5] can occur only where the alleged injury could have been prevented by the injured parties had they known the true facts." Defendants insist that under the language of the Rule there must be reliance by a party with standing before it is applicable. Their reasoning goes this way: a corporation can only act through its agents; all of its agents (directors) here were aware of the true facts, ergo, the corporation was not deceived.

Given evidence sufficient to satisfy the preliminary requirements of the Rule, we think that where, as here, a board of directors is alleged to have caused their corporation to sell its stock to them and others at a fraudulently low price, a violation of Rule 10b–5 is asserted. Certainly a fraud in the act of selling a security of the required kind is asserted. The only question which remains is whether the act of fraud involved is of the type embraced within the statute and the Rule. It is contended that proof of "deception" is required to bring the claim within the statute and implementing Rule. Obviously the definition of "deception" may vary with the circumstances. But if a "deception" is required in the present context, it is fairly found by viewing this fraud as though the "independent" stockholders were standing in the place of the defrauded corporate entity at the time the original resolution authorizing the stock sales was passed. Indeed, as the district court found, that resolution contained at least two material misrepresentations of fact. Certainly the deception of the independent stockholders is no less real because, "formalistically", the corporate entity was the victim of the fraud. The same is true of the fact that the fraud may go unredressed because those in a position to sue lack actual knowledge of the fraud.

The defendants seem to agree that in situations where stockholder approval of a purchase or sale of stock is necessary, material misstatements of fact made or fraud committed by a unanimous board would nevertheless be embraced by Rule 10b–5. They would apparently take a similar position if a minority of the board of directors were misled. We think these references as to their position indicate that their construction of Rule 10b–5 is untenable. It exalts form over substance. Indeed, it seems to suggest that there is an inverse relationship between the application of the Rule and the number of directors participating in a fraud on its corporation. Finally, it restricts the application of the Rule in a way which is at odds with its basic purpose.

In SCHOENBAUM v. FIRSTBROOK, 405 F.2d 200, 215 (2d Cir. 1968), the court faced a situation similar to *Pappas,* in which Acquitaine, the controlling shareholder of Banff, was alleged to have used its controlling influence to cause Banff to issue additional shares to it for an inadequate consideration. The eight directors of Banff were conceded to have known all the material facts at the time the board approved the transaction. Furthermore, the three representatives of Aquitaine on the board abstained from voting on the transaction, which was approved by the five "non-interested" directors. A three-judge panel of the Second Circuit held that there could be no fraud on the corporation under Rule 10b–5, since the knowledge of the "non-interested" directors would be imputed to the corporation. In a rehearing *en banc*, the full Second Circuit reversed this decision. The rationale for its decision was stated somewhat cryptically:

> In the present case it is alleged that Aquitaine exercised a controlling influence over the issuance to it of treasury stock of Banff for a wholly inadequate consideration. If it is established that the transaction took place as alleged it constituted a violation of Rule 10b–5, subdivision (3) because Aquitaine engaged in an "act, practice or course of business which operates or would operate as a fraud or deceit upon any person, in connection with the purchase or sale of any security." Moreover, Aquitaine and the directors of Banff were guilty of deceiving the stockholders of Banff (other than Aquitaine). See Pappas v. Moss, 393 F.2d 865 (3d Cir.1968).

Three years after the Second Circuit's decision in *Schoenbaum*, the Fifth Circuit took a further step, holding that the trustee in bankruptcy of a corporation could sue its promoters under Rule 10b–5 for causing the corporation to issue its stock in exchange for worthless assets when not only all of the officers and directors, but *all of the shareholders* at the time of the transaction, were participants in the deception. The court held that the transaction "was intended to and in fact did operate *in futuro* to deceive and damage various persons," including the purchasers in a subsequent public offering of the company's stock. BAILES v. COLONIAL PRESS, 444 F.2d 1241 (5th Cir.1971).[a]

In 1972, the Second Circuit drew back slightly from its holding in *Schoenbaum* by barring an action under Rule 10b–5 where the plaintiff conceded that defendants had made full disclosure to the shareholders concerning the terms of a merger, and argued that the unfairness of the terms, by itself, constituted fraud on the shareholders. POPKIN v. BISHOP, 464 F.2d 714 (2d Cir.1972). However, in 1976, the Second Circuit followed a different approach and held that overreaching alone could constitute fraud, without the necessity of alleging misstatements or concealment of material facts. This decision brought the matter before the Supreme Court for review.

---

a. The same court followed a similar approach in Miller v. San Sebastian Gold Mines, 540 F.2d 807 (5th Cir.1976). What classic corporate litigation do the facts in these cases resemble?

SANTA FE INDUSTRIES v. GREEN

430 U.S. 462 (1977).

MR. JUSTICE WHITE delivered the opinion of the Court.

The issue in this case involves the reach and coverage of § 10(b) of the Securities Exchange Act of 1934 and Rule 10b–5 thereunder in the context of a Delaware short-form merger transaction used by the majority stockholder of a corporation to eliminate the minority interest.

I

In 1936 petitioner Santa Fe Industries, Inc. ("Santa Fe") acquired control of 60% of the stock of Kirby Lumber Corporation ("Kirby"), a Delaware corporation. Through a series of purchases over the succeeding years, Santa Fe increased its control of Kirby's stock to 95%; the purchase prices during the period 1968–1973 ranged from $65 to $92.50 per share. In 1974, wishing to acquire 100% ownership of Kirby, Santa Fe availed itself of § 253 of the Delaware Corporation Law, known as the "short-form merger" statute. Section 253 permits a parent corporation owning at least 90% of the stock of a subsidiary to merge with that subsidiary, upon approval by the parent's board of directors, and to make payment in cash for the shares of the minority stockholders. The statute does not require the consent of, or advance notice to, the minority stockholders. However, notice of the merger must be given within 10 days after its effective date, and any stockholder who is dissatisfied with the terms of the merger may petition the Delaware Court of Chancery for a decree ordering the surviving corporation to pay him the fair value of his shares, as determined by a court-appointed appraiser subject to review by the court. Del.Gen.Corp.Law §§ 253, 262.

Santa Fe obtained independent appraisals of the physical assets of Kirby—land, timber, buildings, and machinery—and of Kirby's oil, gas, and mineral interests. These appraisals, together with other financial information, were submitted to Morgan, Stanley & Company ("Morgan Stanley"), an investment banking firm retained to appraise the fair market value of Kirby stock. Kirby's physical assets were appraised at $320 million (amounting to $640 for each of the 500,000 shares); Kirby's stock was valued by Morgan Stanley at $125 per share. Under the terms of the merger, minority stockholders were offered $150 per share.

The provisions of the short-form merger statute were fully complied with. The minority stockholders of Kirby were notified the day after the merger became effective and were advised of their right to obtain an appraisal in Delaware court if dissatisfied with the offer of $150 per share. They also received an information statement containing, in addition to the relevant financial data about Kirby, the appraisals of the value of Kirby's assets and the Morgan Stanley appraisal concluding that the fair market value of the stock was $125 per share.

Respondents, minority stockholders of Kirby, objected to the terms of the merger, but did not pursue their appraisal remedy in the Delaware Court of Chancery. Instead, they brought this action in federal court on behalf of the corporation and other minority stockholders, seeking to set aside the merger or to recover what they claimed to be the fair value of their shares. The amended complaint asserted that, based on the fair market value of Kirby's physical assets as revealed by the appraisal included in the Information Statement sent to minority shareholders, Kirby's stock was worth at least $772 per share. The complaint alleged further that the merger took place without prior notice to minority stockholders; that the purpose of the merger was to appropriate the difference between the "conceded pro rata of value of the physical assets" and the offer of $150 per share—to "freez[e] out the minority stockholders at a wholly inadequate price," and that Santa Fe, knowing the appraised value of the physical assets, obtained a "fraudulent appraisal" of the stock from Morgan Stanley and offered $25 above that appraisal "in order to lull the minority stockholders into erroneously believing that [Santa Fe was] generous." This course of conduct was alleged to be "a violation of Rule 10b–5 because defendants employed a 'device, scheme or artifice to defraud' and engaged in an 'act, practice or course of business which operates or would operate as a fraud or deceit upon any person, in connection with the purchase or sale of any security.'" Morgan Stanley assertedly participated in the fraud as an accessory by submitting its appraisal of $125 per share although knowing the appraised value of the physical assets.

The District Court dismissed the complaint for failure to state a claim upon which relief could be granted. As the District Court understood the complaint, respondents' case rested on two distinct grounds. First, federal law was assertedly violated because the merger was for the sole purpose of eliminating the minority from the company, therefore lacking any justifiable business purpose, and because the merger was undertaken without prior notice to the minority shareholders. Second, the low valuation placed on the shares in the cash exchange offer was itself said to be a fraud actionable under Rule 10b–5. In rejecting the first ground for recovery, the District Court reasoned that Delaware law required neither a business purpose for a short-form merger nor prior notice to the minority shareholders who the statute contemplated would be removed from the company, and that Rule 10b–5 did not override these provisions of state corporate law by independently placing a duty on the majority not to merge without prior notice and without a justifiable business purpose.

As for the claim that actionable fraud inhered in the allegedly gross undervaluation of the minority shares, the District Court observed that respondents valued their shares at a minimum of $772 per share, "basing this figure on the pro rata value of Kirby's physical assets." Accepting this valuation for purposes of the motion to dismiss, the District Court further noted that, as revealed by the complaint, the physical asset appraisal, along with other information relevant to

Morgan Stanley's valuation of the shares, had been included with the Information Statement sent to respondents within the time required by state law. It thought that if "full and fair disclosure is made, transactions eliminating minority interests are beyond the purview of Rule 10b–5," and concluded that "the complaint fail[ed] to allege an omission, misstatement or fraudulent course of conduct that would have impeded a shareholder's judgment of the value of the offer." The complaint therefore failed to state a claim and was dismissed.

A divided Court of Appeals for the Second Circuit reversed, 533 F.2d 1283 (1976). It first agreed that there was a double aspect to the case: first, the claim that gross undervaluation of the minority stock itself violated Rule 10b–5; and second, that "without any misrepresentation or failure to disclose relevant facts, the merger constituted a violation of Rule 10b–5" because it was accomplished without any corporate purpose and without prior notice to the minority stockholders. As to the first aspect of the case, the Court of Appeals did not disturb the District Court's conclusion that the complaint did not allege a material misrepresentation or nondisclosure with respect to the value of the stock; and the court declined to rule that a claim of gross undervaluation itself would suffice to make out a Rule 10b–5 case. With respect to the second aspect of the case, however, the court fundamentally disagreed with the District Court as to the reach and coverage of Rule 10b–5. The Court of Appeals' view was that, although the Rule plainly reached material misrepresentations and nondisclosures in connection with the purchase or sale of securities, neither misrepresentation or nondisclosure was a necessary element of a Rule 10b–5 action; the rule reached "breaches of fiduciary duty by a majority against minority shareholders without any charge of misrepresentation or lack of disclosure." The court went on to hold that the complaint taken as a whole stated a cause of action under the Rule:

> "We hold that a complaint alleges a claim under Rule 10b–5 when it charges, in connection with a Delaware short-form merger, that the majority has committed a breach of its fiduciary duty to deal fairly with minority shareholders by effecting the merger without any justifiable business purpose. The minority shareholders are given no prior notice of the merger, thus having no opportunity to apply for injunctive relief, and the proposed price to be paid is substantially lower than the appraised value reflected in the Information Statement."

We granted the petition for certiorari challenging this holding because of the importance of the issue involved to the administration of the federal securities laws. We reverse.

II

Section 10(b) of the 1934 Act makes it "unlawful for any person * * * to use or employ * * * any manipulative or deceptive device or contrivance in contravention of [Securities Exchange Commission rules]"; Rule 10b–5, promulgated by the SEC under § 10(b), prohibits in addition to nondisclosure and misrepresentation, any "artifice to defraud" or any act "which operates or would operate as a fraud or deceit." The court below construed the term "fraud" in Rule 10b–5 by adverting to the use of the term in several of this Court's decisions in contexts other than the 1934 Act and the related Securities Act of 1933. The Court of Appeals' approach to the interpretation of Rule 10b–5 is inconsistent with that taken by the Court last Term in Ernst & Ernst v. Hochfelder.

Ernst & Ernst makes clear that in deciding whether a complaint states a cause of action for "fraud" under Rule 10b–5, "we turn first to the language of § 10(b), for '[t]he starting point in every case involving construction of a statute is the language itself.' " In holding that a cause of action under Rule 10b–5 does not lie for mere negligence, the Court began with the principle that "[a]scertainment of congressional intent with respect to the standard of liability created by a particular section of the [1933 and 1934] Acts must * * * rest primarily on the language of that section," and then focused on the statutory language of § 10(b)—"[t]he words 'manipulative or deceptive' used in conjunction with 'device or contrivance.' " The same language and the same principle apply to this case.

To the extent that the Court of Appeals would rely on the use of the term "fraud" in Rule 10b–5 to bring within the ambit of the Rule all breaches of fiduciary duty in connection with a securities transaction, its interpretation would, like the interpretation rejected by the Court in *Ernst & Ernst,* "add a gloss to the operative language of the statute quite different from its commonly accepted meaning." But as the Court there held, the language of the statute must control the interpretation of the Rule:

> "Rule 10b–5 was adopted pursuant to authority granted the [Securities Exchange] Commission under § 10(b). The rulemaking power granted to an administrative agency charged with the administration of a federal statute is not the power to make law. Rather, it is ' "the power to adopt regulations to carry into effect the will of Congress as expressed by the statute." ' * * * [The scope of the Rule] cannot exceed the power granted the Commission by Congress under § 10(b)." [12]

The language of § 10(b) gives no indication that Congress meant to prohibit any conduct not involving manipulation or deception. Nor have we been cited to any evidence in the legislative history that would

12. The case for adhering to the language of the statute is even stronger here than in *Ernst & Ernst,* where the interpretation of Rule 10b–5 rejected by the Court was strongly urged by the Commission. By contrast, the Commission apparently has not concluded that Rule 10b–5 should be used to reach "going private" transactions where the majority stockholder eliminates the minority at an allegedly unfair price. See SEC Securities Act Release No. 5567 (Feb. 6, 1975) (proposing Rules 13e–3A and 13e–3B dealing with "going private" transactions, pursuant to six sections of the 1934 Act including § 10(b), but stating that the Commission "has reached no conclusions with respect to the proposed rules"). Because we are concerned here only with § 10(b), we intimate no view as to the Commission's authority to promulgate such rules under other sections of the Act.

support a departure from the language of the statute. "When a statute speaks so specifically in terms of manipulation and deception, * * * and when its history reflects no more expansive intent, we are quite unwilling to extend the scope of the statute * * *." Id., at 214 (footnote omitted). Thus the claim of fraud and fiduciary breach in this complaint states a cause of action under any part of Rule 10b–5 only if the conduct alleged can be fairly viewed as "manipulative or deceptive" within the meaning of the statute.

III

It is our judgment that the transaction, if carried out as alleged in the complaint, was neither deceptive nor manipulative and therefore did not violate either § 10(b) of the Act or Rule 10b–5.

As we have indicated, the case comes to us on the premise that the complaint failed to allege a material misrepresentation or material failure to disclose. The finding of the District Court, undisturbed by the Court of Appeals, was that there was no "omission" or "misstatement" in the Information Statement accompanying the notice of merger. On the basis of the information provided, minority shareholders could either accept the price offered or reject it and seek an appraisal in the Delaware Court of Chancery. Their choice was fairly presented, and they were furnished with all relevant information on which to base their decision.[14]

We therefore find inapposite the cases relied upon by respondents and the court below, in which the breaches of fiduciary duty held violative of Rule 10b–5 included some element of deception.[15] Those

14. In addition to their principal argument that the complaint alleges a fraud under clauses (a) and (c) of Rule 10b–5, respondents also argue that the complaint alleges nondisclosure and misrepresentation in violation of clause (b) of the Rule. Their major contention in this respect is that the majority stockholder's failure to give the minority advance notice of the merger was a material nondisclosure, even though the Delaware short-form merger statute does not require such notice. But respondents do not indicate how they might have acted differently had they had prior notice of the merger. Indeed, they accept the conclusion of both courts below that under Delaware law they could not have enjoined the merger because an appraisal proceeding is their sole remedy in the Delaware courts for any alleged unfairness in the terms of the merger. Thus the failure to give advance notice was not a material nondisclosure within the meaning of the statute or the Rule. Cf. TSC Industries, Inc. v. Northway, Inc., 426 U.S. 438 (1976).

15. The decisions of this Court relied upon by respondents all involved deceptive conduct as part of the Rule 10b–5 violation alleged. Affiliated Ute Citizens v. United States, 406 U.S. 128 (1972) (misstatements of material fact used by bank employees in position of market maker to acquire stock at less than fair value); Superintendent of Insurance v. Bankers Life & Cas. Co., 404 U.S. 6, 9 (1971) ("seller [of bonds] was duped into believing that it, the seller, would receive the proceeds"). Cf. SEC v. Capital Gains Research Bureau, 375 U.S. 180 (1963) (injunction under Investment Advisors Act of 1940 to compel registered investment adviser to disclose to his clients his own financial interest in his recommendations).

We have been cited to a large number of cases in the Courts of Appeals, all of which involved an element of deception as part of the fiduciary misconduct held to violate Rule 10b–5. E.g., Schoenbaum v. Firstbrook, Drachman v. Harvey, Schlick v. Penn–Dixie Cement Corp., Pappas v. Moss, Shell v. Hensley, Rekant v. Dresser. See Note, 89 Harv.L.Rev. 1917, 1926 (1976) (stating that no appellate decision before that of C.A.2 in this case and in Marshel v. AFW Fabric Corp., 533 F.2d 1277, "had

cases forcefully reflect the principle that "[s]ection 10(b) must be read flexibly, not technically and restrictively" and that the statute provides a cause of action for any plaintiff who "suffer[s] an injury as a result of deceptive practices touching its sale [or purchase] of securities. * * *" Superintendent of Insurance v. Bankers Life & Casualty Co., 404 U.S. 6, 12–13 (1971). But the cases do not support the proposition, adopted by the Court of Appeals below and urged by respondents here, that a breach of fiduciary duty by majority stockholders, without any deception, misrepresentation, or nondisclosure, violates the statute and the Rule.

It is also readily apparent that the conduct alleged in the complaint was not "manipulative" within the meaning of the statute. Manipulation is "virtually a term of art when used in connection with securities markets." Ernst & Ernst, 425 U.S., at 199. The term refers generally to practices, such as wash sales, matched orders, or rigged prices, that are intended to mislead investors by artificially affecting market activity. Section 10(b)'s general prohibition of practices deemed by the SEC to be "manipulative"—in this technical sense of artificially affecting market activity in order to mislead investors—is fully consistent with the fundamental purpose of the 1934 Act "to substitute a philosophy of full disclosure for the philosophy of *caveat emptor*. * * *" Indeed, nondisclosure is usually essential to the success of a manipulative scheme. No doubt Congress meant to prohibit the full range of ingenious devices that might be used to manipulate securities prices. But we do not think it would have chosen this "term of art" if it had meant to bring within the scope of § 10(b) instances of corporate mismanagement such as this, in which the essence of the complaint is that shareholders were treated unfairly by a fiduciary.

IV

The language of the statute is, we think, "sufficiently clear in its context" to be dispositive here, but even if it were not, there are additional considerations that weigh heavily against permitting a cause of action under Rule 10b–5 for the breach of corporate fiduciary duty alleged in this complaint. Congress did not expressly provide a private cause of action for violations of § 10(b). Although we have recognized an implied cause of action under that section in some circumstances, we have also recognized that a private cause of action under the antifraud provisions of the Securities Exchange Act should not be implied where it is "unnecessary to ensure the fulfillment of Congress' purposes" in adopting the Act. Piper v. Chris–Craft Industries. As we noted earlier, the Court repeatedly has described the "fundamental purpose" of the Act as implementing a "philosophy of full disclosure"; once full and fair disclosure has occurred, the fairness of the terms of the transaction is at most a tangential concern of the statute. As in Cort v. Ash, 422

permitted a 10b–5 claim without some element of misrepresentation or nondisclosure").

U.S. 78, 80 (1975), we are reluctant to recognize a cause of action here to serve what is "at best a subsidiary purpose" of the federal legislation.

A second factor in determining whether Congress intended to create a federal cause of action in these circumstances is "whether 'the cause of action [is] one traditionally relegated to state law. * * *'" Piper v. Chris-Craft Industries, Inc., quoting Cort v. Ash. The Delaware Legislature has supplied minority shareholders with a cause of action in the Delaware Court of Chancery to recover the fair value of shares allegedly undervalued in a short-form merger. Of course, the existence of a particular state law remedy is not dispositive of the question whether Congress meant to provide a similar federal remedy, but as in *Piper* and *Cort,* we conclude that "it is entirely appropriate in this instance to relegate respondent and others in his situation to whatever remedy is created by state law."

The reasoning behind a holding that the complaint in this case alleged fraud under Rule 10b–5 could not be easily contained. It is difficult to imagine how a court could distinguish, for purposes of Rule 10b–5 fraud, between a majority stockholder's use of a short-form merger to eliminate the minority at an unfair price and the use of some other device, such as a long-form merger, tender offer, or liquidation, to achieve the same result; or indeed how a court could distinguish the alleged abuses in these going private transactions from other types of fiduciary self-dealing involving transactions in securities. The result would be to bring within the Rule a wide variety of corporate conduct traditionally left to state regulation. In addition to posing a "danger of vexatious litigation which could result from a widely expanded class of plaintiffs under Rule 10b–5," Blue Chip Stamps v. Manor Drug Stores, 421 U.S. 723, 740 (1975), this extension of the federal securities laws would overlap and quite possibly interfere with state corporate law. Federal courts applying a "federal fiduciary principle" under Rule 10b–5 could be expected to depart from state fiduciary standards at least to the extent necessary to ensure uniformity within the federal system.[16] Absent a clear indication of congressional intent, we are reluctant to federalize the substantial portion of the law of corporations that deals with transactions in securities, particularly where established state policies of corporate regulation would be overridden. As the Court stated in Cort v. Ash, supra, "Corporations are creatures of state law, and investors commit their funds to corporate directors on the under-

16. For example, some States apparently require a "valid corporate purpose" for the elimination of the minority interest through a short-form merger, whereas other States do not. Compare Bryan v. Brock & Blevins Co., 490 F.2d 563 (C.A.5), cert. denied, 419 U.S. 844 (1974) (merger arranged by controlling stockholder for no business purpose except to eliminate 15% minority stockholder violated Georgia short-form merger statute) with Stauffer v. Standard Brands, Inc., 41 Del.Ch. 7, 187 A.2d 78 (Sup.Ct.1962) (Delaware short-form merger statute allows majority stockholder to eliminate the minority interest without any corporate purpose and subject only to an appraisal remedy). Thus to the extent that Rule 10b–5 is interpreted to require a valid corporate purpose for elimination of minority shareholders as well as a fair price for their shares, it would impose a stricter standard of fiduciary duty than that required by the law of some States.

standing that, except where federal law *expressly* requires certain responsibilities of directors with respect to stockholders, state law will govern the internal affairs of the corporation."

We thus adhere to the position that "Congress by § 10(b) did not seek to regulate transactions which constitute no more than internal corporate mismanagement." Superintendent of Insurance v. Bankers Life & Cas. Co., 404 U.S., at 12. There may well be a need for uniform federal fiduciary standards to govern mergers such as that challenged in this complaint. But those standards should not be supplied by judicial extension of § 10(b) and Rule 10b–5 to "cover the corporate universe." [17]

The judgment of the Court of Appeals is reversed, and the case is remanded for further proceedings consistent with this opinion.[a]

MR. JUSTICE BRENNAN dissents and would affirm for substantially the reasons stated in the majority and concurring opinions in the Court of Appeals, 533 F.2d 1283 (1976).

MR. JUSTICE BLACKMUN, concurring in part.

Like MR. JUSTICE STEVENS, I refrain from joining Part IV of the Court's opinion. I, too, regard that part as unnecessary for the decision in the instant case and, indeed, as exacerbating the concerns I expressed in my dissents in Blue Chip Stamps v. Manor Drug Stores, and in Ernst & Ernst v. Hochfelder. I, however, join the remainder of the Court's opinion and its judgment.

MR. JUSTICE STEVENS, concurring in part.

For the reasons stated by Mr. Justice Blackmun in his dissenting opinion in Blue Chip Stamps v. Manor Drug Stores, and those stated in my dissent in Piper v. Chris–Craft Industries, I believe both of those cases were incorrectly decided. I foresee some danger that Part IV of the Court's opinion in this case may incorrectly be read as extending the holdings of those cases. Moreover, the entire discussion in Part IV is unnecessary to the decision of this case. Accordingly, I join only Parts I, II, and III of the Court's opinion. I would also add further emphasis to the fact that the controlling stockholders in this case did not breach any duty owed to the minority shareholders because (a)

17. Cary, Federalism and Corporate Law: Reflections Upon Delaware, 83 Yale L.J. 663, 700 (1974). Professor Cary argues vigorously for comprehensive federal fiduciary standards, but urges a "frontal" attack by a new federal statute rather than an extension of Rule 10b–5. He writes, "It seems anomalous to jig-saw every kind of corporate dispute into the federal courts through the securities acts as they are presently written." See also, Note, Going Private, 84 Yale L.J. 903 (1974) (proposing the application of traditional doctrines of substantive corporate law to problems of fairness raised by "going private" transactions such as short-form mergers).

a. In subsequent proceedings under Delaware law by minority shareholders of Kirby who had objected to the merger and demanded appraisal of their shares, the Delaware Supreme Court upheld an award of $254.40 per share, based 60% on Kirby's earnings and 40% on the value of its assets. The court rejected shareholders' argument that the award should be based on the amount that shareholders would have received on a sale of the entire company, holding that under Delaware law "going concern" value and not liquidation value was the appropriate standard. BELL v. KIRBY LUMBER, 413 A.2d 137 (Del.1980).

there was complete disclosure of the relevant facts, and (b) the minority are entitled to receive the fair value of their shares. The facts alleged in the complaint do not constitute "fraud" within the meaning of Rule 10b–5.

The *Santa Fe* decision is pretty clear in its basic holding: an allegation of "fraud" on a corporation or its outside shareholders under Rule 10b–5 must involve some element of deception or concealment of material information, rather than mere unfairness. What is less clear is how deeply its rationale cuts into the "fraud on the corporation" cases up to and including *Schoenbaum.* There are two aspects to this inquiry: (a) the circumstances under which disclosure to the board of directors will bar the assertion of any claim on behalf of the corporation, and (b) the circumstances under which nondisclosure to the shareholders may still give rise to a cause of action. The Second Circuit has considered both of these questions in cases decided after *Santa Fe.*

MALDONADO v. FLYNN

597 F.2d 789 (2d Cir.1979).

Before KAUFMAN, CHIEF JUDGE, and MANSFIELD and MESKILL, CIRCUIT JUDGES.

MANSFIELD, CIRCUIT JUDGE:

In this stockholders' derivative suit on behalf of Zapata Corporation ("Zapata" or "the Corporation"), a Delaware corporation, against a group of its past and present directors, the complaint alleges that the defendants violated various provisions of the Securities and Exchange Act of 1934, ("the Act") and applicable "common law" in their administration of the Corporation's stock option plan for key employees of Zapata and its subsidiaries. Specifically, it is claimed that defendants (1) violated § 10(b) of the Act and Rule 10b–5 by modifying the stock option plan without obtaining stockholders' approval, resulting in certain directors' using inside information to gain substantial personal benefits at the Corporation's expense, and (2) violated § 14(a) of the Act and Rule 14a–9 thereunder by making statements in proxy solicitations issued to the shareholders by the Corporation in 1975, 1976, and 1977, for the election of directors of the Corporation that were materially misleading with respect to the earlier modification of the stock option plan and the directors' exercise of their options thereunder.

* * *

Since the facts are set out in full in the district court's opinion, we limit ourselves here to a brief summary for convenience. Under a nonqualified stock option plan adopted by Zapata's board of directors in 1970 and by its stockholders in 1971, key employees were granted options to purchase Zapata stock at $12.15 a share. Purchases could be made only in cash, and options became exercisable in five equal installments: 20% 90 days after the date on which the options were granted, July 14, 1970, and an additional 20% on the four successive anniversaries of the date of grant. This plan authorized the board of directors to amend the plan in any way with certain exceptions not relevant here. Pursuant to the plan, options were granted to approximately 130 employees.

In late June 1974 defendant William Flynn, the chief executive officer and a director of Zapata, consulted the Corporation's investment bankers about the possibility of the Corporation's making a cash tender offer in the open market for its own stock. It was decided to go forward with the offer at a price substantially in excess of the market price of the stock. It was then contemplated that Zapata would offer $25 to $30 per share for its shares, which were then trading at approximately $19 per share. By July 1, 1974, the plans for financing and executing the tender offer were complete. All of the directors had discussed the tender offer with Flynn. They were aware that it was likely to occur and that the announcement of the tender offer would trigger a sharp rise in the market price of Zapata stock.

Events came to a head on July 2, 1974. Early in the day trading in Zapata stock on the New York Stock Exchange was suspended at the request of Zapata's management, pending an announcement of the tender offer. When trading was halted, the price for Zapata stood at approximately $18.50 per share. Later that day a special meeting of the board of directors was held, with a quorum consisting of Flynn, Israel, Mackin, Woolcott, and Gueymard in attendance. The balance of the Board's eight members—Harrison, Shiels and Naess—were not present. With Flynn abstaining, the others unanimously adopted three resolutions amending the stock option plan insofar as it applied to Zapata's six "senior officers." One resolution accelerated the exercise date for their final installment of their options from July 14, 1974, to July 2, 1974. The other two resolutions modified the plan to authorize the Corporation to make interest-free loans to these six optionees in the amount of the purchase price for the options exercised and for the tax liability incurred by their exercising the options. Finally, the board adopted a resolution directing that these modifications be submitted to the company's shareholders for approval, with the provision that if the modifications were not approved, the stock purchased would be returned, the loans cancelled, and the option reinstated. Pursuant to these resolutions, each of the six senior officers exercised their options on July 2, 1974, purchasing in the aggregate 151,200 Zapata shares. For reasons not fully explained, the modifications were never submitted to the shareholders.

On July 3, 1974, Zapata's Board met and formally authorized the tender offer at a price between $25 and $30 per share. On July 8, 1974, the Corporation publicly disclosed its intention to make a tender offer for the purchase of 2,300,000 of its shares at $25 per share, whereupon public trading in the stock resumed. The closing price for Zapata on July 8 was $24.50 per share.

The purpose and effect of the eleventh-hour amendments to the stock option plan was to permit the Corporation's six senior officers to benefit at Zapata's expense. Under applicable federal tax laws an employee who exercises stock options such as those received by the six senior officers realizes ordinary income in the amount of the difference between the fair market price of the stock at the time the option is exercised and the option price paid for the stock (the "bargain spread"). The corporation, on the other hand, is entitled to deduct the bargain spread as a business expense, it being considered a form of compensation to its employees. By accelerating the exercise date of the last installment of the options and thus allowing the six officers to exercise their options prior to the foreseen imminent rise in the market price of Zapata stock, the Board permitted the six officers to save themselves a considerable amount of tax liability, and prevented the Corporation from enjoying a correspondingly higher tax deduction, assuming the six officers would have exercised their options on or after the originally scheduled date, July 14, 1974. Given the fact that the market price immediately after the announcement of the tender offer became, as anticipated, more than double the option price, this appears to be a safe assumption.

DISCUSSION

We first turn to appellants' contention that defendants violated Rule 10b–5 by modifying Zapata's stock option plan so that they could exercise their options immediately and profit at the Corporation's expense. The Exchange Act "protects corporations as well as individuals who are sellers of a security," and Zapata's sale of stock pursuant to the stock option plan constituted a sale of securities within the meaning of § 10(b) and Rule 10b–5. However, not every allegation of malfeasance by corporate officers in connection with the sale or purchase of a security states a claim under Rule 10b–5. Since Santa Fe Industries, Inc. v. Green, 430 U.S. 462 (1977), an essential element is that the defendants have engaged in some form of deception.

Appellants contend that deception occurred by reason of the failure of the officers and directors to inform the shareholders of the changes in the option plan. Appellees respond that no deception occurred because, notwithstanding the direction for stockholder approval in the July 2, 1974, resolution, such approval was not required and all material facts were disclosed to the four disinterested directors, who, being a majority of the five directors who met on that date, had the power to act for the Corporation in this matter. Delaware Corp.Law § 141.

When a corporate action requires shareholders' approval, full disclosure of material information must be made to them. Where approval by the shareholders is not necessary, however, full disclosure to a disinterested board of directors is equivalent to full disclosure to the shareholders. Even if some directors have an interest in the transaction, absent domination or control of a corporation or of its board by the officer-beneficiaries, approval of the transaction by a disinterested majority of the board possessing authority to act and fully informed of all relevant facts will suffice to bar a Rule 10b–5 claim that the corporation or its stockholders were deceived. See Goldberg v. Meridor; Schoenbaum v. Firstbrook. The knowledge of the disinterested majority must in such event be attributed to the corporation and its stockholders, precluding deception. For this purpose "disinterest" is defined as lack of any financial stake by a director in the transaction under consideration. Delaware law, although not controlling is to the same effect. 8 Del.Code Ann. § 144.

Applying these principles here, stockholder approval of the modification of Zapata's stock option plan was not required under its charter or by-laws and was not mandated by Delaware law. The four directors who approved the modification had no financial stake in the stock purchases approved by them. It is true that one of them, Mackin, was a partner in a large law firm which annually received substantial fees from Zapata for legal work and that this relationship could have motivated him to curry favor with Flynn and with at least some of the other senior officers benefiting from the amendment of the stock option plan approved by him, since they would in turn be approving his firm's continued employment and its substantial legal fees.[7] However, absent a claim that Mackin voted in favor of the amendments in exchange for the Zapata management's continued retention of his firm as its counsel, or for some other *quid pro quo,* to label him an "interested" director for purposes of Rule 10b–5 because of his relationship as the company's legal counsel would be to open the door to an unworkable standard for determining whether there has been deception practiced upon the corporation. Unless and until board membership on the part of a corporation's outside counsel, or of anyone with a commercial relationship with the corporation, is outlawed, we cannot assume that a counsel-director acts for reasons that are against the corporation's interest, as distinguished from the private interests of its officers. Moreover, the shareholders were aware of Mackin's relationship as legal counsel to the Corporation when they elected him a director, and presumably were willing to trust his judgment notwithstanding this fact.

Another of the four directors who voted to amend the stock option plan, Mr. Woolcott, engaged in his own private profiteering from inside information received by him as a director regarding the impending tender offer by arranging, without the knowledge of other board members, to have a corporation wholly owned by his mother purchase Zapata stock on the market immediately before the news of the tender offer became public.[8] Appellants contend that by thus engaging in

7. During the fiscal year ending September 30, 1974. Mr. Mackin's law firm received over $960,000 in legal fees from Zapata.

8. Mr. Woolcott's trading on inside information was evidently not known to the other directors or to Zapata's management until some time after the events giving rise

conduct similar to that which he was called upon to judge as a director (albeit at the expense of the public rather than the Corporation) he lost his disinterestedness. As in the case of Mackin, his conduct does indicate that he may not have exercised a detached judgment on behalf of Zapata stockholders in deciding whether to approve the proposed amendments to the stock option plan. Although theoretically he could, by approving the tender offer but disapproving modification of the stock option plan, have achieved his own personal objective of using the inside information to gain a private profit at the public's expense, he may also have wanted to gain the favor of the Corporation's senior executives, with a view to protecting himself against their displeasure if they should later learn of his profiteering. In the latter event he may have believed that he could induce the management to cover up his private misuse of inside information by pointing to his cooperation in enabling them to profit at the expense of Zapata's stockholders by his approving modification of the stock option plan.

* * *

We need not reach the question of whether these circumstances would require that Woolcott be classified as an interested director since even if his vote were disregarded, a majority of the disinterested directors present would still have approved the resolutions. See Del. Corp.Law, § 144.

There remains the question of whether appellant should be afforded the opportunity to proceed on the theory that the four directors who voted in favor of the stock option plan amendments, even if they had not had any material personal interest in the matter under consideration, were nevertheless "interested" members of the board for the reason that the Corporation and its board may have been controlled by some or all of the six officers who were the beneficiaries of the amendments. Domination or control of a corporation or of its board by those benefiting from the board's action may under some circumstances preclude its directors from being disinterested. In such a case, since they would be acting as mere pawns of the controlling wrongdoer, their knowledge could hardly be imputed to the corporation or its stockholders. We have so held, for instance, where the "corporation is influenced by its controlling shareholders to engage in a transaction adverse to the corporation's interests * * * and there is a nondisclosure or misleading disclosure," Goldberg v. Meridor; see also Schoenbaum v. Firstbrook; Shell v. Hensley. However, in the present case it is not claimed that Flynn and the five other senior Zapata officers who were the beneficiaries of the modification of the stock option plan were controlling shareholders or that they controlled decision-making by those directors who voted for the amendments (Mackin, Woolcott, Israel and Gueymard).

to this litigation. In September 1975 Woolcott submitted to a consent judgment entered against him in a suit brought by the SEC alleging a 10b-5 violation.

For all of these reasons we adhere to the rule that a director must be deemed to be disinterested for purposes of Rule 10b–5 if he has no material personal interest in the transaction or matter under consideration. Under that test, the knowledge of Mackin, Woolcott, Israel and Gueymard that their July 2 modification of the Corporation's stock option plan would benefit its six senior officers at the stockholders' expense must be attributed to the Corporation and its stockholders, thus precluding deception.

* * *

Is this decision consistent with the decision in *Schoenbaum*? Zapata Corp. had eight directors—four officers, who were beneficiaries of the option plan, and four "outsiders." The fateful meeting was attended by the four "outsiders" and the chief executive officer (whose presence was necessary to establish a quorum). The CEO abstained from voting, and the four "outside" directors (including one who was receiving almost $1 million a year in legal fees from the corporation, and one who was doing some "insider trading" on his own) proceeded to vote a $400,000 giveaway to six senior officers, including their four colleagues on the board. The Second Circuit holds that there was no "fraud" on the corporation, because all the facts were fully disclosed to a "disinterested" board. Is Judge Mansfield simply challenging the courts to deal with this kind of egregious conduct under state law? How should they respond?

In fact, Maldonado brought an additional derivative action in the Delaware courts alleging that the directors had breached their fiduciary duty under Delaware law by their actions in connection with the stock option plan. After 1975, Zapata's business and profitability steadily deteriorated, and in February 1979 another shareholder, Maher, brought a derivative action in the federal court in Texas (where Zapata's principal office was located), alleging that William Flynn, Zapata's chief executive officer, had mismanaged the company and had engaged in a number of self-dealing transactions, including the option transaction attacked in the Maldonado action.

In April 1979, Zapata's board ousted Flynn as chief executive officer and removed him from the board, then elected two new directors and constituted them as an "Independent Investigation Committee" to determine whether prosecution of the New York, Delaware and Texas derivative actions were in the best interests of the corporation. The committee determined that the actions should be dismissed, and the corporation moved for their dismissal. This motion was the occasion for the Delaware Supreme Court to express its view on the weight to be given to the determination of such an "independent committee" in determining whether a shareholder action could go forward. In ZAPATA v. MALDONADO, 430 A.2d 779 (Del.1981), the court held that, in view of the conflicts present when "directors are passing judgment on fellow directors," the action should only be dismissed if (a) the corporation carries the burden of proof of establishing that the committee was independent, acted in good faith, and made a reasonable investigation, and (b) the court is satisfied, "applying its own independent business judgment," that the motion to dismiss should be granted.

In 1981, Maher and Zapata agreed on a settlement of the Texas action, providing for the payment of $250,000 in legal fees to Maher's attorneys, but not requiring any payment by the defendants to Zapata. The court approved the agreement on the ground that the lawsuit "was at least a contributing factor in several major beneficial changes in Zapata," including the removal of Flynn, and the approval was affirmed by the Fifth Circuit over the objections of Maldonado, who argued that it was inadequate and might preclude pursuance of his claims in the New York action. MAHER v. ZAPATA, 714 F.2d 436 (5th Cir.1983). The New York court then held that Maldonado's action was in fact precluded by the Texas settlement, and that "a continuation of the action would be wasteful and contrary to Zapata's interest and impose upon it additional expenses for legal fees without discernible financial or other benefit to the corporation." MALDONADO v. FLYNN, 573 F.Supp. 684, 686 (S.D.N.Y.1983).

GOLDBERG v. MERIDOR

567 F.2d 209 (2d Cir.1977), cert. denied 434 U.S. 1069 (1978).

Before: FRIENDLY, TIMBERS and MESKILL, CIRCUIT JUDGES.

FRIENDLY, CIRCUIT JUDGE:

In this derivative action in the District Court for the Southern District of New York, David Goldberg, a stockholder of Universal Gas & Oil Company, Inc. (UGO), a Panama corporation having its principal place of business in New York City, sought to recover damages and to obtain other relief against UGO's controlling parent, Maritimecor, S.A., also a Panama corporation; Maritimecor's controlling parent, Maritime Fruit Carriers Company Ltd., an Israel corporation; a number of individuals who were directors of one or more of these companies; the investment firm of Hornblower & Weeks, Hemphill, Noyes, Inc.; and the accounting firm of Laventhal & Horwath, with respect to transactions which culminated in an agreement providing for UGO's issuance to Maritimecor of up to 4,200,000 shares of UGO stock and its assumption of all of Maritimecor's liabilities (including a debt of $7,000,000 owed to UGO) in consideration of the transfer of all of Maritimecor's assets (except 2,800,000 UGO shares already held by Maritimecor). It suffices at this point to say that the complaint, filed February 3, 1976, alleged that the contract was grossly unfair to UGO and violated both § 10(b) of the Securities Exchange Act and the SEC's Rule 10b–5 and common law fiduciary duties.

* * *

Defendants filed motions to dismiss the amended complaint for failure to state a claim under § 10(b) of the Securities Exchange Act and Rule 10b–5. In answer to defendants' argument "that deception and non-disclosure is a requirement for a 10b–5 case" which was disputed as a matter of law, plaintiff counsel submitted an affidavit asserting that "insofar as plaintiff Goldberg, a minority shareholder is concerned, there has been no disclosure to him of the fraudulent nature of the transfer of Maritimecor assets and liabilities for stock of UGO".

* * *

On February 11, 1977, Judge Lasker filed an opinion that granted the motions to dismiss. He thought the case was governed by Popkin v. Bishop rather than by our *en banc* decision in Schoenbaum v. Firstbrook * * *. After the [Supreme Court decision in Santa Fe Industries v. Green], the judge filed a memorandum adding to the opinion fn. 4 to the effect that the Supreme Court's decision * * * lent substantial support to the result.

Before proceeding further, we must deal with the district court's refusal to permit amendment of the complaint to include reference to the two press releases or otherwise to claim deception. * * * We are constrained to hold that the refusal of leave to amend was an abuse of discretion and to treat the cases as if an amendment, at least in the two respects noted, had been allowed.

II.

If the complaint were thus amended, we would deem it clear that, so far as this court's decisions are concerned, the case would be governed by *Schoenbaum* rather than by *Popkin*. The August 1 press release held out an inviting picture that

> As a result of the transaction, UGO will replace Maritimecor as the principal operating subsidiary of MFC and, as such, will engage in a diversified line of shipping and shipping related activities including the sale of ships and shipbuilding contracts, the operation of reefers and tankers, and upon their delivery, product carriers and oil drilling rigs, and underwriting marine insurance.

when allegedly the truth was that UGO had entered into a transaction that would ensure its doom. *Popkin* was specifically rested on its special facts. The plaintiff was taken to have conceded that the complaint did not allege misrepresentation or non-disclosure and that he relied solely on the unfairness of the merger terms. * * * The observation in *Popkin* that "our emphasis on improper self-dealing did not eliminate nondisclosure as a key issue in the Rule 10b–5 cases" followed a statement that when, as here, state law does not demand prior shareholder approval of a transaction, "it makes sense to concentrate on the impropriety of the conduct itself rather than on the 'failure to disclose' it because full and fair disclosure in a real sense will rarely occur. It will be equally rare in the legal sense once the view is taken—as we did in *Schoenbaum*—that under federal securities law disclosure to interested insiders does not prevent a valid claim that fraud was committed upon 'outsiders' (such as minority shareholders) whatever the requirements of state corporate law may be." Id. The ruling of *Popkin* was that in the *opposite* situation, where "merger transactions * * *, under state law, must be subjected to shareholder approval * * * if federal law ensures that shareholder approval is fairly sought and freely given, the principal federal interest is at an end." Clearly that is not this case.

III.

The ruling that this case is governed by *Schoenbaum* rather than by *Popkin* by no means ends our inquiry. Rather it brings us to the serious question whether *Schoenbaum* can be here applied consistently with the Supreme Court's decision in Santa Fe Industries, Inc. v. Green, supra. We think it can be and should.

* * *

Schoenbaum has been generally applauded by commentators, even though it may sometimes have been read to mean more than it does or than is needed to call for a reversal here. * * * It likewise is viewed with approval—indeed seemingly would be adopted—by §§ 1303 and 1402(c) of the proposed ALI Federal Securities Code. It has also found favor in other circuits. A notable instance is Shell v. Hensley, 430 F.2d 819, 827 (5 Cir.1970), where the court in a derivative suit rejected a claim that no "causal deceit" existed when the corporation's board knew all the facts, saying:

> When the other party to the securities transaction controls the judgment of all the corporation's board members or conspires with them or the one controlling them to profit mutually at the expense of the corporation, the corporation is no less disabled from availing itself of an informed judgment than if the outsider had simply lied to the board. In both situations, the determination of the corporation's choice of action in the transaction in question is not made as a reasonable man would make it if possessed of the material information known to the other party to the transaction. * * *

Schoenbaum, then, can rest solidly on the now widely recognized ground that there is deception of the corporation (in effect, of its minority shareholders) when the corporation is influenced by its controlling shareholder to engage in a transaction adverse to the corporation's interests (in effect, the minority shareholders' interests) and there is nondisclosure or misleading disclosures as to the material facts of the transaction. Assuming that, in light of the decision in *Green*, the existence of "controlling influence" and "wholly inadequate consideration"—an aspect of the *Schoenbaum* decision that perhaps attracted more attention—can no longer alone form the basis for Rule 10b–5 liability, we do not read *Green* as ruling that no action lies under Rule 10b–5 when a controlling corporation causes a partly owned subsidiary to sell its securities to the parent in an unfair transaction and fails to make a disclosure or, as can be alleged here, makes a misleading disclosure. * * *

Here the complaint alleged "deceit * * * upon UGO's minority shareholders" and, if amendment had been allowed as it should have been, would have alleged misrepresentation as to the UGO–Maritimecor transaction at least in the sense of failure to state material facts "necessary in order to make the statements made, in the light of the circumstances under which they were made, not misleading," Rule 10b–5(b). The nub of the matter is that the conduct attacked in *Green* did not violate the " 'fundamental purpose' of the Act as implementing a 'philosophy of full disclosure' "; the conduct here attacked does.

Defendants contend that even if all this is true, the failure to make a public disclosure or even the making of a misleading disclosure would have no effect, since no action by stockholders to approve the UGO–Maritimecor transaction was required. Along the same lines our brother Meskill, invoking the opinion in *Green,* contends that the defendants' acts were not material since plaintiff has failed adequately to allege what would have been done had he known the truth.

In TSC Industries, Inc. v. Northway, Inc., 426 U.S. 438, 449 (1976), a case arising under Rule 14a–9, the Court laid down the standard of materiality as "a showing of a substantial likelihood that, under all the circumstances, the omitted fact would have assumed actual significance in the deliberations of the reasonable shareholder" or, putting the matter in another way, "a substantial likelihood that the disclosure of the omitted fact would have been viewed by the reasonable investor as having significantly altered the 'total mix' of information made available." When, as in a derivative action, the deception is alleged to have been practiced on the corporation, even though all the directors were parties to it, the test must be whether the facts that were not disclosed or were misleadingly disclosed to the shareholders "would have assumed actual significance in the deliberations" of reasonable and disinterested directors or created "a substantial likelihood" that such directors would have considered the "total mix" of information available to have been "significantly altered." That was the basis for liability in *Schoenbaum;* it was likely that a reasonable director of Banff, knowing the facts as to the oil discovery that had been withheld from minority shareholders, would not have voted to issue the shares to Aquitaine at a price below their true value. This also is the principle recognized in the passage from Judge Ainsworth's opinion in Shell v. Hensley, 430 F.2d at 827, quoted above. Here there is surely a significant likelihood that if a reasonable director of UGO had known the facts alleged by plaintiff rather than the barebones of the press releases, he would not have voted for the transaction with Maritimecor.

Beyond this, Goldberg and other minority shareholders would not have been without remedy if the alleged facts had been disclosed. The doubts entertained by our brother as to the existence of injunctive remedies in New York are unfounded. * * *

The availability of injunctive relief if the defendants had not lulled the minority stockholders of UGO into security by a deceptive disclosure, as they allegedly did, is in sharp contrast to *Green,* where the disclosure following the merger transaction was full and fair, and, as to the pre-merger period, respondents accepted "the conclusion of both courts below that under Delaware law they could not have enjoined the merger because an appraisal proceeding is their sole remedy in the Delaware courts for any alleged unfairness in the terms of the merger." * * * We readily agree that if all that was here alleged was that UGO had been injured by "internal corporate mismanagement", no federal claim would have been stated. But a parent's looting of a subsidiary with securities outstanding in the hands of the public in a securities transaction is a different matter; in such cases disclosure or at least the absence of misleading disclosure is required. It would be incongruous if Rule 10b–5 created liability for a casual "tip" in the bar of a country club, as we held in SEC v. Geon Industries, Inc., 531 F.2d 39 (2 Cir.1976), but would not cover a parent's undisclosed or misleadingly disclosed sale of its overvalued assets for stock of a controlled subsidiary with securities in the hands of the public.

The order dismissing the complaint is reversed and the case is remanded to the district court for further proceedings, including amendment of the complaint, consistent with this opinion.

MESKILL, CIRCUIT JUDGE, concurring in part and dissenting in part:

I concur in Parts I and II of Judge Friendly's opinion, for I agree that the district judge should have allowed amendment of the complaint and that a corporation may be defrauded by some or all of its directors. I part company, however, with the majority's holding that the complaint, as "amended" in the manner suggested by Judge Friendly, to include the press releases, states a cause of action. Assuming that any deception of the minority shareholders took place, the complaint nevertheless fails to establish that the claimed deception was "material." Accordingly, I respectfully dissent from the discussion in Part III of the majority opinion concerning materiality and the impact of Santa Fe Industries, Inc. v. Green.

The test of materiality in securities law has recently been laid out by the Supreme Court. In TSC Industries, Inc. v. Northway, Inc., 426 U.S. 438 (1976), which dealt with an alleged omission under Rule 14a–9, Justice Marshall stated:

> The general standard of materiality that we think best comports with the policies of Rule 14a–9 is as follows: An omitted fact is material if there is a substantial likelihood that a reasonable shareholder would consider it important in deciding how to vote. * * *

Under Panamanian law, no shareholder action was necessary to effect the UGO–Maritimecor merger. Accordingly, the burden is on the plaintiffs to demonstrate a substantial likelihood that they would have acted differently had full disclosure been made.

* * *

Although the majority asserts in a footnote that "state remedies presumably were available," to halt the merger, it does not explain what they were. The principal action suggested by the majority opinion is an injunction against the proposed merger. The theory is apparently that the shareholders, who were led down the primrose path by the misleading press releases, would have raced into court if armed with the full story. It is possible that plaintiffs could have obtained an injunction under New York's Martin Act. In order to prove materiality under this theory, Goldberg will have to demonstrate that he would, as a reasonable stockholder, have sought and obtained an injunction against the proposed action had the facts not been concealed.

Moreover, the plaintiff fails even to mention in his two complaints what course of action he contemplated taking. Under *Green,* such an allegation is required to state a claim under 10b–5. * * * I do not understand the remand to have relieved the plaintiff of his burden of pleading and proving the availability of state relief.

* * *

The final suggested rationale of the majority is the "chastening effect" of full disclosure. The apparent theory is that those about to loot a corporation can be shamed into honesty through a requirement that they reveal their nefarious purposes.

* * *

Those who breach their fiduciary duties seldom disclose their intentions ahead of time. Yet under the majority's reasoning the failure to inform stockholders of a proposed defalcation gives rise to a cause of action under 10b–5. Thus, the majority has neatly undone the holdings of *Green, Piper* and *Cort* by creating a federal cause of action for a breach of fiduciary duty that will apply in all cases, save for those rare instances where the fiduciary denounces himself in advance.

If the defendants have looted UGO in the manner alleged by the plaintiffs, a full recovery should not be difficult to obtain. Under New York state law, this would be a breach of the fiduciary duty imposed upon directors. My dissent is not based upon any desire to insulate such business practices from legal redress, but upon the fact that the plaintiff has chosen the wrong forum.

Under the *Goldberg* approach, is it enough for the plaintiff to allege that he would have *sought* an injunction under state law if the true facts had been revealed, or must he show that he could have *obtained* one? In HEALEY v. CATALYST RECOVERY, 616 F.2d 641, 647 (3d Cir.1980), the court held that "the plaintiff must demonstrate that at the time of the misrepresentation or omission, there was a reasonable probability of ultimate success in securing an injunction had there been no misrepresentation or omission." A similar result was reached in KIDWELL v. MEIKLE, 597 F.2d 1273 (9th Cir.1979).

Note on Rule 10b–5 as Opera

You may by now be somewhat confused about the meaning of Rule 10b–5, as elaborated by recent Supreme Court decisions. Since some lawyers say that it depends on whether one follows the "words" or the "music" of those decisions, it occurred to the author of this casebook that they can really best be understood as scenes in an opera.

The heroine of the opera is Dieci Becinque (10b–5), a beautiful 30-year-old rule, much beloved by securities lawyers everywhere. In the first act, we find her in a marble temple surrounded by nine high priests who sing her praises. First Willio, the eldest priest, sings his famous patter song, "Il Sovrintendente d' Assicurazione" ("The Superintendent of Insurance"), in which he eulogizes 10b–5 as the solution to all the wrongs of mankind. The act closes with Blackmunio's aria "I Uti Affiliati", in which he lauds her as the savior of the oppressed Indian tribes of the American West.

After a three-year intermission, the curtain rises on the second act. We find our heroine in the same marble temple, but the mood has changed dramatically. Two new priests, Paolo and Rehnquistio, are sworn to destroy her. In the opening aria, "La Scheggia Azzurra" ("The Blue Chip"), Rehnquistio tells her that only one who has paid the price may enjoy her affections. This is followed by the rousing "Ride of the Hochfelder," in which Paolo tells her that she was born in manipulation and deception and may only deal with wicked people. Next, in the haunting aria "O Santa Fe" ("Oh, Holy Faith"), Bianco declares that she must have nothing to do with corporate managers, no matter how wicked they are. Finally, in "La Chiarella" ("The Little Printer"), sung again by Paolo, she is told that nobody must have anything to do with her unless he has first breached a specific duty to his fellow man.

We do not yet know how the second act will end but, despite Blackmunio's cry of protest, "Dissento," at the end of each aria, it appears that she will finally be banished from the temple. However, there may yet be a third act in which she is restored to her former position of glory. Time will tell.

Selected References

Hazen, Corporate Mismanagement and the Federal Securities Laws' Antifraud Provisions, 20 B.C.L.Rev. 819 (1979).

Jacobs, Rule 10b–5 and Self–Dealing by Corporate Fiduciaries, 48 U.Cin.L. Rev. 643 (1979).

Jacobs, How *Santa Fe* Affects 10b–5's Proscriptions Against Corporate Mismanagement, 6 Sec.Reg.L.J. 3 (1978).

Sherrard, Federal Judicial and Regulatory Response to *Santa Fe,* 35 W. & L.L.Rev. 695 (1978).

Steinberg & Lindahl, The New Law of Squeeze–Out Mergers, 62 Wash.L.Q. 351 (1984).

Note, *Santa Fe* Revisited: A Critique of Circuit Court Applications of Rule 10b–5 to Breaches of Fiduciary Duty, 28 UCLA L.Rev. 564 (1981).

Note, Causation in Rule 10b–5 Actions for Corporate Mismanagement, 48 U.Chi.L.Rev. 936 (1981).

Note, Suits for Breach of Fiduciary Duty Under Rule 10b–5 After *Santa Fe,* 91 Harv.L.Rev. 1874 (1978).

Note, Goldberg v. Meridor: The Second Circuit's Resurrection of Rule 10b–5, 64 Va.L.Rev. 765 (1978).

B. CORPORATE REPURCHASES AND "GOING PRIVATE"

A corporation's repurchase of its own shares may be subject to attack under state corporation law where the purpose of the repurchase is to preserve the control position of the incumbent management, rather than to serve a legitimate corporate end. Such repurchases may also have a manipulative effect, where the corporate management has a particular interest in maintaining the market price of the shares at a certain level.

SEC v. GEORGIA–PACIFIC CORP.

CCH Fed.Sec.L.Rep. ¶¶ 91,680, 91,692 (S.D.N.Y.1966).

[Excerpts from SEC Complaint]

* * *

11. Since on or about May 26, 1961 GP has merged with other corporations or has acquired substantially all of the stock or assets of other corporations in return for stock in GP pursuant to agreements which provided that the total number of shares of GP stock to be issued in return for the interests in such other corporations would be dependent on the price of GP common stock on the NYSE at certain times or during certain periods of time (hereafter referred to as valuation periods.)

12. During and immediately prior to certain of such valuation periods the defendants GP, Cheatham and Pamplin, (individually and as trustees of the Georgia–Pacific Stock Bonus Trust), and Mrs. Brooks, intentionally caused GP common stock to be bid for and purchased for the Stock Bonus Plan and for the GP treasury on the NYSE in a manner which would and did, directly and indirectly, cause the price of GP common stock on the NYSE to rise in order that GP's obligation to issue additional shares of its common stock in return for the interests in other corporations would be avoided or reduced.

13. In making such purchases for the Stock Bonus Plan the defendants Cheatham, Pamplin, and Mrs. Brooks did not attempt to have them executed in a manner which would have tended to result in

purchases at the lowest prices possible and thus did not act exclusively in the interest of the Stock Bonus Plan participants.

14. The defendants GP, Cheatham, and Pamplin did not disclose to shareholders in the companies being acquired or their representatives or to other investors or prospective investors in GP securities that the NYSE price, which was to determine the total number of shares of GP common stock to be issued to the shareholders of such other corporations, would not reflect an independent consensus reached between buyers and sellers in a course of competitive trading, uninfluenced by the activities of the defendants alleged in paragraphs 12 and 13.

15. In connection with such acts, practices, and course of business said defendants, directly and indirectly, made use of the means and instrumentalities of interstate commerce, of the mails, and of the facilities of the NYSE. Such acts, practices, and course of business are more particularly described in the following four sections (paragraphs 16 through 51).

THE ST. CROIX PAPER COMPANY

16. From January 17, 1963 to about February 27, 1963 GP made an offer to exchange a maximum of 587,714 shares of GP common stock for the common stock of St. Croix Paper Company (St. Croix), a Maine corporation, which then had approximately 2,700 shareholders. The offer provided that up to 470,172 shares of GP common stock would initially be issued to the St. Croix shareholders at the rate of $\frac{8}{10}$ of a GP share for each St. Croix share. The offer further provided that GP was obligated to issue additional GP shares, up to the limit of $\frac{2}{10}$ of a GP share for each St. Croix share exchanged, to make up any difference should the last sale price on the NYSE of GP common stock not average $50 per share for a period of 30 consecutive trading days next preceding any date to be later selected by GP within the next $2\frac{1}{2}$ years. The offer also provided that GP was obligated to issue the additional $\frac{2}{10}$ of a GP share for each St. Croix share exchanged if within $2\frac{1}{2}$ years GP did not select such a date.

17. On March 7, 1963 GP acquired 94.6% of the St. Croix stock under this offer, and on April 10, 1963 GP acquired an additional 4.16% of the St. Croix stock under the same terms.

18. On nine occasions between February 15 and April 9, 1963 the three trustees of the Stock Bonus Plan passed resolutions authorizing purchases of a total of 23,100 shares of GP common stock to be made at the discretion of either Cheatham or Pamplin. Pursuant to these authorizations, 22,900 shares of GP common stock (or 50.66% of the GP common stock purchased for the Stock Bonus Plan in 1963) were purchased for the Stock Bonus Plan on the NYSE on 25 of the 36 trading days from February 21 through April 15, 1963. Such purchases were effected at the discretion of Mrs. Brooks under the general direction of Cheatham.

19. During this period, Cheatham, Pamplin, and Mrs. Brooks did not attempt to have such purchases executed in a manner which would have tended to result in purchases at the lowest prices possible. Instead, such purchases were caused to be executed predominantly through the use of several orders at the market on the same day (on one occasion as many as 11 separate orders on the same day), sometimes through two or more brokerage firms on the same day and at the same times during one day and on most occasions without placing any price limit on such orders. In addition, such purchases were caused to be concentrated near the close of the market on many days during this period.

20. Purchases of 9.6% of the GP stock made for the Stock Bonus Plan from March 28 through April 15, 1963 were executed at prices higher than those of the preceding transactions (on "plus ticks") or at the same price as the preceding transaction, the last change in price having been upward (on "zero-plus ticks"). Consequently, the prices at which such purchases were executed led advances and retarded declines in the price of GP common stock on the NYSE. Between March 28 and April 15, 1963 such purchases accompanied an advance in the market price of GP common stock from 49 to 52¾. When the price of GP common stock appeared to be averaging above the price required to eliminate GP's obligation to issue additional shares under the St. Croix offer, such purchasing was discontinued, although funds still remained in the Stock Bonus Plan. In addition, on April 2, April 9, and April 10 such purchases (on plus and zero-plus ticks) were the last purchases of the day. In summary, such purchases were intentionally effected in a manner which would and did, directly and indirectly, cause the last sale price of GP common stock on the NYSE to rise in order that GP's obligation to issue additional shares of its common stock under the St. Croix offer would be avoided or reduced.

21. Thereafter, on May 4, 1963 GP gave notice to the exchange agent under the St. Croix offer that GP had elected to have the GP common stock valued for purposes of the St. Croix offer on the 30 trading days from March 22 through May 3, 1963. As a result of the average of the last sale prices of GP stock on the NYSE on those 30 trading days, no additional shares of GP common stock were issuable under the terms of the St. Croix offer.

22. At no time was the fact that such purchases were or would be made at the times and in the manner in which they were made disclosed to the St. Croix shareholders or their representatives or to other investors or prospective investors in GP securities.

* * *

Wherefore, plaintiff, the Securities and Exchange Commission, demands:

I. A preliminary injunction and final judgment restraining and enjoining defendant GP, and defendants Cheatham and Pamplin, individually and as trustees of the Georgia–Pacific Stock Bonus Trust, and defendant Mrs. Brooks, and each of them, and their agents, officers, employees, attorneys, and persons or entities having a control relationship with them or any of them, and any other person acting in concert or participation with them from: directly or indirectly, by the use of the means of instrumentalities of interstate commerce of the mails or any facilities of any national securities exchange,

(1) using or employing any manipulative or deceptive device or contrivance in connection with the purchase or sale of any GP security; and particularly

(2) engaging in any act, practice or course of business which operates or would operate as a fraud or deceit upon any person in connection with the purchase or sale of any GP security, including acts, practices or a course of business of the type described in this Complaint;

(3) bidding for or purchasing for any account, in which such defendants, or any of them, have a beneficial interest, including any account of GP, or attempting to induce any other person, including the trustees of the Georgia–Pacific Stock Bonus Trust and their agents, to purchase any GP security which is the subject of a distribution, or any security of the same class or series, or any right to purchase such security, while such defendants, or any of them, are persons on whose behalf such distribution is being made or are otherwise participating in such distribution, until such distribution has been completed including the termination of a valuation period or other such condition upon which the issuance or nonissuance of additional shares as a part of such distribution may depend, unless the activities of such defendants fall within the exemptive provisions of Rule 10b–6 under the Securities Exchange Act of 1934 or an exemptive order therefrom is obtained from the Securities and Exchange Commission;

(4) omitting to state material facts necessary in order to make statements made, in the light of the circumstances under which they were made, not misleading in connection with the sale of any GP security, including the type of omissions described in this Complaint; or

(5) engaging in any act, practice or course of business of similar purport or object. * * *

[Opinion of the Court]

WYATT, DISTRICT JUDGE.

Plaintiff Securities and Exchange Commission, having filed its complaint herein on April 27, 1966, and the defendants having appeared without admitting the substantive allegations thereof and said defendants having consented to the entry of this Final Judgment pursuant to the stipulation appended hereto, without trial or adjudication of any issue of fact or law herein and without this Final Judgment constituting evidence against, or an admission by, said defendants, and this Court having directed the entry of such a Final Judgment;

Now, Therefore, before the taking of any testimony herein and without trial or adjudication of any issue of fact or law herein, and upon the consent of the parties hereto, it is hereby

Ordered, Adjudged and Decreed as follows: * * *

Consenting Defendants are enjoined and restrained from directly or indirectly, by use of the means or instrumentalities of interstate commerce, of the mails, or of any facility of any national securities exchange,

(A) Using or employing any manipulative or deceptive device or contrivance in connection with the purchase or sale of any security of G–P,

(B) Engaging in any act, practice or course of business which operates or would operate as a fraud or deceit upon any Person in connection with the purchase or sale of any security of G–P, including acts and practices affecting the market price of any security of G–P and

(C) Bidding for or purchasing any security of G–P for the purpose of creating actual or apparent active trading in or raising the price of any security of G–P.

V.

G–P and the noncorporate Consenting Defendants, so long as they are associated directly or indirectly with G–P, are enjoined and restrained from directly or indirectly bidding for or purchasing any security of G–P:

(A) Which is the subject of a distribution until such distribution has been completed or abandoned, except as permitted by the provisions of Rule 10b–6 of the Rules and Regulations of the Securities and Exchange Commission promulgated under the Securities Exchange Act of 1934;

(B) When an agreement in principle looking towards the acquisition of securities or assets of another Person for stock of G–P (whether or not such agreement is evidenced by a formal contract or agreement) has been reached between G–P and the other Person as to the terms and conditions of the proposed acquisition until

1. In the case of an acquisition requiring a vote of the stockholders of an acquired company, the vote of such stockholders has been consummated,

2. In the case of an acquisition not requiring a vote of the stockholders of an acquired company, the number of shares of stock of G–P has been fixed in accordance with the terms of a binding contract, and

3. In the case of an exchange offer subject to the registration provisions of the Securities Act of 1933, such exchange offer has been finally terminated;

(C) During, and within ten business days immediately prior to, any time or period of time at or during which the market price of any security of G–P is to be used to determine the amount of securities of G–P to be issued by it as consideration for property or assets acquired by G–P; and

(D) At any other time unless,

1. As to bids or purchases made on the New York Stock Exchange the following conditions are met:

(a) Orders will be placed through only one broker on the same day and G–P shall not employ a different broker from that purchasing for the Trust on the same day; and

(b) No bid or purchase will be made at the opening of the Exchange; and

(c) Each order shall be entered to be executed prior to one hour before the close of the Exchange; and

(d) No bid will be placed and no purchase will be made at a price in excess of the last sale price or the highest current independent bid, whichever is higher; and

(e) The number of shares purchased in any one week will not exceed 10% of the average weekly trading volume on the New York Stock Exchange in the four preceding calendar weeks; the number of shares purchased in any one day will not exceed 15% of the average daily trading volume on the New York Stock Exchange on the four preceding calendar weeks; and the broker employed to effect the purchases will be instructed to endeavor to keep the number of shares purchased during each week equal to or below 10% of such week's volume of trading of the stock and to keep the number of shares purchased during each day equal to or below 15% of that day's volume of trading on the Exchange. In computing the weekly or daily percentages of volume that may be purchased by G–P in accordance with this provision, G–P shall consider purchases made by the Trust as if they had been made by G–P, except that during the period in which the Trust is investing the funds on hand at the date of this Final Judgment each of the foregoing percentages may be increased by 5%.

2. As to purchases made other than on the New York Stock Exchange, such purchases are either,

(a) Unsolicited privately negotiated purchases each involving 1,000 shares or more made from a dealer or broker acting for others at prices not exceeding the current New York Stock Exchange price; or

(b) Unsolicited privately negotiated purchases each involving 1,000 shares or more effected neither on a securities exchange nor from or through a broker or dealer.

VI.

G–P shall, upon commencing serious negotiations (as distinguished from exploratory conversations) looking toward the acquisition of securities or assets of another Person in exchange for securities of G–P, obtain all information respecting the daily volume and prices of purchases of such G–P securities, including any G–P securities into which such G–P securities are or may be convertible, made within the preceding 30 days by:

(A) G–P,

(B) The Trust,

(C) The noncorporate Consenting Defendants, so long as they, respectively, are associated, directly or indirectly with G–P, and they shall furnish such information to G–P, and G–P shall furnish such information to the Persons from whom such securities or assets are to be acquired. G–P shall request similar information from its officers, directors and holders of more than 10% of any class of its equity securities, and shall furnish such information as it may receive to the Persons from which such securities or assets are to be acquired. Each week thereafter, G–P shall continue to furnish the Persons from whom such securities or assets are to be acquired with similar information as to such purchases of G–P securities made during the previous week until such negotiations are broken off or until the amount of G–P securities to be issued for such acquisition, or the formula determining such amount, has been fixed under an agreement binding all parties to the acquisition and approved by the stockholders, if such approval is necessary. * * *

In February 1967, the SEC circulated for informal comment to a limited number of people a preliminary draft of a proposed Rule 10b–10 which would have made generally applicable to all corporations the type of volume and price limitations imposed upon Georgia–Pacific by the foregoing decision. Critical comments were received from the New York and American Stock Exchanges. They argued that extension of such restrictions to all corporations, without any evidence of the type of manipulative or fraudulent intent that was alleged in the Georgia–Pacific case, went beyond the SEC's power under § 10(b) of the 1934 Act.

In 1967 and 1968, hearings were held on the Williams Bill for the regulation of takeover bids and tender offers, described in the preceding chapter. Proposed § 13(e) of that bill, as originally introduced and passed by the Senate, would have prohibited any corporation from repurchasing its own shares "in contravention of such rules and regulations as the Commission may prescribe as necessary or appropriate in the public interest or for the protection of investors *or* in order to prevent such acts or practices as are fraudulent, deceptive or manipulative". As a result of industry opposition to extending the SEC's power to regulate repurchases except as necessary for the prevention of fraud, deception or manipulation, the House Commerce Committee amended the proposed § 13(e) to its present form to "make it clear that such rules and regulations may be adopted only for these purposes." H.Rep. No. 1711, 90th Cong., 2d Sess., at 7 (1968).

Acting with a certain amount of deliberation in exercising its "new" powers under § 13(e), the Commission in July 1970 proposed a new Rule 13e–2 to regulate issuers' repurchases of their own securities. The rule was substantially revised and reproposed in December 1973 and again in October 1980. Finally, in November 1982, the Commission abandoned its effort to write a rule under § 13(e), and instead adopted a "safe harbor" rule under § 10(b). Under this new Rule 10b–18, repurchases by an issuer and its affiliates during any trading day are deemed not to violate the anti-manipulative provisions of § 9(a)(2) and Rule 10b–5 if (a) they are made through only one broker or dealer, (b) none of them are made as the opening transaction or during the last half hour of trading on that day, (c) none of them are made at a price exceeding the highest current independent bid price or the last independent sale price, whichever is higher, and (d) the total of such purchases does not exceed 25% of the average daily trading volume for the preceding four weeks. Sec.Ex. Act Rel. No. 19244 (Nov. 17, 1982).

In an effort to deal with the "going private" phenomenon described in Santa Fe Industries v. Green, the Commission in 1977 proposed a new Rule 13e–3, which would have prohibited any registered company from purchasing its own shares for the purpose of "going private" unless the transaction was "fair to unaffiliated securityholders." Among the criteria of "fairness" were the fairness of the consideration being paid and the other terms of the transaction, whether the transaction had been approved by a majority of unaffiliated shareholders and disinterested directors, the purpose of the transaction, and the anticipated benefits to the company and its affiliates. Sec. Act Rel. No. 5884 (Nov. 17, 1977). Would a rule of this type be within the Commission's authority under § 13(e), in light of the Supreme Court's decision in *Santa Fe?* See note 12 to the opinion.

After consideration of comments on this proposal, the Commission withdrew the proposed substantive fairness requirement, and adopted a final rule requiring any registered company which plans to "go private" to file a detailed schedule of information with the Commission and disseminate such information to its shareholders at least 20 days prior to consummation of the transaction. The 20–day requirement is intended "to permit security holders to make an unhurried and informed choice as to their alternatives," including "utilizing remedies available under state law to challenge the transaction." Among the items of information required to be disclosed are the purpose of the transaction and the basis for management's belief that the terms of the transaction are fair to unaffiliated shareholders in relation to (a) the current and historical market price of the stock, (b) the net book value, going concern value and liquidation value of the company, (c) any outside offers for the stock, and (d) any reports, opinions or appraisals received from outside parties. See Rule 13e–3 and Schedule 13E–3, as adopted in Sec.Act Rel. No. 6100 (Aug. 2, 1979).

Selected References

T. Hazen, Securities Regulation § 11.17 (2d ed. 1990).

Bradley & Rosenzweig, Defensive Stock Repurchases, 99 Harv.L.Rev. 1377 (1986).

Rothwell, Safe Harbor for Repurchases by Corporate Issuers: New SEC Rule 10b–18, 6 Corp.L.Rev. 228 (1983).

Malley, Corporate Repurchases of Stock and the SEC Rules, 29 Bus.Lawyer 117, 879 (1973–74).

Ruder, Dangers in a Corporation's Purchase of Its Own Shares, 13 Practical Lawyer 75 (1967).

Note, Defensive Stock Repurchase Programs: Tender Offers in Need of Regulation, 38 Stan.L.Rev. 535 (1986).

Comment. Corporate Stock Repurchases Under the Federal Securities Laws, 66 Colum.L.Rev. 1292 (1966).

CHAPTER 8

MERGERS AND ACQUISITIONS

A. DISCLOSURE REQUIREMENTS UNDER 1933 AND 1934 ACTS

When two companies combine by means of a statutory merger or consolidation, state corporation law generally requires that the transaction must be approved by the shareholders of one or both of the companies. If one of the companies is a publicly-held company registered under § 12 of the 1934 Act, it must solicit proxies from its shareholders in accordance with the SEC "proxy rules" adopted under § 14 of that Act. These proxy rules require, among other things, the distribution of a "proxy statement" setting forth all the material facts about the merger transaction (see Items 14 and 15 of Schedule 14A). In addition, the transaction may give rise to disclosure requirements under the 1933 Act.

For almost 40 years after the enactment of the Securities Act of 1933, the SEC took the position that the solicitation of shareholder votes for approval of a merger, sale of assets, or reclassification of securities was not a "sale" within the meaning of § 2(3) and therefore did not require registration under that Act. This position led to a number of problems and anomalies in the application of disclosure requirements, as described in the material which follows.

Effective January 1, 1973, the SEC adopted Rule 145, reversing its long-standing position and making the registration requirements of the 1933 Act fully applicable to these kinds of transactions. To coordinate the registration procedures with the proxy solicitation rules under § 14 of the 1934 Act (which continue to apply to such transactions where the company involved has securities registered under § 12 of that Act), the SEC modified its rules and forms so that a single document could serve as the disclosure vehicle under both Acts.

DISCLOSURE TO INVESTORS

(The "Wheat Report") (1969).

6. CHAPTER VII—BUSINESS COMBINATIONS

Business combinations in which payment by the acquiring corporation is made in its own securities are effected in three standard ways: (1) a voluntary exchange of securities, (2) a statutory merger or consolidation, and (3) a sale of the assets of the acquired company in exchange for securities of the acquiring company which are thereupon transferred to the seller's shareholders on its dissolution.

Where method (1) is used, an offer of securities of the acquiring corporation is made directly to the shareholders of the acquired corporation. In methods (2) and (3), the shareholders of the corporation to be acquired are asked to cast their individual votes for or against approval of the acquisition, or, in realistic terms, for or against a legal procedure by which their present shareholdings are exchanged for shares in another company.

The first method subjects the transaction to the disclosure requirements of the '33 Act. The other two do not. The reason for this lies in the existence of a long-standing Commission rule (Rule 133) under which the submission of the acquisition transaction to the vote of shareholders is not deemed to involve a "sale" or "offer to sell" the shares of the acquiring company so far as those shareholders are concerned.

* * *

Assuming that Corporation B's outstanding shares are held by 400 shareholders of record (so that the requirement of registration under Section 12 of the '34 Act is inapplicable) then, if Corporation A wishes to offer its shares in a voluntary exchange for the outstanding shares of B, it must register the shares to be offered under the '33 Act and deliver a prospectus to the offerees. If the transaction can be structured as a merger or sale of assets and Rule 133 applies, however, not only is registration under the '33 Act avoided but, under the laws of many states, the only document which must be sent the shareholders of B in advance of their vote on the transaction is a bare notice of meeting.

The Study questions whether these important distinctions between the Securities Act consequences of different methods of business combination—differences which affect not only the choice of the method to be used but also the interest of public investors—can be justified.

Several possible alternative solutions to the problem were examined. The most promising of these involves the replacement of Rule 133 with a special kind of '33 Act registration procedure adapted to mergers and sales of assets. The new procedure would be consistent with the proposition that where an acquired company is publicly held, a proxy statement under the Commission's rules is both an appropriate and an adequate form of disclosure: nothing additional, by way of a prospectus, is needed. Such a solution would substantially eliminate all distinctions under the '33 Act between the three types of business combinations.

There are, of course, certain practical difficulties in applying the '33 Act registration process to transactions now covered by Rule 133. The Study does not minimize these practical difficulties. It believes, however, that they are surmountable. Under the proposed procedure, one document would serve both as a '34 Act proxy statement (where the acquired company is subject to the proxy rules) and as the '33 Act prospectus. The '33 Act registration statement would consist, essentially, of a proxy statement conforming to the proxy rules. It would be processed in much the same fashion as the proxy statement is now processed and would be made effective prior to mailing. Specific procedures and rules are suggested to authorize appropriate announcements of a forthcoming merger and to deal with prospectus delivery requirements, persons not considered to be "underwriters," the mechanics of registration in a consolidation, and sale-of-assets transactions which do not require registration.

ADOPTION OF RULE 145

Securities Act Release No. 5316 (Oct. 6, 1972).

The Securities and Exchange Commission today announced the adoption of Rule 145 under the Securities Act of 1933 ("Act") and several related proposals and the prospective rescission of Rule 133 under that Act. The effect of this action will be to subject transactions involving business combinations of types described in the new rule to the registration requirements of the Act. * * *

EXPLANATION AND ANALYSIS

I. Rescission of Rule 133. Definition for Purposes of Section 5 of "Sale," "Offer to Sell," and "Offer for Sale."

Rule 133 provides that for purposes only of Section 5 of the Act, the submission to a vote of stockholders of a corporation of a proposal for certain mergers, consolidations, reclassifications of securities or transfers of assets is not deemed to involve a "sale", "offer", "offer to sell", or "offer for sale" of the securities of the new or surviving corporation to the security holders of the disappearing corporation. That rule further provides that persons who are affiliates of the constituent corporation are deemed to be underwriters within the meaning of the Section 2(11) of the Act, and except for certain limited amounts cannot sell their securities in the surviving corporation without registration.

The "no-sale" theory embodied in Rule 133 is based on the rationale that the types of transactions specified in the rule are essentially corporate acts, and the volitional act on the part of the individual stockholder required for a "sale" was absent. The basis of this theory was that the exchange or alteration of the stockholder's security occurred not because he consented thereto, but because the corporate action, authorized by a specified majority of the interests affected, converted his security into a different security.

Based on the Commission's experience in administering the provisions of the Act and Rule 133 thereunder, and having given consideration to the Disclosure Policy Study Report, to the comments received on the Commission's published proposed revision of Rule 133 (Release 33–

5012) and to the comments received on the proposed adoption of Rule 145 (Release 33–5246), the Commission is of the view that the "no-sale" approach embodied in Rule 133 overlooks the substance of the transactions specified therein and ignores the fundamental nature of the relationship between the stockholders and the corporation. The fact that such relationships are in part controlled by statutory provisions of the state of incorporation does not preclude as a matter of law the application of the broad concepts of "sale", "offer", "offer to sell", and "offer for sale" in Section 2(3) of the Act which are broader than the commercial or common law meanings of such terms.

Transactions of the type described in Rule 133 do not, in the Commission's opinion, occur solely by operation of law without the element of individual stockholder volition. A stockholder faced with a Rule 133 proposal must decide on his own volition whether or not the proposal is one in his own best interest. The basis on which the "no-sale" theory is predicated, namely, that the exchange or alteration of the stockholder's security occurs not because he consents thereto but because the corporation by authorized corporate action converts his securities, in the Commission's opinion, is at best only correct in a formalistic sense and overlooks the reality of the transaction. The corporate action, on which such great emphasis is placed, is derived from the individual consent given by each stockholder in voting on a proposal to merge or consolidate a business or reclassify a security. In voting, each consenting stockholder is expressing his voluntary and individual acceptance of the new security, and generally the disapproving stockholder is deferring his decision as to whether to accept the new security or, if he exercises his dissenter's rights, a cash payment. The corporate action in these circumstances, therefore, is not some type of independent fiat, but is only the aggregate effect of the voluntary decisions made by the individual stockholders to accept or reject the exchange. Formalism should no longer deprive investors of the disclosure to which they are entitled.

* * *

In view of the above, the Commission is of the opinion that transactions covered by Rule 133 involve a "sale", "offer", "offer to sell", or "offer for sale" as those terms are defined in Section 2(3) of the Act. The Commission no longer sees any persuasive reason why, as a matter of statutory construction or policy, in light of the broad remedial purposes of the Act and of public policy which strongly supports registration, this should not be the interpretative meaning. * * *

V. *Amendments to Form S–14.*

The Commission believes that registration of securities issued in transactions of the character specified in Rule 145 is practical and not unduly burdensome. However, the Commission is aware that registration of such securities imposes some additional burdens on issuers, and, in order to minimize these burdens to the extent feasible, particularly for small businesses, Form S–14 provides that the prospectus to be used shall consist of a proxy or information statement that meets the requirements of the Commission's proxy or information rules under Section 14 of the Exchange Act. In the case of companies subject to those rules the filing of the registration statement on Form S–14 satisfies the requirement for filing a proxy statement and form of proxy or information statement pursuant to those rules. Thus, registration will involve little additional work on the part of the companies subject to those rules who are required to solicit votes from their security holders, because the informational requirements will be the same for both. Where a company is not subject to the proxy rules, or is subject thereto but is not required to solicit votes from its security holders, the prospectus would contain the same information that would be required by the proxy rules. In this regard, the information requirements under Section 14 of the Exchange Act are not as burdensome to small companies as are those under the Securities Act. * * *

In 1985, Form S–14 was replaced by new Form S–4.

B. LIABILITY FOR MISLEADING PROXY STATEMENTS

The adoption of Rule 145 results in most merger proxy statements also being 1933 Act registration statements, subject to § 11 liabilities in the event they contain any misstatements. However, almost all of the claims involving misleading proxy statements continue to be brought under 1934 Act Rule 14a–9, as to which the Supreme Court recognized an implied private right of action in J.I. Case v. Borak, p. 480 above, although Rule 10b–5 may also be invoked.

MILLS v. ELECTRIC AUTO–LITE CO.

396 U.S. 375 (1970).

MR. JUSTICE HARLAN delivered the opinion of the Court.

This case requires us to consider a basic aspect of the implied private right of action for violation of § 14(a) of the Securities Exchange Act of 1934, recognized by this Court in J.I. Case Co. v. Borak. As in *Borak* the asserted wrong is that a corporate merger was accomplished through the use of a proxy statement that was materially false or misleading. The question with which we deal is what causal relationship must be shown between such a statement and the merger to establish a cause of action based on the violation of the Act.

I

Petitioners were shareholders of the Electric Auto–Lite Company until 1963, when it was merged into Mergenthaler Linotype Company. They brought suit on the day before the shareholders' meeting at which the vote was to take place on the merger against Auto–Lite, Mergenthaler, and a third company, American Manufacturing Company, Inc. The complaint sought an injunction against the voting by Auto–Lite's management of all proxies obtained by means of an allegedly misleading proxy solicitation; however, it did not seek a temporary restraining order, and the voting went ahead as scheduled the following day. Several months later petitioners filed an amended complaint, seeking to have the merger set aside and to obtain such other relief as might be proper.

In Count II of the amended complaint, which is the only count before us, petitioners predicated jurisdiction on § 27 of the 1934 Act. They alleged that the proxy statement sent out by the Auto–Lite management to solicit shareholders' votes in favor of the merger was misleading, in violation of § 14(a) of the Act and SEC Rule 14a–9 thereunder. Petitioners recited that before the merger Mergenthaler owned over 50% of the outstanding shares of Auto–Lite common stock, and had been in control of Auto–Lite for two years. American Manufacturing in turn owned about one-third of the outstanding shares of Mergenthaler, and for two years had been in voting control of Mergenthaler and, through it, of Auto–Lite. Petitioners charged that in light of these circumstances the proxy statement was misleading in that it told Auto–Lite shareholders that their board of directors recommended approval of the merger without also informing them that all 11 of Auto–Lite's directors were nominees of Mergenthaler and were under the "control and domination of Mergenthaler." Petitioners asserted the right to complain of this alleged violation both derivatively on behalf of Auto–Lite and as representatives of the class of all its minority shareholders.

On petitioners' motion for summary judgment with respect to Count II, the District Court for the Northern District of Illinois ruled as a matter of law that the claimed defect in the proxy statement was, in light of the circumstances in which the statement was made, a material omission. The District Court concluded, from its reading of the *Borak* opinion, that it had to hold a hearing on the issue whether there was "a causal connection between the finding that there has been a violation of the disclosure requirements of § 14(a) and the alleged injury to the plaintiffs" before it could consider what remedies would be appropriate.

After holding such a hearing, the court found that under the terms of the merger agreement, an affirmative vote of two-thirds of the Auto–Lite shares was required for approval of the merger, and that the respondent companies owned and controlled about 54% of the outstanding shares. Therefore, to obtain authorization of the merger, respondents had to secure the approval of a substantial number of the minority shareholders. At the stockholders' meeting, approximately 950,000 shares, out of 1,160,000 shares outstanding, were voted in favor of the merger. This included 317,000 votes obtained by proxy from the minority shareholders, votes that were "necessary and indispensable to the approval of the merger." The District Court concluded that a causal relationship had thus been shown, and it granted an interlocutory judgment in favor of petitioners on the issue of liability, referring the case to a master for consideration of appropriate relief.

The District Court made the certification required by 28 U.S.C. § 1292(b), and respondents took an interlocutory appeal to the Court of Appeals for the Seventh Circuit. That court affirmed the District Court's conclusion that the proxy statement was materially deficient, but reversed on the question of causation. The court acknowledged that, if an injunction had been sought a sufficient time before the stockholders' meeting, "corrective measures would have been appropriate." However, since this suit was brought too late for preventive action, the courts had to determine "whether the misleading statement and omission caused the submission of sufficient proxies," as a prerequisite to a determination of liability under the Act. If the respondents could show, "by a preponderance of probabilities, that the merger would have received a sufficient vote even if the proxy statement had not been misleading in the respect found," petitioners would be entitled to no relief of any kind.

The Court of Appeals acknowledged that this test corresponds to the common-law fraud test of whether the injured party relied on the misrepresentation. However, rightly concluding that "[r]eliance by thousands of individuals, as here, can scarcely be inquired into" the court ruled that the issue was to be determined by proof of the fairness of the terms of the merger. If respondents could show that the merger had merit and was fair to the minority shareholders, the trial court would be justified in concluding that a sufficient number of shareholders would have approved the merger had there been no deficiency in the proxy statement. In that case respondents would be entitled to a judgment in their favor.

Claiming that the Court of Appeals has construed this Court's decision in *Borak* in a manner that frustrates the statute's policy of enforcement through private litigation, the petitioners then sought review in this Court. We granted certiorari, believing that resolution of this basic issue should be made at this stage of the litigation and not postponed until after a trial under the Court of Appeals' decision.

II

As we stressed in *Borak*, § 14(a) stemmed from a congressional belief that "[f]air corporate suffrage is an important right that should attach to every equity security bought on a public exchange." H.R.Rep. No. 1383, 73d Cong., 2d Sess., 13. The provision was intended to promote "the free exercise of the voting rights of stockholders" by ensuring that proxies would be solicited with "explanation to the stockholder of the real nature of the questions for which authority to cast his vote is sought." The decision below, by permitting all liability to be foreclosed on the basis of a finding that the merger was fair, would allow the stockholders to be bypassed, at least where the only legal challenge to the merger is a suit for retrospective relief after the meeting has been held. A judicial appraisal of the merger's merits could be substituted for the actual and informed vote of the stockholders.

The result would be to insulate from private redress an entire category of proxy violations—those relating to matters other than the terms of the merger. Even outrageous misrepresentations in a proxy solicitation, if they did not relate to the terms of the transaction, would give rise to no cause of action under § 14(a). Particularly if carried over to enforcement actions by the Securities and Exchange Commission itself, such a result would subvert the congressional purpose of ensuring full and fair disclosure to shareholders.

Further, recognition of the fairness of the merger as a complete defense would confront small shareholders with an additional obstacle to making a successful challenge to a proposal recommended through a defective proxy statement. The risk that they would be unable to rebut the corporation's evidence of the fairness of the proposal, and thus to establish their cause of action, would be bound to discourage such shareholders from the private enforcement of the proxy rules that "provides a necessary supplement to Commission action." [5]

Such a frustration of the congressional policy is not required by anything in the wording of the statute or in our opinion in the *Borak* case. Section 14(a) declares it "unlawful" to solicit proxies in contravention of Commission rules, and SEC Rule 14a–9 prohibits solicitations "containing any statement which * * * is false or misleading with respect to any material fact, or which omits to state any material fact necessary in order to make the statements therein not false or misleading * * *." Use of a solicitation that is materially misleading is itself a violation of law, as the Court of Appeals recognized in stating that injunctive relief would be available to remedy such a defect if sought prior to the stockholders' meeting. In *Borak*, which came to this Court on a dismissal of the complaint, the Court limited its inquiry to whether a violation of § 14(a) gives rise to "a federal cause of action for rescission or damages." Referring to the argument made by petitioners there "that the merger can be dissolved only if it was fraudulent or non-beneficial, issues upon which the proxy material would not bear," the Court stated: "But the causal relationship of the proxy material and the merger are questions of fact to be resolved at trial, not here. We therefore do not discuss this point further." In the present case there has been a hearing specifically directed to the causation problem. The question before the Court is whether the facts found on the basis of that hearing are sufficient in law to establish petitioners' cause of action, and we conclude that they are.

5. The Court of Appeals' ruling that "causation" may be negated by proof of the fairness of the merger also rests on a dubious behavioral assumption. There is no justification for presuming that the shareholders of every corporation are willing to accept any and every fair merger offer put before them; yet such a presumption is implicit in the opinion of the Court of Appeals. * * *

Where the misstatement or omission in a proxy statement has been shown to be "material," as it was found to be here, that determination itself indubitably embodies a conclusion that the defect was of such a character that it might have been considered important by a reasonable shareholder who was in the process of deciding how to vote.[6] This requirement that the defect have a significant *propensity* to affect the voting process is found in the express terms of Rule 14a–9, and it adequately serves the purpose of ensuring that a cause of action cannot be established by proof of a defect so trivial, or so unrelated to the transaction for which approval is sought, that correction of the defect or imposition of liability would not further the interests protected by § 14(a).

There is no need to supplement this requirement, as did the Court of Appeals, with a requirement of proof of whether the defect actually had a decisive effect on the voting. Where there has been a finding of materiality, a shareholder has made a sufficient showing of causal relationship between the violation and the injury for which he seeks redress if, as here, he proves that the proxy solicitation itself rather than the particular defect in the solicitation materials, was an essential link in the accomplishment of the transaction. This objective test will avoid the impracticalities of determining how many votes were affected, and, by resolving doubts in favor of those the statute is designed to protect, will effectuate the congressional policy of ensuring that the shareholders are able to make an informed choice when they are consulted on corporate transactions.[7]

6. * * * In this case, where the misleading aspect of the solicitation involved failure to reveal a serious conflict of interest on the part of the directors, the Court of Appeals concluded that the crucial question in determining materiality was "whether the minority shareholders were sufficiently alerted to the board's relationship to their adversary to be on their guard." 403 F.2d at 434. An adequate disclosure of this relationship would have warned the stockholders to give more careful scrutiny to the terms of the merger than they might to one recommended by an entirely disinterested board. Thus, the failure to make such a disclosure was found to be a material defect "as a matter of law," thwarting the informed decision at which the statute aims regardless of whether the terms of the merger were such that a reasonable stockholder would have approved the transaction after more careful analysis. See also Swanson v. American Consumer Industries, Inc., 415 F.2d 1326 (C.A.7th Cir.1969).

7. We need not decide in this case whether causation could be shown where the management controls a sufficient number of shares to approve the transaction without any votes from the minority. Even in that situation, if the management finds it necessary for legal or practical reasons to solicit proxies from minority shareholders, at least one court has held that the proxy solicitation might be sufficiently related to the merger to satisfy the causation requirement, see Laurenzano v. Einbender, 264 F.Supp. 356 (D.C.E.D.N.Y. 1966); cf. Swanson v. American Consumer Industries, Inc., 415 F.2d 1326, 1331–1332 (C.A.7th Cir.1969); Eagle v. Horvath, 241 F.Supp. 341, 344 (D.C.S.D.N.Y.1965); Globus, Inc. v. Jaroff, 271 F.Supp. 378, 381 (D.C.S.D.N.Y.1967); Comment. Shareholders' Derivative Suit to Enforce a Corporate Right of Action Against Directors Under SEC Rule 10b–5, 114 U.Pa.L.Rev. 578, 582 (1966). But see Hoover v. Allen, 241 F.Supp. 213, 231–232 (D.C.S.D.N.Y.1965); Barnett v. Anaconda Co., 238 F.Supp. 766, 770–774 (D.C.S.D.N.Y.1965); Robbins v. Banner Industries, Inc., 285 F.Supp. 758, 762–763 (D.C.S.D.N.Y.1966). See generally 5 L. Loss, Securities Regulation 2933–2938 (Supp.1969).

III

Our conclusion that petitioners have established their case by showing that proxies necessary to approval of the merger were obtained by means of a materially misleading solicitation implies nothing about the form of relief to which they may be entitled. We held in *Borak* that upon finding a violation the courts were "to be alert to provide such remedies as are necessary to make effective the congressional purpose," noting specifically that such remedies are not to be limited to prospective relief. In devising retrospective relief for violation of the proxy rules, the federal courts should consider the same factors that would govern the relief granted for any similar illegality or fraud. One important factor may be the fairness of the terms of the merger. Possible forms of relief will include setting aside the merger or granting other equitable relief, but, as the Court of Appeals below noted, nothing in the statutory policy "requires the court to unscramble a corporate transaction merely because a violation occurred." In selecting a remedy the lower courts should exercise " 'the sound discretion which guides the determinations of courts of equity,' " keeping in mind the role of equity as "the instrument for nice adjustment and reconciliation between the public interest and private needs as well as between competing private claims."

We do not read § 29(b) of the Act, which declares contracts made in violation of the Act or a rule thereunder "void * * * as regards the rights of" the violator and knowing successors in interest, as requiring that the merger be set aside simply because the merger agreement is a "void" contract. This language establishes that the guilty party is precluded from enforcing the contract against an unwilling innocent party, but it does not compel the conclusion that the contract is a nullity, creating no enforceable rights even in a party innocent of the violation. The lower federal courts have read § 29(b), which has counterparts in the Holding Company Act, the Investment Company Act, and the Investment Advisers Act, as rendering the contract merely voidable at the option of the innocent party. This interpretation is eminently sensible. The interests of the victim are sufficiently protected by giving him the right to rescind; to regard the contract as void where he has not invoked that right would only create the possibility of hardships to him or others without necessarily advancing the statutory policy of disclosure.

The United States, as *amicus curiae,* points out that as representatives of the minority shareholders, petitioners are not parties to the merger agreement and thus do not enjoy a statutory right under § 29(b) to set it aside. Furthermore, while they do have a derivative right to invoke Auto-Lite's status as a party to the agreement, a determination of what relief should be granted in Auto-Lite's name must hinge on whether setting aside the merger would be in the best interests of the shareholders as a whole. In short, in the context of a suit such as this one, § 29(b) leaves the matter of relief where it would be under *Borak* without specific statutory language—the merger should be set aside only if a court of equity concludes, from all the circumstances, that it would be equitable to do so.

Monetary relief will, of course, also be a possibility. Where the defect in the proxy solicitation relates to the specific terms of the merger, the district court might appropriately order an accounting to ensure that the shareholders receive the value that was represented as coming to them. On the other hand, where, as here, the misleading aspect of the solicitation did not relate to terms of the merger, monetary relief might be afforded to the shareholders only if the merger resulted in a reduction of the earnings or earnings potential of their holdings. In short, damages should be recoverable only to the extent that they can be shown. If commingling of the assets and operations of the merged companies makes it impossible to establish direct injury from the merger, relief might be predicated on a determination of the fairness of the terms of the merger at the time it was approved. These questions, of course, are for decision in the first instance by the District Court on remand, and our singling out of some of the possibilities is not intended to exclude others. * * *

On remand, the district court held that, in light of various factors, including particularly the public trading in stock of the merged company, it would be impracticable to rescind the merger, and that "insofar as plaintiffs may have suffered any injury by reason of the merger, they may be adequately compensated by an award of money damages." Mills v. Electric Auto-Lite Co., CCH Fed.Sec.L.Rep. ¶ 93,354 (N.D.Ill. 1972). Comparing the earnings and book values of Auto-Lite and Mergenthaler prior to the merger, the district court found the terms of the merger unfair to the Auto-Lite shareholders, and awarded them damages of $1,234,000. On appeal, the Court of Appeals reversed. It held that the appropriate comparison was between the market prices of Auto-Lite and Mergenthaler shares, and that, giving effect to "the synergism generated by the merger," the terms were fair to the Auto-Lite shareholders, and they were not entitled to any damages. Mills v. Electric Auto-Lite Co., 552 F.2d 1239 (7th Cir.1977). Does this indicate that the Court of Appeals may have been on the right track in its first decision?

One question left open by the Supreme Court in *Mills* (see note 7) was whether causation could be shown where the controlling person owned enough shares to approve the transaction without the votes of any other shareholders.

In SCHLICK v. PENN-DIXIE CEMENT CORP., 507 F.2d 374 (2d Cir.1974), a panel of the Second Circuit (Judge Oakes and two district judges) upheld the sufficiency of a complaint attacking a merger under Rules 10b-5 and 14a-9. Plaintiffs, minority shareholders of Continental, alleged that Penn-Dixie (which owned 53% of Continental's stock) "had manipulated and depressed the market value of Continental stock in relation to that of Penn–Dixie by utilizing Continental's assets for the benefit of Penn–Dixie", had "caused Continental to enter into a merger agreement providing for an unfair exchange ratio based upon manipulated and artificial stock values," and "in connection with the merger * * * [had] issued a materially defective proxy statement which failed to disclose the manner in which Penn–Dixie had inflated the value of its shares at the expense of Continental." The district court dismissed the complaint on the ground that the plaintiff failed to allege any causal connection between the misstatements in the proxy statement and the damage resulting from the "unfair" exchange ratio in the merger, since Penn–Dixie owned enough shares to approve the merger without soliciting the votes of any other shareholders. The Court of Appeals reversed. With respect to the claim under Rule 10b–5, it stated:

* * *

> This is not a case where the 10b–5 claim is based solely upon material omissions or misstatements in the proxy materials. Were it so, concededly there would have to be a showing of both *loss causation*—that the misrepresentations or omissions caused the economic harm—and *transaction causation*—that the violations in question caused the appellant to engage in the transaction in question. The former is demonstrated rather easily by proof of some form of economic damage, here the unfair exchange ratio, which arguably would have been fairer had the basis for valuation been disclosed. Transaction causation requires substantially more. In a misrepresentation case, to show transaction causation a plaintiff must demonstrate that he relied on the misrepresentations in question when he entered into the transaction which caused him harm. In an omission or nondisclosure case based upon Rule 10b–5, a plaintiff need not show reliance in order to show transaction causation but must still show that the facts in question were material "in the sense that a reasonable investor might have considered them important" in making his investment decisions.
>
> Under the 10b–5 count, proof of transaction causation is unnecessary by virtue of the allegations as to the effectuation of a scheme to defraud which includes market manipulation and a merger on preferential terms, of which the proxy omissions and misrepresentations are only one aspect. Thus appellant need only show loss causation with respect to his claim for relief under 10b–5; Judge Metzner found and we agree that this has been shown. Here the complaint clearly alleges that, as a result of the merger, appellant was forced to sell his Continental shares to Penn–Dixie on the basis of an exchange ratio that reflected adversely the manipulated market value of Continental stock, and that he sustained injury accordingly.
>
> * * *
>
> Thus, the complaint completes the showing necessary to state a claim under Rule 10b–5. It alleges a specific scheme to defraud (a scheme which includes the proxy solicitation as a part, but which included substantial collateral conduct as well); the fraud was accomplished in connection with a securities transaction; the appellant was

a seller in that transaction; and as a result of the sale, appellant alleges a loss was sustained.

* * *

With respect to the claim under Rule 14a–9, the court held that the "broad remedial purposes" of the proxy rules to ensure "fair corporate suffrage" made it inappropriate to apply a strict causation rule, under which plaintiff would have to show that the misstatements in the proxy material might have affected the result of the merger vote:

* * *

> The equities call for protection of the minority shareholder when he is the most helpless, as when neither disinterested director nor disinterested shareholder voting exists as a safeguard. To require strict causation would "sanction all manner of fraud and overreaching in the fortuitous circumstance that a controlling shareholder exists." Swanson v. American Consumer Industries, Inc., 415 F.2d at 1331.
>
> * * *
>
> The minority shareholders aside, there are two other purposes served by the disclosure requirements which make a strict causation rule—whether under a 10(b) or a 14(a) claim—antithetical to it:
>
> 1. By disclosure the *market* will be informed, so as to permit well-based decisions about buying, selling and holding the securities involved in the transaction. Thus, had there been full disclosure here, the merger ratio would have been unfair on its face and the shares of Penn–Dixie in the open market would have sold for less.
>
> 2. By virtue of the disclosure either modification or reconsideration of the terms of the merger by those in control might be effectuated. We cannot assume that even a rapacious controlling management would necessarily want to hang its dirty linen out on the line and thereby expose itself to suit or Securities Commission or other action—in terms of reputation and future takeovers.
>
> In short, we refuse to adopt the narrow view of causation for which the appellees argue. Instead, in the light of the *Mills* footnote, *Affiliated Ute,* the Seventh Circuit's *Swanson I* and *Swanson II,* and the other cases in our own circuit above referred to, we are of the view that sufficient causation is alleged so that the complaint must not be dismissed.

A similar result was reached in COLE v. SCHENLEY INDUSTRIES, 563 F.2d 35 (2d Cir.1977) and in SANDBERG v. VIRGINIA BANKSHARES, 891 F.2d 1112 (4th Cir.1989). In April 1990, the U.S. Supreme Court agreed to review the decision in the *Sandberg* case.

If the controlling person owns enough shares to approve a merger or similar transaction without soliciting the votes of any outside shareholders, can it avoid potential 14a–9 liability by simply not soliciting proxies? See § 14(c) of the 1934 Act, which was added in 1964.

GERSTLE v. GAMBLE–SKOGMO, INC.

478 F.2d 1281 (2d Cir.1973).

Before FRIENDLY, CHIEF JUDGE, OAKES, CIRCUIT JUDGE, and DAVIS, JUDGE.

FRIENDLY, CHIEF JUDGE.

This appeal and cross-appeal in a class action by minority stockholders of General Outdoor Advertising Co. (GOA), attacking its merger into defendant Gamble–Skogmo, Inc. (Skogmo), raise a variety of new and difficult questions with respect to the SEC's Proxy Rules, adopted under § 14(a) of the Securities Exchange Act, and the remedy for their violation. * * *

[T]he gravamen of plaintiffs' complaint concerning the Proxy Statement sent to GOA's stockholders was that its disclosure that Skogmo expected to realize large profits from the disposition of such of GOA's advertising plants as had not been sold at the date of the merger was inadequate.

* * * Judge Bartels found the Proxy Statement disseminated by GOA to violate Rule 14a–9 by failing adequately to disclose the market value of GOA's advertising plants remaining unsold at the time of the merger and Skogmo's intent to realize the large profits available from the remaining plants by selling them shortly after the merger.

A. WAS THE PROXY STATEMENT MISLEADING?

One of the plaintiffs' principal attacks on the adequacy of the Proxy Statement was that GOA was bound to disclose its appraisals of the market value of the remaining plants and the existence and amount of the firm offers to purchase the unsold plants that it had received. Skogmo countered that the SEC would not have allowed this. By a stroke of luck it was able to support its position not only by materials generally available but by the SEC staff's reaction in this very case to the suggestion of Minis & Co. that market values be disclosed in the proxy statement. In an attempt to obtain assistance on this issue, the court asked the Commission to file a brief as *amicus curiae.*

The SEC's brief has been the subject of considerable comment.[9] Its first section reaffirms the Commission's longstanding position that "in financial statements filed with the Commission, fixed assets should be carried at historical cost (less any depreciation) in the absence of any statute, rule, or specific Commission authorization to the contrary." A second section is headed, "The narrative or textual portions of a proxy statement must contain whatever additional material is necessary under the circumstances in order to make the proxy statement not

9. See, e.g., Fiflis & Kripke, Accounting for Business Lawyers 473–80 (1971); Manne, Accounting and Administrative Law Aspects of Gerstle v. Gamble–Skogmo, Inc., 15 N.Y.Law Forum 304 (1969).

misleading." So much is hardly controversial. But the heading of the third section reads:

> When a balance sheet in a proxy statement for a merger reflects assets at an amount that is substantially lower than their current liquidating value, and liquidation of those assets is intended or can reasonably be anticipated, the textual or narrative portion of the proxy statement must contain whatever available material information about their current liquidating value is necessary to make the proxy statement not misleading.

The text goes on to elaborate that while the corporation's own asking price may not be disclosed, "good faith offers from unaffiliated third parties to buy corporate assets for more than their book value must be disclosed if their omission would render the proxy statement materially misleading." Similarly, the text states that, although appraisals generally cannot be disclosed because they may be misleading, existing appraisals of current liquidating value must be disclosed if they have been made by a qualified expert and have a sufficient basis in fact. The district judge seemingly adopted the Commission's statement of the governing principles, and found that Skogmo's failure to disclose its appraisals and firm offers made the proxy statement materially misleading.

The assertion that the Commission would have permitted reference to "appraisals" made by GOA's own officials, and the intimation that it would have required them had it known of their existence, must have been as much a surprise to the Commission's branch chief who had refused to insist on a revision of the proxy statement to include appraisals because this was contrary to Commission policy, as it was to Skogmo's counsel. Rule 14a–9 has long carried a note giving examples "of what, depending upon particular facts and circumstances, may be misleading within the meaning of the rule"; the very first is "(a) Predictions as to specific future market values, earnings or dividends." This note does not in terms refer to appraisals of assets at current market value and, indeed, the SEC in this case attempted to distinguish appraisals of present liquidating values from estimates of future earnings or profits in an effort to reconcile its position in favor of disclosure here with the stand it took in Sunray DX Oil Co. v. Helmerich & Payne, Inc., 398 F.2d 447 (10 Cir.1968). The validity of this distinction is far from apparent, see Kripke, The SEC, The Accountants, Some Myths and Some Realities, 45 N.Y.U.L.Rev. 1151, 1200 (1970), particularly in the context of this case, where the appraisals hinged to no small degree on the ability of prospective purchasers to pay for the properties out of future earnings. But, more important, it is clear that the policy embodied in the note to Rule 14a–9 has consistently been enforced to bar disclosure of asset appraisals as well as future market values, earnings or dividends. The Commission acknowledged this in its brief:

> The Commission and its staff have traditionally looked with suspicion upon the inclusion of asset appraisals even in the text or narrative

> portion of proxy statements. It has been our experience that such appraisals are often unfounded or unreliable. For this reason, the Commission's staff, on a case-by-case basis, has usually requested the deletion of appraisals that have been included in proxy statements.

The Commission further acknowledged that its branch chief had enforced this policy in his refusal to consider disclosure of asset appraisals in the Proxy Statement here, admitting that at the meeting recounted above, "a branch chief of the Commission's Division of Corporation Finance did express the staff's general policy against the inclusion of appraisals in a proxy statement."

However, the note to Rule 14a–9 states only that disclosure of appraisals "may be misleading" "depending upon particular facts and circumstances," and the SEC's brief attempts to capitalize upon this and clothe its longstanding policy against disclosure of appraisals with an appearance of flexibility and case-by-case analysis, as some of the foregoing quotations indicate. However desirable such a policy may be, we do not believe this is what it was in 1963. The Commission's examiners "are trained to strike at appraisal values as unacceptable whenever they read them in documents filed with the Commission." Fiflis & Kripke, supra note 9, at 472. See also id. at 470; Manne, supra note 9, at 315, 323. It has long been an article of faith among lawyers specializing in the securities field that appraisals of assets could not be included in a proxy statement.

There is nothing in the authorities cited by the Commission in support of the position taken in its brief which casts serious doubt on this conclusion. The Commission's principal reliance in its brief here was on an *amicus* brief it had filed in the well-known case of Speed v. Transamerica Corp., 99 F.Supp. 808 (D.Del.1951), modified and affirmed, 235 F.2d 369 (3 Cir.1956). While we have no doubt that *Speed* was correctly decided, that case dealt with an inventory of a commodity, tobacco, about to be liquidated by the buyer, which was actively traded and whose market value could be ascertained with reasonable certainty on the basis of actual sales. No "appraisal" of market value was required, and the dangers that the SEC has perceived in the disclosure of appraised values were not present. And, of course, *Speed* did not involve proxy statements or the SEC's policy of not allowing disclosure of appraisals in them. As has been correctly said, "No one, the Commission included, has seriously believed that the *Speed* case stands for the general proposition that appraisals of assets must be disclosed to the shareholders." *Manne,* supra note 9, at 323.

The only other supporting references in the *amicus* brief were to two SEC litigation releases issued in the 1940's. Only one of these, SEC v. Standard Oil Co., Litigation Release No. 388 (Feb. 26, 1947), is of any relevance here. The SEC there brought an action under Rule 10b–5 to enjoin the defendants from purchasing the shares of minority shareholders or soliciting shareholders to exchange their common stock for preferred in connection with a merger without disclosing that the present value of the Company's oil reserves, as appraised by qualified outside engineers, was far greater than the value carried on the firm's balance sheet, and the litigation release reported that the defendants had agreed to entry of a consent order without admitting liability. The other litigation release reported only that the SEC had filed an action under Rule 10b–5 complaining of the failure of a brokerage firm to disclose the value of its marketable securities before repurchasing its debentures.[11] Such bits and pieces, flushed out by industrious research, cannot retroactively overcome the general understanding embodied in the note to Rule 14a–9, regularly given effect by the Commission's able staff in dealing with lawyers who specialize in SEC matters, and repeated in this very case.[12]

The Commission's policy against disclosure of asset appraisals in proxy statements has apparently stemmed from its deep distrust of their reliability, its concern that investors would accord such appraisals in a proxy statement more weight than would be warranted, and the impracticability, with its limited staff, of examining appraisals on a case-by-case basis to determine their reliability. The Commission is now in the process of a thorough re-examination of its policy, and it appears that new rules on the permissible uses of appraisals and projections may shortly be forthcoming. See Statement by the Committee on Disclosure of Projections of Future Economic Performance, CCH Fed.Sec.L.Rep. ¶ 79,211 (Feb. 2, 1973). The SEC may well determine that its policy, while protecting investors who are considering the purchase of a security from the overoptimistic claims of management, may have deprived those who must decide whether or not to sell their securities, as the plaintiffs effectively did here, of valuable information, as Professor Kripke has argued, Rule 10b–5 Liability and "Material Facts", 46 N.Y.U.L.Rev. 1061, 1071 (1971). But we would be loath to impose a huge liability on Skogmo on the basis of what we regard as a substantial modification, if not reversal of the SEC's position on disclosure of appraisals in proxy statements, by way of its *amicus* brief in this case. Indeed, it was to protect against this that Congress enacted section 23(a) of the Securities Exchange Act, which provides that "No provision of this chapter imposing any liability shall apply to any act done

11. SEC v. Greenfield, Litigation Release No. 302 (Nov. 7, 1945). The Commission's brief also cited Millimet v. George F. Fuller Co., CCH Fed.Sec.L.Rep. ¶ 91,570 (S.D.N.Y.1965), complaint dismissed sub nom. Richland v. Crandall, 262 F.Supp. 538, 554–555 (S.D.N.Y.1967), and CMC Corp. v. Kern County Land Co., 290 F.Supp. 695 (N.D.Cal.1968). While these cases involved allegations by private plaintiffs that the failure to disclose appraised values made proxy statements misleading, both complaints were dismissed without considering whether the SEC would have allowed such appraisals to appear in the proxy statement. As Professor Manne has said, supra note 9, at 323, the relevance of these holdings to the present case "is too tenuous to merit the space accorded them."

12. It is argued that Mr. Bodolus' position at the meeting in early October might have been different if the Proxy Statement had made clear that Skogmo had a fixed intention immediately to sell the remaining plants. We are not at all sure of this; in any event the judge's findings could not reasonably go so far. The most that could be found was that Skogmo intended vigorously to pursue the program of sales if adequate prices could be secured and that it had good reason to expect they could be. We are confident that the SEC staff would not have allowed the appraisals to appear in the Proxy Statement even if this intention had been disclosed to it. What a court would have ruled if Minis had chosen to seek an injunction is not determinative here.

or omitted in good faith in conformity with any rule or regulation of the Commission," notwithstanding any later amendment. While defendant's reliance here was on the Commission's consistent interpretation of its own rule, rather than on the terms of the rule itself, it is hard to attach any significance to this distinction when the effect of the Commission's interpretation was to lead counsel reasonably to believe Skogmo would not be allowed to make the references to "appraisals" which plaintiffs now claim were required.

* * *

However, * * * quite apart from the SEC's *amicus* brief, the Proxy Statement must be faulted * * * as failing adequately to disclose that, upon completion of the merger, Skogmo intended to pursue aggressively the policy of selling GOA's plants, which had already yielded such a substantial excess of receipts over book value.

The adequacy of the disclosure in the Proxy Statement, especially in what we have called the fateful paragraph, must be weighed against Judge Bartels' basic factual finding,

> that Skogmo as the controlling stockholder and surviving corporation intended at least by and probably before July 19, 1963, to sell all the remaining outdoor advertising plants of General immediately after the merger.

* * *

Skogmo does not seriously maintain that these findings are clearly erroneous. The only reasonable quarrel would be with the word "immediately" in the finding first quoted, but the result would not be different if this were changed to read "as soon as possible".

In contrast to the court's finding of intention, the affirmative statement in the first sentence of the key paragraph in the Proxy Statement is that Skogmo intended "to continue the business of General Outdoor". The Statement had earlier described this to be just what its name implied, and most stockholders must have understood this sentence to mean that Skogmo intended to remain in the outdoor advertising business. True, earlier portions of the Proxy Statement had noted that part of the "business" consisted of selling plants, and the paragraph under scrutiny did say that the "business" that would be continued included "the policy of *considering* offers for the sale to acceptable prospective purchasers of outdoor advertising branches" (emphasis supplied) and using the proceeds for further diversification. But, particularly with the disclaimer in the final sentence, that "at the present time there are no agreements, arrangements or understandings * * * and no negotiations are presently being conducted with respect to the sale of any branch," only the most sophisticated reader would conclude that Skogmo had the firm intention, which the Judge reasonably found, not simply to "consider" offers but actively to solicit them. While "corporations are not required to address their stockholders as if they were children in kindergarten," Richland v. Crandall, 262 F.Supp. 538, 554 (S.D.N.Y.1967), it is not sufficient that overtones might have been picked up by the sensitive antennae of investment analysts.

* * *

We recognize that, in thus branding the Proxy Statement as misleading, the district judge and we possess an advantage of hindsight that was not available to the draftsman. It would not have been proper to say that Skogmo *was going to sell* all the remaining plants, when, even with the encouragement that had been received, there was no assurance that it could do this on satisfactory terms. But the English language has sufficient resources that the draftsman could have done better than he did and more accurately expressed Skogmo's true intention to the stockholders. If only the first sentence of the fateful paragraph had said something like "including a policy of aggressively seeking to dispose of the remaining outdoor advertising branches or subsidiaries of General Outdoor through sales to acceptable prospective purchasers on advantageous terms in the range of those that have been achieved in the past," we would at least have had a very different case.

B. What Is the Standard of Culpability in Suits for Damages for Violation of Rule 14a–9?

In contrast to the large quantity of ink that has been spilled on the issue whether a plaintiff seeking damages under Rule 10b–5 must make some showing of "scienter" and, if so, what, there has been little discussion of what a plaintiff alleging damage because of a violation of Rule 14a–9(a) must show in the way of culpability on the part of a defendant.[16] Neither of the Supreme Court decisions concerning private actions under section 14(a), J.I. Case Co. v. Borak, or Mills v. Electric Auto–Lite Co., casts light on the problem.

Judge Bartels held that "the basis for incorporating scienter into a Rule 10b–5 action does not exist in a Rule 14a–9 suit," and that "Negligence alone either in making a misrepresentation or in failing to disclose a material fact in connection with proxy solicitation is sufficient to warrant recovery." The judge agreed in substance with Judge Mansfield's analysis in Richland v. Crandall, supra, to the effect that one strong ground for holding that Rule 10b–5 requires a showing of something more than negligence in an action for damages is that the statutory authority for the Rule, section 10(b) of the Securities Exchange Act, is addressed to "any manipulative or deceptive device or contrivance," whereas section 14(a) contains no such evil-sounding language.

We think there is much force in this. Although the language of Rule 14a–9(a) closely parallels that of Rule 10b–5, and neither says in

16. Our discussion of this point is limited to the rights of persons who were invited by a proxy statement to participate in the taking of corporate action involving a change in the character of their securities, as in a sale of assets or a consolidation or merger. It does not include persons who have traded because of information in such a proxy statement, for whom the statement would seem to stand no differently from, say, an annual report to stockholders. We likewise do not pass on the principles that should govern liability of directors and other individuals having some responsibility for such a statement, as distinguished from a controlling corporation which has been the beneficiary of the action that was induced.

so many words that scienter should be a requirement, one of the primary reasons that this court has held that this is required in a private action under Rule 10b–5, is a concern that without some such requirement the Rule might be invalid as exceeding the Commission's authority under section 10(b) to regulate "manipulative or deceptive devices." In contrast, the scope of the rulemaking authority granted under section 14(a) is broad, extending to all proxy regulation "necessary or appropriate in the public interest or for the protection of investors" and not limited by any words connoting fraud or deception. This language suggests that rather than emphasizing the prohibition of fraudulent conduct on the part of insiders to a securities transaction, as we think section 10(b) does, in section 14(a) Congress was somewhat more concerned with protection of the outsider whose proxy is being solicited. Indeed, it was this aspect of the statute that the Supreme Court emphasized in recognizing a private right of action for violation of section 14(a) in *Borak.* We note also that while an open-ended reading of Rule 10b–5 would render the express civil liability provisions of the securities acts largely superfluous, and be inconsistent with the limitations Congress built into these sections, a reading of Rule 14a–9 as imposing liability without scienter in a case like the present is completely compatible with the statutory scheme.[18]

Although this does not mean that scienter should never be required in an action under Rule 14a–9, a number of considerations persuade us that it would be inappropriate to require plaintiffs to prove it in the circumstances of this case. First, many 10b–5 cases relate to statements issued by corporations, without legal obligation to do so, as a result of what the SEC has properly called "a commendable and growing recognition on the part of industry and the investment community of the importance of informing security holders and the public generally with respect to important business and financial developments." Imposition of too liberal a standard with respect to culpability

18. It has been argued that imposing liability for negligent misrepresentations or omissions under Rule 14a–9 would be inconsistent with the congressional intent in enacting section 18 of the 1934 Act, which expressly creates liability in a private civil action for making materially false or misleading statements in any document filed with the Commission but provides that no liability shall be imposed if the defendant "acted in good faith and had no knowledge that such statement was false and misleading." See Gould v. American Hawaiian S.S. Co., supra, 351 F.Supp. at 863. But section 18 applies broadly to any document filed with the Commission, whereas section 14 was specifically directed at proxy regulation. Moreover, most of the documents within the scope of section 18 are not distributed to stockholders for the purpose of inducing action; we see nothing anomalous about applying a different standard of culpability in actions concerning misrepresentations in proxy statements which are so distributed than in those involving reports which were merely filed with the Commission. In short, we see no incompatibility between our holding here and the limitations Congress imposed in section 18.

In any event, we note that a corporation in Skogmo's position would be unable to take advantage of the defenses in section 18. The statute requires that both good faith and lack of knowledge be shown to escape liability under that section. But, as Jennings and Marsh point out, a corporation would be charged with the knowledge of all its agents and it is most unlikely that it could issue a false or misleading proxy statement without "knowledge" of the facts which made it false or misleading.

would deter this particularly in light of the almost unlimited liability that may result. Such considerations do not apply to a proxy statement required by the Proxy Rules, especially to one, like that in the present case, which serves many of the same functions as a registration statement. Rather, a broad standard of culpability here will serve to reinforce the high duty of care owed by a controlling corporation to minority shareholders in the preparation of a proxy statement seeking their acquiescence in this sort of transaction, a consideration which is particularly relevant since liability in this case is limited to the stockholders whose proxies were solicited. While "privity" is not required for most actions under the securities laws, its existence may bear heavily on the appropriate standard of culpability. See Ruder, *Texas Gulf Sulphur*—The Second Round: Privity and State of Mind in Rule 10b–5 Purchase and Sale Cases, 63 Nw.U.L.Rev. 423, 437 (1968).

Furthermore, the common law itself finds negligence sufficient for tort liability where a person supplies false information to another with the intent to influence a transaction in which he has a pecuniary interest. Restatement (Second) of Torts § 552 (Tent.Draft No. 12, 1966); Prosser, Torts § 107, at 706–09 (4th ed. 1971); Gediman v. Anheuser Busch, Inc., 299 F.2d 537, 543–546 (2 Cir.1962). This is particularly so when the transaction redounded directly to the benefit of the defendant, in which case the common law would provide the remedies of rescission and restitution without proof of scienter. See Prosser, supra, § 105, at 687–89; 3 Loss, supra, at 1626–27. It is unlikely that section 14(a) and Rule 14a–9 contemplated less.

We thus hold that in a case like this, where the plaintiffs represent the very class who were asked to approve a merger on the basis of a misleading proxy statement and are seeking compensation from the beneficiary who is responsible for the preparation of the statement, they are not required to establish any evil motive or even reckless disregard of the facts. Whether in situations other than that here presented "the liability of the corporation issuing a materially false or misleading proxy statement is virtually absolute, as under Section 11 of the 1933 Act with respect to a registration statement." Jennings & Marsh, Securities Regulation: Cases and Materials 1358 (3d ed. 1972), we leave to another day.

C. Was the Inadequacy in the Proxy Statement Material?

The first of the two Supreme Court cases dealing with civil liability under Rule 14a–9(a), J.I. Case Co. v. Borak, supra, raised no question with respect to materiality. However, the second, Mills v. Electric Auto-Lite Co., supra, has often been regarded as setting forth a clear definition of "materiality" for purposes of damage suits under Rule 14a–9(a) in Mr. Justice Harlan's statement that:

> Where the misstatement or omission in a proxy statement has been shown to be "material," as it was found to be here, that determination itself indubitably embodies a conclusion that the defect was of

such a character that it might have been considered important by a reasonable shareholder who was in the process of deciding how to vote.

This statement, however, was not in fact intended to establish a definition of materiality. * * *

Moreover, Justice Harlan cited with apparent approval two decisions of this court which set out a somewhat higher standard of materiality. Thus, he cited Judge Waterman's opinion in List v. Fashion Park, Inc., a face-to-face 10b–5 case, where it was held, quoting from the Restatement of Torts § 538(2)(a) (1938), that the basic test of materiality is whether "a reasonable man *would* attach importance [to the fact misrepresented] in determining his choice of action in the transaction in question" (emphasis supplied). The Justice also cited the writer's statement in General Time Corp. v. Talley Industries, Inc., 403 F.2d 159, 162 (2 Cir.1968), that the test was whether "taking a properly realistic view, there is a *substantial* likelihood that the mistatement or omission may have led a stockholder to grant a proxy to the solicitor or to withhold one from the other side, whereas in the absence of this he would have taken a contrary course" (emphasis supplied).

We think that, in a context such as this, the "might have been" standard mentioned by Mr. Justice Harlan sets somewhat too low a threshold; the very fact that negligence suffices to invoke liability argues for a realistic standard of materiality. Justice Harlan's next sentence in *Mills,* that the defect must "have a significant *propensity* to affect the voting process," comes closer to the right flavor. While the difference between "might" and "would" may seem gossamer, the former is too suggestive of mere possibility, however unlikely. When account is taken of the heavy damages that may be imposed, a standard tending toward probability rather than toward mere possibility is more appropriate. We therefore adhere to this court's formulations of the test of materiality quoted above.

We hold, however, that the deficiency in the Proxy Statement was material under this slightly higher standard * * *. At the time of the merger, the minority shareholders of GOA were required to make an investment choice between retaining their shares in GOA, a firm with poor earnings prospects if it remained in the outdoor advertising field but also with the possibility of substantial extraordinary profits from liquidation of that business, or exchanging them for a small premium for the Skogmo convertible preferred, a security involving much less risk but with a correspondingly reduced interest in the profits potentially available through sales of advertising plants. Certainly the intent of those in control of GOA would be a significant factor in a reasonable shareholder's decision whether or not to vote for the merger.

* * *

We thus hold that the district court correctly held Skogmo liable for damages for violating Rule 14a–9(a).

* * *

IV. Damages

Both sides attack the method used by the district judge for computing damages. * * *

Plaintiffs' argument that the district court erred in not awarding them credit for the appreciation in value since the merger of Stedman and Claude Neon takes off from the well-known decision in Janigan v. Taylor, 344 F.2d 781, 786–787 (1 Cir.1965), recently approved and applied in Affiliated Ute Citizens v. United States. These cases hold that a defrauded seller suing the purchaser for violation of the federal securities laws may recover the profits obtained by the purchaser with respect to the securities. Both these cases, however, involved face-to-face dealings wherein the defendant had purchased stock at a low price by misrepresenting its value and had resold it prior to suit at a large profit. Skogmo does not dispute that once liability is established, this principle justifies an award to plaintiffs of the profits it realized on the sales of all the outdoor advertising plants, which were completed within nine months after the merger.

Plaintiffs argue, however, that the rationale of *Janigan* goes beyond this and requires that they be credited with the post-merger appreciation of the unsold holdings as well. The court in *Janigan* reasoned that the wrongdoer should not be allowed to profit from his wrong, and that the courts should require him to disgorge his profits to prevent his unjust enrichment, even if this would give the defrauded plaintiff the benefit of a windfall. Plaintiffs argue that defendants here are profiting from the appreciation of the properties obtained unlawfully through the merger, whether or not this profit has been realized; they argue that these properties could have been sold at a profit during this period, and, indeed, suggest that sale of Claude Neon and Stedman may have been deliberately withheld until after final judgment in this action.[25]

A second rationale supporting the *Janigan* rule in some situations is provided by the Restatement of Restitution § 151, comment c (1937). Reasoning that the defrauded seller is entitled to be put in substantially the same position he would have occupied absent the fraud, it would allow the seller to recover the profits realized or the appreciation in value of the securities on the theory that he would have otherwise been in a position to obtain these profits for himself. See also Zeller v. Bogue Electric Mfg. Corp., 476 F.2d 795, 802 n. 10 (2 Cir.1973). It is primarily this second rationale that provides the support for plaintiffs' further argument that the award should be based on the highest intermediate value of the assets of GOA between the date of the merger and the date of judgment. The argument runs as follows: If the disclosures in the Proxy Statement had been adequate, the GOA stock-

25. We are informed that since the judgment below was entered, Skogmo has sold its interest in Claude Neon to a Canadian subsidiary of Combined Communications Corp. for $18,000,000, of which $16,000,000 was in cash and $2,000,000 in notes. This sale was completed in January 1973.

holders would not have approved the merger. If the merger had not occurred, GOA would have retained the stock of Stedman and Claude Neon and the directors would have been able to sell them at a profit at a later time. Since Skogmo cannot show at what time that would have been or that the sale would have been made at any lower price, it must be charged with the highest intermediate value of each.

* * *

While plaintiffs' argument is simple, it is thus too simple. In the first place, it cannot be said that in the absence of the misrepresentations in the Proxy Statement there was a likelihood that GOA would have realized profits from sale of these holdings. As pointed out in our discussion of materiality, an adequate disclosure would not necessarily have led to an abandonment of the idea of a merger, which had much to recommend itself to the minority stockholders of GOA; the utmost consequences would likely have been a demand for postponement until the plant sales had been effected, a revision of the terms to reflect the potential gains on the sale of the plants, or the exercise of appraisal rights. * * * If the merger had been accomplished, whether in 1963 or a year later, on somewhat better terms for the GOA stockholders, adequately reflecting and disclosing the potential profits from plant sales, they would have had no conceivable claim for the post-merger appreciation of the Stedman or Claude Neon shares. In these circumstances, awarding plaintiffs the profits on the plant sales and the value of the unsold assets, together with pre-judgment interest at a substantial rate, amply deprives Skogmo of profit from its wrong. To go further and hold Skogmo for any appreciation in the value of Stedman or Claude Neon over the long period between the merger and the judgment below—nearly nine years—is not required by this equitable principle.

In TSC INDUSTRIES v. NORTHWAY, 426 U.S. 438, 449 (1976), the Supreme Court agreed with Judge Friendly's formulation of the test of "materiality" in a proxy statement, holding that "an omitted fact is material if there is a substantial likelihood that a reasonable shareholder would consider it important in deciding how to vote. * * * Put another way, there must be a substantial likelihood that the disclosure of the omitted fact would have been viewed by the reasonable investor as having significantly altered the 'total mix' of information made available." The Court stated that materiality was a mixed question of law and fact, and reversed a determination by the court of appeals that certain omissions from a proxy statement were "materially misleading as a matter of law." The omitted facts related to the manner in which the corporation was controlled by the other party to the transaction, the fairness of the terms of the transaction, and certain share purchases which were alleged, but not shown, to have had a manipulative effect on the market.

Despite the SEC's change of position on projections and other types of "soft" information, an appeals court could still hold in 1982 that the SEC's views on appraisals had not changed sufficiently since the time of the *Gerstle* case to warrant requiring a company to include estimates of current market value in a proxy statement soliciting shareholder approval for a sale of the company's assets. SOUTH COAST v. SANTA ANA, 669 F.2d 1265 (9th Cir.1982).

GOULD v. AMERICAN HAWAIIAN STEAMSHIP CO.

351 F.Supp. 853 (D.Del.1972).

CALEB M. WRIGHT, CHIEF JUDGE.

This is a suit challenging certain aspects of a merger of McLean Industries, Inc. (McLean) into R.J. Reynolds Tobacco Company (Reynolds). On September 17, 1971, this Court granted the plaintiffs' motion for summary judgment [against Reynolds and four individual defendants, on the ground that the proxy statement used to solicit the votes of McLean shareholders in favor of the merger contained false and misleading statements and omissions in violation of § 14(a) of the 1934 Act and Rule 14a–9. Three of the individual defendants, Casey, Kroeger and Ludwig, who were non-management or "outside" directors of McLean, assert that they can be held individually liable for monetary damages only on a showing that they acted with *scienter* in approving the McLean proxy material.]

* * * The parties have argued for three separate standards: (1) scienter, or conduct which is intentional or reckless in nature, (2) negligence, and (3) absolute liability.

The Court is unable to accept the plaintiffs' contention that any person who solicits proxies or permits his name to be used for purposes of solicitation is strictly liable in any instance when the proxy materials are held to be materially false or misleading. The plaintiffs have failed to cite a single case in support of their position, and none of the other sections of either the 1933 Act or the 1934 Act have imposed absolute liability on an individual defendant. It is true that the § 14(a) and Rule 14a–9 contain language which might be construed to impose strict liability, and such a result would certainly insure the accomplishment of a Congressional desire to protect stockowners in any instance in which a violation has occurred. Nonetheless, the Court is of the opinion that making directors guarantors of the accuracy of proxy materials would create serious practical problems for directors and would not fulfill other purposes of the Securities Acts. * * * Presumably Congress has the power to impose such burdens on corporate directors; however, the Court cannot agree that Congress has done so absent a clear Congressional mandate which is not contained in § 14(a).

In support of the position that scienter is a requisite element of liability, Casey, Kroeger and Ludwig rely on the statutory or judicially construed standards of conduct imposed under other sections of the Securities Act of 1933 (1933 Act) and the 1934 Act. Stressing that these two Acts embody a comprehensive and interrelated regulatory scheme, these defendants argue that certain of the standards adopted under various sections of the 1933 and 1934 Acts dealing with other forms of securities' fraud ought to be employed under § 14(a). Analyzing the four sections in which Congress specifically authorized the recovery of monetary damages, §§ 11 and 12 of the 1933 Act, and §§ 9 and 18 of the 1934 Act, the defendants contend that although Congress permitted the recovery of monetary damages for negligence or lack of due diligence under the 1933 Act, it premised recovery under the 1934 Act on proof of scienter. Thus, these defendants contend that to avoid negating this evidenced Congressional intent, Courts must require proof of scienter for recovery under § 14(a) and the other sections of the 1934 Act which have been subsequently construed to provide a private remedy for damages.

The three defendants also argue that the federal courts have utilized the scienter requirement in their development of the issue of personal liability under § 10(b) of the 1934 Act and § 17(a)(2) of the 1933 Act. * * *

The Court is unable to accept the conclusion of Casey, et al. that proof of scienter is a prerequisite to establishing individual liability for damages under § 14(a). The appropriate standard of conduct as supported by lower court opinions and the rationale and language of the proxy statute and rule is one of liability for negligence. Thus, an individual who participates in a solicitation which utilizes materially false or misleading statements is liable if he knew or should have known that the statements were false or misleading. * * *

The appropriate standard of conduct for a particular section of the Securities Act should be determined with reference to that section, and not by analogy to generalized considerations pertinent to other, perhaps significantly different sections. An examination of the several sections cited by the defendants evidences that they are designed to accomplish different purposes, that they prohibit diverse types of activity, and that they do not necessarily suggest identical degrees of culpability to establish personal liability. Section 10(b) outlaws manipulative and deceptive devices. While the defendants stress the similarity between the wording of Rule 10b–5(b) and Rule 14a–9 in terms of prohibiting materially false or misleading statements, they avoid the necessity of interpreting each regulation in light of the statutory provision pursuant to which it was adopted. Therefore, although the operative language of Rule 14a–9 is substantially similar to that in Rule 10b–5(b) and in § 17, the substantive legislation does not embody a similar congruence and does not mandate identical standards of culpability. * * * While § 10(b) deals with a type of conduct categorized as deceptive or manipulative and perhaps suggests a requirement of some form of knowledge or fraudulent participation, Section 14(a) refers solely to the accuracy or completeness of a particular form of correspondence, the proxy solicitation. Making no reference to deceit or fraud, § 14(a) authorizes the S.E.C. to designate the necessary standard for proxy disclosures. This the Commission has done in Rule 14a–9 without language connoting fraudulent or deceptive activity or illicit motive on the part of the solicitor.

* * *

The Court cannot accept the contention that awarding damages for negligent conduct and misrepresentations under § 14(a) would undercut and conflict with § 18 of the 1934 Act. Under § 18, any person making a false or misleading statement in any document filed pursuant to the 1934 Act is liable to any individual who, in reliance on the statement, purchased or sold a security at a price which was affected by the statement, unless the person making the statement can prove that he acted in good faith and had no knowledge that the statement was false. As noted previously, Casey, et al. argue that in providing for this type of good faith defense under § 18, Congress expressly rejected the negligence standard for liability for damages predicated on any form of false or misleading statements.

Arguing that proxy materials are within § 18's coverage, the defendants protest that the application of the negligence standard and concomitant recovery for negligent misstatements under § 14(a) and Rule 14a–9 would eliminate the good faith defense in all cases involving proxy statements and nullify Congress's rejection of the negligence standard. However, the defendants have failed to acknowledge that, in spite of portions of overlap, §§ 18 and 14(a) involve the regulation of two fundamentally different types of securities activities. Section 18 provides broad coverage for any document filed pursuant to the 1934 Act and subjects an individual to liability to anyone buying or selling a security in reliance on a misleading statement in such a document. Section 14(a) is considerably more limited as it encompasses solely the solicitation of proxies and proxy materials. In light of the Supreme Court's admonitions concerning the paramount necessity to insure the sanctity of the mechanisms of corporate suffrage and for the dissemination of information to shareholders, see J.I. Case Co. v. Borak, supra, the conclusion that a more demanding standard of conduct might be imposed under § 14(a) than under § 18 is readily acceptable.

* * *

Having determined for the reasons stated above that individual liability for damages under § 14(a) may be predicated on negligence, the Court must reanalyze the contentions of Casey, Kroeger and Ludwig in light of this standard. * * *

The issue is whether the undisputed factual record mandates the conclusion that all three were negligent in their approval of the McLean proxy materials or participation in the McLean proxy solicitation. Prior to an examination of the specific facts applicable to these defendants, it is necessary to deal with one additional issue raised by them. * * * The defendants claim that under the scienter standard not only must the defendants be shown to know the statements were false and misleading, but also they must be shown to know that the statements were material. * * *

The Court does not agree that, at least for affirmative false or misleading statements, the question of a defendant's knowledge regarding materiality is a factor in determining his liability. Proof of actual knowledge of materiality would be almost impossible absent some showing of the defendant's awareness of court rulings concerning equivalent or substantially similar misstatements. * * *

However, the Court is concerned about the appropriate degree of culpability for material omissions about which the proxy materials are completely silent and the noninclusion of which does not render misleading an affirmative statement made in the proxy materials. The Court perceives some problems in holding an individual liable for such an omission absent some evidence showing he knew or ought to have known of its probable importance to a shareholder's decision regarding the questions presented in the proxy statement. Since omitted information could arise from the entire spectrum of corporate activity and a myriad of facts, there are strong reasons supporting the position that a director should not be liable unless the misleading or false statement appears in the proxy materials, or there is some showing that he ought to have known of its importance and the need for its inclusion in the proxy materials. The materiality standard may be an adequate demarcation of those facts of sufficient importance that an individual defendant ought to insure their inclusion in the proxy materials. However, the Court is of the opinion that this additional element of proof regarding the defendant's knowledge of the importance of this type of omission will establish the appropriate degree of culpability with minimal adverse impact on the protections afforded to investors.

Whatever the appropriate standard for the latter form of omission, three of the four statements which the Court determined to be materially false or misleading cannot be classified as that form of omission. The statement concerning the favored defendants' agreement to vote for the merger was false, the omission of Mr. McLean's dual and conflicting role in the negotiations with Reynolds made the statement that the favored defendants had negotiated the sale of their stock to Reynolds misleading, and the omission of the conflict of interest of Casey, Ludwig and Kroeger made the statements regarding the Board of Directors' recommendations misleading. There is no dispute on the present record that Casey, Kroeger and Ludwig knew that (a) there was no agreement to vote for the merger and (b) that McLean had negotiated on behalf of both classes of sellers of McLean stock. There is also ample evidence indicating they knew or should have known there was a conflict of interest.

All three men have categorically denied that they or their respective companies entered into any voting agreements, and the Court so determined in a prior opinion. However, all three individual defendants seek to avoid liability through various arguments directed to the time sequence of the drafting and approval of the proxy materials and their specific awareness of what the proxy materials actually stated at various time periods.

An examination of these arguments insofar as they deal with the voting agreement statement not only shows their inadequacy, but also demonstrates certain of the most obvious infirmities of the scienter standard. Kroeger and Ludwig present the following position in support of their contention that the entry of summary judgment against them is improper on the present record. First, they approved the proxy draft on March 10th prior to the execution of the agreements to sell their company's shares to Reynolds and at that time might have anticipated that these agreements would include agreements to vote in favor of the merger. Second, on March 25th when the sales agreements were signed and did not include an agreement to vote, they argue that it was reasonable for them to expect McLean's expert legal counsel to amend the proxy statement to comport with the actual agreements. Third, they assert that nothing in the record indicates that they ever read the proxy materials after they were disseminated in final form and thereby ascertained that the necessary changes had not been made. In essence, these defendants argue that they cannot be held liable for a materially false proxy statement which they utilized in the solicitation of proxies because (a) they might have relied on others to correct a statement they knew was false and (b) they might not have read the proxy statement. These contentions are without merit. Since § 14(a) imposes liability for the false and misleading McLean proxy materials on the solicitors, the Court cannot accept the contention that these defendant solicitors could avoid liability by relying on McLean counsel to rectify errors in the proxy materials. While it was entirely possible that the McLean lawyers might have remedied the misstatement regarding the agreement to vote, this Court is of the opinion that § 14(a) places a burden on these defendants to at a minimum bring such discrepancies to the lawyers' attention.

* * *

The second contention that a director may escape liability for a materially false proxy statement because he lacked scienter or knowledge of its falsity by reason of his failure to read the statement is almost too disingenuous to believe. To exonerate a director for his failure to peruse the very materials the accuracy of which is his legal responsibility would effectively emasculate the proxy provisions. This is especially true in this instance when a director is attempting to rely on the expertise of persons themselves not liable under § 14(a). Clearly had these defendants read the proxy statement after it was issued on April 10th, they would have ascertained its inaccuracy.

* * *

All three defendants knew that there was no agreement to vote for the merger and would have known that the April 10th proxy materials were false had they read them. The Court is of the opinion that under these facts, Casey, Kroeger and Ludwig are liable for the materially false and misleading McLean proxy statement as a matter of law.

In subsequent proceedings in the *Gould* case, certain defendants sought indemnity or contribution from other defendants who had participated more directly in the preparation of the misleading proxy material. The court denied their claims for indemnification. It distinguished other cases permitting indemnification of defendants whose participation in a fraudulent scheme had been "passive" or "secondary", on the ground that those cases arose under § 10(b), "where the gravamen of the wrong-doing is fraudulent and intentional conduct." Since "§ 14(a) reaches negligent as well as deliberately deceptive conduct, * * * the considerations governing indemnity are somewhat different."

> To allow indemnity to those who have breached responsibilities squarely placed upon them by the statute would vitiate the remedial purposes of § 14(a). Only a realistic possibility of liability for damages will encourage due diligence by those who solicit proxies and will protect the interest of informed corporate suffrage. Consequently, even if one concurrent tort-feasor bears greater responsibility for preparation or approval of false or misleading proxy materials, a person who breaches § 14(a) duties should not thereby be entitled to indemnity.

Cf. Globus v. Law Research Service, p. 220 above. With respect to contribution, the court held that it would be available in appropriate circumstances, but that none of the defendants requesting it in this case had shown that they "have been required to pay an inequitable share of the liability to the plaintiff class." GOULD v. AMERICAN-HAWAIIAN STEAMSHIP CO., 387 F.Supp. 163 (D.Del.1974).

On appeal, the court of appeals affirmed the holding of the district court that negligence was the appropriate standard for determining the liability of an outside director in an action under § 14(a), even though scienter would be required in an action under § 10(b). The court was "confirmed in this view by the very recent case of Ernst & Ernst v. Hochfelder, in which the Supreme Court pointed out that the 'operative language and purpose' of each particular section of the Acts of 1933 and 1934 are important considerations in determining the standard of liability for violations of the section in question." GOULD v. AMERICAN-HAWAIIAN STEAMSHIP CO., 535 F.2d 761 (3d Cir.1976).

A different result was reached in ADAMS v. STANDARD KNITTING MILLS, 623 F.2d 422 (6th Cir.1980), where the court held that an accounting firm could not be held liable in damages for a negligent misstatement in a proxy statement, but must be shown to have acted with scienter. The court could "see no reason for a different standard of liability for accountants under the proxy provisions than under § 10(b)." It drew support from a Senate report on § 14(a), which referred to "*unscrupulous* corporate officials * * * *concealing* and *distorting* facts," implying congressional concern with dishonest, rather than negligent, acts.

Since the adoption of Rule 145 (see Chapter 8.A above), many merger proxy statements are also 1933 Act registration statements. How would the liability of directors of the acquiring and acquired companies under the 1933 Act differ from their liability under the 1934 Act as enunciated in the *Gould* case?

Selected References

Note, Proxy Regulation: Ensuring Accurate Disclosure Through a Negligence Standard, 50 Fordham L.Rev. 1423 (1982).

Note, Causation and Liability in Private Actions for Proxy Violations, 80 Yale L.J. 107 (1970).

CHAPTER 9

TAKEOVERS AND TENDER OFFERS

One of the most significant developments in securities regulation in recent years has been the growing use of the "tender offer" as a technique for one company to acquire another. Starting in the 1960s, aggressively-managed corporations, in increasing numbers, embarked on campaigns to acquire controlling stock interests in other publicly-held corporations. They might acquire the stock for cash, or by issuing their own securities in exchange, or some combination of the two. They might acquire stock in private transactions, by purchases through brokers in the open market, or by making a public offer to the shareholders of the target company to tender their shares, either for a fixed cash price or for a package of securities of the offering corporation. These "takeover bids" were often bitterly opposed by the management of the target corporation, and the contests featured flamboyant public claims and charges on both sides, efforts to manipulate the market, and confusing and coercive approaches to the shareholders of the target corporation. Where the takeover bid involved a public offer of securities of the aggressor corporation in exchange for shares of the target corporation, the securities of course had to be registered under the Securities Act of 1933 and a prospectus delivered to the shareholders being solicited. In the case of a cash tender offer, however, there was no requirement for the filing of any solicitation material with the SEC.

TENDER OFFERS FOR CORPORATE CONTROL

By E. Aranow & H. Einhorn

Pp. 64–68 (1973).*

Federal regulation of cash tender offers was originally proposed in October 1965 by Senator Harrison Williams of New Jersey for the ostensible purpose of protecting incumbent managements from "industrial sabotage" resulting from what were deemed to be reckless corporate raids on "proud old companies." Such regulation, unique in that it represented perhaps the first attempt to enact securities regulation designed primarily for the benefit of the issuer rather than the investor, was inspired by the conglomerate merger mania of the early and mid 1960s. During this period, the cash tender offer, which had previously been resorted to only on infrequent occasions in the United States, emerged with frenetic abandon.[3] The following have been suggested as some of the underlying reasons for the rapid growth of the tender offer phenomenon in this country:

1. Increased corporate liquidity and readily available credit;

2. Comparatively depressed price/earnings ratios, book values, and cash or quick assets ratios, making acquisition via the tender offer more attractive;

3. Greater recognition, sophistication, and knowledge with respect to the takeover via tender technique;

4. Lack of extensive federal or state regulation of tender offers;

5. Quicker and more successful results when compared with a full-dress proxy contest;

6. Greater flexibility—the ability to hedge by reserving certain options against a final and irrevocable commitment;

7. Psychology—the appeal to shareholders in straight dollars and cents language, eliminating the need, as in a proxy contest, to convince the shareholder that the insurgent can do a more efficient job;

8. Notwithstanding the actual capital investment, the reduced costs of effecting a tender offer when compared with a proxy contest;

9. A new "respectability" for cash tender offers.

While no hearings were held on the original Williams Bill, many of its proposals formed the basis for a second bill introduced by Senator Williams in 1967. By the time this second bill was introduced, however, there was a greater recognition of the desirability of providing investors confronted with a tender offer with certain basic substantive protections together with full disclosure of the terms, conditions, and financing of the offer as well as the identity and pertinent background information regarding the offeror. In addition, there was a growing recognition that tender offers might in some cases promote the best interests of society by providing an effective method of removing entrenched but inefficient management. Nonetheless, the view persisted that the motives behind many tender offers did not reflect a desire to improve the management of companies and were but disguised forms of industrial sabotage. References by a co-sponsor of the legislation to attempted takeovers by undisclosed principals financed by Swiss banks, to the "corporate raider," and to the "takeover pirate" helped to generate hearty Congressional support for the second Williams Bill.

While the bill was embraced by the SEC and supported by several managements that had recently fought off cash takeover bids, there were others who opposed such regulation. Opposition to the bill was based primarily on the contention that the legislation was weighted so

3. In 1960 there were only eight cash tender offers involving companies with securities listed on national securities exchanges as compared to 107 in 1966. In 1960 there were tender offers for $200 million of listed securities as compared to approximately $1 billion in 1965. * * *

as to give incumbent management an unfair advantage in defending against a cash takeover bid and would therefore help to promote inefficient management. One commentator went so far as to suggest that the purpose of the legislation was to enhance the powers of the SEC rather than to protect the legitimate interests of the investing public. In addition, it was argued that a tender offer was in essence an open-market transaction and that traditional market forces, powered by individual self-interest, would best promote the interests of investors and our corporate system as a whole.

These objections notwithstanding, the final version of the second Williams Bill, which took the form of amendments to the Securities Exchange Act of 1934, became law on July 29, 1968 and was ostensibly designed to provide investors with full disclosure and other substantive protections within a statutory framework favoring neither the tender offeror nor the management of the target company. To insure adequate disclosure as well as the continued integrity of the securities markets in connection with acquisitions of securities which might cause or affect changes in control of public corporations, the bill also granted the SEC authority to regulate corporate repurchases of their own securities and imposed detailed disclosure requirements on persons acquiring more than 10 percent of certain equity securities other than pursuant to a tender offer. The Commission immediately adopted "temporary regulations" to effectuate those sections of the statute which were not self-operative. * * *

In 1970, the Williams Act was amended, primarily to expand SEC rule-making authority and to extend the coverage of the law to certain types of offers previously exempt from regulation.

The Williams Act amended the 1934 Act by adding §§ 13(d) and (e) and §§ 14(d), (e) and (f). The key provisions regulating takeovers and tender offers are § 13(d), § 14(d) and § 14(e).[a]

Section 13(d) requires any person who acquires more than 5% of any class of equity securities registered under the Act to file a statement with the SEC (with a copy to the issuer) within ten days after the acquisition. The statement must set forth specified information with respect to the person's background and source of funds, the purpose of the acquisition and any plans for major changes in the target company, and any contracts or arrangements with any other person relating to the target company.

Section 14(d) requires any person making a "tender offer" for more than 5% of any class of registered equity security to file a statement with the SEC containing such of the information required by § 13(d),

a. Section 13(e) authorizes the SEC to regulate certain aspects of purchases by corporations of their own shares, and is considered at p. 714 above. Section 14(f) requires certain disclosures to shareholders where there is a sale of a controlling block of stock followed by replacement of a majority of the directors without a shareholders' meeting.

and such other information, as the SEC requires by rule, and to include in all of its advertisements or invitations for tenders such information as the SEC may require. Sections 14(d)(5), (6) and (7) contain provisions regulating the substantive terms of a tender offer requiring that tendered shares be withdrawable for a specified period, that shares be taken up pro rata where more shares are tendered than the offeror has agreed to accept, and that the same price be paid to all shareholders where the price is raised during the pendency of the offer.

Section 14(e) makes it unlawful to make any untrue or misleading statements of material facts, or to engage in any fraudulent, deceptive or manipulative acts or practices, in connection with a tender offer.

In January 1980, the SEC replaced its "temporary" rules under § 14(d) and (e) with a detailed set of regulations relating to (a) the filing, transmittal and dissemination of statements and recommendations, (b) the obligation of the target company's management with respect to shareholder lists and recommendations on the offer, (c) the duration of the offer, and (d) the fairness of the offering terms. See Rules 14d–1 to 10, 14e–1 to 3.

A. DISCLOSURE BY 5% OWNERS

RONDEAU v. MOSINEE PAPER CORP.

422 U.S. 49 (1975).

MR. CHIEF JUSTICE BURGER delivered the opinion of the Court.

We granted certiorari in this case to determine whether a showing of irreparable harm is necessary for a private litigant to obtain injunctive relief in a suit under § 13(d) of the Securities Exchange Act of 1934, as added by § 2 of the Williams Act. The Court of Appeals held that it was not. We reverse.

I

Respondent Mosinee Paper Corp. is a Wisconsin company engaged in the manufacture and sale of paper, paper products, and plastics. Its principal place of business is located in Mosinee, Wis., and its only class of equity security is common stock which is registered under § 12 of the Securities Exchange Act of 1934. At all times relevant to this litigation there were slightly more than 800,000 shares of such stock outstanding.

In April 1971 petitioner Francis A. Rondeau, a Mosinee businessman, began making large purchases of respondent's common stock in the over-the-counter market. Some of the purchases were in his own name; others were in the name of businesses and a foundation known to be controlled by him. By May 17, 1971, petitioner had acquired 40,413 shares of respondent's stock, which constituted more than 5% of those outstanding. He was therefore required to comply with the disclosure provisions of the Williams Act, by filing a Schedule 13D with respondent and the Securities and Exchange Commission within 10 days. That form would have disclosed, among other things, the number of shares beneficially owned by petitioner, the source of the funds used to purchase them, and petitioner's purpose in making the purchases.

Petitioner did not file a Schedule 13D but continued to purchase substantial blocks of respondent's stock. By July 30, 1971, he had acquired more than 60,000 shares. On that date the chairman of respondent's board of directors informed him by letter that his activity had "given rise to numerous rumors" and "seems to have created some problems under the Federal Securities Laws * * *." Upon receiving the letter petitioner immediately stopped placing orders for respondent's stock and consulted his attorney. On August 25, 1971, he filed a Schedule 13D which, in addition to the other required disclosures, described the "Purpose of Transaction" as follows:

> "Francis A. Rondeau determined during early part of 1971 that the common stock of the Issuer [respondent] was undervalued in the over-the-counter market and represented a good investment vehicle for future income and appreciation. Francis A. Rondeau and his associates presently propose to seek to acquire additional common stock of the Issuer in order to obtain effective control of the Issuer, but such investments as originally determined were and are not necessarily made with this objective in mind. Consideration is currently being given to making a public cash tender offer to the shareholders of the Issuer at a price which will reflect current quoted prices for such stock with some premium added."

Petitioner also stated that, in the event that he did obtain control of respondent, he would consider making changes in management "in an effort to provide a Board of Directors which is more representative of all of the shareholders, particularly those outside of present management * * *." One month later petitioner amended the form to reflect more accurately the allocation of shares between himself and his companies.

On August 27 respondent sent a letter to its shareholders informing them of the disclosures in petitioner's Schedule 13D. The letter stated that by his "tardy filing" petitioner had "withheld the information to which you [the shareholders] were entitled for more than two months, in violation of federal law." In addition, while agreeing that "recent market prices have not reflected the real value of your Mosinee stock," respondent's management could "see little in Mr. Rondeau's background that would qualify him to offer any meaningful guidance to a Company in the highly technical and competitive paper industry."

Six days later respondent initiated this suit in the United States District Court for the Western District of Wisconsin. Its complaint named petitioner, his companies, and two banks which had financed some of petitioner's purchases as defendants and alleged that they were engaged in a scheme to defraud respondent and its shareholders in violation of the securities laws. It alleged further that shareholders who had "sold shares without the information which defendants were required to disclose lacked information material to their decision whether to sell or hold," and that respondent "was unable to communicate such information to its stockholders, and to take such actions as their interest required." Respondent prayed for an injunction prohibiting petitioner and his codefendants from voting or pledging their stock and from acquiring additional shares, requiring them to divest themselves of stock which they already owned, and for damages. A motion for a preliminary injunction was filed with the complaint but later withdrawn.

After three months of pretrial proceedings petitioner moved for summary judgment. He readily conceded that he had violated the Williams Act, but contended that the violation was due to a lack of familiarity with the securities laws and that neither respondent nor its shareholders had been harmed. The District Court agreed. It found no material issues of fact to exist regarding petitioner's lack of willfulness in failing to timely file a Schedule 13D, concluding that he discovered his obligation to do so on July 30, 1971, and that there was no basis in the record for disputing his claim that he first considered the possibility of obtaining control of respondent some time after that date. The District Court therefore held that petitioner and his codefendants "did not engage in intentional covert and conspiratorial conduct in failing to timely file the 13D Schedule."

Similarly, although accepting respondent's contention that its management and shareholders suffered anxiety as a result of petitioner's activities and that this anxiety was exacerbated by his failure to disclose his intentions until August 1971, the District Court concluded that similar anxiety "could be expected to accompany any change in management," and was "a predictable consequence of shareholder democracy." It fell far short of the irreparable harm necessary to support an injunction and no other harm was revealed by the record; as amended, petitioner's Schedule 13D disclosed all of the information to which respondent was entitled, and he had not proceeded with a tender offer. Moreover, in the view of the District Court even if a showing of irreparable harm were not required in all cases under the securities laws, petitioner's lack of bad faith and the absence of damage to respondent made this "a particularly inappropriate occasion to fashion equitable relief * * *." Thus, although petitioner had committed a technical violation of the Williams Act, the District Court held that respondent was entitled to no relief and entered summary judgment against it.

The Court of Appeals reversed, with one judge dissenting. The majority stated that it was "giving effect" to the District Court's findings regarding the circumstances of petitioner's violation of the Williams Act, but concluded that those findings showed harm to respondent because it "was delayed in its efforts to make any necessary response to" petitioner's potential to take control of the company. In any event, the majority was of the view that respondent "need not show irreparable harm as a prerequisite to obtaining permanent injunctive relief in view of the fact that as issuer of the securities it is in the best position to assure that the filing requirements of the Williams Act are being timely and fully complied with and to obtain speedy and forceful remedial action when necessary." The Court of Appeals remanded the case to the District Court with instructions that it enjoin petitioner and his codefendants from further violations of the Williams Act and from voting the shares purchased between the due date of the Schedule 13D and the date of its filing for a period of five years. It considered "such an injunctive decree appropriate to neutralize [petitioner's] violation of the Act and to deny him the benefit of his wrongdoing."

We granted certiorari to resolve an apparent conflict among the Courts of Appeals and because of the importance of the question presented to private actions under the federal securities laws. We disagree with the Court of Appeals' conclusion that the traditional standards for extraordinary equitable relief do not apply in these circumstances, and reverse.

II

As in the District Court and the Court of Appeals, it is conceded here that petitioner's delay in filing the Schedule 13D constituted a violation of the Williams Act. The narrow issue before us is whether this record supports the grant of injunctive relief, a remedy whose basis "in the federal courts has always been irreparable harm and inadequacy of legal remedies." Beacon Theatres, Inc. v. Westover, 359 U.S. 500, 506–507 (1959).

The Court of Appeals' conclusion that respondent suffered "harm" sufficient to require sterilization of petitioner's stock need not long detain us. The purpose of the Williams Act is to insure that public shareholders who are confronted by a cash tender offer for their stock will not be required to respond without adequate information regarding the qualifications and intentions of the offering party. By requiring disclosure of information to the target corporation as well as the Securities and Exchange Commission, Congress intended to do no more than give incumbent management an opportunity to express and explain its position. The Congress expressly disclaimed an intention to provide a weapon for management to discourage takeover bids or prevent large accumulations of stock which would create the potential for such attempts. Indeed, the Act's draftsmen commented upon the "extreme care" which was taken "to avoid tipping the balance of regulation either in favor of management or in favor of the person making the takeover bid."

The short of the matter is that none of the evils to which the Williams Act was directed has occurred or is threatened in this case. Petitioner has not attempted to obtain control of respondent, either by a cash tender offer or any other device. Moreover, he has now filed a proper Schedule 13D, and there has been no suggestion that he will fail to comply with the Act's requirement of reporting any material changes in the information contained therein. On this record there is no likelihood that respondent's shareholders will be disadvantaged should petitioner make a tender offer, or that respondent will be unable to adequately place its case before them should a contest for control develop. Thus, the usual basis for injunctive relief, "that there exists some cognizable danger of recurrent violation," is not present here.

Nor are we impressed by respondent's argument that an injunction is necessary to protect the interests of its shareholders who either sold their stock to petitioner at predisclosure prices or would not have invested had they known that a takeover bid was imminent. As observed, the principal object of the Williams Act is to solve the dilemma of shareholders desiring to respond to a cash tender offer, and it is not at all clear that the type of "harm" identified by respondent is redressable under its provisions. In any event, those persons who allegedly sold at an unfairly depressed price have an adequate remedy by way of an action for damages, thus negating the basis for equitable relief. Similarly, the fact that the second group of shareholders for whom respondent expresses concern have retained the benefits of their stock and the lack of an imminent contest for control make the possibility of damage to them remote at best.

We turn, therefore, to the Court of Appeals' conclusion that respondent's claim was not to be judged according to traditional equitable principles, and that the bare fact that petitioner violated the Williams Act justified entry of an injunction against him. This position would seem to be foreclosed by Hecht Co. v. Bowles, 321 U.S. 321 (1944). There, the administrator of the Emergency Price Control Act of 1942 brought suit to redress violations of that statute. The fact of the violations was admitted, but the District Court declined to enter an injunction because they were inadvertent and the defendant had taken immediate steps to rectify them. This Court held that such an exercise of equitable discretion was proper despite § 205(a) of the Act, which provided that an injunction or other order "shall be granted" upon a showing of violation * * *.

This reasoning applies *a fortiori* to actions involving only "competing private claims," and suggests that the District Court here was entirely correct in insisting that respondent satisfy the traditional prerequisites of extraordinary equitable relief by establishing irreparable harm. Moreover, the District Judge's conclusions that petitioner acted in good faith and that he promptly filed a Schedule 13D when his attention was called to this obligation support the exercise of the court's sound judicial discretion to deny an application for an injunction, relief which is historically "designed to deter, not to punish" and to permit the court "to mould each decree to the necessities of the particular case." * * *

Respondent urges, however, that the "public interest" must be taken into account in considering its claim for relief and relies upon the Court of Appeals' conclusion that it is entitled to an injunction because it "is in the best position" to insure that the Williams Act is complied with by purchasers of its stock. This argument misconceives, we think, the nature of the litigation. Although neither the availability of a private suit under the Williams Act nor respondent's standing to bring it has been questioned here, this cause of action is not expressly authorized by the statute or its legislative history. Rather, respondent is asserting a so-called implied private right of action established by cases such as J.I. Case Co. v. Borak, 377 U.S. 426 (1964). Of course, we have not hesitated to recognize the power of federal courts to fashion private remedies for securities laws violations when to do so is consistent with the legislative scheme and necessary for the protection of investors as a supplement to enforcement by the Securities and Exchange Commission. However, it by no means follows that the plaintiff in such an action is relieved of the burden of establishing the traditional prerequisites of relief. Indeed, our cases hold that quite the contrary is true.

In Deckert v. Independence Shares Corp., 311 U.S. 282 (1940), this Court was called upon to decide whether the Securities Act of 1933 authorized purchasers of securities to bring an action to rescind an allegedly fraudulent sale. The question was answered affirmatively on the basis of the statute's grant of federal jurisdiction to "enforce any liability or duty" created by it. The Court's reasoning is instructive:

> "The power *to enforce* implies the power to make effective the right of recovery afforded by the Act. And the power to make the right of recovery effective implies the power to utilize any of the procedures or actions normally available to the litigant according to the exigencies of the particular case. If petitioners' bill states a cause of action when tested by the customary rules governing suits of such character, the Securities Act authorizes maintenance of the suit * * *." 311 U.S., at 288.

In other words, the conclusion that a private litigant could maintain an action for violation of the 1933 Act meant no more than that traditional remedies were available to redress any harm which he may have suffered; it provided no basis for dispensing with the showing required to obtain relief. Significantly, this passage was relied upon in *Borak* with respect to actions under the Securities Exchange Act of 1934.

Any remaining uncertainty regarding the nature of relief available to a person asserting an implied private right of action under the securities laws was resolved in Mills v. Electric Auto–Lite Co., 396 U.S. 375 (1970).

* * *

Mills could not be plainer in holding that the questions of liability and relief are separate in private actions under the securities laws, and that the latter is to be determined according to traditional principles.

Thus, the fact that respondent is pursuing a cause of action which has been generally recognized to serve the public interest provides no basis for concluding that it is relieved of showing irreparable harm and other usual prerequisites for injunctive relief. Accordingly, the judgment of the Court of Appeals is reversed and the case is remanded to it with directions to reinstate the judgment of the District Court.

MR. JUSTICE MARSHALL dissents.

MR. JUSTICE BRENNAN, with whom MR. JUSTICE DOUGLAS joins, dissenting.

I dissent. Judge Pell, dissenting below, correctly in my view, read the decision of the Court of Appeals to construe the Williams Act, as I also construe it, to authorize injunctive relief upon the application of the management interests "irrespective of motivation, irrespective of irreparable harm to the corporation, and irrespective of whether the purchases were detrimental to investors in the company's stock. The violation timewise is * * * all that is needed to trigger this result." In other words, the Williams Act is a prophylactic measure conceived by Congress as necessary to effect the congressional objective "that investors and management be notified at the earliest possible moment of the potential for a shift in corporate control." Id., at 1016. The violation itself establishes the actionable harm and no showing of other harm is necessary to secure injunctive relief. Today's holding completely undermines the congressional purpose to preclude inquiry into the results of the violation.

What must a corporation establish under *Rondeau* to obtain an injunction against shareholders who have violated § 13(d)? In FINANCIAL GENERAL BANKSHARES v. LANCE, CCH Fed.Sec.L.Rep. ¶ 96,403 (D.D.C.1978), the court found that five investors had acted as a "group" in acquiring approximately 25% of a corporation's stock, and had therefore violated § 13(d) by failing to file a report when the group's holdings reached 5%. The corporation asked the court to enjoin them from acquiring any additional shares, voting the shares they held, or exercising any influence or control over the management of the corporation.

> The broad relief sought by plaintiff might be appropriate if defendants had obtained effective control of FG as a result of purchases made while not complying with section 13(d). In that event, both continuing shareholders and shareholders who sold to the purchasers would have been denied the opportunity to make an informed choice about selling to a group attempting a takeover, and a disenfranchisement or divestiture order might be appropriate. In the instant action, however, defendants have not acquired control of FG and they intend to make a tender offer to obtain such control. Thus, it is entirely unclear to the Court that FG shareholders who have not sold to the defendants would be irreparably injured if defendants proceed with a tender offer. In fact, these present shareholders of FG probably would

welcome the opportunity to consider a tender offer at above-market prices. The Court should therefore limit its inquiry to what injunctive relief is necessary to prevent any irreparable injury that will result to shareholders who sold to the defendants if the defendants are now permitted to obtain control of FG.

The Court concludes that the group defendants, pending a trial on the merits, should be enjoined from acquiring FG stock or soliciting proxies until they have offered rescission to those persons from whom they purchased FG stock on the open market during December, 1977, and January, 1978. These shareholders, who sold their stock without knowledge that these purchasers were acquiring a large block of FG stock and were considering seeking control of FG, will be irreparably injured unless defendants offer them rescission before defendants obtain control of FG. The damages remedy will not necessarily compensate these shareholders for having been denied the opportunity to decide whether to sell to a group considering a takeover attempt. Moreover, for shareholders who do not want defendants to obtain control of FG and therefore would not have sold to the defendants, the rescission remedy will be meaningless if not available until after defendants have obtained control of FG.

Is the "limited relief" granted in this case consistent with the decision in *Rondeau,* or is it directed at a type of "harm" which the Supreme Court thought was not redressable under the Williams Act?

For the purposes of § 13(d), two or more persons acting as a "group" in acquiring or holding securities are considered to be a single "person" in determining whether the requisite 5% ownership is present. One difficult question in interpreting this provision has arisen where a group of people owning in the aggregate more than 5% of a class of securities agree to act together for the purpose of gaining control of the issuer. The question is whether the agreement constitutes an "acquisition" by the "group" of the stock owned by its members, triggering the reporting requirement of § 13(d), even though the individual members of the group have not acquired any shares over and above their pre-existing holdings.

The Seventh Circuit, focussing on "the overriding purpose of Congress * * * *to protect the individual investor* when substantial shareholders or management undertake to acquire shares in a corporation", held that § 13(d) applies only when such a group "agree to act in concert *to acquire additional shares.*" BATH INDUSTRIES, INC. v. BLOT, 427 F.2d 97 (7th Cir.1970). The Second Circuit, however, held that § 13(d) applied whether or not such a group acquired additional shares. It relied on specific statements in both the Senate and House Reports that such a group "would be required to file the information called for in § 13(d)(1) within 10 days after they agree to act together, whether or not any member of the group had acquired any securities at that time", and held that the language of § 13(d) "amply reflected * * * the purpose * * * to alert the marketplace to every large, rapid aggregation or accumulation of securities, regardless of technique employed, which might represent a potential shift in corporate control * * *." GAF CORP. v. MILSTEIN, 453 F.2d 709 (2d Cir.1971). The court reached this conclusion despite the fact that the Milstein "group" consisted of members of a single family who had acquired the securities more than a year before in a single merger transaction, and that their holdings consisted of 10.25% of a class of convertible preferred stock, which had only about 2% of the total voting power in the corporation.[a]

Note on Private Relief Under § 13(d)

The Court in the *Rondeau* decision seemed receptive to the granting of private injunctive relief under § 13(d) but for the plaintiff's inability to show any injury resulting from the delay in filing. Courts generally are reluctant to interfere in contested takeover attempts where the issuance of an injunction might have a substantial adverse impact on the market. See University Bank v. Gladstone, 574 F.Supp. 1006 (D.Mass.1983). Courts will, however, issue an injunction in an appropriate case. E.g., Hanna Mining Co. v. Norcen Energy Resources Ltd., 574 F.Supp. 1172 (N.D.Ohio 1982). Filing of a Schedule 13D (or curative amendments to a deficient previous filing) will generally result in the denial of an injunction or lifting of any injunctive relief previously granted. E.g. Hubco v. Rappaport, 628 F.Supp. 345 (D.N.J.1985); Chromalloy v. Sun Chemical, 474 F.Supp. 1341 (E.D.Mo.1979). As discussed below at p. 788, in *Piper v. Chris–Craft,* the Supreme Court has held that a competing tender offeror does not have standing to sue for damages under § 14(e) of the Williams Act. Subsequent decisions by the lower courts have recognized the ability of a competing bidder to sue for injunction. As to the question of when target company management or its shareholders can sue, see *Polaroid v. Disney,* p. 792 below.

B. WHAT IS A "TENDER OFFER"?

Section 14(d) imposes certain disclosure requirements and substantive restrictions on any person making a tender offer, and § 14(e) prohibits fraud or misstatements by any person in connection with such an offer. However, the term "tender offer" is nowhere defined in the Act. While public invitations for tenders are clearly covered, the courts have had considerable difficulty in determining what other kinds of transactions are subject to the requirements of §§ 14(d) and (e).

---

a. While the Milsteins had not purchased any additional preferred stock after the merger, they had purchased an aggregate of 1.6% of the *common* stock of GAF, bringing their total voting power in the corporation to approximately 4%.

KENNECOTT COPPER CORP. v. CURTISS–WRIGHT CORP.

584 F.2d 1195 (2d Cir.1978).

Before OAKES, VAN GRAAFEILAND, and MESKILL, CIRCUIT JUDGES

VAN GRAAFEILAND, CIRCUIT JUDGE:

* * *

In November 1977, Curtiss–Wright, a diversified manufacturing company, decided to acquire an interest in Kennecott [Copper Corp.]. By March 13, 1978, when Curtiss–Wright filed its Schedule 13D with the Securities and Exchange Commission, it had acquired 9.9 per cent of the outstanding Kennecott shares at a cost of approximately $77 million.

* * *

Section 3 of the Williams Act amended section 14 of the Securities Exchange Act of 1934 by adding subsections (d), (e), and (f). Subsection (d) prohibits the making of a tender offer for any class of a registered stock if, after consummation thereof, the offeror would own more than five per cent of the class, unless a Schedule 13D form is first filed with the SEC. If ownership of more than five per cent is obtained through more customary modes of stock acquisition, the Schedule 13D form must be filed within ten days after the five per cent figure is reached. Curtiss–Wright filed its Schedule 13D on March 17, 1978, which was within ten days of the time it had acquired five per cent of Kennecott's stock. Accordingly, unless it had acquired this stock by means of a tender offer, it was not in violation of section 14(d).

The trial court rejected Kennecott's contention that Curtiss–Wright's acquisition had been made by means of a tender offer. The district judge found that Curtiss–Wright had purchased substantially all of the stock on national exchanges; that although one of Curtiss–Wright's brokers had solicited fifty Kennecott shareholders off the floor of the exchange, the sales were consummated on the floor. He also found that another broker had solicited approximately a dozen institutional holders of Kennecott, consummating an unspecified number of sales off the floor of the exchange. He found that the potential sellers were merely asked whether they wanted to sell. They were offered no premium over the market price and were given no deadline by which to make their decision. He also found that the off-market purchases were made largely from sophisticated institutional shareholders who were unlikely to be forced into uninformed, ill-considered decisions. He concluded that Curtiss–Wright had not made a tender offer prior to the filing of its Schedule 13D.

* * *

Although the Williams Act does not define the term "tender offer," the characteristics of a typical offer are well-recognized. They are described in the House Report of the Committee on Interstate and Foreign Commerce, which held hearings on the proposed Act.

The offer normally consists of a bid by an individual or group to buy shares of a company—usually at a price above the current market price. Those accepting the offer are said to tender their stock for purchase. The person making the offer obligates himself to purchase all or a specified portion of the tendered shares if certain specified conditions are met.

This definition of a conventional tender offer has received general recognition in the courts. Several courts and commentators have taken the position, however, that other unique methods of stock acquisition which exert pressure on shareholders to make uninformed, ill-considered decisions to sell, as is possible in the case of tender offers, should be treated as tender offers for purposes of the statute.

Although broad and remedial interpretations of the Act may create no problems insofar as the antifraud provisions of subsection (e) of section 14 are concerned, this may not be true with regard to subsections (d)(5)–(d)(7). Subsection (d)(5) provides that securities deposited pursuant to a tender offer may be withdrawn within seven days of the publication or delivery to shareholders of the tender offer or at any time after sixty days from the date of the original tender offer. Subsection (d)(6) requires offerors to purchase securities on a pro rata basis where more are tendered than the offeror is bound or willing to take. Subsection (d)(7) provides that where the offeror increases the offering price before the expiration of his tender offer, those tenderers whose stock has already been taken up are entitled to be paid the higher price. It seems unlikely that Congress intended "tender offer" to be so broadly interpreted as to make these provisions unworkable.

In any event, we know of no court that has adopted the extremely broad interpretation Kennecott urges upon us in this case. Kennecott's contention, as we understand it, is that whenever a purchaser of stock intends through its purchases to obtain and exercise control of a company, it should immediately file a Schedule 13D. Kennecott conceded in the trial court that no pressure was exerted on sellers other than the normal pressure of the market place and argued there and here that the absence of pressure is not a relevant factor. Kennecott also conceded in the trial court that no cases supported its argument and that it was asking the court to "make new ground." The district court did not err in refusing to do so.

Kennecott's interpretation would render the five per cent filing provisions of section 13(d)(1) meaningless except in cases where the purchaser did not intend to obtain a controlling interest. It would also require courts to apply the withdrawal, pro rata and increased price provisions of section 14(d)(5)–(7) to ordinary stock purchases, a difficult if not impossible task.

The fact that several of Curtiss–Wright's purchases were negotiated directly with financial institutions lends no force to Kennecott's contentions.

If this Court is to opt for an interpretation of "tender offer" that differs from its conventional meaning, this is not the case in which to do it.

In the course of an SEC "public fact-finding investigation" of tender offers in 1974, the Commission received a number of comments suggesting that it adopt rules defining the term "tender offer" or exempting specified types of transactions. However, the Commission concluded in 1976 that

> a definition of the term "tender offer" is neither appropriate nor necessary. This position is premised on the dynamic nature of these transactions and the need of the Commission to remain flexible in determining what types of transactions, either present or yet to be devised, are or should be encompassed by the term. Therefore, the Commission specifically declines to propose a definition of the term "tender offer."
>
> The Commission's position should in no way be construed to mean that the term applies only to so-called conventional tender offers whereby an offer is published by a person requesting that all or a portion of a class of a company's securities be deposited during a fixed period of time so that such person may purchase such securities at a specified price (whether cash and/or securities) and subject to specified conditions. But rather, the term is to be interpreted flexibly and applies to special bids; purchases resulting from widespread solicitations by means of mailings, telephone calls and personal visits; and any transaction where the conduct of the person seeking control causes pressures to be put on shareholders similar to those attendant to a conventional tender offer.[a]

In January 1978, Sun Company, a major oil company, acting through a subsidiary called LHIW, Inc. (reportedly an acronym for "Let's Hope It Works"), made simultaneous secret offers to 28 large shareholders of Becton, Dickinson & Co. (who held in the aggregate 35% of its outstanding shares) to purchase their shares at a price of $45 a share. (The stock was then trading at about $32 a share.) Two of the offerees were directors of Becton; the other 26 were institutional investors. The offerees were given periods ranging from ½ hour to overnight to accept or reject the offer, were not told the identity of the purchaser and in some cases were told that if they did not respond quickly the purchasing program might be oversubscribed, and their shares would be rejected. The two directors and 22 of the 26 institutions accepted Sun's offer, and Sun acquired 6½ million shares, or 34% of Becton's stock, for an aggregate price of $290 million.

The SEC brought an action for an injunction against Sun, alleging that it had made a "tender offer" without complying with the requirements of § 14(d). In WELLMAN v. DICKINSON, 475 F.Supp. 783 (S.D.

a. Sec.Act Rel. No. 5731 (Aug. 2, 1976).

N.Y.1979), the court agreed with the SEC's contention and held that Sun had violated § 14(d).

Recognizing that "privately negotiated transactions" were not intended to be covered by the Williams Act, the court held that this applied only to transactions which *both* parties desired to keep secret. The court then analogized to the standards for "non-public offerings" developed under § 4(2) of the 1933 Act, holding that even though most of the solicitees were sophisticated institutional investors, their supposed sophistication would "not suffice to render the transaction private if they are given no information on which to exercise their skills."

Having held that the transaction was not "private", the court then turned to the question of whether it was a "tender offer." The court found that not only did the transaction have "all the characteristics of a tender offer that were identified by Congress in the debates on consideration of the Williams Act," but, "more important," Sun's acquisition was "infected with the basic evil which Congress sought to cure," namely "a transfer of at least a 20% controlling interest in BD to Sun in a swift, masked maneuver." The court noted that Congress had not defined the term "tender offer," but had

> left to the Commission the task of providing through its experience concrete meaning to the term. The Commission has not yet created an exact definition, but in this case and in others, it suggests some seven elements as being characteristic of a tender offer: (1) active and widespread solicitation of public shareholders for the shares of an issuer; (2) solicitation made for a substantial percentage of the issuer's stock; (3) offer to purchase made at a premium over the prevailing market price; (4) terms of the offer are firm rather than negotiable; (5) offer contingent on the tender of a fixed number of shares, often subject to a fixed maximum number to be purchased; (6) offer open only a limited period of time; (7) offeree subjected to pressure to sell his stock. * * * With the exception of publicity, all the characteristics of a tender offer, as that term is understood, are present in this transaction. The absence of one particular factor, however, is not necessarily fatal to the Commission's argument because depending upon the circumstances involved in the particular case, one or more of the above features may be more compelling and determinative than the others.[b]

Is this holding consistent with the Second Circuit decision in the *Kennecott* case? What will be the consequences of applying § 14(d)? Who will be the major beneficiary of its provisions?

(a) *The Offerees?* Under § 14(d)(5), they would have to be given a minimum of seven days during which they could withdraw shares they had tendered in response to the offer. Do institutions require this kind

b. Having prevailed on the merits, the SEC asked the court (a) to order Sun to divest itself of its Becton stock and (b) to rescind the sales by certain of the sellers or to require them to "disgorge" the $15 million premium over market value that they received on the sale. Wall St. Journal, Sept. 19, 1979, p. 38, col. 6.

of protection when they are offered a cash price about 40% above the current market?

(b) *The Management?* Under § 14(d)(1), Sun would have had to send a copy of its offering statement to the Becton management at the time it first made its offer to the institutions. Is management entitled to notice before the offerees have tendered their shares, so that it can attempt to persuade them not to sell? A recent article notes that about one-third of the companies listed on the New York Stock Exchange have more than 20% of their stock held by institutions, and may therefore be subject to the same kind of "blitzkrieg" attack.[c]

(c) *The Other Shareholders?* Would § 14(d)(6) require Sun to extend its offer to all 13,000 Becton shareholders, and to take all shares on a pro rata basis if it was only willing to buy 35% of the total outstanding? If so, would it therefore become a federal substantive restriction on sale of a controlling block at a premium? Or could Sun, consistently with that section, limit its offer only to specified persons or to all persons holding more than X shares of stock?

In UNOCAL v. MESA PETROLEUM, 493 A.2d 946 (Del.1985), the Delaware Supreme Court upheld an issuer self tender offer that excluded shares owned by a hostile bidder. Shortly thereafter the SEC adopted its all holders rules which declare that such exclusionary tender offers are deceptive and manipulative. See Rule 13e–4(f)(8)(i) for tender offers by issuers for their own shares and Rule 14d–10 for third-party tender offers. In POLAROID v. DISNEY, 862 F.2d 987 (3d Cir. 1988), the court upheld the validity of Rule 14d–10 (see p. 806 below) and also held that the rule supports an implied private right of action (see p. 792 below).

SEC v. CARTER HAWLEY HALE

760 F.2d 945 (9th Cir.1985).

Before: GOODWIN, SNEED, and SKOPIL, CIRCUIT JUDGES.

Opinion of SKOPIL, CIRCUIT JUDGE.

The issue in this case arises out of an attempt by The Limited ("Limited"), an Ohio corporation, to take over Carter Hawley Hale Stores, Inc. ("CHH"), a publicly-held Los Angeles corporation. The SEC commenced the present action for injunctive relief to restrain CHH from repurchasing its own stock in an attempt to defeat the Limited takeover attempt without complying with the tender offer regulations. The district court concluded CHH's repurchase program was not a tender offer. The SEC appeals from the district court's denial of its motion for a preliminary injunction. We affirm.

c. Block & Schwarzfeld, Curbing the Unregulated Tender Offer, 6 Sec.Reg.L.J. 133 (1978). The authors suggest that the SEC adopt a rule making § 14(d) applicable to privately negotiated purchases of 5% or more of the outstanding stock from 10 or more persons within a one-month period.

Facts and Proceedings Below

On April 4, 1984 Limited commenced a cash tender offer for 20.3 million shares of CHH common stock, representing approximately 55% of the total shares outstanding, at $30 per share. Prior to the announced offer, CHH stock was trading at approximately $23.78 per share (pre-tender offer price).

* * *

On April 16, 1984 CHH responded to Limited's offer. CHH issued a press release announcing its opposition to the offer because it was "inadequate and not in the best interests of CHH or its shareholders." CHH also publicly announced an agreement with General Cinema Corporation ("General Cinema"). * * * Finally, CHH announced a plan to repurchase up to 15 million shares of its own common stock for an amount not to exceed $500 million. * * *

* * *

CHH began to repurchase its shares on April 16, 1984. In a one-hour period CHH purchased approximately 244,000 shares at an average price of $25.25 per share. On April 17, 1984 CHH purchased approximately 6.5 million shares in a two-hour trading period at an average price of $25.88 per share. By April 22, 1984 CHH had purchased a total of 15 million shares. It then announced an increase in the number of shares authorized for purchase to 18.5 million.

On April 24, 1984, the same day Limited was permitted to close its offer and start purchasing, CHH terminated its repurchase program having purchased approximately 17.5 million shares, over 50% of the common shares outstanding. On April 25, 1984 Limited revised its offer increasing the offering price to $35.00 per share and eliminating the second-step merger. The market price for CHH then reached a high of $32.00 per share. On May 21, 1984 Limited withdrew its offer. The market price of CHH promptly fell to $20.62 per share, a price below the pre-tender offer price.

On May 2, 1984, two and one-half weeks after the repurchase program was announced and one week after its apparent completion, the SEC filed this action for injunctive relief. The SEC alleged that CHH's repurchase program constituted a tender offer conducted in violation of section 13(e) of the Exchange Act, and Rule 13e–4. On May 5, 1984 a temporary restraining order was granted. CHH was temporarily enjoined from further stock repurchases. The district court denied SEC's motion for a preliminary injunction, finding the SEC failed to carry its burden of establishing "the reasonable likelihood of future violations * * * [or] * * * a 'fair chance of success on the merits' * * *." The court found CHH's repurchase program was not a tender offer because the eight-factor test proposed by the SEC and adopted in Wellman v. Dickinson, 475 F.Supp. 783 (S.D.N.Y.1979), had not been satisfied. The court also refused to adopt, at the urging of the SEC, the alternative test of what constitutes a tender offer as enunciated in S–G Securities, Inc. v. Fuqua Investment Co., 466 F.Supp. 1114

(D.Mass.1978). On May 9, 1984 the SEC filed an emergency application for an injunction pending appeal to this court. That application was denied.

DISCUSSION

* * *

The SEC urges two principal arguments on appeal: (1) the district court erred in concluding that CHH's repurchase program was not a tender offer under the eight-factor *Wellman* test, and (2) the district court erred in declining to apply the definition of a tender offer enunciated in *S–G Securities.* Resolution of these issues on appeal presents the difficult task of determining whether CHH's repurchase of shares during a third-party tender offer itself constituted a tender offer.

1. The Williams Act.

* * *

B. Issuer Repurchases Under Section 13(e)

Issuer repurchases and tender offers are governed in relevant part by section 13(e) of the Williams Act and Rules 13e–1 and 13e–4 promulgated thereunder.

The SEC argues that the district court erred in concluding that issuer repurchases, which had the intent and effect of defeating a third-party tender offer, are authorized by the tender offer rules and regulations. The legislative history of these provisions is unclear. Congress apparently was aware of an intent by the SEC to regulate issuer tender offers to the same extent as third-party offers. At the same time, Congress recognized issuers might engage in "substantial repurchase programs * * * inevitably affect[ing] market performance and price levels." Such repurchase programs might be undertaken for any number of legitimate purposes, including with the intent "to preserve or strengthen * * * control by counteracting tender offer or other takeover attempts * * *." Congress neither explicitly banned nor authorized such a practice. Congress did grant the SEC authority to adopt appropriate regulations to carry out congressional intent with respect to issuer repurchases. The legislative history of section 13(e) is not helpful in resolving the issues.

There is also little guidance in the SEC Rules promulgated in response to the legislative grant of authority. Rule 13e–1 prohibits an issuer from repurchasing its own stock during a third-party tender offer unless it discloses certain minimal information. The language of Rule 13e–1 is prohibitory rather than permissive. It nonetheless evidences a recognition that not all issuer repurchases during a third-party tender offer are tender offers. In contrast, Rule 13e–4 recognizes that issuers, like third parties, may engage in repurchase activity amounting to a tender offer and subject to the same procedural and substantive safeguards as a third-party tender offer. The regulations do not specify when a repurchase by an issuer amounts to a tender offer governed by Rule 13e–4 rather than 13e–1.

We decline to adopt either the broadest construction of Rule 13e–4, to define issuer tender offers as virtually all substantial repurchases during a third-party tender offer, or the broadest construction of Rule 13e–1, to create an exception from the tender offer requirements for issuer repurchases made during a third-party tender offer. Like the district court, we resolve the question of whether CHH's repurchase program was a tender offer by considering the eight-factor test established in Wellman.

To serve the purposes of the Williams Act, there is a need for flexibility in fashioning a definition of a tender offer. The *Wellman* factors seem particularly well suited in determining when an issuer repurchase program during a third-party tender offer will itself constitute a tender offer. *Wellman* focuses, inter alia, on the manner in which the offer is conducted and whether the offer has the overall effect of pressuring shareholders into selling their stock. Application of the *Wellman* factors to the unique facts and circumstances surrounding issuer repurchases should serve to effect congressional concern for the needs of the shareholder, the need to avoid giving either the target or the offeror any advantage, and the need to maintain a free and open market for securities.

2. *Application of the Wellman Factors.*

Under the *Wellman* test, the existence of a tender offer is determined by examining the following factors:

> (1) Active and widespread solicitation of public shareholders for the shares of an issuer; (2) solicitation made for a substantial percentage of the issuer's stock; (3) offer to purchase made at a premium over the prevailing market price; (4) terms of the offer are firm rather than negotiable; (5) offer contingent on the tender of a fixed number of shares, often subject to a fixed maximum number to be purchased; (6) offer open only for a limited period of time; (7) offeree subjected to pressure to sell his stock; [and (8)] public announcements of a purchasing program concerning the target company precede or accompany rapid accumulation of a large amount of target company's securities.

Not all factors need be present to find a tender offer; rather, they provide some guidance as to the traditional indicia of a tender offer.

The district court concluded CHH's repurchase program was not a tender offer under *Wellman* because only "two of the eight indicia" were present. The SEC claims the district court erred in applying *Wellman* because it gave insufficient weight to the pressure exerted on shareholders; it ignored the existence of a competitive tender offer; and it failed to consider that CHH's offer at the market price was in essence a premium because the price had already risen above pre-tender offer levels.

A. *Active and Widespread Solicitation*

The evidence was uncontraverted that there was "no direct solicitation of shareholders." No active and widespread solicitation occurred.

Nor did the publicity surrounding CHH's repurchase program result in a solicitation. The only public announcements by CHH were those mandated by SEC or Exchange rules.

B. Solicitation for a Substantial Percentage of Issuer's Shares

Because there was no active and widespread solicitation, the district court found the repurchase could not have involved a solicitation for a substantial percentage of CHH's shares. It is unclear whether the proper focus of this factor is the solicitation or the percentage of stock solicited. The district court probably erred in concluding that, absent a solicitation under the first *Wellman* factor, the second factor cannot be satisfied, but we need not decide that here. The solicitation and percentage of stock elements of the second factor often will be addressed adequately in an evaluation of the first *Wellman* factor, which is concerned with solicitation, and the eighth *Wellman* factor, which focuses on the amount of securities accumulated. In this case CHH did not engage in a solicitation under the first *Wellman* factor but did accumulate a large percentage of stock as defined under the eighth *Wellman* factor. An evaluation of the second *Wellman* factor does not alter the probability of finding a tender offer.

C. Premium Over Prevailing Market Price

The SEC contends the open market purchases made by CHH at market prices were in fact made at a premium not over market price but over the pre-tender offer price. At the time of CHH's repurchases, the market price for CHH's shares (ranging from $24.00 to $26.00 per share) had risen above the pre-tender offer price (approximately $22.00 per share). Given ordinary market dynamics, the price of a target company's stock will rise following an announced tender offer. Under the SEC's definition of a premium as a price greater than the pre-tender offer price, a premium will always exist when a target company makes open market purchases in response to a tender offer even though the increase in market price is attributable to the action of the third-party offeror and not the target company. The SEC definition not only eliminates consideration of this *Wellman* factor in the context of issuer repurchases during a tender offer, but also underestimates congressional concern for preserving the free and open market. The district court did not err in concluding a premium is determined not by reference to pre-tender offer price, but rather by reference to market price.

D. Terms of Offer Not Firm

There is no dispute that CHH engaged in a number of transactions or purchases at many different market prices.

E. Offer Not Contingent on Tender of Fixed Minimum Number of Shares

Similarly, while CHH indicated it would purchase up to 15 million shares, CHH's purchases were not contingent on the tender of a fixed minimum number of shares.

F. Not Open For Only a Limited Time

CHH's offer to repurchase was not open for only a limited period of time but rather was open "during the pendency of the tender offer of The Limited." The SEC argues that the offer was in fact open for only a limited time, because CHH would only repurchase stock until 15 million shares were acquired. The fact that 15 million shares were acquired in a short period of time does not translate into an issuer-imposed time limitation. The time within which the repurchases were made was a product of ordinary market forces, not the terms of CHH's repurchase program.

G–H. Shareholder Pressure and Public Announcements Accompanying a Large Accumulation of Stock

With regard to the seventh *Wellman* factor, following a public announcement, CHH repurchased over the period of seven trading days more than 50% of its outstanding shares. The eighth *Wellman* factor was met.

The district court found that while many shareholders may have felt pressured or compelled to sell their shares, CHH itself did not exert on shareholders the kind of pressure the Williams Act proscribes.

While there certainly was shareholder pressure in this case, it was largely the pressure of the marketplace and not the type of untoward pressure the tender offer regulations were designed to prohibit. * * *

The shareholder pressure in this case did not result from any untoward action on the part of CHH. Rather, it resulted from market forces, the third-party offer, and the fear that at the expiration of the offer the price of CHH shares would decrease.

The district court did not abuse its discretion in concluding that under the *Wellman* eight factor test, CHH's repurchase program did not constitute a tender offer.

3. *Alternative* S–G Securities *Test.*

The SEC finally urges that even if the CHH repurchase program did not constitute a tender offer under the *Wellman* test, the district court erred in refusing to apply the test in *S–G Securities,* 466 F.Supp. at 1114. Under the more liberal *S–G Securities* test, a tender offer is present if there are

> (1) A publicly announced intention by the purchaser to acquire a block of the stock of the target company for purposes of acquiring control thereof, and (2) a subsequent rapid acquisition by the purchaser of large blocks of stock through open market and privately negotiated purchases.

There are a number of sound reasons for rejecting the *S–G Securities* test. The test is vague and difficult to apply. It offers little guidance to the issuer as to when his conduct will come within the ambit of Rule 13e–4 as opposed to Rule 13e–1. A determination of the existence of a tender offer under *S–G Securities* is largely subjective and made in hindsight based on an ex post facto evaluation of the response in the marketplace to the repurchase program. The SEC's contention that these concerns are irrelevant when the issuer's repurchases are made with the intent to defeat a third-party offer is without merit. * * *

* * *

We decline to abandon the *Wellman* test in favor of the vague standard enunciated in *S–G Securities.* * * *

HANSON TRUST v. SCM

774 F.2d 47 (2d Cir.1985).

Before MANSFIELD, PIERCE and PRATT, CIRCUIT JUDGES.

MANSFIELD, CIRCUIT JUDGE:

Hanson Trust appeals from an order of the Southern District of New York, granting SCM Corporation's motion for a preliminary injunction restraining them, their officers, agents, employees and any persons acting in concert with them, from acquiring any shares of SCM and from exercising any voting rights with respect to 3.1 million SCM shares acquired by them on September 11, 1985. The injunction was granted on the ground that Hanson's September 11 acquisition of the SCM stock through five private and one open market purchases amounted to a "tender offer" for more than 5% of SCM's outstanding shares, which violated §§ 14(d)(1) and (6) of the Williams Act, and rules promulgated by the Securities and Exchange Commission (SEC) thereunder. We reverse.

* * *

Although § 14(d)(1) clearly applies to "classic" tender offers * * *, courts soon recognized that in the case of privately negotiated transactions or solicitations for private purchases of stock many of the conditions leading to the enactment of § 14(d) for the most part do not exist. The number and percentage of stockholders are usually far less than those involved in public offers. The solicitation involves less publicity than a public tender offer or none. The solicitees, who are frequently directors, officers or substantial stockholders of the target, are more apt to be sophisticated, inquiring or knowledgeable concerning the target's business, the solicitor's objectives, and the impact of the solicitation on the target's business prospects. In short, the solicitee in the private transaction is less likely to be pressured, confused, or ill-informed regarding the businesses and decisions at stake than solicitees who are the subjects of a public tender offer.

These differences between public and private securities transactions have led most courts to rule that private transactions or open market purchases do not qualify as a "tender offer" requiring the purchaser to meet the pre-filing strictures of § 14(d). The borderline between public solicitations and privately negotiated stock purchases is not bright and it is frequently difficult to determine whether transactions falling close to the line or in a type of "no man's land" are "tender offers" or private deals. This has led some to advocate a broader interpretation of the term "tender offer" than that followed by us in Kennecott Copper Corp. v. Curtiss–Wright Corp., and to adopt the eight-factor "test" of what is a tender offer, which was recommended by the SEC and applied by the district court in Wellman v. Dickinson and by the Ninth Circuit in SEC v. Carter Hawley Hale Stores.

* * *

Although many of the above-listed factors are relevant for purposes of determining whether a given solicitation amounts to a tender offer, the elevation of such a list to a mandatory "litmus test" appears to be both unwise and unnecessary. As even the advocates of the proposed test recognize, in any given case a solicitation may constitute a tender offer even though some of the eight factors are absent or, when many factors are present, the solicitation may nevertheless not amount to a tender offer because the missing factors outweigh those present.

We prefer to be guided by the principle followed by the Supreme Court in deciding what transactions fall within the private offering exemption provided by § 4(1) of the Securities Act of 1933, and by ourselves in *Kennecott Copper* in determining whether the Williams Act applies to private transactions. That principle is simply to look to the statutory purpose. In S.E.C. v. Ralston Purina Co., the Court stated, "the applicability of § 4(1) should turn on whether the particular class of persons affected need the protection of the Act. An offering to those who are shown to be able to fend for themselves is a transaction 'not involving any public offering.'" Similarly, since the purpose of § 14(d) is to protect the ill-informed solicitee, the question of whether a solicitation constitutes a "tender offer" within the meaning of § 14(d) turns on whether, viewing the transaction in the light of the totality of circumstances, there appears to be a likelihood that unless the pre-acquisition filing strictures of that statute are followed there will be a substantial risk that solicitees will lack information needed to make a carefully considered appraisal of the proposal put before them.

Applying this standard, we are persuaded on the undisputed facts that Hanson's September 11 negotiation of five private purchases and one open market purchase of SCM shares, totalling 25% of SCM's outstanding stock, did not under the circumstances constitute a "tender offer" within the meaning of the Williams Act. Putting aside for the moment the events preceding the purchases, there can be little doubt that the privately negotiated purchases would not, standing alone, qualify as a tender offer, for the following reasons:

(1) In a market of 22,800 SCM shareholders the number of SCM sellers here involved, six in all, was miniscule compared with the numbers involved in public solicitations of the type against which the Act was directed.

(2) At least five of the sellers were highly sophisticated professionals, knowledgeable in the market place and well aware of the essential facts needed to exercise their professional skills and to appraise Hanson's offer, including its financial condition as well as that of SCM, the likelihood that the purchases might block the SCM–Merrill bid, and the risk that if Hanson acquired more than 33⅓% of SCM's stock the SCM–Merrill lockup of the "crown jewel" might be triggered. * * *

(3) The sellers were not "pressured" to sell their shares by any conduct that the Williams Act was designed to alleviate, but by the forces of the market place. Indeed, in the case of Mutual Shares there was no initial solicitation by Hanson; the offer to sell was initiated by Mr. Price of Mutual Shares. Although each of the Hanson purchases was made for $73.50 per share, in most instances this price was the result of private negotiations after the sellers sought higher prices and in one case price protection, demands which were refused. The $73.50 price was not fixed in advance by Hanson. Moreover, the sellers remained free to accept the $74 per share tender offer made by the SCM–Merrill group.

(4) There was no active or widespread advance publicity or public solicitation, which is one of the earmarks of a conventional tender offer. Arbitrageurs might conclude from ticker tape reports of two large anonymous transactions that Hanson must be the buyer. However, liability for solicitation may not be predicated upon disclosures mandated by Stock Exchange Rules.

(5) The price received by the six sellers, $73.50 per share, unlike that appearing in most tender offers, can scarcely be dignified with the label "premium." The stock market price on September 11 ranged from $72.50 to $73.50 per share. Although risk arbitrageurs sitting on large holdings might reap sizeable profits from sales to Hanson at $73.50, depending on their own purchase costs, they stood to gain even more if the SCM–Merrill offer of $74 should succeed, as it apparently would if they tendered their shares to it. Indeed, the $73.50 price, being at most $1 over market or 1.4% higher than the market price, did not meet the SEC's proposed definition of a premium, which is $2.00 per share or 5% above market price, whichever is greater.

(6) Unlike most tender offers, the purchases were not made contingent upon Hanson's acquiring a fixed minimum number or percentage of SCM's outstanding shares. Once an agreement with each individual seller was reached, Hanson was obligated to buy, regardless what total percentage of stock it might acquire. Indeed, it does not appear that Hanson had fixed in its mind a firm limit on the amount of SCM shares it was willing to buy.

(7) Unlike most tender offers, there was no general time limit within which Hanson would make purchases of SCM stock. Concededly, cash transactions are normally immediate but, assuming an inability on the part of a seller and Hanson to agree at once on a price, nothing prevented a resumption of negotiations by each of the parties except the arbitrageurs' speculation that once Hanson acquired 33⅓% or an amount just short of that figure it would stop buying.

In short, the totality of circumstances that existed on September 11 did not evidence any likelihood that unless Hanson was required to comply with § 14(d)(1)'s pre-acquisition filing and waiting-period requirements there would be a substantial risk of ill-considered sales of SCM stock by ill-informed shareholders.

C. REGULATION OF THE TERMS OF TENDER OFFERS

As the court noted in the *Kennecott* case above, subsections (5), (6) and (7) of § 14(d) set forth substantive rules governing the withdrawal rights of shareholders and the manner in which the offeror must pay for tendered shares. The SEC rules under § 14(d) expand and elaborate on those provisions. When there are competing tender offers with different terms and expiration dates, and the parties are modifying their offers to gain a competitive advantage, the interpretation of these provisions can become somewhat difficult, as the following case indicates:

McDERMOTT v. WHEELABRATOR-FRYE

649 F.2d 489 (7th Cir.1980).

Before FAIRCHILD, CHIEF JUDGE, and SWYGERT and PELL, CIRCUIT JUDGES.

FAIRCHILD and SWYGERT, CIRCUIT JUDGES. Defendant-appellant, Wheelabrator-Frye, Inc. ("Wheelabrator") and plaintiff-appellee, McDermott, Inc. ("McDermott"), are engaged in rival tender offers for ownership and control of Pullman Incorporated ("Pullman"). All three are large, highly diversified corporations. Late in the afternoon of September 19, 1980, McDermott moved in the district court for a temporary restraining order, alleging that Wheelabrator had violated certain provisions of the Williams Act, and regulations promulgated thereunder, by increasing the number of Pullman shares it was seeking, without extending the closing date for its tender offer, which was due to expire that midnight. The district court granted McDermott's motion that evening, and ordered Wheelabrator to extend its tender offer until midnight, October 17, 1980 and to provide Pullman shareholders who had already tendered their shares the right to withdraw their shares within 15 business days of September 15, 1980. For reasons hereinafter stated, we vacate the district court's order entered September 19, 1980.

For the purposes of this appeal it is sufficient to note the following facts. McDermott began a hostile tender offer for Pullman on July 3, 1980. On August 22, 1980, Wheelabrator began a rival tender offer with the announced purpose of effecting a merger between it and Pullman. Pullman management welcomed this second offer. During the following weeks, McDermott, Wheelabrator and Pullman engaged in a series of maneuvers now typical of tender offer strategy and defense. Pullman has about 11,150,000 shares outstanding which are listed on the New York Stock Exchange.

As of 7 a.m., Chicago time, September 19, 1980, Wheelabrator's tender offer was to purchase 3,000,000 shares of Pullman at $52.50 per share, reserving the right to purchase an additional 1,000,000 shares. This offer was due to expire at midnight, New York time, September 19. If the offer was successful in the second-stage merger, non-tendering Pullman shareholders were to receive 1.1 Wheelabrator shares for each Pullman share. Some 1,000,000 Pullman shares had been tendered under this Wheelabrator offer.

Also on the morning of September 19, McDermott's tender offer was to purchase 5,400,000 shares of Pullman at $43.50 per share. The McDermott offer was due to expire at midnight, New York time, September 26. McDermott's announced intention was also to seek a business combination between it and Pullman. McDermott had not yet specified what consideration it would offer to the remaining Pullman shareholders in the second stage of their acquisition of Pullman. As of that morning, some 3,882,000 shares had been tendered to McDermott.

On Friday morning, between 7:45 and 8:40, Chicago time, Wheelabrator announced it was increasing the number of securities it was seeking to 5,500,000. Its press announcement stated that no other terms and conditions of its offer were being changed. Between the time this announcement was made until 2:00 p.m., Chicago time, the number of shares tendered to Wheelabrator did not significantly change, in all likelihood because the arbitrageurs who were holding a majority of the outstanding Pullman shares were waiting for an increased bid expected from McDermott. There was no appreciable reaction to the Wheelabrator announcement on the New York Stock Exchange.

Shortly after 2:00 p.m., Chicago time, McDermott announced that it was increasing its offer to $54 a share and that in the second stage combination, non-tendering Pullman shareholders would receive securities valued at about $39 a share. This offer was extended to September 29. Paradoxically, by midnight, New York time, Friday, September 19, Wheelabrator's offer was in fact oversubscribed: some 7,300,000 shares had been irrevocably tendered, although Wheelabrator was only seeking 5,500,000. Nearly all of the shares provisionally tendered to McDermott had been withdrawn. Had the district court not intervened, Wheelabrator's tender offer would have been successful; it would have been able to purchase up to 5,500,000 shares and its 49 percent stake in Pullman would have conferred effective control on Wheelabrator.

However at 4:15 p.m., Chicago time, September 19, after McDermott increased its offer to $54.00 and while shareholders were nevertheless tendering to Wheelabrator, McDermott appeared before the district court seeking a restraining order against Wheelabrator's closing offer. During an extended hearing lasting past 8:00 p.m., McDermott argued that the increase in the amount of securities being sought constituted such a material change in the offer that it was in effect a new tender offer and required an additional time extension. The district court agreed, finding,

> It seems that the withdrawal period was more than the 10-day period so the consequence of my finding has to be that Wheelabrator is obligated to hold the offer open 20 business days because it is a *new offer* with 15 business days to withdraw.

During its consideration of the time extension required, the district court discussed several alternative periods of time during which Wheelabrator would be compelled to keep this new offer open, but ultimately concluded that Rule 14e–1(a) required a full 20 day extension.

* * *

On September 22, Wheelabrator appealed to this court, filing at the same time an emergency motion for stay or in the alternative to vacate the preliminary injunction and for suspension of the rules. On that day we ordered oral argument on the emergency motion and on the appeal to be heard on September 23. In light of the reasons set out hereinafter, we vacate the order issued by the district court.

* * *

The district court's order can only rest upon the proposition that the announcement of the increase in the number of shares Wheelabrator obligated itself to buy created a new tender offer, thereby triggering the time requirements of the statute and regulations attendant upon the commencement of a tender offer. We conclude that this proposition is untenable, based upon our reading of the statute and regulations thereunder. Even an increase in consideration is not treated as a new tender offer. See Rule 14e–1(b). It is illogical to assume that when the SEC, acting under rule-making authority granted by Congress, expressly required a ten day waiting period after a change in the consideration offered, it intended that an increase in the number of shares sought be the commencement of a new tender offer, triggering more extensive requirements than the SEC thought necessary for a change in the price.

It is argued that the regulations treat a change in the number of shares sought as a change in information, requiring the lapse of some reasonable time thereafter during which the tender offer must remain outstanding. Rule 14d–4(c). Under the order appealed from, the offer has remained open while this appeal has been pending. Assuming without deciding that the regulations require the offer to remain outstanding for a reasonable period after the announcement made the morning of September 19, we think that the period of time which has already lapsed since the order of the district court on September 19 has clearly been an adequate period. We therefore see no need to remand to the district court to fix the reasonable time under this theory.

Accordingly, the order appealed from is vacated and this court's mandate shall issue forthwith.

PELL, CIRCUIT JUDGE, dissented.

Following the *McDermott* decision, Congress amended the Act to clarify the interaction of the various time periods. The current rules may be summarized as follows.

In general, a tender offer must be held open for at least twenty days following the date the offer is first published or sent or given to security holders. Rule 14e–1(a). Modification of a tender offer may trigger mandatory extension of the period during which the offer must be held open. If the offeror changes (increases or decreases) the consideration offered or the dealer's solicitation fee, the offer must be held open for at least ten business days from the date of notice of such change. Rule 14e–1(b). The same is true for an increase or decrease in the "percentage of the class of securities being sought." Rule 14e–1(b). The extension of time also applies when the bidder exercises a reservation of the right to acquire additional shares in the original offer. However, the ten-business-day period is not triggered by acceptance of additional securities not exceeding two percent of the class of securities subject to the tender offer. Rule 14e–1(b).

In CRTF v. FEDERATED DEPARTMENT STORES, 683 F.Supp. 422 (S.D.N.Y.1988), CRTF revised its cash offer for all shares of the target company from $61 per share to a two-tiered cash offer of $75 per share for 80% of the target shares and $44 per share for the remainder in a second stage merger. Plaintiff claimed that CRTF's revision of both the percentage of securities sought and the consideration to be offered amounted to a new offer renewing the twenty business day period under Rule 14e–1(a). The court held that the revisions to the percentage of the securities sought and the price to be paid therefor were "covered by Rule 14e–1(b) . . . which only requires[s] that the offer remain open for ten business days." The court reasoned that the twenty day period contemplates allowance of a period in which to evaluate "far more than price and quantity" such as "the form of consideration, the procedures for tendering shares, information on financing, . . . purpose in making the offer, . . . plans for the target company and other information." See Schedule 14D–1.

The ten-business-day period is triggered only by changes effected by the tender offeror. Thus, if the target company increases the number of shares outstanding and the bidder does nothing, the ten-business-day time period will not be triggered despite the fact that the percentage of securities sought by the bidder has decreased. Only if the bidder's own actions cause a decrease or increase in the consideration offered or percentage of securities sought will the ten-business-day time period be triggered. See Sec.Ex.Act Rel. No. 23421 (July 17, 1986).

In that same release, the SEC takes the position that public announcement of the bidder's intent to increase the consideration if a given number of shares are tendered would itself constitute a change in the consideration offered and thereby invoke Rule 14e–1(b).

When "material" changes are made in the terms of the offer, other than those described above, Rule 14d–4(c) requires that notice be "promptly disseminated to security holders in a manner reasonably designed to inform [them] of such change." In interpreting this language, the SEC has promulgated a rule of thumb that an offer should be held open for five business days from the date of notice of a "material" change.

Section 14(d)(5) entitles a tendering shareholder to withdraw tendered shares at any time (a) within seven days from the date notice of the tender offer is given to the security holders; and (b) after sixty days from the date of the original tender offer, except as the Commission may otherwise provide. The Commission has expanded these rights in Rule 14d–7 by permitting withdrawal at any time during the period the tender offer remains open. Note that this period would include any extension in the expiration date of the offer resulting from modification of terms of the offer.

The following table summarizes some of the more important Williams Act requirements:

	Third–Party Tender Offer	Issuer Tender Offer
Best Price Rule	Rule 14d–10(a)(2)—the highest price paid to any tendering security holder must be paid to all tendering security holders.	Rule 13e–4(f)(8)(ii)—the highest price paid to any tendering security holder must be paid to all security holders.
	Rule 14d–10(c) allows different types of consid. to be offered which need not be substantially equivalent in value as long as: 1) security holders are free to elect among the types of consideration offered; and 2) the highest consideration of each type paid to any security holder is paid to any security holder electing that type.	Rule 13e–4(f)(10) (same as third-party offer)
All Holders Rule	Rule 14d–10(a)(1) requires that the tender offer be open to all holders of the class of securities sought.	Rule 13e–4(f)(8)(i) (same as third-party offer)
	Rule 14d–10(b)(2) permits a bidder to exclude holders in a state where the bidder is prohibited by statute from making the offer after a good faith effort to comply with the statute.	Rule 13e–4(f)(9)(ii) (same as third-party offer)

	Third-Party Tender Offer	Issuer Tender Offer
Pro Rata Rule	§ 14(d)(6)—where the offer is for less than for all outstanding securities of a class and the offer is oversubscribed, the bidder must take up the tendered securities on a pro rata basis. The rule only applies to securities tendered w/in 10 days from the original publication of the offer or notice of an increase in consideration the rule does not apply if the bidder's acquisitions of that class of securities during the past 12 months does not exceed 2% of that class	Rule 13e–4(f)(3)—where the offer is for less than all outstanding securities of a class and the offer is oversubscribed, the bidder must take up the tendered securities on a pro rata basis. The rule provides exceptions for odd-lot tender offers and for shares which are tendered on an all or none basis
Duration of the Tender Offer	Rule 14e–1(a)—the tender offer must remain open for at least 20 days. Rule 14e–1(b)—a change in the consideration to be paid, the percentage of securities sought or the dealer's solicitation fee will require that the offer be held open at least 10 days from the date of notice of such change. Exception—acceptance of additional securities not exceeding 2% of the class sought Rule 14d–4(c)—notice of "material" changes in the terms of the offer must be made in a manner reasonably designed to inform security holders of such change. The SEC interprets this rule to mean that a material change would require holding the offer open for at least five days from the date of notice and 10 days when the change approaches the level of a change in consid. or the % of securities sought.	Rule 13e–4(f)(1)(i) (same as third-party offer) Rule 13e–4(f)(1)(ii) (same as third-party offer) (same as third-party offer) Rule 13e–4(e)(2)—notice of a "material" change in the information sent to security holders must be made in a manner reasonably calculated to inform security holders of such change.
Withdrawal Rights	§ 14(d)(5) tendered securities may be withdrawn at any time during the first seven days of the tender offer and at any time after 60 days from the date of the original tender offer. Rule 14d–7—tendered securities may be withdrawn while the tender offer remains open.	Rule 13e–4(f)(2) tendered securities may be withdrawn: (i) at any time while the tender remains open; and (ii) after 40 days from commencement of the offer if the securities have not been accepted.

D. DISCLOSURE REQUIREMENTS

The heart of the disclosure requirements applicable to tender offers is the statement which § 14(d)(1) requires the offeror to file and distribute. The specific disclosure requirements for that statement are spelled out in Schedule 14D–1, but special questions of materiality are raised by the fact that, in most tender offers, what is being offered is cash rather than securities. Under those circumstances, what does a shareholder deciding whether to tender his or her shares really need to know?

PRUDENT REAL ESTATE TRUST v. JOHNCAMP REALTY

599 F.2d 1140 (2d Cir.1979).

Before: MOORE, FRIENDLY and MESKILL, CIRCUIT JUDGES.

FRIENDLY, CIRCUIT JUDGE: On March 28, 1979, we heard a motion by appellant Prudent Real Estate Trust (Prudent), the target of a tender offer by the defendant Johncamp Realty, Inc. (Johncamp), for an injunction pending appeal from an order of the District Court for the Southern District of New York, which had denied Prudent's motion for a temporary injunction against the continuation of a tender offer on the ground that the material filed with the Securities and Exchange Commission (SEC) pursuant to § 14(d) of the Securities and Exchange Act was insufficient and that, because of certain statements and omissions, the offer violated § 14(e) of the Act.

* * * Defendant Johncamp is a Delaware close corporation which was founded by Johncamp Netherlands Antilles, N.V. (Johncamp N.V.) and The Pacific Company, a California corporation (Pacific). Johncamp N.V. owns 60% and Pacific 40% of the common shares of Johncamp. All of the stock of Johncamp N.V. is owned by Campeau Corporation (Campeau), a publicly held Ontario corporation; Robert Campeau, a resident of Canada, is chairman of its board and chief executive officer. John E. Wertin, a resident of California, is president, secretary and a director of Johncamp, president and a director and sole stockholder of Pacific, and president and director of John Wertin Development Corporation (JWDC), a California corporation, 95% of the stock of which is owned by Pacific. * * *

On March 12, 1979, Johncamp filed with the SEC a Schedule 14D–1 as required for a tender offer. The schedule contained the form of offer, which was advertised the following day in the New York Times. The offer, which was to expire on March 23 unless extended, was to purchase any and all of Prudent's outstanding shares at $7 net per share, as against the last available market price of 4⅞, and was not conditioned upon any minimum number of shares being tendered. * * *

The offer went on to state that 80% of the required funds would be furnished by Johncamp N.V. which would obtain them from Campeau, out of the latter's own funds or from a $50,000,000 (Canadian) line of bank credit described in some detail, and that 20% would be supplied by Pacific which would obtain the funds from JWDC and Wertin. The purpose of the offer was to acquire all the shares of Prudent but if this did not occur pursuant to the offer, Johncamp, Campeau, Johncamp

N.V. and Pacific desired to acquire enough shares to exercise control.

* * *

The only portion of the Schedule 14D here relevant is *Item 9. Financial Statements of Certain Bidders.* This was answered: "Not applicable, but see Exhibit 1." Exhibit 1 consisted of the printed annual reports of Campeau for 1976 and 1977 and audited consolidated financial statements for 1978.

On March 16, 1979, Prudent initiated this action to enjoin the defendants from proceeding with the tender offer, and moved for a temporary restraining order and a preliminary injunction on various grounds. One of these, not pressed on this appeal but reserved for future presentation in the district court after further discovery, is that there is a secret undisclosed plan to liquidate Prudent. The three points urged below which continue to be pressed here are the failure to disclose in the Offer or the Schedule any financial information about the Wertin interests, to wit, Pacific, JWDC, and Wertin himself, as Item 9 allegedly requires; the claimed inadequacy of the discussion of the effects of loss of REIT status; and the falsity of the statement that Prudent could be terminated only by a vote of two-thirds of the outstanding shares when Prudent's declaration of trust also allowed this to be done by the board of trustees acting alone.

* * *

The relevant sections of the Securities Exchange Act, § 14(d)(1) and (e), added by the Williams Act of 1968, are too familiar to require extended exposition. It is sufficient here to say that in a case like this § 14(d)(1) prohibits the making of a tender offer by any person "unless at the time copies of the offer or request or invitation are first published or sent or given to security holders, such person has filed with the Commission a statement containing such of the information specified in section 13(d) of this title, and such additional information as the Commission may by rules and regulations prescribe as necessary or appropriate in the public interest or for the protection of investors", and that "[a]ll requests for tender or advertisements making a tender offer or requiring or inviting tenders of such a security shall be filed as a part of such statement and shall contain such of the information contained in such statement as the Commission may by rules and regulations prescribe."

* * *

Faced with the need of quickly issuing regulations, the SEC responded with a set of emergency rules. These made no express requirement for revelation of the financial condition of the offeror. In November and December 1974 the SEC conducted Tender Offer Hearings; these led to the publication of proposed § 14(d) regulations on August 6, 1976.

Meanwhile cases presenting the question whether the maker of a cash offer must furnish information about its financial position were beginning to reach the courts. Since Schedule 14D had not yet been formulated, plaintiffs had to take the harder road of asserting that failure to furnish such information constituted a violation of § 14(e). The first case was Corenco Corp. v. Schiavone & Sons, Inc., 362 F.Supp. 939, 948–50 (S.D.N.Y.1973). Judge Ward held that § 14(e) required the offeror, Schiavone & Sons, Inc., to provide enough information about itself to enable a Corenco shareholder to make an informed decision.[1] * * * Next came Alaska Interstate Co. v. McMillian, 402 F.Supp. 532, 546–49 (D.Del.1975), a case of exceeding complexity. Judge Stapleton framed the issue as being whether "the Williams Act is violated whenever one who tenders for less than all of the stock and proposes an acquisition of the target corporation for its own securities fails to provide its financials in the tender materials." In answering that question in the negative he stressed the large amount of financial information about the offeror that was readily available and the fact that the SEC had not yet required disclosure when the offer was in cash rather than securities of the offeror. Finally, in Copperweld Corporation v. Imetal, 403 F.Supp. 579, 598–602 (W.D.Pa.1975), Judge Miller stated that he was "inclined to agree with Copperweld [the target] that, *under appropriate circumstances,* financials can be required under Section 14(e)" (emphasis in original), but held that the reports filed by a French offeror were sufficient although they did not conform to SEC Regulation S–X but had been prepared in accordance with French requirements.[2]

Meanwhile, the SEC's rulemaking had been proceeding and in a release appearing on July 28, 1977, new regulations were issued, which for the first time adopted a schedule 14D specifically tailored to § 14(d) of the Act. The schedule included as Item 9:

> *Item 9. Financial Statements of Certain Bidders.* Where the bidder is other than a natural person and the bidder's financial condition is material to a decision by a security holder of the subject company whether to sell, tender or hold securities being sought in the tender offer, furnish current, adequate financial information concerning the bidder * * *.

* * *

The parties accept that the test of materiality is that stated in TSC Industries, Inc. v. Northway, although that case arose under Rule 14a–9 concerning proxy contests. * * * The Court's formulation was:

> An omitted fact is material if there is a substantial likelihood that a reasonable shareholder would consider it important in deciding how to vote.

* * *

1. Judge Ward found the following factors to be relevant:

(1) no financial information concerning Schiavone is available; (2) Schiavone seeks control; (3) Schiavone contemplates a merger; and (4) less than all shares are sought.

2. The court also put weight on the fact that Schiavone's offer in *Corenco* had been for less than a third of the shares whereas Imetal offered to purchase all.

In applying this test to a cash tender offer, it is necessary to appreciate the problem faced by a stockholder of the target company in deciding whether to tender, to sell or to hold part or all of his securities. It is true that, in the case of an "any and all" offer such as that here at issue, a stockholder who has firmly decided to tender has no interest in the financial position of the offeror other than its ability to pay—a point not here at issue—since he will have severed all financial connections with the target. It is also true that in the case of such an offer, there is less reason for him to seek to eliminate the risk of being partly in and partly out by selling to arbitrageurs, usually at a price somewhere between the previous market and the offered price, than where the offer is for a stated number or percentage of the shares (with or without the right to accept additional shares) or is conditioned on a minimum number being obtained. Still, the shareholder of the target company faces a hard problem in determining the most advantageous course of action, a problem whose difficulty is enhanced by his usual ignorance of the course other shareholders are adopting. If the bidder is in a flourishing financial condition, the stockholder might decide to hold his shares in the hope that, if the offer was only partially successful, the bidder might raise its bid after termination of the offer or infuse new capital into the enterprise. *Per contra,* a poor financial condition of the bidder might cause the shareholder to accept for fear that control of the company would pass into irresponsible hands. The force of these considerations is diminished but not altogether removed in this case by the fact that the Wertin interests were supplying only 20% of the financing and that Campeau's annual reports for 1976 and 1977 and its financial statements for 1978, which were incorporated in the Schedule 14D, showed it to be a company of substance. As against this, the stockholders' agreement gave Wertin the right to vote all acquired Prudent shares and the district court found that Wertin was to manage the properties.

Johncamp relies on statements by SEC Chairman Cohen before the House Committee at the hearings that led to the Williams Act wherein he analogized the information required by the bill to be provided to stockholders with that required in proxy contests, where Regulation 14A does not require a challenger to file its financial statements unless it proposes a merger or consolidation or the issuance "of securities of another issuer", even if its objective is to gain control. Prudent counters with the language from the House Committee report quoted above, echoing Chairman Cohen's article, that in the case of a cash tender offer "the investment decision—whether to retain the security or sell it—is in substance little different from the decision made on an original purchase of a security, or on an offer to exchange one security for another." In truth the situation is not precisely like any of these models. It differs from the proxy contest *simpliciter* in that an investment decision is being made; it differs from an original purchase of a security or an offer to exchange one security for another in that the stockholder does not have to appraise what he is buying. It differs also from an ordinary sale in that the investment decision is influenced not solely by general factors affecting the prospects of the economy, the market, or the company, but importantly by the particular proposal being made. In any event we must look to some extent to what the Congressional committees said rather than to what the facts are.

From the beginning of litigation under the Williams Act, this court has been conscious of its responsibility not to allow management to "resort to the courts on trumped-up or trivial grounds as a means for delaying and thereby defeating tender offers." However, the issue raised by this appeal seems to us to be one where it does matter that the test of materiality is not the more severe one we proposed in *General Time* and *Gamble–Skogmo,* supra, but the standard fashioned by the Supreme Court in 1976, "substantial likelihood that disclosure of the omitted fact would have assumed actual significance in the deliberations of the reasonable shareholder." An important factor here is the impracticability of obtaining information about the Wertin interests from other sources. At the very least there is "fair ground for litigating" the issue of materiality and the balance of hardships tips heavily in Prudent's favor. We are further influenced by the fact that our decision imposes no serious impediment to cash tender offers. Even in this case the omission can be readily corrected; in future cases presumably it will not be made.

* * *

We therefore reverse the order under appeal and direct the district court to issue a temporary injunction. It will be sufficient if this extends only until Johncamp makes the necessary corrections and allows a reasonable period for withdrawal of stock already tendered; we see no need for the further cooling-off period that Prudent requests. * * *

Are you persuaded by Judge Friendly's reasons for requiring disclosure of additional financial information about the bidder? The authors of one article, after an empirical study of 57 tender offers, found that a cash bid for any and all stock was almost certain to be followed within a year by a "freeze-out" merger in which non-tendering shareholders would be paid off at the tender offer price. They therefore concluded that shareholders faced with such an offer required only the most rudimentary information about the bidder. On the other hand, they found that bids for only a portion of the stock were generally not followed by a merger, and that shareholders faced with that kind of bid would have more concern with the background and finances of the bidder. Borden & Weiner, An Investment Decision Analysis of Cash Tender Offer Disclosure, 23 N.Y.L.S.L.Rev. 553 (1978).

In addition to the detailed disclosure requirements promulgated by the SEC under § 14(d), the SEC has used its rule-making authority under the antifraud provisions of § 14(e) to adopt Rule 14e–2, which requires the management of a company faced with a tender offer to distribute to its shareholders a statement disclosing whether management recommends acceptance or rejection of the offer, or is neutral or unable to express an opinion, and setting forth the reasons for its decision. Since § 14(e) is not limited to companies registered under the 1934 Act, this rule is applicable to all companies, however small or closely held.

One special disclosure problem arises in tender offers in which securities, rather than cash, are offered in exchange for the shares of the target company. The requirement that the offeror make full disclosures may come into conflict with § 5(c) of the 1933 Act which prohibits any statements which could be construed as "offers" prior to the filing of a registration statement. The following materials indicate how the SEC has dealt with this conflict.

CHRIS–CRAFT INDUSTRIES v. BANGOR PUNTA CORP., 426 F.2d 569 (2d Cir.1970), involved a battle between Chris–Craft and Bangor Punta for control of Piper Aircraft. Bangor Punta agreed to purchase the 31% of Piper stock owned by the Piper family and, as part of the deal, agreed to make an exchange offer to all other Piper shareholders under which they would be entitled to exchange each share of Piper "for Bangor Punta securities and/or cash having a value, in the written opinion of The First Boston Corporation, of $80 or more." Bangor Punta issued a press release announcing the agreement and the terms of the proposed exchange offer.

Chris–Craft sued for an injunction, alleging that the press release violated § 5(c) of the Securities Act of 1933 by offering the Bangor Punta securities for sale before any registration statement had been filed with the SEC. Chris–Craft's argument, supported by the SEC, was that the SEC's Rule 135 was the only exception to the prohibition in § 5(c), and that Bangor Punta's announcement did not qualify under Rule 135 because it contained a statement of anticipated value which was not permitted by the Rule.

Bangor Punta responded that, if it did not make public the terms of the agreement, it might be held liable under Rule 10b–5 to Piper shareholders who sold without knowledge of the terms. Furthermore, under § 13(d), it was required to file a copy of the agreement with the SEC, where it would be publicly available for inspection by anyone who wanted to examine it.

The Second Circuit, *en banc,* upheld the SEC–Chris–Craft position that the press release did not comply with Rule 135 and therefore violated § 5(c). The majority felt that "the danger that substantial numbers of investors were misled by the figure's publication" outweighed the "unfair advantage" that might otherwise have been obtained by insiders or by the "few additional sophisticated investors [who] could have discovered the $80 value guarantee in the description of the transaction which Bangor Punta filed with the SEC pursuant to

§ 13(d)." Judges Lumbard and Moore, dissenting, felt that, in view of the countervailing considerations, the court should have construed the announcement as coming within Rule 135(a)(4), which permits a statement of "the basis on which the exchange is to be made." [a]

Technicalities aside, who has the better argument here? Is this like a situation in which a tender offeror agrees to make a cash offer to all shareholders of $80 a share (in which case disclosure would clearly be appropriate)? Or is it more like a situation in which a company planning to issue a new class of shares announces that, in the opinion of its financial adviser, the shares will have a market value of at least $80 (which would clearly be inappropriate)? It is interesting to note that the statement here was in fact misleading; the securities issued by Bangor Punta did not have a market value of $80 a share. Under another provision of the agreement between Bangor Punta and the Piper family, which required Bangor Punta to make up the difference between the value of the securities issued to them and $80 per share, Bangor Punta was subsequently required to pay them $5.3 million.[b]

The problem that gave rise to the *Chris–Craft* case can also appear in other contexts, one of which ultimately required the SEC to rethink the position it had taken in *Chris–Craft.* One company may undertake a friendly two-step acquisition of another company, under which it makes a cash tender offer for a certain percentage of the other company's stock, having already agreed with the management of the acquired company to follow that up with a merger proposal under which the remaining shares of the acquired company will be exchanged for securities of the acquiring company. In April 1978, the SEC analyzed the problem in Securities Act Release No. 5927:

> The issue here is whether the acquiring company's disclosure in its tender offer materials of the negotiations with the acquired company and/or the merger agreement, including the material terms of the statutory merger contemplated subsequent to the tender offer, constitutes an "offer to sell" the securities of the acquiring company to be received by the acquired company's shareholders pursuant to the merger within the meaning of Section 2(3) of the 1933 Act and Rule 145(a) promulgated thereunder. A finding that such disclosure constitutes an "offer to sell" leads to the conclusion that the bidder's tender offer violates Section 5(c) of the 1933 Act if at the time of the tender offer a registration statement for the acquiring company's securities to be exchanged in the merger has not been filed with the Commission.
>
> This issue was addressed in a letter to the Bendix Corporation ("Bendix") from the Division (available November 30, 1976). That letter concerned a proposed merger of Ex–Cell–O Corporation ("Ex–Cell–O") into Bendix. After the agreement was signed but before the distribution of proxy statements and the vote by shareholders on the merger, Bendix proposed to make a tender offer for up to 40% of the outstand-

a. See Note, Preregistration Publicity in an Exchange Offer, 119 U.Pa.L.Rev. 174 (1970).

b. See Wall St. Journal, Mar. 23, 1976, p. 29, col. 2.

ing shares of Ex–Cell–O common stock at $30 per share. The tender offer materials to be delivered to the Ex–Cell–O shareholders would contain a brief description of the principal terms of the merger, including the basis of exchange and a statement that after Bendix and Ex–Cell–O entered into a definitive merger agreement proxy statements concerning the merger would be distributed to the shareholders of both companies. In its letter to Bendix, the Division took the position that the Ex–Cell–O shareholder when confronted with the Bendix tender offer would be making an investment decision to accept either the cash offered in the tender offer or to take the Bendix stock later. On this basis, the Division was unable to conclude that the tender offer did not constitute an "offer to sell" the Bendix common stock to be exchanged in the subsequent merger within the meaning of Section 2(3) of the 1933 Act and Rule 145 thereunder. The implication from the Bendix letter is that, unless the bidder/acquiring company has filed a registration statement at the time the cash tender offer commences, the disclosure in the cash tender offer of the material terms of the subsequent merger violates Section 5(c) of the 1933 Act.

On August 31, 1977, Schedule 14D–1 and the amendments to Rule 14D–1 implementing the filing and disclosure requirements of that Schedule became effective. * * *

One of the new disclosure requirements is Item 3(b) which requires a bidder to describe any contracts, negotiations or transactions which have occurred since the commencement of the subject company's third full fiscal year preceding the filing date of the Schedule between the bidder and the subject company concerning: a merger, consolidation or acquisition, a tender offer or other acquisition of securities; an election of directors; or a sale or other transfer of a material amount of assets. * * *

Item 5(a) of Schedule 14D–1 parallels the former requirement of Item 4 in Schedule 13D by requiring a bidder to describe any plan or proposal it has which relates to or would result in an extraordinary corporate transaction involving the subject company or any of its subsidiaries such as a merger, reorganization, or liquidation. * * *

Additionally, Item 7 of Schedule 14D–1 which represents an expansion of a similar requirement in Schedule 13D requires the bidder to describe any contract, arrangement, understanding or relationship between the bidder and any person with respect to any securities of the subject company. * * *

Not only does Rule 14d–1(a) require the information contained in items 3(b), 5(a) and 7 to be filed with the Commission in Schedule 14D–1, but Rule 14d–1(c)(4) requires these items or a fair and adequate summary thereof to be included in the tender offer which is published, sent or given to the subject company's security holders. Accordingly, disclosure by a bidder of negotiations with the subject company, and/or an agreement in principle or plan of merger entered into with the subject company is required by Section 14(d)(1) of the Exchange Act and the rules and Schedule 14D–1 promulgated thereunder. Indeed, the omission of such disclosure in the Schedule 14D–1 filed with the Commission or the tender offer materials communicated to security holders would constitute a violation of the provisions of the Williams Act.

The disclosure philosophy of the Williams Act is juxtaposed with the "gun jumping" doctrine under the 1933 Act. That doctrine was designed to prevent an issuer from conditioning the market by arousing investor interest before a registration statement covering the securities proposed to be offered has been filed.

In the Division's view, such a doctrine is inappropriate to apply to a cash tender offer subject to Section 14(d) in which the bidder is seeking to buy the securities of the subject company's security holders. The bidder's concern is purchasing the subject company's securities for cash, not priming the market for a subsequent registered offering of securities. Regardless of the bidder's intent, Schedule 14D–1 for compelling policy reasons reflected by the Williams Act requires such information in order to provide full disclosure to investors confronted with an investment decision in the context of a tender offer. In the Division's opinion, to apply the "gun jumping" doctrine to Situation A would not further the policies underlying the 1933 Act and would be inconsistent with the intention of Schedule 14D–1 to require disclosure of information available to the bidder regarding its previous contracts, arrangements or agreements and future plans and proposals with respect to the subject company.

In light of the above, the Division believes on reconsideration that the position it took in the Bendix letter was not necessary for the protection of investors and has withdrawn that letter. In the Division's view, the disclosure required by the Williams Act to be made by a bidder in a cash tender offer concerning the subsequent statutory merger in Situation A should not be deemed to constitute an "offer to sell" the bidder's securities to be exchanged in such merger, and should not therefore require the filing of a registration statement pursuant to the 1933 Act with respect to such securities prior to the commencement of such tender offer. Such disclosure should be viewed under the 1933 Act as are other written communications or published statements permitted prior to the filing of a registration statement.

The Division's position is, however, limited to the disclosure permitted by Rule 145(b) and to the disclosure required to be made by Section 14(d)(1) of the 1934 Act, Schedule 14D–1 promulgated thereunder and Section 14(e) of the 1934 Act. Depending upon the circumstances, statements which are not required by the Williams Act may constitute an "offer to sell" the securities to be exchanged in the subsequent merger and, in the absence of a registration statement filed with the Commission at the commencement of the tender offer, may constitute a violation of Section 5 of the 1933 Act. For example, a bidder should not issue press releases or grant interviews to the press which discuss a possible merger under circumstances where it appears that the decisions of security holders who will be voting on the merger may be unduly influenced without the benefit of the disclosures in a registration statement.

E. LITIGATION UNDER THE WILLIAMS ACT

The Williams Act, in addition to its detailed provisions for regulation of tender offers, described above, also added § 14(e) to the 1934 Act, prohibiting any untrue statements, misleading omissions, or "any fraudulent, deceptive or manipulative acts or practices" in connection with a tender offer. Litigation under § 14(e) has raised many of the same questions as litigation under §§ 10(b) and 14(a), colored by the distinctive attributes of contested takeover bids.

In ELECTRONIC SPECIALTY CO. v. INTERNATIONAL CONTROLS CORP., 409 F.2d 937 (2d Cir.1969), the first appellate court decision interpreting §§ 14(d) and (e), Judge Friendly held that the target corporation had standing to seek an injunction under § 14(e) against allegedly misleading statements by a tender offeror, analogizing to earlier decisions in which a corporation was held to have standing to attack a misleading proxy solicitation by an insurgent group under § 14(a).

A more difficult question, however, was whether the losing party in a contested tender offer could collect damages from the other parties if it could show that they violated § 14(e) by making false or misleading statements in the course of the contest. The Supreme Court's answer came at the conclusion of a protracted legal battle growing out of a contest between Chris–Craft Industries and Bangor Punta Corporation for control of Piper Aircraft Corporation. After a series of cash tender offers and exchange offers, Bangor Punta emerged victorious with 51% of the Piper stock, while Chris–Craft wound up with 44%. Chris–Craft sued Bangor Punta and members of the Piper family, alleging that they had made a number of misstatements in violation of § 14(e) which had deprived Chris–Craft of a fair opportunity to gain control of Piper.

In ruling on two appeals by Chris–Craft from unfavorable district court holdings, the Court of Appeals for the Second Circuit held that (1) members of the Piper family had violated § 14(e) by making material misstatements of fact in their communications with shareholders in opposition to Chris–Craft's offer, (2) Bangor Punta had violated § 14(e) by making material misstatements of fact in the prospectus offering its securities in exchange for Piper shares, (3) these violations were causally related to Chris–Craft's inability to obtain control of Piper (even though there was evidence that Chris–Craft lost out because it lacked the resources to purchase additional shares), (4) Chris–Craft, as a defeated tender offeror, had standing to sue for damages resulting from these violations, and (5) Chris–Craft was entitled to damages measured by the difference between what it paid for the 44% of the Piper shares which it had acquired and what it might expect to receive on a sale of that minority interest in a company in which Bangor Punta owned a 51% controlling interest. This resulted in a judgment for Chris–Craft in the amount of approximately $26 million, plus $10 million in prejudgment interest, for a total of approximately $36 million, the largest amount ever awarded in an action under federal securities law.

The Supreme Court granted certiorari and reversed, holding that a defeated tender offeror has no implied private right of action for damages for a violation of § 14(e). PIPER v. CHRIS–CRAFT INDUSTRIES, 430 U.S. 1 (1977). In reaching its conclusion, the Court applied the four-factor test it had utilized in Cort v. Ash, 422 U.S. 66 (1975), to determine whether a private remedy is implicit in a statute not expressly providing one. The four factors are (1) whether the plaintiff is one of the class for whose especial benefit the statute was enacted, (2) whether there is any indication of legislative intent, explicit or implicit, either to create such a remedy or to deny one, (3) whether it is consistent with the underlying purposes of the legislative scheme to imply such a remedy for the plaintiff, and (4) whether the cause of action is one traditionally relegated to state law.

In a lengthy opinion by Chief Justice Burger, the Court concluded that "the sole purpose of the Williams Act was the protection of investors who are confronted with a tender offer," and that there was "no hint in the legislative history * * * that Congress contemplated a private cause of action for damages by one of several contending offerors against a successful bidder or by a losing contender against the target corporation." It also found the interests of the Piper shareholders, the group which Congress intended to protect, would not be advanced by an award of damages to Chris–Craft; indeed, those who exchanged their shares for Bangor Punta shares would bear a large part of the burden of any judgment against Bangor Punta.

Three justices who dissented on the question of standing argued that the rationale of the *Borak* decision required recognition of a private right of action by contesting offerors. "Once one recognizes that Congress intended to rely heavily on private litigation as a method of implementing the statute, it seems equally clear that Congress would not exclude the persons most interested in effective enforcement from the class authorized to enforce the new law." The dissenters felt that recognizing a right of action in the persons most likely to sue would encourage compliance with the statute and thus serve as a useful supplement to SEC actions to protect the offeree shareholders. The majority decision, like that in *Rondeau,* can therefore be viewed as a withdrawal from the "private attorney general" rationale of the *Borak* and *Mills* decisions.

Because of its decision on the question of standing, the Supreme Court had no occasion to pass on the Second Circuit rulings on other questions. Statements in the concurring and dissenting opinions, however, indicate strongly that the Court would not have accepted the Second Circuit views, at least on causation and damages.

Under the reasoning of *Piper,* should a tender offeror be permitted to sue for *injunctive relief* under § 14(e)?

HUMANA, INC. v. AMERICAN MEDICORP, INC.

445 F.Supp. 613 (S.D.N.Y.1977).

LASKER, DISTRICT JUDGE.

On September 27, 1977, Humana advised Medicorp by letter that it intended to make an offer to acquire up to 75% of the outstanding shares of Medicorp on the basis of an exchange of cash and securities. The offer constituted a clear premium over the then market price of Medicorp stock. Very shortly after receipt of Humana's letter the Medicorp Board of Directors resolved that the offer was not advantageous to its stockholders and informed them to this effect. There has followed a spate of litigation, including this action alleging that Medicorp has made material misrepresentations concerning the offer in violation of § 14(e) of the 1934 Securities and Exchange Act (the "Williams Act") and in which Medicorp has counterclaimed alleging violations of the same statute by Humana.

* * *

On December 21, 1977, Trans World Airways (TWA) and its wholly owned subsidiary, Hilton International Co. (Hilton), announced a competing partial tender offer which also will expire January 10, 1978, unless extended. * * *

On December 27, 1977, Humana moved by Order to Show Cause to file a second amended and supplemental complaint to its action against Medicorp to add TWA and Hilton as defendants; to state new causes of action relating to the TWA–Hilton competitive offer; and to request injunctive relief against TWA and Hilton. * * *

Medicorp opposes the motion on the grounds that Humana does not have standing to sue for violations of the Williams Act by a competing offeror. Its principal reliance is placed on Piper v. Chris–Craft Industries, 430 U.S. 1 (1977). *Piper* shattered the nearly universal holdings of lower courts that competing tender offerors had standing to sue each other for damages under the Williams Act. In *Piper,* Chris–Craft, a losing tender offeror in a consummated tender offer battle, sued both its competing tender offeror and target management for damages, claiming violations of the Williams Act in connection with the tender offer battle. Holding that the primary, if not exclusive, purpose of the Williams Act was to protect shareholders of the target company, the Supreme Court held that a tender offeror did not have standing to sue for damages under the Act. * * *

The question at hand is whether, in the light of *Piper,* an offeror (Humana) has standing to sue a competing offeror (TWA and Hilton) for injunctive relief. I conclude that it does. Analysis of *Piper* requires determining not only what it decided but what it did not decide.

At footnote 33, Chief Justice Burger wrote:

> "We intimate no view upon whether as a general proposition a suit in equity for injunctive relief, as distinguished from an action for

damages, would lie in favor of a tender offeror under either § 14(e) or Rule 10b-6."

Of course, the footnote merely leaves the question open, and one must look for guidance elsewhere as to whether a ruling that an offeror has standing to sue a competing offeror for *injunctive* relief would be consistent with *Piper*.

A large body of material in *Piper* itself points toward allowance of standing when the remedy sought is injunctive relief. First, Chief Justice Burger exercised scrupulous care to use the word "damages" whenever he described the "narrow" issue before the court. Second, the opinion of the Court cites with approval Judge Friendly's observation in Electronic Specialty Co. Inc. v. International Controls Corp., that "in corporate control contests the stage of preliminary *injunctive* relief, rather than post-contest lawsuits, 'is the time when relief can best be given' ". At footnote 26, the opinion states in its own language that " * * * injunctive relief at an earlier stage of the context is apt to be the most efficacious form of remedy." These comments apply to the case at hand. The proposal is in its primary stages. If Humana's allegations that TWA and Hilton have violated the Williams Act are ever to be effectively explored, they must be explored now, since Medicorp's shareholders must have information upon which to act before the expiration of both offers on January 10th.

At least one passage in *Piper* appears affirmatively to suggest that construing the Williams Act to allow a tender offeror the implied right to sue for injunctive relief would be appropriate even though an implied right to sue for damages does not exist. At page 41, the court states:

> "In short, we conclude that shareholder protection, if enhanced at all by damages awards such as Chris-Craft contends for, can more directly be achieved with other, less drastic means more closely tailored to the precise congressional goal underlying the Williams Act."

No remedy can be more "closely tailored" to the needs of the occasion than injunctive relief, when appropriate. The very purpose of injunctive relief is to afford a remedy precisely contoured to the requirements of the situation.

Moreover, as Judge Weinfeld observed in Applied Digital Data Systems v. Milgo Electronic, 425 F.Supp. 1145, 1152 (S.D.N.Y.1977) "allowing [an offeror] to maintain this suit not only provides a remedy to the wronged offeror, but also serves to effectuate the broader purposes of the Williams Act by putting the tools for enforcement of its fair-play provisions into the hands of those most likely and able to make use of them."

The majority opinion in *Piper* does not render consideration of this factor inappropriate. Justice Stevens, dissenting, criticized the court's decision because in his view it excluded tender offerors whom he described as "the persons most interested in effective enforcement." The majority opinion answered this point (at footnote 28), saying "our precise holding disposes of many observations made in dissent. Thus, the argument with respect to the 'exclusion' from standing for 'persons most interested in effective enforcement,' is simply unwarranted in light of today's narrow holding." We read the footnote to mean that tender offerors, described by Justice Stevens as "the persons most interested in effective enforcement" are not necessarily excluded from standing in cases not covered by *Piper's* "narrow holding" and that it is appropriate to consider a tender offeror's particular interest in effective enforcement in determining whether he should be accorded standing to sue for injunctive relief.

* * *

These general observations are strengthened in the case at hand by virtue of the particular allegations made and relief sought. For example, it is alleged that TWA–Hilton and Medicorp "have sought unlawfully to deprive Medicorp public shareholders of a fair opportunity to evaluate and choose whether to accept the Humana offer," that defendants now seek to "force Medicorp shareholders to make an immediate investment decision regarding such competing offer" in violation of the securities laws "contrary to the interest of Medicorp and its shareholders," and "the effect of the competing offer is to require Medicorp shareholders to make an investment decision now concerning the purported value of the [TWA and/or Hilton] equity securities [which TWA announced would be used to purchase remaining Medicorp shares after the consummation of its tender offer] and their desirability as an investment compared with the securities to be offered by Humana even though these equity securities have not been registered" with the result that the stockholders have no information about the equity securities which may be included in such a proposed package. The complaint alleges also that various "sensitive payments" have been made by TWA, Hilton or its affiliate Canteen, of such a nature that the facts relating to the payments are material to the decision which a Medicorp shareholder is called upon to make: that is whether to entrust his future to the TWA management or not.

In sum, the thrust of the complaint is to request increased disclosure of the terms of the TWA offer and the character of the TWA management so that Medicorp stockholders may more intelligently choose between the competing Humana and TWA–Hilton offers. Of course, the amended and supplemental complaint furthers Humana's interest as well but the critical factor is not whether Humana may be benefited by the suit but whether the stockholders of the target company would be benefited if the allegations of the complaint are proven to be true and the relief requested is granted. If so the purposes of the Act will be furthered. This is the test by which a tender offeror's right to sue for injunctive relief must be determined; and by this test Humana does have such standing.

In subsequent proceedings in the *Humana* case, the court held that when the target company, in press releases and letters to shareholders, described the tender offer as "inadequate" and "not in the best interests of" the shareholders, "it was obligated to furnish its stockholders with all the information it had from Humana so that the stockholders would be sufficiently informed to react intelligently to the offer and would not be unfairly influenced by management's subjective presentation." The court enjoined the target company from disseminating "materially false and misleading" statements about the tender offer. CCH Fed.Sec.L.Rep. ¶ 96,286 (S.D.N.Y.1978).

The statements made by the management of the target company may be designed not only to discourage shareholders from tendering their shares, but also to discourage the bidder from continuing its offer. If management succeeds in this second objective by means of misleading statements, does it incur any liability to its shareholders under § 14(e) for depriving them of an opportunity to tender their shares?

As pointed out at p. 776 above, the SEC has adopted Rule 14d–10, which declares that it is a manipulative and deceptive device to make a tender offer without making it available to all holders of the class of shares involved. In POLAROID v. DISNEY, 862 F.2d 987 (3d Cir.1988), the court addressed the availability of an implied private right of action for violation of the "all holders" rule. The court reasoned that "[i]n light of the judicial construction of Rule 10b–5 and *Borak,* it is reasonable to conclude that Congress passed the Williams Act with an understanding that courts would construe the Act as creating private remedies that would enforce the provisions of the Act effectively." However, the court explained that "the All Holders Rule creates a private right of action *for shareholders.* There is no evidence, however, that it creates a private right of action for the target corporation." On that issue, the court concluded:

> [T]he sole purpose of the Williams Act is to protect target company shareholders. In raising a claim under the Williams Act, Polaroid is therefore seeking to vindicate not its own rights but the rights of its shareholders. * * * [T]he inherent conflicts of interest in litigation under the All Holders Rule may take a corporation a poor representative of shareholder interests. * * * *
>
> The first potential conflict is between those shareholders who view litigation to enjoin a tender offer as adversely affecting their opportunity to collect on the tender offer premium and those shareholders who are cut out of the tender offer and thus may want to see it defeated. Even though some shareholders are disadvantaged by their exclusion from the tender offer, a great majority of shareholders will often benefit from the offer. A corporation is thus an uncertain representative for the interests of the disadvantaged shareholders, as it may have an eye to protecting the interests of the majority. This undermines the basis for *jus tertii* standing—that the *jus tertii* advocate will vigorously assert the interests of the right-holder.
>
> The second conflict of interest that may interfere with the proper conduct of the litigation in some cases is that between the management of a corporation and its shareholders. Even shareholders injured by

their exclusion from a tender offer may sometimes profit handsomely from the tender offer and be injured by litigation that defeats it. The market price of the stock of a corporation jumps skyward within minutes after a credible tender offer is made. Excluded holders of the security can thus profit from the tender offer by selling their shares at the market price to third parties. If the excluded holders fail to sell to third parties, they still have the shares they started out with when the tender offer closes; in this sense they are no worse off than if there had been no tender offer. Indeed, they may be better off since they now have a suit for damages against the tender offeror who excluded them from the tender offer.

While shareholders (including those excluded from the offer) thus have a reason to react favorably to many tender offers, those in control of the target corporation have a natural incentive to resist a corporate takeover. Unless protected by "golden parachutes" guaranteeing them a lucrative exit from corporate affairs, the corporation's top officers may suffer a substantial loss in future earnings if the tender offer is successful. As Polaroid's home state of Delaware has recognized, measures adopted to ward off a takeover raise "the omnipresent specter that a board may be acting primarily in its own interests, rather than those of the corporation and its shareholders . . ." *Unocal,* 493 A.2d at 954.

* * *

For all the foregoing reasons, it would appear that Polaroid does not fit within the confines of the associational standing *jus tertii* doctrine. We nonetheless consider a number of possible counterarguments to the conclusion that a target corporation does not have *jus tertii* standing to assert the interests of its shareholders under the All Holders Rule.

* * * The best argument for allowing target corporations standing to sue under the All Holders Rule may thus be that there is no reason to distinguish All Holders Rule standing from misrepresentation standing. There is, however, a reason to draw this distinction. The bar against misrepresentation is meant to protect all shareholders. Shareholder litigation under the aegis of the corporation makes greater sense in this context, where the class of persons whose rights the corporation is vindicating constitutes all of its shareholders. The All Holders Rule, by contrast, protects what are likely to be only a minority of shareholders. Moreover, it may be more difficult to detect fraud than to detect violations of the All Holders Rule, and the possibility of irreparable harm may be greater in the case of fraud because of the greater difficulty in computing monetary loss. The need for target corporation standing in the fraud context may thus be greater than in the context of the All Holders Rule. Finally, the rule that target corporations have standing to sue for fraud was adopted by this Court without discussion; the Court simply reached the merits in such suits. While we do not question the continued efficacy of target corporation standing in fraud suits, the manner in which the rule was adopted

should make us hesitant to construe it as definitively settling the question of target corporation standing outside of the fraud context.

> We therefore hold that, although the All Holders Rule creates a private right of action enabling injured shareholders to sue a tender offeror whose offer violates the Rule, a target corporation has no standing to sue under the Rule. We thus affirm the district court's refusal to grant a preliminary injunction on the basis of Polaroid's All Holders Rule claim. . . .

In another part of the opinion, the court upheld the validity of the all holders rule. See p. 806 below.

LEWIS v. McGRAW

619 F.2d 192 (2d Cir.1980).

Before KAUFMAN, CHIEF JUDGE, MESKILL, CIRCUIT JUDGE, and BRIEANT, DISTRICT JUDGE.

PER CURIAM.

The instant action is a consolidation of five similar lawsuits brought on behalf of McGraw–Hill, Inc. stockholders, alleging that McGraw–Hill and its directors made false statements of material facts in response to two proposals of the American Express Company for the acquisition of substantial amounts of McGraw–Hill stock. The issue before us is whether shareholders may maintain a cause of action for damages under the Williams Act, where they concede that no tender offer has been made to them. We conclude that they may not.

I

On January 8, 1979, American Express proposed to McGraw–Hill what plaintiff describes as a "friendly business combination" of the two companies through payment by American Express of $34 in cash for each McGraw–Hill share. Alternatively, American Express indicated its willingness to acquire 49% of McGraw–Hill's shares for cash or a combination of cash and securities. McGraw–Hill common stock was trading at $26 per share immediately prior to the announcement. On January 15, 1979, McGraw–Hill announced that its Board of Directors had rejected the proposal and made public a letter to American Express characterizing the offer as "reckless," "illegal," and "improper." The following day, American Express filed Schedule 14D–1 with the Securities and Exchange Commission concerning its intention to make a cash tender offer for any and all of McGraw–Hill's stock.

The proposed offer was never made, however, for on January 29, American Express retracted its earlier announcement, and in its place submitted a new proposal to the McGraw–Hill board. This offer, at a price of $40 per share, would not become effective unless McGraw–Hill's incumbent management agreed not to oppose it by "propaganda, lobbying, or litigation." The offer was rejected by the McGraw-Hill board two days later, and expired, by its own terms, on March 1.

Plaintiffs' consolidated, amended complaint charges that:

> Defendants announced publicly that the tender offer price of $40 per share was inadequate, although they knew that the price * * * was fair
>
> * * *
>
> Defendants, in resisting the AMEXCO [American Express Company] tender offer [*sic*], challenged the integrity and honesty of AMEXCO (by indicating that AMEXCO had illegally complied with the Arab boycott), publicly challenged the legality of the tender offer (by indicating that the federal Bank Holding Company [Act] may preclude the tender offer), and publicly stated that the tender offer somehow threatened freedom of expression under the First Amendment of the Constitution (by stating that since the McGraw-Hill [*sic*] was engaged in publishing, its independence would be smothered by a large financial institution such as AMEXCO).

These statements, as well as McGraw-Hill's characterization of the initial proposal as "reckless," "illegal," and "improper," are alleged to be false, as evidenced by the fact that, some months earlier, McGraw-Hill had advised American Express that it considered it to be a proper and desirable merger partner.

Plaintiffs concede that no tender offer ever took place—that no McGraw-Hill shareholder was ever in a position to offer his shares to American Express at a stated price. The $34 proposal was withdrawn before it became effective, and was replaced with a $40 proposal that could have ripened into an offer only upon the acquiescence of the McGraw-Hill board. Nonetheless, plaintiffs claim, "had defendants provided * * * shareholders and the public with complete and truthful information about AMEXCO and its proposed tender offer (i.e. that $40 per share was a fair price, and that AMEXCO was a company with which defendants themselves had wanted to merge), the AMEXCO tender offer would have been consummated." Accordingly, they each seek damages from the company and its directors for the difference between the $40 proposed tender price, and the $25 price to which the stock returned after the expiration of the American Express proposal.

Judge Motley dismissed the consolidated amended complaint pursuant to Fed.R.Civ.P. 12, noting that "plaintiffs fail to allege that McGraw-Hill stockholders, or anyone else for that matter, in fact relied upon the alleged misrepresentations or omissions. While plaintiffs do allege deception on the part of defendants, plaintiffs do not allege that anyone was deceived or that anyone acted in reliance upon the alleged deception to their detriment." Having found plaintiffs' federal claim critically insufficient, the district court dismissed plaintiffs' pendent state claims for want of jurisdiction.

II

The complaint was properly dismissed. Section 14(e) of the Williams Act has as its "sole purpose" the "protection of investors who are confronted with a tender offer." Piper v. Chris-Craft Industries, 430 U.S. 1, 35 (1977). It is designed "to ensure that [investors] will not be required to respond [to a tender offer] without adequate information." Rondeau v. Mosinee Paper Corp., 422 U.S. 49, 58 (1975). Accordingly, one element of a cause of action under § 14(e) is a showing "that there was misrepresentation upon which the target corporation shareholders *relied.*"[2] In the instant case, the target's shareholders simply could not have relied upon McGraw-Hill's statements, whether true or false, since they were never given an opportunity to tender their shares.

Plaintiffs do not contest this indisputable fact, but rather rest upon cases holding that reliance may sometimes be presumed from a showing of materiality. Mills v. Electric Auto-Lite Co.; Affiliated Ute Citizens v. United States. These cases, however, in presuming reliance, did not abolish it as an element of the cause of action. Rather, they held that in cases in which reliance is possible, and even likely, but is unduly burdensome to prove, the resulting doubt would be resolved in favor of the class the statute was designed to protect. We therefore presume reliance only "where it is logical" to do so. Here, where no reliance was possible under any imaginable set of facts, such a presumption would be illogical in the extreme.

We note in closing that our holding today does not place statements made on the eve of a tender offer by target or tendering companies wholly outside the scope of the Williams Act. On the contrary, where the offer ultimately becomes effective, and reliance can be demonstrated or presumed, such statements may well be made "in connection with a tender offer" as required by § 14(e). Otherwise, either party would be free to disseminate misinformation up to the effective date of the tender offer, thus defeating in substantial part the very purpose of the Act—informed decisionmaking by shareholders. Injunctive relief, moreover, may be available to restrain or correct misleading statements made during the period preceding a tender offer where it appears that such an offer is likely, and that reliance upon the statements at issue is probable under the circumstances. Finally, we must bear in mind that many of the wrongs alleged in this complaint

2. We note that the element of reliance has been held "irrelevant" to a cause of action under Rule 10b-5, where material misstatements can be shown to have caused the issuance of securities which, in turn, resulted in losses to plaintiff purchasers. Shores v. Sklar, 610 F.2d 235 (5th Cir. 1980). In *Shores,* plaintiffs could plausibly claim that if defendants had disclosed the truth concerning the financial condition of the issuer, the bond issue in question would never have been marketed. In the case at bar, by contrast, plaintiffs must contend that but for the alleged misstatements and omissions on the part of defendants, American Express would have proceeded with a hostile tender offer, over the opposition of McGraw-Hill. Such a scenario stretches the principle of causation into the realm of mere speculation, for it depends upon proof of an offer that, for all that appears here, American Express never even contemplated.

may be recast as state law claims for breach of the fiduciary duties owed to shareholders by directors. Indeed, we note that several plaintiffs have commenced state court actions arising out of the abortive transactions at issue here. In this case, however, since American Express never made its proposed offer to the shareholders of McGraw-Hill, plaintiffs cannot state a cause of action for alleged misstatements under the Williams Act.

In addition to making statements designed to discourage a tender offer, the management of the target company may also enter into transactions designed to raise the price of its stock and thus make the tender offer less attractive to shareholders. The question arose whether such transactions could be deemed to constitute "manipulative acts or practices" within the meaning of § 14(e). Contested tender offers present similar opportunities for manipulation. The following decision relates to one of the most notorious of such incidents, and indicates the difficulty of invoking the prohibitions against manipulation in light of Supreme Court decisions.

CRANE CO. v. AMERICAN-STANDARD INC.

603 F.2d 244 (2d Cir.1979).

Before: KAUFMAN, CHIEF JUDGE, SMITH and VAN GRAAFEILAND, CIRCUIT JUDGES.

SMITH, CIRCUIT JUDGE:

This is an appeal from a judgment entered in the United States District Court for the Southern District of New York, in favor of defendants American Standard, Inc. ("Standard") and Blyth & Company ("Blyth"), in a securities action brought by Crane Company ("Crane") more than ten years ago. We affirm in part, reverse in part and remand.

This appeal, nine years after our decision in Crane Co. v. Westinghouse Air Brake Co., 419 F.2d 787 (2d Cir.1969), ("*Crane I*"), and five years after our decision in Crane Co. v. American Standard, Inc., 490 F.2d 332 (2d Cir.1973) ("*Crane II*"), follows the second trial on the merits in this action. Although the "Brobdingnagian procedural imbroglio" which delayed this case for so long has been resolved, we are again confronted with the issue which faced us in *Crane I,* whether Crane has standing to bring this action under §§ 9(e) and 10(b) of the Securities Exchange Act of 1934 ("the 1934 Act"). The district court held, contrary to our decision in *Crane I,* that Crane lacks standing.

* * *

The controversy arose from a battle between Crane and Standard for control of Westinghouse Air Brake Company ("Air Brake"). Crane began making substantial purchases of Air Brake stock in 1967. Air

Brake's management informed Crane that their company was not interested in the possibility of merger with Crane. Crane, however, continued to purchase stock on the open market. Air Brake responded by raising the cumulative vote necessary to obtain representation on its board of directors. In late 1967, Blyth, Standard's investment banker, offered Standard's assistance to Air Brake in fending off Crane's takeover efforts.

On February 20, 1968, when Air Brake stock was selling on the New York Stock Exchange ("NYSE") at about $36 per share, Crane filed its 14–B statements with the SEC declaring its intention to solicit proxies for the election of Air Brake directors. Shortly thereafter, Air Brake's directors approved a merger of Air Brake into Standard on the basis of an exchange of one share of Standard convertible preferred stock worth about $100 for every two shares of Air Brake stock. The merger required approval of a majority of the outstanding Air Brake shares in order to be effected. Air Brake stock rose to $44 on the NYSE after announcement of the merger agreement.

Crane countered by making a tender offer of subordinated debentures with face value of $50 for each share of Air Brake stock. This offer was to expire at 5:00 p.m. on April 19, 1968. Air Brake stock rose to about $49 on April 10, shortly after the tender offer was announced. By April 18, however, the stock price had fallen to about $45.

On April 19, the final day of Crane's original offer, Air Brake stock opened at $45.25. During the course of that day, Standard, acting through Blyth, purchased 82,400 shares on the open market in cash transactions at increasing prices up to $60, with an average price of $49.08 per share. But on that same day, Standard made an undisclosed, off-the-market sale of 100,000 shares to Investors Diversified Services, Inc. at $44.50 and a sale of 20,000 shares on the NYSE to Dillon, Read & Co., Inc. at $44.875.

Crane extended its tender offer several times, the last extension expiring on May 24, 1968. Its total holding of Air Brake stock, from the tender offer and its open market purchases, amounted to 1,480,623 shares, or 32.2% of Air Brake's outstanding stock.

Meanwhile, at a May 16 stockholders' meeting, 2,903,869 shares of Air Brake were voted in favor of the merger with Standard and 1,180,298 shares against. The affirmative vote was 602,290 shares more than the 2,301,579 shares which constituted a majority of the outstanding stock and which were needed to approve the merger. The merger became effective on June 7, 1968, at which time Crane's interest in Air Brake was converted into 740,311 shares of Standard convertible preferred stock. On June 13, under threat of an antitrust action to be brought by Standard, Crane sold all but 10,000 of these preferred shares.

Crane I and II

On April 17, 1968, Crane brought suit claiming that Air Brake had made misrepresentations in its proxy statement soliciting votes in favor of the merger. On May 6, Crane filed a second action contending that Standard and Blyth had engaged in fraud and market manipulation in violation of §§ 9, 10 and 14 of the 1934 Act, Rules 10b–5 and 10b–6, and Regulation 14A. These actions, both of which sought equitable relief, were consolidated and tried before Judge Sylvester J. Ryan, who dismissed the consolidated complaint.

This court, in *Crane I,* affirmed part of Judge Ryan's judgment, but we reversed his dismissal of the fraud and market manipulation claims. We held that (1) Crane had standing to sue under §§ 9 and 10(b) of the 1934 Act; (2) Standard had violated §§ 9(a)(2) by engaging in "massive buying [of Air Brake stock] on April 19, coupled with its concealed sales," with the purpose and effect of "deter[ring] Air Brake shareholders from tendering to Crane," thereby "inducing Crane to become a seller," because of antitrust considerations; and (3) Standard had violated § 10(b) and Rule 10b–5 by its failure to disclose its manipulative activities in connection with its transactions in Air Brake stock. We remanded the action to the district court, stating: "The manipulation *may* be found to have deprived Crane of success in its tender offer in the free market to which it was entitled * * *."

* * *

Standing to Sue

A. Decision on Remand

The trial on remand took place before Judge Ward in April and May of 1976. Before the district court had rendered a decision, however, the Supreme Court announced its opinion in Piper v. Chris–Craft Industries, Inc., 430 U.S. 1 (1977), in which it held that "a tender offeror, suing in its capacity as a takeover bidder, does not have standing to sue for damages under § 14(e)." As a result, the district court concluded that the circumstances presented an exception to the general rule that "the lower court simply carries out a mandate as it is received without reexamination." The district court therefore reconsidered the question of standing, previously decided in *Crane I,* in addition to the question whether Crane had demonstrated that it was entitled to any relief. After carefully considering the impact of *Piper,* the district court concluded that "[a]lthough the case is not directly analogous, the reasoning of [*Piper*] appears to preclude suit by Crane."

* * *

C. Section 10(b) and Rule 10b–5

In *Piper,* the Supreme Court held that the plaintiff, "as a defeated tender offeror, has no implied cause of action for damages under § 14(e)" of the 1934 Act. A number of factors compel the conclusion that the same result is required under § 10(b).

A comparison of the statutory provisions at issue here and in *Piper* suggests that Crane does not have standing. As this court previously has observed, the operative language of Rule 10b–5 and § 14(e) is substantially identical. The primary difference is that Rule 10b–5 applies generally to activities "in connection with the purchase or sale of any security," whereas § 14(e) deals specifically with tender offers. This difference suggests that we should be less willing to imply a cause of action for a defeated offeror under the general provisions of Rule 10b–5 than under § 14(e). We stated in *Crane I* that the addition to the 1934 Act of § 14(e) "should serve to resolve any doubts about standing in the tender offer cases. * * *" Although we were in error as to the way in which those doubts would be resolved, we adhere to our original belief that § 14(e) presented a stronger argument for standing than does Rule 10b–5.

Application of the analysis used by the Supreme Court in *Piper* also leads to the conclusion that Crane lacks standing under § 10(b) and Rule 10b–5. * * *

It is clear that Crane does not come before this court as a defrauded investor seeking redress. Crane, as an investor in Air Brake, made a profit of about $10 million when it sold the Standard preferred stock which it received in the merger. Its grievance against Standard arises from actions which it contends prevented it, as a tender offeror, from acquiring control of Air Brake. In that role, Crane does not present itself to us as a member of the class intended to be protected by § 10(b) and Rule 10b–5. Therefore, a private right of action cannot be implied in its favor.

* * *

D. Section 9(e)

Unlike § 10(b), § 9(e) establishes an express cause of action for persons injured by violations of its provisions. That cause of action exists in favor of "any person who shall purchase or sell any security at a price which was affected by such act or transactions. * * *"

The district court based its determination that Crane lacked standing under 9(e) on the Supreme Court's discussion in *Piper* of the relationship of § 9 to Chris–Craft's claim under Rule 10b–6. The Court noted there that § 9 focused upon "the amount actually paid by an investor for stock that had been the subject of manipulative activity." Because Chris–Craft did not claim to be a "hoodwinked investor" seeking recovery of "an improper premium" paid for Piper stock, the Court held that it had no claim under Rule 10b–6. The district court here held that *Piper* mandated the same result for Crane's § 9 claim.

Although we agree that § 9, read in the light of *Piper*, does not provide a cause of action for Crane, we reach that conclusion by a path different from that followed by the district court. The factual circumstances present here and the legal claim advanced by Crane are not identical to those in *Piper*. The cause of action expressly established by

§ 9(e) runs in favor of both those who purchase *and sell* stock at a price affected by a manipulative transaction. In *Piper,* Chris–Craft in fact had not sold the Piper stock that it had purchased previously. Thus it was not necessary that the Court consider a seller's § 9 cause of action. Crane contended, however, and we held in *Crane I,* that "Standard's actions had the intended and inevitable effect of inducing Crane to become a seller within the meaning of section 9(a)(2) * * *." We must determine, therefore, whether Crane's forced sale occurred "at a price which was affected by" Standard's manipulative transactions, so as to bring Crane within the scope of the protection provided by § 9(e). In light of the Supreme Court's guidance in *Piper,* we conclude that Crane has not alleged and could not demonstrate that it satisfied this requirement.

* * *

Crane suggests that either of two transactions might be viewed as the sale of a security within the terms of § 9(e). The first is the exchange of Air Brake common stock for Standard preferred stock; the second is Crane's sale of the Standard preferred stock on the NYSE. Because we conclude that neither of these transactions took place at a price affected by Standard's manipulation of Air Brake common stock, we need not decide which, if either, could constitute a sale for the purposes of § 9(e).

The "price" at which Crane "sold" its Air Brake common stock was established by the terms of the merger agreement between Air Brake and Standard. This agreement was publicly announced on March 4, 1968, more than one month before Standard engaged in its manipulation of Air Brake common stock. The exchange terms of the merger were not amended thereafter. Crane received 740,311 shares of Standard preferred stock in exchange for its 1,480,623 shares of Air Brake common, in accordance with the terms announced on March 4. It is clear that the price at which Crane "sold" the Air Brake stock was not in any way affected by the manipulation which occurred after the terms of the exchange had been established.

Crane similarly has not alleged or established that the price at which it later sold the Standard preferred stock was in any way affected by the manipulation. Crane sold most of that stock on the NYSE on June 13, 1968 at a price of $104.25 per share, the equivalent of $52.125 per original share of Air Brake common. This was an ordinary open-market transaction, notable only for being, as of that date, the largest single transaction (in dollar volume) in the history of the NYSE. Crane has not suggested that the manipulation of Air Brake common in April, 1968 had any effect on the price at which Standard preferred sold in June, 1968, nor does the record contain proof of such effect.

It might be argued that *any* price for the Standard preferred was in a sense an effect of the manipulation because without the manipulation (assuming, *arguendo,* that Crane had proved that the manipulation caused the defeat of its offer) the merger would not have been approved and the preferred stock would never have been issued. But § 9 was not intended to deal with such a generalized complaint. Rather, Congress sought "to give to investors markets where prices may be established by the free and honest balancing of investment demand with investment supply." Crane has not alleged that the market in Standard preferred was not such a free and honest market.

Crane's claim then is not that the prevailing price in the markets in which it bought or sold a security was affected by any manipulative act or transaction. What it seeks to recover is the "control premium" which would have accrued to it had it obtained sufficient Air Brake stock to block the merger and gain control of Air Brake. Crane's appellate brief argues, "the value of that control would have greatly exceeded the price Crane received for its minority position in Standard * * *." Such a claim for the loss of an opportunity to control a target corporation is not within the ambit of the express civil remedy provided in § 9(e).

In the light of *Piper,* we must conclude that the district court was correct in dismissing Crane's § 9(e) claim.

In the following decision the Supreme Court narrowed even further the availability of a remedy to redress manipulative conduct.

SCHREIBER v. BURLINGTON NORTHERN

472 U.S. 1 (1985).

CHIEF JUSTICE BURGER delivered the opinion of the Court.

We granted certiorari to resolve a conflict in the Circuits over whether misrepresentation or nondisclosure is a necessary element of a violation of § 14(e) of the Securities Exchange Act of 1934.

I

On December 21, 1982, Burlington Northern, Inc., made a hostile tender offer for El Paso Gas Co. Through a wholly owned subsidiary, Burlington proposed to purchase 25.1 million El Paso shares at $24 per share. Burlington reserved the right to terminate the offer if any of several specified events occurred. El Paso management initially opposed the takeover, but its shareholders responded favorably, fully subscribing the offer by the December 30, 1982 deadline.

Burlington did not accept those tendered shares: instead, after negotiations with El Paso management, Burlington announced on January 10, 1983, the terms of a new and friendly takeover agreement. Pursuant to the new agreement, Burlington undertook, *inter alia,* to (1) rescind the December tender offer, (2) purchase 4,166,667 shares from El Paso at $24 per share, (3) substitute a new tender offer for only 21 million shares at $24 per share, (4) provide procedural protections against a squeeze-out merger [1] of the remaining El Paso shareholders, and (5) recognize "golden parachute" [2] contracts between El Paso and four of its senior officers. By February 8, more than 40 million shares were tendered in response to Burlington's January offer, and the takeover was completed.

The rescission of the first tender offer caused a diminished payment to those shareholders who had tendered during the first offer. The January offer was greatly oversubscribed and consequently those shareholders who retendered were subject to substantial proration. Petitioner Barbara Schreiber filed suit on behalf of herself and similarly situated shareholders, alleging that Burlington, El Paso, and members of El Paso's board violated § 14(e)'s prohibition of "fraudulent, deceptive or manipulative acts or practices * * * in connection with any tender offer." She claimed that Burlington's withdrawal of the December tender offer coupled with the substitution of the January tender offer was a "manipulative" distortion of the market for El Paso stock. Schreiber also alleged that Burlington violated § 14(e) by failing in the January offer to disclose the "golden parachutes" offered to four of El Paso's managers. She claims that this January nondisclosure was a deceptive act forbidden by § 14(e).

The District Court dismissed the suit for failure to state a claim. The District Court reasoned that the alleged manipulation did not involve a misrepresentation, and so did not violate § 14(e). The District Court relied on the fact that in cases involving alleged violations of § 10(b) of the Securities Exchange Act, this Court has required misrepresentation for there to be a "manipulative" violation of the section.

The Court of Appeals for the Third Circuit affirmed. * * *

1. A "squeeze-out" merger occurs when Corporation A, which holds a controlling interest in Corporation B, uses its control to merge B into itself or into a wholly owned subsidiary. The minority shareholders in Corporation B are, in effect, forced to sell their stock. The procedural protection provided in the agreement between El Paso and Burlington required the approval of non-Burlington members of El Paso's board of directors before a squeeze-out merger could proceed. Burlington eventually purchased all the remaining shares of El Paso for $12 cash and one quarter share of Burlington preferred stock per share. The parties dispute whether this consideration was equal to that paid to those tendering during the January tender offer.

2. Petitioner alleged in her complaint that respondent Burlington failed to disclose that four officers of El Paso had entered into "golden parachute" agreements with El Paso for "extended employment benefits in the event El Paso should be taken over, which benefits would give them millions of dollars of extra compensation." The term "golden parachute" refers generally to agreements between a corporation and its top officers which guarantee those officers continued employment, payment of a lump sum, or other benefits in the event of a change of corporate ownership. As described in the Schedule 14D–9 filed by El Paso with the Commission on January 12, 1983, El Paso entered into "employment agreements" with two of its officers for a period of not less than five years, and with two other officers for a period of three years. The Schedule 14D–9 also disclosed that El Paso's Deferred Compensation Plan had been amended "to provide that for the purposes of such Plan a participant shall be deemed to have retired at the instance of the Company if his duties as a director, officer or employee of the Company have been diminished or curtailed by the Company in any material respect."

II

A

We are asked in this case to interpret § 14(e) of the Securities Exchange Act. * * * Petitioner reads the phrase "fraudulent, deceptive or manipulative acts or practices" to include acts which, although fully disclosed, "artificially" affect the price of the takeover target's stock. Petitioner's interpretation relies on the belief that § 14(e) is directed at purposes broader than providing full and true information to investors.

Petitioner's reading of the term "manipulative" conflicts with the normal meaning of the term. We have held in the context of an alleged violation of § 10(b) of the Securities Exchange Act:

> "Use of the word 'manipulative' is especially significant. It is and was virtually a term of art when used in connection with the securities markets. It connotes intentional or willful conduct *designed to deceive or defraud* investors by controlling or artificially affecting the price of securities." Ernst & Ernst v. Hochfelder, 425 U.S. 185, 199 (1976) (emphasis added).

* * *

She argues, however, that the term manipulative takes on a meaning in § 14(e) that is different from the meaning it has in § 10(b). Petitioner claims that the use of the disjunctive "or" in § 14(e) implies that acts need not be deceptive or fraudulent to be manipulative. But Congress used the phrase "manipulative or deceptive" in § 10(b) as well, and we have interpreted "manipulative" in that context to require misrepresentation. Moreover, it is a " 'familiar principle of statutory construction that words grouped in a list should be given related meaning.' " All three species of misconduct, i.e., "fraudulent, deceptive or manipulative," listed by Congress are directed at failures to disclose. The use of the term "manipulative" provides emphasis and guidance to those who must determine which types of acts are reached by the statute; it does not suggest a deviation from the section's facial and primary concern with disclosure or Congressional concern with disclosure which is the core of the Act.

B

Our conclusion that "manipulative" acts under § 14(e) require misrepresentation or nondisclosure is buttressed by the purpose and legislative history of the provision. Section 14(e) was originally added to the Securities Exchange Act as part of the Williams Act. "The purpose of the Williams Act is to insure that public shareholders who are confronted by a cash tender offer for their stock will not be required to respond without adequate information." Rondeau v. Mosinee Paper Corp., 422 U.S. 49, 58 (1975).

It is clear that Congress relied primarily on disclosure to implement the purpose of the Williams Act. * * *

The expressed legislative intent was to preserve a neutral setting in which the contenders could fully present their arguments.

* * *

To implement this objective, the Williams Act added §§ 13(d), 13(e), 14(d), 14(e), and 14(f) to the Securities Exchange Act. Some relate to disclosure; §§ 13(d), 14(d) and 14(f) all add specific registration and disclosure provisions. Others—§§ 13(e) and 14(d)—require or prohibit certain acts so that investors will possess additional time within which to take advantage of the disclosed information.

Section 14(e) adds a "broad antifraud prohibition," modeled on the antifraud provisions of § 10(b) of the Act and Rule 10b–5. It supplements the more precise disclosure provisions found elsewhere in the Williams Act, while requiring disclosure more explicitly addressed to the tender offer context than that required by § 10(b).

While legislative history specifically concerning § 14(e) is sparse, the House and Senate Reports discuss the role of § 14(e). Describing § 14(e) as regulating "fraudulent transactions," and stating the thrust of the section:

> "This provision would affirm the fact that the persons engaged in making or opposing tender offers or otherwise seeking to influence the decision of investors or the outcome of the tender offer are under an obligation to make *full disclosure* of material information to those with whom they deal."

Nowhere in the legislative history is there the slightest suggestion that § 14(e) serves any purpose other than disclosure,[11] or that the term "manipulative" should be read as an invitation to the courts to oversee the substantive fairness of tender offers; the quality of any offer is a matter for the marketplace.

To adopt the reading of the term "manipulative" urged by petitioner would not only be unwarranted in light of the legislative purpose but would be at odds with it. Inviting judges to read the term "manipulative" with their own sense of what constitutes "unfair" or "artificial" conduct would inject uncertainty into the tender offer process. An essential piece of information—whether the court would deem the fully disclosed actions of one side or the other to be "manipulative"—would not be available until after the tender offer had closed. This uncertain-

11. The Act was amended in 1970, and Congress added to § 14(e) the sentence, "The Commission shall, for the purposes of this subsection, by rules and regulations define, and prescribe means reasonably designed to prevent, such acts and practices as are fraudulent, deceptive, or manipulative." Petitioner argues that this phrase would be pointless if § 14(e) was concerned with disclosure only.

We disagree. In adding the 1970 amendment, Congress simply provided a mechanism for defining and guarding against those acts and practices which involve material misrepresentation or nondisclosure. The amendment gives the Securities and Exchange Commission latitude to regulate nondeceptive activities as a "reasonably designed" means of preventing manipulative acts, without suggesting any change in the meaning of the term "manipulative" itself.

ty would directly contradict the expressed Congressional desire to give investors full information.

* * *

C

We hold that the term "manipulative" as used in § 14(e) requires misrepresentation or nondisclosure. It connotes "conduct designed to deceive or defraud investors by controlling or artificially affecting the price of securities." Without misrepresentation or nondisclosure, § 14(e) has not been violated.

Applying that definition to this case, we hold that the actions of respondents were not manipulative. The amended complaint fails to allege that the cancellation of the first tender offer was accompanied by any misrepresentation, nondisclosure or deception. The District Court correctly found, "All activity of the defendants that could have conceivably affected the price of El Paso shares was done openly."

Petitioner also alleges that El Paso management and Burlington entered into certain undisclosed and deceptive agreements during the making of the second tender offer. The substance of the allegations is that, in return for certain undisclosed benefits, El Paso managers agreed to support the second tender offer. But both courts noted that petitioner's complaint seeks only redress only for injuries related to the cancellation of the first tender offer. Since the deceptive and misleading acts alleged by the petitioner all occurred with reference to the making of the second tender offer—when the injuries suffered by petitioner had already been sustained—these acts bear no possible causal relationship to petitioner's alleged injuries. The Court of Appeals dealt correctly with this claim.

POLAROID v. DISNEY

862 F.2d 987 (3d Cir.1988).

Before BECKER, HUTCHINSON, and COWEN, CIRCUIT JUDGES

BECKER, CIRCUIT JUDGE.

* * *

The All Holders Rule states that a bidder's tender offer must be open to "all security holders of the class of securities subject to the tender offer." Rule 14d–10(a). The SEC promulgated the Rule to ensure "fair and equal treatment of all holders of the class of securities that is the subject of a tender offer." The Rule was responsive to the situation which gave rise to the litigation in *Unocal Corp. v. Mesa Petroleum Co.,* 493 A.2d 946, 949 (Del.1985), in which the Delaware Supreme Court upheld the power of a corporation to effect a self-tender for its shares which excluded shares of a minority shareholder who was attempting to take over the corporation.

Polaroid argues that Shamrock's tender offer violates the Rule because it is not open to all holders of Polaroid common stock; the Polaroid ESOP [Employee Stock Ownership Plan] is a holder (of 9.7 million shares) of Polaroid common stock and Shamrock has not offered to purchase the ESOP shares. Shamrock's argument in response is that its tender offer is "premised on the invalidity of the ESOP shares."

* * *

The district court "assumed . . . *arguendo* that Polaroid does have standing" to raise the issue but found no violation of the Rule. The court reasoned that "Shamrock should not be forced to make its offer to holders of ESOP shares, the issuance of which Shamrock is challenging in another action."

* * *

2. *Is the All Holders Rule properly within the scope of the Williams Act?*

Section 14(e) of the Williams Act proscribes "fraudulent, deceptive, or manipulative acts . . . in connection with any tender offer." A unanimous Court in Schreiber v. Burlington Northern, Inc., held that section 14(e) does not prohibit manipulative conduct unless there has been some element of deception through a material misrepresentation or omission. The Court held that "[i]t is clear that Congress relied primarily on disclosure to implement the purpose of the Williams Act" and characterized all of the Williams Act provisions as disclosure provisions. *Schreiber* characterizes even section 14(d)(6), which mandates the proration of share purchases when the number of shares tendered exceeds the number of shares sought, and section 14(d)(7), which mandates the payment of the same price to all those whose shares are purchased, as "requir[ing] or prohibit[ing] certain acts so that investors will possess additional time within which to take advantage of the disclosed information." It is thus possible to read *Schreiber* to imply that the All Holders Rule is beyond the SEC's authority under the Williams Act, for the Rule's purpose seems to be neither to ensure full disclosure nor to provide for an adequate time period for investors to comprehend disclosed information.

Although *Schreiber* categorizes the proration and best price provisions of the Williams Act as relating to disclosure, these provisions are only tangentially related to ensuring that investors make fully informed decisions. While the All Holders Rule thus has little to do with ensuring complete disclosure, it is no less related to disclosure than are the proration and best price provisions. Moreover, the SEC has articulated a disclosure justification for the Rule:

> [t]he all-holders requirement would realize the disclosure purposes of the Williams Act by ensuring that all members of the class subject to the tender offer receive information necessary to make an informed decision regarding the merits of the tender offer. If tender offer disclosure is given to all holders, but some are barred from participat-

ing in the offer, the Williams Act disclosure objectives would be ineffective.

In light of the loose definition that *Schreiber* itself ascribes to the meaning of a "disclosure" provision, the emphasis in *Schreiber* on characterizing the Williams Act as a disclosure statute *simpliciter* is of small force in an effort to invalidate the All Holders Rule. For the foregoing reasons, we are satisfied that the SEC was acting within its authority in promulgating the All Holders Rule. This conclusion is buttressed by the deference due the agency's interpretation of its enabling statute, the statute being ambiguous on the issue and the agency's interpretation being a permissible one.

The holding of *Schreiber*—that misrepresentation or nondisclosure is a necessary element of a violation of section 14(e)—is not compromised by a determination that the All Holders Rule is a valid exercise of SEC rulemaking authority. The All Holders Rule is not an attempt to proscribe manipulative practices so much as an attempt to ensure that all holders of a class of securities subject to a tender offer receive fair and equal treatment. And, as explained in the SEC's release, this attempt to ensure fair and equal treatment is the purpose behind both the proration and best price provisions.

Selected References

A. *In General*

E. Aranow & H. Einhorn, Tender Offers for Corporate Control (1973).

E. Aranow, H. Einhorn & G. Berlstein, Developments in Tender Offers for Corporate Control (1977).

T. Hazen, Securities Regulation §§ 11.10–11.22 (2d ed. 1990).

Andre, Tender Offers for Corporate Control: A Critical Analysis and Proposals for Reform, 12 Del.J.Corp.L. 865 (1987).

Demott, Comparative Dimensions of Takeover Regulation, 65 Wash. U.L.Q. 69 (1987).

Black & Schwartzfeld, Curbing the Unregulated Tender Offer, 6 Sec.Reg. L.J. 133 (1978).

Fischel, Efficient Capital Market Theory, the Market for Corporate Control, and the Regulation of Cash Tender Offers, 57 Tex.L.Rev. 1 (1978).

Gillen, Economic Efficiency and Takeover Bid Regulation, 24 Osgoode Hall L.J. 919 (1986).

Leebron, Games Corporations Play: A Theory of Tender Offers, 61 N.Y. U.L.Rev. 153 (1986).

Moylan, Exploring the Tender Offer Provisions of the Federal Securities Laws, 43 G.Wash.L.Rev. 551 (1975).

Weiss, A Proposal For Federal Takeover Law, 9 Cardozo L.Rev. 1699 (1988).

B. *Definition of "Tender Offer"*

Andre, Unconventional Offers Under the Williams Act: The Case for Judicial Restraint, 11 J.Corp.L. 49 (1986).

C. *Section 14(e)*

Conard, Tender Offer Fraud: The Secret Meaning of Subsection 14(e), 40 Bus.Law 87 (1984).

Gibson & Campbell, Fundamental Law for Takeovers, 39 Bus.Law 1551 (1984).

Janewicz, The Appropriate Limits of Section 14(e) of the Securities Exchange Act of 1934, 62 Tex.L.Rev. 1171 (1984).

Lowenstein, Section 14(e) of the Williams Act and the Rule 10b–5 Comparisons, 71 Geo.L.J. 1311 (1983).

Note, The Impact of Schreiber on the SEC Tender Offer Timing Rules, 57 Geo.Wash.L.Rev. 77 (1988).

D. *Defensive Tactics*

Easterbrook & Jarrell, Do Targets Gain from Defeating Tender Offers, 59 N.Y.U. L Rev. 277 (1984).

Gordon & Kornhauser, Takeover Defense Tactics: A Comment on Two Models, 96 Yale L.J. 295 (1986).

Greene, Recent Tender Offer Development: On the Edge or Deep in?, 45 Ohio St.L.J. 377 (1985).

Herzel & Shepro, The Changing Fortunes of Takeover Defenses, 15 Sec Reg. L.J. 116 (1987).

Macey, Takeover Defense Tactics and Legal Scholarship: Market Forces Versus the Policymaker's Dilemma, 96 Yale L.J. 342 (1986).

Morrissey, Defensive Tactics in Tender Offers—Does Anything Go?, 53 Tenn.L.Rev. 103 (1985).

Oesterle, The Negotiations Model of Tender Offer Defenses and the Delaware Supreme Court, 72 Cornell L.Rev. 117 (1986).

Rosenzweig, Legality of "Lock–Ups" and Other Responses of Directors to Hostile Takeover Bids or Stock Aggregations, 10 Sec. Reg.L.J. 291 (1983).

Siegel, Tender Offer Defensive Tactics: A Proposal for Reform, 36 Hastings L.J. 377 (1985).

Tyson, The Williams Act After Hanson Trust v. SCM Corp.: Post–Tender Offer Purchases by the Tender Offeror, 61 Tul.L.Rev. 1 (1986).

Weiss, Defensive Responses to Tender Offers and the Williams Act's Prohibition Against Manipulation, 35 Vand.L.Rev. 1087 (1982).

Note, Front–End Loaded Tender Offers: The Application of Federal and State Law to an Innovative Corporate Acquisition Technique, 131 U.Pa.L.Rev. 389 (1982).

F. STATE REGULATION OF TAKEOVERS

Shortly after Congressional enactment of the Williams Act, a number of states adopted laws regulating tender offers, many of which imposed more stringent requirements than the federal law. Questions quickly arose concerning the extent to which the states constitutionally could regulate tender offers. The constitutional issues were framed in terms of whether the Williams Act preempts the field and also whether the state statutes impose an impermissible burden on interstate commerce. A fair summary of the Supreme Court cases is that so long as state legislation does not (1) alter the Williams Act's basic neutrality between tender offerors and target management or (2) impose burdens that conflict with the Williams Act regulations, the state statutes can survive.

The first generation of state tender offer statutes imposed a variety of disclosure requirements, waiting periods, and fairness thresholds for tender offers. In EDGAR v. MITE, 457 U.S. 624 (1982), the Supreme Court struck down an Illinois statute which imposed a twenty day waiting period on any tender offer and also provided for a hearing to determine the fairness of the offer. The Court held that since tender offers have a national impact and the Williams Act has set out a disclosure and filing requirements, the Illinois statute imposed an excessive burden on interstate commerce and was therefore invalid.[1]

Following the Supreme Court decision in *MITE*, a number of states adopted so-called "second generation" takeover statutes in an attempt to continue to regulate tender offers without imposing the undue burden identified by the *MITE* Court. These statutes generally involved amendment of state laws which govern corporations' internal affairs. Two major varieties of statutes began to emerge: control share acts and best price (or fair price) acts. Control share acquisition acts, modeled on legislation that was originally enacted in Ohio,[2] limit a control person's voting rights.[3] As a bidder acquires shares of the target company it may cross different control thresholds.[4] After crossing a threshold, the bidder cannot vote the shares it has acquired unless there has been a favorable vote by a majority of the disinterested shares.[5] Disinterested shares excludes not only those held by the person seeking control but also shares controlled by the target company's management. The other variety of second generation statutes known as "fair price", or more accurately, "best price" statutes provide

1. In relying on the Commerce Clause, the Supreme Court steered away from the preemption approach that had been used by many lower courts.

2. Ohio Rev.Code § 1701.83.2.

3. E.g. Haw.Rev.Stat. §§ 416–171, 172; Ind.Bus.Corp.Law § 23–1–17–1 et seq.; Minn.Stat.Ann §§ 302A.011, 302A.671; Vernon's Ann.Mo.Stat. §§ 351.015, 351.407; Ohio Rev.Code § 1701.83.2; Utah Code Ann. § 64.41.

4. Control thresholds under the Indiana Statue are crossed when a person becomes the owner of 20%, 33⅓%, or 50% of the voting stock. Ind.Bus.Corp.Law § 23–1–42–1.

5. Disinterested shares are shares not owned by any person seeking to acquire control of the corporation, or by the corporation's officers or directors. Ind.Bus.Corp. Law § 23–1–42–3.

that any person acquiring a covered corporation must pay to all shareholders the "best price" paid to any shareholder.[6] The best price requirement can be waived by a shareholder vote.[7] Also, most best price statutes do not apply to friendly takeovers, as they are waivable by the board of directors.

The first of these "second-generation" statutes reached the Supreme Court in 1987:

CTS v. DYNAMICS

481 U.S. 69 (1987).

POWELL, J., delivered the opinion of the Court in which REHNQUIST, C.J., and BRENNAN, MARSHALL, and O'CONNOR, JJ., joined, and in Parts I, III–A, and III–B of which SCALIA, J., joined. Scalia, J., filed an opinion concurring in part and concurring in the judgment. WHITE, J., filed a dissenting opinion, in Part II of which BLACKMUN and STEVENS, JJ., joined.

JUSTICE POWELL delivered the opinion of the Court.

This case presents the questions whether the Control Share Acquisitions Chapter of the Indiana Business Corporation Law is pre-empted by the Williams Act, or violates the Commerce Clause of the Federal Constitution.

I

A

On March 4, 1986, the Governor of Indiana signed a revised Indiana Business Corporation Law, Ind.Code § 23–1–17–1 et seq. (Supp. 1986). That law included the Control Share Acquisitions Chapter (Indiana Act or Act). Beginning on August 1, 1987, the Act will apply to any corporation incorporated in Indiana, unless the corporation amends its articles of incorporation or bylaws to opt out of the Act. Before that date, any Indiana corporation can opt into the Act by resolution of its board of directors. The Act applies only to "issuing public corporations." The term "corporation" includes only businesses incorporated in Indiana. An "issuing public corporation" is defined as:

"a corporation that has:

"(1) one hundred (100) or more shareholders;

"(2) its principal place of business, its principal office, or substantial assets within Indiana; and

6. E.g. Md. Corps & Ass'ns Code §§ 3–602, 3–603 (defining best price to include the price paid during the past two years). In addition to its best price requirement, the Hawaii statute requires that a bidder offer to purchase all of the target company's shares. Haw.Rev.Stat. § 417E–2(3).

7. Md. Corps & Ass'ns Code §§ 3–602 (2/3 shareholder vote); N.C.Gen.Stats. § 55–9–02 (95% vote).

"(3) either:

"(A) more than ten percent (10%) of its shareholders resident in Indiana;

"(B) more than ten percent (10%) of its shares owned by Indiana residents; or

"(C) ten thousand (10,000) shareholders resident in Indiana."

The Act focuses on the acquisition of "control shares" in an issuing public corporation. Under the Act, an entity acquires "control shares" whenever it acquires shares that, but for the operation of the Act, would bring its voting power in the corporation to or above any of three thresholds: 20%, 33⅓%, or 50%. An entity that acquires control shares does not necessarily acquire voting rights. Rather, it gains those rights only "to the extent granted by resolution approved by the shareholders of the issuing public corporation." Section 9 requires a majority vote of all disinterested shareholders holding each class of stock for passage of such a resolution. The practical effect of this requirement is to condition acquisition of control of a corporation on approval of a majority of the pre-existing disinterested shareholders.

The shareholders decide whether to confer rights on the control shares at the next regularly scheduled meeting of the shareholders, or at a specially scheduled meeting. The acquiror can require management of the corporation to hold such a special meeting within 50 days if it files an "acquiring person statement," requests the meeting, and agrees to pay the expenses of the meeting. If the shareholders do not vote to restore voting rights to the shares, the corporation may redeem the control shares from the acquiror at fair market value, but it is not required to do so. Similarly, if the acquiror does not file an acquiring person statement with the corporation, the corporation may, if its bylaws or articles of incorporation so provide, redeem the shares at any time after 60 days after the acquiror's last acquisition.

* * *

II

The first question in this case is whether the Williams Act preempts the Indiana Act. * * *

Because it is entirely possible for entities to comply with both the Williams Act and the Indiana Act, the state statute can be preempted only if it frustrates the purposes of the federal law.

* * *

B

The Indiana Act differs in major respects from the Illinois statute that the Court considered in Edgar v. MITE Corp., 457 U.S. 624 (1982). After reviewing the legislative history of the Williams Act, Justice White, joined by Chief Justice Burger and Justice Blackmun (the plurality), concluded that the Williams Act struck a careful balance between the interests of offerors and target companies, and that any state statute that "upset" this balance was pre-empted.

* * *

C

As the plurality opinion in *MITE* did not represent the views of a majority of the Court, we are not bound by its reasoning. We need not question that reasoning, however, because we believe the Indiana Act passes muster even under the broad interpretation of the Williams Act articulated by Justice White in *MITE*. As is apparent from our summary of its reasoning, the overriding concern of the *MITE* plurality was that the Illinois statute considered in that case operated to favor management against offerors, to the detriment of shareholders. By contrast, the statute now before the Court protects the independent shareholder against both of the contending parties. Thus, the Act furthers a basic purpose of the Williams Act, " 'plac[ing] investors on an equal footing with the takeover bidder.' "

The Indiana Act operates on the assumption, implicit in the Williams Act, that independent shareholders faced with tender offers often are at a disadvantage. By allowing such shareholders to vote as a group, the Act protects them from the coercive aspects of some tender offers. If, for example, shareholders believe that a successful tender offer will be followed by a purchase of nontendering shares at a depressed price, individual shareholders may tender their shares—even if they doubt the tender offer is in the corporation's best interest—to protect themselves from being forced to sell their shares at a depressed price. As the SEC explains: "The alternative of not accepting the tender offer is virtual assurance that, if the offer is successful, the shares will have to be sold in the lower priced, second step." In such a situation under the Indiana Act, the shareholders as a group, acting in the corporation's best interest, could reject the offer, although individual shareholders might be inclined to accept it. The desire of the Indiana Legislature to protect shareholders of Indiana corporations from this type of coercive offer does not conflict with the Williams Act. Rather, it furthers the federal policy of investor protection.

In implementing its goal, the Indiana Act avoids the problems the plurality discussed in *MITE*. Unlike the *MITE* statute, the Indiana Act does not give either management or the offeror an advantage in communicating with the shareholders about the impending offer. The Act also does not impose an indefinite delay on tender offers. Nothing in the Act prohibits an offeror from consummating an offer on the 20th business day, the earliest day permitted under applicable federal regulations. Nor does the Act allow the state government to interpose its views of fairness between willing buyers and sellers of shares of the target company. Rather, the Act allows *shareholders* to evaluate the fairness of the offer collectively.

D

The Court of Appeals based its finding of pre-emption on its view that the practical effect of the Indiana Act is to delay consummation of tender offers until 50 days after the commencement of the offer. As did the Court of Appeals, Dynamics reasons that no rational offeror will purchase shares until it gains assurance that those shares will carry voting rights. Because it is possible that voting rights will not be conferred until a shareholder meeting 50 days after commencement of the offer, Dynamics concludes that the Act imposes a 50–day delay. This, it argues, conflicts with the shorter 20–business–day period established by the SEC as the minimum period for which a tender offer may be held open. We find the alleged conflict illusory.

The Act does not impose an absolute 50–day delay on tender offers, nor does it preclude an offeror from purchasing shares as soon as federal law permits. If the offeror fears an adverse shareholder vote under the Act, it can make a conditional tender offer, offering to accept shares on the condition that the shares receive voting rights within a certain period of time. The Williams Act permits tender offers to be conditioned on the offeror's subsequently obtaining regulatory approval. There is no reason to doubt that this type of conditional tender offer would be legitimate as well.

Even assuming that the Indiana Act imposes some additional delay, nothing in *MITE* suggested that *any* delay imposed by state regulation, however short, would create a conflict with the Williams Act. The plurality argued only that the offeror should "be free to go forward without *unreasonable* delay." In that case, the Court was confronted with the potential for indefinite delay and presented with no persuasive reason why some deadline could not be established. By contrast, the Indiana Act provides that full voting rights will be vested—if this eventually is to occur—within 50 days after commencement of the offer. This period is within the 60–day maximum period Congress established for tender offers. We cannot say that a delay within that congressionally determined period is unreasonable.

Finally, we note that the Williams Act would pre-empt a variety of state corporate laws of hitherto unquestioned validity if it were construed to pre-empt any state statute that may limit or delay the free exercise of power after a successful tender offer. State corporate laws commonly permit corporations to stagger the terms of their directors. By staggering the terms of directors, and thus having annual elections for only one class of directors each year, corporations may delay the time when a successful offeror gains control of the board of directors. Similarly, state corporation laws commonly provide for cumulative voting. By enabling minority shareholders to assure themselves of representation in each class of directors, cumulative voting provisions can delay further the ability of offerors to gain untrammeled authority over the affairs of the target corporation.

In our view, the possibility that the Indiana Act will delay some tender offers is insufficient to require a conclusion that the Williams Act pre-empts the Act. The longstanding prevalence of state regulation in this area suggests that, if Congress had intended to pre-empt all state laws that delay the acquisition of voting control following a tender offer, it would have said so explicitly. The regulatory conditions that the Act places on tender offers are consistent with the text and the purposes of the Williams Act. Accordingly, we hold that the Williams Act does not pre-empt the Indiana Act.

III

As an alternative basis for its decision, the Court of Appeals held that the Act violates the Commerce Clause of the Federal Constitution. We now address this holding. On its face, the Commerce Clause is nothing more than a grant to Congress of the power "[t]o regulate Commerce * * * among the several States * * *". But it has been settled for more than a century that the Clause prohibits States from taking certain actions respecting interstate commerce even absent congressional action. * * *

A

The principal objects of dormant Commerce Clause scrutiny are statutes that discriminate against interstate commerce. The Indiana Act is not such a statute. It has the same effects on tender offers whether or not the offeror is a domiciliary or resident of Indiana. Thus, it "visits its effects equally upon both interstate and local business".

Dynamics nevertheless contends that the statute is discriminatory because it will apply most often to out-of-state entities. This argument rests on the contention that, as a practical matter, most hostile tender offers are launched by offerors outside Indiana. But this argument avails Dynamics little. "The fact that the burden of a state regulation falls on some interstate companies does not, by itself, establish a claim of discrimination against interstate commerce." Because nothing in the Indiana Act imposes a greater burden on out-of-state offerors than it does on similarly situated Indiana offerors, we reject the contention that the Act discriminates against interstate commerce.

B

This Court's recent Commerce Clause cases also have invalidated statutes that adversely may affect interstate commerce by subjecting activities to inconsistent regulations. The Indiana Act poses no such problem. So long as each State regulates voting rights only in the corporations it has created, each corporation will be subject to the law of only one State. No principle of corporation law and practice is more firmly established than a State's authority to regulate domestic corporations, including the authority to define the voting rights of shareholders. Accordingly, we conclude that the Indiana Act does not create an impermissible risk of inconsistent regulation by different States.

C

The Court of Appeals did not find the Act unconstitutional for either of these threshold reasons. Rather, its decision rested on its view of the Act's potential to hinder tender offers. We think the Court of Appeals failed to appreciate the significance for Commerce Clause analysis of the fact that state regulation of corporate governance is regulation of entities whose very existence and attributes are a product of state law. * * * Every state in this country has enacted laws regulating corporate governance. By prohibiting certain transactions, and regulating others, such laws necessarily affect certain aspects of interstate commerce. This necessarily is true with respect to corporations with shareholders in States other than the State of incorporation. Large corporations that are listed on national exchanges, or even regional exchanges, will have shareholders in many States and shares that are traded frequently. The markets that facilitate this national and international participation in ownership of corporations are essential for providing capital not only for new enterprises but also for established companies that need to expand their businesses. This beneficial free market system depends at its core upon the fact that a corporation—except in the rarest situations—is organized under, and governed by, the law of a single jurisdiction, traditionally the corporate law of the State of its incorporation.

These regulatory laws may affect directly a variety of corporate transactions. Mergers are a typical example. In view of the substantial effect that a merger may have on the shareholders' interests in a corporation, many States require supermajority votes to approve mergers. By requiring a greater vote for mergers than is required for other transactions, these laws make it more difficult for corporations to merge. State laws also may provide for "dissenters' rights" under which minority shareholders who disagree with corporate decisions to take particular actions are entitled to sell their shares to the corporation at fair market value. By requiring the corporation to purchase the shares of dissenting shareholders, these laws may inhibit a corporation from engaging in the specified transactions.

It thus is an accepted part of the business landscape in this country for States to create corporations, to prescribe their powers, and to define the rights that are acquired by purchasing their shares. A State has an interest in promoting stable relationships among parties involved in the corporations it charters, as well as in ensuring that investors in such corporations have an effective voice in corporate affairs.

There can be no doubt that the Act reflects these concerns. The primary purpose of the Act is to protect the shareholders of Indiana corporations. It does this by affording shareholders, when a takeover offer is made, an opportunity to decide collectively whether the resulting change in voting control of the corporation, as they perceive it, would be desirable. A change of management may have important effects on the shareholders' interests; it is well within the State's role as overseer of corporate governance to offer this opportunity. The autonomy provided by allowing shareholders collectively to determine whether the takeover is advantageous to their interests may be especially beneficial where a hostile tender offer may coerce shareholders into tendering their shares.

Appellee Dynamics responds to this concern by arguing that the prospect of coercive tender offers is illusory, and that tender offers generally should be favored because they reallocate corporate assets into the hands of management who can use them most effectively. As indicated, Indiana's concern with tender offers is not groundless. Indeed, the potentially coercive aspects of tender offers have been recognized by the Securities and Exchange Commission, and by a number of scholarly commentators. The Constitution does not require the States to subscribe to any particular economic theory. We are not inclined "to second-guess the empirical judgments of lawmakers concerning the utility of legislation." In our view, the possibility of coercion in some takeover bids offers additional justification for Indiana's decision to promote the autonomy of independent shareholders.

Dynamics argues in any event that the State has " 'no legitimate interest in protecting the nonresident shareholders.' " Dynamics relies heavily on the statement by the *MITE* Court that "[i]nsofar as the * * * law burdens out-of-state transactions, there is nothing to be weighed in the balance to sustain the law." But that comment was made in reference to an Illinois law that applied as well to out-of-state corporations as to in-state corporations. We agree that Indiana has no interest in protecting nonresident shareholders *of nonresident corporations.* But this Act applies only to corporations incorporated in Indiana. We reject the contention that Indiana has no interest in providing for the shareholders of its corporations the voting autonomy granted by the Act. Indiana has a substantial interest in preventing the corporate form from becoming a shield for unfair business dealing. Moreover, unlike the Illinois statute invalidated in *MITE,* the Indiana Act applies only to corporations that have a substantial number of shareholders in Indiana. Thus, every application of the Indiana Act will affect a substantial number of Indiana residents, whom Indiana indisputably has an interest in protecting.

D

Dynamics' argument that the Act is unconstitutional ultimately rests on its contention that the Act will limit the number of successful tender offers. There is little evidence that this will occur. But even if true, this result would not substantially affect our Commerce Clause analysis. We reiterate that this Act does not prohibit any entity—resident or nonresident—from offering to purchase, or from purchasing, shares in Indiana corporations, or from attempting thereby to gain control. It only provides regulatory procedures designed for the better protection of the corporations' shareholders. We have rejected the "notion that the Commerce Clause protects the particular structure or methods of operation in a * * * market." The very commodity that is traded in the securities market is one whose characteristics are defined by state law. Similarly, the very commodity that is traded in the "market for corporate control"—the corporation—is one that owes its existence and attributes to state law. Indiana need not define these commodities as other States do; it need only provide that residents and nonresidents have equal access to them. This Indiana has done. Accordingly, even if the Act should decrease the number of successful tender offers for Indiana corporations, this would not offend the Commerce Clause.

IV

On its face, the Indiana Control Share Acquisitions Chapter evenhandedly determines the voting rights of shares of Indiana corporations. The Act does not conflict with the provisions or purposes of the Williams Act. To the limited extent that the Act affects interstate commerce, this is justified by the State's interests in defining the attributes of shares in its corporations and in protecting shareholders. Congress has never questioned the need for state regulation of these matters. Nor do we think such regulation offends the Constitution. Accordingly, we reverse the judgment of the Court of Appeals.

JUSTICE SCALIA, concurring in part and concurring in the judgment.

* * *

I do not share the Court's apparent high estimation of the beneficence of the state statute at issue here. But a law can be both economic folly and constitutional. The Indiana Control Shares Acquisitions Chapter is at least the latter. I therefore concur in the judgment of the Court.

JUSTICE WHITE, with whom JUSTICE BLACKMUN and JUSTICE STEVENS join as to Part II, dissenting.

The majority today upholds Indiana's Control Share Acquisitions Chapter, a statute which will predictably foreclose completely some tender offers for stock in Indiana corporations. I disagree with the conclusion that the Chapter is neither preempted by the Williams Act nor in conflict with the Commerce Clause. The Chapter undermines the policy of the Williams Act by effectively preventing minority shareholders, in some circumstances, from acting in their own best interests by selling their stock. In addition, the Chapter will substantially burden the interstate market in corporate ownership, particularly if other States follow Indiana's lead as many already have done. The Chapter, therefore, directly inhibits interstate commerce, the very economic consequences the Commerce Clause was intended to prevent. The opinion of the Court of Appeals is far more persuasive than that of the majority today, and the judgment of that court should be affirmed.

I

The Williams Act expressed Congress' concern that individual investors be given sufficient information so that they could make an informed choice on whether to tender their stock in response to a tender offer. The problem with the approach the majority adopts today is that it equates protection of individual investors, the focus of the Williams Act, with the protection of shareholders as a group. Indiana's Control Share Acquisitions Chapter undoubtedly helps protect the interests of a majority of the shareholders in any corporation subject to its terms, but in many instances, it will effectively prevent an individual investor from selling his stock at a premium. Indiana's statute, therefore, does not "furthe[r] the federal policy of *investor* protection," as the majority claims.

* * *

The Control Share Acquisitions Chapter, by design, will frustrate individual investment decisions. Concededly, the Control Share Acquisitions Chapter allows the majority of a corporation's shareholders to block a tender offer and thereby thwart the desires of an individual investor to sell his stock. In the context of discussing how the Chapter can be used to deal with the coercive aspects of some tender offers, the majority states, "In such a situation under the Indiana Act, the shareholders as a group, acting in the corporation's best interest, could reject the offer, although individual shareholders might be inclined to accept it." I do not dispute that the Chapter provides additional protection for Indiana corporations, particularly in helping those corporations maintain the status quo. But it is clear to me that Indiana's scheme conflicts with the Williams Act's careful balance which was intended to protect individual investors and permit them to decide whether it is in their best interests to tender their stock. As noted by the plurality in *MITE,* "Congress * * * did not want to deny shareholders 'the opportunities which result from the competitive bidding for a block of stock of a given company,' namely, the opportunity to sell shares for a premium over their market price.

* * *

II

Given the impact of the Control Share Acquisitions Chapter, it is clear that Indiana is directly regulating the purchase and sale of shares of stock in interstate commerce. Appellant CTS's stock is traded on the New York Stock Exchange, and people from all over the country buy and sell CTS's shares daily. Yet, under Indiana's scheme, any prospective purchaser will be effectively precluded from purchasing CTS's shares if the purchaser crosses one of the Chapter's threshold ownership levels and a majority of CTS's shareholders refuse to give the purchaser voting rights. This Court should not countenance such a restraint on interstate trade.

* * *

The Commerce Clause was included in our Constitution by the Framers to prevent the very type of economic protectionism Indiana's Control Share Chapter represents:

> "The few simple words of the Commerce Clause—'The Congress shall have Power * * * To regulate Commerce * * * among the several States * * *'—reflected a central concern of the Framers that was an immediate reason for calling the Constitutional Convention: the conviction that in order to succeed, the new Union would have to avoid the tendencies toward economic Balkanization that had plagued relations among the Colonies and later among the States under the Articles of Confederation."

The State of Indiana, in its brief, admits that at least one of the Chapter's goals is to protect Indiana Corporations. The State notes that the Chapter permits shareholders "to determine * * * whether [a tender offeror] will liquidate the company or remove it from the State." The State repeats this point later in its brief: "The Statute permits shareholders (who may also be community residents or employees or suppliers of the corporation) to determine the intentions of any offeror concerning the liquidation of the company or its possible removal from the State." A state law which permits a majority of an Indiana corporation's stockholders to prevent individual investors, including out-of-state stockholders, from selling their stock to an out-of-state tender offeror and thereby frustrate any transfer of corporate control, is the archetype of the kind of state law that the Commerce Clause forbids.

Unlike state blue sky laws, Indiana's Control Share Acquisitions Chapter regulates the purchase and sale of stock of Indiana corporations in interstate commerce. Indeed, as noted above, the Chapter will inevitably be used to block interstate transactions in such stock. Because the Commerce Clause protects the "interstate market" in such securities, and because the Control Share Chapter substantially interferes with this interstate market, the Chapter clearly conflicts with the Commerce Clause.

With all due respect, I dissent.

Despite the Supreme Court's validation of the Indiana statute involved in the CTS case, the major commercial states have not followed the Indiana approach. Delaware and New York, the two states in which the largest number of New York Stock Exchange-listed companies are incorporated or headquartered, have opted for statutes which do not restrict a bidder from acquiring or voting shares of the target company, but do prohibit it from merging with the acquired company for a specified period of years after the acquisition. This in effect makes it impossible for the bidder to use the target company's assets to secure the debt incurred by the bidder to finance the takeover.

Section 912 of the New York Business Corporation Law, enacted in 1985, prohibits a business combination with an "interested shareholder" (an owner of more than 20% of the company's shares) for a period of five years unless the merger was approved by the board that was in office prior to the acquisition of the 20% interest. At the end of the five-year period, the transaction can still not be consummated unless it meets a "fair price" test. The statute applies to any New York corporation which has its principal place of business and at least 10% of its stock in New York, and continues to apply even if the corporation changes its state of incorporation after the acquisition.

Section 203 of the Delaware General Corporation Law, enacted in 1988, is modeled after the New York statute, but is less stringent. It prohibits a business combination with an "interested stockholder" (an owner of 15% or more of the company's shares) for a period of three years unless either (a) the combination was approved by the board that was in office prior to the bidder's acquisition of the 15% interest, (b) the interested stockholder acquired at least 85% of the target's voting stock (exclusive of shares held by officers or directors or certain types of employee stock plans) at the time it became an interested stockholder, or (c) the transaction is approved by the directors and by the holders of at least two-thirds of the outstanding stock not owned by the interested stockholder. The statute applies to any Delaware corporation (with certain exclusion and opt-out provisions) regardless of whether it conducts any business or has any stockholders in Delaware. A number of other states have adopted similar statutes.[1]

Other third generation statutes have taken different approaches. For example, the Ohio Foreign Business Acquisition Act imposed stricter burdens on foreign bidders but that statute has been invalidated by at least one court.[2] Pennsylvania and a number of other states have adopted constituency statutes (also referred to as stakeholder statutes) which authorize the board of directors in making decisions to consider interests (including those of employees and the community) in addition to those of the shareholders.[3] Pennsylvania has taken yet another approach by expressly sanctioning use of poison pills as a defensive measure.[4]

Would the New York and Delaware statutes be constitutional under the tests laid down in the CTS case? The Delaware statute has withstood challenges at the preliminary injunction stage because of the failure to show a likelihood of success on the merits. RP Acquisition v. Staley Continental, 686 F.Supp. 476 (D.Del.1988). See also BNS v.

1. E.g., Ariz.Rev.Stat.Ann. §§ 10–1221 – 10–1222 (three year delay); Minn.Stat. Ann. § 302A.673 (five year delay); Mo. Ann.Stat. § 351.459(3)(b) (five year delay); N.J.Rev.Stat. § 49.5–1 (five year delay); Wash S.B. No. 6084, 1987 Wash.Leg.Serv. (No. 10) 11 (five year delay); Wis.Stat.Ann. § 180.725 (three year delay).

2. Campeau Corp. v. Federated Department Stores, CCH Fed.Sec.L.Rep. ¶ 97,984 (S.D.Ohio 1988).

3. E.g., Cal.Corp.Code § 309; Pa.Cons. Stat.Ann. § 8363(b).

4. See Pennsylvania Enacts Law Against Hostile Takeovers, 20 BNA Sec. Reg. & L.Rep. 502 (April 1, 1988).

Koppers, 683 F.Supp. 454 (D.Del.1988). The constitutionality of a similar statute was addressed in the following case:

AMANDA ACQUISITION v. UNIVERSAL FOODS

877 F.2d 496 (7th Cir.1989).

Before BAUER, CHIEF JUDGE, EASTERBROOK, CIRCUIT JUDGE, and WILL, SENIOR DISTRICT JUDGE

EASTERBROOK, CIRCUIT JUDGE.

States have enacted three generations of takeover statutes in the last 20 years. * * *

Wisconsin has a third-generation takeover statute. Enacted after *CTS*, it postpones the kinds of transactions that often follow tender offers (and often are the reason for making the offers in the first place). Unless the target's board agrees to the transaction in advance, the bidder must wait three years after buying the shares to merge with the target or acquire more than 5% of its assets. We must decide whether this is consistent with the Williams Act and Commerce Clause.

I

Amanda Acquisition Corporation is a shell with a single purpose: to acquire Universal Foods Corporation, a diversified firm incorporated in Wisconsin and traded on the New York Stock Exchange. Universal is covered by Wisconsin's anti-takeover law. Amanda is a subsidiary of High Voltage Engineering Corp., a small electronics firm in Massachusetts. Most of High Voltage's equity capital comes from Berisford Capital PLC, a British venture capital firm, and Hyde Park Partners L.P., a partnership affiliated with the principals of Berisford.

Chase Manhattan Bank has promised to lend Amanda 50% of the cost of the acquisition, secured by the stock of Universal. In mid-November 1988 Universal's stock was trading for about $25 per share. On December 1 Amanda commenced a tender offer at $30.50, to be effective if at least 75% of the stock should be tendered.[1] This all-cash, all-shares offer has been increased by stages to $38.00.[2] Amanda's financing is contingent on a prompt merger with Universal if the offer succeeds, so the offer is conditional on a judicial declaration that the law is invalid. * * *

No firm incorporated in Wisconsin and having its headquarters, substantial operations, or 10% of its shares or shareholders there may "engage in a business combination with an interested stockholder . . . for 3 years after the interested stockholder's stock acquisition date

1. Wisconsin has, in addition to § 180.726, a statute modeled on Indiana's, providing that an acquiring firm's shares lose their votes, which may be restored under specified circumstances. Wis.Stat. § 180.25(9). That law accounts for the 75% condition, but it is not pertinent to the questions we resolve.

2. Universal contends that an increase after the district court's opinion makes the case moot, or at least requires a remand. It does not.

unless the board of directors of the [Wisconsin] corporation has approved, before the interested stockholder's stock acquisition date, that business combination or the purchase of stock", Wis.Stat. § 180.726(2). An "interested stockholder" is one owning 10% of the voting stock, directly or through associates (anyone acting in concert with it), § 180.726(1)(j). A "business combination" is a merger with the bidder or any of its affiliates, sale of more than 5% of the assets to bidder or affiliate, liquidation of the target, or a transaction by which the target guarantees the bidder's or affiliates debts or passes tax benefits to the bidder or affiliate, § 180.726(1)(e). The law, in other words, provides for almost hermetic separation of bidder and target for three years after the bidder obtains 10% of the stock—unless the target's board consented before then. No matter how popular the offer, the ban applies: obtaining 85% (even 100%) of the stock held by non-management shareholders won't allow the bidder to engage in a business combination, as it would under Delaware law. See BNS, Inc. v. Koppers Co., 683 F.Supp. 458 (D.Del.1988); RP Acquisition Corp. v. Staley Continental, Inc., 686 F.Supp. 476 (D.Del.1988); City Capital Associates L.P. v. Interco, Inc., 696 F.Supp. 1551 (D.Del.), affirmed, 860 F.2d 60 (3d Cir.1988). Wisconsin firms cannot opt out of the law, as may corporations subject to almost all other state takeover statutes. In Wisconsin it is management's approval in advance, or wait three years. Even when the time is up, the bidder needs the approval of a majority of the remaining investors, without any provision disqualifying shares still held by the managers who resisted the transaction, § 180.726(3)(b).[3] The district court found that this statute "effectively eliminates hostile leveraged buyouts". As a practical matter, Wisconsin prohibits any offer contingent on a merger between bidder and target, a condition attached to about 90% of contemporary tender offers.

Amanda filed this suit seeking a declaration that this law is preempted by the Williams Act and inconsistent with the Commerce Clause. It added a pendent claim that the directors' refusal to redeem the poison-pill rights violates their fiduciary duties to Universal's shareholders. The district court declined to issue a preliminary injunction. It concluded that the statute is constitutional and not preempted, and that under Wisconsin law (which the court believed would follow Delaware's) directors are entitled to prevent investors from accepting tender offers of which the directors do not approve. * * *

II

* * *

A

If our views of the wisdom of state law mattered, Wisconsin's takeover statute would not survive. Like our colleagues who decided *MITE* and *CTS*, we believe that antitakeover legislation injures shareholders. Managers frequently realize gains for investors via voluntary

3. Acquirors can avoid this requirement by buying out the remaining shareholders at a price defined by § 180.726(3)(c), but this is not a practical option.

combinations (mergers). If gains are to be had, but managers balk, tender offers are investors' way to go over managers' heads. If managers are not maximizing the firm's value—perhaps because they have missed the possibility of a synergistic combination, perhaps because they are clinging to divisions that could be better run in other hands, perhaps because they are just not the best persons for the job—a bidder that believes it can realize more of the firm's value will make investors a higher offer. Investors tender; the bidder gets control and changes things. The prospect of monitoring by would-be bidders, and an occasional bid at a premium, induces managers to run corporations more efficiently and replaces them if they will not. * * *

B

Skepticism about the wisdom of a state's law does not lead to the conclusion that the law is beyond the state's power, however. We have not been elected custodians of investors' wealth. States need not treat investors' welfare as their summum bonum. Perhaps they choose to protect managers' welfare instead, or believe that the current economic literature reaches an incorrect conclusion and that despite appearances takeovers injure investors in the long run. Unless a federal statute or the Constitution bars the way, Wisconsin's choice must be respected.

Amanda relies on the Williams Act of 1968, incorporated into §§ 13(d), (e) and 14(d)–(f) of the Securities Exchange Act of 1934. The Williams Act regulates the conduct of tender offers. Amanda believes that Congress created an entitlement for investors to receive the benefit of tender offers, and that because Wisconsin's law makes tender offers unattractive to many potential bidders, it is preempted.

Preemption has not won easy acceptance among the Justices for several reasons. First there is § 28(a) of the '34 Act, which provides that "[n]othing in this chapter shall affect the jurisdiction of the securities commission . . . of any State over any security or any person insofar as it does not conflict with the provisions of this chapter or the rules and regulations thereunder." Although some of the SEC's regulations (particularly the one defining the commencement of an offer) conflict with some state takeover laws, the SEC has not drafted regulations concerning mergers with controlling shareholders, and the Act itself does not address the subject. * * *

The Williams Act regulates the process of tender offers: timing, disclosure, proration if tenders exceed what the bidder is willing to buy, best-price rules. It slows things down, allowing investors to evaluate the offer and management's response. Best-price, proration, and short-tender rules ensure that investors who decide at the end of the offer get the same treatment as those who decide immediately, reducing pressure to leap before looking. * * *

Any bidder complying with federal law is free to acquire shares of Wisconsin firms on schedule. Delay in completing a second-stage merger may make the target less attractive, and thus depress the price offered or even lead to an absence of bids; it does not, however, alter any of the procedures governed by federal regulation. Indeed Wisconsin's law does not depend in any way on how the acquiring firm came by its stock: open-market purchases, private acquisitions of blocs, and acquisitions via tender offers are treated identically. Wisconsin's law is no different in effect from one saying that for the three years after a person acquires 10% of a firm's stock, a unanimous vote is required to merge. Corporate law once had a generally applicable unanimity rule in major transactions, a rule discarded because giving every investor the power to block every reorganization stopped many desirable changes. (Many investors could use their "hold-up" power to try to engross a larger portion of the gains, creating a complex bargaining problem that often could not be solved.) Wisconsin's more restrained version of unanimity also may block beneficial transactions, but not by tinkering with any of the procedures established in federal law.

Only if the Williams Act gives investors a right to be the beneficiary of offers could Wisconsin's law run afoul of the federal rule. No such entitlement can be mined out of the Williams Act, however. * * *

Investors have no right to receive tender offers. More to the point—since Amanda sues as bidder rather than as investor seeking to sell—the Williams Act does not create a right to profit from the business of making tender offers. It is not attractive to put bids on the table for Wisconsin corporations, but because Wisconsin leaves the process alone once a bidder appears, its law may co-exist with the Williams Act.

C

The Commerce Clause, Art. I, § 8 cl. 3 of the Constitution, grants Congress the power "[t]o regulate Commerce . . . among the several States". * * *

When state law discriminates against interstate commerce expressly—for example, when Wisconsin closes its border to butter from Minnesota—the negative Commerce Clause steps in. The law before us is not of this type: it is neutral between inter-state and intra-state commerce. Amanda therefore presses on us the broader, all-weather, be-reasonable vision of the Constitution. Wisconsin has passed a law that unreasonably injures investors, most of whom live outside of Wisconsin, and therefore it has to be unconstitutional, as Amanda sees things. * * *

Illinois's law, held invalid in *MITE*, regulated sales of stock elsewhere. Illinois tried to tell a Texas owner of stock in a Delaware corporation that he could not sell to a buyer in California. By contrast, Wisconsin's law, like the Indiana statute sustained by *CTS*, regulates the internal affairs of firms incorporated there. Investors may buy or sell stock as they please. Wisconsin's law differs in this respect not only from that of Illinois but also from that of Massachusetts, which forbade any transfer of shares for one year after the failure to disclose any material fact, a flaw that led the First Circuit to condemn it. Hyde Park Partners, L.P. v. Connolly, 839 F.2d 837, 847–48 (1st Cir.1988).

Buyers of stock in Wisconsin firms may exercise full rights as investors, taking immediate control. No interstate transaction is regulated or forbidden. True, Wisconsin's law makes a potential buyer less willing to buy (or depresses the bid), but this is equally true of Indiana's rule. Many other rules of corporate law—supermajority voting requirements, staggered and classified boards, and so on—have similar or greater effects on some persons' willingness to purchase stock. States could ban mergers outright, with even more powerful consequences. Wisconsin did not allow mergers among firms chartered there until 1947. We doubt that it was violating the Commerce Clause all those years. Every rule of corporate law affects investors who live outside the state of incorporation, yet this has never been thought sufficient to authorize a form of cost-benefit inquiry through the medium of the Commerce Clause.

Wisconsin, like Indiana, is indifferent to the domicile of the bidder. A putative bidder located in Wisconsin enjoys no privilege over a firm located in New York. So too with investors: all are treated identically, regardless of residence. Doubtless most bidders (and investors) are located outside Wisconsin, but unless the law discriminates according to residence this alone does not matter. * * * Blue sky laws may bar Texans from selling stock in Wisconsin, but they apply equally to local residents' attempts to sell. That their application blocks a form of commerce altogether does not strip the states of power.

Wisconsin could exceed its powers by subjecting firms to inconsistent regulation. Because § 180.726 applies only to a subset of firms incorporated in Wisconsin, however, there is no possibility of inconsistent regulation. Here, too, the Wisconsin law is materially identical to Indiana's. This leaves only the argument that Wisconsin's law hinders the flow of interstate trade "too much". *CTS* dispatched this concern by declaring it inapplicable to laws that apply only to the internal affairs of firms incorporated in the regulating state. States may regulate corporate transactions as they choose without having to demonstrate under an unfocused balancing test that the benefits are "enough" to justify the consequences.

To say that states have the power to enact laws whose costs exceed their benefits is not to say that investors should kiss their wallets goodbye. States compete to offer corporate codes attractive to firms. Managers who want to raise money incorporate their firms in the states that offer the combination of rules investors prefer. Laws that in the short run injure investors and protect managers will in the longer run make the state less attractive to firms that need to raise new capital. If the law is "protectionist", the protected class is the existing body of managers (and other workers), suppliers, and so on, which bears no necessary relation to state boundaries. States regulating the affairs of domestic corporations cannot in the long run injure anyone but themselves. * * *

The long run takes time to arrive, and it is tempting to suppose that courts could contribute to investors' welfare by eliminating laws that impose costs in the short run. The price of such warfare, however, is a reduction in the power of competition among states. Courts seeking to impose "good" rules on the states diminish the differences among corporate codes and dampen competitive forces.

The three district judges who have considered and sustained Delaware's law delaying mergers did so in large measure because they believed that the law left hostile offers "a meaningful opportunity for success". BNS, Inc. v. Koppers Co., 683 F.Supp. at 469. See also RP Acquisition Corp., 686 F.Supp. at 482–84, 488; City Capital Associates, 696 F.Supp. at 1555. Delaware allows a merger to occur forthwith if the bidder obtains 85% of the shares other than those held by management and employee stock plans. If the bid is attractive to the bulk of the unaffiliated investors, it succeeds. Wisconsin offers no such opportunity, which Amanda believes is fatal.

Even in Wisconsin, though, options remain. Defenses impenetrable to the naked eye may have cracks. Poison pills are less fatal in practice than in name (some have been swallowed willingly), and corporate law contains self-defense mechanisms. Investors concerned about stock-watering often arranged for firms to issue pre-emptive rights, entitlements for existing investors to buy stock at the same price offered to newcomers (often before the newcomers had a chance to buy in). Poison pills are dilution devices, and so pre-emptive rights ought to be handy countermeasures. So too there are countermeasures to statutes deferring mergers. The cheapest is to lower the bid to reflect the costs of delay. Because every potential bidder labors under the same drawback, the firm placing the highest value on the target still should win. Or a bidder might take down the stock and pledge it (or its dividends) as security for any loans. That is, the bidder could operate the target as a subsidiary for three years. The corporate world is full of partially owned subsidiaries. If there is gain to be had from changing the debt-equity ratio of the target, that can be done consistent with Wisconsin law. The prospect of being locked into place as holders of illiquid minority positions would cause many persons to sell out, and the threat of being locked in would cause many managers to give assent in advance, as Wisconsin allows. (Or bidders might demand that directors waive the protections of state law, just as Amanda believes that the directors' fiduciary duties compel them to redeem the poison pill rights.) Many bidders would find lock-in unattractive because of the potential for litigation by minority investors, and the need to operate the firm as a subsidiary might foreclose savings or synergies from merger. So none of these options is a perfect substitute for immediate merger, but each is a crack in the defensive wall allowing some value-increasing bids to proceed.

At the end of the day, however, it does not matter whether these countermeasures are "enough". The Commerce Clause does not demand that states leave bidders a "meaningful opportunity for success". * * *

Wisconsin's law may well be folly; we are confident that it is constitutional.

The Wisconsin statute involved in the Amanda case, as well as the New York and Delaware statutes on which it was modeled and the Indiana statute involved in the CTS case, apply only to corporations incorporated in the enacting state, and therefore enjoy the presumption of legitimacy accorded to the laws of the state of incorporation under the "internal affairs" doctrine. A number of states, both before and after the CTS decision, enacted anti-takeover laws purporting to apply to corporations organized under the laws of other states, if they had their headquarters, substantial business operations, or a specified number of shareholders in the state. See Hazen, State Antitakeover Legislation: The Second and Third Generations, 23 Wake Forest L.Rev. 77 (1988). Starting with the Supreme Court decision in *MITE,* these statutes have uniformly been struck down by the courts. Tyson Foods v. McReynolds, 865 F.2d 99 (6th Cir.1989) (Tennessee statute); TLX v. Telex, 679 F.Supp. 1022 (W.D.Okla.1987) (Oklahoma statute).

Note on Defensive Maneuvers and Their Treatment Under State Law

The managements of companies faced with hostile tender offers have resorted to a variety of defensive tactics. Among the favorites have been the following:

"Greenmail". The management uses corporate funds to repurchase the bidder's shares at a premium.

"Lock-up". The management enters into an agreement giving an option to a friendly party to purchase the company's prized assets (its "crown jewels") in the event the bidder acquires control.

"White Knight". The management looks for a friendly merger partner who will acquire the company and retain the management in office.

"Poison Pill". The company distributes rights to the shareholders, entitling them, if the company is acquired, to purchase, at a bargain price, a large number of shares of stock of the target company ("flip-in") or the bidder ("flip-over"). The rights are redeemable by the board at a nominal price at any time until they are activated.

Litigation under state law has generally focused on whether management was entitled to the protection of the "business judgment rule" in taking these or other actions to fend off a tender offer, or whether its action was primarily motivated by its self-interest in maintaining itself in office, in which case it would be judged by the "intrinsic fairness" test. Because many large publicly-held companies are incorporated in Delaware, the courts of that state have developed most of the law on that subject. In UNOCAL v. MESA, 493 A.2d 946 (Del.1985), the Delaware Supreme Court stated:

> When a board addresses a pending takeover bid it has an obligation to determine whether the offer is in the best interests of the corporation and its shareholders. In that respect a board's duty is no different from any other responsibility it shoulders, and its decisions should be no less entitled to the respect they otherwise would be accorded in the realm of business judgment. There are, however, certain caveats to a proper exercise of this function. Because of the omnipresent specter that a board may be acting primarily in its own interests, rather than those of the corporation and its shareholders, there is an enhanced duty which calls for judicial examination at the threshold before the protections of the business judgment rule may be conferred.

"In the face of this inherent conflict," the court adopted a "proportionality test" under which the directors would be required to show (a) "that they had reasonable grounds for believing that a danger to corporate policy and effectiveness existed because of another person's stock ownership" and (b) that the "defensive measure [was] reasonable in relation to the threat posed."

When it becomes apparent, however, that control of the company is going to be transferred, the obligations of the board change. As the Court stated in REVLON v. McANDREWS & FORBES, 506 A.2d 173 (Del.1985):

> [W]hen Pantry Pride increased its offer to $50 per share, and then to $53, it became apparent to all that the break-up of the company was inevitable. The Revlon board's authorization permitting management to negotiate a merger or buyout with a third party was a recognition that the company was for sale. The duty of the board had thus changed from the preservation of Revlon as a corporate entity to the maximization of the company's value at a sale for the stockholders' benefit. This significantly altered the board's responsibilities under the *Unocal* standards. It no longer faced threats to corporate policy and effectiveness, or to the stockholders' interests, from a grossly inadequate bid. The whole question of defensive measures became moot. The directors' role changed from defenders of the corporate bastion to auctioneers charged with getting the best price for the stockholders at a sale of the company.

Some of the defensive tactics undertaken by corporate managements have raised significant questions regarding the appropriate scope of state corporation law and federal securities law. For example, in the *Unocal* case, the defense employed was a counter tender offer by the target company to purchase shares from all shareholders other than the bidder. The Delaware courts upheld the validity of this defense under its "proportionality" test in light of the fact that the bidder was "a corporate raider with a national reputation as a 'greenmailer'." However, the SEC, construing its mandate under §§ 14(d) and 13(e) as including an obligation to assure "fair and equal treatment of all holders of the class of securities that is the subject of a tender offer", subsequently adopted Rules 14d–10(a)(1) and 13e–4(f)(8)(i), under which a tender offer must be open to all holders of such class. This "all holders" rule was attacked as not being within the Commission's rule-making authority, by virtue of the Supreme Court's decision in the *Schreiber* case, p. 802 above. The Third Circuit upheld the validity of the rule in POLAROID v. DISNEY, 862 F.2d 987 (3d Cir.1988), p. 806 above.

Some of the defensive tactics undertaken by corporate managements have raised significant questions regarding the appropriate scope of state corporation law and federal securities law. For example, in the *Unocal* case, the defense employed was a counter tender offer by the target company to purchase shares from all shareholders other than the bidder. The Delaware courts upheld the validity of this defense under its "proportionality" test in light of the fact that the bidder was "a corporate raider with a national reputation as a 'greenmailer'." However, the SEC, construing its mandate under §§ 14(d) and 13(e) as including an obligation to assure "fair and equal treatment of all holders of the class of securities that is the subject of a tender offer", subsequently adopted Rules 14d–10(a)(1) and 13e–4(f)(8)(i), under which a tender offer must be open to all holders of such class. In POLAROID v. DISNEY, 862 F.2d 987 (3d Cir.1988), this "all holders" rule was attacked as not being within the Commission's rule-making authority, by virtue of the Supreme Court's decision in the *Schreiber* case, p. 802 above. The Third Circuit upheld the validity of the rule.

Another area of conflict between state and federal law arises with respect to limitations on voting rights. As indicated by the *CTS* case, a number of states have adopted statutes which limit the voting power of persons who acquire more than a specified percentage of a company's stock. Even in states which do not have such provisions, a large number of companies have attempted to block takeover attempts by making it impossible for a bidder to take control simply by acquiring a majority of the common stock. Among the most popular techniques are:

> *Non–Voting Shares.* The company issues voting shares only to the controlling group, and a separate class of non-voting shares to the public. This can be done either at the time of the initial public offering, or by an exchange offer to public shareholders, offering them an economic incentive (e.g., higher dividends) in exchange for giving up their voting rights.
>
> *Super–Voting Shares.* The company issues as a stock dividend a special class of common stock which carries ten votes per share in the hands of its original holder but reverts to one vote per share as soon as it is transferred. The control group plans to retain all its super-voting shares, which acquire a steadily increasing proportion of the voting power as the publicly-held shares are traded.
>
> *"Capped" Voting Rights.* The certificate of incorporation is amended to provide that no shareholder can cast more than a specified percentage or number of the votes cast at any meeting, or to provide that the number of votes per share decrease as the size of the holding increases (e.g., one vote for each share up to 100, then one vote for each ten shares up to 1,000, then one vote for each 100 shares).

"Timed" Voting Rights. Shares cannot be voted, or are entitled to a lesser number of votes, until they have been held for a specified period of time (e.g., one year, three years).

The first two types of plans, which involve different classes of stock with different voting rights, are clearly authorized under state corporation laws. The latter two types, in which the shareholder's voting rights vary with the size of his holding or the length of time he has held the shares, are more questionable, although the Delaware Supreme Court specifically upheld a "capped" voting provision in PROVIDENCE & WORCESTER v. BAKER, 378 A.2d 121 (Del.1977) (the provisions in that case had been in the company's charter since its original incorporation in 1844), and the Delaware Chancery Court upheld a combination of super-voting shares and "timed" voting rights in WILLIAMS v. GEIER, CCH Fed.Sec.L.Rep. ¶ 93,283 (Del.Ch.1987).

The New York Stock Exchange has since 1926 refused to list the common stock of any company which has any non-voting common stock or departs in any way from the rule of "one common share, one vote." (It made an exception in 1956 to permit the listing of Ford Motor Company, which has a class of super-voting shares owned by the Ford family.) The American Stock Exchange and the NASDAQ system had less restrictive rules, and a number of companies have non-voting common shares traded on those two markets. With the threat of takeovers growing, a number of NYSE-listed companies indicated their intention to implement weighted-voting plans, even if this would result in their being delisted from the NYSE and traded in one of the other markets.

In 1984, the NYSE appointed a committee to consider whether to modify its one share, one vote rule, and imposed a moratorium on compliance with the rule. Over the next three years, more than 46 NYSE-listed companies took advantage of the moratorium to adopt various types of "disparate voting rights plans." In September 1986, the NYSE submitted to the SEC a proposal to change its rules to permit a listed company to adopt a disparate voting rights plan, provided the plan was approved by a majority of its independent directors and a majority of its "public" shareholders. The NYSE stated that the change was necessary to maintain its competitive position vis-a-vis the AMEX and NASDAQ.

The SEC declined to approve the NYSE proposal, opting instead to propose its own rule, requiring all exchanges and NASDAQ to amend their rules to bar the listing or continued listing of any company which takes any action which has the effect of "nullifying, restricting, or disparately reducing the per share voting rights of holders of an outstanding class or classes of common stock". The rule was adopted in final form as Rule 19c–4, in July 1988.

Rule 19c–4 raises a number of interesting questions. It was adopted under the authority of § 19(c) of the 1934 Act, which authorizes the Commission, in pursuance of its regulatory power over stock exchanges (discussed more fully in Chapter 12 below) to amend the rules of such exchanges "as the Commission deems necessary or appropriate to insure the fair administration of the [exchange], to conform its rules to the requirements of [the 1934 Act], or otherwise in furtherance of the provisions of [the 1934 Act]". Does Rule 19c–4 fit those criteria? Is it a legitimate exercise of SEC authority to "insure the fair administration of exchanges"? To "further the provisions" of §§ 14(d) and (e) for the protection of shareholders faced with tender offers, or the provisions of § 14(a) dealing with "fair corporate suffrage"? Do those sections authorize the SEC to, in effect, bar public trading of companies which adopt certain kinds of structural features to fend off takeovers? If so, how far does that power extend? Can the SEC order the exchanges to require listed companies to have a majority of outside directors? To provide for cumulative voting? The validity of Rule 19c–4 was challenged in an action brought by The Business Roundtable, an organization of large corporations, in the Court of Appeals for the District of Columbia Circuit:

BUSINESS ROUNDTABLE v. SEC

905 F.2d 406 (D.C.Cir.1990).

Before: EDWARDS, BUCKLEY, and WILLIAMS, CIRCUIT JUDGES.

WILLIAMS, CIRCUIT JUDGE.

In 1984 General Motors announced a plan to issue a second class of common stock with one-half vote per share. The proposal collided with a longstanding rule of the New York Stock Exchange that required listed companies to provide one vote per share of common stock. The NYSE balked at enforcement, and after two years filed a proposal with the Securities and Exchange Commission to relax its own rule. The SEC did not approve the rule change but responded with one of its own. On July 7, 1988, it adopted Rule 19c–4, barring national securities exchanges and national securities associations, together known as self-regulatory organizations (SROs), from listing stock of a corporation that takes any corporate action "with the effect of nullifying, restricting or disparately reducing the per share voting rights of [existing common stockholders]." The rule prohibits such "disenfranchisement" even where approved by a shareholder vote conducted on one share/one vote principles. Because the rule directly controls the substantive allocation of powers among classes of shareholders, we find it in excess of the Commission's authority under § 19 of the Securities Exchange Act of 1934. * * *

Two components of § 19 give the Commission authority over the rules of self-regulatory organizations. First, § 19(b) requires them to file with the Commission any proposed change in their rules. The Commission is to approve the change if it finds it "consistent with the requirements of [the Exchange Act] and the rules and regulations thereunder applicable" to the self-regulatory organization. This provision is not directly at issue here, but, as we shall see, both the procedure and the terms guiding Commission approval are important in understanding the scope of the authority the Commission has sought to exercise. That is found in § 19(c), which allows the Commission on its own initiative to amend the rules of a self-regulatory organization as it

> deems necessary or appropriate [1] to insure the fair administration of the self-regulatory organization, [2] to conform its rules to requirements of [the Exchange Act] and the rules and regulations thereunder applicable to such organization, or [3] *otherwise in furtherance of the purposes of [the Exchange Act].*

(emphasis and enumeration added). As no one suggests that either of the first two purposes justifies Rule 19c–4, the issue before us is the scope of the third, catch-all provision.

* * *

What then are the "purposes" of the Exchange Act? The Commission supports Rule 19c–4 as advancing the purposes of a variety of sections, but we first take its strongest—§ 14's grant of power to regulate the proxy process. The Commission finds a purpose "to ensure fair shareholder suffrage." Indeed, it points to the House Report's declarations that "[f]air corporate suffrage is an important right," and that "use of the exchanges should involve a corresponding duty of according to shareholders fair suffrage." The formulation is true in the sense that Congress's decision can be located under that broad umbrella.

But unless the legislative purpose is defined by reference to the *means* Congress selected, it can be framed at *any* level of generality—to improve the operation of capital markets, for instance. In fact, although § 14(a) broadly bars use of the mails (and other means) "to solicit . . . any proxy" in contravention of Commission rules and regulations, it is not seriously disputed that Congress's central concern was with disclosure.

While the House Report indeed speaks of fair corporate suffrage, it also plainly identifies Congress's target—the solicitation of proxies by well informed insiders "without fairly informing the stockholders of the purposes for which the proxies are to be used." * * *

That proxy regulation bears almost exclusively on disclosure stems as a matter of necessity from the nature of proxies. Proxy solicitations are, after all, only *communications* with potential absentee voters. The goal of federal proxy regulation was to improve those communications and thereby to enable proxy voters to control the corporation as effectively as they might have by attending a shareholder meeting.

We do not mean to be taken as saying that disclosure is necessarily the sole subject of § 14. For example, the Commission's Rule 14a–4(b)(2) requires a proxy to provide some mechanism for a security holder to withhold authority to vote for each nominee individually. It thus bars a kind of electoral tying arrangement, and may be supportable as a control over management's power to set the voting agenda, or, slightly more broadly, voting procedures. But while Rule 14a–4(b)(2) may lie in a murky area between substance and procedure, Rule 19c–4 much more directly interferes with the substance of what the shareholders may enact. It prohibits certain reallocations of voting power and certain capital structures, even if approved by a shareholder vote subject to full disclosure and the most exacting procedural rules.

The Commission noted in the preamble to the Proposed Rule its conviction that collective action problems could cause even a properly conducted shareholder vote (with ample disclosure and sound procedures) to bring about results injurious to the shareholders. We do not question these findings. But we think the Commission's reliance on them is a clue to its stretch of the congressional purposes. In 1934 Congress acted on the premise that shareholder voting could work, so long as investors secured enough information and, perhaps, the benefit of other procedural protections. It did not seek to regulate the stockholders' choices. If the Commission believes that premise misguided, it must turn to Congress.

With its step beyond control of voting procedure and into the distribution of voting power, the Commission would assume an authority that the Exchange Act's proponents disclaimed any intent to grant. Noting that opponents expressed alarm that the bill would give the Commission "power to interfere in the management of corporations," the Senate Committee on Banking and Currency said it had "no such intention" and that the bill "furnish[ed] no justification for such an interpretation."

There are, of course, shadings within the notion of "management." With the present rule the Commission does not tell any corporation where to locate its next plant. But neither does state corporate law; it regulates the distribution of powers among the various players in the process of corporate governance, and the Commission's present leap beyond disclosure is just that sort of regulation. The potpourri of listing standards previously submitted to the Commission under § 19(b), suggests the sweep of its current claim. These govern requirements for independent directors, independent audit committees, shareholder quorums, shareholder approval for certain major corporate transactions, and other major issues traditionally governed by state law. If Rule 19c–4 is closely enough related to the proxy regulation purpose of § 14, then all these issues appear equally subject to the Commission's discretionary control.

Surprisingly, the Commission does not concede a lack of jurisdiction over such issues. When questioned at oral argument as to what state corporation rules are not related to "fair corporate suffrage," SEC counsel conceded only that further intrusions into state corporate governance "would present more difficult situations." In fact the Commission's apparent perception of its § 19 powers has been immensely broad, unbounded even by any pretense of a connection to § 14. In reviewing the previous SRO rule changes on issues of independent directors and independent audit committees, it grounded its review in a supposed mandate to "protect investors and the public interest." * * * If Rule 19c–4 were validated on such broad grounds, the Commission would be able to establish a federal corporate law by using access to national capital markets as its enforcement mechanism. This would resolve a longstanding controversy over the wisdom of such a move in the face of disclaimers from Congress and with no substantive restraints on the power. It would, moreover, overturn or at least impinge severely on the tradition of state regulation of corporate law. As the Supreme Court has said, "[c]orporations are creatures of state law, and investors commit their funds to corporate directors on the understanding that, except where federal law *expressly* requires certain responsibilities of directors with respect to stockholders, state law will govern the internal affairs of the corporation." We read the Act as reflecting a clear congressional determination not to make any such broad delegation of power to the Commission.

If the Commission's one share/one vote rule is to survive, then, some kind of firebreak is needed to separate it from corporate governance as a whole. But the Commission's sole suggestion of such a firebreak is a reference to "the unique historical background of the NYSE's one share, one vote rule." It is true that in the Senate hearings leading to enactment of the Exchange Act there were a few favorable references to that rule. But these few references are culled from 9500 pages of testimony in the Senate hearings. No legislator directly discussed the NYSE's rule and no references were made to it in any of the Committee Reports. The most these references show is that legislators were aware of the rule and that it was an important part of the background. Even if we imputed the statements to a member of Congress, none comes near to saying, "The purposes of this act, although they generally will not involve the Commission in corporate governance, do include preservation of the one share/one vote principle." And even then we doubt that such a statement in the legislative history could support a special and anomalous exception to the Act's otherwise intelligible conceptual line excluding the Commission from corporate governance.

* * *

The petition for review is granted and Rule 19c–4 is vacated.

Selected References

T. Hazen, Securities Regulation §§ 11.21–11.22 (2d ed. 1990).

Booth, The Promise of State Takeover Statutes, 86 Mich.L.Rev. 1635 (1988).

Garrity, Addendum: Post–MITE State Takeover Statutes: Constitutional Issues and Recent Cases, 42 Bus.Law 586 (1987).

Johnson, State Takeover Statutes: Constitution, Community and Heresy, 45 Wash. & Lee L.Rev. 1051 (1988).

Johnson & Millon, Missing the Point About State Takeover Statutes, 87 Mich.L.Rev. 846 (1989).

Lipton, Corporate Governance in the Age of Finance Corporatism, 136 U.Pa.L.Rev. 1 (1987).

Lowenstein, Tender Offer Litigation and State Law, 63 N.C.L.Rev. 493 (1985).

Millon, State Takeover Laws: A Rebirth of Corporation Law, 45 Wash. & Lee L.Rev. 903 (1988).

Pinto, Takeover Statutes: The Dormant Commerce Clause and State Corporate Law, 41 U.Miami L.Rev. 473 (1987).

Pozen, The New Road of State Tender Offer Statutes, 53 Brooklyn L.Rev. 89 (1987).

Romano, The Political Economy of Takeover Statutes, 73 Va.L.Rev. 111 (1987).

Shipman, In Defense of Reasonable State Regulation of Tender Offers, 53 Brooklyn L.Rev. 99 (1987).

Thompson, Defining the Federal and State Realms of Tender Offer Regulation, 64 Wash.U.L.Q. 1057 (1986).

Note, Second Generation State Takeover Statutes and Shareholder Wealth: An Empirical Study, 97 Yale L.J. 1193 (1988).

PART IV

REGULATION OF THE SECURITIES INDUSTRY AND MARKETS

CHAPTER 10

REGULATION OF THE CONDUCT OF SECURITIES FIRMS

A substantial portion of the SEC's activity is devoted to regulation of firms engaged in the securities business. The three principal capacities in which firms act in that business are as broker, dealer, and investment adviser. The 1934 Act defines a "broker" as a "person engaged in the business of effecting transactions in securities for the account of others", § 3(a)(4), while a "dealer" is a "person engaged in the business of buying and selling securities for his own account", § 3(a)(5). An "investment adviser" is defined in § 202(a)(11) of the Investment Advisers Act of 1940 as a "person who, for compensation, engages in the business of advising others * * * as to the advisability of investing in, purchasing or selling securities * * *."

Under § 15(a) of the 1934 Act, no person may engage in business as a broker or dealer in securities (unless he does exclusively intrastate business or deals only in exempted securities) unless he is registered with the Commission. Under § 15(b), the Commission may revoke or suspend a broker-dealer's registration, or impose a censure, if the broker-dealer is found to have violated any of the federal securities laws or committed other specified misdeeds. Section 203 of the Investment Advisers Act of 1940 contains comparable provisions with respect to investment advisers.

In spelling out the substantive obligations of these securities "professionals" in dealing with public investors, the Commission has proceeded largely under the general anti-fraud provisions of §§ 10(b) and 15(c) of the 1934 Act, § 17(a) of the 1933 Act, and § 206 of the Investment Advisers Act. Its attention has been focused on two broad areas: (a) conflicts between the firm's obligations to its customers and its own financial interests, and (b) trading in or recommending securities in the absence of adequate information about the issuer. Violation of the anti-fraud provisions in these two areas has given rise to lawsuits by aggrieved customers as well as disciplinary actions by the SEC.

SEC regulation of the industry is supplemented by a system of "self-regulation". Sections 6 and 15A of the 1934 Act delegate to "national securities exchanges" and "national securities associations", respectively, substantial authority over their members, including the power to expel, suspend or discipline them for certain specified kinds of activities or for "conduct * * * inconsistent with just and equitable principles of trade." In order to exercise such powers, an exchange or association must register with the SEC, which, under § 19 of the Act, is given certain oversight powers with respect to its disciplinary proceedings and adoption and amendment of its rules.

In general, a securities firm must become a member of one or more exchanges in order to execute transactions in listed securities on an exchange, and must become a member of the National Association of Securities Dealers (NASD), the only registered association, to transact business effectively in the over-the-counter market. The financial crisis in the securities industry in 1969–70 raised serious questions as to the overall effectiveness of this "self-regulatory" system, leading to SEC and Congressional reexamination of the appropriate role of industry organizations in the regulatory pattern. In addition, the distinctive features of "self-regulation" have raised a number of difficult legal questions.

Conflicts of interest in the securities business arise from the fact that what is best for the broker-dealer or investment adviser is not always best for the customer. They are complicated by the fact, noted above, that securities firms often engage in several different types of activities, with differing responsibilities.

In considering the following materials, keep in mind an important distinction between securities traded on exchanges and those traded in the over-the-counter (OTC) market. In an exchange transaction, the brokerage firm with which an individual investor deals always acts as his agent in the transaction and charges a commission, while in an OTC transaction the firm may act either as his agent or sell to (or buy from) him as principal for its own account.

The materials in this section indicate the approaches taken by the SEC and the courts in regulating (1) excessive prices for OTC securities; (2) activities of market-makers who deal directly with individual customers; (3) generation of commissions by excessive trading in customers' accounts; and (4) undisclosed interests of investment advisers in the stocks they recommend. In evaluating these approaches, note the emphasis on enforcing "professionalism" among broker-dealers and investment advisers, and consider whether this is a realistic approach in light of the nature of the securities business and the type of people who engage in it.

A. DEALERS AND MARKET MAKERS

1. *Trading Practices*

CHARLES HUGHES & CO. v. SEC

139 F.2d 434 (2d Cir.1943).

Before AUGUSTUS N. HAND, CHASE, and CLARK, CIRCUIT JUDGES.

CLARK, CIRCUIT JUDGE.

This is a petition, pursuant to § 25(a) of the Securities Exchange Act of 1934, to review an order of the Securities and Exchange Commission, entered July 19, 1943, under § 15(b) of that Act, in which petitioner's registration as a broker and dealer was revoked. * * *

Petitioner was incorporated on April 9, 1940, under the laws of New York, and maintains its principal office and place of business in New York City. It is engaged in over-the-counter trading in securities as a broker and dealer, being registered as such with the Commission under the 1934 statute cited above. The dealings which resulted in the revocation were continued sales of securities to customers at prices very substantially over those prevailing in the over-the-counter market, without disclosure of the mark-up to the customers. The Commission concluded that such practices constituted fraud and deceit upon the customers in violation of § 17(a) of the Securities Act, § 15(c)(1) of the Securities Exchange Act, and its own Rule X–15C1–2. * * *

Petitioner's dealings which are here in question were carried out by various of its customers' men. The customers were almost entirely single women or widows who knew little or nothing about securities or the devices of Wall Street. An outline of the sales plan used with Mrs. Stella Furbeck gives a representative picture of how petitioner worked. Stillman, a Hughes & Co. agent, having her name as a prospect, called Mrs. Furbeck on the telephone and told her of a "wonderful" stock that she should buy. She replied that she was not interested. The next day he called again, and he persisted in his calls until she finally relented and made a purchase. From that time on, he and a co-employee of his, one Armstrong, worked their way so completely into her confidence that she virtually placed complete control of her securities portfolio in their hands. Every few days one or the other would have another "marvelous" buy—one that was definitely "beyond the usual"—and she would add it to her collection, selling a more reputable security in order to finance the transaction.

The prices which Mrs. Furbeck and other customers paid for the securities purchased in this manner ranged from 16.1 to 40.9 per cent over market value. In addition, most of the transactions involved little or no risk for petitioner, because an order was usually confirmed before it bought the securities that it was selling. There is conflict in the record as to whether Stillman and Armstrong made any direct representations to Mrs. Furbeck of the relation of the price paid to market value. She claims that every time she made a purchase it was directly induced by the statement that the price would be under that current in the over-the-counter market, while they deny such statements completely. It is unchallenged, however, that at no time did either Stillman or Armstrong reveal the true market price of any security to Mrs. Furbeck or the fact that petitioner's profits averaged around twenty-five per cent. Similar evidence as to other customers all amply furnished the "substantial evidence" required by the statute to make conclusive the Commission's finding of a course of business by petitioner to sell at excessive mark-up prices without disclosure of market values to its customers. * * *

There is evidence in the record to show a threefold violation of § 17(a) of the Securities Act, viz., the obtaining of money "by means of any untrue statement of a material fact"; the "omission to state a material fact" necessary to make statements actually made not misleading; and the engaging in a course of business which operates "as a fraud or deceit upon the purchaser." It is true that the only specific evidence of false statements of a material fact is that of Mrs. Furbeck that the sales price was under the market price, and, as we have noted, these statements were denied by the salesmen. Although the Commission has neglected to make any finding of fact on this point, we need not remand for a specific finding resolving this conflict, for we feel that petitioner's mark-up policy operated as a fraud and deceit upon the purchasers, as well as constituting an omission to state a material fact.

An over-the-counter firm which actively solicits customers and then sells them securities at prices as far above the market as were those which petitioner charged here must be deemed to commit a fraud.[1] It holds itself out as competent to advise in the premises, and it should disclose the market price if sales are to be made substantially above that level. Even considering petitioner as a principal in a simple

1. The Commission points out that the National Association of Securities Dealers, Inc., an organization registered under § 15A of the Securities Exchange Act, of which petitioner was a member at the time of the transaction in question, has a rule limiting mark-up prices in over-counter securities to those which are fair, and calls attention to a decision of the Association's District Business Conduct Committee reported in the NASD News for October, 1943, imposing a fine of $500 and censure upon a member found to have violated rules of the Association by a practice of charging mark-ups of approximately 10 per cent on transactions in listed and unlisted securities. It also cites a decision of the Circuit Court, Sangamon County, Illinois, Matthews, Lynch & Co. v. Hughes, No. 76441. June, 1939, sustaining the revocation of registration of a dealer who took "extremely high" profits, "running in one case to 25%," and a similar interpretation of the Ohio Securities Act by the Ohio Securities Commission, 1 C.C.H. Stocks and Bonds Law Serv., p. 3331.

vendor-purchaser transaction (and there is doubt whether, in several instances at least, petitioner was actually not acting as broker-agent for the purchasers, in which case all undisclosed profits would be forfeited), it was still under a special duty, in view of its expert knowledge and proffered advice, not to take advantage of its customers' ignorance of market conditions. The key to the success of all of petitioner's dealings was the confidence in itself which it managed to instill in the customers. Once that confidence was established, the failure to reveal the mark-up pocketed by the firm was both an omission to state a material fact and a fraudulent device. When nothing was said about market price, the natural implication in the untutored minds of the purchasers was that the price asked was close to the market. The law of fraud knows no difference between express representation on the one hand and implied misrepresentation or concealment on the other.

We need not stop to decide, however, how far common-law fraud was shown. For the business of selling investment securities has been considered one peculiarly in need of regulation for the protection of the investor. "The business of trading in securities is one in which opportunities for dishonesty are of constant recurrence and ever present. It engages acute, active minds, trained to quick apprehension, decision and action." Archer v. Securities and Exchange Commission, 8 Cir., 133 F.2d 795, 803. The well-known "blue sky laws" of 43 states have in fact proved inadequate, so that in 1933 Congress after the most extensive investigations started on a program of regulation, of which this is one of the fruits. In its interpretation of § 17(a) of the Securities Act, the Commission has consistently held that a dealer cannot charge prices not reasonably related to the prevailing market price without disclosing that fact. Had we been in doubt on the matter we should have given weight to these rulings as a consistent and contemporaneous construction of a statute by an administrative body. As we have hitherto said of "the peculiar function" of the Commission: "One of the principal reasons for the creation of such a bureau is to secure the benefit of special knowledge acquired through continuous experience in a difficult and complicated field. Its interpretation of the act should control unless plainly erroneous." But we are not content to rest on so colorless an interpretation of this important legislation.

The essential objective of securities legislation is to protect those who do not know market conditions from the overreachings of those who do. Such protection will mean little if it stops short of the point of ultimate consequence, namely, the price charged for the securities. Indeed, it is the purpose of all legislation for the prevention of fraud in the sale of securities to preclude the sale of "securities which are in fact worthless, or worth substantially less than the asking price." People v. Federated Radio Corp., 244 N.Y. 33, 40, 154 N.E. 655, 658. If after several years of experience under this highly publicized legislation we should find that the public cannot rely upon a commission-licensed broker not to charge unsuspecting investors 25 per cent more than a market price easily ascertainable by insiders, we should leave such legislation little more than a snare and a delusion. We think the Commission has correctly interpreted its responsibilities to stop such abusive practices in the sale of securities.

Petitioner's final contention is that the actual market price of the securities was never satisfactorily proved. We agree, however, with the Commission that the evidence of the quotations published in the National Daily Quotation Sheets, a recognized service giving "daily market indications," as petitioner stipulated, and the prices paid concurrently by petitioner itself sufficiently indicated prevailing market price in the absence of evidence to the contrary.

REGULATION OF THE COMPENSATION OF SECURITIES DEALERS

By David L. Ratner

55 Cornell L.Rev. 348, 368–74 (1970).*

In contrast to stock exchange transactions, no minimum commission rates are applicable to transactions in the over-the-counter (OTC) market. The Exchange Act specifically provides that a national securities association, such as the National Association of Securities Dealers (NASD), may not adopt rules designed "to fix minimum profits, to impose any schedule of prices, or to impose any schedule or fix minimum rates of commissions, allowances, discounts, or other charges." On the other hand, the rules of such an association must be designed "to provide safeguards against unreasonable profits or unreasonable rates of commissions or other charges."

The rules governing compensation for transactions in the OTC market are complicated by the broker-dealer's ability, in many transactions, to choose whether to act as agent or principal. If the broker-dealer maintains an inventory in the particular security, he will normally sell to his customer from that inventory as principal. If he must obtain the security from another dealer, he may either buy for his customer as agent and charge a commission or buy as principal and resell to the customer at a mark-up.

An SEC sampling of sales of 135 OTC stocks on January 18, 1962, showed that in fifty percent of the retail sales transactions the broker-dealers purchased for customers as agents, in twenty-five percent they purchased and resold as principal, and in twenty-five percent they sold as principal from inventory. An NASD sampling of 246 stocks sold on August 11, 1965, showed that in sixty-six percent of such transactions the broker-dealers purchased for customers as agents, in twelve percent they purchased and resold as principal, and in twenty-two percent they sold as principal from inventory.

A. Compensation for Acting as Customer's Agent

When a broker-dealer buys or sells a security for a customer as agent, the NASD requires that

> he shall not charge his customer more than a fair commission or service charge, taking into consideration all relevant circumstances including market conditions with respect to such security at the time of the transaction, the expense of executing the order and the value of any service he may have rendered by reason of his experience in and knowledge of such security and the market therefor.[116]

The amount of the commission must be set forth on the confirmation that the broker-dealer is required to send the customer on completion of the transaction.[117]

* * * A study of agency transactions done for the NASD showed that the average charge on a purchase or sale for a customer in September 1965 was 1.10 percent of the money involved in the transaction.

B. Compensation for Dealing With Customer as Principal

In contrast to the situation where a broker-dealer acts as agent for his customer, a broker-dealer who acts as a principal in the sale of a security to his customer is not required to disclose on the confirmation anything other than the "net" price to be paid by the customer for the security. Without information as to the cost of the security to the dealer or the prices currently being quoted by dealers making a market in the stock, the customer has no way of knowing what he is being charged for the dealer's services.

1. Limitations on Mark–Ups

In 1942 the SEC published for comment a rule that would have required dealers to disclose to their customers in principal transactions the best current independent bid and asked prices for the security. The NASD opposed this proposal, and surveyed its members to determine their mark-up practices. It ascertained that forty-seven percent of the transactions were made at mark-ups of three percent or less and seventy-one percent were made at mark-ups of five percent or less. In October 1943 the NASD distributed the results of the survey to its members, noting that there might be circumstances in which a mark-up of more than five percent would be justified, and that a mark-up of five percent or even lower is not always justified, but the five percent figure would serve as a guide to what constitutes a "fair spread or profit" within the meaning of the NASD's Rules of Fair Practice.[123]

116. NASD Rules, art. III, § 4.

117. Securities Exchange Act of 1934, § 15(c)(1); rule 15c1–4.

123. In 1944, members of the NASD challenged the Board's authority to establish the "5% policy" by interpretation of the Rules of Fair Practice and demanded that the policy statement be considered a rule which must be submitted to a membership vote. The SEC held that the Board's action was "by no means an inflexible limitation on spreads," and thus constituted an interpretation rather than a rule. NASD, Inc., 17 S.E.C. 459 (1944).

This "five percent policy" has been elaborated through interpretation over the years. The amount of the mark-up is to be computed by reference to the "prevailing market price," of which the dealer's contemporaneous cost is the best indication in the absence of other bona fide evidence. A mark-up pattern of five percent or even less may be considered unfair or unreasonable under appropriate circumstances. The fairness of mark-ups may not be justified on the basis of excessive expenses, but should be determined by reference to all relevant factors, including the type and price of the security and its availability in the market, the amount of money involved in the transaction, the nature of the dealer's business, the type of service and facilities provided to customers, the dealer's general pattern of mark-ups, and the type and extent of disclosure he makes to his customers.

A large number of disciplinary proceedings based wholly or partly on excessive mark-ups have been brought against broker-dealers by both the NASD and the SEC. Both the NASD and the SEC require that retail sale and purchase prices be reasonably related to the "current" or "prevailing" market price at the time of the challenged transactions. Usually proceedings are initiated against brokers whose mark-ups are consistently not reasonably related to current market price. Objectionable patterns have consisted of as many as 563 and as few as fourteen transactions, and mark-ups found unfair have ranged from 5.4 percent to 200 percent. Although the decisions generally refer to the NASD's "five percent policy," mark-ups between five percent and ten percent may be justified in some instances. Mark-ups above ten percent are generally considered unjustifiable. In cases that also involve other improper practices, a violation of the mark-up rule may be found on the basis of fewer transactions and lower mark-ups.

When the NASD has shown the existence of a pattern of mark-up violations, the member has the burden of establishing "justifying circumstances" for his action. The following have been held not to be "justifying circumstances": excessive expenses in making a sale; risk in maintaining a large inventory; small total dollar amount of the transaction; reliance on NASD inspection and approval of books; and mark-ups consistent with those customary in the vicinity. In many instances, the dealer claims his mark-up was justified because the sale was of a low-priced security, relying on an NASD statement that a "somewhat higher percentage may sometimes be justified" in the case of a low-priced security; i.e., a security that sells for ten dollars or less. It seems, however, that the "low price factor" alone will not justify a consistent pattern of mark-ups at a level substantially above five percent.

a. *Determination of Prevailing Market Price.* A retail dealer who does not maintain a position in a particular security should, in the absence of countervailing evidence, use his contemporaneous cost—the price paid to other dealers to purchase the same security on the same day—as his mark-up base.

When a dealer who makes a wholesale market in a security sells that security to a retail customer out of inventory, there is a question whether the mark-up should be based on the dealer's contemporaneous cost, normally his *bid* price, or the price at which the stock is then being *offered* by dealers to one another. The *Special Study* found that most integrated firms base their mark-up on the price at which they are then offering the stock to other dealers and recommended that the obligations of an integrated broker-dealer in respect to his retail pricing be "defined * * * more clearly and positively." The 1966 *OTC Study* computed gross income from retail OTC sales as "the difference between the then current interdealer *asked* price and the 'net' price confirmed to the customer."

Recent cases indicate that an integrated dealer is required to use his contemporaneous cost as a mark-up base when the security is not actively traded among dealers, that is, when no independent competitive market exists. This is usually the case where the integrated firm is the dominant factor in either the wholesale or retail market. When an independent competitive retail and wholesale market does exist, the integrated dealer may use the offering prices quoted by other dealers to one another as the basis for his retail mark-ups.

2. *Special Study Recommendations*

Among the sixteen recommendations of the *Special Study* concerning OTC markets, three recommendations relating to dealers' charges for retail transactions were subjects of particular objection by segments of the securities business.

a. *"Riskless" Transactions.* The *Special Study* recommended that "a broker-dealer who neither is a primary market maker nor has a bona fide inventory position should be required (subject to defined exceptions) to execute customers' orders on an agency basis." This proposal was designed to require disclosure of the amount of the retail mark-up in the so-called "riskless transaction" whereby a broker-dealer, after accepting a customer's order, purchases the stock from another dealer as principal and resells at a mark-up to the customer.

In discussions with the SEC in 1964, the NASD argued that this proposal would tend to force firms to execute OTC transactions at commissions roughly equivalent to NYSE minimum commission rates, thus putting an "economic squeeze" on its members and diverting their merchandising efforts away from OTC stocks. The SEC has taken no action to implement the recommendation. The 1966 *OTC Study* showed, however, that the average mark-up on "riskless" principal transactions declined from 2.93 percent in September 1963 to 2.40 percent in September 1965, while, in comparison, average commissions on agency transactions only declined from 1.13 percent to 1.10 percent during the same period. Furthermore, between 1962 and 1965 the proportion of retail OTC sales accounted for by "riskless" principal transactions declined from about twenty-five percent to about twelve percent, while the proportion accounted for by agency transactions increased from about fifty percent to sixty-six percent. These changes are attributable in part to the improvements in disclosure discussed below.

b. *Disclosure.* The *Special Study* recommended changes in the manner in which "retail" quotations were furnished either by or under the supervision of the NASD for publication in newspapers. While the bid prices published at that time generally represented the interdealer bids, the retail asked prices were generally determined by adding to the inter-dealer asked prices a percentage mark-up ranging from about five percent on stocks selling below twenty-five dollars to about two percent on stocks selling above $135. The *Special Study* concluded that this system must be "confusing if not deceptive to many investors" since an investor "may get the impression or actually be told that his security was bought commission free, below the 'high.'" It recommended that the newspaper quotations be revised "to show generally * * * the best prevailing inter-dealer bid and asked quotations that can be reasonably ascertained."

In 1964 the NASD, with the concurrence of the SEC, adopted a plan providing for newspaper publication of representative inter-dealer bid and asked prices for the approximately 1,300 actively traded stocks of larger companies that appear on the "national list." This system was inaugurated "on a test basis" in February 1965, and has been in effect since that time. In 1966 it was extended to the less actively traded securities of smaller companies appearing on the so-called "local lists."

A third controversial recommendation by the *Special Study* was that a broker-dealer selling as principal be required to state in the confirmation the inter-dealer price available at the time of the transaction, thereby showing the customer the approximate amount of the markup. The NASD strongly opposed this recommendation on economic grounds, and it has not been implemented.

Fifteen years after receiving the *Special Study* recommendations with respect to "riskless" principal transactions, the Commission took some action. In October 1978, it amended its Rule 10b–10 (which specifies confirmation requirements for all transactions) to require that dealers disclose, in their confirmations to customers, any mark-up, mark-down, or similar remuneration on a "riskless" transaction. At the same time, it withdrew a proposal it had made a year earlier to require disclosure on confirmations of the best bid and offer prices displayed in the NASDAQ electronic quotation system at the time the transaction was effected. Commentators had objected that the requirement was unnecessary because of the protections provided by the NASD's mark-up and best execution rules and the public availability of quotations, that it would be difficult to enforce, and that it would impose substantial additional costs on the industry. Sec.Ex.Act Rel. No. 15219 (Oct. 6, 1978).

ALSTEAD, DEMPSEY & CO.

Sec.Ex.Act Rel. No. 20825, CCH Fed.Sec.L.Rep. ¶ 83,607 (1984).

I.

Alstead, Dempsey & Company, Incorporated ("registrant"), a registered broker-dealer, appeals from the decision of an administrative law judge. The law judge found that registrant charged retail customers excessive markups in 84 sales of the securities of Flight Transportation Corporation ("FTC") and A.T. Bliss & Company, but dismissed allegations that registrant charged unfair markups in many additional transactions in those securities. He concluded that registrant's broker-dealer registration should be suspended for thirty days.

* * *

II.

This case raises questions concerning the proper pricing practices of an integrated dealer, a market maker who simultaneously makes a wholesale market in an over-the-counter security while selling the same security at retail. Before considering the particular facts at issue, we shall briefly review our policy in the markup area.

As early as 1939, this Commission held that a dealer violates antifraud provisions when he charges retail customers prices that are not reasonably related to the prevailing market price at the time the customers make their purchases. The key issue in cases involving allegations of unfair pricing has always been how to determine the prevailing market price, on the basis of which retail markups are computed. Once that price is determined, we have consistently held that, at the least, markups more than 10% above that level are fraudulent in the sale of equity securities.

The prevailing market price means the price at which dealers trade with one another, i.e., the current inter-dealer market. When a dealer is not simultaneously making a market in a security, we have consistently held that, in the absence of countervailing evidence, a dealer's contemporaneous cost is the best evidence of the current market. That standard, which has received judicial approval, reflects the fact that prices paid for a security by a dealer in actual transactions closely related in time to his retail sales are normally a highly reliable indication of prevailing market price. However, in the case of an integrated dealer, different considerations may be applicable.

In the recent case of *Peter J. Kisch,*[8] we noted that a market maker often purchases stock from other dealers at or around its bid and sells to other dealers at or around its asked or offering price. Thus a rigid application of the "contemporaneous cost" rule (in effect using a dealer's bid as the basis for computing retail markups) may not be appropriate. We indicated that, where a market maker is involved, markups may be computed on the basis of the contemporaneous prices charged by the firm or other market makers in actual sales to other dealers or, if no such prices are available, on the basis of representative asked quotations. But in *Kisch,* as in other cases involving market makers, it is essential to examine the nature of the inter-dealer market in order to determine the extent to which it may legitimately serve as the basis for findings of prevailing market price.

Although the Kisch firm was the dominant market maker in the stock there at issue, Mini Computer Systems, Inc. ("MCS"), Kisch was only one of 14 firms making a market in that security. Moreover, the other 13 firms accounted for more than half the trading volume in that stock during the period in question. On the basis of the evidence, it was clear that Kisch did not control the inter-dealer market in MCS and, accordingly, that the prices paid Kisch for MCS stock by other dealers were an accurate reflection of the prevailing market price. We have consistently used such inter-dealer sales prices as the basis for computing markups in similar situations.

The use of quotations as the basis for computing markups is more problematic. By their very nature, quotations only propose a transaction; they do not reflect the actual result of a completed arms-length sale. Thus, as we have frequently pointed out, quotations for obscure securities with limited inter-dealer trading activity may have little value as evidence of the current market. They often show wide spreads between the bid and ask prices and are likely to be subject to negotiation.

However, there are situations involving a market maker, such as that presented in *Kisch,* where the use of representative asked quotations in the absence of actual inter-dealer sales is appropriate in determining prevailing market price. Where there is an active, independent market for a security, and the reliability of quoted offers can be tested by comparing them with actual inter-dealer transactions during the period in question, such quotations may provide a proper basis for computing markups. Thus, if inter-dealer sales occur with some frequency, and on the days when they occur they are consistently effected at prices at or around the quoted offers, it may properly be inferred that on other days such offers provide an accurate indication of the prevailing market.

8. Securities Exchange Act Release No. 19005 (August 24, 1982), 25 SEC Docket 1533.

With that background, we now turn to a consideration of the particular facts at issue.

III.

A. Our staff alleges that, during the period February 5 through March 21, 1980, registrant charged retail customers unfair markups in the sale of FTC securities. The relevant facts are as follows.

On November 30, 1979, FTC made the first public offering of its securities, 560,000 shares of its common stock at $3.25 per share. Registrant was underwriter of that offering on a "best efforts" basis, and sold 95.7% of the offering, or 537,150 shares, to its own customers. When the offering was completed on February 4, 1980, registrant decided to become a market maker in FTC. It accordingly placed quotations for the stock in the NASDAQ system, as did two other brokerage firms.

During the period at issue, the total trading volume in FTC stock was about 345,000 shares, and registrant's transactions with other dealers and customers amounted to more than 297,000 shares, or 86% of that volume. Since most FTC stock was held by registrant's customers, registrant effectively controlled the supply. And most of its trading volume resulted from principal transactions with its customers who purchased 133,840 shares and sold 130,200 shares during the period in question. The two other dealers who placed quotations in NASDAQ were the only other market makers in FTC, and their combined transactions with dealers other than registrant totaled only 7,750 shares, or 2.2% of the total trading volume.

Under these circumstances, it is clear that there was no independent competitive market in FTC stock. Registrant dominated the market to such a degree that it controlled wholesale prices. Thus the only reliable basis for determining the prevailing market price is the contemporaneous prices that registrant was willing to pay other dealers for the FTC stock it purchased from them. On the basis of the prices registrant paid such dealers on the day before or the same day as its sales to customers, we find that it charged customers excessive markups in 80 transactions. The markups in those sales ranged from 11.1% to 14.7% in 13 transactions, from 15.4% to 19.4% in 41 transactions, and over 20% in the remaining 26 transactions.

B. Our staff alleges that, during the period June 3 through July 31, 1980, registrant charged customers excessive markups in the sale of Bliss securities.

Although several market makers were listed with respect to Bliss in the nationally distributed "pink sheets" published by the National Quotation Bureau, Inc., numerical quotations appeared in those sheets only from July 28 through July 31. Registrant entered numerical quotations for Bliss in regional inter-dealer sheets published in Minneapolis. It argues that its published offers in those sheets should be accepted as the best evidence of prevailing market price. We cannot agree.

During the relevant period, registrant purchased a total of 116,500 shares of Bliss from other dealers and 28,650 shares from its own customers. It sold 138,650 shares to customers, but made only two inter-dealer sales totaling 2,500 shares. Those sales, on June 10 and June 16, 1980, were both made to the same firm. Except for one day during the period in question, registrant's offering price for Bliss was 4. But it never effected any sales at that figure. The two sales it made to another dealer were at prices of 3 7/16 and 3 1/2, and even its sales to retail customers were consistently below its published wholesale offering price. Moreover, on seven occasions when registrant was short and purchased Bliss stock from another dealer, a strong indication that registrant initiated the transactions and thus paid the other dealer's offering price, registrant paid price ranging from about 2 3/4 to 3 3/8.

In view of the foregoing, it is clear that registrant's offering price was wholly illusory, and cannot be accepted as evidence of the prevailing market. Since there is no indication that registrant controlled the market for Bliss, the prices it charged the other dealer in two transactions may properly be used as a basis for computing markups. In all other instances during the period in question, the best evidence of the prevailing market is the price registrant paid for Bliss in contemporaneous transactions.

Accordingly, computing registrant's markups on the basis of the prices it charged in contemporaneous inter-dealer sales, and, in other instances, on the basis of its contemporaneous costs, we find that, in 207 retail sales of Bliss, registrant charged excessive markups ranging from 11.1% to 24% above the prevailing market price.

C. We conclude that, in connection with the retail sales of FTC and Bliss stock cited above, registrant willfully violated the antifraud provisions of Section 17(a)(1) of the Securities Act and Section 10(b) of the Securities Exchange Act and Rule 10b–5 thereunder. We also find that registrant willfully violated the antifraud provisions of Sections 17(a)(2) and 17(a)(3) of the Securities Act.

IV.

Registrant engaged in very serious misconduct. It charged customers excessive prices in nearly 300 transactions, many of which involved markups of more than 20% above the prevailing market price. These blatant overcharges reflect a marked insensitivity on the part of registrant to the obligation of fair dealing borne by all brokerage firms.

As noted above, we ordered review on our own motion of the sanction assessed against registrant by the administrative law judge. The law judge concluded that it was appropriate to suspend registrant's broker-dealer registration for a period of 30 days. However, we have found that registrant charged more than three times the number of unfair markups cited by the law judge in his initial decision. Under the circumstances, we consider that a 90–day suspension of registrant is warranted in the public interest.

By the Commission (CHAIRMAN SHAD and COMMISSIONERS TREADWAY and COX.).

In ETTINGER v. MERRILL LYNCH, 835 F.2d 1031 (3d Cir.1987), the court held that excessive markups on certain kinds of bonds could be attacked under Rule 10b–5, and that SEC rules requiring disclosure of markups in certain kinds of transactions did not mean that price information would not be material in other kinds of transactions not covered by the rules.

NORRIS & HIRSHBERG v. SEC

85 U.S.App.D.C. 268, 177 F.2d 228 (D.C.Cir.1949).

Before CLARK, WILBUR K. MILLER and PRETTYMAN, CIRCUIT JUDGES.

CLARK, CIRCUIT JUDGE. * * *

Petitioner is a securities broker and dealer and has been engaged mainly in what is known as over-the-counter business in Atlanta. Georgia, since September, 1932. It became a registered broker and dealer on January 1, 1936. * * *

Petitioner dealt in both listed and unlisted stocks and bonds. In the case of listed securities that were handled for customers on a brokerage basis, transactions were effected through New York houses with whom petitioner had connections, and petitioner would charge a commission in addition to the commission charged by the exchange member. This seems to have been the customary practice in the community.

We understand that there is substantially no complaint by the Commission or any one else as to this portion of the firm's business. It is the other, and by far the greater, portion of the business of which the Commission complains and which occasioned the hearing and subsequent revocation order now under review. Petitioner's transactions in local, unlisted securities have always constituted the predominant portion of its business and are now, we understand, the sole concern of the firm. The Commission raises no contention as to the financial strength and earning capacity of the issuers of these local securities and, for the purposes of this opinion, it will be assumed that these securities in themselves are sound. In other words, there is no complaint as to the type or intrinsic value of the securities in which petitioner specializes. The case is here because of petitioner's methods of dealing with those securities and with its customers with regard to those securities.

* * * After oral argument before the Commission and the Commission having independently reviewed the record, the Commission, by

opinion dated January 22, 1946, revoked petitioner's registration. * * * Petitioner now seeks review of this Commission action. * * *

It is undisputed that petitioner, during the times here in question, dealt primarily with local, unlisted securities. It is also beyond dispute that petitioner specialized in the issues of the following five local companies: Haverty Furniture Companies, Inc., Southern Spring Bed Company, National Manufacture and Stores Company, Atlantic Steel Company, and Fulton Bag and Cotton Mills. As to these five securities, Hirshberg himself testified that his firm probably sold 75% of what was sold in those securities during the period in question. This is substantial evidence in support of the Commission's finding that petitioner dominated the market in those securities.

All of the fifty customers of petitioner who testified in the proceeding below had margin accounts with petitioner. Many did not know what a margin account was or what a debit balance was or that they were dealing on margin. Thirty-one of the fifty were women—twelve were widows. Fifteen of the customers testifying had given petitioner express discretionary powers over their accounts. One elderly widow of very limited means stated that "everything was put in his [Hirshberg's] hands absolutely and completely." She did not understand that the firm was selling her stock it owned or buying stock from her for itself. Although she was aware that the monthly confirmations referred to petitioner as "principal," she didn't pay any attention to that and never asked for any explanation. She received a letter from Hirshberg expressing distress at her ill health and closing "with fondest love." This witness and many others were obviously under the impression that petitioner acted as agent for them rather than as principal. Most of the witnesses believed that petitioner was dealing *for* them rather than *with* them. Though it was recognized that petitioner was in business for profit, it was very generally believed by petitioner's customers that its income was derived primarily from the commissions it charged rather than mark-ups. The record is replete with evidence that the faith and trust of the customers in petitioner was "absolute," "implicit," "perfect," "sublime," and "blind." Further, though petitioner refuses to admit that it is so, there is substantial evidence in the record in the form of customer testimony to the effect that the great majority of the customers accepted and followed the advice rendered by petitioner in almost every instance. From the facts enumerated above it is apparent, and we believe obvious, that petitioner was not only in a dominant position as to the market for its unlisted securities but that it was in a position to strongly influence and, in fact, control what securities would be bought and what sold and the timing and frequency of such purchases and sales as well as the amount of the mark-ups and mark-downs at which they would be made. The Commission so ruled and we see no basis in the record for overturning that ruling.

But these factors alone, while sufficient to arouse the suspicion of persons informed in these matters, do not necessarily establish that petitioner violated the anti-fraud provisions of the Securities and Securities Exchange Acts. The stage is set, however, for fraudulent activity. It should be noted parenthetically at this point that petitioner has not been charged with or proven guilty of the practice commonly known as "rigging the market" in order to artificially raise the market and unload stock at a price far above its worth. Petitioner's offense against the public interest is more subtle, though no less insidious.

The Commission charged and subsequently concluded that petitioner had violated (1) Section 17(a) of the Securities Act of 1933, (2) Section 15(c)(1) of the Securities Exchange Act of 1934, and (3) Section 10(b) of the latter Act, as well as certain Commission rules promulgated thereunder. The record supports the charges made and the conclusions reached.

Bearing in mind constantly that petitioner had achieved the absolute and blind confidence of its relatively naive customers and that petitioner dominated the market in the five mentioned unlisted securities in which it specialized, the facts of record with respect to petitioner's business methods, as summarized below, become vitally significant. The record shows clearly that petitioner controlled at all times a large percentage of the floating supply of the five specialities. There was no system for collection and publication of market quotations for these specialities. Most of petitioner's customers had margin accounts thus offering the opportunity for greater trading volume as well as providing petitioner a greater degree of control over its customers' accounts. The record offers ample proof that it was an integral part of petitioner's trading system to constantly whip its specialties back and forth in its customers' accounts so that, within a short space of time, one can observe the interesting phenomenon of the same customers selling securities to petitioner and then a few days later buying the same securities back at higher prices. An analysis of one customer account reveals the astonishing proportions which this excessive trading practice of petitioner could, and did, assume.

From October, 1937, through 1941 this account "bought" about $1,400,000 and "sold" about $1,300,000 of securities with an average net investment of only $323,500. The account made 266 purchases and 191 sales during that period. About 170 of those purchases were made on the same day as sales. As applied to the five specialty securities the figures demonstrate that the account made 117 purchases and 67 sales. Of the 117 purchase transactions 37 followed intervening sales of the same security. This means that this individual account went in and out of the five specialties an aggregate of 74 times.

As the Commission put it, "the heart of [petitioner's] business was the continual shuffling of securities back and forth in its customers' accounts." The record fully supports this statement. One illustration taken from the record and summarized in the Commission's opinion below will suffice. This illustration refers only to the month of December, 1935, and the figures represent petitioner's trading in one stock alone. Petitioner opened the month with an inventory short 35 shares and closed the month with an inventory of zero. During the month it dealt exclusively with its customers in that stock, that is, it neither bought nor sold any of these shares on the outside market. During the month it bought a total of 5,105 shares and sold 5,070 shares. It made a total trading profit for the month of $8,273 in that stock alone. This is, in part, how petitioner accomplished that result. On the 3rd, Customer A sold 100 shares to petitioner at 22. During the day those shares were sold to other customers at 24. On the 10th, Customer B sold 500 shares to petitioner at 22½ and petitioner sold back 100 shares to Customer A at 24. On the 4th, Customer C sold 200 shares to petitioner at 22. On the same and next day these and other shares were sold to other customers at 23 and 24. On the 16th, petitioner bought 300 shares from two other customers at 23½ and the same day sold 200 shares to Customer C at 25. On the 6th, Customer D sold to petitioner 200 shares at 22½ and, on the same day, these shares were sold to other customers at 24. On the 11th, Customer D bought back 50 shares from petitioner at 25. On the 18th, Customer D bought back from petitioner another 100 shares at 25.

With this trading practice in mind it is not difficult to perceive why petitioner realized, during the period at issue here, $530,000 in gross trading profits while its customers realized only $53,000. It also helps explain why the securities of customers held long in margin accounts showed unrealized losses of $285,000 at the end of that period. All this occurred, it will be remembered, while the trusting clients were all convinced that petitioner was acting *for* them and in their best interest. We cannot visualize any circumstances to which the statutory phrase "manipulative, deceptive, or other fraudulent device or contrivance" applies more aptly than the present one.

Petitioner's registration was ordered revoked primarily because of petitioner's failure or omission to fully disclose its trading practices and its adverse position to its customers. Petitioner concedes that, except for its confirmations of purchase or sale, it made no disclosure whatever to its customers. Petitioner does, however, assert that its customers were told that petitioner dealt from inventory, but the testimony of the customers themselves belies this assertion.

Reduced to its essence, petitioner's argument in this court with all its many facets amounts to no more than a claim that common law fraud has not been proven and that the registration cannot be revoked without such proof. We must reject such a claim. To accept it would be to adopt the fallacious theory that Congress enacted existing securities legislation for the protection of the broker-dealer rather than for the protection of the public. To say, as petitioner does, that every element of common law fraud must be proven in order to validate the revocation of a broker-dealer registration is to say that Congress had no purpose in enacting regulatory statutes in this field and that its legislation in the field is meaningless. On the contrary, it has long been recognized by the federal courts that the investing and usually naive public needs special protection in this specialized field. We believe that the Securities and the Securities Exchange Act were designed to prevent, among other things, just such practices and business methods as have been shown to have been indulged in by the petitioner in this case. Those practices described above when viewed in the setting portrayed in this record can only be described as manipulative, deceptive, and fraudulent. There is abundant and substantial evidence of record to support the conclusion that this petitioner has completely failed to disclose to its customers the true capacity in which it was acting and the manner in which it dealt with them. This failure constituted violation of federal statute. * * *

Section 11(e) of the 1934 Act directed the Commission to "make a study of the feasibility and advisability of the complete segregation of the functions of dealer and broker, and to report the results of its study and its recommendations to the Congress on or before January 3, 1936." The Commission's report submitted in accordance with this direction noted the many conflicts of interest arising from the combination of functions, but recommended that these be handled by specific rules, rather than a general segregation of functions.

In CHASINS v. SMITH, BARNEY, 438 F.2d 1167 (2d Cir.1970), the court held that a brokerage firm violated Rule 10b–5 by failing to disclose to a customer that the firm was "making a market" in over-the-counter securities which it sold to him, even though the confirmation of sale, as required by SEC rules, disclosed that the firm was selling to him as principal and not acting as his agent.

In May 1977, the SEC replaced Rule 15c1–4, the confirmation rule referred to in the *Chasins* case, with a new Rule 10b–10, setting forth confirmation and disclosure requirements for all types of transactions by brokers or dealers. Sec.Ex.Act Rel. No. 13508 (May 5, 1977). In October 1978, the rule was amended to require specific disclosure of market-maker status. Sec.Ex.Act Rel. No. 11529 (Oct. 6, 1978).

In CANT v. A.G. BECKER & CO., INC., 374 F.Supp. 36 (N.D.Ill. 1974), the court held a broker-dealer firm liable in damages under Rule 10b–5 to a client who had a "unique and special relationship" with the firm over many years, when it failed to make adequate disclosure to him that it was selling him certain securities as principal from its own inventory. Even though the firm disclosed on its confirmation slips the capacity in which it was acting, as required by Rule 15c1–4, the disclosure was held inadequate because the code and terminology used on the confirmation slips were not explained to the client.

SHIVANGI v. DEAN WITTER

825 F.2d 885 (5th Cir.1987).

Before WISDOM, HIGGINBOTHAM and DAVIS, CIRCUIT JUDGES.

PATRICK E. HIGGINBOTHAM, CIRCUIT JUDGE:

Dr. and Mrs. Sampat S. Shivangi sued Dean Witter Reynolds, Inc., under SEC Rule 10b–5 for failing to disclose that Dean Witter's account executives receive higher compensation for principal trades of over-the-counter stocks in which Dean Witter is a market maker than for other sales. * * *

I

A

In 1981, Dean Witter Reynolds, Inc., was a market maker in the over-the-counter market for Keldon Oil stock. As a market maker, Dean Witter held itself out as being willing to buy and sell Keldon Oil stock for its own account on a regular or continuous basis, according to quotations in National Association of Securities Dealers Automated Quotations, a computerized quotations system. NASDAQ lists bid prices and ask prices, or the prices at which a customer can sell and buy a stock, respectively.

Unless a retail customer requests Dean Witter to handle the transaction as an agent, Dean Witter handles as a principal over-the-counter trades in which it is a market maker—that is, Dean Witter sells the stock to its customer from its own account instead of acting as the customer's agent to buy the stock from another.[2] This does not mean that Dean Witter has in inventory the stock at a cost that makes the principal transaction profitable. It means that Dean Witter will acquire the stock long or short, or take it from inventory, and sell it to the customer at the prices quoted on NASDAQ. Dean Witter's Jackson, Mississippi, office handles as a principal approximately 75 to 80 percent of its over-the-counter trades in which Dean Witter makes a market.

When Dean Witter acts as an agent, it receives a commission and passes 30 to 40 percent of the commission to the account executive as his compensation. When Dean Witter acts as a principal, it sells the stock at the inside ask price—the lowest price any market maker asks—and then adds a "mark-up" to the price as its compensation. Dean Witter's mark-up never exceeds the amount the commission would be in an agency transaction. In fact, the customer pays less than he would in an agency transaction because Dean Witter rounds the mark-up to the nearest 1/16 below what the agency commission would have been. Dean Witter pays the account executive thirty to forty

2. Dean Witter generally acts as an agent when trading on a national stock exchange.

percent of the mark-up and also of the spread—the difference between the bid price and the ask price—sometimes resulting in higher compensation for principal transactions than for agency transactions.

B

Dr. Sampat S. Shivangi and his wife, Dr. Udaya S. Shivangi, opened an investment account with Dean Witter in the spring of 1981. On May 13, 1981, Thomas Aitken, the Shivangis' account executive at Dean Witter's Jackson, Mississippi, office, called the Shivangis to recommend that they purchase shares in Keldon Oil. Heeding the recommendation, the Shivangis purchased through Dean Witter 400 shares of Keldon Oil stock for 17½ per share, or $7000.00 total.

At the time of the purchase, Keldon Oil stock had a market price of 15 bid and 17⅛ ask, or a spread of 2⅛.[3] The mark-up was ⅜. Aitken's compensation was forty percent of the mark-up and spread, or $400.00.[4] Dean Witter's normal commission on an agency transaction for 400 shares at 17⅛ is $154.70, of which Aitken would have received thirty to forty percent, or $46.41 to $61.88, rather than the $400 he was paid.

Dean Witter sent the Shivangis a confirmation slip that complied fully with SEC Rule 10b–10, by stating the purchase price, indicating Dean Witter's role as principal, and stating "DWR IS MARKET MAKER." At no time were the Shivangis told the account executive's compensation.[5]

The market price of Keldon Oil stock rose about ten percent shortly after the transaction, then declined steadily. The Shivangis sold their shares in December 1981 at 7¼ per share, or $2,900.00 total.

C

On July 13, 1982, the Shivangis sued Dean Witter, Tom Aitken, and James Palmer, who was the branch manager of Dean Witter's Jackson office, alleging that Aitken made misleading statements of material fact about Keldon Oil stock and omitted other material facts in violation of the Securities Exchange Act of 1934, § 10(b), of SEC Rule 10b–5, and of various state laws. When the Shivangis learned in discovery about the spread and the account executive compensation system, they amended their complaint to allege that the failure to disclose the compensation information violated Rule 10b–5 and state laws. They also sought to represent a class of similarly situated purchasers.

* * *

At the conclusion of the Shivangis' proof in the bench trial, Dean Witter moved to dismiss for the Shivangis' failure to prove scienter. The district court granted Dean Witter's motion. * * * We are not

3. A normal spread in 1981 was ¼ to ⅜. The large spread likely reflected a slow market in the stock.

4. .40 × (400 shares) × $(2⅛ + ⅜)/share = $400.00.

5. Effective March 17, 1986, the SEC amended Rule 10b–10 to require disclosure of the mark-up also.

persuaded that the district court clearly erred in finding that the Shivangis failed to prove scienter.

Dean Witter knowingly failed to disclose the account executive compensation to the Shivangis, but knowledge of omitted facts does not itself establish scienter. Rather, the Shivangis must prove that Dean Witter acted with actual "intent to deceive, manipulate, or defraud." * * *

The record supports the district court's finding of no actual intent to deceive. The record contains no evidence that Aitken or Dean Witter actually intended to deceive the Shivangis by failing to disclose the compensation information, nor does it establish that Aitken recommended the stock because of his unusual compensation. Rather, Aitken recommended Keldon Oil stock because Dean Witter's best analyst considered it a good investment.

The record also supports the district court's determination that the defendants did not know nor should have known the danger of misleading the customers by the omission. At the time of the purchase, neither the SEC nor any court had determined the compensation information to be material. Indeed, the materiality of this information remains an open question today. Dean Witter fully disclosed all that the SEC specifically requires a market maker acting as a principal to disclose under Rule 10b–10. The Shivangis did not introduce evidence establishing that compensation to sales personnel is ordinarily disclosed in the securities industry, a fact that might have indicated to Dean Witter the danger of nondisclosure. Finally, the evidence did not establish that the compensation system affected the price of the stock to the Shivangis, nor the actual value of the stock. Thus, any danger of misleading the customers by the omission was not obvious.

Jeremiah Mullins, head of Dean Witter's Trading Department, testified that Dean Witter intended its compensation system to provide a uniform system for account executive compensation in over-the-counter, principal transactions and also to restore account executive compensation to competitive levels existing before 1980, when an SEC rule requiring NASDAQ display of inside quotation prices and an NASD rule requiring market makers to sell at the inside ask price had the incidental effect of reducing account executives' compensation. Such is not the intent essential to a violation of Rule 10b–5.

* * *

Selected References

S. Goldberg, Fraudulent Broker–Dealer Practices (1978 ed.).

T. Hazen, Securities Regulation ch. 10 (2d ed. 1990).

D. Lipton, Broker–Dealer Regulation (1989).

N. Wolfson, R. Phillips & T. Russo, Regulation of Brokers, Dealers and Securities Markets (1977).

Goforth, Stockbrokers' Duties to their Customers, 33 St. Louis U.L.J. 407 (1989).

Langevoort, Fraud and Deception by Securities Professionals, 61 Texas L.Rev. 1247 (1983).

Ratner, Regulation of the Compensation of Securities Dealers, 55 Cornell L.Rev. 348 (1970).

Scott, Caveat Vendor: Broker–Dealer Liability Under the Securities Exchange Act, 17 Sec.Reg.L.J. 274 (1989).

Note, Broker Dealers, Market Makers and Fiduciary Duties, 9 Loy.–Chi.L.J. 746 (1978).

---

2. *Market Manipulation*

One of the most serious abuses in the securities markets on which Senate investigators focused in their 1933 hearings was the operation of "pools" which ran up the prices of securities on an exchange by series of well-timed transactions, then unloaded their holdings on the public just before the price dropped. Accordingly, §§ 9 and 10(a) of the 1934 Act prohibit a variety of manipulative activities with respect to exchange-listed securities, and § 10(b) contains a catch-all provision permitting the SEC to prohibit by rule any "manipulative or deceptive device or contrivance" with respect to any security.

By and large, these provisions have been effective in preventing a recurrence of the widespread manipulation on exchanges which flourished in the 1920s. The present focus of concern, at least with respect to stocks listed on the New York Stock Exchange, is the extent to which large transactions by "institutional investors", such as pension funds, mutual funds and insurance companies, produce undesirable fluctuations and distortions in the market price of particular securities. This problem, however, results from changes in investment patterns and other economic factors, rather than from the type of deliberate fraud with which the draftsmen of the 1934 Act were concerned.

There is one area, however, in which there have been continuing problems in drawing the line between manipulative activity and legitimate transactions, namely the extent to which securities dealers and others participating in a public offering or "distribution" of securities may simultaneously bid for or purchase the same security.

(a) Purchases or Bids by Persons Involved in a Distribution

The success of a public offering of securities may depend in large measure on whether the market price of the security goes up or down during the period of the distribution. Accordingly, there is a strong incentive for those participating in the distribution to maintain the market price at a high level during that period. The history of the

SEC's efforts to separate legitimate "stabilization" from improper "manipulation" are summarized in the following excerpt:

MARKET ACTIVITIES OF PARTICIPANTS IN SECURITIES DISTRIBUTIONS

By Wm. Ward Foshay

45 Va.L.Rev. 907 (1959).*

In the conventional case, an issuer or security holder enters into a contract with a syndicate of underwriters to purchase and sell a block of securities to the public. The underwriters then offer and sell the securities directly and through other securities dealers, and several days later the underwriters take delivery of the securities and redeliver them to those to whom the sales have been made. Any open market trading during the distribution period of the securities being distributed, or of securities of the same class, obviously can facilitate or impede the distribution of the block. For this reason the problem has been to determine the extent to which market activities of participants or persons otherwise interested in the distribution should be prohibited or permitted. If a participant should trade excessively, or in a manner designed to raise the open market price, solely for the purpose of creating an artificial market conducive to sales of the block, no one would question the unfairness to the investing public or the characterization of the practice as unlawful manipulation. On the other hand, underwriters, as another part of their regular business, engage in day-to-day trading in securities for both their own and their customers' accounts. To the extent that timing, terms, and volume of such trading are determined by customers or others not participating in the distribution, the contrary result should follow. Similarly, trading by an underwriter or other participant for its own account may occur simply in the regular course of business or otherwise as the result of perfectly proper motivation. However, the uncertainty inherent in making intent the criterion gives rise to the question whether such trading should be restricted regardless of purpose to insure protection to the public. Further, market activities of participants which simply stabilize the market price, though in a sense artificial, have been demonstrated to serve a useful public purpose by contributing to orderly distributions, and the question in this regard has concerned the controls to which these activities should be subjected. * * *

For twenty years there were no comprehensive rules on market activities in the course of distributions. The statutory provisions were administered partly through published interpretations and decisions, and partly through unpublished correspondence, conferences, and telephone calls with underwriters' and dealers' representatives and their counsel. Out of these there emerged some definition of the areas for regulation and also many of the principles to be followed in determining the types of activities to be prohibited or permitted.

A. Trading

To be condemned under section 9(a)(2), the excessive trading, raising, or depressing of price must be for the purpose of inducing the purchase or sale of the security by others. This element of intent was alluded to in an early opinion of the Commission's General Counsel in which it was said that during the course of a distribution, any trading transactions by the underwriters "designed" substantially to raise or lower stock exchange prices constituted a violation. The purpose to induce others to purchase was readily inferred, however, from the timing and other circumstances of purchases in contemplation of, or during, a distribution. Finally, in answer to an inquiry whether an underwriter's trading department could continue to function with respect to a security while its retail department was distributing securities of the same issue, the Director of the Commission's Trading and Exchange Division, in effect, eliminated any further necessity of establishing purpose in this context:

> When an underwriter is engaged in the distribution of a security, he obviously has the purpose of inducing the purchase of that security by others, with the result that when he concurrently effects trading transactions which raise the price of the security, or create trading activity beyond that necessary for stabilizing, it is difficult, if not impossible, to give credence to the view that the trading transactions were not also conducted, at least in part, for the purpose of inducing the purchase of the security by others.

It then became the practice to include in agreements among underwriters flat prohibitions against trading for the underwriters' own accounts during distributions.

Further administrative decisions made it clear that the types of transactions considered unlawful would include not only bids or purchases made by underwriters or dealers for their own accounts, or accounts in which they had interests, but also transactions consummated by others at their request or recommendation. * * *

Certain kinds of transactions were excepted. This was true of unsolicited brokerage transactions, and probably also of privately negotiated purchases effected otherwise than in the open market. Exceptions were also made where the security being distributed was traded only in the over-the-counter market and all, or a substantial segment, of the dealers who made the market were to be among the underwriters. * * *

B. Stabilization

Stabilization is the pegging or fixing of the market price of a security for the limited purpose of preventing or retarding a decline in such price. The Commission had to decide whether to permit unregulated stabilization, to regulate it, or to prohibit it. It chose the second alternative and recognized the propriety of stabilization.

In April, 1936, a registration statement under the Securities Act of 1933 with respect to common stock of The Flintkote Company became effective, and approximately 280,000 shares were offered by underwriters to the public at the initial offering price of $47.25. Several days later the Commission was advised that approximately 100,000 of such shares remained unsold, and that the stock was then selling on the New York Curb Exchange at $46.25. The Commission was asked, among other things, whether the underwriters could stabilize on the exchange while they were selling the remaining shares, and, if so, whether they could stabilize at the initial public offering price or were obliged to place bids at $46.25. The Commission's General Counsel replied that "certain stabilizing operations" were not within the prohibitions against manipulation, and that, while "the accepted concept of stabilization does not require that the price of the security be held to one particular quotation," activities designed "substantially to raise or lower stock exchange prices are clearly manipulative."

Thereafter, a sticker supplement to the Flintkote prospectus informing prospective purchasers that stabilizing purchases had been made and were expected to continue was prepared and sent to underwriters and members of the selling group. On April 17, 1936, The New York Times reported:

> For the first time since the passage of the Securities Exchange Act of 1934 an underwriting group yesterday openly notified dealers participating in distribution of a security that the group had supported and might continue to support the market for the issue in the period of public distribution.

The practice of disclosing stabilizing transactions was subsequently formalized, and since 1939 the Commission's rule 426 under the Securities Act of 1933 has required every prospectus to carry on its front cover or inside front cover page the familiar stabilization statement "in capital letters, printed in bold-face roman type at least as large as ten-point modern type and at least two points leaded." There was introduced at about the same time the requirement in rule 17a–2 for the filing with the Commission of specified reports on stabilizing activities.

The first formal regulation of substantive aspects of Stabilization came in 1940 with the adoption of Regulation X–9A6–1, which applied only to stabilization to facilitate an "offering at the market" of a registered security. In the release which announced the adoption of the rule, the Commission adverted to some of the difficulties it was apparently having in attempting to devise rules of more general application. The rule proved to be of little practical significance because of its limited scope [32] and because it "simply put the quietus on market offerings." * * *

32. The term "offering at the market" was defined to mean an offering in which the offering price was represented to be "at the market" or at a price related thereto.

In May, 1954, the Commission announced a proposal to adopt three rules regarding activities of participants in a distribution. The proposed rules were described as a formulation of principles historically applied in considering questions relating to manipulative activity and stabilization, and were said to be part of the Commission's continuing program to set forth in written rules its administrative interpretations wherever possible.

The proposed rules were in principle and structure generally along the lines mapped out by the prior administrative interpretation. Rule 10b–6 would restrict trading activity, rule 10b–7 would set forth the principles to be followed in stabilizing, and rule 10b–8 would deal with the peculiar problems of rights offerings. If rule 10b–7 were to be adopted, Regulation X–9A6–1 would be rescinded as having proved unworkable, and rule 10b–7 would prohibit stabilization in offerings "at the market" because of the inherent contradiction in representing an offering to be "at the market" when the price of the security is being artificially maintained. * * *

In July, 1955, the Commission announced the adoption of rules 10b–6, 10b–7, and 10b–8, and the rescission of Regulation X–9A6. * * *

Rules 10b–7 and 10b–8 have generally worked smoothly in underwritten fixed-price offerings. Difficulties have arisen, however, in applying Rule 10b–6 to unmanaged market-price offerings, as the following cases indicate:

HAZEL BISHOP INC.

40 S.E.C. 718 (1961).

By WOODSIDE, COMMISSIONER.

On June 28, 1960, Hazel Bishop Inc. ("Hazel Bishop," registrant), a company engaged in the cosmetics business, filed a registration statement with us under the Securities Act of 1933 ("Act"), relating to 1,157,200 shares of common stock, all of which were then outstanding. It was stated that these shares which represented approximately 61% of registrant's outstanding common stock were held by 70 named persons, referred to as the selling stockholders, who may offer them from time to time at prices current at the time of sale through brokers on the American Stock Exchange, in the open market, or otherwise. An amendment to the registration statement was filed on October 18, 1960, which, among other things, increased the number of shares to be offered to 1,274,823 and the number of selling stockholders to 112.

It was construed by the Commission not to include an offering at a fixed dollar amount, even though determined by the market price at the date of the offering. Moreover, even though the offering price was changed to reflect the market price, it did not become an offering at the market if the price continued to be expressed in a fixed dollar amount and if it was not changed with every shift in the market.

Shortly thereafter the Commission initiated public proceedings under Section 8(d) of the Act, to determine whether a stop order should issue suspending the effectiveness of the registration statement. * * *

The prospectus, without being specific as to precisely how the proposed offering will in fact be made, conveys the impression that at least some of the shares will be offered through brokers on the American Stock Exchange. * * *

In a conventional distribution of a new issue or a secondary offering (this offering has some of the characteristics of both), the activities of underwriters and other participants in the distribution are governed by carefully drawn underwriting agreements and related contracts providing a controlled procedure designed to bring about an orderly marketing of the security free of practices prohibited by the statutes or rules as manipulative, deceptive or fraudulent, or otherwise unlawful.

In supplying registrant with much needed capital in late 1959 and early 1960, and proposing the resale of the shares thus acquired to the public, the original purchasers and their associates and transferees in fact were and are performing an underwriting function for registrant, a function normally performed by an underwriter-dealer group. However, none of the contractual safeguards designed for the protection of both buyer and seller ordinarily provided in the conventional distribution through professional underwriters and dealers are mentioned in the prospectus. The absence of any indication of these safeguards, the size of the group of selling stockholders, and various relationships among them lead us to be apprehensive that this large group of sellers may not be aware that various statutory provisions and rules which govern the conduct of underwriters and dealers will apply to them and their activities for the duration of the offering of their shares to the public.

There are at least 112 selling stockholders. Apparently no procedures for coordinating their activities or guarding against unlawful practices have been established. Among them are persons who control Hazel Bishop's affairs, including the publication of financial data and other information about registrant and its prospects. Some of these stockholders are linked by agreements among themselves for profit sharing and provisions protecting them against loss. Many of them have options to purchase a large part of Spector's shares at prices below the current market prices. Some of the shares being registered have been pledged as collateral for loans. One of the sellers is the specialist responsible for maintaining an orderly market in the stock on the American Stock Exchange. The shares to be offered amount to approximately 60% of the outstanding stock, almost twice the number of shares heretofore available for trading in the open market.

The terms of the proposed offering in their over-all effect, as stated in the prospectus, amount to a representation by Hazel Bishop that the offering by the selling stockholders will be "at the market." We do not wish to be understood as implying that the statements in the prospectus as to the terms of the proposed offering are inaccurate as of the date of the prospectus. Without intimating that any manipulative or improper purposes exist, we are convinced, on the basis of our experience and the mechanics of the securities markets, that there is grave danger of the development in the course of time of conditions inconsistent with the representations in the prospectus. Should that occur, registrant and the selling stockholders might find themselves participating in serious violations of the Securities Act, the Securities Exchange Act, and the rules under both statutes.

The Commission's Rule 10b–6 under the Exchange Act prohibits, bids or purchases by any person who is an underwriter, prospective underwriter, a broker, dealer or other person who is participating in a distribution, or who is a person on whose behalf a distribution is being made. Each of the selling stockholders and any broker or person acting for any of them will be subject to the provisions of this rule.

Moreover, notwithstanding the potential size of this offering, it will not be possible to stabilize the market for the stock to facilitate the distribution, since stabilizing is prohibited by Rule 10b–7 in connection with an offering "at the market." Rule 10b–2 would also be applicable, thus prohibiting any person who participates or is otherwise financially interested in a distribution of a security from paying or offering to pay any person for soliciting another to purchase any such security on the Exchange.

Underlining the specific requirements referred to above is the basic principle that any representation that a security is being offered "at the market" implies the existence of a free and open market which is not made, controlled or artificially influenced by any person participating in the offering. Any activity which constitutes a violation of the anti-manipulative provisions mentioned or which is otherwise intended to stabilize, stimulate or condition the market would be inconsistent with the representation and would render the registration statement false and misleading.

In addition to the foregoing and other provisions of the Exchange Act and the rules thereunder, it must be borne in mind that this is a registered distribution which must be made in accordance with the prospectus requirements of the Securities Act of 1933. The use by Hazel Bishop or any other participants of written communications which offer its securities will be subject to the prohibitions of Section 5(b)(1) of the Securities Act. Consequently, any such communications would be unlawful unless they are in the form of a statutory prospectus, or the communication was accompanied by or had been preceded by a statutory prospectus. Prior delivery of prospectuses to the Exchange pursuant to Rule 153 would not satisfy this requirement of Section 5(b)(1).

The specialist will be confronted with a most difficult problem. It is his duty to maintain a fair and orderly market on the Exchange for the Hazel Bishop stock. Since the firm is listed in the registration statement as a selling stockholder and is a member of a group whose interest lies in effecting a distribution at the best price obtainable, it is not clear how the specialist can properly discharge his function and at the same time comply with the rules under the Exchange Act.

In summary, we think that under the factual situation here presented the potentialities for violations of the law, witting or unwitting, on the part of those who are about to offer their stock on the basis stated are so grave that consistent with our obligations under the Exchange Act, they should be called to the attention of the selling stockholders, the issuer, the Exchange, the existing stockholders of Hazel Bishop and the general public. * * *

The proposed sale of shares in the *Hazel Bishop* case, involving 61% of the outstanding stock of the company, was clearly a "distribution" within the meaning of Rule 10b–6, as well as a "distribution" causing the sellers to be considered "underwriters" for purposes of the 1933 Act. But, as we saw in Chapter I.B.6, even a relatively small sale of stock by a person who is categorized as an "underwriter" for 1933 Act purposes is considered a "distribution" for purposes of that Act. If every sale which is a distribution for 1933 Act purposes is automatically classified as a distribution for Rule 10b–6 purposes, every dealer who purchases some of the registered stock for resale becomes a "participant in a distribution," and is required to cease bidding for the stock, i.e., to cease making a market. In the case of an over-the-counter stock in which only one or two dealers are making a market, involvement of those dealers in the distribution could therefore cause the "market" to disappear.

In JAFFEE & CO., 44 S.E.C. 285 (1970), the Commission held, with one dissent, that a sale required to be registered under the 1933 Act was also a distribution for Rule 10b–6 purposes. Five years later, in COLLINS SECURITIES CORP., CCH Fed.Sec.L.Rep. ¶ 80,327 (1975), reversed on other grounds, 562 F.2d 820 (D.C.Cir.1977), the Commission reversed its position:

> Rule 10b–6 provides, in pertinent part, that it is a manipulative or deceptive device for a broker-dealer which is participating in a particular distribution of securities to bid for or purchase such securities until it has completed its participation in the distribution.
>
> * * *
>
> Registrant and Collins argue that there was no "distribution" within the meaning of Rule 10b–6. They point to the test we laid down for making that determination in Bruns, Nordeman & Co., 40 S.E.C. 652 (1961)—the magnitude of the offering and the selling efforts and selling methods utilized. Respondents also contend that registrant was not an underwriter as defined in the rule.
>
> Under our holding in Jaffee & Co., the *Bruns, Nordeman* standard would be inapplicable here since an offering registered under the

Securities Act would necessarily be a distribution within the meaning of Rule 10b–6. But we have reconsidered the proposition that registration of an offering *per se* makes Rule 10b–6 applicable. Instead we have concluded, as did Commissioner Smith dissenting in part in the *Jaffee* case, that this proposition does not comport with the intended coverage of the rule. As Commissioner Smith pointed out, the term distribution is not defined either in the Securities Act of 1933 or in the Securities Exchange Act of 1934 and its meaning and applicability to particular persons in each context should be derived from the differing purposes for which it is used.

The purpose of the Securities Act is to provide adequate disclosure about an issuer through the registration process in situations where registration is necessary and practicable. The Securities Act contemplates that registration will be required, absent some special exemption, when securities are publicly offered by or on behalf of an issuer or are purchased from an issuer for public resale, and the term "distribution" as used in the Act has been interpreted to accomplish that purpose. Thus, as Commissioner Smith pointed out, if an individual acquires 200 shares of an actively traded stock from the issuer and promptly sells them on an exchange, it is clear that registration would be required.

Rule 10b–6, on the other hand, is designed to prevent manipulation in the markets. To that end, it precludes a person from buying stock in the market when he is at the same time participating in an offering of securities which is of such a nature as to give rise to a temptation on the part of that person to purchase for manipulative purposes. The term distribution in Rule 10b–6 should therefore be interpreted to identify situations where that temptation may be present. Our opinion in *Bruns, Nordeman* attempted to define distribution so as to identify such circumstances.

If the term distribution in Rule 10b–6 were to be equated with the concept of public offering or distribution in the Securities Act, this would not only extend the restrictions of Rule 10b–6 beyond their intended purpose but could result in unnecessary disruption of the trading markets, particularly where an exchange specialist or other market maker acquires registered stock in the performance of his normal functions. It would obviously make no sense to conclude that a specialist, who happens to acquire some registered stock in the course of his normal activities, has to get out of the market until after he has disposed of that stock. No one has ever thought that such a result was required, even though specialists might well purchase registered stock being sold under a so-called "shelf registration."

We accordingly decline to hold that any offering of securities pursuant to a registration statement automatically constitutes a distribution within the meaning of Rule 10b–6, and the *Jaffee* decision, insofar as it is to the contrary, is overruled.

This does not mean that a requirement that an offering be registered is irrelevant for purposes of determining the applicability of Rule 10b–6. Rule 10b–6 undoubtedly applies to most registered offerings.

> Indeed, that rule, and its companions, Rule 10b–7 and Rule 10b–8, were framed in contemplation of such offerings, although Rule 10b–6, of course, may apply to a distribution which is, for some reason, exempt from registration under the Securities Act. The present case is an example of a registered offering to which Rule 10b–6 does apply. As pointed out above, registrant acquired 75,694 shares of Big Horn stock, issued pursuant to the warrants, and proceeded to distribute 73,460 of those shares at a price of 5⅛, or approximately $360,000, between July 22 and July 25. Considering the activity, or rather lack of it, in the trading market for Big Horn, and the fact that the offering amounted to more than 30% of the outstanding stock, the sales effort was of such magnitude that there was unquestionably a distribution for purposes of Rule 10b–6. Registrant appears to have been an underwriter and certainly was, at least, a participant in that distribution.

In March 1983, the SEC amended Rule 10b–6 to define the term "distribution" to include any offering that is "distinguished from ordinary trading transactions by the magnitude of the offering and the presence of special selling efforts and selling methods."

At the same time, the Commission substantially revised the exceptions in Rule 10b–6(a) to permit prospective underwriters to continue making a market in the stock up to 2 days (rather than 10 days) before the commencement of the offering (provided the stock has a price of at least $5 a share and a public "float" of at least 400,000 shares), and to change the exceptions relating to block purchases, odd lot transactions, sinking fund purchases, option exercises, over allotment options, and other matters. Sec.Ex.Act Rel. No. 19565 (Mar. 4, 1983).

(b) The "Hot Issue" Problem

The preceding materials raised the problem of purchases and bids by underwriters and others which support the price of a security in order to facilitate a distribution. A somewhat different kind of problem is raised by the so-called "hot issue", which has been a recurring source of frustration to securities regulators since the late 1950s.

PRELIMINARY REPORT ON DISTRIBUTION OF "HOT ISSUES"

Securities Act Release No. 4150 (Oct. 23, 1959).

The Securities and Exchange Commission today made public a preliminary report submitted to it by Philip A. Loomis, Jr., Director of its Division of Trading and Exchanges, discussing the results of an inquiry into the circumstances surrounding the distribution of "hot issues", those issues which on the first day of trading, frequently the offering date, sold at a substantial premium.

The text of the preliminary report follows:

"Recently the Commission directed the staff to make a study into the circumstances surrounding price increases following immediately upon the public offering of certain issues registered with the Commission under the Securities Act of 1933 or offered pursuant to Regulation A which conditionally exempts certain small issues from registration. Most of these issues were low priced, had no public market prior to the offering and often involved companies in the electronics, missile and related defense fields. These are so-called 'glamour' stocks for which there has recently been a strong public demand.

"During the course of this study certain practices in connection with the distribution of these issues have been disclosed which, in the opinion of the staff, may involve violations of the federal securities laws. Although the study is continuing, it is believed that these practices should be called to the attention of the financial community in order that violations of laws may be avoided.

"The practices in question involve a combination of some or all of the following elements:

"1. In addition to allotments of the offered securities to his own customers and to selling group dealers, if any, the underwriter may allot a portion of the offering at the public offering price to trading firms active in the over-the-counter market. These firms are expected to commence making a market in such securities at or immediately after the start of the public offering. Some of these firms sell their allotments at prices substantially in excess of the public offering price stated in the prospectus, and in some cases bid for and purchase the security while they are distributing their allotments. The inquiry also discloses that such distributions may be made by these firms without any use of a prospectus.

"In one recent offering, which almost doubled in price on the first day of trading, over thirteen percent of the entire offering was sold by the underwriters at the public offering price to four broker-dealers and one of these broker-dealers sold out its entire allotment in the course of trading activities within three weeks of the offering date at substantially higher prices. In another 'hot issue' offering the principal underwriter sold substantial amounts of its participation at the public offering price of $3 per share to several broker-dealers and on the first day of trading, six of these firms appeared in the 'sheets' of the National Daily Quotation Service with bids and offers ranging from 5¾ to 7¼.

"2. Underwriters and selling group dealers may allot a substantial portion of the securities acquired by them to partners, officers, employees or relatives of such persons ('insiders'), to other broker-dealers with whom they may have reciprocal arrangements or to 'insiders' of such other broker-dealers. Such allotments are made notwithstanding the fact that customers of such firms are unable to obtain a part of the original distribution and therefore could only purchase the securities in the market at the higher price.

"In one recent offering, which more than doubled in price on the offering date, the selling group allotted over twenty-eight percent of its total participation to 'insiders'. One member of that selling group diverted to 'insiders' over seventy-five percent of its 3,000 share allotment of the 100,000 share offering, and another sold almost fifty percent of its 5,000 shares allotment to 'insiders'. Underwriters have indulged in the same practice. The underwriters in a recent offering of an electronics stock diverted almost twenty-two percent of the entire offering to 'insider' accounts. In another offering one of the underwriters diverted over eighty-seven percent of its participation to 'insider' accounts and another sold forty-seven percent to such accounts.

"The foregoing practices may involve violations of several requirements of the federal securities laws:

"(a) The registration statement and prospectus, or the offering circular may be materially misleading because of the failure to disclose the actual plan of distribution and the marketing arrangements for the issue. The usual representations in these documents imply that the securities will be offered to the public by the underwriters and selected dealers at the public offering price. These disclosures are misleading if, in fact, substantial blocks of shares are not to be offered to the public at the prospectus price, but rather are to be allotted to 'insiders', trading firms and others who may be expected to reoffer at a higher price.

"(b) The staff is of the opinion that the functions and activities of the trading firms described above constitute part of the distribution process and are of such a nature as to make them 'underwriters' within the meaning of Section 2(11) of the Securities Act of 1933. The failure to identify them as 'underwriters', to state the profits realized through these activities and to describe the effect of these activities makes the prospectus a misleading document. As participants in a distribution, these firms are required by Section 5(b) of the Act to deliver the prospectus to investors.

"(c) In the above cases, violations of the anti-fraud provisions of the Securities Act and the Securities Exchange Act may be involved. The public is led to believe by the prospectus, selling solicitations and newspaper advertisements that a stated number of shares are being publicly offered at the prospectus price when, in fact, they are not and the initial supply in the market is being restricted. To add to this initial deception statements are circulated that the issue has been heavily oversubscribed. Believing that public demand has exhausted the issue, and observing the market action, produced at least in part by the nature of the distribution arrangements, the public is induced to buy the security in the market at premium prices—the 'market' being one created and under the control of persons actively engaged in a distribution. Purchases by the public raise the price further and give 'insiders' and others an opportunity to make substantial profits at the expense of a public unaware of the actual method of distribution.

"(d) The practice described above of selling stock at the public offering price to trading firms for the purpose of making an over-the-counter market for the security may result in violations of Rule 10b–6 adopted under the Securities Exchange Act of 1934. That rule prohibits, among other things, an underwriter or a participant in a distribution from bidding for or purchasing securities being distributed or any other securities of the same class until he has completed his participation in the distribution. Since these trading firms are participating in a distribution while selling their allotments to the public, any open market purchases while so participating accordingly violate the rule. In this connection, if securities are allotted at the public offering price to 'insiders' of trading firms or others with a view to resale by such persons to or through such firms in the course of trading activities, the distribution of such securities would not have been completed within the meaning of Rule 10b–6.

"(e) If a broker-dealer engaging in the above activities should represent that such security was being sold 'at the market' or at a price related to the market, then his activity could also involve a violation of Rule 15c1–8 unless the broker or dealer knew or had reasonable grounds to believe that there was a market for such security other than that made, created, or controlled by such broker or dealer or by any person associated with him in the distribution.

"The staff also considers it appropriate to point out that pursuant to the authorization of the Commission it has submitted to the National Association of Securities Dealers, Inc., for such disciplinary action as the Association considers to be appropriate, the evidence obtained by the staff with respect to possible 'free riding' by some members of such Association. The staff has been informed by such Association that it is reviewing its policy with respect to 'free riding' and the enforcement of such policy to determine what further steps, if any, it should take in the matter.

"These practices should be called to the attention of the financial community since, in the view of the staff, they may involve violations of the federal securities laws. The staff is continuing its inquiry into these and other arrangements, understandings and practices in connection with the distribution of various issues. The staff will, of course, recommend to the Commission whatever further action it considers to be appropriate under the circumstances as a result of this inquiry."

The SEC's *Special Study of the Securities Markets* devoted considerable attention to the "hot issue" market of 1959–61. As a result of its recommendations, the SEC and the National Association of Securities Dealers (NASD) tightened their regulation of new issue practices by (a) requiring prompt confirmation and delivery of securities to customers, (b) extending prospectus delivery requirements on first-time issues from 40 to 90 days, (c) prohibiting withholding of securities by underwriters, dealers and their associates for subsequent sale at higher prices in the after-market, and (d) prohibiting "excessive" compensation to underwriters, particularly in the form of warrants or "cheap stock." Despite these reforms, the 1968–69 "hot issue" market exhibited many of the same characteristics as its predecessor, as the following excerpt indicates:

CONTROLLING A HOT ISSUE MARKET

By David Clurman †

56 Cornell L.Rev. 74 (1970).*

At the end of May 1969 New York State Attorney General Louis J. Lefkowitz requested that a study be made of the "hot issue" securities market that had caused severe upswings in the prices of certain new issues of stocks sold in New York State. * * * We conducted an inquiry during a ninety-day period ending on September 1, 1969, and analyzed various facets of 103 companies that went public for the first time in 1968–69.

* * *

The study reached the conclusion that, rather than being bona fide new enterprises seeking capital in the securities market, many companies were merely created by underwriters for stock profits. * * *

Public participation and price movement were sometimes shocking. Despite the obviously weak quality of most of the new issues analyzed, they were readily sold out and almost inevitably rose in price in the after-market. For example, the stock of one company with an appropriate space-age name was issued at two dollars per share and ran up to $7.50 per share before severe swings downward. This particular company represented in its prospectus that sixty percent of the proceeds were to be used for such items as past due accounts, repayment of loans, back wages, back rents, and similar items. The issuer was a constant loser in operations and had a working capital deficit. We concluded that the public issue was the method used to delay bankruptcy. Yet the price of the stock more than tripled in a short period of trading.

To determine the motivations of purchasers of these issues, the study interviewed 122 persons who bought initial offerings. Certain patterns of behavior clearly emerged. In only a small minority of cases did investors state that the prospectus had any influence in their decision. In fact, investors largely disregarded the typical "high risk" language of these documents; many were less than certain of what business the company was in.

Investor selection of stock based upon judgment as to merit was rare. The most potent component of the decision to buy was a desire to obtain a new issue—preferably one regarding which they had received an "inside tip." In the great majority of instances, investors purchased at the original offering price with the intent of a quick resale at a

† Special Assistant Attorney General, State of New York.

premium above that price. Approximately seventy-three percent of the group that bought at the original issue price did in fact resell, usually quite soon after the time of purchase.

In part, this investor mentality may have been created by a generally rising market that made cheaply-priced stock attractive. However, what may have begun as a natural economic phenomenon was exploited by issuers and the investment banking community. Members of this group used various techniques to generate interest in these securities to increase their subsequent price moves. They then took full advantage of the rising temperature in the new issue market.

The basic device used to further overheat the market was stimulating demand while simultaneously reducing supply. Brokers increased demand by frequently emphasizing to their customers the difficulty of obtaining shares. Their statements were of course often true, but by playing upon this fact still greater demand was created. Salesmen regularly predicted that the after-market prices would be higher than the original or current prices. Cruder techniques included brokers informing customers that if they did not make additional purchases in the after-market they would be cut off from further new issues. In addition, a steady flow of "tips" was fed into the market, and purchasers often stated that this type of information had stimulated their interest in a particular security. The question of the validity of such information is not even a logical one to ask—these companies were generally in such an early stage of development that all predictions as to their future were unwarranted.

The study group uncovered instances where intra-office brokerage memoranda were inconsistent with offering literature. The former material no doubt provided ammunition for customers' men. One such memo contained the following gem: "OTC initially, NYSE eventually." In another case where the prospectus contained a "substantial-risk" section and a cover legend emphasizing such risks, the confidential underwriter memo contained a section called "Factors Limiting Risks" as an obvious offset. Moreover, some of the names chosen by companies were misleading on their face. Thus, a company with the word "aerosystems" in its title was mainly involved in manufacturing ball point pen parts.

Concurrently, various methods of reducing supply were used. In nearly all of the offerings substantial percentages of shares registered for sale—in certain instances up to twenty-five percent—were reserved for employees, principals, and the like. In some cases, the underwriters held back shares either for their own accounts or for those associated with or related to them. At other times, underwriters made efforts to limit supply after trading began. Thus, some customers were told that if they sold without permission, they would not participate in the underwriters' future distributions. In other instances, underwriters advised customers that a stock had good long-term investment potential and should not be quickly resold. As another means of limiting supply, underwriters made heavy purchases of a new issue for discretionary accounts, thereby gaining a large degree of effective trading control.

The effect of all the increased pressures of demand upon a shortened supply was a sharp upswing in prices in the after-market. * * *

Company insiders and investment bankers took full advantage of the opportunities presented to them by the generally heated situation—a situation that was partially of their own creation. The most obvious method was the acquisition of shares at a low price for resale when the time appeared right. At times, underwriters withheld part of the issue for their own accounts and then sold when they thought the market had reached its peak. Company insiders frequently did the same with stock they received. * * *

Beyond this, both underwriters and issuers fully utilized the opportunity to reward business associates, friends, or favorite customers for either past transactions or anticipated future ones. As new issues grew more difficult to obtain, the ability of issuers and their underwriters to allocate shares became a matter of considerable import. Approximately two-thirds of the new issue purchasers interviewed had prior business or social contacts with either company insiders or the brokers through whom the purchases were made. Several underwriters who were interviewed during the study stated that allocations were based upon the customer's prior business dealings with the firm and the likelihood of a continued relationship.

* * *

Obviously, investors in the favored group received neither threats nor suggestions that they hold the shares for any prolonged period. As noted earlier, most original investors purchased for quick resale, and of those interviewed who did resell, only two percent took a loss on the transaction. While this group was able to quickly turn over shares at substantial profits, members of the public who purchased after the stock had risen in price were not so fortunate. A random sampling of thirty-seven new issues indicated that in a seven-month period the price level in the majority of these companies declined more than forty percent from the original issue price.

* * *

Much of the existing regulation of new issues is aimed principally at curbing old-fashioned "boiler-room" frauds; it has not been adapted to deal with the more sophisticated maneuverings of a hot issue market. * * *

The problems surrounding new issues have tended to recur periodically, usually at five- or six-year intervals, when the securities market is sought out by numerous investors interested in "hot" new issues because of the likelihood of major upswings in prices. Therefore, it would not be appropriate to impose rules or regulations that might endanger or obstruct the free flow of capital to new issue financing during periods of time when the problems uncovered by the study do not exist. Instead, state legislation that would authorize the Attorney General to cool the type of new issue market that existed in 1968–69 may be necessary. Such authorization should specifically include: (a) stand-by power to act when the Attorney General determines that the new issue market is approaching dangerous levels of heated activity, and makes a formal finding to that effect; and (b) authorization to act whenever the price of a specific new issue suddenly begins to spurt in the absence of available financial information about the company or its activities.

This authorization would add to new issue, over-the-counter transactions the "halt in trading" concept now employed by national stock exchanges when unusual price variations in listed stocks are not substantiated by sufficient business information. Just as such regulation by the exchanges has proved helpful in avoiding the untoward effects of rumors and misrepresentations, similar authority vested in the State Attorney General's office would assure adequate disclosure of information about companies involved in heated initial trading based largely on rumors. Furthermore, the Attorney General should be authorized to impose a standard three- to five-day trading hiatus between the issue date and the start of after-market trading (and the receipt of orders) whenever a general pattern of huge differentials between issue price and opening price begins to emerge in market trading, evidencing high pressure activities in the new issue market.

* * *

Following the submission of the study group's report to Attorney General Lefkowitz, remedial legislation was introduced during the New York State Legislature's 1970 session. That legislation failed to be released from committee, perhaps because the depressed condition of the market made the problem appear academic.

Another "hot issue" market in 1971–72 led to a formal SEC investigation of the problem, including several series of public hearings. While the findings of this investigation have never been published, it did lead to a broadening of prospectus disclosure requirements and underwriters' due diligence obligations with respect to first-time registrants.

INSTITUTIONAL SECURITIES OF COLORADO

SEC Admin.Proc.File No. 3–5104 (Aug. 14, 1978).

INITIAL DECISION

WAGNER, ADMINISTRATIVE LAW JUDGE:

* * *

Chemex Corporation (Chemex) was incorporated in the State of Wyoming on June 3, 1975 and is located in and does business out of

Riverton, Wyoming. Chemex was formed to conduct research, either directly or indirectly, to attempt to identify the mechanism of action by which certain constituents of elements of *larrea divaricata* (a perennial evergreen shrub also known as the creosote bush) may have some inhibitory effect on the growth and development of cancerous cells. * * *

Chemex made an offering of 3,000,000 shares of its common stock to the public pursuant to an offering circular dated January 17, 1975 with an offering price of 10¢ per share. The offering was made pursuant to a claimed Regulation A exemption from registration and was purportedly closed on February 18, 1975.

* * *

When the offering was made on January 17, 1975, United Securities Corporation, a Wyoming broker, in which Armor, a long-time personal friend of Hamilton, [the President of Chemex], was employed as a salesman, was named as the underwriter and the participating dealers were M.S. Wien (Harty) and ISOC (Richards). The offering was for 3,000,000 shares at 10¢ a share.

The proposed offering had been presented to the owners of United by Armor. Harty had brought the offering to Wien and Richards had proposed it to ISOC.

Allocations among the selling group were as follows:

a. United — 1,700,000 shares
b. Wien — 950,000 shares
c. ISOC — 350,000 shares

The over-the-counter market in Chemex commenced on February 19, 1975, and on that first day the market rose from a bid of 25¢ to a bid of 37½¢ per share. On February 20, 1975 the bid rose to 48¢ per share and by March 6, 1975 the bid was 68¢ per share.

It is clear that the Chemex offering was a "hot issue" and that the participants were well aware of the fact. The Division produced a number of public investors who testified that they were unable to obtain shares in the quantities they desired. The fact that United, a firm which had little underwriting experience and success, was selected as underwriter is a further indication that the promoters had no doubt that the offering could be easily sold. There is testimony that both Tomlinson and Richards expected from an early date that a "hot deal" would result.

In fact, the offering was largely a dispensation of largesse by the three participating firms, rather than a sale of stock.

Thus, United's Wyoming office sold mainly to persons who were referred to it by the issuer and its promoters. * * * A number of these persons borrowed money to purchase the stock, and all of them may be considered "issuer-directed" in the sense that the promoters of the issuer referred them to Armor at United and Armor willingly sold to them. While Hamilton told Armor prior to the offering that a number of friends would be interested in purchasing Chemex, the record does not indicate that there was any understanding on Armor's part that such prospects would be preferred in that shares would be set aside for them to the exclusion of others.

* * *

There is no direct evidence that the promoters extracted any agreement from these persons respecting the future sale of their stock or brought any influence to bear at any time concerning resale. Certain circumstantial evidence on this point is discussed later.

* * *

The heart of the [SEC] charges against Richards and Harty is that they, singly and in concert, willfully violated antifraud provisions of the Federal securities laws in the Chemex offering by:

> (1) withholding from public distribution Chemex shares while placing a substantial portion of that stock into accounts which Richards and Harty controlled and accounts controlled by the issuer.
>
> (2) reselling some of the shares to members of the investing public at prices in excess of the offering price.
>
> (3) using a misleading offering circular which failed to disclose the above plan of distribution and failed to disclose that, by virtue of such plan, the true public offering price was considerably higher than the designated price of 10¢ per share.

Respondents' motions to dismiss the charges were denied by Commission order, dated February 23, 1977. The order stated at p. 4:

> "Respondents are charged with withholding a substantial portion of the Chemex offering from public distribution, placing the withheld stock in accounts which they and control persons of the issuer controlled, immediately reselling some of the stock to the public at prices in excess of the offering price, and using an offering circular which failed to disclose these facts. These allegations do not break new ground. Taken as a whole they spell out a pattern of fraudulent conduct similar to that which we have dealt with in several prior cases."

It should be noted at the outset that the pattern referred to by the Commission did not occur here. Except for limited instances, the stock purchased by insiders and friends of the issuer and by relatives and friends of the respondents was not sold until more than six months after the offering was closed.

The situation presented is atypical in other respects.

(1) Chemex has proved to be of continuing interest to investors. As of the end of January, 1978 its stock was quoted at $5.25 bid, $6 asked. Accordingly, at least as of this date, the public has not been left holding the bag.

(2) Chemex is fortunate in having the services in its research department of Dr. Russell T. Jordan, a scientist of impeccable credentials.

(3) Demand for Chemex stock during the Regulation A offering and thereafter may be attributable in part to Dr. Jordan's reputation and to the earlier phenomenal record of Vipont Chemical Company, a local company which was also attempting to develop a cancer cure and also employed Dr. Jordan.

(4) A large proportion of the Chemex resales was made through a broker-dealer who was not in the underwriting group and who is not charged as a respondent in the proceeding.

This case, however, has certain typical "hot issue" elements. Thus, there is no real dispute that large portions of the Regulation A offering were placed in the hands of a favored few, i.e., relatives, friends and business associates of the respondents and of principals of the issuer. One facet of the Division's argument is that this, in itself, without disclosure, is a violation of the antifraud provisions.[7] It is as to this contention that counsel for respondent Harty states:

> "No matter how the staff clothes the manipulative aspects of its case, it comes down to no more than the view, that it is somehow a violation of the antifraud provisions for an issue to be allocated unfairly."

It is clear that the promoters and Richards and Harty knew or could reasonably have expected that the Chemex offering would be a "hot issue", and it is further clear that enormous profits were obtained by the insiders—apparently attributable only to their ability to obtain an allocation of Chemex stock through association and friendship with the promoters of the company or with Richards and Harty.

There is no doubt that the distribution was "unfair" in the sense noted, but the leading cases cited by the Division do not establish that unfairness alone violates the antifraud provisions.

For example, in *Holman* [8] there was much more than inequity in the distribution. The period of retention by certain of the controlled insider purchasers was so short that it was apparent that they did not represent true demand but were merely being interposed between the broker-dealer and the public to take a profit without risk to them. Under these circumstances, it could be concluded that the market was being artificially stimulated with manipulative effect.

* * *

I grant the request of counsel for Harty that official notice be taken of certain testimony, set forth in his brief, contained in the transcripts of the "Hot Issue" Hearings [before the SEC in 1971–72].

Generally these hearings tend to show that:

7. The Division Brief states at pp. 8–9:

> "Thus, a distribution is not complete if any part of the offering remains in the hands of broker-dealer or in the hands of persons (such as for example officers, directors, partners, employees and favored friends of broker-dealers, underwriters or issuers) who are not generally members of the public."

As noted above, the Chemex offering circular failed to disclose this plan of distribution and was therefore a false and misleading offering circular.

8. R.A. Holman & Co., Inc. v. SEC, 366 F.2d 446, 450 (2d Cir.1966), aff'g R.A. Holman & Co. Inc., 42 S.E.C. 866 (1965).

(1) Allocations in a "hot issue" underwriting were frequently made on the basis of business considerations, such as the potential of the account.

(2) "Directed" stock frequently accounted for high percentages of a "hot issue" offering, and frequently these people were the first to unload.

(3) Large portions of "hot issue" offerings were placed in discretionary accounts (the ultimate controlled account).

Counsel for Harty notes that as a result of the hearings the Commission amended Form S–1 to require a statement of the extent to which the principal underwriters intended to place the securities being offered in discretionary accounts.

As counsel further notes, the Commission in Securities Act Releases 5274 and 5275 (July 26, 1972) urged the National Association of Securities Dealers (NASD) to improve standards with respect to what constituted a bona fide public offering and indicated that, failing action by the self-regulatory organization, it might take action itself. Now, six years later, the NASD has not taken such action nor has the Commission.

Counsel contends that under these circumstances it would be inappropriate for the Commission to conclude in an administrative proceeding (dealing with events that took place 2½ years after the above releases) that placing the offering in the hands of the "favored few" or even that placing an offering in controlled accounts, without more, violates the antifraud provisions.

I agree not only for these reasons, but because I find no authority for the proposition that such actions by themselves constitute violations.

However, the Division also asserts that the "thrust" of its case is "that there was a pre-arranged plan among insiders of the issuer, Chemex (Tomlinson, Larsen and Hamilton) and respondents Harty and Richards to withhold from distribution the shares of Chemex issued pursuant to a Regulation A offering. The plan was accomplished through an issuer-directed distribution." It charges an alleged scheme "to represent that securities are being sold at a price which is purportedly the market price while failing to disclose restrictive and manipulative practices such as assuring that large blocks of stock are locked up with holders who are withholding the shares from sale." In citing and discussing as support for the last quoted proposition certain cases, the Division further appears to clarify its charges to assert an agreement or arrangement between the insiders and the issuer's promoters to withhold insider purchases from sale and to sell only pursuant to prearrangement. The Division argues that a like arrangement existed between Harty and Richards and their customers.

[The Division of Enforcement also claimed that the subsequent resale of approximately 600,000 shares of Chemex stock through a

Denver broker between November 1975 and June 1976 was "orchestrated" by a promoter of Chemex "for manipulative purposes pursuant to a pre-arranged scheme."]

While the circumstances here are exceedingly suspicious, proof of the charged pre-arranged manipulative scheme must, as noted, be "clear and convincing". In order to find as the Division proposes, it would be necessary to view all of the direct testimony in point as perjured. While I suspect that there may be some animus on the part of the Wyoming group against what is probably viewed as "government interference", I am not prepared to find, in effect, that these persons, who appear to be reputable citizens, have all given perjured testimony.

In *Institutional Securities of Colorado,* the administrative law judge found insufficient evidence of a plan to withhold the offered securities for subsequent sale at a higher price. Compare the following case:

SHEARSON, HAMMILL & CO.

42 S.E.C. 811 (1965).

[Shearson, Hammill & Co. ("Registrant") acted as *de facto* underwriter for an offering of 290,000 shares of common stock of USAMCO. The SEC brought a proceeding against Registrant and a number of its partners and employees, including Dunbar, Teweles, Brum, Troutman, Silver and Wayne, alleging numerous violations of the securities laws in connection with the offering.]

USAMCO commenced a Regulation A offering of 290,000 shares of its common stock at $1 per share about November 8, 1960. Six days later, as more fully discussed below, registrant's Los Angeles office began trading in the stock and made the principal or sole market in it.

* * *

USAMCO allocated the 290,000–share offering to 178 persons who were named on lists submitted by two officers and directors of USAMCO, including Stevens, by USCM's president, and by Troutman, after discussions with Dunbar. Dunbar was listed by Stevens. Troutman's list allocated 194,600 shares to 118 persons, including a resident partner of registrant in another branch office in California, Teweles, Troutman, Brum, Wayne, Silver, and other employees of registrant, seventy-five customers of registrant and twenty-five individuals who did not maintain accounts with registrant but had asked Troutman or Dunbar for shares. Dunbar purchased 10,000 shares, the resident partner, 1,000 shares, and Troutman, 5,000 shares. These purchases, together with those by registrant's employees, accounted for 36,200 shares, or about 13% of the issue, and the seventy-five customers of registrant, all but one of whom were customers of Dunbar and Troutman, acquired 133,300 shares, or about 46% of the issue. Some of the persons who advised USAMCO that they wished to subscribe were not allocated any shares and their checks were returned.

* * *

[I]t is clear that the distribution of the Regulation A offering was not completed when registrant commenced trading in the stock on November 14, 1960, but rather continued until at least June 1961. Not only were new subscriptions accepted between November 14 and 28, 1960, but partners and employees of registrant and insiders of USAMCO and USCM sold their Regulation A shares at prices substantially above the offering price through the first half of 1961. As a result of such sales of stock, the $300,000 limitation under Regulation A was exceeded. During the first eight days beginning on November 14, 1960, Dunbar's secretary sold 200 shares through registrant at 5, Brum sold 1,500 shares at the same price through an account opened with another broker-dealer, Stevens' mother and stepfather sold 1,900 shares through registrant and Dunbar at 4 and 5, and an officer of USCM sold 500 shares through registrant at 4.

Thereafter, during the first half of 1961, partners and employees of registrant liquidated all or large portions of their Regulation A shares at substantial profits. Brum sold 3,000 shares to registrant through another broker-dealer, for a total profit on all his Regulation A shares of $37,119. One of his assistants sold 100 shares through registrant at 13 in February 1961, and another assistant sold 100 shares through registrant at 17 in May 1961. Dunbar, who testified that he followed the practice of selling enough of his holdings of a speculative security to recover his cost plus a profit when the market price reached a sufficiently high level, sold 3,300 of his 10,000 Regulation A shares for a profit on those shares of $49,479 in May 1961, when the stock became "long-term," i.e., when only a portion of any capital gain would be taxable. Similarly, Troutman sold 2,000 of his 5,000 shares in May for a profit on those shares of $31,349, the manager of a branch office in California sold 800 shares in May and June at 14⅞ to 15⅞, Teweles, who had become a partner of registrant on January 1, 1961, sold 6,000 shares, including 4,500 Regulation A shares, in February and June at 12 to 16, and Wayne sold 1,000 shares in June at 15. Other sales of such shares during the period by registrant's personnel included a sale of 1,000 shares by the manager of another California branch office for a profit of $8,321.

* * *

Registrant's opening bid for USAMCO stock in the sheets on November 14, 1960, was 3. Thereafter, throughout the remainder of 1960 and the first half of 1961, registrant entered daily quotations in the sheets at generally increasing prices. On November 18, it quoted the stock at 5 bid—5½ asked, on December 15, at 5¾–6¼, on December 30 at 7–7½, on January 31, 1961, at 12–13, and on March 3 at 14–15. On March 30 registrant's quotes were 16½–17½, although no other broker-dealers had been entering quotations in the sheets since March 23, when registrant's bid was 15. The high of 18 bid–19 asked was reached in April, and sales were made at prices as high as 19⅞. During May and June 1961, when the profits on the Regulation A shares became long-term for tax purposes, and Dunbar and Teweles liquidated portions of their holdings, registrant maintained its quotations at slightly below the April highs and sold the stock at 15 and 16. At the end of June, the price of the stock declined to about 10 and remained at about that level until September 11, when registrant was selling it to customers at 11. On that day, registrant's New York partners ordered the firm's registered representatives to discontinue the solicitation of USAMCO stock buy orders from customers. The market in the stock then collapsed and by December 11, its bid was ¼, after which registrant ceased making a market in the stock.

From November 14, 1960 until the end of 1961, registrant made the principal or sole market in USAMCO stock. Through November 30, 1961 registrant as principal sold 312,449 shares, including 76,098 shares to dealers, and purchased 311,117 shares, including 104,291 shares from dealers. As agent for customers registrant purchased 66,312 shares and sold 83,910 shares.

* * *

On June 12, 1961, Brum reported to Dunbar that he feared that the demand for USAMCO stock was insufficient to cover anticipated orders to sell such stock. On the following day, Dunbar authorized Brum to establish a "work-out" market, in which no sell orders from customers were to be accepted or executed by registrant unless offsetting buy orders for at least an equal number of shares were on hand.[1] During the period of the work-out market, registrant continued to enter both bid and ask quotations and was the only broker-dealer quoting the stock in the sheets. Registrant solicited customers to buy USAMCO stock but, with the exception of one order to sell 100 shares, did not accept or execute customers' sell orders in the absence of an off-setting buy order. The registered representatives who solicited buy orders from customers quoted the market to their customers in the ordinary manner and generally did not disclose that the market was work-out. Registrant sold 8,782 shares during this period, of which 3,500 shares were purchased from Teweles and 90 from his secretary, 3,000 shares were purchased from Wayne, 1,982 shares came from registrant's own inventory, and only 210 shares were purchased from customers. It did not execute any agency transactions nor purchase USAMCO stock from broker-dealers.

* * *

Other registered representatives, including Silver and Wechter, also induced customers to purchase USAMCO stock at between 13¾ and 16 without disclosing, as they knew, that the work-out market was in effect. Since registrant was making the only market in USAMCO

1. A work-out market has been described as one in which the trader acts essentially as broker and attempts to find interest on the other side of the market. S.E.C. Special Study of Securities Markets, 88th Cong., 1st Sess., House Doc. No. 95, Part 2, p. 572 (July 17, 1963).

stock at this time, there was no other outlet through which customers could sell their stock and they were thus "locked in" for the duration of the work-out. After the work-out market was terminated at Dunbar's direction, many of the customers, whose sell orders were not accepted or remained unexecuted because of the preference given to Teweles and Wayne, sold their shares at below 12.

Since registrant was the principal market maker and, as shown, dominated and controlled the market in USAMCO stock, the commencement of the work-out market created a situation which not only was potentially subject to abuse but was in fact used to conduct a one-sided market at an artificial level for the benefit of registrant and its employees while it was through its quotations giving the false appearance of maintaining a normal two-sided market. In view of the fact that registrant had no intention of purchasing USAMCO stock from broker-dealers during the work-out market it is clear that its bid quotations in the sheets during the work-out were not *bona fide* and constituted a manipulative and deceptive device and fraudulent course of business. Dunbar admitted that the work-out market conducted by the Los Angeles office was not a true market, and according to Brum, in a "normal" market the price during that month would have dropped rapidly to about 10, at which price there was some demand for the stock. As noted, after the salesmen were instructed in September 1961 to cease soliciting buy orders from customers, the market in the stock collapsed. Moreover, registrant's failure to execute customers' sell orders that it had accepted, while effecting the purchases from its own employees which as noted were at prices higher than those the customers had asked, constituted a violation of the duty to deal fairly with customers that inheres in the broker-dealer relationship.

* * *

If "unfair allocation" of a new issue to favored customers is not itself a "fraud," as the judge found in *Institutional Securities of Colorado,* is there any other way to deal with it? If the underwriters stimulate demand for a new issue to the point where there is insufficient stock to meet all orders, should they be required to prorate the issue among all customers who place orders? Could they legally do so?

EICHLER v. SEC

757 F.2d 1066 (9th Cir.1985).

Before CHAMBERS, BOOCHEVER and BEEZER, CIRCUIT JUDGES. Opinion of BEEZER, CIRCUIT JUDGE.

Bateman Eichler, Hill Richards, Inc. ("BEHR") is registered as a broker-dealer with the SEC and is a member of NASD. At the time of the events at issue in this case, Eichler was president of BEHR and

Witt was the head of BEHR's trading department. William Walker was BEHR's syndicate manager.

In March 1977, BEHR served as managing underwriter for a syndicate of thirty-one firms that were underwriting a public offering of securities by Jhirmack Enterprises, Inc. ("Jhirmack"). The syndicate offered a total of 385,000 shares of Jhirmack stock. When BEHR and the other firms completed the distribution of Jhirmack shares on March 24, 1977, the syndicate had sold 398,200 shares, leaving the syndicate "short" 13,200 shares. BEHR was responsible for covering its share of the syndicate's short position.

After the syndicate completed the distribution, BEHR began taking orders from its customers for the "aftermarket" for Jhirmack shares. When trading in Jhirmack stock commenced on March 25, BEHR was obligated to purchase a large number of shares for its customers in addition to covering its share of the syndicate's short position. Along with fourteen other brokerage firms, BEHR held itself out as a "market maker" for Jhirmack stock.

The officials at BEHR soon realized that BEHR's bid price would not be sufficient to acquire the number of shares that BEHR needed. Because the demand for Jhirmack shares greatly exceeded the supply, the officials at BEHR feared a dramatic price increase. Walker informed Witt that, under the circumstances, it would not be necessary to fill the syndicate's short position immediately. Rather than raising the bid price to a level that would attract a sufficient number of shares, Witt and Eichler decided to maintain the bid price at or near the market price. Witt and Eichler also decided to purchase only a portion of the shares being offered by other dealers, since excessive purchases would drive up the market price. Instead, Witt and Eichler decided to allocate the available shares among their customers at an average price determined at the close of the trading day.

On March 25, BEHR filled approximately fifty percent of each order at an average price of 13⅛. On March 28, the next trading day, BEHR filled sixty percent of each order at an average price of 14⅞. The allocation system ended at 9:43 a.m. on March 29. Orders received before 9:43 a.m. were partially filled at an average price of 15⅜. Orders received after 9:43 a.m. were completely filled at the market price.

On March 25, 28, and 29, BEHR took fifty-six "market orders." Under a "market order," the broker is expected to fill the order completely at the best available market price, with the customer bearing the risk of price increases. BEHR purchased only 12,375 of the 23,875 shares that were ordered on that basis.

Many of BEHR's customers were not notified of the allocation until after it had been completed. Those who were notified were told only that BEHR could not fill their orders completely. On the three days in question, however, BEHR purchased 11,350 shares to reduce its share of the underwriting syndicate's short position. In addition, BEHR sold 15,612 shares to other firms, rather than to its own customers.

Following a customer complaint, the staff of NASD's District Business Conduct Committee for District No. 2 ("the DBCC") began to investigate BEHR's actions. The staff filed a complaint against BEHR, Eichler, Witt, and Walker ("the BEHR group"). The complaint alleged violations of federal securities law and Article III, section 1 of NASD's Rules of Fair Practice, which states: "A member, in the conduct of his business, shall observe high standards of commercial honor and just and equitable principles of trade." After an evidentiary hearing, the DBCC found that the BEHR group had violated the Rules of Fair Practice, but not federal securities law. On September 27, 1979, the DBCC censured the BEHR group and assessed a joint and several fine of $20,000.

The BEHR group appealed to the Board of Governors of NASD. After a further evidentiary hearing, the Board of Governors affirmed the judgment of the DBCC on October 2, 1980. * * * On March 29, 1984, the SEC affirmed.

II

SUBSTANTIAL EVIDENCE

* * *

The SEC found that BEHR had a duty either to execute its customers' market orders to the greatest extent possible or to obtain their informed consent to a different arrangement. The SEC concluded BEHR had violated that duty.

A. Failure to Execute Transactions

The petitioners contend that the SEC's conclusion that BEHR failed to execute transactions to the greatest extent possible is not supported by substantial evidence. Actually, the petitioners do not challenge the evidentiary basis of the SEC's findings. Instead, the petitioners attempt to justify their failure to fill their customers' market orders. The asserted justifications are without merit.

First, the petitioners argue that raising BEHR's bid price would have inflated the market price, exposing BEHR to customer complaints. While that may be true, it is just as likely that BEHR's failure to fill its customers' orders would have generated complaints if BEHR's customers had known the reasons for BEHR's allocation policy. In any event, the SEC addressed this argument in its second opinion:

> Where an unusual market situation exists, and the immediate execution of market orders would result in significant disruption in the market and, consequently, in executions that would vary significantly from customer expectations at the time the orders were entered, it may well be preferable for a firm to contact its customers promptly, inform them of the change in market conditions, and obtain further instructions from those customers with respect to the execution of their orders. But a firm cannot substitute its own judgment for its custom-

ers' informed consent to changes in their orders' terms or manner of execution. In the absence of such consent, a firm has a duty to execute customer orders fully and promptly.

Second, the petitioners argue that there was no active interdealer market and no adequate supply of stock away from BEHR. The petitioners contend that BEHR therefore "dominated" the market, so that they would have been subject to discipline if they had raised BEHR's bid price. *See* In re Norris & Hirshberg, Inc., 21 S.E.C. 865 (1946), *aff'd*, 177 F.2d 228 (D.C.Cir.1949). It is not clear that BEHR "dominated" the market, especially in light of the presence of fourteen other market makers. In any event, *Norris & Hirshberg* only requires the dominant firm to disclose its position to its customers. 21 S.E.C. at 881–82.

B. Failure to Notify Customers

The petitioners also contend that the SEC's conclusion that BEHR made inadequate disclosure to its customers is not supported by substantial evidence. The petitioners' arguments are largely based on the misconception that the SEC found that BEHR had an independent duty to notify its customers of the conditions in the market for Jhirmack shares. In fact, the SEC found that BEHR had two choices after it accepted market orders for Jhirmack shares: (1) fill the orders, or (2) obtain its customers' informed consent to an allocation system. Because BEHR chose not to fill the orders, the SEC concluded that BEHR had a duty to obtain its customers' informed consent. The SEC found that BEHR had violated that duty. The petitioners challenge that finding on several grounds, all of which are without merit.

* * *

C. The Nature of the Over-the-Counter Market

The petitioners argue that the SEC's opinion is based on a misconception of the over-the-counter ("OTC") market. They contend that BEHR was obligated to maintain an orderly market for Jhirmack shares. The SEC correctly rejected this argument in its second opinion. While a specialist on a stock exchange has a duty to maintain an orderly market, *see* Rule 11b–1, an OTC market maker's sole duty is to its customers. The petitioners also argue that BEHR's allocation system was in the best interests of its customers. While that may be true, BEHR had no authority to implement such a system without the informed consent of its customers. The SEC's conception of the OTC market is correct.

Compare the following memorandum sent out by one of the underwriters of the initial public offering of Apple Computer, which was offered at $25 a share and was expected to be (and was) a "hot issue."

> In anticipation of possible buying interest by customers in the aftermarket for the common shares of Apple Computer ("AAPL") and until further notice, the firm is imposing, effective immediately, the

following restrictions with respect to aftermarket customer transactions in AAPL common shares:

(A) We may not solicit aftermarket purchases in AAPL common stock from the time of the release of the offering until the time that the offering's completion is announced by the Syndicate Department; and

(B) As a matter of firm policy, aftermarket purchase orders entered after completion of the offering is announced by the Syndicate Department may be solicited up to a price not to exceed $27 a share. Accordingly, the firm will only accept unsolicited orders for the purchase of AAPL common stock at any price in excess of $27 per share.

Selected References

T. Hazen, Securities Regulation ch. 6 (2d ed. 1990).

Manning & Miller, The SEC's Recent Revisions to Rule 10b–6, 11 Sec.Reg. L.J. 195 (1983).

Martin, Broker–Dealer Manipulation of the Over–The–Counter Market—Toward a Reasonable Basis for Quotations, 25 Bus.Lawyer 1463 (1970).

Rogoff, Legal Regulation of Over-the-Counter Market Manipulation, 28 Me. L.Rev. 149 (1976).

Wolfson, Rule 10b–6: The Illusory Search for Certainty, 25 Stanford L.Rev. 809 (1973).

Weiss & Leibowitz, Rule 10b–6 Revisited, 39 Geo.Wash.L.Rev. 474 (1971).

Whitney, Rule 10b–6: The Special Study's Rediscovered Rule, 62 Mich.L. Rev. 567 (1964).

Comment, The SEC's Rule 10b–6: Preserving a Competitive Market During Distributions, 1967 Duke L.J. 809.

Comment, Legislative and Administrative Treatment of the "Hot Issue" Phenomenon, 1968 Duke L.J. 1137.

B. BROKERS—"CHURNING" AND "UNSUITABILITY"

When a firm acts as broker—i.e., as agent—for a customer, taking the customer's order to the exchange or over-the-counter market for execution and receiving a commission for its services, there is less opportunity for overreaching than when the firm is selling securities to the customer from its own inventory. Even here, however, the firm or its salesperson may be tempted to cause the customer to engage in excessive or inappropriate trading for the purpose of generating extra commission income. Claims of this nature have been dealt with under the rubrics of "churning" and "unsuitability."

MIHARA v. DEAN WITTER

619 F.2d 814 (9th Cir.1980).

Before CHAMBERS and TANG, CIRCUIT JUDGES, and CAMPBELL, SENIOR DISTRICT JUDGE.

WILLIAM J. CAMPBELL, SENIOR DISTRICT JUDGE:

On April 26, 1974, Samuel Mihara filed this action in United States District Court for the Central District of California. He alleged both federal statutory and California common law fiduciary duty claims arising from the handling of Mihara's securities accounts by defendants. Specifically, plaintiff alleges that the defendants, Dean Witter & Company and its account executive, George Gracis, engaged in excessive trading or "churning" in plaintiff's securities account, and purchased "unsuitable" securities which did not conform to Mihara's stated investment objectives. Plaintiff sought relief under Section 10(b) of the Securities Exchange Act of 1934 and Rule 10b–5 promulgated thereunder, as well as for breach of fiduciary duties. Plaintiff sought both compensatory and punitive damages, and demanded a jury trial.

On February 2, 1978, after a jury trial, a verdict was entered for Mihara and against the defendants on both the Rule 10b–5 claim and the State breach of fiduciary duty claim. Compensatory damages in the amount of $24,600 were awarded to Mihara, a punitive damages award of $66,666 was assessed against Dean Witter & Company, and a $2,000 punitive damage award was assessed against defendant Gracis. Defendants subsequently filed motions for new trial and judgment notwithstanding the verdict, having moved for a directed verdict at trial, which motions were denied. Dean Witter & Company and Gracis (hereinafter appellants) appeal from the denial of those motions, and the plaintiff Mihara appeals from an order disallowing recovery of $1,800 in costs.

On January 6, 1971, plaintiff Mihara opened a joint securities account with the Santa Monica office of Dean Witter. At that time Mihara was employed by the McDonnell–Douglas Corporation as a supervisory engineer. He was 38 years old and possessed a Bachelor of Science and Master's Degree in Engineering. He and his wife were the parents of two daughters. Mihara's assets at the time consisted of approximately $30,000 in savings, an employee's savings account at McDonnell–Douglas of approximately $16,000, and equity in his home for approximately fifteen to seventeen thousand dollars. He also held shares of McDonnell–Douglas stock obtained through an employee payroll deduction plan.

Prior to opening his account with Dean Witter, Mihara had invested in securities for approximately ten years. He had dealt with several other firms during that period, but apparently felt that his account had not received adequate attention, and was looking for a new investment firm. Mihara opened his account with Dean Witter in January of 1971 by telephoning Stuart Cypherd, the office manager for Dean Witter's Santa Monica office, and asking to be assigned an account executive. Cypherd, in turn, instructed defendant Gracis to phone Mihara to set up an appointment.

The evidence as to the content of the initial meeting between Mihara and Gracis is conflicting. Mihara testified that as an engineer he lacked a finance and economics background and was looking for someone with expertise on which he could rely. He also stated that he was concerned about possible cutbacks at McDonnell–Douglas, noting that layoffs were common in that industry. He indicated that he was concerned about the education of his two daughters, and their financial security.

Gracis' testimony with regard to their initial meeting, and specifically relating to Mihara's investment objectives, differs substantially. Gracis testified that Mihara was not concerned about a possible layoff, that he was primarily interested in growth, and that he was knowledgeable about margin accounts and broker call rates.

Mihara invested $30,000 with Dean Witter. This money was to be invested according to Gracis' recommendations but subject to Mihara's approval.

The history of Mihara's investment account with Dean Witter & Company reflects speculative investments, numerous purchases and sales, and substantial reliance on the recommendations of Gracis. The initial recommendations of Gracis were that Mihara purchase shares of companies engaged in the double-knit fabric industry. These stocks included Venice Industries, Devon Apparel, Edmos, Fab Industries, D.H.J. Industries, Leslie Fay, Graniteville, Duplan, and United Piece and Dye. From 1971 to 1973, Mihara's account lost considerable sums of money. Since many of the purchases were on margin, Mihara would often have to come up with additional funds as the equity in his account declined. The final trading losses in the account totaled $46,464. This loss occurred during the period of January 1971 to May 1973.

Mihara first began to complain of the handling of his account when it showed a loss in April 1971. At that time he complained to Gracis because his account was losing money, then about $3,000. Throughout 1971, as Mihara's account lost money, he continued to complain to Gracis. In October of 1971, Mihara went to Mr. Cypherd, the office manager for the Santa Monica office of Dean Witter. Mihara complained to Cypherd about the handling of the account by Gracis. He did not, however, close out the account. As the value of Mihara's securities account continued to dwindle, he visited Cypherd on several occasions to complain further about Gracis. While Cypherd told Mihara he was "on top" of the account, the performance and handling of the account did not improve.

At about the same time that Mihara first contacted him, Cypherd was also made aware of substantial trading in the account by means of a Dean Witter Monthly Account Activity Analysis. This analysis was initiated by the Dean Witter computer whenever an account showed 15 or more trades in one month or commissions of $1,000 or more. Because Mihara's account reflected 16 trades for the month of April 1971, Cypherd was alerted to the problem at that time. In May of 1971, the Dean Witter computer generated another monthly account activity analysis as the result of 21 trades during that month in Mihara's account. Mihara's account in March of 1971 reflected 33 transactions; however, the computer did not generate an account analysis.

In November 1973, Mihara went to the San Francisco office of Dean Witter and complained to Paul Dubow, the National Compliance Director for Dean Witter, Inc. At that point Mihara's account had suffered considerable losses. Apparently not satisfied with the results of that meeting, Mihara filed this suit in April 1974.

At trial plaintiff gave his recollection of the initial meeting with Gracis. He testified that Gracis recommended securities which did not appear to conform to those objectives. He also related the dismal record of the account, and how attempts to remedy the situation through meetings with Gracis' superiors proved fruitless. Plaintiff also introduced the Dean Witter Account Executive Manual which stated that Dean Witter account executives had a "sacred trust to protect" their customers, that Dean Witter customers have confidence in the firm, and "under no circumstances should we violate this confidence."

* * *

Plaintiff's expert, Mr. White, a former attorney with the Securities & Exchange Commission, testified at trial that the pattern of trading in the Mihara account reflected a pattern of churning. Plaintiff's Exhibit 20, Chart G, introduced at trial, indicated the following holding periods for Mihara's securities. In 1971, 50% of the securities were held for 15 days or less, 61% for 30 days or less, and approximately 76% were held for 60 days or less. Through June of 1973, 81.6% of the securities in the Mihara account were held for a period of 180 days or less. White also relied on the "turnover rate" in Mihara's account in reaching his conclusion. The turnover rate for a given period is arrived at by dividing the total dollar amount of stock purchases for a given period by the average monthly capital investment in the account. Plaintiff's Exhibit No. 20, Chart C, indicates that between January 1971 and July 1973, Mihara's average monthly investment of $36,653 was turned over approximately 14 times. On an annualized basis, Mihara's average capital monthly investment in 1971 of approximately $40,000 was turned over 9.3 times. His average capital investment in 1972 was $39,800 and that was turned over approximately 3.36 times. His average monthly capital investment for the first half of 1973 was $23,588 and that was turned over approximately .288 times. White testified that a substantial turnover in the early stages of the account followed by a significant decline in the turnover rate was typical of a churned account.

White also testified that the holding periods for securities in Mihara's account reflected a pattern of churning. He noted that churned accounts usually reflect significant turnover in the early stages, that is, a very short holding period for the securities purchased, followed by longer holding periods in the later stages of the account. Thus, the typical churned account is churned in the early stages of the account generating large commissions at the outset, followed by less trading and longer holding periods in the latter stages of the account, after significant commissions have been generated. Mihara's account reflects precisely that pattern. The cumulative total of commissions earned by Gracis was $12,672, the majority of which came in the early stages of the account.

In addition to the testimony of Mr. White that, in his expert opinion, Mihara's account had been "churned," plaintiff's expert witness McCuen also testified that in his opinion the securities purchased from Mihara's account were not suitable for Mihara's stated investment objectives. Mr. McCuen based his analysis in part on rankings found in reports in the "Value Line" investment service newsletter which rates those stocks poorly. Mr. McCuen noted that the securities in question were rated as high risk securities with below average financial strength.

* * *

The defendant Gracis testified that Mihara was more interested in riskier growth potential investments. He stated he recommended such stocks, but also noted the drawbacks of such investments. Gracis testified that he also warned of the dangers of utilizing a margin account.

* * *

When a securities broker engages in excessive trading in disregard of his customer's investment objectives for the purpose of generating commission business, the customer may hold the broker liable for churning in violation of Rule 10b–5. Hecht v. Harris Upham & Company, 430 F.2d 1202 (9th Cir.1970). In order to establish a claim of churning, a plaintiff must show (1) that the trading in his account was excessive in light of his investment objectives; (2) that the broker in question exercised control over the trading in the account; and (3) that the broker acted with the intent to defraud or with the wilful and reckless disregard for the interests of his client.

Whether trading is excessive is a question which must be examined in light of the investment objectives of the customer. While there is no clear line of demarcation, courts and commentators have suggested that an annual turnover rate of six reflects excessive trading. In Hecht v. Harris Upham & Company, 283 F.Supp. 417 (N.D.Cal., 1968), aff'd at 430 F.2d 1202, 1210 (9th Cir., 1970), this Court affirmed a finding of churning where an account had been turned over 8 to 11.5 times during a six-year ten-month period. In that case, 45% of the securities were held for less than six months, 67% were held for less than nine months, and 82% were held for less than a year. Under this Court's holding in *Hecht,* the evidence in the present case clearly supports a finding of excessive trading.

With regard to the second prerequisite, we believe that Gracis exercised sufficient control over Mihara's account in the present case to support a finding of churning. The account need not be a discretionary account whereby the broker executes each trade without the consent of the client. As the *Hecht* case indicates, the requisite degree of control is met when the client routinely follows the recommendations of the broker. The present case, as in *Hecht,* reflects a pattern of *de facto* control by the broker.

The third requisite element of a 10b–5 violation—scienter—has also been established. The manner in which Mihara's account was handled reflects, at best, a reckless disregard for the client's investment concerns, and, at worst, an outright scheme to defraud plaintiff. Perhaps in recognition of this, appellants have constructed a curious argument as to the scienter element. They suggest that plaintiff must establish an intent to defraud as to each trade executed by the broker. This assertion is entirely without merit. The churning of a client's account is, in itself, a scheme or artifice to defraud within the meaning of Rule 10b–5. With regard to the definition of scienter, this circuit has held that reckless conduct constitutes scienter within the meaning of *Ernst & Ernst v. Hochfelder.* The evidence in the present case reflects, at the very minimum, a reckless disregard for the client's stated interests.

* * * We affirm the judgment below in all respects.

NESBIT v. McNEIL

896 F.2d 380 (9th Cir.1990).

Before WRIGHT, TANG and FERNANDEZ, CIRCUIT JUDGES.

FERNANDEZ, CIRCUIT JUDGE.

Virginia H. Nesbit and the W. Wallace Nesbit Trust ("plaintiffs") brought this action against Steve McNeil and Black & Company, Inc. ("defendants") and alleged that the defendants had churned the plaintiffs' investment accounts. Among other things, plaintiffs sought to recover for violations of the federal securities laws and under the State of Oregon securities laws. The district court directed a verdict against the plaintiffs on the Oregon securities law claim, and submitted the federal securities claim to the jury. The jury brought in a verdict against defendants, and awarded damages in the amount of the excess commissions generated by the churning of the plaintiffs' accounts. The district court denied a motion for judgment notwithstanding the verdict, and entered judgment accordingly.

Defendants now appeal and claim that the district court erred because it did not permit the offset of trading gains against the excess commissions, because the evidence of churning was insufficient to support the verdict, and because the plaintiffs' claims were barred by the statute of limitations in whole or in part. Defendants also claim that they should not have been required to disgorge the full amount of excess commissions, but only their net gain on those commissions.

BACKGROUND FACTS

Virginia H. Nesbit was a retired school teacher and the widow of W. Wallace Nesbit, a businessman. Upon his death, Mr. Nesbit left a portfolio of securities that were rather conservative although not necessarily highly successful. Those, as well as other assets, were divided between Mrs. Nesbit and the W. Wallace Nesbit Trust ("the Trust"). Mrs. Nesbit was the trustee of the Trust. From then until 1974, the investments remained conservative and did not do very well. By 1974, there had been a significant loss of value. Mrs. Nesbit then opened accounts for herself and the Trust at Black & Company, Inc. They were opened through Steve McNeil, who was the son of a friend of Mrs. Nesbit. The equity in Mrs. Nesbit's account was then $167,463, and the equity in the Trust's account was $44,177. Mrs. Nesbit, who was not knowledgeable in these matters, told the defendants that her investment objectives for herself and the Trust were stability, income and growth. Defendants claim that she told them she wanted to recoup the losses that had been suffered previously.

Defendants then embarked on a course of conduct that extended over a period of eleven and one half years. By the time the accounts were closed out in October of 1985, the equity in Mrs. Nesbit's account was $301,711, and the equity in the Trust's account was $92,844. There can be little dispute that this was a substantial increase in value. However, the activities of defendants during those eleven and one half years are called into question in this case.

Plaintiffs have pointed out that defendants first liquidated some of the securities in plaintiffs' portfolio. Mr. McNeil then embarked on a course of trading that involved 150 issues, one thousand trades, and an overall transaction value of $4,400,000. While the plaintiffs' account values did grow by $182,915 during the period in question, the defendants' commissions came to $250,000. Moreover, the investments chosen by defendants were not the kind of investments that one would purchase if one sought a stable, income-producing portfolio. Rather, they were often speculative in nature and were not income-producing. By the time the accounts terminated, many of the investments had accrued losses.

By 1984, Mrs. Nesbit became concerned about the level of activity in the accounts. She kept in closer contact with Mr. McNeil, and the level of trading decreased, but did not end entirely. She became even more concerned in 1985. At that time she discovered losses in the portfolio when calls were made upon her by lenders to whom she had pledged certain of the securities. Her concerns increased when the handling of the accounts was questioned by Ronald Linn, an analyst at Titan Capital, and were not particularly allayed when visits with Mr. McNeil brought forth an apology and an expression of embarrassment at the list of losing stocks. All of this ultimately led to the closing of the accounts in October of 1985. Over one year later, plaintiffs filed this action.

* * *

C. The Measurement of Damages.

As we have already noted, defendants obtained commissions of $250,000 from the plaintiffs. The jury found that $134,000 of that constituted excess commissions. At the same time, the value of plaintiffs' accounts increased in the sum of $182,915. Defendants claimed below, and continue to claim, that the plaintiffs' portfolio gain should be offset against the plaintiffs' commission loss, as a result of which plaintiffs can recover no damages whatever. The district court disagreed, and gave the following instruction to the jury: "If you find that the plaintiffs have proven their claims for churning, excessive trading, plaintiffs may recover as damages any commissions they paid as a result of the churning in excess of commissions that would have been reasonable on transactions during the pertinent time period." The district court did not go on to instruct the jury that it could then offset the trading gains against those commission losses. We agree with the district court.

We begin with the rather straightforward principle announced in Mihara v. Dean Witter, where we said that, "While damages for churning are limited to commissions and interest, plaintiff's claim as to the suitability of the securities purchased would also encompass trading losses." As the Fifth Circuit Court of Appeals explained in Miley v. Oppenheimer & Co., Inc., 637 F.2d at 326, there are two separate and distinct possible harms when an account has been churned, and those are:

> First, and perhaps foremost, the investor is harmed by having had to pay the excessive commissions to the broker. . . . Second, the investor is harmed by the decline in the value of his portfolio . . . as a result of the broker's having intentionally and deceptively concluded transactions, aimed at generating fees, which were unsuitable for the investor. The intentional and deceptive mismanagement of a client's account, resulting in a decline in the value of that portfolio, constitutes a compensable violation of both the federal securities laws and the broker's common law fiduciary duty, regardless of the amount of the commissions paid to the broker.

In the case at hand, the plaintiffs only suffered one of those harms, but there is no reason to find that they should be denied a recovery because their portfolio increased in value, either because of or in spite of the activities of the defendants.

We are mindful of our decision in Hatrock v. Edward D. Jones & Co., 750 F.2d 767 (9th Cir.1984). In that case we pointed out that the investor could recover both the "excessive commissions charged by the broker, and the decline in value of the investor's portfolio resulting from the broker's fraudulent transactions." However, the investor had in fact suffered both of those losses, and nothing in that opinion suggested that we intended to declare that an investor must suffer both harms before he can recover from the broker. It is not surprising that a broker who is guilty of churning—an element of which is the making of unsuitable investment decisions—may also have purchased unsuitable investments. That does not mean that the two concepts should be conflated, and we have never said that they must be. Rather, our decisions are properly harmonized to reach an unremarkable result which ultimately makes the plaintiff whole in any event—a plaintiff may separately recover either or both types of damages, but gains in portfolio will not offset losses in commissions. That is a result that prevents the broker from escaping with improper commissions. Defendants would have us say that a broker who, for example, engages in unsuitable management of the account but actually buys suitable or successful investments cannot be held responsible for his actions. One can easily envision a single successful security which is bought and sold an unreasonable number of times, thereby relieving the client of gains and improperly enriching the broker. We would be remiss if we were to find no redress within the securities law for that kind of wrongdoing. Finally, it would be a poor rule indeed that unnecessarily forced courts and juries to enter into the complex determinations needed to determine whether any gain on a portfolio was due to the improper activities of a broker. Once the trier of fact finds that the trading was excessive it had determined that the trading should not have taken place. It should not be forced to decide whether gains or losses are a result of market forces, luck, good times or intrinsically good stock. Nor should the trier of fact have to decide what part of the loss or gain should be allocated to any given factor. That is one reason we have said that proof of causation is not a necessary element of a plaintiff's case. The broker will have made trades that should not have been made, and he should not retain his ill gotten gain. This salutory rule also informs the brokerage community that churning is a fraud that will violate the securities laws, regardless of the ultimate condition of the client's portfolio. It therefore serves to forward the deterrent policies which underlie the federal securities laws. Randall v. Loftsgaarden, 478 U.S. 647 (1986).

As a final attack on damages, the defendants rely on a portion of the Supreme Court's decision in Randall v. Loftgaarden, for the proposition that the plaintiff must lean upon the concept of unjust enrichment in order to recover. Reasoning from the proposition, defendants ask that the brokers' expenses be deducted from the commissions and that plaintiffs recover, at most, the difference. It is true that *Randall* addresses the question of unjust enrichment, but it does not mandate the theory suggested by defendants. The core of the defendants' position must be that if a broker defrauds a client of a commission, the broker ought to be able to deduct the expenses he incurred in perpetrating the fraud and then return the rest to the client. We believe that the very statement of the proposition refutes it, and not a shard of judicial precedent supports it. *Randall,* on the other hand, merely offers the possibility that even if a plaintiff has not lost as much as a defendant has gained, the plaintiff should recover that gain from the defendant. To apply that to a situation where defendant has not netted as much as he has taken from the plaintiff would stand *Randall* on its head. It takes no hierophant to discover that.

Therefore, we must reject defendants' assault on the damage award in this case.

* * *

In addition to the prohibition against churning, which is based on the SEC's antifraud rules, the rules of the major self-regulatory organizations also affect broker-dealers' relations with their customers.

The most important NASD rule is the so-called "suitability" rule, found in Article III, § 2 of the NASD's Rules of Fair Practice, which provides that a broker-dealer who recommends a security to a customer "shall have reasonable grounds for believing that the recommendation is suitable for such customer upon the basis of the facts, if any, disclosed by such customer as to his other security holdings and as to his financial situation and needs." The NASD's policy statement interpreting this rule offers the following examples of practices which may violate this Rule:

> 1. Recommending speculative low-priced securities to customers without knowledge of or attempt to obtain information concerning the customers' other securities holdings, their financial situation and other necessary data. The principle here is that this practice, by its very nature, involves a high probability that the recommendation will not be suitable for at least some of the persons solicited. This has particular application to high pressure telephone sales campaigns.
>
> * * *
>
> 3. Trading in mutual fund shares, particularly on a short-term basis. It is clear that normally these securities are not proper trading vehicles and such activity on its face may raise the question of rule violation.
>
> * * *
>
> 5. Recommending the purchase of securities or the continuing purchase of securities in amounts which are inconsistent with the reasonable expectation that the customer has the financial ability to meet such a commitment.

The New York Stock Exchange follows a somewhat different approach. NYSE Rule 405, the "know your customer" rule, requires every member firm to "use due diligence to learn the essential facts relative to every customer." While this rule is primarily designed to assure the financial stability of the member firms, it is sometimes interpreted as a kind of "suitability" rule, requiring the firm to know enough about the customer's situation and objectives to avoid making inappropriate recommendations.

While these NASD and NYSE rules have been the basis for numerous disciplinary proceedings against broker-dealers, there is doubt as to whether they give rise to any private right of action on behalf of an aggrieved customer. See Chapter 11.A below.

COMMODITIES REGULATION

By Philip M. Johnson & Thomas L. Hazen

Volume 3, pp. 126–128 (2d Ed.1989).*

Futures and commodity options trading is, by nature, a heavy turnover type of investment. First of all, futures and option contracts (unlike equity securities) have a limited life—usually a year to eighteen months—that necessitates turnover at least that frequently. Moreover, the high leverage available in futures and option contracts means a magnification of gains and losses from price changes and a concomitant desire to cut losses quickly and to add to profitable positions. There is no doubt that turnover of futures and option contracts, for these reasons, far exceeds the frequency with which most securities investors alter their portfolios. Day trading, for instance, is commonplace in futures and options, especially among the professionals, and even the avocational investor may neither want nor be able to sustain a particular position for more than a few days or weeks. Thus, for example, in Hecht v. Harris, Upham & Co. [430 F.2d 1202 (9th Cir.1970)], the court reviewed claims under both the securities and commodity accounts of the plaintiff, and recognized the fact that greater turnover can be expected in a commodity account.

A second relevant feature of futures and options trading, when assessing whether an account has been "churned" (as defined below), is that the same leverage and resultant impact on an account when prices change encourages customers to vest authority in their brokers to make and liquidate trades without express prior approval from the customer in each instance. Sudden price movements, amplified by the contract's leverage, call for quick corrective or exploitive action, and the broker is frequently better situated than the customer to react with the necessary speed. Accordingly, many customers routinely open discretionary trading accounts with the carrying FCM or with a floor broker.

A third factor relevant to churning is that FCMs [i.e. brokers] and their employees handling customer accounts (APs) are commonly compensated by commissions calculated by reference to the volume of trading conducted in customers' accounts. As a result, high-volume accounts are more profitable for both the FCM and its APs than accounts with a modest volume of trading. The temptation exists, therefore, to keep accounts as active as possible and from time to time that temptation may prevail over the duty to protect and preserve the customer's assets.

Churning, defined in its simplest terms, is simply excessive trading of a customer's account—that is, trading that cannot be justified as necessary to fulfill the customer's trading objective or to preserve his or her assets. Ordinarily, churning consists of too much trading by the broker. But it should also be noted—although the case law has not done so—that a form of de facto churning can sometimes be built into an account by consistently taking positions that, by their nature, must be made and liquidated rapidly. If this is the customer's wish, of course, it should not be viewed as unlawful; but where a broker—with or without trading discretion—follows a pattern of either trading or recommending trades that require rapid turnover without the customer's informed concurrence in that practice, the account may well warrant close scrutiny.

Selected References

Baker, Actions Against Broker–Dealers for the Sale of Unsuitable Securities, 13 Stetson L.Rev. 283 (1984).

Brodsky, Measuring Damages in Churning and Suitability Cases, 6 Sec.Reg. L.J. 157 (1978).

Kerr, Suitability Standards: A New Look at Economic Theory and Current SEC Disclosure Policy, 16 Pac.L.J. 805 (1985).

Nichols, The Broker's Duty to His Customer Under Evolving Federal Fiduciary and Suitability Standards, 26 Buffalo L.Rev. 435 (1977).

O'Hara, The Elusive Concept of Control in Churning Claims Under Federal Securities And Commodities Laws, 75 Geo.L.J. 1875 (1987).

Poser, Options Accounts Fraud: Securities Churning In a New Context, 39 Bus.Law. 571 (1984).

Roach, The Suitability Obligations of Brokers: Present Law and the Federal Securities Code, 29 Hast.L.J. 1067 (1978).

Winslow & Anderson, A Model for Determining the Excessive Trading Element in Churning Claims, 68 N.C.L.Rev. 327 (1990).

Note, Measuring Damages in Suitability and Churning Actions Under Rule 10b–5, 25 B.C.L.Rev. 839 (1984).

Note, Private Actions for the Broker's "Churning" of a Securities Account, 40 Mo.L.Rev. 281 (1975).

Note, Churning by Securities Dealers, 80 Harv.L.Rev. 869 (1967).

C. INVESTMENT ADVISERS—"SCALPING"

SEC v. CAPITAL GAINS RESEARCH BUREAU

375 U.S. 180 (1963).

MR. JUSTICE GOLDBERG delivered the opinion of the Court.

We are called upon in this case to decide whether under the Investment Advisers Act of 1940 the Securities and Exchange Commission may obtain an injunction compelling a registered investment adviser to disclose to his clients a practice of purchasing shares of a security for his own account shortly before recommending that security for long-term investment and then immediately selling the shares at a profit upon the rise in the market price following the recommendation. The answer to this question turns on whether the practice—known in the trade as "scalping"—operates as a fraud or deceit upon any client or prospective client" within the meaning of the Act.[2] We hold that it does and that the Commission may "enforce compliance" with the Act by obtaining an injunction requiring the adviser to make full disclosure of the practice to his clients.[2]

The Commission brought this action against respondents in the United States District Court for the Southern District of New York. At the hearing on the application for a preliminary injunction, the following facts were established. Respondents publish two investment advisory services, one of which—"A Capital Gains Report"—is the subject of this proceeding. The Report is mailed monthly to approximately 5,000 subscribers who each pay an annual subscription price of $18. It carries the following description:

> "An Investment Service devoted exclusively to (1) The protection of investment capital. (2) The realization of a steady and attractive income therefrom. (3) The accumulation of CAPITAL GAINS thru the timely purchase of corporate equities that are proved to be undervalued."

2. [Section 206 of the Act] provides in relevant part that:

"It shall be unlawful for any investment adviser, by use of the mails or any means or instrumentality of interstate commerce, directly or indirectly—

"(1) to employ any device, scheme, or artifice to defraud any client or prospective client;

"(2) to engage in any transaction, practice, or course of business which operates as a fraud or deceit upon any client or prospective client;

"(3) acting as principal for his own account, knowingly to sell any security to or purchase any security from a client, or acting as broker for a person other than such client, knowingly to effect any sale or purchase of any security for the account of such client, without disclosing to such client in writing before the completion of such transaction the capacity in which he is acting and obtaining the consent of the client to such transaction. The prohibitions of this paragraph shall not apply to any transaction with a customer of a broker or dealer if such broker or dealer is not acting as an investment adviser in relation to such transaction. * * *"

Between March 15, 1960, and November 7, 1960, respondents, on six different occasions, purchased shares of a particular security shortly before recommending it in the Report for long-term investment. On each occasion, there was an increase in the market price and the volume of trading of the recommended security within a few days after the distribution of the Report. Immediately thereafter, respondents sold their shares of these securities at a profit. They did not disclose any aspect of these transactions to their clients or prospective clients.

On the basis of the above facts, the Commission requested a preliminary injunction as necessary to effectuate the purposes of the Investment Advisers Act of 1940. The injunction would have required respondents, in any future Report, to disclose the material facts concerning, *inter alia,* any purchase of recommended securities "within a very short period prior to the distribution of a recommendation * * *," and "[t]he intent to sell and the sale of said securities * * * within a very short period after distribution of said recommendation * * *."

The District Court denied the request for a preliminary injunction, holding that the words "fraud" and "deceit" are used in the Investment Advisers Act of 1940 "in their technical sense" and that the Commission had failed to show an intent to injure clients or an actual loss of money to clients. The Court of Appeals for the Second Circuit, sitting *en banc,* by a 5–to–4 vote accepted the District Court's limited construction of "fraud" and "deceit" and affirmed the denial of injunctive relief. The majority concluded that no violation of the Act could be found absent proof that "any misstatements or false figures were contained in any of the bulletins"; or that "the investment advice was unsound"; or that "defendants were being bribed or paid to tout a stock contrary to their own beliefs"; or that "these bulletins were a scheme to get rid of worthless stock"; or that the recommendations were made "for the purpose of endeavoring artificially to raise the market so that [respondents] might unload [their] holdings at a profit." The four dissenting judges pointed out that "[t]he common-law doctrines of fraud and deceit grew up in a business climate very different from that involved in the sale of securities," and urged a broad remedial construction of the statute which would encompass respondents' conduct. We granted certiorari to consider the question of statutory construction because of its importance to the investing public and the financial community.

The decision in this case turns on whether Congress, in empowering the courts to enjoin any practice which operates "as a fraud or deceit upon any client or prospective client," intended to require the Commission to establish fraud and deceit "in their technical sense," including intent to injure and actual injury to clients, or whether Congress intended a broad remedial construction of the Act which would encompass nondisclosure of material facts. For resolution of this issue we consider the history and purpose of the Investment Advisers Act of 1940.

I.

* * *

The Public Utility Holding Company Act of 1935 "authorized and directed" the Securities and Exchange Commission "to make a study of the functions and activities of investment trusts and investment companies * * *." Pursuant to this mandate, the Commission made an exhaustive study and report which included consideration of investment counsel and investment advisory services. This aspect of the study and report culminated in the Investment Advisers Act of 1940.

The report reflects the attitude—shared by investment advisers and the Commission—that investment advisers could not "completely perform their basic function—furnishing to clients on a personal basis competent, unbiased, and continuous advice regarding the sound management of their investments—unless all conflicts of interest between the investment counsel and the client were removed." The report stressed that affiliations by investment advisers with investment bankers or corporations might be "an impediment to a disinterested, objective, or critical attitude toward an investment by clients * * *."

This concern was not limited to deliberate or conscious impediments to objectivity. Both the advisers and the Commission were well aware that whenever advice to a client might result in financial benefit to the adviser—other than the fee for his advice—"that advice to a client might in some way be tinged with that pecuniary interest [whether consciously or] subconsciously motivated * * *." The report quoted one leading investment adviser who said that he "would put the emphasis * * * on subconscious" motivation in such situations. It quoted a member of the Commission staff who suggested that a significant part of the problem was not the existence of a "deliberate intent" to obtain a financial advantage, but rather the existence "subconsciously [of] a prejudice" in favor of one's own financial interests. * * *

One activity specifically mentioned and condemned by investment advisers who testified before the Commission was "*trading by investment counselors for their own account in securities in which their clients were interested* * * *."

This study and report—authorized and directed by statute—culminated in the preparation and introduction by Senator Wagner of the bill which, with some changes, became the Investment Advisers Act of 1940. In its "declaration of policy" the original bill stated that

> "Upon the basis of facts disclosed by the record and report of the Securities and Exchange Commission * * * it is hereby declared that the national public interest and the interest of investors are adversely affected—* * * (4) when the business of investment advisers is so conducted as to defraud or mislead investors, or to enable such advisers to relieve themselves of their fiduciary obligations to their clients.
>
> "It is hereby declared that the policy and purposes of this title, in accordance with which the provisions of this title shall be interpreted,

are to mitigate and, so far as is presently practicable, to eliminate the abuses enumerated in this section." S. 3580, 76th Cong., 3d Sess., § 202.

Hearings were then held before Committees of both Houses of Congress. In describing their profession, leading investment advisers emphasized their relationship of "trust and confidence" with their clients and the importance of "strict limitation of [their right] to buy and sell securities in the normal way if there is any chance at all that to do so might seem to operate against the interests of clients and the public." The president of the Investment Counsel Association of America, the leading investment counsel association, testified that the

> "two fundamental principles upon which the pioneers in this new profession undertook to meet the growing need for unbiased investment information and guidance were, first, that they would limit their efforts and activities to the study of investment problems from the investor's standpoint, not engaging in any other activity, such as security selling or brokerage, which might directly or indirectly bias their investment judgment; and second, that their remuneration for this work would consist solely of definite, professional fees fully disclosed in advance."

* * *

The Investment Advisers Act of 1940 thus reflects a congressional recognition "of the delicate fiduciary nature of an investment advisory relationship," as well as a congressional intent to eliminate, or at least to expose, all conflicts of interest which might incline an investment adviser—consciously or unconsciously—to render advice which was not disinterested. It would defeat the manifest purpose of the Investment Advisers Act of 1940 for us to hold, therefore, that Congress, in empowering the courts to enjoin any practice which operates "as a fraud or deceit," intended to require proof of intent to injure and actual injury to clients.

This conclusion moreover, is not in derogation of the common law of fraud, as the District Court and the majority of the Court of Appeals suggested. To the contrary, it finds support in the process by which the courts have adapted the common law of fraud to the commercial transactions of our society. It is true that at common law intent and injury have been deemed essential elements in a damage suit between parties to an arm's-length transaction. But this is not such an action. This is a suit for a preliminary injunction in which the relief sought is, as the dissenting judges below characterized it, the "mild prophylactic," of requiring a fiduciary to disclose to his clients, not all his security holdings, but only his dealings in recommended securities just before and after the issuance of his recommendations.

The content of common-law fraud has not remained static as the courts below seem to have assumed. It has varied, for example, with the nature of the relief sought, the relationship between the parties, and the merchandise in issue. It is not necessary in a suit for equitable or prophylactic relief to establish all the elements required in a suit for monetary damages. * * *

> "Fraud has a broader meaning in equity [than at law] and intention to defraud or to misrepresent is not a necessary element."

We cannot assume that Congress, in enacting legislation to prevent fraudulent practices by investment advisers, was unaware of these developments in the common law of fraud. Thus, even if we were to agree with the courts below that Congress had intended, in effect, to codify the common law of fraud in the Investment Advisers Act of 1940, it would be logical to conclude that Congress codified the common law "remedially" as the courts had adapted it to the prevention of fraudulent securities transactions by fiduciaries, not "technically" as it has traditionally been applied in damage suits between parties to arm's-length transactions involving land and ordinary chattels. * * *

II.

We turn now to a consideration of whether the specific conduct here in issue was the type which Congress intended to reach in the Investment Advisers Act of 1940. It is arguable—indeed it was argued by "some investment counsel representatives" who testified before the Commission—that any "trading by investment counselors for their own account in securities in which their clients were interested * * *" creates a potential conflict of interest which must be eliminated. We need not go that far in this case, since here the Commission seeks only disclosure of a conflict of interests with significantly greater potential for abuse than in the situation described above. An adviser who, like respondents, secretly trades on the market effect of his own recommendation may be motivated—consciously or unconsciously—to recommend a given security not because of its potential for long-run price increase (which would profit the client), but because of its potential for short-run price increase in response to anticipated activity from the recommendation (which would profit the adviser). An investor seeking the advice of a registered investment adviser must, if the legislative purpose is to be served, be permitted to evaluate such overlapping motivations, through appropriate disclosure, in deciding whether an adviser is serving "two masters" or only one, "especially * * * if one of the masters happens to be economic self-interest." Accordingly, we hold that the Investment Advisers Act of 1940 empowers the courts, upon a showing such as that made here, to require an adviser to make full and frank disclosure of his practice of trading on the effect of his recommendations.

III.

Respondents offer three basic arguments against this conclusion. They argue first that Congress could have made, but did not make, failure to disclose material facts unlawful in the Investment Advisers Act of 1940, as it did in the Securities Act of 1933, and that absent specific language, it should not be assumed that Congress intended to include failure to disclose in its general proscription of any practice which operates as a fraud or deceit. But considering the history and chronology of the statutes, this omission does not seem significant. The Securities Act of 1933 was the first experiment in federal regulation of the securities industry. It was understandable, therefore, for Congress, in declaring certain practices unlawful, to include both a general proscription against fraudulent and deceptive practices and, out of an abundance of caution, a specific proscription against nondisclosure. It soon became clear, however, that the courts, aware of the previously outlined developments in the common law of fraud, were merging the proscription against nondisclosure into the general proscription against fraud, treating the former, in effect, as one variety of the latter. * * * In light of this, and in light of the evidence purpose of the Investment Advisers Act of 1940 to substitute a philosophy of disclosure for the philosophy of *caveat emptor,* we cannot assume that the omission in the 1940 Act of a specific proscription against nondisclosure was intended to limit the application of the antifraud and antideceit provisions of the Act so as to render the Commission impotent to enjoin suppression of material facts. The more reasonable assumption, considering what had transpired between 1933 and 1940, is that Congress, in enacting the Investment Advisers Act of 1940 and proscribing any practice which operates "as a fraud or deceit," deemed a specific proscription against nondisclosure surplusage. * * *

Respondents argue, finally, that their advice was "honest" in the sense that they believed it was sound and did not offer it for the purpose of furthering personal pecuniary objectives. This, of course, is but another way of putting the rejected argument that the elements of technical common-law fraud—particularly intent—must be established before an injunction requiring disclosure may be ordered. It is the practice itself, however, with its potential for abuse, which "operates as a fraud or deceit" within the meaning of the Act when relevant information is suppressed. * * * To impose upon the Securities and Exchange Commission the burden of showing deliberate dishonesty as a condition precedent to protecting investors through the prophylaxis of disclosure would effectively nullify the protective purposes of the statute. Reading the Act in light of its background we find no such requirement commanded. * * *

It misconceives the purpose of the statute to confine its application to "dishonest" as opposed to "honest" motives. As Dean Shulman said in discussing the nature of securities transactions, what is required is "a picture not simply of the show window, but of the entire store * * * not simply truth in the statements volunteered, but disclosure." [56] The high standards of business morality exacted by our laws regulating the securities industry do not permit an investment adviser to trade on the market effect of his own recommendations without fully

56. Shulman, Civil Liability and the Securities Act, 43 Yale L.J. 227, 242.

and fairly revealing his personal interests in these recommendations to his clients.

Experience has shown that disclosure in such situations, while not onerous to the adviser, is needed to preserve the climate of fair dealing which is so essential to maintain public confidence in the securities industry and to preserve the economic health of the country.

The judgment of the Court of Appeals is reversed and the case is remanded to the District Court for proceedings consistent with this opinion.

Reversed and remanded.

ZWEIG v. HEARST CORP.

594 F.2d 1261 (9th Cir.1979).

Before ELY and GOODWIN, CIRCUIT JUDGES, and SOLOMON, DISTRICT JUDGE.

GOODWIN, CIRCUIT JUDGE:

Plaintiffs appeal from a judgment denying recovery in their action for damages against a financial columnist who, they allege, purposely used his column to elevate the price of stock in a small company for his own benefit.

Richard Zweig and Muriel Bruno sued Alex Campbell, a financial columnist for the Los Angeles Herald–Examiner; the Hearst Corporation, Campbell's employer; and H.W. Jamieson and E.L. Oesterle, directors of American Systems, Inc. (ASI). Zweig and Bruno alleged violations of Section 10(b) of the Securities Exchange Act of 1934, and of Rule 10b–5, as well as common-law fraud and negligence.

Campbell wrote and the Herald–Examiner published a column that contained a highly favorable description of ASI. The plaintiffs alleged that the directors of ASI had made material misrepresentations and omissions in an interview with Campbell and hoped that he would publish false information "puffing" ASI shares. This is essentially what he did, but only after first buying 5,000 shares from the company at a substantial discount below their market price.

Zweig and Bruno claimed that Campbell's column about ASI caused the price of ASI stock to rise, and that they were damaged when they merged their company with ASI in exchange for a quantity of temporarily inflated ASI stock. The plaintiffs were under a contractual duty to exchange stock at the market price as of a time certain. They alleged that Campbell had violated Rule 10b–5 by publishing his column about ASI without disclosing to his readers that he had bought ASI stock at a discount and intended to sell some of it upon the rise in market price that he knew his column would cause. In addition, plaintiffs contended, Campbell should have revealed to his readers that the column was likely to be republished as an advertisement for ASI in an investment periodical in which Campbell held a substantial ownership interest.

The case against the Hearst Corporation was dismissed by a summary judgment, on the ground that Hearst was not vicariously liable for Campbell's action. Another panel of this court affirmed. Zweig v. Hearst Corp., 521 F.2d 1129 (9th Cir.1975).

The case against Campbell, Jamieson, and Oesterle went to trial without a jury in April of 1975. During the plaintiffs' opening statement and again after the testimony of the plaintiffs' first witness, the trial judge indicated that he did not agree with the plaintiffs' theory of liability under Rule 10b–5 as it applied to Campbell. Realizing that a full trial on the merits might be useless, the plaintiffs made an offer of proof and asked the court to rule on Campbell's motion to dismiss in light of this offer of proof.

After considering the plaintiffs' offer of proof, the trial judge granted the motion to dismiss.

* * *

II. MATERIALITY OF OMITTED FACTS

Campbell wrote four or five columns a week during 1969 as a financial columnist for the Herald–Examiner. In these columns he frequently discussed the financial conditions of small companies in southern California. He often bought the shares of companies that he expected to discuss favorably in forthcoming columns, and then sold the shares at a profit soon after his columns appeared.[4]

In late May or early June of 1969, Campbell interviewed Jamieson, Oesterle, and another ASI officer to obtain information for a column about ASI. The ASI officials did not give Campbell complete or accurate information. They were silent about problems then confronting ASI. There is no claim that Campbell was a knowing party to any fraud by ASI, but Campbell engaged in no independent research before publishing his story. Campbell also purchased directly from ASI 5,000 shares of its stock. While the bid price of the ASI stock on the day of the purchase was 3⅝, Campbell paid only $2.00 per share.[5]

Two days after he bought the ASI shares, Campbell's column about ASI appeared in the Herald–Examiner. The article contained several erroneous statements that cast the company in a more favorable light than it deserved. On this record we assume that Campbell did not know that the misleading parts of his column were false. An inference

4. During the two-year period prior to June 4, 1969, Campbell bought the stock of 21 companies shortly before his columns about those companies were to be published. In almost every case he sold at least some of his recently purchased stock within five days after the publication of the column about the company involved. In 21 of 22 sales occurring within five days of the publication of a column, Campbell made a profit because of an increase in the price of the stock after the publication of his column.

5. The plaintiffs have not presented the question whether Campbell's acceptance of the stock at a bargain price was the receipt of "consideration" for his column, within the meaning of Section 17(b) of the Securities Act of 1933.

is permissible that, while he made no effort to portray the facts accurately, he honestly believed the optimistic opinions of his co-defendants, who were then (perhaps unknown to Campbell) preparing to close the executory plan of merger with plaintiffs' firm, Reading Guidance Center, Inc. (RGC).

Equally reasonable is the inference that Campbell knew that his column would run up the prices of ASI stock for a short time, during which persons who knew the reason for the increase could unload the stock at a profit. Thus, the trial judge's finding that Campbell had no plan to create the price rise and then sell was premature under the summary judgment standard of review. Moreover, unless Campbell can produce more evidence than that already in the record to rebut the strong inference caused by his long history of similar dealings, any "finding" that he did not intend to profit from his stock purchase and concurrent column would be of dubious value under the clearly erroneous standard. We therefore presume an intent to profit, the inference urged by plaintiffs, at this stage of the case.

After Campbell's column appeared, the price of ASI stock rose swiftly. The plaintiffs' offer of proof included the opinion of an expert witness that the Campbell column caused a market increase in the number of investors wanting to buy ASI stock, and that this, combined with the "thin float" of the stock (500,000 shares outstanding), led to the dramatic increase in the bid price of the shares.[6]

On June 5, the day after the article appeared, Campbell sold 2,000 of his 5,000 ASI shares for $5.00 per share, thereby recouping his entire cash investment while retaining 3,000 shares of the stock for future profits.

Plaintiffs Zweig and Bruno did not know of any plan to inflate the price of the stock. Each owned one third of the shares of RGC. In February of 1969, RGC entered into a plan of reorganization by which RGC was to merge into ASI. ASI was to pay the RGC stockholders by transferring enough ASI stock to equal a market value of $1,800,000. The number of shares would be determined by the average closing bid for ASI stock for the five market days preceding the closing date, June 10, 1969.

The plaintiffs were prepared to show that an artificial price rise was caused by the Campbell column and led to a substantial dilution in the interest in ASI that they ultimately received under the merger agreement.

Zweig and Bruno argue that Campbell should be liable under Rule 10b–5 for his omission of these material facts from his column about ASI: (1) that he had invested in ASI stock at a discount price two days before his column was to be published, and intended to sell it on the short-swing rise in price; (2) that he made a practice of "scalping" the

6. According to this expert witness, the price of ASI stock would not have risen above $3.25 before June 10, 1969, without the Campbell column. But instead, the average closing bid price between June 3 and June 9 was $4.35 per share.

stocks of companies about which he wrote by buying their stock shortly before his columns about them were published and then selling the stock at a profit after the columns caused a jump in the market price; and (3) that his favorable columns were often reprinted as advertisements for the subject companies in a financial journal in which Campbell had an interest.[7]

Zweig and Bruno contend that Rule 10b–5 required Campbell to inform his readers of these facts so that the readers could judge for themselves whether Campbell's personal motives for promoting ASI affected his objectivity.

The appropriate test for the materiality of an omitted fact is whether there is a substantial likelihood that a reasonable investor would consider the fact important in making his or her investment decision. The facts revealing Campbell's lack of objectivity were material under this test. Reasonable investors who read the column would have considered the motivations of a financial columnist such as Campbell important in deciding whether to invest in the companies touted. See Affiliated Ute Citizens v. United States, 406 U.S. 128 (1972); Chasins v. Smith, Barney & Co., 438 F.2d 1167, 1172 (2d Cir. 1970).

* * *

III. The Duty to Disclose

Most disclosure cases cited by the parties have involved a corporate insider, or a receiver of a tip, who traded in the corporation's stock without disclosing material facts that, if publicly known, would have affected the stock's market value. In most of these cases, the information withheld was directly relevant to inherent value of the firm's assets and operations or its potential earnings and growth prospects.

In this case, the information withheld from the public was of a slightly different type. Viewing the evidence in the light most favorable to the plaintiffs, Campbell failed to reveal to investor-readers that he expected to gain personally if they followed his advice. He did not tell them that he had purchased the stock at a bargain price knowing that he would write his column and then sell on the rise, as he had done with other stocks before. He did not reveal that his column would also appear as a paid advertisement for ASI in his journal. This withheld information did not relate directly to the company's value and expected performance, but it was necessary to avoid misleading Campbell's audience on the reliance they could place on the column. We hold that in failing to disclose these facts, Campbell violated Section 10(b) and Rule 10b–5 just as corporate insiders do when they withhold material facts about a corporation's prospects while trading its stock.

7. In 1969, Campbell had a financial interest in the California Financial Journal, a weekly publication specializing in news about business ventures in Los Angeles County. It was a regular practice of Journal employees to call companies Campbell had written about and solicit those companies to run copies of the Campbell columns as advertisements in the Journal. On July 1, 1969, the Campbell column on ASI ran as an advertisement in the California Financial Journal.

Zweig and Bruno rely on S.E.C. v. Capital Gains Research Bureau, Inc., 375 U.S. 180 (1963). In *Capital Gains,* the Supreme Court held that the SEC could obtain an injunction under the Investment Advisers Act of 1940 to force a registered advisory service to disclose its practice of profiting from the market effect of its investment recommendations, which it made in a monthly report to subscribers. The Court found the service's failure to disclose this practice a "fraud or deceit" on its clients within the meaning of the Investment Advisers Act of 1940.

The holding in *Capital Gains* was limited to the duties imposed on investment advisers by the 1940 Act. The plaintiffs here do not argue that Campbell was an investment adviser as defined in that statute; thus, *Capital Gains* is not controlling. But the failure to bring the case within the Investment Advisers Act does not mean that the claim under Section 10(b) and Rule 10b–5 should fail. We hold that as applied to the facts we must assume in this case, the Investment Advisers Act was not meant to limit the Securities Exchange Act or Rule 10b–5. Instead, we believe that these provisions complement each other and provide different means to curb slightly different types of "fraud or deceit".

A number of cases since *Capital Gains* suggests that Rule 10b–5 requires the disclosure of conflicts of interest in situations similar to the facts of this case. In Chasins v. Smith, Barney & Co., supra, the court held that a brokerage firm had the duty to disclose its "market making" activities in certain stocks to a client who purchased those stocks on the firm's recommendation. The court upheld a judgment for damages suffered by the client, on the ground that the firm's failure to inform the customer of the possible conflict of interest was an omission of a material fact in violation of Rule 10b–5.

The court's holding in *Chasins* could be interpreted narrowly, as imposing a duty to disclose conflicts of interest only upon brokers acting within a traditional broker-client relationship. However, the Supreme Court's opinion in *Affiliated Ute* illustrated that this duty may be imposed on others as well.

The plaintiffs in *Affiliated Ute* were former shareholders in the Ute Development Corporation (UDC), a corporation formed as part of a plan to distribute the assets of the Ute Indian Tribe among its mixed-blood and full-blood members. Upon its formation, UDC had issued 10 shares of stock in the name of each mixed-blood member and then appointed a Utah bank to act as the UDC stock transfer agent. The plaintiffs sued the bank and two of its employees under Rule 10b–5 when they learned that the bank employees had promoted and participated in sales of Indians' shares to non-Indian buyers at a price that the employees knew was well below the market value of the securities.

We find Campbell's activities sufficiently similar to those of the bank employees in *Affiliated Ute* to impose on him a duty to disclose to his readers his stock ownership, his intent to sell when the market price rose, and the practice of reprinting his articles. Columnists, like transfer agents, ordinarily have no duty to disclose facts about their personal financial affairs or about the corporations on which they report. But there are instances in which Section 10(b) and Rule 10b–5 require disclosure. Here, as in *Affiliated Ute,* the defendant assumed those duties when, with knowledge of the stock's market and an intent to gain personally, he encouraged purchases of the securities in the market. Campbell should have told his readers of his stock ownership, of his intent to sell shares that he had bought at a discount for a quick profit, and of the practice of having his columns reprinted verbatim as advertisements in the financial journal in which he had an interest.

* * *

In order for Campbell to be liable to non-readers Zweig and Bruno, however, a further duty must be shown. To recover damages, these plaintiffs must prove that Campbell owed them a duty. They must show that they were in a relationship with Campbell similar to his readers' relationship with him. We believe that RGC, and its shareholders Zweig and Bruno, were in a position similar to that of Campbell's readers. RGC and the readers had strikingly similar stakes in the processes of the market.

At the time the Campbell column was published, RGC had already contractually committed itself to sell its assets to ASI. ASI agreed to pay at a future date stock worth $1,900,000 for the RGC assets. The number of ASI shares was to be fixed by the market value of ASI stock on given dates. In making this deal, RGC relied on the existence of an honest market. A market presumes the ability of investors to assess all the relevant data on a stock, including the credibility of those who recommend it, in creating a demand for that stock.

In effect, RGC in good faith placed its fate in the hands of market investors, including Campbell's readers. RGC relied on the forces of a fully informed market. Instead, it was forced to sell in a manipulated market. If Campbell was unaware of RGC's reliance on the market, he could have discovered it with minimal effort by asking ASI or RGC about the terms of the merger or by checking the reorganization agreement that had been signed several months before. RGC was a foreseeable plaintiff.

* * *

We are aware that in traditional common-law terms it is difficult to make out a duty owed by Campbell to a corporation that did not, and could not, have read his writings before deciding to purchase ASI stock. But if there had been no RGC merger planned, Campbell would be liable to his readers for losses caused by the $1.10 per share temporary inflation that we must assume was caused by his column. In the unusual fact setting here, someone else, a purchaser of ASI stock that relied on the free and unmanipulated market that the federal securities laws were designed to foster, absorbed part of that loss. That forced purchaser should not be required, in effect, to pay Campbell's damages for him. We believe it fully consistent with the spirit and letter of the securities laws to impose upon Campbell a duty to RGC. As we have illustrated, to extend the obligation of disclosure to the readers but to bar RGC from recovery under the rubrics of reliance or duty would lead to a wholly incongruous result: the more effective Campbell was in elevating the price of the stock for his own benefit, the greater the losses an innocent third party (RGC) would have to absorb.

IV. Conclusion

The other aspects of this cause of action require but brief comment. The Supreme Court has held that Rule 10b–5 will not support a private action for damages in the absence of an allegation of scienter. Ernst & Ernst v. Hochfelder, 425 U.S. 185 (1976). Here, Campbell knew the material facts he failed to reveal. Moreover, there is at the very least a triable issue of fact as to whether Campbell intended to benefit from the column, from which he intentionally omitted any mention of his financial interests. And as the Supreme Court noted in *Affiliated Ute,* when a Rule 10b–5 action is based on nondisclosure, causation of harm is sufficiently proved by a showing of materiality. Thus, we believe the court below should presume on remand that the public purchases of ASI stock that followed the republication of the article were in reliance on it. RGC did not rely specifically on Campbell or his column, but it did rely on the natural process of the market. That market included Campbell's readers, who must be presumed to have relied on his making a full and frank disclosure. We hold that these two legitimate expectations constitute sufficient reliance to establish liability in this case.

While Rule 10b–5 should not be extended to require every financial columnist or reporter to disclose his or her portfolio to all of his or her readers, it does cover the activities of one who uses a column as part of a scheme to manipulate the market and deceive the investing public. On the record in this case there were material questions of motive and method that should be resolved in a trial.

The court below asserted that it saw no harm or impropriety in a columnist's "making a nickel" at the same time he tells his readers of what may truly appear to him to be an enterprise with a bright future. The trial court was apprehensive that compelling disclosure of financial interest in such a situation would provide a disincentive to columnists to report on the merits of worthy companies. This observation is true, but it proves too much. If brokers were permitted to make secret profits by self-dealing in the market, they too would be stimulated to find better stocks, in which they could invest personally while passing along the advice to their customers. Moreover, the judgment of corporate directors and officers and controlling shareholders might similarly be spurred if they could expect short-swing profits in the markets for the stocks of the companies they manage. But the federal securities laws, in guarding the public from abuses, strictly circumscribe the opportunities of persons holding certain positions to profit from their positions. We hold that these laws also require a financial columnist, in recommending a security that he or she owns, to provide the public with all material information he or she has on that security, including his or her ownership, and any intent he or she may have (a) to score a quick profit on the recommendation, or (b) to allow or encourage the recommendation to be published as an advertisement in his or her own periodical.

Reversed and remanded.

ELY, CIRCUIT JUDGE (dissenting):

I respectfully dissent. I agree that causation and reliance may, in certain circumstances, be inferred from materiality. But it is also clear that "affirmative evidence of non-reliance may defeat this inference." The record plainly shows that the appellants' decision to acquire ASI stock, embodied in the merger agreement between ASI and RGC, predated the publication of Campbell's column by several months. Thus, it is, as I see it, *impossible* that a causal relationship could exist between Campbell's wrongful conduct and the appellant's decision to invest. There was not even the possibility of reliance upon Campbell's column in connection with the execution of the merger agreement by the appellants. In these circumstances, we surely have compelling "affirmative evidence of nonreliance," evidence that should thoroughly negate any inference of causation and reliance.

While I agree that Campbell's alleged conduct was reprehensible, the District Court rightly concluded that he was not liable to the appellants in this case. The majority effectively removes the substantive content in the requirement of "in connection with" when it holds that Campbell may be liable in damages under Rule 10b–5 to individuals who decided to acquire stock and executed a merger agreement months before the wrongful conduct occurred. Sincerely believing that my Brothers stretch section 10(b) and Rule 10b–5 beyond their breaking point, I would affirm.

Does the approach taken by the court in *Zweig* survive the Supreme Court decisions on insider trading in the *Chiarella* and *Dirks* cases, set forth in Chapter 5.A? In June 1985, R. Foster Winans, a columnist for *The Wall Street Journal,* was convicted of a criminal violation of Rule 10b–5 for "tipping" a broker to stocks that he intended to recommend in his column, and sharing in the profits from the subsequent rise in price. His conviction was upheld by the Second Circuit under the "misappropriation" theory, see p. 583 above. The Supreme Court unanimously upheld his conviction for mail fraud, but his conviction for violation of Rule 10b–5 was affirmed without opinion by an equally divided court. CARPENTER v. UNITED STATES, 484 U.S. 19 (1987). In its argument to the Supreme Court, the government did not refer to the Court's decision in the *Capital Gains Research Bureau* case, even though the language of § 206 of the Investment Advisers Act is virtually identical to that of Rule 10b–5. Is there any significant difference between what Winans did and what the defendants in *Capital Gains* case did (except that the *Capital Gains* defendants could not have "misappropriated" the information, because they owned it)?

Under § 202(a)(11)(D) of the Investment Advisers Act, the term "investment adviser" does not include "the publisher of any bona fide newspaper, news magazine or business or financial publication of general and regular circulation". In SEC v. WALL STREET TRANSCRIPT CORP., 422 F.2d 1371 (2d Cir.1970), the court held that neither that subsection, nor the First Amendment to the Constitution, barred the SEC from compelling the production of a publication's advertising materials and correspondence, in an investigation to determine whether the publisher was required to register under the Act or was entitled to exemption as a "bona fide" newspaper. After trial, the district court determined that the publication was indeed a bona fide newspaper exempt from the Act. It relied in part on the fact that the publication was basically engaged in reprinting reports issued by brokerage houses and that, "because [it] does not print reports until the brokerage houses have circulated them publicly, the defendants' opportunity to engage in 'scalping' * * * is minimized." CCH Fed.Sec.L.Rep. ¶ 96,440 (S.D. N.Y.1978).

LOWE v. SEC

472 U.S. 181 (1985).

JUSTICE STEVENS delivered the opinion of the Court.

The question is whether petitioners may be permanently enjoined from publishing nonpersonalized investment advice and commentary in securities newsletters because they are not registered as investment advisers under § 203(c) of the Investment Advisers Act of 1940 (Act).

Christopher Lowe is the president and principal shareholder of Lowe Management Corporation. From 1974 until 1981, the corporation was registered as an investment adviser under the Act. During that period Lowe was convicted of misappropriating funds of an investment client, of engaging in business as an investment adviser without filing a registration application with New York's Department of Law, of tampering with evidence to cover up fraud of an investment client, and of stealing from a bank. Consequently, on May 11, 1981, the Securities and Exchange Commission (Commission), after a full hearing before an Administrative Law Judge, entered an order revoking the registration of the Lowe Management Corporation, and ordering Lowe not to associate thereafter with any investment adviser.

In fashioning its remedy, the Commission took into account the fact that petitioners "are now solely engaged in the business of publishing advisory publications." The Commission noted that unless the registration was revoked, petitioners would be "free to engage in all aspects of the advisory business" and that even their publishing activities afforded them "opportunities for dishonesty and self-dealing."

A little over a year later, the Commission commenced this action by filing a complaint in the United States District Court for the Eastern District of New York alleging that Lowe, the Lowe Management Corporation, and two other corporations, were violating the Act, and that Lowe was violating the Commission's order. The principal charge in the complaint was that Lowe and the three corporations (petitioners) were publishing two investment newsletters and soliciting subscriptions for a stock-chart service. The complaint alleged that, through those publications, the petitioners were engaged in the business of advising others "as to the advisability of investing in, purchasing, or selling securities * * * and as a part of a regular business * * * issuing reports concerning securities." Because none of the petitioners was registered or exempt from registration under the Act, the use of the mails in connection with the advisory business allegedly violated § 203(a) of the Act. The Commission prayed for a permanent injunction restraining the further distribution of petitioners' investment advisory publications; for a permanent injunction enforcing compliance with the order of May 11, 1981; and for other relief.

Although three publications are involved in this litigation, only one need be described. A typical issue of the Lowe Investment and Financial Letter contained general commentary about the securities and bullion markets, reviews of market indicators and investment strategies, and specific recommendations for buying, selling, or holding stocks and bullion. The newsletter advertised a "telephone hotline" over which subscribers could call to get current information. The number of subscribers to the newsletter ranged from 3,000 to 19,000. It was advertised as a semimonthly publication, but only eight issues were published in the 15 months after the entry of the 1981 order.

Subscribers who testified at the trial criticized the lack of regularity of publication, but no adverse evidence concerning the quality of the publications was offered. There was no evidence that Lowe's criminal convictions were related to the publications; no evidence that Lowe had engaged in any trading activity in any securities that were the subject of advice or comment in the publications; and no contention that any of the information published in the advisory services had been false or materially misleading.

For the most part, the District Court denied the Commission the relief it requested. * * * After determining that petitioners' publications were protected by the First Amendment, the District Court held that the Act must be construed to allow a publisher who is willing to comply with the existing reporting and disclosure requirements to register for the limited purpose of publishing such material and to engage in such publishing.

A splintered panel of the Court of Appeals for the Second Circuit reversed. The majority first held that petitioners were engaged in business as "investment advisers" within the meaning of the Act. It concluded that the Act does not distinguish between person-to-person advice and impersonal advice given in printed publications. Rather, in its view, the key statutory question was whether the exclusion in § 202(11)(D), for "the publisher of any bona fide newspaper, news magazine, or business or financial publication of general and regular circulation" applied to the petitioners. Relying on its decision in SEC v. Wall Street Transcript Corp., 422 F.2d 1371 (CA2), cert. denied, 398 U.S. 958 (1970), the Court of Appeals concluded that the exclusion was inapplicable.

* * *

The basic definition of an "investment adviser" in the Act reads as follows:

> " 'Investment adviser' means any person who, for compensation, engages in the business of advising others, either directly or through publications or writings, as to the value of securities or as to the advisability of investing in, purchasing, or selling securities, or who, for compensation and as part of a regular business, issues or promulgates analyses or reports concerning securities. * * * "

Petitioners' newsletters are distributed "for compensation and as part of a regular business" and they contain "analyses or reports concerning securities." Thus, on its face, the basic definition applies to petitioners. The definition, however, is far from absolute. The Act excludes several categories of persons from its definition of an investment adviser, lists certain investment advisers who need not be registered, and also authorizes the Commission to exclude "such other person" as it may designate by rule or order.

One of the statutory exclusions is for "the publisher of any bona fide newspaper, news magazine or business or financial publication of general and regular circulation." Although neither the text of the Act nor its legislative history defines the precise scope of this exclusion, two points seem tolerably clear. Congress did not intend to exclude publications that are distributed by investment advisers as a normal part of the business of servicing their clients. The legislative history plainly demonstrates that Congress was primarily interested in regulating the business of rendering personalized investment advice, including publishing activities that are a normal incident thereto. On the other hand, Congress, plainly sensitive to First Amendment concerns, wanted to make clear that it did not seek to regulate the press through the licensing of nonpersonalized publishing activities.

* * *

The exclusion itself uses extremely broad language that encompasses any newspaper, business publication, or financial publication provided that two conditions are met. The publication must be "bona fide," and it must be "of regular and general circulation." Neither of these conditions is defined, but the two qualifications precisely differentiate "hit and run tipsters" and "touts" from genuine publishers. Presumably a "bona fide" publication would be genuine in the sense that it would contain disinterested commentary and analysis as opposed to promotional material disseminated by a "tout." Moreover, publications with a "general and regular" circulation would not include "people who send out bulletins from time to time on the advisability of buying and selling stocks," or "hit and run tipsters." Because the content of petitioners' newsletters was completely disinterested, and because they were offered to the general public on a regular schedule, they are described by the plain language of the exclusion.

The Court of Appeals relied on its opinion in SEC v. Wall Street Transcript Corp., to hold that petitioners were not bona fide newspapers and thus not exempt from the Act's registration requirement. In *Wall Street Transcript,* the majority held that the "phrase 'bona fide' newspapers * * * means those publications which do not deviate from customary newspaper accounts to such an extent that there is a likelihood that the wrongdoing which the Act was designed to prevent has occurred." It reasoned that whether "a given publication fits within this exclusion must depend upon the nature of its practices rather than upon the purely formal 'indicia of a newspaper' which it exhibits on its face and in the size and nature of its subscription list." The court expressed its concern that an investment adviser "might choose to present [information to clients] in the guise of traditional newspaper format." The Commission, citing *Wall Street Transcript,* has interpreted the exclusion to apply "only where, based on the content, advertising material, readership and other relevant factors, a publication is not primarily a vehicle for distributing investment advice."

These various formulations recast the statutory language without capturing the central thrust of the legislative history, and without even mentioning the apparent intent of Congress to keep the Act free of constitutional infirmities. The Act was designed to apply to those persons engaged in the investment-advisory profession—those who provide personalized advice attuned to a client's concerns, whether by written or verbal communication. The mere fact that a publication contains advice and comment about specific securities does not give it the personalized character that identifies a professional investment adviser. Thus, petitioners' publications do not fit within the central purpose of the Act because they do not offer individualized advice attuned to any specific portfolio or to any client's particular needs. On the contrary, they circulate for sale to the public at large in a free, open market—a public forum in which typically anyone may express his views.

The language of the exclusion, read literally, seems to describe petitioners' newsletters. Petitioners are "publishers of any bona fide newspaper, news magazine or business or financial publication." The only modifier that might arguably disqualify the newsletters are the words "bona fide." Notably, however, those words describe the publication rather than the character of the publisher; hence Lowe's unsavory history does not prevent his newsletters from being "bona fide." In light of the legislative history, this phrase translates best to "genuine"; petitioners' publications meet this definition: they are published by those engaged solely in the publishing business and are not personal communications masquerading in the clothing of newspapers, news magazines, or financial publications. Moreover, there is no suggestion that they contained any false or misleading information, or that they were designed to tout any security in which petitioners had an interest. Further, petitioners' publications are "of general and regular circulation." Although the publications have not been "regular" in the sense of consistent circulation, the publications have been "regular" in the sense important to the securities market: there is no indication that they have been timed to specific market activity, or to events affecting or having the ability to affect the securities industry.

The dangers of fraud, deception, or overreaching that motivated the enactment of the statute are present in personalized communications but are not replicated in publications that are advertised and sold in an open market. To the extent that the chart service contains factual information about past transactions and market trends, and the newsletters contain commentary on general market conditions, there can be no doubt about the protected character of the communications, a matter that concerned Congress when the exclusion was drafted. The content of the publications and the audience to which they are directed in this case reveal the specific limits of the exclusion. As long as the communications between petitioners and their subscribers remain entirely impersonal and do not develop into the kind of fiduciary, person-to-person relationships that were discussed at length in the legislative history of the Act and that are characteristic of investment adviser-client relationships, we believe the publications are, at least presumptively, within the exclusion and thus not subject to registration under the Act.

We therefore conclude that petitioners' publications fall within the statutory exclusion for bona fide publications and that none of the petitioners is an "investment adviser" as defined in the Act. It follows that neither their unregistered status, nor the Commission order barring Lowe from associating with an investment adviser, provides a justification for restraining the future publication of their newsletters. It also follows that we need not specifically address the constitutional question we granted certiorari to decide.

The judgment of the Court of Appeals is reversed.

JUSTICE POWELL took no part in the decision of this case.

JUSTICE WHITE, with whom THE CHIEF JUSTICE and JUSTICE REHNQUIST join, concurring in the result.

The issue in this case is whether the Securities and Exchange Commission may invoke the injunctive remedies of the Investment Advisers Act to prevent an unregistered adviser from publishing newsletters containing investment advice that is not specifically tailored to the needs of individual clients. The Court holds that it may not because petitioner's activities do not make him an investment adviser covered by the Act. * * * I disagree with this improvident construction of the statute. In my view, petitioner is an investment adviser subject to regulation and sanction under the Act. I concur in the judgment, however, because to prevent petitioner from publishing at all is inconsistent with the First Amendment. * * *

In SEC v. WALL STREET PUBLISHING INSTITUTE, 851 F.2d 365 (D.C.Cir.1988), the SEC charged that WSPI was violating § 17(b) of the 1933 Act by publishing a magazine containing articles about individual companies without disclosing that the articles were written by the companies themselves or by public relations firms paid by the companies. Section 17(b) prohibits any person from accepting consideration from the issuer for publishing a description of a security, without fully disclosing the receipt of such consideration. The SEC requested an injunction ordering WSPI to make the disclosures required by § 17(b). The district court held that, in light of the Supreme Court's decision in *Lowe,* holding that magazines such as the one published by WSPI are "bona fide publications entitled to First Amendment rights," an injunction ordering WSPI to disclose the consideration it received would be an impermissible prior restraint under the First Amendment.

The Court of Appeals reversed. While conceding that a flat prohibition against publication of an investment newsletter might well violate the First Amendment, as interpreted by the Supreme Court in *Lowe,* it held that the more limited relief sought by the SEC against WSPI would probably pass constitutional muster under Supreme Court decisions recognizing greater leeway for government regulation of speech relating to securities than of other types of speech.

Selected References

Draughan, SEC v. Lowe: Redefining the Bona Fide Newspaper Exclusion, 14 Sec.Reg.L.J. 291 (1987).

Estreicher, Securities Regulation and the First Amendment, 24 Ga.L.Rev. 223 (1990).

Lively, Securities Regulation and the Freedom of the Press: Toward a Marketplace of Ideas in the Marketplace of Investment, 60 Wash.L. Rev. 843 (1985).

Schoeman, The First Amendment and Restrictions on Advertising of Securities Under the Securities Act of 1933, 41 Bus.Law 377 (1986).

Note, Financial Reporters, the Securities Laws and the First Amendment: Where to Draw the Line, 53 Fordham L.Rev. 1035 (1985).

Note, First Amendment and 'Scalping' by a Financial Columnist: May a Newspaper Article be Commercial Speech?, 57 Ind.L.J. 131 (1982).

D. OBLIGATION TO "KNOW THE SECURITY"

The requirements imposed on issuers to provide adequate information about publicly-offered or publicly-traded securities are discussed in the preceding chapters. As an adjunct to these requirements, the SEC has used a variety of techniques to prevent broker-dealers from recommending or trading in securities as to which no such adequate information is available. In this section, we consider SEC sanctions against firms which make unsubstantiated recommendations or trade in securities in the absence of current and reliable information about the issuer.

HANLY v. SEC

415 F.2d 589 (2d Cir.1969).

Before LUMBARD, CHIEF JUDGE, FEINBERG, CIRCUIT JUDGE, and TIMBERS, DISTRICT JUDGE.

TIMBERS, DISTRICT JUDGE:

Five securities salesmen petition to review an order of the Securities and Exchange Commission which barred them from further association with any broker or dealer. The Commission found that petitioners, in the offer and sale of the stock of U.S. Sonics Corporation (Sonics) between September 1962 and August 1963, willfully violated the antifraud provisions of Section 17(a) of the Securities Act of 1933, Sections 10(b) and 15(c)(1) of the Securities Exchange Act of 1934, and Rule 10b–5. Specifically, the Commission held that "the fraud in this case consisted of the optimistic representations or the recommendations * * * without disclosure of known or reasonably ascertainable adverse information which rendered them materially misleading * * *. It is clear that a salesman must not merely avoid affirmative misstatements when he recommends the stock to a customer; he must also disclose material adverse facts of which he is or should be aware." Petitioners individually argue that their violations of the federal securities laws were not willful but involved at most good faith optimistic predictions concerning a speculative security, and that the sanctions imposed by the Commission exceeded legally permissible limits. The Commission, upon an independent review of the record before the hearing examiner, affirmed his findings as to individual violations, rejected his finding of concerted action, and increased the sanctions he had imposed. We affirm in all respects the order of the Commission as to each of the five petitioners.

VIOLATIONS

The primary witnesses before the hearing examiner were customers of each of petitioners and the former president of Sonics. Since the Commission rejected the conclusion of the hearing examiner that petitioners had acted in concert in the conduct of their fraudulent activities, we have considered separately the evidence against each petitioner and have considered the sanctions against each in the light of his specific alleged violations.

While we believe it neither necessary nor appropriate to set forth all of the evidence upon which the Commission's findings and order were based, we shall summarize sufficiently the background of Sonics and petitioners' individual violations to indicate the basis of our holding that there was substantial evidence to support the Commission's underlying finding of affirmative misrepresentations and inadequate disclosure on the part of petitioners.

U.S. Sonics Corporation

Sonics was organized in 1958. It engaged in the production and sale of various electronic devices. From its inception the company operated at a deficit. During the period of the sales of its stock here involved, the company was insolvent.

By 1962 the company had developed a ceramic filter which was said to be far superior to conventional wire filters used in radio circuits. Sonics' inability to raise the capital necessary to produce these filters led it to negotiate with foreign and domestic companies to whom Sonics hoped to grant production licenses on a royalty basis. Licenses were granted to a Japanese and to a West German company, each of which made initial payments of $25,000, and to an Argentine company, which made an initial payment of $50,000. License negotiations with domestic companies continued into 1963 without success; negotiations terminated with General Instrument Corporation on March 20, 1963 and with Texas Instruments, Incorporated, on June 29, 1963. In addition, testing of the filter by prospective customers provided unsatisfactory results.

Merger negotiations with General Instrument and Texas Instruments likewise proved unsuccessful. Sonics' financial condition continued to deteriorate with the cancellation by the Navy of anticipated orders for hydrophones. On December 6, 1963 bankruptcy proceedings were instituted against Sonics, and on December 27, 1963 it was adjudicated a bankrupt.

During most of the relevant period petitioners were employed by Richard J. Buck & Co., a partnership registered as a broker-dealer. Gladstone and Fehr were co-managers of the firm's Forest Hills, N.Y., branch office. Hanly was the manager of its Hempstead, N.Y., office. Stutzmann and Paras were salesmen in the Hempstead office.

Gladstone

Gladstone (along with Paras) first heard of Sonics in September 1962 during a conversation with one Roach who had been a sales manager for his prior employer, Edwards and Hanly. Roach compared Sonics to Ilikon, whose stock he had previously recommended and which had been highly successful. Sonics was praised for its good management, large research and development expenses and, most important, its development of a ceramic filter. In January 1963 Roach told Gladstone of the possibility of a domestic license and furnished him with a copy of an allegedly confidential 14 page report which predicted a bright future for the company.[5] In February Gladstone met with Eric Kolm, Sonics' president, who confirmed most of the statements in the report. During the spring of 1963 Gladstone learned of the licensing and merger negotiations mentioned above.

On the basis of this information and knowing that Sonics had never shown a year end profit since its inception, that it was still sustaining losses, and that the 14 page report was not identified as to source and did not contain financial statements, Gladstone told Hanly, Stutzmann and Paras about the company and made certain representations to his customers.

Evidence of affirmative misrepresentations by Gladstone to his customers regarding Sonics stock included the following: Sonics was a winner and would make money. It had a fabulous potential and would double or triple. It would make Xerox look like a standstill and would revolutionize the space age industry. Gladstone himself had purchased the stock for his own account and he would be able to retire and get rich on it. It had possibilities of skyrocketing and would probably double in price within six months to a year. Although it had not earned money in the past, prospects were good for earnings of $1 in a year. Sonics had signed a contract with General Instrument. The stock would go from 6 to 12 in two weeks and to 15 in the near future. The 14 page report had been written by Value Line. The company was not going bankrupt. Its products were perfected and it was already earning $1 per share. It was about to have a breakthrough on a new product that was fantastic and would revolutionize automobile and home radios.

In addition to these affirmative misrepresentations, the testimony disclosed that adverse information about Sonics' financial difficulties was not disclosed by Gladstone; that some customers had received confirmations for orders they had not placed; and that literature about the company was not provided. Most of the customer-witnesses testified that they had purchased in reliance upon the recommendations of Gladstone. * * *

5. The source of this report was not disclosed to Gladstone. Its source is not disclosed in the record.

[The court here describes the comparable statements and actions of the other petitioners.]

Law Applicable to Violations

In its opinion the Commission quoted from the record in attributing the representations discussed above respectively to each of the petitioners. It concluded that their optimistic representations or recommendations were materially false and misleading. Fraud was found both in affirmative falsehoods and in recommendations made without disclosure of known or reasonably ascertainable adverse information, such as Sonics' deteriorating financial condition, its inability to manufacture the filter, the lack of knowledge regarding the filter's commercial feasibility, and the negative results of pending negotiations.

The Commission found that the sophistication of the customers or prior relationships which many of them had enjoyed with the respective petitioners were irrelevant. It held that the absence of a boiler room did not justify affirmative misrepresentations or a failure to disclose adverse financial information. The relevance of a customer's nonloss of money or a salesman's speculation in the stock likewise was discounted.

The sensitivity of operations in the securities field and the availability of opportunities where those in a position of trust can manipulate others to their own advantage led Congress to pass the antifraud provisions of the statutes with which the instant proceedings are concerned. Congress committed to the Commission the responsibility of supervising the activity of broker-dealers and registered representatives.

When a securities salesman fraudulently violates the high standards with which he is charged, he subjects himself to a variety of punitive, compensatory and remedial sanctions. In the instant proceedings petitioners have not been criminally charged, nor have they been sued for damages by their customers arising from the alleged misrepresentations. Instead, in private proceedings initiated by the Commission, each petitioners' *privilege* of being employed in the securities industry has been revoked. It is in this context that the issues before the Court must be considered. More particularly, we are here concerned with the expertise of the Commission in its assessment of how the public interest best may be protected from various kinds of intentional fraud and reckless misconduct which often threaten securities transactions, especially, as here, in the over the counter market.

Brokers and salesmen are "under a duty to investigate, and their violation of that duty brings them within the term 'willful' in the Exchange Act."[6] Thus, a salesman cannot deliberately ignore that which he has a duty to know and recklessly state facts about matters of which he is ignorant. He must analyze sales literature and must not blindly accept recommendations made therein.[7] The fact that his customers may be sophisticated and knowledgeable does not warrant a

6. Dlugash v. SEC, 373 F.2d 107, 109 (2 Cir.1967).

7. Walker v. SEC, 383 F.2d 344 (2d Cir. 1967) (per curiam).

less stringent standard.[8] Even where the purchaser follows the market activity of the stock and does not rely upon the salesman's statements, remedial sanctions may be imposed since reliance is not an element of fraudulent misrepresentation in this context.[9]

Just as proof of specific intent to defraud is irrelevant for insider violations of Rule 10b–5, it is irrelevant in private proceedings such as these:

> "In an enforcement proceeding for equitable or prophylactic relief, the common law standard of deceptive conduct has been modified in the interests of broader protection for the investing public so that negligent insider conduct has become unlawful * * *. Absent any clear indication of a legislative intention to require a showing of specific fraudulent intent * * * the securities laws should be interpreted as an expansion of the common law both to effectuate the broad remedial design of Congress * * * and to insure uniformity of enforcement * * *."[10]

A securities dealer occupies a special relationship to a buyer of securities[11] in that by his position he implicitly represents he has an adequate basis for the opinions he renders.[12] While this implied warranty may not be as rigidly enforced in a civil action[a] where an investor seeks damages for losses allegedly caused by reliance upon his unfounded representations,[13] its applicability in the instant proceedings cannot be questioned.[14]

8. Lehigh Valley Trust Co. v. Central National Bank, 409 F.2d 989, 992 (5 Cir. 1969).

9. N. Sims Organ & Co., Inc. v. SEC, 293 F.2d 78 (2 Cir.1961). See also Commonwealth Securities Corporation. Securities Exchange Act Release No. 8360, p. 5 (July 23, 1968): "It is irrelevant that customers to whom fraudulent representations are made are aware of the speculative nature of the security they are induced to buy, or do not rely on such representations." * * *

10. SEC v. Texas Gulf Sulphur Co., 401 F.2d 833, 854–55 (2 Cir.1968) (en banc). The applicability of the above quoted language to misrepresentation such as that before the Court in the instant case would appear self-evident.

11. SEC v. Great American Industries, Inc., 407 F.2d 453, 460 (2 Cir.1968) (paralleling the affirmative duty of disclosure imposed upon insiders with that imposed upon broker-dealers).

12. See Kahn v. SEC, 297 F.2d 112, 115 (2 Cir.1961) (concurrence of Judge Clark) for an analysis of the "shingle theory" of implicit representation and its relationship to the antifraud provisions of the securities law. See also Aircraft Dynamics International Corp., 41 S.E.C. 566 (1963); Alexander Reid & Co., Inc., 40 S.E.C. 986, 990 (1962) ("A broker-dealer cannot avoid responsibility for unfounded statements of a deceptive nature, recklessly made, merely by characterizing them as opinions or predictions or by presenting them in the guise of a probability or possibility.")

a. One commentator has criticized this statement and suggested that "a better view is represented by a California decision in a suit brought by a customer to recover damages from a broker who had traded his account excessively. 'It would be inconsistent to suggest that a person should be defrocked as a member of his calling, and yet not be liable for the injury which resulted from his acts or omissions.'" Jacobs, The Impact of Securities Exchange Act Rule 10b–5 on Broker–Dealers, 57 Cornell L.Rev. 869, 880–81 (1972), quoting from the opinion in Twomey v. Mitchum, Jones & Templeton, Inc., 262 Cal.App.2d 690, 721–722, 69 Cal.Rptr. 222, 244 (1968).

13. See, e.g., Phillips v. Reynolds & Co., 294 F.Supp. 1249 (E.D.Pa.1969) (in an action for damages by investors, failure of the broker to disclose a substantial deficit is not a basis for civil liability since a broker is not a virtual insurer of his recommendations even where he does not disclose all material facts; reliance is also required); Weber v. C.M.P. Corp., 242 F.Supp. 321 (S.D.N.Y.1965) (some form of

14. See note 14 on page 924.

Sonics was an over the counter stock. Those who purchased through petitioners could not readily confirm the information given them. In Charles Hughes & Co., Inc. v. SEC, 139 F.2d 434 (2 Cir.1943), this Court recognized the difficulties involved in over the counter stocks and the special duty imposed upon those who sell such stocks not to take advantage of customers in whom confidence has been instilled.

In summary, the standards by which the actions of each petitioner must be judged are strict. He cannot recommend a security unless there is an adequate and reasonable basis for such recommendation. He must disclose facts which he knows and those which are reasonably ascertainable. By his recommendation he implies that a reasonable investigation has been made and that his recommendation rests on the conclusions based on such investigation. Where the salesman lacks essential information about a security, he should disclose this as well as the risks which arise from his lack of information.

A salesman may not rely blindly upon the issuer for information concerning a company, although the degree of independent investigation which must be made by a securities dealer will vary in each case. Securities issued by smaller companies of recent origin obviously require more thorough investigation.

SANCTIONS

The Commission is authorized by Section 15(b)(7) of the Securities Exchange Act to bar any person from association with a broker or dealer "if the Commission finds that such * * * barring * * * is in the public interest * * *," and that such person has willfully violated the Securities Act or the Securities Exchange Act.

Acting pursuant to this statutory authority and upon a finding that it was in the public interest to do so, the Commission, having found that each petitioner had violated the antifraud provisions of the securities laws, ordered that each be barred from further association with any broker or dealer, except that Fehr was barred for only 60 days, after which he may return to the securities business in a non-supervisory

scienter required, more than innocent or negligent misstatements). Cf. SEC v. Van Horn, 371 F.2d 181, 185 (7 Cir.1966), criticizing *Weber*.

14. Petitioners argue that their activities are to be distinguished from those of a "boiler room" and that, absent a finding of boiler room operations here, the Commission's strict standards should not be applied against petitioners.

A boiler room usually is a temporary operation established to sell a specific speculative security. Solicitation is by telephone to new customers, the salesman conveying favorable earnings projections, predictions of price rises and other optimistic prospects without a factual basis. The prospective buyer is not informed of known or readily ascertainable adverse information; he is not cautioned about the risks inherent in purchasing a speculative security; and he is left with a deliberately created expectation of gain without risk. Berko v. SEC, 316 F.2d 137, 139 n. 3 (2 Cir.1963).

Salesmen in a boiler room are held to a high duty of truthfulness which is not met by a claim of lack of knowledge. The Commission having previously refused to condone misrepresentation in the absence of a boiler room, we specifically reject petitioners' argument that absence of boiler room operations here is a defense to a charge of misrepresentation.

capacity and upon an appropriate showing that he will be adequately supervised.[16]

The courts, including ours, uniformly have recognized the fundamental principle that imposition of sanctions necessarily must be entrusted to the expertise of a regulatory commission such as the SEC; and only upon a showing of abuse of discretion—such as the imposition of a sanction unwarranted in law or without justification in fact—will a reviewing court intervene in the matter of sanctions.

For the most part, petitioners' attacks upon the sanctions here imposed do not merit discussion. Their arguments were fully considered by the Commission which, in accordance with its undoubted authority, gave different weight to such arguments than petitioners would like. Moreover, their legal claims on the matter of sanctions so recently have been considered by this Court that we do not believe it either necessary or appropriate further to dilate upon the subject. For example, the obvious disparity in culpability between petitioners, reflected in our summary above of the evidence of violations by each, is not a proper basis for challenging the Commission's sanctions; nor is the fact that in the case of one or more petitioners only one investor-witness testified against him. And of course even the permanent bar order which the Commission in its discretion has imposed as to four of the petitioners is not necessarily an irrevocable sanction; upon application, the Commission, if it finds that the public interest no longer requires the applicant's exclusion from the securities business, may permit his return—usually subject to appropriate safeguards.[21]

There is one aspect of the sanction issue in the instant case which does merit brief mention: the Commission's imposition of *greater* sanctions upon four of the petitioners than ordered by the hearing examiner. This appears to be a matter of first impression, at least in this Court. The Commission clearly has the authority to modify, including the authority to increase, sanctions ordered by a hearing examiner in his initial decision,[23] and we so hold. Moreover, our independent

16. In thus imposing sanctions, the Commission agreed with the hearing examiner's determination that Gladstone should be *barred* from association with any broker or dealer, but it found inadequate the sanctions imposed upon the other petitioners. The examiner had ordered Fehr, Stutzmann and Paras *suspended* from association with any broker or dealer for five months, Hanly for four months; and the reinstatement of Stutzmann and Paras was conditioned upon a showing of adequate supervision in accordance with the Commission's usual practice.

The three sanctions authorized by the statute are *censure, barring,* or *suspension.*

21. The Commission informs us that, since January 1, 1965 (the amendments to the Securities Exchange Act which became effective August 20, 1964, 78 Stat. 565, having first granted to the Commission direct power to bar an individual from being associated with a broker-dealer), of 21 applications for reinstatement by persons who in effect have been barred from the securities business, 16 have been granted (omitting certain refinements in these statistics).

We express the hope that, in the event any of the petitioners before us should apply to reenter the securities business, the Commission will provide for early and speedy consideration of such applications, in contrast to the delay in the instant proceedings.

23. See Section 8(a) of the Administrative Procedure Act, 5 U.S.C. § 557(b). "On appeal from or review of the initial deci-

examination of the record in the instant case satisfies us that there is substantial evidence to support the Commission's finding that the sanctions ordered by the examiner with respect to all petitioners except Gladstone were inadequate to protect the public interest and that there is substantial evidence to support the Commission's imposition of increased sanctions in the public interest with respect to each of the four. We suggest, however, that in the future it would be appropriate for the Commission to make specific findings in support of its conclusion that sanctions ordered by a hearing examiner are inadequate and should be increased. Such practice will facilitate the Court's task of determining whether the findings with respect to increased sanctions are supported by substantial evidence.

Affirmed.

The Second Circuit's opinion in the Hanly case (written by Judge Timbers, a former General Counsel of the SEC), gives great deference to the Commission's discretion in making findings and imposing sanctions. The Court of Appeals for the District of Columbia Circuit, which hears many appeals from administrative agency decisions, subsequently tried to pull the SEC in on a tighter rein. In COLLINS SECURITIES CORP. v. SEC, 562 F.2d 820 (D.C.Cir.1977), the court held that, in an SEC proceeding alleging "fraud" in which the broker-dealer faced the "heavy sanction [of] deprivation of livelihood," the SEC's decision must be based on "clear and convincing evidence" rather than the "preponderance of the evidence" which is the normal standard for judicial review of administrative decisions. In STEADMAN v. SEC, 450 U.S. 91 (1981), however, the Supreme Court rejected this approach, holding that the language of § 7(c) of the Administrative Procedure Act, which requires that an administrative sanction must be "supported by and in accordance with the reliable, probative and substantial evidence," indicated that Congress intended the "preponderance of the evidence" standard to be applied.

As the *Hanly* opinion indicates, the first SEC proceedings against broker-dealers for making unsubstantiated recommendations involved so-called "boiler rooms"—small firms which used long-distance telephone calls and high-pressure sales tactics to peddle the stock of one or a few companies. The firm involved in the *Hanly* case—Richard J. Buck & Co.—was not a "boiler room," but it was hardly a household word either. In June 1973, however, the SEC commenced a proceeding against Merrill Lynch, the nation's largest brokerage firm, alleging similar violations of the antifraud provisions in connection with the recommendation of stock in a small computer company.

sion, the agency has all the powers which it would have in making the initial decision except as it may limit the issues on notice or by rule," and [SEC Rule of Practice] 17(g)(2), "On review the Commission may affirm, reverse, modify, set aside or remand for further proceedings, in whole or in part, the initial decision by the hearing officer and make any findings or conclusions which in its judgment are proper on the record."

Most SEC proceedings against large well-known brokerage firms are settled promptly by the firms to avoid protracted adverse publicity. In this case, however, Merrill Lynch stoutly maintained its innocence of the charges, and vowed to fight the SEC to the finish. Four and a half years later, after more than two years of public hearings, and after Merrill Lynch had agreed to a $1.5 million settlement of suits brought by its customers, the administrative proceeding was also settled. The SEC issued its opinion setting forth its view of the obligations of a broker-dealer in recommending securities:

MERRILL LYNCH, PIERCE, FENNER & SMITH, INC.

Sec.Ex.Act Rel. No. 14149 (Nov. 9, 1977).

FINDINGS, OPINION AND ORDER OF THE COMMISSION

On June 22, 1973, the Commission instituted this proceeding and ordered a public hearing to determine whether Merrill Lynch, Pierce, Fenner & Smith, Inc. ("Merrill Lynch") two employees of its Securities Research Division and forty-seven of its account executives, willfully violated Section 17(a) of the Securities Act and Section 10(b) of the Securities Exchange Act ("Exchange Act") and Rule 10b–5 thereunder in connection with the recommendation and sale of the common stock of Scientific Control Corporation ("Scientific") to its customers during the period March 1, 1968 to November 21, 1969 ("relevant period") and whether Merrill Lynch and one of its employees failed reasonably to supervise its employees with a view to preventing violations of the anti-fraud provisions of the federal securities laws. * * *

Background

Scientific was a small Dallas based corporation engaged in the design, manufacture and sale of computers and data processing equipment. From the date of its incorporation on May 11, 1964 to the date a voluntary petition for an arrangement under Chapter XI of the Bankruptcy Act was filed on November 21, 1969, Scientific never enjoyed a profitable year.

* * *

Merrill Lynch Research

The Securities Research Division of Merrill Lynch maintained a recommendation regarding Scientific during the period from March 1, 1968 through November 10, 1969.[3] That recommendation varied during the period as follows:

1. March 1, 1968 through June 3, 1968—"Buy/Hold";
2. June 4 through December 16, 1968—"Hold/Not O.K. to Exchange";

3. On November 10, 1969 Merrill Lynch changed its position to one of "No–Opinion."

3. December 17, 1968 through October 16, 1969—"Buy/Hold";

4. October 16, 1969 through November 9, 1969—"Hold/O.K. to Exchange";

* * *

Respondent Pierce was primarily responsible for following Scientific and for formulating the research recommendations which were promulgated concerning Scientific. * * *

During the period March 1, 1968 through November 9, 1969 Pierce met personally with representatives of management of Scientific on three occasions. During that same time period, Pierce also spoke with representatives of Scientific by telephone, and reviewed press releases issued by Scientific, the two prospectuses filed by Scientific in connection with its two public offerings of common stock on December 21, 1967 and October 31, 1968, annual reports, a proxy statement dated October 7, 1969 and company brochures. In addition, Pierce received information from an account executive in Dallas, Texas who knew some of the officers of Scientific.

While virtually all of the information which Pierce had concerning Scientific came either directly or indirectly from Scientific, the record of this proceeding supports the finding that Pierce did not subject this information to sufficiently critical evaluation and analysis. Accordingly, the recommendations on Scientific, both in the QRQ opinions and the Wire Flashes, often reflected an undue acceptance of management's statements and projections, many of which were either overly optimistic or simply untrue. These optimistic and misleading statements of management, to the extent that they were simply reiterated (in some instances, without attribution to management), rendered Merrill Lynch's recommendations inadequate and misleading.

* * *

In addition to placing undue reliance on management data, Pierce ignored certain developments, which can be characterized as "red flags" or "warning signals," and which should have suggested to him that management's optimistic statements were suspect and that Scientific's financial condition was worse than that represented. These developments included increasing slippage in management's projections of sales, earnings and product development; an increasing need for financing; and an unrealistically escalating backlog.

* * *

These developments should have constituted clear warning signals, both as to the credibility of Scientific's management and the true financial condition of Scientific itself. Pierce's failure to recognize the significance of these developments and to conduct further investigation resulted in the continuation of recommendations to purchase or hold Scientific which lacked an adequate basis.

In addition, certain of the information received by Pierce from the account executive in Dallas and, to a lesser extent, from the company itself, appears to have been material, non-public information. While that information was never specifically included in the texts of the QRQ opinions or the Wire Flashes, it is reasonable to infer that this information formed, in part, the basis of Pierce's generally optimistic opinion.

* * *

On November 10, 1969, Merrill Lynch changed its rating on Scientific to a "No Opinion" leaving its customers without guidance. At about the time, Merrill Lynch held approximately 27% of the outstanding shares of Scientific on behalf of its customers. Shortly thereafter, Scientific filed a petition for an arrangement under Chapter XI of the Bankruptcy Act.

Applicable Legal Principles

* * *

When a broker-dealer recommends a security to its customer it represents that it has conducted a reasonable investigation of that security and that there exists a reasonable basis for the recommendation. * * *

The quantum of investigation will vary on the facts of each situation. To illustrate, it is clear that an unseasoned company such as Scientific requires a more thorough investigation than a well-established company. In no event will "blind reliance" upon a company's management alone be sufficient to constitute a reasonable investigation. All too frequently, the self-interest of a company's management will color its presentation of the facts in a manner which vitiates the reliability of the information.[11] A recommendation by a broker-dealer is perceived by a customer as (and it in fact should be) the product of independent and objective analysis which can only be achieved when the scope of the investigation is extended beyond the company's management. The fact that Scientific's management disseminated inaccurate and misleading information to Pierce and others will not excuse Pierce's failure to conduct a reasonable investigation.

While the duty to go beyond the self-serving statements of management is present from the initiation of a recommendation, this duty is all the more compelling in the presence of "red flags" or "warning signals". The receipt of information inconsistent with prior information which has been used as the basis for a recommendation necessarily demands a detailed investigation. This is especially true when projections made by a company fail to materialize. Any credence previously given to such projections must be carefully re-evaluated with a jaundiced eye. And, when adverse information becomes known, it must be communicated to customers. Richard J. Buck & Co., 43 S.E.C. 993, aff'd sub nom. Hanly v. S.E.C., 415 F.2d 589 (2d Cir.1969).

Further, we find that some of the information relied upon to form the basis of the Merrill Lynch recommendation which resulted in the purchase and sale of Scientific shares by customers was material

11. We do not suggest that information from management be ignored, but rather that such information be verified.

nonpublic information. Such conduct is also violative of Section 10(b) of the Exchange Act and Rule 10b–5 thereunder. See, e.g., SEC v. Texas Gulf Sulphur Co.

Our conclusion that Merrill Lynch willfully violated the anti-fraud provisions of the securities laws in connection with the recommendation and sale of Scientific does not rest solely on Pierce's inadequate investigation of Scientific. We find that Merrill Lynch is also responsible for the false and misleading statements of twenty-eight of the forty-seven respondent account executives. This conduct is described in a subsequent portion of this opinion.

We recognize that Merrill Lynch is a very large securities firm and that Scientific was but one of the many securities recommended by its salesmen during the relevant period. However, it is clear from the record that Merrill Lynch had more than a passing interest in Scientific. From March 1, 1968 through November 21, 1969, Merrill Lynch traded in excess of 1.4 million shares of Scientific. These transactions had a total dollar value of nearly $100 million and accounted for substantial trading profits and commissions for Merrill Lynch. More than 4,000 of Merrill Lynch's customers purchased shares of Scientific during 1968 and 1969.

* * *

False and Misleading Statements of the Respondent Account Executives

According to the evidence adduced at the hearings the vast majority of Merrill Lynch's customers who purchased shares of Scientific had never heard of the company prior to being introduced to it by their account executive. Common to the testimony of investor witnesses was the fact that their account executives went beyond the Merrill Lynch research opinion by making optimistic representations, varying in nature and degree, which had no reasonable basis in fact and were false and misleading. These representations included statements regarding the future price of Scientific's shares, the comparability of Scientific's growth potential to established, highly successful and well capitalized companies, the likelihood that Scientific's shares would become listed on a national securities exchange, the soundness of an investment in Scientific and the quality of Scientific's management.

* * *

We have consistently held that predictions of specific and substantial increases in the price of a speculative security of an unseasoned company are fraudulent and can not be justified. During the course of the hearings, the respondents frequently contended that if such statements about Scientific's future price were made they were not stated in terms of a guarantee but rather as being contingent upon the company attaining its sales and earnings projections. Even if we were to adopt that view of the evidence, it would matter little because predictions of substantial increases in price, under these circumstances, need not be presented in terms of a guarantee in order to be fraudulent. Further, couching such statements in terms of probability or possibility does not alter the character of the violation.

* * *

Interspersed among the various affirmative misrepresentations made in connection with the recommendation and sale of Scientific's shares to Merrill Lynch customers were omissions by the account executives to state material adverse facts regarding Scientific's true financial condition and the degree of risk involved in the purchase of the company's securities. For example, many customers testified that they were never told that Scientific had a history of losses or that the June 9, 1969 Wire Flash indicated Scientific estimated it would lose $1.55 million for fiscal year 1969. Further, numerous customers were not informed of the highly speculative nature of Scientific's shares or that Merrill Lynch only recommended the purchase of Scientific's shares to those accounts willing to assume major risks. These omissions, considered in the context of recommendations in which optimistic misstatements regarding Scientific were made, were false and misleading.

* * *

Failure of Supervision

A registered broker-dealer has an affirmative obligation to properly supervise the business activities of the firm. * * *

In both the instance of the research department and of the respondent account executives Merrill Lynch failed to exercise reasonable supervision over its employees with a view toward preventing violations. In so doing Merrill Lynch has breached a duty imposed by the Exchange Act.

Public Interest

After consideration of the offer of settlement of Merrill Lynch wherein the firm offers: to accept the imposition of a censure; to pay a sum of up to $1,600,000 pursuant to the terms of its offer to compensate customers of Merrill Lynch who suffered losses resulting from transactions in Scientific; to undertake to review, and, where appropriate, adopt new or modified guidelines relating to its research and sales activities; and, to undertake to review and, where necessary, strengthen its Account Executive Training Programs, the Commission accepts Merrill Lynch's offer of settlement.

In deciding to accept this offer, the Commission has given weight to the fact that the violations occurring herein, although serious in nature, related to a small portion of Merrill Lynch's total business and a relatively small number of the firm's total employees. The Commission recognizes that since the occurrence of the violations found herein Merrill Lynch has improved the quality of its research capability by increasing the number of security analysts the firm employs in its research department and by reducing the number of securities each analyst is assigned to follow. The Commission also recognizes that the violations took place in the somewhat speculative climate of the late 1960's when high technology companies were in vogue. However, the Commission warns that a speculative climate, no matter how rampant, will not attenuate duties imposed by the securities laws.

Twenty nine individual respondents have submitted offers of settlement wherein seven individuals offer to accept suspensions and twenty two individuals offer to accept censures. After consideration of these offers, the Commission has determined to accept them as being in the public interest. * * *

One rather anomalous charge in the SEC's complaint against Merrill Lynch was that the firm violated Rule 10b–5 by recommending Scientific stock on the basis of "inside information" received from the company which was not publicly available. There have been a number of actions against brokerage firms in which the customer alleged that the firm's sales representative induced him to purchase a stock by representing (falsely) that he had inside information about favorable developments in the company. When faced with such an action, the brokerage firm would allege that the customer was *in pari delicto* (equally at fault) for trading on inside information, and therefore not entitled to recover. Some courts accepted this defense; others rejected it. In BATEMAN EICHLER v. BERNER, 472 U.S. 299 (1985), the Supreme Court held that the *in pari delicto* defense was not available to the broker in such a case, since a customer who trades on inside information, while he may have violated Rule 10b–5, is generally not "as blameworthy as a corporate insider or broker-dealer who discloses this information for personal gain." The Court also expressed the view that "denying the *in pari delicto* defense in such circumstances will best promote the primary objective of the federal securities laws—protection of the investing public and the national economy through the promotion of 'a high standard of business ethics in every facet of the securities industry.' "

In addition to bringing proceedings against individual broker-dealers for recommending securities without a reasonable basis, the SEC in 1971 took a major step to prevent trading in the stocks of companies for which there is insufficient information available to serve as a basis for recommendations.

ADOPTION OF RULE 15C2–11

Securities Exchange Act Release No. 9310 (Sept. 13, 1971).

The Securities and Exchange Commission today announced the adoption of Rule 15c2–11 under the Securities Exchange Act of 1934 ("the Act"). In general, Rule 15c2–11 prohibits the initiation or resumption of quotations respecting a security by a broker or dealer who lacks specified information concerning the security and the issuer.

The Commission has discussed on an earlier occasion the practices of some companies and persons in connection with the distribution of the securities of "shell" corporations by means of the "spin off" device. These practices have often resulted in the initiation of market making activities by some brokers and dealers by the submission of quotations, in most cases, at a time when no financial or other information concerning the security or the issuer was available to either the brokers and dealers submitting the quotations or to public investors induced to purchase the security. Frequently, there was a substantial increase in the market price of the securities due, in large measure, to the fraudulent and manipulative activities of the persons involved.

Although the practices discussed in Securities Act Release No. 4982 involved the securities of "shell" corporations, the fraudulent and manipulative potential inherent in those situations also exists when a broker or dealer submits quotations concerning any infrequently-traded security in the absence of certain information.

Therefore, to protect public investors against these occurrences, Rule 15c2–11 (subject to certain exemptions) prohibits a broker or dealer from submitting any quotation (as defined) for any security to any quotation medium unless (a) a registration statement has become effective with respect to such security within 90 days prior to the time of submission or publication of the quotation, and was not subject to a stop order at the time of such submission or publication, and unless the broker or dealer has in his records a copy of the prospectus, or (b) a notification under Regulation A has become effective with respect to such security within 40 days prior to the time of submission or publication of the quotation, and was not the subject of a suspension order at the time of such submission or publication, and unless the broker or dealer has in his records a copy of the offering circular, or (c) the issuer is required to file reports pursuant to Section 13 or 15(d) of the Act, or is the issuer of a security covered by Section 12(g)(2)(B) or (G) of the Act, the broker or dealer has a reasonable basis for believing that the issuer is current in filing the reports or statements required, and the broker or dealer has in his records a copy of the issuer's most recent annual report and any other reports required to be filed at regular intervals which were filed after such annual report, or (d) the broker or dealer has in his records specified information, which he must make reasonably available to any person expressing an interest in entering into a transaction in that security with him, and which he has no reasonable basis for believing is not true and correct, and which was obtained by him from sources which he has a reasonable basis for believing are reliable. As that term is used in the rule, the requirement that the broker or dealer "make reasonably available" the specified information would mean that the broker or dealer must furnish the information to the interested person at the cost of reproduction, if for any reason it is impractical to provide the information in any other manner. * * *

It should be emphasized that this rule is not intended to, and does not, excuse brokers and dealers from their duty to comply with applicable registration and other anti-fraud provisions of the federal securities laws and Commission rules, including their duty to make appropriate inquiry. In this connection, brokers and dealers should be aware that the submission or publication of a quotation at a price which does not bear a reasonable relationship to the nature and scope of the issuer's business or its financial status or experience, may constitute a part of a fraudulent or manipulative scheme. * * *

Is Rule 15c2–11 a valid exercise of the Commission's power under § 15(c)(2) to "define, and prescribe means reasonably designed to prevent, such acts and practices as are fraudulent, deceptive or manipulative and such quotations as are fictitious"?

Pearlstine, New Securities Rule Could Hurt Brokers But Help Many Investors in Small Concerns, Wall St. Journal, Dec. 13, 1971, p. 28, col. 1: *

> Almost unnoticed by the public, the Securities and Exchange Commission has tossed a bomb into an area of securities trading. It is a small bomb and a small area, but a good many brokers and small but publicly held companies may be hurt by the explosion. And a good many shareholders may be helped.
>
> The SEC move is the adoption of Rule 15C2–11, which takes effect today. On the surface, it appears innocuous. The rule simply prohibits market makers—those broker-dealers who keep an inventory of a given stock or stocks and buy or sell on demand from other dealers and the public, thus setting prices on the stock—from publishing price quotes on certain of their stocks without having on file extensive financial and other data about those stocks. * * *
>
> That has been quite enough, however, to give Excedrin headaches to many broker-dealers in the over-the-counter securities industry. There are about 1,000 such firms that make markets in thousands of stocks that will be affected, and about 100 stocks a week are added to the pile, the SEC estimates. All over the country, brokers are scurrying to round up information about the stocks they make markets in, tossing out many they can't get data on and groaning about the new back-office burden.
>
> The functioning of market makers in obscure, low-priced and often highly speculative stocks is a little-known phenomenon. And that may be a good thing, since many investors might be shocked to watch a market maker in, say, Whoopee Uranium & Storm Door Corp. stock at work. Many market makers don't even know where some of their

companies are headquartered, much less who runs them or how much money they make. With some exceptions, market makers in such firms have traditionally viewed themselves as "trading the numbers"—keeping an inventory of the stock, and publishing prices on it, but under no special obligation to know anything about it.

"I'm a real garbage peddler," concedes Robert Green, president of a Los Angeles firm that bears his name and makes a market in at least 350 stocks. "If you went through my files, you'd probably find that the new rule would exclude 25% of my merchandise." Mr. Green believes the new rule will in the long run be good for the industry, but he says, "until I get files on all these companies, it's going to be very difficult for me." Just how difficult is exemplified by a fruitless search among market makers for information, any information, about one little company.

Hello, Out There

Will Seagull Industries Inc. please stand up?

Seagull has been regularly bought and sold by a number of market makers. One in Salt Lake City says he thinks Seagull is based somewhere in California, but he isn't sure. Nor does he know what Seagull does for a living or who runs it. Another market maker in New Jersey says he always thought Seagull was in Salt Lake City. Still another, in New York, says his records indicate Seagull is in Orange, Calif. Another says he recently stopped making a market in Seagull because he couldn't find out anything about it. Seagull's transfer agent, in Reno, Nev., says Seagull's address is a post-office box in Santa Ana, Calif., and its president is Dominick Sfregola, but he knows nothing else.

The California secretary of state's office says Seagull is not incorporated in the state and there is no telephone listing for it, or for Mr. Sfregola, in Orange, Santa Ana or Salt Lake City. Yet investors are still buying and selling the stock every day through the market makers. Though no one can be found who even knows what Seagull is, that hasn't prevented the stock from fluctuating wildly, from 60 cents a share to its current price of three cents a share.

Under the new rule, market makers technically can keep on publishing quotes on Seagull without getting any more information on it, since Seagull was regularly traded for a month before today. "There are still all kinds of companies that neither market makers nor investors know anything about that are going to go along being freely traded," frets one SEC regulator. "That still leaves a lot of potential for fraud."

Cautious Lawyers

That it does, but some attorneys counseling market makers on the impact of 15C2–11 are telling their clients that they'd better start digging up information on companies like Seagull, even though those companies' stock is exempt from the rule. On the theory that the new rule represents a stiffening SEC attitude toward all such trading, the same attorneys are advising market makers to demand that companies in which they make a market file registration statements with the SEC, even though many of them are not legally required to do so. The reasoning: Since the SEC has indicated that market makers have a measure of responsibility for seeing that the information in their files is complete and accurate, what could be safer than having on file a registration statement with audited financial figures that has gone through the SEC itself?

Indeed, as these attorneys, along with some law professors specializing in securities law read it, the new rule is an attempt by the SEC to cement a principle it has consistently tried to establish, albeit without the force of law—that no company be traded except through registration. "Congress has never been willing to legislate a requirement of continuous disclosure by very small publicly held companies (under 500 shareholders), but that's where the SEC is taking the law through its rule-making process," says Alan Bromberg, a Southern Methodist University professor and specialist in securities fraud. * * *

Broker-dealers also have another new worry: civil liability. The rule could result in customers, including other dealers, suing market makers who violate it.

But some market makers say that's the least of their worries. They fear that the reporting requirements of 15C2–11 will result in a number of small companies just taking their stock out of the market altogether. "There are a lot of legitimate small companies with no cash to spend on the simpler required financial statements, let alone an SEC registration" or a court defense, says a New York market maker. "They just won't be able to have a market for their stock." * * *

Be that as it may, it seems clear the new rule will also put a severe crimp in the operations of another group—securities swindlers who practice "the shell game." In that ploy, a promoter seeks a publicly held firm that no longer has any assets, liabilities or operations. (One favorite: now-dormant uranium companies set up in the 1950s) * * *

The shell game has fleeced millions of people of millions of dollars over the years, and until now the SEC's only recourse was costly, time-consuming case-by-case investigations. Now, however, existing shells that want to keep a market going in their stock will have to file hard financial data with market makers—if in the past their stock has been traded only sporadically and thus falls under the purview of the new rule. The regulation should also work to check fraud in new shells created by spin-off or in shells that will likely form over the course of time as companies now traded regularly go dormant, cease to be traded with frequency and get grabbed up by shell operators. * * *

In 1989, the Commission proposed to strengthen Rule 15c2–11 by requiring broker-dealers to review the information specified in the Rule before initiating or resuming quotations for any security, and to have a reasonable basis to believe that the information is true and accurate and obtained from reliable sources. Sec.Ex.Act Rel. No. 27247 (Sep. 25, 1989).

At the same time, the Commission took a major step to attempt to control fraudulent practices in the so-called "penny stock" market, in which broker-dealers utilize high-pressure telephone sales campaigns to sell low-priced speculative securities to large numbers of unsophisticated investors:

SALES PRACTICE REQUIREMENTS FOR CERTAIN LOW-PRICED SECURITIES

Sec.Ex.Act Rel. No. 27160 (Aug. 22, 1989).

The Commission is adopting Rule 15c2–6 ("Rule") to regulate the sales practices of broker-dealers active in the market for low-priced, non-NASDAQ over-the-counter ("OTC") securities. As a means reasonably designed to prevent fraud, the Rule makes it unlawful for a broker-dealer to sell a security subject to the Rule ("Designated Security") to, or to effect the purchase of a Designated Security by, any person unless (1) the transaction is exempt under paragraph (c) of the Rule, or (2) prior to the transaction, the broker-dealer has (i) approved the purchaser's account for transactions in Designated Securities, and (ii) received written agreement to the transaction from the purchaser. In approving an account for transactions in Designated Securities, a broker-dealer must obtain sufficient information from the purchaser to make an appropriate suitability determination, provide the purchaser with a written statement setting forth the basis of the determination, and obtain a signed copy of the suitability statement from the purchaser.

The scope of the Rule is limited in order to exclude transactions that are less likely to be subject to fraudulent, high pressure sales practices. Application of the Rule is limited to transactions in Designated Securities, which are defined as non-NASDAQ OTC equity securities whose issuers have less than $2,000,000 in net tangible assets. In addition, exemptions are provided in paragraph (c) of the Rule for: (1) transactions in which the price of the security is five dollars or more; (2) transactions in which the purchaser is an accredited investor or an established customer of the broker-dealer; (3) transactions that are not recommended by the broker-dealer; and (4) transactions by a broker-dealer who is not a market maker in the Designated Security that is the subject of the transaction, and whose sales-related revenue from transactions in Designated Securities does not exceed five percent of its total sales-related revenue from transactions in securities.

* * *

III. BACKGROUND

A. Broker–Dealer Misconduct Involving Low–Priced Securities

The Commission's proposal of Rule 15c2–6 reflected its growing concern with the widespread incidence of broker-dealer fraud and other misconduct in connection with low-priced stocks that are traded predominantly in the non-NASDAQ OTC market. * * *

Most of the sales practice abuses involving low-priced securities are conducted over the telephone by broker-dealers engaging in "boiler-room" operations. Improved communications technology has enabled an increasing number of this type of broker-dealer to engage in high pressure sales campaigns on a nationwide basis. An essential aspect of a boiler-room operation is the use of numerous salespersons making hundreds of high pressure cold calls each day to generate sales of low-priced securities to new customers. Cold calls are telephone calls made to persons whose names are drawn from a telephone directory or a membership list. Consequently, many of the persons called will have little investment experience and limited financial resources. The salespersons are trained in high pressure sales tactics designed to elicit a buy decision during the course of a telephone call, and typically are compensated solely by commissions generated by sales of securities. Because many of the persons called are inexperienced investors, they are particularly vulnerable to deceptive sales pitches promising high profits made by salespersons willing to disregard the unsuitability of a security for the purchaser.

Broker-dealers engaging in boiler-room operations frequently choose a low-priced, non-NASDAQ OTC security as their sales product for several reasons. First, low-priced securities sold in large volume can generate enormous profits for broker-dealers. Price spreads in these securities, while small in dollar amount, can be very large in percentage terms. For example, if a stock is quoted at five cents bid and ten cents asked, the spread, while only five cents in amount, constitutes a potential 100% profit per share to the broker-dealer. The broker-dealer can attract purchasers to these stocks by touting that a small gain in price will produce large percentage gains in value. Unsophisticated investors may fail to recognize, however, that if they purchase a stock with a 100% spread they will not break even on a sale of their investment until the bid price doubles (assuming that a broker-dealer actually will buy all of the investor's stock at that bid price).

Second, many low-priced securities are issued by smaller, little-known companies that may attract little attention outside that generated by a boiler-room sales campaign. Often, these issuers are not subject to Exchange Act reporting requirements. The scarcity of information about the issuer is further aggravated by the lack of information on transactions in the issuer's securities. The non-NASDAQ OTC market does not have reliable quotation or trade information that the public could use to examine the nature of the market. In contrast, firm quotations are readily available in exchange and NASDAQ markets, and all exchange securities and NASDAQ/National Market System securities have minute by minute trade reports that are disseminated to investors. The availability of this information makes possible ongoing electronic surveillance of exchange and NASDAQ markets by the relevant self-regulatory organization ("SRO"). Many unsophisticated investors may not appreciate the vast difference in the nature, market information, and supervision of the market between the exchange and NASDAQ markets, and the non-NASDAQ OTC market.

B. The Commission's Response

The Commission realizes that only comprehensive action will successfully reduce fraud in the sale of low-priced securities, and therefore has undertaken a broad-based program in this area that includes expanded enforcement efforts, a public education program, and regulatory initiatives. The Commission has begun a concerted enforcement program against broker-dealers and individuals engaging in misconduct in connection with transactions in low-priced securities. Release 34–26529 noted that in 1988 the Commission had initiated more than 25 enforcement actions involving fraud and abuse in the non-NASDAQ OTC market, and that since 1986, the Denver Regional Office alone had initiated more than thirty such actions. Thus far in 1989, the Commission has initiated more than forty additional enforcement actions involving fraud and other misconduct in connection with transactions in low-priced securities, and is investigating many other cases involving similar abuses. In addition, the Commission has cooperated with the SROs, other federal agencies, and state regulatory authorities in proceedings involving penny stock fraud, and these efforts have resulted in a number of criminal prosecutions.

The Commission also has begun a campaign to educate the public concerning the risks of fraud in the market for low-priced securities. Ultimately, the best defense against fraudulent activities by securities salespersons is an informed investing public that recognizes deceptive sales pitches and is not misled. The Commission's public education campaign is intended to increase the number of investors who can guard themselves against fraudulent practices.

Finally, the Commission has developed, and has encouraged the SROs to develop, new regulatory initiatives designed to address fraud and manipulation in connection with transactions in low-priced securities. In a forthcoming release, the Commission will propose amendments to Rule 15c2–11 under the Exchange Act that would emphasize the responsibility of market makers to review information concerning non-NASDAQ OTC securities and take it into account in their market making activities. In addition, the NASD has implemented a program that requires broker-dealers to report to the NASD volume and price information concerning their transactions in non-NASDAQ OTC securities. This program should provide assistance to regulators in monitoring the non-NASDAQ OTC market, and in identifying fraudulent or manipulative trading activities in that market.

In addition to these ongoing efforts, the Commission continues to believe that a comprehensive program to deter fraud in connection with transactions in low-priced securities must address the sales practices of broker-dealers actively involved in selling low-priced securities to new customers. In this connection, the Commission is adopting Rule 15c2–6.

IV. Rule 15c2–6

A. Objectives of the Rule

In adopting the Rule, the Commission has sought to combat the unscrupulous, high pressure sales tactics of certain broker-dealers by imposing objective and readily reviewable requirements that condition the process by which new customers are induced to purchase low-priced stocks. The requirements are intended to assist investors in protecting themselves from fraudulent sales practices, and also to reinforce a broker-dealer's suitability obligations, which historically have been an important standard constraining indiscriminate high pressure sales tactics by broker-dealers.

An essential aspect of high pressure "boiler-room" operations is the constant solicitation of new, and often unsophisticated, customers. The Rule conditions this process by establishing account opening procedures that must be followed before Designated Securities are recommended to unsophisticated new customers. The procedures are intended to provide greater assurance that the broker-dealer will make an appropriate suitability determination by obtaining sufficient information concerning the customer and by considering the customer's previous investment experience, investment objectives, and financial situation.

In addition, the Rule will protect investors from fraudulent sales practices in low-price stocks in two ways. First, the requirement that the customer agree to purchases in writing provides the customer with an opportunity to make an investment decision outside of a pressured telephone conversation with a salesperson. Boiler room salespersons realize the importance of making a sale while on the telephone and use high pressure tactics to close the sale. The written agreement requirement is intended to remove this pressure for an immediate decision. Second, the account opening procedures require the broker-dealer to provide a copy of the broker-dealer's suitability determination to the customer prior to the customer's commitment to purchase a Designated Security. The customer therefore will have the opportunity to review the determination, and decide whether the broker-dealer has made a good faith attempt to consider the customer's financial situation, investment experience, and investment objectives.

The Commission realizes that certain broker-dealers may ignore the requirements of the Rule. The Rule therefore requires records to be kept that will indicate their compliance with each of its provisions.

* * *

B. Effect on Small Business Capital Formation

The Commission recognized in proposing Rule 15c2–6 that, while non-NASDAQ OTC securities issued by smaller companies frequently provide the greatest opportunity for abusive sales practice activity, many securities trading in this market are issued by legitimate small businesses that do not meet the qualifications for quotation on NASDAQ. * * * Accordingly, the Commission has modified the Proposed Rule in several respects to limit its effect on small business capital formation.

First, the Commission has streamlined substantially the paperwork requirements of the Rule. Broker-dealers are no longer required to obtain a manually-executed statement from customers setting forth a number of specific items of information, as required in the Proposed Rule. Instead, a broker-dealer can obtain over the telephone the customer information it needs for a responsible suitability determination, record its basis for this determination, and then send the information and this determination to the customer for verification. * * *

Second, the Rule provides that offerings of securities approved for trading on an exchange or NASDAQ upon notice of issuance are excluded from the Rule. * * *

Third, the Commission has enabled additional issuers to qualify for an exclusion from the Rule by the reformulation of the issuer financial standards in the Proposed Rule. The Rule's definition of Designated Security excludes securities issued by companies with net tangible assets in excess of $2 million. This standard compares with the $10 million total assets and the $8 million capital and surplus alternative standards contained in the Proposed Rule. * * *

Fourth, as discussed below, the Rule contains a new exemption for transactions in Designated Securities at prices of five dollars or more. Thus, issuers can avoid perceived adverse effects of the Rule by adjusting their capital structure and setting the offering price for their securities at five dollars or more, thereby reducing the opportunities for abusive sales practices in their securities. * * *

The Commission believes that the changes incorporated in the Rule substantially reduce the Rule's effect on legitimate broker-dealers and issuers. The Commission also believes that the significant potential for sales practice abuse and manipulation in connection with the transactions covered by the Rule justifies the Rule's adoption as modified.

* * *

In October 1990, Congress enacted the Securities Enforcement Remedies and Penny Stock Reform Act, requiring additional disclosures about "penny stocks," their market value, and the people selling them, requiring the SEC to adopt rules limiting the use of proceeds of "penny stock" sales and providing a right of rescission to purchasers, and directing the SEC to facilitate development of a quotation system providing volume and last sale information.

CHAPTER 11

CIVIL LIABILITIES OF SECURITIES FIRMS

A broker-dealer which violates the antifraud provisions of the securities laws or the rules of the SEC or one of the self-regulatory organizations (SROs) faces revocation or suspension of its registration and, in egregious cases, criminal prosecution. In addition, it may face substantial claims from customers who claim they have been damaged by the violation. Among the issues that frequently arise in such litigation are (a) whether there is an implied private right of action for violation of SEC or SRO rules, (b) the extent to which the firm can be held liable for the wrongful acts of its employees and agents, and (c) the effect of arbitration clauses in customer agreements.

A. LIABILITY FOR VIOLATION OF SEC OR SRO RULES

As indicated in Chapter 4.B above, the courts have consistently recognized the availability of an implied private right of action for violation of the rules promulgated by the SEC under the general antifraud provisions of § 10(b) of the 1934 Act. With respect to the rules promulgated by the SROs, however, there is considerable doubt as to whether any such right of action exists. In the first consideration of this question by an appellate court, Colonial Realty Corp. v. Bache & Co., 358 F.2d 178 (2d Cir.1966), the court declined to hold either that there would always be, or that there would never be, a private right of action for violation of an exchange or NASD rule. The question, said Judge Friendly, was "the nature of the particular rule and its place in the regulatory scheme." The case for implying a private right of action would be strongest where a rule "provides what amounts to a substitute for regulation by the SEC itself" and "imposes an explicit duty unknown to the common law"; it would be weakest in a case, like *Colonial,* where plaintiff was claiming that failure to comply with an alleged oral understanding violated the exchange's "catch-all" prohibition against "conduct inconsistent with just and equitable principles of trade."

This distinction proved difficult to apply in practice. In Buttrey v. Merrill Lynch, 410 F.2d 135 (7th Cir.1969), the court held that a broker, which failed to make adequate inquiry as to the source of the securities which a customer was trading, could be held liable to the persons from whom the securities were fraudulently converted on the basis of a violation of the NYSE's "know your customer" rule, where the broker's conduct was "tantamount to fraud." Other courts, however, applying the *Colonial* approach, refused to recognize an implied private right of action under either the "know your customer" rule or the NASD's "suitability" rule. Nelson v. Hench, 428 F.Supp. 411 (D.Minn.1977); Lange v. H. Hentz, 418 F.Supp. 1376 (N.D.Tex.1976). More recently, most courts have rejected the *Colonial* approach in light of the Supreme Court's more restrictive attitude toward implied private rights of action and held that there is no right of action for violation of any exchange or NASD rules, since there is no evidence that Congress intended to create one.

JABLON v. DEAN WITTER

614 F.2d 677 (9th Cir.1980).

Before: WRIGHT, HUG and SKOPIL, CIRCUIT JUDGES.

WRIGHT, CIRCUIT JUDGE: This is an appeal from an order of dismissal. Appellant Jablon alleges Dean Witter violated New York Stock Exchange (NYSE) Rule 405 (the "know your customer" rule) and Article III, Section 2 of the National Association of Securities Dealers (NASD) Rules of Fair Practice (the "suitability" rule) in its handling of her margin account. She also charges a violation of Securities and Exchange Commission Rule 10b–5. The district court dismissed the complaint, ruling (1) there is no implied private cause of action under NYSE Rule 405 or the NASD suitability rule, and (2) the Rule 10b–5 claim was barred by the statute of limitations. We affirm.

FACTS

In 1946, Jablon opened a "margin account" with Dean Witter. She alleges Sidney Turner, her account salesman at Dean Witter, urged her to open it without first inquiring diligently into her financial position, business expertise, or investment goals. She says she was not advised she could close her margin account and thereby avoid paying interest on funds loaned to her by Dean Witter and avoid placing additional funds in her account to meet "margin calls." Finally, she alleges that Turner improperly recommended that she purchase highly speculative securities on margin.

Jablon made numerous stock purchases between 1946 and 1970, including three purchases allegedly based on Dean Witter's recommendation: (1) additional shares of RCA (1965); (2) an unspecified number of shares of Lockheed stock (1967); and (3) another 100 Lockheed shares (1970). She argues these purchases were too speculative for her financial position.

Although no stock purchases were made after 1970, Jablon alleges she had repeated margin calls made upon her account through 1974. In 1974 she was unable to meet one call and Dean Witter sold her account. She alleges she lost $39,000 as a result of her investment plan; an initial investment of $23,000, plus additional cash to meet margin calls, offset by $800 remaining in her account.

Jablon contends she was not aware of Turner's alleged misconduct until she consulted legal counsel in 1974.

DISCUSSION

The Supreme Court recently enunciated the standard for implying private actions. Touche Ross & Co. v. Redington, 442 U.S. 560 (1979). The Court held that customers of securities brokerage firms had no implied cause of action for damages under § 17(a) of the Securities Exchange Act of 1934. It declared:

> The question of the existence of a statutory cause of action is, of course, one of statutory construction. * * * As we recently have emphasized, "the fact that a federal statute has been violated and some person harmed does not automatically give rise to a private cause of action in favor of that person." Instead, our task is limited solely to determining whether Congress intended to create the private right of action. * * *

This rule of statutory construction was extended by the Court in Transamerica Mortgage Advisors, Inc. v. Lewis, 444 U.S. 11 (1979). The Court ruled that § 206 of the Investment Advisors Act created no private cause of action for damages and explained:

> The question whether a statute creates a cause of action, either expressly or by implication, is basically a matter of statutory construction. * * * While some opinions of the Court have placed considerable emphasis upon the desirability of implying private rights of action in order to provide remedies thought to effectuate the purposes of a given statute, what must ultimately be determined is whether Congress intended to create the private remedy asserted. * * *

The Supreme Court's decisions in *Touche Ross* and *Transamerica* reflect a restrictive approach to implying private rights of action. Although those cases involved statutes rather than stock exchange rules, we think the same approach should apply in this case.

Because the stock exchange rules were not enacted by Congress but by the exchange acting on authority delegated by Congress, a two-step inquiry is necessary: (1) whether Congress intended to delegate authority to establish rules implying a private right of action; (2) whether the stock exchange rules were drafted such that a private action may legitimately be implied. We need not decide today whether the *Transamerica* test should be applied to the second step because we hold that Congress did not intend to create private rights of action for violation of stock exchange rules.

The Stock Exchange Rules

The Securities Exchange Act does not expressly authorize private actions for stock exchange rule violations. Prior to *Transamerica* and *Touche Ross,* courts and commentators found a statutory basis for implying private actions for exchange rule violations under §§ 6(b) and

27 of the Securities Exchange Act. Section 6(b), requiring exchanges to adopt rules promoting "just and equitable principles of trade," was said to create a duty. A private action was recognized in conjunction with § 27 of the Act which provides that an action may be "brought to enforce any liability or duty created by this title or the rules and regulations thereunder." This theory is no longer viable.

The Supreme Court specifically rejected a similar theory in *Touche Ross.* Relying on *Borak,* plaintiffs argued that defendant Touche Ross had breached its duties under § 17(a) and the rules adopted thereunder. They contended the breach was actionable under § 27. The Court rejected this theory, declaring that § 27 could play no part in implying liability:

> The reliance on § 27 is misplaced. Section 27 grants jurisdiction to the federal courts and provides for venue and service of process. It creates no cause of action of its own force and effect; it imposes no liabilities. The source of plaintiffs' rights must be found, if at all, in the substantive provisions of the 1933 Act which they seek to enforce, not in the jurisdictional provision.

Congressional intent to provide a private cause of action must therefore be found in § 6(b) alone. We find no such intent. The Supreme Court has decided that no private cause of action was intended under § 17(a) of the Securities Exchange Act because it neither confers rights on private parties nor proscribes any conduct as unlawful. We believe this reasoning applies with equal force to § 6(b).

Jablon argues that § 6(b) implies a private action because it was intended to protect the public. The Supreme Court rejected a similar public protection argument in *Touche Ross:*

> Certainly, the mere fact that § 17(a) was designed to provide protection for brokers' customers does not require the implication of a private damage action in their behalf.

In *Transamerica,* the Court similarly rejected public protection as a basis for implying a private action under § 206 of the Investment Advisers Act:

> Section 206 of the Act here involved concededly was intended to protect the victims of the fraudulent practices it prohibited. But the mere fact that the statute was designed to protect advisers' clients does not require the implication of a private cause of action for damages on their behalf. * * * The dispositive question remains whether Congress intended to create any such remedy. Having answered that question in the negative, our inquiry is at an end.

Because we find no Congressional intent to provide a private action for violation of stock exchange rules in § 6(b), our inquiry is also at an end.

No provision in the Securities Exchange Act explicitly provides for a private action for violations of stock association rules. Jablon argues that a private right is implicit because § 15A(b)(6) of the Securities

Exchange Act, requiring a stock association to adopt disciplinary rules, establishes an actionable duty under § 27. As we have noted, the Supreme Court has held that an implied private action cannot be predicated upon § 27.

Section 15A(b)(6) does not in itself imply that Congress intended to create a private action. Its language, like that of §§ 6(b) and 17(a) of the Securities Exchange Act, "neither confers rights on private parties nor proscribes any conduct as unlawful." Based upon the standards in *Touche Ross* and *Transamerica,* we conclude there is no implied right of action for an NASD rule violation.

Our conclusion that neither § 6(b) nor § 15A(b)(6) provides private rights of action is further supported by the fact that sections 9(e), 16(b), and 18 of the Securities Exchange Act explicitly provide private rights of action. The Supreme Court found no implied private action under § 17(a) of the Act because "when Congress wished to provide a private damage remedy, it knew how to do so and did so expressly."

We believe the entire statutory scheme makes it "highly improbable that 'Congress absentmindedly forgot to mention an intended private action'" in either § 6(b) or § 15A(b)(6).

* * *

In CLARK v. JOHN LAMULA INVESTORS, INC., 583 F.2d 594 (2d Cir.1978), the court bypassed the problem of finding a private right of action under the NASD suitability rule by holding that a knowing recommendation of unsuitable securities was a fraud under Rule 10b–5. It upheld an instruction by the trial judge to the jury that "the rules of fair practice of the NASD may be considered by you as an expression of the security industry itself concerning what constitutes proper conduct, and the violation of those rules under certain circumstances amounts to fraud under the federal securities laws." One judge concurred on the ground that the trial judge had adequately charged the requirement of scienter, but expressed his "concern over the attempts being made, as in this case, to fit the square peg of the 'suitability' rules into the round hole of § 10(b) and Rule 10b–5."

Section 22(a) of the Commodity Exchange Act provides an express right of action in the courts against commodities brokers and other professionals who violate the Act or the CFTC regulations. There is no counterpart in the securities laws.

Section 14 of the Commodity Exchange Act also provides injured commodities customers with an administrative avenue for relief. Section 14 permits any aggrieved customer to initiate reparations proceedings before the Commodity Futures Trading Commission. In such a proceeding, the customer's claim is adjudicated by a CFTC administrative law judge. The initial decision is appealable to the full Commission and then to a federal court of appeals. Under the Commodity

Exchange Act, the customer may elect a judicial remedy or arbitration as an alternative to the reparations procedure. The streamlined nature of the reparation procedure makes it more economical to litigate small claims against brokers, without being forced to resort to arbitration. The CFTC's reparation procedure provides an efficient, and relatively inexpensive, method of dispute resolution that is not available to injured securities customers. For an analysis of the effectiveness of the CFTC program, see Smythe, The Reparation Program of the CFTC: Reducing Formality in Agency Adjudication, 2 Admin.L.J. 39 (1988).

Selected References

T. Hazen, Securities Regulation § 10.14 (2d ed. 1990).

Hoblin, A Stock Broker's Implied Liability to Its Customers for Violation of a Rule of a Registered Stock Exchange, 39 Fordham L.Rev. 253 (1970).

Lashbrooke, Implying a Cause of Action for Damages: Rule Violations by Registered Exchanges and Associations, 48 U.Cin.L.Rev. 949–67 (1979).

Scott, A Broker–Dealer's Civil Liability to Investors for Fraud: An Implied Private Right of Action Under Section 15(c)(1), 63 Ind.L.J. 687 (1988).

Wolfson & Russo, The Stock Exchange Member: Liability for Violation of Stock Exchange Rules, 58 Calif.L.Rev. 1120 (1970).

Comment, Exchange Liability Under § 6 of the Securities Exchange Act: The Eligible Plaintiff Problem, 78 Colum.L.Rev. 112 (1978).

Comment, Exchange Liability for Improper Enforcement of Its Constitution and Rules, 24 Emory L.J. 865 (1975).

B. RESPONSIBILITY FOR ACTS OF AGENTS

The question of a broker-dealer's civil liability for the acts of its agents is complicated by the existence of three possible bases for liability. The first is the concept of liability for "aiding and abetting" a violation, discussed at pp. 519–21 above. The second is the liability imposed by § 20 of the 1934 Act and § 15 of the 1933 Act on any person who "controls" another person who violates the law. And the third is the common law doctrine of *respondeat superior,* under which a "master" is held liable for torts committed by his "servant," regardless of fault. The interplay of these three approaches is illustrated by the following opinion.

MARBURY MANAGEMENT v. KOHN

629 F.2d 705 (2d Cir.1980).

Before MESKILL and KEARSE, CIRCUIT JUDGES, and DOOLING, DISTRICT JUDGE.

DOOLING, DISTRICT JUDGE:

Marbury Management, Inc., ("Marbury") and Harry Bader sued Alfred Kohn and Wood, Walker & Co., the brokerage house that employed Kohn, for losses incurred on securities purchased through Wood, Walker allegedly on the faith of Kohn's representations that he was a "lawfully licensed registered representative," authorized to transact buy and sell orders on behalf of Wood, Walker. After a non-jury trial before the Honorable Lee P. Gagliardi, District Judge, the court found that Kohn was employed by Wood, Walker as a trainee and that his repeated statements that he was a stock broker and his use of a business card stating that he was a "portfolio management specialist" were undeniably false; the court found further that Kohn made the statements with intent to deceive, manipulate or defraud in making them, and that his misstatements were material. The court found that Kohn's misrepresentations about his employment status caused Marbury and Bader to purchase securities from Kohn between summer 1967 and April 1969. The district court also found that the predictive statements Kohn made about various securities were not fraudulently made, and that there was no evidence that they were made without a firm basis.

* * *

Judge Gagliardi dismissed the plaintiffs' claims against Wood, Walker on the ground of plaintiffs' failure to prove that Wood, Walker participated in the fraudulent manipulation or intended to deceive plaintiffs; treating plaintiffs as basing their claims against Wood, Walker solely on the theory that the firm aided and abetted Kohn's fraud, the court found that the evidence supported neither a finding of conscious wrongful participation by the firm nor a legally equivalent recklessness but at best a finding of negligence in supervision.

* * *

1. The substantial question that the appeal of defendant-appellant Kohn raises is whether Kohn's misrepresentation was the legal cause of the loss for which Marbury and Bader have been allowed recovery. The securities bought did not lose value because Kohn was not a registered representative with Wood, Walker, and this case, accordingly, is not one in which a material misrepresentation of an element of value intrinsic to the worth of the security is shown to be false, and in which it is shown that disclosure of the falsity of the representation results in a collapse of the value of the security on the market. In such cases one induced to buy the security on the faith of the misrepresentation of the value element is obviously damaged, and the chain of causation is clear.

Here the claim and finding are that Kohn's statements by their nature induced both the purchase and the retention of the securities, the expertise implicit in Kohn's supposed status overcoming plaintiffs' misgivings prompted by the market behavior of the securities. * * *

* * *

Although the theory of plaintiffs' case relates their damages to the inaction of retaining the securities on the faith of their belief in Kohn's assertion of his status, the claim is nevertheless one within Section 10(b) and Rule 10b–5 because the representation relied upon was made in connection with the purchase of securities, and both Marbury and Bader sue as purchasers of securities. Cf. Blue Chip Stamps v. Manor Drug Stores. * * *

It follows from what has been said that the judgment against defendant-appellant Kohn must be affirmed.

2. Marbury and Bader have appealed from the judgment in favor of Wood, Walker. Judge Gagliardi considered the case against Wood, Walker as one in which plaintiffs sought recovery against Wood, Walker only "as an aider and abettor of Kohn's securities law violations." Judge Gagliardi found that the evidence did not show that Wood, Walker intended to deceive plaintiffs, or knew of Kohn's violations, or provided substantial assistance to Kohn in violating the securities law, but at most showed only negligence on Wood, Walker's part. Applying the standard of *Rolf v. Blyth, Eastman Dillon & Co.*, 570 F.2d 38, 44–48 (2d Cir.1978), the district court held that plaintiffs had failed to establish essential elements of their claim against Wood, Walker as an aider and abettor of Kohn's securities law violations. The court did not consider Wood, Walker's possible liability under the respondeat superior theory, or as a "controlling person" under Section 20(a) of the Securities Act of 1934. It is concluded, on this branch of the case, that the court's disposition of the "aider and abettor" issues was correct, but that it was error, on the record before the court, not to consider and determine whether Wood, Walker was liable as a controlling person or as Kohn's employer.

* * *

The way in which the case was tried, and the shift in the emphasis of argument on the motion to dismiss arising from the introduction of *Ernst & Ernst* into the discussion may explain Judge Gagliardi's taking the position that he had to consider only the aider and abettor analysis, but the record evidence tending to support the plaintiffs' claim on the other two grounds was before the court, and, on the whole of that evidence, the three theories of liability—aider and abettor, controlling person, and respondeat superior—equally presented themselves for resolution. * * *

It was then error not to pass on the respondeat superior and Section 20(a) issues which lurked in the record, unless resort to respondeat superior is precluded by Section 20(a) and the district court's rejection of the claim that Wood, Walker aided and abetted Kohn's violations implies a finding that Wood, Walker has a "good faith" defense under Section 20(a). That section provides in relevant part:

> Every person who, directly or indirectly, controls any person liable under any provision of this chapter or of any rule or regulation thereunder shall also be liable jointly and severally with and to the same extent as such controlled person to any person to whom such controlled person is liable, unless the controlling person acted in good faith and did not directly or indirectly induce the act or acts constituting the violation or cause of action.

This court has avoided explicit "resolution of the rather thorny controlling person—respondeat superior issue." SEC v. Management Dynamics, Inc., 515 F.2d 801, 812–13 (2d Cir.1975), reasoned, in the light of the legislative history, that the "controlling person" provision of Section 20(a) was not intended to supplant the application of agency principles in securities cases, and that it was enacted to expand rather than to restrict the scope of liability under the securities laws; the court, however, intimated no view as to cases involving minor employees, claims for damages, or respondeat superior which might be broader than the apparent authority involved in *Management Dynamics,* which dealt with actions of a principal executive officer using corporate facilities to create a misleading appearance of activity in the stock in question. A little later, in SEC v. Geon Industries, Inc., 531 F.2d 39, 54–56 (2d Cir.1976), the court, reiterating the view expressed in *Management Dynamics,* again rejected the theory that a brokerage firm called to account for an employee's activities could be liable only as a controlling person under § 20(a). The court, however, declined to enjoin the firm on the theory that as employer it was responsible for the acts of its employee, a registered representative, finding that the firm had exercised reasonable supervision over him, that he had made no special use of his connection with the firm, and that the firm derived only ordinary commissions from his activities. * * *

Cases in other circuits are not in agreement about the relation of respondeat superior to Section 20(a) liability. The Eighth Circuit, in Myzel v. Fields, 386 F.2d 718, 737–739 (8th Cir.1967), imposed Section 20(a) liability in a Rule 10b–5 case in which, on the evidence, the liability of the allegedly controlling persons was governed "neither by principles of agency nor conspiracy," but the court assumed that common law principles of agency would apply to impose liability on a principal for an agent's deceit committed in the business he was appointed to carry out.

The Sixth Circuit, in Armstrong, Jones & Co. v. SEC, 421 F.2d 359, 362 (6th Cir.1970), held, adopting the position of the Securities Exchange Commission, that sanctions may be imposed on a broker-dealer for the wilful violations of its agents under the doctrine of respondeat superior; the court did not refer to Section 20(a). * * *

The Fourth Circuit, in Johns Hopkins University v. Hutton, 422 F.2d 1124 (4th Cir.1970), a case brought under § 12(2) of the '33 Act, held a brokerage house liable "under familiar [agency] principles, for the tortious representations of its agent"; although the partners of the defendant brokerage house were personally blameless, they had clothed their departmental manager with actual and apparent authority to provide the purchaser of the security with information about its yield, the manager acted within the scope of his employment in offering the security to the purchaser, and the firm received compensation based on the manager's sales effort. The court held that Section 15 of the '33 Act, which imposes a controlling person liability parallel to that imposed by Section 20(a) of the '34 Act, was not intended to insulate a brokerage house from the misdeeds of its employees.

The Fifth Circuit in Lewis v. Walston & Co., 487 F.2d 617 (5th Cir. 1973), applied agency principles in imposing liability on a brokerage firm in a suit under Section 12(1) of the '33 Act for an employee's sale of unregistered stock to plaintiffs, notwithstanding that the brokerage house never received a commission or other benefit from the transactions, did not deal in unregistered securities in the course of its own business, and did not perform any of its usual brokerage functions in the completion of the sales transactions. * * * The Seventh Circuit in a "churning" case, Fey v. Walston & Co., 493 F.2d 1036, 1052–53 (7th Cir.1974), held a brokerage house liable for the conduct of one of its officers, on the ground that "the general law rendered the broker liable for any churning conduct by its representative, and foundation for this result need not be sought within the confines of Section 20(a)." The Tenth Circuit in Richardson v. MacArthur, 451 F.2d 35, 41–42 (10th Cir.1971), imposed Section 20(a) liability on an employing corporation in a Rule 10b–5 case, saying, "Liability under § 20(a) is not restricted by principles of agency or conspiracy." The court did not make a respondeat superior analysis of the facts.

The earliest of the cases usually cited for the proposition that Section 20(a) of the '34 Act supplanted the doctrine of respondeat superior in securities cases, Kamen & Co. v. Paul H. Aschkar & Co., 382 F.2d 689, 697 (9th Cir.1967), does not elaborate the point, and Hecht v. Harris, Upham & Co., 430 F.2d 1202, 1210 (9th Cir.1970), which imposed liability in a churning case, did so under Section 20(a) on the basis that the brokerage house had failed to maintain adequate internal controls, and that its failure of diligence constituted failure to act in good faith; the court did not refer to the doctrine of respondeat superior. * * *

(c) While the precise standard of supervision required of broker-dealers to make good the good faith defense of Section 20(a) is uncertain, where, as in the present case, the erring salesman completes the transactions through the employing brokerage house and the brokerage house receives a commission on the transactions, the burden of proving good faith is shifted to the brokerage house, and requires it to show at least that it has not been negligent in supervision, and that it has maintained and enforced a reasonable and proper system of supervision and internal control over sales personnel. That Wood, Walker has successfully met the charge that it aided and abetted Kohn does not establish that it has borne the burden of proving "good faith" under the last clause of Section 20(a). The intimation of Judge Gagliardi's findings of fact is to the contrary; he was very far from finding that Wood, Walker had shown due care in its supervision and control of Kohn's activities.

Different considerations control the application of respondeat superior principles. Here the concern is simply with scope or course of employment and whether the acts of the employee Kohn can fairly be considered to be within the scope of his employment. The evidence of record in the present case presents substantial issues of credibility and interpretation, but it indicates, if taken at face value, that Kohn at all times acted as an employee of Wood, Walker, and accounted to Wood, Walker for the transactions. The evidence contains no indication that he profited by any of the transactions other than by reason of his compensation from Wood, Walker as one of its employees. Whatever the specific limitations on his authority as between him and his employer, the evidence, again, indicates, although with some uncertainty, that it was his function as a trainee to be an intermediary in the making of transactions in securities, but that there were certain limitations on the manner in which he was to carry on his activities. Kohn's deviant conduct, while it may have induced the purchase of securities that would not otherwise have been purchased, did not appear, on the record made at the trial, to mark any deviation from Kohn's services to his employer. Arguably, what he did was done in Wood, Walker's service, though it was done badly and contrary to the practices of the industry and the standing instructions of the firm. The record on the respondeat superior issue more than sufficed to require the trier of the fact to dispose of the issue on the merits.

Where respondeat superior principles are applied, the special good faith defense afforded by the last clause of Section 20(a) is unavailable. Quite apart from the fact that that conclusion was clearly adumbrated in SEC v. Management Dynamics, supra, and has become settled law in other circuits, there is no warrant for believing that Section 20(a) was intended to narrow the remedies of the customers of brokerage houses or to create a novel defense in cases otherwise governed by traditional agency principles. On the contrary Section 28(a) specifically enacts that the rights and remedies provided by the '34 Act shall be in addition to any and all rights and remedies that may exist at law or in equity, and Section 16 of the '33 Act, similarly provides that the rights and remedies of the '33 Act are additional to pre-existing remedies.

The judgment against defendant Kohn is affirmed and the judgment in favor of Wood, Walker & Co. is reversed, and a new trial of the claims of Marbury Management and Harry Bader against Wood, Walker & Co. is granted.

MESKILL, CIRCUIT JUDGE, dissenting:

In straining to reach a sympathetic result, the majority overlooks a fundamental principle of causation which has long prevailed under the common law of fraud and which has been applied to comparable claims brought under the federal securities acts. This is, quite simply, that the injury averred must proceed directly from the wrong alleged and must not be attributable to some supervening cause. This elementary rule precludes recovery in the case at bar since Kohn's misrepresentations as to his qualifications as a broker in no way caused the decline in the market value of the stocks he promoted. * * *

Is imposition of liability under the "no-fault" respondeat superior approach consistent with the Supreme Court's holding in *Hochfelder* [p. 455 above] that no person can be held liable under Rule 10b–5 unless he is found to have acted with scienter?

The standard of culpability under the "controlling person" provisions is also the subject of some disagreement among the circuits, as indicated in ORLOFF v. ALLMAN, 819 F.2d 904 (9th Cir.1987):

> Recent Ninth Circuit cases indicate that, to establish Allen's liability as a controlling person with respect to Allman or any other defendant, the Orloffs must show that: "(1) the defendant [Allen] had actual power or influence over the alleged controlled person, and (2) the defendant was a culpable participant in the alleged illegal activity." The district court granted summary judgment on the ground that the Orloffs had failed to establish a genuine dispute of material fact concerning Allen's "culpable participation."
>
> On appeal, the Orloffs renew their efforts to show that Allen was a culpable participant in the federal securities violations alleged in their complaint: * * * The Orloffs have presented no evidence that Allen actually knew (or culpably refused to see) that fraudulent sales of unregistered securities were being made.
>
> The Orloffs argue at length that they should not have to show Allen's knowing culpability, for two reasons. First, they suggest that Allen may be found liable for his *inaction,* his failure to investigate and exercise control over Allman and the others. This theory of "indirect participation" * * * provides no comfort to the Orloffs. It is applicable only where the control person can be analogized to a broker-dealer, who has a statutory duty to supervise his agents. Even if Allen can be analogized to a broker-dealer, the Orloffs must still show that his inaction was culpable.
>
> Second, the Orloffs recommend that this court adopt the reasoning of the Eighth Circuit in Metge v. Baehler, 762 F.2d 621 (8th Cir.1985). * * * According to the Eighth Circuit, it is enough to allege that the controlling person could have controlled the specific transaction that violated the securities laws. "[G]ood faith and lack of participation are affirmative defenses in a controlling person action."

Metge is inconsistent with the law of this circuit * * * We affirm the district court's decision on controlling person liability, on the ground that the Orloffs failed to show Allen's culpable participation in the frauds perpetrated by Allman.

Selected References

T. Hazen, Securities Regulation §§ 7.7, 13, 15 (2d ed. 1990).

Fitzpatrick & Carman, Respondeat Superior and the Federal Securities Laws: A Round Peg in a Square Hole, 12 Hofstra L.Rev. 1 (1983).

Musewicz, Vicarious Employer Liability and Section 10(b): In Defense of Common Law, 50 G.W.L.Rev. 754 (1982).

Note, Brooding Omnipresence of the Federal Common Law: The Evisceration of the Controlling Persons Provisions of the Federal Securities Acts, 50 Fordham L.Rev. 472 (1981).

Note, Liability of Corporate Directors as "Controlling Persons" Under § 20(a), 28 Drake L.Rev. 437 (1979).

C. ARBITRATION CLAUSES

An additional obstacle to a customer attempting to hold a brokerage firm liable for the wrongdoing of its employees is the standard provision in customer account agreements providing for arbitration of any dispute between the firm and the customer. The question is whether such a provision can be invoked by the firm against a customer who sues it for violations of federal securities law, or whether such an agreement violates the policy expressed in § 29(a) of the 1934 Act that "any condition, stipulation or provision binding any person to waive compliance with any provision of [the Act] or of any rule or regulation thereunder, or of any rule of an exchange required thereby shall be void."

SHEARSON/AMERICAN EXPRESS v. McMAHON

482 U.S. 220 (1987).

JUSTICE O'CONNOR delivered the opinion of the Court.

This case presents two questions regarding the enforceability of predispute arbitration agreements between brokerage firms and their customers. The first is whether a claim brought under § 10(b) of the Securities Exchange Act of 1934 must be sent to arbitration in accordance with the terms of an arbitration agreement. The second is whether a claim brought under the Racketeer Influenced and Corrupt Organizations Act (RICO), 18 U.S.C. § 1961 et seq., must be arbitrated in accordance with the terms of such an agreement.

I

Between 1980 and 1982, respondents Eugene and Julia McMahon, individually and as trustees for various pension and profit-sharing plans, were customers of petitioner Shearson/American Express Inc. (Shearson), a brokerage firm registered with the Securities and Exchange Commission (SEC or Commission). Two customer agreements signed by Julia McMahon provided for arbitration of any controversy relating to the accounts the McMahons maintained with Shearson. The arbitration provision provided in relevant part as follows:

> "Unless unenforceable due to federal or state law, any controversy arising out of or relating to my accounts, to transactions with you for me or to this agreement or the breach thereof, shall be settled by arbitration in accordance with the rules, then in effect, of the National Association of Securities Dealers, Inc. or the Boards of Directors of the New York Stock Exchange, Inc. and/or the American Stock Exchange, Inc. as I may elect."

In October 1984, the McMahons filed an amended complaint against Shearson and petitioner Mary Ann McNulty, the registered representative who handled their accounts, in the United States District Court for the Southern District of New York. The complaint alleged that McNulty, with Shearson's knowledge, had violated § 10(b) of the Exchange Act and Rule 10b–5, by engaging in fraudulent, excessive trading on respondents' accounts and by making false statements and omitting material facts from the advice given to respondents. The complaint also alleged a RICO claim and state law claims for fraud and breach of fiduciary duties.

* * *

II

The Federal Arbitration Act, 9 U.S.C. § 1 et seq., provides the starting point for answering the questions raised in this case. The Act was intended to "revers[e] centuries of judicial hostility to arbitration agreements," by "plac[ing] arbitration agreements 'upon the same footing as other contracts.'" The Arbitration Act accomplishes this purpose by providing that arbitration agreements "shall be valid, irrevocable, and enforceable, save upon such grounds as exist at law or in equity for the revocation of any contract." The Act also provides that a court must stay its proceedings if it is satisfied that an issue before it is arbitrable under the agreement, and it authorizes a federal district court to issue an order compelling arbitration if there has been a "failure, neglect, or refusal" to comply with the arbitration agreement.

* * *

The Arbitration Act, standing alone, therefore mandates enforcement of agreements to arbitrate statutory claims. Like any statutory directive, the Arbitration Act's mandate may be overridden by a contrary congressional command. The burden is on the party opposing arbitration, however, to show that Congress intended to preclude a waiver of judicial remedies for the statutory rights at issue.

* * *

To defeat application of the Arbitration Act in this case, therefore, the McMahons must demonstrate that Congress intended to make an exception to the Arbitration Act for claims arising under RICO and the Exchange Act, an intention discernible from the text, history, or purposes of the statute. We examine the McMahons' arguments regarding the Exchange Act and RICO in turn.

III

When Congress enacted the Exchange Act in 1934, it did not specifically address the question of the arbitrability of § 10(b) claims. The McMahons contend, however, that congressional intent to require a judicial forum for the resolution of § 10(b) claims can be deduced from § 29(a) of the Exchange Act, which declares void "[a]ny condition, stipulation, or provision binding any person to waive compliance with any provision of [the Act]."

First, we reject the McMahons' argument that § 29(a) forbids waiver of § 27 of the Exchange Act. Section 27 provides in relevant part:

> "The district courts of the United States * * * shall have exclusive jurisdiction of violations of this title or the rules and regulations thereunder, and of all suits in equity and actions at law brought to enforce any liability or duty created by this title or the rules and regulations thereunder."

The McMahons contend that an agreement to waive this jurisdictional provision is unenforceable because § 29(a) voids the waiver of "any provision" of the Exchange Act. The language of § 29(a), however, does not reach so far. What the antiwaiver provision of § 29(a) forbids is enforcement of agreements to waive "compliance" with the provisions of the statute. But § 27 itself does not impose any duty with which persons trading in securities must "comply." By its terms, § 29(a) only prohibits waiver of the substantive obligations imposed by the Exchange Act. Because § 27 does not impose any statutory duties, its waiver does not constitute a waiver of "compliance with any provision" of the Exchange Act under § 29(a).

We do not read Wilko v. Swan, 346 U.S. 427 (1953), as compelling a different result. In *Wilko,* the Court held that a predispute agreement could not be enforced to compel arbitration of a claim arising under § 12(2) of the Securities Act. The basis for the ruling was § 14 of the Securities Act, which, like § 29(a) of the Exchange Act, declares void any stipulation "to waive compliance with any provision" of the statute. At the beginning of its analysis, the *Wilko* Court stated that the Securities Act's jurisdictional provision was "the kind of 'provision' that cannot be waived under § 14 of the Securities Act." This statement, however, can only be understood in the context of the Court's ensuing discussion explaining why arbitration was inadequate as a means of enforcing "the provisions of the Securities Act, advantageous to the buyer." The conclusion in *Wilko* was expressly based on the Court's belief that a judicial forum was needed to protect the substantive rights created by the Securities Act: "As the protective provisions of the Securities Act require the exercise of judicial direction to fairly assure their effectiveness, it seems to us that Congress must have intended § 14 * * * to apply to waiver of judicial trial and review." *Wilko* must be understood, therefore, as holding that the plaintiff's waiver of the "right to select the judicial forum," was unenforceable only because arbitration was judged inadequate to enforce the statutory rights created by § 12(2).

Indeed, any different reading of *Wilko* would be inconsistent with this Court's decision in Scherk v. Alberto–Culver Co., 417 U.S. 506 (1974). In *Scherk,* the Court upheld enforcement of a predispute agreement to arbitrate Exchange Act claims by parties to an international contract. The *Scherk* Court assumed for purposes of its opinion that *Wilko* applied to the Exchange Act, but it determined that an international contract "involve[d] considerations and policies significantly different from those found controlling in *Wilko.*" The Court reasoned that arbitration reduced the uncertainty of international contracts and obviated the danger that a dispute might be submitted to a hostile or unfamiliar forum. At the same time, the Court noted that the advantages of judicial resolution were diminished by the possibility that the opposing party would make "speedy resort to a foreign court." The decision in *Scherk* thus turned on the Court's judgment that under the circumstances of that case, arbitration was an adequate substitute for adjudication as a means of enforcing the parties' statutory rights. *Scherk* supports our understanding that *Wilko* must be read as barring waiver of a judicial forum only where arbitration is inadequate to protect the substantive rights at issue. At the same time, it confirms that where arbitration does provide an adequate means of enforcing the provisions of the Exchange Act, § 29(a) does not void a predispute waiver of § 27—*Scherk* upheld enforcement of just such a waiver.

The second argument offered by the McMahons is that the arbitration agreement effects an impermissible waiver of the substantive protections of the Exchange Act. Ordinarily, "[b]y agreeing to arbitrate a statutory claim, a party does not forego the substantive rights afforded by the statute; it only submits to their resolution in an arbitral, rather than a judicial, forum." The McMahons argue, however, that § 29(a) compels a different conclusion. Initially, they contend that predispute agreements are void under § 29(a) because they tend to result from broker over-reaching. They reason, as do some commentators, that *Wilko* is premised on the belief "that arbitration clauses in securities sales agreements generally are not freely negotiated." According to this view, *Wilko* barred enforcement of predispute agreements because of this frequent inequality of bargaining power, reasoning that Congress intended for § 14 generally to ensure that sellers did not "maneuver buyers into a position that might weaken their ability to recover under the Securities Act." The McMahons urge that we should interpret § 29(a) in the same fashion.

We decline to give *Wilko* a reading so far at odds with the plain language of § 14, or to adopt such an unlikely interpretation of § 29(a). The concern that § 29(a) is directed against is evident from the statute's plain language: it is a concern with whether an agreement "waive[s] compliance with [a] provision" of the Exchange Act. The voluntariness of the agreement is irrelevant to this inquiry: if a stipulation waives compliance with a statutory duty, it is void under § 29(a), whether voluntary or not. Thus, a customer cannot negotiate a reduction in commissions in exchange for a waiver of compliance with the requirements of the Exchange Act, even if the customer knowingly and voluntarily agreed to the bargain. Section 29(a) is concerned, not with whether brokers "maneuver[ed customers] into" an agreement, but with whether the agreement "weaken[s] their ability to recover under the [Exchange] Act." The former is grounds for revoking the contract under ordinary principles of contract law; the latter is grounds for voiding the agreement under § 29(a).

The other reason advanced by the McMahons for finding a waiver of their § 10(b) rights is that arbitration does "weaken their ability to recover under the [Exchange] Act." That is the heart of the Court's decision in *Wilko,* and respondents urge that we should follow its reasoning. *Wilko* listed several grounds why, in the Court's view, the "effectiveness [of the Act's provisions] in application is lessened in arbitration." First, the *Wilko* Court believed that arbitration proceedings were not suited to cases requiring "subjective findings on the purpose and knowledge of an alleged violator." *Wilko* also was concerned that arbitrators must make legal determinations "without judicial instruction on the law," and that an arbitration award "may be made without explanation of [the arbitrator's] reasons and without a complete record of their proceedings." Finally, *Wilko* noted that the "[p]ower to vacate an award is limited," and that "interpretations of the law by the arbitrators in contrast to manifest disregard are not subject, in the federal courts, to judicial review for error in interpretation." *Wilko* concluded that in view of these drawbacks to arbitration, § 12(2) claims "require[d] the exercise of judicial direction to fairly assure their effectiveness."

As Justice Frankfurter noted in his dissent in *Wilko,* the Court's opinion did not rest on any evidence, either "in the record * * * [or] in the facts of which [it could] take judicial notice," that "the arbitral system * * * would not afford the plaintiff the rights to which he is entitled." Instead, the reasons given in *Wilko* reflect a general suspicion of the desirability of arbitration and the competence of arbitral tribunals—most apply with no greater force to the arbitration of securities disputes than to the arbitration of legal disputes generally.

It is difficult to reconcile *Wilko*'s mistrust of the arbitral process with this Court's subsequent decisions involving the Arbitration Act.

* * *

Indeed, most of the reasons given in *Wilko* have been rejected subsequently by the Court as a basis for holding claims to be nonarbitrable. In [Mitsubishi v. Soler, 473 U.S. 614 (1985)], for example, we recognized that arbitral tribunals are readily capable of handling the factual and legal complexities of antitrust claims, notwithstanding the absence of judicial instruction and supervision. Likewise, we have concluded that the streamlined procedures of arbitration do not entail any consequential restriction on substantive rights. Finally, we have indicated that there is no reason to assume at the outset that arbitrators will not follow the law; although judicial scrutiny of arbitration awards necessarily is limited, such review is sufficient to ensure that arbitrators comply with the requirements of the statute.

* * *

Thus, the mistrust of arbitration that formed the basis for the *Wilko* opinion in 1953 is difficult to square with the assessment of arbitration that has prevailed since that time. This is especially so in light of the intervening changes in the regulatory structure of the securities laws. Even if *Wilko's* assumptions regarding arbitration were valid at the time *Wilko* was decided, most certainly they do not hold true today for arbitration procedures subject to the SEC's oversight authority.

In 1953, when *Wilko* was decided, the Commission had only limited authority over the rules governing self-regulatory organizations (SROs)—the national securities exchanges and registered securities associations—and this authority appears not to have included any authority at all over their arbitration rules. Since the 1975 amendments to § 19 of the Exchange Act, however, the Commission has had expansive power to ensure the adequacy of the arbitration procedures employed by the SROs. No proposed rule change may take effect unless the SEC finds that the proposed rule is consistent with the requirements of the Exchange Act; and the Commission has the power, on its own initiative, to "abrogate, add to, and delete from" any SRO rule if it finds such changes necessary or appropriate to further the objectives of the Act. In short, the Commission has broad authority to oversee and to regulate the rules adopted by the SROs relating to customer disputes, including the power to mandate the adoption of any rules it deems necessary to ensure that arbitration procedures adequately protect statutory rights.

In the exercise of its regulatory authority, the SEC has specifically approved the arbitration procedures of the New York Stock Exchange, the American Stock Exchange, and the National Association of Securities Dealers, the organizations mentioned in the arbitration agreement at issue in this case. We conclude that where, as in this case, the prescribed procedures are subject to the Commission's § 19 authority, an arbitration agreement does not effect a waiver of the protections of the Act. While *stare decisis* concerns may counsel against upsetting *Wilko's* contrary conclusion under the Securities Act, we refuse to extend *Wilko's* reasoning to the Exchange Act in light of these intervening regulatory developments. The McMahons' agreement to submit to arbitration therefore is not tantamount to an impermissible waiver of the McMahons' rights under § 10(b), and the agreement is not void on that basis under § 29(a).

* * *

IV

Unlike the Exchange Act, there is nothing in the text of the RICO statute that even arguably evinces congressional intent to exclude civil RICO claims from the dictates of the Arbitration Act.

* * *

In sum, we find no basis for concluding that Congress intended to prevent enforcement of agreements to arbitrate RICO claims. The McMahons may effectively vindicate their RICO claim in an arbitral forum, and therefore there is no inherent conflict between arbitration and the purposes underlying § 1964(c).

* * *

JUSTICE BLACKMUN, with whom JUSTICE BRENNAN and JUSTICE MARSHALL join, concurring in part and dissenting in part.

I concur in the Court's decision to enforce the arbitration agreement with respect to respondents' RICO claims and thus join Parts I, II, and IV of the Court's opinion. I disagree, however, with the Court's conclusion that respondents' § 10(b) claims also are subject to arbitration.

* * *

There are essentially two problems with the Court's conclusion that predispute agreements to arbitrate § 10(b) claims may be enforced. First, the Court gives *Wilko* an overly narrow reading so that it can fit into the syllogism offered by the Commission and accepted by the Court, namely, (1) *Wilko* was really a case concerning whether arbitration was adequate for the enforcement of the substantive provisions of the securities laws; (2) all of the *Wilko* Court's doubts as to arbitration's adequacy are outdated; (3) thus *Wilko* is no longer good law. Second, the Court accepts uncritically petitioners' and the Commission's argument that the problems with arbitration, highlighted by the *Wilko* Court, either no longer exist or are not now viewed as problems by the Court. This acceptance primarily is based upon the Court's belief in the Commission's representations that its oversight of the SROs ensures the adequacy of arbitration.

* * *

In sum, the same reasons that led the Court to find an exception to the Arbitration Act for § 12(2) claims exist for § 10(b) claims as well. It is clear that *Wilko,* when properly read, governs the instant case and mandates that a predispute arbitration agreement should not be enforced as to § 10(b) claims.

Even if I were to accept the Court's narrow reading of *Wilko,* as a case dealing only with the inadequacies of arbitration in 1953, I do not think that this case should be resolved differently today so long as the policy of investor protection is given proper consideration in the analysis. Despite improvements in the process of arbitration and changes in the judicial attitude towards it, several aspects of arbitration that were seen by the *Wilko* court to be inimical to the policy of investor protection still remain. Moreover, I have serious reservations about the Commission's contention that its oversight of the SROs' arbitration procedures will ensure that the process is adequate to protect an investor's rights under the securities acts.

* * *

In the *McMahon* decision, the Supreme Court was not clear as to whether it was overruling or distinguishing *Wilko.* In the subsequent case of RODRIGUEZ v. SHEARSON/AMERICAN EXPRESS, 109 S.Ct. 1917 (1989), the Court, in a 5–4 decision, expressly overruled *Wilko* and held that an arbitration agreement with a broker barred a customer from suing the broker under the express liability provisions of § 12 of the 1933 Act. The Court found there was "no sound basis for construing the prohibition in § 14 on waiving 'compliance with any provision' of the Securities Act to apply to [the] procedural [as distinct from the substantive] provisions" of § 12. The dissenters felt that the Court should not overrule a prior construction of the statute "which Congress [had elected] not to amend during the ensuing 3½ decades."

In the wake of the *McMahon* decision, members of Congress put pressure on the SEC to reform industry arbitration procedures. The industry's self-regulatory organizations established a Securities Industry Conference on Arbitration, which worked with the SEC staff over a period of several months to produce a mutually acceptable set of rules. In May 1989, the Commission approved the rules submitted by the NASD and the New York and American Stock Exchanges. See Sec.Ex. Act Rel. No. 26805 (May 10, 1989). In general the rules provide that:

(a) The SRO will prepare a summary of each arbitration proceeding, describing the parties, the issues, and the relief requested and awarded, which will be available for inspection in their public reference rooms;

(b) Each member firm must explain to customers the consequences of signing an arbitration agreement and their rights in arbitration proceedings;

(c) Arbitrators having certain specified connections with the securities industry, including lawyers, accountants and other professionals, will be considered "industry" rather than "public" arbitrators;

(d) Procedures are established for service of pleadings, discovery of information, and replacement of arbitrators, and requiring that a verbatim record of each proceeding be maintained; and

(e) Member firms may not enter into agreements which restrict customers from filing claims, or seeking punitive damages or attorneys' fees, or restrict the situs of an arbitration hearing.

While Congress took no action on bills which would have barred broker-dealers from requiring customers to sign an arbitration agreement as a condition of opening an account, a number of states have adopted such laws. In SECURITIES INDUSTRY ASS'N v. CONNOLLY, 883 F.2d 1114 (1st Cir.1989), the court held that a Massachusetts statute containing such provisions was preempted by the Federal Arbitration Act.

In the wake of the Supreme Court decisions in *McMahon* and *Rodriguez,* securities firms embraced arbitration as the preferred method for dealing with claims by customers. Between 1986 and 1988, the number of arbitration proceedings increased by 115% while the number of securities-related federal lawsuits dropped by 7% . By mid-1990, however, the firms were beginning to have second thoughts about the desirability of arbitration. For one thing, the new rules imposed by the SEC increased the cost and length of the proceedings, and resulted in public announcement of the awards. In addition, arbitration panels learned that they had the right to award punitive awards in appropriate cases, and even to award RICO treble damages. Between May 1989 and May 1990, securities arbitration panels granted 21 punitive damage awards to investors totalling $4.5 million, up from nine awards totaling $1.7 million in the previous year.[1] At the same time, the SEC was pressing the industry to offer investors the choice of having their claims heard in independent arbitration forums, such as the American Arbitration Association, rather than requiring them to use the arbitration systems established by the NASD and the NYSE.[2]

Section 2 of the Federal Arbitration Act (9 U.S.C. § 2) subjects arbitration agreements to challenge upon any grounds that might exist to invalidate contracts in general. A frequent challenge to the validity of predispute arbitration agreements is that they constitute unenforceable contracts of adhesion. Such claims are highly factual and are generally resolved in favor of enforcing the agreement to arbitrate. See, e.g., Coleman v. Prudential Bache Securities, Inc., 802 F.2d 1350 (11th Cir.1986); Webb v. R. Rowland & Co., 800 F.2d 803 (8th Cir.1986); Surman v. Merrill Lynch, 733 F.2d 59 (8th Cir.1984). For discussion of lingering issues regarding predispute agreements to arbitrate claims under the federal securities laws, see T. Hazen, Hornbook on the Law of Securities Regulation § 14.5 (2d ed. 1990). As discussed in the follow-

1. See "Stock Investors Win More Punitive Awards in Arbitration Cases," Wall St. J., June 11, 1990, p. A1, col. 6.

2. See "SEC Urges Firms to Widen Arbitration Options to Include Independent Panels," Wall St.J., June 11, 1990, p. C5, col. 4.

ing excerpt, the Commodity Exchange Act requires that all commodity brokers offer arbitration to their customers. The customer may elect to pursue other remedies, but arbitration is mandatory if the customer elects that route.

COMMODITIES REGULATION

by Philip M. Johnson & Thomas L. Hazen

Vol. 1 pp. 335–344 (2d ed. 1989).*

* * *

In 1974 Congress incorporated into the Commodity Exchange Act, as section 5a(11), an affirmative duty of the contract markets to offer arbitration or similar dispute-settlement procedures in controversies arising between a member and a *customer.* Today, the Act permits contract markets to delegate the arbitration obligation to the National Futures Association. The section is silent with respect to member-to-member claims, but such claims are subject to voluntary arbitration programs. Section 17(a)(10) has a parallel provision for the National Futures Association. Under sections 5a(11) and 17(a)(10), it is mandatory for contract markets and the NFA to have a "fair and equitable procedure" to resolve claims asserted by *customers* against members or their employees. The required procedure, however, must contain three features. First, use of the system by a customer must be voluntary. However, if a customer consents, the procedure is mandatory for the member and employees. Second, compulsory payment may not result unless the parties so agree. Third, the term *customer* does not include another member of the contract market (i.e., a futures commission merchant (FCM), introducing broker (IB), or a floor broker (FB)). Sections 5a(11) and 17(a)(1) make no reference to possible counterclaims by a member against the customer in these proceedings, a right that had clearly existed under the contract markets' earlier arbitration systems. Commission Regulation § 180.4 provides that contract market and National Futures Association rules may permit the presentation of a counterclaim that arises out of the transaction or occurrence that is the subject of the customer's claim.

Sections 5a(11) and 17(a)(1) raise many questions. What is required to assure that the customer's commitment to arbitrate is made voluntarily? If the parties must agree between themselves to be bound by any award that is entered, does this give the member a right to refuse to submit to binding arbitration? Does section 5a(11) mean to bar *all* FCMs and floor brokers from asserting claims, even if they are true customers of other members and even if they do not belong to the host exchange? Does the arbitration program infringe contract members' or NFA members' constitutional right to a jury trial?

* * *

COUNTERCLAIMS

As noted earlier, section 5a(11) is mute on the question whether counterclaims can be asserted in arbitrations governed by it. However, Regulation § 180.4 expressly allows counterclaims (without the customer's assent) if limited to $15,000 and if they arise out of the "transaction or occurrence that is the subject of" the customer's claims. As in the customer's claim, adjudication of a counterclaim will not be entertained if it would require "the presence of essential witnesses, parties or third persons over whom the contract market does not have jurisdiction." Curiously, Regulation § 180.4 does not expressly include the language of Regulation § 180.1—governing the customer's claim—that the arbitration may proceed if such essential persons are "otherwise available." It would be anomalous, indeed, if a counterclaimant able to assure the attendance of essential witnesses were nevertheless precluded from an adjudication of his or her counterclaim merely because those persons are not under the formal jurisdiction of the contract market, that is, are beyond its compulsory powers. The better reading of Regulation § 180.4 would be to construe it as broadly as Regulation § 180.1 by permitting counterclaims when essential witnesses can be *brought within* the jurisdiction of the arbitration panel, by voluntary attendance or otherwise.

The foregoing requirements apply only to nonconsent counterclaims—that is, counterclaims that the customer cannot veto. However, a customer may voluntarily agree to the adjudication of a counterclaim arising out of events that are not the subject of his own claim, and if so, the arbitration panel may hear that unrelated counterclaim.

RIGHT TO JURY TRIAL

As discussed above, the customer arbitration programs are mandatory as far as the FCM, IB, CPO, CTA, floor broker, or associated person is concerned. Accordingly, when a customer invokes his or her right to arbitration, the broker (or other registrant) is deprived of a jury trial. The Court of Appeals for the Seventh Circuit has recently held that the arbitration program is not violative of the registrant's constitutional right to a jury trial.[31] In so ruling, the Court of Appeals reversed a ruling by the district court holding that Seventh Amendment rights had been violated. The Court of Appeals first noted that the registrant consented to the arbitration procedure and thus waived its right to resolution of the dispute by a court established by Article III of the Constitution. In other words, the objection to the lack of a jury trial should have been made before the arbitration proceedings commenced. The court then went on to examine the question of whether there was a right to an Article III court (and therefore a right to a jury trial) even in the absence of a waiver. The court concluded that there was no such right. The absence of a right to trial by jury was based, in part, on

31. Geldermann, Inc. v. CFTC, 836 F.2d 310 (7th Cir.1987).

recent Supreme Court rulings upholding the right to present common law counterclaims in reparations proceedings before the Commission, and upholding the arbitrability of disputes arising under the federal securities laws.

In addition to the arbitration programs, the Commodity Exchange Act provides the option of reparations proceedings before the CFTC as well as an express private remedy in the courts (see Merrill Lynch v. Curran, 456 U.S. 353 (1982) p. 484, above).

Selected References

T. Hazen, Securities Regulation § 14.4 (2d ed. 1990).

Fletcher, Privatizing Securities Disputes Through the Enforcement of Arbitration, 71 Minn.L.Rev. 393 (1987).

Katsoris, Securities Arbitration After McMahon: The Diminishing Role of the Courts, 16 Fordham Urb.L.J. 361 (1987–88).

CHAPTER 12

FINANCIAL AND MARKET REGULATION

In addition to authorizing the SEC to impose sanctions for fraudulent actions by individual firms, the Securities Exchange Act also empowers the agency to regulate the financial structure and practices of such firms, as well as the operation of the markets themselves.

A. FINANCIAL RESPONSIBILITY OF BROKER-DEALERS

Since many broker-dealers maintain custody of funds and securities belonging to their customers, safeguards are required to assure that the customers can recover those funds and securities in the event the broker-dealer becomes insolvent. The three principal techniques that have been utilized are (a) financial responsibility standards for broker-dealers, (b) requirements for segregation of customers' funds and securities, and (c) maintenance of an industry-wide fund to satisfy the claims of customers whose brokerage firms become insolvent.

1. Net Capital Rules

The basic financial responsibility standards for broker-dealers are found in the "net capital" rules adopted by the SEC under authority of § 15(c)(3) of the 1934 Act. Prior to the financial debacle suffered by the securities industry in 1968–70, securities firms belonging to exchanges which had "net capital" rules deemed to be more stringent than those of the SEC were exempt from the SEC's requirements. However, after SEC and Congressional investigations showed how flexibly the exchanges had interpreted their rules to allow member firms to continue in business with inadequate capital, the SEC revoked this exemption and made all broker-dealers subject to its requirements.

Under the SEC net capital rule, Rule 15c3–1, which was substantially revised in 1975, a broker-dealer must maintain "net capital" of at least $25,000 ($5,000 in the case of broker-dealers which do not hold any customers' funds or securities and conduct their business in a specified manner). "Net capital" is defined as "net worth" (excess of assets over liabilities), subject to many special adjustments prescribed in the rule. In addition, a broker-dealer may not let its aggregate indebtedness exceed 1500% of its net capital (800% during its first year of business).

A broker-dealer can alternatively qualify under Rule 15c3–1(f), which is designed to test its general financial integrity and liquidity and its ability to meet its continuing commitments to its customers. Under this alternative, which was significantly liberalized in 1982, a broker-dealer must maintain net capital equal to the greater of $100,000 or 2% of the aggregate debit balances attributable to its transactions with customers.

2. *Customers' Funds and Securities*

Customers leave large amounts of cash and securities with their brokers. The securities are of two types: securities purchased "on margin" (i.e., with the broker advancing part of the purchase price to the customer), which (under the standard margin agreement) the broker is entitled to hold as security for the loan and to repledge to secure its own borrowings; and "fully-paid" securities, which the broker holds solely as a convenience for the customer and is supposed to "segregate" from the broker's own securities. The cash "free credit balances" arise principally from two sources: a deposit of cash by a customer prior to giving his broker a purchase order, and receipt by the broker of proceeds of a sale of securities, or interest or dividend income, which has not yet been reinvested or delivered to the customer.

With respect to fully-paid securities, investigators of the securities industry's operational crises in 1968–70 discovered that many firms had lost control of their records, and did not have in their possession many of the securities which they were supposed to be holding as custodians for their customers. Accordingly, the SEC in 1972 adopted SEA Rule 15c3–3, which requires that all brokers "promptly obtain and * * * thereafter maintain the physical possession or control of all fully-paid securities", and prescribes daily determinations of compliance with the rule.

With respect to cash free credit balances, brokers have traditionally mingled the cash belonging to customers with their own assets used in their business. Since 1964, Rule 15c3–2 has required brokers to notify their customers at least quarterly that such funds (a) are not segregated and may be used in the business, and (b) are payable to the customer on demand. In the wake of the 1968–70 debacle, which revealed that many firms had been using customers' free credit balances as their own working capital, there were demands for complete segregation of these cash balances. The industry argued, however, that it should continue to have interest-free use of these moneys to finance customer-related transactions (principally margin loans). The result was Rule 15c3–3, adopted by the SEC in 1972, which requires each broker to maintain a "Special Reserve Bank Account for the Exclusive Benefit of Customers" in which it holds cash or U.S. government securities in an amount equal to (a) free credit balances in customers' accounts (plus other amounts owing to customers) less (b) debit balances in customers' cash and margin accounts.

3. *The Securities Investor Protection Act*

Following the financial collapse of one of its large member firms in 1963, the NYSE established a "trust fund", financed by assessments on its members, to pay the claims of customers of member firms which failed. This trust fund proved inadequate to deal with the financial crisis of 1969–70, however, and the industry turned to Congress to establish a more secure system of customer protection. Congress responded by passing the Securities Investor Protection Act of 1970 (SIPA).

SIPA § 3(a) created a non-profit membership corporation, called Securities Investor Protection Corporation (SIPC), and requires every broker-dealer registered under § 15 of the Exchange Act (with certain limited exceptions) to be a member. The corporation is managed by a seven-person board of directors, of which one is appointed by the Secretary of the Treasury, one by the Federal Reserve Board, and five by the President, of which three are to be representatives of different segments of the securities industry and two are to be from the general public.

In order to accumulate the funds necessary to enable SIPC to meet its responsibilities, each member of SIPC is required to pay an annual assessment equal to ½ of 1% of the member's gross revenues, until SIPC has accumulated a fund of $150 million, and to pay such further assessments as are necessary to maintain the fund at that level. If this fund proves insufficient, SIPC is authorized to borrow up to $1 billion from the Treasury (through the SEC). The SEC, if it determines that assessments on members will not satisfactorily provide for repayment of the loan, may levy a charge of not more than 1/50 of 1% of all transactions in the exchange and OTC markets to provide for repayment.

Operation of SIPC. If the SEC or a self-regulatory organization determines that a broker or dealer is in or approaching financial difficulty, it must notify SIPC. If SIPC determines that the member has failed or is in danger of failing to meet its obligations to customers, or that certain other conditions exist, it may apply to a court for a decree adjudicating that the customers of the member are in need of the protection provided by the Act. A customer of a SIPC member has no right to apply to a court for an order directing SIPC to take action with respect to that member. SIPC v. Barbour, 421 U.S. 412 (1975).

If the court makes the requisite findings and issues the requested decree, it must then appoint as trustee, and attorney for the trustee, "disinterested" persons designated by SIPC. The functions of the trustee are (a) to return "specifically identifiable property" to customers and to satisfy their other claims out of available funds, (b) to complete the "open contractual commitments" of the firm, and (c) to liquidate the firm's business. If the firm's assets are insufficient to satisfy the claims of all customers, SIPC must advance to the trustee moneys sufficient to satisfy all such claims, up to a maximum of

$500,000 for each customer (but not more than $100,000 in respect of claims for cash). In general, the liquidation proceeding is to be conducted in the same manner as if it were being conducted under Chapter X of the Bankruptcy Act.

In light of problems in the administration of the Act, particularly with respect to prompt settlement of customers' claims, the Act was amended in 1978 to permit the trustee to purchase securities for delivery to customers, to transfer customers' accounts in bulk to another broker-dealer, and to make direct payments to customers without judicial supervision in small liquidations.

B. MARKET REGULATION

In addition to its provisions for the regulation of individual broker-dealers, the Securities Exchange Act regulates the overall operations of the markets in which securities are traded. The principal regulatory provisions included in the original act in 1934 were §§ 7 and 8, governing the extension of credit on listed securities, and § 11, regulating trading by exchange members for their own account. These provisions have been substantially modified over the years. In the Securities Acts Amendments of 1975, Congress also added §§ 11A and 17A, directing the SEC to facilitate the establishment of a "national market system" and a national system for clearing and settlement of transactions.

1. Extension of Credit

"For the purpose of preventing the excessive use of credit for the purchase or carrying of securities," §§ 7 and 8 authorize the Federal Reserve Board (FRB) to limit "the amount of credit that may be initially extended and subsequently maintained on any security," and to regulate borrowing by brokers and dealers. Pursuant to this authority, the FRB has promulgated regulations governing the extension of credit by broker-dealers (Regulation T), banks (Regulation U), and other persons (Regulation G), and the obtaining of credit by purchasers (Regulation X). See 12 C.F.R. Pts. 220, 221, 207, 224.

While § 7 authorizes the FRB to regulate both the initial extension and the subsequent maintenance of credit, the FRB rules, or "margin regulations," as they are generally known, in fact regulate only the initial extension of credit on a new purchase. This is done by specification of a "maximum loan value" of securities, expressed as a percentage of current value, which the FRB changes from time to time in response to increases and decreases in the amount of speculative activity and the availability of credit. For example, if the current "maximum loan value" is 50%, a customer who wants to buy securities with a current market value of $4,000 must put up $2,000 in cash and may borrow the remaining $2,000 from his broker "on margin." If the securities subsequently decline in value to $2,500, the FRB margin regulations would not require the customer to pay an additional $750 to the broker to reduce his debt to $1,250. However, certain stock exchanges do impose "margin maintenance" rules on their members, requiring that customers maintain a "margin," or equity, in their accounts equal to at least 25% of current market value. Thus, if the broker in this example was an NYSE member, it would be required to make a "margin call" on the customer to reduce his loan by $125, thus raising his "margin" to $625, or 25% of current market value. If the customer then wanted to buy another $2,500 worth of securities, the FRB margin regulations would require him to put up $1,875 in cash, since he could only borrow an additional $625 from the broker—the difference between the maximum loan value of the account ($2,500) and his outstanding loan to the broker ($1,875).

The FRB restrictions apply only to extension of credit on equity securities; there are no limitations on the amount of credit that may be extended for the purchase of U.S. government bonds, state and local government bonds, or non-convertible corporate debt securities. As originally enacted, § 7 permitted extension of credit only on equity securities listed on a stock exchange; over-the-counter stocks had no "loan value." However, the statute was amended in 1968 to permit extension of credit on OTC stocks meeting criteria established by the FRB, which maintains a list of such securities. Section 11(d) bars broker-dealers from extending any credit to customers for the purchase of newly-issued securities with respect to which the broker-dealer is acting as an underwriter or selling group member.

While the power to regulate extensions of credit under §§ 7 and 8 is vested in the FRB, enforcement of the rules with respect to broker-dealers is the responsibility of the SEC and the self-regulatory organizations. A large number of proceedings have been brought against broker-dealers for violations of the margin rules, which bar them not only from extending credit in violation of FRB limitations but also from arranging for the extension of such credit by others.

Although the basic purpose of the margin regulations is to restrict stock market speculation, rather than to protect individual customers, some courts have allowed customers to sue their brokers for losses on transactions in which the brokers extended credit in violation of the rules, even where the illegal extension of credit was not shown to have induced the customer to enter into the transaction. Pearlstein v. Scudder & German, 429 F.2d 1136 (2d Cir.1970), modified at 527 F.2d 1141 (2d Cir.1975). However, the addition in 1970 of § 7(f), prohibiting *customers* from obtaining credit in violation of the FRB rules, coupled with the Supreme Court's current reluctance to imply new private rights of action, has led the courts in the more recent cases to deny customers any right to recover in these circumstances. The opinion in GILMAN v. FDIC, 660 F.2d 688 (6th Cir.1981), illustrates the current approach:

The District Court decided, and Gilman contends on appeal, that a private right of action exists for violation of the margin requirements. We disagree.

Since neither the Act nor the Regulation expressly provides for borrowers' suits, the District Court relied principally on two earlier cases of this court, Spoon v. Walston, 478 F.2d 246 (6th Cir.1973) (per curiam) and Goldman v. Bank of the Commonwealth, 467 F.2d 439 (6th Cir.1972), to support an implied right of action against the FDIC. These cases found an implied right of action under section 7(c) and Regulation T, which prohibit stockbrokers from extending credit to their customers in excess of the margin requirements.

This court has recently repudiated *Spoon* and its predecessor Pearlstein v. Scudder & German, to the extent these decisions permit the inference of private actions on the theory that Congress intended brokers to bear the entire burden of margin compliance. In Gutter v. Merrill Lynch, 644 F.2d 1194 (6th Cir.1981), Judge Brown stated that the private cause of action rule sanctioned by *Spoon, Pearlstein,* and their progeny was no longer "viable" in light of a 1970 amendment to the '34 Act. Section 7(f) subjects borrowers themselves to the margin requirements, and prohibits customers from accepting credit that exceeds the maximum permitted by the regulations. Because borrowers now share with lenders the burden of observing margin requirements, the rationale for inferring a private cause of action has disappeared.

* * * As we noted in *Gutter,* we must follow the tests the Supreme Court outlined in Cort v. Ash, to determine whether a regulatory statute implies a private cause of action. The first factor *Cort* identifies is whether the plaintiff is one "for whose *especial* benefit the statute was enacted;" the second, and most important, is whether there is any indication of congressional intent to create a private remedy; the third is whether a private remedy is consistent with the legislative scheme; and the fourth is whether it would be inappropriate to infer a federal cause of action in an area traditionally relegated to state law. * * *

The language and legislative history of section 7 convince us that Congress did *not* intend to create a remedy in favor of borrowers. Section 7's language expressly announces the aim of "preventing the excessive *use* of credit for the purchase or carrying of securities" and of accommodating "commerce and industry, having due regard to the general credit situation of the country." Thus section 7 presaged section 7(f) and Regulation X, for it implies by its very terms an intention to regulate those who *use* credit, namely borrowers.

Nothing in the legislative history indicates to us that Congress intended to provide a remedy for borrowers. * * *

Disclosure. Loans by securities firms to their customers are specifically exempted from the federal Truth in Lending Act. 15 U.S.C. § 1603(2). However, the exemption was premised on a Congressional understanding that the SEC would promulgate substantially similar disclosure rules under its existing authority. Rule 10b–16, adopted by the SEC in 1969, requires broker-dealers to disclose to their margin customers (a) the rate and method of computing interest on their indebtedness, and (b) the nature of the firm's interest in the customer's securities and the circumstances under which additional collateral may be required. A firm which fails to disclose its policy with respect to requirement of additional collateral may be liable to a customer for damages resulting from the customer's failure to meet a margin call. Liang v. Dean Witter, 540 F.2d 1107 (D.C.Cir.1976).

2. *Trading by Exchange Members*

The principal function, and purpose, of a national securities exchange is to provide a marketplace in which member firms, acting as brokers, can purchase and sell securities for the account of their customers. The question addressed in § 11 is the extent to which stock exchange members and their firms should be permitted to trade in listed securities for their own account, in view of the possibly unfair advantages they may have over public customers when engaging in such trading.

Section 11(a), as amended in 1975, prohibits an exchange member from effecting any transactions on the exchange for its own account, or any account with respect to which it exercises investment discretion, with certain specified exceptions, including transactions as a market maker (specialist) or odd-lot dealer, stabilizing transactions in connection with distributions, bona fide arbitrage transactions, and other transactions which the SEC concludes should be exempt from the prohibition.

Traditionally, the inquiry has focused on three special categories of transactions: (a) "floor trading" and "off-floor trading" by members and their firms, (b) transactions by "odd-lot dealers," and (c) transactions by specialists. More recently, the increasing domination of NYSE trading by institutional customers has focused attention on two additional categories: (d) "block positioning" by member firms, and (e) transactions for "managed institutional accounts."

"Floor Trading" and "Off-Floor Trading." The principal purpose of § 11(a), as originally enacted, was to authorize the SEC to write rules (1) "to regulate or prevent floor trading" by exchange members, and (2) to prevent excessive off-floor trading by members if the Commission found it "detrimental to the maintenance of a fair and orderly market."

"Floor trading" was the speciality of a small percentage of NYSE members who maintained their memberships for the sole or primary purpose of roaming around the exchange floor and trading for their own account in whatever securities caught their fancy. The SEC adopted some mild restrictions on floor trading in 1945, but nothing significant was done until 1963, when the Commission's Special Study of the Securities Markets concluded that floor trading was a vestige of the pre–1934 "private club" atmosphere of the exchanges, and should be abolished. In 1964, the Commission adopted Rule 11a–1, prohibiting all floor trading by members, unless conducted in accordance with a plan adopted by an exchange and approved by the Commission. The NYSE simultaneously adopted a plan, which was then approved by the Commission, requiring floor traders to register with the exchange, to maintain minimum capital and pass a qualifying examination, and to comply with special restrictions on their trading activity.

In 1978, the NYSE established a new category of "registered competitive market makers" with certain responsibilities to assist the specialist in maintaining an orderly market. As floor traders have switched over to this new category, traditional floor trading has continued to diminish in importance, amounting to only 0.02% of NYSE trading in 1989.

"Off-floor" trading by member firms (i.e. transactions initiated by decisions at the firm's offices, rather than on the floor), accounts for a much greater proportion of activity than floor trading, having amounted to roughly 14% of total NYSE volume in 1989. This type of activity has not been thought to give rise to the same kind of problems as floor trading, and the SEC has never undertaken to impose any direct restrictions on it. However, after an SEC study of off-floor trading in 1967, the NYSE adopted rules designed to prevent member firms from transmitting orders to the floor ahead of their customers at times when they might be privy to "inside information."

Specialists. The specialist firm occupies a unique dual role in the operation of the NYSE and other exchanges. First, it acts as a "broker's broker," maintaining a "book" on which other brokers can leave customers' "limit orders" (i.e., orders to buy or sell at a price at which they cannot currently be executed). Second, it acts as the exclusive franchised dealer, or "market maker" in its assigned stocks, buying and selling shares from other brokers when there are no customer orders on its book against which they can be matched.

The functions of the specialist can be illustrated by the following example. A firm is the specialist in an actively-traded stock, in which the market is 40–40⅛. This means that customer orders are on the specialist's book to buy specified numbers of shares at $40 or less, and other orders are on his book to sell at $40⅛ or more (for historical reasons, shares are quoted in halves, quarters and eighths, rather than cents, and the minimum unit is ⅛ point, or 12½ cents). A broker who comes to the specialist with an order to sell "at the market" will sell to the customer with the first buy order on the book at $40, and a broker who comes with a market order to buy will buy from the customer with the first sell order on the book at 40⅛. The specialist acts solely as a subagent, receiving a portion of the "book" customer's commission to his broker.

Now assume the same firm is also specialist in an inactively traded stock. The only orders on the book are an order to buy at 38 and an order to sell at 42. If the specialist acted solely as agent, a broker who came in with a market order to sell would receive 38, and another broker who came in an hour later with a market order to buy would pay 42. The report of these two trades on the "tape" would indicate the stock had risen 4 points, or 10%, in an hour. The exchange therefore imposes an obligation on the specialist to maintain an "orderly market" in his assigned stocks, buying and selling for his own account to even out swings which would result from buyers and sellers not appearing at his post at the same time. In this case he might make his market at 40–40¼, trading for his own account as long as necessary, but yielding priority to customers' orders on his book whenever they provide as good a price to the party on the other side.

While this combination of functions has obvious advantages, it also offers possibilities for abuse. With his monopoly trading position and knowledge of the "book," the specialist, by moving the price of his specialty stocks up and down, can guarantee himself profits in both his "broker" and "dealer" functions. The SEC has from time to time studied, and expressed its concern about, this problem, but has never undertaken direct regulation of specialists' activities. In 1965, it adopted Rule 11b–1, requiring the principal exchanges to maintain and enforce rules designed to curb abuses by specialists, but recent SEC and Congressional studies have expressed continuing dissatisfaction with NYSE surveillance and regulation of specialist activities. In recent years, however, the NYSE has disciplined a number of specialists for improper trades or reports of trades, failure to maintain orderly markets, and other violations.

In 1975, Congress amended § 11(b) to make clear that the SEC had authority to limit specialists to acting either as brokers or dealers, but not both, but the Commission has not yet taken any action pursuant to this authority.

"Block Positioning." Institutional investors (principally pension funds, mutual funds, and insurance companies) have increased their investments in common stocks to the point that they currently account for 60–70% of the trading on the New York Stock Exchange. Institutions often trade in large blocks (10,000 shares or more), which in 1989 accounted for 51% of total NYSE trading volume. These block transactions put special strains on exchange market-making mechanisms. If a member firm which specializes in institutional business has a customer which wishes to sell 100,000 shares of a particular stock, but can only find buyers for 80,000, the firm itself will "position" the remaining 20,000 shares, and then sell them off over a period of time as the market can absorb them. Section 11(a)(1)(A) recognizes this "market making" function as a legitimate exception to the prohibition against trading by members for their own account.

"Institutional Membership." Another question raised by the growth of institutional trading was whether an institution (or an affiliated broker) should be permitted to become a member of an exchange to effect transactions for the institution's account. The NYSE had consistently barred institutions and their affiliates from

membership. However, a number of institutions, in the pre–1975 period when fixed minimum commissions were charged on all stock exchange transactions, joined "regional" exchanges (which serve as alternative markets for most NYSE-listed stocks) to achieve greater flexibility in the use of their commission dollars, or to recover a portion of the commissions for the benefit of the institutions.

The brokerage firms, alarmed at the potential loss of their biggest customers, persuaded Congress in the 1975 amendments to prevent "institutional membership" by prohibiting any exchange member from effecting any transaction on the exchange for any institutional account over which it or an affiliate exercises investment discretion. However, since the elimination of fixed rates in 1975 eliminated virtually all incentive for institutions to join exchanges, the brokerage firms discovered that they (or those of them that manage institutional accounts) were the principal victims of the new prohibition, which became effective in February 1979.

3. *Market Structure*

The fixed minimum commission rates maintained by the New York Stock Exchange prior to 1975 resulted in the diversion of a substantial portion of institutional trading to the "regional" exchanges or to the "third market" (an over-the-counter market in NYSE-listed stocks, maintained by non-member market makers). This "fragmentation" results in orders for a single stock being routed to different markets, with customers in some cases receiving less favorable prices than they would have received if all orders met in a single place.

Accordingly, in the Securities Acts Amendments of 1975, Congress directed the SEC to "use its authority to facilitate the establishment of a national market system" to link all markets for particular securities. The first result of this effort was the 1976 replacement of the old NYSE "tape" with a "consolidated tape" which records all transactions in a listed security, wherever effected. In 1978, the exchanges introduced an "intermarket trading system" (ITS) which permits electronic transfer of orders from one exchange floor to another when a better price is available on the other exchange. In 1980, about 3½% of total exchange trading was routed through ITS.

The exchanges have continued to resist the development of a competing over-the-counter market in listed stocks by barring their members from "effect[ing] any transaction in any listed stock in the over-the-counter market, either as principal or agent." NYSE Rule 390. The SEC took a small first step against this prohibition in 1980, when it adopted Rule 19c–3, barring any exchange from enforcing the prohibition with respect to any stock which was first listed on an exchange after April 26, 1979. However, NYSE member firms have made very little use of this exception.

4. *Clearing and Settlement of Transactions*

Congressional and SEC investigations of the securities industry's "paperwork crisis" during the period from 1968 to 1970 revealed that a substantial cause of the problem was the obsolete and inefficient method of completing transactions by the delivery (and, in some cases, cancellation and reissuance) of stock certificates. Accordingly, in the Securities Acts Amendments of 1975, Congress directed the SEC to "use its authority to facilitate the establishment of a national system for the prompt and accurate clearance and settlement of transactions in securities." In furtherance of this objective, the SEC was given direct regulatory power over clearing agencies and transfer agents, as well as the power to prescribe the format of securities registered under the 1934 Act.

Since the crisis, transfers of certificates have been reduced somewhat by the establishment of a depository through which certain major brokers and banks can effect transfers among themselves without movement of certificates. Also the SEC in 1977 prescribed a set of minimum performance standards for transfer agents. See Rules 17Ad–1 et seq.

5. *The 1987 Market Break*

The 1980s were a period of enormous activity and volatility in the stock market. The volume of stock trading by institutions soared, and the stock market averages rose to successive new highs. The Dow Jones Industrial average rose from 777 in August 1982 to a peak of 2722 in August 1987. At the same time there was an explosion of trading in options on individual stocks and futures contracts on stock market averages, as institutions and broker-dealers developed new and complex techniques for hedging their stock positions with offsetting transactions in the options and futures markets. Some institutions, accepting the contention of efficient market theorists that it was impossible to outperform the market, "indexed" large portions of their portfolios, i.e., invested in a broad "basket" of stocks designed to duplicate the performance of the stock market as a whole. These institutions would then seek to improve their yield and limit their risk by undertaking a variety of sophisticated trading techniques such as:

> Index arbitrage—buying stocks and selling futures (or vice versa) when there is a disparity between the prices on the stock exchanges and the options or futures markets;
>
> Program trading—Installing computer programs which automatically generate massive orders to buy or sell large amounts of stock or futures when the market moves a specified amount;
>
> Portfolio insurance—Using computer programs to generate orders to sell futures when the market drops a specified amount.

In October 1987, the stock market, in a one-week period, experienced the largest percentage drop in its history. In the wake of this "market break," the SEC and a special task force appointed by the

President (the "Brady Commission") undertook studies of what had happened and how to prevent it from happening again.[1] The following are excerpts from the report of the Brady Commission:

REPORT OF THE PRESIDENTIAL TASK FORCE ON MARKET MECHANISMS

(Jan. 1988).

All major stock markets began an impressive period of growth in 1982. Spurred by the economic turnaround, the growth in corporate earnings, the reduction in inflation and the associated fall in interest rates, the Dow rose from 777 to 1,896 between August 1982 and December 1986. Other factors contributing to this dramatic bull market included: continuing deregulation of the financial markets; tax incentives for equity investing; stock retirements arising from mergers, leveraged buyouts and share repurchase programs; and an increasing tendency to include "takeover premiums" in the valuation of a large number of stocks.

Despite the dramatic rise in the market, stock valuation at the end of 1986 was not out of line with levels achieved in past periods.

1987

Stocks in the U.S. continued to appreciate rapidly during the first eight months of 1987, despite rapidly increasing interest rates (see Figure 5). When the Dow reached its peak of 2,722 in August, stocks were valued at levels which challenged historical precedent and fundamental justification. Factors which contributed to this final rise included, in addition to those listed earlier, increased foreign investment in U.S. equities and growing investment in common stock mutual funds.

The rapid rise in the popularity of portfolio insurance strategies also contributed to the market's rise. Pension fund managers adopting these strategies typically increased the funds' risk exposure by investing more heavily in common stock during this rising market. The rationale was that portfolio insurance would cushion the impact of a market break by allowing them to shift quickly out of stocks.

* * *

From the close of trading on Tuesday, October 13, 1987, to the close of trading on October 19, 1987, the Dow Jones Industrial Average ("Dow") fell 769 points or 31 percent. In those four days of trading, the value of all outstanding U.S. stocks decreased by almost $1.0 trillion. On October 19, 1987, alone, the Dow fell by 508 points or 22.6 percent. Since the early 1920's, only the drop of 12.8 percent in the Dow on October 28, 1929 and the fall of 11.7 percent the following day, which

1. The October 1987 Market Break: A Report by the SEC Division of Market Regulation (Feb. 1988); Report of the Presidential Task Force on Market Mechanisms (Jan. 1988).

together constituted the Crash of 1929, have approached the October 19 decline in magnitude.

* * *

The Market Break

The precipitous market decline of mid-October was "triggered" by specific events: an unexpectedly high merchandise trade deficit which pushed interest rates to new high levels, and proposed tax legislation which led to the collapse of the stocks of a number of takeover candidates. This initial decline ignited mechanical, price-insensitive selling by a number of institutions employing portfolio insurance strategies and a small number of mutual fund groups reacting to redemptions. The selling by these investors, and the prospect of further selling by them, encouraged a number of aggressive trading-oriented institutions to sell in anticipation of further market declines. These institutions included, in addition to hedge funds, a small number of pension and endowment funds, money management firms and investment banking houses. This selling, in turn, stimulated further reactive selling by portfolio insurers and mutual funds.

Portfolio insurers and other institutions sold in both the stock market and the stock index futures market. Selling pressure in the futures market was transmitted to the stock market by the mechanism of index arbitrage. Throughout the period of the decline, trading volume and price volatility increased dramatically. This trading activity was concentrated in the hands of a surprisingly few institutions. On October 19, sell programs by three portfolio insurers accounted for just under $2 billion in the stock market; in the futures market three portfolio insurers accounted for the equivalent in value of $2.8 billion of stock. Block sales by a few mutual funds accounted for about $900 million of stock sales.

The stock and futures market handled record volume of transactions and had a generally good record of remaining available for trading on October 19 and 20. However, market makers were unable to manage smooth price transitions in the face of overwhelming selling pressure.

Clearing and credit system problems further exacerbated the difficulties of market participants. While no default occurred, the possibility that a clearinghouse or a major investment banking firm might default, or that the banking system would deny required liquidity to the market participants, resulted in certain market makers curtailing their activities and increased investor uncertainty. Timely intervention by the Federal Reserve System provided confidence and liquidity to the markets and financial system.

One Market

Analysis of market behavior during the mid-October break makes clear an important conclusion. From an economic viewpoint, what have been traditionally seen as separate markets—the markets for stocks, stock index futures, and stock options—are in fact one market. Under ordinary circumstances, these marketplaces move sympathetically, linked by financial instruments, trading strategies, market participants and clearing and credit mechanisms.

To a large extent, the problems of mid-October can be traced to the failure of these market segments to act as one. Confronted with the massive selling demands of a limited number of institutions, regulatory and institutional structures designed for separate marketplaces were incapable of effectively responding to "intermarket" pressures. The New York Stock Exchange's ("NYSE") automated transaction system ("DOT"), used by index arbitrageurs to link the two marketplaces, ceased to be useful for arbitrage after midday on October 19. The concern that some clearinghouses and major market participants might fail inhibited intermarket activities of other investors. The futures and stock markets became disengaged, both nearly going into freefall.

The ability of the equity market to absorb the huge selling pressure to which it was subjected in mid-October depended on its liquidity. But liquidity sufficient to absorb the limited selling demands of investors became an illusion of liquidity when confronted by massive selling, as everyone showed up on the same side of the market at once. Ironically, it was this illusion of liquidity which led certain similarly motivated investors, such as portfolio insurers, to adopt strategies which call for liquidity far in excess of what the market could supply.

Regulatory Implications

Because stocks, futures and options constitute one market, there must be in place a regulatory structure designed to be consistent with this economic reality. The October market break illustrates that regulatory changes, derived from the one-market concept, are necessary both to reduce the possibility of destructive market breaks and to deal effectively with such episodes should they occur. The guiding objective should be to enhance the integrity and competitiveness of U.S. financial markets.

Analysis of the October market break demonstrates that one agency must have the authority to coordinate a few critical intermarket issues cutting across market segments and affecting the entire financial system; to monitor activities of all market segments; and to mediate concerns across marketplaces. The specific issues which have an impact across marketplaces and throughout the financial system include: clearing and credit mechanisms; margin requirements; circuit breaker mechanisms, such as price limits and trading halts; and information systems for monitoring activities across marketplaces.

The single agency required to coordinate cross-marketplace issues must have broad and deep expertise in the interaction of the stock, stock option and stock index futures marketplaces, as well as in all financial markets, domestic and global. It must have broad expertise in the financial system as a whole.

The Task Force compared these requirements with possible alternative regulatory structures, including: existing self-regulatory organizations, such as the exchanges; existing government regulatory agencies, namely the Securities and Exchange Commission and the Commodity Futures Trading Commission; the Department of the Treasury; the Federal Reserve Board; a combination of two or more of these; and a new regulatory body.

The issuance of the SEC and Brady Commission reports generated many suggestions for change. Institutions and securities firms voluntarily curbed some of their more aggressive trading practices, but proposals for specific restrictions or prohibitions were by and large rejected.

On October 13, 1989, the market suffered another sharp jolt when the Dow Jones Industrial Average dropped 190 points in one day. An SEC staff report on this incident [2] drew the following conclusions:

> On October 13, 1989, the nation's securities markets experienced extraordinary price volatility, losing $190 billion in value, $160 billion of which was lost in the last 90 minutes. This decline continued into the opening on Monday, October 16, 1989, when the Dow Jones Industrial Average fell an additional 63.16 points (2.46%) in a steep sell-off in the first 40 minutes of trading, followed by an even sharper up-swing to close up 88.12 points (3.43%) from the October 13 close. This price volatility was accompanied by hourly trading volume levels that rivalled those of the 1987 market break. Even more violent price swings were experienced in the stock index futures markets on both days.
>
> In response to the events of October 1989, Chairman Richard C. Breeden directed the Commission's Division of Market Regulation ("Division") to reconstruct trading on October 13 and 16, 1989. The results of this reconstruction are presented in this report. The Division's trading reconstruction of October 13 and 16, 1989, indicates that:
>
> Futures selling was focused in small and large speculative accounts, foreign accounts (which the Division has identified as mostly speculative short-term trading accounts), options market makers and major broker-dealers that were hedging large institutional options put in writing;
>
> * * *
>
> Unlike the 1987 market break, futures selling was not dominated by a few institutions. Instead, institutions were net buyers;
>
> Index arbitrage and other program selling significantly accelerated and exacerbated the market decline. From 2:40 to the close on October 13, index arbitrage and other program selling on the NYSE was significant, accounting for nearly 27% of S & P 500 stock volume. Moreover, program selling accounted for 36% of S & P volume when

2. Trading Analysis of October 13 and 16, 1989: A Report by the SEC Division of Market Regulation (May 1990).

the futures were not subject to price limits. These aggregate levels were higher on a sustained basis than the aggregate index arbitrage levels during the 1987 market break;

Given current market and regulatory structures, there can be no assurance that the extraordinary volatility of October 13 and 16 will not be repeated or surpassed in the future.

In response to these concerns, Congress enacted the Market Reform Act of 1990, which (a) authorizes the SEC to regulate program trading during periods of extreme market volatility; (b) authorizes the Chairman of the SEC, with the permission of the President, to suspend trading on all securities markets in times of market emergency; (c) requires large securities traders to report their market positions to the SEC; (d) mandates the coordination of clearance and settlement procedures for stocks, options and futures contracts; (e) requires annual reports from the Treasury, the Federal Reserve Board, the SEC and the CFTC on their efforts to protect the integrity of the markets; and (f) authorizes the SEC to review the financial condition of holding companies which own broker-dealers.

Selected References

Molinari & Kibler, Broker Dealers' Financial Responsibility Under the Uniform Net Capital Rule—A Case for Liquidity, 72 Geo.L.J. 1 (1983).

Climan, Civil Liability Under the Credit–Regulation Provisions of the Securities Exchange Act of 1934, 63 Cornell L.Rev. 206 (1978).

Note, Implied Private Actions for Federal Margin Violations: The Cort v. Ash Factors, 47 Ford.L.Rev. 242 (1978).

Guttman, Broker–Dealer Bankruptcies, 48 N.Y.U.L.Rev. 887 (1973).

Mofsky, SEC Financial Requirements for Broker–Dealers: Economic Implications of Proposed Revisions, 47 Ind.L.J. 272 (1972).

C. "SELF-REGULATION"

The scheme of regulation of the securities business is complicated by the fact that regulatory authority is not lodged solely in the SEC, but is divided between the SEC and a number of "self-regulatory organizations" (SRO). These are private associations of broker-dealers to which Congress has delegated (a) authority to adopt and enforce rules for the conduct of their members and (b) responsibility to assure compliance by their members with provisions of the federal securities laws.

Stock Exchanges. When Congress created the SEC in 1934, stock exchanges, as private associations, had been regulating their members for up to 140 years. Rather than displace this system of "self-regulation", Congress superimposed the SEC on it as an additional level of regulation. Section 5 requires every "national securities exchange" to register with the SEC. Under § 6(b), an exchange cannot be registered unless the SEC determines that its rules are designed, among other things, to "prevent fraudulent and manipulative acts and practices, to promote just and equitable principles of trade," and to provide for appropriate discipline of its members for any violations of its own rules or the securities laws.

Under this authority, the various exchanges, of which the New York Stock Exchange (NYSE) is by far the largest and most important, have maintained and enforced a large body of rules for the conduct of their members. These rules fall into two categories: rules relating to transactions on the particular exchange, and rules relating to the internal operations of the member firms and their dealings with their customers.

In the first group are found rules governing: criteria for listing securities on the exchange and provisions for delisting or suspension of trading in particular securities; obligations of issuers of listed securities; bids and offers on the exchange floor; activities of "specialists" (designated market-makers in listed securities); transactions by members in listed securities for their own account; conditions under which transactions in listed securities may be effected off the exchange; clearing and settlement of exchange transactions; and rules for the governance and operation of the exchange itself.

In the second category are generally found rules governing: the form of organization of member firms and qualifications of their partners or officers; qualifications of salesmen and other personnel; handling of customers' accounts; advertising; and financial statements and reports. In the case of firms which are members of more than one exchange, there is a kind of "pecking order" with respect to regulatory responsibility: the NYSE has principal responsibility for regulation of the internal affairs of all of its members (which includes almost all of the largest firms in the industry), the American Stock Exchange has principal responsibility for those of its members that are not also NYSE members, and the various "regional" exchanges in cities other than New York have responsibility over their "sole" members.

Section 19, as originally enacted, gave the SEC power to suspend or withdraw the registration of an exchange, to suspend or expel any member of an exchange, to suspend trading in listed securities, and to require changes in exchange rules with respect to a wide range of matters. However, it did not require SEC approval for changes in stock exchange rules, nor did it provide for SEC review of disciplinary actions by exchanges against their members.

National Association of Securities Dealers. When Congress decided to extend federal regulation over the nonexchange, or over-the-counter (OTC) market, it followed the pattern already established with respect to exchanges. Section 15A, added by the "Maloney Act" of 1938, authorized the establishment of "national securities associations" to be registered with the SEC. Like an exchange, any such association must have rules designed "to prevent fraudulent and manipulative acts and practices [and] to promote just and equitable principles of trade" in transactions in the OTC market. Only one such association has been established, the National Association of Securities Dealers (NASD). The NASD has adopted a substantial body of "Rules of Fair Practice," dealing with various problems in the OTC markets. Among the most important are: its rule that a dealer may not recommend a security unless it has reason to believe the security is "suitable" to the customer's financial situation and needs; its interpretation of its "fair spread or profit" rule to bar markups in excess of 5% on principal transactions; its procedures for reviewing underwriting compensation and provisions for assuring that members make a bona fide public offering of underwritten securities; and its rules with respect to execution of orders in the OTC market and disclosure in confirmations to customers.

Prior to 1971, the NASD was a purely regulatory organization, since the OTC market had no central facility comparable to an exchange floor. Trading was effected by telephone calls between dealers on the basis of quotations published in commercial "sheets" by broker-dealers who chose to make markets in particular securities. However, in 1971, the NASD put into operation an electronic automated quotation system (NASDAQ) for selected OTC securities, in which dealers can insert, and instantaneously update, bid and asked quotations for securities in which they are registered with the NASD as market makers. The NASD thus now combines the dual functions of an exchange: regulating access to and operation of NASDAQ, and regulating the internal affairs of those of its members which are not members of any exchange (generally the smaller firms.)

Under Section 15(b)(8), as amended in 1983, a broker-dealer cannot do business in over-the-counter securities unless it becomes a member of the NASD.

Securities Acts Amendments of 1975. Between 1968 and 1970, the securities industry passed through an operational and financial crisis which ultimately led to extensive Congressional modification of the self-regulatory scheme. The Securities Acts Amendments of 1975 made important changes in the powers of the SRO's and the SEC's role in supervising them.

Section 19, as amended in 1975, expanded and consolidated the SEC's authority over *all* self-regulatory organizations. The SEC's new authority with respect to exchanges and the NASD is roughly comparable to, but even broader than, its previous authority over the NASD. In particular, the SEC must now give advance approval for any exchange rule changes, and has review power over exchange disciplinary actions. The 1975 amendments also confirmed the SEC action terminating the power of exchanges to fix minimum rates of commission (which both Congress and the SEC found to have been a major cause of market distortion) and directed the SEC to eliminate any other exchange rules which imposed unwarranted restraints on competition.

In addition to these policy questions, the authority delegated by Congress to non-governmental entities to adopt rules having the force of law has given rise to two difficult questions relating to the legal liabilities of those entities. The first question is whether a self-regulatory organization can be held liable in damages for failure to enforce its rules. The second question is whether it can be held liable for actions taken to enforce those rules, if a member or non-member injured by the action can show that the SRO lacked legal authority for the action it took.

---

1. SRO Liability for Failure to Enforce Rules

In the early case of BAIRD v. FRANKLIN, 141 F.2d 238 (2d Cir. 1944), a customer of an NYSE member firm sued the Exchange, alleging that losses which she suffered when the firm went bankrupt resulted from the Exchange's failure to enforce its rules against the firm. The court said that an exchange could be held liable under those circumstances, holding that § 6(b) of the 1934 Act, under which the rules of an exchange must provide for appropriate sanctions against members who engage in conduct inconsistent with just and equitable principles of trade, "places a duty upon the Stock Exchange to enforce the rules and regulations prescribed by that section." However, the court denied recovery to the plaintiff on the ground that she had not shown that the Exchange's failure to enforce its rules had caused the loss that she suffered.

Section 19(g)(1) of the 1934 Act, added in 1975, now explicitly imposes a duty on SROs to enforce their rules. However, recent court decisions, following the lead of the Supreme Court, have declined to recognize an implied private right of action for breach of that duty.

WALCK v. AMERICAN STOCK EXCHANGE

687 F.2d 778 (3d Cir.1982).

Before ALDISERT and WEIS, CIRCUIT JUDGES, and RE, CHIEF JUDGE.

ALDISERT, CIRCUIT JUDGE.

The plaintiff appeals from a judgment on the pleadings in favor of the defendants, the New York Stock Exchange and the American Stock Exchange, in an action under federal securities law. The major questions presented are whether §§ 6 and 7 of the Securities Exchange Act of 1934 implicitly authorize private civil actions for damages against a registered stock exchange based on failure to enforce its own rules and federal margin requirements. * * * We hold that Congress did not create private rights of action by implication in §§ 6 and 7, * * * and we affirm the judgment below in all respects.

I.

* * * Appellant Lynn G. Walck was a customer of the securities brokerage firm of Edwards & Hanly (E & H), now bankrupt, which was a member of the appellee New York and American Stock Exchanges. E & H in 1969 began to promote aggressively the purchase of Trans–Lux Corporation common stock, recommending to Walck and other customers that they utilize the full amount of margin purchasing power available in their accounts for this purpose. E & H sold numerous shares of Trans–Lux; between March 1971 and June 1973 the number of Trans–Lux shares in E & H accounts increased from 151,637 to 500,406, and its share of Trans–Lux equity from 14.95% to 24.6%.

The price of Trans–Lux stock began an extended and steady decline in early 1973, causing a number of E & H accounts to become undermargined. E & H requested additional margin deposits of numerous customers in May 1973, but several customers, including Walck, failed to meet the call. E & H continued to send margin calls, but it liquidated none of the accounts holding Trans–Lux. In August 1973, as the market for Trans–Lux continued to decline, E & H began searching for a buyer to purchase in a block the shares in its under-margined accounts; and in January 1974 it sold 146,300 shares to the Trans–Lux Corporation at a substantial loss. After E & H credited its customers' accounts with the proceeds of the sale, there remained an aggregate $506,429 debit balance in the accounts sold out; and E & H thereafter attempted to collect the deficiencies from its customers.

Walck filed an action against E & H in March 1974, alleging violations of the Securities Act of 1933, the Securities Exchange Act of 1934, SEC Rule 10b–5, Federal Reserve Board Regulation T, and common law. In September 1975, before the case came to trial, E & H petitioned for reorganization under Chapter XI of the Bankruptcy Code. The Bankruptcy Court then stayed further prosecution of Walck's action against E & H.

Frustrated in his attempt to obtain relief from E & H, Walck commenced the present action against the appellee Exchanges, seeking actual and punitive damages on January 13, 1977. He alleges *inter alia* that appellees violated § 6 of the Exchange Act by failing to enforce their own rules against E & H, that they violated § 7 by failing to enforce Regulation T, and that they violated and aided and abetted violations by E & H of §§ 9 and 10(b) and Rule 10b–5. The complaint avers that the Exchanges were aware of the "enormous concentration in Trans–Lux shares in [E & H] customer accounts" as early as January 1971; and it charges that between 1971 and 1974 E & H and appellees "intentionally, willfully and deliberately with scienter" failed to notify and "affirmatively concealed" from E & H's customers that E & H was accumulating a large and illiquid block of Trans–Lux stock in their accounts, that many of the accounts were under-margined because of the concentrations of Trans–Lux stock therein, that Trans–Lux was in violation of several Exchange Rules relating to margin collateral and supervision and suitability of customer purchases, and that the market price of Trans–Lux stock was being further depressed by E & H's efforts to liquidate its under-margined accounts in a block.

The district court granted appellant's motion for class certification but thereafter, by orders entered May 15 and December 18, 1981, granted appellees' motion for judgment on the pleadings and dismissed the complaint. Citing recent Supreme Court decisions, the court rejected Walck's arguments that §§ 6 and 7 of the Exchange Act and the Rules of the Exchanges implicitly authorize private damages actions. * * *

II.

The first question is whether an investor has an implied right of action for damages against a registered stock exchange under § 6 of the Exchange Act, based on the failure of the exchange to enforce its own rules. Because all relevant events concluded in 1974, we apply the statute as it then existed and not as amended in 1975. The central inquiry is whether Congress intended to create a private damages remedy by implication, "not one of whether this Court thinks that it can improve upon the statutory scheme that Congress enacted into law," and our primary tool for determining congressional intent is the four-factor test enunciated in *Cort v. Ash,* 422 U.S. 66.

A.

Section 6 provides for SEC registration of any securities exchange that complies with stated requirements, upon a finding that it "is so organized as to be able to comply with the provisions of this title and the rules and regulations thereunder and that the rules of the exchange are just and adequate to insure fair dealing and to protect investors." The exchange's rules must provide "for the expulsion, suspension, or disciplining of a member for conduct or proceeding inconsistent with just and equitable principles of trade," and it must agree "to comply, and to enforce so far as is within its powers compliance by its members, with the provisions of this title * * * and any rule or regulation * * * thereunder." Compliance with § 6 is mandated by § 5, which forbids securities transactions on an unregistered exchange.

Appellant contends that an investor injured by an exchange's violation of the registration requirements of § 6—more precisely, by the exchange's failure to enforce its own rules against an errant member broker—has an implied right of action under that section to recover his damages from the exchange. We turn to that contention.

B.

In *Cort v. Ash* the Court stated that "several factors are relevant" in determining whether Congress has created a private remedy by implication:

First, is the plaintiff "one of the class for whose *especial* benefit the statute was enacted,"—that is, does the statute create a federal right in favor of the plaintiff? Second, is there any indication of legislative intent, explicit or implicit, either to create such a remedy or to deny one? Third, is it consistent with the underlying purposes of the legislative scheme to imply such a remedy for the plaintiff? And finally, is the cause of action one traditionally relegated to state law, in an area basically the concern of the States, so that it would be inappropriate to infer a cause of action based solely on federal law?

* * *

1.

The first factor unambiguously supports appellant's position; there can be no doubt that § 6 was enacted for the "*especial* benefit" of investors. * * * This factor alone is insufficient to maintain the inference, however, no matter how clearly it favors the plaintiff. * * *

2.

Turning to the second factor, we look for evidence of "legislative intent, explicit or implicit, either to create such a remedy or to deny one." Both sides concede that the 1934 legislative history offers no express evidence of Congress' intent. Congress in 1934 did, however, expressly create private rights of action in §§ 9(e), 16(b), and 18 of the Exchange Act. "Obviously, then, when Congress wished to provide a private damages remedy, it knew how to do so and did so expressly." We do not treat this factor alone as conclusive, but we must recognize that the express provision of private remedies has been treated in numerous decisions as strong evidence of congressional intent not to create additional private remedies by implication.

3.

The third *Cort* factor is less clear, but we think it also weighs against the inference. We note preliminarily that although *Cort* inquired whether an implied remedy was "consistent with the underlying purposes of the statutory scheme," later decisions demonstrate that more than mere "consistency" is required to lend much support to an inference. * * *

Appellant advances the thesis that a private right of action against a stock exchange for failure to enforce its own rules is a necessary adjunct to SEC enforcement if the congressional objective of protecting investors is to be achieved. He points out that prior to 1975 the only sanctions available to the Commission to enforce § 6 were withdrawal or suspension for up to twelve months of an exchange's registration and expulsion or suspension of a member or officer of the exchange. These sanctions are so severe that they are not likely to be imposed in the absence of a serious default. Therefore, appellant suggests, SEC enforcement is inadequate and Congress' purposes will be undermined if we refuse to authorize injured investors to seek damages from the exchanges in the event of a lesser violation.

a.

The argument fails for two distinct but related reasons. First, the major premise of appellant's position, that the sanctions available to the SEC are so draconian as to be insufficient to serve the purposes of the legislation, was presented to and carefully examined by Congress itself during its extensive consideration of the 1975 Exchange Act amendments. The SEC in 1971 recommended to Congress that it be given authority to enforce a self-regulatory body's rules by proceeding directly against its members, arguing that "[t]he Commission's power to withdraw the registration of a stock exchange or of the NASD in the event that they do not enforce their rules is so extreme that it does not present a viable regulatory tool." Congress, however, was not persuaded by this argument. The Subcommittee on Securities, relying in part on an earlier SEC study, found the proposal unnecessary because "the Commission already ha[d] the power to accomplish much of what this new authority would allow" by virtue of its existing rule-making powers under the Act.

* * *

b.

An even more fundamental difficulty with appellant's position, however, is that he asks us to adopt too simplistic a reading of the legislative purposes. Certainly Congress sought to protect investors by enacting § 6; but it specifically declined to enact a comprehensive regulatory code or to authorize detailed governmental oversight of the workings of the exchanges. It instituted instead a system of exchange "self-regulation" subject to limited governmental oversight.

* * *

Congress deliberately chose self-regulation over governmental preemption to serve several important policies. In addition to the primary consideration that wide-scale government regulation would be expensive and ineffective, Congress found that "self-regulation has significant advantages in its own right."

* * *

The clear implication of the legislative history is that Congress has carefully studied and "balanced" the competing considerations and enacted the statutory schema that in its view would best serve its various goals of promoting transactional efficiency, fair dealing, and investor protection, and of limiting expensive and ineffective federal intervention. We cannot infer in the face of all this evidence that Congress nonetheless authorized by implication authority in the federal courts to intervene in the self-regulatory system at the instance of an injured investor and grant redress in the form of a monetary award against an exchange, conditioned on its failure to enforce its own rules, for the purpose of coercing or encouraging enforcement.

C.

We therefore conclude that application of the *Cort v. Ash* standards demonstrates a clear congressional intent not to create a private damages remedy in § 6. "[T]he inquiry ends there: The question whether Congress, either expressly or by implication, intended to create a private right of action, has been definitely answered in the negative."

III.

Appellant also argues, relying on Merrill Lynch, Pierce, Fenner & Smith, Inc. v. Curran, 102 S.Ct. 1825 (1982), that we should recognize in the 1975 Securities Acts Amendments an intent to preserve an implied remedy in § 6 previously recognized in "numerous court decisions." This argument fails for several reasons. First, as we have noted, all of the events underlying this action occurred prior to enactment of the 1975 Amendments, so that this case is controlled by the unamended statute. Although the 1975 debate is a matter of relevant historical fact and thus appropriate to our consideration of Congress' evaluation of SEC sanctions, we do not think it proper to find by reference to the actions of its 1975 successor that Congress in 1934 intended to create a remedy by implication.

Second, even if we held the "preservation" theory of *Curran* applicable to pre-amendment transactions such as these, this case lacks the factual predicate necessary for its application. In *Curran* the Court found that "the federal courts routinely and consistently had recognized an implied private cause of action" prior to the amendments in question, and therefore that the inference that the unamended statute authorized private actions was "a part of the 'contemporary legal context' in which Congress legislated." Here, however, notwithstanding appellant's assertion that "numerous court decisions" have recognized an implied remedy in § 6, his citations of authority and our own research have disclosed only one appellate decision prior to 1975 recognizing such a remedy. Baird v. Franklin, 141 F.2d 238 (2d Cir. 1944). Indeed, we have found only one other reported decision permitting a plaintiff to go to trial on a § 6 claim. Pettit v. American Stock Exchange, 217 F.Supp. 21 (S.D.N.Y.1963). Under these circumstances it would be inappropriate for us to say, as the Supreme Court said in *Curran,* that before 1975 "the consensus of opinion concerning the existence of a private cause of action under [§ 6] * * * was equally [as] uniform and well understood" as that concerning § 10(b) and Rule 10b–5.

Third, the Court in *Curran* relied on affirmative evidence, found in the legislative history of the pertinent amendments, that Congress was aware of and intended to preserve the implied remedy in question. Here, by contrast, appellant has not cited and we have not discovered any affirmative indication in the records of the extensive seven-year study and evaluation of the Exchange Act that led to the 1975 Amendments that Congress was even aware of—much less intended to preserve—the remedies inferred in the *Baird* and *Pettit* decisions.

Given the dearth of judicial authority and the absence of any evidence in the legislative history that Congress was even aware of the *Baird* and *Pettit* decisions, we cannot find that an implied right of action under § 6 was "a part of the 'contemporary legal context' in which Congress legislated" in 1975. Thus the inference that "Congress intended to preserve the preexisting remedy," even if it were applicable to pre-amendment transactions, would not be available in this case.

IV.

Appellant next contends that he has an implied right of action under the Exchanges' Rules themselves, without regard to § 6, arguing that Congress so intended. We reject this contention for the reasons stated in Part II. See also Jablon v. Dean Witter & Co., 614 F.2d 677, 679–81 (9th Cir.1980). In addition, appellant overlooks the reality that the Exchanges and not Congress promulgated the rules; and we perceive no basis for an inference that the Exchanges in their quasi-legislative capacity intended to subject themselves to damages for non-enforcement.

As the *Walck* decision indicates, the Supreme Court in MERRILL LYNCH v. CURRAN, 456 U.S. 353 (1982) recognized implied rights of action under the Commodity Exchange Act, including the right to sue a commodities exchange for a bad faith refusal to enforce its own rules. See also, e.g., Sam Wong v. New York Mercantile Exchange, 735 F.2d 653 (2d Cir.1984). In 1983 Congress codified the Commodity Exchange Act remedies that had been recognized in *Curran.* Thus, under § 22(b) there is now an explicit private right of action against commodities exchanges, their clearing agencies, and registered futures associations which in bad faith refuse to enforce their own rules. Liability also exists for enforcement of a rule in a manner that violates the Commodity Exchange Act or a CFTC rule. Does this Congressional action in amending the Commodity Exchange Act support or undermine the court's reasoning in *Walck?*

Selected References

Lashbrooke, Implying a Cause of Action for Damages: Rule Violations by Registered Exchanges and Associations, 48 U.Cin.L.Rev. 949–67 (1979).

Hoblin, A Stock Broker's Implied Liability to Its Customers for Violation of a Rule of a Registered Stock Exchange, 39 Fordham L.Rev. 253 (1970).

Wolfson & Russo, The Stock Exchange Member: Liability for Violation of Stock Exchange Rules, 58 Calif.L.Rev. 1120 (1970).

Comment, Exchange Liability Under § 6 of the Securities Exchange Act: The Eligible Plaintiff Problem, 78 Colum.L.Rev. 112 (1978).

Comment, Exchange Liability for Improper Enforcement of Its Constitution and Rules, 24 Emory L.J. 865 (1975).

---

2. *Antitrust and Due Process Limitations on SRO Actions*

As noted above, an SRO generally cannot be held civilly liable for failure to enforce its rules. However, it may be held civilly liable for action taken to enforce those rules, if a member or non-member injured by the action can show that the SRO lacked legal authority for the action it took.

Prior to the 1975 amendments, there was no statutory means of obtaining SEC or court review of an exchange disciplinary action (NASD disciplinary actions were subject to SEC review). The principal vehicle for attacking exchange actions in the courts, therefore, was federal antitrust law, particularly the prohibition in § 1 of the Sherman Act against "contracts, combinations or conspiracies in restraint of trade." The theory of such attacks was that, since an exchange is an association of competing broker-dealers, any action it takes which limits the ability of members to compete with one another, or the ability of non-members to compete with members, is a *per se* violation of the Sherman Act, unless the exchange is exempted from the antitrust laws by the provisions of the federal securities laws.

SILVER v. NYSE, 373 U.S. 341 (1963), involved an NYSE order to its members to terminate their wire connections with plaintiff, a broker-dealer who dealt solely in unlisted securities. The district court held that the NYSE action was a *per se* violation of the antitrust laws, since the NYSE had no statutory power to regulate trading in unlisted securities. The court of appeals reversed, holding that the NYSE had statutory power to regulate all transactions by its members, including their transactions in unlisted securities, and that since the NYSE action was "within the general scope of its authority" under the 1934 Act, that action was exempt from the antitrust laws. The Supreme Court rejected both extremes. It held that the NYSE did have statutory authority to regulate its members' transactions in unlisted securities, but that the 1934 Act did not automatically repeal the antitrust laws with respect to any action which the Exchange had authority to take. "Repeal is to be regarded as implied only if necessary to make the [Act] work, and even then only to the minimum extent necessary. This is the guiding principal to reconciliation of the [antitrust laws and securities laws]."

With respect to the specific situation before it, the Court said that since the SEC had no power to review Exchange disciplinary actions, there was "nothing built into the regulatory scheme which performs the antitrust function of insuring that an exchange will not in some cases apply its rules so as to do injury to competition which cannot be justified as furthering legitimate self-regulative ends." And since the NYSE had refused to tell the plaintiff the nature of the charges against him or afford him an opportunity to explain or refute them, the NYSE had no basis for justifying its action in that case as "necessary to make the Exchange Act work."

This "antitrust-due process" approach has been followed in a number of subsequent cases, see, e.g., Zuckerman v. Yount, 362 F.Supp. 858 (N.D. Ill.1973), and also held applicable to the NASD. Harwell v. Growth Programs, Inc., 451 F.2d 240 (5th Cir.1971) modified, 459 F.2d 461 (5th Cir.1972). However, the need to resort to antitrust law to attack SRO disciplinary actions is substantially lessened by § 19(d), added in 1975, which makes all SRO disciplinary actions reviewable by the SEC (and thus ultimately by the courts). In addition, an aggrieved party may go directly to court to challenge the validity of SRO action on constitutional or statutory grounds.

FIRST JERSEY SECURITIES v. BERGEN

605 F.2d 690 (3d Cir.1979).

Before ADAMS, ROSENN, and HIGGINBOTHAM, CIRCUIT JUDGES.

ROSENN, CIRCUIT JUDGE.

We are presented with a petition for a writ of mandamus, urging us to direct the district court to dismiss a suit for want of subject matter jurisdiction. The suit was filed in the United States District Court for the District of New Jersey, by First Jersey Securities, Inc., and some of its officers and personnel ("First Jersey"), seeking to enjoin the National Association of Securities Dealers, Inc., (NASD) and George J. Bergen, vice president of NASD and District Director for NASD District 12, from proceeding with a disciplinary hearing.

* * *

I. BACKGROUND

NASD is a securities association registered with the Securities and Exchange Commission pursuant to the provisions of the Maloney Act. The purpose of the voluntary association is to provide self-regulation of the over-the-counter securities market. * * * Furthermore, the statute gives the association the power to discipline its members who fail to conform to the standard of conduct established by the organization. "The Act also authorizes the SEC to exercise a significant oversight function over the rules and activities of the registered associations."

The NASD is headed by a Board of Governors. Its certificate of incorporation and by-laws divide the organization into thirteen geographical districts, each headed by a District Committee. The District Committee is required to appoint a District Business Conduct Committee, which assumes primary responsibility for enforcing the NASD rules.

In November 1977, NASD staff examiners began investigating First Jersey Securities, Inc., a New Jersey corporation. First Jersey, a registered member of NASD, has fourteen offices located in four states and Puerto Rico employing approximately 350 people. NASD claims that its investigators uncovered "a pattern of market domination and price manipulation used to perpetrate a massive fraud on First Jersey's public customers." On February 1, 1979, the Business Conduct Committee of District 12 began a disciplinary proceeding by issuing a complaint against First Jersey, Robert E. Brennan (its president), six branch managers, and the supervisor of the trading department. As of yet, no hearing has been held by the NASD on this matter.

On April 17, 1979, First Jersey filed suit in the United States District Court for the District of New Jersey against NASD and George Bergen. The complaint sought damages, declaratory relief, and an injunction enjoining NASD from proceeding further with its disciplinary action against First Jersey. It alleged that Bergen had a longstanding bias against Brennan and that he influenced and corrupted the entire Business Conduct Committee to hold a similar bias, the effect of which was to deny First Jersey's constitutional rights to a fair hearing before an impartial tribunal. The complaint further alleged that the NASD had violated or would violate the Administrative Procedure Act, the Maloney Act, and various internal rules, resulting in a gross abuse of power; that the Maloney Act is an unconstitutional delegation of legislative power to the NASD; and that Bergen had maliciously and willfully caused a deprivation of First Jersey's constitutional rights and interfered with its contractual and business relations. First Jersey moved, and was granted, leave to take early depositions pursuant to Fed.R.Civ.P. 30(a). The district court refused a subsequent request by NASD for a stay of discovery.

First Jersey requested a preliminary injunction, and at the same time, NASD moved for dismissal of the suit. On June 4, 1978, the district judge delivered an oral opinion denying both motions without prejudice. During the pendency of these motions, two developments occurred. First, the SEC instituted its own independent proceeding by issuing a complaint against First Jersey. Second, NASD decided to transfer its proceedings to District 8 headquarters in Chicago in order to vitiate the accusations of bias.

* * *

a. Unconstitutional Delegation

First Jersey claims that the Maloney Act is an unconstitutional delegation of legislative power to a private institution. In Todd & Co. v. SEC, 557 F.2d 1008 (3d Cir.1977), we found no merit to this argument, because the SEC

> (1) has the power, according to reasonably fixed statutory standards, to approve or disapprove the Association's rules; (2) must make *de novo* findings aided by additional evidence if necessary, and (3) must make an independent decision on the violation and penalty * * *.

First Jersey points out, however, that the statute was amended in 1975 and the *Todd* court specifically refused to rule on the constitutionality of the amendment. Prior to 1975, the review provision of the statute called for the SEC to render its decision "upon consideration of the record before the association and such other evidence as it may deem relevant * * *." The statute now provides that the SEC hearing "may consist solely of consideration of the record before the self-regulatory organization and opportunity for the presentation of supporting reasons to affirm, modify, or set aside the sanction * * *." We need not now decide whether this statutory change effects a significant alteration in the SEC's power to review NASD disciplinary proceedings. It suffices to say that to the extent the amendment restricts the SEC's ability to receive additional evidence not presented below, this does not alter our conclusion in *Todd* that there is no unconstitutional delegation of legislative authority.

b. Bias

The major thrust of First Jersey's contentions of unconstitutionality deal with the alleged bias of NASD and its inability to conduct a fair hearing before an impartial tribunal. This attack is carried at two levels: 1) because the Business Conduct Committee is composed of members of the industry, any panel of judges, as competitors of First Jersey, will have a personal pecuniary interest in seeing sanctions imposed against First Jersey; and 2) specific allegations portray Bergen's and the NASD staff's long-standing bias against Brennan and First Jersey.

(1.) Structural Bias

The first, which amounts to an allegation of structural bias and was expounded for the first time in a supplemental brief requested by the Court at oral argument, relies primarily on the Supreme Court decision in Gibson v. Berryhill, 411 U.S. 564 (1973). In *Gibson,* the Alabama Board of Optometry intended to revoke the licenses which were required to practice of all optometrists employed by corporations, a group comprising about one-half of all the optometrists in the state. Members of the Board were drawn exclusively from the Alabama Optometric Association, whose membership was limited to independent practitioners. The district court found that the Board members, along with other private practitioners of optometry, would fall heir to the corporate practices if the licenses were revoked. The Supreme Court affirmed the district court's conclusion that this amounted to a deprivation of due process, holding that "those with substantial pecuniary interest in legal proceedings should not adjudicate these disputes."

Reliance on *Gibson* cannot provide First Jersey with a clear and unambiguous constitutional violation in this case. We believe that the NASD system of self-regulation is sufficiently dissimilar in crucial respects from the Alabama Board of Optometry's method of regulation to render the former constitutionally sound. NASD is a voluntary association, not a state agency. Unlike the Alabama Board of Optometry, NASD approval is not required to practice the trade. Neither NASD nor the industry it regulates is divided into factions or identifiable groups in a manner comparable to the independent practitioners versus the optometrists employed by corporations in *Gibson.* Neither First Jersey nor firms like it are excluded from membership in the association and, unlike the optometrists in Alabama, they were not denied participation in the governance of their own profession. In Wall v. American Optometric Association, 379 F.Supp. 175, 189 (N.D.Ga.), aff'd, 419 U.S. 888 (1974), the court pointed out that "[e]very member of the tribunal is a member of a group which opposes the continuation of the plaintiffs' businesses." That division is not present here.

Furthermore, the NASD hearing has been transferred to District 8, meaning that members of the panel will be drawn from the Chicago area. First Jersey does not have any offices in that area, but if it believed that one or more members of the panel were direct competitors with a personal interest in the outcome, it could file a motion to have those members disqualified through the administrative process. In addition, the basis for the disciplinary proceeding is not a status violation, similar to *Gibson* or *Wall,* which could lead to the demise of a substantial block of the industry; it stems instead from specific allegations of misconduct applicable only to First Jersey.

Finally, to uphold First Jersey's contention would destroy the valuable congressional scheme for self-regulation in the securities area and the destruction could very well extend to other areas employing intramural controls. The Maloney Act expresses Congress's thoughtful view that self-regulation is the best "first-line" defense against unethical or illegal securities practices. It allows the industry to set its own standards of proper conduct and permits their members to discipline themselves applying their own expertise and experience.

Although Congress preferred self-regulation by a private body over direct involvement of a governmental agency, it established safeguards to prevent abuse of the system. The Maloney Act requires specific procedural protections, some of which are drafted by the association. For example, the NASD Code of Procedure, unlike the proceedings before the Alabama Optometric Board in *Gibson,* requires the disqualification of any panel member who may have a personal interest in the outcome of the case. Further insurance against abuse is provided by the supervisory role of the SEC. The SEC is required to approve all the NASD rules and regulations, including those concerning discipline of NASD members. This oversight function also encompasses review of specific cases imposing sanctions. We believe that the intrinsic benefits of a system of self-regulation, insulated with extensive procedural and substantive protections and subject to judicial review, renders insignificant objections of bias to the system which inherently involves disciplining by potential competitors. We therefore reject First Jersey's contention that the NASD scheme for self-regulation is unconstitutional.

(2.) Specific Bias

The second prong of First Jersey's assault for bias against NASD deals with specific allegations of animosity on the part of Bergen and the NASD against First Jersey. The evidence of bias recited in First

Jersey's complaint includes among other things the allegations that Bergen has said that he is out to "get Brennan," that he has called Brennan "slippery," that he has "personally devote[d] his full concentration and energies to First Jersey and Brennan," that NASD agents have referred to Brennan as a crook and have threatened uncooperative witnesses with reprisals. Regardless of the merit of First Jersey's claim, we hold that absent a showing of irreparable harm, allegations of personal bias are insufficient to excuse a plaintiff from the requirements of the exhaustion doctrine.

In SCHULTZ v. SEC, 614 F.2d 561 (7th Cir.1980), the court held that a securities exchange is not an "authority of the government" and that its procedures are therefore not subject to the provisions of the Administrative Procedure Act which prohibit commingling of prosecutorial and adjudicatory functions.

The more significant question raised by the Supreme Court decision in *Silver,* p. 991 above, was whether the antitrust laws applied to exchange *rules* which operated to restrict competition, particularly the exchange rules which required members to charge fixed minimum rates of commission on all transactions. This situation was distinguishable from *Silver,* since the SEC had explicit statutory power to order changes in exchange rules governing commission rates.

GORDON v. NEW YORK STOCK EXCHANGE, INC.

422 U.S. 659 (1975).

MR. JUSTICE BLACKMUN delivered the opinion of the Court.

This case presents the problem of reconciliation of the antitrust laws with a federal regulatory scheme in the particular context of the practice of the securities exchanges and their members of using fixed rates of commission. The United States District Court for the Southern District of New York and the United States Court of Appeals for the Second Circuit concluded that fixed commission rates were immunized from antitrust attack because of the Securities and Exchange Commission's authority to approve or disapprove exchange commission rates and its exercise of that power.

I

In early 1971 petitioner Richard A. Gordon, individually and on behalf of an asserted class of small investors, filed this suit against the New York Stock Exchange, Inc. (NYSE), the American Stock Exchange, Inc. (Amex), and two member firms of the exchanges. The complaint challenged a variety of exchange rules and practices and, in particular, claimed that the system of fixed commission rates, utilized by the exchanges at that time for transactions less than $500,000, violated §§ 1 and 2 of the Sherman Act. * * *

Respondents moved for summary judgment on the ground that the challenged actions were subject to the overriding supervision of the Securities and Exchange Commission (SEC) under § 19(b) of the Securities Exchange Act of 1934, and, therefore, were not subject to the strictures of the antitrust laws. The District Court granted respondents' motion as to all claims. 366 F.Supp. 1261 (1973). * * *

On appeal, the Second Circuit affirmed. 498 F.2d 1303 (1974). * * *

II

* * *

Commission rates for transactions on the stock exchanges have been set by agreement since the establishment of the first exchange in this country. The New York Stock Exchange was formed with the Buttonwood Tree Agreement of 1792, and from the beginning minimum fees were set and observed by the members. That Agreement itself stated:

> "We the Subscribers, Brokers for the Purchase and Sale of Public Stock, do hereby solemnly promise and pledge ourselves to each other, that we will not buy or sell from this day for any person whatsoever, any kind of Public Stock at a less rate than one-quarter percent. Commission on the Specie value, and that we will give a preference to each other in our Negotiations." F. Eames, The New York Stock Exchange 14 (1968 ed.).

* * *

These fixed rate policies were not unnoticed by responsible congressional bodies. For example, the House Committee on Banking and Currency, in a general review of the stock exchanges undertaken in 1913, reported that the fixed commission rate rules were "rigidly enforced" in order "to prevent competition amongst the members."[5] The report, known as the Pujo Report, did not recommend any change in this policy, for the Committee believed

> "the present rates to be reasonable, except as to stocks, say, of $25 or less in value, and that the exchange should be protected in this respect

5. See, for example, the comments of the Report in reviewing evidence on fixed commissions:

> "As stated by Mr. Sturgis, a former president of the exchange, since 1876 a governor, and now the chairman of the law committee * * *:
>
> " 'The violation of the commission law we regard as one of the most infamous crimes that a man can commit against his fellow members in the exchange, and as a gross breach of good faith and wrongdoing of the most serious nature, and we consider it a crime that we should punish as severely as, in the judgment of the governing committee, the constitution permits.
>
> * * *
>
> " 'Q. * * * But the reach of that rule (referring to the rule for uniform commissions) by a broker you consider the most heinous crime he can commit?
>
> " 'A. It is absolute bad faith to his fellow men.'
>
> "The rule is rigidly enforced by suspension from one to five years for a first violation and expulsion for a second. * * * The acknowledged object is to prevent competition amongst the members."

H.R.Rep. No. 1593, 62d Cong., 3d Sess., 39 (1913).

by the law under which it shall be incorporated against a kind of competition between members that would lower the service and threaten the responsibility of members. A very low or competitive commission rate would also promote speculation and destroy the value of membership."

Despite the monopoly power of the few exchanges, exhibited not only in the area of commission rates but in a wide variety of other aspects, the exchanges remained essentially self-regulating and without significant supervision until the adoption of the Securities Exchange Act of 1934. At the lengthy hearings before adoption of that Act, some attention was given to the fixed commission rate practice and to its anticompetitive features.

Perhaps the most pertinent testimony in the hearings preparatory to enactment of the Exchange Act was proffered by Samuel Untermyer, formerly Chief Counsel to the committee that drafted the Pujo Report. In commenting on proposed S. 2693, Mr. Untermyer noted that although the bill would provide the federal supervisory commission with

> "the right to prescribe uniform rates of commission, it does not otherwise authorize the Commission to fix rates, which it seems to me it should do and would do by striking out the word 'uniform.' That would permit the Commission to fix rates.
>
> "The volume of the business transacted on the exchange has increased manyfold. Great fortunes have been made by brokers through this monopoly. The public has no access to the exchange by way of membership except by buying a seat and paying a very large sum for it. Therefore it is a monopoly. Probably it has to be something of a monopoly. But after all it is essentially a public institution. It is the greatest financial agency in the world, and should be not only controlled by the public but it seems to me its membership and the commissions charged should either be fixed by some governmental authority or be supervised by such authority. As matters now stand, the exchange can charge all that the traffic will bear, and that is a burden upon commerce."

As finally enacted, the Exchange Act apparently reflected the Untermyer suggestion, for it gave the SEC the power to fix and insure "reasonable" rates. Section 19(b) provided:

> "(b) *The Commission is further authorized, if* after making appropriate request in writing to a national securities exchange that such exchange effect on its own behalf specified changes in its rules and practices, and after appropriate notice and opportunity for hearing, *the Commission determines* that such exchange has not made the changes so requested, and that *such changes are necessary or appropriate for the protection of investors or to insure fair dealing in securities traded in* upon such exchange or to insure fair administration of such exchange, by rules or regulations or by order *to alter or supplement the rules of such exchange* (insofar as necessary or appropriate to effect such changes) *in respect of such matters as * * ** (9) *the fixing of reasona-*

ble rates of commission, interest, listing, and other charges." (Emphasis added.)

This provision conformed to the Act's general policy of self-regulation by the exchanges coupled with oversight by the SEC. The congressional reports confirm that while the development of rules for the governing of exchanges, as enumerated in § 19(b), was left to the exchanges themselves in the first instance, the SEC could compel adoption of those changes it felt were necessary to insure fair dealing and protection of the public.

III

With this legislative history in mind, we turn to the actual post-1934 experience of commission rates on the NYSE and Amex. * * *

This lengthy history can be summarized briefly: In enacting the Securities Exchange Act of 1934, the Congress gave clear authority to the SEC to supervise exchange self-regulation with respect to the "fixing of reasonable rates of commission." Upon SEC determination that exchange rules or practices regarding commission rates required change in order to protect investors or to insure fair dealing, the SEC was authorized to require adoption of such changes as were deemed necessary or appropriate. This legislative permission for the fixing of commission rates under the supervision of the SEC occurred seven years *after* this Court's decision in United States v. Trenton Potteries Co., 273 U.S. 392 (1927), to the effect that price fixing was a *per se* violation of the Sherman Act. Since the Exchange Act's adoption, and primarily in the last 15 years, the SEC has been engaged in thorough review of exchange commission rate practices. The committees of the Congress, while recently expressing some dissatisfaction with the progress of the SEC in implementing competitive rates, have generally been content to allow the SEC to proceed without new legislation. As of May 1, 1975, the SEC, by order, has abolished fixed rates. And new legislation, enacted into law June 5, 1975, codifies this result, although still permitting the SEC some discretion to reimpose fixed rates if warranted.

IV

This Court has considered the issue of implied repeal of the antitrust laws in the context of a variety of regulatory schemes and procedures. Certain axioms of construction are now clearly established. Repeal of the antitrust laws by implication is not favored and not casually to be allowed. Only where there is a "plain repugnancy between the antitrust and regulatory provisions" will repeal be implied. * * *

The starting point for our consideration of the particular issue presented by this case, *viz,* whether the antitrust laws are impliedly repealed or replaced as a result of the statutory provisions and administrative and congressional experience concerning fixed commission rates, of course, is our decision in *Silver.* * * *

In *Silver,* the Court concluded that there was no implied repeal of the antitrust laws in that factual context because the Exchange Act did not provide for SEC jurisdiction or review of particular applications of rules enacted by the exchanges. * * *

* * * The Court in *Silver,* cautioned, however, that "[s]hould review of exchange self-regulation be provided through a vehicle other than the antitrust laws, a different case as to antitrust exemption would be presented."

It is patent that the case presently at bar is, indeed, that "different case" to which the Court in *Silver* referred. In contrast to the circumstances of *Silver,* § 19(b) gave the SEC direct regulatory power over exchange rules and practices with respect to "the fixing of reasonable rates of commission." Not only was the SEC authorized to disapprove rules and practices concerning commission rates, but the agency also was permitted to require alteration or supplementation of the rules and practices when "necessary or appropriate for the protection of investors or to insure fair dealings in securities traded in upon such exchange." Since 1934 all rate changes have been brought to the attention of the SEC, and it has taken an active role in review of proposed rate changes during the last 15 years. Thus, rather than presenting a case of SEC impotence to affect application of exchange rules in particular circumstances, this case involves explicit statutory authorization for SEC review of all exchange rules and practices dealing with rates of commission and resultant SEC continuing activity.

Having determined that this case is, in fact, the "different case," we must then make inquiry as to the proper reconciliation of the regulatory and antitrust statutes involved here, keeping in mind the principle that repeal of the antitrust laws will be "implied only if necessary to make the Securities Exchange Act work, and even then only to the minimum extent necessary." We hold that these requirements for implied repeal are clearly satisfied here. To permit operation of the antitrust laws with respect to commission rates, as urged by petitioner Gordon and the United States as *amicus curiae,* would unduly interfere, in our view, with the operation of the Securities Exchange Act.

As a threshold matter, we believe that the determination of whether implied repeal of the antitrust laws is necessary to make the Exchange Act provisions work is a matter for the courts, and in particular for the courts in which the antitrust claims are raised. *Silver* exemplifies this responsibility. In some cases, however, the courts may defer to the regulatory agency involved, in order to take advantage of its special expertise. The decision in the end, however, is for the courts. Ricci v. Chicago Mercantile Exchange, 409 U.S. 289 (1973).

* * *

The United States appears to suggest that only if there is a pervasive regulatory scheme, as in the public utility area, can it be concluded that the regulatory scheme ousts the antitrust laws. It is true that in some prior cases we have been concerned with the question of the pervasiveness of the regulatory scheme as a factor in determining whether there is an implied repeal of the antitrust laws. In the present case, however, respondents do not claim that repeal should be implied because of a pervasive regulatory scheme, but because of the specific provision of § 19(b)(9) and the regulatory action thereunder. Hence, whether the Exchange Act amounts to pervasive legislation ousting the antitrust acts is not a question before us.

We agree with the District Court and the Court of Appeals, and with respondents, that to deny antitrust immunity with respect to commission rates would be to subject the exchanges and their members to conflicting standards. It is clear from our discussion in Part III, supra, that the commission rate practices of the exchanges have been subjected to the scrutiny and approval of the SEC. If antitrust courts were to impose different standards or requirements, the exchanges might find themselves unable to proceed without violation of the mandate of the courts or of the SEC. Such different standards are likely to result because the sole aim of antitrust legislation is to protect competition, whereas the SEC must consider, in addition, the economic health of the investors, the exchanges, and the securities industry. Given the expertise of the SEC, the confidence the Congress has placed in the agency, and the active roles the SEC and the Congress have taken, permitting courts throughout the country to conduct their own antitrust proceedings would conflict with the regulatory scheme authorized by Congress rather than supplement that scheme.

* * *

In sum, the statutory provision authorizing regulation, § 19(b)(9), the long regulatory practice, and the continued congressional approval illustrated by the new legislation, point to one, and only one, conclusion. The Securities Exchange Act was intended by the Congress to leave the supervision of the fixing of reasonable rates of commission to the SEC. Interposition of the antitrust laws, which would bar fixed commission rates as per se violations of the Sherman Act, in the face of positive SEC action, would preclude and prevent the operation of the Exchange Act as intended by Congress and as effectuated through SEC regulatory activity. Implied repeal of the antitrust laws is, in fact, necessary to make the Exchange Act work as it was intended; failure to imply repeal would render nugatory the legislative provision for regulatory agency supervision of exchange commission rates.

Affirmed.

MR. JUSTICE DOUGLAS, concurring.

The Court relies upon three factors—statutory authorization for regulation by the Securities and Exchange Commission (SEC), a long history of actual SEC oversight and approval, and continued congressional affirmation of the SEC's role—in holding that the system of fixed commission rates employed on the securities exchanges is immune from antitrust attack. While I join that opinion, I write separately to emphasize the single factor which, for me, is of prime importance.

The mere existence of a statutory power of review by the SEC over fixed commission rates cannot justify immunizing those rates from antitrust challenges. The antitrust laws are designed to safeguard a strong public interest in free and open competition, and immunity from those laws should properly be implied only when some equivalent mechanism is functioning to protect that public interest. Only if the SEC is actively and aggressively exercising its powers of review and approval can we be sure that fixed commission rates are being monitored in the manner which Congress intended.

The Court reviews at length the history of the SEC's involvement with fixed commission rates. In light of that history, I am satisfied to join the opinion of the Court and affirm the judgment below.

MR. JUSTICE STEWART, with whom MR. JUSTICE BRENNAN, joins, concurring.

While joining the opinion of the Court, I add a brief word. The Court has never held, and does not hold today, that the antitrust laws are inapplicable to anticompetitive conduct simply because a federal agency has jurisdiction over the activities of one or more of the defendants. An implied repeal of the antitrust laws may be found only if there exists a "plain repugnancy between the antitrust and regulatory provisions."

* * *

As the Court's opinion explains, when Congress enacted the Securities Exchange Act of 1934, it was fully aware of the well-established exchange practice of fixing commission rates, which had existed continuously since 1792. Nevertheless, Congress chose not to prohibit that practice. Instead, in § 19(b)(9) of the 1934 Act, Congress specifically empowered the Commission to exercise direct supervisory authority over exchange rules respecting "the fixing of reasonable rates of commission." Congress thereby unmistakably determined that, until such time as the Commission ruled to the contrary, exchange rules fixing minimum commission rates would further the policies of the 1934 Act. Accordingly, although the Act contains no express exemption from the antitrust laws for exchange rules establishing fixed commission rates, under *Silver* that particular instance of exchange self-regulation is immune from antitrust attack.

As the Supreme Court notes in *Gordon,* there were two other major developments in 1975. First, the SEC ordered the end of fixed rates, effective May 1, thus eliminating the specific practice attacked in *Gordon.* Second, Congress amended the 1934 Act to confirm the SEC's elimination of fixed rates. The 1975 legislation contains two other relevant provisions. It makes all exchange disciplinary actions subject to review by the SEC, on its own motion or on the application of a person aggrieved by the action. § 19(d). And it provides that the SEC shall not approve any exchange rules or rule changes that "impose any burden on competition not necessary or appropriate in furtherance of the purposes of" the Act. §§ 6(b)(8), 19(b)(2). These provisions should reduce the incidence of resort to the antitrust laws and the courts to protest a lack of "due process" (as in *Silver*) or unwarranted economic restraints (as in *Gordon*).

The antitrust attack on fixed stock exchange commission rates has also raised questions about the validity of the arrangements in firm-commitment underwritings binding each underwriter to offer and sell the securities to the public at a fixed price, less a specified discount [a] to selected dealers. In May 1979, the SEC announced a public hearing on proposed revisions in the NASD rules on this subject: [b]

> The growth of institutional participation in the securities markets has exerted increasing pressure on the fixed price offering system. In connection with distributions, a number of practices have developed which may have the economic effect of granting to institutional and other large purchasers a rebate of some portion of the gross spread in fixed price offerings. Such practices include both direct discounting techniques, such as "over-trading" in swap transactions and certain types of underwriting fee recapture, and indirect compensation arrangements, such as the provision of goods and services in return for so-called "syndicate soft dollars."
>
> In swap transactions, securities are taken in trade from a customer, in lieu of cash, in exchange for the offered securities. A discount from the fixed offering price may be granted to the purchaser of the offered securities where the syndicate member purchases the securities taken in trade at a price exceeding their market value. This "over-trade" is economically equivalent to paying less than the stated offering price for the securities being distributed.
>
> A customer may seek to recapture underwriting fees by designating a broker-dealer affiliate to be included in the selling group. The customer may then purchase the offered security through its affiliate, thereby recapturing the selling concession. Such concession payments to an affiliate enable the customer to obtain direct discounts from the fixed offering price.
>
> A broker-dealer providing research or other services to a customer may be compensated for those services, at least in part, through purchases by the customer in a fixed price offering. The customer can either purchase the securities directly through the broker-dealer or can contact the managing underwriter and "designate" the dealer to receive credit for the order. In these instances, the dealer is compensated indirectly by receiving "soft dollar" concessions for the research or other services it has provided.

a. See pp. 25–29 above.

b. Sec.Ex.Act Rel. No. 15807 (May 9, 1979).

Since the registration of the NASD in 1939 pursuant to the Maloney Act, the NASD has regulated, particularly under Article III, Section 24 of its Rules of Fair Practice, the circumstances in which concessions, discounts or other allowances may be given in fixed price offerings. Section 24, which until filing of the proposed rule change had not been the subject of revision during the 40 years of its existence, provides that:

> [s]elling concessions, discounts, or other allowances, as such, shall be allowed only as consideration for services rendered in distribution and in no event shall be allowed to anyone other than a broker or dealer actually engaged in the investment banking or securities business; provided, however, that nothing in this rule shall prevent any member from selling any security owned by him to any person at any net price which may be fixed by him unless prevented therefrom by agreement.

During this period, Section 24 has received little interpretive attention from the courts or the Commission. In 1941, the NASD imposed sanctions on several member firms that violated the terms of a fixed price underwriting agreement by selling debt securities of Public Service Company of Indiana during the distribution at prices below the public offering price. The NASD charged those members with a violation of Article III, Section 1 of its Rules of Fair Practice, which requires members to "observe high standards of commercial honor and just and equitable principles of trade." In reviewing those sanctions, the Commission held, in *National Association of Securities Dealers, Inc. ("PSI")*,[12] that Section 15A(b)(7) of the Act did not permit the NASD to use its disciplinary authority to enforce contracts "designed to restrict a free and open market, even though such contracts may under given conditions fall within an exception to the general public policy against restraints on commerce." [14] In *PSI*, the Commission rejected the NASD's argument that Section 24 supported its interpretation of Article III, Section 1, but noted that the meaning and validity of Section 24 were not directly at issue.[15]

The Commission, however, also expressly rejected any implication that, by invalidating the NASD's rule interpretation, it would similarly seek as a general matter to invalidate or otherwise question the private enforceability of customary underwriting agreements to make fixed price offerings. To the contrary, the Commission in *PSI* concluded:

> Thus, if in this case we were faced with the question whether we should or should not prohibit the use of the price-maintenance provisions in question, we would reach the same conclusion that we did with respect to stabilization, i.e., that we should not prohibit such provisions. * * *

12. 19 SEC 424 (1954).

14. 19 SEC at 444. The Commission's conclusion, in *dictum*, that agreements among underwriters to fix the price at which an offering is to be distributed do not generally violate the Sherman Act, 15 U.S.C. 1, was later judicially confirmed in U.S. v. Morgan, 118 F.Supp. 621 (S.D.N.Y. 1953).

15. 19 SEC at 445–446.

Neither the Commission nor the courts has been called upon to deal directly with the proper interpretation and general applicability of Section 24, until recently. A number of cases in the last few years have considered the recapture of commissions by investment companies in a variety of contexts. One of these cases, Papilsky v. Berndt ("*Papilsky*"),[18] dealt directly with the recapture of underwriting discounts. In *Papilsky,* a shareholder derivative action was brought against an investment company and its adviser/underwriter for failure to seek such recapture. The court concluded that, in the absence of a contrary ruling from the Commission or the NASD, underwriting recapture was available and legal under Section 24.

As a result of the *Papilsky* decision, several requests were made to the NASD on behalf of investment advisers and investment companies for a ruling on the propriety of recapture under Section 24. The NASD responded to these requests, in November and December 1976, by stating that, in its opinion, Section 24 prohibits underwriting recapture. The Commission, however, wrote to the NASD, in February 1977, stating that the NASD "interpretation" of Section 24 raised important issues of general applicability with regard to the public interest, the protection of investors and the appropriateness of burdens on competition, and that prior Commission decisions, including *PSI,* cast doubt on the NASD authority to adopt a rule having the effect the NASD interpretation would give to Section 24. For those reasons, the Commission stated that the NASD interpretation should be filed as a proposed rule change. After a public meeting with the Commission on May 26, 1977, the NASD agreed to prepare and file the proposed rule change. In July 1978, the NASD made the Papilsky filing following circulation of two exposure drafts to its membership. Pursuant to Section 19(b) of the Act, the proposed rule change cannot become effective unless approved by the Commission after affirmatively finding that it is consistent with the requirements of the Act and Commission rules thereunder applicable to the NASD.

The NASD's proposed rule changes in effect reaffirmed the ban on discounts in fixed price offerings, and specified the kinds of reciprocal arrangements that would violate the rule.

As might be predicted, the Antitrust Division of the Justice Department opposed the rule change, arguing that the appearance of discounting or rebating indicated that the amount of compensation set by the underwriters may often be excessive, and that the rule changes "may be aptly characterized as an effort to compel adherence * * * by regulatory coercion" to agreements which the underwriters would otherwise be unable to enforce.[c]

Equally predictably, the Securities Industry Association challenged the Antitrust Division's approach, arguing that it "displays little knowledge of the workings of underwritten public offerings" and "fails to

18. Papilsky v. Berndt, CCH Fed.Sec.L. Rep. ¶ 95,627 (S.D.N.Y.1976). [See Loomis, Paulette Papilsky's Deadly Threat to Wall Street, Fortune, Apr. 23, 1979, p. 90—Ed.]

c. See BNA Sec.Reg. & L.Rep. No. 489, at A-13 (Feb. 7, 1979).

appreciate the vital part that the syndicate system and limited price maintenance play in this nation's capital-raising process." [d]

After a year of hearings, the SEC approved the rule changes, which continue to sanction fixed-price offerings and purport to restrict underwriters from using portions of the underwriting discount to reward dealers and others for unrelated services. Sec.Ex.Act Rel. No. 17371 (Dec. 12, 1980).

Selected References

Karmel, Securities Industry Self–Regulation Tested by the Crash, 45 Wash. & Lee L.Rev. 1297 (1988).

Linden, A Reconciliation of Antitrust Law with Securities Regulation: The Judicial Approach, 45 G.W.L.Rev. 179 (1977).

Mazo, Antitrust Courts Versus the SEC: A Functional Allocation of Decisionmaking Roles, 12 Harv.J.Legis. 63 (1974).

Pozen, Competition and Regulation in the Stock Markets, 73 Mich.L.Rev. 317 (1974).

Smythe, Government Supervised Self–Regulation in the Securities Industries and the Antitrust Laws: Suggestions for an Accommodation, 62 N.C.L.Rev. 475 (1984).

---

d. Id. No. 494, at A–2 (Mar. 14, 1979).

CHAPTER 13

INTER-INDUSTRY COMPETITION

As indicated in the Introduction, the financial services industry is presently experiencing an unprecedented degree of competition between entities which had previously limited themselves to more closely-defined areas of activity. The players in the field include banks, thrift institutions, insurance companies and securities firms, but companies from other specialties are also getting into the act. An indication of the interpenetration of markets is that four of the leading competitors are Citicorp (banking), Merrill Lynch (securities), Sears (retailing) and American Express (credit cards and travelers' checks).

At the same time, the financial markets have been further fragmented by the development of an active market in "futures" on debt and equity instruments, conducted on commodity exchanges rather than stock exchanges. In addition, the securities markets are becoming increasingly multinational, with firms conducting both their trading activities and public offerings in a number of different countries simultaneously. The regulatory and policy problems posed by these developments are the subject matter of this chapter.

A. SECURITIES FIRMS AND BANKS

While securities firms compete with a number of different types of entities, their competition with banks has been an especially contentious area, because of the arbitrary separation of their activities imposed by Congress when it passed the Glass–Steagall Act in 1933. That Act bars banks from underwriting or dealing in securities, and bars securities firms from making loans and accepting deposits. While efforts are continually being made to persuade Congress to redraw the lines to better reflect current conditions, Congress has so far not acted. As a result, there is continuous litigation to define the boundaries of permissible activities. The following decisions handed down by the U.S. Supreme Court in 1984 give an idea of the manner in which the issues are currently being resolved.

SECURITIES INDUSTRY ASS'N v. BOARD OF GOVERNORS

468 U.S. 137 (1984).

JUSTICE BLACKMUN delivered the opinion of the Court.

This case involves a challenge to the efforts of a state commercial bank to enter the business of selling third-party commercial paper. The Board of Governors of the Federal Reserve System (Board) concluded that such activity by state member banks is not prohibited by the Banking Act of 1933 (Act), ch. 89, 48 Stat. 162 (commonly known as the Glass–Steagall Act) because commercial paper is neither a "security" nor a "note" within the meaning of that Act and therefore falls outside the Act's proscriptions. The District Court disagreed with the Board, but the Court of Appeals deferred to the Board's interpretation and reversed the judgment of the District Court. Because commercial paper falls within the plain language of the Act, and because the inclusion of commercial paper within the terms of the Act is fully consistent with the Act's purposes, we conclude that commercial paper is a "security" under the Glass–Steagall Act, and we reverse the judgment of the Court of Appeals.

I

During 1978 Bankers Trust Company (Bankers Trust), a New York-chartered member bank of the Federal Reserve System, began serving as agent for several of its corporate customers in placing their commercial paper [1] in the commercial-paper market. Petitioners, the Securities Industry Association (SIA), a national securities-industry trade association, and A.G. Becker, Inc. (Becker), a dealer in commercial paper, informally expressed concern to the Board about Bankers Trust's commercial-paper activities. SIA and Becker subsequently petitioned the Board for, among other things, a ruling that Bankers Trust's activities are unlawful under §§ 16 and 21 of the Act, 12 U.S.C. §§ 24 Seventh and 378(a)(1). Section 16 prohibits commercial banks from underwriting "stocks and securities," while § 21 prohibits them from marketing "stocks, bonds, debentures, notes, or other securities." Petitioners asserted that Bankers Trust's activities violated both §§ 16 and 21.

On September 26, 1980, the Board responded to petitioners' request for enforcement of §§ 16 and 21 against Bankers Trust. See Federal Reserve System, Statement Regarding Petitions to Initiate Enforcement Action (1980), App. 122A (Board Statement). The Board acknowledged that Congress enacted the Act to prevent commercial banks from

1. "Commercial paper" refers generally to unsecured, short-term promissory notes issued by commercial entities. Such a note is payable to the bearer on a stated maturity date. Maturities vary considerably, but typically are less than nine months. See generally, Hurley, The Commercial Paper Market, Fed.Res.Bull. 525 (1977); Comment, The Commercial Paper Market and the Securities Acts, 39 U.Chi.L.Rev. 362, 363–364 (1972).

engaging in certain investment-banking activities, but explained that Congress did not intend the Act's prohibitions to cover every instrument that could be characterized as a "note" or "security." The Board expressed concern that such a broad interpretation might preclude commercial banks from maintaining many of their traditional activities. Accordingly, the Board took the position that "if a particular kind of financial instrument evidences a transaction that is more functionally similar to a traditional commercial banking operation than to an investment transaction, then fidelity to the purposes of the Act would dictate that the instrument should not be viewed as a security." Applying this "functional analysis" to commercial paper, the Board concluded that such paper more closely resembles a commercial bank loan than an investment transaction and that it is not a "security" for purposes of the Glass–Steagall Act. Because of this determination, the Board did not consider whether Bankers Trust's involvement with commercial paper constitutes "underwriting," within the meaning of the Act.

Petitioners challenged the Board's ruling in the United States District Court for the District of Columbia under, *inter alia,* the judicial-review provisions of the Administrative Procedure Act, claiming that the ruling was contrary to law. The District Court reversed the ruling, finding that commercial paper falls within the scope of § 21's reference to "notes * * * or other securities." * * *

The United States Court of Appeals for the District of Columbia Circuit, by a divided vote, reversed the judgment of the District Court. The Court of Appeals' majority acknowledged that § 21's reference to "notes" was broad enough to include commercial paper, which is a promissory note. The court explained, however, that the term "note" was also susceptible of a narrower reading, limited to long-term debt securities closely resembling a bond or debenture but of shorter maturity. * * *

Because of the importance of the issue for the Nation's financial markets, we granted certiorari.

II

The Board is the agency responsible for federal regulation of the national banking system, and its interpretation of a federal banking statute is entitled to substantial deference. * * * We also have made clear, however, that deference is not to be a device that emasculates the significance of judicial review. Judicial deference to an agency's interpretation of a statute "only sets 'the framework for judicial analysis; it does not displace it.'" * * *

Although these principles establish in general terms the appropriate standard of review, this case presents an additional consideration that counsels against full deference to the Board. At the administrative level, the Board took the position that commercial paper was not a "security" within the meaning of the Act, and that, therefore, it did "not appear necessary to examine the dangers that the Act was intended to eliminate." Before this Court, however, the Board appears to have changed somewhat the nature of its argument. The Board's counsel now insists that the activities of Bankers Trust "involv[e] none of the 'hazards' that this Court identified" as the concerns at which the Act is aimed. We previously have stated that *post hoc* rationalizations by counsel for agency action are entitled to little deference: "It is the administrative official and not appellate counsel who possesses the expertise that can enlighten and rationalize the search for the meaning and intent of Congress." Investment Company Institute v. Camp, 401 U.S. 617 (1971) (*Camp*). * * * To the extent that the Board has changed its position from that adopted at the administrative level, its interpretation is entitled to less weight.

III

A

In *Camp* this Court explored at some length the congressional concerns that produced the Glass–Steagall Act. Congress passed the Act in the aftermath of the banking collapse that produced the Great Depression of the 1930's. The Act responded to the opinion, widely expressed at the time, that much of the financial difficulty experienced by banks could be traced to their involvement in investment-banking activities both directly and through security affiliates. At the very least, Congress held the view that the extensive involvement by commercial banks had been unwise; some in Congress concluded that it had been illegal. Senator Glass stated bluntly that commercial-bank involvement in securities had made "one of the greatest contributions to the unprecedented disaster which has caused this almost incurable depression."

Congressional worries about commercial-bank involvement in investment-bank activities reflected two general concerns. The first was the inherent risks of the securities business. Speculation in securities by banks and their affiliates during the speculative fever of the 1920's produced tremendous bank losses when the securities markets went sour. In addition to the palpable effect that such losses had on the assets of affected banks, they also eroded the confidence of depositors in the safety of banks as depository institutions. This crisis of confidence contributed to the runs on the banks that proved so devastating to the solvency of many commercial banks.

But the dangers that Congress sought to eliminate through the Act were considerably more than the obvious risk that a bank could lose money by imprudent investment of its funds in speculative securities. The legislative history of the Act shows that Congress also focused on "the more subtle hazards that arise when a commercial bank goes beyond the business of acting as fiduciary or managing agent and enters the investment banking business." The Glass–Steagall Act reflects the 1933 Congress' conclusion that certain investment-banking activities conflicted in fundamental ways with the institutional role of commercial banks.

The Act's legislative history is replete with references to the various conflicts of interest that Congress feared to be present when a single institution is involved in both investment and commercial banking. Congress observed that commercial bankers serve as an important source of financial advice for their clients. They routinely advise clients on a variety of financial matters such as whether and how best to issue equity or debt securities. Congress concluded that it was unrealistic to expect a banker to give impartial advice about such matters if he stands to realize a profit from the underwriting or distribution of securities.

* * *

Congress also expressed concern that the involvement of a commercial bank in particular securities could compromise the objectivity of the bank's lending operations. Congress feared that the pressure to dispose of an issue of securities successfully might lead a bank to use its credit facilities to shore up a company whose securities the bank sought to distribute. Some in Congress feared that a bank might even make unsound loans to companies in whose securities the bank has a stake or to a purchaser of securities that the bank seeks to distribute. * * *

The Act's design reflects the congressional perception that certain investment-banking activities are fundamentally incompatible with commercial banking. After hearing much testimony concerning the appropriate form of a legislative response to the problems, Congress rejected the view of those who preferred legislation that simply would regulate the underwriting activities of commercial banks. Congress chose instead a broad structural approach that would "surround the banking business with sound rules which recognize the imperfection of human nature that our bankers may not be led into temptation, the evil effect of which is sometimes so subtle as not to be easily recognized by the most honorable man." Through flat prohibitions, the Act sought to "separat[e] as completely as possible commercial from investment banking." * * *

B

Sections 16 and 21 of the Act are the principal provisions that demarcate the line separating commercial and investment banking. Section 16 limits the involvement of a commercial bank in the "business of dealing in stock and securities" and prohibits a national bank from buying securities, other than "investment securities," for its own account. In addition, the section includes the general provision that a national bank "shall not underwrite any issue of securities or stock." Section 5(c) of the Act makes § 16's limitations applicable to state banks that are members of the Federal Reserve System. It is therefore clear that Bankers Trust may not underwrite commercial paper if commercial paper is a "security" within the meaning of the Act.

Section 21 also separates investment and commercial banks, but does so from the perspective of investment banks. Congress designed § 21 to prevent persons engaged in specified investment-banking activities from entering the commercial-banking business. The section prohibits any person "engaged in the business of issuing, underwriting, selling, or distributing * * * stocks, bonds, debentures, notes, or other securities" from receiving deposits. Bankers Trust receives deposits, and it therefore is clear that § 21's prohibitions apply to it.

Because § 16 and § 21 seek to draw the same line, the parties agree that the underwriting prohibitions described in the two sections are coextensive, and we shall assume that to be the case. In any event, because both §§ 16 and 21 apply to Bankers Trust, its activities in this case are unlawful if prohibited by either section. The language of § 21 is perhaps the more helpful, however, because that section describes in greater detail the particular activities of investment banking that Congress found inconsistent with the activity of commercial banks.

It is common ground that the terms "stocks," "bonds" and "debentures" do not encompass commercial paper. The dispute in this case focuses instead on petitioners' claims that commercial paper constitutes a "note" within the meaning of § 21, and, if not, that it is nevertheless encompassed within the inclusive term "other securities." Thus, petitioners claim that the plain language of the Act makes untenable the Board's conclusion that commercial paper is not a "security" within the meaning of the Act. Petitioners contend further that the role played by Bankers Trust in placing the commercial paper of third parties is precisely what the Glass–Steagall Act sought to prohibit.

C

Neither the term "notes" nor the term "other securities" is defined by the statute. "This silence compels us to 'start with the assumption that the legislative purpose is expressed by the ordinary meaning of the words used.'" Respondents do not dispute that commercial paper consists of unsecured promissory notes and falls within the general meaning of the term "notes." Respondents assert, however, that the context in which the term is used suggests that Congress intended a narrower definition. Because the term appears in a phrase that includes "stocks, bonds, [and] debentures," the Board insists that the Act's prohibitions apply only to "notes [and] other securities" that resemble the enumerated financial instruments. The Board's position seems to be that because "stocks, bonds, [and] debentures" normally are considered "investments," the Act is meant to prohibit the underwriting of only those notes that "shar[e] that characteristic of an investment that is the common feature of each of the other enumerated instruments." Applying that criterion to commercial paper, the Board maintains that commercial paper more closely resembles a commercial loan and that it is therefore not an investment of the kind that qualifies as a "security" under the Act.

For a variety of reasons, we find unpersuasive the notion that Congress used the terms "notes * * * or other securities" in the narrow sense that respondents suggest. First, the Court noted in *Camp* that "there is nothing in the phrasing of either § 16 or § 21 that suggests a narrow reading of the word 'securities.' To the contrary, the breadth of the term is implicit in the fact that the antecedent statutory language encompasses not only equity securities but also securities representing debt."

There is, moreover, considerable evidence to indicate that the ordinary meaning of the terms "security" and "note" as used by the 1933 Congress encompasses commercial paper. Congress enacted the Glass–Steagall Act as one of several pieces of legislation collectively designed to restore public confidence in financial markets. See the Banking Act of 1933, the Securities Act of 1933, the Securities Exchange Act of 1934, and the Public Utility Holding Company Act of 1935. In each of these other statutes, the definition of the term "security" includes commercial paper, and each statute contains explicit exceptions where Congress meant for the provisions of an act not to apply to commercial paper. These explicit exceptions demonstrate congressional cognizance of commercial paper and Congress' understanding that, unless modified, the use of the term "security" encompasses it.

* * *

The difficulty with the Board's attempt to narrow the ordinary meaning of the statutory language is evidenced by the Board's unsuccessful efforts to articulate a meaningful distinction between notes that the Act purportedly covers and those it does not. In other statutes in which commercial paper is exempted from securities regulation, Congress either has identified a particular feature, such as maturity period, that defines the exempted class of "notes," or it has authorized a federal agency to define it through regulation. The Glass–Steagall Act does neither, and the efforts by the Board and the Court of Appeals to provide a workable definition that excludes commercial paper have been fraught with uncertainty and inconsistency. The Court of Appeals concluded that the Act applies only to notes that are issued "to raise money available for an extended period of time as part of the corporation's capital structure." It is not clear that such a distinction finds support even with reference to the statutory language from which it purportedly derives. There is no requirement, for example, that stocks, bonds, and debentures be used only to meet the capital requirements of a corporation, and, even if there were, the legislative history provides little evidence to suggest that such a distinction was one that Congress found significant.

* * * Without some clearer directive from Congress that it intended the statutory terms to involve the nebulous inquiry described by the Board, we cannot endorse the Board's departure from the literal meaning of the Act. * * *

In this respect, we find ourselves in substantial agreement with petitioners' suggestion that the Board's interpretation effectively converts a portion of the Act's broad prohibition into a system of administrative regulation. By concluding that commercial paper is not covered by the Act, the Board in effect has obtained authority to regulate the marketing of commercial paper under its general supervisory power over member banks. The Board acknowledges that "the sale of third party commercial paper by a commercial bank could involve, at least in some circumstances, practices that are not consistent with principles of safe banking." In response to these concerns, the Board issued guidelines for state member banks explaining the circumstances in which they properly may place the commercial paper of third parties.

Although the guidelines may be a sufficient regulatory response to the potential problems, Congress rejected a regulatory approach when it drafted the statute, and it has adhered to that rejection ever since. * * *

* * *

In the face of Congress' refusal to give the Board any rulemaking authority over the activities prohibited by the Act, we find it difficult to imagine that Congress intended the Board to engage in the subtle and ad hoc "functional analysis" described by the Board.

D

By focusing entirely on the nature of the financial instrument and ignoring the role of the bank in the transaction, moreover, the Board's "functional analysis" misapprehends Congress' concerns with commercial bank involvement in marketing securities. Both the Board and the Court of Appeals emphasized that Congress designed the Act to prevent future bank losses arising out of investments in speculative, long-term investments. This description of the Act's underlying concerns is perhaps accurate but somewhat incomplete. "[I]n enacting the Glass–Steagall Act, Congress contemplated other hazards in addition to the danger of banks using bank assets in imprudent securities investments." The concern about commercial-bank underwriting activities derived from the perception that the role of a bank as a promoter of securities was fundamentally incompatible with its role as a disinterested lender and advisor.

* * *

The 1933 Congress also was concerned that banks might use their relationships with depositors to facilitate the distribution of securities in which the bank has an interest, and that the bank's depositors might lose confidence in the bank if the issuer should default on its obligations. This concern would appear fully applicable to commercial-paper sales, because banks presumably will use their depositor lists as a prime source of customers for such sales. To the extent that a bank sells commercial paper to large bank depositors, the result of a loss of confidence in the bank would be especially severe.

By giving banks a pecuniary incentive in the marketing of a particular security, commercial-bank dealing in commercial paper also seems to produce precisely the conflict of interest that Congress feared would impair a commercial bank's ability to act as a source of disinterested financial advice. Senator Bulkley, during the debates on the Act, explained:

> "Obviously, the banker who has nothing to sell to his depositors is much better qualified to advise disinterestedly and to regard diligently the safety of depositors than the banker who uses the list of depositors in his savings department to distribute circulars concerning the advantages of this, that, or the other investment on which the bank is to receive an originating profit or an underwriting profit or a distribution profit or a trading profit or any combination of such profits."

This conflict of interest becomes especially acute if a bank decides to distribute commercial paper on behalf of an issuer who intends to use the proceeds of the offering to retire a debt that the issuer owes the bank.

In addressing these concerns before this Court, the Board focuses primarily on the extremely low rate of default on prime-quality commercial paper. We do not doubt that the risk of default with commercial paper is relatively low—lower perhaps than with many bank loans. For several reasons, however, we find reliance on this characteristic misplaced. First, it is not clear that the Board's exemption of commercial paper from the proscriptions of the Act is limited to commercial paper that is "prime." The statutory language admits of no distinction in this respect, and the logic of the Board's opinion must exempt all commercial paper from the prohibition on underwriting by commercial banks. Second, as described above, it appears that a bank can make a particular issue "prime" simply by extending back-up credit to the issuer. Such a practice would seem to fit squarely within Congress' concern that banks would use their credit facilities to aid in the distribution of securities.

More importantly, however, there is little evidence to suggest that Congress intended the Act's prohibitions on underwriting to depend on the safety of particular securities. Stocks, bonds, and debentures exhibit the full range of risk; some are less risky than many of the loans made by a bank. And while the risk features of a security presumably affect whether it qualifies as an "investment security" that a commercial bank may purchase for its own account, the Act's underwriting prohibition displays no appreciation for the features of a particular issue; the Act just prohibits commercial banks from underwriting any of them, with an exception for certain enumerated governmental obligations that Congress specifically has chosen to favor. The Act's prophylactic prohibition on underwriting reflects Congress' conclusion that the mere existence of a securities operation, " 'no matter how carefully and conservatively run, is inconsistent with the best interests' " of the bank as a whole.

* * *

The Board also seeks comfort in the fact that commercial paper is sold largely to "sophisticated" investors. Once again, however, the Act leaves little room for such an ad hoc analysis. In its prohibition on commercial-bank underwriting, the Act admits of no exception according to the particular investment expertise of the customer. The Act's prohibition on underwriting is a flat prohibition that applies to sales to both the knowledgeable and the naive.

Finally, it is certainly not without some significance that Bankers Trust's commercial-paper placement activities appear to be the first of that kind since the passage of the Act. The history of commercial-bank involvement in commercial paper prior to the Act is not well documented; evidently, commercial banks occasionally dealt in commercial paper, but their involvement was overwhelmingly in the role of discounter rather than dealer. Since enactment of the Act, however, there is no evidence of commercial-bank participation in the commercial-paper market as a dealer. The Board has not offered any explanation as to why commercial banks in the past have not ventured to test the limits of the Act's prohibitions on underwriting activities. Although such behavior is far from conclusive, it does support the view that when Congress sought to "separat[e] as completely as possible commercial from investment banking," the banks regulated by the Act universally recognized that underwriting commercial paper falls on the investment-banking side of the line.

IV

For the foregoing reasons, the judgment of the Court of Appeals is reversed and the case is remanded for further proceedings consistent with this opinion.

JUSTICE O'CONNOR, with whom JUSTICE BRENNAN and JUSTICE STEVENS join, dissenting.

The question in this case is whether the Board of Governors of the Federal Reserve System (Board) adopted an erroneous interpretation of law when it concluded that commercial paper is not a "security" under, and hence is not subject to the proscriptions of, §§ 16 and 21 of the Glass–Steagall Act. The area of banking law in which this question arises is as specialized and technical as the financial world it governs, and the relevant statutes are far from clear or easy to interpret. The question is accordingly one on which this Court must give substantial deference to the Board's construction. Because of the Board's expertise and experience in this complicated area of law, and because of its extensive responsibility for administering the federal banking laws, the Board's interpretation of the Glass–Steagall Act must be sustained unless it is unreasonable.

* * *

The Board's own careful and thorough opinion, I believe, amply demonstrates the reasonableness—perhaps the inevitability—of its construction of the critical statutory language. Moreover, the Court's construction of the statute and petitioners' objections to the Board's position are unpersuasive. In these circumstances, the Court should defer to the Board and uphold its ruling. Because the Court does not do so, I respectfully dissent.

I

The language of §§ 16 and 21 of the Glass–Steagall Act makes it clear that, in considering whether the Act prohibits a covered bank from selling third-party commercial paper, the threshold issue is whether commercial paper is a "security" within the meaning of those two sections.

It is apparent from the statutory language that there is no "plain meaning" of the key terms in either § 16 or § 21 that forecloses the Board's interpretation. The Glass–Steagall Act nowhere defines the term "securities," and the term is not so well-defined, either generally or as a legal term of art, that commercial paper is plainly included within its meaning. In particular, nothing on the face of the Glass–Steagall Act reveals whether "securities" refers to the class of all written instruments evidencing a financial interest in a business or, alternatively, to a narrower class of capital-raising investment instruments, as opposed to instruments evidencing short-term loans used to fund current expenses. The term "notes" in § 21, on which petitioners rest their argument that the Glass–Steagall Act covers commercial paper, is likewise susceptible to different meanings. Although "note" is often used generically to refer to any written promise to pay a specified sum on demand or at a specified time, it is also used, more narrowly, to refer to a particular kind of capital-raising debt instrument distributed under an indenture agreement, like bonds or debentures but of shorter maturity. Commercial paper, which consists of "prime quality, negotiable, usually unsecured short-term promissory notes issued by business organizations to meet part of their short-term credit needs," does not come within the narrower interpretations of either "securities" or "notes." Thus, the words "securities" and "notes" in §§ 16 and 21, considered alone, are susceptible to the Board's construction.

Not only do the key terms of §§ 16 and 21, read in isolation, admit the Board's interpretation, but the provisions as a whole lend strong, perhaps decisive, support to the Board's view. A reading of §§ 16 and 21 reveals that petitioners' interpretation, like any other interpretation that treats commercial paper as a "security," does violence to the statutory language. And the Board's interpretation makes sense of the statutory language and of its history.

SECURITIES INDUSTRY ASS'N v. BOARD OF GOVERNORS

468 U.S. 207 (1984).

JUSTICE POWELL delivered the opinion of the Court.

This case presents the question whether the Federal Reserve Board has statutory authority under § 4(c)(8) of the Bank Holding Company Act of 1956 to authorize a bank holding company to acquire a nonbanking affiliate engaged principally in retail securities brokerage.

I

BankAmerica Corp. (BAC) is a bank holding company within the meaning of the Bank Holding Company Act.[1] In March 1982, BAC applied to the Federal Reserve Board (Board) for approval under § 4(c)(8) of the Act to acquire 100 percent of the voting shares of The Charles Schwab Corp., a company that engages through its wholly-owned subsidiary, Charles Schwab & Co. (Schwab), in retail discount brokerage.[2] The Board ordered that formal public hearings be held before an Administrative Law Judge (ALJ) to consider the application. The Securities Industry Association (SIA), a national trade association of securities brokers, and petitioners here, opposed BAC's application and participated in those hearings. After six days of hearings, the ALJ recommended that BAC's application be approved. After reviewing the evidentiary record, the Board adopted, with modifications, the findings and conclusions of the ALJ and authorized BAC to acquire Schwab. SIA petitioned the Court of Appeals for the Second Circuit for judicial review under 12 U.S.C. § 1848.

The Court of Appeals held that the Board had acted within its statutory authority in authorizing BAC's acquisition of Schwab under § 4(c)(8) of the BHC Act. The Court accordingly affirmed the Board's order. We granted SIA's petition for certiorari, and now affirm.

II

Section 4 of the Bank Holding Company Act (BHC Act) prohibits the acquisition by bank holding companies of the voting shares of nonbanking entities unless the acquisition is specifically exempted. The principal exemption to that prohibition is found in § 4(c)(8). That provision authorizes bank holding companies, with prior Board approval, to engage in nonbanking activities that the Board determines are "so closely related to banking * * * as to be a proper incident thereto."

1. BAC operates one subsidiary bank, Bank of America. That bank is a member of the Federal Reserve System, and the parties inform us that it is the largest commercial bank in the United States.

2. Schwab is known as a "discount" broker because of the low commissions it charges. Schwab can afford to charge lower commissions than full-service brokerage firms because it does not provide investment advice or analysis, but merely executes the purchase and sell orders placed by its customers.

Application of the § 4(c)(8) exception requires the Board to make two separate determinations. First, the Board must determine whether the proposed activity is "closely related" to banking. If it is, the Board may amend its regulations to include the activity as a permissible nonbanking activity. Next, the Board must determine on a case-by-case basis whether allowing the applicant bank holding company to engage in the activity reasonably may be expected to produce public benefits that outweigh any potential adverse effects.

A

In this case, the Board held that the securities brokerage services offered by Schwab were "closely related" to banking within the meaning of § 4(c)(8). Relying on record evidence and its own banking expertise, the Board articulated the ways in which the brokerage activities provided by Schwab were similar to banking. The Board found that banks currently offer, as an accommodation to their customers, brokerage services that are virtually identical to the services offered by Schwab. Moreover, the Board cited a 1977 study by the Securities and Exchange Commission that found that

> "bank trust department trading desks, at least at the largest banks, perform the same functions, utilize the same execution techniques, employ personnel with the same general training and expertise, and use the same facilities * * * that brokers do."

Finally, the Board concluded that the use by banks of "sophisticated techniques and resources" to execute purchase and sell orders for the account of their customers was sufficiently widespread to justify a finding that banks generally are equipped to offer the type of retail brokerage services provided by Schwab. On the basis of these findings, the Board held that a securities brokerage business that is "essentially confined to the purchase and sale of securities for the account of third parties, and without the provision of investment advice to the purchaser or seller" is "closely related" to banking within the meaning of § 4(c)(8) of the BHC Act.

B

The Board next determined that the public benefits likely to result from BAC's acquisition of Schwab outweighed the possible adverse effects. Specifically, the Board identified as public benefits the increased competition and the increased convenience and efficiencies that the acquisition would bring to the retail brokerage business. As to possible adverse effects, the Board determined that the proposed acquisition would not result in the undue concentration of resources, decreased competition, or unfair competitive prices.

Finally, the Board concluded that BAC's acquisition of Schwab was not prohibited by the Glass–Steagall Act. The Board observed that the proposed acquisition would make Schwab an affiliate of BAC's banking subsidiary and thus subject to the provisions of the Glass–Steagall Act. It held, however, that Schwab was "not engaged principally in any of the activities prohibited to member bank affiliates by the Glass–Steagall Act," and thus concluded that the acquisition was "consistent with the letter and spirit of that act."

SIA challenges the Board's order in this case on two grounds. First, it argues that the Board may not approve an activity as "closely related" to banking unless it finds that the activity will facilitate other banking operations. Second, it argues that § 20 of the Glass–Steagall Act prohibits a bank holding company from owning any entity that is engaged principally in retail securities brokerage and thus that the Board lacked statutory authority under § 4(c)(8) to approve BAC's acquisition of Schwab.

III

A

There is no express requirement in § 4(c)(8) that a proposed activity must facilitate other banking operations before it may be found to be "closely related" to banking. Indeed, the relevant statutory language does not specify any factors that the Board must consider in making that determination. The general nature of the statutory language, therefore, suggests that Congress vested the Board with considerable discretion to consider and weigh a variety of factors in determining whether an activity is "closely related" to banking. In this case, the Board concluded that Schwab's brokerage services were "closely related" to banking because it found that the services were "operationally and functionally very similar to the types of brokerage services that are generally provided by banks and that banking organizations are particularly well equipped to provide such services." The Board acted well within its discretion in ruling on such factors. * * *

B

The Board expressly considered and rejected SIA's argument that BAC's acquisition of Schwab violates the Glass–Steagall Act. That Act comprises four sections of the Banking Act of 1933. Only one of those four sections is applicable here. That provision, § 20, provides in relevant part:

> "[N]o member bank shall be affiliated in any manner described in subsection (b) of section 221a of this title with any corporation, association, business trust, or other similar organization *engaged principally in the issue, flotation, underwriting, public sale, or distribution* at wholesale or retail or through syndicate participation of stocks, bonds, debentures, notes, or other securities * * *." (emphasis added).

A bank holding company's subsidiaries are bank affiliates within the meaning of § 20. Section 20, therefore, prohibits BAC's proposed acquisition if Schwab is "engaged principally" in any of the activities listed therein.

SIA concedes that Schwab is not engaged in the "issue, flotation, underwriting, * * * or distribution" of securities. It argues, however, that the term "public sale" of securities as used in § 20 applies to Schwab's brokerage business. * * *

"Public sale" is used in conjunction with the terms "issue," "flotation," "underwriting," and "distribution" of securities. None of these terms has any relevance to the brokerage business at issue in this case. Schwab does not engage in issuing or floating the sale of securities, and the terms "underwriting" and "distribution" traditionally apply to a function distinctly different from that of a securities broker. An underwriter normally acts as principal whereas a broker executes orders for the purchase or sale of securities solely as agent. Under the "familiar principle of statutory construction that words grouped in a list should be given related meaning," the term "public sale" in § 20 should be read to refer to the underwriting activity described by the terms that surround it, and to exclude the type of retail brokerage business in which Schwab principally is engaged.

* * *

The legislative history demonstrates that Congress enacted § 20 to prohibit the affiliation of commercial banks with entities that were engaged principally in "activities such as underwriting." In 1933, Congress believed that the heavy involvement of commercial banks in underwriting and securities speculation had precipitated "the widespread bank closings that occurred during the Great Depression." * * *

Congressional concern over the underwriting activities of bank affiliates included both the fear that bank funds would be lost in speculative investments and the suspicion that the more "subtle hazards" associated with underwriting would encourage unsound banking practices. None of the more "subtle hazards" of underwriting identified in *Camp* is implicated by the brokerage activities at issue here. Because Schwab trades only as agent, its assets are not subject to the vagaries of the securities markets. Moreover, Schwab's profits depend solely on the volume of shares it trades and not on the purchase or sale of particular securities. Thus, BAC has no "salesman's stake" in the securities Schwab trades. It cannot increase Schwab's profitability by having its bank affiliate extend credit to issuers of particular securities, nor by encouraging the bank affiliate improperly to favor particular securities in the management of depositors' assets. Finally, the fact that § 16 of the Glass–Steagall Act allows banks to engage directly in the kind of brokerage services at issue here, to accommodate its customers, suggests that the activity was not the sort that concerned Congress in its effort to secure the Nation's banks from the risks of the securities market.

* * *

IV

The Board determined in this case that a securities brokerage business that is essentially limited to the purchase and sale of securities for the account of customers, and without provision of investment advice to purchaser or seller, is "closely related" to banking. We hold that the Board's determination is consistent with the language and policies of the BHC Act. We also hold that the Board's determination that the Glass–Steagall Act permits bank holding companies to acquire firms engaged in such a brokerage business is reasonable and supported by the plain language and legislative history of the Act. We therefore affirm the judgment of the Court of Appeals.

Selected References

T. Hazen, Securities Regulation § 19.5 (2d ed. 1990).

Butler & Macey, The Myth of Competition in the Dual Banking System, 73 Cornell L.Rev. 677 (1988).

DiLorenzo, Public Confidence and the Banking System: The Policy Basis for Continued Separation of Commercial and Investment Banking, 35 Am.U.L.Rev. 647 (1986).

Garten, Regulatory Growing Pains: A Perspective On Bank Regulation In A Deregulatory Age, 57 Fordham L.Rev. 501 (1989).

Isaac & Fein, Facing the Future—Life Without Glass–Steagall, 37 Cath. U.L.Rev. 281 (1988).

Norton, Up Against "the Wall": Glass–Steagall and the Dilemma of a Deregulated ("Reregulated") Banking Environment, 42 Bus.Law 327 (1987).

O'Brien, Securities Industry Continues to Support the Principles of Glass–Steagall, 8 Ann.Rev.Banking L. 457 (1989).

Pitt & Williams, The Glass–Steagall Act: Key Issues for the Financial Services Industry, 11 Sec.Reg.L.J. 234 (1983).

Saba, Regulation of State Nonmember Insured Banks' Securities Activities: A Model for the Repeal of Glass–Steagall?, 23 Harv.J.Legis. 211 (1986).

Note, Glass–Steagall Reform: It's Time to Replace the Crumbling Wall, 14 J.Corp.L. 973 (1989).

Note, The Transparency Theory: An Alternative Approach to Glass–Steagall Issues, 97 Yale L.J. 603 (1988).

Note, Requiem on the Glass–Steagall Act: Tracing the Evolution of the Current Status of Bank Involvement in Brokerage Activities, 63 Tul.L. Rev. 157 (1988).

Note, Security Under the Glass–Steagall Act: Analyzing the Supreme Court's Framework for Determining Permissible Bank Activity, 70 Cornell L.Rev. 1194 (1985).

Comment, Securities Activities Under the Glass–Steagall Act, 35 Emory L.J. 463 (1986).

Note, A Banker's Adventures in Brokerland: Looking Through Glass–Steagall at Discount Brokerage Services, 81 Mich.L.Rev. 1498 (1983).

B. SECURITIES AND COMMODITIES MARKETS

COMMODITIES REGULATION

by Philip M. Johnson & Thomas L. Hazen.

Vol. 1 pp. 9–12 (2d ed. 1989).*

Section 2(a)(1) of the [Commodity Exchange] Act defines *contracts of sale* as "sales, agreements of sale, and agreements to sell." The words *future delivery* are not affirmatively defined, but section 2(a)(1) excludes from their meaning "any sale of a cash commodity for deferred shipment or delivery." Thus, a contract of sale appears to embrace any form of sales arrangement, but the phrase *future delivery* eliminates transactions where an immediate sale occurs but where, for the convenience of the parties or otherwise, the actual transfer of the commodity is deferred. The primary focus of this exclusion, in historical context, was on a common practice in agriculture trade of making binding sales with postponed delivery; these arrangements frequently are referred to as *forward contracts.* For example, grain merchants would often commit to buy a portion of farmers' plantings in advance of harvest. The sales price was fixed immediately, both parties contemplated that the grain or produce would eventually be transferred, but delivery would have to await harvesting. In most cases, the commitment was personal to the parties, and the obligation to deliver could be excused only with the other party's consent.

Although futures contracts are not defined with particularity in the Act, business usage permits a general description to be made. This description, however, is not intended to exclude other arrangements of comparable nature, and the Commodity Futures Trading Commission has made clear its intent to construe very broadly the meaning of the phrase "contracts of sale of a commodity for future delivery." [1]

The traditional futures contract is an agreement between a seller and a buyer that the seller (called a *short*) will deliver to the buyer (called a *long*), at a price agreed to when the contract is first entered,

1. It is clear that designation does not dictate whether a contract is a forward or a futures contract. In the Matter of First Natl. Monetary Exch., [1984–1986 Transfer Binder] Comm.Fut.L.Rep. (CCH) ¶ 22,698 (CFTC 1985).

In determining whether a contract for delayed delivery is a futures contract, a number of factors come into play. Standardization of terms is a key feature of publicly traded futures contracts. With a futures contract most customers do not expect to take delivery and probably lack the facilities to do so. There is an opportunity to offset, and the customer has a right to liquidate in the face of adverse price movements rather than take delivery. Another indicia of a futures contract is that the commodity generally has no business use for the customer but rather is traded for profit. The customer can take a *long* or a *short* position and controls the position in a futures contract with a partial deposit (*margin*). With a futures as opposed to a forward contract the customer does not acquire a specific right to a particular lot of the commodity.

and the buyer will accept and pay for a specified quantity and grade of an identified commodity during a defined period in the future.

[I]t has been held that traditional domestic futures contracts can be acquired lawfully *only* on the designated contract markets. The contracts, in fact, are designed and sponsored by the commodities markets where they are traded. A key feature of these futures contracts is their standardized, uniform terms. Thus, for example, a corn futures contract designed and sponsored by the Chicago Board of Trade calls for the delivery of No. 2 (grade) yellow corn in the quantity of 5,000 bushels during one of a number of specified future months. Similarly, financial futures call for cash settlement based on a predetermined formula. Thus, for example, a stock index future based on the Standard and Poor 500 Stock Index sponsored by the Chicago Mercantile Exchange calls for the delivery of cash based on the index number times $500 during one of a number of specified future months. The terms of a futures contract are not negotiable between the parties; they must be accepted by both. The only item open to negotiation is the contract's *price,* which is established through competitive bidding on the exchange floor. The sponsoring market also sets the procedures for delivery: where, when, and how. If variations in quality (grade) are allowed, it is the exchange—not the parties—that fixes applicable price premiums and discounts.

The importance of exchange sponsorship of futures contracts cannot be overstated. It permits the development of uniform contracts that would be impossible through private negotiation. It makes possible the design of contracts of maximum utility to commercial firms seeking price hedging protection or a useful reference point for commercial pricing decisions. It brings certainty to the understanding between the parties. And, of great importance, it achieves the *fungibility* of contracts necessary to engage in *offset.* * * *

There are two consequences of an investment contract being characterized as a "contract for future delivery." First, trading of such instruments must take place on a "contract market." Under § 4 of the Commodity Exchange Act, futures contracts, may be traded only through a "contract market." Contract markets and boards of trade are regulated by the CFTC in much the same manner as securities exchanges are regulated by the SEC. See CEA §§ 5, 5a. The prohibition against off-exchange trading of futures contracts means that there is a contract market monopoly and thus there is no over-the-counter trading analogous to that which takes place in securities.

As explained in the decision that follows, the second consequence of an instrument being designated a futures contract is that the jurisdiction of the CFTC is exclusive. Although originally established as a means for hedging positions in agricultural commodities, the futures markets rapidly became an investment forum. In addition to agricultural commodities, futures contracts have traditionally existed for precious metals and energy-related commodities. In the 1970s, there was increased investor interest in financial futures. Futures contracts can be found for foreign currencies. The increasing proliferation of hybrid instruments has led to several jurisdictional battles between the CFTC and the SEC.

The SEC initially took the position that futures contracts on securities were subject to its jurisdiction since such a derivative instrument clearly fell within the statutory definition of "security." However, the commodities exchanges wanted to list futures contracts on government securities. The battle was first fought over futures on GNMA certificates.

In 1981, representatives of the SEC and CFTC met with the hopes of eliminating the confusion concerning the jurisdictions of the two agencies. The resulting Johnson–Shad accord (See CCH Comm.Fut.L. Rep. ¶ 21,332) was incorporated into § 2(a)(1)(B) of the Commodity Exchange Act, § 2 of the 1933 Act, and § 3 of the 1934 Act. Under the terms of the accord and resulting legislation, the SEC retains jurisdiction over options on securities while the CFTC is granted exclusive jurisdiction over futures contracts and options on futures contracts where the underlying commodity is either (1) a government security that is exempt from registration under the securities acts or (2) an index based on a group of securities.

The CFTC now has jurisdiction over futures contracts on individual government securities,[1] on indices of stocks and municipal bonds, and options on such futures contracts. Futures and commodity option contracts on other individual securities are prohibited. The SEC has jurisdiction over stock index *options* while the CFTC presides over stock index *futures*. Although conceptually they are commodities instruments, the SEC has jurisdiction over options on foreign currencies if they are traded on a national securities exchange[2] while the CFTC regulates foreign currency futures and options that are not traded on a national securities exchange. As shown by the following chart from the House Report, the allocation of jurisdiction is based on political compromise rather than functional differences between the financial futures and options in question:

1. See, e.g., Messer v. E.F. Hutton & Co., 847 F.2d 673 (11th Cir.1988) (neither federal nor state securities laws applied to United States Treasury Bill futures contracts; the CFTC has exclusive jurisdiction).

2. See Exch. Act Rel. No. 34–22853, 51 Fed.Reg. 5129; (Feb. 3, 1986). Cf. Hiden & Crawshaw, New Instruments, Foreign Currency Warrants and Section 4c(f) of the Commodity Exchange Act, 7 Commod. Law Letter 11 (April/May 1988).

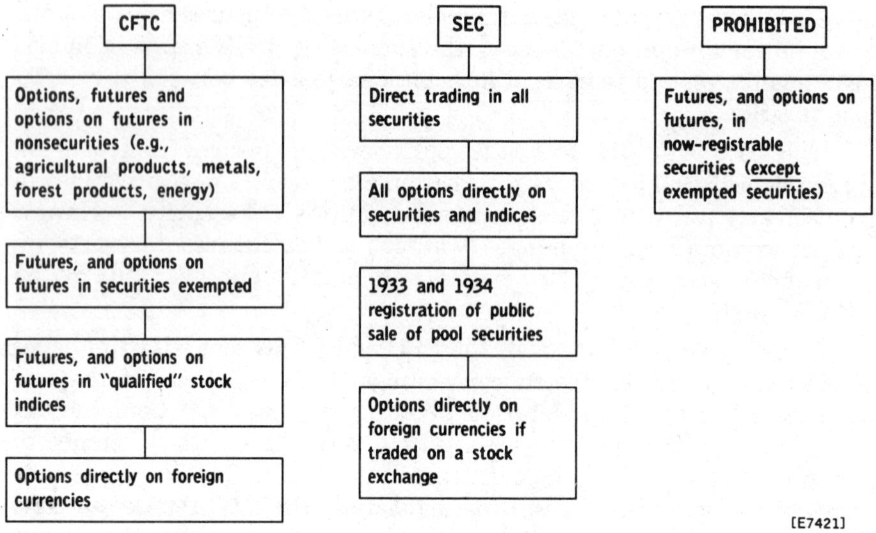

[E7421]

CHICAGO MERCANTILE EXCHANGE v. SEC

883 F.2d 537 (7th Cir.1989).

Before BAUER, CHIEF JUDGE, EASTERBROOK, CIRCUIT JUDGE and FAIRCHILD, SENIOR CIRCUIT JUDGE.

EASTERBROOK, CIRCUIT JUDGE.

The Commodity Futures Trading Commission has authority to regulate trading of futures contracts (including futures on securities) and options on futures contracts. The Securities and Exchange Commission has authority to regulate trading of securities and options on securities. If an instrument is both a security and a futures contract, the CFTC is the sole regulator because "the Commission shall have exclusive jurisdiction with respect to . . . transactions involving . . . contracts of sale (and options on such contracts) for future delivery of a group or index of securities (or any interests therein or based upon the value thereof)", 7 U.S.C. § 2a(ii). See also 7 U.S.C. § 2 ("the Commission shall have exclusive jurisdiction, except to the extent otherwise provided in section 2a of this title"); Chicago Board of Trade v. SEC, 677 F.2d 1137 (7th Cir.), vacated as moot, 459 U.S. 1026, 103 S.Ct. 434, 74 L.Ed.2d 594 (1982) (*GNMA Options*). If, however, the instrument is both a futures contract and an option on a security, then the SEC is the sole regulator because "the [CFTC] shall have no jurisdiction to designate a board of trade as a contract market for any transaction whereby any party to such transaction acquires any put, call, or other option on one or more securities . . . including any group or index of such securities, or any interest therein or based on the value thereof."

The CFTC regulates futures and options on futures; the SEC regulates securities and options on securities; jurisdiction never overlaps. Problem: The statute does not define either "contracts . . . for future delivery" or "option"—although it says that " 'future delivery' . . . shall not include any sale of any cash commodity for deferred shipment or delivery." Each of these terms has a paradigm, but newfangled instruments may have aspects of each of the prototypes. Our case is about such an instrument, the index participation (IP). We must decide whether tetrahedrons belong in square or round holes.

I

Index participations are contracts of indefinite duration based on the value of a basket (index) of securities. The seller of an IP (called the "short" because the writer need not own the securities) promises to pay the buyer the value of the index as measured on a "cash-out day." Any index, such as the Standard & Poor's 500, can be used. The buyer pays for the IP in cash on the date of sale and may borrow part of the price (use margin) on the same terms the Federal Reserve sets for stock—currently 50%. The exchange designates a conversion ratio between the index and the IP, so that (say) each IP unit entitles the holder on cash-out day to the value of the index times 100. Until cash-out the IP may trade on the exchange just like any other instrument. At the end of each quarter the short must pay the buyer (the "long") a sum approximating the value of dividends the stocks in the index have paid during the quarter. From the perspective of the long, then, an IP has properties similar to those of a closed-end mutual fund holding a value-weighted portfolio of the securities in the index: the IPs last indefinitely, pay dividends, and may be traded freely; on cash-out day the IP briefly becomes open-end, and the investor can withdraw cash without making a trade in the market.

Things differ from the short's perspective. Unlike the proprietor of a mutual fund, the short need not own the securities in the index; it will own them (equivalently, a long futures contract based on the same index) only to reduce risk. The short receives the long's cash but must post margin equal to 150% of the value of the IP, similar to the margin required for a short sale of stock. The short sees the IP as a speculative or hedging instrument scarcely distinguishable from a futures contract that terminates on the cash-out day, plus an option held by the long to roll over the contract to the next cash-out date. Cash-out days for an IP generally are the third Friday of March, June, September, and December, the expiration dates of the principal stock-index futures contracts, making the link even more apparent.

Long and shorts do not deal directly with each other. After the parties agree on the price, the Options Clearing Corporation (OCC) issues the IP to the long, receiving the cash; at the same time the OCC pays the short and "acquires" the short's obligation to pay at cash-out time. OCC guarantees the short's obligations to the long, to secure which it holds the short's 150% margin. As the quarter progresses the short must pony up cash to cover dividend-equivalent obligations. When a long exercises the cash-out privilege, the OCC chooses a short at random to make the payment. Any link between the original buyer and seller of an IP thus does not extend beyond the formation of the instrument; after that instant, each person's rights and obligations run to the OCC exclusively. This arrangement also permits either party to close its position by making an offsetting transaction. If the seller of an IP buys an identical contract in the market, the OCC cancels the two on its books.

The Philadelphia Stock Exchange asked the SEC in February 1988 for permission to trade IPs. The American Stock Exchange and the Chicago Board Options Exchange later filed proposals of their own. Each exchange's IP differs slightly from the others. * * *

On April 11, 1989, the SEC granted the exchanges' requests. At the same time, its Division of Market Regulation, acting with delegated authority, allowed the OCC to change its rules so that it could issue, settle, and clear IPs. The SEC concluded that IPs are "stock" within the meaning of § 3(a)(10) of the Securities Exchange Act of 1934. IPs are negotiable, pay dividends, may appreciate in value, and may be hypothecated; the only attribute of stock missing from IPs is voting rights, which the SEC thought unimportant. If not stock, the SEC concluded, IPs are "certificates of interest or participation in" stock, another of the instruments defined as "securities" in § 3(a)(10). Next the SEC found that IPs are not "futures," because they lack two features the SEC thought essential: "futurity" and "bilateral obligation." "Futurity" means that value is set in the future, while as the SEC observed the buyer of an IP pays a price fixed at the time of sale; "bilateral obligation" means that the contract is executory on both sides until expiration or settlement, while the long on an IP performs at the time of purchase, leaving only the short with executory obligations. The SEC went on to say that the OCC need not register under the Investment Company Act because there is no "issuer" within the meaning of § 3(a)(1) of that statute. Concluding that IPs may serve as substitutes for "program trading," provide "an additional layer of liquidity to the market," and afford "an alternative vehicle for retail customers to invest in 'the market,' " the SEC allowed the exchanges to proceed with their plans. We denied the futures markets' request for a stay but accelerated the hearing of the case on the merits. IPs have been trading on the three exchanges since May.

* * *

III

A

A futures contract, roughly speaking, is a fungible promise to buy or sell a particular commodity at a fixed date in the future. Futures contracts are fungible because they have standard terms and each side's obligations are guaranteed by a clearing house. Contracts are entered into without prepayment, although the markets and clearing house will set margin to protect their own interests. Trading occurs in "the contract", not in the commodity. Most futures contracts may be performed by delivery of the commodity (wheat, silver, oil, etc.). Some (those based on financial instruments such as T-bills or on the value of an index of stocks) do not allow delivery. Unless the parties cancel their obligations by buying or selling offsetting positions, the long must pay the price stated in the contract (e.g., $1.00 per gallon for 1,000 gallons of orange juice) and the short must deliver; usually, however, they settle in cash, with the payment based on changes in the market. If the market price, say, rose to $1.50 per gallon, the short would pay $500 (50 per gallon); if the price fell, the long would pay. The extent to which the settlement price of a commodity futures contract tracks changes in the price of the cash commodity depends on the size and balance of the open positions in "the contract" near the settlement date. When the contract involves financial instruments, though, the price is fixed by mechanical computation from the instruments on which the contracts are based.

The SEC consistently has taken the position that options on securities should be regulated as securities. For some years the CFTC maintained that options on securities should be regulated as futures because options are extrinsic to capital formation and because it is almost always possible to devise an option with the same economic attributes as a futures contract (and the reverse). Matters came to a head in 1980, when both agencies asserted jurisdiction over options on securities based on pools of notes. The Government National Mortgages Association (GNMA) sold pass-through certificates representing proceeds of mortgage notes, and persons started writing options on them to allow hedging against movements in interest rates. The SEC observed that options written on securities are securities under § 3(a)(10) of the '34 Act; indeed the SEC contended that because options are securities it should regulate all options. The CFTC countered that options on financial instruments are futures under § 4c(b) of the CEA, and added that because its jurisdiction is exclusive, it is the sole lawful regulator. When the SEC allowed stock exchanges to start trading GNMA options, the futures markets sought review in this court and the CFTC howled bloody murder.

While the case was pending, the agencies reached a pact, which the SEC calls the Shad–Johnson Agreement and the CFTC calls the Johnson–Shad Agreement. (John Shad was the SEC's Chairman at the time, and Phillip Johnson the CFTC's). This Accord (as we shall call it to avoid offending either agency) provided that jurisdiction over options follows jurisdiction over the things on which the options are written. So the SEC received jurisdiction of options on securities, while the CFTC got jurisdiction of options on futures contracts. Things were not quite done, though, because we held in *GNMA Options* that the agencies could not alter their jurisdiction by mutual agreement. 677 F.2d at 1142 n. 8. Starting from the proposition that options on GNMAs are both securities and futures, we held that the CFTC's jurisdiction is exclusive in light of 7 U.S.C. §§ 2 and 2a.

Congress then enacted the Accord almost verbatim, producing the explicit reference to options in § 3(a)(10) of the '34 Act, the SEC savings clause in § 2a(i) of the CEA, and a small change in 7 U.S.C. § 6n to implement an understanding about pools. The legislature thought that this Accord would resolve things and restore a regime in which the SEC supervises capital formation and the CFTC hedging.

The legislation implementing the Accord left in place the premise on which *GNMA Options* was founded: if an instrument is *both* a security and a futures contract, then the CFTC's jurisdiction is exclusive. Section 2a(ii) has no other possible meaning. Like many an agreement resolving a spat, the Accord addressed a symptom rather than the problem. Options are only one among many instruments that can have attributes of futures contracts as well as securities. Financial markets work best when they offer every possible combination of risk and return—a condition financial economists call "spanning"—so that investors can construct a portfolio to each need and taste. Exchanges and professional investors therefore continually devise financial products to fill unoccupied niches. These products are valuable to the extent that they do *not* match the attributes of instruments already available. New products, offering a new risk-return mixture, are designed to depart from today's models.

Which means that the dispute of 1980–82 about options will be played out—is being played out—about each new instrument. Today's case repeats the conflict. Other novel instruments are being handled by regulation. For example, on July 17, 1989, the CFTC adopted rules exempting from its regulation certain hybrid instruments combining equity or debt with payments based on the price of commodities. 17 C.F.R. Part 34. Only merger of the agencies or functional separation in the statute can avoid continual conflict. Functional separation is hard to achieve (new instruments will appear at any border). The SEC favors merger; it has asked Congress repeatedly for jurisdiction over all products (including stock-index and financial futures) based on securities, which would relegate the CFTC to its original role as superintendent of commodities futures. The CFTC has so far defended its position, in part with the argument that multiple regulatory bodies allow greater competition and experimentation—a new product can reach market if either agency approves the variant within its domain. * * *

B

* * *

Despite the congruence of futures and IPs on the short side, the SEC and the stock exchanges say that both "futurity" and "bilateralism" are missing. According to the SEC, IPs lack "futurity" because an IP is the "present obligation to pay current value." And IPs are not bilateral because the long performs in full by paying up front, although in a futures contract both sides must perform on settlement or expiration.

With respect to bilateralism, the SEC's point is inescapable. With respect to futurity, the SEC is wrong. IPs are no more a "present obligation to pay current value" than are futures contracts. The holder of either an IP or a stock-index futures contract may go to market and trade it; the price necessarily tracks current value. * * * Both the futures contract and the IP are settled quarterly (the same dates for both kinds of instrument, except for the CBOE's omission of two of the four dates). The short's obligation is to pay the value of the index *on that date*—which lies in the future to the same extent as the settlement date of any futures contract. Even from the long's point of view, IP and futures contract ultimately look the same. The long pays up front for the IP, but the long on a futures *promises* up front to make a defined payment on the settlement date; the difference in the timing of the payment does not affect the fact that valuation comes at the defined future date.

So the IP has futurity but not bilateralism. It looks like a futures contract to the short—except that it is of indefinite duration, carries a dividend-equivalent obligation, and requires higher margin. It looks like a mutual fund to the long—except that it has no voting rights, does not represent any interest in an underlying pool of stock, and may be settled by executing an offsetting transaction. Fact is, it is no less a future than it is a security, and no more. It just doesn't fit. Which is the whole point. It isn't supposed to be just like something else; the IP was designed as a novel instrument so that it could offer attributes previously missing in the market.

The only thing of which we are sure is that an IP is not an option on a security. The AMEX contends that it is a prepaid option, with a premium equal to the full value and an exercise price of zero. The SEC did not accept this contention, writing:

> [W]hile IPs contain some characteristics of stock index options (e.g., the issuance and clearance and settlement features of IPs are analogous to those of stock index options), the Commission believes that IPs predominantly have the attributes of a portfolio of common stock.

The only "characteristics of stock index options" that either the AMEX or the SEC identified are those introduced by the presence of a clearing house—characteristics that the IP shares with stock-index futures to the last detail. Unless we were to say that all futures are also options (they aren't), these features do not make IPs options. The very features that the SEC emphasizes to show that IPs are securities—indefinite duration, payment up front in cash, dividend equivalency, and so on—show that IPs cannot be options. Options are written out of the money, limited in time, and establish a careful balance among premium, strike price, and duration; the writer retains dividends. IPs possess none of these distinguishing features. * * * IPs are not options.

C

Having concluded that neither the '34 Act nor the CEA addresses the status of IPs in a straightforward way, the logical thing to do is to defer to the agency's resolution of the problem. But which agency? Each claims to be exercising its discretion; each claims entitlement to deference on a subject within its domain.

* * * Perhaps a court could say that because the agencies disagree, neither is entitled to deference. Yet disagreement doesn't make the court the recipient of interpretive powers. One or the other agency is still in charge. Courts readily could accept both the SEC's application of the '34 Act to IPs and the CFTC's application of the CEA. Our difficulty is not any logical conundrum in deferring to both agencies when they disagree. It is instead that a dispute about the agencies' jurisdiction is a zero-sum game because of the exclusivity clauses in the CEA. * * *

We may assume without deciding that even in this jurisdictional dispute, each agency is entitled to leeway in applying its own statute to IPs.

D

If each agency's interpretation of its own statute is entitled to some deference, then the IP is both a security and a futures contract. It has some attributes of both, and all attributes of neither, as we have laid out in excessive detail. Neither characterization can be called wrong.

The only element of financial futures contracts that is missing is "bilateralism." Yet bilateralism is not essential to a futures contract. CFTC v. Co Petro Marketing Group, Inc., 680 F.2d 573 (9th Cir.1982), held that a contract that imposes performance obligations only on the short may be a futures contract. Co Petro sold interests in gasoline that were designed to look like forward contracts, which under the CEA are not futures contracts. Buyers put down deposits to obtain Co Petro's promise to deliver gasoline on future dates. These contracts could not be traded on any market, but Co Petro promised to pay the investor in cash if the market price should rise (that is, the investor could sell the contract back to Co Petro). The investor risked no more than 95% of his deposit; if the price of gasoline fell, the investor's position would be closed. Thus buyers of Co Petro's contracts performed fully on the date they posted the deposit; thereafter only Co Petro had obligations. Despite that, and despite the fact that the contracts were illiquid, the court of appeals concluded that they were futures contracts because their value depended entirely on the price of the commodity at their expiration date, and they were not formed in contemplation of physical delivery.

* * * Recall the statutory scope of the CEA: contracts "for future delivery." Commodity futures contracts may be settled by delivery; financial futures contracts are settled exclusively in cash. One might have thought the prospect of "future delivery" the *sine qua*

non of "futures" contract. Yet no one, not even the SEC, doubts that a contract may be a futures contract even though it provides for cash settlement. If delivery is not essential, then the "traditional" elements of futures contracts are not invariable ingredients of the CFTC's jurisdiction.

[T]he SEC's orders approving the applications of the stock exchanges and the OCC are set aside.

Note on Commodities Professionals

Although the commodities brokerage relationship functions in much the same way as securities brokerage, the nomenclature and regulatory structure is quite different. The Commodity Exchange Act defines various categories of trading professionals who must register with the National Futures Association (NFA), a self regulatory agency analogous to the NASD for securities dealers. While the Act speaks in terms of registration with the CFTC, these registration functions have for the most part been delegated to the NFA.

In the commodities world, the primary retail brokerage unit is known as a futures commission merchant (FCM). Section 2(a)(1)(A) of the Commodity Exchange Act defines "futures commission merchant" as including "individuals, associations, partnerships, corporations, and trusts engaged in soliciting or in accepting orders for the purchase or sale of [commodity futures and options] . . ."). FCMs must be registered with the NFA. Employees of a futures commission merchant who function as account executives are classified as "associated persons" (APs) of the FCM, and similarly must be registered with the NFA. Sales representatives may elect to be registered as "introducing brokers" (IBs). Introducing brokers, who must also register with the NFA, act as agents of the FCM.

As noted at p. 1024 above, generally speaking, all futures trading must take place on an exchange. Floor traders are known as floor brokers (FBs) and, as is the case with other commodity trading professionals, they must be registered with the NFA.

The commodities world's counterparts to investment companies are known as commodity pools. Commodity pools are managed by commodity pool operators (CPOs). Unless they can find an exemption in the Commodity Exchange Act or the CFTC regulations promulgated thereunder, commodity pool operators must register with the National Futures Association. In addition to the various exemptions, entities that are registered as investment companies under the Investment Company Act of 1940 are excluded from the Commodity Exchange Act's CPO registration requirements. 17 C.F.R. § 4.5(a)(1).

Investment advisors who render advice with regard to commodities investments are known as commodity trading advisors (CTAs). Unless an exemption is available, commodity trading advisors are subject to registration requirements similar to those applicable to commodity pool operators.

Two other varieties of commodities trading professionals deserve mention. Prior to exchange trading for commodity options, off-exchange options that originated from registered option grantors could be traded through commodity option dealers. Although off-exchange commodity options may soon become a thing of the past in light of exchange trading, commodity option grantors that operated prior to exchange trading continue to operate subject to the Act's registration requirements. Additionally, leverage transaction merchants (LTMs) who are registered under the Act, may deal in leverage commodity contracts.

Selected References

P. Johnson & T. Hazen, Commodities Regulation (2d ed. 1989).

Anderson, The Regulation of Futures Contracts Innovations in the United States, 4 J. Futures Markets 297 (1984).

Carlton, Futures Markets: Their Purposes, Their History, Their Growth, Their Successes and Failures, 4 J. Futures Markets 237 (1984).

Clark, Genealogy and Genetics of contract of Sale of a commodity for Future Delivery in the commodity Exchange Act, 27 Emory L.J. 1175 (1978).

Fischel, Regulatory Conflict and Entry Regulation of New Futures Contracts, 59 J. Business S85 (1986).

Markham & Gilberg, Stock and Commodity Options—Two Regulatory Approaches and Their Conflicts, 47 Albany L.Rev. 741 (1983).

Silber, Innovation, Competition and New Contract Design in Futures Markets, 1 J. Futures Markets 123 (1981).

Smythe, The Reparation Program of the CFTC: Reducing Formality in Agency Adjudication, 2 Admin. L.J. 39 (1988).

Stein, The Exchange–Trading Requirement of the Commodity Exchange Act, 41 Vand.L.Rev. 473 (1988).

C. TRANSNATIONAL COMPETITION AND REGULATION

The increasing internationalization of the securities markets has raised difficult questions as to when, and to what extent, U.S. securities laws apply to transnational transactions. The transactions fall into three categories: U.S. transactions in foreign securities; foreign transactions in U.S. securities; and foreign transactions in foreign securities which have some impact on U.S. investors or markets.

Many of the provisions of the U.S. securities laws speak in terms of "the use of facilities of interstate commerce or of the mails." The term "interstate commerce" is defined in 1933 Act § 2(7) and 1934 Act § 3(a)(17) to include commerce between any foreign country and the U.S. 1934 Act § 30(b) provides that the Act does "not apply to any person insofar as he transacts a business in securities without the jurisdiction of the United States." In this context, what is meant by "jurisdiction"?

Once jurisdiction has been established, problems may still exist with regard to service of process. Section 22(a) of the 1933 Act and 1934 Act § 27 both provide that process may be served on any defendant "wherever the defendant may be found." However, in order to satisfy due process requirements, "the person sought to be charged must know, or have good reason to know, that his conduct will have effect in the state seeking to assert jurisdiction over him." Leasco v. Maxwell, 468 F.2d 1326 (2d Cir.1972).

---

1. U.S. Transactions in Foreign Securities

Problems arise with regard to securities of foreign issuers which are purchased by U.S. investors in secondary transactions and come to be traded on U.S. exchanges or in the over-the-counter markets. As the securities become traded in the U.S. they may become subject to the registration requirements of 1934 Act § 12 and the reporting, disclosure, and other requirements of §§ 12, 13, 14, and 16. However, since in many such situations, the foreign issuer has not made any offering in the United States and is not subject to U.S. jurisdiction, the only way for the SEC to enforce the registration and reporting requirements is to suspend trading. After much deliberation and delicate international negotiations, the SEC in 1967 adopted Rule 12g3–2, which exempts securities of foreign issuers from the registration provisions of 1934 Act § 12(g) if the issuer, or the government of its home country, furnishes the Commission each year with copies of all information material to investors which it has made public in its home country during the preceding year.

U.S. Public Offerings by Foreign Issuers. Public offerings to U.S. investors by foreign issuers are of course subject to the registration requirements of the 1933 Act to the same extent as offerings by domestic issuers. Indeed, Schedule B to the Act sets forth special disclosure requirements for the registration of securities issued by foreign governments (which do not share in the exemption for U.S. federal, state, and local government securities).

Foreign issuers are also entitled to the same exemptions as domestic issuers (except for Regulation A, which under Rule 252(a)(1) is available only to U.S. and Canadian issuers). However, the entire offering must meet the terms of the exemption; a foreign issuer cannot claim the "private offering" exemption under § 4(2) for a single sale to a U.S. purchaser in conjunction with a general public offering in another country.

Rule 144A. In 1990, the SEC adopted Rule 144A which permits sales of unregistered securities to qualified institutional investors. At the same time, the Commission approved the PORTAL system developed by the NASD which provides an electronic quotation medium for institutional trading of unregistered securities. This secondary market for unregistered securities has created increased opportunities for trading of foreign securities in the U.S.

MULTIJURISDICTIONAL DISCLOSURE

Sec. Act Rel. No. 6841 (August 4, 1989).

The Securities and Exchange Commission (the "Commission") is publishing for comment proposed Rules, Forms and Schedules intended to facilitate cross-border offerings of securities by specified Canadian issuers. The Rules, Forms and Schedules will provide a foundation for a multijurisdictional disclosure system (the "system") that can be expanded to encompass a wider class of issuers and be extended to additional jurisdictions.

As currently proposed, the multijurisdictional disclosure system would permit Canadian issuers that, depending on the nature of the offering, meet market value, public float and Canadian reporting history tests to register securities in the United States using disclosure documents prepared according to the requirements of Canadian regulatory authorities. Issuers meeting tests of market value and public float also would be able to use such documents to meet U.S. periodic disclosure requirements. Companies subject to U.S. proxy requirements could use their Canadian documents for certain solicitations. In addition, insiders of companies subject to Section 16 of the Securities Exchange Act could meet the reporting requirements by filing Canadian forms.

The multijurisdictional disclosure system further would permit third-party and issuer exchange and cash tender offers for securities issued by a Canadian company to be made in compliance with the provisions of applicable Canadian tender offer regulation where less than 20 percent of the class of securities subject to the offer were held of record by U.S. residents.

Concurrently with the publication of this Release, the Ontario Securities Commission ("OSC") and the Commission des valeurs mobilieres du Quebec ("CVMQ") are issuing for comment proposals that would provide for the implementation of the multijurisdictional disclosure system in Canada and would permit U.S. issuers to make public offerings and tender offers in Canada using disclosure documents prepared in accordance with Commission requirements. Such proposals are published as an appendix to this Release.

II. BACKGROUND

A. Developments in International Securities Markets

In recent years, there has been substantial growth in both U.S. investors' purchases of foreign securities and offerings by U.S. issuers outside the United States. In 1988, gross transactions by U.S. investors in foreign corporate stocks totalled over $151 billion, representing almost nine times the total of such transactions in 1980. Gross U.S. transactions in foreign debt securities totalled $445 billion in 1988, reflecting a more than twelve-fold increase since 1980. There are 150 foreign securities traded on U.S. securities exchanges, and 291 quoted in NASDAQ (99 in the National Market System). Many others are traded over-the-counter. In all, the securities of over 2000 foreign issuers are traded in the United States.

Part of the growth in cross-border securities transactions has consisted of an increase in the number of offerings made simultaneously in two or more countries, one of which may be the country of the issuer. Such offerings typically are made when the size of the offering is such that it cannot be absorbed by the issuer's domestic market (for example, in the case of large issuers from the comparatively small Scandinavian markets, or the recent British and French government privatizations), when the issuer desires to expand the geographic base of its security holders, when the issuer wishes to increase the market for its securities internationally, or when strategic reasons exist (for example, to protect against takeover attempts). The issues raised by transnational capital formation became most apparent in the course of such multinational offerings, and were the impetus for the Concept Release.

The number of multinational offerings including a U.S. public tranche has increased significantly in recent years, due in large part to the increase in privatization offerings. The first such major offering was by British Petroleum Company PLC in 1977. Since then, major public multinational offerings have increased significantly, especially in connection with privatizations of various foreign industries. The significance of the privatization offerings lies not only in their increasing frequency and international impact, but also in their enormous size.

In the past few years non-governmental companies also have made multinational offerings involving a public U.S. tranche. Although these offerings usually are substantial in size, to date they have not been as large as the industry privatizations. They can be expected to continue to increase in size and number, especially in view of developments such as the creation of a single market in Europe in 1992.

With increasing U.S. interest in and holding of foreign securities, the impact of registration obligations and tender offer regulation on the willingness of foreign issuers to extend rights and exchange offers or cash tender offers to U.S. shareholders has become increasingly significant. Frequently, U.S. investors are denied participation in such offers, or cashed out, because foreign issuers decide not to subject themselves to U.S. registration and continuous reporting requirements. Consequently, while rights offers are very common in Europe and exchange offers are not uncommon in non-U.S. markets, rights and exchange offers by foreign companies into the United States are rare, while cash tender offers are much more frequent.

B. Canadian Issuers in the United States Market

Canadian companies are frequent issuers in the U.S. capital markets. In 1987 and 1988, Canadian issuers made a total of 124 public offerings in the United States, registering approximately $10 billion of securities, of which $8 billion was equity . . . Canadian companies also have made use of the U.S. shelf registration system. Over $1.7 billion in debt securities have been registered by Canadian issuers for sale under Rule 415 in the last three years.

Of the 516 foreign issuers filing periodic reports with the Commission under the Exchange Act, more than half are Canadian. As of June 30, 1989, there were 21 Canadian issuers listed on the New York Stock Exchange, 38 on the American Stock Exchange and 146 quoted in NASDAQ.

C. Accommodations Made to Foreign Issuers; Issues Raised by Multijurisdictional Offerings

1. Disclosure Issues

The Commission traditionally has accommodated various foreign disclosure policies and business practices, recognizing the differences in foreign disclosure and reporting requirements, and making available special forms for use by foreign issuers.

In 1977, the Commission adopted a new form, Form 20–F, for registration statements and annual reports filed under the Exchange Act. This form may be used by non-Canadian foreign private issuers and Canadian issuers that are not listed on a U.S. securities exchange and have not offered their securities publicly in the United States. Although the form requires substantial disclosure by foreign private issuers, it makes several concessions based on a recognition of foreign disclosure practices. The form permits preparation of financial statements in accordance with GAAP in the registrant's home country, with reconciliation to U.S. GAAP attached thereto. The form also calls for less detail regarding related-party transactions than is required for domestic registrants, and management remuneration may be presented on an aggregate basis. Additionally, the time frame for filing annual reports on Form 20–F is designed to accommodate foreign issuers.

Quarterly reports are not required to be filed by foreign private issuers. Rather, current information that is made public or required to be filed in the home country of a foreign issuer must be provided to the Commission on Form 6–K. Until 1982, foreign issuers making a public offering in the United States were required to use the same forms as domestic issuers. The system was revised that year with the adoption of the foreign integrated disclosure system. This system parallels the integrated disclosure system for domestic issuers, but extends the accommodations made to foreign issuers in Form 20–F to registration statements under the Securities Act.

Foreign issuers with fewer than 300 U.S. shareholders are exempt from the reporting requirements of Section 12(g) of the Exchange Act pursuant to Rule 12g3–2(a) thereunder. Additionally, foreign private issuers not listed on an exchange or quoted in NASDAQ or subject to reporting requirements under Section 15(d) of the Exchange Act may qualify for the "information supplying-exemption" provided by Rule

12g3–2(b). Under this rule, foreign issuers that furnish the Commission with current information required in their home jurisdiction are exempt from the reporting requirements of Section 12(g).

Foreign governmental issuers and foreign private issuers eligible to use Form 20–F are exempt from the proxy and short-swing profit regulations of Sections 14 and 16 of the Exchange Act.

Notwithstanding the accommodations made to foreign issuers, U.S. requirements reportedly continue to deter foreign companies from entering the U.S. markets. When a multinational offering includes a public U.S. tranche, the disclosure requirements established by the Commission usually dictate the addition of information to selling documents prepared in accordance with another jurisdiction's rules.

2. Distribution Issues

Problems of timing also often arise in multijurisdictional offerings as a result of different offering practices and regulatory schemes. This has been a significant issue in recent offerings that included public tranches in the United States and the United Kingdom, because the price is set at different times in relation to the offering in the two jurisdictions. Timing problems also arise from the different regulatory clearances required in multijurisdictional offers. While Canadian offerings have not involved the first difficulty, they have involved the second.

In light of the different distribution techniques used by U.S. and foreign underwriters, the application of Rules 10b–6, 10b–7, and 10b–8 under the Exchange Act also affects the process of bringing a multinational offering to market.

In an increasing number of contexts, the Commission has crafted relief from these and other applicable Exchange Act provisions in order to accommodate the structure and regulatory pattern of foreign jurisdictions, and to permit non-U.S. distribution participants to continue certain customary activities in foreign markets.

The multijurisdictional disclosure system was designed to mitigate the problems posed by multinational offerings. Canada is the first partner for the United States in this effort because of the sophistication of its markets, and the similarities between U.S. and Canadian securities laws, in terms of both their investor protection mandate and the structure of the regulatory scheme established to effect that mandate.

D. Mutual Recognition and Harmonization

Efficiency of the capital-raising process would be enhanced greatly by permitting an issuer to prepare one disclosure document for use in each jurisdiction in which it chooses to sell securities. There are two primary approaches to achieve this goal: Harmonization of disclosure standards worldwide and mutual recognition of disclosure standards established in other countries. The multijurisdictional registration system proposed today includes aspects of both of these approaches.

Under a harmonization approach, participating jurisdictions would agree upon a set of disclosure requirements that would be the same in each jurisdiction, with the result that a prospectus prepared pursuant to the requirements of one participating jurisdiction would comply automatically with the requirements of all other participating jurisdictions. In addition to reducing costs, a prime benefit of such a system would be providing comparability of information from issuer to issuer and country to country.

Mutual recognition, on the other hand, would enable an issuer to prepare a disclosure document according to the requirements of its home jurisdiction, and to have that document accepted for securities offerings in every other participating jurisdiction. Mutual recognition may sacrifice comparability in order to facilitate the offering process.

As proposed, the multijurisdictional disclosure system is a hybrid of the two approaches. While it is based on the concept of mutual recognition, the participants will be those jurisdictions whose disclosure systems, while different in detail, provide investors with information to make an informed investment decision and financial statements of relevance and reliability. The existence of a well-developed, sophisticated and reliable system for administering these requirements is also critical, as the Commission will rely on foreign definitions and application of disclosure standards, and day-to-day enforcement of those standards.

The Commission recognizes that the success of the multijurisdictional approach is contingent upon the ability of the relevant regulators to enforce effectively their securities laws as applied to cross-border securities offerings. As a result, in the Commission's view, Memoranda of Understanding, which provide mechanisms for comprehensive cooperation and enforcement assistance among regulators, are a key component of this approach. The SEC's MOU [Memoranda of Understanding] with British Columbia, Ontario and Quebec exemplifies such a comprehensive mechanism.

III. Canadian Securities Regulation

Canadian securities law has two distinct, yet related purposes: (1) To ensure full and fair disclosure to the capital markets through the registration of securities and continuous reporting of all material information necessary for informed investment decision making; and (2) to maintain fairness and equality of treatment of investors in these markets through the promulgation and enforcement of substantive rules.

Like the United States, Canada requires the registration of securities intended to be offered to the public, the provision of information adequate to enable investors to make informed investment decisions, and continuous disclosure by issuers of publicly sold securities.

A. Canada's Regulatory System

Within the framework of Canada's federal system, securities regulation falls primarily under the legislative authority of that country's ten provinces and two territories. Each provincial legislature has enacted its own securities laws and regulations applicable to all nonexempt securities transactions occurring within the borders of the particular province, which typically are administered and enforced by a commission empowered to license brokers and securities dealers and to compel full disclosure to the investing public. Due in major part to the location of Canada's principal stock exchanges in Toronto and Montreal, the OSC and the CVMQ are very influential in the regulation of securities markets.

While there is neither a federal securities commission nor a comprehensive federal statute governing the Canadian capital markets, the national Parliament has enacted a body of corporate law, known as the Canada Business Corporations Act ("CBCA"), which is administered by the Department of Consumer and Corporate Affairs (the "Department"). Many of Canada's largest reporting companies are incorporated under the CBCA, and therefore are subject to regulation by the Department. Because these companies must comply with securities laws of all provinces in which their securities are distributed or traded, provincial jurisdiction also exists over transactions in such securities.

B. The Registration Process

Subject to statutory exemptions, any distribution of securities in Canada must be registered through the filing of a prospectus with the appropriate securities commission. An identical prospectus, which meets the most stringent provincial disclosure requirements, must be filed with the securities commissions of any province in which securities will be distributed. Virtually all distributions by major issuers are regulated by the OSC and CVMQ, given that most securities offerings include residents of Ontario and Quebec.

---

2. Foreign Transactions in U.S. Securities

A foreign investor who purchases securities in an offering registered under the 1933 Act has the same right of action as a U.S. purchaser in the event there is a material misstatement or omission in the registration statement. However, the SEC has taken the position that, since the principal purpose of the 1933 Act is to protect U.S. investors, it will not make any objection to a U.S. corporation making a public offering of its securities abroad, solely to foreign investors, without registration under the Act, provided that the offering is made under circumstances reasonably designed to preclude redistribution of securities within the U.S. or to American Investors. Sec.Act.Rel. No. 4708 (1964). In 1990, the Commission took a major step toward codifying the scope of this exemption by adopting Regulation S. The following are excerpts from the releases announcing the proposal and adoption of the Regulation.

OFFSHORE OFFERS AND SALES

Sec.Act Release No. 6779 (June 10, 1988).

The Securities and Exchange Commission (the "Commission") is publishing for comment a proposed Regulation intended to clarify the extraterritorial application of the registration provisions of the Securities Act of 1933. The Regulation would provide that any offer or sale that occurs within the United States is subject to section 5 of the Securities Act and any offer or sale that occurs outside the United States is not subject to section 5. The Regulation would set forth factors considered to be important in determining whether an offer or sale occurs outside the United States. Additionally, the Regulation would provide "safe harbors" for specified transactions. Offers and sales meeting all of the conditions of the applicable safe harbor would be deemed to be outside the United States and, therefore, not subject to section 5. The Regulation, as proposed, would not be available with respect to offers and sales or securities issued by investment companies required to register under the Investment Company Act of 1940.

The Commission is proposing Regulation S to clarify the extraterritorial application of the registration provisions of the Securities Act of 1933 (the "Securities Act"). The Regulation would consist of a general statement of applicability of the registration provisions ("General Statement") and safe harbors. The General Statement would provide that section 5 of the Securities Act does not apply to offers or sales of securities that occur outside the United States. In order for a transaction to fall within the provisions of the General Statement, both the sale and the offer relating to that sale would have to be made outside the United States. The General Statement would provide that the elements to be examined in determining whether an offer or sale is made outside the United States include the locus of the offer or sale, the absence of directed selling efforts in the United States, the likelihood of the securities sold coming to rest outside the United States, and the justified expectations of the parties to the transaction as to the applicability of the registration requirements of the U.S. securities laws. * * * *

A. Section 5 and Release No. 33–4708

The registration requirements of the Securities Act apply to any offer or sale of a security involving interstate commerce or use of the mails, unless an exemption is available. The term "interstate commerce" includes "trade or commerce in securities or any transaction or communication relating thereto * * * between any foreign country and any State, Territory or the District of Columbia * * *." The registration requirements thus literally apply to any offer or sale of securities to any person if the means of interstate commerce or the mails are used.[7]

The Commission, however, historically has recognized that registration obligations should not be imposed on offerings with only incidental jurisdictional contacts. In Securities Act Release No. 4708,[8] the Commission stated that it would not take any enforcement action for failure to register securities of U.S. corporations distributed abroad solely to foreign nationals, even though the means of interstate commerce are used, if the distribution is effected in a manner that will result in the securities coming to rest abroad.[9]

Numerous procedures have been employed since the issuance of Release 4708 to ensure that securities sold in reliance upon the Release are sold to non-U.S. persons and "come to rest" abroad. These procedures frequently have been the subject of no-action letters issued by the Commission's staff. In the case of non-convertible debt securities, the staff has granted a number of no-action letters involving, in addition to other restrictions, a 90–day period during which no sales would be permitted to be made in the United States or to U.S. nationals.[10] The staff has also granted no-action letters involving equity securities and convertible securities where more stringent offering procedures were employed.

While the Commission did not define the term "U.S. person" in Release 4708, the staff has construed this term in the no-action and interpretative process. As a general matter, the term "U.S. persons" has been considered to include citizens and residents of the United States as well as organizations formed under the laws of the United States or any political subdivision thereof. Foreign agencies and

7. Leasco Data Processing Equipment Corp. v. Maxwell, 468 F.2d 1326, 1335 (2d Cir.1972); cf. SEC v. United Financial Group, Inc., 474 F.2d 354, 357 (9th Cir. 1973).

8. Release No. 33–4708 (July 9, 1964) (29 FR 9828) ("Release 4708"); cf. IIT v. Vencap Ltd., 519 F.2d 1001, 1016 (2d Cir. 1975), quoting Steele v. Bulova Watch Co., Inc., 344 U.S. 280, 282–283 (1952) (resolution of jurisdictional questions in the securities area "depends on construction of exercised congressional power not the limitations upon that power itself").

9. Although Release 4708 specifically refers only to domestic issuers, the staff also has applied it to offerings by foreign issuers. See, e.g., no-action letters to Vizcaya International N.V. (Apr. 4, 1973); Republic of Iceland (Mar. 19, 1971).

10. E.g., Procter & Gamble Co. (Feb. 21, 1985). The request for no-action treatment proposed the following procedures designed to ensure that the securities would come to rest abroad: Provisions would be placed in agreements with underwriters and dealers in any selling group requiring observation of restrictions on sales to U.S. persons for 90 days after completion of the distribution; a statement regarding the restrictions on sales to U.S. persons would be placed in invitation telexes, the prospectus, press releases and tombstones; confirmations would be delivered in sales to other dealers restating these restrictions; a statement would be placed in requests for all-sold telexes requiring confirmation from underwriters and dealers that the securities were sold outside the United States to persons other than U.S. persons; and at the closing, a temporary global security would be delivered, which would be exchangeable for definitive securities only after at least 90 days following completion of the distribution and certification of non-U.S. beneficial ownership. See also, Fairchild Camera and Instrument International Finance N.V. (Dec. 15, 1976); Raymond International Inc. (June 28, 1976); The Singer Company (Sept. 3, 1974).

branches of U.S. banks and insurance companies are not treated as "U.S. persons" if operating for valid business reasons as locally regulated entities.

Although sales generally were not made to U.S. persons, including U.S. citizens residing overseas, in an offering made in reliance upon Release 4708, the staff recently has taken no-action positions with respect to such sales under narrow circumstances * * *

The staff traditionally has not expressed any view as to when or under what circumstances securities issued pursuant to Release 4708 could be resold in the United States or to U.S. persons. Rather, the staff has indicated that resales may only be made in compliance with the registration requirements of the Securities Act or an exemption therefrom. * * *

In 1970 the Commission adopted guidelines concerning the offer and sale outside the United States of shares of registered open-end investment companies. The Commission indicated that the position taken in Release 4708 would not be applied to foreign sales of investment company securities.

B. Developments in the International Capital Markets

Since the issuance of Release 4708 in 1964, dramatic changes have occurred in the international capital markets. The most significant of these changes is the tremendous growth of the Eurobond market and the recent development of the Euroequity market. Many factors have contributed to these developments.

The Interest Equalization Tax Act of 1964 ("IET"), which was intended to address the United States' balance of payment deficit by discouraging U.S. investors from investing in foreign securities, caused foreign borrowers to turn to foreign markets for capital. The imposition in 1965 of voluntary restraints on capital formation by multinational corporations resulted in United States corporations financing their foreign operations from abroad and when this program became mandatory in 1968, an immediate surge of dollar-denominated Eurobonds issued by United States corporations occurred. The passage of the Tax Reform Act of 1984 further facilitated Eurobond financings by United States issuers by repealing the 30 percent withholding tax on payments of "portfolio interest" on debt securities issued after July 18, 1984 to non-U.S. holders.

More recent regulatory developments have also contributed to the tremendous growth of world financial markets. Capital market restrictions have been relaxed in many countries, as have other economic restrictions such as exchange controls, foreign investment restrictions, and fixed commission rates.

Technological advances have facilitated the internationalization of the securities markets, with transactions taking place through an increasingly electronic and computerized global financial network. Automated quotation, collection and dissemination systems already are in extensive use.

The revolutionary changes in the international market are reflected in the volume of international offerings and global trading. The international bond market grew at a compound annual rate of 21 percent from 1976–1986. Between 1980 and 1986, international bond issues increased from $38.3 billion to $225.4 billion, followed by a decline in 1987 to $177 billion due to effects from the October market break and other economic factors.

In recent years, U.S. issuers have been among the largest borrowers in the international bond markets. In 1986, U.S. issuers tapped the international bond market for a record $43.7 billion, or 19 percent of gross bond offerings in international markets. Eurobond issues accounted for 88 percent of the proceeds raised by U.S. issuers in the international bond markets during 1986. In 1987, U.S. issuers raised approximately $21 billion in the international bond market.

Almost non-existent five years ago, the Euroequity market has recently become established and has shown remarkable growth. Euroequities recently brought to market have included both international issues in the Euromarket as well as foreign tranches of domestic issues directed to particular foreign equity markets. Euroequity offerings of common and preferred stock amounted to approximately $20 billion in 1987 compared to only about $200 million as recently as 1983. International equity offerings have declined in the wake of the October 1987 market break. During the twelve months prior to the market break, Euroequity offerings averaged $2 billion per month, compared to an average of $300 million per month since that time.

The global character of the securities markets also is reflected in the rapid growth of transactions by U.S. and foreign investors in markets outside the investor's home country. U.S. investors' purchases and sales of foreign stocks reached a record $187 billion in 1987, while foreign investors' activity in U.S. domestic corporate stock was a record $481.5 billion. These trends have been even more pronounced with respect to transactions in debt securities. U.S. investors' purchases and sales of foreign debt securities reached a record $404 billion in 1987, while foreign investors' activity in U.S. debt securities was a record $2,832 billion. Larger amounts of capital than ever before are crossing national borders as investors throughout the world increase their purchases of foreign securities.

C. Developments in the U.S. Disclosure System

In the 24 years since the issuance of Release 4708, the disclosure systems under the Securities Act and the Exchange Act also have undergone substantial evolution. In particular, the Exchange Act reporting system has expanded, both with respect to the number of companies covered and the scope of its requirements, to become the primary source of federally mandated information about publicly owned issuers. . . .

OFFSHORE OFFERS—REGULATION S

Securities Act Release No. 6863 (April 24, 1990).

Regulation S [Rules 901 et seq.] as adopted includes two safe harbors. One safe harbor applies to offers and sales by issuers, securities professionals involved in the distribution process pursuant to contract, their respective affiliates, and persons acting on behalf of any of the foregoing (the "issuer safe harbor"), and the other applies to resales by persons other than the issuer, securities professionals involved in the distribution process pursuant to contract, their respective affiliates (except certain officers and directors), and persons acting on behalf of any of the foregoing (the "resale safe harbor"). An offer, sale or resale of securities that satisfies all conditions of the applicable safe harbor is deemed to be outside the United States within the meaning of the General Statement and thus not subject to the registration requirements of Section 5.

Two general conditions apply to the safe harbors. First, any offer or sale of securities must be made in an "offshore transaction," which requires that no offers be made to persons in the United States and that either: (i) the buyer is (or the seller reasonably believes that the buyer is) offshore at the time of the origination of the buy order, or (ii) for purposes of the issuer safe harbor, the sale is made in, on or through a physical trading floor of an established foreign securities exchange, or (iii) for purposes of the resale safe harbor, the sale is made in, on or through the facilities of a designated offshore securities market, and the transaction is not prearranged with a buyer in the United States. Second, in no event could "directed selling efforts" be made in the United States in connection with an offer or sale of securities made under a safe harbor. "Directed selling efforts" are activities undertaken for the purpose of, or that could reasonably be expected to result in, conditioning of the market in the United States for the securities being offered. Exceptions to the general conditions are made with respect to offers and sales to specified institutions not deemed U.S. persons, notwithstanding their presence in the United States.

The issuer safe harbor distinguishes three categories of securities offerings, based upon factors such as the nationality and reporting status of the issuer and the degree of U.S. market interest in the issuer's securities. The first category of offerings has been expanded from the Proposals and includes: securities offered in "overseas directed offerings," securities of foreign issuers in which there is no substantial U.S. market interest, securities backed by the full faith and credit of a foreign government, and securities issued pursuant to certain employee benefit plans. The term "overseas domestic offerings," includes an offering of a foreign issuer's securities directed to any one foreign county, whether or not the issuer's home country, if such offering is conducted in accordance with local laws, offering practices and documentation. It also includes certain offerings of a domestic issuer's non-convertible debt securities, specified preferred stock and asset-backed securities denominated in the currency of a foreign country, which are directed to a single foreign country, and conducted in accordance with local laws, offering practices and documentation. The second category has been revised to include offerings of securities of U.S. reporting issuers and offerings of debt securities, asset-backed securities and specified preferred stock of foreign issuers with a substantial U.S. market interest. The third, residual category has been adopted substantially as reproposed.

The issuer safe harbor requires implementation of procedural safeguards, which differ for each of the three categories, to ensure that the securities offered come to rest offshore. Offerings under the first category may be made offshore under the issuer safe harbor without any restrictions beyond the general conditions. Offerings made in reliance on the other two categories are subject to additional safeguards, such as restrictions on offer and sale to or for the account or benefit of U.S. persons.

The resale safe harbor has been expanded from the Proposals to allow reliance thereon by certain officers and directors of the issuer or distributors. In such a transaction, no remuneration other than customary broker's commissions may be paid. Otherwise, the resale safe harbor is adopted substantially as reproposed. Under the resale safe harbor, dealers and others receiving selling concessions, fees or other remuneration in connection with the offering (such as sub-underwriters) must comply with requirements designed to reinforce the applicable restriction on directed selling efforts in the United States and the offshore transaction requirement. All other persons eligible to rely on the resale safe harbor need only comply with the general conditions.

The safe harbors are not exclusive and are not intended to create a presumption that any transaction failing to meet their terms is subject to Section 5. Reliance on one of the safe harbors does not affect the availability of any exemption from the Securities Act registration requirements upon which a person may be able to rely.

* * *

II. Background and Introduction

* * *

The Regulation adopted today is based on a territorial approach to Section 5 of the Securities Act. The registration of securities is intended to protect the U.S. capital markets and investors purchasing in the U.S. market, whether U.S. or foreign nationals. Principles of comity and the reasonable expectations of participants in the global markets justify reliance on laws applicable in jurisdictions outside the United States to define requirements for transactions effected offshore. The territorial approach recognizes the primacy of the laws in which a market is located. As investors choose their markets, they choose the laws and regulations applicable in such markets.

In view of the objectives of Regulation S and the policies underlying the Securities Act, the Regulation is not available for any transaction or chain of transactions that, although in technical compliance with the rules, is part of a plan or scheme to evade the registration obligations of the Securities Act. In such cases, registration under the Securities Act would be required.

Regulation S relates solely to the applicability of the registration requirements of Section 5 of the Securities Act, and does not limit the scope or extraterritorial application of the antifraud or other provisions of the federal securities laws or provisions of state law relating to the offer and sale of securities. The antifraud provisions have been broadly applied by the courts to protect U.S. investors and investors in U.S. markets where either significant conduct occurs within the United States (the "conduct" test) or the conduct occurs outside the United States but has a significant effect within the United States or on the interests of U.S. investors (the "effects" test). It is generally accepted that different considerations apply to the extraterritorial application of the antifraud provisions than to the registration provisions of the Securities Act. While it may not be necessary for securities sold in a transaction that occurs outside the United States, but touching this country through conduct or effects, to be registered under United States securities laws, such conduct or effects have been held to provide a basis for jurisdiction under the antifraud provisions of the United States securities laws.

Foreign persons who engage in transactions involving securities of U.S. issuers may be subjected to liability under federal securities law, provided there has been the requisite use of the mails of facilities of interstate commerce. For example in ROTH v. FUND OF FUNDS, 405 F.2d 421 (2d Cir.1968) a foreign mutual fund owning more than 10% of the stock in a U.S. company was held liable under 1934 Act § 16(b) for short-swing profits realized on transactions on a U.S. exchange. The court held that liability would exist regardless of where the trades took place, on the exchange since jurisdiction under section 16 is based not on the use of interstate facilities but rather on the fact that the securities are registered under § 12 of the Act. Similarly, 1934 Act § 13(d), which requires certain disclosures to any person or group which acquires more than 5% of the stock of any company registered under § 12, has been held applicable to foreign investors and foreign banks. United States v. Weisscredit, 325 F.Supp. 1384 (S.D.N.Y.1971). With regard to liability under 1934 Act Rule 10b–5, the use of facilities of interstate commerce will support jurisdiction over a foreigner. See, e.g., SEC v. Texas Gulf Sulphur, 258 F.Supp. 262, 287 (S.D. N.Y.1966), affirmed in part, reversed in part 401 F.2d 833 (2d Cir.1968). See also the summary of the cases in the Securities Act Release on Offshore Offers and Sales, p. 1042 above.

Under its margin regulations (see p. 969 above), the Federal Reserve Board limits the amount of credit that can be extended for the purchase of U.S. securities. In 1970, 1934 Act § 7 was amended to prohibit any U.S. person from obtaining credit from a foreign lender in a transaction which would have been prohibited if it had taken place in the U.S. Accordingly, foreign banks have been held subject to margin regulations to the extent they engage in transactions which can be found to constitute doing business as a broker or dealer in the U.S.

---

3. *Foreign Transactions in Foreign Securities*

The courts have frequently applied the antifraud provisions of the federal securities laws to transactions in foreign securities taking place outside the U.S. In some cases, the basis of the jurisdiction has been the harm to the U.S. shareholders who were the alleged victim of the fraud. Schoenbaum v. Firstbrook, 405 F.2d 200 (2d Cir.1968). In other cases, jurisdiction has been predicated upon the fact that some of the acts alleged to constitute the violation occurred within the U.S. Leasco v. Maxwell, 468 F.2d 1326 (2d Cir. 1972); Travis v. Anthes Imperial, 473 F.2d 515 (8th Cir.1973).

In BERSCH v. DREXEL FIRESTONE, 519 F.2d 974 (2d Cir.1975), the court held that the antifraud provisions extend to:

(1) sales to U.S. persons residing in the U.S. whether or not any significant acts occurred in the U.S.;

(2) sales to U.S. persons residing outside the U.S. if acts in the U.S. contributed significantly to their losses; and

(3) sales to foreigners outside the U.S. only if acts in the U.S. caused their losses.

The following case analyzes the current state of the law with regard to the extraterritorial reach of antifraud provisions:

ZOELSCH v. ARTHUR ANDERSEN

824 F.2d 27 (D.C.Cir.1987).

Before WALD, CHIEF JUDGE, BORK, and SILBERMAN, CIRCUIT JUDGES.

BORK, CIRCUIT JUDGE.

* * *

I.

The transactions that led to this lawsuit involved four principal participants. Dr. Loescher und Co. KG ("Loescher") is a West German limited partnership. First American International Real Estate Limited Partnership ("FAIR") is an American limited partnership based in Miami, Florida. Arthur Andersen & Co. GmbH ("GmbH") is a West German limited liability corporation. Arthur Andersen & Co. ("AA–USA"), the sole defendant in this case, is an American general partnership organized under the laws of Illinois.

Zoelsch and the other West Germans invested in an intricate investment and tax shelter plan. Under the plan, their funds were placed either directly with Loescher, or indirectly with another West German entity that is a limited partner of Loescher. In either case, the investors understood that their funds would be channeled through these entities to FAIR. FAIR, in turn, would invest the funds in property and condominium conversions in Memphis, Tennessee, and Atlanta, Georgia.

In April of 1981, Loescher and FAIR entered into an investment agreement. In September of 1981, Loescher commissioned GmbH to prepare an audit report on the entire plan, including an analysis of FAIR's written description of the American investments. Within the month, GmbH issued its report. Loescher then solicited investors by distributing a package of materials to them, which included GmbH's audit report and FAIR's materials. It is undisputed that FAIR's materials were prepared in the United States, that the audit report was prepared in West Germany, and that the package of materials was distributed only in West Germany to West German investors. The investments were not successful, and Zoelsch's complaint alleges that he and the other investors detrimentally relied on a number of false representations and material omissions in the audit report.

Zoelsch has brought a separate suit against GmbH in Munich, West Germany. He brings this suit, however, only against AA–USA, which was not directly involved in the solicitation of these investors or in the preparation of any of the documents that induced these purchases of securities. The sole link between AA–USA and the package of materials distributed by Loescher is one reference to AA–USA in the audit report prepared by GmbH. The reference is in German, and plaintiff's translation reads: "With respect to a number of data and particulars in the prospectus in conjunction with the economic fundamentals we have made inquiries thereabout by way of our branch-establishment Arthur Andersen & Co., Memphis." Defendant's translation is somewhat different: "With respect to some general prospectus data relating to the overall environment we have made inquiries through the office of Arthur Andersen & Co. Memphis." We do not have the original German version but the difference between the two translations does not affect our jurisdictional determination.

Zoelsch's complaint alleged that AA–USA provided false and misleading information to GmbH with ample reason to know that this information would be incorporated in GmbH's audit report and would be relied on by investors such as Zoelsch. Zoelsch alleged fraud in connection with the sale of securities and the aiding and abetting of securities fraud in violation of section 10(b) of the Securities Exchange Act of 1934 and its attendant Rule 10b–5. The district court granted defendant's motion to dismiss for lack of subject matter jurisdiction.

II.

A.

The issue, not previously addressed in this circuit, is American court jurisdiction over securities law claims against a defendant who acted in the United States when the securities transaction occurred abroad and there was no effect felt in this country.

Congress can, of course, prescribe the extent of federal jurisdiction over actions to enforce the federal securities laws, so long as it does not overstep the broad limits set by the due process clause. See, e.g., Leasco Data Processing Equip. Corp. v. Maxwell, 468 F.2d 1326, 1334 (2d Cir.1972). But in the Securities Exchange Act of 1934, Congress said little that bears on this issue. The explicit purposes of the Act are:

> to remove impediments to and perfect the mechanisms of a national system for securities and a national system for the clearance and settlement of securities transactions and the safeguarding of securities and funds related thereto, and to impose requirements necessary to make such regulation and control reasonably complete and effective, in order to protect interstate commerce, the national credit, the Federal taxing power, to protect and make more effective the national banking system and Federal Reserve System, and to insure the maintenance of fair and honest markets in such transactions.

The relevant language of section 10(b) prohibits "any person, directly or indirectly, by the use of any means or instrumentality of interstate commerce or of the mails" from using "in connection with the purchase or sale of any security . . . any manipulative or deceptive device or contrivance" proscribed by the SEC. "Interstate commerce" is broadly defined to include "trade, commerce, transportation, or communication . . . between any foreign country and any State." And the federal district courts are given exclusive jurisdiction of suits brought to enforce the securities laws. These provisions frame a fairly broad grant of jurisdiction, but they furnish no specific indications of when American federal courts have jurisdiction over securities law claims arising from extraterritorial transactions.

A single passage in the statute addresses this issue explicitly. Section 30(b) states that the 1934 Act "shall not apply to any person insofar as he transacts a business in securities without the jurisdiction of the United States, unless he transacts such business in contravention of such rules and regulations as the Commission may prescribe as necessary or appropriate to prevent the evasion of this chapter." But AA–USA is not alleged to have transacted a business in securities anywhere. Nevertheless, section 30(b) gives some reinforcement to the conclusion that there is no jurisdiction to entertain Zoelsch's claims.

If the text of the 1934 Act is relatively barren, even more so is the legislative history. Fifty years ago, Congress did not consider how far American courts should have jurisdiction to decide cases involving predominantly foreign securities transactions with some link to the

United States. The web of international connections in the securities market was then not nearly as extensive or complex as it has become. In this state of affairs, our inquiry becomes the dubious but apparently unavoidable task of discerning a purely hypothetical legislative intent. As Judge Friendly candidly put it in a very similar case:

> We freely acknowledge that if we were asked to point to language in the statutes, or even in the legislative history, that compelled these conclusions, we would be unable to respond. The Congress that passed these extraordinary pieces of legislation in the midst of the depression could hardly have been expected to foresee the development of offshore funds thirty years later. . . . Our conclusions rest on . . . our best judgment as to what Congress would have wished if these problems had occurred to it.

Bersch v. Drexel Firestone, Inc., 519 F.2d 974, 993 (2d Cir.), cert. denied, 423 U.S. 1018, 96 S.Ct. 453, 46 L.Ed.2d 389 (1975).

B.

The courts have not confined federal jurisdiction to securities transactions consummated in the United States. They have deviated from this position in two respects. First, they have asserted jurisdiction over extraterritorial conduct that produces substantial effects within the United States, such as effects on domestic markets or domestic investors. Second, they have asserted jurisdiction in some cases over acts done in the United States that "directly caused" the losses suffered by investors outside this country.

Zoelsch concedes that jurisdiction in this case cannot be premised on domestic "effects" of predominantly foreign conduct, and "[j]urisdiction may not be sustained on a theory that the plaintiff has not advanced." Zoelsch relies on AA–USA's domestic conduct as the basis for jurisdiction.

Several tests have been devised for determining when American courts have jurisdiction over domestic conduct that is alleged to have played some part in the perpetration of a securities fraud on investors outside this country. The Second Circuit has set the most restrictive standard. It has declined jurisdiction over alleged violations of the securities laws based on conduct in the United States when the conduct here was "merely preparatory" to the alleged fraud, that is, when the conduct here did not "directly cause" the losses elsewhere. See, e.g., Bersch, 519 F.2d at 992–93; IIT v. Vencap, Ltd., 519 F.2d 1001, 1018 (2d Cir.1975). In later cases, the line between domestic conduct that is "merely preparatory" and conduct that "directly causes" the losses elsewhere has been significantly clarified. The Second Circuit's rule seems to be that jurisdiction will lie in American courts where the domestic conduct comprises all the elements of a defendant's conduct necessary to establish a violation of section 10(b) and Rule 10b–5: the fraudulent statements or misrepresentations must originate in the United States, must be made with scienter and in connection with the sale or purchase of securities, and must cause the harm to those who claim to be defrauded, even though the actual reliance and damages may occur elsewhere. See IIT v. Cornfeld, 619 F.2d 909, 920–21 (2d Cir. 1980); cf. Vencap, 519 F.2d at 1018 (finding of jurisdiction "is limited to the perpetration of fraudulent acts themselves"); Leasco, 468 F.2d at 1335 ("if defendants' fraudulent acts [occurred] in the United States . . . it would be immaterial . . . that the damage resulted, not from the contract . . . procured in this country, but from interrelated action which he induced in England").

The Third, Eighth, and Ninth Circuits appear to have relaxed the Second Circuit's test. They too have asserted jurisdiction only when the conduct in this country "directly causes" the losses elsewhere. See SEC v. Kasser, 548 F.2d 109, 115 (3d Cir.), cert. denied, 431 U.S. 938, 97 S.Ct. 2649, 53 L.Ed.2d 255 (1977); Continental Grain (Australia) Pty. Ltd. v. Pacific Oilseeds, Inc., 592 F.2d 409, 418–20 (8th Cir.1979); Grunenthal GmbH v. Hotz, 712 F.2d 421, 424 (9th Cir.1983). But in *Continental Grain* the court explicitly repudiated the Second Circuit's requirement that "domestic conduct constitute the elements of a rule 10b–5 violation," 592 F.2d at 418, in favor of a test that would find jurisdiction whenever the domestic conduct "was in furtherance of a fraudulent scheme and was significant with respect to its accomplishment." Id. at 421. The Third Circuit's formulation seems more permissive, allowing subject matter jurisdiction "where at least some activity designed to further a fraudulent scheme occurs within this country." *Kasser,* 548 F.2d at 114. The consequence of these approaches has been a loosening of the jurisdictional requirements; any significant activity undertaken in this country—or perhaps any activity at all—that furthers a fraudulent scheme can provide the basis of American jurisdiction over the domestic actor.

C.

We believe that a more restrictive test, such as the Second Circuit's, provides the better approach to determining when American courts should assert jurisdiction in a case such as this. There is no doubt, of course, that Congress could confer jurisdiction over activity like that alleged to have been engaged in by AA–USA. Moreover, considerations of comity, which will often cause a court to stay its hand, appear to be minimal or nonexistent here. Appellants do not seek to have us assert jurisdiction over West German parties, nor would a judgment about AA–USA's conduct in the United States necessarily or even probably require a pronouncement on the propriety of the behavior of the West German parties. The case going forward in the Federal Republic would likely be unaffected by this case. Nevertheless, we think we should not assert jurisdiction.

We begin from the established canon of construction that "legislation of Congress, unless a contrary intent appears, is meant to apply only within the territorial jurisdiction of the United States," which "is based on the assumption that Congress is primarily concerned with domestic conditions." And even aside from this presumption, it is quite clear that the Securities Exchange Act of 1934 had as its purpose the protection of American investors and markets. That is the inference to be drawn from section 30(b) as well, for it states that the statute does not apply to persons transacting business in securities abroad unless the Securities and Exchange Commission issues rules and regulations making the statute applicable to such persons because that is "necessary or appropriate to prevent the evasion" of the statute. That rather clearly implies that Congress was concerned with extraterritorial transactions only if they were part of a plan to harm American investors or markets. The Commission has never issued such rules or regulations and there is no allegation in this case that AA–USA's conduct was engaged in to evade American law.

Courts have also been concerned to preserve American judicial resources for the adjudication of domestic disputes and the enforcement of domestic law. *Bersch,* 519 F.2d at 985 ("When, as here, a court is confronted with transactions that on any view are predominantly foreign, it must seek to determine whether Congress would have wished the precious resources of the United States courts and law enforcement agencies to be devoted to them rather than leave the problem to foreign countries."). It is far from clear that these resources would be well spent on all the potential disputes in which domestic conduct makes a relatively small contribution to securities fraud that occurs elsewhere.

Were it not for the Second Circuit's preeminence in the field of securities law, and our desire to avoid a multiplicity of jurisdictional tests, we might be inclined to doubt that an American court should ever assert jurisdiction over domestic conduct that causes loss to foreign investors. It is somewhat odd to say, as *Bersch* and some other opinions do, that courts must determine their jurisdiction by divining what "Congress would have wished" if it had addressed the problem. A more natural inquiry might be what jurisdiction Congress in fact thought about and conferred. Congress did not think about conduct here that contributes to losses abroad in enacting the Securities Exchange Act of 1934; it could easily provide such jurisdiction if that seemed desirable today. But, for the reasons just given, we defer to *Bersch* and the later Second Circuit cases and adopt the Second Circuit's approach. We are not persuaded by the reasoning of those circuits that have broadened federal court jurisdiction for reasons that are essentially legislative. In *Continental Grain,* the court said, "[w]e frankly admit that the finding of subject matter jurisdiction in the present case is largely a policy decision." 592 F.2d at 421. Yet Congress is available to make any policy decisions that are required. In *Kasser,* similarly, the court justified its approach in part because "[f]rom a policy perspective, and it should be recognized that this case in a large measure calls for a policy decision, we believe that there are sound rationales for asserting jurisdiction." 548 F.2d at 116 (footnote omitted). Three rationales were offered. "First, to deny such jurisdiction may embolden those who wish to defraud foreign securities purchasers or sellers to use the United States as a base of operations." Id.

Second, "[b]y finding jurisdiction here, we may encourage other nations to take appropriate steps against parties who seek to perpetrate frauds in the United States." Id. Finally, the court's action "will enhance the ability of the SEC to police vigorously the conduct of securities dealings within the United States." Id.; see also *Continental Grain,* 592 F.2d at 421–22 (approving and employing these same policy rationales). *Kasser* concluded: "We are reluctant to conclude that Congress intended to allow the United States to become a 'Barbary Coast,' as it were, harboring international securities 'pirates.'" 548 F.2d at 116.

We, too, are reluctant to conclude that Congress intended any such thing, but we are less reluctant to conclude that Congress in 1934 had no intention at all on the subject because it was concerned with United States investors and markets. That being so, *Kasser*'s policy arguments may provide very good reasons why Congress should amend the statute but are less adequate as reasons why courts should do so. As the Supreme Court has said in another context, "[t]he responsibilities for assessing the wisdom of such policy choices and resolving the struggle between competing views of the public interest are not judicial ones: 'Our Constitution vests such responsibilities in the political branches.'" This is particularly the case since such an amendment providing jurisdiction over aspects of predominantly foreign transactions should take into account considerations of comity and foreign affairs. Those factors do not weigh heavily in this case but they may in others.

For these reasons we adopt what we understand to be the Second Circuit's test for finding jurisdiction based on domestic conduct: jurisdiction is appropriate when the fraudulent statements or misrepresentations originate in the United States, are made with scienter and in connection with the purchase or sale of securities, and "directly cause" the harm to those who claim to be defrauded, even if reliance and damages occur elsewhere. Indeed, we believe this test is only a slight recasting, if at all, of the traditional view that jurisdiction will lie in American courts only over proscribed acts done in this country.

III.

The application of these principles to Zoelsch's claims is not difficult. [I]t is clear that any actual defrauding of investors took place in West Germany, so that reliance and damages would have occurred there. We are therefore left to consider whether Zoelsch alleges any tenable theory of liability according to which AA–USA committed acts in this country that are "punishable" in the sense that they satisfy the other elements needed to establish liability under section 10(b) or Rule 10b–5.

One possible theory of liability that can be gleaned from the complaint is that AA–USA and GmbH are "branch establishments," parts of a single world-wide organization, so that one could be held liable for the other's fraudulent misrepresentations. But Zoelsch has not raised this argument on appeal, and appears not to dispute that AA–USA and GmbH are completely separate legal entities.

The only other theory of liability that we find in the complaint, and the essence of Zoelsch's position on appeal, is that AA–USA acted willfully or recklessly by either misrepresenting or omitting to state material facts that it knew, in response to inquiries made by GmbH. The complaint indicates that AA–USA could foresee that its misrepresentations or omissions might affect future purchasers of securities. Zoelsch also alleges that those misrepresentations or omissions were in fact one of the causes of the damage he and the other investors suffered when they were defrauded. These actions by AA–USA form the basis of Zoelsch's claims of securities fraud under section 10(b) and Rule 10b–5 and for aiding and abetting such fraud.

These allegations, even if true, are insufficient to support jurisdiction under the test we have enunciated. At the most, they establish that AA–USA made misrepresentations to GmbH that GmbH credited in drawing up its audit report. AA–USA's statements were not themselves made for distribution to the public, and were not transmitted to the public. AA–USA was merely one of the sources GmbH consulted in conducting the investigations which culminated in its audit report. That report, which was circulated to investors as part of the larger package of materials distributed by Loescher, was prepared and certified by GmbH alone.

On these allegations, any misrepresentations made by AA–USA would not have been made "in connection with the purchase or sale of any security" as required for liability by section 10(b) and Rule 10b–5.

Zoelsch offers one final argument that comes at jurisdiction from a very different angle. He asserts that we should consider all the activity that surrounds any given securities transaction as a single mass, and exercise subject matter jurisdiction over any individual defendant if we find that the sum of all the domestic activities by all participants in a string of transactions seems large enough to support jurisdiction in American federal courts. Thus we should take account of FAIR's domestic conduct in deciding whether to assert jurisdiction over AA–USA, even though FAIR is not even a party to this case, and there is no allegation that AA–USA acted in concert with FAIR to perpetrate a securities fraud. It is obvious that this suggestion is completely antithetical to the approach we have adopted here. It bears no relation to the tests for determining jurisdiction that have been adopted by any of the federal appellate courts. It is a novel theory and appears not to relate to the statute's purpose to protect American investors and securities markets. There seems nothing to recommend it. We therefore find no theory of liability in Zoelsch's complaint that supports American federal jurisdiction over the securities law claims brought against this defendant. The district court's decision is

Affirmed.

WALD, CHIEF JUDGE, concurring

I agree with the majority that the District Court properly dismissed this action for lack of subject matter jurisdiction. In reaching that result, I find it unnecessary, however, to adopt the Second Circuit's restrictive test for determining the extent of federal jurisdiction over securities law claims involving international transactions. It seems clear that, even under the less strict approach adopted by the Third, Eighth, and Ninth Circuits, AA–USA's alleged misrepresentations or omissions of material fact were so insignificant and so indirectly related to the overall fraudulent scheme as set out in the complaint that no federal jurisdiction would exist over Zoelsch's claims.

Furthermore, I cannot accept the majority's rationale for rejecting the jurisdictional standard adopted by the Third, Eighth, and Ninth Circuits. The majority characterizes those courts as having improperly engaged in judicial activism by "broaden[ing] federal court jurisdiction for reasons that are essentially legislative." Those courts were faced, as we are, with a question of statutory interpretation for which the language of the statute and its legislative history provide little guidance. It is clear that "[f]ifty years ago, Congress did not consider how far American courts should have jurisdiction to decide cases involving predominantly foreign securities transactions with some link to the United States." In such circumstances, courts properly look to the overall purposes of the statute in resolving an issue of statutory construction. The majority may disagree with the policy rationales offered by the other circuits, but its criticism of them as engaging in ad hoc judicial legislation is misplaced. The decisions cited by the majority as examples of judicial lawmaking clearly indicate that the policies adopted are those the court perceives as most consistent with the intent of Congress in enacting the federal securities laws. See, e.g., SEC v. Kasser, 548 F.2d 109, 116 (3d Cir.) ("the antifraud provisions of the 1933 and 1934 Acts were designed to insure high standards of conduct in securities transactions within this country in addition to protecting domestic markets and investors from the effects of fraud"). I therefore wish to distance myself from the majority's labeling of these courts' efforts as an attempt to usurp the role of Congress.

Selected References

T. Hazen, Law of Securities Regulation § 14.2 (2d ed. 1990).

Casper, Transnational Offerings and the Problem of Integration, 34 U.Miami L.Rev. 47 (1979).

Evans, Offerings of Securities Solely to Foreign Investors. 40 Bus.Law. 69 (1984).

Harker & Rotunda, Extraterritorial Regulation of Foreign Business Under the U.S. Securities Laws. 59 N.C.L.Rev. 643 (1981).

Levine & Calcott, The SEC and Foreign Policy: The International Securities Enforcement Cooperation Act of 1988. 17 Sec.Reg.L.J. 115 (1989).

Royston, The Regulation of American Depositary Receipts: Americanization of the International Capital Markets. 10 N.C.J.Int'l L. & Com. Reg. 87 (1985).

Roundtable, Problems of Enforcement in the Multinational Securities Market. 9 U.Pa.J.Int'l Bus.L. 307 (1987).

Symposium, Policing Trans–Border Fraud in the United States Securities Markets. 11 Brooklyn J.Int'l L. 475 (1985).

Note, Subject Matter Jurisdiction Over Transnational Securities Fraud: A Suggested Roadmap to the New Standard of Reasonableness, 71 Cornell L.Rev. 919 (1986).

Note, Regulation of Offshore Investment Companies Through Extraterritorial Application of Rule 10b–5. 1982 Duke L.J. 167.

Index

References are to Pages

References are to Pages

References are to Pages

†